Principles of Taxation

for Business and Investment Planning   2024 Edition

Sally M. Jones

Professor Emeritus of Accounting
McIntire School of Commerce
University of Virginia

Shelley C. Rhoades-Catanach

Associate Professor of Accountancy
School of Business
Villanova University

Sandra R. Callaghan

Associate Professor of Accounting
Neeley School of Business
Texas Christian University

Thomas R. Kubick

Professor of Accountancy
College of Business
University of Nebraska-Lincoln

Mc
Graw
Hill

PRINCIPLES OF TAXATION FOR BUSINESS AND INVESTMENT PLANNING, TWENTY-SEVENTH EDITION

This book is printed on acid-free paper.

1 2 3 4 5 6 7 8 9 LWI 28 27 26 25 24 23

ISBN 978-1-265-67409-0 (bound edition)
MHID 1-265-67409-4 (bound edition)
ISBN 978-1-266-83875-0 (loose-leaf edition)
MHID 1-266-83875-9 (loose-leaf edition)
ISSN 1099-5587

Portfolio Manager: *Kathleen Klehr*
Product Developers: *Michele Janicek, Katie Jones-Aiello*
Marketing Manager: *Kaitlin Murray*
Content Project Managers: *Jill Eccher, Angela Norris*
Buyer: *Laura Fuller*
Content Licensing Specialist: *Sarah Flynn*
Cover Image: *©theromb/Shutterstock*
Compositor: *Straive*

mheducation.com/highered

To Zane, Tony, Tom, and Jessica

About the Authors

Sally M. Jones

Sally M. Jones is professor emeritus of accounting at the McIntire School of Commerce, University of Virginia, where she taught undergraduate and graduate tax courses. Before joining the Virginia faculty in 1992, Professor Jones spent 14 years on the faculty of the Graduate School of Business, University of Texas at Austin. She received her undergraduate degree from Augusta College, her MPA from the University of Texas, and her PhD from the University of Houston. She is also a CPA. Professor Jones was the first editor of *Advances in Taxation* (JAI Press) and the *PriceWaterhouse Case Studies in Taxation.* She has published numerous articles in the *Journal of Taxation, The Tax Adviser,* and the *Journal of the American Taxation Association.* Professor Jones is a frequent speaker at tax conferences and symposia, a past president of the American Taxation Association, and the 2000 recipient of the Ray M. Sommerfeld Outstanding Tax Educator Award.

Shelley C.
Rhoades-Catanach

Shelley C. Rhoades-Catanach is an associate professor of accountancy at Villanova University. She teaches a variety of tax courses in Villanova's undergraduate, masters of accounting, and graduate tax programs. Before joining the Villanova faculty in 1998, Professor Rhoades-Catanach spent four years on the faculty of Washington University in St. Louis. She has also served as a visiting faculty member at the Darden Graduate School, University of Virginia, and at INSEAD, an international MBA program in Fontainebleau, France. She received her undergraduate degree in accounting from the University of Nebraska at Lincoln and her PhD from the University of Texas at Austin. Professor Rhoades-Catanach has published articles in numerous journals, including the *Journal of the American Taxation Association, Accounting Review, Issues in Accounting Education, Journal of Accounting Education,* and *Review of Accounting Studies.* She has served as president, vice president, and trustee of the American Taxation Association and on the editorial boards of the *Journal of the American Taxation Association* and the *Journal of International Accounting, Auditing and Taxation.* She is the former co-editor of the *Journal of International Accounting, Auditing and Taxation.* Professor Rhoades-Catanach is the 2010 recipient of the Ray M. Sommerfeld Outstanding Tax Educator Award.

Sandra Renfro Callaghan

Sandra Renfro Callaghan is an associate professor of accounting at the Neeley School of Business at Texas Christian University. She joined the faculty in 1998 after earning her PhD in accounting from Michigan State University. Her current research is primarily focused on topics in taxation, executive compensation, and the Affordable Health Care Act. Professor Callaghan teaches tax and financial accounting courses both at the undergraduate and the graduate level and has earned numerous teaching awards, including the Deans' Teaching Award and Neeley School of Business Alumni Professor of the Year. She has served in various leadership roles, including president of the American Taxation Association and member of the American Accounting Association Council. Professor Callaghan earned a BS from Texas Christian University and an MPA from the University of Texas at Austin. Prior to earning her PhD, she was a tax professional with Ernst & Young.

Thomas R. Kubick

Thomas R. Kubick is a professor of accountancy and Fulk faculty chair at the University of Nebraska–Lincoln, where he teaches undergraduate and graduate tax courses. Prior to joining the University of Nebraska–Lincoln in July 2019, he was an associate professor at the University of Kansas. A native of Lincoln, he received his undergraduate and graduate degrees from the University of Nebraska–Lincoln. He holds numerous professional certifications, including the Chartered Financial Analyst (CFA), Certified Public Accountant (CPA), Chartered Alternative Investment Analyst (CAIA), Certified Management Accountant (CMA), Certified Fraud Examiner (CFE), and Certified Financial Planner (CFP). Professor Kubick's research interests include taxation, corporate finance, and incentives. His research has been published in numerous academic journals such as the *Journal of Accounting and Economics, The Accounting Review, Management Science, Review of Accounting Studies, Journal of Corporate Finance, National Tax Journal,* and the *Journal of the American Taxation Association.* He currently serves on the editorial boards of *Journal of Business Finance and Accounting* and the *Journal of International Accounting Research.*

A Note from the Authors

Principles of Taxation for Business and Investment Planning is a unique approach to the subject of taxation. This text is designed for use in introductory tax courses included in either undergraduate or graduate business programs. Its objective is to teach students to recognize the major tax issues inherent in business and financial transactions. The text focuses on fundamental concepts, the mastery of which provides a permanent frame of reference for future study of advanced tax topics. Unlike traditional introductory texts, *Principles of Taxation for Business and Investment Planning* downplays the technical detail that makes the study of taxation such a nightmare for business students. Traditional texts are heavily compliance oriented and convince many students that the tax law is too complex and specialized to be relevant to their future careers. This text attempts to do just the opposite by convincing students that an understanding of taxation is not only relevant but critical to their success in the business world.

Principles of Taxation for Business and Investment Planning has its origin in the 1989 White Paper titled *Perspectives on Education: Capabilities for Success in the Accounting Profession,* published jointly by the Big Eight public accounting firms. The White Paper expressed disenchantment with the narrow technical focus of undergraduate accounting curricula and called for scholastic emphasis on a broad set of business skills necessary for professional success. The Accounting Education Change Commission (AECC), operating under the aegis of the American Accounting Association, embraced the philosophy reflected in the White Paper. In September 1990, the AECC published its Position Statement No. One, titled *Objectives of Education for Accountants.* This statement reiterated that an undergraduate business education should provide a base for lifelong learning.

Beginning in 1996, the American Institute of CPAs (AICPA) and the American Taxation Association (ATA) developed the Model Tax Curriculum (MTC) as a resource for accounting educators seeking to develop or modify accounting programs or course offerings to best prepare students to enter the accounting profession. The primary objective of the MTC is for students to understand the role taxation plays in business decision making and financial reporting by building a foundation for future learning in tax, even if the student does not plan on becoming a tax professional. The MTC has been updated several times since its inception to provide ongoing support and guidance to tax educators.

The environment in which CPAs operate is changing rapidly as the business world becomes increasingly complex. As a result, entry-level CPAs need skills and competencies that require deeper critical thinking, problem solving and professional judgment.

CPA Evolution is a joint effort between the AICPA and the National Association of State Boards of Accountancy (NASBA) to transform the CPA licensure model to meet the demands of today's profession. The new model starts with a deep and strong core in accounting, auditing, tax and technology that all candidates would be required to complete. Then, each CPA candidate will choose a discipline (business analysis and reporting, information systems and controls, or tax compliance and planning) in which to demonstrate deeper skills and knowledge. As a part of the new model, a new Uniform CPA Examination is expected to launch in January 2024.

As part of the CPA Evolution, the AICPA and NASBA have collaborated to develop a Model Curriculum for educators. Part 1 of this CPA Evolution Model Curriculum covers the content necessary for all future CPAs, regardless of their chosen discipline. Part 2 of the Model Curriculum covers the content relevant for each of the three separate disciplines.

Part 1 of the CPA Evolution Model Curriculum contains a section specific to tax topics covered by the core portion of the new CPA exam. *Principles of Taxation* covers over 90 percent of the detailed tax topics contained in part 1 of the Model Curriculum. In addition, this text addresses a significant portion of the Part 2 topics covered in the tax compliance and planning discipline-specific portion of the Model Curriculum. Finally, the planning and decision-making focus of this text are very appropriate to the goals of CPA Evolution to create entry-level CPAs with skills and competencies that require critical thinking, problem solving and professional judgment.

A Paradigm for the Introductory Tax Course

Principles of Taxation for Business and Investment Planning provides a paradigm for meeting the educational needs of tax students in the 21st century. This paradigm is based on three postulates:

- **Postulate 1: Students should learn the tax law as an integrated component of a complex economic environment.** They should be aware of the role taxes play in financial decision making and should understand how taxes motivate people and institutions to engage in certain transactions.

- **Postulate 2: Students should comprehend the tax law as an organic whole rather than as a fragmented collection of rules and regulations.** They should learn general tax rules rather than the myriad of exceptions that confuse rather than clarify the general rules. They should appreciate how the general rules apply to all taxpaying entities before they learn how specialized rules apply to only certain entities. Finally, they should learn how the law applies to broad categories of transactions rather than to a particular transaction.

- **Postulate 3: Students who learn fundamental concepts have a permanent frame of reference into which they can integrate the constant changes in the technical minutiae of the law.** The rapid evolution of the tax law results in a short shelf life for much of the detailed information contained in undergraduate tax texts. Yet the key elements of the law—the statutory and judicial bedrock—do not change with each new revenue act. Students who master these key elements truly are prepared for a lifetime of learning.

We authors know that traditional paradigms die hard and educational reform is difficult. Nevertheless, we believe that change in the way college and university professors teach tax is both inevitable and worthwhile. Our responsibility to our students is to prepare them to cope in a business world with little tolerance for outdated skills or irrelevant knowledge. Our hope is that *Principles of Taxation for Business and Investment Planning* is a tool that can help us fulfill that responsibility.

Using This Text in a First-Semester Tax Course

Principles of Taxation for Business and Investment Planning is designed for use in a one-semester (15-week) introductory tax course. Instructors can choose which of the 18 chapters deserve a full week's coverage and which can be covered in less than a week. Instructors may even decide to omit chapters that seem less relevant to the educational needs of their students. Business students who complete a one-semester course based on this text will be well prepared to function in the modern tax environment. If they are required (or may elect) to take a second tax course, they will have a solid, theoretical foundation on which to build.

This is the 27th annual edition of *Principles of Taxation for Business and Investment Planning.* Adopters of the text will certainly have many excellent suggestions to improve the next edition. We welcome any and all comments and encourage fellow teachers to e-mail us with their input (shelley.rhoades@villanova.edu, s.callaghan@tcu.edu, and tkubick@unl.edu).

Sally M. Jones
Shelley C. Rhoades-Catanach
Sandra R. Callaghan
Thomas R. Kubick

Changes in *Principles of Taxation*, 2024 edition

In addition to the content changes listed below, McGraw Hill Connect offers new assignable and auto-gradable Applying Alteryx Exercises, in addition to Integrated Excel problems and Tableau Dashboard Activities. Please see the Online Assignments section for additional information.

Chapter 1

- Updated all Tax Talks, examples, and end-of-chapter problems as needed.
- Updated all references to state income tax, sales tax, and excise tax rates.

Chapter 2

- Updated federal deficit and national debt data on page 2–3.
- Updated discussion of payroll and self-employment taxes for changes to inflation-adjusted Social Security tax threshold on page 2–3.
- Updated Tax Talk to reflect new CBO projection of public debt to GDP on page 2–8.
- Updated Share of Income/Share of Taxes discussion on page 2–17 to reflect most current data available.

Chapter 3

- Updated the cost of private letter ruling on page 3–12.

Chapter 4

- Revised the Tax Talk on page 4-2.
- Revised Global Tax Costs example on page 4–10.

Chapter 5

- New Tax Talk added on page 5-2.

Chapter 6

- Updated 2023 threshold for use of cash method of accounting.
- Updated 2023 excess business loss thresholds.

Chapter 7

- Updated discussion of Section 179 deduction for 2023 thresholds.
- Revised example of interaction of Section 179 and bonus depreciation on page 7-21 to incorporate 2023 phase-down of bonus depreciation to 80 percent.
- Updated passenger automobile limits to 2022 amounts.

Chapter 8

- Updated all Tax Talks, examples, and end-of-chapter problems as needed.

Chapter 9

- Updated all Tax Talks, examples, and end-of-chapter problems as needed.

Chapter 10

- Updated filing statistics in Tax Talks throughout.
  Updated Schedule C, Form 1065, Form 1120-S, and Schedule K-1s to 2022 versions.
- Updated discussion of payroll and self-employment taxes for changes to inflation-adjusted Social Security tax threshold on pages 10–11 through 10–15.
- Updated QBI thresholds for 2023 inflation adjustments.

Chapter 11

- Updated filing statistics in Tax Talks throughout.
- Replaced the Tax Talks on pages 11-4 and 11-15.
- Updated Form 1120 to 2022 version.
- Removed discussion of pre-2018 minimum tax credit carryforwards.
- Added discussion and examples of new 15 percent corporate minimum tax on large corporations.
- Added new Tax Talk on page 11-13.

Chapter 12

- Updated filing statistics in Tax Talk on page 12–8.

Chapter 13

- Updated filing statistics in Tax Talks throughout.
  Updated discussion of Ohio CAT and Texas TMT to include exemption thresholders, on page 13-3.
- Significantly revised comprehensive state income tax example to reflect reduction in North Dakota tax rate and changes in apportionment formulas for both North Dakota and Montana.
- Added new Tax Talk on page 13–24.

Chapter 14

- Updated for inflation adjustments including tax rate tables, standard deductions, and AMT exemption amounts.
- Added Tax Talk related to the online marketplace on page 14-7.
- Updated earned income credit to reflect 2023 inflation adjustments on page 14–19.
- Updated Volpe family examples throughout chapter to reflect 2023 law.
- Updated Form 1040 to reflect revised version of the 1040 and supporting schedules.
- Added additional scenarios to select Application Problems.

Chapter 15

- Updated all Tax Talks, examples, and end-of-chapter problems.
- Updated data from Bureau of Labor and Statistics in Tax Talk on page 15–2.
- Updated examples on pages 15–3 and 15–4 to include 2022 Form W-2 and Form 1099-NEC on page 15–3.
- Updated Tax Talk discussion of retirement savings on page 15–19.
- Replaced Tax Talk on page 15-22
- Updated Tax Talk on page 15-27
- Updated coverage of employer-provided plans to reflect 2023 inflation adjustments.
- Updated coverage of individual retirement accounts to reflect 2023 inflation adjustments.

Chapter 16

- Updated all Tax Talks, examples, and end-of-chapter problems as needed.
- Updated Exhibits 16.1, 16.2, and 16.3 to include 2022 Form 1040, Schedule B, Schedule D, and Schedule E.
- Updated coverage of the gift and estate taxes to reflect 2023 inflation adjustments.
- Revised Appendix 16-A to include 2022 Form 8949, Form 1040, Schedule D, and Qualified Dividends and Capital Gain Tax Worksheet.

Chapter 17

- Updated all Tax Talks, examples, and end-of-chapter problems as needed.

Chapter 18

- Added reference to Form 1065 and Form 1120-S filing deadlines on page 18-4.
- Added introduction to SSTS No. 1 and Interpretation 1-1 on page 18-5.
- Added a Tax Talk on privileged communications on page 18-15.
- Added discussion of common law duty of tax preparer on page 18-5.
- Updated all Tax Talks, examples, and end-of-chapter problems.

Content Organization

The content and organization of this text are highly compatible with the tax core of the CPA Evolution Model Curriculum proposed by the American Institute of Certified Public Accountants and the National Association of State Boards of Accountancy. According to the AICPA, the introductory tax course should expose students to a broad range of tax concepts and emphasize the role of taxation in the business decision-making process. Under the model curriculum, students learn to measure taxable income from business and property transactions, and are introduced to different types of business entities and the tax considerations unique to each type. Individual tax topics are covered by the Model Curriculum but are not the primary focus. Because *Principles of Taxation for Business and Investment Planning* reflects this recommended pedagogical approach, the text is ideal for courses based on the tax core of the Model Curriculum.

PART ONE

Exploring the Tax Environment

PART TWO

Fundamentals of Tax Planning

Part One consists of two chapters that familiarize students with the global tax environment. Chapter 1 describes the environment in terms of the legal relationship between taxes, taxpayers, and governments. Definitions of key terms are developed, and the major taxes are identified. Chapter 2 considers the tax environment from a normative perspective by asking the question: "What are the characteristics of a good tax?" Students are introduced to the notions of tax efficiency and tax equity and learn how contrasting political beliefs about efficiency and equity continue to shape the tax environment.

Part Two concentrates on developing a methodology for incorporating tax factors into business decisions. Chapter 3 introduces the pivotal role of net present value of cash flows in evaluating financial alternatives. Students learn how to compute tax costs and tax savings and how to interpret them as cash flows. Chapter 4 covers the maxims of income tax planning. The characteristics of the tax law that create planning opportunities are explained, and the generic techniques for taking advantage of those opportunities are analyzed. Chapter 5 provides a succinct overview of the tax research process and prepares students to solve the research problems included at the end of each chapter. The chapter explains the six steps in the tax research process and contains a cumulative example of the application of each step to a research case.

Part Three focuses on the quantification of business taxable income. Chapter 6 covers the computation of income or loss from ongoing commercial activities, with special emphasis on differences between taxable income and net income for financial statement purposes. Chapters 7 and 8 explore the tax implications of acquisitions and dispositions of business property, while Chapter 9 is devoted to nontaxable exchanges.

Part Four teaches students how to calculate the tax on business income. Chapter 10 describes the function of sole proprietorships, partnerships, LLCs, and S corporations as conduits of income, while Chapter 11 discusses corporations as taxable entities in their own right. Chapter 12 builds on the preceding two chapters by exploring the tax planning implications of the choice of business entity. Chapter 13 broadens the discussion by considering the special problems of businesses operating in more than one tax jurisdiction. This chapter introduces both multistate and international tax planning strategies.

Part Five concentrates on the tax rules and regulations unique to individuals. Chapter 14 presents the individual tax formula and acquaints students with the complexities of computing individual taxable income. Chapter 15 covers compensation and retirement planning. Chapter 16 covers investment and rental activities and introduces wealth transfer planning. Finally, Chapter 17 analyzes the tax consequences of personal activities, with particular emphasis on home ownership.

Part Six consists of Chapter 18, which presents the important procedural and administrative issues confronting taxpayers. It covers the basic rules for paying tax and filing returns, as well as the penalties on taxpayers who violate the rules. Chapter 18 also describes the judicial process through which taxpayers and the IRS resolve their differences.

Key Learning Tools

Learning Objectives

The chapters begin with learning objectives that preview the technical content and alert students to the important concepts to be mastered. These objectives appear again as marginal notations marking the place in the chapter where each learning objective is addressed.

LO 4-3
Explain how the assignment of income doctrine constrains income-shifting strategies.

Assignment of Income Doctrine

The federal courts have consistently held that our income tax system cial shifts of income from one taxpayer to another. Over 80 years ago decided that income must be taxed to the person who earns it, even if legal right to the wealth represented by the income.[4] Thus, a business a $10,000 check in payment for services rendered to a client can't avo income by simply endorsing the check over to his or her child. In the of the Court, the tax law must disregard arrangements "by which the f a different tree from that on which they grew."

Examples and Cases

The chapters contain numerous examples and cases illustrating or demonstrating the topic under discussion.

Conflicting Maxims

Firm MN operates as two separate taxable entities, Entities M and N. The firm is nego a transaction that will generate $25,000 cash in year 0 and $60,000 cash in year 1. If M undertakes the transaction, taxable income will correspond to cash flow (i.e., Entity report $25,000 and $60,000 taxable income in years 0 and 1). If Entity N undertake transaction, it must report the entire $85,000 taxable income in year 0. Entity M has percent marginal tax rate, while Entity N has a 21 percent marginal tax rate. Firm MN 5 percent discount rate to compute NPV.

	Entity M		Entity N	
Year 0:				
Before-tax cash flow		$25,000		$25
Taxable income	$25,000		$85,000	
	.32		.21	

Tax Talk

Each chapter includes items of "Tax Talk." These items highlight new tax planning strategies, tax facts, legislative proposals, or innovative transactions with interesting tax implications reported in the business press.

Tax Talk
Several of Europe's smallest countries, such as Luxembourg, Switzerland, and Ireland, offer very low corporate tax rates to attract multinational corporations. Case in point: Amazon.com channels the profits earned across the 27-nation European Union through its Luxembourg subsidiary.

Both firms face a 21 percent federal tax rate. Under these facts, Firms Y and Z have lowing after-tax cash flows:

	Firm Y	Firm Z
Before-tax cash/income	$5,000	$5,000
State income tax cost	(200)	(500)
Federal taxable income	$4,800	$4,500
Federal tax cost		
(Taxable income × 21%)	(1,008)	(945)
After-tax cash flow	$3,792	$3,555

A comparison of these after-tax cash flows gives us our third income tax planning
Tax costs decrease (and cash flows increase) when income is generated in a jurisdictio low tax rate.

Key Terms

Key terms are indicated in boldface in the text. A list of key terms is also supplied at the end of the chapter with page references for easy review. Definitions of key terms from all the chapters are compiled in a Glossary for the text.

Key Terms

accrual method of accounting *6-15*
all-events test *6-19*
allowance method *6-23*
business interest limitation *6-9*
calendar year *6-5*

cash method of accounting *6-11*
constructive receipt *6-12*
deferred tax asset *6-17*
deferred tax liability *6-17*
direct write-off method *6-23*

econom
perfor
excess
limita
fiscal y
general
princi

Sources of Book/ Tax Differences

Chapters 6, 7, 8, 9, 11, 13, and 15 provide a list of the sources of book/tax differences introduced in the chapter.

Sources of Book/Tax Differences

Permanent
- Interest on state and local bonds
- Key-person life insurance proceeds and premiums
- Fines and penalties
- Political contributions and lobbying expense
- Meals and entertainment expenses
- Sexual harassment settlements subject to nondisclosure agreements

Temporary
- Prepaid income
- Bad debts
- Accrued expenses f test
- Compensation accr
- Related party accru
- NOL carryforwards
- Business interest ex

Questions and Problems for Discussion

The questions and problems challenge students to think critically about conceptual and technical issues covered in the chapter. These problems tend to be open-ended and are designed to engage students in debate. Many problems require students to integrate material from previous chapters in formulating their responses.

Questions and Problems for Discussion

LO 6-1   1. Firm LK bought a warehouse of used furniture to equip several of its c
An employee discovered a cache of gold coins in a desk drawer. A local
Firm LK the rightful owner of the coins, which have a $72,000 fair marke
Does Firm LK recognize income because of this lucky event?

LO 6-2   2. Discuss the choice of a taxable year for the following businesses:
   a. Retail plant and garden center.
   b. French bakery.
   c. Chimney cleaning business.
   d. Moving and transport business.
   e. Software consulting business.

LO 6-3   3. Corporation DB operates three different lines of business. Can the corp
different overall method of accounting for each line, or must the corpora
overall method?

Application Problems

Application problems give students practice in applying the technical material covered in the chapter. Most of the problems are quantitative and require calculations to derive a numeric solution.

Issue Recognition Problems

These issue recognition problems develop students' ability to recognize the tax issues suggested by a set of facts and to state those issues as questions. The technical issues buried in these problems typically are *not* discussed in the chapter. Consequently, students must rely on their understanding of basic principles to analyze the problem, spot the tax concern or opportunity, and formulate the question to be resolved. In short, students must take the first steps in the tax research process.

Research Problems

Research problems provide further opportunity for students to develop their analytic skills. These problems consist of short scenarios that suggest one or more tax issues. The scenarios conclude with explicit research questions for the students to answer. To find the answers, they need access to either a traditional or an electronic tax library.

Tax Planning Cases

These cases give students an opportunity to integrate their tax knowledge into a business planning framework. Most cases involve taxpayers who must decide whether to undertake a certain transaction or who must choose between alternative transactions. Students must assume the role of tax adviser by recommending a course of action to maximize the after-tax value of the transaction.

Application Problems

LO 6-1 1. Nello Company owed $23,400 overdue rent to its landlord, Bonview, Nello is a desirable tenant, Bonview agreed to settle the overdue account cash payment from Nello. Both Nello and Bonview are accrual basis taxpa

   a. What is the tax consequence to Nello of the settlement of its $23,400 able to Bonview? Compute Nello's net cash outflow from the settleme its tax rate is 35 percent.

   b. What is the tax consequence to Bonview of the settlement of its $23, receivable from Nello? Compute Bonview's net cash inflow from th assuming its tax rate is 21 percent.

Issue Recognition Problems

Identify the tax issue or issues suggested by the following situations, and state the form of a question.

LO 4-1 1. Dr. Phan is a physician with his own medical practice. For the past seve marginal income tax rate has been 37 percent. Dr. Phan's daughter, who is dent, has no taxable income. During the last two months of the year, Dr. P his patients to remit their payments for his services directly to his daughte

LO 4-1 2. Mr. and Mrs. Knight own rental property that generates $4,000 monthly couple is in the highest marginal tax bracket. For Christmas, Mr. and Mrs the uncashed rent checks for October, November, and December to the grandson as a gift.

Research Problems

LO 6-1, 6-6 1. Bontaine Publications, an accrual basis, calendar year corporation, publis weekly and monthly magazines to retail bookstores and newsstands. The sa provides that the retailers may return any unsold magazines during the one- after purchase. Bontaine will refund one-half of the purchase price of each re zine. During December 2023, Bontaine recorded $919,400 of magazine January 2024, Bontaine refunded $82,717 to retailers that returned magazin during December. Can Bontaine reduce its 2023 income by the refund paid

LO 6-1, 6-6 2. CheapTrade, an accrual basis, calendar year corporation, operates a disco brokerage business. CheapTrade accepts orders to buy or sell marketable se customers and charges them a commission fee for effecting the transactio low-cost manner. CheapTrade executes an order on the "trade" date, but titl

---

Tax Planning Cases

LO 4-4 1. Mrs. Oliver is negotiating to purchase a tract of land from DC Compan year taxpayer. DC bought this land six years ago for $480,000. Accordin appraisal, the land is worth $800,000 in the current real estate market. DC's director of tax, the company's profit on the sale will be taxed at 35 sale occurs this year. However, this tax rate will definitely decrease to 21 sale occurs next year. Mrs. Oliver is aware that DC would prefer the sale c However, Mrs. Oliver needs the land immediately to begin construction c outlet. She offers to pay $875,000 for the land with the stipulation that th December 31. Should DC accept Mrs. Oliver's offer?

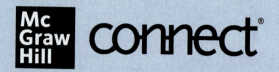

Instructors
The Power of Connections

A complete course platform

Connect enables you to build deeper connections with your students through cohesive digital content and tools, creating engaging learning experiences. We are committed to providing you with the right resources and tools to support all your students along their personal learning journeys.

65%
Less Time Grading

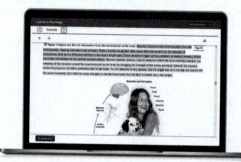

Laptop: Getty Images; Woman/dog: George Doyle/Getty Images

Every learner is unique

In Connect, instructors can assign an adaptive reading experience with SmartBook® 2.0. Rooted in advanced learning science principles, SmartBook 2.0 delivers each student a personalized experience, focusing students on their learning gaps, ensuring that the time they spend studying is time well-spent.
mheducation.com/highered/connect/smartbook

Affordable solutions, added value

Make technology work for you with LMS integration for single sign-on access, mobile access to the digital textbook, and reports to quickly show you how each of your students is doing. And with our Inclusive Access program, you can provide all these tools at the lowest available market price to your students. Ask your McGraw Hill representative for more information.

Solutions for your challenges

A product isn't a solution. Real solutions are affordable, reliable, and come with training and ongoing support when you need it and how you want it. Visit **supportateverystep.com** for videos and resources both you and your students can use throughout the term.

Students
Get Learning that Fits You

Effective tools for efficient studying

Connect is designed to help you be more productive with simple, flexible, intuitive tools that maximize your study time and meet your individual learning needs. Get learning that works for you with Connect.

Study anytime, anywhere

Download the free ReadAnywhere® app and access your online eBook, SmartBook® 2.0, or Adaptive Learning Assignments when it's convenient, even if you're offline. And since the app automatically syncs with your Connect account, all of your work is available every time you open it. Find out more at **mheducation.com/readanywhere**

"I really liked this app—it made it easy to study when you don't have your text-book in front of you."

- Jordan Cunningham, Eastern Washington University

iPhone: Getty Images

Everything you need in one place

Your Connect course has everything you need—whether reading your digital eBook or completing assignments for class—Connect makes it easy to get your work done.

Learning for everyone

McGraw Hill works directly with Accessibility Services Departments and faculty to meet the learning needs of all students. Please contact your Accessibility Services Office and ask them to email accessibility@mheducation.com, or visit **mheducation.com/about/accessibility** for more information.

Online Assignments

NEW! Applying Alteryx Exercises in Connect

Build students' data analytics skills while introducing them to real-world application using Alteryx, a cutting edge data analytics tool. Students will learn to address technical tax issues by downloading and manipulating data to build Alteryx workflows and then interpreting the data to answer auto-graded questions in Connect.

Integrated Excel

Our new Integrated Excel assignments pair the power of Microsoft Excel with the power of Connect. A seamless integration of Excel within Connect, Integrated Excel questions allow students to work in live, auto-graded Excel spreadsheets–no additional logins, no need to upload or download files. Instructors can choose to grade by formula or solution value, and students receive instant cell-level feedback via integrated Check My Work functionality.

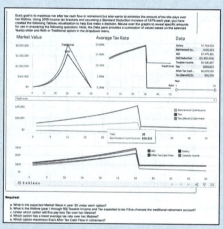

Source: Internal Revenue Service

Tableau Dashboard Activities

Tableau Dashboard Activities allow students to explore live Tableau dashboards directly integrated into *Connect* through interactive filters and menus as well as auto-graded questions focused on both calculations and analysis. Students can check their understanding and apply what they are learning within the framework of analytics and critical thinking.

Auto-Graded Tax Form Simulations

The auto-graded tax form simulation, assignable within *Connect,* provides a much-improved student experience when solving the tax form–based problems. The tax form simulation allows students to apply tax concepts by completing the actual tax forms online with automatic feedback and grading for both students and professors.

Auto-Graded Tax Planning Cases and Application Problems

Connect helps students learn more efficiently by providing feedback and practice material when they need it, where they need it. *Connect* grades homework automatically and gives immediate feedback on any questions students may have missed. The extensive assignable, gradable end-of-chapter content includes static and algorithmic versions of tax planning cases (some in the form of auto-graded tax form problems) and application problems. Also, select questions have been redesigned to test students' knowledge more fully. They now include tables for students to work through rather than requiring that all calculations be done offline.

UWorld CPA

UWorld CPA Review content is integrated directly into your Connect course and provides the highest quality CPA Exam multiple-choice questions, helping students master key concepts they will see on the CPA Exam. In addition to access throughout Connect,

UWorld provides a wide variety of options for you to integrate their entire suite of CPA Review resources directly into your program. To learn more visit: **https://accounting.uworld.com/cpa-review/partner/university/**.

TaxAct

Users of *Principles of Taxation for Business and Investment Planning* now have access to TaxAct, one of the leading preparation software companies in the market today.

Please note, TaxAct is compatible only with PCs and not Macs. However, we offer easy-to-complete licensing agreement templates that are accessible within *Connect* and the Instructor Resources Center to enable school computer labs to download the software onto campus hardware for free.

Test Builder in *Connect*

Available within *Connect,* Test Builder is a cloud-based tool that enables instructors to format tests that can be printed or administered within a LMS. Test Builder offers a modern, streamlined interface for easy content configuration that matches course needs, without requiring a download.

Test Builder allows you to:

- Access all test bank content from a particular title.
- Easily pinpoint the most relevant content through robust filtering options.
- Manipulate the order of questions or scramble questions and/or answers.
- Pin questions to a specific location within a test.
- Determine your preferred treatment of algorithmic questions.
- Choose the layout and spacing.
- Add instructions and configure default settings.

Test Builder provides a secure interface for better protection of content and allows for just-in-time updates to flow directly into assessments.

Tegrity Campus: Lectures 24/7

Tegrity in *Connect* is a tool that makes class time available 24/7 by automatically capturing every lecture. With a simple one-click start-and-stop process, you capture all computer screens and corresponding audio in a format that is easy to search, frame by frame. Students can replay any part of any class with easy-to-use, browser-based viewing on a PC, Mac, iPod, or other mobile device.

Educators know that the more students can see, hear, and experience class resources, the better they learn. In fact, studies prove it. Tegrity's unique search feature helps students efficiently find what they need, when they need it, across an entire semester of class recordings.

Help turn your students' study time into learning moments immediately supported by your lecture. With Tegrity, you also increase intent listening and class participation by easing students' concerns about note-taking. Using Tegrity in Connect will make it more likely you will see students' faces, not the tops of their heads.

Remote Proctoring and Browser-Locking Capabilities

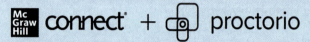

Remote proctoring and browser-locking capabilities, hosted by Proctorio within *Connect,* provide control of the assessment environment by enabling security options and verifying the identity of the student.

Seamlessly integrated within *Connect,* these services allow instructors to control students' assessment experience by restricting browser activity, recording students' activity, and verifying students are doing their own work.

Instant and detailed reporting gives instructors an at-a-glance view of potential academic integrity concerns, thereby avoiding personal bias and supporting evidence-based claims.

ReadAnywhere

Read or study when it's convenient for you with McGraw Hill's free ReadAnywhere app. Available for iOS or Android smartphones or tablets, ReadAnywhere gives users access to McGraw Hill tools including the eBook and SmartBook 2.0 or Adaptive Learning Assignments in Connect. Take notes, highlight, and complete assignments offline—all of your work will sync when you open the app with WiFi access. Log in with your McGraw Hill Connect username and password to start learning—anytime, anywhere!

Writing Assignment

Available within Connect and Connect Master, the Writing Assignment tool delivers a learning experience to help students improve their written communication skills and conceptual understanding. As an instructor you can assign, monitor, grade, and provide feedback on writing more efficiently and effectively.

Create

Your Book, Your Way

McGraw Hill's Content Collections Powered by Create® is a self-service website that enables instructors to create custom course materials—print and eBooks—by drawing upon McGraw Hill's comprehensive, cross-disciplinary content. Choose what you want from our high-quality textbooks, articles, and cases. Combine it with your own content quickly and easily, and tap into other rights-secured, third-party content such as readings, cases, and articles. Content can be arranged in a way that makes the most sense for your course and you can include the course name and information as well. Choose the best format for your course: color print, black-and-white print, or eBook. The eBook can be included in your Connect course and is available on the free ReadAnywhere app for smartphone or tablet access as well. When you are finished customizing, you will receive a free digital copy to review in just minutes! Visit McGraw Hill Create®—**www.mcgrawhillcreate.com**—today and begin building!

Acknowledgments

We want to thank the many friends and colleagues who continue to share their ideas for this textbook. We particularly want to acknowledge the contribution of Professor Pat Wilkie (University of Virginia) and Professor Jim Young (Northern Illinois University). Their article titled "Teaching the Introductory Tax Course: A Template of the Federal Income Tax Formula, Taxpayer Activities, and Taxpayer Entities," in the *Journal of the American Taxation Association* (Fall 1997), profoundly influenced the organization of this book. Thank you to our accuracy checker who worked on the 26th edition: Matt Lowenkron of Glendale Community College–Arizona. Special thanks to J.T. Eagan of Purdue University Northwest for developing the data analytics problems available in *Connect*. Thank you also to J.T. Eagan and Temple University instructors Wayne Williams, David Jones, and Ronald Unger for the development of the Tableau Dashboard Activities. Thanks also to the individuals who reviewed the 2021 and previous editions of the text. Their expert comments were invaluable, and this edition is significantly improved because of their involvement:

Joe Assalone, *Rowan College at Gloucester County*

Valeriya Avdeev, *William Paterson University*

Robyn Barrett, *St. Louis Community College*

Jeanne Bedell, *Keiser University*

Marcia Behrens, *Nichols College*

David Berman, *Community College of Philadelphia*

Cynthia Bird, *Tidewater Community College*

Lisa Blum, *University of Louisville*

Cindy Bortman Boggess, *Babson College*

Esther Bunn, *Stephen F. Austin State University*

Alisa Carini, *University of California–San Diego (Extension)*

Ernest Carraway, *North Carolina State University*

Ronald Carter, *Patrick Henry Community College*

Cynthia Caruso, *Endicott College*

Max Chao, *University of California–Irvine*

Eric Chen, *Saint Joseph College*

Christine Cheng, *Louisiana State University*

Marilyn Ciolino, *Delgado Community College*

Wayne Clark, *Southwest Baptist University*

Bradrick Cripe, *Northern Illinois University*

Rick Crosser, *Metropolitan State University of Denver*

Nichole Dauenhauer, *Lakeland Community College*

Susan Davis, *Green River College*

Julie Dilling, *Moraine Park Technical College*

Reed Easton, *Seton Hall University*

Elizabeth Ekmekjian, *William Paterson University*

Ann Escarco, *McHenry County College*

Michael Fagan, *Raritan Valley Community College*

Brian Fink, *Danville Area Community College*

Micah Frankel, *California State University-East Bay*

R. Thomas Godwin, *Purdue University*

David Golub, *Northeastern University*

Marina Grau, *Houston Community College*

Patrick Griffin, *Lewis University*

John Grigsby, *Philadelphia University*

Sandy Grunewald, *California State University-Monterey Bay*

Joe Holdren, *Muskingum University*

Carol Hughes, *Asheville Buncombe Technical Community College*

Paul Johnson, *Mississippi Gulf Coast Community College*

Andrew Junikiewicz, *Temple University*

Edmund Keim, *Colorado Technical University*

Janice Klimek, *University of Central Missouri*

Pamela Knight, *Columbus Technical College*

Dawn Konicek, *Idaho State University*

Teresa Lightner, *University of North Texas*

Gwendolyn McFadden, *North Carolina A&T State University*

Lois McWhorter, *Somerset Community College*

Michele Dawn Meckfessel, *University of Missouri-St. Louis*

Richard Mole, *Hiram College*

Mike Nee, *Cape Cod Community College*

Jamie O'Brien, *University of Notre Dame*

Ronald Pearson, *Bay College*

Martina Peng, *Franklin University*

Susan Porter, *University of Virginia*

Ian Redpath, *Canisius College*

John Robertson, *Arkansas State University*

Morgan Rockett, *Moberly Area Community College*

Ray Rodriguez, *Southern Illinois University-Carbondale*

Deanna Sharp, *University of Missouri*

Georgi Smatrakaleve, *Florida Atlantic University*

Angela Sneed, *Saint Leo University*

Adam Spoolstra, *Johnson County Community College*

A.J. Stagliano, *Saint Joseph's University*

Jason Stanfield, *Ball State University*

George Starbuck, *McMurry University*

Randall Stone, *East Central University*

Ron Unger, *Temple University*

George Violette, *University of Southern Maine*

Cassandra Weitzenkamp, *Peru State College*

Xiaoli Yuan, *Elizabeth City State University*

We are grateful to the entire McGraw Hill team for their professional support. In particular, we want to acknowledge Tim Vertovec; Kathleen Klehr; Michele Janicek; Jill Eccher; Kaitlin Murray; Angela Norris; and Katie Jones-Aiello of Agate Publishing.

Sally M. Jones
University of Virginia

Shelley C. Rhoades-Catanach
Villanova University

Sandra R. Callaghan
Texas Christian University

Thomas R. Kubick
University of Nebraska–Lincoln

Introduction to Students

Principles of Taxation for Business and Investment Planning explores the role that taxes play in modern life. The book is written for business students who have completed introductory courses in accounting and finance and are familiar with basic business concepts. Those of you who fit this description, regardless of your future career path, will make decisions in which you must evaluate the effect of taxes. At the most fundamental level, all business decisions have the same economic objective: maximization of long-term wealth through cash flow enhancement. The cash flow from any transaction depends on the tax consequences. Therefore, businessmen and -women must appreciate the role of taxes before they can make intelligent decisions, whether on behalf of their firm or on their personal behalf.

Taxes as Business Costs

When businesspeople are asked to identify the common goal of all business decisions, their immediate response tends to be that the goal is to increase profits. When prompted to think past the current year, most eventually conclude that the long-term goal of business decisions is to maximize the value of the firm. In this text, a **firm** is a generic business organization. Firms include sole proprietorships, partnerships, limited liability companies, subchapter S and regular corporations, and any other arrangement through which people carry on a profit-motivated activity. Firm managers know that short-term profits and long-term value are enhanced when operating costs, including taxes, are controlled. Experienced managers never regard taxes as fixed or unavoidable costs. As you will soon discover, opportunities abound for controlling the tax cost of doing business.

The preceding paragraph suggests that tax planning means reducing tax costs to maximize the value of the firm. Firms can reduce taxes by any number of strategies. However, tax cost is only one variable that managers must consider in making business decisions. A strategy that reduces taxes may also have undesirable consequences, such as reducing revenues or increasing nontax costs. Because of nontax variables, the strategy with the least tax cost may not be the best strategy. Therefore, tax minimization in and of itself may be a short-sighted objective. This point is so elementary yet so important: *Effective tax planning must take into account both tax and nontax factors.* When faced with competing strategies, managers should implement the strategy that maximizes firm value, even when that strategy has a higher tax cost than the alternatives. In other words, managers should never let the tax tail wag the business dog.

Taxes as Household Expenditures

Principles of Taxation for Business and Investment Planning concentrates on the income taxation of business activities and organizations. This doesn't mean that the tax rules applying to individuals are ignored. Quite the contrary. For income tax purposes, individuals and the profit-making activities in which they engage are entwined. As we will observe over and over again, the ultimate taxpayers in every business are the people who own and operate that business.

As you study this text, consider your own role as a lifelong taxpayer. Regardless of who you are, where you live, or how you earn and spend your money, you will pay taxes on a regular basis to any number of governments. In fact, in the United States, taxes are the single largest household expenditure. According to data from the Tax Foundation, Americans devote about 2 hours and 15 minutes of every 8-hour workday to earn enough to pay their local, state, and federal taxes.

People who are clueless about taxes must take a passive role, participating in a tax system they don't understand and over which they exercise no control. In contrast, if you understand how taxes relate to your life, you can take an active role. You can take positive steps to minimize your personal tax to the fullest extent allowed by law. You can make informed financial decisions to take advantage of tax-saving opportunities. You can draw rational conclusions about the efficiency and fairness of existing tax laws and can assess the merit of competing tax reform proposals. Finally, you can change the tax system by participating as a voter in the democratic process.

The Text's Objectives

Principles of Taxation for Business and Investment Planning has three objectives that motivate the overall design of the text, the selection and ordering of topics, and the development of each topic: (1) introducing tax policy issues, (2) bridging the gap between finance and tax, and (3) teaching the framework of the income tax.

Introducing Tax Policy Issues

The first objective is to acquaint you with the economic and social policy implications of the tax systems by which governments raise revenues. Most of the subject matter of the text pertains to today's tax environment and how successful businesses adapt to and take advantage of that environment. But the text also raises normative issues concerning the efficiency and equity of many features of the tax environment. You will learn how certain provisions of the tax law are intended to further the government's fiscal policy goals. You are invited to evaluate these goals and to question whether the tax system is an appropriate mechanism for accomplishing the goals.

The text identifies potentially negative aspects of the tax environment. It explains how taxes may adversely affect individual behavior or cause unintended and undesirable outcomes. You will be asked to consider whether certain provisions of the tax law favor one group of taxpayers over another and whether such favoritism is justifiable on any ethical grounds. After probing both the strengths and the weaknesses of the current tax system, you can draw your own conclusions as to how the system can be improved.

Bridging the Gap between Finance and Tax

The second objective of the text is to bridge the academic gap between the study of financial theory and the study of tax law. Finance courses teach students how to make decisions on the basis of after-tax cash flows. However, these courses give only rudimentary instruction on determining the tax consequences of transactions and overlook the possibilities for controlling tax costs to maximize cash flows. In extreme cases, financial models simply ignore tax consequences by assuming that business decisions are made in a tax-free environment.

Traditional tax law courses err in the opposite direction. These courses teach students to apply statutory rules to well-defined, closed-fact situations to determine the tax consequences. Correct application of the rule is the learning objective. Students are not required to integrate the tax consequences of transactions into a business decision-making framework. In other words, they don't translate tax outcomes into cash flows. Traditional law courses may fail to encourage students to consider how closed-fact situations can be restructured to change the tax outcome and improve financial results. Consequently, students often develop the habit of analyzing transactions from a backward-looking *compliance* perspective rather than a forward-looking *planning* perspective.

The focus of *Principles of Taxation for Business and Investment Planning* is the common ground shared by financial theory and tax law. The connecting links between the two disciplines are stressed throughout the text. You will learn how effective business planning depends on an accurate assessment of relevant tax factors. Tax rules and regulations are presented and illustrated in the context of a decision-making framework. Admittedly, these rules and regulations are tough to master. Two observations should give you reassurance. First, while the tax law is extremely technical and complex, the application of its underlying principles to business decision making is relatively straightforward. Second, you can learn to appreciate tax planning strategies without becoming a tax-compliance expert.

Teaching the Framework of the Income Tax

The third objective of *Principles of Taxation for Business and Investment Planning* is to teach the framework of the federal income tax, the dominant feature of the modern tax environment. This framework has been remarkably stable over time, even though the details of the law change every year. Students who learn the framework needn't worry that their knowledge will be outdated when Congress enacts its next revenue bill.

The federal income tax system has a bad reputation as an impenetrable, intractable body of law. While the income tax law is every bit as complicated as its critics suggest, its framework consists of a manageable number of basic principles. The principles are internally consistent and underlie many technical provisions. By concentrating on these principles, you can attain a sufficient level of tax knowledge in a single introductory course. You will not be a tax expert, but you will be tax literate. You may not be capable of implementing sophisticated tax planning strategies, but you will appreciate how those strategies can improve cash flows and maximize wealth.

Because this text takes a conceptual approach to the tax law, narrowly drawn provisions, exceptions, limitations, and special cases are deemphasized. Details with the potential to confuse rather than clarify tax principles are usually relegated to footnotes. When we do examine a detailed provision of the law, the detail should illuminate an underlying concept. Or we may discuss a thorny technical rule just to emphasize the practical difficulties encountered by tax professionals who don't have the luxury of dealing with concepts.

The conceptual approach should sensitize you to the tax implications of transactions and cultivate your ability to ask good tax questions. This approach downplays the importance of the answers to these questions. Knowing the answers or, more precisely, *finding* the answers to tax questions is the job of accountants and attorneys who devote long hours in their research libraries to that end. A tax-sensitive business manager knows when to consult these experts and can help formulate the tax issues for the expert to resolve. The text's emphasis on issue recognition rather than issue resolution is reflected in the problems at the end of each chapter. Many of these problems ask you to analyze a fact situation and simply identify tax concerns or opportunities. Other problems present you with facts suggesting tax issues with no correct solution.

A Word to Accounting Majors

Principles of Taxation for Business and Investment Planning is an ideal introductory text for those of you who are concentrating in accounting and who may even plan to specialize in taxation. You will benefit enormously from mastering the framework of the income tax as the first step in your professional education. This mastery will be the foundation for the future study of advanced topics. You will gain a command of basic principles on which to rely as you develop an instinct for your subject—a facility for diagnosing the tax issues suggested by unfamiliar and unusual transactions.

The conceptual approach is appropriate for the first tax course because it concentrates on broad issues concerning most taxpayers instead of narrow problems encountered by only a few taxpayers. If you learn these issues, you will be well prepared to expand and deepen your tax knowledge through professional experience. You will understand that taxes are only one aspect of the economic decision-making process. Because of this understanding, those of you who become tax professionals will be equipped to serve your clients not just as tax specialists but as business advisers.

The text also examines the interrelation of taxes and financial reporting. Taxes are a major cost of doing business. That cost and related assets and liabilities are reported in business financial statements in accordance with the requirements of generally accepted accounting principles. While your financial accounting courses will likely cover these requirements in detail, this text approaches these issues from a tax perspective. You will become very familiar with the types of book/tax differences that are common in typical business operations. An understanding of these differences is critical for both tax reporting and financial reporting.

CPA Exam Preparation

This text provides excellent preparation for the CPA exam. The text covers approximately 90 percent of the specified federal tax content of the Regulation portion of the current exam and a similar portion of the tax content in the Core of the CPA Evolution Model Curriculum proposed for the new exam expected to launch in 2024. The 10 percent remaining content consists of advanced topics usually covered in a second semester undergraduate tax course.

The CPA exam includes a variety of interactive problems designed to test your knowledge of the tax law and your ability to apply the law in realistic situations. Many of the problems are in the form of *simulations:* short cases in which you must demonstrate your tax research and analytic skills. These are the exact skills that you will learn, practice, and refine as you work your way through *Principles of Taxation for Business and Investment Planning*.

If your instructor is using *Connect*'s auto-graded homework for this course, he/she has the ability to assign Roger CPA Review multiple-choice questions and task-based simulations, providing you with even more opportunities to prepare for the CPA exam.

Conclusion

The authors hope this introduction has conveyed the message that people who decide on a particular course of action without considering the tax outcomes are making an uninformed, and possibly incorrect, decision. By proceeding with the course of study contained in this text, you will learn to recognize the tax implications of a whole spectrum of transactions. Upon entering the business world, you will be prepared to make decisions incorporating this knowledge. You will spot tax problems as they arise and will call in a tax professional before, rather than after, a transaction with profound tax consequences. Finally, you will understand that effective tax planning can save more money than the most diligent tax compliance.

Brief Contents

Contents

Exploring the Tax Environment

Chapter One

Taxes and Taxing Jurisdictions

Learning Objectives

After studying this chapter, you should be able to:

LO 1-1. Define *tax, taxpayer, incidence,* and *jurisdiction.*

LO 1-2. Express the relationship between tax base, rate, and revenue as a formula.

LO 1-3. Describe the taxes levied by local governments.

LO 1-4. Describe the taxes levied by state governments.

LO 1-5. Describe the taxes levied by the federal government.

LO 1-6. Explain the structure of the value-added tax levied by foreign governments.

LO 1-7. Summarize why different jurisdictions compete for revenues from the same taxpayer.

LO 1-8. Discuss the reasons why governments modify their tax systems.

LO 1-9. Identify the three primary sources of federal tax law.

An explorer planning a journey through unknown territory prepares by inspecting a map of the territory. The explorer becomes familiar with topographic features such as major highways, mountain ranges, lakes and rivers, and population centers, and gathers information about the climate of the region and the language and customs of its inhabitants. This preliminary knowledge helps the explorer chart the course and reduces the danger that progress will be impeded by unforeseen circumstances.

For students who are just beginning their study of taxation, the tax environment in which individuals and organizations must function is unknown territory. Chapter 1 serves as a map of this territory. The chapter begins by describing the environment in terms of the relationship between taxes, taxpayers, and governments. It identifies the major types of taxes that businesses routinely encounter and examines how governments with overlapping jurisdictions compete for tax revenues. The chapter also describes how data analytics is often used by tax authorities and businesses to respond to the complexity inherent in the tax environment. By reading the chapter, you will gain a familiarity with the tax environment that will help you understand the role of taxes in the business decision-making process.

The chapter should alert you to two important features of the tax environment. First, taxes are *pervasive* because they are so widespread, come in so many varieties, and affect virtually every aspect of modern life. Second, taxes are *dynamic* because the tax laws change so frequently. The rate of change reflects the fact that the economic and political assumptions on which tax structures are based are constantly evolving. While these two features make the tax environment a challenging one for business managers, they also create a vitality that makes the study of tax planning so fascinating.

SOME BASIC TERMINOLOGY

LO 1-1

Define *tax, taxpayer, incidence*, and *jurisdiction*.

Before beginning our exploration of the tax environment, we must define some basic terminology. A **tax** can be defined as a payment to support the cost of government. A tax differs from a fine or penalty imposed by a government because a tax is not intended to deter or punish unacceptable behavior. On the other hand, taxes are compulsory rather than voluntary on the part of the payer. A tax differs from a user's fee because the payment of a tax doesn't entitle the payer to a specific good or service in return. In the abstract, citizens receive any number of government benefits for their tax dollars. Nevertheless, the value of government benefits received by any particular person isn't correlated to the tax that person must pay. As the Supreme Court explained

> A tax is not an assessment of benefits. It is . . . a means of distributing the burden of the cost of government. The only benefit to which the taxpayer is constitutionally entitled is that derived from his enjoyment of the privileges of living in an organized society, established and safeguarded by the devotion of taxes to public purposes.[1]

A **taxpayer** is any person or organization required by law to pay a tax to a governmental authority. In the United States, the term *person* refers to both natural persons (individuals) and corporations. Corporations are entities organized under the laws of one of the 50 states or the District of Columbia. These corporate entities generally enjoy the same legal rights, privileges, and protections as individuals. The taxing jurisdictions in this country uniformly regard corporations as entities separate and distinct from their shareholders. Consequently, corporations are taxpayers in their own right.

The **incidence** of a tax refers to the ultimate economic burden represented by the tax. Most people jump to the conclusion that the person or organization that makes a direct tax payment to the government bears the incidence of such tax, but in some cases, the payer can shift the incidence to a third party. Consider the following examples:

Income Tax Incidence	Government G enacts a new tax on corporate business profits. A manufacturing corporation with a monopoly on a product in great demand by the public responds to the new tax by increasing the retail price at which it sells the product. In this case, the corporation is nominally the taxpayer and must remit the new tax to the government. The economic burden of the tax falls on the corporation's customers who indirectly pay the tax in the form of a higher price for the same product.

Property Tax Incidence	Mr. Blaire owns an eight-unit apartment building. Currently, the tenants living in each unit pay $9,600 annual rent. The local government notifies Mr. Blaire that his property tax on the apartment building will increase by $5,400 for the next year. Mr. Blaire reacts by informing his tenants that their rent for the next year will increase by $675. Consequently, Mr. Blaire's total revenue will increase by $5,400. Although Mr. Blaire is the taxpayer who must remit the property tax to the government, the incidence of the tax increase is on the tenants who indirectly pay the tax through higher rent.

[1] Source: *Carmichael v. Southern Coal & Coke Co.*, 301 U.S. 495, 522 (1937).

The right of a government to levy tax on a specific person or organization is referred to as **jurisdiction.** Jurisdiction exists because of some rational linkage between the government and the taxpayer. For instance, our federal government has jurisdiction to tax any individual who is a U.S. citizen or who permanently resides in this country.

U.S. Jurisdiction over Citizens	Mrs. Fowler was born in Kentucky and is a U.S. citizen. However, she has lived her entire adult life in Cape Town, South Africa. Even though Mrs. Fowler is a permanent resident of a foreign country, the United States claims jurisdiction to tax her entire income.

U.S. Jurisdiction over Permanent Residents	In 2022, Francoise Benet, a citizen of Algeria, was issued a Green Card authorizing her to reside and work in the United States. Because Ms. Benet is a permanent resident, the United States claims jurisdiction to tax her entire income.

The government also claims jurisdiction to tax individuals who are neither U.S. citizens nor residents (nonresident aliens) but who earn income from a source within the United States.

U.S. Jurisdiction over Nonresident Aliens	Mr. Kohala is a citizen of Spain and resides in Madrid. He owns an interest in a partnership formed under Florida law that conducts a business within the state. Even though Mr. Kohala is a nonresident alien, the United States claims jurisdiction to tax him on his share of the partnership income because the income was earned in this country.

The Relationship between Base, Rate, and Revenue

Taxes are usually characterized by reference to their base. A **tax base** is an item, occurrence, transaction, or activity with respect to which a tax is levied. Tax bases are usually expressed in monetary terms.[2] For instance, real property taxes are levied on the ownership of land and buildings, and the dollar value of the property is the tax base. When designing a tax, governments try to identify tax bases that taxpayers can't easily avoid or conceal. In this respect, real property is an excellent tax base because it can't be moved or hidden, and its ownership is a matter of public record.

The dollar amount of a tax is calculated by multiplying the base by a tax rate, which is usually expressed as a percentage. This relationship is reflected in the following formula:

$$\text{Tax (T)} = \text{Rate (r)} \times \text{Base (B)}$$

A single percentage that applies to the entire tax base is described as a **flat rate.** Many types of taxes use a **graduated rate** structure consisting of multiple percentages that apply to specified portions or **brackets** of the tax base.

Graduated Rate Structure	Jurisdiction J imposes a tax on real property located within the jurisdiction. The tax is based on the market value of the real property and consists of three rate brackets:

Percentage Rate	Bracket
1%	Value from –0– to $100,000
2%	Value from $100,001 to $225,000
3%	Value in excess of $225,000

(continued)

[2] A per capita, or head, tax requires each person subject to the tax to pay the same amount to the government. This antiquated type of tax does not have a monetary base.

Company C owns a tract of real property worth $500,000. The tax on this property is $11,750:

1% of $100,000 (first bracket of base)	$ 1,000
2% of $125,000 (second bracket of base)	2,500
3% of $275,000 (third bracket of base)	8,250
Total tax on $500,000 base	$11,750

The term **revenue** refers to the total tax collected by the government and available for public use. Note that in the equation T = r × B, the tax is a function of both the rate and the base. This mathematical relationship suggests that governments can increase revenues by increasing either of these two variables in the design of their tax systems.

Transaction- or Activity-Based Taxes

Taxes can be characterized by the frequency with which they are levied. A tax can be **event or transaction based** so that the tax is triggered only when an event occurs or a transaction takes place. A familiar example is a sales tax levied on the purchase of retail goods and services. A second example is an estate tax levied on the transfer of property from a decedent to the decedent's heirs. Taxpayers may have some degree of control over the payment of these types of taxes. By avoiding the event or transaction on which the tax is based, a person avoids the tax. With certain taxes, such as excise taxes levied on the purchase of liquor and cigarettes, people have total discretion as to whether they ever pay the tax. By choosing not to drink alcoholic beverages or not to smoke, they are also choosing not to pay the excise tax. In contrast, no individual can avoid an estate or inheritance tax levied on the transfer of property at death by indefinitely postponing the event that triggers the tax!

A tax can be described as **activity based** when it is imposed on the cumulative result of an ongoing activity. Taxpayers must maintain records of the activity, summarize the result at periodic intervals, and pay tax accordingly. An annual income tax is a prime example of an activity-based tax.

An **income tax** is imposed on the periodic inflow of wealth resulting from a person's economic activities. For persons who engage in a limited number or variety of economic transactions, the measurement of taxable income is relatively simple. For persons who engage in complex activities involving many economic transactions, the measurement of taxable income can be a challenging process.

Earmarked Taxes

Tax Talk
Washington, D.C., levies a five-cent-per-bag tax on disposable plastic and paper bags. All revenue from the tax is earmarked for the Anacostia River Clean Up and Protection Fund. In fiscal year 2021, over $1.9 million in bag fees were collected from regulated businesses.

Another way to characterize taxes is to link them to government expenditures. The revenues from some taxes are **earmarked** to finance designated projects. For instance, revenues from local real property taxes are typically earmarked to support public school systems. Revenues generated by the federal payroll and self-employment taxes fund the Social Security system (Old-Age, Survivors, and Disability Insurance Trust Fund) and Medicare (Hospital and Supplementary Medical Insurance Trust Funds). Revenues from so-called environmental excise taxes on businesses are appropriated to the Environmental Protection Agency's Hazardous Substance Superfund, which subsidizes the cleanup and disposal of toxic wastes. In contrast to these earmarked taxes, revenues from taxes that pour into a general fund may be spent for any public purpose authorized by the government.

THE PERVASIVE NATURE OF TAXATION

Supreme Court Justice Potter Stewart perfectly described the U.S. tax environment by observing

> Virtually all persons or objects in this country . . . may have tax problems. Every day the economy generates thousands of sales, loans, gifts, purchases, leases, wills, and the like, which suggest the possibility of tax problems for somebody. Our economy is "tax relevant" in almost every detail.[3]

Why are taxes so pervasive in our modern world? One reason is the multiplicity of jurisdictions in which people conduct business. Every firm operates in some geographic location within the taxing jurisdiction of one or more local governments. Local governments include townships, cities, municipalities, counties, and school districts, all of which have operating budgets financed by tax revenues. Local governments are subject to the authority of state governments, and state constitutions or statutes typically regulate the nature and extent of local taxation.

The governments of each of the 50 states and the District of Columbia levy taxes on firms conducting business within their geographic territory. In turn, the states' taxing jurisdiction is subject to federal constitutional and statutory constraints. The federal government represents still another jurisdiction that taxes business activities conducted within the United States. Consequently, even the smallest domestic enterprise is usually required to pay taxes to support at least three different levels of government. If a domestic enterprise conducts any business in a foreign country, the number of potential taxing jurisdictions is even higher.

Business managers who want to control tax costs must be aware of any local, state, federal, or foreign tax for which the firm is, or might become, liable. In the next section of Chapter 1, we will survey the types of taxes levied by different jurisdictions to finance their governments.

Local Taxes

Local governments depend heavily on real property taxes and personal property taxes, which are frequently referred to as **ad valorem taxes.** According to the most recent census data, these two taxes account for more than 70 percent of local government tax revenues.[4]

Real Property Taxes

All 50 states allow local jurisdictions to tax the ownership of real property sited within the jurisdiction. Real property, or **realty,** is defined as land and whatever is erected or growing on the land or permanently affixed to it. This definition encompasses any subsurface features such as mineral deposits.

Real property taxes are levied annually and are based on the market value of the property as determined by the local government. Elected or appointed officials called **tax assessors** are responsible for deriving the value of realty and informing the owners of the assessed value. Property owners who disagree with the assessed value may challenge the assessment in an administrative or judicial proceeding. A unique feature of real property taxes is that the tax rate is determined annually, according to the jurisdiction's need for revenue for that particular budget year.

Property Tax Rates	Springfield's city council decides that the city must raise $12 million of real property tax revenues during its next fiscal year. Because Springfield's tax assessor determines that the total value of real property located within the city limits is currently $230 million, the council sets the tax rate for the upcoming year at 5.22 percent ($12 million ÷ $230 million). This rate can be adjusted each year, depending on Springfield's future revenue needs and the fluctuating value of its real property tax base.

[3] Source: *United States* v. *Bisceglia,* 420 U.S. 141, 154 (1975).

[4] These and subsequent data are obtained from *Quarterly Summaries of Federal, State, and Local Tax Revenues,* Bureau of the Census, U.S. Department of Commerce.

Local governments may establish different tax rates for different classifications of property. For instance, a township may choose to tax commercial realty at a higher rate than residential realty, or a county might tax land used for agricultural purposes at a higher rate than land maintained for scenic purposes. Governments may grant permanent tax-exempt status to realty owned by charitable, religious, or educational organizations and publicly owned realty. They may also grant temporary tax exemptions called **abatements** for limited periods of time. Governments usually grant abatements to lure commercial enterprises into their jurisdiction, thereby creating jobs and benefiting the local economy. From a business manager's point of view, the tax savings from abatements can be significant. Consequently, firms contemplating expansion into new jurisdictions frequently negotiate for property tax abatements before acquiring or beginning construction of realty within the jurisdiction.

Tax Incentives for Boeing	In 2014, Boeing selected a site in Washington State for a new facility to manufacture its 777X airliners. In return, Boeing received a tax incentive package from the state expected to be worth over $8 billion to the aerospace giant. Good Jobs First, a group that tracks government subsidies to business, says the state's new Boeing package is the biggest tax subsidy in U.S. history.

Personal Property Taxes

Most states permit localities to tax the ownership of **personalty,** defined as any asset that is not realty. Like real property taxes, personal property taxes are based on the value of the asset subject to tax. However, such value isn't usually assessed by a government official. Instead, individuals and organizations must determine the value of their taxable personalty and render (i.e., report) the value to the tax assessor.

There are three general classes of taxable personalty: household tangibles, business tangibles, and intangibles.[5] Household tangibles commonly subject to tax include automobiles and recreational vehicles, pleasure boats, and private airplanes. Taxable business tangibles include inventory, furniture and fixtures, machinery, and equipment. The most common intangible assets subject to personal property tax are marketable securities (stocks and bonds).

During the last century, personal property taxation has declined steadily as a revenue source. One reason for the decline is that this tax is much more difficult to enforce than other taxes. Personalty is characterized by its mobility; owners can easily hide their assets or move them to another jurisdiction. Any governmental attempt to actively search for personalty, particularly household tangibles, could violate individual privacy rights. Governments have responded to these practical problems by linking the payment of personal property tax to asset registration or licensing requirements.

Boat Tax Linked to State Registration	All motorboats used on the public waters of Virginia must be registered and titled with the state's Department of Game and Inland Fisheries. Each year, this department provides a list of registered watercraft to the city of Virginia Beach, which then imposes a $1.50 tax on each $100 of value of watercraft permanently garaged, docked, or parked in the city.

---

[5] Tangible property has physical substance that can be perceived by sight or touch. Intangible property has no physical substance.

State Taxes

LO 1-4
Describe the taxes levied by state governments.

In the aggregate, state governments rely in almost equal measure on sales taxes and income taxes as major sources of funds. These two kinds of taxes account for approximately 90 percent of total state tax revenues.

Retail Sales, Use, and Excise Taxes

Tax Talk
On average, one-third of state and local government spending is devoted to public education.

Forty-five states and the District of Columbia impose a tax on in-state sales of tangible personal property and selected services. (The exceptions are Alaska, Delaware, Montana, New Hampshire, and Oregon.) Moreover, 38 states (including Alaska and Montana) allow local governments to levy sales taxes. Sales taxes have been the great growth taxes of state governments during the past century.[6] In 1930, only two states had a general sales tax. During the depression era, revenue-starved states began enacting temporary sales taxes as an emergency measure. These taxes proved to be both simple and effective and soon became a permanent feature of state tax systems. Sales taxes produce about $290 billion of annual revenue, roughly one-third of all state tax collections. Sales taxes also have become an important revenue source for local governments, although property taxes remain their primary revenue source.

A **sales tax** is typically based on the retail price of tangible personalty. State and local sales tax rates range from 1.76 percent of the dollar amount in Alaska to 9.55 percent in Louisiana. Sales taxes are broad-based and apply to most types of consumer goods and even to selected consumer services, such as telephone and cable television service.[7] The tax may take the form of a business tax levied on the seller or, more commonly, a consumption tax levied on the purchaser who is the final user of the goods or services. Regardless of the form, the seller is responsible for collecting the tax at point of sale and remitting it to the state government.

Tax Talk
Louisiana residents bear the heaviest state and local tax burden (9.55 cents of every dollar of income) while Alaska residents bear the lightest (1.76 cents of every dollar of income). The national average state and local tax burden is 6.57 cents of every dollar of income.

Every state with a sales tax imposes a complementary **use tax** on the ownership, possession, or consumption of tangible goods within the state. The use tax applies only if the owner of the goods didn't pay the state's sales tax when the goods were purchased. A use tax acts as a backstop to a sales tax by discouraging residents from purchasing products in neighboring jurisdictions with lower sales tax rates. The one-two punch of a sales and use tax theoretically ensures that state residents are taxed on all purchases of consumer goods, regardless of where the purchase occurred. As a result, merchants operating in high-tax states are not at a competitive disadvantage with respect to merchants operating in low-tax states.

As a general rule, consumers may take a credit for out-of-state sales taxes against their in-state use tax liability.

Use Tax Calculation

Ms. Goode is a resident of Rhode Island, which has a 7 percent sales and use tax. While on vacation in Hawaii, Ms. Goode purchased a diamond bracelet for $7,600 and paid $337 (4.44 percent) Hawaiian sales tax. Because Ms. Goode didn't pay her own state's sales tax on the purchase, she owes $195 use tax to Rhode Island. The use tax equals $532 (7 percent of $7,600) minus a $337 credit for the Hawaiian sales tax. If Ms. Goode had vacationed in California and paid that state's 8.82 percent sales tax on her jewelry purchase, she would not owe any Rhode Island use tax.

[6] Jerome Hellerstein and Walter Hellerstein, *State Taxation,* vol. II (Boston: Warren, Gorham & Lamont, 1993), p. 12–1.

[7] Many states provide sales tax exemptions for items considered necessities of life, such as food and prescription drugs.

Tax Talk
The 20 states in which recreational marijuana is legal are experimenting with ways to tax this new base. For example, Colorado imposes a 15 percent tax on the sale of marijuana from a cultivator to a retailer plus an additional 10 percent tax on retail sales to customers, 2.9 percent general sales tax, local sales taxes, and local marijuana taxes (such as a 3.5 percent tax in Denver).

Millions of people are unaware of their responsibility for paying use tax on goods purchased out of state or through mail-order catalogs, or they ignore their self-assessment responsibility. States have recently become much more aggressive in collecting use taxes directly from their residents and have entered into cooperative agreements to share sales and use tax audit information. Twenty-seven states and the District of Columbia have added lines to their personal income tax returns on which individuals are instructed to report the use tax due on their out-of-state and catalog purchases for the year.

An **excise tax** is imposed on the retail sale of specific goods, such as gasoline, cigarettes, and alcoholic beverages, or on specific services, such as hotel and motel accommodations. States may impose an excise tax in addition to or instead of the general sales tax on a particular good or service. In either case, the seller is responsible for collecting and remitting the excise tax. Excise taxes can be extremely heavy. Washington levies a 37.5 cents excise tax on each gallon of gasoline, New York levies a $4.35 excise tax on one pack of cigarettes, and Virginia levies a $19.89 excise tax per gallon of distilled liquor.

A Not-So-Sweet Tax

In 2017, Philadelphia became the first major city to levy an excise tax on nonalcoholic sugar-sweetened beverages. This controversial 1.5-cent-per-ounce "soda tax" was enacted primarily as a revenue-raiser with a side benefit of reducing childhood obesity. A number of other local jurisdictions, including Boulder, Colorado, have followed Philadelphia's lead by enacting taxes on sugary soft drinks. Needless to say, the beverage industry opposes these new taxes, arguing that such taxes won't make people healthier, just poorer.

Personal Income Taxes

Forty-three states and the District of Columbia levy some form of personal income tax on individuals who reside in the state and nonresidents who earn income within the state. (The exceptions are Alaska, Florida, Nevada, South Dakota, Texas, Washington, and Wyoming.) The technical details of the computation of taxable income vary considerably from state to state, but the tax rates are uniformly modest. Currently, the maximum rates range from 2.9 percent in North Dakota to 13.3 percent in California.

Corporate Income Taxes

Forty-four states and the District of Columbia tax corporations on their net income attributable to the state. Nevada, Ohio, Texas, and Washington have no corporate income tax; instead, these four states impose a corporate gross receipts tax. Only South Dakota and Wyoming do not have corporate income or gross receipts tax. Many states authorize their cities and counties to tax either the income or gross receipts of both incorporated and unincorporated businesses operating within the locality.

Tax Talk
The IRS is spearheading an effort to allow corporations to file combined electronic federal and state tax returns. Officials anticipate a flood of returns from corporations taking advantage of the simplicity of joint e-filing.

The computation of corporate taxable income is prescribed by state law. Conceptually, each state could have its own unique set of computational rules so that one corporation operating in all 44 income-taxing jurisdictions would be required to make 44 different calculations of taxable income. Fortunately for corporate America, differences in the computations are the exception rather than the rule. All states with a net income tax refer to the *federal* definition of taxable income as the starting point for calculating state taxable income. "The outstanding characteristic of state corporate net income measures is their broad conformity to the measure of the federal corporation income tax."[8]

[8] Source: Walter R. Hellerstein, Jerome Hellerstein, and John Swain, *State Taxation,* 3rd ed. (Carrollton, TX: Thomson Reuters, 2014), p. 7.3.

The major advantage of state conformity to federal income tax law is simplicity. State legislatures don't have to reinvent the wheel by enacting a comprehensive income tax statute. State agencies responsible for administering their state's income tax can refer to regulatory and judicial interpretations of the federal law. A second advantage is that state conformity to federal tax law eases the compliance burdens of corporate taxpayers. The major disadvantage is the states' lack of control over their corporate income tax revenues. Each time the U.S. Congress changes the federal definition of taxable income, the income tax base of conforming states is increased or decreased.

Corporate income tax rates vary from state to state. The majority of states use a flat rate, while the remainder use a mildly progressive graduated rate structure. Currently, the maximum rates range from 2.5 percent in North Carolina to 11.5 percent in New Jersey.

Federal Taxes

LO 1-5
Describe the taxes levied by the federal government.

The U.S. government depends almost exclusively on the income tax as a source of general revenues. The federal income tax applies to both individuals and corporations, as well as trusts and estates. The structure and operation of the federal income tax are discussed in considerable detail in Parts Three, Four, and Five of this text. At this point, suffice it to say that the federal income tax predominates in the business environment.

History of the Income Tax

The modern income tax doesn't have a particularly long history in this country. The federal government enacted the first personal income tax in 1861 to raise money to support the Union armies during the Civil War. Even though Congress allowed the tax to expire in 1872, its revenue-generating capability made a lasting impression on the legislative memory. In 1894, Congress needed a permanent source of funds and decided to resurrect the personal income tax. However, in the landmark case of *Pollock* v. *Farmers' Loan and Trust Company*,[9] the Supreme Court held that the U.S. Constitution did not authorize the federal government to levy a national income tax. Determined to have its way, Congress launched a campaign to change the Constitution, a campaign that ended victoriously on February 25, 1913, when Wyoming became the 36th state to ratify the Sixteenth Amendment:

> The Congress shall have the power to lay and collect taxes on incomes from whatever source derived, without apportionment among the several states, and without regard to any census or enumeration.
>
> Source: U.S. Constitution

Congress immediately exercised its new power by passing the Revenue Act of 1913, and the income tax became a permanent feature of American life. In 1939, Congress organized all of the federal tax laws then in effect (income and otherwise) into the first Internal Revenue Code. This compilation was substantially revised as the Internal Revenue Code of 1954 and again as the Internal Revenue Code of 1986. Although Congress has not changed the title of the Internal Revenue Code since 1986, it enacts new legislation each year to amend the Code.

On December 22, 2017, President Trump signed the Tax Cuts and Jobs Act into law. This major legislation made sweeping changes to the tax rules that apply to both individual and corporate taxpayers. Many changes affecting individual taxpayers are temporary; the changes apply only for tax years beginning after December 31, 2017, and before January 1, 2026. The changes affecting corporations are permanent.

Tax Talk
In response to the economic crisis brought on by the coronavirus, the CARES Act of 2020 temporarily suspended a number of the tax provisions enacted in 2017 as part of the Tax Cuts and Jobs Act.

[9] 157 U.S. 429 (1895).

Employment and Unemployment Taxes

The two largest programs sponsored by the federal government are the Social Security system, which provides monthly old-age, survivors, and disability benefits to qualifying citizens and residents, and Medicare, which provides hospital insurance for people who are elderly or disabled. These programs aren't funded from the general revenues generated by the income tax. Instead, the revenues from the federal **employment taxes** are earmarked to pay for Social Security and Medicare. These taxes are based on annual wages and salaries paid by employers to their employees and on the net income earned by self-employed individuals. The details of these important taxes are discussed in Chapter 10.

The federal and state governments act in coordination to provide monetary benefits to individuals who are temporarily unemployed through no fault of their own. This national unemployment insurance system is administered by the states and financed by federal and state taxes imposed directly on employers. These **unemployment taxes** are based on the annual compensation paid to employees. Virtually every business in this country pays unemployment taxes with respect to its workforce, and significant planning opportunities do exist for controlling this particular cost. Nevertheless, because of the narrow scope of the unemployment taxes, we will not discuss them further in this text.

Tax Talk
According to a 2019 report by the Joint Committee on Taxation, 67.8 percent of individual taxpayers pay more in Social Security and Medicare taxes than federal income tax.

Other Federal Taxes

The federal government raises general revenues from excise taxes imposed on the retail purchase of specific goods and services such as tobacco products, luxury automobiles, and firearms. The federal **transfer taxes,** which are based on the value of an individual's wealth transferred by gift or at death, are also a source of general revenues. Transfer taxes play a key role in family tax planning and are described in detail in Chapter 16. As Exhibit 1.1 shows, these two types of taxes are an insignificant source of federal funds. In fiscal year 2020, excise taxes accounted for only 2.1 percent of federal tax revenues, while transfer taxes accounted for just .5 percent.

Tax Talk
In 1934, excise taxes raised 46 percent of federal revenues.

Taxes Levied by Foreign Jurisdictions

LO 1-6
Explain the structure of the value-added tax levied by foreign governments.

The types of foreign taxes that firms encounter when expanding from domestic to international operations are as varied as the languages, politics, and cultures characterizing the global environment. Many foreign taxes have a familiar structure. National governments and their political subdivisions the world over levy income taxes, property taxes, and retail sales taxes. Other taxes have no counterpart in the United States and are therefore less familiar to domestic companies operating abroad. For instance, many industrialized nations depend heavily on some type of **value-added tax (VAT)** as a revenue source. Value-added taxes are levied on firms engaged in any phase of the production of goods and are based on the incremental value that the firm adds to the goods.

[10] Source: National Commission on Economic Growth and Tax Reform, quote from "Unleashing America's Potential: A Pro-Growth, Pro-Family Tax System for the 21st Century," 70 *Tax Notes* 413, 418. Originally appeared in a 1909 editorial in *The New York Times*.

EXHIBIT 1.1
Fiscal Year 2020
Federal Tax Revenues

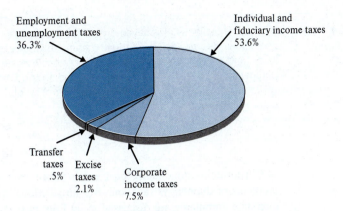

Employment and
unemployment taxes
36.3%

Individual and
fiduciary income taxes
53.6%

Transfer
taxes
.5%

Excise
taxes
2.1%

Corporate
income taxes
7.5%

Value-Added Tax	Firm M and Firm W operate in a jurisdiction that imposes a 5 percent VAT. Firm M manufactures small electronic appliances. M's material cost per unit is $40, and M sells each unit to Firm W, a regional distributor, for $46. The $6 difference represents the incremental value that M added to the production process. Therefore, M must pay a 30-cent VAT (5 percent of $6) for each unit sold.
	Firm W sells the appliances purchased from Firm M to various unrelated retailers for $50 per unit. Firm W's $4 gross profit on the sale of each unit represents the incremental value that W added to the production process by providing distribution services. Consequently, Firm W must pay a 20-cent VAT (5 percent of $4) for each unit sold.

This example is extremely simplistic because it ignores the possibility that both Firm M and Firm W can shift the economic incidence of the VAT by increasing the price at which they sell their product to the next business in the production sequence. To the extent that a VAT is shifted along the entire production sequence to the final purchaser (the customer who buys the product for personal consumption), the VAT resembles a retail sales tax.

Jurisdictional Competition

LO 1-7
Summarize why
different jurisdictions
compete for revenues
from the same taxpayer.

Domestic businesses pay tax to state and local governments, as well as to the federal government. International businesses pay tax to any number of foreign jurisdictions. Governments understand that their taxing jurisdictions overlap and that, as a result, they are competing for revenues from the same businesses. They also understand that taxpayers are mobile and that business managers make location decisions with an eye on comparative tax costs. Thus, jurisdictional competition creates an interesting tension. On the one hand, a government that fails to protect its jurisdictional turf may lose revenues to more assertive taxing authorities. On the other hand, a government that is overly aggressive may drive businesses away from its jurisdiction.

In the United States, the competing levels of government have traditionally accommodated each other by relying on different taxes as their primary source of funding. As we learned earlier in the chapter, property taxes are the mainstay of local governments, while retail sales taxes are used almost exclusively by state governments. Our federal government doesn't levy either property taxes or a national sales tax but instead relies on income and employment taxes for its revenues.

Ready for a National Sales Tax?

A group of business executives organized as Americans for Fair Taxation (AFT) are publicly campaigning to replace the federal income tax, Social Security and Medicare employment taxes, and transfer taxes with a 23 percent national sales tax. The tax would apply to retail purchases of all goods and services, including food, medicine, and housing. According to AFT, this new tax would raise the same federal revenue as existing taxes, while stimulating economic growth.

Corporations conducting business in more than one state face particularly difficult problems of duplicative taxation. The jurisdictional concerns of corporations engaged in interstate commerce are discussed more fully in Chapter 13. Of course, the potential for jurisdictional conflict is greatest when corporations operate on a global scale. Industrialized nations assume that it is in their self-interest to promote the growth of international business operations. These nations understand that if they fail to adapt their tax systems to the needs of the worldwide marketplace, their economies will be at a competitive disadvantage. Consequently, the industrialized nations have created a network of bilateral and multilateral tax treaties to minimize friction among their respective tax systems and to reduce duplicative taxation of international businesses. The role of these treaties and other unique features of international tax planning are covered in Chapter 13.

DYNAMIC NATURE OF TAXATION

LO 1-8
Discuss the reasons why governments modify their tax systems.

Business managers must understand not only that taxes are pervasive in the modern world but that tax systems are in a constant state of flux. Tax systems are dynamic because they must be attuned to the fiscal condition of their respective jurisdictions. In every jurisdiction, individual citizens and organizations continually reevaluate the nature and level of services they want from their governments. Governments, in turn, must reassess the tax systems that pay for those services.

Tax Base Changes

Tax Talk
States often devote gambling revenues to popular public services. A member of Congress boasted that Oregon residents "are gambling for education, salmon restoration, parks, and economic activity. It's an amazing phenomenon."

Any government dependent on a tax system that fails to raise sufficient revenues will sooner or later be forced to change the system. The loss of revenue-generating power is often attributable to an eroding tax base. For instance, cities that depend on real property taxes experience a decline in revenues when their populations decrease. As families and businesses move away from urban areas, residential and commercial properties located within the city lose value. Owners can no longer afford to maintain the properties and, in extreme cases, they may simply abandon them. Cities only worsen this cycle of deterioration if they raise their property tax rates. The only solution may be to identify an alternative tax base or a source of nontax revenue.

Legalized Gambling

One important source of nontax revenue is legalized gambling. About 40 years ago, a few states experimented with lotteries as a means of raising money. Lotteries proved so lucrative that 44 states and the District of Columbia are now sponsoring these betting games. In the late 1980s, states in the Midwest and the South decided to shore up their tax bases by going into the casino business and gave private gambling corporations legal monopolies to operate within the state. Today, casinos are legal in more than half the states, and all but two states (Hawaii and Utah) depend on some form of gambling as a source of revenue.

A Gambler's Worst Bet	According to recent census data, state lotteries on average pay back only 62 percent of the money received from ticket sales—the smallest share of the take of any legal gambling game. In contrast, slot machines, which offer the worst odds of any private casino game, generally pay back a minimum of 80 percent of the money fed into them.

Sales Tax Expansion

State and local governments are aggressive in exploiting new tax bases that develop in the economy. Historically, state sales taxes apply to retail purchases of tangible property but not to purchases of retail services. Because of the dramatic growth in the service sector over the past several decades, an increasing number of states are adding selected services, such as utilities, cable television, parking, and theater tickets, to their sales tax base. Currently, Hawaii, New Mexico, North Dakota, and South Dakota are the most aggressive in taxing services.

Sales Tax on Rentals	Beginning on September 1, 2017, Airbnb began collecting and remitting South Dakota's state and local sales tax from vacationers who rent lodging in the Mount Rushmore state. The tax is based on the rental fee and is billed when the lodging is booked. Because South Dakota has no personal or corporate income tax, the state depends heavily on its sales tax to generate revenue.

Tax Talk
A poll by the National Taxpayers Union found that 65 percent of the people surveyed oppose new Internet sales taxes.

For the past 26 years, states have lobbied the federal government to enact legislation permitting them to collect sales tax on mail-order and Internet sales to in-state customers. In 1992, the Supreme Court ruled that states lacked jurisdiction to tax these so-called remote sales unless the seller had a physical presence, such as an office or storefront, in the state.[11] In 2018, the Court issued a landmark decision overturning this physical presence requirement.[12] This decision frees state governments to enact legislation compelling catalog and online retailers to collect sales tax based on the residence of the purchaser. According to the states, such legislation will level the fiscal playing field between remote retailers and brick-and-mortar retailers, while raising enormous amounts of additional sales tax revenue.

Taxes and the Political Process

Tax Talk
According to Otto von Bismarck, the "Iron Chancellor" of 19th-century Germany, "The less people know about how sausages and laws are made, the better they'll sleep at night."

The political process by which tax law is made contributes to the dynamic nature of taxes. In this country, local, state, and federal tax laws are the result of democratic systems in which elected or appointed representatives decide on the appropriate tax structure. These representatives are sensitive to the political climates of their respective constituencies. As these climates change over time, representatives may decide that the tax structure should change as well. Many of these changes have little to do with revenues. Instead, the changes are philosophic in nature, reflecting a shift in the public attitude concerning the proper role of taxes in society.

Special-interest groups have a significant effect on the tax legislative process. Thousands of organizations have pet provisions in the existing law or wish lists for new provisions. These organizations use their own emissaries or hire professional lobbyists to communicate their point of view to government officials. The constant pressure from powerful

[11] *Quill Corporation v. North Dakota*, 504 U.S. 298 (1992).
[12] *South Dakota v. Wayfair*, 138 S.Ct. 1543 (2018).

organizations with competing and even conflicting political objectives adds to the vibrant nature of the tax law.

People don't enjoy paying taxes and are willing to devote considerable money and effort to avoid doing so. Each time taxpayers or their advisers devise a new tactic to reduce their tax burdens, governments respond by enacting a new rule to render the tactic ineffective. This constant gamesmanship is another reason why the tax environment is dynamic. As humorist Dave Barry explains, "[Tax laws] are constantly changing as our elected representatives seek new ways to ensure that whatever tax advice we receive is incorrect."*

Taxes and Data Analytics

The increasing complexity of tax systems across multiple taxing jurisdictions creates considerable challenges for large businesses operating across the United States and globally. Meeting tax compliance requirements demands sophisticated data reporting systems. Effective tax planning to minimize the costs of these diverse tax systems often requires analysis of large amounts of tax data, both across jurisdictions and across time. Today's business professionals increasingly turn to data analytics to meet these compliance and planning needs.

A number of sophisticated data analytics tools have developed over the past two decades. Although Excel remains a stalwart of data analysis, spreadsheet data solutions are often time-consuming to create and maintain. Data programs such as Alteryx, Power BI, Python, STATA, SQL, and Tableau offer greater efficiency when dealing with large data sets.

Data analytics tools can assist taxpayers and tax professionals with tasks such as responding to tax authority audit requests, analyzing sales and use tax data for multi-state businesses, accumulating country-by-country reporting information for global businesses, forecasting future tax costs, analyzing uncertain tax position reporting, computing tax depreciation, identifying and analyzing book–tax differences, and many more.

Data Analytics	Large public accounting firms are champions of data analytics in the tax function. As EY notes, tax authorities are relying more and more on data to make compliance and audit determinations. As a result, companies face risks and exposure if their people, processes, and systems are dated or out of sync with government requirements and expectations. The tax department has an opportunity to deliver value by harnessing data analytics to manage risk, control costs, and inform communications and business decisions.
	EY Global, 2019. How data analytics is transforming tax administration. Available at: https://www.ey.com/en_gl/tax/how-data-analytics-is-transforming-tax-administration

SOURCES OF FEDERAL TAX LAW

LO 1-9
Identify the three primary sources of federal tax law.

Throughout this text, we will constantly refer to the **tax law.** For modern tax systems, this term encompasses three sources of authority: statutory law, administrative pronouncements, and judicial decisions. In combination, these sources provide the rules of the game by which both taxpayers and governments must abide. This final section of Chapter 1 describes the primary sources of authority that constitute our federal tax law. In subsequent chapters of the text, you will encounter much technical information originating from this body of law. You should have a much easier time understanding this information if you are familiar with the underlying sources from which the information is derived.

* Source: Dave Barry

Statutory Authority

In its narrowest sense, federal tax law means the **Internal Revenue Code of 1986,** the voluminous compilation of statutory rules enacted by Congress. The Internal Revenue Code is a dynamic document; at least once a year, Congress passes legislation that adds to, deletes from, or modifies its provisions.

Legislative Process

According to the U.S. Constitution, the tax legislative process must begin in the House of Representatives. The original version of a new tax bill is drafted by the **House Ways and Means Committee** and is then considered by the full House. If the House votes to approve the bill, it moves to the **Senate Finance Committee.** That committee can make revisions, additions, or deletions to the House bill before presenting its amended bill to the full Senate for approval.

Oftentimes, the amended bill approved by the Senate is quite different from the original bill approved by the House. In such case, both versions of the tax bill are considered by a **Conference Committee** composed of members from both the House and Senate committees. This committee reconciles the differences between the two versions and drafts a compromise bill. If both the House and Senate vote to approve the Conference Committee's final version, the bill is submitted to the president for signature or veto. If the president signs the bill, it is redesignated as a tax act and becomes law.

Referencing Code Sections

The Internal Revenue Code consists of numerically ordered **sections,** beginning with Section 1 and ending (at last count) with Section 9834. Each section contains an operational, definitional, or procedural rule relating to one of the federal taxes. Code section numbers have become the language in which tax experts communicate, and accountants and lawyers have incorporated many of them into their professional jargon. (Bob, I think our client has a real Section 469 problem.) Sections are divided into subsections, paragraphs, subparagraphs, and so on. In the footnotes to the text, a reference such as §469(f)(3)(B) is citing the precise statutory rule under discussion.

Administrative Authority

The Department of the Treasury is responsible for writing regulations to interpret and illustrate the rules contained in the Internal Revenue Code. These **Treasury regulations** provide tremendous guidance to taxpayers and their advisers. The Treasury regularly publishes new regulations or amends existing regulations to keep abreast of legislative developments. While Treasury regulations carry great authority as the government's official explanation of the law, they are not laws in and of themselves. On rare occasions, taxpayers have convinced the federal courts that a regulation was an incorrect interpretation of statute and was therefore invalid.[13]

The citation to a Treasury regulation consists of a sequence of numbers, the first of which identifies the type of federal tax under consideration. For instance, a regulation beginning with 1 is an income tax regulation. The next number identifies the Code section to which the regulation relates. The last number in the sequence is the number of the regulation itself. The citation Reg. §1.469-4 refers to the fourth Treasury regulation relating to Section 469 of the Internal Revenue Code. Some sections have only one regulation, while others have dozens, and some Code sections have no interpretive regulations at all!

---

[13] The Internal Revenue Code occasionally empowers the Treasury to write regulations that have the force and effect of law. These so-called legislative regulations have the same authority as statutory law.

The **Internal Revenue Service (IRS),** the subdivision of the Treasury responsible for the enforcement of the law and collection of tax, provides still more guidance in the form of revenue rulings and revenue procedures. A **revenue ruling** explains how the IRS applies the tax law to a particular set of facts. A **revenue procedure** advises taxpayers how to comply with IRS procedural or administrative matters. While these pronouncements carry much less authority than the Code and regulations, they do represent the IRS's official position and provide valuable insight on specific issues. Rulings and procedures are published in weekly **Internal Revenue Bulletins (I.R.B.).** Until 2009, the IRS compiled I.R.B.s into semiannual **Cumulative Bulletins (C.B.).** Footnote references such as Rev. Rul. 2019-11, 2019-17 I.R.B. 1041, and Rev. Proc. 89-17, 1989-1 C.B. 118 are citing these sources of authority.

Goodbye to the Penny	In one of the first revenue rulings published after Congress enacted the Internal Revenue Code of 1954, the IRS authorized taxpayers to eliminate the penny from their bookkeeping by rounding numbers up or down to the nearest dollar.

Judicial Authority

The third primary source of tax law is the federal judicial system. Taxpayers who disagree with the IRS's interpretation of the law as it applies to their own situations may take their cases to federal court. The hundreds of legal decisions handed down every year clarify the correct implementation of the tax law. The weight of authority of a particular case depends on the court that rendered the verdict. Trial court verdicts have less authority than verdicts by an appellate court. A Supreme Court verdict is the equivalent of law and becomes the final word in any tax dispute. Chapter 18 discusses the process by which a federal judge or jury resolves a controversy between a taxpayer and the IRS. When this text refers to a judicial decision, an accompanying footnote provides the complete legal cite. You can use the citation to locate the decision in any law library or commercial tax service.

Conclusion

Business managers engaged in effective tax planning take into account the variety of taxes that exist in the modern economic environment. When making strategic decisions, managers must consider their firm's total tax burden rather than any tax in isolation. A strategy that decreases the cost of one tax could easily increase the cost of another. The primary focus of this text is the federal income tax; as a result, other taxes that affect business and investment decisions will be mentioned only occasionally. Even so, many income tax planning strategies are valid in other tax contexts. Decision makers should remember that every tax represents a controllable cost of conducting business.

As greater numbers of U.S. firms expand their operations across national boundaries, jurisdictional tax planning becomes crucial. Managers must decide which tax systems are attractive and which systems are inhospitable to foreign investors. They must be aware of differences between competing tax regimes and how those differences can be exploited to the firm's advantage. In today's tax environment, successful tax planning must be conducted on a global scale.

Key Terms

abatement *1-8*

activity-based tax *1-6*

ad valorem tax *1-7*

bracket *1-5*

Conference Committee *1-17*

Cumulative Bulletin (C.B.) *1-18*

earmarked tax *1-6*

employment tax *1-12*

event- or transaction-based tax *1-6*

excise tax *1-10*

flat rate *1-5*

graduated rate *1-5*

House Ways and Means Committee *1-17*

incidence *1-4*

income tax *1-6*

Internal Revenue Bulletin (I.R.B.) *1-18*

Internal Revenue Code of 1986 *1-17*

Internal Revenue Service (IRS) *1-18*

jurisdiction *1-5*

personalty *1-8*

real property tax *1-7*

realty *1-7*

revenue *1-6*

revenue procedure *1-18*

revenue ruling *1-18*

sales tax *1-9*

section *1-17*

Senate Finance Committee *1-17*

tax *1-4*

tax assessor *1-7*

tax base *1-5*

tax law *1-16*

taxpayer *1-4*

transfer tax *1-12*

Treasury regulation *1-17*

unemployment tax *1-12*

use tax *1-9*

value-added tax (VAT) *1-12*

Questions and Problems for Discussion

LO 1-1 1. How do tax payments differ from other payments that people or organizations make to governmental agencies?

LO 1-1 2. The Green River, which is heavily polluted by industrial waste, flows through State S. Eighty-five companies operate manufacturing facilities that border the river. State S recently enacted legislation requiring each company to pay $50,000 annually into a special fund to clean up the Green River. Does this payment meet the definition of a tax?

LO 1-1, 1-2 3. Custer County is considering raising revenues by imposing a $25 fee on couples who obtain a marriage license within the county. Does this fee meet the definition of a transaction-based tax?

LO 1-1 4. Mr. Powell owns a residential apartment complex in a suburban area. This year, the local jurisdiction increased the property tax rate on the apartment complex. To offset this additional cost, Mr. Powell decreased the amount he usually spends on maintaining the exterior of the building and the landscaping. Who bears the incidence of the increased property tax?

LO 1-1 5. Mr. and Mrs. Ahern pay $18,000 annual tuition to a private school for their three children. They also pay $2,300 property tax on their personal residence to support the local public school system. Should Mr. and Mrs. Ahern be exempt from this property tax?

LO 1-1 6. A local government imposed a new 2 percent tax on the gross receipts of businesses operating within its jurisdiction. XYZ Company, which manufactures soap and other toiletries, responded to the tax by reducing the size of its bars of soap and purchasing a cheaper grade of ingredients. By making these changes, XYZ maintained its before-tax level of profits. Who bears the incidence of the new gross receipts tax?

LO 1-2, 1-3 7. Why is real property a better tax base than personal property?

LO 1-2, 1-3 8. Many local jurisdictions apply a low property tax rate to land owned by privately operated golf courses. What is the economic justification for such a preferential rate?

LO 1-3 9. Churchill University is located in a small town that depends on real property taxes for revenue. Over the past decade, the university has expanded by purchasing a number of commercial buildings and personal residences and converting them to classrooms and dormitories. In what way could this expansion result in a decline in the town's revenues?

LO 1-4   10. Why can people avoid paying an excise tax more readily than they can avoid paying a sales tax?

LO 1-3, 1-4, 1-8   11. A city government increased its local sales tax from 1 percent to 2 percent of the dollar value of consumer goods purchased in the city. However, the city's sales tax revenues increased by only 30 percent after the doubling of the tax rate. What factors might account for this result?

LO 1-4, 1-5   12. Both the federal government and many states impose so-called sin taxes: excise taxes levied on the retail sale of liquor and cigarettes. Discuss the reasons why sales of these particular items make a good tax base.

LO 1-5   13. Does the federal income tax or the federal payroll tax have the broader tax base?

LO 1-3, 1-7   14. Differentiate between a property tax and a transfer tax.

LO 1-5, 1-7   15. One way for the federal government to increase tax revenues would be to enact either a VAT or a national retail sales tax. The U.S. sales tax could be collected in the same manner and at the same time as state and local sales taxes. Which tax would be less costly for the federal government to implement and administer? Which tax would be less likely to cause jurisdictional conflict?

LO 1-9   16. The Internal Revenue Code and Treasury regulations are two major sources of federal tax law. Differentiate between the Code and the regulations in terms of their relative weight of authority.

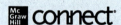   All applicable Application Problems are available with *Connect.*

Application Problems

LO 1-1   1. Mr. Josh Kenney, a U.S. citizen and resident of Vermont, owns 100 percent of the stock of JK Services, which is incorporated under Vermont law and conducts business in four counties in the state. JK Services owns 100 percent of the stock of JK Realty, which is incorporated under Massachusetts law and conducts business in Boston.
   a. How many taxpayers are identified in the given statement of facts?
   b. Identify the governments with jurisdiction to tax each of these taxpayers.

LO 1-1, 1-5   2. In each of the following cases, determine if the United States has jurisdiction to tax Mrs. May.
   a. Mrs. May is a citizen of Brazil but is a permanent resident of Orlando, Florida.
   b. Mrs. May is a citizen and resident of Brazil. She owns Manhattan real estate that generates $100,000 net rental income annually.
   c. Mrs. May is a citizen and resident of Brazil. She owns no property and conducts no business in the United States.
   d. Mrs. May is a U.S. citizen but is a permanent resident of São Paulo, Brazil.

LO 1-1, 1-5   3. In each of the following cases, determine if the United States has jurisdiction to tax Mr. Tompkin.
   a. Mr. Tompkin is a U.S. citizen but has been a permanent resident of Belgium since 1993.
   b. Mr. Tompkin is a citizen and resident of Canada. He owns an apartment building in Buffalo, New York, that generates $18,000 annual net rental income.
   c. Mr. Tompkin is a citizen of Singapore but is a permanent resident of St. Louis, Missouri.
   d. Mr. Tompkin, a citizen and resident of Greece, is a partner in Sophic Partnership, which conducts business in 12 countries, including the United States.

LO 1-2   4. This year, State A raised revenues by increasing its general sales tax rate from 5 percent to 6 percent. Because of the increase, the volume of taxable sales declined from $800 million to $710 million. In contrast, State Z raised revenues from its 5 percent sales tax by expanding the tax base to include certain retail services. The volume of services subject to tax was $50 million. Compute the additional revenue raised by State A and by State Z.

LO 1-2, 1-3   5. The city of Springvale levies a tax on the value of real property located within its city limits. The tax equals 2 percent of the property's assessed value up to $500,000 plus 4 percent of the value in excess of $500,000.
   a. Compute the tax on real property valued at $415,000.
   b. Compute the tax on real property valued at $725,000.

LO 1-2, 1-3   6. Monroe County levies a tax on the value of real property located within the county. The tax equals 3 percent of the property's assessed value up to $2 million plus 1 percent of the value in excess of $2 million.
   a. Compute the tax on real property valued at $1.3 million.
   b. Compute the tax on real property valued at $4.5 million.

LO 1-3   7. This year, Lexon Company built a light industrial facility in County G. The assessed property tax value of the facility is $20 million. To convince Lexon to locate within its jurisdiction, the county abated its 4 percent property tax for the year. Because of the local economic boom created by the new facility, the aggregate assessed value of County G's property tax base (including the Lexon facility) increased by $23 million. Compute the net effect on County G's current year tax revenue from the abatement.

LO 1-4   8. Heliot Company operates its business in State H, which levies a 6 percent sales and use tax. This year, Heliot purchased a $600,000 item of tangible property in State K and paid $18,000 sales tax to the state. It also purchased a $750,000 item of tangible property in State L and paid $48,750 sales tax to the state. Firm H transported both items of property into State H for use in its business.
   a. Compute the use tax that Heliot owes to State H for the property purchased in State K.
   b. Compute the use tax that Heliot owes to State H for the property purchased in State L.

LO 1-4   9. TR Company conducts business exclusively in State V, which levies a 5 percent sales and use tax on goods purchased or consumed in-state. This year, TR bought equipment in State B. The cost of the equipment was $90,000, and TR paid $5,400 sales tax to State B. TR also bought machinery in State D. The cost of the machinery was $200,000, and TR paid $7,000 sales tax to State D.
   a. How much use tax does TR Company owe to State V with respect to the equipment bought in State B?
   b. How much use tax does TR Company owe to State V with respect to the machinery bought in State D?

LO 1-4   10. Mrs. Palencia, a resident of Rhode Island, traveled to Delaware to purchase an oil painting from a local artist. The cost of the painting was $9,400. Rhode Island has a 7 percent sales and use tax, while Delaware has no sales and use tax.
   a. How much Rhode Island use tax does Mrs. Palencia owe on the purchase she made in Delaware?
   b. How much Rhode Island use tax would Mrs. Palencia owe if she purchased the painting from a gallery in New York City and paid 8.75 percent state and local sales tax on the transaction?
   c. How much Rhode Island use tax would Mrs. Palencia owe if she purchased the painting from a dealer in Milwaukee and paid Wisconsin's 5 percent sales tax on the transaction?

LO 1-4   11. Ms. Pike, who lives in California, traveled to Oregon to purchase gold jewelry for $20,000. California has a 7.25 percent sales and use tax, while Oregon has no sales and use tax.

    a. Compute the use tax that Ms. Pike owes to California on the jewelry purchased in Oregon.

    b. Compute the use tax that Ms. Pike owes to California if she purchased the jewelry in New Mexico and paid that state's 5.125 percent sales tax on the transaction.

LO 1-4   12. Correll Company, which operates a mail-order clothing business, is physically located in State L. This year, the firm shipped $18 million of merchandise to customers in State R. State R imposes a 6 percent sales and use tax on the purchase and consumption of retail goods within the state.

    a. Do State R residents who purchased Correll merchandise owe use tax on their purchases?

    b. If State R could legally require Correll to collect a 6 percent tax on mail-order sales made to residents of the state, how much additional revenue would the state collect? Explain the reasoning behind your answer.

LO 1-3, 1-4   13. Mr. and Mrs. Ruiz operate a hardware store in a jurisdiction that levies both a sales tax on retail sales of tangible personalty and an annual personal property tax on business tangibles. The personal property tax is based on book value as of December 31. This year, Mr. and Mrs. Ruiz purchased $840,000 of inventory for their store.

    a. Are Mr. and Mrs. Ruiz required to pay sales tax on the purchase of the inventory?

    b. How can Mr. and Mrs. Ruiz minimize their personal property tax by controlling the timing of their inventory purchases?

LO 1-6   14. Querrey Inc. and Ronno Inc. conduct business in a foreign country that imposes a 3 percent VAT. Querrey produces entertainment videos at a $6 material cost per unit and sells the videos to Ronno for $9 per unit. Ronno sells the videos at retail for $10 per unit. This year, the combined efforts of Querrey and Ronno resulted in sales of 12.4 million videos to the public. Compute the VAT for each corporation.

LO 1-6   15. Wallis Company produces circuit boards in a foreign country that imposes a 15 percent VAT. This year, Wallis manufactured 8.3 million boards at a $5 material cost per unit. Wallis's labor and overhead added $1 to the cost per unit. Wallis sold the boards to various customers for $7.50 per unit for a net profit of $1.50 per unit. How much VAT does Wallis Company owe?

Issue Recognition Problems

Identify the tax issue or issues suggested by the following situations, and state each issue in the form of a question.

LO 1-1, 1-3   1. A local government levies an annual real property tax on the personal residence located at 123 Maple Drive. This tax is assessed on a calendar year basis, and the homeowner must pay the tax before December 31. In November, Mr. and Mrs. Julius received the annual tax bill for $2,900. The couple purchased the home on October 6.

LO 1-3   2. Firtex Company operates in a jurisdiction that levies real property tax but no personal property tax. This year, the company spent $6 million to add an exterior lighting system and security fences to the parking lot adjacent to its corporate headquarters.

LO 1-3   3. Bailey Company, which has offices in six states, owns an airplane that company executives use to travel from office to office. When the plane is not in use, it is stored in a hangar located in a jurisdiction that doesn't levy a personal property tax on business tangibles. When the plane is in use, it is stored on a temporary basis in hangars located in jurisdictions that tax business tangibles.

LO 1-1, 1-4, 1-5 4. For the past 22 years, Mrs. Otis contributed part of her salary to a retirement plan sponsored by her corporate employer. Under federal law, Mrs. Otis did not pay tax on the income she contributed. She will, however, pay federal income tax on the distributions from the plan when she retires. Mrs. Otis has resided in State A for her entire life. Because State A's personal income tax is based on taxable income for federal purposes, Mrs. Otis never paid State A tax on her retirement contributions. This year, Mrs. Otis retires and moves to State K, which has no personal income tax.

LO 1-4 5. Yarrow Company orders $500,000 of office furniture from Vendor V, which ships the furniture by rail from its manufacturing facility in State V to Yarrow's corporate headquarters in State Q. State V imposes a 6.5 percent sales tax, while State Q imposes only a 4 percent sales tax.

LO 1-4 6. Acme Corporation was formed under the laws of State X and has its corporate headquarters in that state. Acme operates a manufacturing plant in State Y and sells goods to customers in States X, Y, and Z. All three states have a corporate income tax. This year, Acme's net profit from its tristate operation was $14 million.

LO 1-4 7. Mr. Wycomb is a professional golfer who played 23 tournaments in 14 different states and earned $893,000 total prize money for the year. When he is not traveling, Mr. Wycomb lives with his family in Tucson, Arizona.

LO 1-3 8. Eighteen months ago, BBB Company opened a manufacturing facility in County K. As an incentive for BBB to locate within its jurisdiction, County K abated all local property taxes for the first two years of operation. BBB recently announced that it will shut down the facility before the end of the year.

LO 1-1, 1-5 9. Dempsey Corporation is organized under Canadian law and has its corporate headquarters in Montreal. This year, Dempsey sold $28 million of goods to customers who live in the United States. However, Dempsey doesn't maintain any type of office in the United States.

LO 1-1, 1-5 10. Mr. Imhoff, age 72, has lived in Los Angeles his entire life. His net worth is estimated at $95 million. Mr. Imhoff is considering renouncing his U.S. citizenship, selling his home in Los Angeles, and permanently relocating to the Cayman Islands. The Cayman Islands impose no tax of any kind on their residents.

Research Problems

LO 1-4 1. Visit the website for the Federation of Tax Administrators (**www.taxadmin.org**) to find out if your state has either an individual or a corporate income tax. If so, what is the maximum tax rate?

LO 1-5 2. Visit the website for the Internal Revenue Service (**www.irs.gov**). What is the name of the commissioner of the IRS? Can you locate the IRS Taxpayer Assistance Center closest to your hometown?

LO 1-5 3. Conduct a search on the Internet to find a brief description of the flat tax. Write a short paragraph describing the flat tax and explaining how it differs from the federal individual income tax.

LO 1-4 4. The next time you buy groceries in a supermarket, study your receipt. Which items that you purchased were subject to your state's sales tax, and which items were exempt from sales tax?

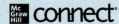 **All applicable Tax Planning Cases are available with *Connect*.**

Tax Planning Cases

LO 1-7   1. The management of Nixon Company must decide between locating a new branch office in foreign Jurisdiction F or foreign Jurisdiction G. Regardless of location, the branch operation will use tangible property (plant and equipment) worth $10 million and should generate annual gross receipts of $2 million. Jurisdiction F imposes an annual property tax of 4 percent of the value of business property and a 15 percent gross receipts tax. Jurisdiction G imposes no property tax but imposes a 30 percent gross receipts tax. Solely on the basis of these facts, should Nixon locate its new branch in Jurisdiction F or Jurisdiction G?

LO 1-7   2. KTR Company earns a $10 profit on each unit of manufactured goods, and it sells 20 million units each year. KTR's income tax rate is 20 percent. However, the jurisdiction in which KTR operates just increased the tax rate to 22 percent for next year. KTR's owners are considering two alternatives. They could simply accept the $4 million tax increase as a reduction in their after-tax profit, or they could raise the price of each unit by 20 cents, thereby increasing the profit per unit to $10.20. However, the marketing department estimates that the price increase could reduce annual sales to 19 million units. Which alternative is better for KTR's owners?

Chapter Two

Policy Standards for a Good Tax

Learning Objectives

After studying this chapter, you should be able to:

LO 2-1. Explain the concept of sufficiency of a good tax.

LO 2-2. Differentiate between the income effect and the substitution effect.

LO 2-3. Describe the characteristics of a convenient tax.

LO 2-4. Contrast the classical and the modern concepts of tax efficiency.

LO 2-5. Define *horizontal* and *vertical equity*.

LO 2-6. Differentiate between regressive, proportionate, and progressive rate structures.

LO 2-7. Explain the difference between marginal and average tax rates.

LO 2-8. Discuss distributive justice as a tax policy objective.

In Chapter 1, we identified the various taxes that characterize the modern tax environment. In this chapter, we will consider a more qualitative dimension of the environment as we identify the *normative* standards by which politicians, economists, social scientists, and individual taxpayers evaluate the merit of a tax.

Governments are aware of and influenced by these standards as they formulate tax policy. **Tax policy** can be defined as a government's attitude, objectives, and actions with respect to its tax system. Presumably, tax policy reflects the normative standards that the government deems most important. After reading this chapter, you can draw your own conclusions as to the relative importance of the standards by which tax systems are judged. You will be able to evaluate the current federal tax system in light of these standards. When you are asked as a voter to choose between competing tax policy proposals, the material covered in this chapter will help you make an informed decision.

Business managers and their tax advisers share a keen interest in tax policy. They know that many complex rules in the Internal Revenue Code have an underlying policy rationale. If they can understand this rationale, the rule itself is easier to interpret and apply. Moreover, business managers know that today's policy issues shape tomorrow's tax environment. By paying close attention to the current policy debate, managers can anticipate developments that might affect their firm's long-term strategies. Their familiarity with policy issues helps them assess the probability of changes in the tax law and develop contingent strategies to deal with such changes.

STANDARDS FOR A GOOD TAX

The American jurist Oliver Wendell Holmes, Jr., is quoted as saying, "I like to pay taxes. With them I buy civilization." Few people in modern society seem to share this sentiment. In fact, many people regard taxes as a necessary evil and consider the notion of a good tax as a contradiction in terms. Nonetheless, theorists maintain that every tax can and should be evaluated on certain basic standards.[1] These standards can be summarized as follows:

- A good tax should be sufficient to raise the necessary government revenues.
- A good tax should be convenient for the government to administer and for people to pay.
- A good tax should be efficient in economic terms.
- A good tax should be fair.

Source: Adam Smith, author of *The Wealth of Nations.*

In this chapter, we will discuss these four standards in detail. We will also identify the reasons why standards that are easy to describe in the abstract can be so difficult to put into practice.

TAXES SHOULD BE SUFFICIENT

LO 2-1
Explain the concept of sufficiency of a good tax.

The first standard by which to evaluate a tax is its **sufficiency** as a revenue raiser. A tax is sufficient if it generates enough funds to pay for the public goods and services provided by the government. After all, the reason that governments tax their citizens in the first place is to raise revenues needed for specific purposes. If a tax (or combination of taxes) is sufficient, a government can balance its budget. Tax revenues equal government spending, and the government has no need to raise additional funds.

What is the consequence of an insufficient tax system? The government must make up its revenue shortfall (the excess of current spending over tax receipts) from some other source. In Chapter 1, we learned that state governments now depend heavily on legalized gambling as an alternative source of funds. Governments may own assets or property rights that they can lease or sell to raise money. For example, the U.S. government raises minuscule revenues by selling energy generated by federally owned dams and mineral and timber rights with respect to federal lands.

Another option is for governments to borrow money to finance their operating deficits. In the United States, the federal, state, and local governments sell debt obligations in the capital markets. By selling both short-term instruments (such as U.S. Treasury bills) and long-term bonds, governments with insufficient tax systems can make ends meet. Debt financing isn't a permanent solution to an insufficient tax system. Like other debtors, governments must pay interest on borrowed funds. As the public debt increases, so does the annual interest burden. At some point, a government may find itself in the untenable position of borrowing new money not to provide more public goods and services but merely to pay the interest on existing debt.

In a worst-case scenario, a government may be forced to default on its debt obligations, damaging its credibility and creating havoc in its capital markets.

Tax Talk
In 2017, the Tax Policy Center director testified before the Senate Finance Committee and described the principles that should guide tax reform as "(1) the tax code is designed to raise revenue for government goods and services, (2) people who earn the same amount of income should be taxed equally, (3) people who make more should pay more, and (4) taxes should be as simple as possible."

Source: R. Zaretsky, *Tax Reform To-Dos,* Tax Policy Center, 2017.

---

[1] Adam Smith, author of *The Wealth of Nations,* was one of the first economists to suggest such standards. Smith's four canons were that a good tax should be equitable, certain in application, convenient for people to pay, and economical for the government to collect.

The National Debt

According to Congressional Budget Office data, the federal government operated at a deficit for every fiscal year from 1970 through 1999. After generating small surpluses in 2000 and 2001, the government returned to chronic deficit spending in 2002. In 1970, the national debt was about $380 billion and interest payments totaled $14 billion. In 2022, the debt is over $31 trillion, with the related interest payments on this debt estimated at about $305 billion.

These data suggest that our federal tax system is insufficient to support the level of government spending. Yet politicians continue to tell their constituencies that taxes are too high, and few people seem inclined to disagree. But the arithmetic is inescapable. If we want to pay less tax and at the same time curb the growth of the national debt, the federal government must cut spending. If we want our government to maintain its level of spending without incurring additional debt, we should be prepared to pay the necessary federal tax.[2]

How Much Deficit?	In the first 11 months of 2022, the CBO estimated a budget deficit of $944 billion. This was $1.8 trillion less than the same time in the previous year. The decline can largely be attributed to declines in spending related to the COVID-19 pandemic.

How to Increase Tax Revenues

Taxing jurisdictions can increase revenues in at least three ways. One way is to exploit a new tax base. For instance, the legislature of one of the seven states without a personal income tax could enact such a tax. Another way is to increase the rate of an existing tax. A jurisdiction with a 5 percent corporate income tax could increase the rate to 7 percent. Still a third way is to enlarge an existing tax base. A jurisdiction with a retail sales tax applying to tangible goods could expand the tax to apply to selected personal services, such as haircuts or dry cleaning. A jurisdiction that exempts land owned by private charities from real property tax could simply eliminate the exemption.

From a pragmatic perspective, the enactment of a tax on a new base is the most radical and politically sensitive way to increase revenues. Consequently, elected officials tend to favor the less drastic alternative of enhancing the revenue-raising capability of a tax that people are accustomed to paying. When focusing on existing tax structures, an increase in the percentage rate can be very obvious and therefore is likely to anger the greatest number of voters. In contrast, an expansion of the tax base is more subtle and less likely to attract public attention. It is hardly surprising that many significant tax increases in recent years have been accomplished through the base-expansion method.

Social Security Tax Increases	The 6.2 percent rate for the federal Social Security payroll tax has not increased since 1990. However, the tax base (the annual amount of wages or salary subject to tax) has increased almost every year. In 1990, this wage base was $51,300. In 2023, the base is $160,200. In 1990, an employee with a $150,000 salary paid $3,181 Social Security tax (6.2 percent of $51,300). In 2023, that employee would pay $9,932 Social Security tax (6.2 percent of $160,200).

[2] As another author so eloquently describes the situation, "Elected representatives must eventually confront the political reality of an electorate with an apparently insatiable appetite for 'public goods' that at the same time harbors a deep-rooted intolerance for the levels of taxation sufficient to support its own proclivities." Sheldon D. Pollack, "The Failure of U.S. Tax Policy: Revenue and Politics," 73 *Tax Notes* 341, 348.

Static versus Dynamic Forecasting

In Chapter 1, we expressed the amount of tax as an arithmetic function of the tax rate and base: $T = r \times B$. This equation suggests that an increase in the rate should increase government revenues by a proportionate amount. For instance, if the tax rate is 5 percent and the base is $500,000, a rate increase of one percentage point should generate $5,000 additional tax. This straightforward math represents a **static forecast** of the incremental revenue resulting from a change in the rate structure. The forecast is static because it assumes that B, the base variable in the equation, is independent of r, the rate variable. Accordingly, a change in the rate has no effect on the tax base.

Economic theory suggests that in many cases the two variables in the equation $T = r \times B$ are correlated. In other words, a change in the rate actually causes a change in the base.

Effect of a Rate Change on Base	For the past 10 years, the city of Fairview has levied a hotel occupancy tax equal to 10 percent of the price of a room. In the prior fiscal year, this tax yielded $800,000 in revenue.

Total annual hotel receipts subject to tax	$8,000,000
Prior year rate	.10
Prior year revenue	$ 800,000

At the beginning of the fiscal year, the city increased the tax rate to 12 percent. On the basis of a static forecast, the city expected revenue to increase to $960,000.

Forecasted hotel receipts subject to tax	$8,000,000
Current year rate	.12
Forecasted current year revenue	$ 960,000

Unfortunately, business travelers and tourists reacted to the additional cost represented by the higher room tax by purchasing fewer accommodations from Fairview hotels. Occupancy rates fell, and annual hotel receipts declined by $500,000. Consequently, the room tax yielded only $900,000 current year revenue.

Actual hotel receipts subject to tax	$7,500,000
Current year rate	.12
Actual current year revenue	$ 900,000

In the Fairview example, the increase in the tax rate caused a decrease in the tax base. Because Fairview failed to anticipate this effect, it overestimated the incremental revenue from the rate increase.

If a jurisdiction can predict the extent to which a change in tax rates will affect the tax base, it can incorporate the effect into its revenue projections. These projections, which assume a correlation between rate and base, are called **dynamic forecasts.** The accuracy of dynamic forecasts depends on the accuracy of the assumptions about the correlation. In a complex economic environment, a change in tax rates may be only one of many factors contributing to an expansion or contraction of the tax base. Economists may be unable to isolate the effect of the rate change or to test their assumptions empirically. Consequently, governments have generally relied on static forecasting to estimate the revenues gained or lost because of a tax rate change.

Behavioral Responses to Rate Changes

LO 2-2
Differentiate between
the income effect and
the substitution effect.

In the case of an income tax, the incremental revenue generated by a rate increase depends on whether (and to what extent) the increase affects the aggregate amount of income subject to tax. Specifically, the increment depends on the ways that individuals modify their economic behavior in response to higher tax rates.

Income Effect

An increase in income tax rates might induce people to engage in more income-producing activities. Consider the case of Mr. Spivey, who earns $25,000 a year as a factory worker and pays 20 percent of that income ($5,000) in tax. Mr. Spivey spends every penny of the $20,000 in after-tax income to make ends meet. How might Mr. Spivey react if the government increases the tax rate to 30 percent, thereby reducing disposable income to $17,500? Mr. Spivey might decide to work more hours or even take a second job to increase before-tax income to at least $28,600. Under the new rate structure, Mr. Spivey will pay $8,580 in tax on this income, leaving the same disposable income of $20,020 enjoy before the rate increase. This reaction (akin to running faster just to stay in the same place) has been labeled the **income effect** of a rate increase.[3]

If Mr. Spivey responds to the higher tax rate by working longer to generate more income, the government will enjoy a revenue windfall. A static forecast indicates that the government should collect an additional $2,500 in revenue from Mr. Spivey because of the 10 percent rate increase.

Static Forecast	
Revenue after rate increase (30% × $25,000 base)	$7,500
Revenue before rate increase (20% × $25,000 base)	(5,000)
Additional revenue from Mr. Spivey	$2,500

However, if Mr. Spivey reacts by increasing income from $25,000 to $28,600, the government will actually collect $3,580 additional revenue.

Income Effect	
Revenue after rate increase (30% × $28,600 base)	$8,580
Revenue before rate increase (20% × $25,000 base)	(5,000)
Additional revenue from Mr. Spivey	$3,580

Substitution Effect

If we change the financial circumstances of our hypothetical taxpayer, we might expect a different behavioral response to an income tax rate increase. Assume Ms. Hoover works 60 hours a week as a self-employed management consultant, earning $350,000 annual income. At a 20 percent tax rate, after-tax income is $280,000—more than enough to support a comfortable lifestyle. If the government increases the tax rate to 30 percent, Ms. Hoover may devote less time and effort to income-producing activity. Such a reaction

---

[3] Richard A. Musgrave and Peggy B. Musgrave, *Public Finance in Theory and Practice,* 5th ed. (New York: McGraw-Hill, 1989), p. 663.

makes sense if the after-tax value of an hour of additional labor is now worth less to Ms. Hoover than an additional hour of leisure. This behavioral reaction to a rate increase is called the **substitution effect.**[4]

If Ms. Hoover responds to the higher tax rate by working fewer hours and generating less income, the government will suffer a revenue shortfall. On the basis of a static forecast, the government is anticipating an additional $35,000 revenue from Ms. Hoover.

Static Forecast

Revenue after rate increase (30% × $350,000 base)	$105,000
Revenue before rate increase (20% × $350,000 base)	(70,000)
Additional revenue from Ms. Hoover	$ 35,000

If Ms. Hoover's income falls to $325,000 because the tax increase dampened the entrepreneurial spirit, the additional revenue from Ms. Hoover will be only $27,500.

Substitution Effect

Revenue after rate increase (30% × $325,000 base)	$97,500
Revenue before rate increase (20% × $350,000 base)	(70,000)
Additional revenue from Ms. Hoover	$ 27,500

The probability of a substitution effect varies across taxpayers. The degree of personal control that individuals exercise over their careers determines the extent to which they can replace an hour of work with an hour of relaxation. Consequently, the substitution effect is more potent for self-employed persons than for salaried employees with rigid 9 A.M. to 5 P.M. schedules. The financial flexibility necessary to curtail work effort is more characteristic of a family's secondary wage earner than of the primary wage earner. Finally, ambitious career-oriented people who are highly motivated by nonmonetary incentives such as prestige and power may be impervious to the substitution effect.

Whether an income tax will goad a person to extra effort or whether it will be a disincentive to work depends on that person's economic circumstances. Theoretically, the income effect is most powerful for lower-income taxpayers who may already be at a subsistence standard of living and do not have the luxury of choosing leisure over labor. The substitution effect becomes stronger as an individual's disposable income rises and the financial significance of each additional dollar declines. From a macroeconomic viewpoint, these contradictory behavioral reactions have important tax policy implications. Conventional wisdom suggests that governments needing more revenue should increase the tax rate on people with the highest incomes. However, if the tax rate climbs too high, the substitution effect may become so strong that the projected revenues never materialize as more and more people are discouraged from working because the after-tax return on their labor is too small.

Supply-Side Economics

Faith in the substitution effect is the foundation for **supply-side economic theory,** which holds that a decrease in the highest income tax rates should ultimately result in an increase in government revenues. The logic underlying this theory is that a rate cut increases the value of income-generating activities (work and investment) relative to the value of

[4] Ibid.

non–income-generating activities (leisure and consumption). Accordingly, people who benefit directly from the rate reduction will invest their tax windfall in new commercial ventures rather than simply spend it. This influx of private capital will stimulate economic growth and job creation. An expanding economy will result in prosperity across the board so that everyone, regardless of income level, indirectly benefits from the tax rate reduction. People will earn more income for the government to tax, and revenues attributable to this enlarged tax base will swell.

Tax Talk
The emergence of the COVID-19 pandemic in 2020 had a significant impact on the U.S. economy. In response, the U.S. Government passed three stimulus packages from April 2020 to July 2021 to curb the economic hardships experienced in both the public and private sectors.

Does this supply-side theory hold true? In 1981, the Reagan administration, acting on its belief in the theory, convinced Congress to enact the Economic Recovery Tax Act. This legislation lowered the highest marginal individual tax rates from 70 percent to 50 percent on ordinary income and from 28 percent to 20 percent on capital gains. The Tax Reform Act of 1986 went even further by reducing the highest marginal rate for individuals to 28 percent. These deep rate cuts were just one of many dramatic factors affecting the U.S. economy during the 1980s. The price of oil dropped by half, and the double-digit inflation of the late 1970s fell to less than 4 percent. Federal spending on many domestic programs declined, but defense spending soared. Congress increased the federal payroll tax rates significantly to keep pace with the explosive growth in Social Security and Medicare outlays. The government borrowed money at an unprecedented rate, creating deficits of record peacetime magnitude.[5]

Supply-side economics fell out of favor during the Clinton administration when Congress raised the highest individual tax rate to 39.6 percent. However, the spirit of "Reaganomics" was revived in George W. Bush's first term by the Economic Growth and Tax Relief Reconciliation Act of 2001. This legislation decreased the highest individual rate on ordinary income to 35 percent. The next year, Congress followed up by reducing the individual rate on capital gains and dividend income to 15 percent. Theoretically, the stimulative effect of these tax cuts should have increased federal revenues and reduced the federal deficit. However, the economic convulsion following the September 11, 2001, terrorist attacks and the unanticipated cost of the wars in Afghanistan and Iraq pushed annual deficits to ever-higher levels. The 2008 collapse of the housing industry and the meltdown of global financial markets forced the Bush and Obama administrations to spend enormous sums to stave off a depression. More often than not, a complex tangle of events make it difficult to assess the efficacy of supply-side economic theory. As economists continued to debate the issue, in December 2017 the Trump administration passed the Tax Cuts and Jobs Act, yet another example of reform based on supply-side economics.

TAXES SHOULD BE CONVENIENT

LO 2-3
Describe the characteristics of a convenient tax.

Our second standard for evaluating a tax is **convenience.** From the government's viewpoint, a good tax should be convenient to administer. Specifically, the government should have a method for collecting the tax that most taxpayers understand and with which they routinely cooperate. The collection method should not overly intrude on individual privacy but should offer minimal opportunity for noncompliance. States that levy retail sales taxes use a collection method under which sellers are responsible for collecting the tax from buyers at a point of sale and remitting the tax to the state. This method is effortless for buyers and offers them no opportunity to evade the tax. States can concentrate their enforcement efforts on retail businesses, which are much easier to audit than individual consumers.

---

[5] Isabel V. Sawhill, "Reaganomics in Retrospect: Lessons for a New Administration," *Challenge,* May–June 1989, p. 57.

In contrast, states have yet to develop a workable collection mechanism for use taxes; consequently, these taxes generate almost no revenue.

A good tax should be economical for the government. The administrative cost of collecting and enforcing the tax should be reasonable in comparison with the total revenue generated. At the federal level, the Internal Revenue Service (IRS) is the agency responsible for administering the income, payroll, excise, and transfer taxes. For its 2021 fiscal year, the IRS operated at a cost of $13.7 billion and collected more than $4.1 trillion tax revenue. Thus, the federal government's cost of collecting $100 in tax was a modest 30 cents in 2021.[6]

From the taxpayer's viewpoint, a good tax should be convenient to pay. The convenience standard suggests that people can compute their tax with reasonable certainty. Moreover, they do not have to devote undue time or incur undue costs in complying with the tax law. A retail sales tax receives high marks when judged by these criteria. People can easily compute the sales tax on a purchase and can pay the tax as part of the purchase price with no effort whatsoever.

In contrast, the federal income tax is denounced as both uncertain and costly. Because the income tax laws are so complex and change with such frequency, even tax professionals are often unsure how the law should apply to a particular transaction. Millions of Americans are bewildered by the income tax and have no confidence in their ability to compute the amount they owe. As a result, the majority pay someone else to prepare their income tax returns. By any measure, the cost to society of complying with the federal tax law is high; according to IRS estimates, individual taxpayers devote more than 2.6 billion hours each year to this inconvenient task.[7]

Aspects of the Tax Cuts and Job Act of 2017 likely simplified the filing process for many individual taxpayers. At the same time, the new law added complexities for other taxpayers such as those with pass-through businesses. No doubt researchers and lawmakers will attempt to quantify the overall impact in the coming years.

Notable Quote: "The hardest thing in the world to understand is the income tax."

—Albert Einstein

> **Tax Talk**
> *According to the Tax Foundation, the Internal Revenue Code is 2,652 pages, with well over 1 million words. For comparison, the entire Harry Potter series contains just over 1 million words.*
>
> *Source:* Tax Foundation

TAXES SHOULD BE EFFICIENT

Our third standard for a good tax is economic **efficiency.** Tax policymakers use the term *efficiency* in two different ways. Sometimes the term describes a tax that does not interfere with or influence taxpayers' economic behavior. At other times, policymakers describe a tax as efficient when individuals or organizations react to the tax by deliberately changing their economic behavior. In this section of the chapter, we will compare these two competing concepts of efficiency.

The Classical Standard of Efficiency

LO 2-4
Contrast the classical and the modern concepts of tax efficiency.

Policymakers who believe that competitive markets result in the optimal allocation of scarce resources within a society define an efficient tax as one that is *neutral* in its effect on the free market. From this perspective, a tax that causes people to modify their economic behavior is inefficient because it distorts the market and may result in suboptimal allocations of goods and services.

---

[6] IRS 2020 Data Book.
[7] https://taxfoundation.org/compliance-costs-irs-regulations/.

Classical economist Adam Smith believed that taxes should have as little effect as possible on the economy. In his 1776 masterwork, *The Wealth of Nations,* Smith concluded the following:

> A tax . . . may obstruct the industry of the people, and discourage them from applying to certain branches of business which might give maintenance and employment to great multitudes. While it obliges the people to pay, it may thus diminish, or perhaps destroy, some of the funds which might enable them more easily to do so.
>
> Source: Smith, A. *The Wealth of Nations,* 1776.

The laissez-faire system favored by Adam Smith theoretically creates a level playing field on which individuals and organizations, operating in their own self-interest, freely compete. When governments interfere with the system by taxing certain economic activities, the playing field tilts against the competitors engaging in those activities. The capitalistic game is disrupted, and the outcome may no longer be the best for society.

Of course, every modern economy has a tax system, and firms functioning within the economy must adapt to that system. Business managers become familiar with the existing tax laws and make decisions based on those laws. To return to the sports metaphor, these managers have adjusted their game plan to suit the present contours of the economic playing field.

When governments change their tax structures, firms are forced to reevaluate their tax situations in light of the change. Some may find that they benefit from the change, while others may conclude that the new tax structure puts them at a competitive disadvantage. Managers must reassess how the tax laws affect their particular business operations. They may discover that traditional planning strategies no longer work, while the efficacy of new strategies is uncertain. In short, every time the government changes its tax structure, the contours of the economic playing field shift. Because these shifts are both costly and unsettling to the business community, many economists conclude that "an old tax is a good tax."

Taxes as an Instrument of Fiscal Policy

Tax Talk

According to John Maynard Keynes, "Capitalism is the astounding belief that the most wickedest of men will do the most wickedest of things for the greatest good of everyone."

Source: John Maynard Keynes

The British economist John Maynard Keynes disagreed with the classical notion that a good tax should be neutral. Keynes believed that free markets are effective in organizing production and allocating scarce resources but lack adequate self-regulating mechanisms for maintaining economic stability.[8] According to Keynes, governments should protect their citizens and institutions against the inherent instability of capitalism. Historically, this instability caused cycles of high unemployment, severe fluctuations in prices (inflation or deflation), and uneven economic growth. Lord Keynes believed that governments could counteract these problems through *fiscal policies* to promote full employment, price-level stability, and a steady rate of economic growth.

In the Keynesian schema, tax systems are a primary tool of fiscal policy. Rather than trying to design a neutral tax system, governments should deliberately use taxes to move the economy in the desired direction. If an economy is suffering from sluggish growth and high unemployment, the government could reduce taxes to transfer funds from the public to the private sector. The tax cut should both stimulate demand for consumer goods and services and increase private investment. As a result, the economy should expand and new jobs should be created. Conversely, if an economy is overheated so that wages and prices are in an inflationary spiral, the government could raise taxes. People will have less money to spend, the demand for consumer and investment goods should weaken, and the upward pressure on wages and prices should be relieved.

[8] John Maynard Keynes, *The General Theory of Employment, Interest and Money* (New York: Harcourt, Brace, 1936).

The U.S. government formally embraced its fiscal policy responsibilities when Congress enacted the Employment Act of 1946. This legislation charged the Executive Branch with promoting full employment and a stable dollar and resulted in the formation of the President's Council of Economic Advisers. Since 1946, both political parties have regarded the federal income tax as a legitimate instrument of fiscal policy and have advocated changes in that system to further their respective economic agendas. Changes that have the intended macroeconomic effect are touted as enhancing the efficiency of the tax system, while changes that have no effect on the national economy are branded as inefficient. This Keynesian concept of efficiency is far removed from the classic concept of economic neutrality.

Economic Booster Shot	On December 22, 2017, President Trump signed the Tax Cuts and Jobs Act. The tax changes included in this far-reaching legislation impact virtually every American household and business owner. A stated goal of this tax act was to make corporate America more competitive and to discourage companies from relocating abroad.

Taxes and Behavior Modification

Modern governments use their tax systems to address not only macroeconomic concerns but also social problems. Many such problems could be reduced if people or organizations could be persuaded to alter their behavior. Governments can promote behavioral change by writing tax laws to penalize undesirable behavior or reward desirable behavior. The penalty takes the form of a higher tax burden, whereas the reward is some type of tax relief.

Some of the social problems that the federal income tax system tries to remedy are by-products of the free enterprise system. Economists refer to these by-products as **negative externalities.** One of the most widely recognized is environmental pollution. The tax system contains provisions that either pressure or entice companies to clean up their act, so to speak. One example of a provision that discourages environmentally unfriendly behavior is the excise tax on ozone-depleting chemicals manufactured in or exported into the United States.[9] An example of a provision that encourages the private sector to be more environmentally responsible is the lucrative tax break for the construction of pollution-control facilities such as wastewater purification plants.[10]

Disposable Bag Tax	In 2010, Washington, D.C., instituted a five-cent-per-bag tax on consumer use of plastic bags. According to the city's chief financial officer, the "bag tax" resulted in an 80 percent reduction in the use of disposable bags. The success did not go unnoticed. In 2020, the Virginia General Assembly passed a bill authorizing any county or city in Virginia to impose a similar tax starting in 2021.

Tax systems may also promote activities that are undervalued by the free market but that the government believes are socially desirable. By bestowing a tax benefit on the activity, the government is providing a financial "carrot." This carrot should induce more taxpayers to engage in the activity and thus result in a greater level of the activity across society. An example of an activity that the federal government promotes is the rehabilitation of historic buildings. The law allows firms to reduce their annual tax bill by a percentage of the cost of renovating a certified historic structure.[11] Without this tax break, firms might find it

[9] §4681.
[10] §169.
[11] §47.

cheaper to build or purchase modern buildings than to invest in historic structures requiring extensive renovation. At the margin, the tax break could make the investment in the historic structure the more cost-effective business decision.

Governments use tax breaks to subsidize targeted activities, thereby making those activities less costly or more profitable. An excellent example of such a subsidy is the provision in the Internal Revenue Code making the interest paid on state and local debt obligations nontaxable.[12] Because investors pay no tax on the income generated by these tax-exempt bonds, they are willing to accept a lower before-tax interest rate than if the interest was taxable. Consequently, state and local governments can pay less interest than other debtors and still compete in the financial markets. By providing this tax break, the federal government subsidizes state and local governments by reducing their cost of borrowed capital.

Income Tax Preferences

Provisions in the federal income tax system designed as incentives for certain behaviors or as subsidies for targeted activities are described as **tax preferences.** These provisions do not contribute to the accurate measurement of the tax base or the correct calculation of the tax. Tax preferences do not support the primary function of the law, which is to raise revenues. In fact, tax preferences do just the opposite. Because they allow certain persons or organizations to pay less tax, preferences lose money for the Treasury. In this respect, preferences are indirect government expenditures.

Like any other government outlay, a tax preference is justifiable only if the intended result has merit and deserves public support. But a tax preference should be subject to a second level of scrutiny: Is a tax incentive the best way to accomplish the intended result, or would direct government support be more effective? This question can be hard to answer in any objective manner. Preferences are based on assumptions about how taxpayers react to the law. In a complex economy consisting of well over 100 million taxpayers, measuring the aggregate reaction to a tax preference is extremely difficult.

A Call for Tax Neutrality

On November 1, 2005, the President's Advisory Panel on Federal Tax Reform released a 271-page report recommending an overhaul of the Internal Revenue Code. The report proposed repealing many tax preferences that benefit only certain persons or organizations. Supporters of the report were enthusiastic about a return to a level playing field: "The whole idea behind tax reform is getting the government out of the business of encouraging or discouraging any activity, however worthwhile. To the extent that this 'tax neutrality' hurts anyone, the pain consists of losing the right to continue picking the pockets of other taxpayers."[13]

The Tax Expenditures Budget

Opponents of tax preferences maintain that they are too well hidden within the Internal Revenue Code and, as a result, their cost to the government is easily overlooked. In response to this criticism, the Congressional Joint Committee on Taxation publishes an annual **Tax Expenditures Budget** that quantifies the revenue loss from each major tax preference.[14] Prior to the Tax Cuts

[12] §103.

[13] Source: S. Pearlstein, "Tax Reform That's Bold and Beautiful," *The Washington Post,* November 11, 2005.

[14] A tax expenditure is measured by the difference between tax liability under present law and the tax liability that would result from a recomputation of tax without benefit of the tax expenditure. This measurement is static because taxpayer behavior is assumed to remain unchanged for tax expenditure estimate purposes.

and Jobs Act (TCJA), the government lost about $68 billion each year because of the ability to deduct home mortgage interest payments and another $10 billion because tax provisions permitted certain individuals to deduct medical expenses. The total revenue lost from tax expenditures exceeded $1.5 trillion annually. Provisions of the TCJA sharply reduced the number of individuals who can benefit from these and similar deductions. At the same time, more individuals will benefit from a significantly increased standard deduction. The overall impact of these tax expenditures on net tax revenue is yet to be understood.

The Tax Expenditures Budget sheds light on the cost of specific preferences and their aggregate cost to the government. However, tax expenditures are not included in the calculation of any federal operating deficit. Another troubling aspect of tax preferences is that they add enormously to the length and complexity of the tax law. If the Internal Revenue Code could be stripped of every provision that is not strictly necessary to measure taxable income and compute tax, it would be far simpler to understand and apply.

TAXES SHOULD BE FAIR

Tax Talk

A survey by the Tax Foundation revealed that the local property tax is the most unpopular tax. "People hate the property tax because it is visible. One of the great ironies of tax policy is that people hate the tax that is easiest to see, not necessarily the tax that costs them the most."

Source: Tax Foundation

The fourth standard by which to evaluate a tax is whether the tax is fair to the people who must pay it. While no economist, social scientist, or politician would ever argue against fairness as a norm, there is precious little agreement as to the exact nature of tax equity. Many people believe that their tax burden is too heavy, while everyone else's burden is too light. As former U.S. Senator Russell Long expressed it, the attitude of the man on the street about tax equity is "Don't tax you, don't tax me; tax the fellow behind the tree." Clearly, any meaningful discussion of the standard of fairness must rise above this sentiment.

Ability to Pay

A useful way to begin our discussion of equity is with the proposition that each person's contribution to the support of government should reflect that person's **ability to pay.** In the tax policy literature, ability to pay refers to the economic resources under a person's control. Each of the major taxes used in this country is based on some dimension of ability to pay. For instance, income taxes are based on a person's inflow of economic resources during the year. Sales and excise taxes are based on a different dimension of ability to pay: a person's consumption of resources represented by the purchase of goods and services. Real and personal property taxes complement income and sales taxes by focusing on a third dimension of ability to pay: a person's accumulation of resources in the form of property. Transfer taxes capture a fourth dimension: the accumulated wealth that a person gives to others during life or at death.

Horizontal Equity

LO 2-5
Define *horizontal equity.*

If a tax is designed so that persons with the same ability to pay (as measured by the tax base) owe the same amount of tax, that system can be described as horizontally equitable. This standard of **horizontal equity** is consistent with the principle of equal protection under the law guaranteed by the U.S. Constitution. In the federal income tax system, the tax base is annual taxable income. Consequently, the income tax is horizontally equitable if the taxable income calculation accurately reflects the ability to pay. Let's explore this notion in more depth by comparing two people, Ms. Buell and Mr. Deetz—both unmarried and both earn a $65,000 annual salary. Neither has any additional inflows of economic resources. Do Ms. Buell and Mr. Deetz have the same ability to pay an income tax? If we consider only their identical marital status and salaries, the answer must be yes, and the two should pay an equal tax.

But what additional facts might be relevant in measuring the ability to pay? Suppose that Ms. Buell suffers from a chronic illness and has $7,000 of uninsured medical expenses each year while Mr. Deetz is in perfect health. Suppose that Mr. Deetz is the sole provider for two young children while Ms. Buell has no children. On the basis of this new evidence, should we still conclude that Ms. Buell and Mr. Deetz have the same ability to pay an income tax? To ask the question another way, should medical expenses and child support enter into the computation of taxable income? Certainly our two individuals would argue that it is only fair to consider these variables.

The horizontal equity of the income tax is enhanced by refining the calculation of taxable income to include the significant variables affecting a person's economic circumstances. But refining the tax base has its price: Every refinement adds another page to the Internal Revenue Code. Increased precision in the measurement of ability to pay may improve the horizontal equity of the income tax, but it also increases the complexity of the law.

Annual versus Lifetime Horizontal Equity

Federal taxable income is computed on a 12-month basis. This annual measurement of the ability to pay may bear little or no relationship to a person's lifetime ability to pay.

Annual versus Lifetime Horizontal Equity	This year, a blue-collar laborer wins a $300,000 lottery jackpot and, as a result, has the same taxable income as the scion of a wealthy family who lives off the interest and dividends from a trust fund. With the exception of this lucky year, the laborer's taxable income averages $35,000 per year, while the trust fund beneficiary's income averages $300,000 every year. Nevertheless, both individuals owe the same tax this year.

Tax Preferences and Horizontal Equity

In the previous section of this chapter, we introduced the concept of tax preferences. These income tax provisions are designed as incentives or subsidies and favor people who arrange their affairs to take advantage of the preference. Consequently, the tax benefit represented by preferences is not distributed impartially across taxpayers.

Preferences and Equity	Two unrelated individuals, Mr. Doh and Ms. Hernandez, invested in two different businesses this year. Both businesses earned $20,000 profit for their respective investors. Mr. Doh's business qualifies for several tax preferences. As a result, Mr. Doh must report only $14,000 of the profit on his income tax return. In contrast, Ms. Hernandez must report her entire profit. While their businesses increased our two individuals' economic ability to pay by $20,000, the tax preferences available to Mr. Doh result in taxable income that is $6,000 less than Ms. Hernandez's taxable income.

This example suggests that tax preferences can distort the horizontal equity of the income tax. Certainly the public perception is that the law is riddled with preferences that allow a privileged few to avoid paying their fair share of tax. We will examine the validity of this perception in later chapters of this text. Even if the perception is false and preferences don't undermine horizontal equity, the perception nonetheless erodes civic confidence in the fairness of the income tax system.

Vertical Equity

LO 2-5
Define *vertical equity*.

A tax system is vertically equitable if persons with a greater ability to pay owe more tax than persons with a lesser ability to pay. While horizontal equity is concerned with a rational and impartial measurement of the tax base, **vertical equity** is concerned with a fair rate structure by which to calculate the tax.

Horizontal and Vertical Equity	A local government enacted a real property tax and established a board of assessors to determine the market values of the properties in its jurisdiction. The board completes its task in a conscientious manner so that each resident's tax base (assessed value of their real property) is fairly measured. The property tax system has a two-bracket rate structure.

Percentage Rate	Bracket
2%	Assessed value from –0– to $1 million
1%	Assessed value in excess of $1 million

Mr. Foley owns real property with an assessed value of $500,000, resulting in property tax of $10,000 (2 percent of $500,000). Ms. Mugabi owns real property with an assessed value of $1.5 million, resulting in property tax of $25,000 (2 percent of $1 million + 1 percent of $500,000).

This property tax is horizontally equitable because the base is fairly measured, and taxpayers with equal bases (assessed value) bear an equal tax burden. The tax is also vertically equitable because taxpayers with a greater base (such as Ms. Mugabi) owe more tax than taxpayers with a lesser base (such as Mr. Foley).

Regressive Taxes

LO 2-6
Differentiate between regressive, proportionate, and progressive rate structures.

The property tax described in the preceding example meets a strict definition of vertical equity because Mr. Foley pays less tax than Ms. Mugabi: $10,000 versus $25,000 in tax. However, Mr. Foley's average tax rate of 2 percent ($10,000 tax ÷ $500,000 base) is *more than* Ms. Mugabi's average tax rate of 1.667 percent ($25,000 tax ÷ $1,500,000 base).

This inversion in average rates occurs because the property tax has a **regressive rate structure:** graduated rates that decrease as the base increases. Tax policymakers agree that regressive rates are inequitable because they place a proportionally greater tax burden on persons with smaller tax bases. However, the regressive nature of a tax is not always obvious from its rate structure.

Retail sales taxes consist of only a single rate and therefore are not *explicitly* regressive. Even so, many economists criticize these taxes are *implicitly* regressive in operation, bearing most heavily on people with the least economic resources.

Regressive Sales Tax Rates	James and Kim live in Maryland, which has a 5 percent sales tax on all retail purchases. James earns $20,000 annual disposable income and spends this entire amount on taxable purchases. James pays $1,000 sales tax, resulting in an average tax rate (with respect to disposable income) of 5 percent.

$1,000 tax ÷ $20,000 base = 5% average tax rate

In contrast, Kim earns $100,000 annual disposable income, spends only $75,000, and invests the remaining $25,000. Kim pays $3,750 sales tax, resulting in an average tax rate of 3.75 percent.

$3,750 tax ÷ $100,000 base = 3.75% average tax rate

According to a 2009 study, "Sales and excise taxes are very regressive. Poor families pay almost eight times more of their incomes in these taxes than the best-off families, and middle-income families pay more than five times the rate of the wealthy."[15] The majority of states mitigate the *implicit* regressivity of sales taxes by legislating broad exemptions for groceries purchased for home consumption, prescription medicines, and residential utilities.

[15] Source: Institute on Taxation and Economic Policy, *Who Pays? A Distributional Analysis of the Tax Systems in All 50 States,* 5th ed., January 2015, p. 6.

Income Tax Rate Structures

In an income tax system, the simplest rate structure consists of a single rate applied to taxable income. To illustrate this **proportionate rate structure,** consider a group of three individuals, A, B, and C, who have respective incomes of $20,000, $45,000, and $100,000. A proportionate 10 percent income tax results in the following tax for each individual:

Proportionate Rate (10%)

	Taxable Income	Tax
Taxpayer A	$ 20,000	$2,000
Taxpayer B	45,000	4,500
Taxpayer C	100,000	10,000
		$16,500

Under this rate structure, individual C, who has the most taxable income and presumably the greatest ability to pay, owes the most tax, while B, who has more income than A, owes more tax than A. Despite this result, many theorists believe that a single rate fails to fairly apportion the tax burden across people with different incomes. They argue that the 10 percent tax is relatively less of a hardship on C than on A and B. Although the tax rate is proportionate, the economic sacrifice is disproportionate.

This argument is based on the theory of the **declining marginal utility of income.** This theory presumes that the financial importance of each dollar of income diminishes as total income increases. In other words, people value the subsistence income spent on necessities, such as food and shelter, more than they value incremental income spent on luxury items. According to this theory, a **progressive rate structure** in which the rates increase as income increases results in an equality of sacrifice across taxpayers.[16]

Assume that individuals A, B, and C compute their income tax under a progressive rate structure consisting of three rate brackets:

Percentage Rate	Bracket
5%	Income from –0– to $20,000
10%	Income from $20,001 to $50,000
16%	Income in excess of $50,000

This rate structure results in the following:

Progressive Rates

	Taxable Income	Tax Computation	Tax
Taxpayer A	$ 20,000	5% of 20,000	$1,000
Taxpayer B	45,000	5% of 20,000	
		+10% of 25,000	3,500
Taxpayer C	100,000	5% of 20,000	
		+10% of 30,000	
		+16% of 50,000	12,000
			$16,500

[16] See Walter J. Blum and Harry Kalven, Jr., *The Uneasy Case for Progressive Taxation* (Chicago: University of Chicago Press, 1953), for a provocative analysis of the arguments for and against progressive tax rates.

Note that this rate structure raises the same $16,500 revenue as the 10 percent proportionate rate structure, and the aggregate tax burden is unchanged. However, A and B are paying fewer dollars, while C's tax has increased by $2,000.

Is the proportionate or the progressive rate structure more equitable for our three individuals? If the progressive rate structure seems fairer than the proportionate structure, would a more progressive structure—perhaps with a top rate of 25 percent—be even fairer? There are no objective answers to these questions. Progressivity has an intuitive appeal to many people, and the U.S. income tax has always used a progressive rate structure. Nonetheless, while it may be plausible that individuals value income less as their economic resources increase, this proposition cannot be tested empirically. To refer to our illustration, the taxing authorities have no idea how A, B, or C personally values income, or whether the economic sacrifices each makes by paying tax are even remotely comparable. Until economists discover how to measure the utility of income and to compare utilities across individuals, the extent to which any progressive rate structure achieves equality of sacrifice is a matter of opinion.

Marginal and Average Tax Rates

LO 2-7
Explain the difference between marginal and average tax rates.

Before leaving the subject of income tax rate structures, we must distinguish between marginal and average tax rates. The **marginal rate** is the rate that applies to the *next* dollar of income. In the progressive rate structure in our example, individual C with $100,000 taxable income owed $12,000 tax. If C earns one more dollar, that dollar is subject to a 16 percent tax rate. Nevertheless, the fact that C is in the 16 percent marginal tax bracket does not mean the taxpayer is paying 16 percent of their income to the government. The $12,000 tax divided by $100,000 taxable income is an **average rate** of only 12 percent. Similarly, individual B has a 10 percent marginal rate, but the average rate is only 7.8 percent ($3,500 tax divided by $45,000 taxable income).

Under a proportionate rate structure, the marginal and average rates are the same for all levels of taxable income. Under a progressive rate structure, the marginal rate is higher than the average rate for incomes in excess of the first rate bracket. The graphs in Exhibit 2.1 illustrate the relationship between marginal and average rate for the proportionate and progressive tax structures in our examples. In both graphs, the marginal rate is represented by a solid line and the average rate is represented by a broken line.

Tax Talk
In 1935, the top marginal rate of 79 percent on income in excess of $5 million applied to only one person: John D. Rockefeller.

EXHIBIT 2.1A
Marginal and Average Tax Rates under a Proportionate Rate Structure

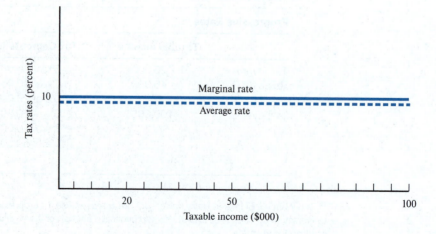

EXHIBIT 2.1B
Marginal and Average Tax Rates under a Progressive Rate Structure

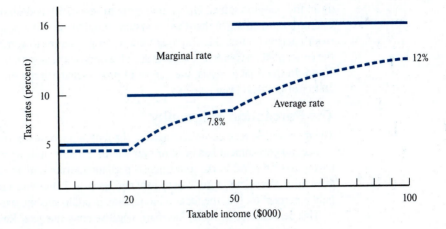

LO 2-8
Discuss distributive justice as a tax policy objective.

Distributive Justice

In a social sense, a tax is equitable if it redresses inequities existing in a capitalistic system. A vastly uneven distribution of private wealth across households, characterized by extremes of poverty and affluence, is one such inequity. By definition, taxes appropriate private wealth for public use, and they appropriate more from the rich than from the poor. Consequently, taxes become mechanisms for the redistribution of wealth across society. Wealth transfer taxes, such as the federal estate and gift taxes, are prime examples of taxes with strong distributional implications. These taxes were enacted early in this century to allow the government to tap into the immense personal fortunes amassed during America's "gilded age." Some policymakers believe that the justification for a progressive income tax is its potential for rectifying distributive inequity. "The case for drastic progression in taxation must be rested on the case against inequality—on the ethical or aesthetic judgment that the prevailing distribution of wealth and income reveals a degree (and/or kind) of inequality that is distinctly evil or unlovely."[17]

Share of Income/Share of Taxes

In 2019 (the most recent year that data is available), the top 1 percent of U.S. taxpayers (with incomes in excess of $546,434) accounted for 20.41 percent of the total income reported on all individual tax returns filed for that year. This highest income group also accounted for 39 percent of the total individual tax paid in 2019.

In contrast, the bottom 50 percent of U.S. taxpayers (with incomes less than $44,269) accounted for just 11.61 percent of total income reported. However, this lowest income group accounted for only 3.06 percent of the total tax paid.

Many social commentators view the current distribution of wealth across American households as unjust.[18] These commentators suggest that the federal government could combat this injustice by making the income tax rate structure more progressive. But once

[17] Source: H. Simons, *Personal Income Taxation* (Chicago: University of Chicago Press, 1938), pp. 18–19.

[18] In 2013, the richest 1 percent of Americans owned 36.7 percent of the national wealth, the richest 20 percent owned 88.9 percent of the wealth, and the poorest 40 percent owned negative .9 percent of the wealth. Edward N. Wolff, *Household Wealth Trends in the United States, 1962–2013: What Happened Over the Great Recession?* (National Bureau of Economic Research, December 2014).

again the question arises: How much more progressivity is desirable? Only the most fanatic egalitarian would argue that the tax system should result in a perfectly equal distribution of wealth across households. Although many people agree (to a greater or lesser extent) with the concept of distributive justice, many also oppose the notion of Uncle Sam playing Robin Hood. In the final analysis, the degree of progressivity in the income tax system remains a matter of political taste.

The Perception of Inequity

The most widespread complaint against the federal income tax system is that it is unfair. Of course, no government has been or ever will be capable of designing a tax that people enjoy paying. As Edmund Burke, the English parliamentarian and social scientist, observed, "To tax and to please, no more than to love and be wise, is not given to man." Nevertheless, the public perception that the federal income tax is unfair has increased in recent decades.

This perception of inequity has many negative consequences. Research has shown that individuals who believe that the income tax system is unfair are more likely to deliberately underreport their incomes than individuals who believe the system is fair. This result suggests that as public confidence in the equity of the federal tax system erodes, the level of compliance will decline. As greater numbers of citizens regard tax evasion as acceptable, and even rational, behavior, the tax system will place an increasingly unfair burden on the honest remainder who comply with the law. The philosopher Plato reinforces this idea: "When there is an income tax, the just man will pay more and the unjust less on the same amount of income."

> Taxpayer morale ultimately depends on the belief that taxes are fair. If the basis for this belief comes under suspicion, voluntary compliance with the tax laws is jeopardized. Thus, the perceived lack of fairness of the income tax may be as important as actual complexities, economic distortions, and inequities.[19]

Many individuals believe that the income tax system is unfair because it is so complicated. They are convinced that the system is full of exotic loopholes benefiting only the rich who can afford expert legal advice. As you will learn, this conviction is unfounded. Many of the complexities of the law were designed to ensure that high-income taxpayers *cannot* manipulate the system to unwarranted advantage. Affluent individuals undeniably use the tax planning strategies discussed throughout this text on a routine basis to maximize the net present value of their business and investment transactions. However, most of these strategies derive from commonplace features of the law rather than from closely guarded secrets known only to tax professionals.

Conclusion

The late Jack Kemp, 1996 Republican vice presidential candidate, provided this summary description of a good tax:

> Surely, a tax code which is simple and fair must generate sufficient revenue so that the federal government may carry out its legitimate tasks. Second, it must not place a tax burden on those members of society least able to bear one. And, perhaps most important of all, it must not restrict the innovative and entrepreneurial capacities of Americans upon which rising living standards and our general prosperity so greatly depend.[20]

[19] Source: Department of the Treasury, *Tax Reform for Fairness, Simplicity, and Economic Growth,* vol. 1 (Washington, D.C.: U.S. Government Printing Office, 1984), p. 9.

[20] Source: National Commission on Economic Growth and Tax Reform, "Unleashing America's Potential: A Pro-Growth, Pro-Family Tax System for the 21st Century," 70 *Tax Notes* 413, 415.

This summary remains relevant and touches on the four normative standards discussed in this chapter: sufficiency, convenience, efficiency, and equity. In our discussions, we learned that people interpret these standards in different ways and hold varying opinions as to how each should be achieved.

The standards for a good tax are not necessarily in harmony, and reconciling them can be a tricky proposition. A government's attempt to improve the sufficiency of its tax system by raising rates or expanding the base could make the tax less efficient in terms of its economic effect. The introduction of a preferential rule to enhance economic efficiency might damage the equity of the tax. Conversely, the enactment of a provision making a tax fairer may create complexity that makes it more difficult to administer. Tax policymakers are well aware of the frictions between the standards for a good tax. They know that trade-offs may be necessary in the design and implementation of the tax system that best serves the needs of their governments.

Key Terms

ability to pay *2-12*	marginal rate *2-16*	substitution effect *2-6*
average rate *2-16*	negative externality *2-10*	sufficiency *2-2*
convenience *2-7*	progressive rate	supply-side economic
declining marginal utility of	structure *2-15*	theory *2-6*
income *2-15*	proportionate rate	Tax Expenditures
dynamic forecast *2-4*	structure *2-15*	Budget *2-11*
efficiency *2-8*	regressive rate	tax policy *2-1*
horizontal equity *2-12*	structure *2-14*	tax preferences *2-11*
income effect *2-5*	static forecast *2-4*	vertical equity *2-13*

Questions and Problems for Discussion

LO 2-1, 2-2, 2-3, 2-4, 2-5, 2-6, 2-7
1. Identify the tax policy issue that you believe is the most important in today's society.

LO 2-1
2. What evidence suggests that the federal tax system receives a low grade when evaluated on the standard of sufficiency?

LO 2-1
3. Identify three ways that governments can alter their tax system to increase revenues.

LO 2-1
4. National governments have the authority to print their own currency. Why might governments be reluctant to finance an operating deficit (excess of spending over revenues) simply by printing more money?

LO 2-2
5. In each of the following cases, discuss how the taxpayers might respond to a tax rate increase in a manner consistent with the income effect.
   a. Mr. Edwards earns $32,000 a year as an employee, and Mrs. Edwards doesn't work.
   b. Mr. Frank earns $22,000 a year as an employee, and Mrs. Frank earns $10,000 a year as a self-employed worker.
   c. Mrs. George earns $22,000 a year as an employee, and Mr. George earns $10,000 a year as an employee.

LO 2-2
6. In each of the following cases, discuss how the taxpayers might respond to a tax rate increase in a manner consistent with the substitution effect.
   a. Ms. Akai earns $195,000 a year as a salaried employee, and Mr. Akai doesn't work.
   b. Ms. Junga earns $195,000 a year as a salaried employee, and Mr. Junga earns $38,000 a year as a salaried employee.
   c. Ms. Kahn is single and earns $195,000 a year as a self-employed consultant.

LO 2-2   7. Ms. Vincent resides in a jurisdiction with a 35 percent income tax. Ms. Vincent is considering two options: invest $40,000 in bonds paying 8 percent annual interest or spend the $40,000 on a new luxury automobile. Ms. Vincent is having a hard time deciding between these two alternatives. Why might the decision be easier if the jurisdiction increases its income tax rate to 50 percent?

LO 2-2   8. What nonmonetary incentives affect the amount of time and energy people devote to income-generating activities?

LO 2-2   9. The U.S. Congress has occasionally considered enacting a federal tax on the sale of consumer goods and services. This national sales tax would be in addition to any state and local sales tax. Would this new source of federal revenue affect the revenues of state and local governments?

LO 2-3   10. The federal government levies a gift tax on the value of property that people give away during their life and an estate tax on the value of property that people transfer at death. From the government's perspective, which tax is more convenient?

LO 2-3   11. Discuss the tax policy implications of the saying "an old tax is a good tax."

LO 2-3   12. Jurisdiction R and Jurisdiction S both impose a personal income tax on their residents. Under Jurisdiction R's system, employers are required to withhold income tax from their employees' paychecks and remit the tax to the government. Jurisdiction S's system has no such withholding requirement. Instead, residents must compute their income tax and pay the tax directly on a monthly basis. Which tax system is more convenient for the government and for the taxpayer?

LO 2-4   13. Jurisdiction E spends approximately $7 million each winter on snow removal. The jurisdiction is considering adding a new income tax provision that would allow people to deduct the cost of snow removal equipment purchased during the year.

   a. Does this proposed change in Jurisdiction E's tax law meet the definition of a tax preference? Explain briefly.

   b. Jurisdiction E forecasts that the proposed change will decrease its annual tax revenues by $250,000 but will improve the jurisdiction's financial condition by $300,000. On what assumptions is this forecast based?

LO 2-5   14. The federal income tax is criticized as being both inequitable across individuals and overly complicated. Discuss why equity and simplicity can be considered conflicting tax policy goals.

LO 2-5   15. Jurisdiction W has decided to enact a personal income tax on its residents. Policymakers are considering the following alternatives:

   a. No tax on income up to $35,000, and a 15 percent tax on all income in excess of $35,000.

   b. A 10 percent tax on all income.

   c. A 15 percent tax on all income up to $80,000, and no tax on any income in excess of $80,000.

   Identify the rate structure of each of the three alternatives.

LO 2-5   16. Corporation R and Corporation T conduct business in Jurisdiction Q. The corporations' financial records for last year show the following:

	Corporation R	Corporation T
Gross receipts from sales	$ 5,000,000	$5,000,000
Cost of goods sold	(3,200,000)	(3,670,000)
Gross profit	$ 1,800,000	$1,330,000
Annual operating expenses	(1,000,000)	(400,000)
Charitable contributions	–0–	(300,000)
Net profit	$ 800,000	$ 630,000

Jurisdiction Q decided to enact a tax on corporations conducting business within its jurisdiction but has not decided on the tax base. Identify four different tax bases suggested by the corporations' financial records and discuss each base in terms of horizontal equity.

LO 2-7   17. Ms. Valdez is considering investing $20,000 in a new business and projects that this investment should generate $3,000 income each year. In estimating the tax on this future income stream, should Ms. Valdez use marginal or average tax rate?

All applicable Application Problems are available with *Connect*.

Application Problems

LO 2-1   1. Country M levies a 10 percent excise tax on the retail price of any automobile purchased in the country. This year, the aggregate purchase price subject to tax was $8 million, so current year revenue was $800,000. Country M plans to increase the tax rate next year to 11 percent. Compute next year's excise tax revenue assuming

   a. Next year's tax base equals the current year base.

   b. Next year's tax base increases to $9.3 million.

   c. Next year's tax base decreases to $7 million.

LO 2-1   2. The city of Lakeland levies a 2 percent tax on the value of all restaurant meals served to the public within the city limits. This year, the aggregate value subject to tax was $29.4 million, so current year revenue was $588,000. Lakeland plans to decrease the tax rate next year to 1.5 percent. Compute next year's restaurant tax revenue assuming

   a. Next year's tax base equals the current year base.

   b. Next year's tax base increases to $36 million.

   c. Next year's tax base increases to $41 million.

LO 2-1   3. The city of Clement levies a 5 percent tax on the base price of rooms provided by hotels and motels located within the city limits. This year, the aggregate room price subject to tax was $25 million, so current year revenue was $1.25 million. Clement's city council recently voted to increase the hotel tax rate to 6 percent for the next fiscal year. Compute next year's hotel tax revenue assuming

   a. Next year's tax base equals the current year base.

   b. Next year's tax base decreases to $22 million.

   c. Next year's tax base decreases to $19 million.

LO 2-1, 2-2   4. Mrs. King, a single taxpayer, earns a $42,000 annual salary and pays 15 percent in state and federal income tax. If tax rates increase so that Mrs. King's annual tax rate is 20 percent, how much additional income must Mrs. King earn to maintain the same after-tax disposable income?

LO 2-2   5. Mrs. Esposito, a petroleum engineer, earns an $83,000 annual salary, while Mr. Esposito has no earned income. Under current law, the couple pays 20 percent in state and federal income tax. Because of recent tax law changes, the couple's future tax rate will increase to 28 percent. If Mrs. Esposito decides to take a part-time job because of the rate increase, how much income must she earn to maintain the couple's after-tax disposable income?

LO 2-2   6. Mr. and Mrs. Jerald own a dry cleaning business that generates $125,000 taxable income each year. For the past few years, the couple's federal tax rate on this income has been 32 percent. Congress recently increased the tax rate for next year to 40 percent.

   a. Based on a static forecast, how much additional revenue will the federal government collect from Mr. and Mrs. Jerald next year?

   b. How much additional revenue will the government collect if Mr. and Mrs. Jerald respond to the rate increase by working harder and earning $140,000 next year?

   c. How much additional revenue will the government collect if Mr. and Mrs. Jerald respond to the rate increase by working less and earning only $110,000 next year?

LO 2-2   7. Ms. Benoit is a self-employed architect who earns $300,000 annual taxable income. For the past several years, the tax rate on this income has been 35 percent. Because of recent tax law changes, Ms. Benoit's tax rate for next year will decrease to 25 percent.

   a. Based on a static forecast, how much less revenue will the government collect from Ms. Benoit next year?

   b. If Ms. Benoit responds to the rate decrease by working more hours and earning $375,000 taxable income, how much less tax revenue will the government collect from Ms. Benoit next year?

   c. If Ms. Benoit responds to the rate decrease by working fewer hours and earning only $275,000 taxable income, how much less tax revenue will the government collect from Ms. Benoit next year?

LO 2-6, 2-7   8. Jurisdiction B levies a flat 7 percent tax on the first $5 million of annual corporate income.

   a. Jersey Inc. generated $3.9 million income this year. Compute Jersey's income tax and determine its average and marginal tax rate on total income.

   b. Leray Inc. generated $9.6 million income this year. Compute Leray's income tax and determine Leray's average and marginal tax rate on total income.

   c. What type of rate structure does Jurisdiction B use for its corporate income tax?

LO 2-6, 2-7   9. Jurisdiction X levies a flat 14 percent tax on individual income in excess of $35,000 per year. Individuals who earn $35,000 or less pay no income tax.

   a. Mr. Hill earned $98,750 income this year. Compute Mr. Hill's income tax, and determine average and marginal tax rate.

   b. Ms. Lui earned $47,900 income this year. Compute Ms. Lui's income tax and determine average and marginal tax rate.

   c. Ms. Archer earned $34,100 income this year and paid no income tax. Describe Ms. Archer's average and marginal tax rate.

   d. What type of rate structure does Jurisdiction X use for its individual income tax?

LO 2-7   10. Government G levies an income tax with the following rate structure:

Percentage Rate	Bracket
6%	Income from –0– to $30,000
10	Income from $30,001 to $70,000
20	Income from $70,001 to $200,000
28	Income in excess of $200,000

    a. Taxpayer A's taxable income is $119,400. Compute A's income tax liability and average tax rate. What is A's marginal tax rate?

    b. Taxpayer B's taxable income is $383,900. Compute B's income tax liability and average tax rate. What is B's marginal tax rate?

LO 2-5, 2-7   11. Refer to Government G's rate structure described in the preceding problem. Taxpayer O earns $50,000 annually during years 1 through 10. Taxpayer P earns $20,000 annually during years 1 through 5 and $80,000 annually during years 6 through 10.

    a. How much total income does each taxpayer earn over the 10-year period?

    b. Compute each taxpayer's average tax rate for the 10-year period.

LO 2-7   12. Country A levies an individual income tax with the following rate structure:

Percentage Rate	Bracket
10%	Income from –0– to $20,000
15	Income from $20,001 to $75,000
25	Income from $75,001 to $160,000
30	Income in excess of $160,000

    a. Mr. Levi's taxable income is $69,200. Compute Mr. Levi's tax on this income as well as average and marginal tax rate.

    b. Ms. Jinn's taxable income is $184,400. Compute Ms. Jinn's tax on this income as well as average and marginal tax rate.

LO 2-7   13. Refer to Country A's rate structure described in the preceding problem. Ms. Slattery's annual taxable income for years 1 through 5 is $150,000. Ms. Ochoa's taxable income for years 1 through 4 is $20,000. In year 5, Ms. Ochoa wins a lottery, resulting in taxable income of $670,000 for this one year.

    a. How much total income does each individual earn over the five-year period?

    b. Compute each individual's average tax rate for the five-year period.

LO 2-5, 2-6, 2-7   14. Jurisdiction Z levies an excise tax on retail purchases of jewelry and watches. The tax equals 3 percent of the first $1,000 of the purchase price plus 1 percent of the purchase price in excess of $1,000.

    a. Individual C purchases a watch for $500. Compute C's excise tax and average excise tax rate.

    b. Individual D purchases a watch for $5,000. Compute D's excise tax and average excise tax rate.

    c. Is Jurisdiction Z's excise tax vertically equitable? Explain briefly.

Issue Recognition Problems

Identify the tax issue or issues suggested by the following situations, and state each issue in the form of a question.

LO 2-1
1. Country O imposes just two taxes on its citizens. The first tax is a 20 percent excise tax on motor fuel and motor oil. This tax is earmarked for Country O's Highway Improvement Trust Fund, and the revenues can't be spent for any other purpose. The second tax is a 10 percent general sales tax on consumer goods and services (excluding retail purchases of motor fuel and motor oil). Sales tax revenues can be spent for any authorized public purpose. This year, Country O collected $185 million in excise tax and spent only $77 million from the Highway Improvement Trust Fund. It collected $718 million in sales tax and spent $800 million for public purposes.

LO 2-2
2. County M imposes a 1 percent tax on the gross receipts earned by firms operating within its jurisdiction. For the past year, gross receipts subject to tax totaled $400 million. The county government is considering raising the tax rate to 2 percent because it needs $400,000 additional revenue to improve its road system.

LO 2-5
3. Mrs. Kinsolver is completely blind, while Mr. Lu is paralyzed from the waist down. Both individuals have the same income. The Internal Revenue Code provides a preferential deduction for individuals who are blind, and as a result, Mrs. Kinsolver's income tax liability is less than Mr. Lu's income tax liability.

LO 2-3, 2-5
4. Four years ago, the citizens of Country C complained that the national tax system was too uncertain because the government changed the tax laws so frequently. In response to this criticism, the government enacted a 10-year moratorium on change: No existing tax law can be modified and no new tax law can be enacted for a decade. This year, Country C is experiencing a severe recession. Economic growth is at a standstill, and the national unemployment rate is 18 percent.

LO 2-3, 2-5
5. Two years ago, the government of State P decided to improve the horizontal equity of its individual income tax by allowing families to deduct the cost of heating and air conditioning their homes. This modification necessitated an additional tax form and three additional pages of instructions. For the past two years, only one-third of the families eligible for the deduction actually claimed it on their returns.

LO 2-4
6. Jurisdiction J decides to clean up its streets, parks, and waterways by providing a tax break for businesses that assign employees to pick up trash for a minimum number of hours each month. The annual revenue loss from this tax break is $1.9 million.

Research Problems

LO 2-1
1. Visit the website for the Congressional Budget Office (**www.cbo.gov**), follow the link to Budget and Economic Information, and look up the most current Monthly Budget Review. What is the CBO's estimate of the U.S. government's total budget surplus or deficit for fiscal year 2023? Does this estimate include or exclude the surplus in the Social Security Trust Fund?

LO 2-1
2. Visit the website for the Tax Foundation (**www.taxfoundation.org**). Select the link "About Us" to read the organization's mission statement. Select the link "Tax Topics" to research the following:

    a. What and when was Tax Freedom Day in 2022?

    b. How many additional days would Americans have to work to pay off the 2022 federal budget deficit?

LO 2-1
3. Visit the U.S. Treasury's Public Debt website (**https://fiscaldata.treasury.gov/national-debt/**) to find out today's total national debt to the penny!

Tax Planning Case

LO 2-1   Jurisdiction B's tax system consists of a 6.5 percent general sales tax on retail goods and selected services. Over the past decade, the average annual volume of sales subject to this tax was $500 million. The jurisdiction needs to increase its tax revenues by approximately $5 million each year to finance its spending programs. The taxing authorities are considering two alternatives: a 1 percent increase in the sales tax rate or a new 2 percent tax on the net income of corporations doing business in the jurisdiction. Based on recent economic data, the annual net income subject to the new tax would be $275 million. However, the jurisdiction would have to create a new agency responsible for enforcing and collecting the income tax. The estimated annual cost of the agency is $500,000. Jurisdiction B borders four other taxing jurisdictions, all of which have a general sales tax and two of which have a corporate income tax.

1. Based on a static forecast, how much incremental revenue would Jurisdiction B raise under each alternative?
2. Assume that the taxing authorities in Jurisdiction B want a dynamic forecast of the incremental revenues under each alternative. What additional facts would be important in making such a forecast, and why?

Part **Two**

Fundamentals of Tax Planning

Chapter **Three**

Taxes as Transaction Costs

Learning Objectives

After studying this chapter, you should be able to:

LO 3-1. Compute a transaction's net present value (NPV).

LO 3-2. Compute the tax cost of an income item and the tax savings from a deduction.

LO 3-3. Integrate tax costs and savings into NPV calculations.

LO 3-4. Identify the uncertainties concerning future tax costs and savings.

LO 3-5. Explain why tax minimization may not be the optimal business strategy.

LO 3-6. Explain why bilateral tax planning is important in private market transactions.

LO 3-7. Distinguish between arm's-length and related party transactions.

In the introduction to this text, we established the premise that the overall objective of business decisions is to maximize the value of the firm. The premise is relevant to managers who are employed to make decisions on behalf of the owners of the firm. Managers who make good decisions that increase the value of owners' equity can expect to be well compensated for their success. Managers who make bad decisions that decrease value can expect to lose their jobs. A variation of the premise holds true for individuals acting in their own economic self-interest. Individuals want to make personal financial decisions that further their goal of wealth maximization.

In this chapter, we will explore the business decision-making process. It begins with a review of the concept of net present value of cash flows as the cornerstone of this process. This chapter then focuses on how the tax consequences of business transactions affect net present value and how these consequences must be integrated into the decision-making framework. We will consider how managers can structure transactions to control tax consequences and maximize net present value. This chapter concludes by discussing the extent to which the various parties to a business transaction can negotiate to reduce the tax burden on the transaction and to share the tax savings among themselves.

THE ROLE OF NET PRESENT VALUE IN DECISION MAKING

Every business activity consists of a series of transactions intended to generate profit and create value. Business managers need a method for evaluating whether an isolated transaction or an integrated sequence of transactions will contribute to or detract from the profitability of the activity. The method should be useful to managers who must choose between alternative transactions that accomplish the same result for the firm.

Quantifying Cash Flows

Financial theorists agree that the first step in evaluating a business transaction is to quantify the cash flows from the transaction. Some transactions result in the receipt of cash by the firm. The sale of merchandise to a customer and the rental of property to a lessee are examples of transactions generating cash inflows. Other transactions require the firm to disburse cash. The purchase of business assets and the hiring of employees are common transactions requiring cash outflows. Of course, many transactions involve both inflows and outflows and must be evaluated on the basis of **net cash flow** (the difference between cash received and cash disbursed).

The various revenue-generating transactions in which firms engage typically result in positive net cash flows that increase the value of the firm. If managers must choose between alternative revenue-generating opportunities, they should choose the opportunity with the greatest positive net cash flow. The various costs that firms incur can be expressed as negative net cash flows. Viewed in isolation, negative net cash flows decrease the value of the firm. However, costs are essential components of an integrated business activity and contribute to short-term and long-term profitability. If managers conclude that a particular cost is unnecessary because it doesn't enhance profitability, the cost should be eliminated. If a cost is justified, managers should reduce the negative net cash flow associated with the cost as much as possible.

In summary, managers want to make decisions that enhance profitability by increasing revenues and controlling costs. More precisely, *managers want to make decisions that maximize the value of the firm by maximizing positive cash flow or minimizing negative cash flow.*

Business Perspective	Entrepreneurs believe that profit is what matters most in a new enterprise. But profit is secondary. Cash flow matters most.[1]

The Concept of Present Value

LO 3-1
Compute a transaction's net present value (NPV).

When cash flows from a transaction occur at different times, the quantification of net cash flow should take into account the **time value of money.** Time value refers to the fact that a dollar available today is worth more than a dollar available tomorrow because the current dollar can be invested to start earning interest immediately.[2] A dollar available today has a present value of a dollar. The present value of a dollar available in the future is based on a **discount rate**—the after-tax rate of interest on invested funds for the deferral period. A transaction's **net present value (NPV)** is the sum of the present values of cash inflows and outflows from the transaction.

---

[1] Gendron George, "Flashes of Genius: An Interview with Peter F. Drucker," *Inc.,* May 15, 1996.

[2] This proposition is the first basic principle of finance. Richard A. Brealey and Stewart C. Myers, *Principles of Corporate Finance,* 5th ed. (New York: McGraw-Hill, 1996).

The next several paragraphs review the mathematical derivation of present value. If you are already familiar with this material, please feel free to jump ahead to the issue of risk.

Present Value

The algebraic expression of the present value (PV) of a dollar available at the end of one period based on the discount rate (r) for that period is

$$PV(\$1) = \frac{1}{1 + r}$$

PV Calculation	At an annual 10 percent discount rate, the present value of $1 to be received at the end of one year is $.9091:

$$\$.9091 = \frac{1}{1.10}$$

If the availability of the dollar is deferred for a number of periods (n) over which the discount rate is constant, the algebraic expression of present value is

$$PV(\$1) = \frac{1}{(1 + r)^n}$$

PV Calculation	At an annual 10 percent discount rate, the present value of $1 to be received at the end of three years is $.7513:

$$\$.7513 = \frac{1}{1.331} = \frac{1}{(1.10)^3}$$

In other words, $.7513 invested today to earn 10 percent compounded annually will accumulate to $1 at the end of three years.

Present Value of an Annuity

A cash flow consisting of a constant dollar amount available at the end of the period for a specific number of equal time periods is called an **annuity.** Examples include monthly rent payments over the term of a lease agreement and equal annual payments to retire the principal of an outstanding loan. The algebraic expression of the present value (PV) of an annuity of $1 for a number of periods (n) based on the discount rate (r) over the period is

$$PV(\$1 \text{ for n periods}) = \frac{1}{r} - \frac{1}{r(1 + r)^n}$$

PV of an Annuity	At a 10 percent annual discount rate, the present value of $1 to be received at the end of years 1 through 4 is $3.1699:

$$PV(\$1 \text{ for 4 years}) = \frac{1}{.10} - \frac{1}{.10(1.10)^4}$$

$$PV(\$1 \text{ for 4 years}) = 10 - \frac{1}{.10(1.4641)}$$

$$\$3.1699 = 10 - 6.8301$$

The present value of the annuity is the sum of the present values of the four $1 payments. Note that this formula works only for a series of *equal* payments.

Present Value Tables

The algebraic formulas in the preceding paragraphs can be used to derive tables of discount factors for computing the present value of cash receipts or payments deferred for any given number of periods. Appendix A of this text is a table of discount factors for computing the present value of $1 available at the end of 1 through 20 years at annual discount rates ranging from 3 percent to 20 percent. Appendix B is a table of discount factors for computing the present value of a $1 annuity for a period of 1 through 20 years at annual discount rates ranging from 3 percent to 20 percent. Throughout the text, computations of the net present value of cash flows are based on factors from these tables.

The net present value of cash flows can also be computed by using a financial calculator or a spreadsheet computer program such as Microsoft Excel. Remember that discount factor tables, calculators, and electronic spreadsheets are all means to the same end. Business managers can use whichever tool is the most convenient for computing net present value.

The Issue of Risk

The quantification of cash flows and calculation of their net present value are based on assumptions concerning future events. In projecting the cash inflows and outflows from a proposed transaction, business managers research pertinent industry and economic data, consult professionals who have expertise relevant to the transaction, and rely on their experience with past transactions of a similar nature. Nonetheless, even the most carefully developed projections can be inaccurate, and unexpected events can alter the actual cash flows from a transaction.

Financial forecasters must accept the possibility that one or more of the assumptions on which their cash flow projections are based will be wrong. Of course, some assumptions are more certain than others. The assumption that the U.S. government will pay the interest on its debt obligations is more certain than the assumption that the value of an initial public offering (IPO) of stock will double in value over the next 12 months. This difference in certainty makes a decision to invest in U.S. Treasury bills less risky than a decision to invest in the IPO.

Business managers must be sensitive to the uncertainties and the resultant degree of risk inherent in any transaction. When calculating net present value, they should invoke the financial principle that a safe dollar is worth more than a risky dollar. In other words, the present value of a highly speculative future dollar should be based on a higher discount rate than the present value of a guaranteed future dollar.

High Risk and Low Risk

Firm Z has the opportunity to invest $200,000 in a new business venture. The promoters of the venture provide Firm Z with a 10-year projection of net cash flows. Firm Z determines that the venture has a high degree of risk and therefore uses a 10 percent discount rate to calculate the net present value of the projected cash flows. With the high discount rate, the net present value is a *negative* number. Consequently, Firm Z decides not to make the investment. In contrast, assume that Firm Z determines that the venture has a low degree of risk and uses a 4 percent discount rate to calculate net present value. With the lower discount rate, the net present value is a positive number, and Firm Z decides to make the investment.

Because this text concentrates on the tax aspects of business decisions, the cash flow examples throughout the text incorporate two simplifying assumptions about financial risk. First, they assume that the discount rate in the example accurately reflects the risk of the transaction under consideration. Second, the examples assume that such risk is stable over time so that the appropriate discount rate does not change from period to period.

Net Present Value Example

Let's summarize our discussion of net present value and its role in business decision making by working through a simple example. Suppose a consulting firm must decide between two engagements, either of which would require the firm's complete attention for two years. Engagement 1 will generate $40,000 revenue in the current year and $185,000 revenue in the next year. The firm estimates that this engagement will require $15,000 of expenses in the current year and $10,000 of expenses in the next year. Engagement 2 will generate $200,000 revenue in the current year and $85,000 revenue in the next year. The firm estimates that Engagement 2 will require $45,000 of annual expenses. Based on a 5 percent discount rate and *without considering the effect of any type of tax,* the net present values of the competing engagements are computed as follows:

	Engagement 1	Engagement 2
Current year:		
Cash revenues	$ 40,000	$200,000
Cash expenses	(15,000)	(45,000)
Net cash flow	$ 25,000	$155,000
Next year:		
Cash revenues	$185,000	$ 85,000
Cash expenses	(10,000)	(45,000)
Net cash flow	$175,000	$ 40,000
Present value of current year cash flow	$ 25,000	$155,000
Present value of next year cash flow (cash flow × .952 discount factor)	166,600	38,080
NPV	$191,600	$193,080

While the total net cash flow (current year plus next year) is higher for Engagement 1 ($200,000) relative to Engagement 2 ($195,000), the timing of the cash flows differs, resulting in a higher NPV for Engagement 2 relative to Engagement 1. The firm now has a rational basis for choosing between the two consulting opportunities. All else equal, it should accept Engagement 2 because Engagement 2 has a greater net present value than Engagement 1.

In this example, the net cash flow received in the current year was not discounted, and the net cash received in the next year was discounted for one period. This treatment is based on an assumption that cash flows attributable to the current year (year 0) are available immediately and are not discounted. Cash flows attributable to the next year (year 1) are available one year hence and are discounted for one period, and so forth. *This assumption is used consistently throughout the NPV examples in the text and for the solutions to the problems and cases at the end of each chapter.*

TAXES AND CASH FLOWS

Calculations of net present value must reflect all cash flows, including any tax costs or tax savings resulting from the transaction. In the business decision-making process, cash flows *before* tax have no relevance.

Words of Wisdom	Legendary investor Warren Buffett made the following observation: "What is one really trying to do in the investment world? Not pay the least taxes, although that may be a factor to be considered in achieving the end. Means and end should not be confused, however, and the end is to come away with the largest after-tax rate of compound." Source: Warren Buffett

Tax Costs

LO 3-2
Compute the tax cost of an income item and the tax savings from a deduction.

If a transaction results in an increase in any tax for any period, the increase (**tax cost**) is a cash outflow. A tax cost may be incremental to a nontax cost. For instance, a firm that purchases machinery may pay a sales tax; the cash outflow from the transaction includes both the purchase price and the sales tax. In the context of an income tax, tax cost can be a direct result of the receipt of taxable income; the cash outflow represented by the tax is linked to any cash inflow represented by the income item.

Income Tax Cost	Firm F sells a unit of inventory for $50 cash. If the unit cost was $40, the sales transaction generates $10 taxable income. If the firm is subject to a 30 percent income tax, the tax cost of the transaction is $3. The *sales transaction* generates both $50 cash inflow and $3 cash outflow, resulting in a positive net cash flow of $47.

Tax Savings

If a transaction results in a decrease in any tax for any period, the decrease (**tax savings**) is a cash inflow. In the income tax system, tax liability is based on net business profits rather than gross revenues. Accordingly, many business expenditures can be subtracted, or deducted, in the computation of taxable income. The **deduction** reduces taxable income and causes a corresponding reduction in tax. Hence, the deductible expenditure results in a tax savings.[3]

Income Tax Savings	Firm F leases office space for $1,000 monthly rent. Each $1,000 expenditure is deductible in computing the firm's taxable income; in other words, the expenditure shields $1,000 income from tax. If the firm is subject to a 30 percent tax rate, the deduction causes a $300 tax savings. The monthly rent transaction involves both a $1,000 cash outflow and a $300 cash inflow, resulting in a negative net cash flow of $700.

Note that in both of these examples, the tax cost or tax savings from a transaction is treated as a cash flow *in the year that the transaction occurs.* This timing of the cash flow reflects the reality that taxpayers must pay the tax on their current income *during the current year* and not when they file their tax return in the following year. (The tax payment requirements for corporations are discussed in Chapter 11, and the tax payment requirements for individuals are discussed in Chapter 14.) If a taxpayer engages in a transaction with tax consequences in 2023, the taxpayer's tax cost or savings is a 2023 cash flow.

The Significance of Marginal Tax Rate

The income tax cost or savings from a transaction is a function of the firm's marginal tax rate. In Chapter 2, we defined marginal rate as the rate that applies to the next dollar of taxable income. In an analysis of transactions that either increase or decrease taxable income, the marginal rate is the rate at which the increase or decrease would be taxed. If this rate is constant over the increase or decrease, the computation of the tax cost or savings from the transaction is simple.

Constant Marginal Rate	Firm F is subject to a progressive income tax consisting of two rates: 15 percent on the first $50,000 taxable income and 30 percent on taxable income in excess of $50,000. The firm's taxable income to date is $100,000. If Firm F engages in a transaction that generates $10,000 additional income, the entire increment is subject to a 30 percent tax rate. Therefore, the transaction has a $3,000 tax cost.

[3] In the accounting and finance literature, the tax savings from deductible business expenditures are often described as *tax shields.*

The computation of tax cost or savings is more complex if the marginal tax rate is not constant over the change in taxable income.

Changing Marginal Rate	Firm G is subject to a progressive income tax consisting of two rates: 15 percent on the first $50,000 taxable income and 30 percent on taxable income in excess of $50,000. The firm's taxable income to date is $44,000. If Firm G engages in a transaction that generates $10,000 additional income, the marginal rate on the first $6,000 increment is 15 percent and on the next $4,000 increment is 30 percent. Thus, the transaction has a $2,100 tax cost. If Firm G engages in a transaction that generates a $10,000 deduction, the marginal tax rate on the entire income shielded by the deduction is 15 percent. Thus, the transaction results in a $1,500 tax savings.

Obviously, managers must know their firm's marginal tax rate to compute the tax cost or savings from a transaction.

Net Present Value Example Revisited

LO 3-3
Integrate tax costs and savings into NPV calculations.

Let's integrate income tax consequences into the net present value example developed earlier in the chapter. Remember that our consulting firm must choose between two engagements with different revenues and expenses over a two-year period. Now assume that the revenues are taxable, the expenses are deductible, and the marginal income tax rate is 40 percent. Based on these assumptions, the net present values of the competing engagements are computed as follows:

	Engagement 1	Engagement 2
Current year:		
Taxable revenues	$ 40,000	$200,000
Deductible expenses	(15,000)	(45,000)
Before-tax cash flow/taxable income	$ 25,000	$155,000
Income tax cost at 40%	(10,000)	(62,000)
After-tax cash flow	$ 15,000	$ 93,000
Next year:		
Taxable revenues	$185,000	$ 85,000
Deductible expenses	(10,000)	(45,000)
Before-tax cash flow/taxable income	$175,000	$ 40,000
Income tax cost at 40%	(70,000)	(16,000)
After-tax cash flow	$105,000	$ 24,000
Present value of current year cash flow	$ 15,000	$ 93,000
Present value of next year cash flow (after-tax cash flow × .952 discount factor)	99,960	22,848
NPV	$114,960	$115,848

The introduction of an income tax reduced the NPV of each engagement but did not change the proportionate difference between the values. Because the income tax applies in the same manner to each engagement and because the marginal rate does not change over the two-year period, the tax is neutral. In other words, income tax consequences are not a factor affecting the decision as to which engagement to accept. Now consider two examples in which the income tax consequences become an important factor in the decision-making process.

Different Tax Treatments across Transactions

Tax costs are not neutral if the income tax law applies differentially to the two engagements. Assume that the law allows the firm to deduct 100 percent of the expenses of Engagement 1 but only 75 percent of the expenses of Engagement 2. Observe how the NPV computations change:

		Engagement 1		Engagement 2
Current year:				
Taxable revenues			$ 40,000	$200,000
Deductible expenses			(15,000)	(33,750)
Nondeductible expenses			–0–	(11,250)
Before-tax cash flow			$ 25,000	$155,000
Income tax cost:				
Taxable income	$ 25,000		$166,250	
	.40		.40	
Tax cost			(10,000)	(66,500)
After-tax cash flow			$ 15,000	$ 88,500
Next year:				
Taxable revenues			$185,000	$ 85,000
Deductible expenses			(10,000)	(33,750)
Nondeductible expenses			–0–	(11,250)
Before-tax cash flow			$175,000	$ 40,000
Income tax cost:				
Taxable income	$175,000		$ 51,250	
	.40		.40	
Tax cost			(70,000)	(20,500)
After-tax cash flow			$ 105,000	$ 19,500
Present value of current year cash flow			$ 15,000	$ 88,500
Present value of next year cash flow (after-tax cash flow × .952 discount factor)			99,960	18,564
NPV			$114,960	$107,064

The fact that the tax law limits the deduction for the Engagement 2 expenses increases the tax cost of the engagement and decreases after-tax cash flow. As a result, the NPV of Engagement 2 is less than that of Engagement 1, and Engagement 1 is the superior opportunity. In this case, tax consequences are a factor in the decision.

Different Tax Rates over Time

Calculations of net present value are sensitive to changes in tax rates over time. To illustrate this point, modify the example again by returning to the initial assumption that the firm can deduct 100 percent of the expenses of both engagements. But now assume that Congress recently enacted legislation reducing the income tax rate from 40 percent in the current year to 35 percent in the next year.

	Engagement 1	Engagement 2
Current year:		
Taxable revenues	$ 40,000	$200,000
Deductible expenses	(15,000)	(45,000)
Before-tax cash flow/taxable income	$ 25,000	$155,000
Income tax cost at 40%	(10,000)	(62,000)
After-tax cash flow	$ 15,000	$ 93,000
Next year:		
Taxable revenues	$185,000	$ 85,000
Deductible expenses	(10,000)	(45,000)
Before-tax cash flow/taxable income	$175,000	$ 40,000
Income tax cost at 35%	(61,250)	(14,000)
After-tax cash flow	$113,750	$ 26,000
Present value of current year cash flow	$ 15,000	$ 93,000
Present value of next year cash flow		
(after-tax cash flow × .952 discount factor)	108,290	24,752
NPV	$123,290	$117,752

The fact that a lower tax rate applies next year decreases the tax cost for that year relative to the tax cost for the current year. Engagement 1 generates more of its taxable income in the next year than Engagement 2. Consequently, Engagement 1 has a lower overall tax cost and a greater NPV than Engagement 2 and is the superior opportunity.

The Uncertainty of Tax Consequences

LO 3-4
Identify the uncertainties concerning future tax costs and savings.

A net present value calculation is incomplete unless it includes cash flows attributable to the current and future tax consequences of the proposed transaction. However, assumptions concerning tax consequences have their own unique uncertainties.

Audit Risk

Oftentimes the correct application of the tax law to a proposed transaction is unclear or unresolved. In such cases, business managers must decide on the most probable tax consequences to incorporate into their net present value calculations. Whenever a firm enters into a transaction involving ambiguous tax issues, it runs the risk that the Internal Revenue Service (or state and local tax authorities) will challenge the tax treatment on audit. The IRS may conclude that the transaction resulted in a greater tax cost or a smaller tax savings than the manager originally projected. The firm can dispute the unfavorable result of the audit in court.[4] Even if the firm wins its case, the cost of litigation can be substantial. Accordingly, actual cash flows from a contested transaction may vary from the estimated cash flows in the NPV calculation.

---

[4] Historically, the burden of proof in a federal tax case was on the taxpayer, not the government. In other words, taxpayers had to convince the court that the IRS was wrong in its conclusions. In the IRS Reform and Restructuring Act of 1998, Congress modified this long-standing rule. Section 7491(a) provides that the burden of proof *with respect to any factual issue* shifts to the IRS if the taxpayer introduces credible evidence concerning the facts, meets any statutory substantiation requirements, and has cooperated with the IRS in establishing the facts of the case. Corporations, trusts, and partnerships with net worth in excess of $7 million are ineligible for the benefits of the burden-shifting provision.

Managers can reduce the risk of an IRS challenge by engaging a tax professional, such as a CPA or an attorney, to analyze questionable transactions and render an expert opinion as to the proper tax treatment. Managers can even ask the IRS to analyze a proposed transaction and to conclude how the tax law should be applied. The IRS will communicate its conclusion in the form of a **private letter ruling (PLR)** to the firm. Obtaining a private letter ruling can be expensive; firms typically require professional help in drafting a ruling request, and the basic IRS fee is $38,000 for a ruling but can be as little as $3,000 if the taxpayer's income is less than $250,000.[5] Despite the cost, a private letter ruling can be invaluable when thousands or even millions of tax dollars are at stake. If a firm reports the tax consequences of a transaction in accordance with a private letter ruling, it has a guarantee that the consequences will not be challenged by the IRS upon subsequent audit.[6]

Tax Law Uncertainty

A second source of uncertainty is the possibility that tax laws may change during the time period of the NPV computation. Of course, the potential for change varies greatly with the particular tax under consideration. The federal income tax system is notorious for the frequency with which Congress changes the rules of the game. But even within this volatile tax system, some provisions are quite stable. The tax consequences of a proposed transaction to which a stable tax provision applies are more predictable than the consequences of a transaction subject to a provision that Congress modifies every year. As a result, the NPV of the former transaction can be calculated with greater certainty than the NPV of the latter.

Stable and Unstable Tax Provisions	The Internal Revenue Code allows firms to deduct "all interest paid or accrued within the taxable year on indebtedness." This provision was included in the Internal Revenue Code of 1939 and has been substantially unchanged for more than 70 years. In contrast, the provision requiring corporate taxpayers to pay an alternative minimum tax in addition to regular income tax was added to the Internal Revenue Code in 1986, then amended in 1988, 1993, 1996, 1998, 2001, 2003, 2010, 2013, and 2017 until the corporate alternative minimum tax (AMT) was repealed altogether in December 2017 under the Tax Cuts and Jobs Act.

Marginal Rate Uncertainty

The estimated tax cost or savings from a transaction are a function of the firm's projected marginal tax rate. This marginal rate may change in future years because the government changes the statutory rates for all taxpayers. This was certainly the case following passage of the Tax Cuts and Jobs Act, which significantly changed the marginal tax rate for many taxpayers. The marginal rate may also change because of a change in the firm's circumstances. In the income tax context, marginal rate depends on the amount of annual taxable income. If taxable income for a future year is significantly more or less than anticipated, the actual marginal rate for that year may vary from the projected rate. If the actual rate is higher than projected, the tax cost or savings in that year will be more than expected. Conversely, if the rate is lower than projected, the tax cost or savings will be less than expected.

[5] Rev. Proc. 2022-1, Appendix A, 2022-1 IRB 1.

[6] A taxpayer may rely on a ruling unless the ruling request misstated or omitted material facts concerning the proposed transaction or the actual transaction differs substantially from the proposed transaction. No taxpayer may rely on a ruling issued to another taxpayer. Rev. Proc. 2015-1, Section 11, 2015-1 IRB 1.

Marginal Rate Increase	Last year, Company N had to choose between two business opportunities in different tax jurisdictions. The company projected that Opportunity 1 would generate $100,000 income taxed at 30 percent, while Opportunity 2 would generate $90,000 income taxed at 20 percent. Company N chose Opportunity 2 because its $72,000 projected after-tax income ($90,000 − $18,000 tax) exceeded the $70,000 projected after-tax income ($100,000 − $30,000 tax) from Opportunity 1. Because of an unexpected change in circumstances, the marginal tax rate on the income from Opportunity 2 increased to 25 percent this year. As a result, Company N's after-tax income was only $67,500 ($90,000 − $22,500) and, in retrospect, Opportunity 2 was not the best choice.

STRUCTURING TRANSACTIONS TO REDUCE TAXES

The tax consequences of business transactions depend on the legal and financial structure of the transaction. Firms often can change the tax consequences by changing the structure. For instance, a firm that needs an additional worker to perform a certain task could hire a part-time employee. As a result of this employment transaction, the firm is liable for federal and state payroll taxes on the salary paid to the employee.[7] Alternatively, the firm could engage an independent contractor to perform the same task. The firm is not liable for payroll taxes on the fee paid to the independent contractor. Thus, by changing the legal structure of the transaction, the firm eliminates the payroll tax cost of adding personnel.

Let's add some numbers to compute the after-tax cost of each alternative.

Cost of Employee	Firm W plans on hiring an employee to perform a certain task. The firm would pay a $15,000 salary and $1,148 payroll tax on the salary. Both the salary and the payroll tax are deductible in computing taxable income. If the firm's marginal income tax rate is 35 percent, the after-tax cost of the transaction is $10,496:

Cash flows:	
Salary	$(15,000)
Payroll tax cost	(1,148)
Income tax savings	
($16,148 × 35%)	5,652
Net cash flow	$(10,496)

Cost of Independent Contractor	If Firm W engages an independent contractor to perform the task and pays the contractor a $15,000 fee, the after-tax cost of the transaction is only $9,750:

Cash flows:	
Fee	$(15,000)
Income tax savings	
($15,000 × 35%)	5,250
Net cash flow	$ (9,750)

[7] An independent contractor is a self-employed individual who performs services for compensation. Unlike an employee, an independent contractor significantly controls the manner in which the services are performed.

In this simple example, Firm W can eliminate the payroll tax cost without affecting any nontax cash flow. The income tax applies in the same manner to both alternatives and thus is a neutral consideration. Consequently, Firm W can minimize the after-tax cost of the transaction by engaging an independent contractor instead of hiring an employee.

An Important Caveat

LO 3-5
Explain why tax minimization may not be the optimal business strategy.

Business managers who decide to change the structure of a transaction to reduce tax costs must consider the effect of the change on nontax factors. If a change that saves tax dollars adversely affects other factors, the change may be a bad idea. In financial terms, a strategy that minimizes the tax cost of a transaction may not maximize net present value and may not be the optimal strategy for the firm.

To demonstrate this important point, reconsider the example in which Firm W can either hire an employee or engage an independent contractor to perform a task. The firm can hire the employee for a $15,000 salary and a $10,496 after-tax cost. But what if the independent contractor demands a $17,500 fee to do the job?

Cost of Independent Contractor

If Firm W engages an independent contractor to perform the task and pays the contractor a $17,500 fee, the after-tax cost of the transaction is $11,375:

Cash flows:	
Fee	$ (17,500)
Income tax savings	
($17,500 × 35%)	6,125
Net cash flow	$(11,375)

Now the alternative that eliminates the payroll tax cost increases the compensation that Firm W must pay. As a result, the after-tax cost of engaging an independent contractor ($11,375) exceeds the after-tax cost of hiring an employee ($10,496). Firm W should hire the employee, even though this alternative doesn't minimize the payroll tax cost of the transaction.

Transactional Markets

The extent to which managers can control the tax consequences of transactions depends on the nature of the market in which the transaction occurs. A **market** is a forum for commercial interaction between two or more parties for the purpose of exchanging goods or services. One or both parties may want to customize the terms of the exchange to obtain a certain tax result. Their ability to do so depends on the flexibility of the particular market.

Private Market Transactions

LO 3-6
Explain why bilateral tax planning is important in private market transactions.

Many business transactions involve private parties who deal directly with each other. The parties have flexibility in designing a transaction that accommodates the needs of both. The legal and financial characteristics of the transaction are specified in the contract to which both parties finally agree. In negotiating such **private market** transactions, each party should evaluate the tax consequences not only to itself but also to the other party. By doing so, the parties can work together to minimize the aggregate tax cost of the transaction and share the tax savings between them.

To illustrate this bilateral approach to tax planning, consider the case of Firm M and key employee Mr. Grant and their negotiation of a new employment contract. For simplicity's sake, the case disregards payroll tax costs and focuses on the income tax consequences of the contract. Firm M and Mr. Grant have respective marginal income tax rates of 35 percent and 30 percent. Salary payments are deductible by Firm M and taxable to Mr. Grant.

Initial Compensation Package

Firm M and Mr. Grant begin their negotiation by analyzing the consequences of a $120,000 salary payment. The firm's after-tax cost of the $120,000 payment would be $78,000.

Cash flows:	
Salary	$(120,000)
Income tax savings ($120,000 × 35%)	42,000
Net cash flow	(78,000)

Mr. Grant's after-tax cash flow would be $84,000.

Cash flows:	
Salary	$120,000
Income tax cost ($120,000 × 30%)	(36,000)
Net cash flow	$ 84,000

Both parties know that Mr. Grant spends $10,000 each year to pay the premiums on his family's health insurance policy. Mr. Grant cannot deduct this expense in computing taxable income; therefore, the premium payments do not result in any tax savings to him.[8] After this expense, Mr. Grant's after-tax cash flow is only $74,000.

Health Insurance Factor

Cash flows:	
Salary	$120,000
Income tax cost ($120,000 × 30%)	(36,000)
Insurance premium	(10,000)
Net cash flow	$ 74,000

Both parties also know that Firm M could pay a $5,000 premium for comparable health insurance for Mr. Grant under its group plan. Moreover, Firm M could deduct the premium payment. The compensatory fringe benefit (employer-provided health insurance) would be nontaxable to Mr. Grant.[9] On the basis of this mutual knowledge, the parties agree to a final compensation package.

[8] The tax consequences of an individual's personal expenses are discussed in Chapter 17.
[9] Nontaxable employee fringe benefits are discussed in Chapter 15.

Final Compensation Package

Firm M agrees to pay Mr. Grant a $110,000 salary and provide health insurance coverage under its group plan. The firm's after-tax cost of this compensation package is $74,750:

Cash flows:	
Salary	$(110,000)
Insurance premium	$ (5,000)
Income tax savings	
($115,000 × 35%)	40,250
Net cash flow	$ (74,750)

Based on this compensation package, Mr. Grant's after-tax cash flow is $77,000:

Cash flows:	
Salary	$110,000
Income tax cost	
($110,000 × 30%)	(33,000)
Insurance premium	–0–
Net cash flow	$ 77,000

By considering the tax consequences to both parties, Firm M and Mr. Grant structured their contract to improve both their after-tax positions. Specifically, Firm M decreased the after-tax cost of employing Mr. Grant by $3,250, and Mr. Grant's after-tax cash flow increased by $3,000.

Tax Cost to Government

	Initial Compensation Package	Final Compensation Package	Increase (Decrease) in Tax Revenue
Firm M's tax savings	$42,000	$40,250	$ 1,750
Mr. Grant's tax cost	36,000	33,000	(3,000)
Net decrease in tax revenue			$(1,250)

The Arm's-Length Presumption

An important presumption about market transactions is that the parties are negotiating at arm's length. In other words, each party is dealing in its own economic self-interest, trying to obtain the most advantageous terms possible from the other party. In an **arm's-length transaction,** the parties' consideration of the mutual tax consequences is just one element of their bargaining strategy. If one party suggests a modification to the transaction that directly improves its tax outcome, the other party may not agree unless it can indirectly capture some part of the tax benefit for itself. To do so, the other party might demand more favorable terms with respect to another aspect of the transaction.

This *quid pro quo* is exemplified in the employment contract between Firm M and Mr. Grant. The fact that Mr. Grant's compensation package includes a nontaxable fringe benefit (the insurance coverage) results in a direct tax savings to Mr. Grant. However, the firm captures part of this tax savings by paying less salary to Mr. Grant. In the final analysis, Firm M agreed to a compensation package that includes the fringe benefit because the package minimizes its after-tax cost, not because the package saves income tax for Mr. Grant.

The only interested party worse off because of the final terms of the employment contract is the federal government. The inclusion of a nontaxable fringe benefit in the compensation package costs the Treasury $1,250 in tax revenue.

In spite of potential revenue loss, the IRS (and state and local tax authorities) generally accepts the tax consequences of arm's-length transactions because those consequences reflect economic reality. The IRS understands that parties negotiate to further their respective business objectives and that any favorable tax outcomes are legitimate by-products of these negotiations.

Public Market Transactions

Some business transactions occur in **public markets** that are too large, too impersonal, or too regulated to allow parties to communicate privately and to customize their transactions. Firms entering such markets must accept the terms dictated by the market. For instance, if a firm decides to invest excess working capital in short-term U.S. government bonds, it must purchase the bonds through a federal bank for the prevailing market price. The firm can't negotiate with the selling party (the government) to buy the bonds at a different price. Similarly, the financial characteristics of the bonds such as the interest rate and maturity date are nonnegotiable.

Firms have limited flexibility in tailoring public market transactions to control the tax results. Because buyers and sellers are not involved in direct negotiation, they cannot develop a bilateral strategy to improve their joint tax consequences. Any tax planning that does occur must be one-sided.

Fictitious Markets: Related Party Transactions

LO 3-7
Distinguish between arm's-length and related party transactions.

The arm's-length presumption is unreliable for transactions between related parties, such as family members or subsidiary corporations owned by the same controlling parent corporation. **Related party transactions** lack the economic tension characteristic of transactions between unrelated parties. In commercial dealings, unrelated parties typically have competing objectives; related parties may have compatible objectives or even share a single objective. Unrelated parties are motivated by self-interest to drive the hardest possible bargain; related parties may be eager to accommodate each other in their negotiations.

If related parties are not dealing at arm's length, no true market exists, and any transaction between them may not reflect economic reality. In this fictitious market setting, related parties are unconstrained by many of the financial considerations that normally drive arm's-length transactions. As a result, they enjoy significant flexibility in controlling the tax consequences of their transactions. The IRS is well aware that related party transactions lack arm's-length rigor and regards the tax consequences with suspicion. If the IRS concludes that a transaction is bogus, it may disallow any favorable tax outcome claimed by the related parties.

Let's examine a related party transaction with a favorable tax outcome.

Related Party Transaction	The Bowens are business owners with a 25 percent marginal tax rate. The couple has a 17-year-old child, Bobby, who is interested in taking over the business at some future date. The Bowens decide to give Bobby some experience by hiring Bobby as a full-time employee. If the Bowens pay Bobby a $20,000 annual salary, this deductible payment saves them $5,000 a year in federal income tax.[10] Because Bobby has so little taxable income, the marginal tax rate on Bobby's salary is only 10 percent, resulting in a tax cost of $2,000 to Bobby. As a result of this related party transaction, the Bowen family saves $3,000 income tax.

While the federal tax laws don't explicitly prohibit the Bowens from deducting the salary payment to their son, Bobby, the IRS will carefully scrutinize the employment transaction if it audits the parents' tax return. The familial relationship of the transacting parties suggests that the salary was not negotiated at arm's length. If the IRS examines all the relevant facts, it may discover that Bobby did not actually perform any valuable services whatsoever for the parents' business. In this extreme case, the employment transaction had no purpose other than tax avoidance, and the IRS may recast the $20,000 payment from parents to child as a gift.[11] Consequently, the Bowens lose their $20,000 tax deduction, Bobby has no salary income, and the family's anticipated income tax savings disappear.

On the other hand, the relevant facts may indicate that the son is a genuine employee and that his salary is comparable to the salary an unrelated person could have negotiated at arm's length. In this case, the IRS should respect the transaction and accept the favorable tax consequences of the $20,000 salary payment. Whatever the outcome, the lesson from this example should be clear. Whenever related parties transact, they must be aware that the tax authorities may challenge the validity of the transaction. If the related parties cannot offer convincing evidence that the terms of the transaction approximate an arm's-length standard, they may forfeit control of the tax consequences altogether.

Conclusion

Estimating cash flows and calculating the net present value of those cash flows are central to the business decision-making process. A manager's ability to determine after-tax cash flows depends on his or her skill in quantifying the tax cost or savings from the transaction. Managers must be familiar with current tax law and must be prepared to make informed assumptions concerning how that law might change in future periods. Managers involved in business negotiations should evaluate the tax implications for all parties to the transaction in formulating an optimal tax strategy.

Although managers should view all business taxes as controllable costs, they should understand that the transaction with the least tax cost may not maximize net present value. Business transactions consist of any number of interrelated tax and nontax variables, all of which must be considered in the decision-making process. In the next chapter, we will concentrate on strategies that manipulate the income tax variable. As we focus on tax planning ideas, remember the basic lesson of this chapter—cash flows cannot be analyzed in a meaningful way until they are stated as after-tax numbers.

[10] Federal payroll taxes are not an issue in this example because such taxes are not levied on wages paid by parents to their children under age 18. §3121(b)(3)(A).

[11] When a related party transaction is a blatant tax avoidance scheme, the IRS may impose monetary penalties on the taxpayers. See the discussion of taxpayer negligence and fraud in Chapter 18.

Key Terms

annuity *3-5*
arm's-length
 transaction *3-16*
deduction *3-8*
discount rate *3-4*
market *3-14*

net cash flow *3-4*
net present value
 (NPV) *3-4*
private letter ruling
 (PLR) *3-12*
private market *3-14*

public market *3-17*
related party
 transaction *3-17*
tax cost *3-8*
tax savings *3-8*
time value of money *3-4*

Questions and Problems for Discussion

LO 3-1   1. Does the NPV of future cash flows increase or decrease as the discount rate increases?

LO 3-1   2. Explain the relationship between the degree of financial risk associated with future cash flows and the discount rate used to compute NPV.

LO 3-2   3. Does the after-tax cost of a deductible expense increase or decrease as the taxpayer's marginal income tax rate increases?

LO 3-2   4. Firm A and Firm Z are in the same business. Both firms considered spending $10,000 for the same reason. The expenditure would be deductible for both firms. Firm A decided that the expenditure was worthwhile and spent the money, but Firm Z rejected the expenditure. Can you provide a tax explanation for these apparently inconsistent decisions?

LO 3-2   5. In what circumstance is the before-tax cost of an expenditure equal to its after-tax cost?

LO 3-3   6. Corporation N must decide between two opportunities that will generate different cash flows over a five-year period. Describe the circumstances in which the tax cost of the opportunities is a neutral factor in the corporation's decision-making process.

LO 3-4   7. Which assumption about the tax consequences of a future transaction is more uncertain: an assumption based on a provision that has been in the Internal Revenue Code for 25 years or an assumption based on a provision that Congress added to the Internal Revenue Code 2 years ago?

LO 3-4   8. Which type of tax law provision should be more stable and less uncertain as to its future application: a provision relating to the proper measurement of taxable income or a provision designed to encourage individual taxpayers to engage in a certain economic behavior?

LO 3-4   9. In the U.S. system of criminal justice, a person is innocent until proven guilty. Does this general rule apply to disputes between a taxpayer and the IRS?

LO 3-4   10. Identify two reasons why a firm's actual marginal tax rate for a year could differ from the projected marginal tax rate for that year.

LO 3-6   11. Firm F is negotiating to purchase a multimillion-dollar computer system from the manufacturer. Under applicable state law, Firm F is exempt from sales tax on the purchase. Because the manufacturer discovered this fact, it increased its selling price for the system by $25,000. Is this transaction taking place in a private or a public market?

LO 3-7   12. Corporation P owns 85 percent of the outstanding stock of Corporation R. This year, employees of Corporation R performed extensive management services for Corporation P. In return for the services, Corporation P paid a $250,000 fee to Corporation R, which Corporation P reported as a deductible business expense.

   a. Is the consulting arrangement an arm's-length transaction?

   b. If the IRS challenges the validity of Corporation P's deduction, what facts might the corporation offer as evidence of the validity of the payment?

Application Problems

LO 3-1   1. Use the present value tables in Appendices A and B to compute the NPV of each of the following cash inflows:

    a. $18,300 received at the end of 15 years. The discount rate is 5 percent.

    b. $5,800 received at the end of four years and $11,600 received at the end of eight years. The discount rate is 7 percent.

    c. $1,300 received annually at the end of each of the next seven years. The discount rate is 6 percent.

    d. $40,000 received annually at the end of each of the next three years and $65,000 received at the end of the fourth year. The discount rate is 3 percent.

LO 3-1   2. Use the present value tables in Appendices A and B to compute the NPV of each of the following cash inflows:

    a. $89,000 received at the end of six years. The discount rate is 4 percent.

    b. $3,400 received annually at the end of each of the next 15 years. The discount rate is 9 percent.

    c. A 10-year annuity of $5,000 per annum. The first $5,000 payment is due immediately. The discount rate is 6 percent.

    d. $20,000 received annually at the end of years 1 through 5 followed by $13,000 received annually at the end of years 6 through 10. The discount rate is 15 percent.

LO 3-1   3. Use the present value table in Appendices A and B to compute the NPV of each of the following cash outflows:

    a. $22,000 paid at the end of four years. The discount rate is 5 percent.

    b. $2,000 paid at the end of three years and $5,000 paid at the end of five years. The discount rate is 8 percent.

    c. $7,000 paid annually at the end of each of the next four years. The discount rate is 4 percent.

    d. $1,500 paid annually at the end of each of the next four years and $3,000 paid at the end of the fifth year. The discount rate is 6 percent.

LO 3-1   4. Use a 5 percent discount rate to compute the NPV of each of the following series of cash receipts and payments:

    a. $6,200 received now (year 0), $1,890 paid in year 3, and $4,000 paid in year 5.

    b. $10,000 paid now (year 0), $12,690 paid in year 2, and $31,000 received in year 8.

    c. $20,000 received now (year 0), $13,500 paid in year 5, and $7,500 paid in year 10.

LO 3-1   5. Consider the following opportunities: Opportunity 1 requires a $4,000 cash payment now (year 0) but will result in $14,000 cash received in year 5. Opportunity 2 requires no cash outlay and results in $3,500 cash received in years 3 and 5.

    a. Use a 6 percent discount rate and determine whether Opportunity 1 or Opportunity 2 results in a greater NPV.

    b. Use a 10 percent discount rate and determine whether Opportunity 1 or Opportunity 2 results in a greater NPV.

LO 3-2   6. Business J operates in a jurisdiction that levies an income tax with the following rate structure:

Percentage Rate	Bracket
7%	Income from –0– to $75,000
10	Income from $75,001 to $150,000
15	Income in excess of $150,000

Business J has the opportunity to invest in a project that should generate $35,000 additional taxable income for the year. Compute the tax cost of this additional income assuming that

a. Business J's taxable income before considering the additional income is $92,000.

b. Business J's taxable income before considering the additional income is $400,000.

c. Business J has a $16,000 loss before considering the additional income.

LO 3-2   7. Refer to the income tax rate structure in the preceding problem. Company K incurs a $22,000 deductible expense. Compute the current year tax savings from the deduction assuming that

a. Company K's taxable income before considering the additional deduction is $65,000.

b. Company K's taxable income before considering the additional deduction is $168,000.

c. Company K has a $4,000 loss before considering the additional deduction.

LO 3-2   8. Company P must choose between two alternate transactions. The cash generated by Transaction 1 is taxable, and the cash generated by Transaction 2 is nontaxable. Determine the marginal tax rate at which the after-tax cash flows from the two transactions are equal assuming that

a. Transaction 1 generates $100,000 of income and Transaction 2 generates $60,000 of income.

b. Transaction 1 generates $160,000 of income and Transaction 2 generates $120,000 of income.

LO 3-3   9. Company N will receive $100,000 of taxable revenue from a client. Compute the NPV of the $100,000 in each of the following cases:

a. Company N will receive $50,000 now (year 0) and $50,000 in year 1. The company's marginal tax rate is 30 percent, and it uses a 6 percent discount rate.

b. Company N will receive $50,000 in year 1 and $50,000 in year 2. The company's marginal tax rate is 40 percent, and it uses a 4 percent discount rate.

c. Company N will receive $20,000 now (year 0) and $20,000 in years 1, 2, 3, and 4. The company's marginal tax rate is 10 percent, and it uses a 9 percent discount rate.

LO 3-3   10. Keyshawn Vonte, who has a 30 percent marginal tax rate, invested $65,000 in a bond that pays 8 percent annual interest. Compute Vonte's annual net cash flow from this investment assuming that

a. The interest is tax-exempt income.

b. The interest is taxable income.

LO 3-3   11. Lin Vu has $100,000 in an investment paying 9 percent taxable interest per annum. Each year Vu incurs $825 of expenses relating to this investment. Compute Vu's annual net cash flow assuming the following:

a. Vu's marginal tax rate is 10 percent, and the annual expense is not deductible.

b. Vu's marginal tax rate is 35 percent, and the annual expense is deductible.

c. Vu's marginal tax rate is 25 percent, and the annual expense is not deductible.

d. Vu's marginal tax rate is 40 percent, and only $500 of the annual expense is deductible.

LO 3-3   12. Firm E must choose between two alternative transactions. Transaction 1 requires a $9,000 cash outlay that would be nondeductible in the computation of taxable income. Transaction 2 requires a $13,500 cash outlay that would be a deductible expense. Determine which transaction has the lesser after-tax cost, assuming that

   a. Firm E's marginal tax rate is 20 percent.

   b. Firm E's marginal tax rate is 40 percent.

LO 3-3   13. Company J must choose between two alternate business expenditures. Expenditure 1 would require an $80,000 cash outlay, and Expenditure 2 requires a $60,000 cash outlay. Determine the marginal tax rate at which the after-tax cash flows from the two expenditures are equal assuming that

   a. Expenditure 1 is fully deductible and Expenditure 2 is nondeductible.

   b. Expenditure 1 is 50 percent deductible and Expenditure 2 is nondeductible.

   c. Expenditure 1 is fully deductible and Expenditure 2 is 50 percent deductible.

LO 3-3   14. Firm Q is about to engage in a transaction with the following cash flows over a three-year period:

	Year 0	Year 1	Year 2
Taxable revenue	$13,000	$16,250	$23,400
Deductible expenses	(3,900)	(6,000)	(8,100)
Nondeductible expenses	(350)	(2,000)	–0–

If the firm's marginal tax rate over the three-year period is 30 percent and its discount rate is 6 percent, compute the NPV of the transaction.

LO 3-3   15. Corporation ABC invested in a project that will generate $60,000 annual after-tax cash flow in years 0 and 1 and $40,000 annual after-tax cash flow in years 2, 3, and 4. Compute the NPV of these cash flows assuming that

   a. ABC uses a 10 percent discount rate.

   b. ABC uses a 7 percent discount rate.

   c. ABC uses a 4 percent discount rate.

LO 3-3, 3-5   16. Firm W has the opportunity to invest $150,000 in a new venture. The projected cash flows from the venture are as follows:

	Year 0	Year 1	Year 2	Year 3
Initial investment	$(150,000)			
After-tax cash flow		$5,000	$8,000	$10,000
Return of investment				150,000
Net cash flow	$(150,000)	$5,000	$8,000	$160,000

Determine if Firm W should make the investment, assuming that

   a. It uses a 6 percent discount rate to compute NPV.

   b. It uses a 3 percent discount rate to compute NPV.

LO 3-3, 3-5   17. Margaret Daniels has the opportunity to invest $500,000 in a new venture. The projected cash flows from the venture are as follows:

	Year 0	Year 1	Year 2	Year 3	Year 4
Initial investment	$(500,000)				
Taxable revenue		$ 62,500	$ 57,500	$ 47,500	$ 42,500
Deductible expenses		(10,000)	(10,000)	(12,000)	(12,000)
Return of investment					500,000
Before-tax net cash flow	$(500,000)	$ 52,500	$ 47,500	$ 35,500	$530,500

Margaret uses a 7 percent discount rate to compute NPV. Determine if Margaret should make this investment assuming that

a. Margaret's marginal tax rate over the life of the investment is 15 percent.

b. Margaret's marginal tax rate over the life of the investment is 20 percent.

c. Margaret's marginal tax rate in years 1 and 2 is 10 percent and in years 3 and 4 is 25 percent.

LO 3-3, 3-5   18. Firm X has the opportunity to invest $200,000 in a new venture. The projected cash flows from the venture are as follows:

	Year 0	Year 1	Year 2	Year 3
Initial investment	$(200,000)			
Revenues		$ 40,000	$ 40,000	$ 40,000
Expenses		(25,000)	(7,000)	(7,000)
Return of investment				200,000
Before-tax net cash flow	$(200,000)	$ 15,000	$33,000	$233,000

Firm X uses an 8 percent discount rate to compute NPV, and its marginal tax rate over the life of the venture will be 35 percent. Determine if Firm X should make the investment, assuming that

a. The revenues are taxable income, and the expenses are deductible.

b. The revenues are taxable income, but the expenses are nondeductible.

LO 3-3, 3-5   19. Company DL must choose between two business opportunities. Opportunity 1 will generate $14,000 before-tax cash in years 0 through 3. The annual tax cost of Opportunity 1 is $2,500 in years 0 and 1 and $1,800 in years 2 and 3. Opportunity 2 will generate $14,000 before-tax cash in year 0, $20,000 before-tax cash in years 1 and 2, and $10,000 before-tax cash in year 3. The annual tax cost of Opportunity 2 is $4,000 in years 0 through 3. Which opportunity should Company DL choose if it uses a 10 percent discount rate to compute NPV?

LO 3-3, 3-5   20. Firm E must choose between two business opportunities. Opportunity 1 will generate an $8,000 deductible loss in year 0, $5,000 taxable income in year 1, and $20,000 taxable income in year 2. Opportunity 2 will generate $6,000 taxable income in year 0 and $5,000 taxable income in years 1 and 2. The income and loss reflect before-tax cash inflow and outflow. Firm E uses a 5 percent discount rate to compute NPV and has a 40 percent marginal tax rate over the three-year period.

a. Which opportunity should Firm E choose?

b. Would your answer change if Firm E's marginal tax rate over the three-year period is 15 percent?

c. Would your answer change if Firm E's marginal tax rate is 40 percent in year 0 but only 15 percent in years 1 and 2?

LO 3-3, 3-5 21. Firm Y has the opportunity to invest in a new venture. The projected cash flows are as follows:

Year 0: Initial cash investment in the project of $300,000.

Years 1, 2, and 3: Generate cash revenues of $50,000.

Years 1, 2, and 3: Incur fully deductible cash expenditures of $30,000.

Year 3: Incur nondeductible cash expenditure of $10,000.

Year 3: Receive $300,000 cash as a return of the initial investment.

Assuming a 6 percent discount rate and a 30 percent marginal tax rate, compute the NPV of the cash flows resulting from investment in this opportunity.

Issue Recognition Problems

Identify the tax issue or issues suggested by the following situations, and state each issue in the form of a question.

LO 3-2, 3-4 1. Mr. and Mrs. Khalid's taxable income from their business has been stable for the past five years, and their average federal income tax rate has ranged between 22 and 24 percent. Because of a boom in the local economy, the couple estimates that their business will generate an additional $100,000 taxable income next year. In making their cash flow projections, they estimate that their federal income tax cost with respect to this incremental income will be $24,000.

LO 3-2, 3-4 2. Firm V must choose between two alternative investment opportunities. On the basis of current tax law, the firm projects that the NPV of Opportunity 1 is significantly less than the NPV of Opportunity 2. The provisions in the tax law governing the tax consequences of Opportunity 1 have been stable for many years. In contrast, the provisions governing the tax consequences of Opportunity 2 are extremely complicated and have been modified by Congress several times during the past five years.

LO 3-4 3. Company WB is evaluating a business opportunity with uncertain tax consequences. If the company takes a conservative approach by assuming the least beneficial tax consequences, the tax cost is $95,000. If the company takes an aggressive approach by assuming the most beneficial tax consequences, the tax cost is only $86,000. If the company takes the aggressive approach, the IRS will certainly challenge the approach on audit.

LO 3-4 4. Refer to the facts in problem 3. Company WB is considering engaging a CPA to prepare a request for a private letter ruling from the IRS concerning the tax consequences of the business opportunity.

LO 3-5 5. Ms. Olsen is the chief financial officer for Firm XYZ. The marketing department requested approval for an $80,000 cash expenditure. The request points out that the expenditure would be deductible. Therefore, the marketing department concludes that Ms. Olsen should approve the expenditure because it would reduce XYZ's tax cost.

LO 3-4 6. Earlier in the year, Ms. Girabaldi, a business manager for Company RW, evaluated a prospective opportunity that could generate $20,000 additional taxable income. Ms. Girabaldi determined that the company's marginal tax rate on this income would be 25 percent. Later in the year, a different manager evaluated another opportunity that could generate $100,000 additional taxable income. This manager referred to Ms. Girabaldi's earlier evaluation and used the same 25 percent marginal rate in an analysis of after-tax cash flows.

LO 3-5   7. Firm UW is about to enter into a venture that will generate taxable income for the next six to eight years. The director of tax has come up with an idea to restructure the venture in a way that will reduce tax costs by at least 5 percent.

LO 3-6   8. DLT's chief operating officer is negotiating the acquisition of a controlling interest in the stock of AA, Inc. from Mr. and Mrs. Alvarez. The director of tax suggested that the acquisition be structured as a nontaxable transaction to Mr. and Mrs. Alvarez. The CEO rejected the suggestion by saying, "Since DLT is the purchaser, our negotiating team doesn't really care if the structure of the acquisition saves taxes for the seller."

LO 3-7   9. Ms. Sun is the sole shareholder and chief executive officer of SMJ Corporation. Ms. Sun's college roommate is recently unemployed, is in financial difficulty, and has asked Ms. Sun for a loan. Instead of a loan, Ms. Sun offered the roommate a job with SMJ at a $35,000 annual salary.

All applicable Tax Planning Cases are available with *Connect*.

Tax Planning Cases

LO 3-1, 3-6   1. Firm B wants to hire Ms. Ali to manage its advertising department. The firm offered Ms. Ali a three-year employment contract under which it will pay her an $80,000 annual salary in years 0, 1, and 2. Ms. Ali's projected tax rate is 25 percent in year 0 and 40 percent in years 1 and 2. Firm B's tax rate for the three-year period is 34 percent.

   a. Assuming an 8 percent discount rate for both Firm B and Ms. Ali, compute the NPV of Ms. Ali's after-tax cash flow from the employment contract and Firm B's after-tax cost of the employment contract.

   b. To reduce her tax cost, Ms. Ali requests that the salary payment for year 0 be increased to $140,000 and the salary payments for years 1 and 2 be reduced to $50,000. How would this revision in the timing of the payments change your NPV computation for both parties?

   c. Firm B responds to Ms. Ali's request with a counterproposal. Firm B will pay Ms. Ali $140,000 in year 0 but only $45,000 in years 1 and 2. Compute the NPV of Firm B's after-tax cost under this proposal. From the firm's perspective, is this proposal superior to its original offer ($80,000 annually for three years)?

   d. Should Ms. Ali accept the original offer or the counterproposal? Support your conclusion with a comparison of the NPV of each offer.

LO 3-1, 3-5   2. Firm D is considering investing $400,000 cash in a three-year project with the following cash flows:

	Year 0	Year 1	Year 2
(Investment)/return of investment	$(400,000)	–0–	$400,000
Revenues	80,000	$65,000	35,000
Expenses	(25,000)	(25,000)	(10,000)
Before-tax net cash flow	$(345,000)	$40,000	$425,000

   Under each of the following assumptions, determine if Firm D should make the investment. In each case, use a 10 percent discount rate to compute NPV.

   a. The revenue is taxable, the expenses are deductible, and the marginal tax rate is 15 percent.

   b. The revenue is taxable, the expenses are deductible, and the marginal tax rate is 40 percent.

    c. The revenue is taxable, only one-half of the expenses are deductible, and the marginal tax rate is 15 percent.

    d. Firm D can deduct the expenses in the year paid (against other sources of income) but can defer recognizing the $180,000 total income until year 2. (It will *collect* the revenues as indicated in years 0, 1, and 2 so that before-tax cash flows don't change.) The marginal tax rate is 40 percent.

Chapter Four

Maxims of Income Tax Planning

Learning Objectives

After studying this chapter, you should be able to:

LO 4-1. Describe the difference between tax avoidance and tax evasion.

LO 4-2. Explain why an income shift or a deduction shift from one entity to another can affect after-tax cash flows.

LO 4-3. Explain how the assignment of income doctrine constrains income-shifting strategies.

LO 4-4. Determine the effect on after-tax cash flows of deferral of a tax cost.

LO 4-5. Discuss why the jurisdiction in which a business operates affects after-tax cash flows.

LO 4-6. Contrast the tax character of ordinary income, capital gain, and tax-exempt income.

LO 4-7. Distinguish between an explicit tax and an implicit tax.

LO 4-8. Summarize the four tax planning maxims.

LO 4-9. Describe the legal doctrines that the IRS uses to challenge tax planning strategies.

In Chapter 3, we learned that the concept of net present value (NPV) plays a key role in the business decision-making process and that the computation of NPV incorporates tax costs as cash outflows and tax savings as cash inflows. With these lessons in mind, we begin this chapter by defining **tax planning** as the structuring of transactions to reduce tax costs or increase tax savings to maximize the NPV of the transaction.

Why does the structure of a transaction matter in the tax planning process? Specifically, what are the variables that determine the tax outcome of the transaction? These questions are addressed in the first section of the chapter. Our study of the variables leads to the development of *income tax planning maxims*—basic principles that are the foundation for many planning techniques discussed in subsequent chapters. We will analyze how these maxims improve the tax outcomes of transactions. We will also identify the limitations on their use in the planning process. In the final section of the chapter, we will consider how managers use the maxims to develop tax strategies for their firms and why managers must be cognizant of how the Internal Revenue Service (IRS) may react to their strategies.

TAX AVOIDANCE—NOT EVASION

LO 4-1
Describe the difference between tax avoidance and tax evasion.

Our discussion in this and subsequent chapters is restricted to tax planning ideas that are entirely legal. Legitimate means of reducing taxes are described as **tax avoidance;** illegal means to the same end constitute **tax evasion.** Tax evasion is a federal crime—a felony offense punishable by severe monetary fines and imprisonment.[1] The qualitative difference between avoidance and evasion is in the eye of the beholder. Many aggressive tax plans involve major questions of judgment. Taxpayers eager to implement these plans run the risk that the IRS will conclude that the plan crosses the line between a good-faith effort to reduce tax and a willful attempt to defraud the U.S. government. Business managers should always exercise caution and consult a tax professional before engaging in any transaction with profound tax consequences.

Tax Evasion in Hollywood	Actor Wesley Snipes served a 3-year prison sentence and was fine $5 million for willfully failing to file millions of dollars of past due tax returns. Other well-known actors and performers, such as Willie Nelson, Nicholas Cage, and Lil Wayne, have also been accused of tax evasion.

Tax Talk
In 1998, the U.S. Patent Office began granting patents for innovative tax planning strategies. In 2011, Congress responded to pressure from the American Institute of Certified Public Accountants by enacting legislation that stopped the granting of patents for any "strategy for reducing, avoiding, or deferring tax liability."

Even if tax avoidance strategies are legal, are they ethical? In 1947, federal Judge Learned Hand answered this question in the following way:

> Over and over again courts have said that there is nothing sinister in so arranging one's affairs as to keep taxes as low as possible. Everybody does so, rich or poor; and all do right, for nobody owes any public duty to pay more than the law demands: taxes are enforced exactions, not voluntary contributions. To demand more in the name of morals is mere cant.[2]

This spirited defense of planning makes the point that every person has the civic responsibility of paying the legally required tax and not a penny more. Business managers should be reassured that when they engage in effective tax planning, they are engaging in proper behavior from the perspective of their firm, their government, and society.

WHAT MAKES INCOME TAX PLANNING POSSIBLE?

The federal income tax system applies to every entity conducting business in the United States. If the tax law applied uniformly to every transaction by every entity in every time period, it would be neutral and therefore irrelevant in the business decision-making process. However, as we will observe over and over again, the income tax is anything but neutral. The tax system is replete with rules affecting only particular transactions, entities, or time periods. In every case in which the law applies differentially to a certain dollar of business profit or cost, a planning opportunity is born.

---

[1] The civil and criminal penalties for tax evasion are discussed in Chapter 18.

[2] Source: *Commissioner* v. *Newman,* 159 F.2d 848, 850 (CA-2, 1947).

Tax Planning Driver	According to former New York State Tax Commissioner James W. Wetzler, "tax planning is driven by the fact that under a nonneutral tax law, transactions or arrangements whose economic differences are minor can have significantly different tax consequences." Source: James W. Wetzler

The tax consequences of a transaction depend on the interaction of four variables common to all transactions:

1. The entity variable: Which entity undertakes the transaction?
2. The time period variable: During which tax year or years does the transaction occur?
3. The jurisdiction variable: In which tax jurisdiction does the transaction occur?
4. The character variable: What is the tax character of the income from the transaction?

We will focus on each variable in turn to learn why the variable matters and how it can be manipulated to change the tax outcome of the transaction.

THE ENTITY VARIABLE

LO 4-2
Explain why an income shift or a deduction shift from one entity to another can affect after-tax cash flows.

In the federal tax system, individuals and corporations are the two entities that pay tax on business income. While trusts and estates are also taxable entities, they don't routinely engage in the active conduct of a business. For this reason, this text doesn't address the specialized rules governing the income taxation of trusts and estates. Businesses can be organized as sole proprietorships, partnerships, limited liability companies (LLCs), or S corporations, but these organizational forms are not taxable entities. Income generated by a proprietorship, partnership, LLC, or S corporation is taxed to the proprietor, partners, members, or shareholders. The operation of these passthrough entities is examined in detail in Chapter 10.

For the most part, the provisions in the Internal Revenue Code governing the computation of taxable income apply uniformly across organizational forms.[3] In other words, the *amount of taxable income* from a business activity doesn't depend on the type of entity conducting the business; the tax law is essentially neutral across entities with respect to the tax base. So why do the tax consequences of business transactions depend on which entity undertakes the transaction? The answer lies in the potential difference between applicable *tax rates*.

Section 1 of the Internal Revenue Code provides the tax rate structure for individuals, which currently consists of seven income brackets with rates ranging from 10 percent to 37 percent. Section 11 provides a completely different rate structure for corporations; corporate earnings are taxed at a flat rate of 21 percent. (The rates for individuals are provided in Appendix C.) The individual rate structures are progressive, so that the tax on a given dollar of income depends on the marginal rate of the entity earning that dollar. An entity with a lower marginal rate will pay less tax on a dollar of income than an entity with a higher marginal rate. Consequently, the after-tax value of the dollar is greater to the low-tax entity than to the high-tax entity.

---

[3] The few special provisions applying only to businesses operated in the corporate form are discussed in Chapter 11. Additional special provisions applying only to noncorporate business are discussed in Chapter 10.

Tax Rate Differential

Entity H has a 37 percent marginal tax rate while Entity L has a 21 percent marginal tax rate. Both receive $100 cash that represents taxable income. The after-tax cash available to each entity is computed as follows:

	Entity H	Entity L
Cash received	$100	$100
Tax cost ($100 income × marginal rate)	(37)	(21)
After-tax cash	$ 63	$ 79

A comparison of the tax consequences to Entities H and L suggests our first income tax planning maxim: *Tax costs decrease (and cash flows increase) when income is generated by an entity subject to a low tax rate.*

This maxim is especially important when entrepreneurs are starting a new venture and must decide which organizational form to adopt. The choice of organizational form determines whether the business income will be taxed at the individual rates or the corporate rates. Chapter 12 provides an in-depth discussion of the tax implications of the choice of organizational form for new businesses.

Income Shifting

The first maxim implies that the tax on business income can be reduced if that income is shifted from an entity with a high tax rate to an entity with a low tax rate. Assume that Entity H in the previous example could redirect its $100 cash receipt (and the income represented by the cash) to Entity L.

Income Shift

Entity H and Entity L both expect to receive $100 cash that represents taxable income. Entity H arranges to shift its $100 to Entity L. The after-tax cash available to each entity is computed as follows:

	Entity H	Entity L
Cash received	–0–	$200
Tax cost (taxable income × marginal rate)	–0–	(42)
After-tax cash	–0–	$158

Tax Talk

The Tax Cuts and Jobs Act of 2017 reduced corporate tax rates from 35 percent to 21 percent. As a result, many tax planners encouraged their clients to accelerate deductions into the final weeks of 2017, and defer income recognition into 2018.

This income shift reduces the tax on the shifted $100 from $37 to $21 and increases the after-tax cash from $63 to $79. However, that after-tax cash now belongs to Entity L rather than to Entity H. From Entity H's perspective, the income shift *reduces* its after-tax cash flow from $63 to zero. On the presumption that Entity H makes rational decisions, this transaction makes sense only if Entity H controls, enjoys, or benefits from the shifted cash in some manner. One possible explanation is that Entity L is a corporation and Entity H is its sole shareholder. In such a case, any cash shifted from Shareholder H to Corporation L increases the value of Corporation L's stock and still belongs indirectly to Shareholder H. Although Shareholder H holds less cash, Shareholder H's wealth (which includes the value of Corporation L stock) increases by the $16 tax savings from the income shift.

Deduction Shifting

Entities with different marginal rates can save tax not only by shifting income but also by shifting deductible expenses. To illustrate a deduction shift, let's use Entities H and L again.

Deduction Shift	Entity L expects to pay an $80 expense that is fully deductible in computing taxable income. Because Entity L is in a 21 percent marginal tax bracket, the $80 deduction would save $17 in tax, and the after-tax cost of the payment is $63:

Cash expended by Entity L	$(80)
Tax savings ($80 deduction × 21%)	17
After-tax cost	$(63)

If Entity H could make the $80 payment on behalf of Entity L and claim the $80 deduction on its own tax return, the tax savings would increase to $30 and the after-tax cost would decrease to $50:

Cash expended by Entity H	$(80)
Tax savings ($80 deduction × 37%)	30
After-tax cost	$(50)

Because the deduction is shifted from the entity with the low tax rate to the entity with the high tax rate, the cash outflow with respect to the expense decreases by $13; the shift actually increases Entity H's cash outflow by $50. Entity H would never agree to this strategy unless it derives some indirect economic benefit from the tax savings.

Constraints on Income Shifting

Because income-shifting transactions involve transfers of value from one party to another, they usually occur between related parties. After the income shift, the parties *in the aggregate* are financially better off by the tax savings from the transaction. Congress has long recognized that income-shifting techniques lose revenue for the Treasury. Many effective techniques that were once widely used by related parties have been abolished by legislation; in subsequent chapters, we will consider a number of powerful statutory restrictions on income shifting. The IRS is vigilant in policing related party transactions involving beneficial income shifts. If a transaction serves no genuine purpose besides tax avoidance, the IRS may disallow the tax consequences intended by the parties.

Assignment of Income Doctrine

LO 4-3
Explain how the assignment of income doctrine constrains income-shifting strategies.

The federal courts have consistently held that our income tax system cannot tolerate artificial shifts of income from one taxpayer to another. Over 80 years ago, the Supreme Court decided that income must be taxed to the person who earns it, even if another person has a legal right to the wealth represented by the income.[4] Thus, a business owner who receives a $10,000 check in payment for services rendered to a client can't avoid reporting $10,000 income by simply endorsing the check over to his or her child. In the picturesque language of the Court, the tax law must disregard arrangements "by which the fruits are attributed to a different tree from that on which they grew."

[4] *Lucas v. Earl*, 281 U.S. 111 (1930).

The Supreme Court elaborated on this theme in the case of a father who detached negotiable interest coupons from corporate bonds and gave the coupons to his son as a gift.[5] When the coupons matured, the son collected the interest and reported it as income on his own tax return. The Court concluded that the interest income was taxable to the father because he continued to own the underlying asset (the bonds) that created the right to the interest payments. The holdings in these two cases have melded into the **assignment of income doctrine:** Income must be taxed to the entity that renders the service or owns the capital with respect to which the income is paid. Over the years, the IRS has frustrated many creative income-shifting schemes by invoking this simple, but potent, doctrine.

THE TIME PERIOD VARIABLE

LO 4-4
Determine the effect on after-tax cash flows of deferral of a tax cost.

Because both federal and state income taxes are imposed annually, the tax costs or savings from a transaction depend on the year in which the transaction occurs. In Chapter 3, we learned that these costs and savings are a function of the firm's marginal tax rate. If that rate changes from one year to the next, the tax costs and savings fluctuate accordingly. We've also discussed the fact that the technical details of the federal and state income tax systems change periodically. A tax benefit available in one year may disappear in the next. Conversely, a statutory restriction causing a tax problem this year may be lifted in the future. Managers must be aware of annual changes in the tax laws pertaining to their business operations. By controlling the timing of transactions, they may reduce the tax cost or increase the tax savings for their firm.

Even if marginal tax rates and the tax law were absolutely stable over time, the tax costs and savings from transactions would still vary with the time period during which the transaction occurs. This variation is because of the time value of money. In present value terms, a tax dollar paid this year costs more than a tax dollar paid in a future year. Conversely, a tax dollar saved this year is worth more than a tax dollar saved in the future.

Consider a transaction that takes place over two taxable years. In the first year (year 0), Firm R receives $220 in revenues and pays $40 in expenses. In the next year (year 1), it receives $280 in revenues and pays $80 in expenses. If the revenues are taxable when received and the expenses are deductible when paid, Firm R has $180 taxable income in the first year and $200 taxable income in the next year. If it has a 21 percent tax rate for the two-year period and uses a 6 percent discount rate, the NPV of the cash flows is $291.

Tax Talk
The CARES Act of 2020 delayed the filing deadline for 2019 federal income tax returns from April 15, 2020, until July 15, 2020. Payment of the related tax liability was also deferred without interest cost. This legislation gave scores of taxpayers three months of time period variable tax savings.

		Year 0	Year 1
Revenues		$220	$280
Expenses		(40)	(80)
Income tax cost:			
Taxable income	$180	$200	
	.21	.21	
Tax cost		(38)	(42)
After-tax net cash flow		$142	$158
Present value of year 0 cash flow		$142	
Present value of year 1 cash flow			
($158 × .943 discount factor)		149	
NPV		$291	

[5] *Helvering v. Horst,* 311 U.S. 112 (1940).

Now assume that Firm R could restructure the transaction in a way that *doesn't affect before-tax cash flows* but allows it to report the entire $380 taxable income (and pay the $80 tax thereon) in year 1.[6]

	Year 0		Year 1
Revenues	$220		$280
Expenses	(40)		(80)
Income tax cost:			
Taxable income	–0–	$380	
		.21	
Tax cost	–0–		(80)
After-tax net cash flow	$180		$120
Present value of year 0 cash flow	$180		
Present value of year 1 cash flow			
($120 × .943 discount factor)	113		
NPV	$293		

The NPV of Firm R's restructured transaction is $2 more than that of the original transaction. This entire increase is attributable to the deferral of a $38 tax cost for one year. The only difference in the transactions is timing. This observation suggests our second income tax planning maxim: *In present value terms, tax costs decrease (and cash flows increase) when a tax is deferred until a later taxable year.*

Income Deferral and Opportunity Costs

The restructured transaction in the preceding example represents an ideal situation in which a firm defers the payment of tax without affecting before-tax cash flows. Realistically, firms can defer tax only by deferring the taxable income generated by the transaction, which may be difficult to do without affecting cash flows. A tax deferral strategy that does affect before-tax cash flows may not improve NPV. To illustrate this possibility, assume that Firm R avoids taxable income in year 0 by delaying the receipt of $180 of revenue until year 1. Let's recompute the NPV of the transaction based on this assumption:

	Year 0		Year 1
Revenues	$ 40		$460
Expenses	(40)		(80)
Income tax cost:			
Taxable income	–0–	$380	
		.21	
Tax cost	–0–		(80)
After-tax net cash flow	–0–		$300
Present value of year 0 cash flow	–0–		
Present value of year 1 cash flow			
($300 × .943 discount factor)	$283		
NPV	$283		

[6] For purposes of computing NPV, before-tax cash flows, tax costs, and tax savings in the same taxable year are assumed to occur at the same point in time.

In this transaction, the NPV is $8 *less* than that of the original transaction. While Firm R defers a $38 tax cost for one year, it also delays the receipt of $180 cash. The net result is that Firm R loses the use of $142 for one year at an opportunity cost of $8 [$142 − ($142 × .943 discount factor)].

Instead of delaying the receipt of revenues, what if Firm R could defer taxable income by paying all the expenses in the first year?

	Year 0		Year 1
Revenues		$220	$280
Expenses		(120)	–0–
Income tax cost:			
Taxable income	$100	$280	
	.21	.21	
Tax cost		(21)	(59)
After-tax net cash flow		$ 79	$221
Present value of year 0 cash flow		$ 79	
Present value of year 1 cash flow			
($221 × .943 discount factor)		208	
NPV		$287	

Tax Talk

Taxpayers suffering casualty losses in a federally declared disaster area have the option to claim such losses on their income tax return for the year of the event or the prior year. Thus, victims of Hurricane Ida in August 2021 could claim losses on their 2020 tax returns and receive expedited refunds. This timing rule accelerated the tax savings from the deduction by one year.

This alternative method for deferring taxable income has exactly the same negative effect on NPV. By deferring a $17 tax cost and accelerating the payment of $80 of expenses, Firm R deprives itself of the use of $63 for one year at an opportunity cost of $4. In both transactions, the advantage of tax deferral is overwhelmed by a disadvantageous change in before-tax cash flows. Consequently, we can conclude that our second tax planning maxim holds true only when a tax payment can be deferred independently of before-tax cash flows or when the value of the deferral exceeds any opportunity cost of a coinciding change in before-tax cash flows.

Income Deferral and Rate Changes

The deferral of taxable income into future years creates uncertainty as to the marginal rate that will apply to that income. The value of the deferral could be reduced if Congress were to increase the statutory rates or if the firm were to move unexpectedly into a higher tax bracket. The risk that deferred income will be taxed at a higher rate escalates with the length of the deferral period. To illustrate this problem, assume that Firm N, which is in a 21 percent marginal tax bracket, generates $30,000 profit on a transaction. It has the choice of reporting the entire profit as current year income or reporting the profit as income ratably over the next three years at no opportunity cost. Firm N chooses the deferral strategy based on the following projection (which uses a 5 percent discount rate).

	Year 0	Year 1	Year 2	Year 3
Without deferral:				
Taxable income	$30,000	–0–	–0–	–0–
Tax cost at 21%	6,300	–0–	–0–	–0–
NPV of tax costs	$ 6,300			

	Year 0	Year 1	Year 2	Year 3
With deferral:				
Taxable income	–0–	$10,000	$10,000	$10,000
Tax cost at 21%	–0–	2,100	2,100	2,100
Discount factors		.952	.907	.864
		$ 1,999	$ 1,905	$ 1,814
NPV of tax costs	$ 5,718			

Now assume that Firm N's marginal tax rate in years 1 through 3 jumps to 30 percent because of a change in the tax law. As a result, the tax costs in years 1 through 3 are much higher than projected.

	Year 0	Year 1	Year 2	Year 3
Taxable income	–0–	$10,000	$10,000	$10,000
Tax cost at 30%	–0–	3,000	3,000	3,000
Discount factors		.952	.907	.864
		$ 2,856	$ 2,721	$ 2,592
Actual NPV of tax costs	$8,169			

Because the value of deferring the tax cost is insufficient to compensate for the higher rate at which the deferred income is taxed, Firm N's choice to defer the income *increased* the tax cost of the transaction by $1,869 in present value terms.

Actual NPV of tax costs	$ 8,169
NPV of tax cost without deferral	(6,300)
	$ 1,869

THE JURISDICTION VARIABLE

LO 4-5
Discuss why the jurisdiction in which a business operates affects after-tax cash flows.

Every domestic business is subject to the tax jurisdiction of the federal government. Therefore, the geographic location of a firm within the United States is a neutral factor in the computation of its federal income tax. However, most states and the District of Columbia also tax business income. Because of the differences in state tax systems, a firm's aggregate income tax liability (federal, state, and local) is very much a function of the jurisdictions in which it conducts business.

Consider two domestic firms that each receive $5,000 cash, all of which is taxable income. Firm Y operates in State Y, which imposes a flat 4 percent tax on business income. Firm Z operates in State Z, which imposes a flat 10 percent tax on business income. For federal purposes, state income tax payments are deductible in the computation of taxable income.[7]

---

[7] §164(a).

Both firms face a 21 percent federal tax rate. Under these facts, Firms Y and Z have the following after-tax cash flows:

	Firm Y	Firm Z
Before-tax cash/income	$5,000	$5,000
State income tax cost	(200)	(500)
Federal taxable income	$4,800	$4,500
Federal tax cost		
(Taxable income × 21%)	(1,008)	(945)
After-tax cash flow	$3,792	$3,555

A comparison of these after-tax cash flows gives us our third income tax planning maxim: *Tax costs decrease (and cash flows increase) when income is generated in a jurisdiction with a low tax rate.*

The comparison between the after-tax cash flows of Firms Y and Z would be more complex if these firms operated in any foreign country that taxes business income. Clearly, managers must be aware of the income tax laws of every locality in which their firm operates or plans to operate in the future. Managers should appreciate that they can often minimize the total tax burden by conducting business in jurisdictions with favorable tax climates. The intricacies of tax planning in a multijurisdictional setting are the subject of Chapter 13.

Global Tax Costs

In 2022, the United Arab Emirates had the highest corporate income tax rate—55 percent! However, this rate only applies to oil and gas companies. The UAE's general corporate income tax rate is zero.

The country with the lowest corporate income tax rate, zero, is a tie between Anguilla, the Bahamas, Bermuda, the British Virgin Islands, and the Cayman Islands.

THE CHARACTER VARIABLE

The fourth variable that determines the tax consequences of transactions is the tax character of the income generated by the transaction. The tax character of any item of income is determined strictly by law; it is not intuitive and may bear no relationship to any financial or economic attribute of the income. In addition, the character of income and the ramifications of that characterization can change with each new tax bill passed by Congress or each new regulation published by the Treasury. Because the character variable is artificial, it is the hardest one to discuss in a generalized manner.

Every item of income is ultimately characterized for tax purposes as either **ordinary income** or **capital gain.** The income generated by routine sales of goods or services to customers or clients is ordinary income. The yield on certain types of invested capital, such as interest and rents, is also ordinary in character. As the label implies, most ordinary income is taxed at the regular individual or corporate rates. The sale or exchange of certain types of property, referred to as capital assets, gives rise to capital gain. The term *capital asset* is defined in detail in Chapter 8. Historically, capital gain has enjoyed favorable treatment under the federal tax law, usually in the form of a preferential tax rate. Currently, individuals pay tax on their capital gains at a 28, 25, 20, 15, or 0 percent rate. In some circumstances, dividend income qualifies for these same preferential rates.

In contrast, capital gains and dividend income reported by a corporation are taxed at the same rates as ordinary income.[8] Many items of ordinary income and capital gain have additional characteristics that affect the tax on the income. For example, the ordinary income earned by firms conducting business both in the United States and foreign countries is characterized as either U.S. source income or foreign source income. As we will discuss in Chapter 13, this characterization is crucial in determining how much federal income tax the firms must pay on ordinary income. For another example, the ordinary business income earned by individuals is characterized as either active income or passive income. As we will discuss in Chapter 16, only passive income is subject to the Medicare contribution tax.

To demonstrate the effect of the character variable, let's compare the cash flow consequences of three different items of income received by Mr. Thompson, who has a 35 percent regular marginal tax rate. Each item consists of $1,000 cash. The first item is ordinary income with no other special characteristic; the second item is capital gain eligible for the 15 percent rate; and the third item is interest on a bond issued by the City of New York. While interest generically is ordinary income, municipal bond interest has a very special character—it is exempt from federal income tax. In other words, municipal bond interest is taxed at a preferential rate of zero.

	Ordinary Income	Capital Gain	Tax-Exempt Income
Before-tax cash/income	$1,000	$1,000	$1,000
Tax cost	(350)	(150)	–0–
After-tax cash flow	$ 650	$ 850	$1,000

The fact that the character of income determines whether the income is taxed at the regular rate or at a special rate suggests our fourth tax planning maxim: *Tax costs decrease (and cash flows increase) when income is taxed at a preferential rate because of its character.*

Determining the Value of Preferential Rates

The value of a preferential rate to a particular taxpayer can be quantified only by reference to that taxpayer's regular marginal rate. In the previous example, the $200 difference between the after-tax cash flow from the ordinary income and the capital gain is due to the 20 percentage point spread between Mr. Thompson's 35 percent regular tax rate and the 15 percent preferential rate on the capital gain. If Mr. Thompson's marginal rate on ordinary income is only 24 percent, the 9 percentage point spread between the regular rate and the preferential rate results in only a $90 difference in after-tax cash flow.

	Ordinary Income	Capital Gain
Before-tax cash/income	$1,000	$1,000
Tax cost (24% regular rate)	(240)	(150)
After-tax cash flow	$ 760	$ 850

---

[8] The preferential rates apply only to long-term capital gains. Chapter 16 includes a detailed discussion of the individual preferential rates.

Constraints on Conversion

For many years, taxpayers and their advisers have heeded the fourth tax planning maxim by structuring transactions to result in capital gain rather than ordinary income. The more aggressive have devised ingenious techniques for converting the potential ordinary income from a transaction to capital gain. In response, Congress has worked hard to protect the integrity of the distinction between the two types of income. The Internal Revenue Code contains dozens of prohibitions against artificial conversions of ordinary income into capital gain, many of which we will examine in later chapters. In fact, the preferential treatment of capital gains is responsible for more complexity in the federal income tax system than any other feature. Why then does Congress persist in maintaining the capital gains preference? This tax policy question is addressed in Chapter 16.

Implicit and Explicit Taxes

LO 4-7
Distinguish between an explicit tax and an implicit tax.

The decision to engage in a transaction generating income taxed at a preferential rate should be based on the NPV of the transaction rather than the fact of the preferential rate. The tax cost may not be the only cash flow affected by the tax-favored character of the income. Suppose that Ms. Crowe has $40,000 to invest in either a tax-exempt municipal bond or a corporate bond of identical risk. The interest from the latter would be ordinary income taxed at 32 percent. Let's make an initial assumption that both bonds pay 5 percent interest per year. A comparison of the annual after-tax cash flows indicates that the municipal bond is the superior investment:

	Corporate Bond Interest	Municipal Bond Interest
Before-tax cash/income	$2,000	$2,000
Tax cost	(640)	–0–
After-tax cash flow	$1,360	$2,000

The assumption that the two bonds offer identical before-tax yields is unrealistic. State and local governments take advantage of the tax-exempt status of their debt obligations by offering lower interest rates than their competitors in the capital markets. They know that many investors will accept the lower rate because of the tax-favored status of the bonds. Let's change our example by assuming that the municipal bond would pay only 4 percent interest on Ms. Crowe's $40,000 investment:

	Corporate Bond Interest	Municipal Bond Interest
Before-tax cash/income	$2,000	$1,600
Tax cost	(640)	–0–
After-tax cash flow	$1,360	$1,600

While the municipal bond is still a better investment than the corporate bond, the value of the preferential tax rate to Ms. Crowe has decreased because of the difference in the bonds' respective before-tax yields. Ms. Crowe would pay no direct **explicit tax** on the interest from the municipal bond, but she must accept a reduced market rate of return to take advantage of the tax preference. In the tax literature, this reduction is referred to as an **implicit tax.**[9] As previously defined in Chapter 2, an implicit tax represents a reduction in the pretax return available from investment in a tax-favored asset. In this example, the municipal bonds bear an implicit tax of $400, the difference between the $2,000 of interest available from the corporate bond investment and the $1,600 payable by the municipal bonds.

What if the municipal bond would pay only 3 percent interest on the $40,000 investment?

	Corporate Bond Interest	Municipal Bond Interest
Before-tax cash/income	$2,000	$1,200
Tax cost	(640)	–0–
After-tax cash flow	$1,360	$1,200

Now the $800 implicit tax that Ms. Crowe would incur by purchasing the municipal bond (the reduction in the before-tax yield) is greater than the $640 explicit tax on the interest from the corporate bond. Consequently, the after-tax cash generated by the corporate bond exceeds the after-tax cash generated by the tax-favored municipal bond, and Ms. Crowe should invest accordingly.

Municipal bond interest has no inherent financial characteristic that creates a natural immunity to taxation.[10] Congress granted tax-exempt status to this type of income to help state and local governments compete in the capital markets. The loss in revenues attributable to the tax preference represents an indirect federal subsidy to these governments. Whether this tax preference (or any other preference) is worth anything to a given investor depends on the investor's marginal tax rate and any implicit tax on the investment.

DEVELOPING TAX PLANNING STRATEGIES

LO 4-8
Summarize the four tax planning maxims.

Our analysis of the variables that determine the tax consequences of transactions resulted in the following maxims:

- *Tax costs decrease (and cash flows increase) when income is generated by an entity subject to a low tax rate.*
- *In present value terms, tax costs decrease (and cash flows increase) when a tax is deferred until a later taxable year.*
- *Tax costs decrease (and cash flows increase) when income is generated in a jurisdiction with a low tax rate.*
- *Tax costs decrease (and cash flows increase) when income is taxed at a preferential rate because of its character.*

Tax planning strategies that enhance cash flows typically reflect at least one of these maxims. Many strategies combine two or more maxims working together to minimize taxes. Other strategies may adhere to one maxim but violate another. In such cases, business managers must carefully assess the overall tax consequences to determine if the strategy improves NPV. The following example demonstrates the problem of conflicting maxims.

[9] This term was popularized by Myron S. Scholes and Mark A. Wolfson in *Taxes and Business Strategy: A Planning Approach* (Englewood Cliffs, NJ: Prentice Hall, 1992).

[10] For state income tax purposes, interest on state and local bonds is generally taxable.

Conflicting Maxims

Firm MN operates as two separate taxable entities, Entities M and N. The firm is negotiating a transaction that will generate $25,000 cash in year 0 and $60,000 cash in year 1. If Entity M undertakes the transaction, taxable income will correspond to cash flow (i.e., Entity M will report $25,000 and $60,000 taxable income in years 0 and 1). If Entity N undertakes the transaction, it must report the entire $85,000 taxable income in year 0. Entity M has a 32 percent marginal tax rate, while Entity N has a 21 percent marginal tax rate. Firm MN uses a 5 percent discount rate to compute NPV.

	Entity M		**Entity N**	
Year 0:				
Before-tax cash flow		$25,000		$25,000
Taxable income	$25,000		$85,000	
	.32		.21	
Tax cost		(8,000)		(17,850)
After-tax net cash flow		$17,000		$ 7,150
Year 1:				
Before-tax cash flow		$60,000		$60,000
Taxable income	$60,000		–0–	
	.32			
Tax cost		(19,200)		–0–
After-tax cash flow		$40,800		$60,000
Present value of year 0 cash flow		$17,000		$ 7,150
Present value of year 1 cash flow				
(.952 discount factor)		38,842		57,120
NPV		$55,842		$64,270

Tax Talk

Investopedia defines tax planning as "the analysis of finances from a tax perspective, with the purpose of ensuring maximum tax efficiency."

On the basis of an NPV comparison, Firm MN should undertake the transaction through Entity N. This strategy adheres to the tax planning maxim that cash flows increase when income is generated by an entity with a low tax rate. However, the strategy accelerates the entire tax on the transaction into year 0, thus violating the maxim that calls for tax deferral.

Additional Strategic Considerations

The four tax planning maxims offer general guidance to the tax planning process. Like all generalizations, each one is subject to conditions, limitations, and exceptions depending on the specific tax strategy under consideration. Even though the maxims focus on the reduction of tax costs, managers should remember that their strategic goal is not tax minimization per se but maximization of after-tax value. Consequently, they must consider factors other than tax costs in formulating a winning strategy. One obvious factor is the expense of implementing the strategy. Firms may require professional advice in designing, executing, and monitoring a sophisticated tax plan, and the cost of the advice must be weighed against the potential tax savings from the strategy.

Tax Savings versus Additional Costs

Firm B has a choice between two strategies for reducing its tax with respect to a line of business. The simpler of the two strategies would reduce the annual tax by $50,000 and wouldn't cost anything to implement. The more complex of the two strategies would reduce the annual tax by $70,000 but would require additional legal and accounting fees with an after-tax cost of $25,000. Firm B should choose the simpler strategy because it has the greater value even though it saves less tax.

Managers must consider the economic consequences of tax strategies to all parties. In Chapter 3, we learned that firms negotiating in private markets can work together to maximize the after-tax value of the transaction to both parties. A manager intent on implementing a unilateral tax strategy may miss an opportunity for effective multilateral planning. Even worse, if a manager fails to consider the repercussions of a strategy on other interested parties, those parties might retaliate in ways that reduce the overall value of the strategy to the firm.

Multilateral Planning	Corporation F and Corporation D plan to form a joint venture to conduct a new business. Corporation F's tax cost would be minimized if the business is conducted in Germany. Corporation D's tax cost would be minimized if the business is conducted in the United States. Corporation F agrees to locate the business in the United States, provided that it receives 60 percent of the profit and Corporation D receives only 40 percent. This compromise increases Corporation F's tax cost and decreases Corporation D's before-tax profit. Nevertheless, the corporations agree to the compromise because it maximizes the after-tax value of the joint venture to both corporations.

Tax strategies must be evaluated on the basis of flexibility: the extent to which the strategy can be adapted to unforeseen circumstances. Every strategy's anticipated effect on cash flows is based on assumptions about the future. The more uncertain the assumptions, the greater the risk that the strategy could backfire and have a detrimental effect on cash flows. If the firm can quickly modify or even reverse a failed strategy at minimal cost, this risk may be slight. However, if the strategy is irreversible or would be expensive to fix, the cost of potential failure may outweigh the benefit of success.

The Flexibility Factor	Four years ago, Firm D formed a Brazilian corporation to operate its business in South America. Firm D selected the corporate form to take advantage of generous tax preferences available only to Brazilian corporations. This year, Brazil repealed the preferences and substantially increased its corporate tax rate. If Firm D had not formed the corporation, it could easily avoid the tax increase by restructuring its South American operation. But Firm D can't dissolve the Brazilian corporation without incurring prohibitively high legal and political costs. With hindsight, Firm D would have maximized the after-tax value of its South American operation by choosing a more flexible tax strategy.

Tax Legal Doctrines

LO 4-9
Describe the legal doctrines that the IRS uses to challenge tax planning strategies.

Managers must be confident that they have identified the correct tax consequences of the strategies implemented by their firm. If a manager makes a technical error in applying the tax law and the IRS discovers the error on audit, the planning strategy could unravel, with disastrous effects on cash flows. Even when managers believe that a strategy is technically sound, they must consider the government's reaction to the overall propriety of the strategy. Over the years, both the IRS and the federal courts have made taxpayers adhere not only to the letter but also to the spirit of the law. Consequently, four important common law doctrines have evolved in the tax planning area. The IRS can invoke these doctrines when a firm seems to be bending the rules to gain an unjustified tax advantage.

Tax Talk

The Supreme Court recently declined to review a decision in which the Third Circuit Court used the economic substance doctrine to deny over $1 billion in tax credits to an investor in the rehabilitation of an historic convention center in Atlantic City, New Jersey.

The **economic substance doctrine** holds that a transaction that doesn't change the taxpayer's economic situation except by the tax savings from the transaction can be disregarded by the IRS. This doctrine is closely aligned with the **business purpose doctrine** that a transaction should not be effective for tax purposes unless it has a business purpose other than tax avoidance. In 2010, Congress codified these common law doctrines by enacting Section 7701(o) of the Internal Revenue Code. This subsection states that a transaction has economic substance only if it "changes in a meaningful way (apart from federal income tax effects) the taxpayer's economic position, and the taxpayer has a substantial purpose (apart from federal income tax effects) for entering into such transaction." A transaction that is devoid of economic substance will not be respected for tax purposes.[11]

Lack of Economic Substance	Mr. Early planned to sell developed real estate held in his own name to raise cash to fund a new investment opportunity. The proposed sale would generate a substantial gain, which would be taxed to Mr. Early at a 25 percent rate. Instead of selling the real estate directly, Mr. Early contributed the real estate to a corporation in which he was the sole shareholder. The corporation sold the real estate, paid tax on the gain at a much lower rate, and then made an interest-free loan of the after-tax cash proceeds to Mr. Early. If the IRS concludes that Mr. Early's contribution of the real estate to the corporation had no economic effect or business purpose other than reducing the tax cost of the sale, it could disregard the transaction and require Mr. Early to pay tax on the gain at his 25 percent rate.[12]

The **substance over form doctrine** holds that the IRS can look through the legal formalities to determine the economic substance (if any) of a transaction. If the substance differs from the form, the IRS will base the tax consequences of the transaction on the reality rather than the illusion.[13]

Substance over Form	The sole shareholder and president of Corporation JKL negotiated a leasing contract with a local businessman. Under the terms of the contract, JKL paid $35,000 for the use of equipment for one year and deducted this payment as a business expense. The revenue agent who audited JKL's tax return uncovered two additional facts. First, the local businessman who received the $35,000 was a candidate for state political office and was enthusiastically endorsed by JKL's owner. Second, the corporation had no apparent need for the leased equipment. If these facts convince the agent that the substance of the leasing arrangement was a disguised political contribution (which is completely nondeductible), JKL may lose its $35,000 deduction and the tax savings therefrom.

[11] Source: These doctrines originated with the case of *Gregory* v. *Helvering,* 293 U.S. 465 (1935).

[12] This example is based on the facts in *Paymer* v. *Commissioner,* 150 F.2d 334 (CA-2, 1945).

[13] *Commissioner* v. *Danielson,* 378 F.2d 771 (CA-3, 1967), *cert. denied* 389 U.S. 858 (1967).

The **step transaction doctrine** allows the IRS to collapse a series of intermediate transactions into a single transaction to determine the tax consequences of the arrangement in its entirety.[14] The IRS applies the doctrine when transactions are so obviously interdependent that the parties involved wouldn't have initiated the first transaction without anticipating that the whole series of transactions would occur. Transactions occurring within a short period of time are more vulnerable to the step transaction doctrine than those occurring over a longer interval. As a rule of thumb, the IRS considers transactions occurring within a 12-month period as suspect.[15] Transactions separated in time by more than 12 months are presumed to be independent. In tax parlance, the first transaction is "old and cold" with no connection to the second transaction.

Potential Step Transactions	ABC Corporation sells property to an unrelated purchaser who subsequently resells the property to ABC's wholly owned subsidiary. If these two sales occur within the same month, the IRS would certainly question their autonomy. Unless ABC could present evidence to the contrary, the IRS could collapse the two transactions into a direct sale of property from ABC to its subsidiary and recast the tax consequences of this related party transaction. On the other hand, if the first sale occurs five years before the second sale, the substantial length of time between the sales should make them immune to the step transaction doctrine.

There is considerable overlap in the scope of the common law doctrines, and the IRS frequently uses them in combination to challenge an offending transaction. Of course, the courts may or may not uphold the IRS's challenge. Judges or juries may side with the taxpayer by concluding that a transaction has economic substance that matches its legal form. Business managers should understand that the doctrines seem to be the exclusive property of the IRS; taxpayers can't invoke them to undo the consequences of their own ill-fated tax strategies.[16] Managers should be aware that the IRS's application of these doctrines is subjective. Given the threat of these doctrines, managers can never be absolutely certain that a creative tax plan will work, even if it seems to comply with the letter of the law.

Conclusion

Tax planning is the structuring of transactions to reduce tax costs or increase tax savings to maximize after-tax value. This chapter introduced the four structural variables (entity, time period, jurisdiction, and income character) that affect the tax consequences of transactions. To the extent that taxpayers can control these variables, they can structure transactions to achieve the most advantageous tax outcome. But before taxpayers can properly structure their transactions, they must understand exactly how the tax law pertains to the facts and circumstances of the transaction. Each transaction is unique and may raise any number of tax questions that must be answered before the outcome of the transaction can be determined with certainty. The art of asking and answering tax questions is called *tax research,* which is the subject of the next chapter.

[14] *Helvering* v. *Alabama Asphaltic Limestone Co.,* 315 U.S. 179 (1942).
[15] Reg. §1.368-2(c).
[16] *Durkin,* T.C. Memo 1992-325.

Key Terms

assignment of income
   doctrine *4–6*
business purpose
   doctrine *4–16*
capital gain *4–10*
economic substance
   doctrine *4–16*

explicit tax *4–12*
implicit tax *4–13*
ordinary income *4–10*
step transaction
   doctrine *4–17*
substance over form
   doctrine *4–16*

tax avoidance *4–2*
tax evasion *4–2*
tax planning *4–1*

Questions and Problems for Discussion

LO 4-1

1. For each of the following situations, discuss whether the individual is engaging in tax avoidance or tax evasion.

   a. Mr. Lewis performed minor construction work for a number of people who paid him in cash. Because Mr. Lewis knows that there is almost no chance that the IRS could learn of these payments, he reports only half the payments as income on his federal tax return.

   b. Mr. Pagor, who is in the 37 percent tax bracket, recently had the opportunity to invest $50,000 in a new business that should yield an annual return of at least 17 percent. Rather than invest himself, Mr. Pagor gave $50,000 cash to his son, who then made the investment. The son's marginal tax rate is only 12 percent.

   c. Mrs. Quinn sold an asset during January. Her $12,000 profit on the sale is ordinary income. After preparing her income tax return for the prior year, Mrs. Quinn realized that her marginal tax rate for that year was 24 percent. She also realized that her marginal rate for this year will be 37 percent. Mrs. Quinn decides to report the profit on her prior year return to take advantage of the lower tax rate.

LO 4-2

2. Mrs. Zhang is about to begin a new business activity and asks you if she can reduce taxable income by operating the activity as a corporation rather than as a sole proprietorship. How do you answer Mrs. Zhang?

LO 4-2

3. Is every business organization a taxable entity for federal income tax purposes? Explain briefly.

LO 4-2

4. On the basis of the discussion in this chapter and the rates schedules in Appendix C, determine the marginal tax rate for

   a. A corporation with $23,000 taxable income.

   b. A corporation with $250,000 taxable income.

   c. A single (unmarried) individual with $53,000 taxable income.

   d. A single (unmarried) individual with $625,000 taxable income.

LO 4-2

5. Compare the potential tax savings of an income shift from one entity to another if the entities are subject to

   a. A progressive income tax system with rates from 5 percent to 19 percent.

   b. A progressive income tax system with rates from 10 percent to 50 percent.

   c. A 20 percent proportionate income tax system.

LO 4-2, 4-9

6. Why do income shifts and deduction shifts usually occur between taxpayers who are related parties?

LO 4-2

7. Corporation P owns a controlling stock interest in Subsidiary S and Subsidiary T. Corporation P's marginal tax rate is 21 percent. It engages in one transaction that shifts $10,000 income to Subsidiary S and a second transaction that shifts a $15,000 deduction to Subsidiary T. Based on these facts, what conclusions can you draw about marginal tax rates of the two subsidiaries?

LO 4-4 8. Firm A expects to receive a $25,000 item of income in August and a second $25,000 item of income in December. The firm could delay the receipt of both items until January. As a result, it would defer the payment of tax on $50,000 income for one full year. Firm A decides to receive the August payment this year (and pay current tax on $25,000 income) but delay the receipt of the December payment. Can you offer an explanation for this decision?

LO 4-4 9. Tax planners often tell their clients that "a tax delayed is a tax not paid." Can you provide a more formal explanation of this bit of wisdom?

LO 4-6 10. Assume that Congress amends the tax law to provide for a maximum 18 percent rate on rental income generated by single-family residences. What effect might this preferential rate have on the market value of this category of real estate?

LO 4-8 11. Identify the reasons managers should evaluate the flexibility of a tax planning strategy before implementing the strategy.

LO 4-8 12. In June, Congress enacts legislation that increases income tax rates for all entities effective for the next calendar year.
   a. Why might such legislation result in an increase in federal tax revenues for this year?
   b. In what way would this legislation create a conflict between tax planning maxims?

LO 4-8 13. Mr. Tanis is considering a strategy to defer $10,000 income for five years with no significant opportunity cost. Discuss the strategic implications of the following independent assumptions:
   a. Mr. Tanis is age 24. He graduated from law school last month and accepted a position with a prominent firm of attorneys.
   b. Mr. Tanis is age 63. He plans to retire from business at the end of this year and devote his time to volunteer work and sailing.

LO 4-1 14. Assume that the U.S. Congress replaces the current individual and corporate income tax rate structures with a proportionate rate that applies to both types of taxpayers. Discuss the effect of this change in the federal law on tax strategies based on
   a. The entity variable.
   b. The time period variable.
   c. The jurisdiction variable.
   d. The character variable.

McGraw Hill connect All applicable Application Problems are available with *Connect.*

Application Problems

LO 4-2 1. Using the 2023 corporate tax rate,
   a. What are the tax liability, the marginal tax rate, and the average tax rate for a corporation with $248,300 taxable income?
   b. What are the tax liability, the marginal tax rate, and the average tax rate for a corporation with $39,253,000 taxable income?

LO 4-2 2. Refer to the 2023 individual rate schedules in Appendix C.
   a. What are the tax liability, the marginal tax rate, and the average tax rate for a married individual filing separately with $42,500 taxable income?
   b. What are the tax liability, the marginal tax rate, and the average tax rate for a single individual with $150,500 taxable income?

    c. What are the tax liability, the marginal tax rate, and the average tax rate for a head of household individual with $275,000 taxable income?

    d. What are the tax liability, the marginal tax rate, and the average tax rate for a married couple filing jointly with $630,000 taxable income?

LO 4-2   3. Refer to the 2023 individual rate schedules in Appendix C.

    a. What are the tax liability, the marginal tax rate, and the average tax rate for a married couple filing jointly with $51,900 taxable income?

    b. What are the tax liability, the marginal tax rate, and the average tax rate for a single individual with $197,200 taxable income?

    c. What are the tax liability, the marginal tax rate, and the average tax rate for a head of household with $446,300 taxable income?

LO 4-2   4. Ms. Jolly recently made a gift to her 19-year-old daughter, Alison. Ms. Jolly's marginal income tax rate is 37 percent, and Alison's marginal income tax rate is 12 percent. In each of the following cases, compute the annual income tax savings resulting from the gift.

    a. The gift consisted of rental property generating $19,100 annual rental income to its owner.

    b. The gift consisted of a $4,625 interest coupon from a corporate bond owned by Ms. Jolly.

    c. The gift consisted of a $2,200 rent check written by the tenants who lease rental property owned by Ms. Jolly.

    d. The gift consisted of a corporate bond paying $13,300 annual interest to its owner.

LO 4-2   5. Firm A has a 21 percent marginal tax rate, and Firm Z has a 28 percent marginal tax rate. Firm A owns a controlling interest in Firm Z. The owners of Firm A decide to incur a $9,500 deductible expense that will benefit both firms. Compute the after-tax cost of the expense assuming that

    a. Firm A incurs the expense.

    b. Firm Z incurs the expense.

LO 4-2, 4-3   6. Company G, which has a 30 percent marginal tax rate, owns a controlling interest in Company J, which has a 21 percent marginal tax rate. Both companies perform engineering services. Company G is negotiating a contract to provide services for a client. Upon satisfactory completion of the services, the client will pay $85,000 cash. Compute the after-tax cash from the contract assuming that

    a. Company G is the party to the contract and provides the services to the client.

    b. Company J is the party to the contract and provides the services to the client.

    c. Company J is the party to the contract, but Company G actually provides the services to the client.

LO 4-2   7. BPK, Inc. and OPK, Inc. are owned by the same family. BPK's marginal tax rate is 21 percent, and OPK's marginal tax rate is 32 percent. BPK is about to incur a $72,000 deductible expense that would benefit both corporations. OPK could obtain the same mutual benefit by incurring an $82,500 deductible expense. Which corporation should incur the expense?

LO 4-2   8. Firm M and Firm N are related parties. For the past several years, Firm M's marginal tax rate has been 30 percent and Firm N's marginal tax rate has been 21 percent. Firm M is evaluating a transaction that will generate $10,000 income in each of the next three years. Firm M could restructure the transaction so that the income would be earned by Firm N. Because of the restructuring, the annual income would decrease to $9,000. Should Firm M restructure the transaction?

LO 4-4 9. Company K has a 30 percent marginal tax rate and uses a 7 percent discount rate to compute NPV. The company started a venture that will yield the following before-tax cash flows: year 0, $12,000; year 1, $21,000; year 2, $24,000; year 3, $17,600.

   a. If the before-tax cash flows represent taxable income in the year received, compute the NPV of the cash flows.

   b. Compute the NPV if Company K can defer the receipt of years 0 and 1 cash flows/income until year 2. (It would receive no cash in years 0 and 1 and would receive $57,000 cash in year 2.)

   c. Compute the NPV if Company K can defer paying tax on years 0 and 1 cash flows until year 2. (It would receive $24,000 cash in year 2 but would pay tax on $57,000 income.)

LO 4-4 10. Firm H has the opportunity to engage in a transaction that will generate $100,000 cash flow (and taxable income) in year 0.

   a. Calculate the after-tax cash flow from the transaction described above.

   b. How does the NPV of the transaction change if the firm could restructure the transaction in a way that doesn't change before-tax cash flow but results in no taxable income in year 0, $50,000 taxable income in year 1, and the remaining $50,000 taxable income in year 2? Assume a 6 percent discount rate and a 21 percent marginal tax rate for the three-year period.

LO 4-4 11. What is the effect on the NPV of the restructured transaction in the preceding problem if Firm H's marginal tax rate in year 2 increases to 30 percent?

LO 4-4 12. French Corporation wishes to hire Leslie as a consultant to design a comprehensive staff training program. The project is expected to take one year, and the parties have agreed to a tentative price of $60,000. French Corporation has proposed payment of one-half of the fee now, with the remainder paid in one year when the project is complete.

   a. If Leslie expects her marginal tax rate to be 24 percent this year and 35 percent next year, calculate the after-tax NPV of this contract to Leslie, using a 6 percent discount rate.

   b. French Corporation expects its marginal tax rate to be 21 percent both years. Calculate the NPV of French's after-tax cost to enter into this contract using a 6 percent discount rate.

   c. Given that Leslie expects her tax rate to increase next year, she would prefer to receive more of the income from the project upfront. Consider an alternative proposal under which French pays Leslie $42,000 this year, and $16,000 in one year when the contract is complete. Calculate the after-tax benefit of this counterproposal to Leslie and the after-tax cost to French. Are both parties better off under this alternative than under the original plan?

LO 4-4 13. Corporation R signed a contract to undertake a transaction that will generate $360,000 total cash to the corporation. The cash will represent income in the year received and will be taxed at 21 percent. Corporation R will receive $200,000 in year 0 and $160,000 in year 1. The other party to the contract now wants to restructure the transaction in a way that would increase the total cash to $375,000 ($215,000 received in year 0 and $160,000 received in year 1). However, Corporation R would recognize the entire $375,000 taxable income in year 0. If Corporation R uses an 8 percent discount rate to compute NPV, should it agree to restructure the transaction?

LO 4-6, 4-7 14. Firm W, which has a 32 percent marginal tax rate, plans to operate a new business that should generate $40,000 annual cash flow/ordinary income for three years (years 0, 1, and 2). Alternatively, Firm W could form a new taxable entity (Entity N) to operate the business. Entity N would pay tax on the three-year income stream at a 21 percent rate. The nondeductible cost of forming Entity N would be $5,000. If Firm W uses a 6 percent discount rate, should it operate the new business directly or form Entity N to operate the business?

LO 4-5 15. Lardo, Inc. plans to build a new manufacturing plant in either Country X or Country Y. It projects gross revenue in either location of $4 million per year. Operating expenses would be $1.5 million in Country X and $1.8 million in Country Y. Country X levies income tax at a rate of 20 percent on net business income. Country Y does not have an income tax, but assesses a 10 percent tax on gross revenue, without allowance for any deductions. In which country should Lardo build its new plant?

LO 4-5 16. Company EJ plans to build a new plant to manufacture bicycles. EJ sells its bicycles in the world market for $400 per bike. It could locate the plant in Province P, which levies a 20 percent tax on business income. On the basis of the cost of materials and labor in Province P, EJ estimates that its manufacturing cost per bike would be $212. Alternatively, EJ could locate the plant in Province W, which levies a 16 percent tax on business income. On the basis of the cost of materials and labor in Province W, EJ estimates that its manufacturing cost per bike would be $230. In which province should Company EJ build its new plant?

LO 4-5 17. Moto, Inc. pays state income tax at a 6 percent rate and federal income tax at a 21 percent rate. Moto recently engaged in a transaction in Country N, which levied a $97,300 tax on the transaction. This year, Moto generated $2.738 million net income before consideration of any tax. Compute Moto's total tax burden (federal, state, and foreign) assuming that

 a. The tax paid to Country N is deductible for both state and federal tax purposes.

 b. The tax paid to Country N is not deductible for state tax purposes but is deductible for federal tax purposes.

 c. The tax paid to Country N is not deductible for either state or federal tax purposes.

LO 4-3, 4-6 18. Vern plans to invest $100,000 in a growth stock in year 0. The stock is not expected to pay dividends. However, Vern predicts that it will be worth $135,000 when he sells it in year 3. The $35,000 increase in value will be taxable at the preferential capital gains rate of 15 percent.

 a. Using a 4 percent discount rate, calculate the NPV of after-tax cash flows from this investment.

 b. Which two of the four basic tax planning variables increase the value of Vern's investment?

LO 4-6 19. Mr. Fuentes has $15,000 to invest. He is undecided about putting the money into tax-exempt municipal bonds paying 3.5 percent annual interest or corporate bonds paying 4.75 percent annual interest. The two investments have the same risk.

 a. Which investment should Mr. Fuentes make if his marginal tax rate is 32 percent?

 b. Would your conclusion change if Mr. Fuentes's marginal tax rate is only 12 percent?

LO 4-6 20. At the beginning of the year, Mr. Lanier put $50,000 cash into Investment X. At the end of the year, he received a check for $2,800, representing his annual return on the investment. Mr. Lanier's marginal tax rate on ordinary income is 37 percent. However, his return on Investment X is a capital gain taxed at 20 percent. Compute the value of the preferential rate to Mr. Lanier.

LO 4-6, 4-7 21. Refer to the facts in the preceding problem. At the beginning of the year, Mr. Lanier could have invested his $50,000 in Business Z with an 8 percent annual return. However, this return would have been ordinary income rather than capital gain.

    a. Considering the fact that Mr. Lanier could have invested in Business Z, how much implicit tax did he pay with respect to Investment X described in the preceding problem?

    b. Did Mr. Lanier make the correct decision by putting his $50,000 into Investment X instead of Business Z?

LO 4-2, 4-4, 4-5, 4-6 22. For each of the following scenarios, indicate which of the four basic tax planning variables (entity, character, time period, jurisdiction) affects after-tax value. Note that more than one variable may apply to any scenario; identify all that are relevant.

    a. Aloha Corporation is considering building a new manufacturing facility in either State U or State P. State U has a 10 percent state income tax rate. State P has a 15 percent state income tax rate but offers a tax holiday for new business investment that would exempt up to $250,000 of Aloha's earnings from state income tax for the first five years of operations in State P.

    b. Mary wishes to help her nephew, Gill, pay his college tuition. Instead of giving Gill cash, Mary gives him bonds earning $10,000 annual interest income. Mary's marginal tax rate is 35 percent and Gill's marginal tax rate is 12 percent.

    c. Congress has recently enacted a decrease in corporate tax rates that will take effect at the beginning of next year. Grant Company, a cash basis taxpayer, is planning to pay expenses prior to year-end in order to maximize its tax savings in the current year.

    d. Will has $50,000 to invest in the stock market. He is considering two alternatives. Stock A pays annual qualifying dividends of 6 percent. Stock B pays no dividends but is expected to increase in value at a rate of 5 percent per year. Will would hold either investment for a minimum of four years. Will's marginal tax rate on ordinary income is 35 percent.

LO 4-2, 4-6 23. Assume that Congress amends the tax law to provide for a maximum 20 percent rate on royalty income. Calculate the annual tax savings from this new preferential rate to each of the following taxpayers.

    a. Ms. Able, who is in a 37 percent marginal tax bracket and receives $8,000 royalty income each year.

    b. Mr. Bencic, who is in a 32 percent marginal tax bracket and receives $15,000 royalty income each year.

    c. Mr. Christian, who is in a 10 percent marginal tax bracket and receives $3,000 royalty income each year.

    d. Mrs. Daughtry, who is in a 24 percent marginal tax bracket and receives $70,000 royalty income each year.

LO 4-6, 4-7 24. Firm L has $500,000 to invest and is considering two alternatives. Investment A would pay 6 percent ($30,000 annual before-tax cash flow). Investment B would pay 4.8 percent ($24,000 annual before-tax cash flow). The return on Investment A is taxable, while the return on Investment B is tax exempt. Firm L forecasts that its 21 percent marginal tax rate will be stable for the foreseeable future.

    a. Compute the explicit tax and implicit tax that Firm L will pay with respect to Investment A and Investment B.

    b. Which investment results in the greater annual after-tax cash flow?

Issue Recognition Problems

Identify the tax issue or issues suggested by the following situations, and state each issue in the form of a question.

LO 4-1 1. Dr. Phan is a physician with his own medical practice. For the past several years, his marginal income tax rate has been 37 percent. Dr. Phan's daughter, who is a college student, has no taxable income. During the last two months of the year, Dr. Phan instructs his patients to remit their payments for his services directly to his daughter.

LO 4-1 2. Mr. and Mrs. Knight own rental property that generates $4,000 monthly revenue. The couple is in the highest marginal tax bracket. For Christmas, Mr. and Mrs. Knight give the uncashed rent checks for October, November, and December to their 19-year-old grandson as a gift.

LO 4-4 3. Mrs. Young owns 1,800 shares of Acme common stock, which she purchased for $10 per share in 2002. In October of this year, she decides to sell her Acme stock for the market price of $27 per share, the highest price at which the stock has traded in the past 22 months. A friend advises her to hold the Acme stock until next January so that her gain from the sale will be taxed next year rather than this year.

LO 4-5 4. Company QP must decide whether to build a new manufacturing plant in Country B or Country C. Country B has no income tax. However, its political regime is unstable and its currency has been devalued four times in three years. Country C has both a 20 percent income tax and a stable democratic government.

LO 4-7 5. Mr. and Mrs. Tram own an investment yielding a 4.25 percent after-tax return. Their friend, Ms. Kay, is encouraging them to sell this investment and invest the proceeds in her business, which takes advantage of several favorable tax preferences. Consequently, Ms. Kay's after-tax return from this business is 7 percent.

LO 4-8 6. Firm Z is considering implementing a long-term tax strategy to accelerate the deduction of certain business expenses. The strategy has an opportunity cost because it decreases before-tax cash flows, but the tax savings from the strategy should be greater than this opportunity cost. The strategy is aggressive, and the IRS might disallow the intended tax outcome if it audits Firm Z's tax returns.

LO 4-9 7. Ms. Laguna plans to structure a transaction as a legal sale of property, even though the economic substance of the transaction is a lease of the property. In her current position, the tax consequences of a sale are much more favorable than those of a lease. Ms. Laguna believes that if her position unexpectedly changes so that she would prefer a lease to a sale, she can ignore the legal formalities and report the transaction as a lease.

LO 4-9 8. Firm HR is about to implement an aggressive long-term strategy consisting of three phases. It is crucial to the success of the strategy that the IRS accepts Firm HR's interpretation of the tax consequences of each distinct phase. The firm could implement the first phase in November 2022 and the second phase in August 2023. Alternatively, it could delay the second phase until January 2024.

Research Problems

LO 4-1 1. Using an electronic library such as Checkpoint, CCH IntelliConnect, or LexisNexis, find a federal tax case in which the taxpayer is found guilty of tax evasion. After reading the case, list the behaviors of the taxpayer that convinced the court that the taxpayer was evading (rather than legally avoiding) tax.

LO 4-9   2. Using an electronic library such as Checkpoint, CCH IntelliConnect, or LexisNexis, determine how many federal tax cases decided in 2022 contain the phrase *step transaction.*

LO 4-9   3. Using an electronic library such as Checkpoint, CCH IntelliConnect, or LexisNexis, find a case that discusses the step transaction doctrine in the opinion and prepare a written summary (brief) of the case.

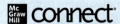 **All applicable Tax Planning Cases are available with *Connect*.**

Tax Planning Cases

LO 4-4   1. Mrs. Oliver is negotiating to purchase a tract of land from DC Company, a calendar year taxpayer. DC bought this land six years ago for $480,000. According to a recent appraisal, the land is worth $800,000 in the current real estate market. According to DC's director of tax, the company's profit on the sale will be taxed at 35 percent if the sale occurs this year. However, this tax rate will definitely decrease to 21 percent if the sale occurs next year. Mrs. Oliver is aware that DC would prefer the sale close next year. However, Mrs. Oliver needs the land immediately to begin construction of a new retail outlet. She offers to pay $875,000 for the land with the stipulation that the sale close by December 31. Should DC accept Mrs. Oliver's offer?

LO 4-5   2. Firm DFG plans to open a foreign subsidiary through which to sell its manufactured goods in the European market. It must decide between locating the subsidiary in Country X or Country Z. If the subsidiary operates in Country X, its gross receipts from sales will be subject to a 3 percent gross receipts tax. If the subsidiary operates in Country Z, its net profits will be subject to a 42 percent income tax. However, Country Z's tax law has a special provision to attract foreign investors: No foreign subsidiary is subject to the income tax for the first three years of operations.

DFG projects the following annual operating results for the two locations (in thousands of dollars):

	Country X	Country Z
Gross receipts from sales	$110,000	$110,000
Cost of sales	(60,000)	(60,000)
Operating expenses	(22,000)	(15,000)
Net profit	$ 28,000	$ 35,000

DFG projects that it will operate the foreign subsidiary for 10 years (years 0 through 9) and that the terminal value of the operation at the end of this period will be the same regardless of location. Assuming a 5 percent discount rate, determine which location maximizes the NPV of the foreign operation.

LO 4-4, 4-6   3. Mr. Kato, who has a 35 percent marginal tax rate, must decide between two investment opportunities, both of which require a $50,000 initial cash outlay in year 0. Investment 1 will yield $8,000 before-tax cash flow in years 1, 2, and 3. This cash represents ordinary taxable income. In year 3, Mr. Kato can liquidate the investment and recover his $50,000 cash outlay. He must pay a nondeductible $200 annual fee (in years 1, 2, and 3) to maintain Investment 1.

4—26 Part Two   *Fundamentals of Tax Planning*

Investment 2 will not yield any before-tax cash flow during the period over which Mr. Kato will hold the investment. In year 3, he can sell Investment 2 for $75,000 cash. His $25,000 profit on the sale will be capital gain taxed at 15 percent.

Assuming a 6 percent discount rate, determine which investment has the greater NPV.

LO 4-5, 4-6   4. Ms. Zelda has decided to invest $75,000 in state bonds. She could invest in State A bonds paying 5 percent annual interest or in State R bonds paying 5.4 percent annual interest. The bonds have the same risk, and the interest from both is exempt from federal income tax. Because Ms. Zelda is a resident of State A, she wouldn't pay State A's 8.5 percent personal income tax on the State A bond interest, but she would pay this tax on the State R bond interest. Ms. Zelda can deduct any state tax payments in the computation of her federal taxable income, and her federal marginal rate is 32 percent. Should Ms. Zelda invest in the State A or the State R bonds?

Chapter **Five**

Tax Research

Learning Objectives

After studying this chapter, you should be able to:

LO 5-1. Explain and apply the six steps of the tax research process.

LO 5-2. Identify and interpret primary sources of tax law.

LO 5-3. Identify secondary sources of tax law and utilize them to locate primary authorities.

Tax Talk
The AICPA Core Competency Framework defines research skill *as the ability "to access relevant guidance or other information, understand it, and apply it."*

Tax research is the process of determining the most probable tax consequences of a course of action undertaken by an individual or organization. Because of the complexity of state, local, and federal tax laws, most taxpayers are unable to conduct research on their own behalf. Consequently, they engage professionals such as certified public accountants (CPAs) or attorneys to investigate the tax consequences of their business, investment, and financial transactions. Taxpayers expect to receive fair value in return for the substantial fees paid to their tax advisers. Specifically, they expect their advisers to provide accurate, useful, and complete tax information on a timely basis.

A client may engage a tax adviser to research a transaction (or series of transactions) that has already occurred. In such a case, the adviser must identify the consequences of the transaction and the proper reporting of the transaction on the client's tax return. Because the transaction is complete, the facts surrounding the transaction are a matter of record and are no longer subject to the client's control. The tax consequences of such a closed-fact transaction can't be changed, even if they are not to the client's liking. Thus, the adviser is limited to providing a tax compliance service to the client.

Alternatively, a client may engage a tax adviser to research a transaction that the client proposes to undertake at some future date. In this case, the adviser not only can determine the tax consequences of the prospective transaction, but also can suggest ways in which the transaction can be modified to result in a more favorable outcome. The facts surrounding a prospective transaction have yet to be established and, therefore, are subject to the client's control. In such an open-fact transaction, the adviser can help the client create facts that will influence the tax consequences. Clearly, this tax planning service can be extremely valuable to clients who want to maximize the after-tax value of their transactions.

DEVELOPING TAX RESEARCH SKILLS

Tax research is an intellectual skill that is developed through both education and experience. Men and women who enter the tax profession have completed many hours of formal study as part of their undergraduate and graduate education. During their careers, they will devote many more hours to maintaining the currency of their technical tax knowledge. Tax professionals also learn by doing. As with any skill, proficiency comes with practice, and tax professionals become more proficient with every research project they undertake.

Students enrolled in an introductory tax class are struggling to learn the rudiments of the tax law. Their knowledge of the subject is limited, and they have no professional experience on which to draw. Nonetheless, even beginning tax students can benefit from an introduction to the tax research process. By studying this process, students gain insight into the nature of the work performed by tax professionals. They learn how CPAs and attorneys identify tax problems, solve those problems, and communicate the solutions to their clients. They gain an appreciation of the expertise necessary to perform these tasks. Finally, students start to develop their own analytic framework for determining the tax consequences of business, investment, and financial transactions.

Several textbooks are devoted entirely to tax research. Most graduate accounting and law programs offer a course on the subject. Obviously, this chapter provides only a brief discussion of the fundamentals of a complex subject. However, after reading this chapter, students should be ready to try their hand at solving the Research Problems provided at the end of the subsequent chapters. Students who do so will enjoy an intellectual challenge that will increase their understanding of the fascinating subject of taxation.

The Tax Research Process

LO 5-1
Explain and apply the six steps of the tax research process.

The tax research process can be broken down into six steps. This chapter provides a description of each research step, followed by an example of the application of the step to a research case. Students who are just starting to develop their research skills should focus on and complete each distinct step in sequence. By doing so, students will establish good research habits. As they become more proficient, students will gradually integrate the steps into a seamless research process. Those students who become accomplished researchers will automatically perform the six steps for every research project they undertake.

The six steps of the tax research process are presented in summary form in Exhibit 5.1.

EXHIBIT 5.1
The Tax Research Process

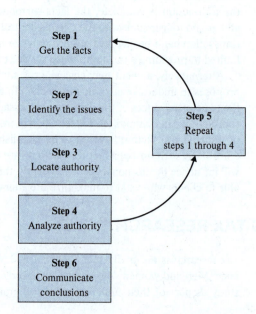

1. Understand the client's transaction and get the facts.
2. Identify the tax issues, problems, or opportunities suggested by the facts and formulate specific research questions.
3. Locate relevant tax law authority.
4. Analyze relevant authority and answer the research questions.
5. Repeat steps 1 through 4 as many times as necessary.
6. Document your research and communicate your conclusions.

STEP 1: GET THE FACTS

Before a researcher can analyze the tax consequences of a transaction, they must thoroughly understand the transaction itself. Specifically, the researcher should discuss the details of the transaction with their client to ascertain the client's motivation. What are the client's economic objectives in undertaking the transaction? What does the client foresee as the desired outcome? What risks has the client identified? By asking these types of questions, the researcher acquaints themselves with the nontax features of the transaction before considering any tax implications.

The researcher must discover all the facts concerning the client's transaction. Like a newspaper reporter, the researcher should question the client about the precise "who, when, where, why, and how" of the transaction. The researcher should not assume that the client's initial summary of the transaction is factually accurate and complete. Perhaps the client hasn't determined all the facts that the researcher needs. Or the client may have discounted the significance of certain facts and omitted them from the initial summary. The researcher should encourage the client to be objective in stating the facts. Oftentimes a client will unwittingly present the researcher with the client's subjective conclusions about the facts rather than with the facts themselves.

When a researcher is working with a client to uncover the relevant facts, the researcher must take into account the level of the client's tax knowledge. If the client has some knowledge of the tax law, the researcher can ask questions that presume such knowledge. On the other hand, if the client is unsophisticated in tax matters, the researcher should ask only questions that the client can answer without reference to the tax law.

Applying Step 1

Sara Colter, a professional photographer, is a new client who has engaged your accounting firm to determine the tax consequences of a proposed transaction: Sara's sale of a 12-acre tract of land to CCM, Inc. Sara provides the following facts in her initial summary of the transaction:

- Sara purchased the land from Mr. and Mrs. Bianca in 2012 for $400,000 cash.
- Sara and CCM, Inc. have reached a tentative agreement under which CCM will pay $325,000 in cash for the land and will pay all transaction expenses.

As a tax professional, you know that the tax consequences of a transaction may depend on whether the parties involved are "related parties" for federal tax purposes. You also know that the tax consequences of the sale of an asset depend on the classification of the asset as capital or noncapital. Because Sara is unsophisticated in tax matters, you cannot ask her directly if she and CCM, Inc. are related parties. Nor can you ask Sara if the land is a capital asset. Because of her lack of tax knowledge, such questions would be meaningless to your client. Accordingly, you decide to ask Sara the following series of questions:

- Do you have any personal relationship with Mr. and Mrs. Bianca? Did you know them in any capacity other than as the sellers of the land that you purchased in 2012?

(continued)

- What was your reason for purchasing the land? Have you made any improvements to the land since 2012? Have you purchased or sold any other real estate during the past 10 years?
- How did you and CCM, Inc. reach an agreement that the land is worth only $325,000? Why has the land declined in value since you purchased it?
- Do you own any stock in CCM, Inc.? Who are CCM, Inc.'s stockholders?

In response to your questions, Sara provides the following additional facts:

- She has no personal relationship with the Biancas and did not know them prior to her purchase of their land. The purchase was arranged through a professional real estate broker.
- She purchased the land because she thought that its value would increase over time and she could eventually sell it at a profit. She has not made any improvements to the land; it is in the same condition today as the day she purchased it. She has never purchased or sold any other real estate other than her personal residence.
- Two months ago, Sara obtained two independent appraisals of the value of the land. Both appraisals concluded that the current market value of the land is $325,000. CCM, Inc. performed its own appraisal that confirmed this value. The $75,000 decline in value is attributable to local zoning restrictions on the land that were put in place in 2014.
- Sara does not own CCM, Inc. stock. Twenty-four individual stockholders own the 1,000 outstanding CCM shares. Two of these stockholders are Sara's brother, Jack, and Jack's son, Robert. Sara is not acquainted with any of the other stockholders.

STEP 2: IDENTIFY THE ISSUES

After a researcher is satisfied that they understand their client's transaction and know all the relevant facts, they can proceed to the second step in the research process. In this step, the researcher identifies the tax issue or issues suggested by the transaction. The ability to recognize tax issues is the product of technical education and professional experience. Consequently, this step is usually the most challenging for students in an introductory tax course.

The identification of issues leads to the formulation of tax research questions. The tax researcher should be as precise as possible in formulating questions. A precise question is narrowly stated and provides clear parameters for the remaining steps in the research process. An imprecise question that is vague or overly broad in scope may provide insufficient parameters and result in wasted time and effort.

If the tax issues suggested by a transaction lead to multiple research questions, the researcher must determine the order in which the questions should be answered. In our complex tax system, the answer to a question often depends on the answer to one or more preliminary questions. Tax researchers who understand the hierarchy of their research questions can address each question in the right order and conduct their research with maximum efficiency.

Applying Step 2

After studying the facts, you conclude that Sara's proposed transaction involves one basic tax issue: Will Sara's sale of the land to CCM, Inc. result in a loss that she can deduct on her individual income tax return? This issue suggests four research questions, which you decide to address in the following order:

Will Sara realize a loss on the sale of her land to CCM, Inc.?

Can Sara recognize her realized loss?

What is the character of any recognized loss?

Given the character of the loss, to what extent can Sara deduct the loss in the computation of taxable income for the year of sale?

Students should note that the research problems provided at the end of the chapters do not require students to perform the first two steps in the tax research process. These problems are deliberately written to contain all the facts necessary to solve the problem. Moreover, the problems provide the specific research question or questions for students to answer. Such is the nature (and weakness) of textbook research problems! But in the real world of tax practice, the first two tasks are not performed by anyone but the researcher. If the researcher fails to get the key facts, identify the important issues, and ask the right questions, all their subsequent efforts are futile.

STEP 3: LOCATE AUTHORITY

As the third step in the research process, the researcher heads for a tax library. Their mission is to locate authority providing answers to the research questions. Traditional libraries consist of shelves filled with books, loose-leaf binders, magazines, and other published materials containing all the technical minutiae of the tax law. Today, traditional libraries are disappearing as professional tax advisers gain access to the electronic libraries available on the Internet. One obvious advantage of electronic libraries is the speed at which researchers can access sources of authority and move among the sources. A second advantage is the ease with which electronic databases can be updated to include current developments. A third advantage is that an electronic library is portable. A tax researcher with a laptop computer can access the library at any time and from any location.

Regardless of whether a tax researcher is working in a traditional or electronic library, they must be knowledgeable about the content and organization of the reference materials in that library. The researcher must know how to locate references pertaining to the problem at hand. The researcher must also be able to distinguish between the two main categories of reference materials: **primary authorities** and **secondary authorities**.

Primary Authorities

LO 5-2
Identify and interpret primary sources of tax law.

Chapter 1 introduced the three sources of authority that comprise the federal tax law: statutory authority, administrative authority, and judicial authority. Recall that statutory tax rules enacted by Congress are compiled in the **Internal Revenue Code of 1986**. Administrative authority is provided by the Treasury Department in the form of written **Treasury regulation** interpreting the Internal Revenue Code.

Tax Talk
IRS Interactive Tax Assistant (ITA) offers interactive question-and-answer sessions to determine the solution to a variety of common tax questions. Find a list of ITA topics at irs.gov/help/ita.

The Internal Revenue Service provides additional administrative guidance in a variety of forms. **Revenue ruling** and **revenue procedure** were introduced in Chapter 1. The IRS also issues two types of administrative guidance that are authoritative only for the specific taxpayer to whom they are issued and cannot be relied on as authority by any other taxpayer. A taxpayer may request a **private letter ruling (PLR)** from the IRS regarding the appropriate tax treatment of a proposed transaction or a completed transaction for which a tax return has not yet been filed. The request must detail all relevant facts surrounding the transaction and requires the payment of a user's fee that could be as high as several thousand dollars. The PLR controls the tax treatment of the transaction for that taxpayer if it is completed in the manner described in the ruling request. A revenue agent or appeals officer can request a **technical advice memorandum (TAM)** during the examination or appeal of a taxpayer's return. The TAM represents the IRS position on a disputed item in the return and applies only to the taxpayer for whom it was issued.

When conflicts between taxpayers and the IRS cannot be resolved administratively, federal courts often hear tax cases. Their decisions represent judicial authority that interprets the tax law and often expands it beyond the narrow language of the Code. For researchers, the decisions rendered by these courts are important sources of primary authority in addition to the Code and the administrative pronouncements of the IRS and Treasury.

In federal tax matters, one of three trial courts has original jurisdiction. A taxpayer may refuse to pay the deficiency determined by the IRS and file a petition with the **U.S. Tax Court** to hear the case. Alternatively, the taxpayer may pay the deficiency and then immediately sue the government for a refund in either the local **U.S. District Courts** or the **U.S. Court of Federal Claims** located in Washington, D.C. The losing party at the trial court level (taxpayer or government) may appeal the verdict to 1 of 13 **U.S. Circuit Courts of Appeals**. The geographic location of the trial court determines which appellate court has jurisdiction. These courts generally do not review findings of fact by a lower court, but they will consider it if the lower court properly applied the relevant law to the facts. After the appellate court has either affirmed or reversed the trial court's decision, the losing party may appeal the case to the **U.S. Supreme Court**. This Court may agree to hear the case (grant *certiorari*) or refuse to hear it (deny *certiorari*). When the Supreme Court denies *certiorari,* the decision of the appellate court is final. During an average term, the Supreme Court hears no more than a dozen federal tax cases, which are selected either because the Court believes that the case involves a significant principle of law or because two or more appellate courts have rendered conflicting opinions on the proper resolution of a tax issue.

> **Tax Talk**
> *The AICPA provides a quick reference chart to the hierarchy of U.S. federal tax law at the following link: https://future. aicpa.org/resources/ article/u-s-federal-tax- law-hierarchy. This chart ranks the weight of authorities from highest to lowest.*

Evaluating Related Judicial Decisions

The legal decision rendered by a trial court or circuit court of appeals may be invalidated if a subsequent appeal reverses that decision. For example, consider the case of *Frank Lyons Co.* v. *U.S.* Lyons entered into a transaction involving the sale and leaseback of real estate. The company deducted depreciation on the real estate as the owner and lessor of the building. The IRS disallowed the deduction, asserting that under the substance over form doctrine, depreciation should be taken by the lessee because it was the true owner of the building.

The trial court in this case, the District Court for Eastern Arkansas [36 AFTR 2d 75-5154 (DC AR, 6/11/1975)], ruled in favor of the taxpayer. The IRS appealed the decision, and the Eighth Circuit Court of Appeals [38 AFTR 2d 76-5060 (CA-8, 5/26/1976)] reversed the district court decision, ruling in favor of the government. Lyons appealed to the U.S. Supreme Court [41 AFTR 2d 78-1142 (US, 4/18/1978)], which reversed the Eighth Circuit Court's decision, finally ruling in favor of the taxpayer.

A tax researcher should rely on only the final decision in this sequence as valid legal authority. However, it might be necessary to read all three decisions to fully understand the facts and reasoning of the courts.

Exhibit 5.2 provides examples of citations to each type of statutory, administrative, and judicial authority discussed previously. Because court cases are published in several different sources, multiple citations are possible for a single case. The exhibit lists alternative citations to sample decisions and the reporters in which they are published.

Secondary Authorities

LO 5-3
Identify secondary sources of tax law and utilize them to locate primary authorities.

While primary authorities are required to adequately support tax conclusions and recommendations, they are written in detailed legal and technical language and are often difficult to understand and interpret. Secondary authorities, such as textbooks, treatises, professional journals, and commercial tax services, attempt to explain and interpret the tax law. Commercial tax services also organize information about primary authorities in a manner that facilitates tax research. These resources are an excellent starting point in the tax research process, but the researcher should always ensure that any conclusions drawn from secondary resources are adequately supported by the underlying primary authority. Our discussion of secondary authorities will focus on describing the content of the more popular electronic commercial tax services. In the next section, we'll explore how these services can be used to guide the tax research process.

EXHIBIT 5.2
Sample Citations to
Primary Authorities

Type of Authority	Citation(s)	Explanation
Internal Revenue Code	Section 1250(d)(1) Sec. 1250(d)(1) §1250(d)(1)	Three alternative citations to the first paragraph, subsection d of Section 1250.
Treasury Regulations	Reg. Sec. 1.267-5(b) Reg. 1.267-5(b) Reg. §1.267-5(b)	Three alternative citations to the fifth subpart of the regulations under Section 267.
Revenue Rulings	Rev. Rul. 89-257, 1989-1 C.B. 221	Citation to the 257th revenue ruling issued in 1989, appearing in the first volume of the 1989 Cumulative Bulletin, page 221.
Revenue Procedures	Rev. Proc. 2002-32, 2002-1 C.B. 959	Citation to the 32nd revenue procedure issued in 2002, appearing in the first volume of the 2002 Cumulative Bulletin, page 959.
U.S. Tax Court memorandum decisions	*Jack D. Carr,* T.C. Memo 1985-19 *Jack D. Carr,* PH TCM ¶85019 *Jack D. Carr,* 49 TCM 507	Three alternative citations to a Tax Court memorandum decision. The first is published by the U.S. government, the second by Thomson Reuters (formerly RIA), and the third by CCH.
U.S. Tax Court regular decisions	*Teleservice Co. of Wyoming Valley,* 27 T.C. 722 (1957)	Citation to a regular Tax Court decision, published by the U.S. government.
U.S. District Court decisions	*Montgomery Engineering Co.* v. *U.S.,* 64-2 USTC ¶9618 (D. Ct. N.J., 1964) *Montgomery Engineering Co.* v. *U.S.,* 13 AFTR2d 1747 (D. Ct. N.J., 1964) *Montgomery Engineering Co.* v. *U.S.,* 230 F. Supp. 838 (D. Ct. N.J., 1964)	Three alternative citations to a 1964 district court case for New Jersey. The first is published by CCH, the second by Thomson Reuters, and the third by West.
U.S. Courts of Appeals	*Lengsfield* v. *Comm.,* 57-1 USTC ¶9437 (CA-5, 1957) *Lengsfield* v. *Comm.,* 50 AFTR 1683 (CA-5, 1957) *Lengsfield* v. *Comm.,* 241 F.2d 508 (CA-5, 1957)	Three alternative citations to a 1957 case before the Fifth Circuit Court of Appeals. The first is published by CCH, the second by Thomson Reuters, and the third by West.
U.S. Supreme Court	*U.S.* v. *Donruss Co.,* 69-1 USTC ¶9167 (USSC, 1969) *U.S.* v. *Donruss Co.,* 23 AFTR2d 69-418 (USSC, 1969) *U.S.* v. *Donruss Co.,* 89 S. Ct. 501 (USSC, 1969)	Three alternative citations to a 1969 case before the Supreme Court. The first is published by CCH, the second by Thomson Reuters, and the third by West.

Tax Talk
The AICPA Tax Section provides a variety of publications and resources for tax practitioners. Much of this information is freely available to nonmembers. See the AICPA Tax home page at https://future .aicpa.org/topic/tax.

Traditionally, tax services are multivolume publications in loose-leaf form, containing a wealth of tax information. Most services are now also available electronically over the Internet. Although each service has its own organizational format and special features, there are commonalities in the type and scope of information presented. In paper format, tax services are organized either topically or by Code section. The popular Code-arranged tax services are *United States Tax Reporter* (published by Thomson Reuters) and *Standard Federal Tax Reporter* (published by CCH). The popular topically arranged tax services are *Federal Tax Coordinator 2d* (published by Thomson Reuters), *CCH Federal Tax Service* (published by CCH), *Law of Federal Income Taxation* (also called Mertens, published by West), and *Tax Management Portfolios* (published by BNA).

Electronic Research Databases

Electronic tax research databases provide the researcher access to a wide variety of both primary and secondary authorities. The Checkpoint online tax research platform (published by Thomson Reuters) and the CCH AnswerConnect software (formerly CCH IntelliConnect, published by Wolters Kluwer) are two popular tax research databases used by tax professionals in the United States.

While the format differs, the Checkpoint and CCH AnswerConnect services contain similar information. These services reproduce the text of each Code section and related Treasury regulations. Each service also provides some legislative history for each Code section. Accompanying each Code section and its regulations is an editorial explanation written by the publisher. The explanation attempts to clarify application of the Code section. While these editorial explanations are often helpful to researchers in locating primary authority, they do not themselves constitute primary authority and should not be cited. In addition to the editorial explanation, each service provides a citation listing and a brief summary of court cases, revenue rulings, and other primary authorities relevant to the Code section under discussion. These summaries are helpful to the researcher in locating a primary authority. Finally, each service attempts to highlight current developments and incorporates new information into the text of the service on an almost daily basis.

Electronic tax research databases offer significant advantages over paper-based research. Keyword searching (discussed in more detail shortly) is an efficient means of accessing electronic resources. Documents within the database are typically hyperlinked, allowing the researcher to easily access related results. Information in the database can be updated more frequently and new resources or new tax legislation released to users within hours of enactment. In addition, the volume of information available in an electronic database is significantly greater than what could reasonably be accessed in paper format.

The major electronic research databases continue to expand the scope and nature of content they offer, seeking to become the primary search engine for tax professionals. For example, the Checkpoint research platform provides the ability to search tax-related materials on other websites, including IRS.gov, the AICPA website, the Tax Executives Institute website, and the online tax publications of the Big 4 public accounting firms. Note that these resources, while useful, would all be considered secondary authorities.

The IRS website, **https://www.irs.gov/**, provides access to numerous tax-related resources, including tax forms and instructions. The IRS also produces a series of IRS publications on specific topical issues, which can be accessed electronically on the IRS website and through commercial tax services. Although IRS publications contain useful summaries of tax information, they are NOT considered a primary authority. They typically do not provide citations to the Code, regulations, or other primary authorities on which the statements in IRS publications are based. In fact, the IRS itself does not consider them authoritative. Thus, while IRS publications are often helpful when taxpayers seek basic information on a particular issue, tax professionals should not rely on or cite IRS publications in conducting professional tax research.

IRS Publication 535	Publication 535 is entitled Business Expenses. It discusses common business expenses and explains which expenses are deductible for federal income tax purposes and which are not. This publication is typically updated annually, providing current information useful to taxpayers in preparing business income tax returns. Although the publication is quite detailed (57 pages in length in 2021), the IRS has publicly cautioned that such publications are for guidance only and should not be relied on as the sole authority for tax conclusions.

Strategies for Locating Relevant Authority

The materials used for tax research will depend on both the nature of the research question and the experience level of the researcher. Skilled researchers tend to rely on those materials they can use most efficiently to find answers to their questions in minimal time. They may bypass many of the following suggested steps as they find a research approach that works best for them. The novice researcher will tend to examine more materials in a methodical manner to maximize her opportunities to find all relevant information. The following suggested strategies are just that—suggestions!

Let's suppose you have completed steps 1 and 2 of the research process, as described previously, and are now ready to identify a relevant authority. Research using paper references would typically begin by using the table of contents or a topical index. However, in today's digital environment, a keyword search using an online research database is the most likely approach to this step.

Keyword Searching

In an electronic service, the researcher has the option of searching the entire database or a specified portion of the database for user-defined keywords. This type of search allows the researcher to combine words and phrases to target the search. Although keyword searching can be very efficient, the researcher must take care to ensure that important information is not missed because the keywords were defined too narrowly or the search was restricted to too limited a number of resources.

For example, suppose you are researching an issue related to the deductibility of losses incurred by an individual taxpayer involved in horse breeding. You know from your study of taxation that such losses are potentially deductible if the activity is considered a trade or business rather than a hobby. We will use this situation to demonstrate potential search strategies in an electronic database.

One option would be a keyword search of the Internal Revenue Code to find the relevant Code section. For some research questions, this approach may be sufficient to answer the question. However, what if this approach does not uncover a clear solution? In some cases, more than one Code section may seem to apply. In other cases, the Code may be very general, and the researcher may wish to find another authority that seems to match the specific facts at hand and more clearly supports the research conclusions. It may also be challenging to find keywords that match the specific technical language in which the Code is written, resulting in an unsuccessful search. In our horse breeding example, a search of the Internal Revenue Code using the key words "hobby loss" would produce zero search results! A broader search is needed to address this and many research questions.

Keyword Search Options	Checkpoint (and other online research databases) now offers two types of keyword searching: Terms & Connectors and Intuitive Search. The Intuitive Search method uses regular language phrases to generate search results. For example, you could enter Can I deduct utility costs for my home office? *(continued)*

> The Terms & Connectors method lets you search for documents by specifying words and phrases that describe your search. Specialized search connectors allow you to customize the search for more specific results. For example, you could enter
>
> Utilities & "home office"

A broader keyword search could easily consider all primary authorities and all secondary authorities (editorial materials) found in the electronic database. For example, Checkpoint allows the researcher to choose the sources to be searched, with *All Primary Source Materials* and *All Editorial Materials* as broad options that will capture results in a large number of potentially relevant documents. When searching a large number of sources, specification of keywords is critical. The researcher seeks to capture relevant information while not locating so many documents that they are overwhelmed.

In our horse-breeding scenario, a Checkpoint keyword search on the phrase "hobby loss" locates 159 results in *Primary Source Materials* and 155 results in *Editorial Materials.* While this total is manageable, that is still a lot of documents to review. A more focused keyword search might allow the researcher to narrow down the search results further.

To return to our horse-breeding example, a Terms & Connectors keyword search could combine the phrase "hobby loss" and the word "horse" to narrow the identification of potential authorities. Using the keyword search function in Checkpoint, the search "hobby loss & horse" identifies 63 results in *Primary Source Materials* and 84 results in *Editorial Materials.* Given that our search did not find results in the Internal Revenue Code, Editorial Materials may be a good place to begin analyzing our results. Each of these documents can then be examined by the researcher to determine their usefulness in answering the research question.

For our example involving horse breeding, the *Federal Tax Coordinator Analysis* lists "¶M-5800 Activities Not Engaged in for Profit—Hobby Losses." This portion of the service would seem a useful starting point in the search for information relevant to the research question. Within this source document, the researcher would find a reference to Code Section 183, Activities not engaged in for profit, the relevant codes section defining limits on deductibility of hobby losses.

Once a promising starting point is located, the researcher can examine related material in the service. For example, if the search term is found within an editorial explanation, the researcher should read the related Code section, scan the regulations, and examine any references to court cases or other primary authorities to determine whether that material addresses the tax issue at hand. Cross-references within the material initially examined can also lead the researcher in promising directions for further exploration. When primary authorities have been identified that appear relevant, the researcher should read those sources carefully.

In our horse-breeding example, a review of the documents identified in the Checkpoint keyword search uncovers a reference to a U.S. Tax Court memorandum decision *Herbert C. Sanderson,* T.C. Memo 1964-284. In this case, a doctor and his wife were allowed a deduction for losses incurred in breeding, raising, showing, racing, and selling horses. This case should be examined further as possible authority to support a deduction for horse-breeding expenses.

Before relying on a judicial opinion to support research conclusions, one final step is needed to ensure that the opinion remains a valid interpretation of the law. In particular, has the decision been appealed and, if so, what was the result? The researcher might also want to determine whether other courts have supported the conclusion of the court in the opinion in question. These issues can be assessed using an important resource called the **Citator**. The Citator may be used to determine the status of tax judicial decisions, revenue rulings, and revenue procedures. Citators are published by Thomson Reuters, CCH, and Shepard's and are available through the major computerized tax services. For each case reported, the

Citator provides a list of subsequent rulings that have referenced the case and a brief indication of the nature of the subsequent reference. For example, a review of the Thomson Reuters Citator listing for *Herbert C. Sanderson,* T.C. Memo 1964-284, reveals that the case was not appealed (no appellate court decision is listed), the case has been cited favorably in four subsequent cases, and the case has been distinguished (the cited case is distinguished either in law or on the facts) in one subsequent case. The Citator listing provides complete citations to each of these subsequent cases, which the researcher may want to examine further.

If the first application of the process described fails to provide an answer to the tax research question, additional iterations will be necessary. The researcher might proceed by trying other search terms, defining the search either more broadly or more narrowly, and combining use of the topical index, table of contents, and various keywords to discover useful information. The researcher may also want to consult more than one service.

Applying Step 3

Return to the example involving Sara Colter's sale of land (in *Applying Step 1*). To begin your search for authority, you conduct a keyword search of the *Federal Tax Coordinator Analysis.* You locate "¶I-2500 Amount of Gain or Loss on Sale or Exchange," which refers you to Section 1001 of the Internal Revenue Code. When you examine this section, you determine that subsections (a) and (c) seem relevant.

Section 1001. Determination of amount of and recognition of gain or loss

a. Computation of gain or loss. The gain from the sale or other disposition of property shall be the excess of the amount realized therefrom over the adjusted basis provided in section 1011 for determining gain, and the loss shall be the excess of the adjusted basis provided in such section for determining loss over the amount realized.

b. OMITTED.

c. Recognition of gain or loss. Except as otherwise provided in this subtitle, the entire amount of the gain or loss, determined under this section, on the sale or exchange of property shall be recognized.

Source: Internal Revenue Service

Section 1001(c) reminds you that gain or loss realized on a sale or exchange is not always recognized. Further examination of search results in the *Federal Tax Coordinator Analysis* reveals "¶I-3500 Losses Resulting from Sales and Exchanges between Related Taxpayers." This subchapter points you to Section 267, which provides that a taxpayer cannot recognize a loss realized on a sale to a related party.

STEP 4: ANALYZE AUTHORITY

Tax Talk

Walter B. Wriston, former chairman and CEO of Citicorp, says, "All the Congress, all the accountants and tax lawyers, all the judges, and a convention of wizards all cannot tell for sure what the income tax law says."

Source: Walter B. Wriston

Regardless of whether a researcher is reading from a printed page or a computer screen, they must have the skill to interpret and evaluate the authority at hand. In some cases, the authority may provide an unambiguous answer to the researcher's question. In other cases, the answer may be equivocal because the authority is inconclusive or subject to interpretation. Or perhaps different sources of authority provide conflicting answers. In these cases, the researcher must bring their judgment to bear in analyzing the authority and answering the question.

As part of the analytic process, the researcher should decide if the authority requires them to make a factual judgment or an evaluative judgment. In making a factual judgment, the researcher compares the authority to a set of facts. Assuming that the facts are complete and accurate, the researcher can provide a definitive answer to the research question. For example, consider the following research problem:

Mr. Johnson provides 100 percent of the financial support for his 12-year-old granddaughter, Cassie, who has lived in Mr. Johnson's home since 2015. Does Cassie qualify as Mr. Johnson's dependent?

Section 152 provides the relevant statutory authority for this research question.

Section 152 Dependent defined

a. In general

For purposes of this subtitle, the term "dependent" means—
1. a qualifying child, or
2. a qualifying relative.

b. OMITTED

c. qualifying child. For purposes of this section—
1. In general

The term "qualifying child" means, with respect to any taxpayer for any taxable year, an individual—

A. who bears a relationship to the taxpayer described in paragraph (2),
B. who has the same principal place of abode as the taxpayer for more than one-half of such taxable year,
C. who meets the age requirements of paragraph (3), and
D. who has not provided over one-half of such individual's own support for the calendar year in which the taxable year of the taxpayer begins.

2. Relationship

For purposes of paragraph (1)(A), an individual bears a relationship to the taxpayer described in this paragraph if such individual is—

A. a child of the taxpayer or a descendant of such a child, or
B. a brother, sister, stepbrother, or stepsister of the taxpayer or a descendant of any such relative.

3. Age requirements

A. In general. For purposes of paragraph (1)(C), an individual meets the requirements of this paragraph if such individual—

    i. has not attained the age of 19 as of the close of the calendar year in which the taxable year of the taxpayer begins, or
    ii. is a student who has not attained the age of 24 as of the close of such calendar year.

Source: Internal Revenue Service

By comparing the facts of this research problem to the relevant authority, a researcher can conclude that Cassie qualifies as Mr. Johnson's dependent. Therefore, the answer to the research questions is an unqualified yes.

Researchers are required to make evaluative judgments when the relevant authority relates to a conclusion inferred from a set of facts, rather than to the facts themselves. By definition, conclusions are subjective; different observers may draw different conclusions from the same facts. A researcher who must draw a conclusion to complete a research project can never be sure that such conclusion will go unchallenged by the IRS. Therefore, the researcher should never give an unqualified answer to a research question requiring an evaluative judgment. This point is illustrated by the following research problem:

Mrs. Clancy operates a business as a sole proprietorship. Last week, she traveled to New York for an important meeting with a major client. Mrs. Clancy paid $2,615 for a first-class airline ticket and paid $340 per night for her hotel room. Can Mrs. Clancy deduct these business expenses on her Schedule C, Form 1040?

Section 162 provides the relevant statutory authority for this research question.

Sec. 162. Trade or business expenses

a. In general

There shall be allowed as a deduction all the ordinary and necessary expenses paid or incurred during the taxable year in carrying on any trade or business, including—

1. a reasonable allowance for salaries or other compensation for personal services actually rendered;

2. traveling expenses (including amounts expended for meals and lodging other than amounts which are lavish or extravagant under the circumstances) while away from home in the pursuit of a trade or business.

Source: Internal Revenue Service

This authority requires the researcher to evaluate the circumstances surrounding Mrs. Clancy's travel expenses. If the expenses were not lavish and extravagant, the entire amount is deductible. However, if some amount was lavish or extravagant, such amount is nondeductible. Note that the term "lavish or extravagant" is a matter of opinion, and reasonable persons might disagree as to whether the term describes Mrs. Clancy's expenses. If the researcher believes that the facts and circumstances support a conclusion that the travel expenses were not lavish or extravagant, the researcher could advise Mrs. Clancy to deduct the expenses. But the researcher should qualify this advice by explaining the risk that an IRS agent might draw the opposite conclusion and disallow the deduction.

Applying Step 4

Return to the example involving Sara Colter's sale of land. On the basis of your reading of Section 1001(a), you determine that Sara will realize a $75,000 loss if she sells her land to CCM, Inc. for $325,000 cash. According to the general rule of Section 1001(c), realized losses are recognized "except as otherwise provided in this subtitle." Therefore, Sara can recognize the loss and report it on her tax return for the year of sale unless Section 267 disallows the loss. The portions of Section 267 that seem applicable to Sara's case read as follows:

Sec. 267. Losses, expenses, and interest with respect to transactions between related taxpayers

a. In general
  1. Deduction for losses disallowed
     No deduction shall be allowed in respect of any loss from the sale or exchange of property, directly or indirectly, between persons specified in any of the paragraphs of subsection (b).

b. Relationships
   The persons referred to in subsection (a) are:

  2. An individual and a corporation more than 50 percent in value of the outstanding stock of which is owned, directly or indirectly, by or for such individual;

c. Constructive ownership of stock
     For purposes of determining, in applying subsection (b), the ownership of stock—
  3. An individual shall be considered as owning the stock owned, directly or indirectly, by or for his family;
  4. The family of an individual shall include only his brothers and sisters (whether by the whole or half blood), spouse, ancestors, and lineal descendants; and
  5. . . . stock constructively owned by an individual by reason of the application of paragraph (2) or (3) shall not be treated as owned by him for the purpose of again applying either of such paragraphs in order to make another the constructive owner of such stock.

Source: Internal Revenue Service

According to Section 267(a)(1), Sara cannot recognize her realized loss if she and CCM, Inc. are related parties. According to Section 267(b)(2), Sara and CCM, Inc. are related parties if Sara directly or indirectly owns more than 50 percent in value of CCM's outstanding stock. You know that Sara does not own CCM stock directly, but you are uncertain as to whether she owns *any* stock indirectly. Section 267(c)(2) provides that Sara is considered to own any CCM stock owned by her "family." When you refer to the facts you established during your first meeting with Sara, you discover that you do not know how many shares of CCM stock are owned by Sara's brother, Jack, and nephew, Robert.

STEP 5: REPEAT STEPS 1 THROUGH 4

At some point in the research process, even an expert may discover that they failed to ascertain all the facts necessary to complete the analysis of the client's transaction. In such a case, the researcher must repeat step 1 by obtaining additional information from the client. Oftentimes the additional information suggests further tax issues and research questions that the researcher must address. A researcher may have to repeat steps 1 through 4 several times before they are satisfied with the analysis.

Applying Step 5

You contact Sara to ask one more question: How many shares of CCM stock do Jack and Robert each own? She replies that Jack owns 350 shares and Robert owns 200 shares of the 1,000 outstanding shares of CCM stock. With this additional fact, you can complete your analysis of Section 267 as it applies to Sara's proposed sale.

According to Section 267(c)(2), Sara's family includes her brother, Jack, but does not include her nephew, Robert. Therefore, Sara indirectly owns the 350 CCM shares directly owned by Jack. However, Jack also indirectly owns the 200 CCM shares owned by his son, Robert. Section 267(c)(5) states that Jack's indirect ownership of these shares is disregarded for the purpose of determining Sara's ownership. On the basis of these statutory rules, you conclude that Sara directly and indirectly owns only 350 (35 percent) of CCM's 1,000 outstanding shares of stock. Thus, she and CCM, Inc. are not related parties; Section 267(a) will not apply to her sale of the land to the corporation; and Sara can recognize her $75,000 realized loss.

You continue to analyze sources of information and sources of authority that pertain to your last two research questions. Sara's recognized loss is considered a capital loss if the land is considered a capital asset under Section 1221. The land is not a capital asset if it is considered property held for sale to customers under Section 1221(a)(1). This determination has been the topic of numerous judicial decisions. One recent case, *James E. Zurcher Jr.* v. *Commissioner,* T.C. Memo 1997-203, states in part:

> Whether the Property is a capital asset or was instead held primarily for sale in the ordinary course of petitioner's business is a factual determination. . . . Courts have developed the following nonexclusive factors to assist in this determination: (1) The nature of the taxpayer's business; (2) the taxpayer's purpose in acquiring and holding the property; (3) subdivision, platting, and other improvements tending to make the property more marketable; (4) the frequency, number, and continuity of sales; (5) the extent to which the taxpayer engaged in the sales activity; (6) the length of time the property was held; (7) the substantiality of income derived from the sales, and what percentage the income was of the taxpayer's total income; (8) the extent of advertising and other promotional activities; and (9) whether the property was listed directly or through brokers.

Sara's stated purpose in acquiring the land was to hold it as a long-term investment. She has made no improvements to the property, engaged in no other real estate sales (other than of her personal residence), does not derive a substantial portion of her income from such sales, and does not advertise or promote real estate activities. On the basis of these facts, you conclude that Sara did not hold the land for sale in the ordinary course of business and, thus, the land is a capital asset and her loss is a long-term capital loss. She can deduct this loss in the year of sale to the extent of any capital gains recognized during the year. If the capital loss exceeds her capital gains, Sara is allowed to deduct $3,000 of the excess in the computation of adjusted gross income. Any nondeductible loss becomes a long-term capital loss carryforward into subsequent taxable years.

STEP 6: COMMUNICATE YOUR CONCLUSIONS

The tax researcher's task is to find an accurate, useful, and complete answer to the research question(s) concerning the client's situation. This task is not finished until the researcher documents their work by preparing a written summary of the research process. Such summary usually takes the form of a research memo that includes (1) a statement of the pertinent facts, (2) a statement of the research issue or issues, (3) an analysis of the relevant sources of authority, (4) an explanation of the researcher's conclusions, and (5) the details of any advice given to the client as part of the research engagement. Although the content of a tax research memo is fairly standard, the order in which such content is presented can vary. For example, some researchers prefer to present their research conclusions immediately following statement of the issues and before the detailed analysis of legal authorities. This memo becomes a permanent record of the research process—a record to which the researcher (or any other professional) can refer at a future date.

The analysis section of the research memo should explain in simple, direct language, but with sufficient detail, the analysis that led to the conclusions. As you write this section, remember the audience and the purpose of the memo. A list of jargon-filled citations does nothing to communicate your thought process.

A logical argument begins with references to higher authorities and progresses as necessary through references to lesser authorities. Begin your argument by analyzing how the relevant Code section or sections apply in the given fact situation. If necessary to support your conclusion, expand your argument to include an analysis of applicable Treasury regulations and case law. Compare and contrast your fact situation with the facts of any case you reference. Finally, as necessary analyze other administrative authorities such as revenue rulings or revenue procedures that support your conclusions.

The researcher also must communicate their conclusions to the client. Typically, the researcher writes a client letter containing information similar to that in the research memo. However, the client letter may contain less detail and instead summarize the information contained in the research memo. In writing the client letter, the researcher should tailor both the contents and the writing style to accommodate the client. For example, a letter to a client who has extensive tax knowledge may contain technical references that would be inappropriate in a letter to a client with minimal tax knowledge. Similarly, a letter to an individual who has been both a client and a friend for many years may be written in an informal style that would be inappropriate for a letter to the chief financial officer of a new corporate client.

Applying Step 6	You write the following research memo for your permanent record:

March 5, 2023

TAX FILE MEMORANDUM

From: Bridget McGuffin
Subject: Sara Colter
Engagement Research Conclusions

Summary of Facts

Sara Colter is considering a sale of 12 acres of undeveloped land to CCM, Inc. at a proposed price of $325,000. The land was purchased in 2012 for $400,000 as a long-term investment from unrelated sellers, Mr. and Mrs. Bianca. Ms. Colter has made no improvements to the land since the date of purchase and has neither purchased nor sold any other real estate with the exception of her personal residence. CCM, Inc. is a closely held corporation with 1,000 shares of stock outstanding. Ms. Colter is not a shareholder of CCM; however, her brother, Jack Colter, and his son, Robert Colter, own 350 and 200 shares, respectively. Ms. Colter is not acquainted with any other CCM shareholders.

Research Issue

Is Ms. Colter entitled to recognize any realized loss on sale of the land?

(continued)

Law and Analysis

Under Section 1001 of the Internal Revenue Code of 1986, Ms. Colter will realize a $75,000 loss on the proposed sale of the land equal to the excess of her adjusted basis in the land ($400,000 purchase price) over the amount realized on the sale ($325,000 proposed sales price). However, Section 267(a)(1) provides that no deduction is allowed for a loss from the sale or exchange of property between related parties, as defined in Section 267(b). For this purpose, related parties include an individual and a corporation more than 50 percent in value of the outstanding stock of which is owned, directly or indirectly, by or for such individual. Although Ms. Colter does not directly own any stock in CCM, Inc., we must consider whether ownership of CCM stock by her brother and nephew constitutes indirect ownership of more than 50 percent of the value of CCM stock.

Section 267(c)(2) provides that, in determining indirect ownership for purposes of Section 267(b), an individual is considered as owning the stock owned, directly or indirectly, by or for his family. Under Section 267(c)(4), family includes an individual's brothers, sisters, spouse, ancestors, and lineal descendants. Thus, Sara Colter is considered to own indirectly the stock owned by her brother, Jack Colter, but not the stock owned by her nephew, Robert Colter. Note that Jack Colter would be considered to indirectly own the stock owned by his son, Robert Colter. However, under Section 267(c)(5), Jack's indirect ownership of these shares is disregarded in determining Sara's ownership. Thus, Sara Colter indirectly owns 350 shares of CCM, Inc., equaling 35 percent of its 1,000 outstanding shares of stock. Because Ms. Colter's ownership of CCM is less than 50 percent, the related party loss disallowance rule of Section 267(a) does not apply.

Ms. Colter's recognized loss is considered a capital loss if the land is considered a capital asset under Section 1221. The land is not a capital asset if it is considered property held for sale to customers [Section 1221(a)(1)]. This determination has been the topic of numerous judicial decisions. One recent case, *James E. Zurcher Jr.* v. *Commissioner,* T.C. Memo 1997-203, states in part:

> Whether the Property is a capital asset or was instead held primarily for sale in the ordinary course of petitioners business is a factual determination. . . . Courts have developed the following nonexclusive factors to assist in this determination: (1) The nature of the taxpayer's business; (2) the taxpayer's purpose in acquiring and holding the property; (3) subdivision, platting, and other improvements tending to make the property more marketable; (4) the frequency, number, and continuity of sales; (5) the extent to which the taxpayer engaged in the sales activity; (6) the length of time the property was held; (7) the substantiality of income derived from the sales, and what percentage the income was of the taxpayer's total income; (8) the extent of advertising and other promotional activities; and (9) whether the property was listed directly or through brokers.

Source: *James E. Zurcher Jr.* v. *Commissioner,* T.C. Memo 1997-203

Ms. Colter's stated purpose in acquiring the land was to hold it as a long-term investment. She has made no improvements to the property, engaged in no other real estate sales (other than of her personal residence), does not derive a substantial portion of her income from such sales, and does not advertise or promote real estate activities. These facts support the conclusion that Ms. Colter did not hold the land for sale in the ordinary course of business and, thus, the land is a capital asset.

Conclusions

Ms. Colter will recognize a $75,000 capital loss. Because she held the land for more than one year, the loss will be a long-term capital loss. If the loss exceeds any recognized capital gains, under Section 1211(b) she may deduct $3,000 of the excess in computing adjusted gross income. Any nondeductible loss may be carried forward into subsequent taxable years.

You also write the following letter to Sara Colter:

March 5, 2023
Ms. Sara Colter
1812 Riverbend Place
Kirkwood, MO 63112

Dear Ms. Colter:

This letter is in response to your inquiry concerning the tax consequences of a proposed sale of 12 acres of undeveloped land to CCM, Inc. Before stating my conclusions, I'd like to summarize the facts of your case. You purchased the land in 2012 as a long-term investment. The purchase price was $400,000, and the sellers of the property, Mr. and Mrs. Bianca, are unrelated to you. You have not improved the land in any way since the date of purchase and have neither purchased nor sold any other real estate with the exception of your personal residence. CCM, Inc. is a closely held corporation with 1,000 shares of outstanding stock. Although you do not own any shares, your brother, Jack Colter, and his son, Robert Colter, own 350 and 200 shares, respectively. You are not acquainted with any other CCM stockholders. The accuracy of my conclusions depends entirely on my understanding of these facts. Consequently, if the statement of facts is in any way incorrect or incomplete, please notify me immediately.

If you sell your land to CCM, Inc. for the proposed contract price of $325,000, you will realize a $75,000 loss. This loss equals the excess of your $400,000 investment in the land over the $325,000 in cash you will receive at closing. You are allowed to report this loss on your individual tax return in the year of sale unless you and CCM, Inc. are "related parties" within the meaning of the tax law. According to my research, you and CCM, Inc. do not meet the statutory definition of "related parties," even though your brother and nephew own an aggregate 55 percent interest in CCM, Inc. Therefore, you can report your $75,000 loss for tax purposes. Because you held the land for investment and owned it for more than one year, the loss is classified as a long-term capital loss. You can deduct a long-term capital loss to the extent of your capital gains for the year. If your capital loss exceeds your capital gains, you can deduct only $3,000 of the excess loss against other sources of income.

Thank you for giving my firm the opportunity to advise you in this matter. If you have any questions about my conclusions, please don't hesitate to call me. If you proceed with your plans to sell the land, I would be glad to meet with you to develop a strategy to maximize your deduction for the projected $75,000 capital loss.

Sincerely,

Bridget McGuffin

Conclusion

Given the length and complexity of existing tax law, tax research is a critical skill for the tax practitioner. Tax research often occurs as part of tax compliance and is also important to the tax planning process by allowing the researcher to identify and explore the tax consequences of alternative investment and business choices. The six steps reviewed in this chapter provide a guide to the novice tax researcher in formulating research questions, identifying and analyzing relevant authority, and communicating research results. As the tax researcher gains experience and familiarity with the variety of legal resources available, the tax research process will become a natural part of strategic tax planning.

Now that you've completed Part Two of *Principles of Taxation for Business and Investment Planning,* you should appreciate how tax planning strategies can reduce costs and increase the NPV of business transactions. In addition, you have learned the basics of tax research necessary to analyze the tax consequences of tax planning alternatives. The framework for a thorough understanding of the tax planning process is in place. Parts Three and Four of the text build on this framework by presenting the basics of the income tax law: how firms compute annual taxable income and the federal tax on that income. As you integrate this legal knowledge into your understanding of taxes as financial costs, your appreciation of the tax planning process will progress from the abstract to the specific.

Key Terms

Citator *5-10*	revenue ruling *5-5*	U.S. Circuit Courts of Appeals *5-6*
Internal Revenue Code of 1986 *5-5*	secondary authorities *5-5*	U.S. Court of Federal Claims *5-6*
primary authorities *5-5*	technical advice memorandum (TAM) *5-5*	U.S. District Courts *5-6*
private letter ruling (PLR) *5-5*		U.S. Supreme Court *5-6*
revenue procedure *5-5*	Treasury regulation *5-5*	U.S. Tax Court *5-6*

Questions and Problems for Discussion

LO 5-1   1. Why is tax research necessary? In other words, why is it not possible for experienced tax professionals to answer all tax questions without performing tax research?

LO 5-1   2. Why is it important for a tax researcher to understand the client's motivation in undertaking a transaction? How will this knowledge assist the tax professional in serving their client?

LO 5-1   3. Explain the difference between a tax issue and a research question.

LO 5-1, 5-2, 5-3   4. Explain the difference between primary and secondary authorities as sources of tax information. On which type of authority should professional tax research conclusions be based?

LO 5-3   5. Discuss why and how a researcher might use secondary authorities in performing tax research.

LO 5-2   6. If a trial court decision has been appealed and the appellate court reversed the trial court's decision, which of the two court decisions is considered authoritative? Briefly explain your answer.

LO 5-3   7. Explain why a researcher should consult the Citator before relying on a judicial opinion to support research conclusions.

LO 5-1, 5-2   8. Describe two advantages of using an online database to conduct tax research.

LO 5-1   9. Explain why, in the course of tax research, it may be necessary for the researcher to gather more facts.

LO 5-1   10. Discuss potential differences in content and style between a research memo and a client letter communicating research results.

Mc Graw Hill **connect**   All applicable Application Problems are available with *Connect*.

Application Problems

LO 5-1   1. Following are the six steps of the tax research process, in random order. Please rearrange these steps into the correct order.

    a. Locate authority.

    b. Identify the issues.

    c. Get the facts.

    d. Communicate conclusions.

    e. Repeat steps 1 through 4.

    f. Analyze authority.

LO 5-1 2. Which of the following statements regarding the tax research process is FALSE?

    a. A tax researcher should be as precise as possible in formulating tax research questions.

    b. Judicial decisions resulting from conflicts between taxpayers and the IRS represent an important source of secondary authority.

    c. The Citator may be used to determine the status of tax judicial decisions, revenue rulings, and revenue procedures.

    d. Researchers are required to make evaluative judgments when the relevant authority relates to a conclusion inferred from a set of facts, rather than to the facts themselves.

LO 5-1 3. For each of the following actions, indicate in which of the six steps (1 through 6) of the tax research process the action would occur.

    a. Write an email to the client, requesting additional information and clarification of information previously received.

    b. Use the Citator to determine the status of a judicial decision.

    c. Compare the facts of two similar court decisions that reach different conclusions.

    d. Write a memorandum documenting research conclusions.

    e. Interview the client to obtain details of the transaction to be analyzed.

LO 5-1 4. For each of the following actions, indicate in which of the six steps (1 through 6) of the tax research process the action would occur.

    a. Discuss the details of the transaction with the client to ascertain the client's motivation.

    b. Obtain additional information from the client to clarify details of the facts.

    c. Write a letter to the client detailing the research conclusions.

    d. Evaluate a judicial decision to reach a conclusion.

    e. Conduct a keyword search in an electronic tax research database.

    f. Determine the order in which multiple related research questions should be answered.

LO 5-1 5. Indicate whether each of the following statements regarding the tax research process is TRUE or FALSE.

    a. In performing step 2 of the tax research process, research questions should be stated as broadly as possible.

    b. Step 5 of the tax research process is typically performed only by novice tax researchers.

    c. If a taxpayer fact situation suggests multiple research questions, the research must consider the order in which the questions should be answered.

    d. Tax research is most often associated with tax planning activities and is rarely conducted as part of the tax compliance process.

LO 5-2, 5-3 6. Indicate whether each of the following items is considered a primary authority or a secondary authority.

    a. *Fin Hay Realty Co.* v. *U.S.,* 22 AFTR2d 5004 (CA-3, 1968).

    b. §702(a).

    c. Rev. Proc. 77-37, 1977-2 C.B. 568.

    d. J. Erickson, B. O'Connor, and B. Rimmke, 2014. "Proposed Regulations under Section 704(c), 734(b), 743(b) and 755: A Basis Shell Game," *Journal of Taxation* 121, no. 2 (2014).

    e. *Nick R. Hughes,* T.C. Memo, 2009-94.

    f. *Federal Tax Coordinator 2d,* Chapter M, Deductions.

LO 5-2, 5-3   7. Indicate whether each of the following items is considered a primary authority or a secondary authority.

     a. Reg. §1.305-1(b).

     b. Rev. Rul. 67-225, 1967-2 C.B. 238.

     c. S.M. Jones, S.C. Rhoades-Catanach, and S. Callaghan, *Principles of Taxation for Business and Investment Planning* (New York: McGraw-Hill Education, 2017).

     d. PLR 201240007.

     e. Helvering v. *Alabama Asphaltic Limestone Co.,* 315 U.S. 179 (1942).

     f. United States Tax Reporter Code Arranged Explanations ¶614 Gross income defined.

LO 5-2, 5-3   8. Indicate whether each of the following items is considered a primary authority or a secondary authority.

     a. Private letter ruling from the IRS.

     b. CCH *Federal Tax Service.*

     c. BNA *Tax Management Portfolios.*

     d. Treasury regulations.

     e. IRS revenue procedure.

     f. U.S. Tax Court memorandum decision.

     g. U.S. Tax Court regular decision.

     h. U.S. Supreme Court decision.

     i. Internal Revenue Code section.

     j. Article published in *Journal of Corporate Taxation.*

LO 5-2   9. Use the legend provided to identify the type of primary authority indicated by each of the following citations.

Legend	
C = Internal Revenue Code Section	RR = IRS Revenue Ruling
R = Treasury Regulation	RP = IRS Revenue Procedure
N = Other	

     a. §351.

     b. Rev. Rul. 86-55, 1986-1 C.B. 373.

     c. Rev. Proc. 2001-10, 2001-1 C.B. 272.

     d. Reg. §301.7701-2.

     e. §1250.

     f. PLR 201432030.

     g. 11 T.C. 836 (1948).

LO 5-2   10. Use the legend provided to identify the court issuing the decision in each of the following judicial citations.

Legend	
T = U.S. Tax Court	A = U.S. Court of Appeals
D = U.S. District Court	S = U.S. Supreme Court

     a. James E. Zurcher Jr. v. *Commissioner,* T.C. Memo 1997-203.

     b. Walter v. *United States,* 148 F.3d 1027 (CA-8, 1996).

   c. *Thor Power Tool Co.* v. *Comm.,* 99 S. Ct. 773 (USSC, 1979).

   d. *Turner* v. *U.S.,* 2004-1 USTC ¶60,478 (D. Ct. Tex., 2004).

   e. *Frazier,* 11 T.C. No. 11 (1998).

LO 5-2 11. Which of the following statements regarding the U.S. Supreme Court is FALSE?

   a. The Supreme Court may agree to hear an appeal (grant *certiorari*) or refuse to hear it (deny *certiorari*).

   b. The Supreme Court generally agrees to hear tax cases only when the case involves a significant principle of law or because two or more appellate courts have rendered conflicting opinions on the proper resolution of a tax issue.

   c. During an average term, the Supreme Court generally hears no more than a dozen federal tax cases.

   d. Decisions of the U.S. Tax Court may be appealed directly to the Supreme Court, without being heard by one of the U.S. Courts of Appeals.

LO 5-3 12. Which of the following statements regarding secondary authorities is FALSE?

   a. Secondary authorities are an excellent starting point in the tax research process.

   b. Secondary authorities attempt to explain and interpret primary authorities.

   c. Secondary authorities are helpful to the tax researcher in locating relevant primary authorities.

   d. Secondary authorities often provide sufficient support for tax research conclusions.

LO 5-2, 5-3 13. Indicate whether each of the following items of IRS administrative guidance should be cited and relied on in researching a tax issue for a taxpayer to whom the item was not directly issued.

   a. Revenue ruling.

   b. IRS publication.

   c. Technical advice memorandum.

   d. Private letter ruling.

   e. Revenue procedure.

Issue Recognition Problems

Identify the tax issue or issues suggested by the following situations and state each issue in the form of a question.

LO 5-2 1. In researching the taxability of noncash compensation, a tax researcher identifies a judicial decision that seems to address the issue at hand. However, the decision was rendered in 1979, and the researcher knows that the tax law has changed many times in the past 44 years.

LO 5-2 2. Guenther is researching a tax issue involving the deductibility of costs to remodel an office building. He has found several authorities permitting such costs to be deducted, and several others requiring that remodeling costs be capitalized and depreciated for tax purposes.

LO 5-2, 5-3 3. Kenji is researching the tax rules related to Individual Retirement Accounts. He is very confused by the information he has found in the IRC and Treasury regulations regarding deductibility of IRA contributions. However, he has found an IRS publication on the IRS website that provides a much clearer explanation of the rules.

LO 5-1 4. Allison works full time as a dental hygienist. She devotes her spare time to designing and creating stained glass pieces. During the past year, she has sold 10 of her pieces at local craft fairs and was recently commissioned to create three stained glass windows for the home of a new customer. She has incurred a number of expenses for taking stained glass classes, purchasing materials and tools, and participating in craft fairs.

LO 5-1   5. John is a dentist. His neighbor, Wade, is a carpenter. John has agreed to perform dental work for Wade and his wife in exchange for Wade's installing a new laminate floor in John's dental office.

LO 5-1   6. Nadira works as a financial analyst at a brokerage firm. At night, she is taking courses to complete her MBA degree. Her firm pays 50 percent of her tuition cost for these courses, and Nadira pays the remainder personally.

LO 5-1   7. Argonaut Corporation sustained considerable damage to one of its warehouses during a recent hurricane. It expects to pay $200,000 to replace the roof of the building and repair other damage. It is unclear at this point whether any of the loss will be compensated by insurance.

LO 5-1   8. Natalie appeared on a game show last year and won a car valued at $30,000. After driving it for six months, she sold it for $24,000.

Research Problems

LO 5-2   1. As discussed in Chapter 3, the IRS carefully scrutinizes transactions between related parties. Several different Code sections define which taxpayers are considered related parties. Suppose that Marsha and Jan are sisters. Are they considered family members and, therefore, related parties under Section 318(a)(1)? How about under Section 267(b)(1)?

LO 5-1   2. One of your clients is planning to sell a piece of raw land and expects to incur a substantial gain on the sale. He has asked you to determine whether this gain will be considered capital gain or ordinary income. List five specific questions you should ask your client to gather more information prior to beginning your research.

LO 5-1   3. One of your clients is planning to start a business. She has incurred costs to investigate potential locations for the business and hired a consultant to conduct a feasibility study. She wishes to know whether such costs will be currently deductible. List five specific questions you should ask your client to gather more information prior to beginning your research.

LO 5-2   4. Find and provide a citation for the IRC section that defines taxable income. Be precise in your reference [e.g., Section 61(a)(1), not Section 61].

LO 5-2   5. Find and provide a citation for the IRC section that provides an exclusion from gross income for interest earned on investments in state and local bonds. Be precise in your reference [e.g., Section 61(a)(1), not Section 61].

LO 5-2   6. Find and provide a citation for the IRC section that defines a capital asset. Be precise in your reference [e.g., Section 61(a)(1), not Section 61].

LO 5-2   7. Find Rev. Rul. 72-542, 1972-2 C.B. 37, and answer the following questions. The purpose of these questions is to enhance your skills in reading and interpreting authorities that you locate while doing tax research.

   a. What are the basic tax issues addressed in the revenue ruling?

   b. Which of the basic tax legal doctrines discussed in Chapter 4 is applied in this ruling?

   c. From the ruling, identify the IRC section defining gross income.

   d. From the ruling, identify the IRC section permitting a charitable contribution deduction.

   e. Has this ruling been cited in other rulings or cases? If so, how many times?

LO 5-2   8. Find a 2006 10th Circuit Court of Appeals decision involving *Roger L. Watkins* and answer the following questions. The purpose of these questions is to enhance your skills in reading and interpreting authorities that you locate while doing tax research.

    a. What is the complete citation to the case?

    b. What is the citation to the original trial court decision to which this appeal relates?

    c. In your own words, explain the basic tax issues addressed in the case.

    d. Which of the four basic tax planning variables described in Chapter 4 is at issue in this case?

    e. Has this case been cited in other cases? If so, how many times?

LO 5-1   9. Asma owns an antique car that she inherited from her father. She is planning to sell it online and is wondering about the tax consequences of such a sale. If you were to research this question using a keyword search in an electronic library, what keywords would you use? Propose three distinct keyword searches that could get you started researching this issue.

LO 5-1, 5-2, 5-3   10. Refer to the facts in problem 9. Using an electronic research database such as Checkpoint or CCH AnswerConnect, run the keyword searches you proposed in problem 9. Include both primary sources and editorial materials in your search. How many documents did each search locate? Explain which of your searches you feel would be most useful in researching this issue.

LO 5-2, 5-3   11. Using an electronic research database such as Checkpoint or CCH AnswerConnect, do a keyword search that includes both the phrase *capital gain* and the keyword *livestock*. Include both primary sources and editorial materials in your search.

    a. How many documents did your search find that meet these search criteria?

    b. Of the documents found, how many represent primary authorities and how many are secondary authorities?

    c. Of the documents found, provide citations to two primary authorities and two secondary authorities.

LO 5-2   12. IRC Section 117 provides that qualified educational scholarships are not taxable in certain circumstances. Included in this exclusion are both scholarships and fellowship grants.

    a. Use Section 117 and the related regulations to find definitions of the terms *scholarship* and *fellowship grant* and provide precise citations to the code and/or regulation sections containing these definitions.

    b. In your own words, explain the distinction between a scholarship and a fellowship grant.

LO 5-2   13. Find the IRS Revenue Procedure that gives the standard deduction amounts for the 2022 tax year. Prepare a table reporting the standard deduction amounts and their associated filing statuses. Also report the full citation for your source, in the form of the following example: Rev. Proc. 98-1, 1998-1 C.B. 7.

LO 5-2, 5-3   14. Using an electronic research database such as Checkpoint or CCH AnswerConnect, do a keyword search on the phrase *hobby loss* to find secondary authorities discussing the tax treatment of losses incurred in pursuing activities as a hobby.

    a. Provide citations to three of the secondary authorities you located.

    b. Provide citations to three primary authorities referenced in the secondary authorities found in your search, including the IRC section that addresses the tax treatment of hobby losses.

    c. Does the IRC section identified in *part (b)* contain the phrase *hobby loss*? What phrase does the IRC section use to refer to activities considered a hobby?

LO 5-2   15. In researching a tax issue, you locate the case *Stern, Sidney B. & Vera L.,* 77 T.C. 614, which seems relevant to your issue. However, before completing your research, check the Citator for subsequent information about the case. What do you find in the Citator for this case that indicates you should not rely on it as judicial authority?

LO 5-2, 5-3   16. Find a tax glossary on any freely accessible website and provide the URL. Also find and provide a citation for the IRC section that defines a long-term capital gain.

    a. What is the tax glossary's definition of a long-term capital gain?

    b. How does the IRC define a long-term capital gain?

    c. Of the two definitions, which would a taxpayer without extensive tax knowledge find easier to understand? Why?

    d. Which of the two definitions is relevant for a tax researcher? Why?

LO 5-2   17. Find Rev. Rul. 83-163, 1983-2 C.B. 26, and answer the following questions. The purpose of these questions is to enhance your skills in reading and interpreting authorities that you locate while doing research.

    a. To which Code section(s) does this revenue ruling relate?

    b. *In your own words,* briefly explain why the taxpayers were required to include the value of barter club services received in their gross incomes.

    c. Find the most recent court case citing this revenue ruling and provide the citation to the case.

LO 5-2   18. Using an electronic research database such as Checkpoint or CCH AnswerConnect, find the case *Mortex Manufacturing Co., Inc.,* T.C. Memo 1994-110, and answer the following questions. The purpose of these questions is to enhance your skills in reading and interpreting authorities that you locate while doing research.

    a. What is the general controversy being litigated in this case?

    b. Which party—the taxpayer or the government—won the case?

    c. What is the relationship between Max Deason, the founder of the business, and Carlene Deason, the vice president?

    d. For the 1988 and 1989 tax years, how much salary did Carlene Deason receive from the corporation? What did the court decide was a reasonable amount of compensation for her for those years?

    e. Why did the court conclude that the salary paid to Carlene Deason was excessive?

    f. Was this case appealed? How did you determine your answer?

LO 5-2   19. Using an electronic research database such as Checkpoint or CCH AnswerConnect, find the case *Thomas A. Curtis, M.D., Inc.,* 1994 T.C. Memo ¶94,015, and answer the following questions. The purpose of these questions is to enhance your skills in reading and interpreting authorities that you locate while doing research.

    a. What is the general controversy being litigated in this case?

    b. Which party—the taxpayer or the government—won the case?

    c. Why is the plaintiff the corporation instead of Dr. or Mrs. Curtis?

    d. What is the relationship between Ellen Barnett Curtis and Dr. Thomas A. Curtis?

    e. For the fiscal year ended in 1989, how much salary did Ms. Curtis receive from the corporation? What did the court decide was a reasonable amount of compensation for her for that year?

    f. Was this case appealed? How did you determine your answer?

LO 5-3   20. Find the IRS website and locate the following items:

       a. Find the IRS publication dealing with moving expenses. What is its publication number?

       b. Find the IRS publication providing tax information relevant to divorced or separated individuals. What is its publication number?

       c. Find the IRS publication dealing with charitable contributions. What is its publication number?

       d. Find the tax form for reporting depreciation deductions for business assets. What is the form number?

       e. Find form 6251. What is the title of this form?

LO 5-2   21. Find the Internal Revenue Code on any freely accessible website and provide the URL. Do you consider the site reliable? Why or why not? What assurance, if any, does the site provide that its information is accurate and up to date?

LO 5-3   22. Find the website for the U.S. Treasury Department and report its URL. Who is the current secretary of the Treasury? Find the equivalent of the U.S. Treasury Department for one of the following countries: Western Australia, Germany, Japan, or Spain. Report that URL.

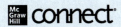 **All applicable Tax Planning Cases are available with *Connect*.**

Tax Planning Cases

LO 5-1, 5-2, 5-3   1. Art likes to invest his spare cash in the stock market. In the past, he has focused on growth stocks and long-term value to take advantage of the preferential tax rate on long-term capital gains. He recently learned that this rate is also available for dividend income. However, he is confused by his brokerage statement, which lists both qualifying dividends and nonqualifying dividends.

       For Art's benefit, investigate the requirements under which dividends qualify for the preferential tax rate. Write a letter to Art communicating the results of your research.

LO 5-1, 5-2, 5-3   2. Lance Strongarm, a recently retired professional athlete, is writing his memoirs. He intends to direct any royalties received on the book to his favorite charitable organization. He has not yet signed a contract with a publisher.

       Will the future royalties be included in Lance's taxable gross income? Why or why not? If your answer is yes, is any alternative arrangement available that Lance might make to avoid gross income recognition? Prepare a written memorandum stating the research issue(s); your conclusions concerning the issue(s); and the specific statutory, regulatory, or judicial authority supporting your conclusions.

LO 5-1, 5-2, 5-3   3. Lucille is an avid boater living near Gotham City. Gotham has recently created a harbor improvement special assessment district to oversee renovations to the public boat docks and boardwalk area surrounding the city harbor. The special assessment district plans to issue bonds to fund a portion of the planned improvements. Lucille is considering an investment in these bonds but is unsure whether the interest income she would earn qualifies as a tax exemption. Prepare a written memorandum stating the research issue(s); your conclusions concerning the issues(s); and the specific statutory, regulatory, or judicial authority supporting your conclusions.

Part **Three**

The Measurement of Taxable Income

Chapter **Six**

Taxable Income from Business Operations

Learning Objectives

After studying this chapter, you should be able to:

LO 6-1. Define *gross income* and *taxable income*.

LO 6-2. Describe the relationship between business operating cycle and taxable year.

LO 6-3. Identify the permissible methods of accounting for tax purposes.

LO 6-4. Explain why tax policy objectives affect the taxable income computation.

LO 6-5. Apply the cash method of accounting to compute taxable income.

LO 6-6. Apply the accrual method of accounting to compute taxable income.

LO 6-7. Differentiate between a permanent and a temporary book/tax difference.

LO 6-8. Explain the difference between tax expense per books and tax payable.

LO 6-9. Apply the tax accounting rules for prepaid income and accrued expenses.

LO 6-10. Explain how the NOL deduction smooths taxable income over time.

LO 6-11. Apply the excess business loss limitation.

The keynote of the text to this point has been the role of taxes in the business decision-making process. We've been concerned with income and deductions only in the generic sense and have worked through a series of hypothetical transactions demonstrating how income and deductions result in tax costs and tax savings. We have incorporated these costs and savings into cash flow models for computing the net present value (NPV) of the transactions.

In Part Three, our attention turns to the statutory, regulatory, and judicial rules governing the measurement of taxable income. This chapter examines the effect of a firm's choice of a taxable year and a method of accounting on the measurement process, with emphasis on the differences between the computation of financial statement income and taxable income. In contrast to earlier chapters, this chapter contains references to the Internal Revenue Code, Treasury regulations, and court cases pertaining to the computation of taxable income. We will analyze this technical material in terms of its effect on cash flows and its relevance to the tax planning process. In doing so, we will accomplish one of the objectives of *Principles of Taxation for Business and Investment Planning*—bridging the gap between finance courses that assume knowledge of the tax law and traditional law courses that ignore the role of taxes in the larger context of financial decision making.

BUSINESS PROFIT AS TAXABLE INCOME

LO 6-1

Define *gross income* and *taxable income.*

The base for the federal income tax is **taxable income**, defined as gross income minus allowable deductions.[1] The Internal Revenue Code defines **gross income** by stating that "gross income means all income from whatever source derived."[2] In a business context, gross income consists primarily of revenues from the sale of goods or performance of services in the regular course of a commercial activity. Gross income from the sale of tangible goods by a manufacturer, wholesaler, or retailer equals gross receipts less cost of goods sold.[3] Gross income from the performance of services includes all charges, fees, commissions, and bonuses received as compensation. Gross income also includes rents received for the occupancy of real estate or the use of tangible personalty, royalties received for the use of intellectual properties (copyrights, trademarks, formulas, patents, and software), and interest and dividends received as a return on invested capital.

Gross Income

Calzo Company sells lighting and plumbing fixtures to wholesale and retail customers and provides installation and repair services for its products. Calzo owns a warehouse and sublets surplus space to another company. It invests its excess working capital in a money market account. This year, Calzo derived the following items of gross income from its commercial activities:

Gross receipts from sales	$ 2,436,100	
Cost of goods sold	(1,606,400)	
Gross income from sales		$ 829,700
Gross receipts from services		512,900
Rent revenue		38,100
Interest on money market account		1,010
Gross income from commercial activities		$1,381,710

The federal courts have consistently ruled that the concept of gross income *from whatever source derived* is broad enough to include any accession to wealth or increase in net worth.[4] Consequently, firms may derive gross income from events or transactions occurring outside the course of their routine commercial activities.

Discharge of Debt Income

Calzo Company had an $18,000 overdue account payable to a major supplier. The supplier needed to settle the account as quickly and as advantageously as possible. After some negotiation, Calzo paid $14,000 cash to the supplier in full settlement of the account payable. Because Calzo extinguished an $18,000 liability with only $14,000 of assets, its net worth increased by $4,000, an increase that Calzo must include in gross income.[5]

---

[1] §63(a).

[2] §61(a).

[3] Reg. §1.61-3(a).

[4] *Commissioner* v. *Glenshaw Glass Co.,* 348 U.S. 426 (1955).

[5] §61(a)(12).

Tax Talk
The courts have consistently held in multiple decisions that proceeds from the sale of illegal drugs are included in gross income, even when the government confiscates the proceeds in a drug enforcement action.

The Internal Revenue Code allows a deduction for "all the ordinary and necessary expenses paid or incurred during the taxable year in carrying on any trade or business."[6] According to judicial interpretation, an expense is ordinary if it is customary for a particular type of trade or business and is commonly or frequently incurred. An expense is necessary if it is appropriate and helpful for the development of the business and the generation of revenue.[7] Because of this broad authorization, firms can deduct most routine operating expenses in the computation of taxable income. They can also deduct the various state, local, and foreign taxes incurred in carrying on their business activities.[8] Firms can even deduct the cost of assets acquired for long-term use in their business; these cost recovery deductions (such as depreciation) are typically spread over some extended period of years. Cost recovery deductions are discussed in detail in Chapter 7. Because the tax law allows firms to deduct expenses and costs incurred in revenue-generating activities, the federal income tax is imposed on *net profit* rather than gross receipts.

Taxable Income

This year, Calzo Company incurred $722,900 deductible operating expenses and was allowed a $30,114 depreciation deduction. Consequently, Calzo's taxable income was $632,696.

Gross income from commercial activities	$1,381,710
Gross income from discharge of debt	4,000
Deductible operating expenses	(722,900)
Depreciation deduction	(30,114)
Taxable income	$ 632,696

THE TAXABLE YEAR

LO 6-2
Describe the relationship between business operating cycle and taxable year.

A firm must measure its taxable income every year and pay tax on an annual basis. Firms have considerable latitude with respect to the 12-month period over which to measure income. A firm's taxable year generally corresponds to its annual accounting period for financial statement purposes.[9] If a firm keeps its financial books and records on a **calendar year**, it measures taxable income over the same January through December period. If a firm keeps its financial records on a **fiscal year** (any 12-month period ending on the last day of any month except December), it uses this fiscal year as its taxable year.[10]

The choice of a calendar or fiscal year is usually dictated by the firm's operating cycle; firms want to close their books and calculate their profit at the end of a natural cycle of business activity. A retail clothing store might find that a February 28 fiscal year-end most accurately reflects an operating cycle that peaks during the holiday season and reaches its lowest point before the beginning of the spring season. A ski resort might use a May 31 fiscal year-end so that its financial statements reflect the profit from an operating cycle that ends when the snow melts off the slopes.

---

[6] Source: Internal Revenue Code section 162(a).

[7] *Daniel E. Fuhrman,* T.C. Memo 2011-236.

[8] §164(a). Firms may forgo a deduction for foreign income taxes paid to claim a credit for these taxes against their federal income tax liability. The foreign tax credit is discussed in Chapter 13.

[9] §441(b) and (c).

[10] Firms may also use a 52- to 53-week year for financial statement and tax return purposes. A 52- to 53-week year is an annual period that is either 52 or 53 weeks long and that always ends on the same day of the week. §441(f).

Changing a Taxable Year

As a general rule, a new business entity establishes its taxable year by filing an initial tax return on the basis of such year.[11] The initial return reflects taxable income or loss from the date business began until the end of the year. As a result, an initial return typically reflects a short period of less than 12 months. After establishing a taxable year, a firm can't change its year unless it formally requests and receives permission to do so from the IRS.[12] This requirement has particular significance when an individual begins a new business as a sole proprietor and wants to keep records on a fiscal year basis. In all likelihood, the individual has always filed a calendar year tax return. Although the business itself is new, the taxable entity (the owner) is already established as a calendar year taxpayer. Consequently, the individual must request permission from the IRS to change to a fiscal year conforming to the sole proprietorship's accounting records.

When a firm has a convincing reason for changing its annual accounting period, the IRS usually grants permission for the firm to change its taxable year. If the firm lacks a convincing reason, the IRS may withhold permission for the change. In those cases in which the IRS grants permission, the firm files a **short-period return** to accomplish the change.

Changing a Taxable Year	Porto Corporation, a calendar year taxpayer since 1995, recently developed a new line of business with an annual operating cycle ending in midsummer. The corporation requests and receives permission from the IRS to change to a fiscal year ending July 31. To move from a calendar year to a fiscal year, the corporation files a return for the 7-month period from January 1 through July 31. Porto's returns for future years will reflect a 12-month taxable year from August 1 through July 31. This change in taxable years is illustrated by the following timeline:

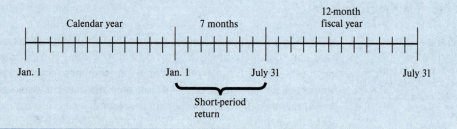

METHODS OF ACCOUNTING

LO 6-3
Identify the permissible methods of accounting for tax purposes.

After establishing its taxable year, a firm must assign the items of income and deduction from its transactions to a particular year. To do this, the firm must adopt a **method of accounting**: a consistent system for determining the point in time at which items of income and deduction are *recognized* (taken into account) for tax purposes. The Internal Revenue Code permits firms to use the cash receipts and disbursements (cash) method, the accrual method, or a combined (hybrid) method as their overall method of computing taxable income. We will discuss each of these three methods later in the chapter. The Code also provides specialized methods of accounting that apply only to particular transactions. For example, firms that contract to manufacture an item of property that will take more than 12 months to complete

---

[11] Reg. §1.441-1(c)(1).

[12] §442. Rev. Proc. 2006-45, 2006-45 C.B. 851, provides that certain corporations that have not changed their taxable year within a 48-month period ending with the close of the proposed year can change their year without IRS approval.

Tax Talk

VERITAS Software Corp. recently won a huge victory when the Tax Court struck down the IRS's attempt to allocate $1.5 billion income from an Irish subsidiary to the U.S. parent corporation. The court concluded that the IRS's application of Section 482 was "arbitrary, capricious, and unreasonable."

(e.g., an oceangoing oil tanker) must use the Section 460 percentage-of-completion method of accounting to measure the annual taxable income from the contract.

The tax law acknowledges that "no uniform method of accounting can be prescribed for all taxpayers. Each taxpayer shall adopt such forms and systems as are, in his judgment, best suited to his needs."[13] Moreover, a taxpayer engaged in more than one business may use a different method of accounting for each business.[14] This permissive attitude is tempered by a caveat: "No method of accounting is acceptable unless, in the opinion of the Commissioner [of the IRS], it clearly reflects income."[15] Thus, the IRS has the right to satisfy itself that a firm's method of income **recognition** accurately measures its ability to pay federal tax.

When related parties enter into business transactions, the IRS has particular reason to scrutinize the methods of accounting used to report the tax consequences, and it has broad authority to challenge these methods. Section 482 of the Internal Revenue Code states that in the case of two or more businesses under common ownership or control, the IRS may "distribute, apportion, or allocate gross income, deduction, credits, or allowances" among the businesses to clearly reflect the income of each.

The IRS typically invokes Section 482 when a method of accounting results in a beneficial shift of income between related parties. The following example illustrates this situation.

Using an Accounting Method to Shift Income	ABC, Inc. and XYZ, Inc. are owned by the same group of investors. ABC operates a manufacturing business, and XYZ is a regional wholesaler that purchases its inventory from a number of suppliers, including ABC. ABC's marginal tax rate is 21 percent, and XYZ's marginal tax rate is only 10 percent. As a result, the owners have an incentive to shift income from ABC to XYZ. They accomplish this shift by having ABC sell its product to XYZ at cost instead of the market price charged to unrelated wholesalers. When XYZ sells ABC's product to its customers, the entire profit with respect to the manufacture and sale of the product is included in XYZ's income.

In this example, ABC's method of accounting for sales to XYZ distorts the taxable income of both corporations. If a revenue agent discovers the questionable accounting method during an audit, the IRS could use its Section 482 authority to allocate income from XYZ to ABC to correct the distortion.

Section 482 Allocation	During its audit of ABC, Inc.'s 2019 tax return, the IRS determined that ABC would have recognized $670,000 more gross income if it had charged an arm's-length market price for the inventory sold to XYZ, Inc. Accordingly, the IRS allocated $670,000 gross income from XYZ to ABC to accurately measure the 2019 taxable income of both corporations.

Once a firm adopts a method of accounting, it may not change the method unless it formally requests and receives permission to do so from the IRS.[16] The request must state the reason the firm wants to change and provide a detailed description of its present and proposed

---

[13] Source: Internal Revenue Service. *The Code of Federal Regulations of the United States of America.* U.S. Government Printing Office, 1997.

[14] §446(d).

[15] Source: Internal Revenue Service. *The Code of Federal Regulations of the United States of America.* U.S. Government Printing Office, 1997.

[16] §446(e). Firms must file Form 3115 Application for Change in Accounting Method during the tax year for which the change is requested.

method of accounting. The IRS does not rubber-stamp these requests. When the IRS does grant permission, it carefully monitors the change to make sure that the firm doesn't omit income or duplicate deductions in the year of conversion to the new method of accounting.[17]

A Request Denied	In 1987, American Express requested the IRS's permission to change its method of accounting for the annual fees received from credit card holders. Until 1987, American Express recorded these fees as income in the month that they were billed. It requested a change to a "ratable inclusion" method under which fees would be recorded as income in equal monthly portions over the 12-month period beginning on the date of billing. The IRS took the position that the proposed method didn't clearly reflect the corporation's taxable income and denied permission to make the change. American Express took its case to federal court, but after 14 years of litigation, the U.S. Court of Appeals held for the government. As a result, American Express incurred $199 million additional tax in 1987.[18]

Tax Policy Objectives

LO 6-4
Explain why tax policy objectives affect the taxable income computation.

The accurate measurement of income is not the sole objective of the tax law. Congress wants the law to be consistent with public policy and political concerns, and the tax rules that achieve this consistency have nothing to do with income measurement. For instance, contributions to political parties or candidates for public office and lobbying expenses are not deductible.[19] Firms must report these expenses in their financial statements, but because Congress doesn't want to subsidize political activities, these expenses don't reduce taxable income.

Tax Talk
Walmart recently pleaded guilty to charges that its California stores dumped hazardous waste in violation of the federal Clean Water Act. The $816 million fine that Walmart must pay to the federal government is nondeductible.

Firms can't deduct illegal bribes and kickbacks or fines and penalties paid to any government for a violation of law because Congress doesn't want to subsidize bad behavior with a tax deduction.[20] For similar reasons, beginning in 2018, no deduction is permitted for any settlement, payout, or attorney fees related to sexual harassment or sexual abuse if such payments are subject to a nondisclosure agreement. The recent wave of sexual harassment scandals in Hollywood and Washington has made its mark on tax policy through this new provision.

The tax treatment of meals and entertainment expenses is intended to make the law more equitable. Many firms incur these expenses to improve their relationships with customers, clients, investors, and employees. While these expenses may have a good business purpose, they may also result in personal enjoyment for the participants. The "three-martini lunch" has become a catchphrase for lavish meals and entertainment that involve more pleasure than business. In response to criticism that the tax law should not underwrite such activities, Congress allows firms to deduct only 50 percent of most business meals.[21] Many exceptions exist, but 50 percent deductibility is the general rule. Beginning in 2018, no deduction is permitted for entertainment expenses, eliminating the subjective determination of whether such expenses are sufficiently business-related to warrant the previous 50 percent deduction allowance.

The Consolidated Appropriations Act of 2021 (CAA) temporarily modified the tax treatment of certain business meals. For expenses incurred after December 31, 2020, and before January 1, 2023, 100% of the cost of business food or beverage provided by a restaurant is deductible. Given the focus of this provision on items "provided by a restaurant," implementation guidance will be critical. What providers are considered restaurants for this purpose?

---

[17] §481(a).

[18] *American Express Company* v. *United States,* 262 F.3d 1376 (CA FC, 2001), *aff'm* 47 Fed Cl 127 (2000).

[19] §276 and §162(e).

[20] §162(c) and (f).

[21] §274(n). Section 274 includes many complicated restrictions on the deduction of business travel and meal expenses.

While it appears that take-out and delivery from restaurants would be included in the provision, what about food and beverage provided by caterers, or acquired from a grocery store?

In April 2021, the IRS issued Notice 2021-25, 2021-17 IRB 1118, addressing many questions regarding meals provided by a restaurant. Under the Notice, a restaurant is defined as a business that prepares and sells food or beverages to retail customers for immediate consumption, regardless of whether the food or beverages are consumed on the business's premises. Thus, take-out or delivery items from an establishment otherwise qualifying as a restaurant would fall within the temporary 100% deduction. However, a restaurant does not include a business that primarily sells pre-packaged food or beverages not for immediate consumption, such as a grocery store; specialty food store; beer, wine, or liquor store; drug store; convenience store; newsstand; or vending machine or kiosk. In addition, most eating facilities on an employer's premises providing free food or beverages to employees are not considered a restaurant for purposes of the temporary 100% deduction.

Nondeductible Expenses	Firm PLW operates a manufacturing business. This year, PLW paid a $2,000 fine to the city of Memphis for violating a local zoning law, contributed $3,500 to a candidate for state office, spent $8,200 on meals, and paid $5,000 for entertainment. While these items were recorded as expenses on PLW's books, the fine, political contribution, and entertainment expense were nondeductible. Only $4,100 of the meal expense was deductible, if these meal costs occurred during 2021 or 2022 and were not provided by a restaurant. If the meal costs occurred during 2021 or 2022 and were provided by a restaurant, the full amount of $8,200 would be deductible. If these meal costs are provided in 2023 or later, only $4,100 would be deductible, regardless of whether they were provided by a restaurant.

Business Financing

For decades, federal tax law has favored debt financing over equity financing by allowing businesses to deduct interest paid on debt. Payments to equity holders, however, are not deductible. The policy rationale behind this disparity in tax treatment of business financing has been hotly debated for years. For tax years beginning after December 31, 2017, Congress has partially addressed this issue by imposing a new **business interest limitation**. A current deduction is not allowed for net interest expense in excess of 30 percent of the business's adjusted taxable income. Net interest expense is business interest expense in excess of business interest income. For 2018–2021 tax years, adjusted taxable income is computed without regard to any nonbusiness income, loss, gain, or deduction; any business interest expense or business interest income; any net operating loss deduction; and any deduction for depreciation, amortization, or depletion. For 2022 tax years and beyond, adjusted taxable income is reduced by depreciation, amortization, or depletion.

Business Interest Limit	Gizmo Corporation has substantial business debt, incurring $4 million of interest expense this year. Gizmo earned $150,000 of business interest income, resulting in net business interest of $3.85 million. If Gizmo's adjusted taxable income is $9.5 million, its maximum deduction for net business interest is $2.85 million ($9.5 million × 30 percent). Of its $4 million of interest expense, Gizmo can deduct $2.85 million under the limitation and is permitted to deduct $150,000 against its business interest income for a total business interest deduction of $3 million. Thus, $1 million of Gizmo's business interest expense is not currently deductible.

Any interest not deductible as a result of this limitation can be carried forward to succeeding taxable years as business interest. The interest expense limitation applies only to taxpayers with average gross receipts of $29 million or more over the three preceding tax years. Thus, smaller taxpayers are exempt from this limitation.

Carryforward of Nondeductible Business Interest	Recall from the previous example that Gizmo Corporation has $1 million of nondeductible business interest this year. Suppose that next year, Gizmo incurs $3 million of net business interest and earns $12 million of adjusted taxable income. Gizmo's maximum deduction for business interest next year is $3.6 million ($12 million × 30 percent). Thus, $600,000 of Gizmo's business interest carryforward will be deductible next year. The remainder will continue to carry forward into subsequent taxable years.

Tax Preferences

The tax law contains many provisions to encourage certain economic behaviors or activities. In Chapter 4, we learned that the interest paid on state and local debt obligations is exempt from federal income tax. Firms that earn tax-exempt interest record it as revenue on their books but don't recognize it as gross income for tax purposes. The law provides a similar preference for the proceeds of life insurance policies: The proceeds are excluded from the recipient's gross income.[22] Many firms insure the lives of their officers and top-level management to protect against business disruption if one of these essential personnel dies. The firm itself (rather than the insured employee's family) is the beneficiary of such **key-person life insurance policies**. When a key person dies and the firm receives payment from the insurance company, the payment is recorded as revenue but is not taxable.

A corollary to the tax-exempt status of municipal bond interest and key-person life insurance proceeds is that expenses related to these income items are nondeductible. Accordingly, a firm can't deduct the interest paid on a debt if the borrowed funds were used to purchase or carry tax-exempt bonds.[23] Nor can a firm deduct the annual premiums paid on key-person life insurance policies.[24]

Key-Person Life Insurance	Migas Company owns insurance policies on the lives of its CEO and five other corporate officers and paid $14,300 premiums on these policies this year. In November, the CEO was killed in a boating accident, and Migas received $750,000 of insurance proceeds. Migas can't deduct the $14,300 premium expense, and it doesn't include the $750,000 proceeds in gross income.

As discussed in Chapter 4, the rate of taxation on income depends on the marginal tax rate of the entity earning that income. As part of the Tax Cuts and Jobs Act (TCJA) of 2017, Congress dramatically reduced the corporate tax rate to 21 percent. To provide similar tax savings to businesses operated in noncorporate forms, Congress also enacted new Section 199A. In general, this section provides taxpayers other than corporations a 20 percent deduction against **qualified business income (QBI)**. This deduction effectively lowers the marginal tax rate on business income earned through sole proprietorships, partnerships, and S corporation. Chapter 10 describes the QBI deduction in more detail.

Marginal Tax Rate after the QBI Deduction	Milo Jones has a marginal tax rate of 37 percent. This year, he earned $100,000 of qualified business income through his sole proprietorship. After the 20 percent QBI deduction, Mr. Jones will pay tax on only $80,000 of business profit ($100,000 − $100,000 × 20 percent). Thus, Mr. Jones owes $29,600 of tax on his business income ($80,000 × 37 percent), an effective tax rate of 29.6 percent ($29,600 ÷ $100,000).

---

[22] §101(a).

[23] §265(a)(2).

[24] §264(a).

THE CASH METHOD

LO 6-5
Apply the cash method of accounting to compute taxable income.

Under the **cash method of accounting,** firms record revenue from the sale of goods or the performance of services in the year that payment is received, regardless of when the sale occurred or the services were performed.

Cash Method for Revenues	Casa Company, a calendar year, cash basis consulting business, completed an engagement late in the year. On December 12, the firm mailed a bill to the client for its $20,000 consulting fee. If Casa doesn't receive a check in payment before year-end, it doesn't record revenue for the year, even though the services were performed during the year. Casa will record $20,000 revenue when it receives payment in the following year.

Under the cash method, firms record expenses in the year the expense is paid, regardless of when the liability for the expense was incurred.

Cash Method for Expenses	Casa Company hired a temporary employee to help the secretarial staff with year-end paperwork. The temp completed the assignment on December 28, but Casa didn't issue their $950 paycheck until January 15. Casa incurred the $950 liability when the employee completed the job in a satisfactory manner. Even so, it will record the $950 expense when it makes payment in the following year.

The Cash Method and Cash Flows

The term *cash method* should not be taken too literally. In the first place, the receipt of non-cash forms of payment creates revenue equal to the value of the payment. The fact that no money is received is irrelevant.

Noncash Receipts	Casa Company billed a client for a $12,000 consulting fee, and the client settled the bill by transferring $12,000 worth of marketable securities to the firm. Casa records $12,000 revenue on the receipt of the securities, even though the transaction didn't involve the receipt of money.

As this example suggests, the net income computed under the cash method doesn't equate to net cash flows. In other words, the terms *income* and *cash* are not synonymous, even for a cash basis taxpayer.

Income and Cash Flow	Casa Company lends $25,000 to an unrelated party at a 10 percent annual interest rate. Three years later, the debtor pays $33,275 ($25,000 principal + $8,275 interest) to Casa in satisfaction of the debt. Casa's income, expense, and cash flow from this transaction are as follows.

	Income/Expense	Cash Flow
Year of loan	–0–	$(25,000)
Year of repayment	$8,275	33,275

Constructive Receipt

Under the cash method of accounting, income is received when a person has unrestricted access to and control of the income, even if it is not in the person's actual possession. Treasury regulations state that this doctrine of **constructive receipt** applies when income is credited to a taxpayer's account, set apart for them, or otherwise made available so the taxpayer can draw on it during the taxable year.[25] For instance, interest accumulating in a savings account is constructively received on the day the owner has the right to withdraw the interest. The owner doesn't avoid income recognition merely because they decline to make the withdrawal.

In litigation between cash basis firms and the IRS, the courts have generally concluded that constructive receipt occurred if no substantial barrier to the firm's control and possession of the income existed. In other words, a calendar year, cash basis firm can't defer income from one year to the next by holding the checks received from its customers in December and cashing the checks the following January.[26]

The Lost Check

Horace and Donna Walter used the cash method to account for the income from their cattle ranch. During an audit of the Walters' 1996 tax records, an IRS agent found the top half of a business document indicating that Mr. Walter sold 115 steers to a customer for $77,442. The document apparently had been attached to a check from the customer. However, the Walters' bank records didn't show a deposit of $77,442 during 1996. Mr. Walter contacted the customer, who advised him that the check issued in 1996 had never been cashed. The customer then issued a new check, which Mr. Walter received and deposited in 1998. The Walters argued that they were not in constructive receipt of the income represented by the original check in 1996 because they had obviously lost the check instead of cashing it. The IRS contended that the fact that the Walters failed to cash the check was irrelevant, and they must include the $77,442 payment in 1996 income. The federal court that decided the case agreed with the IRS, stating, "Losing the check was a restriction on collection imposed by the Walters, the payees. No tax case has recognized an exception to the rule that receipt of a check is constructive receipt of the income when the restrictions on the disposition of the proceeds were the payees' own."[27]

Prepaid Expenses and Interest

Under the cash method of accounting, an expense is recorded in the year when payment is made. Cash basis firms can accelerate a deduction by paying an expense before the year in which the expense contributes to the generation of revenues. If the tax savings from the deduction are greater than the opportunity cost of the early payment, the firm has implemented a successful tax planning strategy. This strategy is limited by the well-established principle that any business expenditure creating a benefit with a useful life extending substantially beyond the close of the year is not deductible but must be capitalized and amortized over its useful life.[28] The tax law provides a "12-month rule" for determining whether an expenditure is currently deductible or must be capitalized to an intangible asset account. If the expenditure results in a benefit with a duration of 12 months or less *and* that benefit doesn't extend beyond the end of the taxable year *following* the year of payment, the expenditure is deductible in the year of payment. If the expenditure results in a benefit with a duration of more than 12 months, it must be capitalized.[29]

[25] Reg. §1.451-2(a).

[26] Ibid.

[27] Source: *Walter* v. *United States,* 148 F.3d 1027 (CA-8, 1996).

[28] *Welch* v. *Helvering,* 290 U.S. 111 (1933).

[29] Reg. §1.263(a)-4(f). This 12-month rule applies to both cash and accrual basis taxpayers.

Prepaid Insurance	On November 28, 2022, Firm Luo, a calendar year taxpayer, paid a $9,930 premium to acquire a casualty insurance policy on its business equipment. • If the insurance policy has a one-year term from December 1, 2022, through November 30, 2023, its benefit has a duration of only 12 months and doesn't extend beyond 2023. Therefore, Firm Luo can deduct the $9,930 premium in 2022. • If the insurance policy has a one-year term from February 1, 2023, through January 31, 2024, its benefit has a duration of only 12 months, but this benefit extends beyond 2023. Therefore, Firm Luo must capitalize the $9,930 premium. It can amortize and deduct $9,103 (11/12 × $9,930) of the cost in 2023 and $827 (1/12 × $9,930) of the cost in 2024. • If the insurance policy has a three-year term from January 1, 2023, through December 31, 2025, its benefit has a three-year duration. Therefore, Firm Luo must capitalize the $9,930 premium and can amortize and deduct $3,310 (1/3 × $9,930) of the cost in 2023, 2024, and 2025.

For many years, cash basis firms with excess liquidity toward the end of the year could generate a deduction by prepaying interest expense to cooperative creditors. Congress forestalled this planning technique by enacting a statutory requirement that prepaid interest be capitalized and deducted in the future year or years for which the interest is actually charged.[30]

Prepaid Interest	On October 1, Nassif Company, a calendar year, cash basis taxpayer, borrowed $100,000 from a local bank at 4.2 percent interest per annum. On December 19, the company paid $4,200 to the bank for the first year's interest on the loan. Even though Nassif is a cash basis taxpayer, it can deduct only $1,050 (the interest for October, November, and December). The $3,150 interest for January 1 through September 30 of the following year is deductible in the following year.

Merchandise Inventories

Firms that sell merchandise to their customers must use the accrual method to account for purchases and sales of the merchandise.[31] In other words, they must capitalize the cost of merchandise as an inventory asset and can expense only the cost of inventory sold during the year. Moreover, they must record revenue from the sale of inventory when the sale occurs instead of when payment is received. Firms that sell merchandise can use an overall **hybrid method of accounting** in which they account for purchases and sales of inventories under the accrual method and all other transactions under the cash method.

Hybrid Method of Accounting	Litz Company, a retail sporting goods store, uses a hybrid method of accounting under which it accounts for all transactions that don't involve inventory under the cash method. It accounts for inventory transactions under the accrual method by capitalizing all merchandise purchases to inventory, performing a physical count at year-end to determine ending inventory and cost of goods sold, and recording revenues from inventory sales when the sales occur.

For tax years beginning after 2017, the Tax Cuts and Jobs Act exempts smaller taxpayers from the requirement to account for inventory transactions under the accrual method. For 2023, taxpayers with average annual gross receipts of $29 million or less may either (1) treat inventories as nonincidental materials and supplies, or (2) conform to their financial

[30] §461(g).
[31] Regs. §1.446-1(a)(4)(i) and §1.471-1.

accounting treatment of inventory. In general, the costs of nonincidental materials and supplies are deductible as used or consumed, with amounts on hand at year-end treated as an asset.[32]

Small Business Exception	Jamestown Animal Hospital's principal business activity is the provision of veterinarian services, but it also sells pet supplies to its patients' owners. Jamestown's average annual gross receipts are $3 million. Consequently, it can use the cash method to account for its sales of both services and supplies. During the last month of this taxable year, Jamestown purchased $6,580 of pet supplies to restock its shelves. At year-end, it had $4,110 of these supplies on hand, so it could deduct only $2,470 of the cost this year. Jamestown can deduct the $4,110 capitalized cost in the year when it sells the supplies.

Limitations on Use of the Cash Method by Corporations

The cash method of accounting is both simple and objective because the measurement of income is based on cash receipts (bank deposits) and disbursements (checks written). The cash method also provides some control over the timing of income recognition.

Year-End Tax Planning under the Cash Method	Ebersall Company is a calendar year, cash basis service business. At the end of each year, the firm delays billing its clients for work performed in December until the following January to defer taxable income. It also prepays as many expenses as possible to accelerate tax deductions.

Because the cash method can be manipulated to defer income and accelerate deductions, the tax law limits its use by large corporations. Corporations that average more than $29 million annual gross receipts (2023 threshold amount) can't use the cash method for tax purposes.[33] This prohibition extends to partnerships with corporate partners. However, it doesn't apply to **personal service corporations**, defined as corporations that offer professional services (medical, legal, accounting, etc.) performed by individual shareholders or employees for the corporate clients. Any corporation, no matter how large, that is a personal service corporation can use the cash method to compute taxable income.

Goodbye to the Cash Method	Walsham Partnership, which operates a construction business, has 18 individual partners. The partnership has used the cash method of accounting since it was organized in 2003. Since its organization, Walsham's annual gross receipts have averaged $33 million a year. For compelling legal reasons, the partners have decided to incorporate their partnership. Once Walsham is converted to a taxable corporation, it must switch to the accrual method of accounting for tax purposes.

THE ACCRUAL METHOD

LO 6-6
Apply the accrual method of accounting to compute taxable income.

According to **generally accepted accounting principles (GAAP)**, only the accrual method of accounting correctly measures annual income.[34] Firms that provide audited financial statements to external users are typically required to use the accrual method. The Securities and Exchange Commission (SEC) requires every publicly held corporation to prepare accrual basis financial statements in accordance with GAAP.

[32] Section 471(c) as amended by the Tax Cuts and Jobs Act.

[33] §448. For tax years prior to 2018, the threshold was $5 million annual gross receipts.

[34] Generally accepted accounting principles are developed by the Financial Accounting Standards Board (FASB) and adhered to by the public accounting profession.

Under the **accrual method of accounting**, firms record revenue when the revenue is realized. **Realization** occurs when the earnings process with respect to the provision of goods or services is complete, regardless of when payment for the goods or services is received.

Accrual Method for Revenues	Azziz Company, a calendar year, accrual basis consulting business, performed client services during October and November and billed the client for $9,200 on December 8. Azziz recorded a $9,200 account receivable and $9,200 revenue even though it didn't receive payment from the client until January 10 of the following year.

Accrual basis firms match expenses against revenue in the year the liability for the expense is incurred, regardless of when payment of the expense is made.

Accrual Method for Expenses	Azziz Company hired a plumber to repair some leaky pipes in the executive washroom. The plumber completed repairs on December 19 and submitted a bill for $550. Azziz recorded a $550 account payable and a $550 expense even though it didn't pay the bill until January 20 of the following year.

If a firm uses the accrual method for both financial accounting (book) purposes and tax purposes, doesn't its annual income per books equal its taxable income? The answer to this question is usually no. For most accrual basis firms, book income and taxable income are different numbers. Discrepancies between the two income computations occur because certain transactions are treated one way under GAAP and another way for tax accounting purposes. One explanation for the inconsistent treatment is the contrast in perspectives on income measurement that shape financial accounting principles and the tax law.

Contrasting Perspectives on Income Measurement

Business managers have one attitude toward income measurement for financial statement purposes and a different attitude toward income measurement for tax purposes. Managers have incentives to report as much book income as possible. Their compensation and even their job security may depend on the level of earnings reported to existing and potential investors. However, GAAP is based on a principle of conservatism: When in doubt, financial statements should delay the realization of income and accelerate the realization of losses. In theory at least, GAAP curbs any tendency of management to *inflate* book income by overstating revenues or understating expenses.

In contrast to their expansive attitude toward book income, managers want to *deflate* the taxable income (and resultant tax cost) reported to the government. Congress and the Treasury are well aware of this measurement bias. Consequently, the federal tax law also embraces a principle of conservatism, but one that operates to prevent managers from understating gross income and overstating deductions. The contrasting principles of conservatism reflected by GAAP and the federal tax law lead to many of the book/tax differences described in Part Three of the text. To help readers keep track, a list of the sources of book/tax differences introduced in each chapter is provided at the end of the chapter.

Different Goals and Responsibilities	According to the Supreme Court, "The primary goal of financial accounting is to provide useful information to management, shareholders, creditors, and others properly interested; the major responsibility of the accountant is to protect these parties from being misled. The primary goal of the income tax system, in contrast, is the equitable collection of revenue; the major responsibility of the Internal Revenue Service is to protect the public fisc."[35]

[35] Source: *Thor Power Tool Co. v. Comm.*, 439 U.S. 522 (1979).

Permanent versus Temporary Differences

LO 6-7
Differentiate between a permanent and a temporary book/tax difference.

Differences between book income and taxable income are either permanent or temporary. A **permanent difference** results when income or gain is realized for book purposes but *never* recognized for tax purposes. Tax-exempt interest is an example of this type of permanent difference. Permanent differences also result when an expense or loss is realized for book purposes but *never* recognized for tax purposes. Nondeductible fines and penalties, entertainment costs, and the nondeductible 50 percent of business meals are good examples. Finally, permanent differences result when the tax law provides for a deduction that *never* corresponds to a book expense or loss. The dividends-received deduction that we will study in Chapter 11 is a prime example. Firms that have permanent book/tax differences never recoup the tax cost or repay the tax savings attributable to the differences.

Permanent Book/Tax Differences

Kalvoni, Inc. earned $114,000 tax-exempt interest, incurred $386,400 nondeductible expenses, and was allowed a $767,000 dividends-received deduction this year. If these were Kalvoni's only book/tax differences and its book income before tax was $4,712,000, its taxable income would be computed as follows:

Book income before tax	$4,712,000
Income never recognized	(114,000)
Expenses never deducted	386,400
Deduction never expensed	(767,000)
Taxable income	$4,217,400

Kalvoni's $494,600 permanent excess of book income over taxable income represents a $103,866 permanent tax saving ($494,600 excess × 21 percent) for the corporation.

A permanent book/tax difference affects only the year in which it occurs. Consequently, income tax expense for *financial statement purposes* is based on book income adjusted for all permanent differences.[36]

Tax Expense per Books

Kalvoni's audited financial statements must include its federal income tax expense for the year. The tax expense per books is based on Kalvoni's book income adjusted for its permanent book/tax differences:

Book income before tax	$4,712,000
Income never recognized	(114,000)
Expenses never deducted	386,400
Deduction never expensed	(767,000)
Adjusted book income	$4,217,400
Tax rate	.21
Tax expense per books	$ 885,654

Temporary differences occur when an item of income, gain, expense, or loss is taken into account in a different year (or years) for book purposes than for tax purposes. Any excess of taxable income over book income from a temporary difference turns around to become an excess of book income over taxable income in some future year, and vice versa. The tax cost or tax savings from temporary differences are recouped or repaid in the future year in which the difference reverses.

[36] This approach ignores unrecognized tax benefits and other accounting for income tax issues that are beyond the scope of our introductory coverage.

Reversal of Temporary Book/Tax Difference	In year 1, Questa Corporation engages in a transaction that generates $100,000 income for financial accounting purposes. For tax purposes, the transaction generates $60,000 income in year 1, $35,000 income in year 2, and $5,000 income in year 3. The following table shows the computation of the book/tax difference each year and the tax savings (cost) at a 21 percent rate.

	Book Income	Taxable Income	Difference	Tax Savings (cost)
Year 1	$100,000	$ 60,000	$ 40,000	$ 8,400
Year 2	–0–	35,000	(35,000)	(7,350)
Year 3	–0–	5,000	(5,000)	(1,050)
Total	$100,000	$100,000	–0–	–0–

Tax Expense versus Tax Payable

LO 6-8
Explain the difference between tax expense per books and tax payable.

Firms compute total tax expense for financial statement purposes based on book income adjusted for permanent book/tax differences. In contrast, temporary book/tax differences don't affect total tax expense per books. According to GAAP, the tax effects of temporary differences are captured as deferred tax assets or liabilities on the balance sheet.

A temporary difference between book income and taxable income generates either a deferred tax asset or a deferred tax liability equal to the difference multiplied by the firm's tax rate.[37] A temporary excess of taxable income over book income generates a **deferred tax asset**.[38] Because a deferred tax asset is analogous to a prepaid tax, temporary differences generating deferred tax assets are described as *unfavorable*. A temporary excess of book income over taxable income generates a **deferred tax liability**. Because a deferred tax liability is analogous to a delayed tax, temporary differences generating deferred tax liabilities are described as *favorable*.

Deferred Tax Asset	In year 1, Holmes, Inc. engaged in a transaction resulting in a $19,000 expense but only an $11,500 tax deduction. This $7,500 unfavorable book/tax difference generated a $1,575 deferred tax asset ($7,500 × 21 percent) on Holmes's balance sheet. This difference reversed in year 4 when Holmes reported a $7,500 tax deduction and no book expense. To account for this reversal, Holmes reduced the deferred tax asset from the original transaction to zero.

Deferred Tax Liability	In year 1, Holmes, Inc. engaged in a second transaction generating $50,000 book income but only $27,200 taxable income. This $22,800 favorable book/tax difference generated a $4,788 deferred tax liability ($22,800 × 21 percent) on Holmes's balance sheet. This difference partially reversed in year 2 when Holmes reported $10,000 taxable income but no book income. To account for this partial reversal, Holmes reduced the deferred tax liability from the original transaction to $2,688 [$4,788 – ($10,000 × 21 percent)].

Firms compute their federal tax payable based on their taxable income, which reflects both permanent and temporary differences from book income. Let's conclude our discussion of tax expense versus tax payable with a comprehensive example.

---

[37] This approach assumes no change in the firm's tax rate from the prior year.

[38] If the realization of a deferred tax asset is questionable, the asset may be reduced by a valuation allowance on the balance sheet.

Permanent and Temporary Differences

Zia Corporation engages in many transactions that result in permanent and temporary differences between book income and taxable income. This year, Zia's financial records show the following:

Book income before tax	$712,000
Net permanent differences	(19,000)
Net temporary differences	63,000
Taxable income	$756,000

Zia's tax expense for financial statement purposes is $145,530:

Book income before tax	$712,000
Permanent differences	(19,000)
	$693,000
Tax rate	.21
Tax expense per books	$145,530

Zia's tax payable is $158,760:

Taxable income	$756,000
Tax rate	.21
Tax payable	$158,760

The $13,230 excess of tax payable over tax expense equals 21 percent of Zia's $63,000 net temporary book/tax difference. This unfavorable difference results in a $13,230 net increase in Zia's deferred tax assets.

Temporary Book/Tax Accounting Differences
Prepaid Income

LO 6-9
Apply the tax accounting rules for prepaid income and accrued expenses.

According to GAAP, income from the sale of goods or performance of services is realized in the year the goods and services are provided to customers and clients and the earnings process is complete. This rule applies even if customers or clients pay for the goods and services in advance. For tax purposes, income is recognized when all events have occurred that fix the taxpayer's right to receive the income and the amount of income can be determined with reasonable accuracy. In addition, the all-events test is considered met no later than when the income is recognized in the taxpayer's financial statements. According to the IRS, a taxpayer's right to receive income generally is fixed when the earnings process is complete *or* when the taxpayer receives payment, *whichever happens first.* Because of this tax accounting rule, accrual basis firms must recognize gross income for many types of **prepaid income** in the year of receipt.[39]

Prepaid Rent Income

Cristal Company leases real estate to a tenant for $30,000 annual rent. At the beginning of the year, Cristal received a $90,000 payment from the tenant for three years' rent. For financial statement purposes, it reported $30,000 rent revenue on its income statement and $60,000 unearned revenue as a liability on its balance sheet. For tax purposes, Cristal must recognize the entire $90,000 prepayment as income. The $60,000 excess of taxable income over book income is a temporary difference that will reverse over the next two years.[40]

[39] Reg. §1.451-1(a). See also Rev. Rul. 84-31, 1984-1 C.B. 127.
[40] Reg. §1.61-8(b).

Accrual basis firms that receive prepayments for *services* to be performed for clients or customers may recognize income under a one-year deferral method authorized by the IRS. Under this special elective method of accounting, only the portion of the prepayment allocable to services performed in the year of receipt is included in taxable income for such year. The remaining prepayment is included in taxable income for the following year.[41] This special one-year deferral rule is also available for advance payments related to the sale of merchandise inventory, the use of intellectual property, and payments for the sale, license, or use of computer software. Prepayments received for rent, insurance premiums, and warranty contracts are specifically excluded from deferral and thus remain taxable on receipt.

Prepaid Service Income	SueLee Company, a calendar year taxpayer, offers ballroom dancing lessons to its clients. In October 2022, SueLee entered into a contract that entitles Ms. Jax to take 60 lessons over the next 36 months. Each lesson costs $40, and Ms. Jax was required to prepay the entire $2,400 contract price. By the end of 2022, Ms. Jax had taken 9 lessons. Under the one-year deferral method, SueLee includes $360 of the $2,400 prepayment (9 lessons × $40) in 2022 income. SueLee must include the $2,040 remaining prepayment in 2023 income, *regardless* of when Ms. Jax takes the 51 lessons remaining under the contract.

Advanced Payment for Inventory	Unsler Products, a calendar year taxpayer, manufactures and sells paper products. On November 16, 2022, Unsler received a $75,000 advanced payment from a customer for an order of paper that Unsler shipped from its warehouse on February 20, 2023. For financial statement purposes, Unsler reports advanced payments for inventory as revenue when the inventory is shipped. Consequently, Unsler can elect, under the one-year deferral method, to include the $75,000 payment in taxable income in 2023, the year in which it is included in book income.

Accrued Expenses

At the close of the year, GAAP requires firms to identify any liability for an unpaid expense and accrue both the expense and the liability on the firm's financial statements. According to GAAP, this requirement results in a proper match of the accrued expense against current year revenue. Even so, the tax law doesn't allow a deduction for the expense unless the accrual satisfies the **all-events test**.[42] This test consists of three requirements. First, the liability for the unpaid expense must be *fixed* because all events establishing the fact of the liability have occurred. Second, the amount of the liability must be *determinable* with reasonable accuracy. Third, *economic performance* with respect to the liability has occurred. Let's begin our discussion of the all-events test by looking at some examples of the first two requirements.

Fixed and Determinable Liability	Drago, Inc., a calendar year taxpayer, hired 113 temporary employees to work during the last two weeks of December 2023 but didn't receive a bill for their services from the employment agency before year-end. On the basis of its record of hours worked, Drago calculated that the bill would be $121,500. Consequently, Drago accrued a $121,500 expense and a $121,500 liability for temporary services payable for financial statement purposes. Because Drago's liability to pay for the services is *fixed* and the amount is *determinable* with reasonable accuracy, the accrual satisfies the first two requirements of the all-events test.

[41] Rev. Proc. 2004-34, 2004-1 C.B. 991 for tax years prior to 2018. These provisions were codified by the Tax Cuts and Jobs Act in Section 451(c)(1)(B).

[42] §461(h)(1) and (4).

Liability Not Fixed and Determinable	Salem, Inc. provides a medical reimbursement plan for its 4,800 employees. At the end of each year, Salem estimates the reimbursable expenses incurred during the year for which employees have not yet filed written claims. On the basis of this estimate, Salem accrues a medical reimbursement expense and a corresponding liability for financial statement purposes. Because Salem's liability for a claim is not fixed until the written claim is filed, the accrual fails the all-events test.[43]

Liability Not Fixed and Determinable	SkyHigh Airlines issues travel vouchers to customers who voluntarily surrender their reserved seats on overbooked flights. The vouchers are for a stated dollar amount and can be used to purchase future tickets. The vouchers are valid for only one year, and many expire without being used. At the end of each year, SkyHigh accrues an unused travel voucher expense and a corresponding liability for financial statement purposes. Because SkyHigh's liability for a voucher is not fixed until the customer uses it to purchase a ticket, the accrual fails the all-events test.[44]

Even when the liability for an accrued expense is fixed and determinable, the expense is not deductible until **economic performance** with respect to the liability has occurred. If a liability relates to the provision of services, property, or the use of property *to* the taxpayer *by* another party, economic performance occurs when the other party provides the services, property, or the use of property.

Provision of Services to Taxpayer	Refer to the earlier example in which Drago accrued a $121,500 expense for temp services. Drago's liability to pay for the services is fixed and determinable, and the employees provided the services to Drago in December 2023. Therefore, economic performance occurred in December, and the accrual meets the three requirements of the all-events test. As a result, Drago can deduct the $121,500 accrued expense in 2023.

Provision of Property to Taxpayer	On November 18, 2023, Drago ordered $4,400 of supplies from a vendor, who delivered the supplies on December 4. Drago didn't pay the vendor before year-end. Consequently, Drago accrued a $4,400 expense and a $4,400 liability for supplies payable for financial statement purposes. The liability is fixed and determinable, and economic performance occurred on December 4. Because the accrual meets the three requirements of the all-events test, Drago can deduct the $4,400 accrued expense in 2023.

If a liability relates to the provision of services or property *by* the taxpayer *to* another party, economic performance occurs when the taxpayer provides the services or property.

Provision of Services by Taxpayer	Bearden, Inc., a calendar year corporation, sells tractors under a three-year warranty obligating Bearden to repair the tractors during the warranty period. In 2023, Bearden sold 218 tractors with warranty periods extending into 2026. At the end of 2023, Bearden accrued a $60,000 expense and a $60,000 liability for future warranty costs. This liability is fixed and determinable with reasonable accuracy. However, economic performance hasn't occurred because Bearden hasn't provided the repair service. Consequently, the accrued liability fails the all-events test and the $60,000 accrued expense is not deductible in 2023. Bearden can deduct its warranty cost in any future year in which it does provide the service.[45]

---

[43] *United States* v. *General Dynamics Corp.*, 481 U.S. 239 (1987).

[44] IRS Letter Ruling 200203004 (January 18, 2002).

[45] Reg. §1.461-4(d)(7), Example 2.

In the case of a few specific liabilities, economic performance occurs only when the taxpayer makes payment to the person to whom the liability is owed. These so-called **payment liabilities** include liabilities arising under any workers' compensation act or out of a tort, breach of contract, or violation of law; liabilities for customer rebates or refunds; liabilities for awards, prizes, or jackpots; and liabilities for taxes imposed by a governmental authority.[46]

Payment Liability	Solange, Inc., a calendar year taxpayer, was sued in 2021 by a customer who was injured on Solange's premises because of the corporation's alleged negligence. Solange accrued a $2 million estimated settlement expense and a $2 million contingent liability for 2021 financial statement purposes. In 2022, Solange and the customer agreed to a $1.5 million out-of-court settlement. Solange actually paid $1.5 million to the customer on April 6, 2023. Solange could not deduct any settlement expense in 2021 when the liability was accrued or in 2022 when the liability became fixed and determinable. Solange could deduct the $1.5 million settlement in 2023 when it made payment to the customer.

The tax law moderates the effect of the economic performance requirement on standard accounting practices by providing a **recurring item exception**.[47] Taxpayers may adopt this exception as a method of accounting for liabilities of a type regularly incurred from year to year and properly accrued at year-end under GAAP. Under this exception, if economic performance occurs within eight and one-half months after the close of the year, the business can deduct the corresponding expense in the year of accrual.

Recurring Item Exception	Omero Company, a calendar year taxpayer, sells digital cameras. Omero refunds the full purchase price of a camera to any customer who requests the refund in writing within 90 days of purchase. At the end of 2023, Omero accrued a $17,600 expense and a $17,600 liability for refunds payable with respect to 88 refund requests received but unpaid. Omero paid all of these requests by September 15, 2024. If Omero hasn't adopted the recurring item exception as its method of accounting for refunds, economic performance (payment) occurred in 2024, and the $17,600 expense is deductible in 2024. If Omero has adopted this method of accounting, it can deduct the $17,600 accrued expense in 2023.[48]

Recurring Item Exception	Refer to the previous example in which Bearden, Inc. sold 218 tractors with warranty periods extending into 2026. At the end of 2023, Bearden accrued a $60,000 warranty expense. By September 15, 2024, Bearden had provided $9,045 worth of repairs under its 2023 warranties. If Bearden has adopted the recurring item exception as its method of accounting for warranty costs, it can deduct $9,045 of the accrued warranty expense in 2023.

Compensation Accruals

The tax law includes a particular rule governing the timing of an employer's deduction for employee compensation. The deduction is allowed in the employer's taxable year in which the compensation is included in the employee's gross income.[49] In other words, compensation is deductible in the year of payment to cash basis employees. Consequently, an accrued

---

[46] Reg. §1.461-4(g).

[47] §461(h)(3). The recurring item exception doesn't apply to liabilities for workers' compensation, tort, breach of contract, or violation of law. Reg. §1.461-5(c).

[48] Reg. §1.461-5(e), Example 1.

[49] §404(a)(5) and (b)(1). According to Reg. §1.461-4(d)(2)(iii), the economic performance requirement is satisfied to the extent an employee benefit is deductible under Section 404.

expense for compensation payable is not deductible in the year of accrual but in the year the liability is paid. There is an important exception to this timing rule: An accrued compensation expense is deductible if payment is made to the employee within two and one-half months after the close of the employer's taxable year.[50]

Compensation Accruals

Panok, a calendar year corporation, pays its employees on a monthly basis and distributes paychecks on the fourth business day after the close of each month. At the end of 2023, Panok accrued a $639,200 expense and a $639,200 liability for December wages payable. Panok paid these wages on January 6, 2024. Because payment occurred by March 15, 2024, Panok could deduct the $639,200 accrued expense in 2023.

On December 28, 2023, Panok's board of directors authorized a $15,000 year-end bonus for each of the six corporate executives. Consequently, Panok accrued a $90,000 expense and a $90,000 liability for bonuses payable. Because of cash flow problems, Panok was unable to pay these bonuses until April 3, 2024. Consequently, Panok could not deduct the $90,000 accrued expense in 2023 but could deduct the payment in 2024.

Panok's employees are compensated with two to six weeks of paid vacation each year. Employees accumulate any unused vacation indefinitely. At the end of 2023, Panok accrued a $144,900 expense and a $144,900 liability for vacation pay accumulated by its employees for the year. Panok paid $28,700 of this liability to employees who took vacation between January 1 and March 15, 2024. Consequently, Panok could deduct $28,700 of its accrued vacation pay expense in 2023. Panok will deduct the remaining expense in the future year when the employees take their remaining accrued vacation.

Related Party Accruals

The two parties to a transaction may use different methods to account for the tax consequences of the transaction. As a result, the two sides of the transaction may be reported in different years.

Different Accounting Methods: Arm's-Length Transaction

Company AB, an accrual basis taxpayer, hires Firm CB, a cash basis taxpayer, to provide professional services. Firm CB performs the services in year 1 and bills Company AB for $10,000. Company AB pays this bill in year 2. For financial statement purposes, the two parties record the following.

	Year 1	Year 2
Company AB's accrued expense	$(10,000)	–0–
Firm CB's realized income	–0–	$10,000

If Company AB and Firm CB are not related parties, the tax consequences of the transaction are consistent with the financial accounting treatment. Company AB reaps the tax savings from a $10,000 deduction in year 1, while Firm CB bears the tax cost of $10,000 income in year 2. In present value terms, the tax savings exceed the tax cost, even if both parties have the same marginal tax rate. Although the Treasury is being whipsawed because of the difference in the parties' accounting methods, the tax law tolerates the result because it arises from an arm's-length transaction.

[50] Reg. §1.404(b)-1T, Q&A 2.

Now assume that Firm CB owns a controlling interest in Company AB. Because the transaction occurs between related parties, the tax law doesn't allow Company AB to deduct the accrued expense in year 1. Instead, Company AB must defer the $10,000 deduction until year 2 when Firm CB recognizes $10,000 income from the transaction.[51]

Different Accounting Methods: Related Parties	If Company AB and Firm CB are related parties, Company AB accrues the $10,000 expense in year 1 but reports a $10,000 deduction in year 2.

	Year 1	Year 2
Company AB's:		
Accrued expense	$(10,000)	–0–
Tax deduction	–0–	$(10,000)
Firm CB's realized income	–0–	10,000

Business Bad Debts

It is well established that the tax law doesn't allow deductions based on reserves or allowances for future or contingent liabilities.[52] Additions to reserves or allowances are based on estimates that fail the crucial all-events test for deductibility. The disallowance of a deduction for such additions causes a temporary difference between book income and taxable income. The most common example of this book/tax difference results from a firm's method of accounting for its bad debts.

When an accrual basis firm sells goods or services and the purchaser doesn't pay cash at the point of sale, the firm records an account receivable for the sales price. Firms anticipate that some portion of their accounts receivable will never be collected because of defaults by customers to whom the firm extended credit. According to GAAP, firms should use the **allowance method** to account for bad debts. Under this method, firms estimate the portion of their accounts receivables that will be uncollectible and establish a bad debt allowance or reserve for this portion. The annual addition to the allowance is recorded as a bad debt expense and matched against sales revenue. For tax purposes, firms must use the **direct write-off method** to account for bad debts. Under this method, firms can deduct accounts receivable (and any other business debts) actually written off as uncollectible during the year.[53]

Accounting for Bad Debts	ABC, Inc. began the year with a $298,000 balance in its allowance for bad debts. During the year, it wrote off $155,000 uncollectible accounts receivable against this allowance. On the basis of ABC's year-end accounts receivable, the independent auditors determined that a $173,000 addition to the bad debt allowance was necessary. As a result, the year-end balance in the allowance increased to $316,000.

Beginning allowance for bad debts	$298,000
Actual write-offs during the year	(155,000)
Addition to allowance	173,000
Ending allowance for bad debts	$316,000

(continued)

[51] §267(a)(2). Under this section, a controlling interest is generally more than a 50 percent ownership interest.
[52] *Lucas* v. *American Code Co.,* 280 U.S. 445 (1930).
[53] §166(a).

ABC's income statement shows a bad debt expense of $173,000, while its tax return shows a bad debt deduction of only $155,000. If ABC's book income before tax is $6,700,000 and it has no other book/tax differences, its taxable income is computed as follows.

Book income before tax	$6,700,000
Nondeductible bad debt expense	173,000
Deductible bad debt write-offs	(155,000)
Taxable income	$6,718,000

Firms occasionally receive payment of an account receivable that was written off as uncollectible in a previous year. For financial statement purposes, this recovery is credited to the allowance for bad debts and has no effect on income. The tax consequences of the recovery are dictated by a long-standing **tax benefit rule**. Under this rule, the recovery of an amount deducted in an earlier year must be included in gross income in the year of recovery.[54] Because the write-off of an account receivable resulted in a bad debt deduction in a previous year, the payment must be included in taxable income.

Recovery of Bad Debt

Two years ago, Sela Company wrote off a $57,000 account receivable as uncollectible. The $57,000 write-off was included in Sela's $589,200 bad debt deduction for that year. This year, the debtor paid $57,000 cash to Sela to settle the old receivable. This recovery has no effect on Sela's book income but increases its taxable income by $57,000.

NET OPERATING LOSSES AND EXCESS BUSINESS LOSSES

LO 6-10
Explain how the NOL deduction smooths taxable income over time.

In this chapter, we've learned that firms must choose a method of accounting to divide a continuous stream of income into 12-month segments. The choice of accounting method has nothing to do with the measurement of taxable income *over the life* of a firm, but everything to do with the measurement of income for each taxable year. The final section of this chapter focuses on one possible outcome of this annual measurement process: a net operating loss. This section also addresses a new limitation, imposed by the Tax Cuts and Jobs Act of 2017, on deductibility of excess business losses.

The Problem of Excess Deductions

If a taxpayer's annual business operation results in an excess of deductible expenses over gross income, this excess is labeled a **net operating loss (NOL)**. Because the taxpayer reports no taxable income, it incurs no tax cost in the year of the NOL. But a subtler fact is that the excess deductions yield no current tax savings; the taxpayer has the same zero tax cost with or without these deductions. If the excess deductions are wasted because they never yield any tax savings, the taxpayer's average tax rate *over time* could be distorted.

[54] Section 111 is a codification of the tax benefit rule. A recovery of a previously deducted amount is taxable only to the extent that the deduction actually reduced the tax base in the year the deduction was allowed.

<table>
<tr><td rowspan="6" valign="top">*Excess Deductions and Average Tax Rate*</td><td colspan="4">TUV, Inc. conducts a business with a 24-month operating cycle. Its most recent operating cycle generated $300,000 profit:</td></tr>
<tr><td></td><td>Year 1</td><td>Year 2</td><td>Total</td></tr>
<tr><td>Gross income</td><td>$100,000</td><td>$625,000</td><td>$725,000</td></tr>
<tr><td>Deductible expenses</td><td>(300,000)</td><td>(125,000)</td><td>(425,000)</td></tr>
<tr><td>Profit</td><td></td><td></td><td>$300,000</td></tr>
</table>

If TUV had to report its income and pay tax based on strict 12-month intervals, it would report a $200,000 NOL for year 1 and $500,000 taxable income for year 2. At a 21 percent rate, it would owe no tax in year 1 and $105,000 tax in year 2. Thus, TUV's overall tax rate on its profit would be 35 percent:

$$\$105{,}000 \text{ tax} \div \$300{,}000 \text{ profit} = 35\%$$

This inflated rate reflects the fact that $200,000 of TUV's deductible expenses (year 1 NOL) generated no tax savings for the corporation.

Solution: The NOL Deduction

The tax law prevents the rate distortion that could result from an inflexible one-year reporting period by permitting taxpayers to smooth income over time by deducting excess deductions in one year against income in another. Specifically, a taxpayer may carry an NOL forward indefinitely as a deduction against taxable income reported in succeeding taxable years. However, the amount deductible in such carryforward years is limited to 80 percent of taxable income before such deduction.[55] A taxpayer reports an **NOL carryforward** as a deduction on future tax returns until the NOL has been fully utilized.

NOL Carryforward

In 2022, Narda Corporation generated a $612,000 NOL. The following schedule shows the years in which it used the NOL as a deduction against taxable income:

	2023	2024	2025	2026	2027	2028
Taxable income before NOL deduction	$165,000	$110,000	$138,000	$99,000	$54,000	$210,000
NOL deduction	(132,000)	(88,000)	(110,400)	(79,200)	(43,200)	(159,200)
Taxable income	$ 33,000	$ 22,000	$ 27,600	$19,800	$10,800	$ 50,800

In tax years 2023 through 2027, Narda's NOL deduction equals 80 percent of taxable income before the NOL deduction. In 2028, the 80 percent limitation is not applicable because the 80 percent limitation is greater than the remaining NOL carryforward.

Tax Talk
The CARES Act also provides that NOLs arising in the 2018, 2019, and 2020 tax years can be carried back five years and deducted against taxable income reported in those carryback years. Any losses not deductible through carryback can be carried forward.

The Coronavirus Aid, Relief, and Economic Security (CARES) Act of 2020, provided important modifications to the 80 percent deduction limitation for NOL carryforwards. First, the CARES Act suspended the 80 percent limitation for tax years before 2021. Second, for tax years after 2020, taxpayers will be able to take a 100 percent deduction for NOLs that arose from pre-TCJA tax years and a deduction limited to 80 percent of taxable income for NOLs that arose from post-TCJA tax years. NOLs not subject to the 80 percent limitation are deducted first, and post-TCJA NOL deductions are limited to 80 percent of remaining taxable income.

[55] §172 as amended by the Tax Cuts and Jobs Act. Prior to 2018, corporate NOLs could be carried back 2 years and forward 20, without an 80 percent limitation.

Pre-TCJA NOL Carryovers under CARES Act	Starter Corporation began business in 2017. It incurred NOLs of $(1.7 million) and $(1 million) in 2017 and 2018, respectively. In 2019, Starter earned $2.8 million of taxable income before any net NOL deduction. Starter's 2017 NOL is fully deductible, reducing its 2019 taxable income to $1.1 million. Under pre-CARES Act law, deduction of its 2018 NOL would have been limited to $880,000 ($1.1 million × 80%), resulting in 2019 taxable income of $220,000. Under the CARES Act, Starter may deduct all $1 million of its 2018 NOL, reducing its 2019 taxable income to $100,000.

Let's incorporate an NOL deduction into the earlier example involving TUV, Inc.

NOL Deduction	Assuming that year 1 was TUV's first taxable year, the NOL in year 1 is carried forward as a deduction into year 2. TUV's tax returns for the two years show the following:

	Year 1	Year 2
Gross income	$ 100,000	$625,000
Deductible expenses	(300,000)	(125,000)
NOL	$(200,000)	
NOL carryforward deduction		(200,000)
Taxable income		$300,000

At a 21 percent rate, TUV owes $63,000 tax in year 2. Because of the NOL carryforward, TUV's taxable income in year 2 equals the $300,000 profit for the 24-month operating cycle, and TUV's tax rate on this profit is 21 percent.

Valuing an NOL Deduction

The value of a deduction equals the tax savings from the deduction. In the case of an NOL deduction, the tax savings (and cash flows) depend on the year (or years) in which the taxpayer takes the deduction against taxable income. Under current law for tax years after 2020, NOLs can only be carried forward, with potential limits on the annual deduction in carryforward years. The present value of the deduction depends on the corporation's projection of its future income stream.

NPV of an NOL Carryforward	Corporation C incurred a $700,000 net operating loss in 2023. It projects that it will generate $350,000 annual income over the next three years. Given the annual deduction limitation, the maximum NOL that could be deducted against $350,000 of income is $280,000. Based on a 5 percent discount rate, the value in 2023 of the NOL carryforward is only $134,730:

	2024	2025	2026
Projected income	$350,000	$350,000	$350,000
NOL carryforward from 2020	(280,000)	(280,000)	(140,000)
Taxable income	$ 70,000	$ 70,000	$210,000
Tax on projected income at 21%	$ 73,500	$ 73,500	$ 73,500
Actual tax	(14,700)	(14,700)	(44,100)
Tax savings from NOL	$ 58,800	$ 58,800	$ 29,400
Present value of tax savings	$ 56,000	$ 53,333	$ 25,397
NPV of tax savings	$134,730		

Because the tax savings from the NOL deduction are deferred into future years, the present value of the deduction decreases. Had Corporation C's $700,000 loss been immediately deductible, it would have generated $147,000 of tax savings ($700,000 × 21 percent). Clearly, the longer the period of time over which a taxpayer deducts an NOL carryforward, the less the present value of the deduction.

Accounting for NOLs

According to GAAP, firms that generate a current net operating loss must report the tax benefit represented by the NOL carryforward on their current financial statements. The anticipated benefit is reported as a deferred tax asset.[56]

Accounting for NOL Carryforward	Groh, Inc. generated a $492,000 NOL in 2023. Groh accounted for the anticipated tax savings from the carryforward by recording a $103,320 deferred tax asset ($492,000 × 21 percent) and a matching $103,320 decrease in 2023 tax expense. In 2024, Groh, Inc. generated $1,316,000 taxable income before consideration of its NOL carryforward. Groh could deduct the entire $492,000 carryforward, thereby reducing its 2024 tax payable by $103,320 ($492,000 × 21 percent). Groh accounted for the use of the carryforward by reducing the $103,320 deferred tax asset to zero and recording a matching $103,320 increase in 2024 tax expense.

Excess Business Losses

LO 6-11
Apply the excess business loss limitation.

For tax years beginning after 2017, the Tax Cuts and Jobs Act has added a new limitation on excess business losses.[57] The CARES Act of 2020 temporarily suspended this limitation for losses arising in 2018, 2019, and 2020. Thus, 2021 was the first tax year for which this limitation now applies.

Before exploring the computation of this limit, let's consider to whom it applies. First, the **excess business loss limitation** applies only to noncorporate taxpayers: individuals, trusts, and estates. For passthrough entities, the limitation applies to noncorporate owners of the entity. Second, the limitation applies only to aggregate excess business losses exceeding a threshold amount. For 2023, these thresholds are $578,000 (married filing jointly taxpayers) and $289,000 (all other taxpayers). The 2022 thresholds are $540,000 (married filing jointly taxpayers) or $270,000 (all other taxpayers).

Taxpayers Subject to Excess Business Loss Limitation	ABC LLC is a partnership with two equal partners, Alice and Beta Corporation. This year, ABC incurred an overall business loss of $(800,000), allocating $(400,000) of such loss to each partner. Beta's share of the loss is not subject to the excess business loss limitation, since Beta is a corporation. If Alice is married filing a joint return and the loss allocated from ABC is her only business activity, the excess business loss limitation will not apply because her loss is below the $578,000 threshold. If Alice is single, $111,000 of her loss exceeds the $289,000 threshold and is subject to the excess business loss limitation.

A taxpayer's excess business loss equals the aggregate of deductions from the taxpayer's trades and businesses over the sum of aggregate business gross income and business gains plus the $578,000 or $289,000 (2023) threshold amount. Thus, a taxpayer involved in multiple trades and businesses is allowed to net losses from one business against profits from another in applying the limitation.

[56] If the firm's prospect of deducting an NOL carryforward is uncertain, the deferred tax asset may be reduced by a valuation allowance on the balance sheet.

[57] New Section 461(l), added by the Tax Cuts and Jobs Act. The excess business loss limitation applies after the Section 469 passive activity loss limitation discussed in Chapter 16.

Calculating the Excess Business Loss	Graham is single and operates two businesses. This year, Business A generated $450,000 of taxable profit. Business B generated a $(975,000) loss. Graham's excess business loss is $(236,000) ($450,000 profit from Business A–$975,000 loss from Business B + $289,000 threshold amount for single taxpayers).

Excess business losses are not deductible in the current year. Instead, such losses carry forward and are treated as part of the taxpayer's net operating loss carryforward in subsequent years. As such, future deductions are subject to the 80 percent limit on NOL deductions, discussed earlier in this section.

Carryforward of Excess Business Loss	Recall that Graham's excess business loss this year is $(236,000). Graham must treat this loss as an NOL carryforward into future tax years. Next year, if Graham's taxable income before any NOL deduction is $280,000, only $(224,000) of his loss carryforward ($280,000 × 80 percent) will be deductible. The remaining $(12,000) will continue to carry forward into the future.

Conclusion	The computation of taxable income depends on the taxable year and the method of accounting adopted by the firm. Firms often use the same overall method for both financial reporting and tax purposes. Even so, many discrepancies exist between the computations of book and taxable income. In subsequent chapters, we'll encounter many more of these book/tax differences. To make sense of these differences, it may help to keep the following in mind. The goal of generally accepted accounting principles (and financial statements prepared in accordance with GAAP) is to provide useful and pertinent information to management, shareholders, creditors, and other business decision makers. In contrast, the primary (but certainly not the only) goal of the Internal Revenue Code (and the responsibility of the IRS) is to generate and protect federal tax revenues.

Sources of Book/Tax Differences	**Permanent**	**Temporary**
	• Interest on state and local bonds	• Prepaid income
	• Key-person life insurance proceeds and premiums	• Bad debts
		• Accrued expenses failing the all-events test
	• Fines and penalties	
	• Political contributions and lobbying expense	• Compensation accruals
		• Related party accruals
	• Meals and entertainment expenses	• NOL carryforwards
	• Sexual harassment settlements subject to nondisclosure agreements	• Business interest expense limitation

Key Terms

accrual method of accounting *6-15*
all-events test *6-19*
allowance method *6-23*
business interest limitation *6-9*
calendar year *6-5*

cash method of accounting *6-11*
constructive receipt *6-12*
deferred tax asset *6-17*
deferred tax liability *6-17*
direct write-off method *6-23*

economic performance *6-20*
excess business loss limitation *6-27*
fiscal year *6-5*
generally accepted accounting principles (GAAP) *6-14*

Questions and Problems for Discussion

LO 6-1   1. Firm LK bought a warehouse of used furniture to equip several of its clerical offices. An employee discovered a cache of gold coins in a desk drawer. A local court declared Firm LK the rightful owner of the coins, which have a $72,000 fair market value (FMV). Does Firm LK recognize income because of this lucky event?

LO 6-2   2. Discuss the choice of a taxable year for the following businesses:

   a. Retail plant and garden center.

   b. French bakery.

   c. Chimney cleaning business.

   d. Moving and transport business.

   e. Software consulting business.

LO 6-3   3. Corporation DB operates three different lines of business. Can the corporation elect a different overall method of accounting for each line, or must the corporation adopt one overall method?

LO 6-3   4. Lester, Inc. owns 55 percent of the outstanding stock of Marvin Corporation. The two corporations engage in numerous intercompany transactions that must be accounted for on both their financial statements and their tax returns. Discuss the circumstances in which the IRS might challenge the method of accounting used to record these intercompany transactions.

LO 6-4   5. For many years, Mr. Kane, the president of KJ, Inc., took the corporation's most important clients golfing at The Links Golf Club several times a year. However, after the tax law was amended to disallow a deduction for business entertainment, Mr. Kane and his clients golf together much less frequently. What does this scenario suggest about the incidence of the indirect tax increase represented by the entertainment disallowance rule?

LO 6-4   6. If a corporation purchases insurance on the life of its chief executive officer and the corporation is named the policy beneficiary, the premium payments are nondeductible. If the officer's spouse and children are named as beneficiaries, the premium payments are deductible. Can you provide a reason for this inconsistent tax treatment?

LO 6-4, 6-7   7. Describe the book/tax difference resulting from each of the following transactions:

   a. Firm A spent $430 on a business dinner attended by the firm's vice president and a potential client.

   b. Firm B borrowed $50,000 and invested the loan proceeds in tax-exempt City of Los Angeles bonds. This year, Firm B paid $2,800 interest on the loan and earned $3,500 interest on the bonds.

   c. Firm C sent its president and several other key employees to Washington, D.C., to lobby a group of senators to enact legislation that would be extremely beneficial for the firm's business. The cost of this trip was $7,400. While in the capital city, the president attended a "$10,000 a plate" fundraising dinner sponsored by one senator's reelection committee.

LO 6-5   8. Firm NB, which uses the cash method of accounting, recently received two cases of French wine from a client in settlement of a $1,300 bill. Does Firm NB avoid income recognition because it received a noncash item as payment?

LO 6-5, 6-6   9. Ms. Hussain is the manager of Firm Z, a new business that anticipates a steady growth in profits over the next decade, must decide between the cash method and the accrual method as the overall method for tax purposes. She understands that the difference between the two methods is essentially one of timing and that, over the life of the firm, either method should result in the same taxable income. What she doesn't understand is why the cash method might improve the NPV of the firm's cash flows over the next decade. Can you provide an explanation?

LO 6-6   10. Discuss the various circumstances in which a firm is required to prepare financial statements in accordance with GAAP.

LO 6-7   11. Why do tax preferences often result in differences between book income and taxable income? Would a book/tax difference from a tax preference be a permanent difference or a temporary difference? Which type of difference is more valuable in NPV terms?

LO 6-8   12. Firms generally prefer to engage in transactions that create assets instead of liabilities. However, firms prefer transactions generating deferred tax liabilities to transactions generating deferred tax assets. Can you explain this apparent contradiction?

LO 6-9   13. Describe the contrasting treatment of prepaid income under GAAP and under the tax law, and explain how each treatment reflects a different principle of conservatism.

LO 6-10   14. Net operating losses can be carried forward indefinitely. Why would a taxpayer prefer to use such losses sooner rather than later?

Mc Graw Hill connect®   All applicable Application Problems are available with *Connect*.

Application Problems

LO 6-1   1. Nello Company owed $23,400 overdue rent to its landlord, Bonview, Inc. Because Nello is a desirable tenant, Bonview agreed to settle the overdue account for a $15,000 cash payment from Nello. Both Nello and Bonview are accrual basis taxpayers.

  a. What is the tax consequence to Nello of the settlement of its $23,400 account payable to Bonview? Compute Nello's net cash outflow from the settlement assuming its tax rate is 35 percent.

  b. What is the tax consequence to Bonview of the settlement of its $23,400 account receivable from Nello? Compute Bonview's net cash inflow from the settlement assuming its tax rate is 21 percent.

LO 6-2   2. For each of the following businesses, indicate the choice of taxable year corresponding to the end of each business's natural business cycle. Your choices should match one of the following options: February 28 year-end, May 31 year-end, September 30 year-end, December 31 year-end.

  a. An upholstery business whose activity is not seasonal.

  b. A ski and snowboard training facility.

  c. A retail clothing and accessories shop.

  d. A beach-front bar and restaurant in New Jersey.

LO 6-1, 6-4   3. Assuming a 21 percent marginal tax rate, compute the after-tax cost of the following business expenses:

   a. $5,600 premium on business property and casualty insurance.

   b. $1,200 fine paid for business entertainment.

   c. $3,700 premium on key-person life insurance.

   d. $50,000 political contribution.

   e. $7,800 client meals not provided by a restaurant.

LO 6-1, 6-4   4. Northwest Company has average gross receipts of $50 million annually. This year, Northwest incurred $10.5 million of net business interest and has adjusted taxable income of $29 million. Compute Northwest's current deduction for business interest and the amount of any business interest carryforward.

LO 6-1, 6-4   5. FruAgro Company has average annual gross receipts of $30 million annually. This year, FruAgro earned $1 million of business interest income, incurred $7 million of business interest expense and has adjusted taxable income of $17 million. Compute FruAgro's current deduction for business interest and the amount of any business interest carryforward.

LO 6-5   6. Besito Company, a calendar year, cash basis taxpayer, leases lawn and garden equipment. During December, it received the following cash payments. To what extent does each payment represent current taxable income to Besito?

   a. $522 repayment of a loan from an employee. Besito loaned $500 to the employee six months ago, and the employee repaid the loan with interest.

   b. $600 deposit from a customer who rented mechanical equipment. Besito must return the entire deposit when the customer returns the undamaged equipment.

   c. $10,000 short-term loan from a local bank. Besito gave the bank a written note to repay the loan in one year at 5 percent interest.

   d. $888 prepaid rent from the customer described in part(b). The rent is $12 per day for the 74-day period from December 17 through February 28.

LO 6-5   7. Firm F is a cash basis legal firm. In 2021, it performed services for a client, mailed the client a bill for $6,150, and recorded a $6,150 receivable. In 2022, Firm F discovered that the client was under criminal indictment and had fled the country. After learning this news, it wrote off the receivable.

   a. What was the effect of the recording of the account receivable on Firm F's taxable income?

   b. What was the effect of the write-off on Firm F's taxable income?

LO 6-5   8. Firm Q operates a cash basis consulting business. In October, Firm Q billed a client for $23,400 of consulting services. In November, the client settled the bill by paying $10,000 cash and transferring marketable securities worth $13,400 to Firm Q. How much taxable income does Firm Q recognize on settlement of the bill?

LO 6-5, 6-6   9. RTY is a calendar year corporation. On December 12, RTY billed a client $17,800 for services rendered during October and November. It had not received payment by December 31. On December 10, RTY received a $4,000 check from a tenant that leases office space from the corporation. The payment was for next year's January and February rent.

   a. If RTY is a cash basis taxpayer, how much income should it recognize from the given transactions this year?

   b. If RTY is an accrual basis taxpayer, how much income should it recognize from the given transactions this year?

LO 6-5, 6-6   10. Malo, Inc. uses a fiscal year ending June 30. On May 29, Malo received a check for $3,900 from a business that leases parking spaces in Malo's parking garage. This payment was for the three-month period beginning June 1. On June 15, Malo sent an invoice for $5,500 to a customer for services rendered during May and June. Malo received payment from the customer on July 3.

    a. If Malo is a cash basis taxpayer, how much income should it recognize from the given transactions in the current fiscal year?

    b. If Malo is an accrual basis taxpayer, how much income should it recognize from the given transactions in the current fiscal year?

LO 6-5   11. Brillo Company uses the calendar year and the cash method of accounting. On December 29, 2023, Brillo made the following cash payments. To what extent can Brillo deduct the payment in 2023?

    a. $50,000 for a two-year office lease beginning on February 1, 2024.

    b. $79,000 of inventory items held for sale to customers.

    c. $1,800 to purchase a new refrigerator for the employees' lounge. The refrigerator was delivered on January 8, 2024.

    d. $4,800 retainer to a consultant who spent three weeks in January 2024 analyzing Brillo's internal control system.

    e. $22,300 property tax to the local government for the first six months of 2024.

LO 6-5, 6-6   12. Nunez Company, a retail hardware store, began business in August and elected a calendar year for tax purposes. From August through December, Nunez paid $319,000 for inventory to stock the store. According to a physical inventory count on December 31, Nunez had $64,600 of inventory on hand. Compute Nunez's cost of goods sold for its first year assuming

    a. Nunez adopted the cash method as its overall method of accounting.

    b. Nunez adopted the accrual method as its overall method of accounting.

LO 6-5   13. LSG Company is a calendar year, cash basis taxpayer. On November 1, 2023, LSG paid $9,450 cash to the janitorial service firm that cleans LSG's administrative offices and retail stores. How much of this expenditure can LSG deduct in 2023 assuming that

    a. The expenditure is a prepayment for six months of cleaning services from November 2023 through April 2024?

    b. The expenditure is a prepayment for 18 months of cleaning services from November 2023 through April 2025?

LO 6-5   14. Warren Company is a calendar year, cash basis firm. On December 6, 2023, Warren paid $7,200 cash to a landscape service business that maintains the lawns and gardens around Warren's headquarters. How much of this expenditure can Warren deduct in 2023 assuming that

    a. The expenditure is a prepayment for four months of landscape maintenance beginning May 1, 2024?

    b. The expenditure is a prepayment for 12 months of landscape maintenance beginning May 1, 2024?

LO 6-5, 6-6   15. Firm F, a calendar year taxpayer, owes a $200,000 long-term debt to an unrelated creditor. In December, it paid $14,160 to the creditor as interest for the 12-month period from the prior September 1 through August 31 of the following year. Compute the deduction for this payment assuming that

    a. Firm F uses the cash method of accounting for tax purposes.

    b. Firm F uses the accrual method of accounting for tax purposes.

LO 6-5, 6-6   16. Wahoo, Inc., a calendar year taxpayer, leases equipment to a customer for $4,500 monthly rent. On November 27, 2023, Wahoo received a $36,000 rent payment for the eight-month period beginning on December 1. How much of the payment must Wahoo recognize as 2023 taxable income assuming that

    a. Wahoo uses the cash method of accounting for tax purposes?

    b. Wahoo uses the accrual method of accounting for tax purposes?

LO 6-7, 6-9   17. EFG, an accrual basis, calendar year corporation, reported $500,000 net income before tax on its financial statements prepared in accordance with GAAP. EFG's records reveal the following information:

- The allowance for bad debts as of January 1 was $58,000. Write-offs for the year totaled $13,800, and the addition to the allowance for the year was $12,500. The allowance as of December 31 was $56,700.

- EFG paid a $17,500 fine to the state of Delaware for a violation of state pollution control laws.

- EFG was sued by a consumers' group for engaging in false advertising practices. Although EFG's lawyers are convinced that the suit is frivolous, its independent auditors insisted on establishing a $50,000 allowance for contingent legal liability and reporting a $50,000 accrued expense on the income statement.

- EFG received a $165,000 advanced payment for 10,000 units of inventory on October 20. EFG reported the payment as revenue the following February when the units were shipped.

Compute EFG's taxable income.

LO 6-8   18. Using a 21 percent rate, compute the deferred tax asset or deferred tax liability (if any) resulting from the following:

    a. A transaction resulting in a $31,000 temporary excess of book income over taxable income.

    b. A transaction resulting in an $18,400 permanent excess of book income over taxable income.

    c. A transaction resulting in a $55,000 temporary excess of taxable income over book income.

LO 6-8   19. GT, Inc.'s net income before tax on its financial statements was $700,000, and its taxable income was $810,000. The $110,000 difference is the aggregate of temporary book/tax differences. GT's tax rate is 21 percent.

    a. Compute GT's tax expense for financial statement purposes.

    b. Compute GT's tax payable.

    c. Compute the net increase in GT's deferred tax assets or deferred tax liabilities (identify which) for the year.

LO 6-8   20. Corporation H's auditors prepared the following reconciliation between book and taxable income. H's tax rate is 21 percent.

Net income before tax	$600,000
Permanent book/tax differences	15,000
Temporary book/tax differences	(76,000)
Taxable income	$539,000

    a. Compute Corporation H's tax expense for financial statement purposes.

    b. Compute Corporation H's tax payable.

    c. Compute the net increase in Corporation H's deferred tax assets or deferred tax liabilities (identify which) for the year.

LO 6-8   21. Yount, Inc.'s auditors prepared the following reconciliation between book and taxable income. Yount's tax rate is 21 percent.

Net income before tax	$378,200
Permanent book/tax differences	(33,500)
Temporary book/tax differences	112,400
Taxable income	$457,100

    a. Compute Yount's tax expense for financial statement purposes.

    b. Compute Yount's tax payable.

    c. Compute the net increase in Yount's deferred tax assets or deferred tax liabilities (identify which) for the year.

LO 6-7, 6-8, 6-9   22. Micro, an accrual basis corporation, reported $505,100 net income before tax on its financial statements prepared in accordance with GAAP. Micro's records reveal the following information:

- Micro paid $25,000 in legal fees and $100,000 to a former employee to settle a claim of sexual harassment. To avoid negative publicity, Micro insisted that the settlement include a confidentiality agreement.

- Late in the year, Micro entered into a five-year licensing agreement with an unrelated firm. The agreement entitles the firm to use a Micro trade name in marketing its own product. In return, the firm will pay Micro an annual royalty of 1 percent of gross revenues from sales of the product. The firm paid a $40,000 advanced royalty to Micro on the day the agreement was finalized. For financial statement purposes, this prepayment was credited to an unearned revenue account.

- In December of the current year, Micro received a $5,000 advance payment on rental income from a tenant to whom Micro sublets some of its unused office space. The payment relates to use of the rented space in January and February of the coming year. For financial accounting purposes, this prepayment was credited to an unearned revenue account.

- At its final meeting for the year, Micro's board of directors authorized a $15,500 salary bonus for the corporation's president as a reward for outstanding performance. Micro paid the bonus on January 12. The president doesn't own enough Micro stock to be considered a related party for federal tax purposes.

- Micro was incorporated last year. On its first tax return, it reported a $21,400 net operating loss.

Compute Micro's taxable income.

LO 6-9   23. GreenUp, a calendar year, accrual basis taxpayer, provides landscaping installation and maintenance services to its customers. In August 2023, GreenUp contracted with a university to renovate its lawns and gardens. GreenUp agreed to complete the entire renovation by May 31, 2025, and the university prepaid the entire $100,000 fee. GreenUp completed 20 percent of the work in 2023, 65 percent in 2024, and 15 percent in 2025.

    a. How much revenue should GreenUp report on its financial statements for 2023, 2024, and 2025?

    b. How much taxable income must GreenUp recognize in 2023, 2024, and 2025?

LO 6-9   24. Cornish, Inc. is an accrual basis, calendar year taxpayer. In December, a flood damaged one of Cornish's warehouses, and Cornish contracted with a construction company to repair the damage. The company estimated that the cost of the repairs could range from $20,000 to $100,000, depending on the severity of the damage. The contract provides that the maximum amount that the company will charge is $100,000. On December 19, the company sent Cornish its first progress bill for $7,200, which Cornish paid on January 8. Cornish's auditors required Cornish to accrue $65,000 of estimated repair expense on its current year financial statements. Compute Cornish's current year tax deduction for repairs.

LO 6-9 25. KLP, a calendar year corporation, sponsored a contest for its customers with a grand prize of $100,000 cash. Contestants could enter the contest from June 1 through November 30. KLP selected the winner and announced their name on December 20. However, it didn't present a $100,000 check to the winner until January 13. In which year can KLP deduct the $100,000 payment assuming

    a. KLP uses the cash method of accounting?

    b. KLP uses the accrual method of accounting?

LO 6-9 26. Ernlo is an accrual basis corporation with a June 30 fiscal year-end. On June 2, 2023, Ernlo entered into a binding contract to purchase a six-month supply of heating oil from a local distributor at the current market price of $12,450. This price is guaranteed regardless of the market price on the delivery date. Ernlo didn't pay its $12,450 bill from the supplier until July 8, and the distributor delivered the oil on October 15.

    a. In which taxable year can Ernlo deduct its $12,450 cost of heating oil if it doesn't elect the recurring item exception as its method of accounting for this annual expense?

    b. In which taxable year can Ernlo deduct its $12,450 cost for heating oil if it elects the recurring item exception?

LO 6-9 27. HomeSafe, an accrual basis, calendar year corporation, sells and installs home alarm systems. The contract price of a system includes four free service calls. HomeSafe's cost of each call is $75. At the end of 2023, HomeSafe accrued a $48,900 expense and a $48,900 liability for future service calls for systems sold in 2023. By September 15, 2024, HomeSafe had made 362 service calls for 2023 systems; from September 16 through December 31, 2024, HomeSafe made 122 additional service calls for 2023 systems.

    a. If HomeSafe has not adopted the recurring item exception as its method of accounting for service calls, how much of the $48,900 accrued expense can it deduct in 2023 and 2024?

    b. If HomeSafe has adopted the recurring item exception as its method of accounting for service calls, how much of the $48,900 accrued expense can it deduct in 2023 and 2024?

LO 6-9 28. BZD, a calendar year corporation, made the following year-end accruals for 2023 financial statement purposes. In each case, determine how much of the accrued expense is deductible on BZD's 2023 federal tax return.

    a. $55,000 expense and $55,000 liability for unpaid December salaries. BZD paid the entire liability to its employees before the end of January 2024.

    b. $40,000 expense and $40,000 liability for the CEO's 2023 bonus. BZD paid $20,000 to the CEO on March 1, 2024, and the remaining $20,000 on May 1, 2024. BZD and the CEO are not related parties.

    c. $219,700 expense and $219,700 liability for accumulated vacation pay. No employees took vacation between January 1 and March 15, 2024.

LO 6-9 29. Parmco, a calendar year corporation, made the following accruals for 2023 financial statement purposes. In each case, determine how much of the accrued expense is deductible on Parmco's 2023 federal tax return.

    a. $30,000 expense and $30,000 liability for Henry Parmenter's 2023 performance bonus. Henry is Parmco's president and sole shareholder. The corporation paid the bonus on January 20, 2024.

b. $10,000 expense and $10,000 liability for Susan Colter's 2023 performance bonus. Susan is Parmco's treasurer; she is not a relative of Henry Parmenter. The corporation paid the bonus on April 1, 2024.

c. $591,000 expense and $591,000 liability for unpaid December salaries. Parmco paid the entire amount to its workforce on January 5, 2024.

LO 6-9 30. In 2022, AS, an accrual basis corporation, contracted with a nationally prominent artist to paint a mural in the lobby of the new corporate headquarters under construction. The artist's commission was $180,000, payable on completion of the mural. The artist finished the work and received the $180,000 commission in 2024. AS has a 21 percent marginal tax rate and uses a 7 percent discount rate to compute NPV.

a. Compute AS's after-tax cost of the commission if it can deduct the $180,000 accrued expense in 2022.

b. Compute AS's after-tax cost of the commission if the economic performance requirement delays the deduction until 2024.

LO 6-9 31. Extronic, a calendar year, accrual basis corporation, reported a $41,900 liability for accrued 2022 state income tax on its December 31, 2022, balance sheet. Extronic made the following state income tax payments during 2023:

March 8	Balance due of 2022 tax	$41,900
April 14	1st estimate 2023 state tax	58,000
June 12	2nd estimate 2023 state tax	58,000
September 15	3rd estimate 2023 state tax	58,000
December 13	4th estimate 2023 state tax	58,000

On December 27, Extronic's tax department calculated that the corporation's actual 2023 state income tax liability was $251,200. Consequently, Extronic accrued a $19,200 liability for state tax payable at year-end. Extronic paid this balance due on March 11, 2024.

a. If Extronic has not adopted the recurring item exception as its method of accounting for state income tax, compute its 2023 deduction for state income tax.

b. If Extronic has adopted the recurring item exception as its method of accounting for state income tax, compute its 2023 deduction for state income tax.

LO 6-9 32. Company N, an accrual basis taxpayer, owes $90,000 to Creditor K. At the end of 2022, Company N accrued $7,740 interest payable on this debt. It didn't pay this liability until March 3, 2023. Both Company N and Creditor K are calendar year taxpayers. For each of the following cases, determine the year in which Company N can deduct the $7,740 interest expense:

a. Creditor K is a cash basis taxpayer, and Company N and Creditor K are related parties.

b. Creditor K is an accrual basis taxpayer, and Company N and Creditor K are related parties.

c. Creditor K is a cash basis taxpayer, and Company N and Creditor K are unrelated parties.

LO 6-9 33. Acme is an accrual basis corporation. Mrs. Torres, Acme's chief financial officer, is a cash basis individual. In December 2022, Acme's board of directors decided that Mrs. Torres should receive a $20,000 bonus as additional compensation. Acme paid the $20,000 bonus to Mrs. Torres on January 12, 2023. In which year can Acme deduct the $20,000 bonus assuming that

a. Mrs. Torres owns no Acme stock?

b. Mrs. Torres owns 63 percent of Acme stock?

LO 6-9 34. GK Company, a calendar year, accrual basis taxpayer, made the following adjustments to its allowance for bad debts this year:

January 1 allowance for bad debts	$86,100
Actual write-offs of accounts receivable	(77,300)
Addition to allowance at year-end	90,000
December 31 allowance for bad debts	$98,800

    a. Compute GK's bad debt expense for financial statement purposes.

    b. Compute GK's tax deduction for bad debts.

LO 6-9 35. ZEJ, a calendar year, accrual basis taxpayer, made the following adjustments to its allowance for bad debts this year:

January 1 allowance for bad debts	$895,000
Actual write-offs of accounts receivable	(840,000)
Addition to allowance at year-end	770,000
December 31 allowance for bad debts	$825,000

    a. Compute ZEJ's bad debt expense for financial statement purposes.

    b. Compute ZEJ's tax deduction for bad debts.

LO 6-9 36. MG is an accrual basis corporation. In 2022, it wrote off a $65,000 account receivable as uncollectible. In 2023, it received a $65,000 check from the creditor in full payment of this receivable.

    a. What was the effect of the write-off on MG's 2022 financial statement income and taxable income?

    b. What was the effect of the collection of the receivable on MG's 2023 financial statement income and taxable income?

LO 6-10 37. TRW, Inc. began business in 2021 and incurred net operating losses for its first two years. In 2023, it became profitable. The following table shows TRW's taxable income *before consideration of these NOLs:*

	2021	2022	2023	2024	2025	2026	2027	2028
Taxable income	$(420,000)	$(358,000)	$81,000	$41,000	$210,000	$298,000	$387,000	$905,000

Recompute TRW's taxable income for 2023 through 2028 after its allowable net operating loss deduction.

LO 6-10 38. For its first taxable year, Rony, Inc.'s accounting records showed the following:

Operating loss per books	$(800,000)
Temporary book/tax difference	90,000
Net operating loss for tax	$(710,000)

    a. Use a 21 percent rate to compute Rony's deferred tax asset with respect to the $90,000 book/tax difference.

    b. Use a 21 percent rate to compute Rony's deferred tax asset with respect to its $710,000 NOL carryforward.

    c. Compute Rony's tax benefit (negative tax expense) reported on its first income statement.

LO 6-10   39. Refer to the facts in the preceding example. For its second taxable year, Rony, Inc.'s accounting records showed the following:

Net income before tax	$1,200,000
Reversal of year 1 book/tax difference	(90,000)
Taxable income before NOL deduction	$1,110,000
NOL deduction	(710,000)
Taxable income	$ 400,000

   a. Use a 21 percent rate to compute Rony's tax expense for financial statement purposes.

   b. Use a 21 percent rate to compute Rony's tax payable.

   c. Compute Rony's reduction in its deferred tax assets.

LO 6-11   40. Margaret, a married taxpayer filing a joint return, engaged in two business activities this year. Business A earned $400,000 of profit. Business B incurred a loss of $(995,000). How much of Margaret's net business loss is not currently deductible?

LO 6-11   41. Jahlil is a 10 percent partner in a partnership that incurred a $4 million business loss this year. Jahlil has no other business activities. How much of Jahlil's partnership loss can he deduct this year if he is single? What if he is married filing jointly?

LO 6-10   42. Grimes Corporation began business in 2017 and incurred losses for its first two years. In 2019, it became profitable. The following table shows Grimes's taxable income before consideration of its NOLs:

	2017	**2018**	**2019**	**2020**	**2021**	**2022**
Taxable income	$(820,000)	$(254,000)	$320,000	$541,000	$210,000	$298,000

Recompute Grimes's taxable income for 2019 through 2022 after its allowable net operating loss deduction.

Issue Recognition Problems

Identify the tax issue or issues suggested by the following situations, and state each issue in the form of a question.

LO 6-1, 6-6   1. In October 2018, Firm G completed a consulting engagement and received a $200,000 cash payment for its services. In December, the client notified Firm G that it was unsatisfied with the work and demanded that Firm G refund $50,000 of the payment. Firm G refused and referred the matter to its attorney. In 2023, Firm G settled the dispute by paying the client $30,000. Firm G's 2017 marginal tax rate was 39 percent, and its 2023 marginal tax rate was 21 percent.

LO 6-1   2. Corporation DS owns assets worth $550,000 and has $750,000 outstanding debts. One of DS's creditors just informed DS that it is writing off a $15,000 account receivable from DS because it believes the receivable is uncollectible. However, even with this debt discharge, DS is insolvent and has no net worth.

LO 6-1   3. Two years ago, a professional theater company paid $300 to an antique dealer for an old oil painting that the company used as a prop. This year, the company's prop manager was cleaning the painting and discovered an older painting hidden beneath the top coat of pigment. To the company's delight, the older painting was signed by Paul Cézanne. Two independent appraisers determined that the painting is worth at least $250,000.

LO 6-3   4. BL, Inc. has been in business since 2000. This year, BL's new CPA discovered that it is using an incorrect accounting method for a certain expense. BL is willing to change to the correct accounting method recommended by the CPA.

LO 6-5, 6-6   5. Company A, a calendar year taxpayer, has always used the cash method of accounting. It completed an engagement for a major client in November 2022 and submitted a bill for its $160,000 fee. Because Company A didn't receive payment before year-end, it recognized no income from the engagement on its 2022 tax return. In January 2023, Company A received permission from the IRS to change from the cash method to the accrual method. This change is effective for 2023. On February 2, 2023, Company A received a $160,000 check from the client in payment of the bill.

LO 6-5   6. Mr. Rathore owns a consulting firm that uses a calendar year and the cash method. In November, Mr. Rathore billed a client $3,500 for services performed in September. After waiting several weeks, he called the client to remind her of the bill. The embarrassed client promised to telephone Mr. Rathore as soon as she prepared a check for $3,500. Mr. Rathore left his business office on December 23 and didn't return until January 2. A message on his answering machine said that he could pick up his check from the client's receptionist. The message was dated December 30.

LO 6-6   7. Every December, Maxo, Inc., an accrual basis, calendar year corporation, purchases 3,500 calendars from a publisher and mails them to its customers as a holiday gift. This year, Maxo received a $14,420 bill from the publisher, which represented a sizable price increase from prior years. Maxo scheduled a January meeting with the publisher to discuss the contested bill.

LO 6-6   8. In 2021, Firm K paid $129,000 real property tax to Jurisdiction J and deducted the payment. In 2023, it successfully contested the property tax assessment. As a result, Jurisdiction J refunded $18,000 of the property tax.

LO 6-10   9. ABC Partnership owns 100 percent of the stock of two corporations, HT (an advertising firm) and LT (a commercial real estate development firm). HT is in a 35 percent marginal tax bracket. LT has an NOL carryforward deduction and will pay no tax this year. HT recently developed a new advertising campaign for LT and charged $75,000 for its services.

LO 6-11   10. Corporation WJ began business in 2022 and elected S corporation status. This year, it operated at a significant loss, flowing through $(624,000) of ordinary business loss to its sole shareholder, William Jones.

LO 6-10   11. BL and TM are both calendar year corporations. On January 1, 2023, BL purchased TM's entire business (all TM's balance sheet assets), and TM's shareholders dissolved the corporation under state law. As of January 1, TM had a $190,000 NOL carryforward. BL's business for 2023 (which includes the business purchased from TM) generated $600,000 taxable income.

Research Problems

LO 6-1, 6-6   1. Bontaine Publications, an accrual basis, calendar year corporation, publishes and sells weekly and monthly magazines to retail bookstores and newsstands. The sales agreement provides that the retailers may return any unsold magazines during the one-month period after purchase. Bontaine will refund one-half of the purchase price of each returned magazine. During December 2023, Bontaine recorded $919,400 of magazine sales. During January 2024, Bontaine refunded $82,717 to retailers that returned magazines purchased during December. Can Bontaine reduce its 2023 income by the refund paid?

LO 6-1, 6-6   2. CheapTrade, an accrual basis, calendar year corporation, operates a discount securities brokerage business. CheapTrade accepts orders to buy or sell marketable securities for its customers and charges them a commission fee for effecting the transaction in a timely, low-cost manner. CheapTrade executes an order on the "trade" date, but title to the securities is not legally transferred, and payment to or from the customer is not due until the "settlement date." In the normal five-day interval between the trade and settlement dates, CheapTrade performs administrative and accounting functions to record the transaction. During the last week of 2023, CheapTrade effected over 18,000 transactions with a trading date in 2023 but a settlement date in 2024. CheapTrade's commission from these transactions was $1,712,400. In which year should CheapTrade recognize this income?

LO 6-6   3. Moleri, an accrual basis corporation with a fiscal taxable year ending on July 31, owns real estate on which it pays annual property tax to Madison County, Texas. The county assesses the tax for the upcoming calendar year on January 1, and the tax becomes a lien on the property as of the assessment date. Property owners have until March 31 to pay the tax without penalty. Moleri paid its 2023 property tax of $29,820 on March 11, 2023. How much of this tax payment is deductible on Moleri's tax return for the fiscal year ending July 31, 2023?

LO 6-6, 6-9   4. Jetex, an accrual basis, calendar year corporation, engages in the business of long-distance freight hauling. Every year, Jetex is required to purchase several hundred permits and licenses from state and local governments in order to legally operate its fleet of trucks. During 2023, the cost of these permits and licenses totaled $1,119,200. Even though none of the permits and licenses was valid for more than 12 months, a substantial number of them didn't expire until sometime in 2024. In fact, Jetex calculated that $612,000 of the total cost incurred in 2023 actually benefited the company in 2024. For financial statement purposes, Jetex capitalized this amount as an asset and expensed only the $507,200 remainder on its 2023 income statement. As an accrual basis taxpayer, is Jetex limited to a $507,200 deduction in 2023?

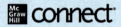 **All applicable Tax Planning Cases are available with *Connect*.**

Tax Planning Cases

LO 6-5   1. Company Y began business in February 2023. By the end of the calendar year, it had billed its clients for $3.5 million of services and had incurred $800,000 of operating expenses. As of December 31, it had collected $2.9 million of its billings and had paid $670,000 of its expenses. It expects to collect the remaining outstanding bills and pay the remaining expenses by March 2024. Company Y adopted a calendar year for federal tax purposes. It may use either the cash method or the accrual method of accounting on its first tax return, and it has asked you to quantify the value of using the cash method for the first year. In doing so, assume Company Y uses a 5 percent discount rate to compute NPV.

LO 6-10   2. Corporation VB was formed in 2023. Immediately prior to year-end, VB is considering a $500,000 deductible expenditure. It can either make the expenditure before the end of 2023, or wait until 2024. However, if it waits, the cost of the expenditure will increase to $525,000. Before considering this expenditure, VB has the following projected pre-tax cash flows and taxable income for 2023, 2024, and 2025:

	2023	*2024*	*2025*
Taxable income and pretax cash flow	$120,000	$400,000	$700,000

   a. Using a 5 percent discount rate, compute the NPV of VB's after-tax cash flows if the expenditure is in 2023.

   b. Using a 5 percent discount rate, compute the NPV of VB's after-tax cash flows if the expenditure is in 2024.

   c. Based on your calculations, when should VB make this expenditure?

Chapter **Seven**

Property Acquisitions and Cost Recovery Deductions

Learning Objectives

After studying this chapter, you should be able to:

LO 7-1. Decide if a business expenditure should be deducted or capitalized.

LO 7-2. Define *tax basis* and *adjusted basis*.

LO 7-3. Explain how leverage can reduce the after-tax cost of assets.

LO 7-4. Compute cost of goods sold for tax purposes.

LO 7-5. Describe and apply the MACRS framework.

LO 7-6. Determine the limitation on depreciation of passenger automobiles.

LO 7-7. Calculate the Section 179 deduction and bonus depreciation.

LO 7-8. Incorporate depreciation deductions into the NPV computation.

LO 7-9. Explain how the cost of intangibles is recovered through amortization.

LO 7-10. Distinguish between cost depletion and percentage depletion.

LO 7-11. Explain cost recovery–related book/tax differences and their effect on GAAP financial statements.

In Chapter 6, we learned that taxable income equals the excess of gross income over allowable deductions. We also learned that firms are allowed to deduct their business expenditures over the period of time that the expenditures create value for the firm. If an expenditure benefits the firm only in the current year, the expenditure is generally allowed as a current deduction. If an expenditure will benefit the firm for more than one taxable year, the deduction for the expenditure must be properly matched against future gross income.

In this chapter, we address this timing issue: In which taxable year or years can a firm deduct its expenditures? This chapter begins with a discussion of the tax rules that distinguish between deductible expenditures and expenditures that must be capitalized. The discussion then turns to the concept of capitalized costs as the tax basis of business assets. The relationship between basis and cost recovery deductions is explored, and the effect of cost recovery deductions on cash flows is examined. The second part of this chapter focuses on the various methods by which firms recover basis as cost of goods sold or through depreciation, amortization, and depletion deductions.

DEDUCTIBLE EXPENSE OR CAPITALIZED COST?

When a firm expends resources as part of its income-generating activity, the financial cost of the expenditure is reduced by any tax savings from the expenditure. In present value terms, tax savings are usually maximized (and after-tax cost is minimized) if the expenditure is deductible in the current year. The present value of the tax savings decreases if the firm must capitalize the expenditure and postpone its deduction until some future year. For tax accounting purposes, **capitalization** means that an expenditure is recorded as an asset on the balance sheet rather than as a current expense. If the firm is never allowed any tax deduction for the capitalized expenditure, the before-tax cost of the expenditure equals its after-tax cost.

Absent any restrictions, firms would immediately deduct every business expenditure. However, a basic premise of the federal income tax is that *no expenditure is deductible* unless the Internal Revenue Code authorizes the deduction. The Supreme Court has elaborated on this premise by observing that "an income tax deduction is a matter of legislative grace" and "the burden of clearly showing the right to the claimed deduction is on the taxpayer."[1] These observations are consistent with the tax law's conservative attitude toward the measurement of taxable income.

The Internal Revenue Code does allow firms to deduct all "ordinary and necessary expenses paid or incurred during the taxable year in carrying on any trade or business."[2] Because of this generic rule, firms deduct routine operating expenses in the year incurred under the firm's method of accounting. But the Code also prohibits a deduction for payments for "permanent improvements or betterments made to increase the value of any property."[3] As we will learn later in this chapter, the law relaxes this prohibition by allowing firms to recover many capital expenditures in the form of *future* deductions. In these cases, the difference in the tax consequences of current expenses and capitalized costs is the timing of the deduction for each. Even so, in cash flow terms, future deductions are worth less than current deductions, and firms minimize their cost of operations by deducting expenditures as soon as possible.

LO 7-1
Decide if a business expenditure should be deducted or capitalized.

What factors determine whether a particular business expenditure is treated as a current deduction or a capital cost? If the expenditure creates or enhances a distinct asset with a useful life substantially beyond the current year, the expenditure must be capitalized.[4] Even if the expenditure does not create or enhance a specific asset, the expenditure must be capitalized if it results in a significant long-term benefit to the firm.[5] Moreover, if the tax treatment of an expenditure is uncertain, capitalization is the norm while deductibility is the exception.[6]

The following example quantifies the difference between deduction and capitalization in cash flow terms.

---

[1] *Interstate Transit Lines v. Commissioner*, 319 U.S. 590, 593 (1943).

[2] 26 U.S. Code §162(a).

[3] 26 U.S. Code §263(a).

[4] *Commissioner v. Lincoln Savings & Loan Assn.*, 403 U.S. 345 (1971).

[5] *Indopco Inc. v. Commissioner*, 503 U.S. 79 (1992).

[6] Ibid.

Current Deduction versus Capitalized Cost

This year, Corporation M raised $1 million of new capital by issuing preferred stock to a group of private investors.[7] The corporation incurred $40,000 of legal and other professional fees related to this transaction. Corporation M's marginal tax rate is 21 percent. Compare the after-tax cash flows under two different assumptions concerning the tax treatment of the $40,000 expenditure:

	Current Deduction	Capitalized Cost
Proceeds of stock issue	$1,000,000	$1,000,000
Professional fees	(40,000)	(40,000)
Tax savings ($40,000 deduction × 21%)	8,400	–0–
After-tax cash flow	$ 968,400	$ 960,000

In this example, the $40,000 expenditure did not create or enhance a new asset for Corporation M. However, the federal courts have consistently ruled that expenses related to raising capital or reorganizing a firm's capital structure benefit the firm for the duration of its existence and are not deductible.[8] On the basis of this rule of law, Corporation M must charge the $40,000 expenditure against the proceeds of the stock sale, which nets $960,000 for the corporation on an after-tax basis.

Repairs and Cleanup Costs

Every firm that owns tangible operating assets must make incidental repairs and perform routine maintenance to keep the assets in good working order. Repair and maintenance costs that are regular and recurring in nature and do not materially add to either the value or the useful life of an asset are deductible.[9] In contrast, expenditures that substantially increase the value or useful life of an asset are nondeductible capital improvements. Similarly, the expense of adapting an existing asset to a new or different use must be capitalized to the cost of the asset.[10] The distinction between a repair and a capital improvement is not always obvious and is frequently a matter of dispute between taxpayers and the Internal Revenue Service.

Repair or Capital Improvement

Out of concern for earthquake safety, the city of San Francisco required the Fairmont Hotel to either remove or replace the concrete parapets and cornices that had decorated the hotel's exterior since 1907. The hotel spent $3 million to replace the old parapets and cornices with replicas made of lightweight fiberglass. The Fairmont Hotel deducted the expenditure as a repair. The IRS concluded that the expenditure was a capital improvement to the building and disallowed the deduction. In court, the Fairmont's owners argued that the $3 million expenditure was necessary to maintain the classical appearance of the building and to preserve its identity as a "grand hotel of the world." Moreover, the expenditure was not voluntary but was required by city ordinance. In spite of these arguments, the court agreed with the IRS that the expenditure materially prolonged the life and increased the value of the Fairmont Hotel and was not deductible.[11]

---

[7] Corporations do not recognize gain on the receipt of cash in exchange for stock. §1032.

[8] See *General Bancshares Corp.* v. *Commissioner,* 326 F.2d 712 (CA-8, 1964) and *Mills Estate, Inc.* v. *Commissioner,* 206 F.2d 244 (CA-2, 1953).

[9] Reg. §1.162-4.

[10] Reg. §1.263(a)-3(l).

[11] *Swig Investment Co.* v. *United States,* 98 F.3d 1359 (CA-FC, 1996).

The business community and the IRS are constantly debating the proper treatment of environmental cleanup costs. Many firms, either voluntarily or because of government mandate, are spending millions of dollars to clean up pollutants, toxic wastes, and other dangerous substances unleashed on the environment as industrial by-products. The firms argue that cleanup costs should be currently deductible, while the IRS maintains that many such costs must be capitalized.

Deductible Cleanup Costs	Lako Transport, Inc. purchased farmland in 1980 and constructed a trucking depot on the land. Over the next two decades, the depot generated hazardous wastes that were buried on the land. Three years ago, Lako began the process of remediating the soil and groundwater contaminated by the waste. It excavated and disposed of the contaminated soil and then backfilled the excavation with clean soil. Lako also constructed a groundwater treatment plant to cleanse the contaminated groundwater. The IRS ruled that the costs of remediating the soil did not prolong the land's useful life or increase its value. Instead, the costs merely returned the land to its original condition. The costs are analogous to repairs, and Lako can deduct them as ordinary and necessary expenses. In contrast, the costs of constructing the groundwater treatment plant are capital expenditures that create a new asset for Lako.[12]
Capitalized Cleanup Costs	PNT Company purchased real property from a dry cleaning business. Two months later, PNT discovered that the soil and groundwater were contaminated with dry cleaning fluid that had been improperly stored by the former owners. PNT incurred substantial costs, including legal and consulting fees, laboratory testing fees, supplies, and labor to decontaminate the land. PNT could not use the real property in its own business until the cleanup process was complete. Unlike Lako in the previous example, PNT acquired the property *in its contaminated state*. Therefore, the IRS ruled that the remediation of the soil and groundwater represented a permanent improvement that increased the value of the land to PNT. Consequently, PNT had to capitalize the cleanup costs as part of the cost of the land.[13]
Asbestos Replacement	Company NM replaced the asbestos insulation in all its manufacturing equipment with non-hazardous insulation and deducted the replacement expense. The company justified the deduction because the replacement was made to protect the health of its employees and did not improve the operating efficiency or increase the value of the equipment. Furthermore, the replacement expense remedied a historic problem and was not related to the generation of future income. Upon audit, the IRS concluded that the asbestos replacement did, in fact, result in a long-term benefit to Company NM by permanently improving the work environment. Therefore, the IRS required the company to capitalize the replacement expense to the cost of the reinsulated equipment.[14]

In September 2013, the IRS issued final regulations providing a framework for distinguishing capital expenditures from supplies, repairs, maintenance, and other deductible business expenses. In addition, the regulations provide important safe harbors permitting deductibility of (1) *de minimis* expenditures, (2) routine maintenance, and (3) certain building improvements by qualifying small taxpayers.

[12] Rev. Rul. 94-38, 1994-1 C.B. 35.

[13] IRS Letter Ruling 200108029 (February 23, 2001).

[14] IRS Letter Ruling 9240004 (July 29, 1992).

Safe Harbor Deduction for De Minimis Expenditures	Granite Corporation is a public company preparing audited financial statements and filing Form 10-K with the SEC. For book purposes, Granite has adopted a written accounting policy of expensing purchases of tangible property with a per-item cost of $5,000 or less.
	During the current year, Granite purchased items costing $267,000 with a per-item cost below the $5,000 threshold. It expensed these costs in preparing its financial statements.
	For tax purposes, Granite may elect to deduct these costs under the *de minimis* safe harbor, which provides a deduction for expenditures not exceeding a per-item amount. For corporations producing public financial statements, the per-item maximum is $5,000. For taxpayers without such financials, the per-item maximum is $2,500. Thus, Granite may deduct the entire $267,000 on its current year tax return.

Building Improvement Deduction by Qualifying Small Taxpayers	Ranger Corporation has average annual gross receipts less than $10 million. During the current year, it paid $8,000 for improvements to a building used in its business. The building originally cost $450,000.
	For tax purposes, Ranger may deduct the cost of such improvements, not to exceed the lesser of (a) $10,000 or (b) 2 percent of the building's unadjusted basis. Thus, Ranger is permitted a current deduction for the $8,000 of building improvements.

Deductions of Capital Expenditures as Subsidies

The tax law contains special rules permitting firms to deduct expenditures that clearly are capital in nature. These preferential rules reduce the firm's after-tax cost of the expenditure and thereby represent an indirect federal subsidy. For instance, firms may deduct the first $15,000 of the annual cost of the removal of architectural and transportation barriers from buildings or transportation equipment to make such facilities more accessible to handicapped or elderly people.[15] A more significant preference is the deduction for **research and experimental expenditures.** This deduction is available even if the research leads to the development of an identifiable asset with an extended useful life to the firm.[16] This valuable preference reflects the federal government's belief that basic research is crucial to economic growth and should be encouraged through the tax law. However, taxpayers must always remember that such preferential treatment is a matter of legislative grace. The Tax Cuts and Jobs Act of 2017 provides that, for tax years beginning after 2021, specified research and experimentation costs must be capitalized and amortized over 5 years for domestic research or 15 years for research conducted outside the United States. Computation of the amortization deduction is addressed later in this chapter in our discussion of amortizable intangible assets.

Self-Created Patent	CPT's research laboratory spent $2 million (prior to 2022) in the development of a chemical process that eliminates cholesterol from dairy products. CPT applied for and received a patent on the process from the U.S. Patent Office. The patent gave CPT the exclusive right to exploit the process for commercial purposes for 17 years. Even though the patent is an identifiable asset with long-term value, CPT deducted the $2 million cost of this "self-created asset" as a research and experimental expenditure. Consequently, its capitalized cost of the patent is zero.

Many preferential deductions benefit only certain industries. For instance, farmers are allowed to deduct soil and water conservation expenditures, which include the cost of leveling, grading, and terracing land; constructing drainage ditches and earthen dams; and

[15] §190.
[16] §174(a).

planting windbreaks to inhibit soil erosion.[17] Farmers get a second tax break in the form of a deduction for the cost of fertilizers or other materials used to enrich farmland.[18]

Oil and gas producers can deduct **intangible drilling and development costs (IDCs)** associated with locating and preparing wells for production.[19] Expenditures such as wages, fuel, repairs to drilling equipment, hauling, and supplies that contribute to the development of a productive well undeniably result in a long-term benefit to the producer and are usually capitalized for financial statement purposes. By allowing a deduction for such IDCs, the tax law provides an incentive for producers to undertake new drilling projects.

Advertising costs are deductible, even though a firm's successful advertising campaign can increase its market share and improve its competitive position for years to come.[20] While the IRS acknowledges that the advertising of a particular product or advertising intended to promote name recognition or goodwill may enhance a firm's profitability, it does not require capitalization of advertising costs except in unusual circumstances.[21]

Graphic Design Costs	R.J. Reynolds Tobacco Company deducted $2.2 million of graphic design costs related to its cigarette packs and cartons. Graphic design comprises the verbal information, styles of print, pictures or drawings, shapes, patterns, and colors displayed on the packs and cartons. The IRS disallowed the deduction because the design costs created intangible "brand equity" assets that were distinguishable from the goodwill created by advertising. In court, R.J. Reynolds argued that its graphic designs fit the textbook definition of advertising as any "presentation and promotion of ideas, goods, or services by an identified sponsor, which involves the use of mass media."[22] The judge accepted this argument and held that R.J. Reynolds could deduct the graphic design costs as advertising expenses.

THE CRITICAL ROLE OF TAX BASIS

LO 7-2
Define *tax basis* and *adjusted basis*.

When a firm capitalizes an expenditure to a new asset account, the amount of the expenditure becomes the firm's **tax basis** in the asset. Basis can be defined as a taxpayer's investment in any asset or property right—the measure of *unrecovered dollars* represented by the asset. An asset's basis plays a key role in the calculation of cash flows because taxpayers are entitled to recover this basis at no tax cost. This recovery occurs either through a series of future deductions or when the taxpayer disposes of the asset. Cost recovery deductions are covered in this chapter, while the tax consequences of asset dispositions are the subject of Chapter 8.

Basis, Cost Recovery, and Cash Flow

When a firm deducts a portion of the capitalized cost of an asset, the deduction has two consequences. The first consequence is that the asset's initial tax basis is reduced by the deduction.[23] The reduced basis is called the asset's **adjusted basis.** The second consequence is that the deduction generates tax savings that reduce the after-tax cost of the asset.

---

[17] §175. This preferential deduction may not exceed 25 percent of the gross income derived from farming during the taxable year.

[18] §180.

[19] §263(c).

[20] Regs. §1.162-1(a) and §1.162-20(a)(2).

[21] Rev. Rul. 92-80, 1992-2 C.B. 57.

[22] American Marketing Association, *AMA Dictionary,* Chicago, IL, 1948.

[23] §1016(a)(2).

Basis, Cost Recovery, and After-Tax Cost

Firm J pays $5,000 cash for a business asset. The tax law allows Firm J to deduct the capitalized cost of the asset ratably over five years. In the year of purchase and in each of the four subsequent years, the firm deducts $1,000 and reduces its basis in the asset by this deduction. If the firm has a 21 percent marginal tax rate and uses a 7 percent discount rate to compute net present value (NPV), the after-tax cost of the asset (NPV of cash flows) is $4,080:

Year	Year-End Adjusted Basis	Annual Deduction
0	$4,000	$(1,000)
1	3,000	(1,000)
2	2,000	(1,000)
3	1,000	(1,000)
4	–0–	(1,000)

Cash Flows	Year 0	Year 1	Year 2	Year 3	Year 4
Initial payment	$(5,000)				
Tax savings from deduction	$ 210	$210	$210	$210	$210
Discount factor		.935	.873	.816	.763
NPV	$(4,790)	$196	$183	$171	$160
Total NPV	$(4,080)				

Firm J's adjusted basis in its asset at the end of each year is the $5,000 cost less the accumulated cost recovery deductions. By the end of the fifth year, the firm has recovered its entire investment in the asset, leaving the asset with a zero tax basis. A zero tax basis does not imply anything about the *value* of the asset to the firm; it simply indicates that Firm J has deducted the entire $5,000 expenditure that created the asset.

The difference between Firm J's $5,000 before-tax cost and $4,080 after-tax cost results from the stream of tax savings generated by the cost recovery deductions. If the firm could have recovered its tax basis over a shorter period of time, the present value of this stream would increase and the after-tax cost of the asset would decrease. Conversely, if the recovery period were longer, the present value of the tax savings would decrease and the after-tax cost of the asset would increase.[24]

Cost Basis

The majority of assets reported on a firm's balance sheet have an initial **cost basis**—the price paid to acquire the asset.[25] Cost basis includes any sales tax paid by the purchaser and any incidental costs related to putting the asset into production. While firms acquire many assets in straightforward cash transactions, they also acquire assets in exchange for property or services. In such cases, the cost basis of the asset equals the fair market value (FMV) of the property surrendered or the services performed.[26]

---

[24] This calculation of after-tax cost implies that the asset has no residual value after five years. If the firm could sell the asset for cash, the present value of this after-tax cash would reduce the after-tax cost of the asset. The cash flow implications of asset sales are addressed in the next chapter.

[25] §1012.

[26] Fair market value is the price at which property or services would change hands between a willing buyer and a willing seller, neither being under any compulsion to buy or to sell and both having reasonable knowledge of the relevant facts. Reg. §20.2031-1(b). Although this definition is in the estate tax regulations, it is the accepted definition for income tax purposes.

Cost Basis: Exchange for Property	BT Corporation, a manufacturer of heavy equipment, sold inventory to an unrelated land developer. BT agreed to let the developer pay for the inventory by transferring five acres of land to the corporation. The inventory has an FMV of $139,000. BT's cost basis in its new asset (the land) is $139,000, the FMV of the inventory that BT exchanged for the asset.

Cost Basis: Exchange for Note	Modify the previous example by assuming that BT sold the inventory for the developer's written interest-bearing note to pay $139,000 in three years' time. BT's cost basis in its new asset (the note receivable) is $139,000, the FMV of the inventory that BT exchanged for the asset.

Cost Basis: Exchange for Services	Firm C, a consulting business, performed professional services for an unrelated corporation and billed the corporation for $17,500. The corporation paid its bill by issuing 1,000 shares of its own common stock to the firm. Firm C recognizes $17,500 gross income and takes a $17,500 cost basis in its new asset (1,000 shares of corporate stock). This basis represents Firm C's investment in these shares—the dollar amount that the firm can recover tax-free when it disposes of the stock.

Leveraged Cost Basis

When a firm acquires an asset through debt financing, the cost basis of the asset equals its entire cost, not just the firm's equity in the asset. Refer to the example in which Firm J purchased a business asset for $5,000. Assume that the firm financed the purchase by paying $1,500 from its bank account and borrowing $3,500 from a commercial lender. Firm J gave the lender a lien on the asset to secure the debt. Although the firm's initial investment in the asset is only $1,500, its cost basis is the full $5,000 purchase price.[27] The firm's repayment of the debt will create additional equity in the asset but will have no effect on the tax basis.

LO 7-3
Explain how leverage can reduce the after-tax cost of assets.

Tax planners refer to the use of borrowed funds to create tax basis as **leverage.** The use of leverage can reduce the purchaser's after-tax cost of the asset. Let's expand on the Firm J example to demonstrate how the after-tax cost of the $5,000 asset is reduced by the use of borrowed funds.

After-Tax Cost of Leveraged Purchase	Under the terms of its agreement with the commercial lender, Firm J must pay $245 interest (7 percent) at the beginning of each year and repay the $3,500 principal amount at the beginning of the fifth year. The annual interest payments are deductible expenses, while the principal payment is charged against (and retires) the $3,500 debt. The following table reflects each year's net cash flows based on Firm J's 21 percent marginal tax rate and 7 percent discount rate:[28]

---

[27] *Crane* v. *Commissioner,* 331 U.S. 1 (1947).

[28] This calculation of after-tax cost assumed that Firm J's interest deduction is not limited by the business interest limitation discussed in Chapter 6.

	Year 0	Year 1	Year 2	Year 3	Year 4
Initial payment and debt repayment	$(1,500)				$(3,500)
Interest payment		$(245)	$(245)	$(245)	(245)
Tax savings from:					
Cost recovery deduction	210	210	210	210	210
Interest deduction		51	51	51	51
Net cash flow	$(1,290)	$ 16	$ 16	$ 16	$(3,484)
Discount factor		.935	.873	.816	.763
NPV	$(1,290)	$ 15	$ 14	$ 13	$(2,658)
Total NPV	$(3,906)				

By leveraging its purchase of the asset, Firm J reduced the after-tax cost from $4,080 to $3,906. The cash flow data explain this result. Firm J's initial cash outflow to buy the asset was only $1,500. By borrowing the balance of the purchase price, it deferred paying $3,500 cash until the fifth year. This beneficial change in cash flows did not affect the $5,000 tax basis in the asset, the annual cost recovery deductions, or the timing of the stream of tax savings from those deductions. The annual cost of the leverage was $194, which is the after-tax interest on the note ($245 interest payment − $51 tax savings). However, even considering this additional cost, leverage saved the firm $174.[29]

INTRODUCTION TO COST RECOVERY METHODS

All the topics covered in the first part of this chapter relate to a key tax planning concept: The after-tax cost of a capitalized expenditure depends on the time period over which the firm can recover the expenditure as a deduction. Thus, time period variable tax savings are achieved when the cost of a capitalized expenditure is recovered over the shortest possible time period. The remainder of the chapter examines the four basic methods of periodic cost recovery: cost of goods sold, depreciation, amortization, and depletion. If none of these recovery methods is applicable, a cost is recoverable only when the firm disposes of the asset or when that asset ceases to exist.

INVENTORIES AND COST OF GOODS SOLD

In Chapter 6, we learned that firms maintaining inventories of goods for sale to customers must account for their inventory using the accrual method. In other words, firms can't deduct the cost of manufactured or purchased inventory but must capitalize the cost to an asset account. At the end of each year, the firm ascertains how much inventory is still on hand and how much has been sold during the year. The cost of the inventory on hand is carried on the balance sheet, while the **cost of goods sold** reduces gross income from sales. The following formula summarizes this accounting procedure:

[29] The leverage was beneficial in this example because Firm J's after-tax interest rate on borrowed funds was 5.54 percent ($194 after-tax interest ÷ $3,500 debt), while its discount rate was 7 percent. If Firm J's after-tax interest rate was higher than its discount rate, the leverage would be detrimental and would increase the after-tax cost of the asset in NPV terms.

Cost of inventory on hand at the beginning of the year
Cost of inventory manufactured or purchased during the year

Total cost of inventory available for sale
(Cost of inventory on hand at the end of the year)

Cost of goods sold

LO 7-4
Compute cost of goods sold for tax purposes.

This formula is based on two assumptions. The first assumption is that all expenditures that contributed to the value of inventory are capitalized to the inventory account. The second assumption is that the total cost of inventory is properly allocated between the inventory on hand at the end of the year and the inventory sold during the year. Let's examine the tax rules underlying each of these assumptions.

The UNICAP Rules

Firms typically prefer to treat expenditures as deductible *period costs* rather than *product costs* that must be capitalized to inventory. Not surprisingly, the tax law contains explicit rules about the expenditures that must be included in inventory. These **uniform capitalization (UNICAP) rules** are as strict as they are complicated.[30] Under UNICAP, firms must capitalize all direct costs of manufacturing, purchasing, or storing inventory (direct materials and direct labor) and any indirect costs that "benefit or are incurred by reason of the performance of production or resale activities."[31] Examples of indirect costs that must be capitalized *to the extent they relate to a firm's production or resale function* include:[32]

Tax Talk
A retailer selling cigarettes in New York was required under New York law to pay a cigarette stamp tax to legally sell this product. The Second Circuit Court of Appeals affirmed the Tax Court's ruling that the stamp tax should be capitalized as an inventory cost under the UNICAP rules. City Line Candy & Tobacco Corp. v. Commissioner, 116 AFTR 2d 2015-6285.

- Officer's compensation.
- Pension, retirement, and other employee benefits.
- Rents paid on buildings and equipment used in a manufacturing process.
- Premiums paid to carry property insurance on production assets.
- Repair and maintenance of production assets.
- Cost recovery deductions for production assets.

For tax years beginning after 2017, the Tax Cuts and Jobs Act exempts from the UNICAP rules any producer or reseller with average annual gross receipts of $29 million (2023 threshold) or less. As discussed in Chapter 6, such taxpayers are also exempt from the requirement that inventory transactions be accounted for under the accrual method of accounting.

Computing Cost of Goods Sold

The allocation of costs between ending inventory and cost of goods sold is based on the method of accounting by which a firm tracks the flow of inventory items through its system. If a firm knows the actual cost of each item, it can use the **specific identification method** to value ending inventory and compute cost of goods sold. Real estate developers and antique dealers are good examples of businesses in which specific identification of inventory is possible.

For manufacturing and retail businesses that deal with thousands, if not millions, of inventory items, specific identification of each item is impossible. These firms must use a costing convention that is not based on the physical movement of inventory through the system. The two most commonly used costing conventions are **FIFO** (first-in, first-out) and **LIFO** (last-in, first-out).

---

[30] The UNICAP rules are found in §263A and the accompanying regulations.
[31] Reg. §1.263A-1(e)(3)(i).
[32] Reg. §1.263A-1(e)(3)(ii).

The selection of an inventory costing convention may have a substantial effect on annual taxable income. During a period of rising prices, it is generally to a firm's advantage to adopt LIFO because the convention assumes that the last goods manufactured or purchased are the first goods sold. In an inflationary economy, the most recently acquired goods are the most expensive. If a firm assumes these goods are the first to be sold, it maximizes the cost of goods sold and minimizes the cost of ending inventory. While the LIFO convention can offer substantial tax savings, its popularity is diminished by the fact that any firm electing LIFO for tax purposes must also use LIFO to prepare financial statements.[33] Because of this forced conformity, any reduction in taxable income attributable to LIFO is mirrored by a reduction in accounting income and earnings per share reported to the firm's investors.

DEPRECIATION OF TANGIBLE BUSINESS ASSETS

Book and Tax Concepts of Depreciation

Tax Talk
An animated film director/producer wasn't entitled to cost recovery deductions for his extensive research library of vintage magazines and archival photographs of classic film stars. The items weren't shown to have limited economic useful life or be subject to wear and tear, decay, or obsolescence (Darrell Rooney, T.C. Memo 2011-14).

Under generally accepted accounting principles (GAAP), firms write off, or *depreciate,* the capitalized cost of tangible assets over their estimated useful lives.[34] As a result, the cost of an asset is expensed over the years in which the asset contributes to the firm's revenue-generating activity. The concept of **depreciation** applies only to wasting assets that

- Lose value over time because of wear and tear, physical deterioration, or obsolescence.
- Have a reasonably ascertainable useful life.

Nonwasting tangible assets lacking these characteristics, such as land and works of art acquired for display, are nondepreciable. For financial statement purposes, firms may calculate their annual depreciation expense under a variety of methods and may choose the method resulting in the best matching of the cost of an asset against revenue.

Before 1981, depreciation for tax purposes was also based on the estimated useful life of business property. Because the useful life of any asset is a matter of conjecture, taxpayers and the IRS were constantly wrangling over the question of asset lives. Firms argued for the shortest life over which to recover the tax basis of their assets, while the IRS asserted that a longer recovery period was more realistic. In 1981, Congress enacted a radically new cost recovery system to replace the old depreciation rules. In 1986, Congress refined this system into the **Modified Accelerated Cost Recovery System (MACRS),** which is in effect today.[35] Under MACRS, the estimated useful life of an asset is irrelevant in computing tax depreciation. Because the MACRS computation is independent of the computation of book depreciation, the depreciation deduction on a firm's tax return and depreciation expense on its financial statements are usually different numbers. The final section of this chapter explores the resulting book/tax differences in more detail.

The MACRS Framework

LO 7-5
Describe and apply the MACRS framework.

This section presents the MACRS framework: the general rules for computing depreciation for federal tax purposes. Business managers who understand this framework can appreciate the role of MACRS in the tax planning process. They do not need to master the system's fine technical points; consequently, many details of MACRS are omitted from our discussion.

---

[33] §472(c).

[34] The depreciable cost is reduced by the asset's estimated residual or salvage value.

[35] §168.

TABLE 7.1
Recovery Periods for Tangible Business Assets

MACRS Recovery Period	Assets Included
3 years	Small manufacturing tools, racehorses and breeding hogs, special handling devices used in food manufacturing.
5 years	Cars, trucks, buses, helicopters, computers, typewriters, duplicating equipment, breeding and dairy cattle, cargo containers, new farming machinery and equipment.
7 years	Office furniture and fixtures, railroad cars and locomotives, most machinery and equipment.
10 years	Single-purpose agricultural and horticultural structures; assets used in petroleum refining, vessels, barges, and other water transportation equipment; fruit- or nut-bearing trees and vines.
15 years	Certain building improvements; land improvements such as fencing, roads, sidewalks, bridges, irrigation systems, and landscaping; telephone distribution plants; pipelines; billboards; and service station buildings.
20 years	Certain farm buildings, municipal sewers.
25 years	Commercial water utility property.
27.5 years	Residential rental real property (duplexes and apartments).
39 years	Nonresidential real property (office buildings, factories, and warehouses).
50 years	Railroad grading or tunnel bore.

Recovery Periods

MACRS applies to both depreciable realty (buildings, improvements, and other structures permanently attached to the land) and personalty (any tangible asset not part of a building or other permanent structure) used in a trade, business, or income-producing activity. Every depreciable asset is assigned to 1 of 10 **recovery periods.** Table 7.1 lists these periods and gives examples of assets assigned to each. For the most part, the MACRS recovery period is shorter than the asset's estimated useful life. The shortened time frame over which firms may deduct their investment in operating assets reduces the after-tax cost of the assets and acts as an incentive for firms to make capital acquisitions.

As previously discussed, expenditures that increase the value or extend the useful life of an existing asset must be capitalized as improvements. How then is the cost of such improvements recovered? In general, the cost of improvements is treated as a separate asset from the existing asset being improved. The improvement cost is depreciated beginning in the year of improvement, regardless of the age or remaining recovery life of the original asset.

Improvements to Residential Rental Property

Vista Corporation owns and operates an apartment complex it acquired in 2002. This year, Vista completed extensive renovations of the property, including new roofing, new exterior stucco, new doors, and new windows. The cost of these improvements is treated as new residential rental real property, with a 27.5-year recovery life. Although the original cost of the apartment complex will be fully depreciated in 10 more years, the improvement costs cannot be depreciated over this remaining useful life.

Under the Tax Cuts and Jobs Act, Congress intended that certain building improvements placed in service after 2017 qualify for a 15-year recovery life. Unfortunately, a drafting error in the final legislation did not specify the 15-year life. Although the error was quickly identified, Congress waited until early 2020 to pass the necessary technical corrections to fix the issue. Under the CARES Act, all qualified improvement property is now given a 15-year life. This modification is retroactive to all assets placed in service as of January 1, 2018. Thus, the cost of the qualified improvement property placed in service after December 31, 2017, is depreciable over 15 years, beginning in the year the improvements are completed.

For purposes of this provision, **qualified improvement property** is an improvement to the interior of nonresidential real property, placed in service after the date the building was first placed in service. Costs of enlarging the building, elevators, escalators, and improvements that are structural do not qualify.

Improvements to Nonresidential Real Property	Ortiz, Inc. owns and operates an office building it acquired in 1997. This year, a new tenant signed a 10-year lease on three floors of the building. As part of the lease contract, Ortiz agreed to pay for new flooring, lighting, nonstructural partitions, and other interior improvements to the space subject to this lease. These improvements are qualified improvement property with a 15-year recovery life, beginning in the year the improvements are completed. The building itself is a 39-year property, with a remaining recovery life of 13 years.

Depreciation Methods

The method by which annual depreciation is calculated is a function of the recovery period. Assets with a 3-year, 5-year, 7-year, or 10-year recovery period are depreciated using a 200 percent (i.e., double) declining-balance method. Assets with a 15-year or 20-year recovery period are depreciated using a 150 percent declining-balance method. In each case, the depreciation method switches to straight line when a straight-line computation over the remaining recovery period results in a greater deduction than the declining-balance method. For these six classes of business personalty, MACRS lives up to its name—depreciation deductions are indeed accelerated into the early years of the recovery period. Such front-end loading of depreciation further reduces the after-tax cost of tangible personalty.[36]

Before 1987, buildings and other types of realty could be depreciated using accelerated declining-balance methods. Since 1987, properties with a 25-year, 27.5-year, 39-year, or 50-year recovery period must be depreciated using the straight-line method. For real property, MACRS is an *accelerated* cost recovery system in name only.

Depreciation Conventions

The depreciation computation requires some assumption about how much depreciation is allowed in the year of an asset's acquisition or disposition. Under MACRS, all personalty (assets with recovery periods from 3 to 20 years) are assumed to be placed in service or disposed of exactly halfway through the year. This **half-year convention** means that in the first year of the recovery period, six months of depreciation is allowed, regardless of when the asset was actually placed in service. The same convention applies in the year in which an asset is disposed of. Regardless of the actual date of disposition, the firm may claim six months of depreciation.[37]

The half-year convention is subject to an important exception. If more than 40 percent of the depreciable personalty acquired during a taxable year is placed in service during the last three months of the year, the firm must use a **midquarter convention** with respect to *all*

---

[36] Under §168(b)(5), taxpayers may elect the straight-line method (rather than an accelerated method) for any class of property placed in service during the year.

[37] No MACRS depreciation is allowed for property placed in service and disposed of in the same year. Reg. §1.168(d)-1(b)(3)(ii).

personalty placed in service during the year. Under this convention, assets placed in service during any quarter (three months) of the year are assumed to be placed in service midway (one and one-half months) through the quarter. When an asset subject to this convention is disposed of, the disposition is treated as occurring at the midpoint of the quarter in which the disposition occurs. The midquarter requirement constrains a taxpayer that might be tempted to accelerate future-year property acquisitions into the last quarter of the current year to take advantage of cost recovery deductions available under the midyear convention.

Half-Year and Midquarter Conventions

During its calendar taxable year, Company P purchased the following depreciable personalty:

Date Placed in Service	Depreciable Basis
February 27	$ 68,000
July 8	20,000
November 19	55,000
	$143,000

Only 38 percent of the depreciable personalty was placed in service during the last three months of the year. Therefore, Company P uses the half-year convention and calculates six months of depreciation for each asset.

Now assume that Company P purchased a $19,000 depreciable asset on December 4. In this case, 46 percent of the depreciable personalty ($74,000 ÷ $162,000) was placed in service in the last three months of the year. For this reason, Company P must use the midquarter convention with the following result:

Quarter Placed in Service	Quarter Basis	Months of Depreciation Allowed
First quarter	$ 68,000	10.5 months
Second quarter	–0–	7.5
Third quarter	20,000	4.5
Fourth quarter	74,000	1.5
	$162,000	

A **midmonth convention** applies to the year in which depreciable realty (assets with recovery periods of 25, 27.5, 39, or 50 years) is placed in service or disposed of. Under this convention, realty placed in service (or disposed of) during any month is treated as placed in service (or disposed of) midway through the month.

Midmonth Convention

Company RS placed three buildings into service during its calendar taxable year. It can claim the following months of depreciation for each building:

	Date Placed in Service	Months of Depreciation Allowed
Building 1	April 2	8.5 months
Building 2	July 30	5.5 months
Building 3	December 18	.5 month

Comprehensive Examples

The next two examples illustrate the MACRS calculation.

MACRS Calculation	Firm P, a calendar year taxpayer, buys a computer for $38,000 and places it in service on September 19. The computer has a five-year recovery period, so the firm uses the 200 percent declining-balance method to compute depreciation. Under this method, the straight-line rate of depreciation (20 percent) is doubled, and the resulting rate (40 percent) is applied each year to the unrecovered basis. Firm P will depreciate the computer according to the following schedule:

Year	Unrecovered Basis at Beginning	Recovery Method	Convention	MACRS Depreciation
1	$38,000	200% DB	Half-year	$ 7,600
2	30,400	200 DB		12,160
3	18,240	200 DB		7,296
4	10,944	200 DB		4,378
5	6,566	SL*		4,378
6	2,188	SL		2,188
				$38,000

*$364.78 per month.

- Because only one-half year of depreciation is allowed in year 1, one-half year of depreciation is necessary in year 6 to complete the five-year recovery period.
- The declining-balance method is changed to the straight-line method in year 5 so that the $6,566 unrecovered basis is depreciated ratably over the remaining one and one-half years (18 months) in the recovery period.
- The basis of the computer is reduced to zero. For MACRS purposes, depreciable assets are assumed to have no residual value.

MACRS Calculation in Year of Sale	Refer to the facts in the previous example but assume that Firm P sells the computer on May 3 in year 4. In this case, the half-year convention also applies in the year of disposition.

Year	Unrecovered Basis at Beginning	Recovery Method	Convention	MACRS Depreciation
1	$38,000	200% DB	Half-year	$ 7,600
2	30,400	200 DB		12,160
3	18,240	200 DB		7,296
4	10,944	200 DB	Half-year	2,189

The computer's adjusted basis immediately prior to sale is $8,755 ($10,944 unrecovered basis at beginning of year 4 − $2,189 depreciation in year 4).

IRS Depreciation Tables

To allow taxpayers to avoid the MACRS math process, the IRS publishes a set of convenient tables incorporating the MACRS computational rules. The tables consist of a series of annual percentages that are multiplied against the *initial undepreciated* basis of the asset to calculate depreciation for the year. Table 7.2 contains the annual percentages for the six recovery periods for business personalty, based on the half-year convention. The IRS tables that provide the annual percentages for personalty depreciated under a midquarter convention are included in Appendix 7–A.

TABLE 7.2
MACRS for Business Personalty (Half-Year Convention)

	Recovery Period					
	3-Year	**5-Year**	**7-Year**	**10-Year**	**15-Year**	**20-Year**
Year	Depreciation Rate					
1	33.33%	20.00%	14.29%	10.00%	5.00%	3.750%
2	44.45	32.00	24.49	18.00	9.50	7.219
3	14.81	19.20	17.49	14.40	8.55	6.677
4	7.41	11.52	12.49	11.52	7.70	6.177
5		11.52	8.93	9.22	6.93	5.713
6		5.76	8.92	7.37	6.23	5.285
7			8.93	6.55	5.90	4.888
8			4.46	6.55	5.90	4.522
9				6.56	5.91	4.462
10				6.55	5.90	4.461
11				3.28	5.91	4.462
12					5.90	4.461
13					5.91	4.462
14					5.90	4.461
15					5.91	4.462
16					2.95	4.461
17						4.462
18						4.461
19						4.462
20						4.461
21						2.231

MACRS Calculation Using IRS Tables

Refer to the facts in the previous two examples. If Firm P holds the equipment until fully depreciated, using Table 7.2 it can compute its annual depreciation deduction for its $38,000 computer as follows:

Year	Initial Basis	Table Percentage	MACRS Depreciation
1	$38,000	20.00%	$ 7,600
2	38,000	32.00	12,160
3	38,000	19.20	7,296
4	38,000	11.52	4,378
5	38,000	11.52	4,378
6	38,000	5.76	2,188
			$38,000

Note that the table percentage in year 1 is one-half the declining-balance rate. In other words, the half-year convention for the year of acquisition is built into this table. However, the table percentages for the remaining years reflect a full year of depreciation. If an asset is disposed of before it is fully depreciated, the MACRS deduction for the year is only one-half the amount indicated by the table. If Firm P sells the computer on May 3 of year 4, MACRS depreciation for that year is computed by multiplying the otherwise applicable table percentage by 50 percent, as follows:

Year 4 sale $38,000 × 11.52% × 50% = $2,189

TABLE 7.3   MACRS for Residential Real Property (27.5-year property)

	Month Placed in Service											
Year	**1**	**2**	**3**	**4**	**5**	**6**	**7**	**8**	**9**	**10**	**11**	**12**
	Depreciation Rate											
1	3.485%	3.182%	2.879%	2.576%	2.273%	1.970%	1.667%	1.364%	1.061%	0.758%	0.455%	0.152%
2–27	3.636	3.636	3.636	3.636	3.636	3.636	3.636	3.636	3.636	3.636	3.636	3.636
28	1.970	2.273	2.576	2.879	3.182	3.458	3.636	3.636	3.636	3.636	3.636	3.636
29	0.000	0.000	0.000	0.000	0.000	0.000	0.152	0.455	0.758	1.061	1.364	1.667

TABLE 7.4   MACRS for Nonresidential Real Property (39-year property)

	Month Placed in Service											
Year	**1**	**2**	**3**	**4**	**5**	**6**	**7**	**8**	**9**	**10**	**11**	**12**
	Depreciation Rate											
1	2.461%	2.247%	2.033%	1.819%	1.605%	1.391%	1.177%	0.963%	0.749%	0.535%	0.321%	0.107%
2–39	2.564	2.564	2.564	2.564	2.564	2.564	2.564	2.564	2.564	2.564	2.564	2.564
40	0.107	0.321	0.535	0.749	0.963	1.177	1.391	1.605	1.819	2.033	2.247	2.461

Tables 7.3 and 7.4 are abridged versions of the IRS tables for computing annual depreciation for 27.5-year and 39-year recovery property. Because these real properties are depreciated by the straight-line method, the tables are really helpful only for the years of acquisition and retirement in which the midmonth convention applies.

MACRS Depreciation for Commercial Building

Bulona Company, a calendar year taxpayer, purchased commercial real property for $3 million and allocated $200,000 cost to the land and $2.8 million to the building. The property was placed in service on June 4 (month 6). According to the IRS table, Bulona can recover the $2.8 million cost of the building as follows:

Year 1 ($2.8 million × 1.391 percent)	$38,948
Years 2 to 39 ($2.8 million × 2.564 percent)	71,792
Year 40 ($2.8 million × 1.177 percent)	32,956

Under a straight-line calculation, Bulona's annual depreciation is $71,795 ($2.8 million cost ÷ 39 years), which corresponds to the rounded number generated by the IRS table for years 2 through 39. In year 1, Bulona can deduct only 6.5 months of depreciation, while in year 40, it can deduct the residual 5.5 months of depreciation.

MACRS and FMV

It is important to understand that MACRS deductions do not represent cash outflows, and they do not correlate to any decline in the FMV of the asset. While operating assets typically lose value as they age, the annual MACRS deduction in no way reflects such loss. Moreover, firms may claim depreciation deductions for assets that may actually appreciate in value over time.[38] The adjusted tax basis in a business asset is the capitalized cost that the firm has not yet deducted and conveys no information concerning FMV.

[38] *Noyce,* 97 T.C. 670 (1991).

Depreciation for an Appreciating Asset?	Richard and Fiona Simon purchased two 100-year-old antique violin bows for $51,500. The couple used the bows in their business as professional violinists and claimed depreciation deductions based on a five-year recovery period. The IRS denied the deductions because the bows were treasured works of art that had actually appreciated in value since they were acquired by the Simons. A federal court concluded that the violin bows met the definition of depreciable property because they suffered "wear and tear" in the taxpayers' business activity. Thus, the Simons could recover their cost and reduce their tax basis in the violin bows to zero even though the bows continued to increase in value.[39]

Limited Depreciation for Passenger Automobiles

LO 7-6
Determine the limitation on depreciation of passenger automobiles.

The tax law contains a major exception to MACRS for depreciation allowed for passenger automobiles held for business use.[40] **Passenger automobiles** are defined as four-wheeled vehicles manufactured primarily for use on public roads with an unloaded gross vehicle weight of 6,000 pounds or less. Vehicles directly used in the business of transporting people or property for compensation—such as taxicabs, limousines, hearses, ambulances, and delivery vans and trucks—are excluded from the definition of passenger automobiles.

The annual depreciation deduction for passenger automobiles may not exceed the limits provided under a special schedule, which is adjusted annually for inflation. For automobiles placed in service during 2022, annual depreciation was limited to the following:[41]

2022	$11,200
2023	18,000
2024	10,800
2025 and subsequent years	6,460

Passenger Automobile Depreciation	In 2022 WRP, Inc. paid $60,000 for a passenger automobile for exclusive business use by its employees. For MACRS purposes, automobiles are five-year recovery property. The following schedule contrasts MACRS depreciation with limited depreciation:

Year	MACRS Depreciation	Limited Depreciation
2022	$12,000	$11,200
2023	19,200	18,000
2024	11,520	10,800
2025	6,912	6,460
2026	6,912	6,460
2027	3,456	6,460
2028		620
	$60,000	$60,000

---

[39] *Simon,* 103 T.C. 247 (1994).

[40] §280F(a).

[41] The annual depreciation limits are increased for trucks, vans, and electric automobiles. See Rev. Proc. 2022-17, 2022-13 IRB. As this book goes to press, the 2023 passenger automobile limitations have not yet been released.

Because MACRS depreciation would exceed the annual limits in each year of the normal MACRS recovery period, WRP must use limited depreciation for all years. Consequently, WRP will recover its $60,000 cost over seven years rather than over the normal six years in the MACRS recovery period.

Firms that use passenger automobiles in their business cannot avoid the limitation on depreciation by leasing automobiles rather than purchasing them. The tax law provides that deductions for lease payments on passenger automobiles must be limited in a manner that is "substantially equivalent" to the depreciation limitation.[42] IRS Publication 463, *Travel, Entertainment, Gift, and Car Expenses,* includes the complicated procedure by which firms compute their limited deduction for lease payments on passenger automobiles.

Section 179 Expensing Election

LO 7-7
Calculate the Section 179 deduction and bonus depreciation.

Section 179 allows firms to elect to expense (rather than capitalize) a limited dollar amount of the cost of certain property placed in service during the year. The limited dollar amount has varied substantially in recent years. The maximum deduction was $250,000 for assets placed in service in 2008 and 2009. Beginning in 2010, the maximum deduction was increased to $500,000. After indexing for inflation, the maximum deduction was $510,000 in 2017. For qualifying assets placed in service in tax years beginning after 2017, the Tax Cuts and Jobs Act increased the maximum deduction to $1 million. This maximum deduction is indexed for inflation. The 2023 maximum deduction amount is $1,160,000 ($1,080,000 in 2022).

Property that qualifies for the **Section 179 election** includes tangible depreciable personalty and off-the-shelf computer software, the cost of which is amortizable over 36 months.[43] Under the Tax Cuts and Jobs Act, the Section 179 election is also available for certain improvements to nonresidential real property placed in service after 2017. Specifically, the election applies to (1) qualified improvement property as defined earlier in this chapter (in our discussion of recovery periods) and (2) other improvements for roofs; heating, ventilation, and air-conditioning property; fire protection and alarm systems; and security systems placed in service after the date the improved nonresidential real property was placed in service.

The Section 179 election allows many small firms to simply deduct the cost of their newly acquired assets and avoid the burden of maintaining depreciation or amortization schedules. Firms that purchase qualifying property with an aggregate cost in excess of the limited dollar amount may expense part of the cost of a specific asset or assets. The unexpensed cost is capitalized and recovered through depreciation or amortization.[44]

Section 179 Expensing	In July 2023, Firm B purchased two new items of tangible property. Item 1 was qualified improvement property with a 15-year recovery life costing $903,200, and item 2 was a 5-year recovery property costing $468,000. These were the only items that qualified for the Section 179 election. Firm B elected to expense the entire $903,200 cost of item 1 (because of its longer recovery period) and $256,800 of the cost of item 2, for a total Section 179 deduction of $1,160,000. Firm B's cost recovery deduction for item 2 is $299,040.

(continued)

[42] §280F(c)(3).

[43] §179(d)(1).

[44] In the case of passenger automobiles, any Section 179 deduction is treated as depreciation subject to the limitations of §230F(a).

		Recovery Deductions
Initial cost	$468,000	
Section 179 expense	(256,800)	$256,800
Adjusted basis for MACRS	$211,200	
Percentage from Table 7.2	20.00%	
MACRS depreciation	$ 42,240	42,240
		$299,040

Firm B's 2023 cost recovery deductions for items 1 and 2 total $1,202,240 ($903,200 for item 1 + $299,040 for item 2). At the end of 2023, the adjusted tax basis in item 1 is zero, and the adjusted tax basis in item 2 is $168,960 ($468,000 − $299,040).

The Section 179 expense election has two limitations. If a firm purchases more than a threshold amount of qualifying property in a year, the annual dollar amount is reduced by the excess of the total cost of the property over the threshold.[45] For 2023, the threshold is $2,890,000 ($2,700,000 in 2022 and $2,030,000 in 2017). Because of this *excess property limitation,* a firm that purchases more than $4,050,000 of qualifying property in 2023 cannot benefit from a Section 179 election because its limited dollar amount is reduced to zero.

Excess Property Limitation

Firm R purchased $2,896,000 of equipment in 2023. Consequently, its excess amount of qualifying property was $6,000 ($2,896,000 − $2,890,000 threshold). Because of the excess property limitation, Firm R may expense only $1,154,000 of the cost of its qualifying property ($1,160,000 2023 limited dollar amount − $6,000). It must capitalize the remaining $1,742,000 cost and recover it through MACRS depreciation.

Once a firm elects to expense the cost of qualifying property, the expense is generally deductible. However, the *deduction* (not the expense) is limited to taxable business income computed without regard to the deduction. Any nondeductible expense resulting from this *taxable income limitation* carries forward to succeeding taxable years.[46]

Taxable Income Limitation

Firm X purchased $447,800 of tangible personalty in 2022 and elected to expense the entire cost. The firm's taxable income without regard to any Section 179 deduction was $429,600. Because of the taxable income limitation, Firm X could deduct only $429,600, thereby reducing taxable income to zero. The $18,200 nondeductible expense carried forward into 2023.

Firm X purchased $336,250 of tangible personalty in 2023 and elected to expense the entire cost. The firm's taxable income without regard to any Section 179 deduction was $1,194,100. Because the taxable income limitation was inapplicable, the firm's Section 179 deduction was $354,450 ($336,250 + $18,200 carryforward), and its taxable income was $839,650.

The carryforward of a nondeductible expense to a succeeding taxable year does not increase the limited dollar amount for such year. Assume that Firm X in the previous example purchased $1,154,000 of qualifying property in 2023. In this case, its Section 179 deduction is limited to $1,160,000 ($1,074,000 + 6,000 carryforward from 2022), and the firm has a $12,200 remaining carryforward to 2024.

[45] §179(b)(2).

[46] §179(b)(3) and Reg. §1.179-3.

Bonus Depreciation

Tax Talk

Bonus depreciation has come and gone from the tax law several times in the past two decades. For qualifying property placed in service between September 11, 2001, and May 5, 2003, 30 percent bonus depreciation applied. For property placed in service between May 6, 2003, and December 31, 2004, 50 percent bonus depreciation applied.

Several recent congressional acts (2008 Economic Stimulus Act, 2009 Recovery Act, Small Business Jobs Act of 2010, 2010 Tax Relief Act, American Taxpayer Relief Act of 2012, Tax Increase Prevention Act of 2014, Protecting Americans from Tax Hikes Act of 2015, and the Tax Cuts and Jobs Act of 2017) have provided for accelerated cost recovery via first-year bonus depreciation for qualified property acquisitions.[47] For this provision, qualified property includes most tangible property with a recovery life of 20 years or less; computer software; and certain property used in film, television, or live theater production. Prior to September 28, 2017, bonus depreciation was available only for new acquisitions. After September 27, 2017, acquisitions of used property qualify, as long as the property was acquired by purchase from an unrelated taxpayer.

The adjusted basis of the property is reduced by the amount of bonus depreciation for purposes of computing regular MACRS depreciation over the recovery life of the asset. Congress hopes this valuable deduction will provide stimulus for both purchasers and producers of business assets.

The available bonus depreciation percentage varies, depending on the time period in which the property is placed in service:

1/1/2008 through 9/8/2010	50%
9/9/2010 through 12/31/2011	100%
1/1/2012 through 9/27/2017	50%
9/28/2017 through 12/31/2022	100%

For acquisitions after December 31, 2022, bonus depreciation is scheduled to phase down and is eliminated for acquisitions after December 31, 2026. During this phase-down period, the following bonus depreciation percentages apply:

1/1/2023 through 12/31/2023	80%
1/1/2024 through 12/31/2024	60%
1/1/2025 through 12/31/2025	40%
1/1/2026 through 12/31/2026	20%

If property qualifies both for the Section 179 deduction and **bonus depreciation,** Section 179 is applied first.[48] The following example illustrates the joint application of these two stimulus provisions.

Recovery Deductions in 2023 versus 2018 through 2022

In March 2023, Firm N purchased new tangible personalty costing $1,750,000. Assume the asset was a five-year recovery property and was the firm's only qualifying asset acquisition for the year. If Firm N elects both Section 179 and 80 percent bonus depreciation for this acquisition, its total 2023 recovery deduction for the asset is $1,655,600.

		Recovery Deductions
Initial cost	$1,750,000	
Section 179 expense (2023 amount)	(1,160,000)	$1,160,000
Adjusted basis for bonus depreciation	$ 590,000	
80% bonus depreciation	(472,000)	472,000
Adjusted basis for MACRS	$ 118,000	
Percentage from Table 7.2	20.00%	
MACRS depreciation	$ 23,600	23,600
		$1,655,600

(continued)

[47] §168(k).

[48] Reg. §1.168(k)-1(a)(2)(iii).

As a result of these incentive provisions, Firm N is able to deduct 95 percent ($1,655,600 ÷ $1,750,000) of the cost of the acquisition in 2023 The remaining unrecovered basis of the asset will be depreciated under the normal MACRS rules for the remainder of its recovery life.

What if the acquisition took place after 2017 but before 2023? Firm N could deduct the entire cost of the asset through 100 percent bonus depreciation (or the combination of Section 179 and bonus depreciation) in the year of acquisition.

Under circumstances in which 100 percent bonus depreciation is permitted, one might reasonably ask whether Section 179 is still relevant. While there is considerable overlap between these two incentive provisions, important differences remain. Recall that Section 179 is targeted at smaller businesses, while bonus depreciation is available to taxpayers of all sizes. The Section 179 deduction cannot exceed current taxable income; bonus depreciation has no such limit. For acquisitions prior to September 28, 2017, bonus depreciation applies only to new property; Section 179 applies to new and used property. Finally, the definition of qualified property for these two provisions is similar, but important differences exist. For example, Section 179 is available for certain improvements to nonresidential real property after 2017 (roofs; heating, air conditioning, and ventilation property; fire protection, alarm, and security systems) that are not eligible for bonus depreciation. The CARES Act provision allowing a 15-year recovery life for other qualified improvement property means that such property is also eligible for bonus depreciation.

Section 179 versus Bonus Depreciation	Smart, Inc. owns a large office building acquired in 2005. This year, it made numerous improvements to the building, at a total cost of $1 million. These improvements relate to the heating, air conditioning, fire protection, and security systems, and have a 39-year MACRS recovery life.

Smart also refurnished the office building with new desks, shelving, conference tables and chairs, and other furnishings at a total cost of $300,000. These assets have a seven-year MACRS recovery life.

The $300,000 of furnishings are eligible for both bonus depreciation and the Section 179 deduction. The $1 million of systems improvements are not eligible for bonus depreciation, but qualify under Section 179. To maximize its recovery deductions, Smart should elect Section 179 for the systems improvements, deducting the entire $1 million cost since it is less than the 2023 maximum $1,160,000 Section 179 deduction. Of the $300,000 cost of furnishings, $160,000 can be deducted under Section 179 ($1,160,000 threshold − $1 million cost of system improvements). Bonus depreciation will allow a deduction of $112,000 [($300,000 cost − $160,000 Section 179 deduction) x 80 percent] of the cost of the furnishings. Thus, Smart is able to deduct $1.272 million of the total $1.3 million cost of furnishings and systems improvements in 2023. The remaining cost of $28,000 will be deducted through MACRS over the recovery life of the furnishings.

Purchase versus Leasing Decision

LO 7-8
Incorporate depreciation deductions into the NPV computation.

Business managers routinely make decisions concerning the acquisition of operating assets. One of the more common decisions is whether the firm should purchase an asset or lease it. Both options provide the firm with the use of the asset over time, but the cash flows associated with each option are different. Managers should choose the option that minimizes the after-tax cost of the acquisition in present value terms. The following example illustrates how depreciation deductions are incorporated into a cash flow analysis.

Purchase versus Leasing

SGM must acquire a piece of heavy machinery for use in its construction business. SGM could purchase the machine for $75,000 cash. The machine would be a seven-year recovery property. SGM's engineers estimate that the machine would actually last for 10 years, after which time it would have no residual value. Alternatively, SGM could lease the machine for 10 years for $11,300 annual rent. SGM is in a 21 percent marginal tax bracket and uses a 7 percent discount rate to compute NPV. To decide whether to purchase or to lease the machine, SGM must calculate and compare the after-tax cost of each option. (Use Table 7.2.)

Purchase Option

Purchase price	$(75,000)
Present value of tax savings from depreciation (see following table)	13,317
After-tax cost of purchase option	$(61,683)

Year	MACRS Depreciation	Tax Savings at 21%	Discount Factor	Present Value of Tax Savings
0	$10,717	$2,251	—	$ 2,251
1	18,367	3,857	.935	3,606
2	13,118	2,755	.873	2,405
3	9,367	1,967	.816	1,605
4	6,698	1,407	.763	1,074
5	6,690	1,405	.713	1,002
6	6,698	1,407	.666	937
7	3,345	702	.623	437
	$75,000			$13,317

Lease Option

Annual lease payment	$(11,300)
Tax savings ($11,300 deduction × 21%)	2,373
After-tax annual payment	$ (8,927)
Present value of year 0 payment	$ (8,927)
Present value of years 1–9 payment ($8,927 × 6.515 discount factor)	(58,159)
After-tax cost of rent option	$(67,086)

A comparison of after-tax cash flows provides SGM with the information necessary to make its decision. SGM should purchase the machine (after-tax cost $61,683) rather than lease it (after-tax cost $67,086) to minimize after-tax cost.

AMORTIZATION OF INTANGIBLE ASSETS

LO 7-9
Explain how the cost of intangibles is recovered through amortization.

Firms may own a variety of assets that have no physical substance but that represent a valuable property right or economic attribute. The tax basis in such intangible assets may be recoverable under some type of **amortization** method allowed by the Internal Revenue Code. As a general rule, amortization is allowed only if the intangible asset has a determinable life.[49] For instance, a firm that purchases a patent or copyright can deduct the cost ratably over the number of months during which the patent or copyright confers an exclusive legal right on the owner.[50]

[49] Reg. §1.167(a)-3.
[50] Reg. §1.197–2(c)(7) and Reg. §1.167(a)-14(c)(4).

Determinable Life	Refer to the example in which CPT created and patented a chemical process that eliminates cholesterol from dairy products. Hanover, a manufacturer of frozen foods, wanted to use the process to develop a new line of healthy ice cream. Thus, Hanover purchased the patent from CPT for $10 million. At date of purchase, the patent had a remaining legal life of 157 months. Hanover must capitalize the cost of the patent and can amortize the cost at the rate of $63,694 per month ($10 million ÷ 157 months).

The cost basis in an intangible asset with an indeterminable life generally is not amortizable but can be recovered only upon disposition of the asset.

Indeterminable Life	This year, Forman Group purchased 16,000 shares of common stock in ABC, Inc. and a 10 percent interest in KLM Partnership. Forman Group must capitalize the cost of both these intangible equity interests. Because the interests represent permanent investments, Forman Group cannot recover the capitalized costs through amortization.

The tax law requires that the capitalized cost basis of a few particular intangible assets be amortized over an arbitrary 15-year period, beginning in the month in which the asset is acquired. This amortization rule applies regardless of how the asset was acquired (self-created or purchased) or the period of time during which the asset confers a legal right or benefit to the owner. The assets subject to this 15-year amortization rule are licenses, permits, and similar rights granted by a government, franchises, trademarks, and trade names.[51]

15-Year Amortization	Perry's Restaurant has been in operation for 12 years. This year, the owners decided to expand their menu to offer wine and beer. They paid $31,500 to the state government for a liquor license that will remain in effect indefinitely. Perry's must capitalize the cost of the license and can amortize the cost over 15 years at the rate of $175 per month ($31,500 ÷ 180 months).

In the following paragraphs, we will analyze four types of intangible assets subject to cost recovery through amortization: organizational and start-up costs, leasehold costs and improvements, research and experimentation costs incurred after 2021, and business acquisition intangibles.

Organizational and Start-Up Costs

The tax law contains a specific rule for the tax treatment of the **organizational costs** of forming a partnership or corporation. These costs include legal and accounting fees attributable to the formation and any filing or registration fees required under state or local law. A new partnership or corporation can deduct the *lesser* of its actual organizational costs or $5,000. This $5,000 maximum is reduced by the amount by which total costs exceed $50,000. The entity must capitalize any nondeductible organizational cost and may elect to amortize such cost over a 180-month period starting with the month in which business begins.[52]

The tax law includes a similar rule for the **start-up expenditures** of any new business, regardless of organizational form. Start-up expenditures include both the up-front costs of investigating the creation or purchase of a business and the routine expenses incurred during the preoperating phase of a business. This preoperating phase ends only when the business has

[51] §197(a) and (d)(1)(D) and (F).
[52] §709 and §248.

matured to the point that it can generate revenues. A firm may deduct the *lesser* of its actual start-up expenditures or $5,000 (reduced by the amount by which total expenditures exceed $50,000). The firm must capitalize any nondeductible start-up expenditures and may elect to amortize such cost over a 180-month period starting with the month in which business begins.[53]

Organizational and Start-Up Costs	Mr. Dugan and Mrs. Guffman went into partnership to start a new business. Their first step was to engage an attorney to draft a partnership agreement and a CPA to set up an accounting system. The total cost of these professional services was $10,580. DG Partnership spent three months locating and renting suitable office space, hiring and training staff, publicizing the new business on radio and television, and applying for the operating license required under local law. These preoperating expenses totaled $61,200. The partnership received an operating license in late August and opened its doors for business on September 8. DG Partnership can deduct $5,000 of its organizational costs and must capitalize the $5,580 remainder. Because its start-up expenditures exceeded $55,000, its deduction for these expenditures is reduced to zero, and it must capitalize the entire $61,200. On its first Form 1065 (U.S. Partnership Return of Income), the partnership makes a written election to amortize the $66,780 total of these capitalized costs over 180 months.[54] If the partnership reports on a calendar year basis, its amortization deduction for its first taxable year is $1,484: $66,780 ÷ 180 months = $371 monthly amortization $371 × four months (September through December) = $1,484 DG Partnership will amortize the $65,296 remaining capitalized costs over the next 176 months.

The capitalization requirement for start-up expenditures does not apply to the **expansion costs** of an existing business.[55] Once DG Partnership in the previous example begins operations, it has established an active business. If DG Partnership expands to a second location, it will repeat the process of renting a facility, hiring and training additional staff, and advertising the new location. Although the expenses with respect to these activities are functionally identical to the $61,200 start-up expenditures, DG Partnership can deduct these expenses because they are incurred in the conduct of an existing business.

Business Start-Up or Expansion?	TresChic Company manufactures and imports perfumes, cosmetics, clothing, and accessories. For many years, TresChic sold its goods only at wholesale. However, three years ago, the company decided to move into the retail market and opened its first BeBe Boutique. The success of the first boutique prompted the company to open 11 more boutiques nationwide. The boutiques operate in the same manner, have a standardized décor, and carry the same merchandise. TresChic handles the accounting, financing, management, purchasing, and advertising for all the boutiques. The IRS ruled that TresChic's retail operation is a substantially different activity from its wholesale operation. Consequently, the first BeBe Boutique represented a new business, and TresChic had to capitalize its start-up expenditures accordingly. However, the next 11 boutiques represented the expansion of TresChic's existing retail operation. Therefore, TresChic could deduct all the operating expenses associated with each new boutique in the year incurred.[56]

[53] §195. According to §195(c)(1), (B), interest expense, taxes, and research and experimentation costs are not start-up expenditures and may be deducted even if incurred during the preoperating phase of a business venture.

[54] The two partners, not the partnership itself, will pay tax on the income generated by the partnership business. Nevertheless, the partnership is required to file an information return on which any elections that affect the computation of taxable income are made. See §703(b).

[55] §195(c)(1)(B).

[56] IRS Letter Ruling 9331001 (April 23, 1993).

Leasehold Costs and Improvements

When a firm rents tangible property for use in its business, it may incur up-front costs to acquire the lease on the property. Such **leasehold costs** must be capitalized and amortized over the term of the lease.[57] In contrast, if a firm pays for physical improvements to leased property, the cost of the **leasehold improvements** must be capitalized to an asset account, assigned to a MACRS recovery period, and depreciated under the MACRS rules. This cost recovery rule applies even when the term of the lease is shorter than the MACRS recovery period.[58]

Leasehold Costs and Improvements	Early in the year, VB Corporation entered into a lease agreement for commercial office space. VB's cost of negotiating the lease was $3,120, and it spent $28,000 to construct cabinets, bookshelves, and lighting fixtures to conform the leased space to its needs. The term of the lease is 48 months, beginning on May 1. VB Corporation must capitalize the $3,120 lease acquisition cost and amortize it over 48 months ($65 per month for a current year amortization deduction of $520). It must also capitalize the $28,000 cost of the lease-hold improvements. These improvements qualify as seven-year recovery property, and VB will recover its cost basis through MACRS depreciation.[59]

Research and Experimentation Costs after 2021

As discussed earlier in this chapter, the Tax Cuts and Jobs Act of 2017 requires that research and experimentation costs incurred after 2021 be capitalized and amortized over 5 years if domestic or 15 years if incurred outside the United States.

Amortization of Research and Experimentation Costs	During 2023, Farnsworth Labs incurred $10 million of domestic research and experimentation costs. Tax amortization will apply the midyear convention and straight-line method over a five-year life. Farnsworth can deduct the following amounts:

	Amortization Deduction
2023	$1 million
2024	2 million
2025	2 million
2026	2 million
2027	2 million
2028	1 million

Business Acquisition Intangibles

A firm that purchases an entire business is usually acquiring more than just the monetary and operating assets recorded on the business's balance sheet. A substantial portion of the value of the business may consist of intangible assets that may or may not appear on the balance sheet. If the purchaser pays a lump-sum price for the business, it must allocate a portion of the price to each balance sheet asset acquired. The price allocated to each asset equals that asset's FMV and becomes the purchaser's cost basis in the asset.[60]

[57] Reg. §1.162-11(a).

[58] §168(i)(8).

[59] Unless VB Corporation renews its lease on the commercial office space after 48 months, it will not have recovered its entire cost basis in the leasehold improvements when it surrenders the space back to the lessor. The tax consequences of this situation are discussed in the next chapter.

[60] Reg. §1.1060-1.

Tax Talk

Johnson & Johnson purchased Pfizer's consumer healthcare division for $16.6 billion cash. Almost the entire cost is allocable to Pfizer's brand names such as Visine, Listerine, Neosporin, and Sudafed. According to J&J's CEO, the brand names are "extraordinary assets that will bring sustainable long-term value to the shareholders." For tax purposes, J&J can amortize the cost of these intangibles over 15 years.

If the lump-sum price exceeds the value of the balance sheet assets, the excess is allocated to the unrecorded intangible assets of the business. Such assets include **goodwill** (value created by the expectancy that customers will continue to patronize the business) and **going-concern value** (value attributable to the synergism of business assets working in coordination). Other common acquisition intangibles follow:

- Information-based intangibles such as accounting records, operating systems or manuals, customer lists, and advertiser lists.
- Customer-based or supplier-based intangibles such as favorable contracts with major customers or established relationships with key suppliers.
- Know-how intangibles such as designs, patterns, formulas, and other intellectual properties.
- Workforce intangibles such as the specialized skills, education, or loyalty of company employees and favorable employment contracts.
- Covenants not to compete and similar arrangements with prior owners of the business.

For tax purposes, firms recover the cost of acquisition intangibles over a 15-year period, regardless of the actual length of time that the intangible asset is expected to yield any commercial benefit.[61] Amortization begins in the month in which the intangible asset is acquired.

Amortization of Acquisition Intangibles

On March 9, BV Company (a calendar year taxpayer) paid $2 million to acquire a business from Mr. Lopez. The sales contract stated that $1.7 million of the lump-sum price was attributable to the appraised value of monetary and tangible operating assets. An additional $50,000 was attributable to the business's customer list, $150,000 was attributable to goodwill, and $100,000 was attributable to a covenant not to compete. Under this covenant, Mr. Lopez cannot engage in a similar business for the next three years. BV Company must capitalize the $300,000 cost of these intangibles and amortize the cost over 15 years at a rate of $1,667 per month ($300,000 ÷ 180 months). Its amortization deduction in the year of purchase is $16,670 ($1,667 for 10 months).

Patents and copyrights are treated as acquisition intangibles *only if* they are acquired as part of the purchase of an *entire business*. In such cases, the purchaser must amortize the cost allocated to the patent or copyright over 15 years, regardless of the remaining legal life of the asset.

Patent as Acquisition Intangible

Refer to the example in which Hanover purchased a patent for a chemical process for use in its manufacturing business. This year, Crown Food purchased Hanover's entire business operation. Consequently, Crown Food acquired all of Hanover's tangible and intangible assets, including the patent. At date of purchase, the patent had a remaining legal life of only eight years (96 months). But because the patent is included as one of Crown Food's acquisition intangibles, it must recover its cost allocated to the patent over a 15-year amortization period.

Comprehensive Example of a Lump-Sum Purchase

Firms that pay a lump-sum price to purchase a business must determine the cost basis of each tangible and intangible asset included in the purchase as well as any cost recovery method allowed for each asset. The next example illustrates this important process.

[61] §197(a). The 15-year amortization rule does not apply to equity interests in other businesses, debt instruments, existing leases of tangible property, and computer software available for purchase by the general public. Under §167(f)(1), the cost of such off-the-shelf software is amortizable over 36 months.

Firm RT's Lump-Sum Purchase

Firm RT purchased the business operated by SW, Inc. for a lump-sum price of $1 million. At the date of purchase, the appraised values of SW's business assets were as follows:

	Appraised FMV
Accounts receivable	$120,000
Supplies	25,000
Inventory	325,000
Furniture and fixtures	360,000
Lease on real property (8-year remaining term)	40,000
	$870,000

RT was willing to pay $1 million because the business has such an excellent reputation in the local community. The cost basis in each of its newly acquired business assets follows:

	Initial Cost Basis
Accounts receivable	$ 120,000
Supplies	25,000
Inventory	325,000
Furniture and fixtures	360,000
Lease on real property	40,000
Purchased goodwill	130,000
	$1,000,000

- RT will recover its basis in the accounts receivable as the receivables are collected.
- RT will recover its basis in the supplies as a deduction when the supplies are consumed.
- RT will recover its basis in the inventory through cost of goods sold.
- RT will recover its basis in the furniture and fixtures through MACRS depreciation.
- RT will recover its basis in the lease through amortization deductions over the eight-year remaining term of the lease.
- RT will recover its basis in the goodwill through amortization deductions over 15 years.

DEPLETION OF NATURAL RESOURCES

LO 7-10
Distinguish between cost depletion and percentage depletion.

Firms engaged in the business of extracting minerals, oil, gas, and other natural deposits from the earth incur a variety of up-front costs to locate, acquire, and develop their operating mines and wells. Some of these costs must be capitalized and recovered over the period of years that the mine or well is productive.[62] The method for recovering a firm's investment in an exhaustible natural resource is called **cost depletion.** The annual cost depletion deduction is based on the following formula:[63]

$$\frac{\text{Units of production sold during the year}}{\begin{array}{c}\text{Estimated total units in the ground}\\\text{at the beginning of the year}\end{array}} \times \text{Unrecovered basis in the mine or well}$$

[62] Oil and gas producers may deduct many intangible drilling and development costs, thereby minimizing the capitalized basis of productive wells.

[63] Reg. §1.611-2(a).

Cost Depletion	Company M, which operates a mining business, spent $500,000 for geological surveys, mineral rights, and excavation costs, all of which were capitalized as the basis of a new copper mine. At the beginning of the first year of production, the company's engineers estimated that the mine should produce 80,000 tons of copper ore. During the first year, 20,000 tons of ore were extracted and sold. The company's cost depletion deduction was $125,000:

$$\frac{20,000 \text{ tons}}{80,000 \text{ tons}} \times \$500,000 \text{ initial basis} = \$125,000$$

At the beginning of the second year, the engineers revised their estimate of the mine's remaining productivity to 65,000 tons; during the second year, 32,000 tons of copper ore were extracted and sold. The cost depletion deduction was $184,615:

$$\frac{32,000 \text{ tons}}{65,000 \text{ tons}} \times \$375,000 \text{ unrecovered basis} = \$184,615$$

By the year in which the copper deposit is exhausted and the mine is no longer productive, Company M will have recovered its entire $500,000 tax basis through cost depletion deductions.

Percentage Depletion

To encourage the high-risk activity of exploration and extraction, Congress invented **percentage depletion,** an annual deduction based on the gross income generated by a depletable property multiplied by an arbitrary depletion rate. For instance, the statutory depletion rate for sulfur and uranium is 22 percent; the rate for gold, silver, copper, iron ore, and crude oil is 15 percent; and the rate for asbestos, coal, and lignite is 10 percent. In any year, a firm is allowed to deduct the *greater* of the cost depletion or percentage depletion attributable to its properties.[64]

Let's highlight the relationship between cost depletion and percentage depletion by returning to our example of Company M and its copper mine.

Percentage Depletion	Company M can sell its copper ore for $40 per ton, and its percentage depletion equals 15 percent of gross income from sales of the ore. The following table shows the computation of the annual depletion deduction (indicated by bold type):

Year	Estimated Tons/ Beginning of Year	Tons Sold during Year	Gross Income	Unrecovered Basis/ Beginning of Year	Cost Depletion	Percentage Depletion*
1	80,000	20,000	$ 800,000	$500,000	**$125,000**	$120,000
2	65,000	32,000	1,280,000	375,000	184,615	**192,000**
3	30,000	17,000	680,000	183,000	**103,700**	102,000
4	15,000	18,500	740,000	79,300	79,300	**111,000**
5	5,000	4,000	160,000	–0–	–0–	**24,000**
6	2,500	2,000	80,000	–0–	–0–	**12,000**

*15 percent of gross income.

Note that in years 1 through 4, Company M deducted the *greater* of cost depletion or percentage depletion and reduced the tax basis in the mine accordingly, but in year 4, a curious thing occurred. Company M claimed a $111,000 depletion deduction that exceeded its unrecovered basis in the mine by $31,700! In years 5 and 6, it deducted $36,000 percentage depletion even though it had a zero basis in the copper mine.

---

[64] §613(a) and (b).

The magic of the percentage depletion deduction is that it is not limited to the capitalized cost of the mine or well. Percentage depletion is available in every year that the property generates gross income, regardless of the fact that the tax basis has been reduced to zero. In such cases, percentage depletion is not a cost recovery deduction at all but an indirect preferential tax rate on the income earned by the extractive industries.

Not surprisingly, this highly beneficial deduction is subject to restrictions. Annual percentage depletion may not exceed 50 percent of the taxable income from the depletable property (100 percent for oil and gas property).[65] In the oil and gas industry, only independent producers and royalty owners are entitled to percentage depletion. This tax break is denied to the giant integrated companies that extract, refine, and sell oil and gas to retail customers.[66] Even with these restrictions, percentage depletion is a valuable government subsidy.

COST RECOVERY–RELATED BOOK/TAX DIFFERENCES

LO 7-11
Explain cost recovery–related book/tax differences and their effect on GAAP financial statements.

Tax cost recovery amounts often differ from those computed in the preparation of GAAP-based financial statements. Varying recovery lives and methods typically produce temporary book/tax differences that reverse over time or on disposition of the related assets. This final section of the chapter details four common sources of cost recovery book/tax differences related to (1) depreciation, (2) inventory, (3) organizational and start-up costs, and (4) goodwill.

Depreciation Book/Tax Differences

MACRS depreciation for tax purposes typically exceeds book depreciation in the early years of an asset's recovery life. This favorable temporary difference will reverse over time. In addition, the availability of bonus depreciation and the Section 179 deduction often cause tax depreciation to significantly exceed book depreciation in the year of acquisition of qualifying assets.

Book/Tax Difference for Depreciation

Porter, Inc. purchased a depreciable asset for $200,000. First-year depreciation for book purposes was $19,000, whereas MACRS depreciation was $28,580. The $9,580 excess tax depreciation is a favorable book/tax difference resulting in a $2,012 deferred tax liability ($9,580 × 21 percent tax rate). The temporary difference will reverse in future years when book depreciation exceeds MACRS depreciation. As the difference reverses, the deferred tax liability will be reduced. By the year in which book basis and tax basis of the asset are depreciated to zero, the deferred tax liability will be eliminated.

Inventory Book/Tax Differences

The UNICAP rules for calculating tax basis of inventory may require indirect costs that were expensed for financial statement purposes to be capitalized for tax purposes. For example, the UNICAP rules require capitalization of indirect payroll department costs, to the extent related to the production function. Such costs would normally be expensed as a period cost under GAAP. The resulting book/tax difference is temporary and will reverse in the year in which the capitalized costs are deducted as cost of goods sold.

[65] Ibid.
[66] §613A(c).

Book/Tax Difference for UNICAP	In year 1, Company MN constructed an inventory item that was on hand at year-end. It incurred $100,000 indirect costs in the construction process. For financial statement purposes, Company MN capitalized $80,000 as inventory product costs and expensed $20,000 as period costs. Under the UNICAP rules, it had to capitalize $88,000 to inventory and could deduct only $12,000 on its tax return. In year 2, Company MN sold the inventory item. For the two-year period, this temporary book/tax difference resulted in the following:

	Book		Tax		Taxable Income over
Year 1	**Expense**	**Inventory Cost**	**Deduction**	**Inventory Cost**	**Book Income**
	$20,000	$80,000	$12,000	$88,000	$8,000

Year 2	**Cost of Goods Sold**	**Cost of Goods Sold**	**Book Income over Taxable Income**
	$80,000	$88,000	$8,000

Book/Tax Difference for Organizational and Start-Up Costs

For financial reporting purposes, firms generally expense organizational and start-up costs when incurred. Thus, the tax requirement to capitalize and amortize a portion of such costs creates a temporary book/tax difference.

Book/Tax Difference for Organizational Costs	Crandall Corporation was formed January 1 of year 1 and incurred $40,000 of organizational costs. All of these costs were expensed in preparing Crandall's year 1 financial statements.
	For tax purposes, Crandall may deduct $5,000 of its organizational costs in year 1. It may also deduct year 1 amortization of $2,333 ($35,000 × 12/180). The difference in book and tax treatment of these costs results in a year 1 unfavorable book/tax difference of $32,667 [$40,000 book expense − ($5,000 + $2,333 tax deductions)]. Crandall will record a year 1 deferred tax asset related to organizational costs of $6,860 ($32,667 × 21 percent tax rate).
	In years 2 through 15, Crandall will continue to deduct amortization of its organizational costs without further book expense. These future favorable book/tax differences will reduce its deferred tax asset at a rate of $490 per year ($2,333 tax deduction × 21 percent tax rate).

Book/Tax Difference for Goodwill

The tax treatment of purchased goodwill is very different from the treatment under GAAP. Firms are not required to amortize the cost of goodwill for financial reporting purposes. Accordingly, the annual deduction for goodwill amortization is a favorable temporary difference between book income and taxable income. For financial reporting purposes, firms must test their purchased goodwill annually for any impairment to its value. If the value of the goodwill is impaired, the firm must record an impairment expense and write down the value of the goodwill reported on its balance sheet.[67] This expense, which is based on an estimate, is not deductible. Consequently, an impairment expense is an unfavorable temporary difference between book income and taxable income.

[67] SFAS No. 142, *Goodwill and Other Intangible Assets* (2000).

| *Book/Tax Difference for Goodwill* | Five years ago, Grant, Inc. purchased a business for a lump-sum price of $12 million. Grant allocated $3.5 million to the goodwill of the acquired business. For tax purposes, Grant is amortizing the capitalized cost of the goodwill at a rate of $19,444 per month ($3.5 million ÷ 180 months). The goodwill is not amortizable for book purposes, so the annual $233,328 amortization deduction is a favorable book/tax difference resulting in an annual $48,999 deferred tax liability ($233,328 × 21 percent tax rate).

This year, Grant's auditors required the corporation to write the goodwill down to $3 million and record a $500,000 goodwill impairment expense. This nondeductible expense is an unfavorable book/tax difference resulting in a $105,000 reduction ($500,000 × 21 percent tax rate) in Grant's deferred tax liability with respect to its goodwill. |

Conclusion

The after-tax cost of a business expenditure is a function of the time period over which the firm can deduct the expenditure. If an expenditure is not deductible in the current year but must be capitalized to an asset account, its after-tax cost depends on the method (if any) by which the firm can compute cost recovery deductions with respect to the asset. Exhibit 7.1 summarizes the tax treatment of business expenditures and should help you appreciate the key roles that cost of goods sold, depreciation, amortization, and depletion play in the tax planning process.

EXHIBIT 7.1
Tax Treatment of Business Expenditures

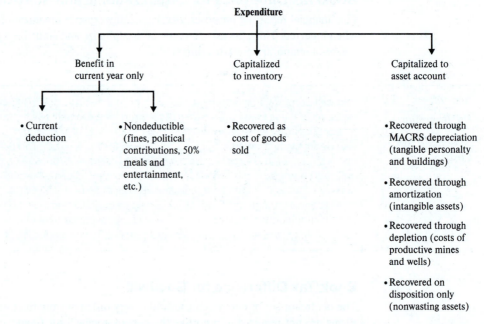

Sources of Book/Tax Differences

Permanent
- Percentage depletion in excess of cost depletion

Temporary
- Intangible drilling costs (IDCs)
- Inventory costs capitalized under UNICAP

- MACRS depreciation
- Section 179 deduction
- Bonus depreciation
- Amortization of organizational and start-up costs
- Amortization of purchased intangibles (goodwill)
- Goodwill impairment expense

Key Terms

adjusted basis *7-6*	leasehold costs *7-26*	percentage depletion *7-29*
amortization *7-23*	leasehold	qualified improvement
bonus depreciation *7-21*	improvements *7-26*	property *7-13*
capitalization *7-2*	leverage *7-8*	recovery period *7-12*
cost basis *7-7*	LIFO *7-10*	research and experimental
cost depletion *7-28*	midmonth	expenditures *7-5*
cost of goods sold *7-9*	convention *7-14*	Section 179 election *7-19*
depreciation *7-11*	midquarter	specific identification
expansion costs *7-25*	convention *7-13*	method *7-10*
FIFO *7-10*	Modified Accelerated	start-up expenditures *7-24*
going-concern value *7-27*	Cost Recovery System	tax basis *7-6*
goodwill *7-27*	(MACRS) *7-11*	uniform capitalization
half-year convention *7-13*	organizational costs *7-24*	(UNICAP) rules *7-10*
intangible drilling and	passenger	
development costs	automobiles *7-18*	
(IDCs) *7-6*		

Questions and Problems for Discussion

LO 7-1   1. How is the principle of conservatism reflected in the tax law's premise concerning the deductibility of business expenditures?

LO 7-1   2. Assume that Congress enacted legislation requiring firms to capitalize advertising costs and amortize them over 20 years. Discuss the potential effects of such legislation on the amount of advertising that firms purchase and the price that advertising companies charge for their product.

LO 7-7   3. Discuss the relationship between cost recovery deductions and cash flows.

LO 7-2, 7-7   4. To what extent do cost recovery deductions based on the capitalized cost of a tangible asset reflect a decline in the economic value of that asset?

LO 7-2   5. Can a firm have a negative tax basis in an asset?

LO 7-1, 7-2   6. If the tax law did not allow farming businesses to deduct soil and water conservation expenditures but required capitalization of these costs, in what year or years would farmers recover these costs?

LO 7-1, 7-4   7. Corporation J manufactures electrical appliances. Corporation K provides architectural services. During the year, both corporations paid $56,000 annual premiums to carry fire and casualty insurance on their tangible assets. Corporation J was required to capitalize the $56,000 cost for tax purposes, while Corporation K was allowed a $56,000 deduction. Can you explain this difference in tax treatment between the two corporations?

LO 7-4   8. Identify the tax and nontax issues that firms must consider in adopting the LIFO method of accounting for inventories.

LO 7-11   9. Identify four possible differences in the computation of depreciation expense for financial statement purposes and MACRS depreciation.

LO 7-5   10. What is the purpose of the MACRS half-year, midquarter, and midmonth conventions?

LO 7-5   11. Why do the MACRS tables published by the IRS incorporate a depreciation convention for the first year during an asset's recovery period but not for the year of disposition?

LO 7-7   12. Discuss the reasons the Section 179 election is more valuable to small firms than to large firms.

LO 7-7   13. Firm O purchased two items of business personalty this year. The first item cost $1,035,000 and has a five-year recovery period, and the second item cost $1,061,500 and has a seven-year recovery period. Firm O wants to make the Section 179 election for one of its new assets. Which asset should the firm choose and why?

LO 7-9   14. Discuss the strengths and weaknesses of the tax rule providing for 15-year amortization of the cost of business acquisition intangibles.

LO 7-9   15. Describe the difference in tax treatment between start-up costs of a new business and expansion costs of an existing business.

LO 7-4, 7-5, 7-9   16. On February 1, Mr. Barnes purchased a business from Mr. and Mrs. Sanchez for a lump-sum price of $750,000. The business included the following balance sheet assets:

	Appraised FMV
Accounts receivable	$ 27,600
Inventory	195,000
Office supplies (4 months' worth)	8,500
Furniture and fixtures	395,000

By buying the business, Mr. Barnes acquired a favorable lease on office space with a remaining term of 31 months; he estimates that the value of this lease is $20,000. The purchase contract stipulates that Mr. and Mrs. Sanchez will not engage in a competitive business for the next 36 months. Discuss how Mr. Barnes can recover the cost of each of the business assets acquired in this purchase.

LO 7-9   17. Firm W and Firm X both have goodwill and going-concern value worth approximately $1 million. However, only Firm X reports an amortization deduction with respect to its goodwill and going-concern value on its tax return. Can you explain this difference in tax treatment between the two firms?

LO 7-10   18. Under what circumstances is percentage depletion not a true cost recovery deduction?

LO 7-9   19. The Tax Cuts and Jobs Act of 2017 changed the tax treatment of research and experimentation costs incurred after 2021. This change requires capitalization and amortization of costs that previously were deductible when incurred. How does this change affect the after-tax cost of these expenditures?

 **All applicable Application Problems are available with *Connect*.**

Application Problems

LO 7-1   1. Assuming a 21 percent tax rate, compute the after-tax cost of the following business expenditures:
  a. $14,200 cost of a survey capitalized to land.
  b. $44,750 research and experimental expenditure incurred prior to 2022.
  c. $23,000 advertising cost.
  d. $120,000 cost of grading land used in a nonfarming business.
  e. $120,000 cost of grading land used in a farming business.

LO 7-1   2. Assuming a 21 percent tax rate, compute the after-tax cost of the following business expenditures:
  a. $20,000 cost of equipment subject to Section 179 election.
  b. $17,500 business expansion costs.
  c. $125,000 cost of land held for investment.
  d. $34,500 intangible drilling costs.

LO 7-2 3. Determine the tax basis of the business asset acquired in each of the following cases:

    a. Firm L paid $5,950 cash plus $416 sales tax plus a $500 installation charge for a satellite dish.

    b. TTP, Inc. acquired inventory in exchange for 800 shares of TTP common stock listed on Nasdaq at $212 per share on the date of exchange.

    c. Firm Q acquired machinery in exchange for architectural drawings rendered by Firm's Q's junior partner. The partner spent 20 hours on the drawings, and their hourly billing rate is $350.

    d. Company C purchased equipment by paying $2,000 cash at date of purchase and financing the $18,000 balance of the price under a three-year deferred payment plan.

LO 7-2 4. ABC Company purchased business property several years ago, paying $25,000 cash and borrowing $80,000 to fund the acquisition. ABC also incurred $2,000 of freight costs for shipping the property to its business location. Over time, ABC has incurred $12,000 of repair costs for the property and made $7,000 of capital improvements. ABC has also deducted $56,000 of MACRS depreciation on the property to date. Calculate ABC's adjusted tax basis in this asset.

LO 7-11 5. Early this year, ZeZe, Inc. paid a $52,000 legal fee in connection with a dispute over ZeZe's title to investment land. ZeZe's auditors required the corporation to expense the payment on this year's financial statements. According to ZeZe's tax adviser, the payment is a nondeductible capital expenditure. ZeZe's tax rate is 21 percent.

    a. Compute the deferred tax asset or a deferred tax liability (identify which) resulting from this difference in accounting treatment.

    b. When will the temporary difference reverse?

LO 7-2 6. In year 1, Firm A paid $50,000 cash to purchase a tangible business asset. In year 1 and year 2, it deducted $3,140 and $7,200 depreciation with respect to the asset. Firm A's marginal tax rate in both years was 21 percent.

    a. Compute Firm A's net cash flow attributable to the asset purchase in each year.

    b. Compute Firm A's adjusted basis in the asset at the end of each year.

LO 7-3 7. Refer to the facts in problem 6. Now assume that Firm A borrowed $50,000 to purchase the asset. In each year, it paid $3,800 annual interest on the debt. The interest payments were deductible.

    a. How does this change in facts affect Firm A's net cash flow attributable to the asset purchase in each year?

    b. How does this change in facts affect Firm A's adjusted basis in the asset at the end of each year?

LO 7-3 8. Hansen Company, a cash basis taxpayer, paid $50,000 for an asset in year 0. Assume it can deduct one-half of the cost in year 0 and the remainder in year 1. Assume a 21 percent tax rate and 8 percent discount rate.

    a. Calculate the net present value of Hansen's after-tax cost of the asset.

    b. Now assume Hansen borrows the $50,000 needed to purchase the asset. It repays the loan in year 2, with interest of $10,000. Calculate the net present value of Hansen's after-tax cost of the asset under these new facts.

LO 7-8 9. In year 0, Jarmex paid $55,000 for an overhaul of a tangible operating asset. Jarmex has a 21 percent marginal tax rate and uses a 7 percent discount rate to compute NPV.

    a. Compute the after-tax cost of the overhaul if Jarmex can deduct the $55,000 payment as a repair in year 0.

    b. Compute the after-tax cost of the overhaul if Jarmex must capitalize the $55,000 payment to the asset account and can recover it on a straight-line basis in years 0, 1, 2, and 3.

LO 7-4   10. Company XYZ manufactures a tangible product and sells the product at wholesale. In its first year of operations, XYZ manufactured 1,000 units of product and incurred $200,000 direct material cost and $130,000 direct labor costs. For financial statement purposes, XYZ capitalized $85,000 indirect costs to inventory. For tax purposes, it had to capitalize $116,000 indirect costs to inventory under the UNICAP rules. At the end of its first year, XYZ held 260 units in inventory. Compute XYZ's cost of goods sold for book purposes and for tax purposes.

LO 7-4, 7-11   11. Refer to the facts in problem 10. In its second year of operations, XYZ manufactured 2,000 units of product and incurred $410,000 direct material cost and $275,000 direct labor costs. For financial statement purposes, XYZ capitalized $139,000 indirect costs to inventory. For tax purposes, it had to capitalize $193,000 indirect costs to inventory under the UNICAP rules. At the end of its second year, XYZ held 300 items in inventory. Compute XYZ's cost of goods sold for book purposes and for tax purposes assuming that

a. XYZ uses the FIFO costing convention.

b. XYZ uses the LIFO costing convention.

LO 7-4, 7-11   12. In its first year of operations, Lima Company manufactured 1,000 widgets, incurring direct materials and labor costs of $227,000. For book purposes, Lima capitalized $260,000 of indirect manufacturing costs. For tax purposes, it had to capitalize $315,000 of indirect costs under the UNICAP rules. At the end of the year, Lima had 170 widgets remaining in inventory.

a. For book purposes, compute Lima's ending inventory cost and cost of goods sold for the year.

b. For tax purposes, compute Lima's ending inventory cost and cost of goods sold for the year.

c. Compute Lima's inventory book/tax difference and indicate if such difference is favorable or unfavorable.

LO 7-5   13. Firm J purchased a depreciable business asset for $62,500. Assuming the firm uses the half-year convention, compute its first-year MACRS depreciation if the asset is

a. A land irrigation system.

b. Duplicating equipment.

c. An oceangoing barge.

d. Small manufacturing tools.

LO 7-5   14. Herelt, Inc., a calendar year taxpayer, purchased equipment for $383,600 and placed it in service on April 1, 2023. The equipment was seven-year recovery property, and Herelt used the half-year convention to compute MACRS depreciation.

a. Compute Herelt's MACRS depreciation with respect to the equipment for 2023 and 2024.

b. Compute Herelt's adjusted basis in the equipment on December 31, 2024.

c. Compute Herelt's MACRS depreciation for 2025 if it disposes of the equipment on February 9, 2025.

LO 7-5   15. Knute Company purchased only one asset during its calendar taxable year. The asset cost $650,000 and has a three-year recovery period. Compute MACRS depreciation with respect to this asset over the recovery period assuming that

a. The asset was placed in service on August 18.

b. The asset was placed in service on November 9.

LO 7-5 16. Erwin Company, a calendar year taxpayer, made only two purchases of depreciable personalty this year. The first purchase was five-year recovery property costing $312,800, and the second purchase was seven-year recovery property costing $574,000. Compute Erwin's first-year MACRS depreciation with respect to the personalty assuming that

a. The first purchase occurred on February 2, and the second purchase occurred on June 18.

b. The first purchase occurred on February 2, and the second purchase occurred on October 13.

LO 7-5, 7-11 17. Suber, Inc., a calendar year taxpayer, purchased equipment for $800,000 and placed it in service on March 1. Suber's chief engineer determined that the equipment had an estimated useful life of 120 months and a $50,000 residual value. For financial statement purposes, Suber uses the straight-line method to compute depreciation.

a. Compute book depreciation for the year.

b. Assuming that the equipment has a seven-year recovery period and is subject to the half-year convention, compute MACRS depreciation for the year.

c. Compute Suber's book basis and tax basis in the equipment at the beginning of next year.

LO 7-5 18. Ryland Company, a calendar year taxpayer, purchased commercial realty for $2 million and allocated $200,000 cost to the land and $1.8 million cost to the building. Ryland placed the real estate in service on May 21.

a. Compute Ryland's MACRS depreciation with respect to the realty for the year of purchase.

b. How would your answer change if Ryland placed the realty in service on September 2 instead of May 21?

c. How would your answer to (*a*) change if the building was a residential apartment complex instead of a commercial office?

LO 7-5 19. AP constructed a new manufacturing plant for a total cost of $9,465,000 and placed it in service on March 2. To finance the construction, AP took out a $6 million, 30-year mortgage on the property. Compute AP's MACRS depreciation for the manufacturing plant for the first, second, and third years of operation.

LO 7-6 20. On May 12, 2022, Nelson, Inc. purchased eight passenger automobiles for its business. Nelson did not make a Section 179 election to expense any portion of the cost of the automobiles, which are five-year recovery property subject to the half-year convention. Assuming no bonus depreciation or Section 179 deduction, compute Nelson's depreciation deduction with respect to the automobiles for 2022 and 2023 assuming

a. The automobiles were Mini Coopers costing $14,300 each.

b. The automobiles were Cadillacs costing $60,000 each.

LO 7-6 21. In March 2022, Jones Company purchased a Mercedes for use in its business at a cost of $73,000. Assuming no bonus depreciation or Section 179 deduction, calculate the allowable tax depreciation on this asset for 2022, 2023, and 2024.

LO 7-5, 7-7 22. Margo, a calendar year taxpayer, paid $1,580,000 for new machinery (seven-year recovery property) placed in service on August 1, 2023.

a. Assuming that the machinery was the only tangible property placed in service during the year, compute Margo's maximum cost recovery deduction.

b. How would your computation change if Margo paid $3,100,000 for the machinery?

    c. How would your computation change if Margo paid $4,750,000 for the machinery?

    d. How would your answer to part (*a*) change if the machinery was purchased in 2022 instead of 2023?

LO 7-7 23. In 2023, Firm L purchased machinery costing $21,300 and elected to expense the entire cost under Section 179. How much of the expense can Firm L deduct in each of the following cases?

    a. Its taxable income before the deduction was $58,000.

    b. Its taxable income before the deduction was $19,200.

    c. Its net operating loss (NOL) before the deduction was $5,016.

LO 7-7 24. In 2022, Company W elected under Section 179 to expense $19,300 of the cost of qualifying property. However, it could deduct only $15,000 of the expense because of the taxable income limitation. In 2023, Company W's taxable income before any Section 179 deduction was $1,812,000. Compute its 2023 Section 179 deduction if

    a. The total cost of qualifying property purchased in 2023 was $13,600.

    b. The total cost of qualifying property purchased in 2023 was $1,158,000.

LO 7-7 25. Loni Company paid $1,167,000 for tangible personalty in 2022 and elected to expense $1,080,000 of the cost (the limited dollar amount for 2022). Loni's taxable income before a Section 179 deduction was $894,100. Loni paid $23,700 for tangible personalty in 2023 and elected to expense the entire cost. Loni's taxable income before a Section 179 deduction was $228,000.

    a. Compute Loni's Section 179 deduction and taxable income for 2022.

    b. Compute Loni's Section 179 deduction and taxable income for 2023.

LO 7-5, 7-7 26. At the beginning of its 2023 tax year, Hiram owned the following business assets:

	Date Placed in Service	Initial Cost	Accumulated Depreciation	Recovery Period	Depreciation Convention
Furniture	6/19/21	$30,750	$11,925	7-year	Half-year
Equipment	5/2/20	70,000	49,840	5-year	Half-year
Machinery	9/30/20	58,000	41,296	5-year	Half-year

On July 8, Hiram sold its equipment. On August 18, it purchased and placed in service new tools costing $589,000; these tools are three-year recovery property. These were Hiram's only capital transactions for the year. Compute Hiram's maximum cost recovery deduction for 2023. In making your computation, assume that taxable income before depreciation exceeds $2,000,000.

LO 7-5, 7-7 27. In April 2023, Lenape Corporation completed security, fire, and heating system improvements to existing nonresidential real property with a total cost of $1,285,000. Assuming these improvements are 39-year recovery property and qualify for the Section 179 deduction, calculate Lenape's total cost recovery on the improvements for 2023.

LO 7-9 28. Ajax, Inc. was formed on April 25 and elected a calendar year for tax purposes. Ajax paid $11,200 to the attorney who drew up the articles of incorporation and $5,100 to the CPA who advised the corporation concerning the accounting and tax implications of its organization. Ajax began business operations on July 15. To what extent can Ajax deduct its $16,300 organizational costs on its first tax return?

LO 7-9 29. Mr. and Mrs. Fabrizio, a retired couple, decided to open a family restaurant. During March and April, they incurred the following expenses:

Prepaid rent on commercial real estate	$18,900
($2,100 per month from April through December)	
Prepaid rent on restaurant equipment	8,910
($990 per month from April through December)	
Advertising of upcoming grand opening	900
Staff hiring and training	11,500
	$40,210

Mr. and Mrs. Fabrizio served their first meal to a customer on May 1. Determine the tax treatment of the given expenses on their tax return.

LO 7-9 30. Mr. Zan, a calendar year taxpayer, opened a new car wash. Prior to the car wash's grand opening on October 8, Mr. Zan incurred various start-up expenditures (rent, utilities, employee salaries, supplies, and so on). In each of the following cases, compute Mr. Zan's first-year deduction with respect to these expenditures.

a. The start-up expenditures totaled $4,750.

b. The start-up expenditures totaled $27,320.

c. The start-up expenditures totaled $53,120.

d. The start-up expenditures totaled $88,380.

LO 7-5, 7-9 31. MNO is a calendar year taxpayer. On March 1, MNO signed a 36-month lease on 2,100 square feet of commercial office space. It paid a $3,240 fee to the real estate agent who located the space and negotiated the lease and $8,800 to install new overhead lighting in the office space. Lighting equipment is seven-year recovery property. Compute MNO's first-year cost recovery deduction with respect to the $12,040 cost relating to the lease space, assuming no Section 179 deduction or bonus depreciation.

LO 7-5, 7-9 32. On April 23, Mrs. Yu purchased a taxi business from Mr. Mann for a $60,000 lump-sum price. The business consisted of a two-year-old taxicab worth $19,000, Mr. Mann's license to operate a taxi business in Baltimore, his list of regular customers, and his registered business name "On Time Any Time Taxi." Mrs. Yu operated the business from April 24 through the end of the year.

a. Compute Mrs. Yu's taxable income from the taxi business if her taxable income *before any cost recovery deductions* was $36,890. Assume Mrs. Yu wants to minimize taxable income.

b. Compute Mrs. Yu's taxable income from the taxi business if her taxable income *before any cost recovery deductions* was $17,100. Assume Mrs. Yu wants to minimize taxable income but does not wish to take bonus depreciation.

LO 7-5, 7-9 33. On November 13, Underhill, Inc., a calendar year taxpayer, purchased a business for a $750,000 lump-sum price. The business's balance sheet assets had the following appraised FMV:

Accounts receivable	$ 38,000
Inventory	177,000
Tangible personalty	400,000
	$615,000

    a. What is the cost basis of the goodwill acquired by Underhill on the purchase of this business?

    b. Compute Underhill's goodwill amortization deduction for the year of purchase.

    c. Assuming a 21 percent tax rate, compute the deferred tax asset or deferred tax liability (identify which) resulting from Underhill's amortization deduction.

LO 7-1, 7-5, 7-9, 7-11

34. SEP, a calendar year corporation, reported $918,000 net income before tax on its current year financial statements prepared in accordance with GAAP. The corporation's records reveal the following information:

- SEP incurred $75,000 of domestic research costs that resulted in a new 17-year patent for the corporation. SEP expensed these costs for book purposes.

- SEP's depreciation expense per books was $98,222, and its MACRS depreciation deduction was $120,000.

- SEP was organized two years ago. For its first taxable year, it capitalized $27,480 start-up costs and elected to amortize them over 180 months. For book purposes, it expensed the costs in the year incurred.

Compute SEP's taxable income.

LO 7-4, 7-5, 7-9, 7-11

35. TGW, a calendar year corporation, reported $3,908,000 net income before tax on its financial statements prepared in accordance with GAAP. The corporation's records reveal the following information:

- TGW's depreciation expense per books was $448,000, and its MACRS depreciation deduction was $377,900.

- TGW capitalized $678,000 indirect expenses to manufactured inventory for book purposes and $802,000 indirect expenses to manufactured inventory for tax purposes.

- TGW's cost of manufactured goods sold was $2,557,000 for book purposes and $2,638,000 for tax purposes.

- Four years ago, TGW capitalized $2,250,000 goodwill when it purchased a competitor's business. This year, TGW's auditors required the corporation to write the goodwill down to $1,500,000 and record a $750,000 goodwill impairment expense.

Compute TGW's taxable income.

LO 7-10

36. A&Z incurred $450,000 of capitalized costs to develop a uranium mine. The corporation's geologists estimated that the mine would produce 900,000 tons of ore. During the year, 215,000 tons were extracted and sold. A&Z's gross revenues from the sales totaled $689,000, and its operating expenses for the mine were $200,000. Calculate A&Z's depletion deduction.

LO 7-10

37. Jonson Corporation incurred $150,000 in capitalized acquisition costs to develop an oil well. The corporation's geologists estimated that there were 200,000 barrels of oil in the well at the beginning of the year. Jonson produced and sold 20,000 barrels this year, earning $140,000 of gross revenue. Its operating expenses for the well totaled $25,000. Calculate Jonson's allowable depletion deduction.

Issue Recognition Problems

Identify the tax issue or issues suggested by the following situations, and state each issue in the form of a question.

LO 7-1

1. Corporation J paid $500,000 for six acres of land on which it plans to build a new corporate headquarters. Four months after the purchase, Corporation J paid $20,000 to a demolition company to tear down an old warehouse located on the land and haul away the rubble from the demolition site.

LO 7-5   2. Mr. Rey lived in a two-bedroom, one-bath residence until August when he moved to a new home and converted his old residence into residential rent property. He had no trouble finding tenants, who signed a one-year lease and moved in on September 1. As of this date, the market value of the old residence was $120,000. Mr. Rey purchased the residence six years ago for $180,000.

LO 7-7   3. Mrs. Kim owns her own consulting firm, and her husband, Mr. Kim, owns a printing business. This year, Mrs. Kim's consulting business generated $89,000 taxable income. Mr. Kim's business operated at a loss. In July, Mr. Kim bought new office furniture for $16,000. This was the only purchase of tangible business personalty by either spouse for the year. Mr. and Mrs. Kim always file a joint tax return.

LO 7-2, 7-9   4. ROJ, Inc. purchased a 20-acre industrial complex consisting of three warehouses and two office buildings surrounded by parking lots. About 12 acres of the land is undeveloped. ROJ paid a lump-sum purchase price of $19.4 million.

LO 7-1, 7-2   5. Firm PY purchased industrial equipment from a Canadian vendor. The firm paid $12,800 to transport the equipment to its manufacturing plant in Florida and a $1,700 premium for insurance against casualty or theft of the equipment while en route.

LO 7-1, 7-9   6. WRT owns a chain of retail bookstores. It recently decided to add coffee bars in each store to sell gourmet coffee drinks and pastries to the bookstore customers. WRT has not yet obtained the necessary licenses required under local law to serve food to the public. However, it has incurred almost $30,000 in up-front expenditures on the coffee bars.

LO 7-1   7. In 2018, Firm Z elected to expense the $8,000 cost of a machine, which it reported as the only item of equipment placed in service that year. This year, the IRS audited Firm Z's 2018 return and discovered that it had incorrectly deducted a $10,000 expenditure. According to the IRS, Firm Z should have capitalized this expenditure as the cost of depreciable equipment with a five-year recovery period.

LO 7-5   8. Company JJ, a calendar year corporation, bought an airplane for use in its oil and gas business in December. The manufacturer delivered the plane to the company's hangar on December 19. Because of severe winter weather, JJ's pilot was unable to fly the plane on company business until February 16 of the next year.

LO 7-1   9. TCJ bought a 10-acre tract of undeveloped land that it intends to improve and subdivide for sale to real estate customers. This year, TCJ paid $4,300 to a local company to clean up the land by hauling away trash, cutting down dead trees, and spraying for poison ivy.

LO 7-1, 7-5   10. Firm D paid a $500,000 lump-sum price for a commercial office building. A local consulting company approached Firm D with a proposal. For a $15,000 fee, the company would analyze the components of the building (shelving, lighting fixtures, floor coverings, plumbing, etc.) to determine how much of the $500,000 price is attributable to five-year or seven-year recovery property rather than to the building itself.

Research Problems

LO 7-5   1. Elsworthy Company operates a number of public golf courses in Florida. This year, Elsworthy constructed six new greens of a type described as "modern" greens. Modern greens contain sophisticated drainage systems that include subsurface drainage tiles and interconnected pipes. These tiles and pipes require replacement about every 20 years. The cost of each modern green was $115,000: $30,000 for earthmoving, grading, and shaping of the land in preparation for construction and $85,000 for construction of the green itself. What is the correct tax treatment of the total cost of each modern green?

LO 7-1 2. On January 1 of every year since 1993, Lanier Corporation has paid a $35,000 retainer fee to the law firm of Myer and Weeble (MW). MW specializes in structuring corporate mergers and acquisitions. In return for the annual payment, MW guarantees that it will represent Lanier for one year. Moreover, MW will not provide legal assistance to any business that Lanier attempts to acquire during the year. MW is entitled to keep the annual retainer regardless of the actual amount of legal work performed for Lanier. On January 1, Lanier paid the annual $35,000 retainer to MW. In August, MW structured Lanier's acquisition of Carstron Manufacturing. MW sent Lanier a bill for $100,000 of additional legal fees in connection with this acquisition.

The tax law clearly requires Lanier to capitalize the $100,000 additional legal fees as part of the cost of Carstron Manufacturing. But can Lanier deduct (rather than capitalize) the $35,000 retainer paid in January?

LO 7-9 3. Last year, Manabee, Inc. leased a computer system from ICS Company for five years. After using the system for only 10 months, Manabee realized that it was no longer adequate for its expanding business needs. As a result, Manabee negotiated with ICS to terminate the original lease and enter into a new five-year lease under which ICS would provide Manabee with an expanded, upgraded computer system. ICS would not agree to the arrangement unless Manabee paid a $200,000 lease cancellation fee. Can Manabee deduct this fee as a current expense, or must Manabee capitalize the fee as a leasehold cost and amortize it over the five-year term of the new lease?

LO 7-7 4. Peter Nelson is employed full time as an accountant by an insurance company. In his spare time, he operates a secondary business as a self-employed wedding photographer. On January 3 of the current year, Peter purchased new video recording equipment for $22,600. Throughout this year, he used this equipment for personal enjoyment (filming his family members on holidays and during vacations). He also used the equipment for business purposes when a client wanted video coverage of a wedding. Peter did not purchase any other property for business use during the year. Peter kept a careful written record of the time that he used the video recording equipment for either personal or business reasons during the year. This record substantiates that he used the equipment 59 percent of the time for personal reasons and 41 percent of the time for business reasons. Can Peter elect to expense any of the cost of the video recording equipment under Section 179?

Mc Graw Hill **connect** All applicable Tax Planning Cases are available with *Connect*.

Tax Planning Cases

LO 7-5 1. MRT, a calendar year corporation, placed the following assets in service this year:

Asset	Initial Cost	Recovery Period	Date Placed in Service
Manufacturing equipment	$259,000	7 years	April 23
Furniture and fixtures	56,000	7 years	May 2
Transportation equipment	225,000	5 years	September 3
Office equipment	120,000	7 years	December 1

a. Compute MRT's MACRS depreciation with respect to the assets placed in service this year. Assume MRT does not elect to use first-year bonus depreciation or Section 179.

    b. In December, MRT decided to purchase $285,000 of additional equipment. The corporation could buy the equipment and place it in service before year-end, or it could postpone the purchase until January. What effect does this decision have on MRT's depreciation with respect to the assets already in service?

LO 7-5, 7-8

2. Company C has a 21 percent marginal tax rate and uses an 8 percent discount rate to compute NPV. The company must decide whether to lease or purchase equipment to use for years 0 through 7. It could lease the equipment for $21,000 annual rent, or it could purchase the equipment for $100,000. The seller would require no money down and would allow Company C to defer payment until year 4 at 11.5 percent simple interest ($11,500 interest payable in years 1, 2, 3, and 4). The equipment would be seven-year MACRS recovery property with no residual value. Should Company C lease or purchase the equipment to minimize the after-tax cost of the use of the property for eight years?

LO 7-5, 7-7, 7-8

3. MG, a corporation in the 21 percent marginal tax bracket, owns equipment that is fully depreciated. This old equipment is still operating and should continue to do so for four years (years 0, 1, 2, and 3). MG's chief financial officer estimates that repair costs for the old equipment will be $1,300 in year 0, $1,400 in year 1, $1,500 in year 2, and $1,600 in year 3. At the end of year 3, the equipment will have no residual value.

    MG could junk the old equipment and buy new equipment for $5,000 cash. The new equipment will have a three-year MACRS recovery period, should not require any repairs during years 0 through 3, and will have no residual value at the end of year 3.

    a. Assume MG cannot make a Section 179 election to expense the $5,000 cost of the new equipment. Which option (keep old or buy new) minimizes MG's after-tax cost? In making your calculations, use a 10 percent discount rate.

    b. Assume MG can make a Section 179 election to expense the entire $5,000 cost of the new equipment. Under this change in facts, which option (keep old or buy new) minimizes MG's after-tax cost?

LO 7-5, 7-8

4. KP, Inc. is negotiating a 10-year lease for three floors of space in a commercial office building. KP can't use the space unless a security system is installed. The cost of the system is $50,000, and it will qualify as seven-year recovery property under MACRS. The building's owner has offered KP a choice. The owner will pay for the installation of the security system and charge $79,000 annual rent. Alternatively, KP can pay for the installation of the security system, and the owner will charge only $72,000 annual rent. Assuming that KP has a 21 percent marginal tax rate, cannot make a Section 179 election to expense the $50,000 cost, and uses a 9 percent discount rate to compute NPV, which alternative should it choose?

Appendix 7–A

Midquarter Convention Tables

Midquarter Convention for Business Personalty Placed in Service in First Quarter

Depreciation Rate for Recovery Period

Year	3-Year	5-Year	7-Year	10-Year	15-Year	20-Year
1	58.33%	35.00%	25.00%	17.50%	8.75%	6.563%
2	27.78	26.00	21.43	16.50	9.13	7.000
3	12.35	15.60	15.31	13.20	8.21	6.482
4	1.54	11.01	10.93	10.56	7.39	5.996
5		11.01	8.75	8.45	6.65	5.546
6		1.38	8.74	6.76	5.99	5.130
7			8.75	6.55	5.90	4.746
8			1.09	6.55	5.91	4.459
9				6.56	5.90	4.459
10				6.55	5.91	4.459
11				0.82	5.90	4.459
12					5.91	4.460
13					5.90	4.459
14					5.91	4.460
15					5.90	4.459
16					0.74	4.460
17						4.459
18						4.460
19						4.459
20						4.460
21						0.557

Midquarter Convention for Business Personalty Placed in Service in Second Quarter

Depreciation Rate for Recovery Period

Year	3-Year	5-Year	7-Year	10-Year	15-Year	20-Year
1	41.67%	25.00%	17.85%	12.50%	6.25%	4.688%
2	38.89	30.00	23.47	17.50	9.38	7.148
3	14.14	18.00	16.76	14.00	8.44	6.612
4	5.30	11.37	11.97	11.20	7.59	6.116
5		11.37	8.87	8.96	6.83	5.658
6		4.26	8.87	7.17	6.15	5.233
7			8.87	6.55	5.91	4.841
8			3.33	6.55	5.90	4.478
9				6.56	5.91	4.463
10				6.55	5.90	4.463
11				2.46	5.91	4.463
12					5.90	4.463
13					5.91	4.463
14					5.90	4.463
15					5.91	4.462
16					2.21	4.463
17						4.462
18						4.463
19						4.462
20						4.463
21						1.673

Midquarter Convention for Business Personalty Placed in Service in Third Quarter

Depreciation Rate for Recovery Period

Year	3-Year	5-Year	7-Year	10-Year	15-Year	20-Year
1	25.00%	15.00%	10.71%	7.50%	3.75%	2.813%
2	50.00	34.00	25.51	18.50	9.63	7.289
3	16.67	20.40	18.22	14.80	8.66	6.742
4	8.33	12.24	13.02	11.84	7.80	6.237
5		11.30	9.30	9.47	7.02	5.769
6		7.06	8.85	7.58	6.31	5.336
7			8.86	6.55	5.90	4.936
8			5.53	6.55	5.90	4.566
9				6.56	5.91	4.460
10				6.55	5.90	4.460
11				4.10	5.91	4.460
12					5.90	4.460
13					5.91	4.461
14					5.90	4.460
15					5.91	4.461
16					3.69	4.460
17						4.461
18						4.460
19						4.461
20						4.460
21						2.788

Midquarter Convention for Business Personalty Placed in Service in Fourth Quarter

Depreciation Rate for Recovery Period

Year	3-Year	5-Year	7-Year	10-Year	15-Year	20-Year
1	8.33%	5.00%	3.57%	2.50%	1.25%	0.938%
2	61.11	38.00	27.55	19.50	9.88	7.430
3	20.37	22.80	19.68	15.60	8.89	6.872
4	10.19	13.68	14.06	12.48	8.00	6.357
5		10.94	10.04	9.98	7.20	5.880
6		9.58	8.73	7.99	6.48	5.439
7			8.73	6.55	5.90	5.031
8			7.64	6.55	5.90	4.654
9				6.56	5.90	4.458
10				6.55	5.91	4.458
11				5.74	5.90	4.458
12					5.91	4.458
13					5.90	4.458
14					5.91	4.458
15					5.90	4.458
16					5.17	4.458
17						4.458
18						4.459
19						4.458
20						4.459
21						3.901

Chapter **Eight**

Property Dispositions

Learning Objectives

After studying this chapter, you should be able to:

LO 8-1. Calculate and distinguish between gain or loss realization and recognition.

LO 8-2. Apply the installment sale method of accounting.

LO 8-3. Explain why the tax law disallows losses on related party sales.

LO 8-4. Identify the two components of the capital gain or loss definition.

LO 8-5. Apply the limitation on the deduction of capital losses.

LO 8-6. Identify Section 1231 assets.

LO 8-7. Apply the Section 1231 netting process.

LO 8-8. Incorporate the recapture rules into the Section 1231 netting process.

LO 8-9. Describe the tax consequences of dispositions other than sales or exchanges.

LO 8-10. Explain disposition-related book/tax differences and their effect on GAAP financial statements.

This chapter continues our investigation of the tax consequences of property transactions. We will discuss how taxpayers account for gains or losses from property dispositions. This discussion centers on three basic questions:

• What is the gain or loss recognized on the disposition of property?
• In what taxable year does the recognition occur?
• What is the tax character of the recognized gain or loss?

The answers to these questions determine the tax cost or savings and, in turn, the after-tax cash flows from the property disposition.

For taxpayers disposing of several assets during the tax year, determining the tax consequences of these dispositions is a multistep process. First, the taxpayer computes gain or loss realized on each asset disposition and the amount of such gain or loss recognized in the current year. Second, the character of the recognized gain or loss must be identified. Character is critical to determining the ultimate impact of property transactions on taxable income and tax liability. As we discussed in our exploration of tax planning variables in Chapter 4, the character of income determines whether it is taxed at preferential rates or at the taxpayer's ordinary income rate. In particular, individuals often qualify for preferential tax rates on capital gains from the disposition of capital assets. When property dispositions result in a loss, the character of the loss is important in determining its deductibility. Capital losses can only be deducted against capital gains, while ordinary losses are fully deductible against any type of income.

For sales of business assets, the ultimate character of gain or loss is controlled by Section 1231. When Section 1231 assets are sold at a gain, depreciation recapture treats some or all of that gain as ordinary income. Any remaining Section 1231 gain is combined with Section 1231 losses as part of a year-end netting process. The net Section 1231 gain or loss is then characterized as either ordinary or capital. Only after the Section 1231 netting process is complete can the taxpayer determine whether net capital gain exists (with potential preferential rates) or net capital loss results (with limits on deductibility). This chapter explores the details of each of these steps.

COMPUTATION OF GAIN OR LOSS RECOGNIZED

The Internal Revenue Code specifies that gross income includes "gains derived from dealings in property"[1] and allows a deduction for "any loss sustained during the taxable year and not compensated for by insurance or otherwise."[2] These two rules of law mean that firms account for gains and losses from property transactions in the computation of taxable income. The **realized gain or loss** from the disposition of property is computed as follows:[3]

> Amount realized on disposition
> (Adjusted tax basis of property)
> Realized gain or (loss)

This computation reflects the realization principle of accounting. Under this principle, increases or decreases in the value of assets are not accounted for as income. Such increases or decreases are not taken into account until an asset is converted to a different asset through an external transaction with another party. As a simple illustration of this principle, suppose that Firm F bought an asset four years ago for $25,000. Although the market value of the asset has steadily increased, the firm has not reported any of this accrued economic gain on either its financial statements or its tax returns. This year, Firm F sells the asset for $60,000 cash, finally realizing a $35,000 gain.

LO 8-1
Calculate and distinguish between gain or loss realization and recognition.

A third general rule of law is that the gain or loss realized on a property disposition is taken into account for tax purposes.[4] In other words, realized gain or loss becomes **recognized gain or loss** for the year.

> Amount realized on disposition
> (Adjusted tax basis of property)
> Realized gain or (loss)
> ↓
> Recognized gain or (loss)

Most of the property transactions examined in this chapter reflect this linkage between realization and recognition. In Chapter 9, we will explore the exceptions to the general rule: transactions in which realized gain or loss is not recognized in the same year.

[1] §61(a)(3).
[2] §165(a).
[3] §1001(a).
[4] §1001(c).

The realization principle has important planning implications because it gives property owners some control over the timing of gain or loss recognition. Owners of appreciated property can defer gain recognition and the related tax cost for as long as they hold the property. Owners of devalued property can accelerate the deduction of loss and the related tax savings by disposing of the property as soon as possible.

Deferring Gains and Accelerating Losses	Firm K has a $15,000 basis in Asset A and a $141,000 basis in Asset B. Near the end of its taxable year, Firm K has the opportunity to sell each asset for $100,000. It decides to hold Asset A to avoid recognizing its $85,000 economic gain and sell Asset B to recognize its $41,000 economic loss. Firm K can deduct this loss against income that would be taxed at 21 percent. Thus, the loss results in an $8,610 tax savings this year.

Sales and Exchanges

Owners can dispose of property through a sale for cash (including the purchaser's obligation to pay cash in the future) or through an exchange for other property. The owner's **amount realized** on the disposition equals any cash received plus the fair market value (FMV) of any property received.[5] For example, if Company J exchanges equipment for marketable securities and the securities are worth $50,000, Company J's amount realized on the disposition of the equipment is $50,000. While the amount realized equals the value of the cash or property received by the seller, the amount realized also equals the value of the property surrendered. In our example, both parties to the transaction must agree that the equipment is also worth $50,000. Why is this so? In an economic setting, no rational person would sell property for less than its value, nor would any purchaser pay more than the property's value. The private market created between seller and purchaser establishes the equal values of the properties changing hands.

Relief of Debt as Amount Realized

In Chapter 7, we learned that the tax basis of property includes any amount that the owner borrowed to acquire the property. In other words, tax basis encompasses both the owner's equity in the property and any debt to which the property is subject. If the owner sells the property and is relieved of debt in the transaction, the owner must include the debt relief in the amount realized on sale.

Relief of Debt	TG Corporation purchased investment land 15 years ago for $450,000. It put $100,000 of its own money into the investment and borrowed the remaining $350,000 from a bank, which took a mortgage on the property. TG's cost basis in the land is $450,000. Each year as TG paid down the principal of the mortgage, the payments increased its equity in the land but had no effect on TG's basis. This year, TG sold the land for $875,000. The purchaser assumed the $200,000 principal balance of the mortgage and paid the $675,000 remaining sales price in cash. TG's realized gain is computed as follows:

Amount realized on sale:	
Cash received	$ 675,000
Relief of debt	200,000
	$ 875,000
Basis of land	(450,000)
Realized gain	$ 425,000

[5] §1001(b). The amount realized is reduced by selling costs such as sales commissions and title transfer fees.

Tax-Free Recovery of Basis and Cash Flow

On a sale or exchange of property, only the excess of amount realized over adjusted basis is taxable income. Accordingly, sellers recover their investment in the property at no tax cost.

Realized Gain and Basis Recovery	Firm R owns an asset with a $5,000 basis. If it sells the asset for $8,000 cash, it realizes a taxable gain of only $3,000. The first $5,000 cash received represents a nontaxable recovery of Firm R's investment in the asset. Assuming that Firm R has a 21 percent marginal tax rate, the sale generates $7,370 cash flow:

	Tax Result	Cash Flow
Amount realized on sale	$ 8,000	$8,000
Basis	(5,000)	
Gain realized	$ 3,000	
	.21	
Tax cost of gain	$ 630	(630)
After-tax cash flow		$7,370

If a seller realizes a loss on a sale or exchange, the entire amount realized is a tax-free recovery of the seller's investment. Moreover, the seller may be allowed to deduct the *unrecovered* investment (realized loss) in the computation of taxable income.

Realized Loss and Basis Recovery	Refer to the facts in the preceding example. If Firm R sells the asset for only $4,000, it realizes a $1,000 loss. *Assuming that this loss is fully deductible,* the firm recovers its $5,000 investment in the asset in the form of $4,000 cash plus a $1,000 deduction. Because of the tax savings from the deduction, the sale generates $4,210 cash flow:

	Tax Result	Cash Flow
Amount realized on sale	$ 4,000	$4,000
Basis	(5,000)	
Loss realized	$(1,000)	
	.21	
Tax savings from loss	$ (210)	210
After-tax cash flow		$4,210

Tax Talk
In early 2019, President Trump announced a proposal to index capital gains for inflation. While proponents argue such a change helps the economy by encouraging investment, opponents protest that the change is simply another tax cut for the wealthy.

In these two examples, the realized gain or loss does not enter into the computation of Firm R's net cash flow. Only the tax cost or savings resulting from the gain or loss are cash items.

Taxation of Inflationary Gains

As the preceding examples demonstrate, taxpayers who sell property can recover their basis at no tax cost. In financial terms, a return of investment does not represent income.

Only the amount realized in excess of the investment—a return *on* investment—should be recognized as income. This return is overstated if the value of the dollar has changed between the date an asset is purchased and the date that asset is sold. In a period of inflation, the dollars that the taxpayer invested in the asset were worth more in terms of purchasing power than the dollars the taxpayer receives on sale.

Inflationary Gain	Refer to the first example in which Firm R sells an asset with a $5,000 cost basis for an $8,000 amount realized. Because of inflation, a dollar in the year the firm acquired the asset was worth $1.25 of today's dollars. In current dollar terms, Firm R's investment in its asset is $6,250 ($5,000 basis × $1.25), and its economic gain on sale is only $1,750 ($8,000 amount realized − $6,250 inflation-adjusted basis). However, because the tax system fails to account for changes in the dollar's purchasing power over time, Firm R pays tax on a $3,000 gain, $1,250 of which is not economic income but a return of its original investment.[6]

Seller-Financed Sales

In many sale transactions, the seller accepts the purchaser's debt obligation (note) as part of the sale price. Such a note represents the purchaser's promise to pay cash to the seller over a specified future period rather than on the date of sale. In an arm's-length **seller-financed sale,** the seller charges the purchaser a market rate of interest on the note. As a general rule, the seller includes the principal amount of the purchaser's note in the amount realized on sale and computes gain or loss accordingly.

Seller-Financed Sale	Company Q sold property with a $195,000 basis for $300,000. The purchaser paid $30,000 cash on the date of sale and gave Company Q a note for the $270,000 balance of the price. The note obligated the purchaser to pay the $270,000 principal over the next 10 years and carried a 7 percent annual interest rate. Company Q realized a $105,000 gain on this seller-financed sale, even though it received only $30,000 cash in the year of sale.

Installment Sale Method

LO 8-2
Apply the installment sale method of accounting.

Taxpayers may use a statutory method of accounting for gains realized on seller-financed sales of certain types of property. Under the **installment sale method,** the seller does not recognize the entire realized gain in the year of sale. Instead, gain recognition is linked to the seller's receipt of cash over the term of the purchaser's note.[7] The seller calculates the gain recognized in the year of sale and each subsequent year by multiplying the cash received during the year by a **gross profit percentage.** This percentage is calculated by dividing the gain realized by the sale price.

Installment Sale Method	In year 1, Firm B sold a five-acre tract of investment land with a $150,000 basis for $214,500. The purchaser paid $14,500 cash on the date of sale and gave Firm B a note for the $200,000 balance of the price. The note provides for annual principal payments of $50,000 in years 2 through 5 plus 6 percent annual interest on the unpaid balance. Firm B's realized gain and gross profit percentage are computed as follows:

Amount realized on sale:	
Cash received	$ 14,500
Purchaser's note	200,000
	$214,500
Basis of land	(150,000)
Realized gain	$ 64,500

(continued)

[6] Congress and the Treasury are well aware of this problem. The theoretically sound solution is to allow taxpayers to adjust the basis in their assets for inflation. Lawmakers have been reluctant to enact this solution into law because of the potential revenue loss and the enormous complexity it would add to the computation of basis, cost recovery deductions, and recognized gains and losses.
[7] §453.

$$\frac{\$64{,}500 \text{ realized gain}}{\$214{,}500 \text{ sale}} = 30.07 \text{ gross profit percentage}$$

Firm B will recognize the following taxable gain each year:

Year	Cash Received	Gross Profit Percentage	Taxable Gain Recognized
1	$14,500	30.07%	$ 4,360
2	50,000	30.07	15,035
3	50,000	30.07	15,035
4	50,000	30.07	15,035
5	50,000	30.07	15,035
			$64,500

Tax Talk

The installment method was allowed in recognizing gain on the sale of industrial parts from a business discontinued 13 years earlier. The parts had become capital assets and were no longer inventory held for sale to customers in the ordinary course of business. Glisson, W. F. (1981) T.C. Memo 1981-379.

The annual interest payments that Firm B receives on the installment note do not enter into the computation of recognized gain under the installment method. The firm must recognize these interest payments as ordinary income under its overall method of accounting.

Taxpayers can use the installment sale method to defer gain recognition on the sale of many types of business and investment property. (The method does not apply to realized losses.) However, the installment method is not permitted to defer gains realized on the sale of stocks or securities traded on an established market.[8] Nor does the method apply to gains realized on the sale of inventory to customers in the ordinary course of the seller's business.[9] The ordinary income created by any of the depreciation recapture rules discussed later in this chapter is not eligible for deferral under the installment method and must be recognized in the year of sale.[10]

Installment Sale of Inventory

Refer to the preceding example. If Firm B is a real estate developer that buys and sells land in the ordinary course of business, it cannot use the installment sale method to account for the gain realized on sale of the five-acre tract. Thus, Firm B would recognize the entire $64,500 gain in the year of sale.

Taxpayers generally benefit from the use of the installment sale method to defer gain recognition. In cases in which deferral is not beneficial, taxpayers may make a written election not to use the installment sale method.[11]

Seller's Basis in Purchaser's Note

When a seller receives the purchaser's note in a seller-financed sale, the seller generally takes a basis in the note equal to its face value. This basis represents the dollars that the seller will recover as tax-free principal payments.

[8] §453(k)(2)(A). Established securities markets include the New York Stock Exchange (NYSE), the American Stock Exchange (AMEX), and Nasdaq.
[9] §453(b)(2).
[10] §453(i).
[11] §453(d).

	Note Receivable	Basis	

Note Receivable Basis

Refer to the example in which Company Q sold property for $300,000, accepted the purchaser's note for $270,000, and realized a $105,000 gain. If Company Q recognized the entire gain in the year of sale, its basis in the note receivable is the note's $270,000 face value. The principal payments that Company Q will receive over the next 10 years will reduce both the face value and the tax basis of this note to zero.

In the case of an installment sale, the seller is not entitled to a tax-free recovery of the dollars represented by the purchaser's note. Instead, the seller will recognize a percentage of every dollar received as taxable income. Consequently, the seller's tax basis in the installment note is reduced by the deferred gain represented by the note.[12]

Note Receivable Basis— Installment Sale Method

Refer to the example in which Firm B sold a five-acre tract of land for $214,500, accepted the purchaser's note for $200,000, and used the installment sale method to defer gain recognition. Firm B's basis in the note receivable is only $139,860 ($200,000 face value − $60,140 deferred gain). As Firm B receives each $50,000 principal payment, it will recognize a portion of the deferred gain and reduce the face value and tax basis of the note according to the following schedule:

Year	Note Receivable Face Value	Deferred Gain	Note Receivable Basis
1	$200,000	$60,140	$139,860
2	150,000	45,105	104,895
3	100,000	30,070	69,930
4	50,000	15,035	34,965
5	–0–	–0–	–0–

If a taxpayer converts a note receivable to cash, the taxpayer must immediately recognize any deferred gain represented by the note.[13] Assume that Firm B in the preceding example collected only two $50,000 principal payments and then sold the note to a financial institution for its $100,000 face value. Because Firm B accelerated its receipt of cash from the installment sale, it must recognize the remaining $30,070 deferred gain. What if Firm B tried the more subtle technique of pledging the note as collateral for a $100,000 loan from the financial institution? In this case, Firm B still owns the note. Nonetheless, Firm B must recognize the $30,070 deferred gain. The installment sale rules stipulate that a pledge of an installment note is treated as a disposition of the note for cash.[14]

Disallowed Losses on Related Party Sales

Earlier in the chapter, we focused on the general rule that the entire gain or loss realized on a property disposition is recognized for tax purposes. Consequently, firms can usually deduct losses realized on the sale of business assets. One important exception to the general rule is that losses realized on the sale or exchange of property between related parties are nondeductible.[15] For purposes of this exception, the Internal Revenue Code defines related parties as people who are members of the same family, an individual and a corporation if

[12] §453B(b).
[13] §453B.
[14] §453A(d).
[15] §267(a)(1).

the individual owns more than 50 percent of the value of the corporation's outstanding stock, and two corporations controlled by the same shareholders.[16]

Disallowed Loss	Firm M sold a business asset to Purchaser P for $75,000. Firm M's basis in the asset was $90,000, and it reported a $15,000 realized loss on its financial statements. Firm M and Purchaser P are related parties for federal tax purposes. Consequently, Firm M may not deduct the $15,000 loss in the computation of taxable income. Even though Firm M's loss is disallowed, Purchaser P takes a $75,000 cost basis in the asset.

LO 8-3
Explain why the tax law disallows losses on related party sales.

This disallowance rule is based on the theory that a related party loss may not represent an economic loss to the seller. For instance, when a corporation realizes a loss on the sale of an asset to an unrelated purchaser, the loss corresponds to the corporation's unrecovered investment in the asset—a permanent reduction in net worth. If the corporation sells that asset to its controlling shareholder, the underlying ownership of the asset doesn't change. If the value of the asset increases after the sale, the shareholder may eventually recover the corporation's entire investment. In this case, the corporation's loss has no economic substance and should not be deductible in computing taxable income.

A second explanation for the disallowance rule is that related party transactions occur in a fictitious market in which seller and purchaser may not be negotiating at arm's length. Because of this possibility, the government has no assurance that the sale price equals the market value at which the asset would change hands between unrelated parties. If the price is unrealistically low, the seller's loss is inflated and results in an unwarranted tax deduction. Thus, the loss disallowance rule applies to every related party sale, regardless of the actual bargaining stance between the parties. For instance, if a brother realizes a loss on the sale of a business asset to his sister, the loss is nondeductible, even if the brother can prove that the siblings have been estranged for years, and the transaction between them was strictly at arm's length.

Offset of Gain by Previously Disallowed Loss

From the seller's perspective, the loss disallowance rule causes a permanent difference between loss realized and loss recognized on the sale of property. Thus, the seller never receives the benefit of a tax deduction for the disallowed loss. However, in the right set of circumstances, the *purchaser* may receive some or all of the benefit. If the purchaser subsequently sells the property acquired in the related party transaction and realizes a gain, the purchaser can offset this gain by the previously disallowed loss.[17]

Use of Seller's Disallowed Loss by Purchaser	Refer to the preceding example in which Firm M realized a $15,000 disallowed loss on the sale of an asset to Purchaser P. Assume that the asset was nondepreciable in P's hands. Several years after the related party transaction, Purchaser P sells the asset to an *unrelated buyer*. The tax consequences based on three different assumptions as to the sale price are presented in the following table:

[16] §267(b)(1), (2), and (3). A person's family includes a spouse, brothers and sisters, ancestors, and lineal descendants. §267(c)(4).
[17] §267(d).

	Assumption 1	Assumption 2	Assumption 3
Amount realized on sale	$ 93,000	$ 81,000	$ 70,000
Basis of asset	(75,000)	(75,000)	(75,000)
Gain (loss) realized	$ 18,000	$ 6,000	$ (5,000)
Previously disallowed loss	(15,000)	(6,000)	–0–
Gain (loss) recognized	$ 3,000	–0–	$ (5,000)

This example demonstrates that Purchaser P can use Firm M's previously disallowed loss only to *reduce* the gain recognized on a subsequent sale of the asset. The disallowed loss cannot *create* a recognized loss or *increase* the recognized loss on a subsequent sale.

TAX CHARACTER OF GAINS AND LOSSES

LO 8-4
Identify the two components of the capital gain or loss definition.

Taxpayers must compute the gain or loss realized on a property disposition and determine the taxable year (or years) in which the gain or loss is recognized. In addition, they must determine the character of the recognized gain or loss. In the tax world, every gain or loss is ultimately characterized as either ordinary or capital. A **capital gain or loss** results from the sale or exchange of a capital asset.[18] Any gain or loss that does not meet this definition is **ordinary** in character.[19]

The capital gain/loss definition has two distinct components. First, the transaction resulting in the gain or loss must be a sale or exchange. Second, the asset surrendered must be a capital asset. If a firm disposes of a capital asset in some way other than a sale or exchange, the realized gain or loss is ordinary in character. Several of these dispositions are discussed later in the chapter. At this point, let's focus our attention on the second component of the capital gain/loss definition: the capital asset requirement.

Capital Asset Defined

The Internal Revenue Code defines the term **capital asset** by exception.[20] For tax purposes, *every* asset is a capital asset unless it falls into one of eight categories:

1. Inventory items or property held by the taxpayer primarily for sale to customers in the ordinary course of business.
2. Accounts or notes receivable acquired in the ordinary course of business (i.e., acquired through the sale of inventory or the performance of services).
3. Supplies used or consumed in the ordinary course of business.
4. Real or depreciable property used in a business (including rental real estate) and intangible business assets subject to amortization.[21]
5. A patent, invention, model, or design; secret formula or process; copyright; literary, musical, or artistic composition; a letter or memorandum; or similar property held by a taxpayer whose personal efforts created the property or a person receiving the property from the creator by gift or through a nontaxable exchange.[22]

[18] §1222.

[19] §64 and §65.

[20] §1221.

[21] Reg. §1.167(a)-3 and §197(f)(7).

[22] In the case of a letter or memorandum, the exclusion from capital asset treatment also applies to a taxpayer for whom such letter or memorandum was prepared.

6. Certain publications of the U.S. government.

7. Commodities derivative financial instruments held by a dealer.

8. Hedging transaction properties.

While the last three categories of capital assets are listed for the sake of completeness, they are not discussed in this text.

Capital asset status is not determined by the intrinsic nature of the asset itself but by the use for which the asset is held by its owner.

Capital Asset Defined

Ms. Helm, a professional sculptor, purchased $50 worth of clay and created a work of art that she sold for $5,000 to BVC Corporation. BVC uses the sculpture as decoration in the lobby of its corporate headquarters. The work of art is not a capital asset in the hands of its creator, so Ms. Helm's $4,950 gain recognized on the sale is ordinary income. In contrast, the sculpture is a capital asset to BVC because it is not a *depreciable* business asset. As a result, if the corporation ever sells the sculpture, its recognized gain or loss will be capital in character.

Capital Loss Limitation

LO 8-5
Apply the limitation on the deduction of capital losses.

The federal income tax system contains a subset of rules applying to capital gains and losses. One logical way to analyze these rules is to begin with the limitation on capital losses: *Capital losses can be deducted only to the extent of capital gains.*[23] In other words, if the combined result of all sales and exchanges of capital assets during the year is a net loss, the net loss is nondeductible. If the combined result is a net gain, the net gain is included in taxable income. The following diagram depicts the result of this netting process:

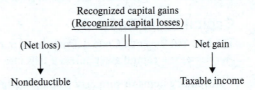

The capital loss limitation has a major effect on the tax savings generated by a capital loss. The next three examples demonstrate this effect.

Fully Deductible Capital Loss

Firm SD sold a capital asset with a $100,000 basis for $25,000. If the firm's marginal tax rate is 21 percent, how much tax savings does this $75,000 capital loss generate? If Firm SD recognized at least $75,000 capital gain during the year, the capital loss generates $15,750 current tax savings, and the after-tax loss on the sale is $59,250:

Loss on sale of capital asset	$(75,000)
Current tax savings	
($75,000 deductible loss × 21%)	15,750
After-tax loss	$(59,250)

---

[23] §1211. This strict limitation is relaxed very slightly for individual taxpayers. See the discussion of individual capital losses in Chapter 16.

Partially Deductible Capital Loss	Assume that Firm SD recognized only $40,000 capital gain during the year. In this case, the firm can deduct only $40,000 capital loss; its $35,000 **net capital loss** (excess of current year capital loss over capital gain) is nondeductible. The current tax savings generated by the capital loss decreases to $8,400, and the after-tax loss increases to $66,600:

Loss on sale of capital asset	$(75,000)
Current tax savings	
($40,000 deductible loss × 21%)	8,400
After-tax loss	$(66,600)

Nondeductible Capital Loss	In the worst-case scenario, Firm SD recognized no capital gains during the year. Consequently, none of the $75,000 net capital loss is deductible, and the before-tax and after-tax loss are both $75,000:

Loss on sale of capital asset	$(75,000)
Current tax savings	–0–
After-tax loss	$(75,000)

The strict rule that capital losses are deductible only against capital gains is relaxed somewhat for individuals. Individual taxpayers are permitted an annual deduction of up to $3,000 for capital losses in excess of capital gains.

Individual Capital Loss Limitation	Janelle Jones recognized $40,000 of capital gains and $47,000 of capital losses during the current year. Janelle is permitted to deduct $43,000 of her capital losses, resulting in a net capital loss for the year of $3,000.

Loss Carrybacks and Carryforwards

The previous examples are incomplete because they show the effect of the capital loss limitation only for an isolated year. If a taxpayer has a nondeductible net capital loss for the year, the law provides a mechanism by which the loss can be deducted in a previous or future year. For no obvious policy reason, the tax law differentiates between capital losses incurred by individuals and those incurred by corporations:

- A nondeductible net capital loss incurred by an *individual* is carried forward indefinitely.[24] In any future year in which the individual recognizes net capital gain (excess of capital gain over capital loss), the loss carryforward is deductible to the extent of such gain.

[24] §1212(b)(1).

- A net capital loss incurred by a *corporation* is carried back three years and forward five years, but only as a deduction against net capital gains recognized during this eight-year period.[25] Let's look at an example of the corporate rule:

Capital Loss Carryback	RO Corporation sold two capital assets in 2023, recognizing a $50,000 gain on the first sale and an $85,000 loss on the second. RO included the $50,000 gain in gross income and deducted $50,000 of the loss on its 2023 tax return; its nondeductible net capital loss is $35,000. RO's taxable income for the three previous years is as follows:

	2020	*2021*	*2022*
Ordinary income	$600,000	$400,000	$730,000
Net capital gain	–0–	10,000	12,000
Taxable income	$600,000	$410,000	$742,000

- Because RO had no net capital gain in the earliest year of its carryback period, it can't deduct any of its 2023 net capital loss against 2020 income.
- RO may deduct $10,000 and $12,000 of the 2023 loss against the capital gains reported in 2021 and 2022, recompute its tax accordingly, and file for a tax refund.
- RO will carry the $13,000 remaining net capital loss forward for five years to deduct against future capital gains.

Taxation of Capital Gains

Under the federal income tax system, capital gains have the unique capacity to absorb capital losses. As a result, both corporate and individual taxpayers always prefer capital gains to ordinary income. In a year in which a taxpayer recognizes a net capital gain (excess of capital gain over capital loss), the net gain is included in taxable income. If the taxpayer is a corporation, this net gain is taxed at the same rates as ordinary income. If the taxpayer is an individual, the net capital gain may be taxed at preferential rates ranging from zero to 31.8 percent.[26] Given that the highest marginal rate on ordinary income is 37 percent, the preferential rates on capital gains are extremely valuable to high-income individuals. The details of the preferential rate structure are discussed in Chapter 16.

Capital Asset Definition Revisited

Now that you understand the tax consequences of capital gains and losses, you can appreciate why gain and loss characterization is so important in the tax planning process. As a general rule, taxpayers prefer capital gains to ordinary income, and they prefer ordinary losses to capital losses. As we discussed earlier in this section, the characterization of gain and loss depends on whether the property was a noncapital or a capital asset in the hands of the seller. More specifically, does the property fit into one of the categories of noncapital assets listed in the Internal Revenue Code? If the property does not fit into one of these

---

[25] §1212(a)(1).

[26] §1(h). These rates apply only to long-term capital gains, which are derived from the sale of capital assets held for more than one year. See §1222.

eight categories, the property is a capital asset.[27] This classification scheme is presented in the following diagram:

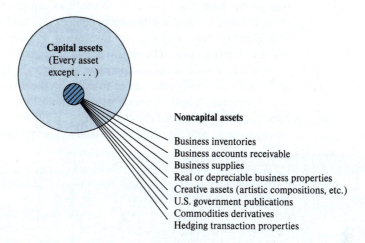

DISPOSITIONS OF NONCAPITAL ASSETS

The expansive definition of a capital asset as every asset except for those specifically excepted may be misleading. In the business context, capital assets are the exception rather than the rule. Most properties listed on a firm's balance sheet fall into one of the first four categories of noncapital assets. In this section of the chapter, we will analyze the tax consequences of the dispositions of these noncapital business assets.

What types of business properties are capital in character? Any asset held by a firm for long-term investment rather than for active business or commercial use is a capital asset. Similarly, equity and creditor interests in other firms, such as stocks, bonds, and partnership interests, are capital in character. Finally, the goodwill and going-concern value *created* by a profitable business is a capital asset.[28]

Other self-created intangibles are specifically excluded from capital asset treatment. The following assets, when held by their creator, are considered ordinary income assets: patents, inventions, models or designs, secret formulas or processes, and copyrights. If such assets are transferred by their creator to another taxpayer through gift or nontaxable exchange, ordinary income treatment still applies.[29]

Inventory

The first category of noncapital assets includes any property held as inventory or primarily for sale to customers. When firms sell inventory assets as part of their everyday operations, the recognized gain or loss is the quintessence of ordinary income or loss. For firms engaged in the manufacture, production, wholesaling, distribution, or retailing of tangible goods, the identification of inventory assets is fairly straightforward. Disputes between taxpayers and the IRS concerning the status of property as inventory most frequently arise when the asset in question is land.

---

[27] *Arkansas Best Corp.* v. *Commissioner,* 485 U.S. 212 (1988).

[28] See IRS Letter Ruling 200243002 (October 25, 2002). Purchased goodwill/going-concern value is not a capital asset to the purchaser. Purchased intangibles fall into the fourth category of noncapital assets, and the tax consequences of their disposition are governed by the specialized rules of §197(f)(1).

[29] §1221(a)(3) and §1235.

Land Sales

If a taxpayer sells a tract of land at a profit, the taxpayer usually prefers to categorize the tract as an investment asset and the profit as capital gain. The IRS might challenge this result if it believes that the taxpayer acquired and held the land primarily for sale to customers rather than as a long-term investment. From this perspective, the profit from the sale is ordinary income. The federal courts have been called on many times to resolve this particular difference of opinion. In cases in which the land sale was an unusual or isolated occurrence, the courts have tended to side with the taxpayer. In cases in which the taxpayer sold other tracts of land on a regular and continual basis, subdivided and improved the land prior to sale, or advertised the availability of the land to the general public, the courts have tended to agree with the IRS that the land was an inventory asset.

Land Sales	Six years ago, Penro Company paid $175,000 to purchase a seven-acre tract of land. Penro, which operates a service business, held the land as a long-term investment. Last year, Penro sold the land to Medoc Development, Inc. for $340,000. Because Penro held the land as a capital asset, it recognized the $165,000 gain on sale as capital gain. Medoc subdivided the seven-acre tract into one-third-acre lots and constructed paved streets and sidewalks, sewers, and utilities. The cost of these improvements totaled $124,800. Medoc advertised the lots in local newspapers and trade journals, and by the end of the current year, it had sold all 21 lots for a total of $647,500. Because Medoc held the land primarily for sale to customers, it recognized its $182,700 gain on sale as ordinary income.

As noted in the section that follows, land could also qualify as a Section 1231 asset, if used in the taxpayer's trade or business. The taxpayer's motives when acquiring the land and use of the land during the period held must be carefully scrutinized to determine the character of any gain or loss on disposition.

Business Accounts Receivable and Supplies

The second category of noncapital assets includes business accounts receivable from the sale of goods or performance of services. Accrual basis firms realize ordinary income from the transactions that create their receivables. Therefore, the tax basis in their accounts receivable equals face value. Cash basis firms do not realize ordinary income until they collect their receivables. Thus, the tax basis in their *unrealized* accounts receivable is zero. Firms usually either collect their receivables or write off any uncollectible accounts as bad debts. In an unusual case, a firm that needs immediate cash might sell or *factor* its accounts receivable to a third party (typically a financial institution). The difference between the amount realized and the tax basis of the receivables is ordinary income or loss.

Factoring Accounts Receivable	SP Company has $400,000 accounts receivable that it expects to collect over the next 120 days. To meet a cash emergency, SP factors the receivables with First City Bank for $383,000. If SP uses the accrual method of accounting, it has a $400,000 basis in its accounts receivable and recognizes a $17,000 ordinary loss on their disposition. If SP uses the cash method of accounting, it has a zero basis in its accounts receivable and recognizes $383,000 ordinary income on their disposition.

The third category of noncapital assets includes business supplies. Depending on their method of accounting, firms deduct the cost of supplies either in the year of purchase or in the year in which the supplies are consumed. In an unusual case, a firm with unneeded or excess supplies on hand might sell the supplies to a third party. The difference between the amount realized and the tax basis of the supplies is ordinary income or loss.

Selling Unwanted Supplies	Firm EQP is moving its home office to a new location and does not want to transport its stock of office supplies for which it paid $6,000. EQP sells the supplies to a neighboring business for $5,600. If EQP deducted the $6,000 cost, it has a zero basis in the supplies and recognizes $5,600 ordinary income on their disposition. If EQP capitalized the $6,000 cost, it recognizes a $400 ordinary loss on their disposition.

Section 1231 Assets

LO 8-6

Identify Section 1231 assets.

The fourth category of noncapital assets includes real or depreciable property used in a business (including rental real estate) and intangible business assets subject to amortization (such as *purchased* goodwill). In other words, the operating assets on a balance sheet are noncapital assets. The tax consequences of a sale of an operating asset depend on the length of time the seller held the asset. If the holding period is a year or less, gain or loss recognized on sale is ordinary in character. If the holding period exceeds one year, the gain or loss is characterized under the complicated rules provided in Section 1231 of the Internal Revenue Code. Consequently, the assets subject to these rules are labeled **Section 1231 assets.**

Section 1231 Assets	Tunley, Inc. has the following noncash assets on its tax-basis balance sheet:

Accounts receivable	$ 44,210
Marketable securities	11,400
Merchandise inventory	293,100
Furniture and fixtures	85,800
Machinery and equipment	112,700
Production facility:	
Land	200,000
Building	394,000
Purchased goodwill	150,000

The accounts receivable and inventory are noncapital assets by statutory definition. Tunley's holding periods for all operating assets used in its business exceed one year. Consequently, the furniture and fixtures, machinery and equipment, production facility (both land and building), and amortizable goodwill meet the definition of Section 1231 assets. Tunley's only capital assets are its marketable securities.

LO 8-7

Apply the Section 1231 netting process.

The basic rule of Section 1231 is simple. If the *combined result* of all sales and exchanges of Section 1231 assets during the year is a net loss, the loss is treated as an ordinary loss. On the other hand, if the result is a net gain, the gain is treated as a capital gain.[30] The following diagram depicts the Section 1231 netting process and the two possible results:

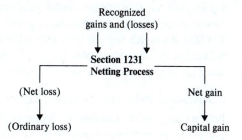

---

[30] §1231(a)(1).

Note that this asymmetric rule offers the best of both worlds to the business community—ordinary loss or capital gain on the sale of operating assets. However, the tax result of any particular Section 1231 asset sale cannot be fully determined until year-end, after application of the netting process. Let's work through two examples of the basic Section 1231 netting process.

Section 1231 Net Loss	During 2023, Company RC sold three Section 1231 assets with the following result:

	Gain or (Loss) Recognized
Asset sale 1	$ 45,000
Asset sale 2	(35,000)
Asset sale 3	(16,000)
Section 1231 net loss	$ (6,000)

Company RC's $6,000 Section 1231 net loss is an ordinary loss, fully deductible in the computation of taxable income. Note that ordinary treatment applies to all three asset sales, NOT just the two sales producing a loss.

Section 1231 Net Gain	Assume that asset sale 2 generated only a $5,000 (rather than a $35,000) loss for Company RC. In this case, the company has a net gain on the sale of its Section 1231 assets.

	Gain or (Loss) Recognized
Asset sale 1	$ 45,000
Asset sale 2	(5,000)
Asset sale 3	(16,000)
Section 1231 net gain	$ 24,000

Under Section 1231, Company RC treats the $24,000 net gain as a capital gain. Note that in this circumstance capital treatment applies to all three sales, NOT just the sale producing a gain. As a result of this net capital gain, the company can deduct up to $24,000 of capital losses or capital loss carryforwards. If the company's capital loss deduction is less than $24,000, the excess Section 1231 gain is treated as net capital gain. If the company's income is taxed at the individual rates (e.g., if Company RC is a sole proprietorship), this gain is taxed at the preferential capital gains rates.

Recapture of Prior Year Ordinary Losses

LO 8-8
Incorporate the recapture rules into the Section 1231 netting process.

Before Company RC can treat its Section 1231 net gain as a capital gain, it must consider an exception to the basic characterization rule. This exception applies if a taxpayer has a Section 1231 net gain in the current year but had a Section 1231 net loss in any of the five preceding taxable years. In such cases, the taxpayer must **recapture** the prior year loss (which was deductible as ordinary loss) by characterizing an equivalent amount of current year gain as ordinary income.[31] The next diagram incorporates this recapture rule:

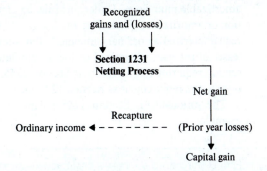

| | **Recapture of Prior Year Losses** | In our previous example, Company RC recognized a $24,000 net Section 1231 gain in 2023. Before Company RC can characterize this gain, it must look back for five years to identify any **nonrecaptured Section 1231 loss.** Here is a schedule of prior year information: |

	2018	**2019**	**2020**	**2021**	**2022**
Section 1231 gains	–0–	$1,350	$ 5,200	$–0–	–0–
Section 1231 losses	–0–	–0–	(11,400)	(900)	–0–
Net gain or (loss)	–0–	$1,350	$ (6,200)	$(900)	–0–

In 2020 and 2021, Company RC deducted a total of $7,100 of net Section 1231 losses against ordinary income. So in 2023, the company must recapture these losses by characterizing $7,100 of its $24,000 net Section 1231 gain as ordinary income. The $16,900 remaining gain is treated as capital gain.

Once a taxpayer has recaptured a prior year Section 1231 loss, the loss is not recaptured again. If Company RC has a Section 1231 net gain in 2024, the entire gain is treated as capital gain because the company no longer has any *nonrecaptured* losses for the preceding five-year period.

Depreciation Recapture

The pro-business rule of Section 1231 is modified when applied to gains recognized on the sale of depreciable or amortizable property. The modification requires that gains attributable to prior year depreciation or amortization deductions be characterized as ordinary income rather than Section 1231 gain. Thus, **depreciation recapture** merely changes the character of gain on the sale of Section 1231 property. It does not create additional gain. This depreciation recapture rule has three components: full recapture, partial recapture, and 20 percent recapture. Before analyzing each component, let's add the basic recapture rule to our diagram:

Recognized
gains and (losses)

Recapture
Ordinary income ◀ – – – – – – – (Depreciation/
amortization)

Section 1231
Netting Process

[31] §1231(c).

Full Recapture Rule

The full recapture rule applies to gains recognized on sales of depreciable personalty and amortizable intangibles. Under this rule, an amount of gain equal to accumulated depreciation or amortization (including any Section 179 expense deduction) through date of sale is recharacterized as ordinary income.[32] Put another way, depreciation recapture equals the lesser of the gain recognized or the accumulated depreciation or amortization. The Code section requiring full recapture is Section 1245. Consequently, tax professionals commonly refer to the requirement as **Section 1245 recapture.**

The rationale for Section 1245 recapture can best be explained through a numeric example:

Rationale for Recapture	Firm D purchased a tangible asset several years ago for $100,000 and has accumulated $40,000 MACRS depreciation through date of sale. As a result, its adjusted basis in the asset is $60,000. If the firm sells the asset for $100,000, it recognizes a $40,000 gain. Absent a *recapture requirement,* this gain is a Section 1231 gain with the potential for capital gain treatment. However, the entire gain is attributable to previous years' cost recovery deductions, which reduced *ordinary income* in those years by $40,000.

Section 1245 recapture prevents this conversion of ordinary income into capital gain. In our example, Firm D must characterize its $40,000 gain as ordinary income. If we modify the example by changing the amount realized on sale, the amount of recaptured ordinary income also changes. The following table illustrates the recapture computation based on four different amounts realized:

	Assumption 1	Assumption 2	Assumption 3	Assumption 4
Amount realized	$100,000	$ 90,000	$105,000	$ 48,000
Cost of asset	$100,000			
Depreciation	(40,000)			
Adjusted basis	(60,000)	(60,000)	(60,000)	(60,000)
Gain (loss) recognized	$ 40,000	$ 30,000	$ 45,000	$(12,000)
Section 1245 recapture	$ 40,000	$ 30,000	$ 40,000	–0–
Section 1231 gain (loss)	–0–	–0–	5,000	$(12,000)
	$ 40,000	$ 30,000	$ 45,000	$(12,000)

- Assumption 1 reflects the original facts in the Firm D example. The $40,000 gain recognized equals the $40,000 accumulated depreciation, and the entire gain is recaptured as ordinary income.
- Under Assumption 2, the $30,000 gain recognized *is less than* accumulated depreciation. In this case, the entire gain is recaptured as ordinary income.
- Under Assumption 3, the $45,000 gain *is more than* accumulated depreciation. In this case, only $40,000 of the gain (an amount equal to accumulated depreciation) is recaptured, and the remaining $5,000 gain (appreciation in the value of the asset) is Section 1231 gain.
- Under Assumption 4, Firm D recognizes a $12,000 loss on the sale. This is a Section 1231 loss; the recapture rules don't apply to losses.

[32] §1245 and §197(f)(7).

Partial Recapture Rule for Realty

The recapture rule applying to gains recognized on sales of depreciable realty (buildings, improvements, and other permanent attachments to land) is less stringent than the full recapture rule.[33] Although Congress has changed the details of this rule many times over the past decades, the essential concept is that only *accelerated depreciation in excess of straight-line depreciation* is recaptured. Tax professionals commonly refer to the partial recapture requirement as **Section 1250 recapture.**

<table>
<tr><td rowspan="2" valign="top">*Section 1250 Recapture*</td><td colspan="3">Company NB sold a residential apartment complex for $1 million: $200,000 for the underlying land and $800,000 for the building. NB purchased the property in 1986 for $1,120,000 and allocated $170,000 and $950,000 of this cost basis to the land and building, respectively. NB deducted $700,000 accelerated depreciation with respect to the building through date of sale. Straight-line depreciation over the same period would have been $628,000; consequently, NB deducted $72,000 excess accelerated depreciation. The computation of NB's recognized gain on sale and characterization of that gain is as follows:</td></tr>
<tr><td align="center">**Land**</td><td></td><td align="center">**Building**</td></tr>
<tr><td>Amount realized</td><td align="right">$200,000</td><td></td><td align="right">$800,000</td></tr>
<tr><td>Cost of asset</td><td align="right">$170,000</td><td align="right">$950,000</td><td></td></tr>
<tr><td>Depreciation</td><td align="right">–0–</td><td align="right">(700,000)</td><td></td></tr>
<tr><td>Adjusted basis</td><td align="right">(170,000)</td><td></td><td align="right">(250,000)</td></tr>
<tr><td>Gain recognized</td><td align="right">$ 30,000</td><td></td><td align="right">$550,000</td></tr>
<tr><td>Section 1250 recapture</td><td align="right">–0–</td><td></td><td align="right">$ 72,000</td></tr>
<tr><td>Section 1231 gain</td><td align="right">$ 30,000</td><td></td><td align="right">478,000</td></tr>
<tr><td></td><td align="right">$ 30,000</td><td></td><td align="right">$550,000</td></tr>
</table>

In Chapter 7, we learned that buildings placed in service after 1986 *must* be depreciated under the straight-line method. Consequently, Section 1250 recapture applies only to buildings placed in service before 1987. By 2023, any such building has been depreciated for more than 30 years. During the later years of a cost recovery period, the excess of accelerated over straight-line depreciation diminishes and eventually disappears when the building is fully depreciated (adjusted tax basis is zero). So with each passing year, the significance of Section 1250 recapture diminishes and eventually will disappear.

Twenty Percent Recapture by Corporations

Corporate taxpayers must contend with a special recapture rule for gain recognized on sales of depreciable realty.[34] Corporations must compute the excess of the gain that would be characterized as ordinary income under the Section 1245 full recapture rule over any gain characterized as ordinary income under the Section 1250 partial recapture rule. The corporation must then recapture 20 percent of this excess as additional ordinary income. Tax professionals commonly refer to the 20 percent recapture requirement as Section 291 recapture.

[33] Nonresidential realty (commercial buildings, warehouses, and so on) placed in service after 1980 and before 1987 and depreciated under an accelerated method is subject to the full recapture rule. See §1245(a)(5) before its amendment by the Tax Reform Act of 1986.

[34] §291(a)(1).

Section 1250 and 20 Percent Recapture

If Company NB in the preceding example is a corporation, it must apply the 20 percent recapture rule to the $550,000 gain recognized on the sale of the building. This gain is less than the $700,000 accumulated depreciation through the date of sale. Consequently, the entire gain would be recaptured as ordinary income under the Section 1245 full recapture rule. However, only $72,000 of the gain was actually recaptured under the Section 1250 partial recapture rule. So Corporation NB must recapture an additional $95,600 ordinary income computed as follows:

Section 1245 recapture	$550,000
Section 1250 recapture	(72,000)
Excess	$478,000
	.20
20 percent recapture	$ 95,600

In summary, Corporation NB recognized a $550,000 gain on sale of the building—$167,600 of which was ordinary income ($72,000 + $95,600) and $382,400 of which was Section 1231 gain.

The **20 percent recapture** rule is particularly significant for sales of buildings placed in service after 1986. Because such buildings are depreciated under the straight-line method, Section 1250 recapture does not apply. Even so, corporate sellers must recapture 20 percent of the gain that would be ordinary income under a full recapture rule.

Twenty Percent Recapture

Enwerd, Inc. purchased a building for use in its business and placed it in service in 1997. This year, it sold the building for $1,975,000. Enwerd's adjusted basis at date of sale was $790,750 ($1,400,000 cost − $609,250 accumulated straight-line depreciation), so the corporation recognized a $1,184,250 gain on sale:

Amount realized	$1,975,000
(Adjusted basis)	(790,750)
Gain recognized	$1,184,250

The gain is not subject to Section 1250 recapture because the building was depreciated under the straight-line method. However, the gain is subject to 20 percent recapture.

Section 1245 recapture	$609,250
Section 1250 recapture	–0–
Excess	$609,250
	.20
Twenty percent recapture	$121,850

In summary, Enwerd recognized a $121,850 ordinary gain and a $1,062,400 Section 1231 gain on sale of the building.

Summary

Exhibit 8.1 provides a summary of the depreciation recapture rules. Remember that recapture applies to only recognized gain on the sale of a Section 1231 asset. If a Section 1231 asset is sold at a loss, the recognized loss is characterized as a Section 1231 loss subject to the Section 1231 netting process.

EXHIBIT 8.1
Summary of Recapture
Rules

Recognized GAIN on Sale or Exchange of Section 1231 Asset	Recapture Rule
• Tangible personalty	Section 1245 recapture of depreciation
• Amortizable intangibles	Section 1245 recapture of amortization
• Nondepreciable realty [land]	No recapture
• Depreciable realty [buildings] placed in service before 1987	Section 1250 recapture of excess accelerated depreciation and 20 percent recapture by corporations
• Depreciable realty [buildings] placed in service after 1986	20 percent recapture by corporations

Comprehensive Example

The tax rules governing the character of gains and losses recognized on the sale or exchange of business operating assets are quite difficult. Before leaving this subject, let's review the rules by working through a comprehensive example.

Characterizing Gains and Losses

In 2023, BC, a calendar year corporation, recognized a $145,000 capital loss on the sale of marketable securities. The corporation did not sell any other capital assets during the year. Therefore, BC cannot deduct any of the capital loss *unless* it recognized a Section 1231 net gain for the year.

BC recognized the following gains and losses on 2023 sales of operating assets. The column headed *Accumulated Depreciation* reflects the correct MACRS depreciation through date of sale.

	Date Placed in Service	Date Sold	Initial Basis	Accumulated Depreciation	Sale Price	Gain (Loss)
Office equipment	11/3/22	2/14	$ 8,200	$ 2,300	$ 5,100	$ (800)
Copying equipment	8/16/19	5/14	4,000	3,650	2,350	2,000
Furniture	12/19/21	5/31	18,000	4,900	20,400	7,300
Hauling equipment	2/12/22	8/28	32,000	12,000	19,250	(750)
Real property:						
Land	4/12/18	11/3	100,000	–0–	125,000	25,000
Building	4/12/18	11/3	500,000	62,000	550,000	112,000

These gains and losses are characterized as follows:

	Gain (Loss)	Ordinary Income or (Loss)	Section 1231 Gain or (Loss)
Office equipment	$ (800)	$ (800)	
Copying equipment	2,000	2,000	
Furniture	7,300	4,900	$ 2,400
Hauling equipment	(750)		(750)
Real property:			
Land	25,000		25,000
Building	112,000	12,400	99,600
Current year totals		$18,500	$126,250

- BC owned the office equipment for less than a year. Therefore, this asset is neither a capital asset nor a Section 1231 asset, and the loss recognized on the sale is ordinary.
- Gain recognized on the sale of the copying equipment is less than accumulated depreciation. Therefore, the entire gain is recaptured as ordinary income.
- Gain recaptured as ordinary income on the sale of the furniture is limited to accumulated depreciation. The rest of the gain is Section 1231 gain.

(continued)

- Loss recognized on the sale of the hauling equipment is Section 1231 loss.
- Gain recognized on the sale of the land is Section 1231 gain.
- Gain recognized on the sale of the building is subject to 20 percent recapture. Therefore, $12,400 (20 percent of $62,000 accumulated depreciation) is recaptured as ordinary income. The rest of the gain is Section 1231 gain.

BC's tax returns for the previous five years show $8,400 nonrecaptured Section 1231 net losses. Thus, the final step in characterizing the corporation's gains and losses is to recapture this loss.

	Ordinary Income or (Loss)	Section 1231 Gain or (Loss)
Current year totals	$18,500	$126,250
Prior year loss recapture	8,400	(8,400)
	$26,900	$117,850

In summary, BC's sales of operating assets generated $26,900 ordinary income and $117,850 Section 1231 gain. BC treats the Section 1231 gain as capital gain. As a result, the corporation can deduct $117,850 of its $145,000 capital loss from the security sale. The $27,150 nondeductible capital loss can be deducted only on a carryback or carryforward basis.

The following diagram summarizes the steps discussed in this chapter for determining the tax consequences of property dispositions:

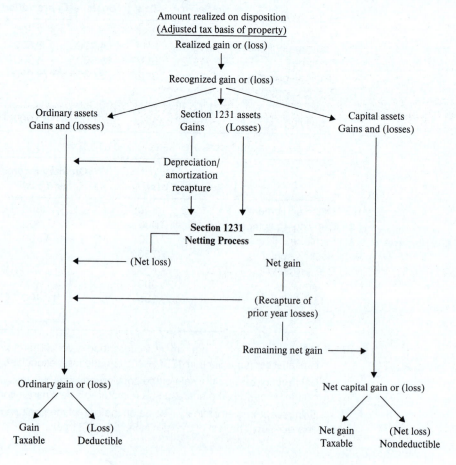

OTHER PROPERTY DISPOSITIONS

LO 8-9
Describe the tax consequences of dispositions other than sales or exchanges.

To this point in the chapter, our consideration of the tax consequences of property dispositions has been limited to the consequences of sales and exchanges. While sales and exchanges are the most common ways to dispose of assets, they are not the only ways. In this section, we consider three other property dispositions and their effect on taxable income.

Abandonment and Worthlessness

If a firm formally relinquishes its ownership interest in an asset, any unrecovered basis in the asset represents an **abandonment loss**.[35] An abandonment loss is an ordinary deduction even if the abandoned asset is a Section 1231 or capital asset because the loss is not realized on a sale or exchange. To claim a loss, a firm must take overt action to indicate that it has no intention of reviving its interest or reclaiming the asset in the future.[36] Firms typically don't abandon property unless the property no longer has any value and is worthless to the firm.

Abandonment Loss

Firm WB occupied leased office space for eight years. During this time, it capitalized the cost of several leasehold improvements to an asset account. This year, WB had a serious dispute with its landlord, broke its lease, and relocated to a new office. Unfortunately, the leasehold improvements were not portable, so WB had to leave them behind. WB's adjusted basis in these improvements was $28,200, so it can claim a $28,200 abandonment loss as an ordinary deduction.

Tax Talk
In order to abandon a security, the taxpayer must permanently relinquish all rights in it without receiving any consideration in exchange.

The Internal Revenue Code contains a special rule for securities that become worthless during the taxable year.[37] The owner must treat the securities as if they were sold on the last day of the year for a price of zero. This fictitious sale triggers a realized loss equal to the owner's basis in the securities. If the securities were capital assets in the owner's hands, the loss is characterized as a capital loss because it resulted from a deemed sale. For purposes of this rule, securities include corporate stocks and bonds, debentures, or other corporate or government debt instruments that bear interest coupons or are in registered form.

Worthless Securities

Colbert Company owns 1,400 shares of stock in NewHigh, Inc., a publicly held corporation. Colbert purchased the stock as an investment 10 years ago for $5,500. This year, NewHigh declared bankruptcy and made a public announcement that its stock is worthless. Colbert must treat the NewHigh shares as if they were sold on the last day of Colbert's taxable year for a price of zero. Colbert recognizes a $5,500 capital loss from the deemed sale of worthless securities.

An important modification to the worthless securities rule applies if a corporation owns worthless securities in an **affiliated corporation**.[38] An affiliated corporation is any 80 percent or more controlled domestic subsidiary that has always derived more than 90 percent of its annual gross receipts from the conduct of an active business. In this case, the corporation can treat the securities as a noncapital asset. Accordingly, the corporation's loss is not subject to the capital loss limitation but is fully deductible.

[35] Regs. §1.165-1(b), §1.165-2, and §1.167(a)-8.
[36] *Echols* v. *Commissioner,* 950 F.2d 209 (CA-5, 1991).
[37] §165(g)(1).
[38] §165(g)(3).

Securities in an Affiliated Corporation	BGH, a calendar year corporation, owns XYZ bonds with a $290,000 tax basis. BGH also owns 90 percent of the outstanding stock of Subsidiary S, a domestic corporation deriving all its gross receipts from a manufacturing business. BGH's basis in this stock is $500,000. Both the bonds and the stock are capital assets.
	This year, BGH's chief financial officer determined that the XYZ bonds and the Subsidiary S stock are worthless. For tax purposes, BGH recognizes a loss as if it sold both securities on December 31 for an amount realized of zero. The $290,000 loss from the deemed bond sale is a capital loss. However, the $500,000 loss from the deemed stock sale qualifies as an ordinary loss because Subsidiary S qualifies as an affiliated corporation.

Foreclosures

If a firm owns property that is collateral for a debt, the firm will lose the property if it fails to service the debt and the creditor forecloses. The tax consequences of a foreclosure depend on whether the debt is recourse or nonrecourse in nature. A **recourse debt** is one for which the debtor is personally liable; the debtor is obligated to repay the debt out of any and all of its assets. A **nonrecourse debt** is secured by only the specific property pledged as collateral; the debtor is not personally liable for repayment of the debt.

Recourse Debt Foreclosure	Company T owned a tract of land for which it paid $400,000 and which was subject to a $275,000 recourse mortgage. Because of financial difficulties, Company T failed to make the required payments on the mortgage. As a result, the creditor foreclosed and took possession of the land. As part of the foreclosure proceedings, Company T and the creditor agreed that the FMV of the land was $240,000.[39] Therefore, Company T was obligated to pay $35,000 cash to the creditor in full satisfaction of the $275,000 recourse mortgage.
	For tax purposes, Company T treats the foreclosure as if it sold the land for its $240,000 FMV, thereby realizing a $160,000 loss.[40] The character of the loss depends on Company T's use of the land. If Company T operates a real estate business and held the land as inventory, the loss is ordinary. If it used the land in the operation of its business, the loss is a Section 1231 loss. If it held the land as an investment, the loss is a capital loss.

Now change the facts in the preceding example by assuming that Company T is in such poor financial condition that it could not pay the $35,000 cash to fully satisfy the mortgage. If the creditor decides not to pursue its legal claim to such payment, Company T must recognize $35,000 ordinary cancellation-of-debt income.[41] This subsequent development does not affect the tax consequences of the land foreclosure itself.

Nonrecourse Debt Foreclosure	Refer to the facts in the preceding example but assume that the $275,000 mortgage on the land was a nonrecourse debt. The creditor's only right when Company T defaulted on the debt was to foreclose on the land. From the creditor's perspective, it received an asset worth only $240,000 in full settlement of a $275,000 debt and, as a result, incurred a $35,000 bad debt loss. Company T treats the foreclosure as a deemed sale for an amount realized of $275,000—the full amount of the nonrecourse debt—and recognizes a $125,000 loss.[42]

[39] FMV is frequently established by the creditor's subsequent sale of the property at public auction.

[40] Reg. §1.1001-2(c), Example 8.

[41] §61(a)(11). If Company T is insolvent, only the cancellation-of-debt income in excess of the insolvency is taxable. If Company T is involved in bankruptcy proceedings, none of the cancellation-of-debt income is taxable. §108(a). See *Frazier,* 111 T.C. No. 11 (1998).

[42] Reg. §1.1001-2(c), Example 7, and *Commissioner* v. *Tufts,* 461 U.S. 300 (1983).

Casualties and Thefts

In this uncertain world, firms may dispose of assets involuntarily because of a sudden, destructive event such as a fire, flood, earthquake, or other act of nature, or through some human agency such as theft, vandalism, or riot. If a firm is adequately insured, the reimbursement from the insurance company should compensate for the economic loss from such casualties. If the insurance reimbursement is less than the adjusted basis of the destroyed property, the firm can claim the unrecovered basis as an ordinary deduction.[43]

If the reimbursement exceeds the adjusted basis, the firm must recognize the excess as taxable income unless it takes advantage of a deferral opportunity, which is discussed in the next chapter.

Casualty Loss

Firm JBJ recently suffered a casualty loss when a flood destroyed four automobiles used in its business. The firm carried property insurance and received a $42,000 reimbursement after filing a claim with its insurance company. The adjusted basis of the four automobiles was $53,800. JBJ can deduct its $11,800 unrecovered basis as an ordinary loss in the computation of taxable income.

Theft Loss

Firm W operates a construction company. Over a recent weekend when one of the firm's job sites was unoccupied, thieves stole construction materials with a total cost of $5,000 and construction tools with an original cost of $4,000 and accumulated tax depreciation of $1,550. The loss was not reimbursed by insurance. Firm W is entitled to an ordinary loss deduction for the cost of the stolen materials and the adjusted tax basis of the tools. The total deductible loss is $7,450 ($5,000 + $4,000 − $1,550).

BOOK/TAX DIFFERENCES ON ASSET DISPOSITIONS

LO 8-10
Explain disposition-related book/tax differences and their effect on GAAP financial statements.

As explored in this chapter, asset dispositions may have significant tax consequences. In addition, such tax consequences may differ from the financial statement results of asset dispositions, resulting in book/tax differences. Such differences relate to two primary issues: (1) gain or loss differences and (2) the capital loss limitation.

Gain or Loss Book/Tax Differences

The amount of gain or loss that a taxpayer recognizes for tax purposes may not be the same amount reported on the taxpayer's financial statements. If an asset's adjusted tax basis does not equal its book basis, the tax gain or loss realized on disposition will not equal the book gain or loss.

Book/Tax Difference on Asset Disposition

Orlof, Inc. purchased a depreciable asset four years ago for $87,400 and sold it this year for $72,000. Orlof's book and tax gain on the sale are computed as follows:

	Book	Tax
Initial cost basis	$87,400	$87,400
Accumulated depreciation	(18,000)	(33,900)
Adjusted basis at date of sale	$69,400	$53,500
Amount realized on sale	$72,000	$72,000
Adjusted basis	(69,400)	(53,500)
Gain realized	$ 2,600	$18,500

(continued)

[43] Reg. §1.165-7(b). This general statement disregards the complex casualty gain/loss netting rule of §1231(a)(4)(C).

> The $15,900 excess tax gain over book gain is a reversal of the temporary differences between Orlof's book income and taxable income caused by excess tax depreciation over book depreciation during the four years that Orlof held the asset.

For taxpayers preparing their financial statements according to GAAP, use of the installment sale method generally results in a favorable temporary difference between book income and taxable income. The difference originates in the year of sale and reverses over the years when the taxpayer receives principal payments on the purchaser's note.

Book/Tax Difference from Installment Sale Method	Assume that Firm B in the example on page 8-5 prepares its financial statements in accordance with GAAP. In the year of the land sale, Firm B included its entire $64,500 realized gain in book income but only $4,360 recognized gain in taxable income. This $60,140 excess of book income over taxable income will reverse over the next four years as Firm B recognizes taxable income on receipt of the $50,000 annual principal payments on the purchaser's note.

	Book Gain	**Tax Gain**	**Difference**
Year 1	$64,500	$ 4,360	$(60,140) favorable
Year 2	0	15,035	15,035 unfavorable
Year 3	0	15,035	15,035 unfavorable
Year 4	0	15,035	15,035 unfavorable
Year 5	0	15,035	15,035 unfavorable
Total	$64,500	$64,500	

Book/Tax Difference for Nondeductible Capital Loss

The characterization of a gain or loss as capital is relevant only for tax purposes. For financial reporting purposes, gains and losses realized during the year generally are included in the computation of book income. Consequently, a nondeductible capital loss results in an excess of tax income over book income. This unfavorable difference is considered temporary because of the loss carryback and carryforward rules.

Book/Tax Difference for Capital Loss	In 2021, Beco, Inc. realized a $46,900 loss on the sale of an investment asset. The loss was included in 2021 book income but was a nondeductible capital loss for tax purposes. Beco was unable to deduct any of the capital loss as a carryback to earlier years. Because of the unfavorable book/tax difference attributable to the loss, Beco recorded a $9,849 deferred tax asset ($46,900 × 21 percent).
	In 2022, Beco realized a $31,000 gain on sale of an investment asset. The gain was included in both book and tax income. The gain was a capital gain, so Beco could deduct $31,000 of its capital loss carryforward. Because this favorable book/tax difference was a partial reversal of the 2021 unfavorable difference, Beco reduced the deferred tax asset recorded in 2021 by $6,510 ($31,000 × 21 percent). The balance of the deferred tax asset was $3,339.
	In 2023, Beco realized a $47,500 gain on the sale of an investment asset. The gain was included in both book and tax income. The gain was a capital gain, so Beco could deduct its remaining $15,900 capital loss carryforward ($46,900 − $31,000 deducted in 2022). Because this favorable book/tax difference completely reversed the 2021 unfavorable difference, Beco reduced the deferred tax asset by $3,339 ($15,900 × 21 percent) to zero.

Conclusion

The rules governing the tax consequences of property transactions are among the most complicated in the tax law. Nevertheless, business managers must understand how these rules operate to determine the taxable gain or deductible loss triggered by sales, exchanges, and other dispositions of assets. The rules relate both the timing of the gain or loss recognition and the character of the gain or loss. The critical distinction between ordinary and capital gain or loss can result in significant differences in tax cost or tax savings. Managers who do not understand this distinction may miss tax planning opportunities that can dramatically improve after-tax cash flows from asset dispositions. In the next chapter, we continue our discussion of property transactions by examining still another type of asset disposition—a nontaxable exchange.

Sources of Book/Tax Differences

Permanent
- Loss on related party sale

Temporary
- Disposition of asset with different book/tax basis
- Seller-financed sale eligible for installment sale method
- Net capital loss

Key Terms

abandonment loss *8-23*
affiliated
  corporation *8-23*
amount realized *8-3*
capital asset *8-9*
capital gain or loss *8-9*
depreciation recapture *8-17*
gross profit
  percentage *8-5*

installment sale
  method *8-5*
net capital loss *8-11*
nonrecaptured Section 1231
  loss *8-17*
nonrecourse debt *8-24*
ordinary gain or loss *8-9*
realized gain or loss *8-2*
recapture *8-16*

recognized gain or loss *8-2*
recourse debt *8-24*
Section 1231 asset *8-15*
Section 1245
  recapture *8-18*
Section 1250
  recapture *8-19*
seller-financed sale *8-5*
20 percent recapture *8-20*

Questions and Problems for Discussion

LO 8-4, 8-6 1. BBB Company, which manufactures industrial plastics, owns the following assets. Characterize each asset as either a capital, ordinary, or Section 1231 asset.

    a. A computer system used in BBB's main office.

    b. A 50 percent interest in a business partnership organized to conduct a mining operation in Utah.

    c. Heavy equipment used to mold BBB's best-selling plastic item.

    d. BBB's customer list developed over 12 years of business.

    e. BBB's inventory of raw materials used in the manufacturing process.

    f. An oil painting of BBB's founder and first president that hangs in the boardroom. The painting was commissioned by the company from a local artist and paid for in cash.

    g. A patent developed by BBB's research and development department.

    h. BBB's company airplane.

LO 8-1 2. For tax purposes, what is the difference between a sale of property and an exchange of property?

LO 8-9 3. Under what circumstances could a taxpayer have an amount realized on the disposition of an asset without any inflow of cash or property?

LO 8-2 4. Under what circumstances would a taxpayer elect not to use the installment sale method of reporting gain?

LO 8-4, 8-10   5. Does the characterization of gain or loss as either ordinary or capital have any effect on the computation of net income per books?

LO 8-1   6. Distinguish between a firm's tax basis in an asset and its equity in that asset.

LO 8-4, 8-6   7. Both Corporation A and Corporation Z have business goodwill worth approximately $1 million. The goodwill is a capital asset to Corporation A and a Section 1231 asset to Corporation Z. Can you explain this apparently inconsistent tax characterization?

LO 8-4   8. Mrs. Carly called her accountant with a question. She is planning to sell nine acres of land for $380,000 cash. She purchased the land eight years ago for $195,000. She asked her accountant if her gain on sale would be a capital gain, and his answer was, "It depends." Can you explain why the accountant could not answer Mrs. Carly's simple question?

LO 8-1   9. Two years ago, Firm OP bought a tract of land for $600,000, paying $50,000 down and borrowing the balance of the purchase price from a commercial lender. The land is the collateral for OP's debt. To date, OP has not repaid any of the loan.

   a. If the debt is recourse, to what extent do OP and the commercial lender bear the risk of loss if the FMV of the land decreases to $475,000?

   b. How does your answer change if the debt is nonrecourse?

LO 8-3   10. Mr. Kyle realized a loss on the sale of an asset to Mr. Payne, his best friend for 20 years. Does this sale represent an arm's-length transaction? Are Mr. Kyle and Mr. Payne related parties for tax purposes?

LO 8-4   11. Why do both corporate and noncorporate taxpayers prefer capital gains to ordinary income? Why is the preference stronger for noncorporate taxpayers?

LO 8-8   12. Why is Section 1250 recapture inapplicable to sales of realty subject to MACRS depreciation?

LO 8-9   13. Does a taxpayer always realize a loss on the involuntary disposition of property because of a casualty or a theft?

LO 8-1   14. Firm F's adjusted basis in operating asset A is $75,000. If the firm carries $75,000 of property insurance on this asset, is it adequately protected against risk of loss?

McGraw Hill connect   **All applicable Application Problems are available with *Connect*.**

Application Problems

LO 8-1, 8-10   1. Lento, Inc. owned machinery with a $30,000 initial cost basis. Accumulated book depreciation with respect to the machinery was $12,000, and accumulated tax depreciation was $19,100. Lento sold the machinery for $13,000 cash. Lento's marginal tax rate is 21 percent.

   a. Compute Lento's book gain or loss on the sale.

   b. Compute Lento's tax gain or loss on the sale.

   c. Compute Lento's after-tax cash flow from the sale.

LO 8-1, 8-10   2. Several years ago, PTR purchased business equipment for $50,000. PTR's accumulated book depreciation with respect to the equipment is $37,200, and its accumulated tax depreciation is $41,000.

   a. Compute PTR's book and tax basis in the equipment.

   b. Using a 21 percent tax rate, compute PTR's deferred tax asset or liability (identify which) resulting from the difference between accumulated book and tax depreciation.

   c. Compute PTR's book and tax gain if it sells the equipment for $14,750.

   d. Explain the effect of the sale on the deferred tax asset or liability computed in part (b).

LO 8-1, 8-4 3. Firm CS performed consulting services for Company P. The two parties agreed that Company P would pay for the services by transferring investment securities to Firm CS. At date of transfer, the securities had a $38,500 FMV. Company P's tax basis in the securities was $25,000.

    a. How much income must Firm CS recognize on receipt of the securities? What is the character of this income? What is Firm CS's tax basis in the securities?

    b. How much income must Company P recognize on disposition of the securities? What is the character of the income?

    c. Does disposition of the securities result in a deduction for Company P? If so, what is the amount of the deduction?

LO 8-1 4. Company L sold an inventory item to Firm M for $40,000. Company L's marginal tax rate is 21 percent. In each of the following cases, compute Company L's after-tax cash flow from the sale:

    a. Firm M's payment consisted of $10,000 cash and its note for $30,000. The note is payable two years from the date of sale. Company L's basis in the inventory item was $15,700.

    b. Firm M's payment consisted of $5,000 cash and its note for $35,000. The note is payable two years from the date of sale. Company L's basis in the inventory item was $47,000.

    c. Firm M's payment consisted of $40,000 cash. Company L's basis in the inventory item was $18,000.

    d. Firm M's payment consisted of $40,000 cash. Company L's basis in the inventory item was $44,000.

LO 8-1 5. KNB sold real property to Firm P for $15,000 cash and Firm P's assumption of the $85,000 mortgage on the property.

    a. What is KNB's amount realized on the sale?

    b. Compute KNB's after-tax cash flow from the sale if its adjusted basis in the real property is $40,000 and its marginal tax rate is 35 percent.

LO 8-1 6. Firm UT sold realty to an unrelated buyer for $40,000 cash plus the buyer's assumption of a $166,700 mortgage on the property. UT's initial cost basis in the realty was $235,000, and accumulated tax depreciation through date of sale was $184,200.

    a. Compute UT's gain recognized on the sale.

    b. Assuming a 21 percent marginal tax rate, compute UT's after-tax cash flow from the sale.

LO 8-1, 8-2 7. TPW, a calendar year taxpayer, sold land with a $535,000 tax basis for $750,000 in February. The purchaser paid $75,000 cash at closing and gave TPW an interest-bearing note for the $675,000 remaining price. In August, TPW received a $55,950 payment from the purchaser consisting of a $33,750 principal payment and a $22,200 interest payment.

    a. Compute gain realized on the sale.

    b. Compute gain recognized in the year of sale if TPW elects not to use the installment sale method of accounting. Compute TPW's tax basis in the note at the end of the year.

    c. Compute gain recognized in the year of sale if TPW uses the installment sale method of accounting. Compute TPW's tax basis in the note at the end of the year.

LO 8-2, 8-10 8. Refer to the facts in the preceding problem and assume that TPW uses the installment sale method of accounting.

    a. Compute the difference between TPW's book and tax income resulting from the installment sale method.

    b. Is this difference favorable or unfavorable?

    c. Using a 21 percent tax rate, compute PTR's deferred tax asset or liability (identify which) resulting from the book/tax difference.

LO 8-2   9. Refer to the facts in problem 7. In the first year after the year of sale, TPW received payments totaling $106,900 from the purchaser. The total consisted of $67,500 principal payments and $39,400 interest payments.

    a. Compute TPW's gain recognized under the installment sale method.

    b. Compute TPW's tax basis in the note at the end of the year.

LO 8-2, 8-10   10. Refer to the facts in the preceding problem.

    a. Compute the difference between TPW's book and tax income resulting from the installment sale method.

    b. Is this difference favorable or unfavorable?

    c. Using a 21 percent tax rate, determine the effect of the difference on the deferred tax asset or liability generated in the year of sale.

LO 8-2   11. In year 1, Maxim sold investment land with a tax basis of $77,000. Payment consisted of $10,000 cash down and the purchaser's note for $90,000. The note is payable in equal installments of $45,000 in years 2 and 3.

    a. Compute Maxim's realized gain on the sale of the land.

    b. Compute Maxim's gross profit percentage on the sale of the land under the installment sale method.

    c. Compute Maxim's recognized gain under the installment sale method in years 1, 2, and 3.

LO 8-2   12. In year 1, Aldo sold investment land with a $61,000 tax basis for $95,000. Payment consisted of $15,000 cash down and the purchaser's note for $80,000. The note is being paid in 10 annual installments of $8,000, beginning in year 2.

    a. Compute Aldo's recognized gain under the installment sale method in years 1 and 2.

    b. In year 4, Aldo pledged the note as partial collateral for a $75,000 bank loan. The unpaid principal at date of pledge was $56,000. Determine the tax consequences of this pledge to Aldo.

LO 8-1   13. Refer to the facts in the preceding problem but assume that Aldo's basis in the investment land was $100,000 rather than $61,000.

    a. Compute Aldo's recognized loss in year 1.

    b. In year 4, Aldo pledged the note received from the purchaser as partial collateral for a $75,000 bank loan. The unpaid principal at date of pledge was $56,000. Determine the tax consequences of this pledge to Aldo.

LO 8-1, 8-3   14. Firm J sold marketable securities to Company B. Firm J's tax basis in the securities was $45,250. Compute Firm J's recognized gain or loss if

    a. The selling price was $60,000, and Firm J and Company B are unrelated parties.

    b. The selling price was $60,000, and Firm J and Company B are related parties.

    c. The selling price was $38,000, and Firm J and Company B are unrelated parties.

    d. The selling price was $38,000, and Firm J and Company B are related parties.

LO 8-3   15. Silo, Inc. sold investment land to PPR, Inc. for $110,000 cash. Silo's basis in the land was $145,000. Mr. and Mrs. Jersey own 100 percent of the stock of both corporations.

    a. What is PPR's tax basis in the land purchased from Silo?

    b. PPR holds the land as an investment for seven years before selling it to an unrelated buyer. Compute the gain or loss recognized if the amount realized on sale is (1) $100,000, (2) $116,000, or (3) $150,000.

LO 8-1, 8-2 16. Firm J, an accrual basis taxpayer, recorded a $40,000 account receivable on the sale of an asset on credit. Its basis in the asset was $33,000. Two months after the asset sale, Firm J sold the receivable to a local bank for $38,000.

 a. Assuming that the asset was an inventory item, determine the amount and character of Firm J's gain or loss recognized on the sale of (1) the asset and (2) the receivable.

 b. Assuming that the asset was a capital asset, determine the amount and character of Firm J's gain or loss recognized on the sale of (1) the asset and (2) the receivable.

LO 8-4 17. Four years ago, Firm RD paid $468,000 for 12 acres of undeveloped land. This year, the firm sold the land for $1 million. What is the character of RD's $532,000 recognized gain under each of the following assumptions?

 a. RD improved the land by adding roads and utilities and then subdivided the land into 36 one-third-acre tracts that RD held for sale to local builders.

 b. RD made no improvements to the land and sold the entire 12 acres to a Japanese purchaser.

LO 8-4 18. On July 8, Divo Company sold office supplies for $13,000. Determine the amount and the character of Divo's gain or loss on sale under each of the following assumptions:

 a. Divo is a retail store that sells office supplies to customers. Under the LIFO method of accounting, Divo's cost basis in the supplies was $11,900.

 b. Divo is a law firm. Divo sold the supplies because it was overstocked and needed the storage space for a different purpose. Under its method of accounting, Divo expenses the cost of office supplies when purchased.

 c. Divo is an accounting firm. Divo sold the supplies because it is liquidating its business. Divo's capitalized cost of the supplies was $14,250.

LO 8-4 19. *Shenandoah Skies* is the name of an oil painting by artist Kara Lee. In each of the following cases, determine the amount and character of the taxpayer's gain or loss on sale of the painting:

 a. The taxpayer is Kara Lee, who sold her painting to the Reller Gallery for $6,000.

 b. The taxpayer is the Reller Gallery, who sold the painting purchased from Kara to a regular customer for $10,000.

 c. The taxpayer is Lollard, Inc., the regular customer that purchased the painting from the Reller Gallery. Lollard displayed the painting in the lobby of its corporate headquarters until it sold *Shenandoah Skies* to a collector from Dallas. The collector paid $45,000 for the painting.

LO 8-5 20. Koil Corporation generated $718,400 ordinary income from the sale of inventory to its customers. It also sold three noninventory assets during the year. Compute Koil's taxable income assuming that

 a. The first sale resulted in a $45,000 capital gain, the second sale resulted in a $12,000 capital loss, and the third sale resulted in a $19,000 capital loss.

 b. The first sale resulted in a $17,000 ordinary gain, the second sale resulted in a $22,300 capital gain, and the third sale resulted in a $58,000 capital loss.

 c. The first sale resulted in a $9,000 capital gain, the second sale resulted in a $16,100 capital loss, and the third sale resulted in an $8,800 ordinary loss.

LO 8-5 21. This year, PRS Corporation generated $300,000 income from the performance of consulting services for its clients. It sold two assets during the year, recognizing a $36,000 gain on the first sale and a $49,000 loss on the second sale. Compute PRS's taxable income assuming that

 a. Both the gain and the loss were capital.

 b. Both the gain and the loss were ordinary.

c. The gain was ordinary, and the loss was capital.

d. The gain was capital, and the loss was ordinary.

LO 8-5 22. Alto Corporation sold two capital assets this year. The first sale resulted in a $13,000 capital gain, and the second sale resulted in a $41,000 capital loss. Alto was incorporated five years ago. Four years ago, Alto recognized $5,000 of net capital gain. Three years ago, Alto recognized $10,000 of net capital gain. Two years ago and last year, Alto recognized no net capital gains.

a. Using a 21 percent tax rate, compute Alto's tax refund from the carryback of its current year capital loss.

b. Compute Alto's capital loss carryforward into next year.

LO 8-5 23. Zeno, Inc. sold two capital assets in 2023. The first sale resulted in a $53,000 capital loss, and the second sale resulted in a $25,600 capital gain. Zeno was incorporated in 2019, and its tax records provide the following information:

	2019	2020	2021	2022
Ordinary income	$443,000	$509,700	$810,300	$921,000
Net capital gain	22,000	–0–	4,120	13,600
Taxable income	$465,000	$509,700	$814,420	$934,600

a. Compute Zeno's tax refund from the carryback of its 2023 nondeductible capital loss. Zeno's marginal tax rate was 21 percent for each prior year.

b. Compute Zeno's capital loss carryforward into 2024.

LO 8-7, 8-10 24. In its first taxable year, Band Corporation recognized $957,500 ordinary business income and a $5,500 capital loss. In its second taxable year, Band recognized $1,220,000 ordinary business income, a $12,500 Section 1231 loss, and a $2,000 capital gain.

a. Compute Band's book and taxable income for its first year.

b. Using a 21 percent tax rate, compute Band's deferred tax asset or liability (identify which) on its balance sheet on the last day of the year.

c. Compute Band's book and taxable income for its second year.

d. Using a 21 percent tax rate, compute Band's deferred tax asset or liability (identify which) on its balance sheet on the last day of the second year.

LO 8-7, 8-10 25. In its first year, Firm KZ recognized $427,300 ordinary business income and a $13,590 loss on the sale of an investment asset. In its second year, Firm KZ recognized $500,800 ordinary business income, a $19,300 Section 1231 gain, and a $7,400 Section 1231 loss on two sales of operating assets.

a. Compute KZ's book and taxable income for its first year.

b. Using a 21 percent tax rate, compute KZ's deferred tax asset or liability (identify which) on its balance sheet on the last day of the year.

c. Compute KZ's book and taxable income for its second year.

d. Compute KZ's deferred tax asset or liability (identify which) on its balance sheet on the last day of the second year.

LO 8-8 26. Firm OCS sold business equipment with a $20,000 initial cost basis and $7,315 accumulated tax depreciation. In each of the following cases, compute OCS's recaptured ordinary income and Section 1231 gain or loss on the sale.

a. Amount realized was $10,000.

b. Amount realized was $13,000.

  c. Amount realized was $17,500.

  d. Amount realized was $22,500.

LO 8-5, 8-7   27. Lemon Corporation generated $324,600 of income from ordinary business operations. It also sold several assets during the year. Compute Lemon's taxable income under each of the following alternative assumptions about the tax consequences of the asset sales.

  a. Lemon recognized a $5,500 capital gain and a $7,400 net Section 1231 loss.

  b. Lemon recognized a $6,500 capital loss and a $4,700 net Section 1231 gain.

  c. Lemon recognized a $2,500 capital gain, a $3,900 capital loss, and a $3,000 net Section 1231 gain.

  d. Lemon recognized $4,000 of depreciation recapture, a $2,000 Section 1231 gain, and a $4,200 Section 1231 loss.

LO 8-5, 8-7   28. This year, Zeron Company generated $87,200 income from the performance of services for its clients. It also sold several assets during the year. Compute Zeron's taxable income under each of the following alternative assumptions about the tax consequences of the asset sales.

  a. Zeron recognized $1,000 recaptured ordinary income, a $2,400 net Section 1231 gain, and a $7,000 capital loss.

  b. Zeron recognized a $6,600 net Section 1231 loss and a $1,700 capital loss.

  c. Zeron recognized $3,900 recaptured ordinary income, a $1,510 net Section 1231 gain, and a $1,200 capital gain.

  d. Zeron recognized a $10,300 net Section 1231 loss and a $4,000 capital gain.

  e. Zeron recognized a $2,800 net Section 1231 gain, a $5,200 capital gain, and a $6,300 capital loss.

LO 8-1, 8-6, 8-7, 8-8   29. This year, QIO Company generated $192,400 income from its routine business operations. In addition, it sold the following assets, all of which were held for more than 12 months. Compute QIO's taxable income.

	Initial Basis	Acc. Depr.*	Sale Price
Computer equipment	$ 22,400	$ 18,600	$ 4,500
Construction equipment	175,000	121,700	50,000
Furniture	6,000	1,500	4,750
Transportation equipment	83,200	26,000	55,000

* Through date of sale.

LO 8-1, 8-4, 8-5, 8-7, 8-8   30. This year, Sigma, Inc. generated $612,000 income from its routine business operations. In addition, the corporation sold the following assets, all of which were held for more than 12 months:

	Initial Basis	Acc. Depr.*	Sale Price
Marketable securities	$144,000	–0–	$ 64,000
Production equipment	93,000	$76,000	30,000
Business realty:			
Land	165,000	–0–	180,000
Building	200,000	58,300	210,000

* Through date of sale.

    a. Compute Sigma's taxable income assuming that it used the straight-line method to calculate depreciation on the building and has no nonrecaptured Section 1231 losses.

    b. Recompute taxable income assuming that Sigma sold the securities for $150,000 rather than $64,000.

LO 8-1, 8-4, 8-5, 8-7, 8-8   31. EzTech, a calendar year accrual basis corporation, generated $994,300 ordinary income from its business this year. It also sold the following assets, all of which were held for more than 12 months:

	Initial Basis	Acc. Depr.*	Sale Price
Machinery	$ 97,500	$39,660	$ 70,000
Office equipment	50,000	12,470	57,500
Warehouse	163,500	21,620	125,000
Investment securities	72,700	n/a	83,100
Investment land	350,000	n/a	328,000

* Through date of sale.

EzTech used the straight-line method to calculate depreciation on the warehouse and has no nonrecaptured Section 1231 losses.

    a. Compute EzTech's taxable income.

    b. Recompute taxable income assuming that EzTech used the land in its business instead of holding it for investment.

LO 8-7   32. Since its formation, Roof Corporation has incurred the following net Section 1231 gains and losses:

Year 1	$(12,000)	Net Section 1231 loss
Year 2	10,500	Net Section 1231 gain
Year 3	(14,000)	Net Section 1231 loss

    a. In year 4, Roof sold only one asset and recognized a $7,500 net Section 1231 gain. How much of this gain is treated as capital gain, and how much is ordinary?

    b. In year 5, Roof sold one asset and recognized a $9,000 net Section 1231 gain. How much of this gain is treated as capital, and how much is ordinary?

LO 8-7   33. Corporation Q, a calendar year taxpayer, has incurred the following Section 1231 net gains and losses since its formation in 2019:

	2019	2020	2021
Section 1231 gains	$ 14,800	$ 5,700	–0–
Section 1231 losses	(13,000)	(9,000)	$(3,100)
Net gain or (loss)	$ 1,800	$(3,300)	$(3,100)

    a. In 2022, Corporation Q sold only one asset and recognized a $4,000 Section 1231 gain. How much of this gain is treated as capital gain, and how much is ordinary?

    b. In 2023, Corporation Q recognized a $16,700 Section 1231 gain on the sale of one asset and a $2,000 Section 1231 loss on the sale of a second asset. How much of the $14,700 net gain is treated as capital gain, and how much is ordinary?

LO 8-1, 8-8 34. Eleven years ago, Lynn, Inc. purchased a warehouse for $315,000. This year, the corporation sold the warehouse to Firm D for $80,000 cash and D's assumption of a $225,000 mortgage. Through date of sale, Lynn deducted $92,300 straight-line depreciation on the warehouse.

    a. Compute Lynn's gain recognized on the sale of the warehouse.

    b. What is the character of this gain?

    c. How would your answers change if Lynn was a noncorporate business?

LO 8-1, 8-8 35. Firm P, a noncorporate taxpayer, purchased residential realty in 1985 for $1 million. This year it sold the realty for $450,000. Through date of sale, Firm P deducted $814,000 accelerated depreciation on the realty. Straight-line depreciation would have been $625,000.

    a. Determine the amount and character of Firm P's recognized gain on sale.

    b. How would your answer change if Firm P was a corporation?

LO 8-6, 8-8 36. Six years ago, Corporation CN purchased a business and capitalized $200,000 of the purchase price as goodwill. Through this year, CN has deducted $74,000 amortization with respect to this goodwill. At the end of the year, CN sold the business for $2 million, $250,000 of which was allocable to goodwill. Determine the amount and character of CN's gain from its sale of goodwill.

LO 8-1, 8-8 37. Company B disposed of obsolete computer equipment with a $32,000 initial cost basis and $27,000 accumulated depreciation. Determine the amount and character of Company B's recognized gain or loss if

    a. It sold the equipment for $7,000.

    b. It sold the equipment for $1,000.

    c. It dumped the equipment in a local landfill.

LO 8-9 38. Firm L owns a commercial building that is divided into 23 offices. Several years ago, it leased an office to Company K. As part of the lease agreement, Firm L spent $29,000 to construct new interior walls to conform the office to Company K's specifications. It capitalized this expenditure to an asset account and has deducted $6,200 depreciation with respect to the asset. Early this year, Company K broke its lease and vacated the office. Firm L has found a prospective tenant that wants Firm L to demolish the interior walls before it will sign a lease. What are the tax consequences to Firm L if it agrees to the demolition?

LO 8-9 39. A taxpayer owned 1,000 shares of common stock in Barlo Corporation, which manufactures automobile parts. The taxpayer's cost basis in the stock was $82,700. Last week, Barlo declared bankruptcy, and its board of directors issued a news release that Barlo common stock should be considered worthless. Determine the character of the $82,700 loss if the taxpayer is

    a. An individual who purchased the stock as an investment.

    b. A corporation that purchased the stock as an investment.

    c. Barlo's parent corporation that owned 96 percent of Barlo's outstanding common stock.

LO 8-9 40. Lyle Company owns commercial real estate with a $360,000 initial cost basis and $285,000 accumulated straight-line depreciation. The real estate is subject to a $120,000 recourse mortgage and has an appraised FMV of only $100,000. The mortgage holder is threatening to foreclose on the real estate because Lyle failed to make the last four mortgage payments. Determine the tax consequences of foreclosure assuming that *a.* Lyle must pay $20,000 cash to the mortgage holder in full satisfaction of its recourse debt.

    b. The mortgage holder agrees to accept the real estate in full satisfaction of the recourse debt.

LO 8-9   41. Change the facts in the preceding problem by assuming that the $120,000 mortgage on Lyle's real estate is nonrecourse. Determine the tax consequence to Lyle if the mortgage holder forecloses on the real estate.

LO 8-1, 8-9   42. Five years ago, Firm SJ purchased land for $100,000 with $10,000 of its own funds and $90,000 borrowed from a commercial bank. The bank holds a recourse mortgage on the land. For each of the following independent transactions, compute SJ's positive or negative cash flow. Assume that SJ is solvent, any recognized loss is fully deductible, and SJ's marginal tax rate is 21 percent.

    a. SJ sells the land for $33,000 cash and the buyer's assumption of the $80,000 principal balance of the mortgage.

    b. SJ sells the land for $113,000 cash and pays off the $80,000 principal balance of the mortgage.

    c. SJ sells the land for $82,000 cash and pays off the $80,000 principal balance of the mortgage.

    d. SJ defaults on the $80,000 mortgage. The bank forecloses and sells the land at public auction for $64,000. The bank notifies SJ that it will not pursue collection of the $16,000 remaining debt.

    e. SJ defaults on the $80,000 mortgage. The bank forecloses and sells the land at public auction for $64,000. The bank requires SJ to pay off the $16,000 remaining debt.

LO 8-9   43. Firm R owned depreciable real property subject to a $300,000 nonrecourse mortgage. The property's FMV is only $250,000. Consequently, the firm surrendered the property to the creditor rather than continuing to service the mortgage. At date of surrender, Firm R's adjusted basis in the property was $195,000. Determine Firm R's cash flow consequences of the disposition, assuming that the gain recognized is taxed at 21 percent.

LO 8-9   44. A fire recently destroyed a warehouse owned by Company J. Its adjusted basis in the warehouse was $489,000. However, the warehouse's replacement value (cost to rebuild) was $610,000. Determine the tax consequences of this property disposition assuming that

    a. The building was insured, and Company J received a $450,000 reimbursement from the insurance company.

    b. The building was uninsured.

LO 8-9   45. Calvin Corporation's office was burglarized. The thieves stole 10 laptop computers and other electronic equipment. The lost assets had an original cost of $35,000 and accumulated tax depreciation of $19,400. Calvin received an insurance reimbursement of $10,000 related to the theft loss. Determine the amount and character of gain or loss recognized as a result of this theft.

LO 8-10   46. Bali, Inc. reported $605,800 net income before tax on this year's financial statements prepared in accordance with GAAP. The corporation's records reveal the following information:

- Depreciation expense per books was $53,000, and MACRS depreciation was $27,400.
- Bali sold business equipment for $100,000 cash. The original cost of the equipment was $125,000. Book accumulated depreciation through date of sale was $48,000, and MACRS accumulated depreciation through the date of sale was $63,000.
- Bali sold investment land to Coroda, a corporation owned by the same person that owns Bali. The amount realized on the sale was $115,000, and Bali's basis in the land was $40,000.
- Bali sold marketable securities to its sole shareholder. The amount realized on the sale was $51,450, and Bali's basis in the securities was $75,000.

Compute Bali's taxable income.

LO 8-10 47. St. George, Inc. reported $711,800 net income before tax on this year's financial statement prepared in accordance with GAAP. The corporation's records reveal the following information:

- Four years ago, St. George realized a $283,400 gain on the sale of investment property and elected the installment sale method to report the sale for tax purposes. Its gross profit percentage is 50.12, and it collected $62,000 principal and $14,680 interest on the installment note this year.
- Five years ago, St. George purchased investment property for $465,000 cash from an LLC. Because St. George and the LLC were related parties, the LLC's $12,700 realized loss on the sale was disallowed for tax purposes. This year, St. George sold the property to an unrelated purchaser for $500,000.
- A flood destroyed several antique carpets that decorated the floors of corporate headquarters. Unfortunately, St. George's property insurance does not cover damage caused by rising water, so the loss was uninsured. The carpets' adjusted book basis was $36,000, and their adjusted tax basis was $28,400.

Compute St. George's taxable income.

LO 8-1, 8-7, 8-8 48. Ms. Drake sold a business that she had operated as a sole proprietorship for 18 years. On the date of sale, the business balance sheet showed the following assets:

	Tax Basis
Accounts receivable	$ 32,000
Inventory	125,000
Furniture and equipment:	
Cost	45,800
Accumulated depreciation	(38,000)
Leasehold improvements:	
Cost	29,000
Accumulated amortization	(5,100)

The purchaser paid a lump-sum price of $300,000 cash for the business. The sales contract stipulates that the FMV of the business inventory is $145,000, and the FMV of the remaining balance sheet assets equals adjusted tax basis. Assuming that Ms. Drake's marginal tax rate on ordinary income is 35 percent and her rate on capital gain is 15 percent, compute the net cash flow from the sale of her business.

LO 8-1, 8-4, 8-7, 8-8   49. Twelve years ago, Mr. and Mrs. Chang purchased a business. This year, they sold the business for $750,000. On the date of sale, the business balance sheet showed the following assets:

		Tax Basis
Accounts receivable		$ 41,200
Inventory		515,000
Furniture and fixtures:		
Cost	$ 395,500	
Accumulated depreciation	(321,800)	73,700
Purchased goodwill:		
Cost	$ 250,000	
Accumulated amortization	(203,600)	46,400
Total tax basis		$676,300

The sales contract allocated $40,000 of the purchase price to accounts receivable, $515,000 to inventory, and $70,000 to furniture and fixtures. Assuming that the Changs' marginal tax rate on ordinary income is 32 percent and their rate on capital gain is 15 percent, compute the net cash flow from the sale of their business.

Issue Recognition Problems

Identify the tax issue or issues suggested by the following situations, and state each issue in the form of a question.

LO 8-4, 8-5, 8-7   1. On March 1, DS Company, a calendar year taxpayer, recognized a $15,000 loss on sale of marketable securities. On May 12, it recognized an $85,000 Section 1231 gain on sale of an office building. In forecasting current taxable income, DS's chief financial officer plans to deduct the $15,000 loss against the $85,000 gain.

LO 8-9   2. Firm LD, a calendar year taxpayer, owns 20,000 shares of MXP stock with a $160,000 basis. In November, LD's chief financial officer learned that MXP had just declared bankruptcy. The CFO was unable to determine if MXP's board of directors intend to try to save the corporation or dissolve it under state law.

LO 8-9   3. A fire-damaged industrial equipment used by Firm L in its manufacturing process. Immediately before the fire, the equipment was worth $40,000. After the fire, the equipment was worth only $15,000. Firm L's adjusted basis in the equipment was $14,000, and it received only $10,000 insurance reimbursement for its loss.

LO 8-9   4. Company LR owns a commercial office building. Four years ago, LR entered into a long-term lease with Lessee M for 2,400 square feet of office space. LR spent $13,600 to finish out the space to meet Lessee M's requirements. The leasehold improvements included several interior walls and special-purpose electrical wiring. This year, Lessee M terminated the lease and moved out of the office space. To make the space more marketable, LR tore down the interior walls and removed the special-purpose wiring.

LO 8-1 5. Two years ago, Corporation M loaned $80,000 to its employee Mr. Erzan. The corporation received Mr. Erzan's properly executed note in which he promised to repay the loan at the end of seven years and to pay annual interest of 9 percent (the market interest rate on the date of the loan). This year, when interest rates were 6 percent, Corporation M sold the $80,000 note to an unrelated party for $92,700.

LO 8-5 6. In its first taxable year, Corporation NM generated a $25,000 net operating loss and recognized an $8,000 net capital loss. The corporation's tax return for its second year reported $15,000 taxable income, $10,000 of which was capital gain.

LO 8-1 7. Firm WD sold depreciable realty for $225,000. The firm purchased the realty 12 years earlier for $350,000 and deducted $155,000 MACRS depreciation through date of sale. During an audit of the tax return on which the sale was reported, the IRS determined that WD had incorrectly computed its depreciation with respect to the realty. The correct depreciation through the date of sale should have been $200,000.

LO 8-4 8. Corporation AD operates four antique dealerships. Last year, it sold a 200-year-old desk to its sole shareholder, Mr. Cramer, for $35,000. AD reported its $2,700 gain as ordinary income from the sale of inventory. This year, Mr. Cramer sold the desk to an unrelated collector for $60,000 and reported a $25,000 capital gain on his tax return.

LO 8-9 9. Mr. Vela sold his sole proprietorship to an unrelated party for a lump-sum price of $900,000. The contract of sale specifies that $100,000 is for a covenant not to compete—Mr. Vela's promise not to operate a similar business anywhere in the state for the next four years.

LO 8-9 10. Corporation TJ ceased business operations and was dissolved under state law. On the last day of its existence, TJ's balance sheet showed $2,200 unamortized organizational costs and $12,000 unamortized goodwill.

LO 8-9 11. At the beginning of the year, Firm GH owned 8,200 shares of common stock in LSR, a publicly held corporation. GH's basis in these shares was $290,000. On a day when LSR stock was trading at $1.14 per share, GH delivered the 8,200 shares to its broker with a letter stating that it was formally abandoning ownership of its LSR equity interest.

Research Problems

LO 8-1, 8-9 1. For the past 12 years, George Link has operated his appliance repair business out of a 1,000-square-foot, ground-floor office in a four-story commercial building called 129 Main. Last year, George signed a five-year lease with Kramer Management, the owner of 129 Main. This year, Kramer decided to convert the building into condominiums and is negotiating with all its tenants to surrender their leasehold rights and vacate their space in 129 Main. Kramer has offered George a $50,000 cash payment and the use of a 1,200-square-foot office in a new shopping center recently constructed by Kramer. If George accepts Kramer's offer, he can use the new office rent free for 36 months. The fair rental value of this office is $1,300 per month. What are the tax consequences to George if he accepts Kramer's offer and moves his business location?

LO 8-2 2. Six years ago, Graham, Inc., an accrual basis corporation, sold investment land (basis $562,250) to Jervil LLC and accepted Jervil's note for the entire $865,000 sale price. The land was the collateral for the note, and Graham used the installment sale method of reporting its taxable gain on sale. This year, Jervil defaulted on the note, and Graham repossessed the land. At the date of repossession, the principal of the note was $644,000. Graham also had $40,800 accrued interest receivable on the note. How much gain must Graham recognize on repossession, and what is its new tax basis in the repossessed land?

LO 8-4

3. In 1998, Big Skye Partnership paid $695,500 for a Christmas tree farm in northern Arizona. In 1991, over 300 farms and ranches in the area were granted allocations of water from a newly completed irrigation project funded by the U.S. Department of the Interior. This year, Big Skye Partnership discontinued its tree farming operation and converted the property to a sheep ranch. Because the property no longer needed irrigation, Big Skye sold its federal water rights to a neighboring farm for $175,000. What is the amount and character of Big Skye's gain or loss on disposition of its water rights?

LO 8-4, 8-5

4. The BPL Corporation is considering selling investment land to Kaier Partnership for the land's independently appraised FMV of $1.2 million. BPL purchased the land 20 years ago for $1.32 million cash. Mr. Larry Bass is the largest shareholder in BPL; he owns 892 of 2,000 BPL shares outstanding. Larry's sister, Mrs. Ann Olsen, owns 165 BPL shares, and various investors who are unrelated to Larry and Ann own the remaining shares outstanding. Ann is a limited partner in Kaier Partnership; she owns a 35 percent interest in Kaier's profits and capital. Ann's daughter, Suzanne Olsen, owns a 22 percent limited interest in Kaier's profits and capital. Ann and Suzanne are unrelated to any other Kaier partner and are not involved in any aspect of the management of the partnership. If BPL sells its land to Kaier Partnership, can it recognize the $120,000 loss that it will realize on the sale?

   **All applicable Tax Planning Cases are available with *Connect*.**

Tax Planning Cases

LO 8-1, 8-4

1. Firm Z, a corporation with a 21 percent tax rate, has $100,000 to invest in year 0 and two investment choices. Investment 1 will generate $12,000 taxable cash flow annually for years 1 through 5. In year 5, the firm can sell the investment for $100,000. Investment 2 will not generate any taxable income or cash flow in years 1 through 5, but in year 5, the firm can sell Investment 2 for $165,000.

   a. Assuming a 6 percent discount rate, which investment has the greater NPV?

   b. Would your answer change if Firm Z were a noncorporate taxpayer with a 35 percent tax rate and the gain on sale of Investment 2 were eligible for the 15 percent capital gains rate?

LO 8-1, 8-4

2. Mr. Renaldo purchased 30 acres of undeveloped ranch land 10 years ago for $935,000. He is considering subdividing the land into one-third-acre lots and improving the land by adding streets, sidewalks, and utilities. He plans to advertise the 90 lots for sale in a local real estate magazine. Mr. Renaldo projects that the improvements will cost $275,000 and that he can sell the lots for $20,000 each. He is also considering an offer from a local corporation to purchase the 30-acre tract in its undeveloped state for $1.35 million. Assuming that Mr. Renaldo makes no other property dispositions during the year and has a 35 percent tax rate on ordinary income and a 15 percent tax rate on capital gain, which alternative (develop or sell as is) maximizes his cash flow?

LO 8-2, 8-5   3. Olno, Inc. has a $52,100 capital loss carryforward into its current taxable year that will expire at the end of the year. During the year, Olno realized a $141,900 capital gain on the sale of land. The purchaser paid 10 percent down and gave Olno an interest-bearing note for the 90 percent remainder of the sale price. Under the installment sale method, Olno will recognize $14,190 gain this year and $14,190 in each of the following nine years. If Olno's marginal tax rate is 21 percent and it uses a 6 percent discount rate to compute NPV, should Olno elect out of the installment sale method?

LO 8-4, 8-5   4. Rocky Corporation is experiencing cash flow problems. It needs to generate an additional $60,000 of working capital and is considering selling off assets to meet this need. Rocky's marginal tax rate is 21 percent, and it has no prior year capital gains. It is considering three alternatives, as follows:

Alternative 1: Sell land for $60,000. The land was acquired three years ago as an investment at a cost of $90,000. Ground contamination caused by industrial dumping has caused the property value to decline.

Alternative 2: Sell land and a building used in Rocky's business. The two assets together could be sold for $60,000, of which $20,000 is attributable to the building and $40,000 is attributable to the land. The building has an adjusted tax basis of $23,000; the land has an adjusted tax basis of $17,000.

Alternative 3: Sell obsolete business machinery and equipment. The machinery has an adjusted basis of $100,000 and can be sold for $60,000.

Determine the impact of each of these alternatives on current year cash flow. Which alternative or alternatives provide the needed cash flow?

Chapter **Nine**

Nontaxable Exchanges

Learning Objectives

After studying this chapter, you should be able to:

LO 9-1. Explain the underlying tax concepts of a nontaxable exchange transaction.

LO 9-2. Compute the substituted basis of property received in a nontaxable exchange.

LO 9-3. Compute gain recognized when boot is received in a nontaxable exchange.

LO 9-4. Explain book/tax differences related to nontaxable exchanges.

LO 9-5. Identify properties that qualify for like-kind exchange treatment.

LO 9-6. Describe the effect of the relief and assumption of debt in a like-kind exchange.

LO 9-7. Compute gain recognized and the basis of replacement property in an involuntary conversion.

LO 9-8. Explain the tax consequences of the exchange of property for equity in a corporation or partnership.

LO 9-9. Describe the tax consequences of a wash sale.

In our analysis of property dispositions thus far, we've been working under the premise that any realized gain or loss is recognized (taken into account for tax purposes) in the year of disposition. In this chapter, we will examine a number of transactions that trigger gain or loss realization but do not result in current recognition of some or all of that gain or loss. These transactions are called **nontaxable exchanges**, and each one is authorized by a provision of the Internal Revenue Code. Congress enacted these provisions for particular tax policy reasons, which we will discuss as we look at the details of selected provisions.

TAX NEUTRALITY FOR ASSET EXCHANGES

LO 9-1
Explain the underlying tax concepts of a nontaxable exchange transaction.

The nontaxable exchange provisions are extremely useful because they allow taxpayers to convert property from one form to another without a tax cost. In other words, a nontaxable exchange provision makes the tax law *neutral* with respect to certain business and investment decisions.

Neutrality of Nontaxable Exchange

Firm T, which has a 21 percent marginal tax rate, owns an investment asset with a $50,000 basis and a $110,000 fair market value (FMV). The asset generates $6,600 annual income, which represents a 6 percent return on FMV. Firm T is considering selling this asset and reinvesting the proceeds in a new venture that promises a 6.7 percent return on capital. If the sale of the investment asset is taxable, Firm T will have only $97,400 after-tax proceeds to reinvest.

Amount realized on sale	$110,000
Basis in investment asset	(50,000)
Gain realized and recognized	$ 60,000
	.21
Tax cost	$ 12,600
After-tax cash ($110,000 − $12,600)	$ 97,400

The annual income from a $97,400 investment at a 6.7 percent rate of return is only $6,526. Therefore, Firm T should not undertake the sale/reinvestment because of the front-end tax cost.

On the other hand, if the conversion of the investment to an equity interest in the new venture can be accomplished with no front-end tax cost, the new investment is superior to the old, and Firm T should undertake the sale/reinvestment.

Unfortunately for taxpayers in the same strategic position as Firm T, tax neutrality for asset exchanges is the exception rather than the rule. An asset exchange is taxable unless it meets the requirements of one of the nontaxable exchange provisions scattered throughout the Internal Revenue Code. These requirements vary substantially across provisions. Some nontaxable exchange provisions are mandatory, while others are elective on the part of the taxpayer. Some apply only to realized gains, yet others apply to both realized gains and losses. Certain provisions require a direct exchange of noncash assets, while others allow the taxpayer to be in a temporary cash position. Nevertheless, all the nontaxable exchanges share several characteristics. We begin the chapter by analyzing these common characteristics in the context of a generic exchange. By doing so, we can focus on the structure of nontaxable exchanges before considering the details of any particular exchange.

A GENERIC NONTAXABLE EXCHANGE

Exchanges of Qualifying Property

Every nontaxable exchange transforms one property interest into another. The type of property that can be swapped tax free depends on the unique qualification requirements of the relevant IRC section. But only the disposition and receipt of **qualifying property** can be a nontaxable exchange. Consider the diagram of a nontaxable exchange between Firm A and Firm B in Exhibit 9.1. Given that the exchange involves only qualifying property, it is nontaxable to both firms. What else do we know about this exchange? Assuming that Firms A and B are unrelated parties dealing at arm's length, they must have agreed that the properties are of equal value.

To quantify the respective tax consequences of the exchange to each firm, we must know the FMV of the property received and the tax basis in the property surrendered. This information

EXHIBIT 9.1

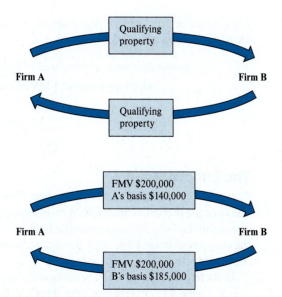

EXHIBIT 9.2

is presented in Exhibit 9.2. Because Firm A disposed of property with a $140,000 basis in return for property worth $200,000, it realized a $60,000 gain. Because the exchange involved qualifying property, Firm A does not recognize any gain in the current year. Similarly, Firm B's disposition of qualifying property with a $185,000 basis in return for qualifying property worth $200,000 resulted in a $15,000 realized but unrecognized gain.

The Substituted Basis Rule

LO 9-2
Compute the substituted basis of property received in a nontaxable exchange.

The nontaxable exchange label is a misnomer. The tax law does not intend that gains and losses realized on nontaxable exchanges should escape recognition permanently. Instead, the exchange provisions are designed so that unrecognized gains and losses are merely deferred until some future year in which the qualifying property is disposed of in a taxable transaction. This deferral is accomplished through the rule for calculating the tax basis of qualifying property acquired in the exchange: The basis of this property equals the basis of the qualifying property surrendered. In the Firm A/Firm B exchange, each firm expended $200,000 (FMV of the property surrendered) to acquire their new properties. Because the exchange was nontaxable, the firms did not take a cost basis. Instead, Firm A's basis in its new property is $140,000, while Firm B's basis in its new property is $185,000.

This **substituted basis** rule causes the unrecognized gain or loss on a nontaxable exchange to be embedded in the basis of the qualifying property acquired. The gain or loss remains dormant as long as the taxpayer holds the property.[1] If and when the taxpayer makes a taxable disposition of the property, the deferral ends, and the unrecognized gain or loss on the nontaxable exchange is finally recognized.

To demonstrate this important concept, return to the facts in the Firm A/Firm B exchange. If Firm A eventually sells its new property for $200,000 cash, it will recognize a $60,000 gain, even though the property has not appreciated in value since Firm A acquired it. Similarly, if Firm B sells its new property for $200,000, it will recognize the $15,000 gain deferred on the exchange. This observation suggests an alternate method for computing the basis of qualifying property acquired in a nontaxable exchange: Basis equals the property's

---

[1] If the qualifying property is depreciable or amortizable, the embedded gain or loss is recognized over the recovery period for the substituted basis.

FMV *minus* deferred gain or *plus* deferred loss on the exchange. The substituted basis rule for nontaxable exchanges is summarized as follows:

$$\text{Basis of property surrendered} = \underline{\text{Basis of qualifying property acquired}}$$

Alternate method: FMV of qualifying property acquired

$$
\begin{array}{r}
- \text{ Deferred gain or} \\
+ \text{ Deferred loss} \\
\hline
\text{Basis of qualifying property acquired}
\end{array}
$$

The Effect of Boot

The facts of our generic exchange between Firm A and Firm B are contrived because the FMVs of the properties are equal. A more realistic scenario is that the FMVs of the properties qualifying for nontaxable exchange treatment are unequal. In this case, the party owning the property of lesser value must transfer additional value in the form of cash or nonqualifying property to make the exchange work.

LO 9-3
Compute gain recognized when boot is received in a nontaxable exchange.

In tax terminology, any cash or nonqualifying property included in a nontaxable exchange is called **boot**. The presence of boot does not disqualify the entire exchange. Instead, the party receiving the boot must recognize a portion of realized gain equal to the FMV of the boot. Refer to Exhibit 9.3 in which the FMV of the property surrendered by Firm B was only $192,000. For Firm A to agree to the exchange, Firm B had to pay $8,000 cash so that Firm A received $200,000 total value in exchange for its asset worth $200,000. In this case, Firm A received $8,000 boot and must recognize $8,000 of its $60,000 realized gain.

Because Firm A must recognize an $8,000 gain, it can increase its basis in its new assets by this amount. In other words, Firm A's investment in the new assets has increased to $148,000 ($140,000 basis in the surrendered property plus $8,000 gain recognized). Firm A must allocate this $148,000 basis between the two assets acquired: $8,000 cash and the qualifying property. Cash always takes a basis equal to monetary value. Consequently, only $140,000 of basis is allocated to the qualifying property. This $140,000 basis can also be derived by subtracting Firm A's $52,000 deferred gain from the $192,000 FMV of the qualifying property. The modification to the substituted basis rule when boot is *received* in a nontaxable exchange is summarized as follows:

$$
\begin{array}{r}
\text{Basis of qualifying property surrendered} \\
+ \text{ Gain recognized} \\
- \text{ FMV of boot received} \\
\hline
\text{Basis of qualifying property acquired}
\end{array}
$$

The fact that Firm B *paid* boot in the exchange did not cause it to recognize gain. Firm B surrendered property with an aggregate basis of $193,000 ($8,000 cash + $185,000 basis of surrendered property) to acquire property worth $200,000. As a result, Firm B realized a $7,000 gain, none of which is recognized. Firm B's basis in the new property is $193,000,

EXHIBIT 9.3

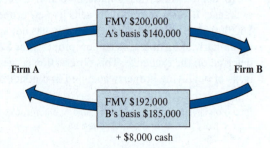

FMV $200,000
A's basis $140,000

Firm A   Firm B

FMV $192,000
B's basis $185,000

+ $8,000 cash

the aggregate basis of the cash and property surrendered. This $193,000 basis equals the $200,000 FMV of the new property less $7,000 deferred gain. The substituted basis rule when boot is *paid* in a nontaxable exchange is summarized as follows:

$$\frac{\text{Basis of qualifying property surrendered}}{\text{Basis of qualifying property acquired}} \begin{array}{l} \\ + \text{ FMV of boot paid} \\ \hline \end{array}$$

Tax Talk

A company that exchanged gold mines for coal mines subject to long-term supply contracts treated the exchange as nontaxable. The IRS argued that the contracts were boot, so the company must recognize gain equal to the contracts' FMV. The Tax Court ruled in favor of the company because the contracts and the coal mines were "inseparable" and represented a single qualifying property.

Two more facts concerning boot should be mentioned. First, the receipt of boot can never trigger recognition of more gain than the recipient realized on the exchange. For example, if Firm A received $70,000 cash and qualifying property worth $130,000, the receipt of $70,000 boot would trigger recognition of the entire $60,000 gain realized. (After all, Firm A would recognize only $60,000 gain if it sold the property for $200,000 cash!) In this case, Firm A's basis in the qualifying property would be $130,000 ($140,000 basis of qualifying property surrendered + $60,000 gain recognized − $70,000 boot received).

Second, the receipt of boot does not trigger loss recognition. Consider the new set of facts in Exhibit 9.4 in which Firm A surrendered qualifying property with a $230,000 basis in exchange for $8,000 cash and qualifying property worth $192,000. As a result, it realized a $30,000 loss, none of which is recognized. Firm A's $230,000 basis in the surrendered property must be allocated between the $8,000 cash received and the new property. Because the cash absorbed $8,000 of the substituted basis, Firm A's basis in the qualifying property is $222,000 ($230,000 basis of qualifying property surrendered − $8,000 boot received). This basis can also be derived by *adding* Firm A's $30,000 deferred loss to the $192,000 FMV of the property.

EXHIBIT 9.4

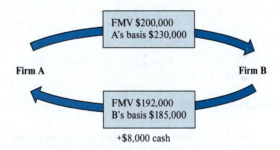

Book/Tax Difference from Nontaxable Exchange

LO 9-4
Explain book/tax differences related to nontaxable exchanges.

For financial reporting purposes, gains and losses realized on property exchanges often are included in book income.[2] In such cases, nontaxable exchanges cause a difference between book income and taxable income. The book basis of the property received in the exchange (the property's FMV) is different from the property's tax basis. Consequently, the book/tax difference caused by the exchange is temporary and will reverse as the newly acquired property is depreciated or when it is disposed of in a taxable transaction.

Book/Tax Difference from Nontaxable Exchange

Hogan, Inc. exchanged old property ($138,200 book and tax basis) for new property ($210,000 FMV). Hogan's $71,800 realized gain was included in book income but was not recognized as taxable income because the old and new properties qualified for nontaxable exchange treatment. Hogan's depreciable book basis in the new property is $210,000, and its depreciable tax basis is only $138,200. Therefore, the $71,800 excess of book income over taxable income resulting from the exchange will reverse as future excesses of book depreciation over MACRS depreciation.

[2] See ASC 845, *Nonmonetary Transactions.*

Summary

The Internal Revenue Code contains an assortment of nontaxable exchange provisions with different definitional and operational rules. Nonetheless, these provisions share the following generic characteristics:

- The exchange must involve qualifying property, as defined in the provision.
- The gain or loss realized on the exchange is deferred.
- The basis of the qualifying property received equals the basis of the qualifying property surrendered (substituted basis rule).
- The receipt of boot triggers gain recognition to the extent of the boot's FMV.

The remainder of the chapter focuses on four nontaxable exchanges with particular relevance in the business world: like-kind exchanges, involuntary conversions, formations of business entities, and wash sales. Before proceeding, refer to the diagram on page 8–22 that links gain or loss realization and gain or loss recognition. Let's expand the diagram to include the possibility of gain or loss deferral on a nontaxable exchange:

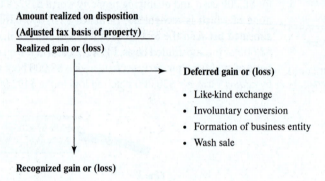

LIKE-KIND EXCHANGES

No gain or loss is recognized on the exchange of business or investment real property for property of a like-kind.[3] Nonrecognition is mandatory for qualifying exchanges. This rule allows firms to convert one asset to another asset with the same function or purpose at no tax cost. The rule's scope, however, is limited: For exchanges after 2017, it does not apply to exchanges of personalty, intangibles, inventory property, equity or creditor interests (stocks, bonds, notes, etc.), or partnership interests.[4]

Like-Kind Realty

LO 9-5
Identify properties that qualify for like-kind exchange treatment.

Virtually all types of business and investment real estate are considered **like-kind property**. As a result, any swap of realty for realty can be structured as a nontaxable exchange, other than real property held primarily for sale.[5]

---

[3] §1031.

[4] Prior to the Tax Cuts and Jobs Act of 2017, business personalty and intangibles could be exchanged tax free under Section 1031. Under transition rules, such exchanges are still nontaxable if the taxpayer either disposed of the relinquished property or acquired the replacement property on or before December 31, 2017.

[5] Reg. §1.1031(a)-1(b).

Like-Kind Realty

An Arizona firm that owned undeveloped investment land in Tucson negotiated with a New York firm that owned an apartment in Manhattan to trade their properties. This exchange is diagrammed in Exhibit 9.5. The investment land has an $800,000 FMV, while the apartment has a $925,000 FMV. As a result, the Arizona firm paid $125,000 cash to the New York firm to equalize the values exchanged. The tax consequences of this exchange are summarized as follows:

	Arizona Firm	New York Firm
Amount realized:		
FMV of realty acquired	$925,000	$800,000
Boot received	–0–	125,000
	$925,000	$925,000
Basis of property surrendered:		
Realty	(500,000)	(485,000)
Boot paid	(125,000)	–0–
Gain realized	$300,000	$440,000
Gain recognized*	–0–	$125,000
Gain deferred	$300,000	315,000
	$300,000	$440,000

*Lesser of FMV of boot received or gain realized.

The final step in the analysis of this like-kind exchange is to determine each party's basis in its newly acquired realty.

	Arizona Firm	New York Firm
Basis of realty surrendered	$500,000	$485,000
Boot paid	125,000	–0–
Gain recognized	–0–	125,000
Boot received	–0–	(125,000)
Basis of realty acquired	$625,000	$485,000

Note that the Arizona firm's basis in its Manhattan property equals the $925,000 FMV less the $300,000 gain deferred in the exchange. The New York firm's basis in its Tucson property equals the $800,000 FMV less the $315,000 gain deferred in the exchange.

EXHIBIT 9.5

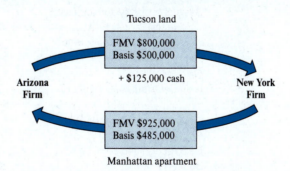

Tax Talk
The professional association for qualified intermediaries is the Federation of Exchange Accommodators (FEA), which grants the professional designation Certified Exchange Specialist (CES).

This example suggests a practical question. How did the Arizona firm and the New York firm find each other? Most like-kind exchanges of realty are arranged by *qualified intermediaries:* real estate professionals who specialize in *three-party* exchanges. In a prototype three-party exchange, a taxpayer that wants to sell property without recognizing gain and a prospective buyer use a qualified intermediary to locate replacement property that is suitable to the seller. The seller relinquishes its property to the intermediary who transfers it to the buyer, the buyer transfers cash to the intermediary, and the intermediary uses the cash to purchase the replacement property for the seller. The tax law governing like-kind exchanges is flexible enough so that the seller is treated as exchanging the relinquished property directly for the replacement property.[6]

Three-Party Exchange

Talmadge Partnership wants to dispose of rental property with a $900,000 FMV, and Vernon, Inc. is willing to buy the property for cash. However, Talmadge's tax basis in the property is only $100,000, and it does not want to recognize gain on the disposition. Talmadge and Vernon work through a qualified intermediary to facilitate a three-party exchange. Talmadge relinquishes its property to the intermediary who transfers it to Vernon for $900,000 cash. The intermediary then uses the cash to purchase replacement property on Talmadge's behalf. For tax purposes, Talmadge has made a nontaxable exchange of the relinquished property for the replacement property.

Exchanges of Mortgaged Properties

LO 9-6
Describe the effect of the relief and assumption of debt in a like-kind exchange.

Many real property interests involved in like-kind exchanges are subject to mortgages that are transferred along with the property and become the legal liability of the new owner. As we learned in Chapter 8, a taxpayer who is relieved of debt on a property disposition must treat the relief as an amount realized from the disposition. In the like-kind exchange context, a party that surrenders mortgaged property receives boot equal to the debt relief. In other words, the relief of debt is treated exactly like cash received in the exchange, while the assumption of debt is treated as cash paid.

Exchange of Mortgaged Property

ABC Inc. and XYZ Partnership exchanged a Chicago shopping mall and a commercial office building located in St. Louis. This exchange is diagrammed in Exhibit 9.6. The net value of the shopping mall is $500,000 ($730,000 FMV – $230,000 mortgage), and the FMV of the office building is $500,000. The tax consequences of this exchange are summarized as follows:

	ABC Inc.	XYZ Partnership
Amount realized:		
FMV of realty acquired	$500,000	$730,000
Boot received (debt relief)	230,000	–0–
	$730,000	$730,000
Basis of property surrendered:		
Realty	(295,000)	(413,000)
Boot paid (debt assumed)	–0–	(230,000)
Gain realized	$435,000	$ 87,000
Gain recognized*	$230,000	–0–
Gain deferred	205,000	$ 87,000
	$435,000	$ 87,000
Basis of realty surrendered	$295,000	$413,000
Boot paid	–0–	230,000
Gain recognized	230,000	–0–
Boot received	(230,000)	–0–
Basis of realty acquired	$295,000	$643,000

*Lesser of FMV of boot received or gain realized.

[6] Regs. §1.1031(b)-2 and §1.1031(k)-1(g)(4). The various steps in a three-party exchange must be completed within a 180-day time period.

EXHIBIT 9.6

Tax Talk

Normally, a three-party, like-kind exchange requires that replacement property be acquired within 180 days of disposition of the transferred property. However, a 120-day extension may be available if the taxpayer is adversely affected by a federally declared disaster.

In a like-kind exchange in which both properties are subject to a mortgage so that both parties are relieved of debt, only the *net* amount of debt is treated as boot given and boot received.[7]

Net Debt Relief as Boot	Firm O and Firm R entered into a like-kind exchange of realty. The property surrendered by Firm O was subject to a $120,000 mortgage, and the property surrendered by Firm R was subject to a $100,000 mortgage. Firm O was relieved of a $20,000 net amount of debt and therefore received $20,000 boot in the exchange. Firm R assumed a $20,000 net amount of debt and therefore paid $20,000 boot in the exchange. Consequently, Firm O must recognize $20,000 of realized gain, while Firm R has a totally nontaxable exchange.

INVOLUNTARY CONVERSIONS

LO 9-7
Compute gain recognized and the basis of replacement property in an involuntary conversion.

Firms generally control the circumstances in which they dispose of property. Occasionally, a disposition is involuntary; property may be stolen or destroyed by a natural disaster such as a flood or a fire. If the property is not insured or if the insurance proceeds are less than the property's adjusted basis, the owner can deduct the unrecovered basis as an ordinary casualty loss. However, if the property is insured and the insurance proceeds are more than the adjusted basis, the disposition actually results in a realized gain. Another example of an **involuntary conversion** is a condemnation of private property by a government agency that takes the property for public use. If a government has the right of eminent domain, it can compel an owner to sell property to the agency for its FMV. If the condemnation proceeds exceed the basis of the condemned property, the owner realizes a gain.

A taxpayer who realizes a gain on the involuntary conversion of property can elect to defer the gain if two conditions are met.[8] First, the taxpayer must reinvest the amount realized on the conversion (the insurance or condemnation proceeds) in **property similar or related in service or use**. This condition requires taxpayers to replace their original property to avoid paying tax on the realized gain.[9] Both the IRS and the courts have been strict in their interpretation of the concept of similar or related property. For instance, the IRS ruled that a taxpayer who owned a land-based seafood processing plant that was destroyed by fire and who used the insurance proceeds to purchase a floating seafood processing vessel was ineligible for nonrecognition treatment because the properties were not similar in function.[10]

---

[7] Reg. §1.1031(b)-1(c).

[8] §1033.

[9] If real property held for business or as an investment is condemned by a government agency, the owner may replace it with like-kind property (any realty held for business or as an investment) rather than realty similar or related in service or use to the property so condemned. §1033(g).

[10] Rev. Rul. 77-192, 1977-1 C.B. 249.

Tax Talk

A beekeeper whose beehives were destroyed when pesticides were sprayed on an adjacent property suffered an involuntary conversion. Gain from the receipt of compensation for his loss was eligible for deferral.

The second condition is that replacement of the involuntarily converted property must occur within the two taxable years following the year in which the conversion took place. If the property is lost due to condemnation, the replacement must occur within three taxable years following the year in which the condemnation took place. Thus, taxpayers making the deferral election usually have ample time to locate and acquire replacement property.

If the cost of replacement property equals or exceeds the amount realized on an involuntary conversion, none of the taxpayer's realized gain is recognized. If the taxpayer does not reinvest the entire amount realized in replacement property (i.e., the taxpayer uses some of the insurance or condemnation proceeds for other purposes), the amount not reinvested is treated as boot, and the taxpayer must recognize gain accordingly. In either case, the basis of the replacement property is its cost less unrecognized gain. As a result, unrecognized gain is deferred until the taxpayer disposes of the replacement property in a future taxable transaction.

Gain Recognized on Involuntary Conversion

Company UL owned equipment that was completely destroyed in a recent California earthquake. The equipment's adjusted basis was $80,000. The company collected $100,000 of insurance proceeds, thereby realizing a $20,000 gain on the involuntary conversion. Company UL purchased identical equipment in the year after the disaster. The following table shows the tax consequences under four different assumptions about the cost of the replacement property:

Insurance Proceeds	Cost of Replacement Property	Unreinvested Proceeds	Gain Recognized	Gain Deferred	Basis of Replacement Property*
$100,000	$135,000	–0–	–0–	$20,000	$115,000
100,000	100,000	–0–	–0–	20,000	80,000
100,000	92,000	$ 8,000	$ 8,000	12,000	80,000
100,000	77,000	23,000	20,000	–0–	77,000

*Costless gain deferred.

The involuntary conversion rule provides relief to taxpayers deprived of property through circumstances beyond their control and who want nothing more than to return to the status quo by replacing that property. The rule applies to the involuntary conversion of any type of asset.[11] Moreover, the rule is elective; taxpayers who would benefit by recognizing the entire gain realized on an involuntary conversion may do so.

FORMATIONS OF BUSINESS ENTITIES

LO 9-8

Explain the tax consequences of the exchange of property for equity in a corporation or partnership.

In the early days of the federal income tax, Congress decided that the tax law should be neutral with respect to the formation of business entities. If entrepreneurs wanted to organize a new business as a corporation or partnership for legal or financial reasons, they should not be discouraged from doing so because of a front-end tax cost. Congress achieved this neutrality with a pair of nontaxable exchange provisions that the business community has relied on for decades. These provisions allow organizers to transfer assets to a corporation or a partnership in exchange for an equity interest without the recognition of gain. In this section of the chapter, we will examine the basic operation of these two extremely useful nontaxable exchanges.

---

[11] The involuntary conversion rules apply to business and investment assets, as well as assets owned by individuals and used for personal enjoyment and consumption.

Corporate Formations

No gain or loss is recognized when property is transferred to a corporation solely in exchange for that corporation's stock if the transferors of property are in control of the corporation immediately after the exchange.[12] In this context, the term *property* is defined broadly to include cash, tangible, and intangible assets. Personal services are not property; individuals who perform services in exchange for corporate stock must recognize the FMV of the stock as compensation income. To satisfy the control requirement for this nontaxable exchange, the transferors of property *in the aggregate* must own at least 80 percent of the corporation's outstanding stock immediately after the exchange.[13]

Corporate Formation	Mr. Jiang and Ms. Kirt each owned a business. The two individuals combined forces by transferring their respective operating assets to newly incorporated J&K Inc. Based on recent appraisals, Mr. Jiang's assets have a $375,000 FMV, and Ms. Kirt's assets have a $250,000 FMV. Therefore, the corporation's beginning balance sheet reflected operating assets with a $625,000 total FMV. The articles of incorporation authorize J&K to issue 100 shares of voting common stock. These shares were issued in proportion to the FMV of the contributed assets: 60 shares to Mr. Jiang and 40 shares to Ms. Kirt. This corporate formation is diagrammed in Exhibit 9.7.

EXHIBIT 9.7

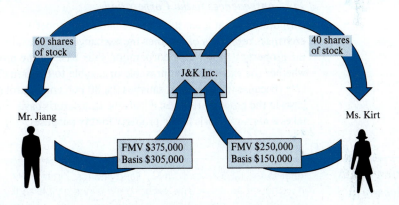

Tax Consequences of Formation	Mr. Jiang's adjusted basis in the assets transferred to J&K was $305,000. Ms. Kirt's adjusted basis in the assets transferred to J&K was $150,000. Consequently, the two transferors realized the following gains on the exchange of property for stock:

	Mr. Jiang	Ms. Kirt
Amount realized (FMV of stock)	$375,000	$250,000
Basis of property transferred	(305,000)	(150,000)
Gain realized	$ 70,000	$100,000

(*continued*)

---

[12] §351.

[13] More precisely, the transferors must own stock possessing at least 80 percent of the voting power represented by all outstanding voting shares and at least 80 percent of the total number of shares of all nonvoting classes of stock. §368(c) and Rev. Rul. 59-259, 1959-2 C.B. 115.

Because Mr. Jiang and Ms. Kirt *in the aggregate* own 100 percent of J&K's stock immediately after the exchange, they are in control of J&K, and neither recognizes any gain. Each shareholder takes a substituted basis in the shares of stock received ($305,000 stock basis for Mr. Jiang and $150,000 stock basis for Ms. Kirt).[14] Thus, their unrecognized gains on the corporate formation are deferred until they dispose of the stock in a taxable transaction.

The nontaxable exchange provision governing corporate formations also applies to transfers of property to an existing corporation. However, if the transferor fails to satisfy the 80 percent control requirement, the exchange of property for stock is taxable.

Taxable Exchange of Property for Stock	Two years after J&K is formed, a third individual, Mr. Larkin, contributes real property with a $285,000 FMV and a $240,000 adjusted basis in exchange for 50 shares of newly issued stock. Immediately after the exchange, Mr. Larkin (the only transferor in the transaction) owns only 33 percent of J&K's stock. Because he does not satisfy the control requirement, Mr. Larkin must recognize the $45,000 gain realized on the exchange. Because the exchange is taxable, Mr. Larkin takes a $285,000 cost basis in his J&K shares.

Tax Consequences to the Corporation

Corporations that issue stock in exchange for property never recognize gain or loss on the exchange, regardless of whether the exchange is nontaxable or taxable to the transferor of the property.[15] However, a corporation's tax basis in the property received does depend on whether the exchange is nontaxable or taxable to the transferor. If the exchange is nontaxable (because the transferor satisfies the 80 percent control requirement), the corporation's basis in the property received equals the transferor's basis.[16] In other words, the corporation takes a **carryover basis** in the property for tax purposes.

Carryover Basis of Property	Refer to Exhibit 9.7, in which Mr. Jiang and Ms. Kirt transferred operating assets to J&K Inc. in exchange for stock. This exchange was nontaxable to the two transferors because they satisfied the control requirement immediately after the exchange. The exchange also was a nontaxable event to J&K. The corporation's carryover tax basis in the assets received from Mr. Jiang is $305,000, and its carryover tax basis in the assets received from Ms. Kirt is $150,000.
	For financial reporting purposes, J&K, Inc. recorded the assets received in the exchange at FMV. Consequently, the corporation has a $375,000 book basis in the assets received from Mr. Jiang and a $250,000 book basis in the assets received from Ms. Kirt. The difference in J&K's book and tax basis will be eliminated over time as the corporation depreciates or amortizes the assets or when it disposes of the assets.

If a corporation issues stock in exchange for property and the exchange is taxable to the transferor (because the transferor does not satisfy the 80 percent control requirement), the corporation takes a cost basis in the property.[17]

---

[14] §358(a)(1).

[15] §1032.

[16] §362(a).

[17] Reg. §1.1032-1(d).

Cost Basis of Property	Again, refer to the example in which Mr. Larkin transfers real property to J&K Inc. in exchange for stock. The exchange is taxable to Mr. Larkin because he does not satisfy the control requirement immediately after the exchange. However, J&K does not recognize any gain on the issuance of its stock in exchange for Mr. Larkin's real property. The corporation's tax basis in the real property is its $285,000 cost (FMV of the shares issued to Mr. Larkin), which equals the book basis of the property for financial reporting purposes.

In rare circumstances, a corporation might receive a contribution to its capital without issuing stock. For example, occasionally a governmental entity might contribute real property to a corporation as enticement for the corporation to locate within its jurisdiction. Governments view this contribution as an investment in future economic stimulus. Prior to 2018, such contributions were nontaxable to the corporation, which then had a zero tax basis in the contributed property. The Tax Cuts and Jobs Act includes such contributions in the corporation's taxable income if received after 2017.

Partnership Formations

The tax law treats partnership formation in a similar manner to corporate formations. Specifically, neither the partners nor the partnership recognizes gain or loss when property is exchanged for an equity interest in the partnership.[18] If Mr. Jiang and Ms. Kirt in our earlier example had decided to become partners, they could have transferred their appreciated assets to J&K Partnership in exchange for a 60 percent and 40 percent interest without recognizing gain. Mr. Jiang's basis in his partnership interest would be a $305,000 substituted basis, and Ms. Kirt's basis in her partnership interest would be a $150,000 substituted basis.[19] The partnership would take a carryover basis in their contributed assets of $305,000 and $150,000, respectively.[20]

While this nontaxable exchange provision is clearly a first cousin to the corporate provision, it lacks any control requirement and is more flexible. For example, if our third individual, Mr. Larkin, wants to become a partner in some future year, he can do so without recognizing gain. If he contributes appreciated real property ($285,000 FMV and $240,000 adjusted basis) for a one-third equity interest in J&K Partnership, the transaction qualifies as a nontaxable exchange, and his $45,000 realized gain escapes current taxation. Of course, Mr. Larkin's substituted basis in his new interest and the partnership's carryover basis in its new property would be only $240,000.

WASH SALES

LO 9-9
Describe the tax consequences of a wash sale.

The **wash sale** rule is a nontypical, nontaxable exchange provision because it defers only the recognition of *losses* realized on certain sales of marketable securities.[21] Realized gains are not deferred. A wash sale occurs when an investor sells securities at a loss and reacquires substantially the same securities within 30 days before or 30 days after the sale. This rule prohibits investors from selling securities to generate a tax loss, while simultaneously buying the stock back to keep their investment portfolio intact. If the wash sale rule applies, the cost of the reacquired securities is increased by the unrecognized loss realized on the sale.

---

[18] §721.
[19] §722.
[20] §723.
[21] §1091.

Wash Sale

BNJ Company owns 10,000 shares of Acme stock with an $85,000 basis. The stock is trading at $6 per share so that BNJ's holding is worth only $60,000. BNJ believes that the stock is an excellent long-term investment and that the depression in the market price is temporary. Nonetheless, it sells the stock on July 13 to trigger a $25,000 tax loss. If BNJ purchases 10,000 shares of Acme stock during the period beginning on June 13 and ending on August 12, it cannot recognize the $25,000 loss. If BNJ purchases Acme stock during this time and pays $61,000 for the replacement shares, its basis in these shares is $86,000 ($61,000 cost + $25,000 unrecognized loss).

Tax Talk

For purposes of the wash sale rules, the term stock or securities includes options to acquire or sell stock or securities.

What if BNJ's 10,000 shares of Acme stock were worth $10 per share when sold? In that case, BNJ would realize and recognize a gain on sale of the Acme shares of $15,000 ($10 × 10,000 – $85,000). Replacement of the shares does not defer the gain, and Acme's tax basis in the replacement shares is their cost of $61,000.

Taxpayers who sell stock at a loss can easily avoid the wash sale rule by waiting more than 30 days to reestablish their investment position. The risk, of course, is that in the time between sale and repurchase, the market value of the securities rebounds, and the taxpayer must pay a higher price for the same securities. This additional cost could easily exceed the tax benefit of the recognized loss.

Conclusion

Business managers may defer the recognition of gain realized on the conversion of property from one form to another by structuring the conversion as a nontaxable exchange. The deferral reduces the tax cost of the conversion and increases the value of the transaction. While the advantages offered by the various nontaxable exchange provisions are considerable, these transactions require careful planning and a respect for the technical nuances differentiating one from the other.

This is the final chapter in Part Three, in which we focused on the measurement of taxable income from business operations. You've learned how firms account for their routine activities and how that accounting can differ under generally accepted accounting principles (GAAP) and the tax law. You've been introduced to the tax consequences of asset acquisitions and dispositions and determined how property transactions affect taxable income. In Part Four of the text, we turn to the next issue: how the tax on that income is calculated and paid to the federal government.

Sources of Book/Tax Differences

Permanent	Temporary
None	• Like-kind exchange
	• Involuntary conversion
	• Nontaxable exchange of property for equity
	• Wash sale of securities

Key Terms

Questions and Problems for Discussion

LO 9-1, 9-2   1. Four years ago, Company PJ acquired 1,000 acres of undeveloped land. On the date of the exchange, the land's FMV was $700,000. During the past four years, the land appreciated in value by $600,000; a recent appraisal indicated that it is worth $1.3 million today. However, if Company PJ sells the land for $1.3 million, the taxable gain will be $825,000. Can you explain this result?

LO 9-1   2. In a nontaxable exchange between unrelated parties, are the amounts realized by the parties always equal?

LO 9-1   3. In a nontaxable exchange, do the tax consequences to one party in any way depend on the tax consequences to the other party?

LO 9-2   4. Is the substituted basis of the qualifying property received in a nontaxable exchange more or less than the cost of that property?

LO 9-5, 9-8   5. Determine if each of the following transactions qualifies as a nontaxable exchange:

    a. Firm A exchanges a 2 percent interest in MG Partnership for a 10 percent interest in KLS Partnership.

    b. Mr. Basu exchanges investment land for common stock in RV, Inc. Immediately after the exchange, Mr. Basu owns 42 percent of RV's outstanding stock.

    c. Corporation C exchanges business equipment for a 25 percent interest in a residential apartment complex.

    d. Company D exchanges 15,000 units of inventory for a new computer system.

LO 9-5   6. Firm Q, a real estate broker, exchanged 16 acres of land for a commercial warehouse owned by Company M. Company M, a light industrial business, plans to hold the land as a long-term investment. Is this exchange nontaxable to Firm Q and Company M?

LO 9-5   7. Company W exchanged the following assets for Blackacre, investment land worth $2 million.

	Company W's Basis	FMV
Real property used in Company W's business	$800,000	$1,750,000
Marketable securities	30,000	250,000

Does Company W recognize any gain on this exchange?

LO 9-7   8. Under what conditions can the destruction of property by casualty or theft result in an economic loss but a realized gain?

LO 9-8   9. In what way is the nontaxable exchange rule for partnership formations more flexible than the nontaxable exchange rule for corporate formations?

LO 9-2   10. Explain the difference between a substituted basis in an asset and a carryover basis in an asset.

LO 9-4   11. If a corporation engages in a nontaxable exchange of assets, could the transaction result in a book/tax difference? Is this difference a permanent or a temporary difference?

LO 9-8   12. When a taxpayer transfers appreciated property to a corporation in exchange for newly issued stock and the exchange is nontaxable, the gain deferred on the exchange actually doubles. Can you explain this?

LO 9-9   13. Why doesn't Congress extend the wash sale rule to apply to realized gains?

LO 9-9   14. This year, Firm B recognized a $100,000 capital gain on the sale of investment land. Toward the end of the year, the firm plans to sell stock from its investment portfolio to generate a $100,000 capital loss. It has two blocks of stock that are candidates for sale (basis exceeds FMV by $100,000). However, Firm B plans to reacquire whichever block it sells on the 31st day after the sale. How should it decide which block of stock to sell and reacquire?

LO 9-1, 9-2 15. Why is the label "nontaxable exchange" a misnomer?

All applicable Application Problems are available with *Connect*.

Application Problems

LO 9-1, 9-2 1. Company Z exchanged an asset (FMV $16,000) for a new asset (FMV $16,000). Company Z's tax basis in the old asset was $9,300.

a. Compute Company Z's realized gain, recognized gain, and tax basis in the new asset assuming the exchange was a taxable transaction.

b. Compute Company Z's realized gain, recognized gain, and tax basis in the new asset, assuming the exchange was a nontaxable transaction.

c. Six months after the exchange, Company Z sold the new asset for $16,850 cash. How much gain does Company Z recognize if the exchange was taxable? How much gain if the exchange was nontaxable?

LO 9-1, 9-2 2. Business K exchanged an old asset (FMV $95,000) for a new asset (FMV $95,000). Business K's tax basis in the old asset was $107,000.

a. Compute Business K's realized loss, recognized loss, and tax basis in the new asset assuming the exchange was a taxable transaction.

b. Compute Business K's realized loss, recognized loss, and tax basis in the new asset, assuming the exchange was a nontaxable transaction.

c. Six months after the exchange, Business K sold the new asset for $100,000 cash. How much gain or loss does Business K recognize if the exchange was taxable? How much gain or loss if the exchange was nontaxable?

LO 9-2, 9-3 3. Rufus, Inc. and Hardy Company are negotiating a nontaxable exchange of business properties. Rufus's property has a $50,000 tax basis and a $77,500 FMV. Hardy's property has a $60,000 tax basis and a $90,000 FMV.

a. Which party to the exchange must pay boot to make the exchange work? How much boot must be paid?

b. Assuming the boot payment is made, how much gain or loss will Rufus realize and recognize on the exchange, and what tax basis will Rufus take in the property acquired?

c. Assuming the boot payment is made, how much gain or loss will Hardy realize and recognize on the exchange, and what tax basis will Hardy take in the property acquired?

LO 9-1, 9-2, 9-3 4. Firm A exchanged an old asset with a $20,000 tax basis for a new asset with a $32,000 FMV. Under each of the following assumptions, apply the generic rules to compute A's realized gain, recognized gain, and tax basis in the new asset.

a. Old asset and new asset are not qualified property for nontaxable exchange purposes.

b. Old asset and new asset are qualified property for nontaxable exchange purposes.

c. Old asset and new asset are not qualified property for nontaxable exchange purposes. To equalize the values exchanged, Firm A paid $1,700 cash to the other party.

d. Old asset and new asset are qualified property for nontaxable exchange purposes. To equalize the values exchanged, Firm A paid $1,700 cash to the other party.

e. Old asset and new asset are not qualified property for nontaxable exchange purposes. To equalize the values exchanged, Firm A received $4,500 cash from the other party.

f. Old asset and new asset are qualified property for nontaxable exchange purposes. To equalize the values exchanged, Firm A received $4,500 cash from the other party.

LO 9-1, 9-2, 9-3   5. Firm Q exchanged old property with an $80,000 tax basis for new property with a $65,000 FMV. Under each of the following assumptions, apply the generic rules to compute Q's realized loss, recognized loss, and tax basis in the new property.

a. Old property and new property are not qualified property for nontaxable exchange purposes.

b. Old property and new property are qualified property for nontaxable exchange purposes.

c. Old property and new property are not qualified property for nontaxable exchange purposes. To equalize the values exchanged, Firm Q paid $2,000 cash to the other party.

d. Old property and new property are qualified property for nontaxable exchange purposes. To equalize the values exchanged, Firm Q paid $2,000 cash to the other party.

e. Old property and new property are not qualified property for nontaxable exchange purposes. To equalize the values exchanged, Firm Q received $8,000 cash from the other party.

f. Old property and new property are qualified property for nontaxable exchange purposes. To equalize the values exchanged, Firm Q received $8,000 cash from the other party.

LO 9-2, 9-3   6. Firm M exchanged an old asset with a $9,100 tax basis and a $21,000 FMV for a new asset worth $18,500 and $2,500 cash.

a. If the exchange is nontaxable, compute Firm M's realized and recognized gain and tax basis in the new asset.

b. How would your answers change if the new asset were worth only $7,000, and Firm M received $14,000 cash in the exchange?

LO 9-2, 9-4   7. This year, Neil, Inc. exchanged a business asset for an investment asset. Both assets had a $932,000 appraised FMV. Neil's book basis in the business asset was $604,600, and its tax basis was $573,000.

a. Compute Neil's book gain and tax gain assuming the exchange was a taxable transaction.

b. Determine Neil's book and tax basis of the investment asset acquired in the taxable exchange.

c. Compute Neil's book gain and tax gain assuming the exchange was a nontaxable transaction.

d. Determine Neil's book and tax basis of the investment asset acquired in the nontaxable exchange.

LO 9-2, 9-4   8. Refer to the facts in the preceding problem. Three years after the exchange, Neil sold the investment asset for $1 million cash.

a. Compute Neil's book gain and tax gain on sale assuming Neil acquired the investment asset in a taxable exchange.

b. Compute Neil's book gain and tax gain on sale assuming Neil acquired the investment asset in a nontaxable exchange.

LO 9-1, 9-2, 9-3   9. CC Company exchanged a depreciable asset with a $17,000 initial cost and a $10,000 adjusted basis for a new asset priced at $16,000.

 a. Assuming that the assets do not qualify as like-kind property, compute the amount and character of CC's recognized gain and its basis in the new asset.

 b. Assuming that the assets qualify as like-kind property, compute the amount and character of CC's recognized gain and its basis in the new asset.

LO 9-2, 9-3   10. XYZ exchanged an old building for a new like-kind building. XYZ's adjusted basis in the old building was $13,000 ($30,000 initial cost − $17,000 accumulated deprecia-tion), and its FMV was $20,000. Because the new building was worth $28,500, XYZ paid $8,500 cash in addition to the old building.

 a. Compute XYZ's realized gain, and determine the amount and character of any rec-ognized gain.

 b. Compute XYZ's basis in its new building.

LO 9-2, 9-3, 9-5   11. OCD exchanged old realty for new like-kind realty. OCD's adjusted basis in the old realty was $31,700 ($60,000 initial cost − $28,300 accumulated depreciation), and its FMV was $48,000. Because the new realty was worth only $45,000, OCD received $3,000 cash in addition to the new realty.

 a. Compute OCD's realized gain, and determine the amount and character of any rec-ognized gain.

 b. Compute OCD's basis in its new realty.

LO 9-2, 9-3, 9-5   12. Firm ML, a noncorporate taxpayer, exchanged residential rental property plus $15,000 cash for 20 acres of investment land with a $200,000 FMV. ML used the straight-line method to compute depreciation on the rental property.

 a. Assuming that ML's exchange was negotiated at arm's length, what is the FMV of the rental property?

 b. If the adjusted basis of the rental property is $158,000, compute ML's realized and recognized gain. What is the character of the recognized gain?

 c. Compute ML's basis in the 20 acres of investment land.

LO 9-2, 9-3, 9-5   13. Refer to the facts in the preceding problem, but assume that ML exchanged the residen-tial rental property for the 20 acres of investment land plus $22,000 (i.e., ML *received* cash in the exchange).

 a. Assuming that ML's exchange was negotiated at arm's length, what is the FMV of the rental property?

 b. If the adjusted basis of the rental property is $158,000, compute ML's realized and recognized gain. What is the character of the recognized gain?

 c. Compute ML's basis in the 20 acres of investment land.

LO 9-2, 9-6   14. Alice and Brendan exchanged the following business real estate:

	Undeveloped Land (exchanged by Alice)	Commercial Building (exchanged by Brendan)
FMV	$975,000	$1,570,000
Mortgage	–0–	(595,000)
Equity	$975,000	$ 975,000

 a. If Alice's adjusted basis in the undeveloped land was $360,000, compute Alice's realized gain, recognized gain, and basis in the commercial building received in the exchange.

b. If Brendan's adjusted basis in the commercial building was $790,000, compute Brendan's realized gain, recognized gain, and basis in the undeveloped land received in the exchange.

LO 9-2, 9-6 15. Firm PO and Corporation QR exchanged the following business real estate:

	Marvin Gardens (exchanged by PO)	Boardwalk (exchanged by QR)
FMV	$1,040,000	$325,000
Mortgage	(715,000)	–0–
Equity	$ 325,000	$325,000

a. If PO's adjusted basis in Marvin Gardens was $403,000, compute PO's realized gain, recognized gain, and basis in Boardwalk.

b. If QR's adjusted basis in Boardwalk was $78,000, compute QR's realized gain, recognized gain, and basis in Marvin Gardens.

LO 9-2, 9-6 16. Company B and Firm W exchanged the following business real estate:

	Blackacre (exchanged by B)	Whiteacre (exchanged by W)
FMV	$400,000	$525,000
Mortgage	(100,000)	(225,000)
Equity	$300,000	$300,000

a. If B's adjusted basis in Blackacre was $240,000, compute B's realized gain, recognized gain, and basis in Whiteacre.

b. If W's adjusted basis in Whiteacre was $100,000, compute W's realized gain, recognized gain, and basis in Blackacre.

LO 9-7 17. On June 2, 2022, a tornado destroyed the building in which FF operated a fast-food franchise. FF's adjusted basis in the building was $214,700. In each of the following cases, determine FF's recognized gain or loss on this property disposition and FF's basis in the replacement building. Assume that FF would elect to defer gain recognition when possible.

a. On September 8, 2022, FF received a $250,000 reimbursement from its insurance company. On August 10, 2023, it completed construction of a replacement building for a total cost of $300,000.

b. On September 8, 2022, FF received a $250,000 reimbursement from its insurance company. On August 10, 2023, it completed construction of a replacement building for a total cost of $235,000.

c. On September 8, 2022, FF received a $200,000 reimbursement from its insurance company. On August 10, 2023, it completed construction of a replacement building for a total cost of $300,000.

LO 9-7 18. On January 10, 2020, a fire destroyed a warehouse owned by NP Company. NP's adjusted basis in the warehouse was $530,000. On March 12, 2020, NP received a $650,000 reimbursement from its insurance company. In each of the following cases, determine NP's recognized gain on this property disposition. Assume that NP would elect to defer gain recognition when possible.

a. NP's board of directors decided not to replace the warehouse.

b. On January 2, 2022, NP paid $700,000 to acquire a warehouse to store its inventory.

c. On February 8, 2023, NP paid $700,000 to acquire a warehouse to store its inventory.

LO 9-7   19. RP owned residential real estate with a $680,000 adjusted basis that was condemned by City Q because it needed the land for a new convention center. RP received $975,000 condemnation proceeds for the real estate. Assume that RP would elect to defer gain recognition when possible.

  a. Assume RP spent $200,000 of the proceeds to expand its inventory and the remaining $775,000 to purchase new residential real estate. Calculate RP's gain or loss realized, gain or loss recognized, and tax basis in the inventory and new real estate.

  b. How would your answer to part (*a*) change if RP's basis in the condemned real estate were $850,000 rather than $680,000?

  c. How would your answer to part (*a*) change if RP invested the entire condemnation proceeds plus an additional $100,000 cash in new residential real estate?

LO 9-7   20. On October 18 of last year, a flood washed away heavy construction equipment owned by Company K. The adjusted tax basis in the equipment was $416,000. On December 8 of last year, Company K received a $480,000 reimbursement from its insurance company. On April 8 this year, Company K purchased new construction equipment for $450,000.

  a. How much of last year's gain must Company K recognize because of the involuntary disposition of the equipment?

  b. What is Company K's tax basis in the new equipment?

  c. How would your answers change if Company K paid $492,000 for the new equipment?

LO 9-7   21. Calvin Corporation's office was burglarized. The thieves stole 10 laptop computers and other electronic equipment. The lost assets had an original cost of $35,000 and accumulated tax depreciation of $19,400. Calvin received an insurance reimbursement of $20,000 related to the theft loss and immediately purchased new replacement computer equipment. In each of the following cases, determine Calvin's recognized gain, if any, and the tax basis of the replacement property. Assume that Calvin would elect to defer gain recognition when possible.

  a. The replacement property cost $27,000.

  b. The replacement property cost $18,000.

LO 9-8   22. Mr. Boyd and Ms. Tuck decide to form a new corporation named BT, Inc. Mr. Boyd transfers $10,000 cash and business inventory ($20,000 FMV; adjusted tax basis $3,200), and Ms. Tuck transfers business equipment (FMV $60,000; adjusted tax basis $41,500) to BT. In exchange for their cash and property, BT issues 1,200 shares of common stock to its two shareholders.

  a. How many shares should Mr. Boyd and Ms. Tuck each receive?

  b. Compute Mr. Boyd's realized and recognized gain on his exchange of property for stock, and determine his tax basis in his BT common shares.

  c. Compute Ms. Tuck's realized and recognized gain on her exchange of property for stock, and determine her tax basis in her BT common shares.

  d. Determine BT, Inc.'s book and tax basis in the inventory transferred by Mr. Boyd and the equipment transferred by Ms. Tuck.

LO 9-8   23. PV, Inc. transferred the operating assets of one of its business divisions into newly incorporated SV, Inc. in exchange for 100 percent of SV's stock. PV's adjusted basis in the operating assets was $4 million, and its FMV was $10 million.

  a. Discuss the business reasons why a parent corporation like PV operates a business through a subsidiary like SV.

  b. Compute PV's realized gain, recognized gain, and basis in its SV stock.

LO 9-8   24. Mr. Zhao owns a sole proprietorship. The business assets have a $246,000 aggregate adjusted basis. According to an independent appraisal, the business is worth $400,000. Mr. Zhao transfers his business to ZJL Corporation in exchange for 1,000 shares of ZJL stock. In each of the following cases, compute Mr. Zhao's recognized gain on the exchange of assets for stock.

   a. Immediately after the exchange, ZJL has 20,000 shares of outstanding stock, of which Mr. Zhao owns 1,000 shares.

   b. Immediately after the exchange, ZJL has 1,500 shares of outstanding stock, of which Mr. Zhao owns 1,000 shares.

   c. Immediately after the exchange, ZJL has 1,200 shares of outstanding stock, of which Mr. Zhao owns 1,000 shares.

LO 9-8   25. Refer to the facts in the preceding problem. Assume that Mrs. Ladd, who is Mr. Zhao's business colleague, transfers $200,000 cash to ZJL Corporation in exchange for 500 shares of ZJL stock. Mr. Zhao and Mrs. Ladd's transfers occur on the same day and, after the exchange, ZJL has 1,500 shares of outstanding stock (1,000 owned by Mr. Zhao and 500 owned by Mrs. Ladd).

   a. Compute Mr. Zhao's recognized gain on the exchange of assets for stock.

   b. Compute Mr. Zhao and Mrs. Ladd's tax basis in their ZJL stock.

   c. Compute ZJL's tax basis in the assets transferred from Mr. Zhao.

LO 9-8   26. Lydia and Oliver want to form a partnership to conduct a new business. They each contribute the following assets in exchange for equal interests in LO Partnership. Lydia's tax basis in the contributed equipment is $22,000, and Oliver's tax basis in the contributed equipment is $57,000.

	Lydia	**Oliver**
Cash	$50,000	$70,000
Business equipment (FMV)	50,000	30,000

   a. Compute each individual's realized and recognized gain or loss on the formation of LO Partnership.

   b. Compute each individual's tax basis in their half interest in LO Partnership.

   c. Compute the partnership's tax basis in the equipment contributed by each individual partner.

LO 9-8   27. Corporation A and Corporation Z go into partnership to develop, produce, and market a new product. The two corporations contribute the following properties in exchange for equal interests in AZ Partnership:

	Corporation A	**Corporation Z**
Cash	$100,000	$50,000
Business equipment (FMV)	30,000	80,000

Corporation A's tax basis in the contributed equipment is $34,000, and Corporation Z's tax basis in the contributed equipment is $12,000.

   a. Compute each corporation's realized and recognized gain or loss on the formation of AZ Partnership.

   b. Compute each corporation's tax basis in its half interest in AZ Partnership.

   c. Compute the partnership's tax basis in the equipment contributed by each corporate partner.

LO 9-9 28. Ten years ago, Ms. Dee purchased 1,000 shares of Fox common stock for $124 per share. On June 2 of the current year, she sold 500 shares for $92 per share. Compute Ms. Dee's recognized loss on sale assuming that

    a. She purchased 600 shares of Fox common stock on June 28 for $94 per share.

    b. She purchased 600 shares of Fox common stock on August 10 for $99 per share.

    c. Compute Ms. Dee's tax basis in the 600 shares purchased in part (*a*).

    d. Compute Ms. Dee's tax basis in the 600 shares purchased in part (*b*).

LO 9-9 29. Eight years ago, SW purchased 1,000 shares of Delta stock. On May 20 of the current year, it sold these shares for $90 per share. In each of the following cases, compute SW's recognized gain or loss on this sale:

    a. SW's cost basis in the 1,000 shares was $104 per share. It did not purchase any other Delta shares during this year.

    b. SW's cost basis in the 1,000 shares was $104 per share. It purchased 1,200 shares of Delta on May 1 for $92 per share.

    c. SW's cost basis in the 1,000 shares was $104 per share. It purchased 1,200 shares of Delta on June 8 for $92 per share.

    d. SW's cost basis in the 1,000 shares was $79 per share. It purchased 1,200 shares of Delta on June 8 for $92 per share.

LO 9-9 30. Refer to the facts in the preceding problem. In each case in which SW purchased 1,200 Delta shares, compute its tax basis in the shares.

LO 9-9 31. Ten years ago, Janine purchased 100 shares of Mega stock for $245 per share. On September 10 of the current year, she sold all 100 shares for $200 per share.

    a. Compute Janine's realized and recognized loss on sale assuming that she purchased 200 shares of Mega on October 1 for $190 per share.

    b. Compute Janine's realized and recognized loss on sale assuming that she purchased 100 shares of Mega on November 1 for $180 per share.

    c. Compute Janine's tax basis in the 200 shares of Mega purchased in part (*a*).

    d. Compute Janine's tax basis in the 100 shares of Mega purchased in part (*b*).

LO 9-4 32. Watson, a calendar year corporation, reported $1,250,000 net income before tax on its financial statements prepared in accordance with GAAP. During the year, Watson exchanged one piece of commercial real estate for another. The real estate given in the exchange had an original cost of $550,000, accumulated book depreciation of $350,000, and accumulated tax depreciation of $410,000. The real estate received in the exchange has a $650,000 FMV.

    a. Calculate Watson's book gain on the exchange.

    b. Calculate Watson's tax gain realized and recognized on the exchange.

    c. Assuming no other book/tax differences, calculate Watson's taxable income.

LO 9-4 33. KAI, a calendar year corporation, reported $500,000 net income before tax on its financial statements prepared in accordance with GAAP. The corporation's records reveal the following information:

    • KAI received an $80,000 insurance reimbursement for the theft of equipment with a $62,000 book basis and a $58,000 tax basis. KAI used $75,000 to replace the equipment and the remaining $5,000 to pay Christmas bonuses.

    • KAI exchanged investment real estate with a $250,000 book and tax basis for commercial real estate with a $600,000 FMV.

Compute KAI's taxable income. In making your computation, assume that the corporation defers the recognition of gain when possible.

LO 9-4   34. Alfix, a calendar year corporation, reported $789,300 net income before tax on its financial statements prepared in accordance with GAAP. The corporation's records reveal the following information:

- Depreciation expense per books was $15,890, and MACRS depreciation was $40,120.
- Two years ago, Alfix exchanged one tract of investment land (Whiteacre) for a different tract of investment land (Greenacre). Alfix's tax basis in Whiteacre was $500,000, and Greenacre's FMV was $835,000. This year, Alfix sold Greenacre for $820,000 cash.
- Alfix transferred business property worth $112,000 to Dundee, Inc. in exchange for 400 shares of Dundee stock. After the exchange, Dundee had 800 shares of stock outstanding. Alfix had a $91,000 book basis and a $68,200 tax basis in the business property.

Compute Alfix's taxable income.

Issue Recognition Problems

Identify the tax issue or issues suggested by the following situations, and state each issue in the form of a question.

LO 9-3, 9-5   1. ST, Inc. and Firm WX are negotiating an exchange of the following business properties:

	Office Building (owned by ST)	Warehouse (owned by WX)
FMV	$2,000,000	$1,700,000
Mortgage	(450,000)	–0–

ST agrees to pay $150,000 cash to WX to equalize the value of the exchange. ST's adjusted basis in the office building is $700,000, and WX's adjusted basis in the warehouse is $500,000.

LO 9-3, 9-5   2. Company JK disposed of the following items of business realty in a like-kind exchange:

	Initial Cost	Acc. Depr.	FMV
Item 1	$75,000	$38,000	$45,000
Item 2	30,000	16,000	10,000

In exchange for the two items, JK received like-kind realty worth $50,000 and $5,000 cash.

LO 9-5   3. NBV, a California corporation, exchanged commercial real estate located in San Francisco for commercial real estate located in Tokyo, Japan. NBV's gain realized was $16.3 million.

LO 9-7   4. FM, Inc. operates a dairy farm. The local government required the corporation to destroy 150 head of cattle because the herd had been exposed to mad cow disease. None of the cattle displayed any symptoms of the disease before they were destroyed. The local government paid $150,000 to FM as compensation for the loss. FM's adjusted basis in the herd was $105,000.

LO 9-7   5. Company T operated a drive-in movie theater for over a decade. Three years ago, the company ceased operations because so few people were attending the outdoor facility. This year, the entire facility (movie screen, projection building, snack bar, 15 picnic tables, and playground equipment) was destroyed by a tornado. Company T received a $360,000 insurance reimbursement. The aggregate-adjusted basis in the destroyed properties was $200,000. Four months after the twister, Company T purchased a new four-screen movie theater complex located in an urban shopping mall.

LO 9-7   6. In 2020, an office building owned by Firm F was completely destroyed by fire. Firm F's adjusted basis in the building was $485,000, and its insurance reimbursement was $550,000. On its 2020 tax return, F elected to defer the $65,000 gain realized on the involuntary conversion. In 2022, F invested $560,000 in another office building. In 2023, F settled a dispute with its insurance company concerning the 2020 claim. Pursuant to the settlement, it received a $25,000 additional reimbursement.

LO 9-7   7. In 2020, an industrial plant owned by Company C, a calendar year taxpayer, was destroyed in a flood. Company C's adjusted basis in the plant was $1.65 million, and the company received a $2 million insurance reimbursement. On its 2020 tax return, C elected to defer the gain realized on the involuntary conversion. C promptly began construction of a new plant on the site of the old plant. However, because of unexpected delays, construction was not completed until January 2022, and C did not place the new industrial plant into service until March 2023. The total construction price was $3 million.

LO 9-7   8. In 2022, transportation equipment owned by Corporation ABC was stolen. The adjusted basis in the equipment was $105,000, and ABC received a $400,000 insurance reimbursement. It immediately paid $440,000 for replacement transportation equipment. On its 2022 tax return, ABC elected to defer the $295,000 gain realized on the involuntary conversion. In 2023, ABC generated a $7 million net operating loss—the first in its history. ABC's aggregate taxable income on its 2021 and 2022 returns was $3.2 million.

LO 9-8   9. Mr. Pitt, a professional architect, entered into an agreement with Partnership M under which he designed three buildings for the partnership and transferred a copyright for design software to the partnership. Mr. Pitt had no tax basis in this software. In exchange for the services and computer software, Mr. Pitt received a 35 percent interest in Partnership M.

LO 9-9   10. On May 19, WJ realized a $48,000 loss on the sale of 10,000 shares of voting common stock in XZY Corporation. On May 30, WJ purchased 3,200 shares of XZY nonvoting preferred stock.

Research Problems

LO 9-5, 9-7   1. Mr. Bryan Olgivie owned an indoor roller-skating rink as a sole proprietorship. On April 9, a flood completely destroyed the rink. Mr. Olgivie's adjusted basis in the rink was $833,400. On May 15, he received a check for $1.1 million from his insurance company in complete settlement of his damage claim. Mr. Olgivie is planning to use the entire insurance settlement to purchase 100 percent of the outstanding stock of IceMagic, Inc., a corporation that owns an indoor ice-skating rink. Can he defer the recognition of gain on the involuntary conversion of his roller-skating rink by purchasing the IceMagic stock?

LO 9-8   2. On February 2, Mr. Eugene Pomeroy transferred all the assets of his sole proprietorship (Pomeroy's Ski Shop) to a newly created corporation, Pomeroy Ski, Inc. In exchange for the business assets, Mr. Pomeroy received all 1,000 shares of the corporation's newly issued voting common stock. On February 3, Mr. Pomeroy gave 100 shares of this stock to each of his five children and three grandchildren, leaving him with 200 shares. Does Mr. Pomeroy's exchange of business assets for corporate stock qualify as a nontaxable exchange even though he reduced his ownership interest from 100 percent to only 20 percent on the day after Pomeroy Ski, Inc. was incorporated?

LO 9-8   3. On April 1, 2023, Bullen Company transferred machinery used in its business to Eaton, Inc. in exchange for Eaton common stock. Both Bullen and Eaton use the calendar year for tax purposes. Bullen's exchange of property for stock qualified as a nontaxable exchange under Section 351. Consequently, Bullen's adjusted tax basis in the machinery carried over to become Eaton's tax basis. Bullen purchased the machinery in 2021 for $413,000 cash. The machinery was seven-year recovery property, and Bullen deducted a total of $160,161 MACRS depreciation in 2021 and 2022. Compute the 2023 MACRS depreciation deduction with respect to the machinery allowed to Bullen Company and to Eaton, Inc.

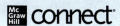

All applicable Tax Planning Cases are available with *Connect*.

Tax Planning Cases

LO 9-8   1. Firm NS owns 90 percent of Corporation T's outstanding stock. NS also owns business realty that T needs for use in its business. The FMV of the realty is $4 million, and NS's adjusted basis is $5.6 million. Both NS and T are in the 21 percent tax bracket. Discuss the tax implications of each of the following courses of action, and decide which course you would recommend to NS.

   a. NS could exchange the realty for newly issued shares of T stock worth $4 million.

   b. NS could sell the realty to T for $4 million cash.

   c. NS could lease the realty to T for its annual fair rental value of $600,000.

LO 9-5   2. Firm K, a noncorporate taxpayer, has owned investment land with a $600,000 basis for four years. Two unrelated parties want to acquire the land from K. Party A has offered $770,000 cash, and Party B has offered another tract of land with a $725,000 FMV. If K accepts Party B's offer, it would hold the new land for no more than two years before selling it. The FMV of this land should appreciate 10 percent annually. K's tax rate on capital gain is 15 percent, and it uses a 7 percent discount rate to compute NPV. Which offer should K accept to maximize the NPV of the transaction?

LO 9-7   3. DM, Inc. incurred a $25,000 net capital loss last year that has carried forward into the current year. During the current year, a hurricane destroyed business assets with a $120,000 basis. DM received a $150,000 insurance reimbursement, which it immediately used to purchase replacement assets. The new assets have a three-year MACRS recovery period. Should DM elect to defer the gain recognized on the involuntary conversion?

Comprehensive Problems for Part Three

1. Croyden is a calendar year, accrual basis corporation. Mr. and Mrs. Croyden (cash basis taxpayers) are the sole corporate shareholders. Mr. Croyden is president of the

corporation, and Mrs. Croyden is vice president. Croyden's financial records, prepared in accordance with GAAP, show the following information for the year:

Revenues from sales of goods	$12,900,000
Cost of goods sold (LIFO)	(9,260,000)
Gross profit	$ 3,640,000
Bad debt expense	$ 24,000
Administrative salaries and wages	612,000
State and local business taxes	135,000
Interest expense	33,900
Advertising	67,000
Annual property insurance premiums	19,800
Annual life insurance premiums	7,300
Depreciation expense	148,800
Repairs, maintenance, utilities	81,000

Croyden's records reveal the following facts:

- Under the UNICAP rules, Croyden had to capitalize $142,800 of administrative wages to inventory. These wages were expensed for financial statement purposes.

- Because of the UNICAP rules, Croyden's cost of goods sold for tax purposes exceeds the cost of goods sold for financial statement purposes by $219,000.

- Bad debt expense equals the addition to the corporation's allowance for bad debts. Actual write-offs of uncollectible accounts during the year totaled $31,200.

- Administrative salaries include an accrued $50,000 year-end bonus to Mr. Croyden and an accrued $20,000 year-end bonus to Mrs. Croyden. These bonuses were paid on January 17 of the following year.

- The life insurance premiums were on key-person policies for Mr. and Mrs. Croyden. The corporation is the policy beneficiary.

- Croyden disposed of two assets during the year. (These dispositions are *not* reflected in the financial statement information shown.) It sold office furnishings for $45,000. The original cost of the furnishings was $40,000, and accumulated MACRS depreciation through date of sale was $12,700. It also exchanged transportation equipment for a 15 percent interest in a partnership. The original cost of the transportation equipment was $110,000, and accumulated MACRS depreciation through date of exchange was $38,900.

- MACRS depreciation for assets placed in service in prior years (including the office furnishings and transportation equipment disposed of this year) is $187,600. The only asset acquired this year was new equipment costing $275,000. The equipment has a seven-year recovery period and was placed in service on February 11. Assume that Croyden does not elect Section 179 or bonus depreciation with respect to this acquisition.

- Croyden's prior-year tax returns show no nonrecaptured Section 1231 losses and a $7,400 capital loss carryforward.

Solely on the basis of these facts, compute Croyden's taxable income.

2. LN Consulting is a calendar year, cash basis unincorporated business. The business is not required to provide audited financial statements to any external user. LN's accounting records show the following:

Cash receipts:	
Revenues from service contracts	$292,000
Proceeds from sale of mutual fund shares	18,000
Insurance reimbursement for fire loss	7,000
Cash disbursements:	
Administrative salaries	$ 32,000
Professional fees	800
Business meals not provided by a restaurant	1,090
Business entertainment costs	2,000
State and local business taxes	5,000
Interest expense	7,600
Advertising	970
Office expense	1,200
Office rent	14,400
New office equipment	8,300

LN's records reveal the following facts:

- In December, the bookkeeper prepaid $1,500 interest on a business debt. This interest is related to the next taxable year.
- LN disposed of two assets during the year. It exchanged computer equipment for office furniture. (These assets are not like-kind for federal tax purposes.) The original cost of the computer equipment was $13,000, and accumulated MACRS depreciation through date of exchange was $9,700. The office furniture has a $6,000 FMV. It sold 1,200 shares in a mutual fund for $18,000. LN purchased the shares as a short-term investment of excess working capital. The cost of the shares was $16,600.
- An electrical fire completely destroyed a company car. The adjusted basis of the car was $9,100, and LN's property insurance company paid $7,000 in complete settlement of its damage claim. LN used the insurance money to pay various operating expenses.
- MACRS depreciation for assets placed in service in prior years (including the computer equipment and company car) is $4,600. The only asset acquired this year (in addition to the office furniture) was office equipment costing $8,300. The equipment was placed in service on August 19.

Based on these facts, compute the taxable income generated by LN Consulting's activities, before any 20 percent (QBI) deduction that might be available to LN's owners.

The Taxation of Business Income

Chapter Ten

Sole Proprietorships, Partnerships, LLCs, and S Corporations

Learning Objectives

After studying this chapter, you should be able to:

LO 10-1. Compute net profit or loss from a sole proprietorship.

LO 10-2. Compute the FICA payroll taxes and the federal SE tax.

LO 10-3. Explain how limited liability companies (LLCs) are treated for federal tax purposes.

LO 10-4. Explain the flow-through of partnership items to the partners.

LO 10-5. Differentiate between a distributive share of partnership income and cash flow.

LO 10-6. Adjust the tax basis in a partnership interest.

LO 10-7. Apply the basis limitation on the deduction of partnership losses.

LO 10-8. Determine if a corporation is eligible to be an S corporation.

LO 10-9. Identify similarities and differences in the tax treatment of S corporations versus partnerships.

LO 10-10. Apply the basis limitation on the deduction of S corporation losses.

In Part Three, we learned that taxable income from business transactions and activities equals gross income minus allowable deductions.[1] In Part Four, we will learn how to compute the tax on business income. Throughout Part Three, we used the labels *firm* and *company* to refer to business organizations. We could get by with these generic labels because we were concentrating on the *measurement of taxable income*. The measurement process does not depend on the type of legal entity operating the business. As stated in Chapter 4, the tax law is essentially neutral across business entities with respect to the tax base. But to make the actual *tax computation,* we must focus on the specific organizational form of the business.

[1] §63(a).

EXHIBIT 10.1
Categories of Business Organizations

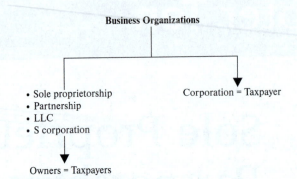

For tax purposes, business organizations fall into one of two categories. The first category consists of organizations that are not taxable entities. The income generated by the organization is taxed directly to the owners. This category includes sole proprietorships, partnerships, limited liability companies (LLCs), and S corporations, all of which are discussed in this chapter. The second category consists of corporations (often referred to as regular or C corporations), which are both persons under the law and taxpayers in their own right. Corporations pay tax on their income at the entity level. If a corporation distributes after-tax earnings to its owners, the distributed income is taxed a second time at the owner level. This potential for double taxation, as well as other characteristics of corporate taxpayers, is examined in detail in Chapter 11. Exhibit 10.1 contrasts the two categories of business organizations in terms of the identity of the taxpayer.

Part Four includes two more chapters that complete our discussion of the taxation of business income. Chapter 12 compares the tax advantages and disadvantages of the various business entities and identifies tax planning strategies unique to each. Finally, Chapter 13 introduces the complexities that develop when business entities operate in more than one taxing jurisdiction.

SOLE PROPRIETORSHIPS

The simplest form of business organization is a **sole proprietorship,** defined as an unincorporated business activity owned by one individual.[2] A sole proprietor owns the business assets in their own name and is personally liable for the business debts. In other words, the business has no legal identity separate from that of its owner. Sole proprietorships are the most common form of business entity in the United States. According to recent Internal Revenue Service data, more than 27 million nonfarm sole proprietorships operate in this country, and nearly three of every four businesses that report to the IRS are operated by sole proprietors.[3]

Overview of Schedule C

LO 10-1
Compute net profit or loss from a sole proprietorship.

The taxable income from a sole proprietorship is reported on Schedule C (Profit or Loss From Business) of the proprietor's Form 1040 (U.S. Individual Income Tax Return).[4] This schedule is the proprietorship's income statement for the year. Gross income from the sale of goods to customers or the performance of services for clients is accounted for in Part One. The proprietorship's deductible operating expenses and cost recovery deductions are listed in Part Two. An excess of gross income over deductions is reported as net profit, while an excess of deductions over gross income is reported as net loss.

---

[2] This definition includes businesses in which the owner's spouse has an equity interest in the business under state property law. As discussed later in this chapter, a single-member LLC whose owner is an individual is treated as a sole proprietorship.

[3] *IRS Statistics of Income Bulletin,* Spring 2018.

[4] Agricultural business operations are reported on Schedule F (Profit or Loss From Farming).

Faux Antiques—Sole Proprietorship	Tom Owen owns and operates a firm that manufactures reproductions of antique furniture. The business name for this sole proprietorship is Faux Antiques. For 2022, the business records reflect the following items of revenue and expense:

Revenue from furniture sales	$1,117,300
Sales returns	(21,000)
Expenses: Advertising	6,200
Accounts written off as uncollectible	8,800
Attorney and CPA fees	2,150
Business license tax	2,500
Cost of goods sold	599,700
Interest to credit union	7,300
MACRS depreciation	3,600
Payroll taxes	9,250
Property and liability insurance	5,600
Rent on workroom	23,200
Repairs to tools and equipment	17,900
Supplies	18,000
Utilities	14,000
Wages	73,200

Mr. Owen used this information to prepare the Schedule C included in his Form 1040. Page 1 of this Schedule C is shown in Exhibit 10.2. The $304,900 net profit reported on Schedule C was included in Mr. Owen's 2022 taxable income.

Note that the tax on net profit is not computed on Schedule C. Instead, the net profit carries to the first page of Form 1040 as ordinary income and is combined with all other income items recognized during the year. Consequently, the individual's business income is just one component of the total income on which tax is computed.

QBI Deduction

As mentioned in Chapter 6, the Tax Cuts and Jobs Act of 2017 enacted new Section 199A, creating a new deduction for noncorporate businesses. The goal of this deduction is to lower the effective tax rate on the business profit earned by pass-through entities.

In February 2019, the Treasury issued new regulations providing a detailed definition of a **qualified business income (QBI).** In general, only ordinary income associated with a qualified trade or business is included in QBI. The regulations also provide a general rule that deductions attributable to a trade or business are taken into account for purposes of computing QBI. In particular, QBI is reduced by (1) the deductible portion of self-employment taxes, (2) the self-employed health insurance deduction, and (3) the deduction for contributions to qualified retirement plans, to the extent the individual's trade or business income is taken into account in calculating the allowable deduction.[5]

The following example illustrates the calculation of qualified business income for purposes of the QBI deduction.

Defining Qualified Business Income	Jana Khan is a single individual with salary income of $30,000 and earnings from self-employment of $65,000. Ms. Khan paid $5,000 for self-employed health insurance. Based on her earnings, Ms. Khan will owe $9,184 of self-employment tax ($65,000 × .9235 × .153), of which $4,592 will be deductible.

(continued)

[5] The calculation of self-employment tax is explained later in the chapter. The self-employed health insurance deduction and deductions to qualified retirement plans are discussed in more detail in Chapter 15.

Ms. Khan contributes to a qualified retirement plan based on her self-employment earnings. This year, she will make the maximum contribution permitted of $12,082 [($65,000 − $4,592 deductible self-employment tax) × 20%].

Assume that Ms. Khan's self-employment activity is a qualified trade or business. Ms. Khan's QBI is $43,326 ($65,000 −$4,592 deductible self-employment tax − $5,000 self-employed health insurance − $12,082 qualified retirement contribution).

EXHIBIT 10.2

Internal Revenue Service

SCHEDULE C (Form 1040)

Department of the Treasury
Internal Revenue Service

Profit or Loss From Business
(Sole Proprietorship)

Go to *www.irs.gov/ScheduleC* for instructions and the latest information.
Attach to Form 1040, 1040-SR, 1040-NR, or 1041; partnerships must generally file Form 1065.

OMB No. 1545-0074

20**22**

Attachment Sequence No. **09**

Name of proprietor	Social security number (SSN)
Tom G. Owen	497-45-9058

A Principal business or profession, including product or service (see instructions)
Manufacturing - furniture

B Enter code from instructions
3 3 7 0 0

C Business name. If no separate business name, leave blank.
Faux Antiques

D Employer ID number (EIN) (see instr.)

E Business address (including suite or room no.) _____
City, town or post office, state, and ZIP code

F Accounting method: (1) ☐ Cash (2) ☑ Accrual (3) ☐ Other (specify) _____

G Did you "materially participate" in the operation of this business during 2022? If "No," see instructions for limit on losses ☑ Yes ☐ No

H If you started or acquired this business during 2022, check here ☐

I Did you make any payments in 2022 that would require you to file Form(s) 1099? See instructions ☐ Yes ☑ No

J If "Yes," did you or will you file required Form(s) 1099? ☐ Yes ☑ No

Part I   Income

1	Gross receipts or sales. See instructions for line 1 and check the box if this income was reported to you on Form W-2 and the "Statutory employee" box on that form was checked ☐	**1** 1,117,300
2	Returns and allowances	**2** 21,000
3	Subtract line 2 from line 1	**3** 1,096,300
4	Cost of goods sold (from line 42)	**4** 599,700
5	**Gross profit.** Subtract line 4 from line 3	**5** 496,600
6	Other income, including federal and state gasoline or fuel tax credit or refund (see instructions)	**6**
7	**Gross income.** Add lines 5 and 6	**7** 496,600

Part II   Expenses. Enter expenses for business use of your home **only** on line 30.

8	Advertising	**8** 6,200	18	Office expense (see instructions)	**18**	
9	Car and truck expenses (see instructions)	**9**	19	Pension and profit-sharing plans	**19**	
10	Commissions and fees	**10**	20	Rent or lease (see instructions):		
11	Contract labor (see instructions)	**11**	a	Vehicles, machinery, and equipment	**20a**	
12	Depletion	**12**	b	Other business property	**20b** 23,200	
13	Depreciation and section 179 expense deduction (not included in Part III) (see instructions)	**13** 3,600	21	Repairs and maintenance	**21** 17,900	
			22	Supplies (not included in Part III)	**22** 18,000	
			23	Taxes and licenses	**23** 11,750	
			24	Travel and meals:		
14	Employee benefit programs (other than on line 19)	**14**	a	Travel	**24a**	
15	Insurance (other than health)	**15** 5,600	b	Deductible meals (see instructions)	**24b**	
16	Interest (see instructions):		25	Utilities	**25** 14,000	
a	Mortgage (paid to banks, etc.)	**16a**	26	Wages (less employment credits)	**26** 73,200	
b	Other	**16b** 7,300	27a	Other expenses (from line 48)	**27a** bad debts 8,800	
17	Legal and professional services	**17** 2,150	b	Reserved for future use	**27b**	
28	**Total expenses** before expenses for business use of home. Add lines 8 through 27a				**28** 191,700	
29	Tentative profit or (loss). Subtract line 28 from line 7				**29** 304,900	

30 Expenses for business use of your home. Do not report these expenses elsewhere. Attach Form 8829 unless using the simplified method. See instructions.
Simplified method filers only: Enter the total square footage of (a) your home: _____
and (b) the part of your home used for business: _____ . Use the Simplified Method Worksheet in the instructions to figure the amount to enter on line 30 **30**

31 **Net profit or (loss).** Subtract line 30 from line 29.
• If a profit, enter on both **Schedule 1 (Form 1040), line 3,** and on **Schedule SE, line 2.** (If you checked the box on line 1, see instructions.) Estates and trusts, enter on **Form 1041, line 3.**
• If a loss, you **must** go to line 32.   **31** 304,900

32 If you have a loss, check the box that describes your investment in this activity. See instructions.
• If you checked 32a, enter the loss on both **Schedule 1 (Form 1040), line 3,** and on **Schedule SE, line 2.** (If you checked the box on line 1, see the line 31 instructions.) Estates and trusts, enter on **Form 1041, line 3.**
• If you checked 32b, you **must** attach **Form 6198.** Your loss may be limited.

32a ☐ All investment is at risk.
32b ☐ Some investment is not at risk.

For Paperwork Reduction Act Notice, see the separate instructions.   Cat. No. 11334P   Schedule C (Form 1040) 2022

In general, the tentative QBI deduction equals 20 percent of qualified business income earned by an individual taxpayer through a sole proprietorship, partnership, or S corporation. However, various limits and exclusions complicate what is otherwise a simple calculation. Specifically, the deduction is subject to both a wage limitation and a taxable income limitation, described further below.

First, the **QBI deduction** cannot exceed the greater of (1) 50 percent of W-2 wages paid by a qualified trade or business or (2) the sum of 25 percent of W-2 wages plus 2.5 percent of the unadjusted basis of qualified property used by the business. W-2 wages include most types of taxable compensation paid to business employees. Qualified property is defined as tangible business property subject to depreciation.

QBI Deduction after Applying the Wage Limitation	Maria Wilson operates a sole proprietorship with qualified business income (after all applicable deductions) of $1.2 million. Her business paid W-2 wages of $400,000 and owns depreciable tangible property with an unadjusted basis of $900,000. Ms. Wilson's QBI deduction (before any taxable income limitation) is computed as follows:

Tentative deduction prior to wage limitation ($1.2 million × 20%)		$240,000
Deduction limited to greater of:		
$400,000 × 50% or	$200,000	$200,000
$400,000 × 25% + $900,000 × 2.5%	122,500	
QBI deduction before taxable income limitation		$200,000

Second, the final QBI deduction is subject to an overall limitation based on taxable income. The final deduction cannot exceed 20 percent of taxable income computed without regard to (1) the QBI deduction and (2) any net capital gain.

QBI Deduction after Applying the Taxable Income Limit	Refer to the preceding example in which Ms. Wilson has qualified business income of $1.2 million and an allowable QBI deduction after the wage limitation of $200,000. Consider two alternative scenarios regarding her taxable income and final QBI deduction.

	Scenario A	Scenario B
Taxable income before QBI deduction, excluding net capital gains	$1,400,000	$ 900,000
Overall limitation percentage	.20	.20
Taxable income limitation	$ 280,000	$ 180,000
Final QBI deduction	$ 200,000	$ 180,000

Ms. Wilson's final QBI deduction is the lesser of the taxable income limitation or the $200,000 QBI deduction after the wage limitation (as computed above). Thus, in Scenario B, the taxable income limitation lowers her allowable deduction.

Third, a qualified business does not include service businesses in the fields of health, law, accounting, actuarial science, performing arts, consulting, athletics, financial services, brokerage services, investing, and investment management. Qualified business income also excludes investment-related income, gains, losses, and deductions, as well as amounts earned as an employee or received from a partnership by a partner in exchange for services (guaranteed payments).

Finally, an important simplification exempts lower-income taxpayers from both the W-2 wage limitation and the exclusion of service businesses. If the taxpayer's 2023 taxable income (prior to the QBI deduction) does not exceed $364,200 (married filing jointly) or $182,100 (all other individuals), the QBI deduction is simply 20 percent of business income, including income from service businesses. For 2022, the related thresholds are $340,100 (married filing jointly), or $170,050 (all other individuals).

If taxable income exceeds the $364,200 (if married filing jointly or $182,100 for all other individuals) threshold by not more than $100,000 ($50,000 other than married filing jointly), the deduction for service businesses is phased down by 1 percent for every thousand dollars of taxable income over the $364,200 threshold amount (2 percent other than married filing jointly).

For both service and nonservice businesses, the W-2 wage limitation is phased in when taxable income is within the phase-in range. This phase-in also equals 1 percent for every thousand dollars of taxable income over the $364,200 threshold amount (2 percent other than married filing jointly). The interplay of these phase-in provisions can result in a complex and often confusing computation. To facilitate the application of these rules, we provide a worksheet in Appendix 10–A. This appendix should be utilized when the taxpayer has an income within the phase-in range, whether from a service business or other qualified trade or business.

QBI Deduction for a Service Business

Levi Krase is a self-employed consultant with 2023 business income (after all applicable deductions) of $230,000. His business pays no W-2 wages and has minimal depreciable property. Mr. Krase is married filing a joint return and has taxable income of $290,000, prior to the QBI deduction.

Mr. Krase's consulting business would be considered a service business, normally not producing qualified business income. In addition, the W-2 wage limitation, if applied, would reduce any deduction to zero. However, because Mr. Krase's taxable income is below the $364,200 threshold, he is permitted a QBI deduction of $46,000 ($230,000 × 20 percent), reducing his taxable income to $244,000 ($290,000 − $46,000). Note that the taxable income limitation would not apply, since the Krases' pre-QBI taxable income of $290,000 is greater than the qualified business income of $230,000.

What if the Krases' taxable income is $370,000? Because they exceed the $364,200 threshold by $5,800, their allowable QBI deduction is reduced by 5.8 percent to $43,332 ($46,000 − 5.8 percent × $46,000) by the phase-in of the income limitation on service businesses. In addition, the phase-in of the W-2 wage limitation reduces their QBI deduction by an additional 5.8 percent to $40,819 ($43,332 − 5.8 percent × $43,332). See Appendix 10–A for a detailed walk-through of the calculation.

Phase-in of Wage Limitation on QBI Deduction of a Nonservice Business

Sam Jensen is self-employed with 2023 qualified business income of $140,000. Mx. Jensen's business paid $48,000 of W-2 wages and has no depreciable property. Mx. Jensen is single and has taxable income of $190,000, prior to the QBI deduction.

Without regard to the wage limitation, Mx. Jensen's QBI deduction would be $28,000 ($140,000 QBI × 20 percent). If the wage limitation is applied in full, the QBI deduction would be limited to $24,000 ($48,000 × 50 percent), a reduction of $4,000.

Mx. Jensen's taxable income exceeds the threshold by $7,900 ($190,000 − $182,100 threshold), resulting in a reduction percentage of 15.8 percent [($7,900 × 2)/1,000]. Mx. Jensen's allowable QBI deduction is $27,368 ($28,000 − 15.8 percent × $4,000).

The QBI deduction does not appear on Schedule C and does not reduce the taxpayer's adjusted gross income. Instead, it is a deduction from adjusted gross income, reducing final taxable income. Chapter 14 discusses this presentation issue in more detail.

Sole Proprietorship Losses

If a sole proprietorship operates at a loss and that loss is deductible, it carries to the first page of Form 1040 to be deducted against other income for the year. However, a current deduction for the loss may be limited. Recall from Chapter 6 that excess business losses of a noncorporate taxpayer are not currently deductible. An excess business loss is an overall net loss from all the taxpayer's business activities in excess of $578,000 (married filing jointly) or $289,000 (all other individuals). These thresholds relate to 2023 tax years. As discussed in Chapter 6, the CARES Act suspended the excess business loss limitation for tax years 2018 through 2020.

Deductible Business Loss	Luis Griffin is a single individual earning salary income of $300,000. He also conducts business through a sole proprietorship. The following are two alternate scenarios regarding deductibility of a 2023 loss sustained by his business:

	Scenario A	Scenario B
Overall business loss	$ (210,000)	$ (320,000)
Salary income	$ 300,000	$ 300,000
Deductible business loss	(210,000)	(289,000)
Net earnings on Form 1040	$ 90,000	$ 11,000

Note that in Scenario A, Mr. Griffin's business loss is fully deductible. In Scenario B, his business loss exceeds the loss threshold for a single taxpayer. His nondeductible $(31,000) excess business loss [$(320,000) − $(289,000)] carries forward to the future as a net operating loss (NOL).

If a deductible business loss exceeds other income, the individual can carry the excess loss forward as an NOL deduction. Recall from Chapter 6 that NOLs carry forward indefinitely, but the deduction in future years is limited to 80 percent of taxable income in each carryforward year.

Individual Net Operating Loss	Avi Zeller reported the following items on his Form 1040 for 2023:

Salary from employer	$21,600
Interest and dividend income from investments	1,200
Business loss from sole proprietorship	(26,810)
Net operating loss	$ (4,010)

Mr. Zeller can use his $4,010 net operating loss as a carryforward deduction in future years, subject to the 80 percent of taxable income limitation.[6]

Cash Flow Implications

The after-tax cash generated by a sole proprietorship belongs to the individual owner. The individual can retain the cash for use in the business, spend it for personal consumption, or invest it in other income-producing property. In the latter case, earnings from the owner's investments (interest, dividends, rents, etc.) are not considered business income and are not reported on Schedule C.[7]

---

[6] This example ignores the computational details of the individual NOL deduction. In general, the following items are not allowed when computing the individual NOL: personal exemptions, net capital losses, nonbusiness deductions in excess of nonbusiness income, and the domestic production activities deduction.

[7] Chapter 16 discusses the taxation of investment income earned by an individual taxpayer.

Faux Antiques Cash to Mr. Owen	Refer to the example in which Tom Owen owns and operates Faux Antiques. During 2022, Mr. Owen transferred $261,300 cash from his business bank account to his personal bank account. Mr. Owen and his spouse pay all their household expenses out of the personal account. The transfer of cash has absolutely no effect on the computation of Faux Antiques' net profit reported on Schedule C.

Dispositions of Business Assets

Only the results of the sole proprietorship's routine operations are reported on Schedule C. If the owner disposes of assets used in the business, recognized gains and losses are reported on Form 4797 (Sales of Business Property). The tax consequences of the disposition are based on the rules discussed in Chapters 8 and 9. For instance, if the owner sells business equipment at a gain, they must report Section 1245 depreciation recapture as ordinary income and any additional gain as Section 1231 gain. If they sell the equipment at a loss, the loss is a Section 1231 loss.

Interest Expense

If an individual borrows money for a business purpose relating to their sole proprietorship, the interest paid on the debt is deductible on Schedule C, subject to the net business interest limitation discussed in Chapter 6. The deductibility of business interest is in sharp contrast to the tax treatment of other types of interest expense. For example, individuals can't deduct the interest paid on debt incurred to purchase consumer goods such as a family car or a new wardrobe. If the sole proprietorship fails to generate enough cash to service the business debt, the individual owner is personally liable for repayment, and the business creditors can look to the owner's nonbusiness assets for satisfaction.

Home Office Deduction

If an individual uses a portion of their personal residence as an office for their sole proprietorship, the expenses allocable to the home office may qualify as a business deduction.

Home Office Deduction	Agatha Greer, a self-employed consultant, uses one room of her home as a business office. This room represents 15 percent of the home's square footage. This year, Mrs. Greer incurred the following expenses in connection with her home:

Home mortgage interest	$18,000
Property tax on residence	4,300
Homeowner's insurance	2,950
Utilities	3,600
House cleaning service	2,400
Repairs	1,900
	$33,150

If Mrs. Greer's office meets the tax law requirements, she can deduct $4,973 (15 percent of the total expenses) as a business deduction on her Schedule C.[8] She can also claim a MACRS depreciation deduction based on 15 percent of the cost of the residence.

The possibility of deducting some percentage of monthly household expenses might prompt the conversion of many a spare bedroom into a home office—even if the use of such office is extraneous to the conduct of the homeowner's business. The tax law limits the potential for abuse through a set of tough requirements for qualifying a portion of a

---

[8] Mrs. Greer can deduct the remainder of her home mortgage interest and property tax as itemized deductions (see Chapters 14 and 17).

residence as a home office. Essentially, the office must be *exclusively* used on a regular basis as the principal place of any business operated by the homeowner or as a place to meet with patients, clients, or customers.[9] A home office used exclusively for administrative or management activities qualifies as a principal place of business if the taxpayer has no other fixed location where such activities are conducted.

Principal Place of Business	Cassandra Milby is a self-employed obstetrician who treats patients at three different urban hospitals. Although Dr. Milby spends more than 12 hours during an average week at each hospital, she does not maintain an office in any of the hospitals. She does all medical reading, patient billing and record keeping, and other administrative tasks in her home office, where she spends 2 to 3 hours each day. Patient treatment is the most significant aspect of Dr. Milby's business, and she spends more hours working at the hospitals than in her home office. Nevertheless, her home office qualifies as Dr. Milby's principal place of business, and she can deduct the expenses allocable to the office.

Even when an individual meets the requirements for a home office, the home office deduction is limited to the taxable income of the business before consideration of the deduction.[10] In other words, the home office deduction can't create or increase a net loss. A sole proprietor who claims a home office deduction must isolate the deduction on line 30, Schedule C, and attach a separate Form 8829 to show the detailed computation of the deduction. Clearly, the IRS is very sensitive about home office deductions. Sole proprietors who are entitled to the deduction should carefully document the underlying expenses and be prepared to justify the necessity of a home office if their tax return is audited.

Employment Taxes

A sole proprietor may be the only person working in the business or the proprietor may have any number of employees. In the latter case, the sole proprietor must obtain an **employer identification number** from the IRS and comply with the state and federal employment tax requirements imposed on every business organization.

Unemployment and FICA Tax

LO 10-2
Compute the FICA payroll taxes and the federal SE tax.

Employers must pay both a state and a federal unemployment tax based on the compensation paid to their employees during the year.[11] As we discussed in Chapter 1, these taxes fund the national unemployment benefits program. Employers must also pay the tax authorized by the Federal Insurance Contribution Act (FICA) that funds our national Social Security and Medicare systems. This **employer payroll tax** has two components: a Social Security tax of 6.2 percent of a base amount of compensation paid to each employee and a Medicare tax of 1.45 percent of the employee's total compensation.[12] Congress increases the Social Security base periodically—in 2022, the base was $147,000; for 2023, the base increased to $160,200.

Employer Payroll Tax	Mr. Duong has a full-time employee, Mrs. Stroh, who manages Mr. Duong's sole proprietorship. Mrs. Stroh's 2023 salary was $165,000, and Mr. Duong's employer payroll tax on this salary was $12,324.

Social Security tax (6.2% × $160,200)	$ 9,932
Medicare tax (1.45% × $165,000)	2,392
Employer payroll tax	$12,324

---

[9] §280A(c)(1).
[10] §280A(c)(5). *Michael H. Visin,* T.C. Memo 2003-246.
[11] §3301.
[12] §3111.

In addition to paying unemployment and payroll taxes, employers must collect the FICA tax levied on their employees.[13] For tax years after 2012, this **employee payroll tax** is computed in exactly the same manner as the employer payroll tax.

Employee Payroll Tax Withholding	Based on the facts in the preceding example, Mrs. Stroh's 2023 employee payroll tax was $12,324.[14]

Social Security tax (6.2% × $160,200)	$ 9,932
Medicare tax (1.45% × $165,000)	2,392
Employee payroll tax	$12,324

Mr. Duong withheld this tax from Mrs. Stroh's salary and remitted it, along with his employer payroll tax to the U.S. Treasury for a total payment of $24,648 ($12,324 employer payroll tax + $12,324 employee payroll tax). Thus, Mr. Duong is the collection agent for the federal government with respect to the employee payroll tax.

Employers should take seriously their responsibility to withhold and remit employee payroll tax. If an employer fails to remit the proper FICA tax for an employee, the federal government may collect both halves of the tax (the employer and the employee portions) from the employer.[15]

Additional Medicare Tax on Employees

Beginning in 2013, individuals whose wages exceed a threshold amount must pay an extra .9 percent Medicare tax on a portion of their wage income, in addition to the 1.45 percent Medicare tax withheld on all wages. The threshold amount for this additional tax is $250,000 for married individuals filing jointly ($125,000 for married filing separately) and $200,000 for unmarried individuals. The .9 percent tax applies only to employees, not employers. In addition, the tax applies only to wage income above the threshold. For joint filers, the additional tax applies to combined wages above the threshold amount.

Additional Medicare Tax on Wages	In 2023, Mr. Ortega earned wage income of $220,000, and his spouse, Mr. Fox, earned wage income of $115,000. On their joint return, they will owe additional Medicare tax on wages of $765 [.9 percent × ($220,000 + $115,000 − $250,000)].

Employers must withhold the additional Medicare tax only after an employee's wages reach $200,000 for the year. However, this withholding may not prove sufficient to cover the tax due, if the employee had additional wage income from another job or the employee's spouse has wage income. Any amount due in excess of withholding will be owed on the tax return when filed. Individuals may wish to request extra income tax withholding by their employer to meet this obligation, or consider this tax in calculating estimated tax payments.

---

[13] §3102.

[14] §3101. The employee payroll tax is nondeductible for federal income tax purposes.

[15] The employer is not technically liable for an employee's payroll tax. However, an employer that fails to "collect, truthfully account for, and pay over" this tax is subject to a penalty equal to 100 percent of such tax. In other words, the penalty on the employer equals the uncollected employee tax. §6672. This penalty has been described as the "iron fist" of the FICA tax system.

Additional Medicare Tax Withholding	As stated previously, in 2023, Mr. Ortega earned wage income of $220,000, and his spouse, Mr. Fox, earned wage income of $115,000. Mr. Ortega's employer will be required to withhold additional Medicare tax of $180 [.9 percent × ($220,000 − $200,000)] on his wages in excess of $200,000. Mr. Fox's employer is not required to withhold this tax because his total wages for the year do not exceed $200,000. The remaining tax not withheld, $585 ($765 − $180), will be owed on their 2023 joint return.

Income Tax Withholding on Employee Compensation

Employers are required to withhold federal income tax (and possibly state income tax) from the compensation paid to their employees.[16] Employers must remit the withholding to the U.S. Treasury periodically throughout the year. The withholding for each employee is based on the information on the employee's Form W-4 (Employee's Withholding Allowance Certificate) and computed by reference to withholding tables provided by the IRS.

Gross and Net Compensation	Refer to the examples *Employer Payroll Tax* and *Employee Payroll Tax Withholding* involving Mr. Duong and Mrs. Stroh. During 2023, Mr. Duong also withheld $22,900 federal income tax from Mrs. Stroh's $165,000 gross salary. Therefore, Mrs. Stroh received only $129,776 after-tax (net) compensation.

Gross salary	$165,000
FICA tax withheld	(12,324)
Federal income tax withheld	(22,900)
Net salary received	$129,776

At the end of each year, employers are required to provide information concerning the gross wages or salary paid to each employee during the year and the payroll and income tax withheld from that gross income. This information is summarized on the familiar Form W-2 (Wage and Tax Statement).

Income Tax Consequences to the Employer

Business organizations can deduct the gross compensation paid to their employees.[17] They can also deduct state and federal unemployment taxes and the employer payroll tax because these taxes are ordinary and necessary expenses incurred in the conduct of an active business.[18] Let's summarize the relationship between these deductible expenses, the employer's withholding requirements, and the net compensation paid to employees by referring again to Mr. Duong's sole proprietorship.

Compensation and Cash Disbursements	For 2023, Mr. Duong deducted $165,000 compensation expense and $12,324 employer payroll tax on that compensation. He withheld $12,324 employee payroll tax and $22,900 income tax from Mrs. Stroh's compensation ($35,224 total) and remitted $47,548 tax to the U.S. Treasury.

(continued)

[16] §3402.

[17] Unless some or all the compensation must be capitalized to inventory under the uniform capitalization (UNICAP) rules discussed in Chapter 7.

[18] See Rev. Rul. 80-164, 1980-1 C.B. 109.

	Deductible Business Expense	Cash Disbursed to:	
		Mrs. Stroh	U.S. Treasury
Salary	$165,000	$129,776	$35,224
Employer FICA tax	12,324		12,324
	$177,324	$129,776	$47,548

Self-Employment Tax

Tax Talk

Recent "tax gap" projections estimate that self-employment tax liability is underreported by as much as $45 billion annually.

While sole proprietors are responsible for collecting and remitting payroll and income taxes from their employees, sole proprietors themselves are not employees and do not receive a salary from the business. Sole proprietors are self-employed and must pay the federal **self-employment (SE) tax** on their business income.[19] Refer to Schedule C in Exhibit 10.2, and note how line 31 instructs the sole proprietor to carry net profit to Schedule SE. The self-employment tax is computed on this schedule and paid along with the individual's income tax for the year. Also note that the self-employment tax base is not reduced by any allowable 20 percent deduction for qualified business income reported by a sole proprietorship.

The SE tax has two components: a Social Security tax of 12.4 percent of a base amount of net earnings from self-employment and a Medicare tax of 2.9 percent of total net earnings. For 2022 and 2023, the Social Security base is $147,000 and $160,200, respectively.

Note that the SE tax rates equal the *combined* employer/employee payroll tax rates, and the Social Security base is the same for both taxes. The SE tax was enacted to complement the FICA tax; the federal government collects the same tax on a sole proprietor's self-employment income as it would collect on an identical amount of compensation. To complete the parallel, sole proprietors can claim as an income tax deduction that portion of the SE tax equivalent to the employer payroll tax. For tax years other than 2011 or 2012, the tax deduction is simply one-half of the SE tax.[20] The CARES Act deferral of the employer portion of the Social Security tax, described above in our discussion of payroll taxes, also applies to this portion of the self-employment tax.

In calculating after-tax business income, sole proprietors must factor in both the income tax and the SE tax levied on that income.

Self-Employment Tax 2023

Mr. Duong's sole proprietorship generated $225,000 net profit in 2023. If his marginal income tax rate is 37 percent, the after-tax income from the business is $136,341.

Schedule C net profit		$225,000
Self-employment tax:		
Self-employment tax base[21]	$207,788	
Social Security tax (12.4% × $160,200)	19,865	
Medicare tax (2.9% × $207,788)	6,026	
Total SE tax		(25,891)

---

[19] §1401. Self-employed individuals are not eligible to receive unemployment benefits and, therefore, are not subject to state and federal unemployment taxes.

[20] §164(f). For 2011 and 2012, the tax deduction equals 59.6 percent of the Social Security tax and 50 percent of the Medicare tax.

[21] The statutory base for the SE tax equals net profit minus a deduction equal to 7.65 percent of such profit. §1402(a)(12). Schedule SE builds this deduction into its computation of net earnings by defining that number as 92.35 percent of Schedule C net profit.

Income tax:		
Schedule C net profit	$225,000	
One-half of self-employment tax	(12,945)	
	$212,055	
20% deduction for qualified business income ($212,055 × 20%)*	(42,411)	
Net profit subject to income tax	$169,644	
	.37	
		(62,768)
After-tax business income		$136,341

* The 20 percent deduction is computed on Mr. Duong's Schedule C net profit, after reduction for the deductible portion of self-employment taxes. The example assumes the taxable income limitation and W-2 wage limitations do not apply. Also note that the 20 percent deduction is not a cash outflow, and therefore does not reduce Mr. Duong's after-tax cash flow.

Note that the SE tax is not a progressive tax because the combined 15.3 percent rate applies to the first dollar of self-employment income. For sole proprietors who earn modest incomes, the SE tax can be a heavier burden than the income tax.

Beginning in 2013, the .9 percent additional Medicare tax also applies to self-employment income when the combination of self-employment income and wages exceeds a threshold amount. The threshold amount for this additional tax is $250,000 for married individuals filing jointly ($125,000 for married filing separately) and $200,000 for unmarried individuals. Unlike the self-employment tax, this additional .9 percent Medicare tax is not deductible for income tax purposes.

Additional Medicare Tax on Self-Employment Income

Recall that Mr. Duong's sole proprietorship generated $225,000 of net profit in 2023, resulting in net earnings from self-employment of $207,788. If Mr. Duong is single and has no wage income, he will owe additional Medicare tax of $70 [.9 percent × ($207,788 − $200,000)]. If Mr. Duong files a joint return with his spouse who has no wage or self-employment income, he owes no additional Medicare tax because his self-employment income is below the $250,000 threshold for married filing jointly.

PARTNERSHIPS

Entrepreneurs who pool their resources by becoming co-owners of a business can organize the business as a partnership. **Partnerships** are unincorporated entities created by contractual agreement among two or more business associates.[22] Such associates can be individuals, corporations, and even other partnerships. All 50 states and the District of Columbia have enacted statutes (generally patterned after the Revised Uniform Partnership Act and the Revised Uniform Limited Partnership Act) to define the characteristics and requirements for partnerships operating within their jurisdiction.

Forming a Partnership

The first step in the formation of a partnership is the drafting of an agreement by the prospective partners.[23] A partnership agreement is a legal contract stipulating both the rights

[22] The term *partnership* encompasses syndicates, groups, pools, joint ventures, or any other unincorporated business organization. §761(a).

[23] See the discussion of organizational and start-up costs in Chapter 7.

Tax Talk

Recent IRS statistics indicate more than 4.7 million partnership returns are filed each year.

and the obligations of the partners and the percentage of profits and losses allocable to each. The agreement gives the partners flexibility to customize their business arrangement to suit their unique situation. The partners can agree to share all profits and losses equally, or they can decide on different sharing ratios for special items of income, gain, deduction, or loss. Ideally, a partnership agreement should be drafted by an attorney, should be in writing, and should be signed by all the partners. However, even oral partnership agreements have been respected as binding contracts by the courts.[24]

A partnership can be a **general partnership** in which all partners have unlimited personal liability for debts incurred by the partnership. Alternatively, a partnership can be a **limited partnership** in which one or more limited partners are liable for partnership debt only to the extent of their capital contributions to the partnership. Limited partnerships must have at least one general partner. The role of a limited partner in partnership activities must be carefully defined to maintain protection from liability for partnership debts. The Revised Uniform Limited Partnership Act (RULPA), adopted by most states, identifies safe harbor activities in which a limited partner may engage without compromising liability protection. Such activities include (1) working for the limited partnership, (2) advising a general partner regarding the partnership business, and (3) voting on partnership matters. Although many limited partners are content to act as passive investors, RULPA permits an expanded role where desired.

Individuals who perform professional services for patients or clients, such as doctors, attorneys, and CPAs, often form **limited liability partnerships (LLPs).** General partners in an LLP are not personally liable for malpractice-related claims arising from the professional negligence of any other partner. However, they are personally liable for other debts of the LLP.[25]

Limited Liability Partnership	Doctors Jeff Batson, Susan Li, and Cary Chen formed an LLP to conduct their medical practice. The three doctors are general partners. This year, the LLP is the defendant in two lawsuits. The first lawsuit was initiated by a former LLP employee who claims that she was fired from her job because of age discrimination. Consequently, the ex-employee is suing the LLP for $600,000 damages. The second lawsuit was initiated by the family of a patient who died shortly after Dr. Chen performed a routine surgical procedure. Because the family believes that Dr. Chen was grossly negligent, it is suing the LLP for $1.2 million in damages. If the LLP loses the first lawsuit, the three general partners are personally liable for any portion of the $600,000 settlement not covered by the LLP's insurance. If the LLP loses the second lawsuit, only Dr. Chen is personally liable for any portion of the $1.2 million settlement not covered by the LLP's or his own malpractice insurance.

Limited Liability Companies

LO 10-3
Explain how limited liability companies (LLCs) are treated for federal tax purposes.

Business owners often prefer the partnership form to the corporate form because partnership income is not taxed at the entity level but only at the owner level. The partnership form also provides the greatest flexibility in the manner in which business income can be divided among the co-owners. The major disadvantage of the partnership form is the unlimited personal liability of the general partners for business debt.

---

[24] See, for example, *Elrod,* 87 T.C. 1046 (1986) and *Kuhl* v. *Garner,* 894 p. 2d 525 (Oregon, 1995).

[25] The Big Four public accounting firms are LLPs.

Tax Talk
The Second Circuit Court of Appeals held the owner of a single-member LLC personally liable for the LLC's unpaid payroll tax. The court held that under the check-the-box regulations, the LLC was treated as a "sole proprietorship" for federal tax purposes and "disregarded as an entity separate from its owner." The court rejected the taxpayer's argument that the regulations wrongfully ignored the limited liability provided to LLC owners under state law. McNamee v. U.S., 99 AFTR 2d 2007-2871 (CA-2, 2007).

Every state (and the District of Columbia) permits business owners to organize as a **limited liability company (LLC)** as an alternative to a general or limited partnership. An LLC is an unincorporated legal entity owned by one or more *members*. In contrast to a partnership, every member has limited liability for the LLC's debts. This limited liability protects even those members who are actively involved in the LLC's business. State laws do not limit the number of members or the type of entity that can be a member in an LLC. Thus, an LLC's membership can include individuals, partnerships, corporations, and even other LLCs.

Under Treasury regulations that classify business entities for federal tax purposes (the check-the-box regulations), an LLC with two or more members is classified as a partnership.[26] Consequently, income earned by an LLC is not taxed at the entity level but passes through to the various members. An LLC with only one member (i.e., one owner) is a *disregarded entity* for federal tax purposes. If the single member is an individual, the LLC is treated as a sole proprietorship. If the single member is an entity, the LLC is treated as a division or branch of the entity.

LLCs offer business owners a terrific combination: one owner-level tax on income and limited liability for business debt. Moreover, LLCs are not subject to many of the bothersome restrictions that apply to S corporations. As a result, LLCs are an attractive option for business ventures.

One major unresolved issue is the extent to which members are subject to self-employment tax on their LLC income. The self-employment tax statute was written before the advent of LLCs and is silent as to whether distributive shares of LLC business income are net earnings from self-employment. In 1997, the Treasury attempted to resolve this issue through proposed regulations.[27] The regulations contain elaborate rules for determining whether an LLC member may be regarded as a limited partner. If so, the member's share of LLC income is not self-employment income. If a member may not be regarded as a limited partner, both guaranteed payments and any share of LLC income are self-employment income. The tax professional community's reaction to these proposed regulations was extremely critical. Congress responded to the criticism by issuing a moratorium that prevented the Treasury from finalizing the 1997 regulations. To date, the Treasury has declined to make a second attempt to resolve this issue.

Self-Employment Income or Not?	Danika Miller is a member in Wooster LLC. She does not work for Wooster on a daily basis and does not receive guaranteed payments. However, last year she worked about 175 hours during October and November on a special marketing campaign for Wooster. Ms. Miller's share of Wooster's ordinary business income last year was $38,170. Because she is not involved in Wooster's business on a regular basis, Ms. Miller could argue that she should be regarded as a limited partner and should not pay SE tax on her share of LLC income. However, the IRS could argue that Ms. Miller did perform substantial personal services for the LLC and therefore should treat her LLC income as earned income subject to SE tax.

Tax Basis in Partnership Interests

Partnerships are both legal entities (title to property can be held and conveyed in the partnership name) and accounting entities (financial books and records are maintained by the partnership). An equity interest in a partnership is an intangible asset, the value of which depends on the underlying value of the partnership business. Partnership interests are considered illiquid assets because partnership agreements usually prevent partners from

---

[26] Reg. §301.7701-3(b)(1). Under this regulation, an LLC can elect to be classified as a corporation for federal tax purposes. There is no obvious reason a domestic LLC would make such an election.

[27] Prop. Reg. §1.1402(a)-2(h).

disposing of their interests without the consent of the other partners. A partner's initial tax basis in a partnership interest equals the cash plus the adjusted basis of any property transferred to the partnership in exchange for the equity interest.[28]

As legal entities, partnerships can borrow money in their own name. Nonetheless, general partners have unlimited liability for repayment of debt to the partnership's creditors. If the partnership business does not generate enough cash to service its debts, the general partners must contribute funds to satisfy any unpaid liabilities.[29] As a result, a partner's economic investment consists of the initial investment of cash or property *plus* the share of partnership debt for which the partner may ultimately be responsible. The tax law acknowledges this responsibility by providing that a partner's share of partnership debt is included in the basis in their partnership interest.[30]

Basis in Partnership Interest	Three individuals each contributed $10,000 cash to a new partnership in which they are equal general partners. The partnership immediately borrowed $24,000 from a local bank and used the money to purchase equipment and supplies. Each partner's basis in his partnership interest is $18,000: the initial cash contribution plus an equal share of partnership debt.[31]

Partnership Reporting Requirements

LO 10-4

Explain the flow-through of partnership items to the partners.

The Internal Revenue Code states that "a partnership as such shall not be subject to the income tax. . . . Persons carrying on a business as partners shall be liable for income tax only in their separate or individual capacities."[32] Although partnerships are not taxable entities, they are required to file an annual Form 1065 (U.S. Partnership Return of Income) with the IRS.[33]

The taxable income generated by partnership activities is measured and characterized at the entity level. All items of gross income and deduction relating strictly to business operations are reported on page 1 of Form 1065. The net of these items is reported on line 22 as ordinary income or loss. This income or loss is allocated among the partners according to the sharing ratio specified in the partnership agreement. The partners report their share of income or loss on their respective returns and include it in the calculation of taxable income. Accordingly, net profit from a partnership business is taxed directly to the partners; the tax rate depends on whether the partner is an individual or a corporation.[34] Because partnerships serve only as conduits of income, they are described as **passthrough entities.**

---

[28] The exchange of property for a partnership interest is nontaxable to both the partner and the partnership (§721). See the discussion of partnership formations in Chapter 9.

[29] In this respect, a general partner's risk with respect to the partnership business is equivalent to a sole proprietor's business risk.

[30] §752(a).

[31] The regulatory rules for calculating a partner's share of partnership debt are extremely complex. The simplest summary of these rules is that recourse debt is shared only by general partners on the basis of their relative loss-sharing ratios and nonrecourse debt is shared by all partners on the basis of their profit-sharing ratios. Regs. §1.752-2 and §1.752-3.

[32] 26 U.S. Code §701.

[33] As a general rule, partnerships are required to use the same taxable year as that used by their partners. Under this rule, a partnership consisting of individual partners who are calendar-year taxpayers files its Form 1065 on a calendar year basis. §706(b).

[34] If partnership income is allocated to a partner that is a passthrough entity (another partnership, LLC, or S corporation), the income is passed through again until it is finally allocated to a taxable entity (an individual or corporation).

Faux Antiques–Partnership	Refer to our earlier example in which Mr. Tom Owen operates a furniture business (Faux Antiques) as a sole proprietorship. Let's change the facts by assuming that Mr. Owen and two co-owners organized Faux Antiques as a partnership. Mr. Owen owns a 60 percent equity interest as a general partner. Faux Antiques generated $304,900 ordinary business income for 2022. Page 1 of the partnership's Form 1065 is shown as Exhibit 10.3.

Partnerships frequently recognize items of income, gain, expense, or loss that don't relate to business operations. For example, a partnership might invest excess cash in marketable securities that pay dividends and interest. The partnership might recognize gain or loss on the sale of one of these securities. Or the partnership could make a contribution to a

EXHIBIT 10.3

Internal Revenue Service

Form 1065 — U.S. Return of Partnership Income

OMB No. 1545-0123

2022

For calendar year 2022, or tax year beginning _____, 2022, ending _____, 20 ____

Go to www.irs.gov/Form1065 for instructions and the latest information.

Department of the Treasury Internal Revenue Service

A Principal business activity: Manufacturing
B Principal product or service: Furniture
C Business code number: 337000

Name of partnership: **Faux Antiques**
Number, street, and room or suite no. If a P.O. box, see instructions. **1012 East Main**
City or town, state or province, country, and ZIP or foreign postal code **Widener, NY 42714**

Type or Print

D Employer identification number: **81-1138419**
E Date business started: **February 1, 1990**
F Total assets (see instructions): $ **1,136,460**

G Check applicable boxes: (1) ☐ Initial return (2) ☐ Final return (3) ☐ Name change (4) ☐ Address change (5) ☐ Amended return
H Check accounting method: (1) ☐ Cash (2) ☑ Accrual (3) ☐ Other (specify): _____
I Number of Schedules K-1. Attach one for each person who was a partner at any time during the tax year: **2**
J Check if Schedules C and M-3 are attached ☐
K Check if partnership: (1) ☐ Aggregated activities for section 465 at-risk purposes (2) ☐ Grouped activities for section 469 passive activity purposes

Caution: Include **only** trade or business income and expenses on lines 1a through 22 below. See instructions for more information.

Income

1a	Gross receipts or sales	1a	1,117,300	
b	Returns and allowances	1b	21,000	
c	Balance. Subtract line 1b from line 1a		1c	1,096,300
2	Cost of goods sold (attach Form 1125-A)		2	599,700
3	Gross profit. Subtract line 2 from line 1c		3	496,800
4	Ordinary income (loss) from other partnerships, estates, and trusts (attach statement)		4	
5	Net farm profit (loss) (attach Schedule F (Form 1040))		5	
6	Net gain (loss) from Form 4797, Part II, line 17 (attach Form 4797)		6	
7	Other income (loss) (attach statement)		7	
8	**Total income (loss).** Combine lines 3 through 7		8	496,800

Deductions (see instructions for limitations)

9	Salaries and wages (other than to partners) (less employment credits)		9	73,200
10	Guaranteed payments to partners		10	
11	Repairs and maintenance		11	17,900
12	Bad debts		12	8,800
13	Rent		13	23,200
14	Taxes and licenses		14	11,750
15	Interest (see instructions)		15	7,300
16a	Depreciation (if required, attach Form 4562)	16a	3,600	
b	Less depreciation reported on Form 1125-A and elsewhere on return	16b		16c	
17	Depletion (**Do not deduct oil and gas depletion.**)		17	
18	Retirement plans, etc.		18	
19	Employee benefit programs		19	
20	Other deductions (attach statement)		20	45,960
21	**Total deductions.** Add the amounts shown in the far right column for lines 9 through 20		21	191,700
22	**Ordinary business income (loss).** Subtract line 21 from line 8		22	304,900

Tax and Payment

23	Interest due under the look-back method—completed long-term contracts (attach Form 8697)	23	
24	Interest due under the look-back method—income forecast method (attach Form 8866)	24	
25	BBA AAR imputed underpayment (see instructions)	25	
26	Other taxes (see instructions)	26	
27	**Total balance due.** Add lines 23 through 26	27	
28	Payment (see instructions)	28	
29	**Amount owed.** If line 28 is smaller than line 27, enter amount owed	29	
30	**Overpayment.** If line 28 is larger than line 27, enter overpayment	30	

Sign Here

Under penalties of perjury, I declare that I have examined this return, including accompanying schedules and statements, and to the best of my knowledge and belief, it is true, correct, and complete. Declaration of preparer (other than partner or limited liability company member) is based on all information of which preparer has any knowledge.

Signature of partner or limited liability company member _____ Date _____

May the IRS discuss this return with the preparer shown below? See instructions. ☐ Yes ☐ No

Paid Preparer Use Only

Print/Type preparer's name	Preparer's signature	Date	Check ☐ if self-employed	PTIN
Firm's name			Firm's EIN	
Firm's address			Phone no.	

For Paperwork Reduction Act Notice, see separate instructions. Cat. No. 11390Z Form **1065** (2022)

local charity. These items are not included in the calculation of ordinary business income or loss. Instead, they are reported on Schedule K of Form 1065 and allocated to the partners for inclusion on the partners' returns.[35] These **separately stated items** retain their tax character as they pass through to the partners.[36]

Separately Stated Items	For several years, Faux Antiques partnership invested its excess cash in a mutual fund. In 2022, the partnership received a $1,680 ordinary dividend from the fund and recognized a $3,710 capital gain on a sale of fund shares. During 2022, Faux Antiques made a $3,000 donation to the United Way and distributed $250,000 cash to its partners. The dividend, capital gain, donation, and distribution were not included in the computation of ordinary business income. Instead, these items were separately stated on Schedule K of Form 1065, which is shown in Exhibit 10.4.

EXHIBIT 10.4

Internal Revenue Service

Form 1065 (2022)   Page **4**

Schedule K	Partners' Distributive Share Items			Total amount
Income (Loss)	1	Ordinary business income (loss) (page 1, line 22)	1	304,900
	2	Net rental real estate income (loss) (attach Form 8825)	2	
	3a	Other gross rental income (loss) 3a		
	b	Expenses from other rental activities (attach statement) 3b		
	c	Other net rental income (loss). Subtract line 3b from line 3a	3c	
	4	Guaranteed payments: a Services **4a** b Capital **4b**		
		c Total. Add lines 4a and 4b	4c	
	5	Interest income	5	
	6	Dividends and dividend equivalents: a Ordinary dividends	6a	1,680
		b Qualified dividends **6b** 1,680 c Dividend equivalents **6c**		
	7	Royalties	7	
	8	Net short-term capital gain (loss) (attach Schedule D (Form 1065))	8	
	9a	Net long-term capital gain (loss) (attach Schedule D (Form 1065))	9a	3,710
	b	Collectibles (28%) gain (loss) 9b		
	c	Unrecaptured section 1250 gain (attach statement) 9c		
	10	Net section 1231 gain (loss) (attach Form 4797)	10	
	11	Other income (loss) (see instructions) Type:	11	
Deductions	12	Section 179 deduction (attach Form 4562)	12	
	13a	Contributions	13a	3,000
	b	Investment interest expense	13b	
	c	Section 59(e)(2) expenditures: **(1)** Type: **(2)** Amount:	13c(2)	
	d	Other deductions (see instructions) Type:	13d	
Self-Employ-ment	14a	Net earnings (loss) from self-employment	14a	304,900
	b	Gross farming or fishing income	14b	
	c	Gross nonfarm income	14c	
Credits	15a	Low-income housing credit (section 42(j)(5))	15a	
	b	Low-income housing credit (other)	15b	
	c	Qualified rehabilitation expenditures (rental real estate) (attach Form 3468, if applicable)	15c	
	d	Other rental real estate credits (see instructions) Type:	15d	
	e	Other rental credits (see instructions) Type:	15e	
	f	Other credits (see instructions) Type:	15f	
Inter-national	16	Attach Schedule K-2 (Form 1065), Partners' Distributive Share Items—International, and check this box to indicate that you are reporting items of international tax relevance ☐		
Alternative Minimum Tax (AMT) Items	17a	Post-1986 depreciation adjustment	17a	
	b	Adjusted gain or loss	17b	
	c	Depletion (other than oil and gas)	17c	
	d	Oil, gas, and geothermal properties—gross income	17d	
	e	Oil, gas, and geothermal properties—deductions	17e	
	f	Other AMT items (attach statement)	17f	
Other Information	18a	Tax-exempt interest income	18a	
	b	Other tax-exempt income	18b	
	c	Nondeductible expenses	18c	
	19a	Distributions of cash and marketable securities	19a	250,000
	b	Distributions of other property	19b	
	20a	Investment income	20a	1,680
	b	Investment expenses	20b	
	c	Other items and amounts (attach statement)		
	21	Total foreign taxes paid or accrued	21	

Form **1065** (2022)

[35] More specifically, Reg. §1.702-1(a)(8)(ii) explains that each partner must be able to take into account separately their distributive share of any partnership item that results in an income tax liability different from that which would result if the item were not accounted for separately.

[36] §702(b).

Tax Consequences to Partners

Distributive Shares and Cash Flows

LO 10-5

Differentiate between a distributive share of partnership income and cash flow.

After the close of its taxable year, a partnership issues a Schedule K-1 (Partner's Share of Income, Credits, Deductions, etc.) to each partner. Schedule K-1 provides detailed information concerning the partner's **distributive share** of the partnership's ordinary business income or loss and any separately stated items. The instructions to the schedule tell individual partners how and where to include each item on their tax return. For instance, a partner's distributive share of ordinary income or loss is reported on Schedule E of Form 1040.

Partners must pay tax on their distributive share of partnership taxable income, regardless of the cash flow from the partnership during the year. In an extreme case, partners may decide to retain all available cash in the partnership. As a result, each partner must find another source of funds to pay the tax on their share of partnership income. Alternatively, partners may decide to withdraw enough cash to pay their taxes. Another possibility is that the partners withdraw all available cash for personal consumption. The important point is that the cash flow is irrelevant in determining the partners' taxable income.

Schedule K-1 for Partner

Each partner in Faux Antiques received a 2022 Schedule K-1 showing a distributive share of ordinary business income, dividend income, capital gain, donation, and cash distribution. Tom Owen's Schedule K-1, which reflects his 60 percent share of each partnership item, is shown in Exhibit 10.5. Mr. Owen reported his $182,940 share of Faux Antiques' business income as ordinary income on his Form 1040. He reported his $1,008 share of dividend income as investment income and his $2,226 share of capital gain as capital gain on his Form 1040. He included his $1,800 share of Faux Antiques' donation in his total personal charitable contributions for 2022.[37] His $150,000 share of the cash distribution had no effect on his 2022 taxable income.

Guaranteed Payments

The personal involvement of individual partners in the partnership business can vary greatly across partners. Limited partners, by definition, do not actively participate in the day-to-day operation of the business and, at most, may take part in major management decisions. General partners may have different levels of participation; some may be sporadically involved, while others may devote 100 percent of their workweek to the business.

Partners who work for the partnership on a continual basis expect to be compensated. These partners typically receive **guaranteed payments** from the partnership based on the value of their work. Guaranteed payments to partners are analogous to the salaries paid to partnership employees. The partnership deducts guaranteed payments in computing ordinary income, and partners report guaranteed payments as ordinary income.[38] However, partners can't be employees of their partnerships any more than individuals can be employees of their sole

---

[37] The tax consequences of personal charitable contributions are discussed in Chapter 17.

[38] §707(c).

EXHIBIT 10.5

Internal Revenue Service

651121

☐ Final K-1	☐ Amended K-1

OMB No. 1545-0123

Schedule K-1
(Form 1065)
Department of the Treasury
Internal Revenue Service

2022

For calendar year 2022, or tax year

beginning ___ / ___ / **2022**   ending ___ / ___ / ___

Partner's Share of Income, Deductions, Credits, etc.   See separate instructions.

Part III	**Partner's Share of Current Year Income, Deductions, Credits, and Other Items**

No.	Item	Amount	No.	Item	Amount
1	Ordinary business income (loss)	182,940	14	Self-employment earnings (loss)	182,940
2	Net rental real estate income (loss)				
3	Other net rental income (loss)		15	Credits	
4a	Guaranteed payments for services				
4b	Guaranteed payments for capital		16	Schedule K-3 is attached if checked . . . . . ☐	
4c	Total guaranteed payments		17	Alternative minimum tax (AMT) items	
5	Interest income				
6a	Ordinary dividends	1,008			
6b	Qualified dividends	1,008	18	Tax-exempt income and nondeductible expenses	
6c	Dividend equivalents				
7	Royalties				
8	Net short-term capital gain (loss)				
9a	Net long-term capital gain (loss)	2,226	19	Distributions A	150,000
9b	Collectibles (28%) gain (loss)				
9c	Unrecaptured section 1250 gain		20	Other information A	Inv Inc 1,008
10	Net section 1231 gain (loss)				
11	Other income (loss)				
12	Section 179 deduction		21	Foreign taxes paid or accrued	
13	Other deductions				

Part I   Information About the Partnership

A   Partnership's employer identification number
81-1138419

B   Partnership's name, address, city, state, and ZIP code

Faux Antiques
1012 East Main
Widener, NY 42714

C   IRS center where partnership filed return: Cincinnati

D   ☐ Check if this is a publicly traded partnership (PTP)

Part II   Information About the Partner

E   Partner's SSN or TIN (Do not use TIN of a disregarded entity. See instructions.)
498-45-9058

F   Name, address, city, state, and ZIP code for partner entered in E. See instructions.

Tom G. Owen
330 Aspen Lane
Widener, NY 42714

G   ☒ General partner or LLC member-manager   ☐ Limited partner or other LLC member

H1   ☒ Domestic partner   ☐ Foreign partner

H2   ☐ If the partner is a disregarded entity (DE), enter the partner's:
TIN _____   Name _____

I1   What type of entity is this partner? _____

I2   If this partner is a retirement plan (IRA/SEP/Keogh/etc.), check here . ☐

J   Partner's share of profit, loss, and capital (see instructions):

	Beginning	Ending
Profit	60 %	60 %
Loss	60 %	60 %
Capital	60 %	60 %

Check if decrease is due to sale or exchange of partnership interest . . ☐

K   Partner's share of liabilities:

	Beginning	Ending
Nonrecourse . . $		$
Qualified nonrecourse financing . . . $	13,612	$ 13,612
Recourse . . . $	21,050	$ 21,050

Check this box if item K includes liability amounts from lower-tier partnerships ☐

L   **Partner's Capital Account Analysis**

Beginning capital account . . . $	25,000
Capital contributed during the year . . $	
Current year net income (loss) . . . $	184,374
Other increase (decrease) (attach explanation) $	
Withdrawals and distributions . . . $ (	150,000)
Ending capital account . . . . $	59,374

M   Did the partner contribute property with a built-in gain (loss)?
☐ Yes   ☒ No   If "Yes," attach statement. See instructions.

N   Partner's Share of Net Unrecognized Section 704(c) Gain or (Loss)
Beginning . . . . $
Ending . . . . $

22	☐ More than one activity for at-risk purposes*
23	☐ More than one activity for passive activity purposes*

*See attached statement for additional information.

For IRS Use Only

For Paperwork Reduction Act Notice, see the Instructions for Form 1065.   www.irs.gov/Form1065   Cat. No. 11394R   **Schedule K-1 (Form 1065) 2022**

proprietorships. Because a guaranteed payment is not a salary, neither the partnership nor the partner pays FICA payroll tax. Nor does the partnership withhold any federal income tax from the guaranteed payment. If a partner earns a $10,000 monthly guaranteed payment, that partner receives $10,000 cash each month. At the end of the year, the partnership does not issue a Form W-2 to the partner. Instead, the total guaranteed payments are reported as an ordinary income item on the partner's Schedule K-1.

Self-Employment Income

Individual general partners are considered to be self-employed. Consequently, any guaranteed payments plus their distributive share of ordinary business income are net earnings from self-employment subject to SE tax and the .9 percent additional Medicare tax.[39] Limited partners are not considered self-employed and are not required to pay self-employment tax on their distributive share of ordinary income.[40]

Self-Employment Income	Refer to Mr. Owen's Schedule K-1 from the Faux Antiques partnership (Exhibit 10.5). Line 14 shows that Mr. Owen's $182,940 distributive share of business income represents net earnings from self-employment. Mr. Owen must report these earnings on a Schedule SE and compute his SE tax accordingly.

QBI Deduction and Excess Business Loss Limitation

Partners who are not corporations may be eligible for the QBI deduction with respect to qualified business income earned through a partnership. This deduction is computed by the partner, not by the partnership. However, the partnership is required to report to its partners the information needed to make the computation. Specifically, each partner will need their share of qualified business income, W-2 wages, and the unadjusted basis of qualified property held by the partnership.

Noncorporate partners must also apply the excess business loss limitation to their share of any business losses flowing through from a partnership. As discussed in Chapter 6 and earlier in this chapter in connection with sole proprietorships, aggregate 2023 business losses in excess of $578,000 (married filing jointly) or $289,000 (all other individuals) are not currently deductible. Instead, such excess losses carry forward as part of the taxpayer's NOL carryforward. The limitation is applied by each noncorporate partner, not by the partnership.

We should emphasize that the QBI deduction and the excess business loss limitation are partner-level computations, not partnership allocations. As such, these items do not affect the partner's basis in their partnership interest.

Partnership Losses and Excess Business Loss Limitation	Fatima Gupta is a partner in two partnerships. This year, Ms. Gupta's share of Partnership N's ordinary business income is $193,000. Partnership Q allocated Ms. Gupta $(500,000) of ordinary business loss. If Ms. Gupta is single, her excess business loss of $(18,000) ($193,000 − $500,000 + $289,000 single threshold) is not currently deductible. If Ms. Gupta is married and files a joint return, her loss deduction is not limited. Her net partnership loss of $(307,000) is fully deductible against other sources of income.

Comprehensive Example

To summarize our discussion of the tax consequences of partnerships, consider the case of ABC Partnership. This business is owned by three individual partners. Ms. Aziz and Mr. Bach are general partners who work in the business, and Ms. Cho is a limited partner. The partnership agreement provides that Ms. Aziz and Mr. Bach are each allocated 40 percent of income or loss, while Ms. Cho is allocated the remaining 20 percent. ABC pays a $3,000

[39] §1402(a).
[40] §1402(a)(13).

monthly guaranteed payment to Ms. Aziz and a $1,100 monthly guaranteed payment to Mr. Bach. For 2020, ABC's ordinary business income (after deducting the guaranteed payments) was $90,800. ABC also earned $3,300 interest income from a mutual bond fund investment. On December 24, ABC distributed $20,000 cash to its partners ($8,000 to Ms. Aziz and Mr. Bach and $4,000 to Ms. Cho). ABC reported the following information on each partner's 2020 Schedule K-1:

ABC Partnership 2020 Schedule K-1s			
	Ms. Aziz	**Mr. Bach**	**Ms. Cho**
Guaranteed payments	$36,000	$ 13,200	–0–
Distributive shares:			
Ordinary business income	36,320	36,320	$18,160
Interest income	1,320	1,320	660
Net earnings from self-employment	72,320	49,520	–0–
Cash distribution	8,000	8,000	4,000

The partners included their guaranteed payments and their share of business and interest income in taxable income, and Ms. Aziz and Mr. Bach paid SE tax on their net earnings from self-employment. Assuming that Ms. Aziz was in a 28 percent marginal tax bracket and both Mr. Bach and Ms. Cho were in a 31 percent marginal tax bracket, each partner's after-tax cash flow from ABC is computed as follows:

ABC Partner Cash Flows			
	Ms. Aziz	**Mr. Bach**	**Ms. Cho**
Guaranteed payments	$36,000	$ 13,200	–0–
Cash distribution	8,000	8,000	$ 4,000
SE tax*	(10,218)	(6,997)	–0–
Income tax	(17,441)	(12,641)	(4,708)
After-tax cash flow	$16,341	$ 1,562	$ (708)
Income tax calculation:			
Guaranteed payments	$36,000	$ 13,200	–0–
Ordinary business income	36,320	36,320	$18,160
Interest income	1,320	1,320	660
One-half SE tax	(5,109)	(3,499)	–0–
QBI deduction†	(6,242)	(6,564)	(3,632)
Taxable income	$62,289	$ 40,777	$15,188
	.28	.31	.31
Income tax	$17,441	$ 12,641	$ 4,708

* Self-employment tax based on 92.35 percent of net earnings from self-employment. See footnote 21. Net earnings from self-employment as reported on Schedule K-1 are computed without regard to this reduction.

† QBI deduction equals 20 percent of ordinary business income reduced by the deductible portion of SE tax. This example assumes that the taxable income and wage limitations do not apply.

Ms. Aziz had positive cash flow from the partnership, but both Mr. Bach and Ms. Cho had negative cash flows. This cash flow information reflects the fact that the three partners paid tax on partnership profits that they did not withdraw as cash from the business.

Adjusting the Basis of a Partnership Interest

LO 10-6

Adjust the tax basis in a partnership interest.

When a partner is allocated a share of partnership income but does not receive a cash distribution of that income, the partner is making an additional investment in the partnership. The partner should be entitled to recover this investment tax-free at some future date. When a partner receives a cash distribution, the distribution is treated as a nontaxable return of investment.[41] These investment increases and decreases are captured as positive and negative year-end adjustments to the tax basis in the partner's interest in the partnership.[42] Finally, note that guaranteed payments, self-employment taxes, and the QBI deduction have no impact on a partner's basis in their partnership interest.

Let's continue the comprehensive example by computing the ABC partners' basis adjustments for 2020. The partner's initial basis on January 1, 2020, carries forward from 2019 and is assumed to be as follows:

ABC Partner Basis Adjustments for 2020*			
	Ms. Aziz	Mr. Bach	Ms. Cho
Adjusted basis on January 1	$35,000	$60,000	$100,000
Increased by:			
Ordinary business income	36,320	36,320	18,160
Interest income	1,320	1,320	660
Decreased by:			
Cash distribution	(8,000)	(8,000)	(4,000)
Adjusted basis on December 31	$64,640	$89,640	$114,820

* This comprehensive example ignores any changes in partnership liabilities that would affect the partners' basis.

When a partnership generates an ordinary business loss or a separately stated loss, each partner's share of the loss represents a decrease in the partner's investment that is captured as a negative basis adjustment. Year-end basis adjustments for losses are made after any adjustments for income items or cash distributions.[43]

To illustrate the negative basis adjustment for losses, assume that ABC Partnership generated a $99,200 operating loss (after deducting Ms. Aziz's and Mr. Bach's guaranteed payments) in 2021. ABC earned $2,400 interest income and recognized a $19,600 capital loss on the sale of mutual fund shares. The partnership made no cash distributions to its partners. ABC reported the following information on each partner's 2021 Schedule K-1:

ABC Partnership 2021 Schedule K-1s			
	Ms. Aziz	Mr. Bach	Ms. Cho
Guaranteed payments	$36,000	$13,200	–0–
Distributive shares:			
Ordinary business loss	(39,680)	(39,680)	$(19,840)
Interest income	960	960	480
Capital loss	(7,840)	(7,840)	(3,920)
Net earnings from self-employment	(3,680)	(26,480)	–0–
Cash distribution	–0–	–0–	–0–

[41] §731(a) and §733. If a partner receives a cash distribution that exceeds the partner's basis, the excess distribution is recognized as capital gain.

[42] §705(a). Basis is also increased for a partner's distributive share of tax-exempt income.

[43] Reg. §1.705-1(a). Basis is also decreased by a partner's distributive share of nondeductible expenses.

The partners included their guaranteed payments and their share of interest income in taxable income. They also deducted their share of ordinary business loss and included their share of ABC's capital loss in their net capital gain or loss for 2021.[44] Because Ms. Aziz and Mr. Bach had negative earnings from self-employment, they paid no SE tax for the year.

ABC Partner Basis Adjustments for 2021			
	Ms. Aziz	Mr. Bach	Ms. Cho
Adjusted basis on January 1	$64,640	$ 89,640	$114,820
Increased by:			
Interest income	960	960	480
Decreased by:			
Ordinary business loss	(39,680)	(39,680)	(19,840)
Capital loss	(7,840)	(7,840)	(3,920)
Adjusted basis on December 31	$18,080	$ 43,080	$ 91,540

Basis Limitation on Loss Deductions

LO 10-7

Apply the basis limitation on the deduction of partnership losses.

As a general rule, partners may deduct their distributive share of partnership losses for the year. However, they must reduce the basis in their partnership interest by their share of losses, and the basis cannot be reduced below zero. If a partner's share of losses exceeds basis, the excess is not deductible in the current year.[45] The partner can carry the nondeductible loss forward indefinitely and can deduct it in a future year in which basis in the partnership interest is restored.

Suppose that ABC Partnership had another bad year in 2022. The partnership did not make any guaranteed payments to Ms. Aziz or Mr. Bach. Even with this frugality, ABC's business generated a $160,000 operating loss. ABC did earn $3,000 interest income from its mutual fund and reported the following information on each partner's 2022 Schedule K-1:

ABC Partnership 2022 Schedule K-1s			
	Ms. Aziz	Mr. Bach	Ms. Cho
Guaranteed payments	–0–	–0–	–0–
Distributive shares:			
Ordinary business loss	$ (64,000)	$ (64,000)	$ (32,000)
Interest income	1,200	1,200	600
Net earnings from self-employment	(64,000)	(64,000)	–0–
Cash distribution	–0–	–0–	–0–

Ms. Aziz's and Mr. Bach's deduction for their share of loss is limited to the adjusted basis in their partnership interest immediately before the negative basis adjustment for the loss.

---

[44] This example assumes that the §465 at-risk limitation and the §469 passive activity loss limitation are inapplicable for all three partners. These limitations are discussed in Chapter 16. Each partner would also include their allocable loss from ABC in applying the excess business loss limitation discussed earlier in this chapter.

[45] §704(d).

ABC Partner Basis Adjustments for 2022			
	Ms. Aziz	**Mr. Bach**	**Ms. Cho**
Adjusted basis on January 1	$ 18,080	$ 43,080	$91,540
Increased by:			
Interest income	1,200	1,200	600
Decreased by:			
Deductible loss	(19,280)	(44,280)	(32,000)
Adjusted basis on December 31	–0–	–0–	$60,140
Nondeductible loss carryforward	$(44,720)	$(19,720)	–0–

In 2022, all three partners must include their share of ABC's interest income in taxable income. Ms. Cho can deduct her entire $32,000 share of ABC's ordinary business loss. Ms. Aziz can deduct only $19,280, and Mr. Bach can deduct only $44,280 of their share of loss. Ms. Aziz and Mr. Bach can carry their nondeductible loss into future taxable years, but they must restore basis in their partnership interests to deduct the carryforward. These partners could easily create basis by investing more money in ABC Partnership. But if the partnership's business is failing (as the 2021 and 2022 losses suggest), Ms. Aziz and Mr. Bach could lose their additional investment. In such a case, they would have made the mistake of throwing good money after bad to secure a tax deduction. Of course, if ABC's business becomes profitable again, the partners' shares of future income will create basis against which Ms. Aziz and Mr. Bach can deduct their loss carryforwards.

Let's complete our comprehensive example with one more year of ABC Partnership's operations. In 2023, the partnership generated $64,400 ordinary business income after deducting an $18,000 guaranteed payment to Ms. Aziz and a $6,600 guaranteed payment to Mr. Bach. ABC earned $3,400 interest income and recognized an $11,000 capital gain on the sale of mutual fund shares. ABC reported the following information on each partner's 2023 Schedule K-1:

ABC Partnership 2023 Schedule K-1s			
	Ms. Aziz	**Mr. Bach**	**Ms. Cho**
Guaranteed payments	$18,000	$ 6,600	–0–
Distributive shares:			
Ordinary business income	25,760	25,760	$12,880
Interest income	1,360	1,360	680
Capital gain	4,400	4,400	2,200
Net earnings from self-employment	43,760	32,360	–0–
Cash distribution	–0–	–0–	–0–

The partners included their guaranteed payments and their share of business, interest, and capital gain in taxable income, and Ms. Aziz and Mr. Bach paid SE tax on their net earnings from self-employment. The partners increased the basis in their partnership interests by their share of income, and, as a result, Ms. Aziz could deduct $31,520 and Mr. Bach could deduct $19,720 of their 2021 loss carryforwards in the computation of 2023 taxable income. Ms. Aziz has a $13,200 remaining loss carryforward that she can deduct to the extent of future increases in the basis in her ABC interest.

ABC Partner Basis Adjustments for 2023			
	Ms. Aziz	**Mr. Bach**	**Ms. Cho**
Adjusted basis on January 1	–0–	–0–	$60,140
Increased by:			
Ordinary business income	$25,760	$ 25,760	12,880
Interest income	1,360	1,360	680
Capital gain	4,400	4,400	2,200
	$31,520	$ 31,520	$75,900
Decreased by:			
Deductible loss carryforward	(31,520)	(19,720)	–0–
Adjusted basis on December 31	–0–	$ 11,800	$75,900
Remaining loss carryforward	(13,200)	–0–	–0–

SUBCHAPTER S CORPORATIONS

Tax Talk
Recent IRS statistics indicate that more than 5.3 million S corporation returns are filed each year.

Before the advent of LLCs, business owners who wanted to avoid both the corporate income tax and the risk of unlimited personal liability had only one choice: the **subchapter S corporation.** This form of business organization is a corporate entity, organized as such under state law.[46] A predominant characteristic of corporations is the limited liability of their shareholders. If a corporation gets into financial trouble and can't pay its debts, the corporate creditors have no claim against the personal assets of the shareholders. Thus, the shareholders' risk is limited to their investment in the corporation.

For federal tax purposes, a subchapter S corporation is a passthrough entity; its business income is allocated and taxed directly to the corporation's shareholders.[47] The statutory rules providing for this passthrough are almost identical to the partnership rules. The ordinary income or loss generated by an S corporation's business is reported on page 1 of Form 1120S (U.S. Income Tax Return for an S Corporation). This income or loss is allocated among the shareholders based on their percentage ownership of the corporation's outstanding stock.[48] Recall from our discussion of partnerships that considerable flexibility is allowed in the allocation of income and loss items to partners. This flexibility is not permitted to S corporations and their shareholders. All S corporation allocations are strictly based on percentage ownership of stock.

Faux Antiques—
S Corporation

Refer to our earlier example involving Mr. Tom Owen and his antique furniture restoration business. Let's change the facts again by assuming that Mr. Owen and his two co-owners incorporated the business as Faux Antiques, Inc., which is an S corporation for federal tax purposes. Tom Owen owns 60 percent of the outstanding stock. Faux Antiques, Inc. generated $304,900 ordinary business income in 2022. Page 1 of the S corporation's Form 1120S is shown in Exhibit 10.6.

If an S corporation recognizes items of income, gain, deduction, or loss that don't relate to ordinary business operations, these items are separately stated on Schedule K of Form 1120S and retain their tax character as they flow through to the shareholders.

---

[46] While a partnership must have at least two co-owners as partners, a corporation may be owned by one shareholder.
[47] §1363(a) and §1366.
[48] §1377(a).

EXHIBIT 10.6

Internal Revenue Service

Form **1120-S**	**U.S. Income Tax Return for an S Corporation**	OMB No. 1545-0123
Department of the Treasury Internal Revenue Service	Do not file this form unless the corporation has filed or is attaching Form 2553 to elect to be an S corporation. Go to *www.irs.gov/Form1120S* for instructions and the latest information.	2022

For calendar year 2022 or tax year beginning _____ , 2022, ending _____ , 20 ____

A S election effective date		Name	**D** Employer identification number
February 1, 1990	TYPE OR PRINT	**Faux Antiques**	81-1138419
B Business activity code number (see instructions)		Number, street, and room or suite no. If a P.O. box, see instructions.	**E** Date incorporated
		1012 East Main	**February 1, 1990**
337000		City or town, state or province, country, and ZIP or foreign postal code	**F** Total assets (see instructions)
C Check if Sch. M-3 attached ☐		**Widener, NY 42714**	$ 1,136,640

G   Is the corporation electing to be an S corporation beginning with this tax year? See instructions.   ☐ Yes ☐ No

H   Check if: **(1)** ☐ Final return   **(2)** ☐ Name change   **(3)** ☐ Address change   **(4)** ☐ Amended return   **(5)** ☐ S election termination

I   Enter the number of shareholders who were shareholders during any part of the tax year   . . . . ▸ _____

J   Check if corporation: **(1)** ☐ Aggregated activities for section 465 at-risk purposes   **(2)** ☐ Grouped activities for section 469 passive activity purposes

Caution: Include **only** trade or business income and expenses on lines 1a through 21. See the instructions for more information.

Income	**1a**	Gross receipts or sales	**1a**	1,117,300	
	b	Returns and allowances	**1b**	21,000	
	c	Balance. Subtract line 1b from line 1a		**1c**	1,096,300
	2	Cost of goods sold (attach Form 1125-A)		**2**	599,700
	3	Gross profit. Subtract line 2 from line 1c		**3**	496,600
	4	Net gain (loss) from Form 4797, line 17 (attach Form 4797)		**4**	
	5	Other income (loss) (see instructions—attach statement)		**5**	
	6	**Total income (loss).** Add lines 3 through 5 . . . . ▸		**6**	496,600
Deductions (see instructions for limitations)	**7**	Compensation of officers (see instructions—attach Form 1125-E)		**7**	
	8	Salaries and wages (less employment credits)		**8**	
	9	Repairs and maintenance		**9**	17,900
	10	Bad debts		**10**	8,800
	11	Rents		**11**	23,200
	12	Taxes and licenses		**12**	11,750
	13	Interest (see instructions)		**13**	7,300
	14	Depreciation from Form 4562 not claimed on Form 1125-A or elsewhere on return (attach Form 4562)		**14**	3,600
	15	Depletion **(Do not deduct oil and gas depletion.)**		**15**	
	16	Advertising		**16**	6,200
	17	Pension, profit-sharing, etc., plans		**17**	
	18	Employee benefit programs		**18**	
	19	Other deductions (attach statement)		**19**	39,750
	20	**Total deductions.** Add lines 7 through 19 . . . . ▸		**20**	191,700
	21	**Ordinary business income (loss).** Subtract line 20 from line 6		**21**	304,900
Tax and Payments	**22a**	Excess net passive income or LIFO recapture tax (see instructions) . . .	**22a**		
	b	Tax from Schedule D (Form 1120-S)	**22b**		
	c	Add lines 22a and 22b (see instructions for additional taxes)		**22c**	
	23a	2022 estimated tax payments and 2021 overpayment credited to 2022	**23a**		
	b	Tax deposited with Form 7004	**23b**		
	c	Credit for federal tax paid on fuels (attach Form 4136)	**23c**		
	d	Add lines 23a through 23c		**23d**	
	24	Estimated tax penalty (see instructions). Check if Form 2220 is attached . . . . . ▸ ☐		**24**	
	25	**Amount owed.** If line 23d is smaller than the total of lines 22c and 24, enter amount owed .		**25**	
	26	**Overpayment.** If line 23d is larger than the total of lines 22c and 24, enter amount overpaid . .		**26**	
	27	Enter amount from line 26: **Credited to 2023 estimated tax** _____ Refunded . ▸		**27**	

Sign Here

Under penalties of perjury, I declare that I have examined this return, including accompanying schedules and statements, and to the best of my knowledge and belief, it is true, correct, and complete. Declaration of preparer (other than taxpayer) is based on all information of which preparer has any knowledge.

Signature of officer	Date	Title	May the IRS discuss this return with the preparer shown below? See instructions. ☐ Yes ☐ No

Paid Preparer Use Only

Print/Type preparer's name	Preparer's signature	Date	Check ☐ if self-employed	PTIN
Firm's name ▸			Firm's EIN ▸	
Firm's address ▸			Phone no.	

For Paperwork Reduction Act Notice, see separate instructions.   Cat. No. 11510H   Form **1120-S** (2022)

Separately Stated Items

In 2022, Faux Antiques, Inc. received a $1,680 ordinary dividend from a mutual fund and recognized a $3,710 capital gain on sale of fund shares. During 2022, the corporation made a $3,000 donation to the United Way and distributed $250,000 cash to its shareholders. The dividend, capital gain, donation, and distribution were not included in the computation of ordinary business income. Instead, these items were separately stated on Schedule K of Form 1120S, which is shown in Exhibit 10.7.

EXHIBIT 10.7

Internal Revenue Service

Schedule K		Shareholders' Pro Rata Share Items			Total amount
Income (Loss)	1	Ordinary business income (loss) (page 1, line 21)	1		304,900
	2	Net rental real estate income (loss) (attach Form 8825)	2		
	3a	Other gross rental income (loss)	3a		
	b	Expenses from other rental activities (attach statement) . .	3b		
	c	Other net rental income (loss). Subtract line 3b from line 3a	3c		
	4	Interest income	4		1,680
	5	Dividends: a Ordinary dividends	5a		
		b Qualified dividends	5b		
	6	Royalties	6		
	7	Net short-term capital gain (loss) (attach Schedule D (Form 1120S)) .	7		
	8a	Net long-term capital gain (loss) (attach Schedule D (Form 1120S)) . .	8a		3,710
	b	Collectibles (28%) gain (loss)	8b		
	c	Unrecaptured section 1250 gain (attach statement)	8c		
	9	Net section 1231 gain (loss) (attach Form 4797)	9		
	10	Other income (loss) (see instructions) . . . Type ▶	10		
Deductions	11	Section 179 deduction (attach Form 4562)	11		
	12a	Charitable contributions	12a		3,000
	b	Investment interest expense	12b		
	c	Section 59(e)(2) expenditures (1) Type ▶ _____ (2) Amount ▶	12c(2)		
	d	Other deductions (see instructions) . . . Type ▶	12d		
Credits	13a	Low-income housing credit (section 42(j)(5))	13a		
	b	Low-income housing credit (other)	13b		
	c	Qualified rehabilitation expenditures (rental real estate) (attach Form 3468, if applicable) .	13c		
	d	Other rental real estate credits (see instructions) Type ▶	13d		
	e	Other rental credits (see instructions) . . . Type ▶	13e		
	f	Biofuel producer credit (attach Form 6478)	13f		
	g	Other credits (see instructions) . . . . . Type ▶	13g		
Foreign Transactions	14a	Name of country or U.S. possession ▶ _____			
	b	Gross income from all sources	14b		
	c	Gross income sourced at shareholder level	14c		
		Foreign gross income sourced at corporate level			
	d	Section 951A category	14d		
	e	Foreign branch category	14e		
	f	Passive category	14f		
	g	General category	14g		
	h	Other (attach statement)	14h		
		Deductions allocated and apportioned at shareholder level			
	i	Interest expense	14i		
	j	Other	14j		
		Deductions allocated and apportioned at corporate level to foreign source income			
	k	Section 951A category	14k		
	l	Foreign branch category	14l		
	m	Passive category	14m		
	n	General category	14n		
	o	Other (attach statement)	14o		
		Other information			
	p	Total foreign taxes (check one): ▶ ☐ Paid ☐ Accrued	14p		
	q	Reduction in taxes available for credit (attach statement)	14q		
	r	Other foreign tax information (attach statement)			
Alternative Minimum Tax (AMT) Items	15a	Post-1986 depreciation adjustment	15a		
	b	Adjusted gain or loss	15b		
	c	Depletion (other than oil and gas)	15c		
	d	Oil, gas, and geothermal properties—gross income	15d		
	e	Oil, gas, and geothermal properties—deductions	15e		
	f	Other AMT items (attach statement)	15f		
Items Affecting Shareholder Basis	16a	Tax-exempt interest income	16a		
	b	Other tax-exempt income	16b		
	c	Nondeductible expenses	16c		
	d	Distributions (attach statement if required) (see instructions)	16d		150,000
	e	Repayment of loans from shareholders	16e		
Other Information	17a	Investment income	17a		1,680
	b	Investment expenses	17b		
	c	Dividend distributions paid from accumulated earnings and profits	17c		
	d	Other items and amounts (attach statement)			
Reconciliation	18	**Income/loss reconciliation.** Combine the amounts on lines 1 through 10 in the far right column. From the result, subtract the sum of the amounts on lines 11 through 12d and 14p	18		307,290

Eligible Corporations

LO 10-8
Determine if a corporation is eligible to be an S corporation.

Only domestic corporations formed under the law of one of the 50 states or the District of Columbia are eligible to be S corporations for federal tax purposes. Eligibility is based on three statutory requirements:[49]

1. Only individuals, estates, certain trusts, and tax-exempt organizations may be shareholders, and nonresident aliens (persons who are neither citizens nor permanent residents of the United States) cannot be shareholders. This requirement ensures that the S corporation's income is taxed at the individual rates.

2. The number of shareholders is limited to 100. A family may elect for all family members to be treated as one shareholder.

3. The corporation can have only a single class of outstanding common stock; an S corporation cannot include preferred stock in its capital structure. Because of this requirement, shares of stock in an S corporation carry identical rights to corporate profits and assets. This requirement is not violated if the outstanding shares have different voting rights.

There are no statutory limits on an S corporation's invested capital, volume of sales, or number of employees. Consequently, S corporations can be very large corporate enterprises.

Subchapter S Election

An eligible corporation becomes an S corporation by the unanimous election of its shareholders.[50] The election is permanent for the life of the corporation unless shareholders owning a majority of the stock revoke the election.[51] The election is immediately terminated if the corporation loses its eligibility. For example, if a shareholder sells shares to a partnership (an ineligible shareholder), the election terminates as of the date of sale.[52] The corporation is no longer a passthrough entity and is subject to the corporate income tax.

The inadvertent termination of an S election can be a tax-planning disaster for the shareholders. Moreover, they generally cannot make a new election for five years.[53] Because of the potential severity of the problem, the tax law provides a relief measure. If shareholders discover that an inadvertent termination has occurred and take immediate steps to correct the situation (repurchase the corporate stock from the partnership in our example), the IRS may allow the original S election to remain in effect.[54]

Shareholders of closely held corporations, including S corporations, often enter into shareholder agreements to prevent negative consequences associated with undesirable transfers of stock. Shareholder agreements may provide that the corporation, or other shareholders, has a right of first refusal if one shareholder wants to dispose of their stock. Such an agreement could prevent a transfer to an ineligible shareholder, avoiding an inadvertent termination of the S corporation election.

---

[49] §1361. Corporations that have been operating as regular corporations and that meet the eligibility requirements can be converted to S corporations. Converted S corporations are subject to several troublesome corporate-level taxes that don't apply to original S corporations. See §1374 and §1375. In addition, an LLC that has "checked the box" to be treated as a corporation could also elect S status.

[50] §1362(a). To document consent to the election, each shareholder must file a signed Form 2553 with the IRS.

[51] §1362(d)(1).

[52] §1362(e)(1).

[53] §1362(g).

[54] §1362(f).

Tax Basis in S Corporation Stock

A shareholder's initial tax basis in stock issued by an S corporation equals the cash plus the adjusted basis of any property transferred to the corporation in exchange for the stock.[55] When an S corporation incurs a debt, no shareholder has any personal liability. Accordingly, no S corporation debt is included in a shareholder's stock basis, even if the shareholder has guaranteed the debt.

Basis in S Corporation Stock	Three individuals each contributed $10,000 cash to form a new S corporation. Each individual received 100 shares of the 300 shares of outstanding stock. The S corporation immediately borrowed $24,000 from a local bank and used the money to purchase equipment and supplies. The bank required the shareholders to personally guarantee repayment of the loan. Each shareholder's basis in their S corporation stock is $10,000: the initial cash contribution to the corporation.

Tax Consequences to Shareholders

LO 10-9
Identify similarities and differences in the tax treatment of S corporations versus partnerships.

After the close of its taxable year, an S corporation issues a Schedule K-1 (Shareholder's Share of Income, Credits, Deductions, etc.) to each shareholder. The Schedule K-1 has the same function as a partnership Schedule K-1; it informs the owners of their **pro rata share** of business income or loss and any separately stated items.[56]

The S corporation shareholders must incorporate the information on Schedule K-1 into their individual tax returns. Thus, the corporate income is taxed at the individual rates, and the shareholders pay the tax. The cash (if any) that the shareholders received from the corporation is irrelevant in determining their taxable income.

Schedule K-1 for Shareholder	Each shareholder in Faux Antiques received a 2022 Schedule K-1 showing a pro-rata share of ordinary business income, dividend income, capital gain, donation, and cash distribution. Tom Owen's Schedule K-1, which reflects his 60 percent share of each corporate item, is shown in Exhibit 10.8. Mr. Owen reported his $182,940 share of Faux Antiques' business income as ordinary income on his Form 1040. He reported his $1,008 share of dividend income as investment income and his $2,226 share of capital gain as capital gain on his Form 1040. He included his $1,800 share of Faux Antiques' donation in his total personal charitable contributions for 2022. His $150,000 share of the cash distribution had no effect on his 2022 taxable income.

QBI Deduction and Excess Business Loss Limitation

S corporation shareholders may be eligible for the Section QBI deduction with respect to qualified business income earned through an S corporation. The deduction is computed by the shareholder, not the S corporation. In addition, S corporation shareholders must also apply the excess business loss limitation to their share of any business losses flowing through from an S corporation. This limitation is applied by each shareholder, not by the S corporation.

---

[55] The transfer of property to a corporation in exchange for stock is nontaxable to the transferors if they have at least 80 percent control of the corporation immediately after the transfer. §351. See the discussion of corporate formations in Chapter 9.

[56] As previously discussed, partners are taxed on their distributive share of partnership income. In contrast, S corporation shareholders are taxed on their pro rata share of S corporation income. This difference in terminology is not simply semantics. The partnership allocation rules provide for considerably more flexibility in determining income allocations than the S corporation rules.

EXHIBIT 10.8

Internal Revenue Service

671121

Final K-1 ☐	Amended K-1 ☐	OMB No. 1545-0123

Schedule K-1
(Form 1120-S)
Department of the Treasury
Internal Revenue Service

2022

For calendar year 2022, or tax year

beginning / / 2022   ending / /

Shareholder's Share of Income, Deductions, Credits, etc.   See separate instructions.

Part I	**Information About the Corporation**

A Corporation's employer identification number
81-1138419

B Corporation's name, address, city, state, and ZIP code

Faux Antiques
1012 East Main
Widener, NY 42714

C IRS Center where corporation filed return
Cincinnati

D Corporation's total number of shares
Beginning of tax year 100
End of tax year 100

Part II	**Information About the Shareholder**

E Shareholder's identifying number
487-45-9058

F Shareholder's name, address, city, state, and ZIP code

Tom G. Owen
330 Aspen Lane
Widener, NY 42714

G Current year allocation percentage . . . 60 %

H Shareholder's number of shares
Beginning of tax year 60
End of tax year 60

I Loans from shareholder
Beginning of tax year . . . . . $ _____
End of tax year . . . . $ _____

For IRS Use Only

Part III	**Shareholder's Share of Current Year Income, Deductions, Credits, and Other Items**	
1	Ordinary business income (loss) 182.940	13 Credits
2	Net rental real estate income (loss)	
3	Other net rental income (loss)	
4	Interest income	
5a	Ordinary dividends 1,008	
5b	Qualified dividends 1,008	14 Schedule K-3 is attached if checked . . . . . ☐
6	Royalties	15 Alternative minimum tax (AMT) items
7	Net short-term capital gain (loss)	
8a	Net long-term capital gain (loss) 2,226	
8b	Collectibles (28%) gain (loss)	
8c	Unrecaptured section 1250 gain	
9	Net section 1231 gain (loss)	16 Items affecting shareholder basis
10	Other income (loss)	
		17 Other information
		D Distribution 150,000
11	Section 179 deduction	
12	Other deductions	
A	Charitable Contr 1,800	
18 ☐	More than one activity for at-risk purposes*	
19 ☐	More than one activity for passive activity purposes*	
	* See attached statement for additional information.	

For Paperwork Reduction Act Notice, see the Instructions for Form 1120-S.   www.irs.gov/Form1120S   Cat. No. 11520D   **Schedule K-1 (Form 1120-S) 2022**

Salary Payments

A significant difference between partnerships and S corporations is that an owner (shareholder) can be an employee of the corporation. Shareholders who work in the corporate business receive salaries as compensation for their services. Both the corporation and the employee pay the FICA payroll tax on the salary, and the corporation withholds federal income tax. At the end of the year, the corporation issues a Schedule K-1 and a Form W-2 to any shareholder/employee. S corporation shareholders are not considered to be self-employed. Therefore, their share of corporate business income is not subject to self-employment tax.[57]

[57] Rev. Rul. 59-221, 1959-1 C.B. 225.

Payments to Shareholder/ Employees	Ghani Todd owns 20 percent of the stock in Koroma, Inc., a calendar year S corporation, and is employed as the corporation's CEO. This year, Mr. Todd's salary from Koroma was $75,000, from which Koroma withheld both employee FICA tax and state and local income tax. Koroma's ordinary business income (after deduction of all employee compensation) was $984,000, and Mr. Todd's share of this income was $196,800. Mr. Todd received a $160,000 cash distribution from Koroma with respect to his stock. Mr. Todd must include $271,800 ($75,000 salary + $196,800 share of corporate income) in taxable income. The $160,000 cash distribution has no effect on Mr. Todd's taxable income.

Note that salary payments to S corporation shareholders are generally deductible in computing ordinary income from the business. Thus, a shareholder receiving a salary payment will report greater salary income and less ordinary income. While the net impact on the shareholder's taxable income may be zero, the payroll tax cost of the salary payment creates an incentive for S corporations to understate salary payable to shareholders. As a result, the IRS tends to carefully scrutinize salary payments to S corporation shareholders to ensure that adequate compensation (and adequate payroll tax) is paid given the shareholder's efforts.

Adequate Salary Payments to Shareholder/ Employees	Maxwell owns 100 percent of the stock of Golden, Inc., a calendar year S corporation. Maxwell spends 60 hours a week working for the corporation. During the current year, Golden earned $200,000 of ordinary income, before any salary payments to Maxwell. If Maxwell is paid $100,000 of salary, the corporation will owe $7,650 employer payroll taxes on this income. Remaining corporate ordinary income, allocated and taxable to Maxwell, will be $92,350. Maxwell will pay $7,650 employee payroll tax on his salary income, and personal income tax on $192,350, his salary and income allocated from the S corporation. If Maxwell's marginal tax rate is 37 percent, his income tax on his salary and S corporation earnings is $71,170, and his total tax burden (payroll and income tax) related to his S corporation is $78,820. If Maxwell does not take a salary from Golden, he will report and pay tax on $200,000 total S corporation earnings, resulting in additional tax liability of only $74,000. However, if the IRS audits either Maxwell or Golden, it will likely assert that Maxwell should be reasonably compensated for his work on behalf of the corporation, and assess additional payroll tax liability on both the corporation and the shareholder.

Adjusting the Basis of S Corporation Stock

Shareholders make positive and negative adjustments to the basis in their S corporation stock in much the same way as partners adjust the basis in their partnership interests.[58] Specifically, shareholders increase the basis in their stock by their share of the corporation's income and gain for the year. Conversely, shareholders reduce the basis by their share of any corporate losses. Cash distributed by an S corporation to a shareholder is a nontaxable return of investment that reduces stock basis.[59] Recall, however, that the basis of S corporation stock does not reflect changes in entity debt.

[58] §1367(a).

[59] Salary payments to shareholders/employees have no effect on stock basis. If a shareholder receives a cash distribution that exceeds stock basis, the excess distribution is recognized as a capital gain. §1368.

Basis Limitation on Loss Deductions

LO 10-10
Apply the basis limitation on the deduction of S corporation losses.

The tax law imposes the same limitation on S corporation losses as it does on partnership losses: Such losses are currently deductible only to the extent of the owner's investment. Under the limitation rule for S corporations, a shareholder can deduct an amount of loss that reduces their stock basis to zero.[60] If a shareholder also has basis in any debt obligation from the S corporation, the shareholder may deduct additional loss to reduce the debt basis to zero.[61] In other words, a shareholder's investment that can be recovered through tax deductions includes both their equity investment and their investment as a corporate creditor.

Nondeductible S Corporation Loss

Olivia Jentz owns 25 percent of the outstanding stock of SGM, a calendar year S corporation. At the beginning of 2022, Ms. Jentz's basis in her stock was $81,000. Several years ago, Ms. Jentz loaned $30,000 to SGM in return for its interest-bearing note. For 2022, SGM incurred a $500,000 operating loss. Although Ms. Jentz's Schedule K-1 reflects a $125,000 loss, Ms. Jentz can deduct only $111,000 of the loss on her Form 1040.

	Stock Basis	Note Basis
Beginning of year	$ 81,000	$ 30,000
Deductible loss	(81,000)	(30,000)
End of year	–0–	–0–
Nondeductible loss	$(14,000)	

Ms. Jentz's $14,000 nondeductible loss is carried forward into future years. If she creates a basis by making an additional investment in SGM as either a shareholder or a creditor, she can deduct the loss to the extent of the additional basis. Alternatively, if SGM generates future income, Ms. Jentz's share of *undistributed* income will first increase the basis in her note to its $30,000 face amount and will then increase her stock basis.[62] Ms. Jentz can deduct her loss carryforward to the extent of her restored basis.

Basis Restoration

Ms. Jentz's 25 percent share of SGM's 2023 income is $50,000. The corporation made no cash distributions during the year. The undistributed income increases Ms. Jentz's investment basis and allows her to deduct the $14,000 loss carryforward from 2022 on her 2023 return.

	Stock Basis	Note Basis
Beginning of year	–0–	–0–
Share of income:		
Increase to note basis		$30,000
Increase to stock basis	$20,000	
	$20,000	$30,000
Loss carryforward	(14,000)	
End of year	$ 6,000	$30,000

Because of the deduction for her loss carryforward, Ms. Jentz's 2023 taxable income includes only $36,000 SGM income.

---

[60] §1366(d)(1)(A).
[61] §1366(d)(1)(B).
[62] §1367(b)(2).

If SGM were to repay the $30,000 loan from Ms. Jentz before her basis in the note was restored to its face amount, the repayment would be treated as an amount realized on sale of the note. Because the note is a capital asset to Ms. Jentz, she would recognize a capital gain equal to the excess of the repayment over her basis.[63]

Gain on Repayment of Debt	Change the facts in the previous example by assuming that SGM retired its debt to Ms. Jentz by paying her $30,000 (plus accrued interest) on June 30, 2023. Assume also that SGM distributed $50,000 cash to Ms. Jentz to match her $50,000 share of 2023 income. In this case, Ms. Jentz had no 2023 *undistributed* income to restore basis in either her SGM note or her SGM stock. Consequently, she must recognize a $30,000 long-term capital gain on repayment of the note and cannot deduct any of her 2022 loss carryforward.

Conclusion

In this chapter, we've examined the tax consequences of operating a business as a sole proprietorship or as a passthrough entity. In the case of a sole proprietorship, the business income is included in the owner's taxable income and taxed at the individual rates. In the case of a general or limited partnership, LLC, or S corporation, the business income is allocated to the owners of the entity. The income is taxed directly to the partners, members, or shareholders at their marginal rate. Many owners deliberately use these organizational forms to avoid paying an entity-level tax on business income. This tax strategy is one of the topics covered in Chapter 11. Before we can evaluate this strategy, we must examine the tax consequences of operating a business as a regular corporation.

[63] §1271(a)(1) and Rev. Rul. 64-162, 1964-1 C.B. 304.

Key Terms

distributive share   *10-20*
employee payroll
    tax   *10-12*
employer identification
    number   *10-11*
employer payroll
    tax   *10-11*
general partnership   *10-16*
guaranteed
    payment   *10-21*

limited liability company
    (LLC)   *10-17*
limited liability partnership
    (LLP)   *10-16*
limited partnership   *10-16*
partnership   *10-15*
passthrough entity   *10-18*
pro rata share   *10-32*
QBI deduction   *10-7*

qualified business income
    (QBI)   *10-5*
self-employment (SE)
    tax   *10-14*
separately stated
    item   *10-20*
sole proprietorship   *10-4*
subchapter S
    corporation   *10-28*

Questions and Problems for Discussion

LO 10-1

1. Can a sole proprietorship be described as a passthrough entity?

LO 10-1, 10-2

2. Mrs. Liu owns a business as a sole proprietor. Near the end of her taxable year, she is evaluating a new opportunity that would generate $25,000 additional income for her business. What marginal tax rate should Mrs. Liu use to compute the tax cost of this opportunity?

LO 10-1

3. This year, Mr. Pitt's sole proprietorship generated a $17,000 net loss. Can Mr. Pitt use this loss as a net operating loss carryforward deduction?

LO 10-2 4. This year, Firm Q, a cash basis taxpayer, remitted $26,800 FICA payroll tax to the federal government. However, the firm deducted only $13,400 FICA tax on its income tax return. Can you explain this apparent inconsistency?

LO 10-2 5. Critique the employee payroll tax on the normative standards of convenience to the taxpayer and vertical equity.

LO 10-2 6. Define the tax base for the self-employment tax. When do sole proprietors pay the self-employment tax to the federal government?

LO 10-1, 10-2 7. Why is only half of a sole proprietor's self-employment tax deductible in the computation of taxable income?

LO 10-3 8. Tom, Neha, and Mateo want to become co-owners of a business enterprise. Compare their personal liability for the debts incurred by the enterprise if they organize as

    a. A general partnership.

    b. A limited partnership.

    c. An LLC.

    d. An S corporation.

LO 10-4 9. Why are certain items of income, gain, deduction, or loss separately stated on a partnership or an S corporation tax return?

LO 10-4 10. This year, Soya Partnership disposed of only one operating asset and recognized a $22,000 loss on the disposition. Why must Soya report this net Section 1231 loss as a separately stated item rather than deducting the loss in the computation of ordinary business income?

LO 10-1 11. Both Mx. Aldo and Mr. Zed are sole proprietors. This year, each proprietorship generated $85,000 net cash flow from business operations. Mx. Aldo used the cash to expand their business, while Mr. Zed used the cash to make the down payment on a new home for his family. Discuss how the different uses of cash affect each person's federal income tax for the year.

LO 10-3, 10-4 12. Four years ago, Mr. Bates purchased 1,000 shares of UPF, Inc. for $10,000. These shares represent a 30 percent equity interest in UPF, which is an S corporation. This year, UPF defaulted on a $120,000 unsecured debt to a major creditor.

    a. To what extent can the creditor demand repayment of the debt from Mr. Bates?

    b. Would your answer change if UPF is a partnership in which Mr. Bates is a 30 percent general partner?

    c. Would your answer change if UPF is a partnership in which Mr. Bates is a 30 percent limited partner?

    d. Would your answer change if UPF is an LLC in which Mr. Bates is a 30 percent member?

LO 10-6, 10-9 13. Mr. Yang sold his interest in a business to an unrelated purchaser for $500,000 cash. How does Mr. Yang determine his adjusted basis for purposes of computing gain or loss realized on the sale if the business is

    a. A sole proprietorship?

    b. A partnership?

    c. An S corporation?

LO 10-4, 10-5 14. Corporation ABC sold its interest in KK Partnership on October 9 for $150,000. KK Partnership uses a calendar year for tax purposes. Explain why Corporation ABC cannot compute gain or loss realized on the date that the sale occurs.

All applicable Application Problems are available with *Connect*.

Application Problems

LO 10-1, 10-2

1. Keiji Jones is the owner of a small retail business operated as a sole proprietorship. During 2022, his business recorded the following items of income and expense:

Revenue from inventory sales	$147,000
Cost of goods sold	33,500
Business license tax	2,400
Rent on retail space	42,000
Supplies	15,000
Wages paid to employees	22,000
Payroll taxes	1,700
Utilities	3,600

   a. Compute taxable income attributable to the sole proprietorship by completing Schedule C to be included in Keiji's 2022 Form 1040.

   b. Compute self-employment tax payable on the earnings of Keiji's sole proprietorship by completing a 2022 Schedule SE, Form 1040.

   c. Assume that Keiji's business is not a service business, and that it has $155,000 unadjusted basis in tangible depreciable property. Calculate Keiji's 2022 QBI deduction, before any overall taxable income limitation.

LO 10-1

2. Rhea Xu is a self-employed professional singer. She resides in a rented apartment and uses one room exclusively as a business office. This room includes 225 of the 1,500 square feet of living space in the apartment. Ms. Xu performs in recording studios and concert halls, but she conducts all of the administrative duties with respect to the business in her home office. This year, Ms. Xu's apartment rent was $48,000. She paid $5,200 to a housekeeping service that cleaned the entire apartment once a week and $2,000 for renter's insurance on the apartment furnishings. Compute Ms. Xu's home office deduction assuming that

   a. Her net profit before the deduction was $300,000.

   b. Her net profit before the deduction was $4,000.

LO 10-1

3. Marcia Alvarez, a single individual, has qualified trade or business income after all applicable deductions of $280,000. Her business paid $100,000 of W-2 wages this year and has $50,000 of tangible business property.

   a. Compute Ms. Alvarez's QBI deduction, assuming her overall taxable income before QBI is $350,000.

   b. Compute Ms. Alvarez's QBI deduction, assuming her overall taxable income before QBI is $240,000.

LO 10-1

4. Evan, a single individual, operates a service business that earned $110,000 (after all applicable deductions) in 2023. The business has no tangible property and paid no W-2 wages.

   a. Compute Evan's QBI deduction, assuming his overall taxable income before QBI is $125,000.

   b. Compute Evan's QBI deduction, assuming his overall taxable income before QBI is $185,000.

LO 10-1

5. Colin, a self-employed consultant, uses a room of his home as a business office. This room represents 10 percent of the home's square footage. This year, Colin incurred the following expenses in connection with his home:

Home mortgage interest	$12,980
Property tax on residence	2,200
Homeowner's insurance	1,475
Utilities	2,100
Furnace repairs	300

Colin purchased the home in 2000 for $225,000. For MACRS depreciation purposes, he allocated $185,000 to the building and $40,000 to the land.

   a. If Colin's gross business income exceeded his operating expenses by $75,000, compute his net profit for the year.

   b. If Colin's gross business income exceeded his operating expenses by $1,800, compute his net profit for the year.

LO 10-2   6. Mr. Li is employed by BDF, Inc. Compute BDF's 2023 employer payroll tax with respect to Mr. Li assuming that

   a. His annual compensation is $60,000.

   b. His annual compensation is $200,000.

LO 10-2   7. Refer to the facts in the preceding problem. Assume that in the year 2024, the Social Security base amount increases to $170,000. Compute BDF's 2023 employer payroll tax with respect to Mr. Li assuming that

   a. His annual compensation is $60,000.

   b. His annual compensation is $200,000.

LO 10-2   8. For 2023, Ms. Deming earned wages totaling $225,000. Calculate any .9 percent additional Medicare tax owed, assuming that

   a. Ms. Deming is single.

   b. Ms. Deming files a joint return with her husband who earned $100,000 of wages for 2023.

LO 10-2   9. Calculate the total Social Security and Medicare tax burden on a sole proprietorship earning 2023 profit of $300,000, assuming a single sole proprietor with no other earned income.

LO 10-2   10. Mrs. Singer owns a profitable sole proprietorship. For each of the following cases, use Schedule SE, Form 1040, to compute her 2022 self-employment tax and her income tax deduction for such tax.

   a. Mrs. Singer's net profit from Schedule C was $51,458. She had no other earned income.

   b. Mrs. Singer's net profit from Schedule C was $51,458, and she received a $120,000 salary from an employer.

   c. Mrs. Singer's net profit from Schedule C was $51,458, and she received a $155,000 salary from an employer.

LO 10-1, 10-2   11. In 2023, Wilma Way's sole proprietorship, WW Bookstore, generated $120,000 net profit. In addition, Wilma recognized a $17,000 Section 1231 gain on the sale of business furniture. The business checking account earned $960 interest income.

   a. Which of these income items are subject to self-employment tax?

   b. Compute Wilma's 2023 self-employment tax, assuming Wilma has no other earned income.

   c. Compute Wilma's allowable QBI deduction, assuming $43,000 of W-2 wages and $90,000 unadjusted basis of tangible depreciable property. Further assume the overall taxable income limitation on QBI does not apply and Wilma's overall taxable income is sufficiently high that the W-2 wage limitation applies.

   d. Compute the overall impact of the bookstore activity on Wilma's 2023 taxable income.

LO 10-1, 10-2   12. JC recently graduated from veterinary school and opened their own professional practice. This year, their net profit was $32,000. Assume JC does not qualify for the QBI deduction. Compute JC's after-tax income from their practice assuming

   a. Their self-employment tax is $4,522, and their marginal income tax rate is 22 percent.

   b. What percentage of the federal tax burden on JC's business income is represented by the self-employment tax?

LO 10-2   13. Tanisha is a self-employed attorney. This year, her net profit exceeded $350,000, which put her in the 37 percent tax bracket. Early in the year, Tanisha hired Ben as a paralegal and paid him a $33,000 salary.

   a. Compute the employer payroll tax on Ben's salary.

   b. In addition to the employer payroll tax, Tanisha paid $400 unemployment tax on Ben's salary. The salary and tax expense reduced Tanisha's net earnings from self-employment, thereby saving $962 in self-employment tax. Compute Tanisha's after-tax cost of hiring Ben.

LO 10-6   14. AB Corporation and YZ Corporation formed a partnership to construct a shopping mall. AB contributed $500,000 cash, and YZ contributed land ($500,000 FMV and $430,000 basis) in exchange for a 50 percent interest in ABYZ Partnership. Immediately after its formation, ABYZ borrowed $250,000 from a local bank. The debt is recourse (unsecured by any specific partnership asset). Compute each partner's initial basis in its partnership interest, assuming that

   a. Both AB and YZ are general partners.

   b. AB is a general partner, and YZ is a limited partner.

LO 10-4   15. This year, FGH Partnership generated $600,000 ordinary business income. FGH has two equal partners: Triad LLC and Beta, an S corporation. Triad LLC has three members: Mr. Ty, who owns a 40 percent interest; Mrs. Ude, who owns a 35 percent interest; and V, Inc., which owns a 25 percent interest. Beta has 100 shares of outstanding stock, all of which are owned by Ms. Byrd. Identify the taxpayers who must pay tax on the partnership income, and determine how much income must be reported by each.

LO 10-5   16. Amit is a limited partner in Reynolds Partnership. This year, Amit's Schedule K-1 from Reynolds reflected $50,000 of ordinary income, $1,000 of interest income, and a cash distribution of $35,000. Amit's marginal tax rate is 37 percent. Amit qualifies for the QBI deduction, without regard to the wage or taxable income limitations.

   a. Calculate the tax cost of Amit's partnership earnings this year.

   b. Calculate Amit's after-tax cash flow from his partnership activity this year.

LO 10-5, 10-6   17. Kari is a limited partner in Lizard Partnership. This year, Kari's share of partnership ordinary income is $20,000, and she received a cash distribution of $30,000. Kari's tax basis in her partnership interest at the beginning of the year was $50,000. Her marginal tax rate is 22 percent. Kari qualifies for the QBI deduction, without regard to the wage or taxable income limitations.

   a. Calculate the tax cost of Kari's partnership earnings this year.

   b. Compute Kari's after-tax cash flow from her partnership activity this year.

   c. Compute Kari's tax basis in her partnership interest at the ending of the year. Assume no change in her share of partnership liabilities during the year.

LO 10-4, 10-5 18. Rochelle is a limited partner in Megawatt Partnership. For 2023, her Schedule K-1 from the partnership reported the following share of partnership items:

Ordinary income	$25,000
Section 1231 loss	(3,000)
Nondeductible expense	1,000
Cash distribution	5,000

    a. Calculate the net impact of the given items on Rochelle's 2023 taxable income. Assume that Rochelle does not qualify for the QBI deduction.

    b. Assume that Rochelle's marginal tax rate is 35 percent. Calculate her 2023 after-tax cash flow as a result of her interest in Megawatt.

LO 10-4 19. KLMN Partnership's financial records show the following:

Gross receipts from sales	$670,000
Cost of goods sold	(460,000)
Operating expenses	(96,800)
Business meals not provided by a restaurant	(6,240)
Section 1231 loss on equipment sale	(13,500)
Charitable contribution	(1,500)
Distributions to partners	(10,000)

Compute KLMN's ordinary business income for the year.

LO 10-4, 10-6 20. Refer to the facts in the preceding problem. Mr. Ty is a 10 percent general partner in KLMN. During the year, he received a $1,000 cash distribution from KLMN.

    a. Compute Mr. Ty's share of partnership ordinary income and separately stated items.

    b. If Mr. Ty's adjusted basis in his KLMN interest was $45,000 at the beginning of the year, compute his adjusted basis at the end of the year. Assume that KLMN's debt did not change during the year.

    c. How would your basis computation change if KLMN's debt at the end of the year was $28,000 more than its debt at the beginning of the year?

LO 10-4, 10-6 21. Jayanthi and Krish each own a 50 percent general partner interest in the JK Partnership. The following information is available regarding the partnership's 2022 activities:

Sales revenue	$500,000
Selling expenses	200,000
Depreciation expense	30,000
Long-term capital gain	9,000
Nondeductible expenses	2,000
Partnership debts, beginning of the year	100,000
Partnership debts, end of the year	120,000
Partnership distributions	
Jayanthi	50,000
Krish	50,000

    a. Calculate the partnership's ordinary (nonseparately stated) income, and indicate which items must be separately stated.

    b. Calculate Jayanthi's allocable share of partnership items.

    c. If Jayanthi has no other sources of taxable income, what is her total gross income for 2022?

    d. At the beginning of the year, Jayanthi's adjusted tax basis in her partnership interest was $25,000. Calculate her ending adjusted tax basis in her partnership interest.

LO 10-4 22. Refer to the facts in the preceding problem.

    a. Complete Schedule K, Form 1065, for the partnership.

    b. Complete Schedule K-1, Form 1065, for Jayanthi.

LO 10-6, 10-7 23. This year, individual X and individual Y formed XY Partnership. X contributed $50,000 cash, and Y contributed business assets with a $50,000 FMV. Y's adjusted basis in these assets was only $10,000. The partnership agreement provides that income and loss will be divided equally between the two partners. Partnership operations for the year generated a $42,000 loss. How much loss may each partner deduct currently, and what basis will each partner have in their interest at the beginning of next year? Assume the excess business loss limitation does not apply to either X or Y.

LO 10-7 24. AV, Inc. is a member of an LLC. This year, AV received a Schedule K-1 reporting a $1,200 share of capital loss and a $4,000 share of Section 1231 gain. During the year, AV recognized a $5,000 capital loss on the sale of marketable securities and a $17,000 Section 1231 loss on the sale of business equipment. What effect do the LLC losses have on AV's taxable income?

LO 10-4 25. Bonnie and Giorgio are equal general partners in BG Partnership. Bonnie receives a $4,000 monthly guaranteed payment for services. This year, BG generated $95,000 profit (before consideration of Bonnie's guaranteed payments).

    a. Compute each partner's distributive share of ordinary business income.

    b. Compute each partner's self-employment income.

    c. How would your answers change if BG's profit was only $32,000 instead of $95,000?

LO 10-6, 10-7 26. Zelda owns a 60 percent general interest in YZ Partnership. At the beginning of 2022, the adjusted basis in her YZ interest was $95,000. For 2021, YZ generated a $210,000 business loss, earned $14,600 dividend and interest income on its investments, and recognized a $6,200 capital gain. YZ made no distributions to its partners and had no debt.

    a. How much of her share of YZ's loss can Zelda deduct on her 2022 return? Assume the excess business loss limitation does not apply.

    b. Compute Zelda's adjusted basis in her YZ interest at the end of 2022.

    c. Would your answers change if Zelda received a $5,000 cash distribution from YZ during 2022?

LO 10-6, 10-7 27. Refer to the facts in the preceding problem. In 2023, YZ generated $7,000 ordinary business income and $18,000 dividend and interest income. The partnership made no distributions. At the end of the year, YZ had $21,000 debt.

    a. How much partnership income will Zelda report on her 2023 return? Assume the excess business loss limitation does not apply.

    b. Compute Zelda's adjusted basis in her YZ interest at the end of 2023.

LO 10-6, 10-7, 10-9 28. At the beginning of 2023, Ms. Pope purchased a 20 percent interest in PPY Partnership for $20,000. Ms. Pope's Schedule K-1 reported that her share of PPY's debt at year-end was $12,000, and her share of ordinary loss was $28,000. On January 1, 2024, Ms. Pope sold her interest to another partner for $2,000 cash.

    a. How much of her share of PPY's loss can Ms. Pope deduct on her 2023 return?

    b. Compute Ms. Pope's recognized gain on sale of her PPY interest.

    c. How would your answers to parts (*a*) and (*b*) change if PPY were an S corporation instead of a partnership?

LO 10-6, 10-7 29. On January 1, 2022, Leo paid $15,000 for 5 percent of the stock in BLS, an S corporation. In November, he loaned $8,000 to BLS in return for a promissory note. BLS generated a $600,000 operating loss in 2022.

 a. How much of his share of the loss can Leo deduct on his 2022 return? Assume the excess business loss limitation does not apply.

 b. Compute Leo's basis in his BLS stock and his BLS note at the end of 2022.

LO 10-6, 10-7 30. Refer to the facts in the preceding problem. BLS generated $408,000 ordinary business income in 2023.

 a. How much of Leo's share of this income is included in his 2023 taxable income?

 b. Compute Leo's basis in his BLS stock and his BLS note at the end of 2023.

 c. How would your answers change if BLS's ordinary business income was only $220,000?

LO 10-6 31. Refer to the facts in (*c*) of the preceding problem. In 2024, BLS repaid its $8,000 debt to Leo before he restored any basis in the debt. How much gain or loss, if any, will Leo recognize as a result of the debt repayment?

LO 10-9 32. For each of the following situations, indicate whether the corporation is eligible to elect S corporation status.

 a. Carman Corporation has two shareholders, Carla and Manuel. Carla is a U.S. citizen permanently residing in Mexico. Manuel is a Mexican citizen permanently residing in the United States.

 b. Same given info as in (*a*), except that Manuel resides in Mexico.

 c. Devin Corporation has 110 individual shareholders, of which 12 are members of the same family.

 d. Evans Corporation has two shareholders, Mark and Joan, who are both U.S. citizens and residents. Mark owns all of the 100 shares of Evans's common stock outstanding, and Joan owns all of the 100 shares of Evans's preferred stock outstanding.

 e. Grant Corporation has two shareholders: Shlomo, a U.S. citizen and resident, and ABC Partnership. ABC is a domestic partnership with six individual partners, all of whom are U.S. citizens and residents.

LO 10-9 33. Wanda is a 20 percent owner of Video Associates, which is treated as a passthrough entity for federal income tax purposes. This year, Wanda was allocated $45,000 of ordinary income from Video Associates, $1,000 of tax-exempt interest income, and $2,000 of nondeductible expenses. Wanda also received a $10,000 distribution from Video Associates this year. At the beginning of the year, Video Associates had outstanding debt of $100,000. At the end of the year, the entity's outstanding debts increased to $130,000.

 a. If Video Associates is a partnership, and her basis in her partnership interest at the beginning of the year is $30,000, determine Wanda's tax basis in her partnership interest at year-end.

 b. If Video Associates is an S corporation, and her basis in her S corporation stock at the beginning of the year is $10,000, determine Wanda's tax basis in her corporate stock at year-end.

LO 10-9 34. Mario is the sole shareholder of Magic Roofing Company, a calendar year S corporation. Although Mario spends at least 30 hours per week supervising Magic's employees, he has never drawn a salary from Magic. Magic has been in existence for five years and has earned a profit every year. Mario withdraws $50,000 of cash from the S corporation each year.

   a. Explain the tax consequences of Mario's cash withdrawals from the S corporation and their impact on Mario's taxable income and Magic's ordinary income.

   b. An IRS agent has just begun examining the last three years of tax returns filed by Mario and Magic. He has questioned whether the $50,000 withdrawals should be characterized as salary payments to Mario instead of shareholder distributions. What are the income tax consequences to Mario and Magic if these distributions are characterized as salary payments?

   c. What are the payroll tax consequences to Mario and Magic if the distributions are characterized as salary payments? Calculate the total potential underpayment of both employee and employer payroll tax that could result from this audit.

Issue Recognition Problems

Identify the tax issue or issues suggested by the following situations and state each issue in the form of a question.

LO 10-4 1. Ellie has operated a sole proprietorship for six years during which net profit has been stable and Ellie's marginal tax rate has been a constant 24 percent. Ellie projects that her profit next year will be the same as this year. Consequently, she estimates her tax cost for next year based on a 24 percent rate. Late in the year, Ellie's husband graduated from law school and accepted an excellent offer of employment from a local firm.

LO 10-2 2. Javier is a full-time employee of B, Inc. and operates a sole proprietorship. This year, his salary was $70,000, and his net earnings from self-employment were $60,000.

LO 10-2 3. Mr. and Mrs. Chou file a joint income tax return. Mr. Chou reports the income from his full-time landscaping business on Schedule C, which lists him as the sole proprietor. He also reports 100 percent of the net profit as his self-employment income and pays SE tax accordingly. During the last several years, Mrs. Chou has worked at least 20 hours per week in her husband's business. However, Mr. Chou does not pay her a salary or wage for her services.

LO 10-1 4. Travis is a professional writer who maintains his business office in one room of his personal residence. The office contains Travis's desk, filing cabinets, personal computer and printer, copying machine, phone system, and fax machine. It also contains his family's library of videotapes, music CDs, popular novels, and the set of encyclopedias used by his three children for their schoolwork.

LO 10-4 5. Lola owns a 15 percent limited interest in AF Partnership, which uses a calendar year for tax purposes. On April 12, Lola sold her entire interest to the R Corporation; consequently, she was a partner for only 102 days during the year. AF generated $845,000 ordinary business income this year and recognized a $70,000 capital gain on the November 13 sale of marketable securities.

LO 10-6 6. Nine years ago, Fred paid $20,000 cash for a 2 percent limited interest in a very profitable partnership. Every year Fred has properly included his distributive share of partnership income in taxable income. This year, Fred sold his interest to an unrelated party for $80,000 and computed a $60,000 gain recognized on sale.

LO 10-3 7. The 18 partners in KT Limited Partnership unanimously voted to convert their partnership to an LLC. To make the conversion, each partner will exchange his interest in KT for a membership interest in the newly formed LLC.

LO 10-9 8. Four individuals are evaluating the tax cost of operating their business as an S corporation. They assume that the corporation will pay no tax on its annual business income. They plan to incorporate the business in a state with a 7 percent corporate income tax.

LO 10-7 9. Mr. Pham just sold his entire 20 percent interest in DK Partnership to an unrelated purchaser for $7,500. Mr. Pham's adjusted basis in the interest was zero, and he had a $12,000 carryforward of DK loss.

LO 10-7 10. Paula's Schedule K-1 from an LLC reported a $12,000 share of ordinary loss and a $1,900 share of capital loss. Paula's adjusted basis in her LLC interest before consideration of these losses was $6,200.

LO 10-4 11. Marcus, a cash basis individual, is a general partner in MNOP Partnership. Both Marcus and MNOP use a calendar year for tax purposes. According to the partnership agreement, MNOP pays a $10,000 guaranteed payment to Marcus on the last day of every calendar month. However, because of a bookkeeping error, the partnership did not pay (and Marcus did not receive) his final guaranteed payment for 2022 until January 10, 2023.

LO 10-6, 10-7 12. David's Schedule K-1 from DES, an S corporation, reported $8,900 tax-exempt interest and $4,700 ordinary loss. David's adjusted basis in his stock before consideration of these items was $2,000.

LO 10-9 13. Mr. and Mrs. West are the only shareholders in WW, an S corporation. This year, WW paid $21,000 to the caterers who provided food for the couple's silver wedding anniversary celebration.

LO 10-8 14. The 100 shares of NS's outstanding stock are owned by seven unrelated individuals. NS has an S corporation election in effect. Late in the year, one individual announces to his fellow shareholders that he intends to give his NS shares to his son-in-law, who is a citizen and resident of Canada.

LO 10-4 15. BR, Inc. owns a 20 percent interest in a limited partnership. All the other partners are individual shareholders in BR. This year, BR sold land to the partnership for use in the partnership's business activity. BR's basis in the land was $400,000, and the selling price was $275,000. This price was determined by an independent appraiser.

LO 10-4 16. JKL Partnership uses the calendar year for tax purposes. For the current calendar year, the partnership generated $1 million ordinary business income. Corporation L, a 10 percent limited partner in JKL, uses a fiscal year ending June 30 as its tax year.

LO 10-6, 10-7 17. FG, Inc. owned a 3 percent limited interest in a partnership that has been unprofitable for several years. The partnership recently informed its partners that they must contribute additional capital if the partnership is to survive. FG decided not to contribute any more money and sent written notification to the general partner relinquishing its equity interest. On the date of notification, FG's adjusted basis in the interest was $15,500.

Research Problems

LO 10-4 1. Don Ferris and Lou Lam are the two partners in F&L Partnership. The partnership agreement provides that all income is allocated equally between Don and Lou, but in no case shall the allocation to Don be less than $75,000 per year. (In other words, Don has a minimum guarantee of $75,000.) This year, F&L generated $107,200 net profit. Compute F&L's taxable income for the year and each partner's distributive share of that income.

LO 10-8 2. Herold had been a calendar year S corporation since 1990. On October 10, 2023, Mrs. Hughes sold 18 shares of Herold stock to a foreign partnership, thereby terminating Herold's S election. Herold's taxable income for the entire 2023 calendar year was

$592,030. Describe the federal tax returns that Herold must file for 2023, determine how much income must be reported on each, and compute any corporate income tax that Herold must pay.

LO 10-10   3. At the beginning of the current year, Sandy Brewer had a zero basis in her 38 shares of stock in Lindlee, an S corporation, a zero basis in a $5,000 note from Lindlee, and a $7,400 carryforward of a prior year ordinary loss from Lindlee that she was unable to deduct because of the basis limitation. Early in February of the current year, Sandy was notified by Lindlee's attorney that the corporation was bankrupt. Consequently, Lindlee was defaulting on its $5,000 debt to Sandy, and Sandy's 38 shares of stock were worthless. Describe the consequences to Sandy of the worthlessness of her Lindlee investments.

 **All applicable Tax Planning Cases are available with *Connect*.**

Tax Planning Cases

LO 10-1   1. Mr. Janus and Ms. Hong are a married couple who operate a restaurant business as a sole proprietorship. The couple has decided to purchase $85,000 of new kitchen equipment for the restaurant. They also want to buy two new automobiles—one for their personal use and one for their 19-year-old son's personal use. The two automobiles will cost $65,000. The couple have $70,000 in a savings account that they can use to partially fund these purchases. They intend to borrow the additional $80,000 from a local bank at 7 percent annual interest. What steps should the couple take to minimize the after-tax cost of the borrowed funds?

LO 10-4, 10-6, 10-7   2. On March 1, 2023, Eve and Frank each contributed $30,000 cash to the newly formed EF Partnership in exchange for a 50 percent general interest. The partnership immediately borrowed $50,000 from an unrelated creditor, a debt that it does not have to repay for two years. In November, the partners estimate with reasonable certainty that EF's 2023 operating loss will be $100,000. However, EF's business has started to generate positive cash flow, and the partners estimate that EF will be profitable in 2024, perhaps generating as much as $125,000 ordinary income. In anticipation of these future profits, Eve and Frank are considering withdrawing their initial cash contributions from EF before Christmas. Eve and Frank are both in the 35 percent tax bracket. What tax planning advice can you offer the partners?

LO 10-9, 10-10   3. In the current year (year 0), Amisha became a shareholder in Sultan, Inc., a calendar year S corporation, by contributing $15,000 cash in exchange for stock. Shortly before the end of the year, Sultan's CFO notified Amisha that her pro rata share of ordinary loss for the year would be $55,000. Amisha immediately loaned $40,000 to Sultan in exchange for a two-year, interest-bearing corporate note. Consequently, she had enough stock and debt basis to allow her to deduct the $55,000 loss on her current year return. Compute the NPV of Amisha's cash flow *associated with her loan* in the following three cases. In each case, assume she has a 35 percent marginal tax rate on ordinary income, a 15 percent rate on capital gains, and a 6 percent discount rate.

   a. For the next two years (years 1 and 2), Amisha's share of Sultan's ordinary income totaled $49,000, and Sultan did not distribute cash to its shareholders. However, it did repay the $40,000 loan plus $3,800 interest in year 2.

   b. For the next two years (years 1 and 2), Amisha's share of Sultan's ordinary income totaled $19,100, and Sultan did not distribute any cash to its shareholders. However, it did repay the $40,000 loan plus $3,800 interest in year 2.

  c. For the next two years (years 1 and 2), Amisha's share of Sultan's ordinary loss totaled $11,400. In year 2, the corporation declared bankruptcy and defaulted on all its debts, including the loan from Amisha.

LO 10-9   4. Marla recently inherited $50,000 and is considering two alternatives for investing these funds. Investment A is stock of a C corporation, expected to pay annual dividends of 8 percent. Investment B is stock of an S corporation. Based on income projections, Marla's share of the S corporation's ordinary income would be approximately $10,000 per year. However, the S corporation does not expect to make cash distributions for the foreseeable future. Marla would hold either investment for three years, at which time she believes the C corporation stock could be sold for $60,000 and the S corporation stock could be sold for $90,000.

  Assume that the initial investment would be made in year 0, dividends on the C corporation stock would be received in years 1, 2, and 3; S corporation earnings would be allocated in years 1, 2, and 3; and either investment would be sold in year 3. Assume that Marla's S corporation income would not qualify for the QBI deduction. Also assume that Marla's marginal tax rate on ordinary income is 35 percent. Using a 4 percent discount rate, calculate the net present value of after-tax cash flows attributable to either investment, and make a recommendation to Marla regarding which investment she should choose.

Appendix 10–A

Calculating the QBI Deduction When Taxable Income Is in the Phase-in Range

Part I: If 2023 taxable income is more than $364,200 but not more than $464,200 if married filing jointly (more than $182,100 but not more than $232,100 all other individuals), complete Part I to compute the phase-in percentage. This percentage is used in Part II to determine eligible income from a specified service trade or business, and in Part III to phase in the wage limitation.

1. Taxable income before qualified business income deduction   _____
2. Threshold: Enter $364,200 if married filing jointly or $182,100 otherwise   _____
3. Subtract line 5 from line 4   _____
4. Phase-in range: Enter $100,000 if married filing jointly, or $50,000 otherwise   _____
5. Phase-in percentage: Divide line 6 by line 7   _____

Part II: Complete Part II if a trade or business is a specified service trade or business and taxable income is within the phase-in range noted in Part I. If taxable income is more than the phase-in range, the specified service trade or business does not qualify for the deduction.

6. Qualified business income from specified service trades and businesses   _____
7. W-2 wages from specified service trades and businesses   _____
8. Unadjusted basis of qualified property from specified service trades or businesses   _____
9. Eligible percentage: Subtract Part I, line 5 from 100 percent   _____
10. Eligible portion of qualified business income: Multiply line 6 by line 9. Enter on Part III, line 13b   _____
11. Eligible portion of W-2 wages: Multiply line 7 by line 9. Enter on Part III, line 15b   _____
12. Eligible portion of the unadjusted basis of qualified property: Multiply line 8 by line 9. Enter on Part III, line 18b   _____

Part III: Complete Part III to determine the phase-in of the W-2 wage limitation when taxable income is within the phase-in range noted in Part I.

13a. Qualified business income from nonservice trades and businesses   _____
13b. Eligible portion of qualified business income from specified service trades and businesses: Enter the amount from Part II, line 10   _____
13c. Total qualified business income: Add lines 13a and 13b   _____
14. Tentative QBI deduction: Multiply line 13c by 20%   _____
15a. W-2 wages from nonservice trades and businesses   _____
15b. Eligible portion of W-2 wages from specified service trades and businesses: Enter the amount from Part II, line 11   _____

15c. Total W-2 wages: Add lines 15a and 15b   _____

16. Multiply line 3c by 50%   _____

17. Multiply line 3c by 25%   _____

18a. Unadjusted basis of qualified property from nonservice trades and businesses   _____

18b. Eligible portion of the unadjusted basis of qualified property from specified service trades and businesses: Enter the amount from Part II, line 12   _____

18c. Total unadjusted basis of qualified property: Add lines 18a and 18b   _____

19. Multiply line 18c by 2.5%   _____

20. Add lines 17 and 19   _____

21. Enter the greater of line 16 or line 20   _____

22. Subtract line 21 from line 14. If less than zero, enter zero   _____

23. Total phase-in reduction: Multiply line 22 by Part I, line 5   _____

24. Tentative QBI deduction after phase-in reduction: Subtract line 23 from line 14   _____

Part IV. Compute the final QBI deduction.

25. Enter the smaller of Part III, line 14, or Part III, line 21   _____

26. QBI deduction before taxable income limitation: Enter the greater of line 24 or line 25   _____

27. Taxable income before qualified business income deduction   _____

28. Net capital gain   _____

29. Subtract line 28 from line 27. If less than zero, enter zero   _____

30. Taxable income limitation: Multiply line 29 by 20%   _____

31. QBI deduction: Enter lesser of line 26 or line 30   _____

Note: The worksheets above ignore complexities related to REITs, publicly traded partnerships, and cooperatives that are beyond the scope of this textbook.

Chapter **Eleven**

The Corporate Taxpayer

Learning Objectives

After studying this chapter, you should be able to:

LO 11-1. Identify the four primary legal characteristics of corporations.

LO 11-2. Compute the corporate charitable contribution and dividends-received deductions.

LO 11-3. Prepare a reconciliation of book and taxable income.

LO 11-4. Compute the regular tax on corporate taxable income.

LO 11-5. Discuss the purpose and calculation of the corporate alternative minimum tax.

LO 11-6. Describe the corporate tax payment and return filing requirements.

LO 11-7. Explain why corporate profits distributed as dividends are double-taxed.

LO 11-8. Discuss the incidence of the corporate income tax.

In the previous chapter, we studied business organizations that are not taxable entities: sole proprietorships, partnerships, limited liability companies (LLCs), and S corporations. These organizations are conduits of business income to the owners who are taxed directly on such income. In this chapter, we turn to the rules governing the taxation of business income earned by corporations.[1] In contrast to sole proprietorships and passthrough entities, corporations are taxpayers in their own right. The tax on corporate profits is determined without reference to the tax situations of the shareholders who own the corporation.

We begin with a discussion of the legal characteristics of corporations. The discussion then shifts to the computation of corporate taxable income and the reconciliation of that income with financial statement income. The corporate tax rate structure is examined and the function of tax credits is explained. This chapter concludes by analyzing the tax consequences of distributions of earnings to corporate investors.

---

[1] Corporations for which a subchapter S election is not in effect are referred to as regular corporations or C corporations. In this text, any reference to a corporation means the taxable, rather than the passthrough, variety.

LEGAL CHARACTERISTICS OF CORPORATIONS

LO 11-1
Identify the four primary legal characteristics of corporations.

A corporation is an entity formed under state law to conduct a business enterprise. Ownership of the entity is represented by the outstanding shares of corporate stock. **Closely held corporations** are privately owned by a relatively small number of shareholders. These shareholders are often personally involved in the operation of the corporate business, and their ownership is stable over time. In contrast, the stock in **publicly held corporations** is traded on established securities markets such as the New York Stock Exchange or Nasdaq. The ownership of these corporations may be diffused over thousands of shareholders and may change on a daily basis.

Many entrepreneurs operate in the corporate form because of the advantageous legal and financial characteristics. One important legal characteristic is the **limited liability** of shareholders. The rights of corporate creditors and other claimants extend only to corporate assets and not to the personal assets of the corporation's owners. While this characteristic protects shareholders against many types of business risk, the scope of the protection is narrowed by two facts. First, financial institutions may refuse to lend money to closely held corporate businesses unless the shareholders personally guarantee repayment of the debt. Second, licensed professionals, such as physicians, attorneys, and CPAs, cannot avoid personal liability for their negligence or misconduct by operating in the corporate form. Even if they offer their services to the public as employees of a personal service corporation, professionals typically must protect themselves by carrying personal malpractice insurance.

A second attractive characteristic is the **unlimited life** of a corporation. Under state and federal law, corporations are persons separate and distinct from their owners. Consequently, their legal existence is not affected by changes in the identity of their shareholders. This characteristic gives corporations the vitality and stability so conducive to a successful enterprise. A related characteristic is the **free transferability** of equity interests in corporations. Stock in publicly held corporations is a highly liquid asset; investors can buy and sell this stock with maximum convenience and minimal transaction cost in a regulated market. As a result, publicly held corporations have access to millions of potential investors and can raise large amounts of venture capital.

Tax Talk
For 2021, the corporate income tax accounted for 10.2 percent of gross federal tax collections and less than 1 percent of returns filed with the IRS.

In the context of closely held corporations, the characteristic of free transferability may be conspicuously absent. Shareholders are often family members or colleagues who want to protect the ownership of the business from outsiders. To this end, the stock in closely held corporations is usually subject to some type of **buy–sell agreement.** The agreement may prohibit the owner from disposing of the stock without approval of the other shareholders, or it may restrict the owner from transferring the stock to anyone but the existing shareholders or the corporation itself.

A fourth corporate characteristic is **centralized management.** Unlike a sole proprietorship or a general partnership, a corporation is not directly managed by its owners. Instead, managerial decisions are made by a board of directors appointed by and acting on behalf of the shareholders and by the officers who are hired by the board of directors. This characteristic is crucial to the efficient management of publicly held corporations with thousands of shareholders. In contrast, the shareholders of closely held corporations usually serve on the board of directors and are employed as corporate officers. In such cases, the characteristic of centralized management has little significance.

Affiliated Groups

For various legal, financial, and managerial reasons, a single corporate entity may not be the best organizational form for a multifaceted enterprise. The enterprise may operate more efficiently if it is compartmentalized into several corporate entities that form an **affiliated group.**

Affiliated groups consist of a parent corporation that directly owns 80 percent or more of at least one subsidiary corporation plus all other subsidiaries that are 80 percent owned within the group.[2] Only taxable, domestic corporations are included in an affiliated group. The following diagram illustrates an affiliated group consisting of four corporations:

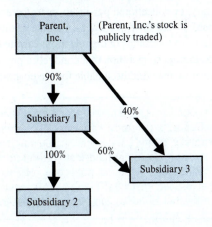

Parent, Inc. is the parent corporation of the affiliated group because of its direct 90 percent ownership of Subsidiary 1. Subsidiaries 2 and 3 are also included in the group because 100 percent of each corporation's outstanding stock is owned within the group.

An affiliated group may consist of just two corporations or a conglomerate with hundreds of subsidiaries. Regardless of an affiliated group's size, the tax law treats it as one entity. For instance, an affiliated group may elect to file a **consolidated tax return**—one return reporting the combined results of the operations of all corporations in the group.[3] The major advantage of consolidated filing is that a net loss generated by one corporate member can offset the taxable income generated by other members.

Consolidated
Return Filing

Refer to the affiliated group illustrated in the previous diagram. This year, the separate operations of the group members resulted in the following:

	Net Income (Loss)
Parent, Inc.	$ 960,000
Subsidiary 1	(750,000)
Subsidiary 2	225,000
Subsidiary 3	114,000

If the corporations file on a separate basis, Parent, Inc., Subsidiary 2, and Subsidiary 3 report their incomes on their respective tax returns, and Subsidiary 1 reports a $750,000 net operating loss on its tax return. This loss will generate no immediate tax benefit but could produce future tax savings to Subsidiary 1 through an NOL carryforward. If the group files a consolidated return, the taxable income on the return is $549,000 (combined net income and loss for the four members). Consequently, Subsidiary 1's loss generates an immediate tax benefit by reducing the affiliated group's taxable income by $750,000.

---

[2] §1504(a)(1).

[3] §1501.

Nonprofit Corporations

Many corporations are formed to conduct philanthropic, rather than profit-motivated, activities. As a general rule, these **nonprofit corporations** are nontaxable entities. Specifically, any corporation formed exclusively for "religious, charitable, scientific, testing for public safety, literary, or educational purposes, or to foster national or international amateur sports competition" is exempt from federal income taxation.[4] The IRS is generous in granting tax-exempt status to thousands of organizations devoted to some aspect of the public good. Nonetheless, a tax-exempt corporation that conducts a profitable sideline activity unrelated to its philanthropic purpose may find itself liable for the corporate tax on unrelated business taxable income.[5]

Unrelated Business Taxable Income

Phi Delta Theta is a national fraternity organized as a tax-exempt corporation. The fraternity published a quarterly magazine, *The Scroll,* that featured articles concerning the achievements of fraternity members and alumni. The publication costs were paid from the earnings from an endowment fund that generated more than $100,000 annual investment income. The IRS determined that publication of *The Scroll* was incidental to the educational purpose that justified Phi Delta Theta's tax-exempt status. Consequently, the annual income from the endowment fund was unrelated business income on which the fraternity must pay tax.[6]

Tax Talk

During 2021, IRS data shows that just 33 universities paid $68 million of excise tax on their investment income, far less than official government estimates of revenue to be generated by this tax.

The Tax Cuts and Jobs Act enacted two new excise taxes that apply to certain tax-exempt organizations for tax years beginning after December 31, 2017. First, the act imposes an excise tax of 1.4 percent on net investment income of certain private colleges and universities. The tax applies only to such tax-exempt institutions with at least 500 students and at least $500,000 of assets per student. Second, a tax-exempt organization is now subject to corporate income tax on compensation in excess of $1 million paid to its five highest compensated employees.

COMPUTING CORPORATE TAXABLE INCOME

LO 11-2
Compute the corporate charitable contribution and dividends-received deductions.

Corporations report their taxable income and calculate the federal tax on that income on Form 1120 (U.S. Corporation Income Tax Return). The information on page 1, Form 1120, is essentially the corporation's income statement for tax accounting purposes.

Form 1120

Movement Plus, Inc., a calendar year, accrual basis corporation, operates aerobics and dance studios. The first page of Movement Plus's Form 1120 is reproduced as Exhibit 11.1. The corporation recognized $834,390 gross profit from fees and memberships (lines 1c and 3) and $1,410 interest income from short-term investments of excess working capital (line 5). These two items represent Movement Plus's total income of $835,800 on line 11. The corporation's deductible operating expenses are listed on lines 12 through 26 and totaled to $510,860. on line 27. Movement Plus had a $6,700 NOL carryforward reported as a deduction on line 29c. The corporation's $318,240. taxable income is reported on line 30.

As discussed in Chapter 6, taxable income equals gross income minus allowable deductions. The rules discussed in Chapters 6 through 9, for determining gross income, ordinary and necessary business deductions, cost recovery deductions, and the tax treatment of property

---

[4] 26 U.S. Code §501(a) and (c)(3).

[5] §511 and §512.

[6] *Phi Delta Theta Fraternity* v. *Commissioner,* 887 F.2d 1302 (CA-6, 1989).

EXHIBIT 11.1

Source: Internal Revenue Service

Form **1120**	U.S. Corporation Income Tax Return		OMB No. 1545-0123

Department of the Treasury
Internal Revenue Service

For calendar year 2022 or tax year beginning _____ , 2022, ending _____ , 20 _____

Go to *www.irs.gov/Form1120* for instructions and the latest information.

2022

A Check if:
1a Consolidated return (attach Form 851)
b Life/nonlife consolidated return .
2 Personal holding co. (attach Sch. PH) .
3 Personal service corp. (see instructions) .
4 Schedule M-3 attached

TYPE OR PRINT

Name — Movement Plus Inc.

Number, street, and room or suite no. If a P.O. box, see instructions. — 48010 Sun Valley Road

City or town, state or province, country, and ZIP or foreign postal code — Albuquerque, NM 87121

B Employer identification number — 28-4288317

C Date incorporated — August 15, 1998

D Total assets (see instructions) — $ 642,212

E Check if: (1) ☐ Initial return (2) ☐ Final return (3) ☐ Name change (4) ☐ Address change

Income

1a	Gross receipts or sales . . .	1a	834,390	
b	Returns and allowances . . .	1b		
c	Balance. Subtract line 1b from line 1a . . .	1c		834,390
2	Cost of goods sold (attach Form 1125-A) . . .	2		
3	Gross profit. Subtract line 2 from line 1c . . .	3		
4	Dividends and inclusions (Schedule C, line 23) . . .	4		1,410
5	Interest . . .	5		
6	Gross rents . . .	6		
7	Gross royalties . . .	7		
8	Capital gain net income (attach Schedule D (Form 1120)) . . .	8		
9	Net gain or (loss) from Form 4797, Part II, line 17 (attach Form 4797) . . .	9		
10	Other income (see instructions—attach statement) . . .	10		
11	**Total income.** Add lines 3 through 10 . . .	11		835,800

Deductions (See instructions for limitations on deductions.)

12	Compensation of officers (see instructions—attach Form 1125-E) . . .	12	40,000
13	Salaries and wages (less employment credits) . . .	13	255,100
14	Repairs and maintenance . . .	14	16,900
15	Bad debts . . .	15	
16	Rents . . .	16	43,300
17	Taxes and licenses . . .	17	24,750
18	Interest (see instructions) . . .	18	
19	Charitable contributions . . .	19	35,360
20	Depreciation from Form 4562 not claimed on Form 1125-A or elsewhere on return (attach Form 4562) . . .	20	42,600
21	Depletion . . .	21	
22	Advertising . . .	22	12,200
23	Pension, profit-sharing, etc., plans . . .	23	
24	Employee benefit programs . . .	24	
25	Reserved for future use . . .	25	
26	Other deductions (attach statement) . . .	26	40,650
27	**Total deductions.** Add lines 12 through 26 . . .	27	510,860
28	Taxable income before net operating loss deduction and special deductions. Subtract line 27 from line 11. .	28	324,940
29a	Net operating loss deduction (see instructions) . . .	29a	6,700
b	Special deductions (Schedule C, line 24) . . .	29b	
c	Add lines 29a and 29b . . .	29c	6,700

Tax, Refundable Credits, and Payments

30	**Taxable income.** Subtract line 29c from line 28. See instructions . . .	30	318,240
31	Total tax (Schedule J, Part I, line 11) . . .	31	66,830
32	Reserved for future use . . .	32	
33	Total payments and credits (Schedule J, Part III, line 23) . . .	33	110,000
34	Estimated tax penalty. See instructions. Check if Form 2220 is attached . . . ☐	34	
35	**Amount owed.** If line 33 is smaller than the total of lines 31 and 34, enter amount owed . . .	35	
36	**Overpayment.** If line 33 is larger than the total of lines 31 and 34, enter amount overpaid . . .	36	33,170
37	Enter amount from line 36 you want: **Credited to 2023 estimated tax** _____ **Refunded**	37	33,170

Sign Here

Under penalties of perjury, I declare that I have examined this return, including accompanying schedules and statements, and to the best of my knowledge and belief, it is true, correct, and complete. Declaration of preparer (other than taxpayer) is based on all information of which preparer has any knowledge.

Signature of officer _____ Date _____ Title _____

May the IRS discuss this return with the preparer shown below? See instructions. ☐ Yes ☐ No

Paid Preparer Use Only

Print/Type preparer's name	Preparer's signature	Date	Check ☐ if self-employed	PTIN
Firm's name			Firm's EIN	
Firm's address			Phone no.	

For Paperwork Reduction Act Notice, see separate instructions. Cat. No. 11450Q Form **1120** (2022)

Tax Talk

IRS statistics indicate that approximately 2.1 million Form 1120 corporate income tax returns were filed for 2021, an increase of 17.8 percent from 2020.

transactions apply in determining corporate taxable income. In addition, a number of special rules apply only to corporate taxpayers. Two such special rules are the limitation on deductibility of corporate charitable contributions and the dividends-received deduction.

Corporations are allowed a deduction for charitable contributions. The annual deduction is limited to 10 percent of taxable income *before* the deduction. Contributions in excess of this limit are carried forward for five years as a deduction against future income.[7]

---

[7] §170(b)(2) and (d)(2). For purposes of this limitation, taxable income is computed without any dividends-received deductions or loss carrybacks into the year.

Limit on Contribution Deduction	Movement Plus, Inc. contributed $40,000 to local charities. However, its deduction for the contribution is limited to $35,360, as shown on line 19, Form 1120. This limitation is computed as follows:

Total income (line 11)	$835,800
Deductions *excluding* line 19 and *including* NOL deduction	(482,200)
Taxable income *before* charitable contribution deduction	$353,600
	.10
Charitable contribution deduction	$ 35,360

Movement Plus has a $4,640 contribution carryforward ($40,000 contribution − $35,360 contribution deduction) into next year.

The Dividends-Received Deduction

The last deduction listed on the first page of Form 1120 (and described on line 29b as a special deduction) is the **dividends-received deduction.**[8] Corporations that receive dividends from other taxable, domestic corporations are entitled to this deduction. Noncorporate shareholders are not eligible for the dividends-received deduction.

Prior to 2018, dividends received from foreign corporations were generally not eligible for the deduction. However, the Tax Cuts and Jobs Act has dramatically altered the treatment of foreign dividends after 2017. In general, dividends received by a domestic corporation from a foreign corporation owned at least 10 percent by domestic corporations are now entitled to a 100 percent dividends-received deduction. This change in tax policy and its implications for global investment are explored in more detail in Chapter 13.

For dividends received from domestic corporations, the dividends-received deduction equals a percentage of the total dividends included in gross income. The percentage depends on the recipient corporation's investment in the corporation paying the dividend, as shown in the following schedule:

- If the recipient corporation owns *less than 20 percent* of the stock of the paying corporation, the deduction equals 50 percent of the dividends received.
- If the recipient corporation owns *at least 20 percent but less than 80 percent* of the stock of the paying corporation, the deduction equals 65 percent of the dividends received.
- If the recipient corporation owns *80 percent or more* of the stock of the paying corporation, the deduction equals 100 percent of the dividends received.

Dividends-Received Deduction	ABC, Inc. owns 5 percent of the stock of Corporation X, 50 percent of the stock of Corporation Y, and 83 percent of the stock of Corporation Z. The three corporations in which ABC invested are taxable, domestic entities. ABC's current year gross income includes the following dividends:

Corporation X dividend	$ 24,000
Corporation Y dividend	8,000
Corporation Z dividend	90,000
	$122,000

[8] §243. If corporate taxable income *before* the dividends-received deduction is less than the corporation's dividend income, the 50 percent and 65 percent deductions are limited to the respective percentages of such taxable income by §246(b)(1).

ABC's dividends-received deduction is $107,200.

Deduction for Corporation X dividend ($24,000 × 50%)	$12,000
Deduction for Corporation Y dividend ($8,000 × 65%)	5,200
Deduction for Corporation Z dividend ($90,000 × 100%)	90,000
	$107,200

The dividends-received deduction percentages were significantly altered by the Tax Cuts and Jobs Act of 2017. The percentages shown apply to dividends received in tax years beginning after December 31, 2017. Prior to 2018, the 50 percent deduction (65 percent) was 70 percent (80 percent).

Because of the dividends-received deduction, only $14,800 of ABC's gross dividend income is included in taxable income. If ABC's marginal tax rate is 21 percent, the tax on this income is $3,108, and ABC's tax rate on its dividend income is only 2.5 percent ($3,108 ÷ $122,000). This low rate is not as generous as it first may seem. The dividends that ABC included in gross income represent after-tax dollars because Corporations X, Y, and Z already paid federal income tax on the earnings distributed as dividends to their investors (including ABC). As we will discuss in a later section of this chapter, ABC's dividends-received deduction simply prevents most of these earnings from being taxed again at the corporate level.

Reconciling Book Income and Taxable Income

LO 11-3
Prepare a reconciliation of book and taxable income.

Because of differences between the measurement of income for federal tax purposes and the measurement of income under generally accepted accounting principles (GAAP), the taxable income reported on page 1, Form 1120, is usually not the same as the net income reported on the corporation's financial statements. The corporation must reconcile the two numbers so that the IRS can identify the differences between financial statement income and taxable income. Until 2004, all corporations provided this reconciliation on Schedule M-1, page 6, Form 1120. In 2004, the IRS developed a new reconciliation Schedule M-3 for use by corporations with total assets of $10 million or more. Schedule M-3 requires much more detailed information than Schedule M-1 and should make the book/tax reconciliation more transparent to revenue agents. According to the IRS, "The new schedule will enable us to focus our

Book/Tax Reconciliation

Diamont, Inc., which has total assets of $6.81 million, reported $343,093 net income after tax on its audited financial statements and $453,364 taxable income on its Form 1120. Here is Schedule M-1 reconciling these numbers:

Schedule M-1	**Reconciliation of Income (Loss) per Books With Income per Return**				
	Note: The corporation may be required to file Schedule M-3. See instructions.				
1	Net income (loss) per books	343,093	7	Income recorded on books this year not included on this return (itemize):	
2	Federal income tax per books	181,474			
3	Excess of capital losses over capital gains	20,500		Tax-exempt interest $	
4	Income subject to tax not recorded on books this year (itemize):			Deferred gain like-kind exchange	71,200
	Prepaid rent	8,100	8	Deductions on this return not charged against book income this year (itemize):	
5	Expenses recorded on books this year not deducted on this return (itemize):		a	Depreciation $ 43,812	
a	Depreciation $		b	Charitable contributions $	
b	Charitable contributions $				
c	Travel and entertainment $ 13,909				43,812
	Bad debts	15,209	9	Add lines 7 and 8	115,012
6	Add lines 1 through 5	568,376	10	Income (page 1, line 28)—line 6 less line 9	453,364

(continued)

- Diamont's net income per books is entered on line 1, and the federal income tax expense per books is entered on line 2.[9] This expense is not deductible in the computation of taxable income.
- Diamont realized a $20,500 net capital loss on the sale of investment securities and included the loss in financial statement income. This nondeductible loss is entered on line 3.
- Diamont received $8,100 prepaid rent that was recorded as a liability for unearned revenues for financial statement purposes. This taxable income is entered on line 4.
- Diamont incurred $27,818 of business meals expense not provided by a restaurant. The nondeductible 50 percent of this expense is entered on line 5(c).
- Diamont's addition to its allowance for bad debts exceeded its actual write-off of uncollectible accounts receivable by $1,300. This nondeductible excess is entered on line 5.

The total on line 6 is financial statement income increased by (1) taxable income items not included in book income and (2) expense items not deducted on the tax return.

- Diamont realized a $71,200 gain on an exchange of commercial real estate. The exchange involved like-kind properties so the realized gain was not recognized for tax purposes. The deferred gain is entered on line 7.
- Diamont's MACRS depreciation deduction exceeded its depreciation expense per books by $43,812. This excess is entered on line 8(a).

The total on line 9 equals (1) book income items not included in taxable income and (2) allowable deductions not reported as expenses for book purposes.

Line 10 is the final number in the reconciliation: taxable income reported on page 1, Form 1120, *before* any NOL deduction and dividends-received deduction. Diamont had neither of these special deductions this year. Consequently, it paid federal tax on $453,364 income.

compliance resources on returns and issues that need to be examined and avoid those that do not." Schedule M-3 is included as Appendix 11–A to this chapter.

Corporations with total assets of less than $10 million may continue to provide their book/tax reconciliation on Schedule M-1. Here is an example of such reconciliation:

Schedule M-1 is organized so that unfavorable book/tax differences (those increasing taxable income) are reported on the left side of the form, while favorable book/tax differences (those decreasing taxable income) are reported on the right side of the form. As noted in the example, line 10 of Schedule M-1 is not bottom-line taxable income. Instead, line 10 equals taxable income before any NOL deduction and the dividends-received deduction. For corporations with such special deductions, Schedule M-1 does not provide a full reconciliation to taxable income.

COMPUTING THE REGULAR CORPORATE TAX

LO 11-4
Compute the regular tax on corporate taxable income.

The final section on the first page of Form 1120 (Exhibit 11.1) is labeled "Tax and Payments." After the corporation has computed taxable income, it must calculate the federal tax on that income. The first step in the calculation is to determine the corporation's regular tax. For earnings after December 31, 2017, corporate tax liability is computed based on a flat tax rate of 21 percent. Prior to that date, the corporate income tax was based on the following rate schedule:[10]

[9] See the discussion of tax expense versus tax payable in Chapter 6.
[10] §11(b)(1), prior to amendment by the Tax Cuts and Jobs Act.

If taxable income is	The tax is
Not over $50,000	15% of taxable income
Over $50,000 but not over $75,000	$7,500 + 25% of the excess over $50,000
Over $75,000 but not over $100,000	$13,750 + 34% of the excess over $75,000
Over $100,000 but not over $335,000	$22,250 + 39% of the excess over $100,000
Over $335,000 but not over $10,000,000	$113,900 + 34% of the excess over $335,000
Over $10,000,000 but not over $15,000,000	$3,400,000 + 35% of the excess over $10,000,000
Over $15,000,000 but not over $18,333,333	$5,150,000 + 38% of the excess over $15,000,000
Over $18,333,333	$6,416,667 + 35% of the excess over $18,333,333

Fiscal year filers are subject to a transition rule for their tax year beginning in 2017 and ending in 2018. The portion of income earned prior to December 31, 2017, is taxed under the old rate structure, and the portion earned after December 31, 2017, is taxed at 21 percent.

Regular Tax Calculation

Corporation M's taxable income is $4 million. For its tax year ended December 31, 2017, based on the corporate rate schedule, the regular tax on this income is $1,360,000:

Taxable income	$4,000,000
	(335,000)
Taxable income in excess of $335,000	$3,665,000
Marginal rate on excess	.34
	$1,246,100
Tax on $335,000 (from rate schedule)	113,900
	$1,360,000

If Corporation M earns the same $4 million for its tax year ended December 31, 2018, regular tax on this income is only $840,000 ($4 million × 21 percent).

What if Corporation M's tax year ended on June 30, 2018? In this case, regular tax liability on $4 million of taxable income is $1,100,000, computed as follows:

Tax on $4 million using 2017 rate schedule	$1,360,000	
Portion of tax year during 2017	.50	$ 680,000
Tax on $4 million using 2018 tax rate	$ 840,000	
Portion of tax year during 2018	.50	420,000
Regular tax liability for June 30, 2018, tax year		$1,100,000

TAX CREDITS

A corporate (or noncorporate) taxpayer's regular tax is offset by any tax credits for which the taxpayer is eligible. A **tax credit** is a direct dollar-for-dollar reduction in tax liability. As a result, the value of a credit is greater than the value of a deduction of the same amount.

Deduction versus Credit

Jodi, Inc.'s taxable income is $600,000, and its regular tax (at 21 percent) is $126,000. If Jodi is allowed an additional $50,000 deduction, the tax decreases to $115,500, and the tax savings from the deduction is $10,500 (21 percent of $50,000). In comparison, if Jodi is

(continued)

entitled to a $50,000 tax credit, the tax decreases to $76,000, and the tax savings from the credit is $50,000.

	Deduction	Credit
Taxable income	$ 600,000	$600,000
Additional deduction	(50,000)	
Recomputed taxable income	$ 550,000	$600,000
	.21	.21
Precredit tax	$ 115,500	$126,000
Tax credit		(50,000)
Recomputed tax	$ 115,500	$ 76,000

Tax credits are generally nonrefundable, which means they can reduce current year tax to zero, but any credit in excess of precredit tax does not generate a refund from the Treasury. However, the tax law may provide that an excess credit can be carried back or forward to reduce tax in a different year.

Because tax credits reduce the regular tax on business income, they are equivalent to a preferential tax rate. Thus, tax credits utilize the character variable, discussed in Chapter 4, to reduce tax liability. To be eligible for a particular credit, taxpayers must engage in very specific activities or transactions that Congress believes are worthy of government support. From this perspective, tax credits are instruments of fiscal policy and are enacted by Congress to increase the efficiency of the tax system as an agent of economic change. Currently, the tax law provides a **general business credit,** which is the sum of 26 different credits for the tax year.[11]

Most of these 26 credits are narrow in scope and are available to relatively few businesses. Moreover, the list of credits changes as Congress experiments with new credits and discards those that fail to produce the intended behavioral result. To learn how a tax credit can induce a certain behavior, we will look at the mechanics of just one credit.

Rehabilitation Credit

Taxpayers who renovate or reconstruct buildings certified as historic structures by the U.S. Department of the Interior are entitled to a **rehabilitation credit.**[12] The credit equals 20 percent of the rehabilitation costs of a certified historic structure. The credit is claimed ratably over a five-year period, beginning in the tax year in which a qualified rehabilitated structure is placed in service. Congress designed this credit to encourage businesses to undertake urban renewal projects that might be financially unfeasible without the tax savings from the credit.

[11] §38. The general business credit that a taxpayer can use each year is limited to $25,000 plus 75 percent of precredit tax in excess of $25,000. §38(c). Any unused credit can be carried back 1 year and forward 20 years. §39(a).

[12] §47. The rehabilitation credit was substantially narrowed by the Tax Cuts and Jobs Act. The discussion here focuses on requirements to claim the credit on projects initiated after December 31, 2017.

Rehabilitation Credit

Quick Corporation must locate a suitable facility to house one of its regional offices and has narrowed its search to two buildings. One building is newly constructed and ready for occupancy. The second building is a certified historic structure in need of extensive renovation. The purchase price of the first building is $10 million, while the purchase price of the second building is only $3 million. Quick estimates that the rehabilitation costs for the second building would be $7.5 million. For tax purposes, Quick's cost basis in either building ($10 million for the new building or $10.5 million for the old building) can be depreciated over the same 39-year recovery period. Assume any rehabilitation credit would be claimed ratably over years 0 through 4. Quick uses a 5 percent discount rate to calculate present value.

Without the rehabilitation credit, the cost of the new building is less than that of the old building, and Quick has no reason to invest in the certified historic structure. However, the credit reduces the cost of the old building to $9,136,200:

Purchase price	$ 3,000,000
Rehabilitation cost	7,500,000
	$10,500,000
Tax savings from credit ($7,500,000 × 20%)	
Year 0 credit ($1,500,000 ÷ 5)	(300,000)
Present value of years 1 to 4 credit	(1,063,800)
($300,000 × 3.546 annuity factor)	
After-tax cost	$ 9,136,200

Because of the rehabilitation credit, Quick minimizes its cost by purchasing the certified historic structure. Note that the tax savings from the credit is not a function of Quick's marginal tax rate. But the savings calculation is based on the assumption that precredit tax is sufficient to allow full use of the credit in years 0 through 4. If this is not the case and Quick must carry forward some of the credit for use in future years, the present value of the carryforward might be insufficient to tip the scale in favor of the rehabilitation project.

Save a Building, Save Tax

The National Park Service released a report summarizing the positive effects of the rehabilitation credit on historic preservation. According to the report, 2,967 historic buildings were preserved in the five-year period of the report, including Chicago office towers, Baltimore row houses, St. Louis warehouses, and Miami art deco hotels. The Park Service concluded that the tax credit "leverages private investment in depressed neighborhoods, creates jobs, promotes community preservation, fosters heritage education, enhances state and local tax revenues, and increases property values."[13] Not bad for a tax credit!

Tax Talk
In 2015, corporations claimed over $14.3 trillion in research activities credits.

Other popular corporate tax credits included in the general business credit include the following: the research activities credit, promoting basic scientific research activities; the empowerment zone employment credit, for hiring employees in designated economically distressed areas; the low-income housing credit, for construction or renovation of multiunit low-income housing; and the tax credit for alternative-fuel vehicles. The details of these credits are beyond the scope of this text. The foreign tax credit, intended to mitigate double taxation of foreign earnings of U.S. taxpayers, is discussed in more detail in Chapter 13.

---

[13] Source: "Tax Matters," *Journal of Accountancy,* September 2001, p. 107.

ALTERNATIVE MINIMUM TAX

LO 11-5
Discuss the purpose and calculation of the corporate alternative minimum tax.

Tax Talk
The Inflation Reduction Act also created a 1 percent excise tax on stock redemptions by domestic corporations whose stock is publicly traded. While the tax was intended to deter stock buybacks, many companies appear to regard it as simply another cost of doing business.

The **alternative minimum tax (AMT)** is a second federal tax system parallel to the regular income tax system described throughout the text. Congress enacted the corporate AMT primarily for political reasons. Under the regular tax system, corporations with substantial economic income can occasionally take advantage of tax exclusions, deductions, or credits to dramatically reduce, or even eliminate, their taxes. In past years, these occasions received a great deal of publicity and caused people to lose respect for a tax system so riddled with "loopholes" that huge companies could escape taxation altogether. In response to this embarrassing public perception, Congress created a backup system to ensure that every corporation pays a "fair share" of the federal tax burden.

For tax years beginning after December 31, 2017, the Tax Cuts and Jobs Act (TCJA) repealed the corporate AMT. As discussed in Chapter 14, the AMT remains in place for individuals. For tax years beginning after December 31, 2022, the Inflation Reduction Act of 2022 imposes a new 15 percent corporate alternative minimum tax based on financial statement income.

The new corporate AMT applies only to very large corporations with average annual adjusted financial statement income (AFSI) in excess of $1 billion over the three preceding years. Once a corporation is subject to the new AMT, it remains subject for all future tax years.

Corporation subject to AMT?

JKL Corporation has the following AFSI amounts for the three years preceding 2023:

Year	AFSI
2020	$ 820,445,000
2021	1,100,332,591
2022	1,345,099,000

JKL's average AFSI over this three-year period is $1,088,625,530. Thus, JKL is subject to the new corporate AMT for 2023 and beyond.

Calculating AFSI

The starting point for computing AFSI is the taxpayer's net income or loss on its applicable financial statement for the tax year, generally a financial statement prepared in accordance with Generally Accepted Accounting Principles (GAAP) or International Financial Reporting Standards (IFRS). Financial statement net income or loss is then adjusted as follows:[14]

- Federal income taxes and foreign income, war profits, and excess profits taxes are disregarded.
- The excess of MACRS depreciation over book depreciation is subtracted (excess of book depreciation over MACRS depreciation is added).
- Financial statement NOL carryforwards are subtracted, limited to 80 percent of AFSI computed without regard to NOL carryforwards.

---

[14] A number of other adjustments, primarily related to affiliated groups and multinational entities, are beyond the scope of this text and thus are omitted from the list of adjustments shown.

Adjusted Financial Statement Income

Mahalo Corporation has GAAP financial statement net income of $2,550,000,000 and no net operating loss carryforwards. For purposes of the corporate AMT, its adjusted financial statement income (AFSI) is computed as follows:

GAAP net income	$2,550,000,000
Plus: federal income tax expense	561,000,000
Minus: excess of MACRS over book depreciation	(221,076,800)
Adjusted financial statement income	$2,889,923,200

Corporations with net losses are permitted to carry those losses forward for purposes of computing AFSI. These financial statement NOL carryforwards are computed with the same adjustments made in calculating AFSI.

AFSI with NOL Carryforwards

Bento Corporation has 2023 adjusted financial statement income of $1,830,000,000 before considering net operating loss carryforwards. If the corporation's financial statement NOL carryforwards total $3 billion, its AFSI is computed as follows:

AFSI before NOL carryforwards	$1,830,000,000
Minus NOL deduction - lesser of	
$3,000,000,000 or	
$1,464,000,000 ($1,830,000,000 x 80%)	(1,464,000,000)
Adjusted financial statement income	$ 366,000,000

Calculating AMT

Calculation of the corporate AMT is a two-step process. First, AFSI is multiplied by a flat 15 percent rate to compute tentative minimum tax. Second, tentative minimum tax is compared to the sum of the corporation's regular tax liability and any **base erosion and anti-abuse tax (BEAT)** owed on cross-border related party transactions.[15] AMT liability equals any excess of tentative minimum tax over regular tax plus BEAT. The AMT is paid in addition to regular tax.

AMT Calculation

Refer to the previous example in which Bento Corporation's 2023 AFSI is $366,000,000. If Bento's regular tax liability is $52,000,000 and it owes no BEAT, Bento's AMT and total tax owed is computed as follows:

AFSI	$366,000,000
	.15
Tentative minimum tax	$ 54,900,000
Regular tax	(52,000,000)
AMT	$ 2,900,000
Total tax (regular tax + AMT)	$ 54,900,000

[15] The BEAT tax is discussed in more detail in Chapter 13.

Minimum Tax Credit

In the preceding example, the fact that Bento's $54,900,000 tax bill consists of both regular tax and AMT may seem to be of little practical importance. Even so, corporations must carefully track their AMT because this payment is transformed into a **minimum tax credit.** This credit is created when AMT is paid, and is usable in the future only against regular tax liability. However, the credit cannot reduce regular tax liability to less than the corporation's tentative minimum tax for the year. The logic behind the credit is that the corporate AMT is not designed as a permanent tax increase. Instead, AMT merely accelerates the payment of tax into years when corporate taxable income is dramatically less than AFSI. Let's extend our Bento example to demonstrate the important function of the minimum tax credit.

Minimum Tax Credit	In 2024, Bento Corporation's AFSI is $350,000,000 and its regular tax liability is $56,000,000. Bento's total tax owed is computed as follows:

AFSI	$350,000,000
	.15
Tentative minimum tax	$ 52,500,000
Regular tax	$ 56,000,000
AMT (regular tax exceeds tentative minimum tax	0
Minimum tax credit from 2023	(2,900,000)
Total tax	$ 53,100,000

In this two-year example, the AMT affected only the timing and not the total amount of Bento's income tax. With or without AMT, Bento pays $108 million total tax for the two years.

	Two-Year Summary for Bento	
	Total Tax with AMT	**Total Tax without AMT**
2023	$ 54,900,000	$ 52,000,000
2024	53,100,000	56,000,000
	$108,000,000	$108,000,000

The effect of the AMT over the two-year period was to accelerate $2,900,000 of tax into the earlier year, not to permanently increase that tax. Realistically, AMT may take any number of years to reverse as minimum tax credits against regular tax. For growing businesses, each successive year's tentative minimum tax may exceed regular tax. In such cases, use of the minimum tax credit is postponed indefinitely. Of course, regardless of the fact that a corporation may recoup AMT in a future year, that AMT always increases the corporation's tax cost in present value terms.

PAYMENT AND FILING REQUIREMENTS

LO 11-6
Describe the corporate tax payment and return filing requirements.

Corporations are required to pay their federal income tax for the year in four installments.[16] Each installment is 25 percent of the annual tax, and the installments are due by the 15th day of the 4th, 6th, 9th, and 12th months of the taxable year. Corporations that fail to make their required installment payments on a timely basis incur an **underpayment penalty.** If the total of the installment payments is less than the actual tax reported on Form 1120, the corporation must pay the balance due by the 15th day of the third month following the close of the taxable year.[17] If the total is more than the actual tax, the corporation is entitled to a refund of the overpayment.

The required installment payments must total to 100 percent of the tax reported on Form 1120. Because corporations can't know their exact tax liability until after year-end, they must base their installment payments on their best estimate. Corporations that underestimate their tax incur the underpayment penalty. The law provides some leeway for small corporations (defined as corporations with less than $1 million taxable income). These corporations escape the underpayment penalty if their total installment payments equal 100 percent of the tax reported on the *previous* year's tax return.[18] This *safe harbor* provision is useful to newly formed corporations with rapidly growing businesses.

Safe Harbor Estimate	In 2022, Corporation DF's taxable income was $400,000, and its tax was $84,000. During 2023, DF made four $22,000 installment payments. Its 2023 taxable income was $930,000, and its tax was $195,300. Although DF paid only $88,000 tax during 2023, it did not incur an underpayment penalty because the payment exceeded 100 percent of its 2022 tax.

Tax Talk
In 2022, Hurricane Ian hit Florida less than two weeks before the October 17 extended due date for calendar-year 2021 tax returns. The IRS granted Hurricane Ian victims in Florida an additional extension of time until February 15, 2023, to file these returns.

The Transportation Act of 2015 made a significant change to corporate filing deadlines for tax years beginning after December 31, 2015. Prior to that date, corporations were required to file their annual income tax returns with the IRS by the 15th day of the third month following the close of the taxable year.[19] For tax years beginning after December 31, 2015, the new due date is the 15th day of the fourth month following the close of the taxable year. Thus, the Transportation Act gives corporations an additional month to meet their filing obligations.[20] In an exception to this change, corporations with June 30 year-ends must file their annual income tax returns by September 15, the 15th day of the third month following the close of the taxable year.

Corporations that are unable to meet this filing deadline may request an automatic six-month extension of time to file their returns, and corporations routinely take advantage of this grace period.[21] Corporations with June 30 year-ends are given a seven-month extension rather than six.

---

[16] §6655.

[17] Corporations do not send tax payments directly to the IRS. Instead, they use the Electronic Federal Tax Payment System (EFTPS) or a Federal Tax Deposit Coupon to deposit their payments in a government account maintained by a qualified depositary, such as a commercial bank.

[18] Large corporations with highly fluctuating patterns of annual income may look to other statutory exceptions to the strict 100 percent requirement for relief from the underpayment penalty.

[19] §6072(b).

[20] Although the Transportation Safety Act specified a five-month extension for calendar year corporations, the IRS has announced it will permit a six-month extension for these corporations.

[21] Reg. §1.6081-3.

It should come as no surprise that corporations that file delinquent returns may incur late-filing penalties.[22] An extension of the filing deadline does *not* extend the payment deadline for any balance of tax due for the year. Corporations must pay any estimated balance due by the initial due date of the return even if they file an extended tax return. Corporations with assets of $10 million or more are required to file their federal tax returns electronically.

Payment and Filing Requirements	Keno, a calendar year corporation, filed a Form 7004 (Application for Automatic Extension of Time to File Corporation Income Tax Return) on March 3, 2016, on which it requested a six-month extension for its 2015 return. On the application, Keno reported that its estimated 2015 tax was $258,500 and its quarterly installment payments of that tax totaled $244,000. Therefore, Keno paid its $14,500 estimated balance due with Form 7004. Keno filed its 2015 return on August 29, 2016, prior to its extended due date of September 15, 2016. The actual tax reported on the return was $255,039, which entitled Keno to a $3,461 refund of 2015 tax ($258,500 total payments − $255,039 actual tax). Under the new filing deadlines, Keno's 2022 return was due April 15, 2023, with a possible six-month extension to October 15, 2023. If Keno had a fiscal year-end of March 31, its tax return for the year ended March 31, 2023, was due July 15, 2023, with a possible six-month extension to January 15, 2024.

DISTRIBUTIONS OF PROFITS TO INVESTORS

LO 11-7
Explain why corporate profits distributed as dividends are double-taxed.

The corporate form of business organization allows an unlimited number of investors to contribute capital to the business. Investors can become creditors, either by lending money directly to the corporation in exchange for a promissory note or by purchasing the corporation's debt instruments traded on a public bond market. Alternatively, investors can become owners by contributing money or property directly to the corporation in exchange for shares of equity stock, purchasing shares from other shareholders, or purchasing shares traded on a public stock market.

Of course, both creditors and shareholders expect a return on their investment. Creditors receive interest income on their corporate notes or bonds. On the other side of the transaction, corporations can deduct the interest paid on their debt obligations, subject to the business interest limitation discussed in Chapter 6. As a result, the business profit flowing through to investors as interest is not taxed at the corporate level but only to the investors. Corporate stockholders may receive a return on their investment in the form of dividends. Corporations *cannot* deduct dividend payments in the computation of taxable income. The business profit flowing through to investors as dividends is taxed both at the corporate level and again to the shareholders receiving the dividends.

This double taxation of corporate earnings is one of the dominant characteristics of the federal income tax system. The fact that dividends are paid with after-tax dollars is a major consideration affecting the choice of organizational form—a consideration we will analyze in the next chapter. This fact also justifies the corporate dividends-received deduction. Without this deduction, business profit would be taxed over and over again as it is distributed through a chain of corporate investors before final distribution to individual shareholders for personal consumption.

---

[22] §6651 describes the penalties for late filing. These penalties are discussed in more detail in Chapter 18.

From the corporate perspective, the nondeductibility of dividend payments creates a bias in favor of debt financing.[23] A corporation that raises capital by borrowing can deduct the interest paid on the debt. At a 21 percent tax rate, the after-tax cost of the capital is only 79 percent of the before-tax cost. In effect, the federal government pays 21 percent of the return on the creditors' investment. If the corporation raises capital by selling stock, the after-tax cost of the dividends paid on that stock equals the before-tax cost. Of course, the choice of debt financing has serious nontax implications, one of the more important of which is that interest and principal payments (unlike dividends paid on common stock) are not discretionary on the part of management. Corporations with high debt-to-equity ratios have more burdensome cash flow commitments and a greater risk of insolvency than corporations with less debt in their capital structures. Companies that break faith with their creditors suffer financial distress that may even lead to bankruptcy. In many situations, the nontax costs associated with debt financing outweigh the tax savings from the corporate interest deduction.[24]

Alternatives to Double Taxation

How could the present income tax system be reformed to eliminate the double taxation of corporate income? One alternative would be to treat corporations as passthrough entities by requiring them to allocate income to their shareholders on an annual basis. Shareholders would include their share of corporate earnings in gross income and pay tax accordingly. This alternative would be administratively cumbersome, if not impossible, for publicly held corporations in which stock ownership changes daily. In addition, this alternative could cause cash flow problems for investors who find themselves owing tax on their share of corporate income but who did not receive a commensurate cash distribution from the corporation.

Another alternative is to make dividends nontaxable to individual investors so that the only tax on corporate income is at the entity level. Congress recently took an unprecedented step in this direction by enacting a 15 percent preferential tax rate for dividend income received by individuals. However, any preferential treatment of dividends is vulnerable to political attack as a tax break for the wealthy who receive much more dividend income than middle- and lower-income individuals. A variation on this alternative would be to allow corporations to deduct dividend payments (in the same way that they deduct interest payments) so that distributed corporate income would be taxed only at the shareholder level.

Still another alternative is a system in which individuals are allowed a tax credit for the corporate tax attributable to the dividends included in their gross income. For example, if a shareholder received a $7,900 dividend, representing $10,000 income on which the corporation already paid $2,100 tax, the shareholder would include the full $10,000 ($7,900 cash received grossed up by $2,100 tax) in income and compute their tax accordingly. The shareholder would then reduce that tax by a $2,100 credit. The end result is that $10,000 income is taxed only once at the individual's rate. Variations of this credit system are currently used in Canada and several western European nations.

Over the past decades, Congress and the Treasury have considered all these alternatives as solutions to the structural problem of double taxation. While the alternatives have theoretical merit, their implementation would result in significant revenue loss. Thus, it is unlikely that any of the alternatives will be enacted into law in the near future.

---

[23] Richard A. Brealey and Stewart C. Myers, *Principles of Corporate Finance,* 5th ed. (New York: McGraw-Hill, 1996), p. 418.

[24] Ibid., p. 421.

INCIDENCE OF THE CORPORATE TAX

LO 11-8
Discuss the incidence of the corporate income tax.

Because corporations are taxpayers in their own right and yet have no human persona, they become easy political targets in any debate on tax reform. People don't enjoy paying taxes and often believe that their tax burden is too heavy because some other taxpayer's burden is too light. Impersonal corporate taxpayers are scapegoats as the hue and cry becomes "raise taxes on the corporate giants, not middle-class Americans." This sentiment ignores the fact that corporations are nothing more than a form in which people organize their business, and that an increase in the corporate tax represents an additional cost of conducting that business.

Just who does pay the corporate income tax? The answer to this question varies across corporations, depending on the nature of the markets in which they compete. In some markets, corporations may shift their tax costs directly to their customers as part of the price of goods and services. In markets in which price competition is fierce, management may offset tax costs by trimming production costs. In such cases, the tax is passed on to the corporation's suppliers (smaller orders for materials), employees (lower compensation or workforce reductions), and even to consumers (lower quality). Still another possibility is that tax costs simply reduce the corporation's net income. In this case, the tax is paid by shareholders in the form of shrinking dividends or reduced market price for their stock. The question of the economic incidence of the corporate tax and whether that tax falls hardest on consumers, suppliers, labor, or capital has been researched and argued for decades without a definitive answer. Nonetheless, one conclusion is inescapable: Corporations do not pay taxes—people do.

Tax Talk
In January 2018, Starbucks announced that it would pass on tax savings from the Tax Cuts and Jobs Act to its employees via salary increases, corporate stock, and expanded benefits worth more than $250 million.

Have You Paid Your Corporate Tax Today?

According to a recent study, in 2019 the average American worked 105 days just to pay their taxes. Included in these estimates are 42 days worked to pay individual income taxes, 26 days worked to cover payroll taxes, and 5 days to pay corporate income taxes![25]

If corporate taxes fall, who reaps the benefits? The Tax Cuts and Jobs Act of 2017 provides a rare opportunity to observe the impact of a corporate tax reduction. That legislation reduced the corporate income tax rate from a top marginal rate of 35 percent to a flat rate of 21 percent. Clearly, such a rate reduction reduces corporate tax costs, and cash outflows to the government. Policymakers hope this tax savings will provide economic stimulus through increased investment and wage increases.

Conclusion

Corporations have many legal and financial characteristics that make them the entity of choice for many enterprises and the only option for publicly held companies. Corporations are taxable entities in their own right, paying tax at a flat 21 percent rate on annual income. When corporations distribute after-tax income as dividends to their shareholders, the income is taxed a second time. In the next chapter, we will consider the impact of this double taxation on the choice of business entity and the entire tax planning process.

---

[25] "Tax Freedom Day 2019," *The Tax Foundation,* April 2019. As this book goes to press, the Tax Foundation has not published a 2020, 2021, or 2022 update on "Tax Freedom Day."

Sources of Book/Tax Differences	**Permanent**	**Temporary**
	• Dividends-received deduction	• Corporate charitable contribution limitation and carryforward

Key Terms

affiliated group   *11-2*
alternative minimum tax (AMT)   *11-12*
base-erosion and anti-abuse tax (BEAT)   *11-13*
buy–sell agreement   *11-2*
centralized management   *11-2*
closely held corporation   *11-2*

consolidated tax return   *11-3*
dividends-received deduction   *11-6*
free transferability   *11-2*
general business credit   *11-10*
limited liability   *11-2*
minimum tax credit   *11-14*

nonprofit corporation   *11-4*
publicly held corporation   *11-2*
rehabilitation credit   *11-10*
tax credit   *11-9*
underpayment penalty   *11-15*
unlimited life   *11-2*

Questions and Problems for Discussion

LO 11-1 1. To what extent does the corporate characteristic of limited liability protect shareholders' employees who perform professional services for corporate clients?

LO 11-1 2. The corporate form of business is characterized by centralized management. Describe this characteristic as it applies to publicly held corporations and closely held corporations.

LO 11-1 3. The corporate form of business is characterized by free transferability of equity interests. Describe this characteristic as it applies to publicly held corporations and closely held corporations.

LO 11-1 4. Mr. and Mrs. Dane and their six children own 100 percent of the stock in three family corporations. Do these corporations qualify as an affiliated group eligible to file a consolidated corporate tax return?

LO 11-1 5. RP, Inc. owns 59 percent of QV's voting stock. RP's board of directors elects the majority of the members of QV's board of directors and thereby controls QV's management. Are RP and QV an affiliated group eligible to file a consolidated corporate tax return?

LO 11-1 6. Libretto Corporation owns a national chain of retail music stores. The corporation wants to expand into a new, extremely competitive, and highly specialized business—the composition and production of rock music videos. Can you identify any nontax reasons why Libretto may want to operate its new business through a controlled subsidiary corporation?

LO 11-2 7. Corporations are allowed a dividends-received deduction for dividends from other domestic, taxable corporations. How does this deduction prevent the same corporate income from potentially three levels of tax?

LO 11-3 8. Corporations are required to detail their book/tax differences on either Schedule M-1 or Schedule M-3 attached to the corporate income tax return. Why is the IRS interested in this information?

LO 11-4 9. In your own words, explain why a tax credit is more valuable than a tax deduction of the same dollar amount.

LO 11-5 10. For 2023, Sevilla Corporation's AFSI exceeds its regular taxable income, yet it owes no AMT. Can you explain this result?

LO 11-7, 11-8 11. In your own words, explain the conclusion that corporations do not pay tax—people do.

 **All applicable Application Problems are available with *Connect*.**

Application Problems

LO 11-1   1. The stock of AB and YZ is publicly traded, and no shareholder owns more than a 1 percent interest in either corporation. AB owns 40 percent and YZ owns 60 percent of the stock of Alpha, which owns 90 percent of the stock of Beta. YZ and Beta each own 50 percent of the stock of Kappa. Which of these corporations form an affiliated group eligible to file a consolidated tax return?

LO 11-1   2. The stock of Grommet Corporation, a U.S. company, is publicly traded, with no single share-holder owning more than 5 percent of its outstanding stock. Grommet owns 95 percent of the outstanding stock of Staple, Inc., also a U.S. company. Staple owns 100 percent of the outstanding stock of Clip Corporation, a Canadian company. Grommet and Clip each own 50 percent of the outstanding stock of Fastener, Inc., a U.S. company. Grommet and Staple each own 50 percent of the outstanding stock of Binder Corporation, a U.S. company. Which of these corporations form an affiliated group eligible to file a consoli-dated tax return?

LO 11-1   3. Corporation P owns 93 percent of the outstanding stock of Corporation T. This year, the corporation's records provide the following information:

	Corporation P	Corporation T
Ordinary operating income (loss)	$500,000	$(200,000)
Capital gain (loss)	(8,300)	6,000
Section 1231 gain (loss)	(1,000)	5,000

a. Compute each corporation's taxable income if each files a separate tax return.

b. Compute consolidated taxable income if Corporation P and Corporation T file a consolidated tax return.

LO 11-2   4. This year, Napa Corporation received the following dividends:

KLP, Inc. (a taxable Delaware corporation in which Napa holds an 8% stock interest)	$ 55,000
Gamma, Inc. (a taxable Florida corporation in which Napa holds a 90% stock interest)	120,000

Napa and Gamma do not file a consolidated tax return. Compute Napa's dividends-received deduction.

LO 11-2   5. This year, GHJ, Inc. received the following dividends:

BP, Inc. (a taxable California corporation in which GHJ holds a 2% stock interest)	$17,300
MN, Inc. (a taxable Florida corporation in which GHJ holds a 52% stock interest)	80,800
AB, Inc. (a taxable French corporation in which GHJ holds a 21% stock interest)	17,300

Compute GHJ's dividends-received deduction.

LO 11-2   6. In its first year, Camco, Inc. generated a $92,000 net operating loss, and it made a $5,000 cash donation to a local charity. In its second year, Camco generated a $210,600 profit, and it made a $10,000 donation to the same charity. Compute Camco's taxable income for its second year.

LO 11-2 7. In its first year, Barsky Corporation made charitable contributions totaling $30,000. The corporation's taxable income before any charitable contribution deduction was $250,000. In its second year, Barsky made charitable contributions of $15,000 and earned taxable income before the contribution deduction of $300,000.

    a. Compute Barsky's allowable charitable contribution deduction and its final taxable income for its first year.

    b. Compute Barsky's allowable charitable contribution deduction and its final taxable income for its second year.

LO 11-2 8. In the current year, Fig Corporation made a $100,000 contribution to charity. In each of the following situations, compute the after-tax cost of this contribution assuming that Fig uses a 6 percent discount rate to compute NPV.

    a. Fig had $8 million taxable income before consideration of the contribution.

    b. Fig had $490,000 taxable income before consideration of the contribution. Next year, Fig's taxable income will be $6 million, and it will make no charitable contributions.

    c. Fig had $190,000 taxable income before consideration of the contribution. For the next five years, Fig's annual taxable income will be $130,000, and it will make no charitable contributions.

LO 11-4 9. Cranberry Corporation has $3,240,000 of current year taxable income.

    a. If the current year is a calendar year ending on December 31, 2017, calculate Cranberry's regular income tax liability.

    b. If the current year is a calendar year ending on December 31, 2018, calculate Cranberry's regular income tax liability.

    c. If the current year is a fiscal year ending on April 30, 2018, calculate Cranberry's regular income tax liability.

LO 11-4 10. Hallick, Inc. has a fiscal year ending June 30. Taxable income was $5,000,000 for its year ended June 30, 2018, and it projects similar taxable income for its 2023 fiscal year.

    a. Compute Hallick's regular tax liability for its June 30, 2018, tax year.

    b. Compute Hallick's projected regular tax liability for its June 30, 2023, tax year.

    c. Compare your results in parts (*a*) and (*b*). Briefly explain why tax liability is so different in these two years even though taxable income is the same.

LO 11-4 11. Landover Corporation is looking for a larger office building to house its expanding operations. It is considering two alternatives. The first is a newly constructed building at a cost of $6 million. It would require only minor modifications to meet Landover's needs, at an estimated cost of $500,000. The second building was constructed in 1910 and is a certified historic structure. It could be purchased for $3 million but would require an additional $4 million in renovations to be suitable for Landover.

    a. Calculate Landover's allowable rehabilitation credit if it chooses to purchase and renovate the certified historic structure, and the after-tax purchase price of the building. Assume Landover would claim the credit ratably over years 0 through 4. Landover uses a 4 percent discount rate to calculate present value.

    b. Based on your analysis, which building should Landover acquire?

    c. How might your analysis and conclusion change if Landover is currently experiencing net operating losses and does not expect to pay regular tax for several years?

LO 11-3, 11-4 12. Luong Corporation, a calendar year, accrual basis corporation, reported $1 million of net income after tax on its financial statements prepared in accordance with GAAP. The corporation's books and records reveal the following information:

- Luong's federal income tax expense per books was $200,000.

- Luong's book income included $10,000 of dividends received from a domestic corporation in which Luong owns a 25 percent stock interest, and $4,000 of dividends from a domestic corporation in which Luong owns a 5 percent stock interest.
- Luong recognized $10,000 of capital losses this year and no capital gains.
- Luong recorded $8,000 of book expense for meals not provided by a restaurant and $10,000 of book expense for entertainment costs.
- Luong's depreciation expense for book purposes totaled $400,000. MACRS depreciation was $475,000.

  a. Compute Luong's federal taxable income and regular tax liability.

  b. Prepare a Schedule M-1, page 6, Form 1120, reconciling Luong's book and taxable income.

LO 11-3, 11-4   13. Western Corporation, a calendar year, accrual basis corporation, reported $500,000 of net income after tax on its financial statements prepared in accordance with GAAP. The corporation's books and records reveal the following information:

- Western's book income included $15,000 of dividends, received from a domestic corporation in which Western owns less than 1 percent of the outstanding stock.
- Western's depreciation expense per books was $55,000, and its MACRS depreciation was $70,000.
- Western earned $5,000 of interest from municipal bonds and $6,000 of interest from corporate bonds.
- Western's capital losses exceeded its capital gains by $2,000.
- Western's federal income tax expense per books was $103,000.

  a. Compute Western's federal taxable income and regular tax liability.

  b. Prepare a Schedule M-1, page 6, Form 1120, reconciling Western's book and taxable income.

LO 11-3, 11-4   14. EFG, a calendar-year, accrual basis corporation, reported $479,900 net income after tax on its financial statements prepared in accordance with GAAP. The corporation's financial records reveal the following information:

- EFG earned $10,700 on an investment in tax-exempt municipal bonds.
- EFG's allowance for bad debts as of January 1 was $21,000. Write-offs for the year totaled $4,400, while the addition to the allowance was $3,700. The allowance as of December 31 was $20,300.
- On August 7, EFG paid a $6,000 fine to a municipal government for a violation of a local zoning ordinance.
- EFG's depreciation expense per books was $44,200, and its MACRS depreciation deduction was $31,000.
- This is EFG's second taxable year. In its first taxable year, it recognized an $8,800 net capital loss. This year, it recognized a $31,000 Section 1231 gain on the sale of equipment. This was EFG's only disposition of noninventory assets.
- In its first taxable year, EFG capitalized $6,900 of organizational costs for tax purposes and elected to amortize the costs over 180 months. For book purposes, it expensed the costs.
- EFG's federal income tax expense per books was $151,000.

  a. Compute EFG's taxable income and regular tax.

  b. Prepare a Schedule M-1, page 6, Form 1120, reconciling EFG's book and taxable income.

LO 11-3 15. Grim Corporation has income and expenses for its current fiscal year, recorded under generally accepted accounting principles, as shown in the following schedule. In addition, a review of Grim's books and records reveals the following information:

- Grim expensed, for book purposes, meals totaling $46,000 and entertainment costs totaling $54,000. Further detail shows that $40,000 of the meals were provided by a restaurant and the remaining $6,000 were not provided by a restaurant. These costs were incurred by Grim sales personnel, are reasonable in amount, and are documented in company records.
- During January of the current year, Grim was sued by one of its employees as a result of a work-related accident. The suit has not yet gone to court. However, Grim's auditors required the company to record a contingent liability (and related book expense) for $50,000, reflecting the company's likely liability from the suit.
- Grim recorded federal income tax expense for book purposes of $80,000.
- Grim used the reserve method for calculating bad debt expenses for book purposes. Its book income statement reflects bad debt expense of $30,000, calculated as 1.5 percent of sales revenue. Actual write-offs of accounts receivable during the year totaled $22,000.
- MACRS depreciation for the year totals $95,000.

a. Complete the following table, reflecting Grim's book/tax differences for the current year, whether such differences are positive (increase taxable income) or negative (decrease taxable income), and the final numbers to be included in the calculation of taxable income on Grim's tax return.

b. Prepare a Schedule M-1, page 6, Form 1120, reconciling Grim's book and taxable income.

	GAAP Book Income	Book/Tax Differences	Taxable income
Sales revenue	$2,000,000		
Cost of goods sold	(1,200,000)		
Gross profit	$ 800,000		
Meals and entertainment expense	(100,000)		
Bad debt expense	(30,000)		
Depreciation expense	(80,000)		
Other operating expenses	(220,000)		
Contingent loss	(50,000)		
Income before taxes	$ 320,000		
Federal income tax expense	(80,000)		
Net income	$ 240,000		

LO 11-4 16. Corporation AB's marginal tax rate is 15 percent, and Corporation YZ's marginal tax rate is 21 percent.

a. If both corporations are entitled to an additional $5,000 deduction, how much tax savings will the deduction generate for each corporation?

b. If both corporations are entitled to a $5,000 tax credit, how much tax savings will the credit generate for each corporation? (Assume that each corporation's precredit tax exceeds $5,000.)

LO 11-4 17. In each of the following cases, compute the corporation's regular tax, average tax rate and marginal tax rate:

 a. Silva Corporation has $160,000 taxable income for its tax year ended December 31, 2017.

 b. Goyal Corporation has $160,000 taxable income for its tax year ended December 31, 2018.

 c. Carver Corporation has $160,000 taxable income for its tax year ended October 31, 2018.

LO 11-5 18. Duka Corporation has the following adjusted financial statement income for the three years preceding 2023:

2020	$1.25 billion
2021	995 million
2022	1.1 billion

 Is Duka subject to the corporate AMT for 2023? Support your answer by computing Duka's average AFSI over the three-year period.

LO 11-4 19. Perkin Corporation has determined that it qualifies for a tax credit in the amount of $120,000. For the current year, it has tax liability before credits of $75,000. It expects at least that amount of tax liability next year.

 a. If the excess credit is not refundable but may be carried forward, calculate the value of the credit. Assume Perkins uses a 4 percent discount rate to calculate present value.

 b. If the excess credit is refundable, what is the value of the credit?

LO 11-5 20. Jahlil Corporation has GAAP net income of $4,670,000,000. To compute Jahlil's AFSI, the following items may require adjustment:

 • Federal income tax expense for book purposes totals $1,074,100,000.

 • MACRS depreciation is $950,000,000; book depreciation is $564,000,000.

 • Book net operating loss carryforwards total $330,000,000.

 a. Compute Jahlil Corporation's AFSI.

 b. If Jahlil's regular tax liability is $747,500,000, compute the corporation's tentative minimum tax, AMT, and total tax liability.

LO 11-3, 11-4, 11-5 21. Camden Corporation, a calendar-year, accrual basis corporation, reported $5 million of net income after tax on its current year financial statements prepared in accordance with GAAP. In addition, the following information is available from Camden's books and records:

 • Federal income tax expense per books was $1.5 million.

 • Camden incurred $30,000 of meals not provided by a restaurant and $25,000 of entertainment expenses.

 • Camden sold two pieces of equipment used in its business for total sales proceeds of $400,000. The equipment's original cost was $2 million. Book depreciation prior to sale totaled $1.2 million; tax depreciation totaled $1.5 million.

 • Camden uses the reserve method of accounting for bad debts. Additions to the reserve during the year totaled $400,000. Accounts receivable actually written off during the year totaled $450,000.

 • Camden's depreciation expense for book purposes totaled $900,000. Tax depreciation computed under MACRS is $1.25 million.

    a. Determine Camden's taxable income and regular tax liability.

    b. Complete Schedule M-1, page 6, Form 1120.

    c. Compute Camden's AFSI, tentative minimum tax, AMT (if any), and final tax due.

LO 11-5 22. Bangura, Inc. has regular taxable income of $932,500,000 and AFSI of $1,437,100,000. Compute Bangura's regular tax liability, tentative minimum tax, AMT (if any) and total tax due.

LO 11-4 23. Hall Corporation plans to invest $5.5 million in rehabilitating a certified historic structure. Calculate the net present value of Hall's allowable rehabilitation credit. Assume Hall has ample taxable income, places the building in service next year (year 1), and uses a 5 percent discount rate to calculate present value.

LO 11-6 24. In 2022, Bartley Corporation's federal income tax due was $147,000. Compute the required installment payments of 2023 tax in each of the following cases:

    a. Bartley's 2023 taxable income is $440,000.

    b. Bartley's 2023 taxable income is $975,000.

    c. Bartley's 2023 taxable income is $2,100,000.

LO 11-6 25. In 2022, NB, Inc.'s federal taxable income was $242,000. Compute the required installment payments of 2023 tax in each of the following cases:

    a. NB's 2023 taxable income is $593,000.

    b. NB's 2023 taxable income is $950,000.

    c. NB's 2023 taxable income is $1,400,000.

LO 11-7 26. Jose, who is in the 35 percent marginal tax bracket with a 15 percent tax rate on dividends, owns 100 percent of the stock of JJ, Inc. This year, JJ generates $500,000 taxable income and pays a $100,000 dividend to Jose. Compute his tax on the dividend under each of the following assumptions:

    a. The federal tax rules currently in effect apply to the dividend payment.

    b. The federal tax system has been amended to allow shareholders to gross up dividend income by the corporate tax paid with respect to the dividend and credit this tax against their individual tax.

LO 11-7 27. Margarita, whose marginal tax rate on ordinary income is 37 percent, owns 100 percent of the stock of Henley Corporation. This year, Henley generates $1 million of taxable income.

    a. If Henley wants to pay all of its after-tax earnings to Margarita as a dividend, calculate the amount of the dividend payment.

    b. Calculate Margarita's tax due on the dividend computed in part (*a*) and her after-tax cash flow from the dividend receipt.

    c. Compute the combined corporate and individual tax burden on Henley's $1 million of current year income, and the effective combined tax rate on this income.

LO 11-8 28. Adams Corporation manufactures appliances. This year, the government increased the corporate tax rate by 5 percent. Adams responded by raising its prices. Customer demand remained steady; therefore, Adams's before-tax profits increased and after-tax profits remained constant.

    a. Who bears the incidence of the increase in Adams's corporate tax?

    b. How would your answer change if Adams did not raise prices, resulting in a decline in its after-tax profits and a drop in the market price of its stock?

LO 11-8 29. Shine, Inc. manufactures laundry detergent and other cleaning products. This year, the government increased the corporate tax rate by 2 percent. The marketing department determined that Shine could not raise its prices and retain its market share. The production department concluded that manufacturing costs cannot be reduced by another penny. Consequently, Shine's before-tax profits remain constant, while after-tax profits decline by the full tax increase. The stock market reaction to the decline in earnings is a fall in Shine's stock price.

    a. Who bears the incidence of the increase in Shine's corporate tax?

    b. How would your answer change if Shine held its after-tax profit constant by shutting down the on-site day care center for its employees' preschool children and eliminating this operating cost from its budget?

LO 11-2   30. Porto Corporation received $50,000 of dividend income from Seville, Inc. Porto owns 5 percent of the outstanding stock of Seville. Porto's marginal tax rate is 21 percent. Assume both companies are U.S. corporations.

    a. Calculate Porto's allowable dividends-received deduction and its after-tax cash flow as a result of the dividend from Seville.

    b. How would your answers to part (*a*) change if Porto owned 55 percent of the stock of Seville?

    c. How would your answers to part (*a*) change if Porto owned 85 percent of the stock of Seville?

Issue Recognition Problems

Identify the tax issue or issues suggested by the following situations, and state each issue in the form of a question.

LO 11-1   1. Greentown Foundation is a nonprofit corporation exempt from federal income tax. Its purpose is to solicit volunteers to plant and tend public gardens and greenbelts located in inner cities. The board of directors is considering publishing a gardener's newsletter that Greentown could sell in retail bookstores to raise money for its various projects.

LO 11-2   2. M&M is a publicly held corporation, and its stock trades on Nasdaq. This year, M&M contributed 15,000 shares of its newly issued common stock to a local charity. At the date of contribution, the stock was selling at $7.12 per share.

LO 11-3   3. Twenty years ago, Chemco Corporation developed, manufactured, and marketed Kepone, a chemical pesticide. As a result of manufacturing practices that violated state environmental standards, harmful levels of Kepone were discharged into the soil and groundwater. A state agency sued Chemco for damages, and the corporation was indicted for criminal negligence for the unlawful discharge of toxic substances. The judge imposed a $1 million fine on Chemco. After extensive meetings with the judge and prosecutors, Chemco created the Midwest Environment Foundation, the purpose of which is to alleviate the effects of Kepone waste. Chemco contributed $950,000 to this nonprofit organization, and the judge promptly reduced the fine to $50,000.

LO 11-4   4. Ferris Corporation is looking to relocate its corporate headquarters to a small, historic town in the northeastern United States. Representatives of the town government have suggested several historic buildings in the town center as options that might meet the company's needs.

LO 11-5   5. Talon Corporation has financial statement net income over $5 billion per year for tax years 2020, 2021, and 2022.

LO 11-6   6. Maya Corporation is a calendar year taxpayer. For the past nine years, its taxable income has been stable, averaging $2 million per year. Through November of this year, its taxable income was $1.81 million. In April, June, and September, Maya made a $175,000 installment payment of tax. In December, it recognized a $5 million gain on the sale of investment land.

LO 11-7 7. TK Enterprises, an accrual basis corporation, needs to raise capital. One idea is for TK to sell bonds to the public for $625 each. These bonds would have no stated rate of interest but would be redeemable from TK in five years for a redemption price of $1,000.

LO 11-7 8. Bandera Corporation has not paid a dividend for six years. This year, the board of directors decides to declare a dividend. It hires a consultant to update the shareholder records so that the dividend can be distributed to the proper people. The consultant's fee for their services is $16,800.

Research Problems

LO 11-8 1. In early 2022, Connor, Inc. announced its intention to construct a manufacturing facility in the Shenandoah Valley. To persuade Connor to locate the facility in Augusta County, the county government contributed a six-acre tract of undeveloped county land to the corporation. The appraised FMV of the land at date of contribution was $280,000. Soon after accepting the contribution, Connor paid $3,300 to an attorney to do a title search to make sure that it had uncontested ownership of the land. Connor also paid $12,900 for a survey and site map of the six acres and $1,360 for two water wells drilled on the land. Did Connor recognize income because of the receipt of the land? What is the proper tax treatment of Connor's $17,560 expenditure with respect to the land?

In 2023, Connor's attorney discovered that the estate of Elsa Reynolds claimed title to the six acres and was preparing to file suit in Virginia state court to regain ownership and possession. The attorney advised Connor that the estate's claim appeared valid and would be upheld. Consequently, Connor informed Augusta County that it was renouncing all claim to the land and would build its new manufacturing facility 200 miles away in Rockingham County. Did Connor recognize a loss when it renounced its claim to the land?

LO 11-2 2. On December 10, 2022, the representative of a national charitable organization contacted the CEO of Wilkie, Inc., a calendar-year, accrual basis corporation, to solicit a $100,000 donation. The CEO presented the solicitation to Wilkie's board of directors on December 19, and the board unanimously authorized the donation. Pursuant to this authorization, Wilkie transferred ownership of 3,973 shares of Gydo, Inc. common stock to the charity on March 20, 2023. Wilkie purchased the Gydo stock in 1998 for $71,800 and held it as an investment. On March 20, Gydo common was selling on the NYSE for $25.17 per share. Before consideration of this donation, Wilkie's taxable income for both 2022 and 2023 exceeded $8 million. In which year is Wilkie allowed a charitable deduction for this donation, and what is the amount of the deduction?

LO 11-2 3. Amira and Lynette Majors own 36 percent of the outstanding stock of Echo Valley, which has approximately $5 million earnings and profits. Echo Valley owns 38 tracts of undeveloped land in central Colorado. Amira and Lynette want to acquire one of the tracts (tract D6) to develop as a campground and recreational park. The appraised FMV of tract D6 is $420,000, although the corporation's tax basis is only $211,000. At the most recent shareholder meeting, Amira and Lynette convinced the other shareholders to distribute tract D6 to them as a dividend. (The other shareholders would receive equivalent cash dividends proportionate to their stock ownership.) Would the distribution of tract D6 as a dividend be a taxable event to Echo Valley? How much dividend income would the Majors recognize, and what would be their tax basis in tract D6?

LO 11-2   4. This year, Prewer, Inc. received a $160,000 dividend on its investment consisting of 16 percent of the outstanding stock of TKS, Inc., a taxable domestic corporation. Before considering this dividend, Prewer had a $43,500 operating loss for the year. It also had a $31,300 NOL carryover deduction from the prior year. What is Prewer's taxable income this year?

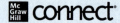 **All applicable Tax Planning Cases are available with *Connect*.**

Tax Planning Cases

LO 11-4   1. Congress recently enacted a nonrefundable credit based on the cost of qualifying alcohol and drug abuse counseling programs provided by any corporate employer to its employees. The credit is limited to 50 percent of the total cost of the program. If a corporation elects the credit, none of the program costs are allowed as a deduction. Any credit in excess of current year tax may not be carried back or forward to another year.

   a. TMM Corporation spent $80,000 for a qualifying counseling program this year. If TMM has $500,000 taxable income before consideration of this expense, should it elect the credit or deduct the program's cost as an ordinary business expense?

   b. Would your answer change if TMM had only $70,000 taxable income before consideration of the expense?

LO 11-7   2. A&Z, Inc. averages $4 million taxable income a year. Because it needs an infusion of cash, the board of directors is considering two options: selling a new issue of preferred stock to the public for a total offering price of $500,000 or borrowing $500,000 from a local bank. The market dividend rate on preferred stock is only 5.6 percent, while the bank's interest rate is 9 percent. Which option minimizes the after-tax cost of the new capital?

Appendix **11–A**

Schedule M-3 for Reconciling Book and Taxable Income

During 2004, the IRS developed Schedule M-3 with the goal of increasing transparency between reported net income for financial accounting purposes and reported net income for tax purposes. The new schedule replaces Schedule M-1 for tax years ending on or after December 31, 2004, for corporations with total assets of $10 million or more. Schedule M-3 reports significantly more detailed information than Schedule M-1, including the temporary versus permanent characterization of book/tax differences and the detail of book income and expense amounts for each line item on Schedule M-3.

Schedule M-3 is divided into three parts. Part I reports the source of the financial information used in the tax return, whether it be from SEC Form 10-K, a certified audited income statement, or simply the corporation's books and records. In addition, for a consolidated group of corporations, Part I reconciles worldwide financial statement net income to the financial statement net income of those corporations permitted to be included in the U.S. consolidated tax return group.

Parts II and III of Schedule M-3 reconcile the elements of financial statement net income to taxable income, using four columns and more than 60 specific categories, many of which require attachment of detailed supporting schedules. Part II focuses on income (loss) items, whereas Part III details expense/deduction items. The end result of the reconciliation process, line 30 of Part II, must equal line 28, page 1, Form 1120.

SCHEDULE M-3
(Form 1120)
(Rev. December 2019)
Department of the Treasury
Internal Revenue Service

Net Income (Loss) Reconciliation for Corporations With Total Assets of $10 Million or More
▶ Attach to Form 1120 or 1120-C.
▶ Go to *www.irs.gov/Form1120* for instructions and the latest information.

OMB No. 1545-0123

Name of corporation (common parent, if consolidated return)

Employer identification number

Check applicable box(es):   (1) ☐ Non-consolidated return   (2) ☐ Consolidated return (Form 1120 only)

(3) ☐ Mixed 1120/L/PC group   (4) ☐ Dormant subsidiaries schedule attached

Part I   Financial Information and Net Income (Loss) Reconciliation (see instructions)

1a Did the corporation file SEC Form 10-K for its income statement period ending with or within this tax year?
  ☐ **Yes.** Skip lines 1b and 1c and complete lines 2a through 11 with respect to that SEC Form 10-K.
  ☐ **No.** Go to line 1b. See instructions if multiple non-tax-basis income statements are prepared.

b Did the corporation prepare a certified audited non-tax-basis income statement for that period?
  ☐ **Yes.** Skip line 1c and complete lines 2a through 11 with respect to that income statement.
  ☐ **No.** Go to line 1c.

c Did the corporation prepare a non-tax-basis income statement for that period?
  ☐ **Yes.** Complete lines 2a through 11 with respect to that income statement.
  ☐ **No.** Skip lines 2a through 3c and enter the corporation's net income (loss) per its books and records on line 4a.

2a Enter the income statement period: Beginning   MM/DD/YYYY   Ending   MM/DD/YYYY

b Has the corporation's income statement been restated for the income statement period on line 2a?
  ☐ **Yes.** (If "Yes," attach an explanation and the amount of each item restated.)
  ☐ **No.**

c Has the corporation's income statement been restated for any of the five income statement periods immediately preceding the period on line 2a?
  ☐ **Yes.** (If "Yes," attach an explanation and the amount of each item restated.)
  ☐ **No.**

3a Is any of the corporation's voting common stock publicly traded?
  ☐ **Yes.**
  ☐ **No.** If "No," go to line 4a.

b Enter the symbol of the corporation's primary U.S. publicly traded voting common stock . . . .

c Enter the nine-digit CUSIP number of the corporation's primary publicly traded voting common stock . . . .

4a Worldwide consolidated net income (loss) from income statement source identified in Part I, line 1 .	**4a**	
b Indicate accounting standard used for line 4a (see instructions): (1) ☐ GAAP (2) ☐ IFRS (3) ☐ Statutory (4) ☐ Tax-basis (5) ☐ Other (specify) _____		
5a Net income from nonincludible foreign entities (attach statement)	**5a**	( )
b Net loss from nonincludible foreign entities (attach statement and enter as a positive amount) . . .	**5b**	
6a Net income from nonincludible U.S. entities (attach statement)	**6a**	( )
b Net loss from nonincludible U.S. entities (attach statement and enter as a positive amount)	**6b**	
7a Net income (loss) of other includible foreign disregarded entities (attach statement)	**7a**	
b Net income (loss) of other includible U.S. disregarded entities (attach statement)	**7b**	
c Net income (loss) of other includible entities (attach statement)	**7c**	
8 Adjustment to eliminations of transactions between includible entities and nonincludible entities (attach statement)	**8**	
9 Adjustment to reconcile income statement period to tax year (attach statement)	**9**	
10a Intercompany dividend adjustments to reconcile to line 11 (attach statement)	**10a**	
b Other statutory accounting adjustments to reconcile to line 11 (attach statement)	**10b**	
c Other adjustments to reconcile to amount on line 11 (attach statement)	**10c**	
11 **Net income (loss) per income statement of includible corporations.** Combine lines 4 through 10 .	**11**	

Note: Part I, line 11, must equal Part II, line 30, column (a), or Schedule M-1, line 1 (see instructions).

12 Enter the total amount (not just the corporation's share) of the assets and liabilities of all entities included or removed on the following lines.

	Total Assets	Total Liabilities
a Included on Part I, line 4 . . . . ▶		
b Removed on Part I, line 5 . . . . ▶		
c Removed on Part I, line 6 . . . . ▶		
d Included on Part I, line 7 . . . . ▶		

For Paperwork Reduction Act Notice, see the Instructions for Form 1120.   Cat. No. 37961C   Schedule M-3 (Form 1120) (Rev. 12-2019)

Schedule M-3 (Form 1120) (Rev. 12-2019) Page **2**

Name of corporation (common parent, if consolidated return) | Employer identification number

Check applicable box(es): (1) ☐ Consolidated group (2) ☐ Parent corp (3) ☐ Consolidated eliminations (4) ☐ Subsidiary corp (5) ☐ Mixed 1120/L/PC group
Check if a sub-consolidated: (6) ☐ 1120 group (7) ☐ 1120 eliminations

Name of subsidiary (if consolidated return) | Employer identification number

Part II Reconciliation of Net Income (Loss) per Income Statement of Includible Corporations With Taxable Income per Return (see instructions)

Income (Loss) Items (Attach statements for lines 1 through 12)	(a) Income (Loss) per Income Statement	(b) Temporary Difference	(c) Permanent Difference	(d) Income (Loss) per Tax Return
1 Income (loss) from equity method foreign corporations				
2 Gross foreign dividends not previously taxed				
3 Subpart F, QEF, and similar income inclusions				
4 Gross-up for foreign taxes deemed paid				
5 Gross foreign distributions previously taxed				
6 Income (loss) from equity method U.S. corporations				
7 U.S. dividends not eliminated in tax consolidation				
8 Minority interest for includible corporations				
9 Income (loss) from U.S. partnerships				
10 Income (loss) from foreign partnerships				
11 Income (loss) from other pass-through entities				
12 Items relating to reportable transactions				
13 Interest income (see instructions)				
14 Total accrual to cash adjustment				
15 Hedging transactions				
16 Mark-to-market income (loss)				
17 Cost of goods sold (see instructions)	( )			( )
18 Sale versus lease (for sellers and/or lessors)				
19 Section 481(a) adjustments				
20 Unearned/deferred revenue				
21 Income recognition from long-term contracts				
22 Original issue discount and other imputed interest				
23a Income statement gain/loss on sale, exchange, abandonment, worthlessness, or other disposition of assets other than inventory and pass-through entities				
b Gross capital gains from Schedule D, excluding amounts from pass-through entities				
c Gross capital losses from Schedule D, excluding amounts from pass-through entities, abandonment losses, and worthless stock losses				
d Net gain/loss reported on Form 4797, line 17, excluding amounts from pass-through entities, abandonment losses, and worthless stock losses				
e Abandonment losses				
f Worthless stock losses (attach statement)				
g Other gain/loss on disposition of assets other than inventory				
24 Capital loss limitation and carryforward used				
25 Other income (loss) items with differences (attach statement)				
26 **Total income (loss) items.** Combine lines 1 through 25				
27 **Total expense/deduction items** (from Part III, line 39)				
28 Other items with no differences				
29a Mixed groups, see instructions. All others, combine lines 26 through 28				
b PC insurance subgroup reconciliation totals				
c Life insurance subgroup reconciliation totals				
30 **Reconciliation totals.** Combine lines 29a through 29c				

Note: Line 30, column (a), must equal Part I, line 11, and column (d) must equal Form 1120, page 1, line 28.

Schedule M-3 (Form 1120) (Rev. 12-2019)

Schedule M-3 (Form 1120) (Rev. 12-2019)   Page **3**

Name of corporation (common parent, if consolidated return)	Employer identification number

Check applicable box(es): **(1)** ☐ Consolidated group **(2)** ☐ Parent corp **(3)** ☐ Consolidated eliminations **(4)** ☐ Subsidiary corp **(5)** ☐ Mixed 1120/L/PC group
Check if a sub-consolidated: **(6)** ☐ 1120 group **(7)** ☐ 1120 eliminations

Name of subsidiary (if consolidated return)	Employer identification number

Part III **Reconciliation of Net Income (Loss) per Income Statement of Includible Corporations With Taxable Income per Return—Expense/Deduction Items** (see instructions)

Expense/Deduction Items	(a) Expense per Income Statement	(b) Temporary Difference	(c) Permanent Difference	(d) Deduction per Tax Return
1 U.S. current income tax expense				
2 U.S. deferred income tax expense				
3 State and local current income tax expense . . .				
4 State and local deferred income tax expense . . .				
5 Foreign current income tax expense (other than foreign withholding taxes)				
6 Foreign deferred income tax expense				
7 Foreign withholding taxes				
8 Interest expense (see instructions)				
9 Stock option expense				
10 Other equity-based compensation				
11 Meals and entertainment				
12 Fines and penalties				
13 Judgments, damages, awards, and similar costs .				
14 Parachute payments				
15 Compensation with section 162(m) limitation . . .				
16 Pension and profit-sharing				
17 Other post-retirement benefits				
18 Deferred compensation				
19 Charitable contribution of cash and tangible property				
20 Charitable contribution of intangible property . .				
21 Charitable contribution limitation/carryforward . .				
22 Domestic production activities deduction (see instructions).				
23 Current year acquisition or reorganization investment banking fees				
24 Current year acquisition or reorganization legal and accounting fees				
25 Current year acquisition/reorganization other costs .				
26 Amortization/impairment of goodwill				
27 Amortization of acquisition, reorganization, and start-up costs				
28 Other amortization or impairment write-offs . . .				
29 Reserved				
30 Depletion				
31 Depreciation				
32 Bad debt expense				
33 Corporate owned life insurance premiums . . .				
34 Purchase versus lease (for purchasers and/or lessees) .				
35 Research and development costs				
36 Section 118 exclusion (attach statement)				
37 Section 162(r)—FDIC premiums paid by certain large financial institutions (see instructions) . . .				
38 Other expense/deduction items with differences (attach statement)				
39 **Total expense/deduction items.** Combine lines 1 through 38. Enter here and on Part II, line 27, reporting positive amounts as negative and negative amounts as positive				

Schedule M-3 (Form 1120) (Rev. 12-2019)

Source: Internal Revenue Service

Chapter Twelve

The Choice of Business Entity

Learning Objectives

After studying this chapter, you should be able to:

LO 12-1. Explain the advantage of start-up losses in a passthrough entity.

LO 12-2. Calculate after-tax cash flow from passthrough entities and taxable corporations.

LO 12-3. Describe how families can use partnerships or S corporations to shift income.

LO 12-4. Explain tax and nontax considerations in choosing a passthrough entity form.

LO 12-5. Define *constructive dividend*.

LO 12-6. Explain why individuals once again can use corporations as tax shelters.

LO 12-7. Explain the purpose of the accumulated earnings tax and the personal holding company tax.

In the two preceding chapters, we identified the basic forms of business organization and learned how the choice of form determines whether business income is taxed at the individual or corporate rates. These chapters concentrated on the tax rules and regulations applying to different business entities. In this chapter, we will build on this technical knowledge as we consider the tax planning implications of the choice of business entity. The first half of the chapter focuses on the potential advantages of conducting a business as a passthrough entity. The second half explains how business owners can control the tax cost of operating in the corporate form. Throughout the chapter, we will analyze how planning strategies affect after-tax cash flow available to the business owners.

No one organizational form is ideal for every business. The tax characteristics of one form may be advantageous in one case and disadvantageous in another. In some cases, a passthrough entity accomplishes the owners' tax objectives, while in other cases, a taxable corporation is the better option. Often, owners have compelling nontax reasons for operating their business in a particular form. As the business matures and the owners' financial situations evolve, the optimal form may change. Finally, business owners must reevaluate the form in which they conduct their business every time Congress amends the Internal Revenue Code. Even minor alterations in the law can affect the tax pros and cons of passthrough entities and taxable corporations. Major law changes, such as those made by the Tax Cuts and Jobs Act of 2017, may significantly alter preferences for the organizational form through which business is conducted.

TAX PLANNING WITH PASSTHROUGH ENTITIES

From Chapter 10, we know that businesses organized as partnerships, LLCs, and S corporations are not subject to federal income tax at the entity level. Instead, income passes through the entity to be reported by and taxed to the owners. If the business operates at a loss, the loss passes through and is reported as a deduction by the owners. Cash distributions from passthrough entities are generally nontaxable. These cash flows represent a return of the owners' investment in the business and do not affect the income or loss reported by the owners. For many individuals, this combination of rules helps them control tax costs and maximize the cash flow from their business. However, recent reductions in the corporate tax rate have narrowed the gap in tax costs when comparing passthrough and corporate forms of doing business.

Tax Benefit of Start-Up Losses

LO 12-1
Explain the advantage of start-up losses in a passthrough entity.

Organizers of a new business may expect to lose money during the start-up phase. If the business is organized as a passthrough entity, these initial losses can generate an immediate tax savings to the owners. If the business is organized as a corporation, the losses do not flow through but are trapped at the entity level as NOL carryforwards. As a result, the tax savings from the start-up losses are deferred until the corporation can deduct them against future income. As discussed in Chapter 6, the future deduction for a NOL carryforward is limited to 80 percent of taxable income before the deduction.[1] Thus, a NOL carryforward cannot reduce future taxable income to zero in any given year. The following examples focus on the difference in timing of the deduction for start-up losses.

Start-Up Losses

A group of individuals owns a business with the following income and deductions for its first three years:

Year	Gross Income	Allowable Deductions	Net Income or Loss
0	$ 420,000	$ (720,000)	$(300,000)
1	800,000	(920,000)	(120,000)
2	1,530,000	(1,000,000)	530,000

If the owners organize the business as a passthrough entity, they can deduct the operating losses in years 0 and 1 (assuming these losses are not subject to the excess business loss limitation discussed in Chapters 6 and 10).[2] In year 2, they pay tax on $530,000 business income. If the owners organize the business as a corporation with no S election, the losses in years 0

Tax Savings and Costs

		Passthrough Entity		
Year	(Deduction) or Taxable Income	Tax Savings or (Cost)	Discount Factor	Present Value of Tax Savings or (Cost)
0	$(300,000)	$ 105,000		$ 105,000
1	(120,000)	42,000	.952	39,984
2	530,000	(185,500)	.907	(168,249)
		$ (38,500)		$ (23,265)

[1] This statement ignores the temporary suspension of the 80 percent limitation provided by the CARES Act for tax years prior to 2021.

[2] If a passthrough loss exceeds the owner's other income for the year, the excess loss is a net operating loss. The owner can carry the NOL forward as a deduction in future tax years.

	Corporation			
Year	(NOL Carryforward) or Taxable Income	Tax Savings or (Cost)	Discount Factor	Present Value of Tax Savings or (Cost)
0	$(300,000)	–0–		–0–
1	(120,000)	–0–		–0–
2	110,000	$(38,500)	.907	$(34,920)
		$(38,500)		$(34,920)

and 1 carry forward and result in $110,000 corporate taxable income in year 2.[3] To isolate the tax effect of the timing difference, let's use a hypothetical 35 percent tax rate for the individual owners and the corporation, and a 5 percent discount rate.

In this simple case, the present value of the tax cost is minimized if the business is organized as a passthrough entity rather than as a corporation. The dramatic difference in tax cost is *entirely attributable* to the timing of the deduction for the first two years of losses. With a passthrough entity, these losses are deductible in the year incurred. Consequently, the owners receive the tax savings from the deduction in years 0 and 1. With a corporate entity, the tax savings from the loss deduction are postponed until year 2, so the savings decrease in present value terms.

The previous example assumes a 35 percent corporate tax rate, consistent with the tax system prior to the Tax Cuts and Jobs Act of 2017. For earnings after 2017, the corporate tax rate drops to 21 percent. Let's rework our example with this revised rate. Tax savings and costs for the passthrough entity do not change. The revised corporate tax costs are as follows:

	Corporation			
Year	(NOL Carryforward) or Taxable Income	Tax Savings or (Cost)	Discount Factor	Present Value of Tax Savings or (Cost)
0	$(300,000)	–0–		–0–
1	(120,000)	–0–		–0–
2	110,000	$(23,100)	.907	$(20,952)
		$(23,100)		$(20,952)

Now the corporate form of doing business minimizes the first level of tax on the business income. Even though the losses do not produce tax savings until year 2, the lower corporate tax rate versus the 35 percent rate on passthrough earnings overshadows deferral of the tax savings. However, as discussed in the next section, a second level of tax will apply to corporate earnings when distributed to shareholders. This second tax should also be considered when choosing an organizational form.

Avoiding a Double Tax on Business Income

LO 12-2
Calculate after-tax cash flow from passthrough entities and taxable corporations.

People who own their own business often depend on the cash flow from the business to meet their household consumption needs. Their basic financial strategy is to maximize the cash transferred from the business bank account to their personal checking account. This strategy usually dictates that they operate their business as a passthrough entity, rather than as a corporation, so that income is taxed only once.

The Tax Cuts and Jobs Act (TCJA) of 2017 significantly reduced the double-tax cost of operating as a corporation, by reducing the corporate tax rate to 21 percent. In addition, the act

[3] Note that the 80 percent limit on deductibility of NOL carryforwards does not apply to this example.

created the QBI deduction for certain noncorporate businesses. The interplay of these two new provisions is an important factor in determining the after-tax cost of each organizational form.

Single versus Double Tax	The Gilberts, a married couple. are the sole shareholders in an S corporation that conducts a restaurant business.[4] The restaurant generates $100,000 taxable income annually and an equal cash flow. The corporation distributes all available cash to the Gilberts each year. Assuming a 35 percent individual tax rate and a 20 percent QBI deduction, the after-tax cash flow from their business is $72,000.

Annual cash from operations	$100,000
Individual tax	
($80,000 taxable income after QBI deduction × 35%)	(28,000)
After-tax cash flow	$ 72,000

If the Gilberts had not elected subchapter S status for their corporation, the $100,000 income would be taxed at the entity level and the corporation itself would pay $21,000 tax. The cash available for distribution would be $79,000. Moreover, the distribution would be a dividend to the Gilberts, and the after-tax cash available for their personal consumption would be only $67,150, assuming a 15 percent tax rate on dividend income.

Annual cash from operations	$100,000
Corporate tax at 21%	(21,000)
Cash distributed to shareholders	$ 79,000
Individual tax	
($79,000 dividend × 15%)	(11,850)
After-tax cash flow	$ 67,150

Tax Talk
The QBI deduction has significantly affected the entity choice decision for new businesses formed after TCJA. Tax professionals can offer their clients significant insights in this area, including detailed analysis of the tax costs of corporate versus passthrough options. As an example, Intuit has developed a "QBI Entity Selection Calculator" to evaluate the type of legal entity a business should consider. See https:// proconnect.intuit.com/ tax-reform/entity-selection-calculator/ to download the calculator.

In the Gilberts' case, the double tax from the corporate form would result in a 32.9 percent effective tax rate on their business income ($32,850 total tax ÷ $100,000 income). With the QBI deduction, the effective tax rate if their business operates through an S corporation is only 28 percent ($28,000 tax ÷ $100,000 income). Clearly, the Gilberts are minimizing their income tax and maximizing the money they can spend by operating their restaurant as a passthrough entity.

The previous example assumed that the Gilberts qualified for the 20 percent QBI deduction discussed in Chapter 10. That deduction provides critical tax savings to businesses operated as passthrough entities. Without the deduction, the Gilberts' S corporation earnings would have resulted in $35,000 of tax cost ($100,000 × 35 percent) and only $65,000 of after-tax cash flow. In this case, even with double taxation, cash flow would be maximized by operating as a regular corporation without an S election.

Income Shifting among Family Members

The creation of a family partnership or S corporation can be an effective way to divide business income among a number of taxpayers. To the extent that this division causes income to be taxed at a lower marginal rate, the total tax burden on the business shrinks. This strategy

---

[4] To keep the example simple, assume that neither shareholder is an employee of the corporation.

is an application of the entity variable, discussed in Chapter 4. Let's illustrate this concept with a simple example:

Shift of Business Income	Mrs. Alm owns a sole proprietorship generating $150,000 annual taxable income. Mrs. Alm is in the 35 percent tax bracket but has two children in the 24 percent tax bracket. If Mrs. Alm could convert her business into a passthrough entity in which she and her children are equal owners, the annual income would be allocated among three individual taxpayers. If the shift of $50,000 business income from Mrs. Alm to each child decreased the tax rate on the income from 35 percent to 24 percent, the tax savings would be $11,000:

Tax on $100,000 at 35%	$ 35,000
Tax on $100,000 at 24%	(24,000)
	$ 11,000

LO 12-3
Describe how families can use partnerships or S corporations to shift income.

Although Mrs. Alm should be impressed with this tax strategy, she must understand that the strategy will not just shift *income* to her children—it will shift *dollars* to them as well. As owners, the children are entitled to an equal share of any cash distributions from the business. When the business eventually terminates or is sold, each child will receive one-third of any remaining property or any amount realized on sale. In other words, if Mrs. Alm wants to shift two-thirds of the business income, she must part with two-thirds of the wealth represented by the business.

Statutory Restrictions

The tax savings achieved through income shifts to family members with low tax rates can be substantial. Not surprisingly, the Internal Revenue Code restricts the use of both partnerships and S corporations as income-shifting devices. Let's first consider the statutory rules pertaining to family partnerships.

If partnership income is primarily attributable to the work performed by individual partners rather than to the property owned by the partnership, any allocation of that income to nonworking partners is an unjustified assignment of earned income. Accordingly, a family member cannot be a partner in a personal service business unless they are qualified to perform services for the business.[5] In contrast, a family member can be a partner in a business in which property is a material income-producing factor.[6] Unlike a service partnership, the mere ownership of an equity interest in a capital-intensive partnership entitles a partner to a share of profits.

Does a Family Partnership Exist?	Elizabeth and Emerson Winkler, who lived on a farm in Illinois, had five children. Emerson was in poor health and was frequently hospitalized. Elizabeth and one or more of her children always drove Emerson to the hospital. During these trips, the family usually purchased three $1 lottery tickets at the gas station where they stopped for fuel. The money was contributed by any family member who happened to have a dollar bill, and Elizabeth kept all the tickets

(continued)

[5] *Commissioner* v. *Culbertson,* 337 U.S. 733 (1949).

[6] §704(e)(1). Property is a material income-producing factor if the business requires substantial inventories or a substantial investment in plant, machinery, or equipment. Reg. §1.704-1(e)(1)(iv).

in her china cabinet. The family often joked about how they would spend their winnings from these "family" tickets. On one trip, Elizabeth used her own money to purchase the three tickets. That night, one of these tickets won $6.5 million. The family agreed that Elizabeth and Emerson should each receive 25 percent of the jackpot, and each child should receive 10 percent. Consequently, when Elizabeth received the $6.5 million, she paid $650,000 to each of her five children. The IRS contended that no family partnership existed among the Winklers and that Elizabeth and Emerson made gifts (the lottery winnings) to the children on which they owed gift tax of more than $116,000. But the federal court disagreed with the IRS. The court concluded that the Winklers formed a family partnership to purchase lottery tickets. Each family member contributed capital to the partnership when they spent a dollar to buy a ticket, and each contributed services by going into the gas station to make the purchase. Consequently, the division of the jackpot was a distribution of profits to partners rather than a taxable gift from Elizabeth and Emerson to their children.[7]

Family partnerships are often created when a business owner makes a gift of an equity interest to a relative, thereby creating a partnership between donor and donee. Alternatively, the owner could sell the equity interest to the relative to create the partnership. In either case, the business income must be allocated among the partners based on their proportionate interests in partnership capital.[8]

Family Partnership	Refer to the *Shift of Business Income* example on page 12-5 involving Mrs. Alm and her two children. Mrs. Alm can convert her sole proprietorship to a family partnership only if capital is a material income-producing factor. In other words, if Mrs. Alm is a self-employed physician earning $150,000 from her medical practice, she can't make her children partners unless they are qualified to provide some type of service to the practice. On the other hand, if Mrs. Alm's business is a retail clothing store, she can transfer the business assets to a partnership and give her children a capital interest in the new entity. If each child receives a one-third interest, the partnership income can be allocated in equal shares to the partners. If Mrs. Alm gives each child only a 10 percent capital interest, only 10 percent of the income can be shifted to each child.

If the partner who gave away or sold an equity interest to a family member provides services to the partnership, the partner must receive a guaranteed payment as compensation.[9] The partnership is allowed to deduct the payment, and the remaining income is allocated in proportion to the capital interests.

Compensation for Services to a Family Partnership	Refer to the preceding example and assume that Mrs. Alm formed a family partnership by giving a one-third equity interest in her retail clothing business to each of her two children. Mrs. Alm works 40 hours a week managing the business. If her services are reasonably worth $60,000 a year, the partnership must pay her a $60,000 guaranteed payment. If partnership income after deduction of this guaranteed payment is $90,000, the maximum allocation to each child is $30,000. Because of this allocation rule, Mrs. Alm can't increase the income shifted to her children by working for free on their behalf.

---

[7] *Estate of Emerson Winkler,* 36 T.C. Memo 1657; T.C. Memo, 1997-4.

[8] In nonfamily partnerships, the allocation of income does not have to be in proportion to each partner's ownership of capital. For example, the partnership agreement could provide that a partner who owns 50 percent of the capital is allocated 80 percent of the business income or loss.

[9] §704(e).

When a business is operated as an S corporation, annual income is allocated pro rata to the outstanding shares of corporate stock. Therefore, the percentage of income allocable to any one individual is based strictly on the number of shares owned. If Mrs. Alm converted her sole proprietorship to an S corporation and gave each child one-third of the stock, each child would be allocated one-third of the business income. If she gave each child only 10 percent of the stock, their pro rata share of the income drops to 10 percent. Before any corporate income is allocated to the shareholders, Mrs. Alm must receive a reasonable salary for any services performed for the corporation.[10]

Transaction Costs

Even with these statutory restrictions, partnerships and S corporations are a viable way to reduce the aggregate income tax burden on a family business. The potential tax savings must be compared to the transaction costs of forming the entity. If an individual creates a family partnership or S corporation by giving an equity interest in an established business to a family member, the donative transfer may be subject to the federal gift tax. This tax is based on the FMV of the transferred interest and must be paid by the *donor* (the individual making the gift). If the business has considerable value, the gift tax may represent a substantial transaction cost.[11] The various nontax transaction costs associated with the formation and operation of a separate legal entity should also be factored into the decision to create a family partnership or S corporation.

Transaction Costs of Partnership Formation	Refer to the preceding example in which Mrs. Alm formed a family partnership by giving a one-third equity interest in her retail clothing business to each of her two children. Immediately before the formation, the business had an appraised FMV of $950,000. Consequently, the FMV of Mrs. Alm's gift to each child was $316,667. If Mrs. Alm has not made prior taxable gifts, she would owe no current gift tax due to the lifetime gift tax exemption. However, if she has fully utilized her lifetime gift tax exemption, the gift tax due on these transfers could be as high as $368,000! The partnership paid $2,750 to the attorney who drafted the partnership agreement and an $800 fee to transfer title in the business real estate to the partnership. Thus, the transaction costs of forming the family partnership could total as much as $371,550. The gift tax is a nondeductible personal expense. The attorney's fee is a deductible organizational cost. The title transfer fee is capitalized to the partnership's basis in the real estate.[12]

Nontax Considerations

Entrepreneurs should carefully determine the extent to which the formation of a family-owned entity will dilute their control of the business. Many business owners who are willing to shift income and dollars to their relatives may be reluctant to give those relatives a voice in management. A limited partnership in which the entrepreneur is the sole general partner can eliminate this concern. Another option is for the entrepreneur to create an S corporation capitalized with both voting and nonvoting stock. The entrepreneur can keep the voting stock and give the nonvoting stock to their family, thereby retaining complete control of the business.

Individuals who transfer equity interests to a family member should understand that the transfer must be complete and legally binding. The recipient becomes the owner of an intangible property right. Absent any restrictions, the recipient is free to dispose of this right,

[10] §1366(e).
[11] The federal gift tax is discussed in more detail in Chapter 16.
[12] Reg. §1.709-2.

with or without the blessing of the other owners. *Buy-sell agreements* among the partners or shareholders are commonly used to restrict family members from selling or assigning their equity interest to an unrelated third party.

Still another important consideration is that the transfer of an equity interest must be irrevocable; the transferor can't simply change their mind and take the interest back. If the transferor becomes estranged from their family, an income-shifting arrangement could turn into a bitterly resented trap. A parent who has an ill-favored child can always disinherit the child. It is another matter entirely if the child owns stock in the family S corporation. A change in the relative economic circumstances of family members can also undermine an income-shifting strategy. Consider a situation in which a high-income taxpayer suffers a severe economic setback. An irreversible arrangement that shifts income away from this taxpayer could cause a personal financial crisis. These unhappy possibilities emphasize a point made earlier in the text: Tax strategies must be evaluated on the basis of flexibility. If a business owner is uneasy about their family's ability to cooperate, a family partnership or S corporation may be a bad idea.

A Family Partnership Gone Wrong	Refer one last time to the family partnership created by Mrs. Alm and her two children. Six years after the partnership was formed, one of the children died in an accident, and their spouse inherited their one-third interest in the partnership. The surviving spouse cannot get along with Mrs. Alm and the surviving child and contests every decision they make concerning the management of the retail clothing business. Because of the continual discord, the three partners finally discontinue the business and terminate the partnership.

PARTNERSHIP OR S CORPORATION?

LO 12-4
Explain tax and nontax considerations in choosing a passthrough entity form.

Entrepreneurs who organize their business as a passthrough entity must choose between some type of partnership and an S corporation. The choice depends on the tax and nontax characteristics that differentiate these two organizational forms. In the next few paragraphs, we will compare and contrast several important characteristics that enter into the decision-making process. Then we will analyze two planning cases.

Contrasting Characteristics

Costs of Entity Formation and Operation

Tax Talk
Although LLCs are increasingly popular, S corporations still dominate the small business landscape. In 2021, the IRS received 5.04 million returns from S corporations and 4.47 million returns from partnerships and LLCs.

The transfer of cash or property to a new partnership or corporation in exchange for a controlling equity interest is generally a nontaxable exchange.[13] Consequently, forming a new business entity has no up-front income tax cost. The owners will incur legal, accounting, and professional fees incidental to the formation. If the owners form a corporation, they must file a timely subchapter S election with the IRS. In addition, they must incur the incremental cost of monitoring the ownership structure to ensure that their S corporation continues to meet the eligibility requirements. If an S corporation loses its eligibility and the election terminates, the corporation automatically reverts to a taxable entity. An S corporation may be more expensive to operate than a partnership because of state tax costs. Several states, including New York, Tennessee, and Texas, impose entity-level income or franchise taxes on S corporations. In contrast, partnerships are typically exempt from state tax at the entity level.

---

[13] See the discussion of §721 and §351 in Chapter 9.

Flexibility of Income and Loss-Sharing Arrangement

Partnerships offer owners the maximum flexibility to tailor their business arrangement to fit their needs. The partnership agreement specifies the amount and type of capital each partner contributes to the business and can create special sharing ratios for different items of income, gain, deduction, and loss. Moreover, the partners can amend their agreement every year. S corporations offer less flexibility because of the statutory restrictions on capital structure. S corporations can have only a single class of stock, and each share must represent an identical claim on the income and assets of the business.

Partnership versus S Corporation Allocations	Ms. Carnes and Mr. Wells plan to form a passthrough entity to operate a new business. They expect the business will generate both ordinary income and capital gains. Because Ms. Carnes has capital loss carryforwards, she would like to be allocated a significant share of the capital gain income generated by the business. If the business is formed as a partnership, the partnership agreement can provide for a special allocation of capital gain income to Ms. Carnes, with a different sharing arrangement for the ordinary business income.[14] If the business is formed as an S corporation, such special allocations are not permitted. All S corporation allocations must be based on relative stock ownership.

Subchapter K versus Subchapter S

Although both partnerships and S corporations are passthrough entities, they are governed by different sections in the Internal Revenue Code. The sections governing partnerships are located in Subchapter K, while the sections governing S corporations are located in Subchapter S. Many provisions of Subchapter K, which originated with the Internal Revenue Code of 1954, are archaic and exceedingly difficult to apply. Subchapter K is particularly outmoded with respect to LLCs, which became widely available as an organizational form 30 years *after* Subchapter K was enacted. In comparison, Subchapter S was completely revised in 1982 to accommodate the modern S corporation and presents few difficulties in its application.

Self-Employment Tax

As we discussed in Chapter 10, general partners and LLC members who work for the LLC must treat their share of the entity's business income as net earnings from self-employment on which they pay self-employment tax. Shareholders in S corporations are not considered to be self-employed and therefore do not pay self-employment tax on their share of corporate income.

SE Tax Comparison	Mr. Biglow is a general partner in a partnership, and Ms. Tippee is a shareholder in an S corporation. Both individuals work full-time for the entity; Mr. Biglow receives a guaranteed payment, while Ms. Tippee receives a salary. This year, both individuals were allocated a $100,000 share of the entity's business income. Mr. Biglow must pay self-employment tax on both his guaranteed payment and his $100,000 share of partnership income. Ms. Tippee must pay employee payroll tax on her salary, but she does not pay self-employment tax on her $100,000 share of S corporation income.

---

[14] This special allocation must satisfy the substantial economic effect requirements of Section 704(b).

Owner Liability

Historically, an S corporation was the only choice for owners who wanted to pay a single tax on business income at the owner level and avoid unlimited personal liability for claims against the business. In contrast, the traditional partnership involved significant financial risk for general partners, who have unlimited liability for business debt. In recent years, traditional partnerships have been supplanted by LLPs and LLCs, both of which offer greater protection against financial risk. In LLPs, a partner is not personally liable for malpractice-related claims arising from the professional misconduct of another partner. In many states, professionals such as CPAs and attorneys organize their practices as LLPs to safeguard themselves against the negligent actions of any one individual partner. In LLCs, every member has limited liability for all debts of or claims against the business. Consequently, the LLC combines the tax advantages of a passthrough entity *and* the legal protection of the corporate form, without the costs or complications of the latter. The number of these organizations is growing at a phenomenal rate, and the LLC is now the entity of choice for many new businesses.

Two Planning Cases

To complete our discussion of the relative advantages and disadvantages of partnerships and S corporations, let's develop two cases in which differences between them are key variables in the planning process.

Leveraged Real Property Venture

Six individuals decide to form a company to purchase, rehabilitate, and manage a hotel. The hotel property is subject to a $3 million nonrecourse mortgage, and the owner is willing to sell their equity in the property for only $50,000. The commercial lender holding the mortgage has agreed to the conveyance of the hotel to the new company. The individuals will each contribute $20,000 cash in exchange for equal ownership interests, and the company will use the cash to buy the hotel and begin the necessary renovations. The individuals forecast that the company will generate a $264,000 tax loss for its first year. Most of this loss is from cost recovery deductions with respect to the hotel building and its furnishings.

The individuals intend to organize the company as a passthrough entity; consequently, each individual will be allocated $44,000 of the first-year loss. The individuals can deduct the loss only to the extent of the tax basis in their equity interest. If the company is organized as an S corporation, each individual's stock basis is $20,000—the cash contributed to the corporation. Therefore, each can deduct only $20,000 of the first-year loss.

If the company is organized as a LLC, the tax basis in each member's interest includes both the contributed cash *and* a portion of the LLC's debts. Because of the $3 million nonrecourse mortgage on the hotel, each individual has an initial basis of $520,000 ($20,000 cash + one-sixth of the mortgage). Because the LLC debt is included in basis, the individuals can deduct their entire shares of the first-year business losses.[15]

With respect to risk of financial loss, the individuals are indifferent between a LLC and an S corporation. In either case, the commercial lender can look only to the hotel property for satisfaction of the mortgage. The choice of entity should not affect the *total* business loss that each individual will eventually deduct. In the S corporation case, each shareholder can carry their $24,000 disallowed loss forward as a deduction against future income from the hotel business. The disadvantage of the S corporation is that the loss deduction is deferred. By operating their company as a LLC, the individuals can deduct the loss in the year incurred, thereby maximizing the value of the tax savings from the loss.

[15] This statement assumes that the mortgage is qualified nonrecourse financing for at-risk purposes and the passive activity loss and excess business loss limitations are inapplicable. The passive activity loss limitation is discussed in Chapter 16. The excess business loss limitation is discussed in Chapter 10.

Transferring Equity to Successive Generations	Amir and David, a married couple, are approaching retirement age and want to begin transferring their business to their three children and, ultimately, to their seven grandchildren. The grandchildren range from 1 year to 18 years of age, and the adults agree that it would be premature to make any grandchild an owner. Amir and David could create a family partnership to give their children an ownership interest in the business. In this case, a legally drafted partnership agreement would create and define the equity interests of each family member. But what happens in four years when one partner wants to transfer a portion of their equity to the eldest grandchild, or in six years when Amir wants to withdraw from the business and divide his equity among their three children? Every time the family modifies the ownership structure, the partnership agreement must be amended and the partnership interests redefined—a procedure that may be both inconvenient and costly. As an alternative, Amir and David could incorporate their business as an S corporation with a specified number of shares of stock. Each share would represent a pro rata interest in the business. Amir and David, and eventually their children, can modify the ownership structure of the corporation by simply giving shares to another relative. By choosing an S corporation rather than a partnership, Amir and David can minimize the transaction costs associated with a systematic transfer of ownership to their offspring.

TAX PLANNING WITH CLOSELY HELD CORPORATIONS

At some point in the life of a small business, the owners may decide to change from a passthrough entity to a corporation. Perhaps the organization has become so complex that the partnership form is unwieldy. Or perhaps the business has grown to the extent that the owners want to sell stock to the public, and the corporate form becomes a legal necessity. Regardless of the size or nature of the enterprise or the number of shareholders, the double taxation of income is the predominant tax challenge associated with the corporate form. In this section of the chapter, we will discuss how the owners of closely held corporations cope with the problem.

Getting Cash out of the Corporation

Owners of closely held C corporations are aware that dividends have a tax cost. Consequently, they can become very creative in devising ways to bail cash out of their corporations. The standard tactic is for an individual shareholder to assume an additional role with respect to the corporation. For instance, shareholders commonly serve as corporate officers or executives. In their role as employees, they are entitled to salaries that create cash flow to them and are deductible by the corporation. As a result, the business dollars paid as compensation are taxed only once at the individual level. Similarly, shareholders can become creditors by lending money to their corporations; the interest paid by the corporation on the debt is a deductible expense. Shareholders may lease property to their corporations for rent payments that the corporation can deduct. In all these cases, the cash received by the shareholder, whether as salary, interest, or rent, is taxable as ordinary income. The critical difference is at the corporate level where dividends are paid with after-tax dollars but salaries, interest, and rent are paid with before-tax dollars.

Qualified dividend income earned by noncorporate (individual) taxpayers is subject to the same preferential rate structure that applies to long-term capital gains. These rates are discussed in greater detail in Chapter 16. In general, the tax rate is zero percent for qualified dividends that would be taxed at a 10 or 12 percent ordinary rate. A 15 percent dividend rate applies to the taxpayers whose ordinary rate is greater than 12 percent up to a threshold amount as shown in Chapter 16. Taxpayers at the very top of the income scale (whose marginal rate on ordinary income would be 37 percent) are subject to a 20 percent rate on qualified dividends. Qualified dividends may also be subject to the additional 3.8 percent Medicare contribution tax, discussed in detail in Chapter 16. Because this preferential rate structure decreases the double-tax burden on dividends, owners of closely held C corporations now have less incentive to pay themselves salaries, interest, and rent instead of dividends.

Constructive Dividends

LO 12-5
Define *constructive dividend.*

The IRS has no quarrel with shareholders who transact with their corporations if the transaction is based on reasonable terms comparable to those that would be negotiated between unrelated parties. Even so, the IRS understands that shareholders have an incentive to violate this arm's-length standard. When revenue agents audit closely held corporations, they pay special attention to any deductions for payments to shareholders. If an agent concludes that the payment is unreasonable in light of the facts and circumstances, the IRS may conclude that the unreasonable portion is a **constructive dividend.**

Unreasonable Compensation

Mr. Maupin, sole shareholder and chief executive officer of MP, Inc., receives a $450,000 annual salary. If other companies comparable in size and function to MP pay salaries to their CEOs ranging from $400,000 to $500,000 and if Mr. Maupin has the talent and experience to merit such compensation, his salary appears reasonable, and MP can deduct it. Conversely, if the CEO salaries paid by comparable firms average only $300,000 and Mr. Maupin spends more time on the golf course than at corporate headquarters, the IRS may conclude that some portion of his salary is unreasonable.[16]

Let's build on the preceding example by assuming that the IRS decides that $150,000 of Mr. Maupin's annual salary is unreasonable and should be treated as a dividend. What are the tax consequences of this decision?

Constructive Dividend

The following table compares the net tax cost of a $450,000 payment from MP, Inc. to Mr. Maupin when the entire payment is treated as salary with the net tax cost when only $300,000 is treated as salary and $150,000 is treated as a dividend. The table assumes that Mr. Maupin's marginal rate on ordinary income is 37 percent, his tax rate on qualified dividends is 20 percent, and MP's tax rate is 21 percent. (The comparison ignores the difference in payroll taxes under the two assumptions.)

	Salary	Salary/ Dividend
Mr. Maupin's salary	$450,000	$300,000
	.37	.37
Mr. Maupin's *tax cost* of salary	$166,500	$111,000
Mr. Maupin's dividend	–0–	$150,000
		.20
Mr. Maupin's *tax cost* of dividend		$ 30,000
MP's deduction for the payment	$450,000	$300,000
	.21	.21
MP's *tax savings* from the deduction	$ 94,500	$ 63,000
Net tax cost of payment (*tax costs less tax savings*)	$ 72,000	$ 78,000

---

[16] The topic of reasonable compensation is discussed in more detail in Chapter 15.

Note that the reduction in Mr. Maupin's tax cost attributable to his 20 percent preferential rate on dividends is not enough to offset the reduction in MP, Inc.'s tax savings attributable to payment of a nondeductible dividend. The $6,000 increase in the net tax cost when $150,000 of the $450,000 payment must be treated as a dividend falls squarely on Mr. Maupin as the sole owner of the corporation.

These next two examples illustrate constructive dividends in two other contexts.

Unreasonable Rent Payments	Mr. Serednesky rented office space from an unrelated third party for $8,000 annual rent and then subleased the office space to his wholly owned corporation for $16,604. The corporation deducted the $16,604 payment as rent expense on its tax return. The IRS determined that only $8,000 of the payment represented a reasonable, arm's-length rent, and $8,604 of the payment was a nondeductible dividend.[17]

Shareholder Expenses	Mr. Leonard was the sole shareholder and employee of a personal service corporation. The corporation paid $1,663 of Mr. Leonard's personal travel and entertainment expenses and deducted the payment as a business expense. The IRS treated the payment as a nondeductible constructive dividend that Mr. Leonard had to include in his taxable income. The federal court agreed with the IRS's evaluation of the transaction. When Mr. Leonard protested that the tax consequences unfairly penalized him for operating a business in corporate form, the court replied, "The corporate bed may have lumps; once chosen, however, a taxpayer must endure a sleepless night every now and then."[18]

Thin Capitalization

The organizers of closely held corporations usually understand that if they invest funds in exchange for a corporate debt obligation, the corporation can deduct the interest paid on the debt. Moreover, a loan is temporary, and the organizers will receive a return of their investment according to a fixed repayment schedule or even on demand. On the other hand, if they invest funds in exchange for equity stock, their investment is permanent, and any dividends paid on the investment are nondeductible. As a result, organizers are motivated to include as much debt as possible in their corporation's capital structure. Congress recognized this motivation when enacting the limitation on deductibility of net business interest discussed in Chapter 6.

If the debt held by shareholders is excessive, the IRS may contend that some or all of the debt is disguised equity. As a result, interest payments are actually nondeductible dividends. Even worse, principal repayments may be reclassified as constructive dividends.[19] Because these repayments were nondeductible to the corporation, their reclassification doesn't affect the corporation's taxable income. However, the shareholders who believed they were receiving a nontaxable return of investment must recognize the repayments as income.

---

[17] *Social Psychological Services, Inc.,* T.C. Memo 1993-565.

[18] Source: *Leonard* v. *Commissioner,* 57 T.C. Memo 1275 (1989), T.C. Memo 1989-423.

[19] This is typically the case when the debt held by the shareholders is in proportion to their stock interests. As a result, principal repayments are treated as distributions under §302(d) and are taxable as dividends to the extent of the corporation's earnings and profits.

Disguised Equity	Mr. and Mrs. Vance formed V&V, Inc. six years ago by contributing $1,000 for 100 shares of common stock (the minimum capitalization under state law). The couple also loaned $25,000 to V&V in exchange for the corporation's note. The note had no fixed repayment schedule but did provide for annual interest. The corporation has never paid a dividend and paid no interest on the note for five years. Late last year, V&V distributed $36,250 to Mr. and Mrs. Vance. According to the corporate financial records, the distribution was a repayment of the original loan plus $11,250 accrued interest. The corporation deducted the $11,250 interest on its tax return, and Mr. and Mrs. Vance reported $11,250 interest income on their tax return. The revenue agent who audited V&V's return concluded that Mr. and Mrs. Vance's loan was, in substance, an equity investment. Thus, the entire $36,250 distribution was a dividend—nondeductible to V&V and taxable to Mr. and Mrs. Vance.

The IRS is most likely to challenge the validity of shareholder debt when a closely held corporation is **thinly capitalized,** with an unusually high ratio of debt to equity. From the government's perspective, the debt-equity ratio is a measure of the business risk borne by the corporation's creditors. A capital structure can become so top heavy with debt that repayment depends on the corporation's continuing profitability rather than on the security of the underlying equity base. In such case, the purported debt has the economic characteristics of common stock. Although the tax law does not contain a safe harbor, a debt-equity ratio of 3 to 1 or less is generally considered immune from IRS attack.[20] Regardless of the corporate debt-equity ratio, shareholders should take care that any loan to their corporation has all the attributes of arm's-length debt. The loan should be evidenced by the corporation's written unconditional promise to repay the principal by a specified date plus a fixed market rate of interest. Ideally, the debt should not be subordinated to other corporate liabilities, and the shareholders should not hold debt in the same proportion as they own the corporate stock. By respecting these formalities, shareholders can minimize the possibility that the IRS will question the capital structure of their corporation.

Under the current tax regime, individual shareholders may prefer dividend treatment to interest treatment (ignoring, of course, recharacterization of principal payments) because dividends are taxed at preferential rates while interest is taxable at ordinary income rates. Corporate shareholders almost always prefer dividend treatment because of the dividends-received deduction. The loss of the corporate-level deduction for interest payments, and the related tax savings, must be balanced against the lower tax cost of dividends to the recipient shareholder.

Rise and Fall of the Corporate Tax Shelter

A Historical Perspective

For most of the history of the federal income tax, the tax rates for individuals were significantly higher than the tax rates for corporations. For example, from 1965 through 1980, the top marginal rate for individuals was 70 percent, while the top marginal rate for corporations hovered around 48 percent. Business owners could take advantage of the rate differential by operating their businesses in the corporate form. Of course, this arbitrage strategy was effective only to the extent that the owners could do without annual dividends from their closely held corporations.

Individual shareholders who had their corporations *accumulate* (i.e., retain) after-tax earnings instead of distributing dividends did not permanently avoid the double tax on such

---

[20] Boris I. Bittker and James S. Eustice, *Federal Income Taxation of Corporations and Shareholders,* 6th ed. (Boston: Warren Gorham Lamont, 1994), pp. 4–35.

earnings. The accumulated earnings increased the shareholders' equity and thus the value of the corporate stock. As long as shareholders held on to their stock, the unrealized appreciation in value was not taxed. But if and when a shareholder disposed of stock in a taxable transaction, the shareholder recognized the appreciation as capital gain and paid an indirect second tax on the corporation's accumulated earnings. Because this second tax was postponed until the year of the stock disposition, its cost was reduced in present value terms. Furthermore, the second tax was computed at the preferential capital gain rate instead of the regular rate on ordinary income. This combination of *deferral* and *conversion* (of ordinary income into capital gain) enhanced the attraction of the corporate tax shelter.

The Classic Corporate Tax Shelter	Many years ago, when the top individual tax rate was 70 percent and the top corporate tax rate was only 48 percent, Mr. and Mrs. Van Sant organized a new business as V&S, Inc. For its first year (year 0), V&S generated $200,000 taxable income, paid $96,000 income tax, and accumulated $104,000. If the Van Sants had organized their business as a passthrough entity, their year 0 individual tax on $200,000 income would have been $140,000. The Van Sants held their V&S stock until year 15 when they sold it to a competitor. Their capital gain on sale, which was taxed at a 20 percent preferential rate, reflected 15 years of appreciation in value attributable to V&S's accumulated earnings. Therefore, the indirect second tax on the $104,000 earnings accumulated in year 0 was $20,800. The NPV of this tax at an 8 percent discount rate was $6,552, and the double tax on the corporate income in present value terms totaled $102,552. By organizing their business as a corporation instead of a passthrough entity, the Van Sants saved $37,448 tax ($140,000 individual tax − $102,552 double tax) on their year 0 income.

The Current Environment

LO 12-6
Explain why individuals once again can use corporations as tax shelters.

In 1981, Congress began to gradually decrease the top marginal rates for both individual and corporate taxpayers and to diminish the spread between the rates. The Jobs and Growth Tax Relief Reconciliation Act of 2003 finally equalized the top marginal rates at 35 percent. Consequently, from 2003 through 2012, the opportunity for individuals to exploit the differences between the individual and the corporate rate structures was exceedingly narrow. Beginning in 2013 through 2017, the top marginal tax rate for individuals increased to 39.6 percent and was once again above the top corporate tax rate of 35 percent. For tax years after 2017, the corporate rate is now 21 percent and the top marginal rate for individuals is 37 percent. Thus, the opportunity once again exists for high-wealth individuals to use corporations as a tax shelter.

Less Shelter	What if the Van Sants were to begin their new business today? Could they save any tax by organizing as a corporation rather than a passthrough entity? If the business generates $200,000 income and is organized as a corporation, the current year corporate tax would be $42,000, and accumulated earnings would be $158,000. If the Van Sants sell their stock after 15 years, their indirect second tax on the $158,000 accumulated earnings at a 20 percent capital gains rate will be $31,600. The NPV of this tax at an 8 percent discount rate is $9,954, and the double tax on the corporate income in present value terms totals $51,954. But if the Van Sants organize their business as a passthrough entity, their current tax on $200,000 *computed at the highest marginal rate* (with a 20 percent QBI deduction) would be $59,200, which is $7,246 more than the corporate alternative. Thus, tax savings are possible today using a corporation as a tax shelter but are certainly smaller than once available.

Penalty Taxes on Corporate Accumulations

LO 12-7
Explain the purpose
of the accumulated
earnings tax and the
personal holding
company tax.

Given the disparity between the top individual and corporate rates, individuals can potentially reduce their tax costs significantly by operating their businesses as corporations. Decades ago, Congress resolved to discourage the use of closely held corporations as tax shelters by enacting two penalty taxes on corporations that fail to distribute dividends to their individual shareholders. These two taxes, the accumulated earnings tax and the personal holding company tax, are still part of the tax law today. A corporation that finds itself liable for either tax must pay it *in addition to* its income tax for the year.

Accumulated Earnings Tax

Tax Talk
*Recent changes in
IRS audit procedure
suggest that the
Service is targeting
for audit corporate
tax returns that show
accumulated earnings
that may have been
accumulated beyond
the reasonable needs
of the business.*

The IRS can impose an **accumulated earnings tax** on any corporation "formed or availed of for the purpose of avoiding the income tax with respect to its shareholders by permitting earnings and profits to accumulate instead of being divided or distributed."[21] This tax avoidance purpose is presumed to exist when a corporation accumulates earnings beyond the reasonable needs of its business. Currently, the penalty tax equals 20 percent of the corporation's *accumulated taxable income* (roughly defined as taxable income less income tax and dividends paid). For example, a corporation with $660,000 after-tax income that pays no dividends and has no business justification to accumulate earnings could owe a $132,000 accumulated earnings tax ($660,000 × 20 percent).

The accumulated earnings tax is clearly intended to coerce corporations to pay dividends. It is not a self-imposed tax but is instead imposed by the IRS on audit. The IRS's application of the tax is uncertain and subjective. Many corporations have accumulated millions of dollars, and their shareholders have never worried about the penalty tax because they have documented reasons justifying the accumulation.[22] The corporate balance sheet may show that retained earnings financed the development of a new product line, the geographic expansion of the business, the retirement of long-term debt, or the construction of a new manufacturing facility. On the other hand, corporations vulnerable to the tax display two common traits. They have a history of minimal or no dividend payments, and their balance sheets reveal an overabundance of nonbusiness assets such as long-term certificates of deposit, marketable securities, investment real estate, and, most damning of all, substantial loans to shareholders.

The tax law gives newly incorporated businesses some leeway to retain after-tax income on a "no-questions-asked" basis. Specifically, every corporation can accumulate $250,000 without establishing business need and without exposure to the penalty tax.[23]

"No-Questions-Asked" Accumulation	Selby, Inc., a calendar year corporate taxpayer, was formed in 2021. On December 31, 2021, Selby's accumulated earnings were $82,700. Consequently, Selby was immune to the accumulated earnings tax for 2021. By December 31, 2022, Selby's accumulated earnings had increased to $204,900. Because this accumulation was still less than $250,000, Selby's immunity continued for 2022. In 2023, Selby's after-tax earnings were $400,000, and the corporation did not pay any dividends. Selby can accumulate only $45,100 ($250,000 − $204,900 prior years' accumulated earnings) in 2023 on a "no-questions-asked" basis. It must be able to demonstrate a reasonable business need for the additional $354,900 accumulation to avoid exposure to a 2023 accumulated earnings tax on these earnings.

---

[21] Source: Internal Revenue Service.

[22] Publicly held corporations are normally immune to the accumulated earnings tax because their dividend policies are not controlled by their shareholders.

[23] Personal service corporations may accumulate only $150,000 without establishing reasonable business need.

Personal Holding Company Tax

Corporations qualifying as personal holding companies may be liable for a **personal holding company tax.**[24] The statutory definition of a **personal holding company** is technically complex—suffice it to say that personal holding companies are owned by a small number of individuals and earn primarily nonbusiness income such as dividends, interest, rents, and royalties. Currently, the penalty tax equals 20 percent of undistributed after-tax corporate income for the year. For example, a personal holding company with $2,450,000 undistributed after-tax income owes a $490,000 personal holding company tax ($2,450,000 × 20 percent). Personal holding companies that distribute 100 percent of after-tax earnings are not liable for any penalty tax.[25]

Congress enacted the personal holding company tax more than 60 years ago. Its purpose was to discourage individuals from incorporating their investment portfolios to take advantage of corporate tax rates that were 45 percentage points less than individual rates. Today, there is less difference between the highest corporate and individual rates, and individuals have less tax incentive to incorporate their portfolios. Nevertheless, a corporation qualifying as a personal holding company must attach a Schedule PH showing the computation of any additional penalty tax to its annual Form 1120.

Conclusion

This chapter concludes our study of the five basic forms of business organization. Four of these forms—sole proprietorships, partnerships, LLCs, and S corporations—are not taxable entities for federal purposes. Individuals who use these forms pay a single tax on their business income. Only the fifth form—the corporation—is taxed at the entity level, and shareholders pay a second tax when they receive dividends from the corporation. Business owners who want to engage in successful tax planning must understand the basic tax rules that differentiate passthrough entities and corporations. By taking advantage of these rules, the owners can control tax costs, maximize after-tax income available for personal consumption, and enhance the value of their investment in the business.

---

[24] §541. Sections 541 through 547 describe the personal holding company tax.

[25] Personal holding companies are not subject to the accumulated earnings tax. §532(b)(1).

Key Terms

accumulated earnings tax *12-16*	personal holding company *12-17*	thinly capitalized *12-14*
constructive dividend *12-12*	personal holding company tax *12-17*	

Questions and Problems for Discussion

LO 12-3   1. The Velottas are self-employed professional musicians. Their average annual income from performance fees and music lessons is $130,000. The couple wants to shift income to their two children, ages 19 and 22. Can the Velottas organize their music business as a family partnership and give each child a 25 percent interest?

LO 12-3   2. The Barnes own a fast-food restaurant that generates $160,000 average annual income. The couple wants to shift some of this income to their two children, ages 19 and 22. Can the Barneses organize their restaurant as a family partnership and give each child a 25 percent interest?

LO 12-3   3. Ms. Johnson is eager to create a family partnership to generate income and cash flow for her three college-aged children. She owns two businesses, either of which could be organized as a partnership. Ms. Johnson established the first business 15 years ago. This business consists of operating assets with a $15 million FMV. Ms. Johnson established the second business only 10 months ago. This business is growing rapidly and already is generating taxable income. However, its operating assets have only a $300,000 FMV. Which business is the better candidate for a family partnership? Explain your reasoning.

LO 12-2   4. Discuss the tax and nontax reasons why the stock in an S corporation is typically subject to a buy-sell agreement.

LO 12-3   5. Mr. Eros operates an antique store located on the first floor of a four-story office building owned by Mr. Eros. The top three stories are leased to business tenants. Mr. Eros is considering giving a one-third interest in both the antique store and the building to each of his two grandchildren and operating the businesses in one passthrough entity. Mr. Eros wants to receive 100 percent of the rent from his tenants for several years but is willing to distribute one-third of the net profit from the antique store to his grandchildren each year. On the basis of this objective, which form of organization should he choose?

LO 12-4   6. Dr. Quinn, Dr. Rose, and Dr. Tanner are dentists who practice as equal owners of QRT Dental Services. A patient of Dr. Rose's recently sued him for medical malpractice and was awarded a $500,000 judgment. Discuss each owner's personal liability for this judgment assuming that

    a. QRT is a general partnership.

    b. QRT is an LLP.

    c. QRT is an LLC.

LO 12-4   7. Refer to the facts in the previous problem. QRT purchased $30,000 of dental equipment on credit. When QRT failed to pay its bill, the seller took it to court and won a judgment for $30,000. Discuss each owner's personal liability for this judgment assuming that

    a. QRT is a general partnership.

    b. QRT is an LLP.

    c. QRT is an LLC.

LO 12-2, 12-6   8. Mrs. Tran and Mrs. Nutter each own a small business that averages $80,000 annual income. Each woman is in the 35 percent marginal tax bracket. Mrs. Tran has decided to incorporate her business as a taxable corporation, while Mrs. Nutter has decided to continue to operate as a sole proprietorship. Both decisions maximize the after-tax value of the business to its owner. How can you explain this apparent contradiction?

LO 12-7   9. BNC, a closely held corporation, was organized in 1987. To date, it has accumulated more than $10 million after-tax income. This year, BNC's taxable income is $750,000, and its federal tax is $255,000. Describe two different ways that BNC can avoid exposure to the accumulated earnings tax for the year.

LO 12-5   10. Describe the FICA payroll tax implications when the IRS classifies a portion of a salary payment to a shareholder/employee as a constructive dividend.

LO 12-5   11. When the IRS classifies a portion of a salary payment to a shareholder/employee as a constructive dividend, which party (corporation or shareholder) bears the economic burden of the tax consequences?

LO 12-5   12. Mx. Knox recently loaned $20,000 to their closely held corporation, which needed the money for working capital. They see no reason to document the loan other than as a "loan payable—shareholder" on the corporate balance sheet. Mx. Knox also sees no reason for the corporation to pay interest on the loan. What advice can you offer Mx. Knox concerning this related-party transaction?

LO 12-7   13. Explain the logic of the tax rate for both the accumulated earnings tax and the personal holding company tax.

LO 12-7   14. In what way does a corporate balance sheet provide information concerning the corporation's exposure to the accumulated earnings tax?

LO 12-7   15. Why are publicly held corporations such as General Motors generally immune from the accumulated earnings tax?

LO 12-6   16. How would the tax shelter potential of closely held corporations be affected by
   a. An increase in the highest individual tax rate to 43 percent?
   b. A decrease in the preferential tax rate on individual capital gains to 5 percent?
   c. Repeal of the accumulated earnings tax?

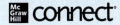 **All applicable Application Problems are available with *Connect*.**

Application Problems

LO 12-1   1. Mr. Tuck and Ms. Under organized a new business as an LLC in which they own equal interests. The new business generated a $4,800 operating loss for the year.
   a. If Mr. Tuck's marginal tax rate before consideration of the LLC loss is 35 percent, compute his tax savings from the first-year LLC loss. Assume the basis and excess business loss limitations do not apply.
   b. Assume that Ms. Under has no taxable income for the year. Does she have any tax savings from the LLC loss? Explain briefly.

LO 12-1   2. Grant and Marvin organized a new business as a corporation in which they own equal interests. The new business generated a $65,000 operating loss for the year.
   a. Assume the corporation expects to generate $500,000 of income next year and has a 21 percent tax rate. Calculate the net present value of the future tax savings associated with the current year operating loss, using a 4 percent discount rate.
   b. Now assume that the corporation makes an election under Subchapter S to be treated as a passthrough entity. If Grant's marginal tax rate is 35 percent and Marvin's marginal tax rate is 37 percent, calculate the tax savings associated with the current year operating loss. Assume the basis and excess business loss limitations do not apply.

LO 12-2   3. Mr. and Mrs. Lund and their two children (Ben and June) are the four equal partners in LBJ Partnership. This year, LBJ generated $36,000 ordinary income. Compute the tax cost for the business if Mr. and Mrs. Lund's marginal rate is 32 percent, Ben's marginal rate is 24 percent, and June's marginal rate is 12 percent. (Ignore SE tax consequences.)

LO 12-2   4. Ms. Kona owns a 10 percent interest in Carlton LLC. This year, the LLC generated $72,400 ordinary income. Ms. Kona's marginal tax rate is 32 percent, and she does not pay SE tax on her LLC income.
   a. Compute the tax cost on Ms. Kona's share of Carlton's income assuming that she received a $35,000 cash distribution this year.
   b. Compute the tax cost on Ms. Kona's share of Carlton's income assuming that she received no cash distribution this year.

LO 12-3 5. Ms. Singh, who is in the 37 percent tax bracket, owns a residential apartment building that generates $80,000 annual taxable income. She plans to create a family partnership by giving each of her two children a 20 percent equity interest in the building. (She will retain a 60 percent interest.) Ms. Singh will manage the building, and the value of her services is $15,000 per year. If Ms. Singh's children are in the 12 percent tax bracket, compute the tax savings from this income-shifting arrangement. (Ignore any payroll tax consequences.)

LO 12-3 6. Delta Partnership has four equal partners. At the beginning of the year, Drew was one of the Delta partners, but on October 1, he sold his partnership interest to Cody. If Delta's ordinary income for the year was $476,000, what portion of this income should be allocated to Drew, and what portion should be allocated to Cody?

LO 12-3 7. WRT, a calendar year S corporation, has 100 shares of outstanding stock. At the beginning of the year, Mr. Wallace owned all 100 shares. On September 30, he gave 25 shares to his brother and 40 shares to his daughter. WRT's ordinary income for the year was $216,000. What portion of this income must each shareholder include in income?

LO 12-4 8. A number of tax and nontax factors should be considered in choosing the type of passthrough entity through which to operate a new business. For each of the following considerations, indicate whether the item favors the partnership form or the S corporation form of passthrough entity:

    a. State taxes, including franchise tax and potential entity-level income taxes.

    b. Flexibility of income and loss sharing arrangements.

    c. Complexity in the application of the relevant tax statutes.

    d. Liability for self-employment tax on allocable shares of the entity's ordinary business income.

LO 12-4 9. Angela and Thomas are planning to start a new business. Thomas will invest cash in the business but not be involved in day-to-day operations. Angela plans to work full time overseeing business operations.

    The two currently project that the business will generate $200,000 of annual taxable income before consideration of any payments to Angela for her services. Both agree that Angela's services are worth $100,000.

    Angela and Thomas plan to form a passthrough entity but are unsure whether to choose a partnership or an S corporation. In either case, they will be equal owners of the entity. Given their other sources of income, both Thomas and Angela have a 37 percent marginal tax rate on ordinary income. (Ignore any payroll or self-employment tax consequences.)

    a. If the business is operated as a partnership, calculate ordinary income allocated to each owner, and explain the treatment by the partnership and by Angela of her $100,000 payment for services.

    b. If the business is operated as an S corporation, calculate ordinary income allocated to each owner, and explain the treatment by the corporation and by Angela of her $100,000 payment for services.

    c. Given your analysis, explain to Angela and Thomas whether and to what extent income tax consequences should control their choice of entity.

LO 12-4 10. Refer to the facts in the preceding problem.

    a. If the business is operated as a partnership, explain the payroll tax/self-employment tax implications for the entity, Thomas, and Angela. (No calculations are required.)

    b. If the business is operated as an S corporation, explain the payroll tax/self-employment tax implications for the entity, Thomas, and Angela. (No calculations are required.)

    c. Given your discussion, how might payroll tax/self-employment taxes influence Thomas and Angela's choice of entity through which to operate their business?

LO 12-4, 12-6   11. Mr. Lion, who is in the 37 percent tax bracket, is the sole shareholder of Toto Inc., which manufactures greeting cards. Toto's average annual net profit (before deduction of Mr. Lion's salary) is $200,000. For each of the following cases, compute the income tax burden on this profit. (Ignore any payroll tax consequences.)

    a. Mr. Lion's salary is $100,000, and Toto pays no dividends.

    b. Mr. Lion's salary is $100,000, and Toto distributes its after-tax income as a dividend.

    c. Toto is an S corporation. Mr. Lion's salary is $100,000, and Toto makes no cash distributions. Assume Toto's ordinary income qualifies for the 20 percent QBI deduction.

    d. Toto is an S corporation. Mr. Lion draws no salary, and Toto makes no cash distributions. Assume Toto's ordinary income qualifies for the 20 percent QBI deduction.

    e. Toto is an S corporation. Mr. Lion draws no salary, and Toto makes cash distributions of all its income to Mr. Lion. Assume Toto's ordinary income qualifies for the 20 percent QBI deduction.

LO 12-2   12. Playa and Quinetta are equal shareholders in Corporation PQ. Both shareholders have a 37 percent marginal tax rate. PQ's financial records show the following:

Gross income from sales of goods	$980,000
Operating expenses	(410,000)
Interest paid on debt to Playa and Quinetta	(62,000)
Dividend distributions:	
Playa	(50,000)
Quinetta	(50,000)

    a. Compute the combined tax cost for PQ, Playa, and Quinetta.

    b. How would your computation change if the interest on the shareholder debt was $162,000 and PQ paid no dividends?

LO 12-2, 12-5   13. American Corporation has two equal shareholders, Mr. Freedom and Brave, Inc. In addition to their investments in American stock, both shareholders have made substantial loans to American. During the current year, American paid $100,000 interest each to Mr. Freedom and Brave, Inc. Assume that American and Brave have 21 percent tax rates, and Mr. Freedom's marginal tax rate on ordinary income is 37 percent.

    a. Calculate American's tax savings from deduction of these interest payments and their after-tax cost.

    b. Calculate Brave's tax cost and after-tax earnings from its receipt of interest income from American.

    c. Calculate Mr. Freedom's tax cost and after-tax earnings from his receipt of interest income from American.

    d. If an IRS agent concludes that American is thinly capitalized and the shareholder loans should be treated as equity, explain the impact on American, Brave, and Mr. Freedom.

    e. Recalculate Brave's tax cost and after-tax earnings assuming its receipt of interest from American is treated as a constructive dividend.

    f. Recalculate Mr. Freedom's tax cost and after-tax earnings assuming his receipt of interest from American is treated as a constructive dividend.

LO 12-6 14. Ms. Xie, who is in the 37 percent tax bracket, is the sole shareholder and president of Xenon. The corporation's financial records show the following:

Gross income from sales of goods	$1,590,000
Operating expenses	(930,000)
Salary paid to Ms. Xie	(300,000)
Dividend distributions	(200,000)

  a. Compute the combined tax cost for Xenon and Ms. Xie. (Ignore payroll tax.)

  b. How would your computation change if Ms. Xie's salary was $500,000 and Xenon paid no dividends?

LO 12-5 15. Mr. Vernon is the sole shareholder of Teva. He also owns the office building that serves as corporate headquarters. Last year, Teva paid $180,000 annual rent to Mr. Vernon for use of the building. Teva's marginal tax rate was 21 percent, and Mr. Vernon's marginal tax rate was 37 percent. The revenue agent who audited Teva's return concluded that the fair rental value of the office building was $125,000.

  a. Calculate any increase or decrease in Mr. Vernon's tax as a result of the agent's conclusion.

  b. Calculate any increase or decrease in Teva's tax as a result of the agent's conclusion.

LO 12-5 16. In 1994, Mr. and Mrs. Adams formed ADC by transferring $50,000 cash in exchange for 100 shares of common stock and a note from the corporation for $49,000. The note obligated ADC to pay 10 percent annual interest and to repay the $49,000 principal on demand. ADC has never declared a dividend or made any interest payments on the note. Last year, it distributed $25,000 cash to Mr. and Mrs. Adams as a principal repayment. When the IRS audited ADC's tax return, the revenue agent determined that this payment was a constructive dividend.

  a. If ADC's marginal tax rate last year was 34 percent, calculate any increase or decrease in ADC's tax as a result of this constructive dividend.

  b. If Mr. and Mrs. Adam's marginal tax rate is 35 percent, calculate any increase or decrease in their tax as a result of this constructive dividend.

LO 12-7 17. During a recent IRS audit, the revenue agent determined that Level Corporation meets the definition of a personal holding company. If Level's undistributed after-tax income last year was $670,000, compute the amount of personal holding company tax it owes.

LO 12-7 18. During a recent IRS audit, the revenue agent decided that the Parker family used their closely held corporation, Falco, to avoid shareholder tax by accumulating earnings beyond the reasonable needs of the business. Falco's taxable income was $900,000, it paid no dividends, and it had no business need to retain income. Falco's marginal tax rate in prior years was 34 percent. Compute Falco's accumulated earnings tax assuming that

  a. It had accumulated $4 million after-tax income in prior years.

  b. It had accumulated $129,000 after-tax income in prior years.

LO 12-5 19. Graham is the sole shareholder of Logan Corporation. For the past five years, Logan has reported little or no taxable income as a result of paying Graham a salary of $500,000 per year. During a recent IRS audit, the revenue agent determined that Graham's educational and business experience, and his time devoted to managing Logan, justified a salary of only $200,000. Thus, the agent recharacterized $300,000 of the payments from the corporation as a dividend.

  a. Calculate the additional income tax liability for Logan as a result of this constructive dividend treatment. Assume Logan's marginal tax rate for the year in question was 34 percent. (Ignore any payroll tax consequences.)

    b. What are the tax consequences to Graham as a result of the constructive dividend treatment? Calculate the change in Graham's income tax liability as a result of this change. Assume that Graham's marginal tax rate on ordinary income is 37 percent. (Ignore any payroll tax consequences.)

    c. Given your calculations, determine the total impact on Treasury tax collections as a result of this audit finding.

LO 12-5 20. Refer to the facts in the preceding problem. Briefly explain the payroll tax consequences of the revenue agent's conclusions.

LO 12-6 21. Megan operates a housecleaning business as a sole proprietorship. She oversees a team of 10 cleaning personnel, markets the business, and provides supplies and equipment. The business has been generating net taxable profits of $50,000 per year, before considering the QBI deduction. As a sole proprietor, Megan qualifies for the 20 percent deduction, reducing taxable income from the business to $40,000.

    a. Assume that Megan's marginal tax rate on ordinary income is 35 percent and that she has no pressing need for cash flow from this business. Should Megan consider incorporating and operating the business through a C corporation? Provide calculations to support your conclusion. (Ignore any payroll or self-employment tax considerations.)

    b. How would your conclusion in part (*a*) change if Megan's marginal tax rate were only 28 percent?

Issue Recognition Problems

Identify the tax issue or issues suggested by the following situations, and state each issue in the form of a question.

LO 12-3 1. Mr. and Mrs. Keck are in the highest marginal tax bracket. Their son, a first-year college student, earns minimal income from his summer job, and his marginal tax rate is 10 percent. Mr. and Mrs. Keck are considering making their son an equal owner in a family business that generates more than $200,000 taxable income each year. They believe that every dollar of income shifted to their son will save more than 25 cents of tax for the family.

LO 12-1 2. Mr. Ortiz owns a 40 percent interest in newly formed MNO Partnership. The partners organized their business as a passthrough entity so that the start-up loss would generate an immediate tax savings. Mr. Ortiz, however, had a substantial loss from another business and has no taxable income against which to deduct his share of the MNO loss.

LO 12-5 3. Mr. and Mrs. Braun own 100 percent of the stock of BB, Inc., which operates a temporary employment business. Late last year, Mr. Braun was short of cash in his personal checking account. Consequently, he paid several personal bills by writing checks on the corporate account and recorded the payments as miscellaneous expenses. Three months later he repaid the corporation in full.

LO 12-5 4. REW, Inc. is closely held by six members of the Rew family. The corporation owns two vans that employees use for various business transportation purposes. However, for at least eight weeks during each year, the shareholders use the vans to take their families on extended vacation trips.

LO 12-3 5. Eight years ago, Mr. and Mrs. Lauffer created a family partnership with their son, the son's spouse, their daughter, and the daughter's spouse. Each of these six individuals owns an equal interest in the partnership. This year, the son and his spouse decide to divorce.

LO 12-7   6. LSN, a calendar year S corporation, has 13 shareholders. Since its incorporation, LSN has retained more than $800,000 income to reinvest in its business. Because LSN is a passthrough entity, the shareholders have paid tax on this undistributed income and increased their stock basis accordingly. The shareholders want to revoke the S election and operate LSN as a regular corporation. LSN has only $69,000 in its corporate bank account.

LO 12-4   7. Last year, Mrs. Kahn and Mrs. Toms each contributed the assets of their respective sole proprietorships to a new corporation. The shareholders believed that by combining their businesses, they could increase profitability. They were encouraged to do so because they could transfer their assets in exchange for stock without recognizing gain. Unfortunately, Mrs. Kahn and Mrs. Toms discovered that they couldn't work together effectively. They agreed to part company by dissolving the corporation and taking back ownership of their respective assets (essentially just reversing the incorporation process).

LO 12-2   8. Taha is closely held by eight family members. Taha purchased investment land 12 years ago for $100,000. The land was recently appraised at an FMV of $3 million. A buyer has offered to pay cash for the land. Because the shareholders need the cash, they plan to have Taha distribute the land to them as a dividend. They will then sell the land and recognize a capital gain taxable at the 15 percent preferential individual rate.

LO 12-5   9. Mr. and Mrs. Crandall own 100 percent of the stock in CR, Inc., which recently hired the couple's nephew at a $30,000 annual salary. The nephew, age 20, has been in several scrapes with the law and needs financial help, and the Crandall family agreed that a low-stress job with the family business is just what he needs for a year or two.

LO 12-7   10. WQ Corporation, a closely held family business, has not paid a dividend for the last seven years. Each year, the minutes of the board of directors' December meeting state that WQ must accumulate after-tax income to pay for a new manufacturing facility. Until plans for construction are finalized, WQ has been investing its excess cash in marketable securities. This year, WQ curtails its manufacturing business and abandons its plan for the new facility.

Research Problems

LO 12-5   1. Fifteen years ago, Mr. and Mrs. Boyer created Brovo, a regular corporation, through which to operate a service business. The Boyers own all of Brovo's 1,000 shares of stock with a $1.6 million aggregate tax basis. The corporate business has been extremely successful; at the beginning of the year, Brovo's balance sheet reflected more than $2 million retained earnings. According to a recent appraisal, its stock is worth $2.5 million. The Boyers want to withdraw $500,000 cash from Brovo for their personal use, but they do not want Brovo to pay them a dividend. Instead, they plan to have Brovo distribute $500,000 in exchange for 200 shares of their stock. The Boyers believe that they will recognize a $180,000 gain on this redemption, which will qualify as capital gain. Are the Boyers correct in their analysis of the tax consequences of the redemption?

LO 12-1   2. On March 1, the Trents formed Trent Properties, Inc. through which to operate a real estate management business. Both of the Trents worked full time for modest, but reasonable, salaries. In early December, the Trents estimated that the corporation would incur a $325,000 net loss for its first 10 months of operation. They decided to adopt a calendar year for Trent Properties, Inc. and make an S election so that they could deduct the loss on their individual tax return. Can the Trents make an S election for Trent Properties, Inc.'s first taxable year?

LO 12-5   3. Fair View, Inc. owns and operates a golf club, which includes two 18-hole courses, a driving range, a restaurant, and a pro shop. The club's facilities can be used only by its membership, which includes all the individual shareholders as well as nonshareholders. All the members are charged a greens fee for each round of play plus an additional fee for use of a golf cart. However, the fees for shareholders are 30 percent less than the fees for nonshareholders. Shareholders also enjoy a 30 percent discount on the price of food and drink purchased in the club restaurant and merchandise purchased in the pro shop. Do these discounts have any income tax consequences to Fair View's shareholders?

LO 12-4   4. Four years ago, Amy Huang contributed four acres of undeveloped land to Richter Company in exchange for a 12 percent equity interest in Richter. Amy's tax basis in the land was $275,000, and the land's appraised FMV on date of contribution was $430,000. The exchange of land for equity was nontaxable to both Amy and Richter. Since the exchange, Richter has held the land as a long-term investment. This year, Richter sold the land to an unrelated purchaser for $550,000. How much capital gain does Richter recognize on the sale? How much of this gain is allocated to Amy if Richter is an LLC? How much gain is allocated to Amy if Richter is an S corporation?

 All applicable Tax Planning Cases are available with *Connect*.

Tax Planning Cases

LO 12-2   1. Mr. and Mrs. Tinker own a sizable investment portfolio of stock in publicly held corporations. The couple has four children—ages 20, 22, 25, and 27—with whom they want to share their wealth. Unfortunately, none of the children has demonstrated an ability to manage money. As a result, Mr. and Mrs. Tinker plan to transfer their portfolio to a new corporation in exchange for 20 shares of voting stock and 400 shares of nonvoting stock. They will give 100 nonvoting shares to each child. The couple will serve as the directors of the corporation, manage the investment portfolio, and distribute cash dividends when their children need money. They estimate that the portfolio will generate $72,000 annual dividend income.

   a. If the Tinker Family Corporation is operated as an S corporation, compute the annual income tax burden on the dividend income generated by the investment portfolio. Assume that Mr. and Mrs. Tinker are in the 37 percent tax bracket, qualify for the 20 percent dividend tax rate, and each child is in the 12 percent tax bracket with a zero percent dividend tax rate. To simplify the case, ignore any value of the couple's management service to the corporation.

   b. Compute the tax burden for the first year if Tinker Family Corporation does not have an S election in effect and distributes a $100 annual dividend per share.

LO 12-2   2. Agatha is planning to start a new business venture and must decide whether to operate as a sole proprietorship or incorporate. She projects that the business will generate annual cash flow and taxable income of $100,000. Agatha's personal marginal tax rate, given her other sources of income, is 37 percent and she qualifies for the 20 percent rate on dividend income. (Ignore any employment tax consequences.)

   a. If Agatha operates the business as a sole proprietorship, calculate the annual after-tax cash flow available for reinvestment in the business venture. Assume the sole proprietorship will qualify for the 20 percent QBI deduction.

   b. If Agatha operates the business as a regular (C) corporation that makes no dividend distributions, calculate the annual after-tax cash flow available for reinvestment in the business.

c. Now suppose that Agatha wishes to withdraw $20,000 per year from the business and will reinvest any remaining after-tax earnings. What are the tax consequences to Agatha and the business of such a withdrawal if the business is operated as a sole proprietorship? How much after-tax cash flow will remain for reinvestment in the business? How much after-tax cash flow will Agatha have from the withdrawal?

d. What are the tax consequences to Agatha and the business of a $20,000 withdrawal in the form of a dividend if the business is operated as a C corporation? How much after-tax cash flow will remain for reinvestment in the business? How much after-tax cash flow will Agatha retain from the dividend?

e. If Agatha wants to operate the business as a corporation but also wants to receive cash flow from the business each year, what would you recommend to get a better tax result?

LO 12-2, 12-6 3. Mr. Young operates a photography studio as a sole proprietorship. His average annual income from the business is $100,000. Because Mr. Young does not need the entire cash flow for personal consumption, he is considering incorporating the business. He will work as a corporate employee for a $40,000 annual salary, and the corporation will accumulate its after-tax income to fund future business expansion. For purposes of this case, assume that Mr. Young's marginal income tax rate is 32 percent and ignore any employment tax consequences.

a. Assuming Mr. Young's sole proprietorship does not qualify for the QBI deduction, would Mr. Young decrease the annual tax burden on the business by incorporating?

b. How would your answer change if Mr. Young's sole proprietorship qualifies for the 20 percent QBI deduction?

Chapter **Thirteen**

Jurisdictional Issues in Business Taxation

Learning Objectives

After studying this chapter, you should be able to:

LO 13-1. Identify factors contributing to state and local tax burden.

LO 13-2. Define *nexus*.

LO 13-3. Apportion corporate taxable income among states according to UDITPA.

LO 13-4. Explain the significance of a permanent establishment.

LO 13-5. Compute a foreign tax credit.

LO 13-6. Describe the tax consequences of export sales, foreign branches, and foreign partnerships.

LO 13-7. Explain when and how U.S. shareholders are taxed on dividends received from foreign corporations.

LO 13-8. Explain the tax consequences of subpart F income and global intangible low-taxed income earned by a CFC.

LO 13-9. Describe limitations on tax benefits from cross-border related party transactions.

This chapter introduces the issues that arise when firms operate in more than one taxing jurisdiction. Firms that span territorial boundaries must understand that an overlap in jurisdictions can cause the same income to be taxed more than once. In this chapter, we will learn how firms can minimize the burden of such duplicative taxation. We will also discover how the differences in tax costs across jurisdictions create planning opportunities. Firms can implement many effective strategies to shift income away from jurisdictions with high tax costs. These strategies relate back to our maxim that tax costs decrease and cash flows increase when income is generated in a jurisdiction with a low tax rate.

We begin with an overview of state and local taxes as a cost of doing business, and then we focus on the key issues involving state income taxation. The first issue concerns the states' right to tax interstate commerce and the federal restrictions on such a right. The concept of income apportionment is introduced, and strategies for reducing the aggregate tax burden on multistate businesses are discussed. The remainder of the chapter deals with the taxation of international business. We will learn that the United States has a global tax system that can result in the double taxation of foreign source income. The major role of the foreign tax credit in mitigating double taxation and the limitations on the credit are covered in some detail. We will consider how U.S. firms can organize overseas operations to control the tax consequences of those operations. Finally, we will discuss how U.S. corporations use foreign subsidiaries to avoid U.S. income recognition and reduce the tax cost of international business.

STATE AND LOCAL TAXATION

LO 13-1
Identify factors contributing to state and local tax burden.

In the United States, even the smallest firm is subject to three taxing jurisdictions: local government, state government, and the federal government. Historically, firms concentrated their tax planning efforts at the federal level and devoted less attention to state and local tax costs. Recently, firms have become more aware of their state and local tax burden. In response to demand by the business community, public accounting firms have specialized state and local tax (SALT) practices to provide expert professional help. More than ever before, firms and their tax advisers are formulating strategies to minimize real and personal property taxes, unemployment taxes, and sales and use taxes.

In the first section of this chapter, we focus on planning opportunities in the area of state income taxation. As we learned in Chapter 1, most states impose both a personal (individual) and a corporate income tax. Consequently, business income is subject to state tax whether the business is organized as a passthrough entity or a corporation. For federal purposes, corporations are allowed to deduct state income tax in the computation of taxable income.[1] The tax savings from this deduction reduce the cost of the state tax.

Federal Deduction for State Income Tax

Zeta, Inc. paid $45,000 state income tax this year. If Zeta's federal tax rate is 21 percent, the after-tax cost of the payment is only $35,550:

State tax paid	$ (45,000)
Federal tax savings ($45,000 deduction × 21%)	9,450
After-tax cost	$ (35,550)

Tax Talk
The Tax Cuts and Jobs Act of 2017 limited the federal deduction for state income taxes taken as an itemized deduction by individuals. This change potentially increases federal income tax costs, particularly for taxpayers in states with high state tax rates.

Nonetheless, Zeta's aggregate tax burden is increased because it must pay income tax at both the state and the federal level. If Zeta's before-tax income is $900,000 and the state tax rate is 5 percent, Zeta's tax rate for the year is 24.95 percent.

State tax[2] ($900,000 taxable income × 5%)	$ 45,000
Federal tax ($855,000 taxable income × 21%)	179,550
Total income tax	$224,550
$224,550 ÷ $900,000 before-tax income = 24.95%	

[1] For individual taxpayers, the state tax on both business and nonbusiness income is allowed as an itemized deduction, with limitations. See Chapter 17 for a full discussion.

[2] State income tax payments are not deductible in the computation of taxable income for state purposes. Three states (Alabama, Iowa, and Missouri) allow corporations to deduct a limited amount of federal tax in the computation of taxable income for state purposes.

Gross Receipts Taxes

Although most states apply a net income tax to business earnings, several states have adopted tax systems that tax gross revenues instead of net earnings. For example, Ohio assesses a commercial activity tax (CAT) for the privilege of doing business in Ohio. The CAT tax rate is generally .26 percent of gross receipts from business operations in excess of $1 million, without reduction for cost of goods sold or other business expenses. Texas assesses the Texas margin tax (TMT) on gross receipts reduced by the greater of cost of goods sold or compensation paid to employees. The TMT tax rate is generally .375 percent for retailers and wholesalers and .75 percent for all others. The TMT applies only to companies whose taxable amount exceeds a $1.23 million threshold. Washington's gross receipts tax is called the business and occupation (B&O) tax. B&O rates vary by industry, taxing gross receipts without reduction for expenses.

Michigan State Taxation—What Next?	Michigan's state tax system has changed dramatically in the past 15 years and continues to evolve. Prior to 2008, Michigan assessed a single business tax (SBT) that was a type of value-added tax. That system was replaced in 2008 with a combined business income tax (BIT) and gross receipts tax (GRT). In addition, a surcharge was assessed on the combined liability under the BIT and the GRT. The BIT, GRT, and surcharge taxes applied to businesses operated by individuals, corporations, and passthrough entities. Effective in 2012, Michigan repealed the BIT, GRT, and surcharge taxes, replacing them with a 6 percent corporate income tax (CIT) levied only on C corporations. Individuals and passthrough entities are exempt from the new system, although Michigan does assess an individual income tax at a rate of 4.25 percent.

Constitutional Restrictions on State Jurisdiction

LO 13-2
Define *nexus*.

A state has jurisdiction to tax all individuals who reside in the state and all corporations formed under the laws of the state. This jurisdiction extends to nonresident individuals and corporations conducting business within the state. Thus, firms engaged in interstate commerce may be subject to tax in any number of states. Given that thousands of U.S. companies conduct business in more than 1 state, if not all 50 states, some degree of national coordination is necessary to avert fiscal anarchy.

Article 1 of the U.S. Constitution grants the federal government the power to "regulate commerce with foreign nations, and among the several states, and with the Indian tribes." This **Commerce Clause** empowers Congress and the federal courts to establish ground rules for state tax laws. For a state tax to be constitutional, it must not discriminate against interstate commerce. For instance, an income tax with a 3 percent rate for resident corporations and a 6 percent rate for nonresident corporations would be blatantly unconstitutional. In addition, state taxes can be levied only on businesses having nexus with the state. **Nexus** means the degree of contact between a business and a state necessary to establish jurisdiction.

The Issue of Nexus

Tax Talk
A New York statute requires online retailers to collect sales tax on sales to New York residents if the retailer pays commissions or other compensation to New York residents for customer referrals. Amazon.com's challenge of the law as violating the Commerce Clause was denied by a New York appellate court. Amazon appealed that ruling to the U.S. Supreme Court, which declined to hear the case.

Let's examine the concept of nexus by considering the regional business conducted by Show-Me, Inc., which is incorporated in Missouri. Show-Me's corporate headquarters are in St. Louis, and its two manufacturing plants are in Kansas and Arkansas. The corporation uses a common carrier to ship its products to customers in Missouri, Kansas, Arkansas, Iowa, Nebraska, and Oklahoma. Show-Me's business is illustrated in Exhibit 13.1.

Because Show-Me is formed and protected under Missouri law and is commercially domiciled in the state, the corporation has nexus with Missouri. Show-Me has employees and owns real and personal property located in Kansas and Arkansas, and these states provide public benefits (fire and police protection, roads and highways, etc.) that add value to

EXHIBIT 13.1
Show-Me, Inc.

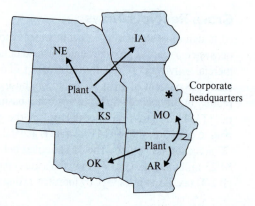

the corporation's business. Thus, Show-Me's physical presence in these two states creates nexus allowing both Kansas and Arkansas to tax the corporation.

But what about the other three states in Show-Me's region? According to the facts, Show-Me has no physical presence in Iowa, Nebraska, or Oklahoma. Under a long-standing federal statute, Public Law 86-272, firms do not establish nexus by simply selling tangible goods to customers residing in a state. Firms can even send traveling salespeople into a state to solicit orders for such goods without creating nexus.[3] Because of this federally mandated immunity, Show-Me is not subject to income tax in Iowa, Nebraska, and Oklahoma.

P.L. 86-272 does not pertain to business activities other than the sale of tangible goods. As a result, nonresident firms providing services (including the leasing of tangible property) or marketing intangible property to in-state residents are not immune to the state's taxing jurisdiction. Currently, the issue of nexus with respect to these in-state activities is unsettled. Several states have taken the aggressive position that any firm conducting a regular commercial activity within the state has established *economic* nexus. Accordingly, the state has jurisdiction to tax the firm regardless of the lack of physical presence in the state.[4] P.L. 86-272 protection applies only to nexus for income tax purposes. Thus, a seller of tangible goods could still be subject to gross receipts taxes and sales taxes in states in which it sells its products.

The issue of economic nexus is being hotly debated by lawmakers, tax policy groups, and taxpayers alike. Several bills have been introduced in Congress attempting to provide a common standard across the states, but to date no legislation has passed.[5] In June 2007, the U.S. Supreme Court declined to hear two taxpayer appeals in cases in which states (West Virginia and New Jersey) assessed income and franchise taxes on companies with no physical presence in the state. Absent federal legislation restricting the economic nexus approach, some commentators predict a surge in state assessment of tax on businesses without a physical presence but with economic presence and earnings in the state.

Tax Talk

In June 2018, the Supreme Court addressed the issue of economic nexus for sales and use tax. In South Dakota v. Wayfair, *the court ruled that a physical presence is not necessary to require an online retailer to collect sales and use tax on sales to in-state customers.*

Economic Nexus

Show-Me's research division recently developed a manufacturing process that the corporation patented with the federal government. Show-Me licensed this patent to a number of companies, three of which operate in South Carolina. The companies pay an annual royalty for use of the patent. Although Show-Me has no physical presence (tangible property or employees) in South Carolina, it does earn revenue from marketing an intangible asset to South Carolina customers. On the basis of this economic nexus, South Carolina claims jurisdiction to tax Show-Me's royalty income.

---

[3] 15 U.S.C. 381-384 (1959).

[4] The landmark case in this area is *Geoffrey, Inc.* v. *South Carolina Tax Commission,* 437 S.E.2d 13 (1993), *cert. denied,* 510 U.S. 992 (1993).

[5] See, for example, H.R. 1083, the Business Activity Tax Simplification Act of 2009.

The nexus issue is particularly uncertain for firms that sell goods and services over the Internet. Traditional nexus concepts make little sense when applied to business conducted in cyberspace. Consequently, firms may be hesitant about expanding their Internet operations for fear of inadvertently creating nexus with states in which they have no physical presence. In turn, state governments are concerned that the anticipated growth in electronic commerce will result in a loss of sales tax and income tax revenues from traditional commercial activities. The business community, the Internet industry, and state governments all acknowledge the need for a workable tax policy with respect to electronic commerce. Such policy should "facilitate, not impede, the growth of new technologies, while ensuring that no unfair tax advantage accrues to companies that develop or utilize such technologies."[6]

No Taxes in Cyberspace	On October 1, 1998, the Internet Tax Freedom Act went into effect. The act included a three-year moratorium on new state and local taxes imposed on Internet access and a congressional declaration that the Internet should be free of all international tariffs, trade barriers, and other restrictions. Supporters of the act maintain that the Internet is still in its infancy and must be protected against unbridled taxation. Critics claim that the act establishes the Internet as a giant tax shelter and that "for a bunch of nerds, computer types have proven to be very effective lobbyists."[7] The act has been extended several times and was made permanent by the Trade Facilitation and Trade Enforcement Act of 2015.

Apportionment of Business Income

LO 13-3

Apportion corporate taxable income among states according to UDITPA.

The federal courts established the principle that states may tax only the income attributable to a firm's in-state business activity; the state may not tax income attributable to the firm's *extraterritorial value.* To comply with this principle, state law must provide a rational and fair method for determining the portion of a firm's total income subject to that state's tax.

In 1957, a National Conference of Uniform State Laws drafted the **Uniform Division of Income for Tax Purposes Act (UDITPA)** as a recommended method for apportioning income among multiple state jurisdictions. Today, most states use an apportionment formula modeled after UDITPA. Firms apply these formulas to derive an **apportionment** percentage, which determines the income taxable by each state. The UDIPTA formula is based on three equally weighted factors: the sales factor, the payroll factor, and the property factor.

$$\frac{\text{Sales factor} + \text{Payroll factor} + \text{Property factor}}{3} = \text{State apportionment percentage}$$

Each factor itself is a percentage computed as follows:

- The sales factor is the ratio of gross receipts from sales to in-state customers divided by total gross receipts from sales.
- The payroll factor is the ratio of compensation paid to employees working in-state divided by total compensation.
- The property factor is the ratio of the cost of real or tangible personal property located in-state divided by the total cost of such property.

---

[6] Kendall L. Houghton and Jeffrey A. Friedman, "Lost in (Cyber) Space?" *State Tax Notes,* September 15, 1997, pp. 173–725.

[7] Lee Sheppard, "What Does 'No New Internet Taxes' Mean?" *State Tax Notes,* July 21, 1997, pp. 141–51.

Tax Talk

State-level definitions of the apportionment factors often vary. A recent trend in sales factor sourcing, called market-based sourcing, treats revenue from services as sourced to the state in which the customer is located. California and New York are among the states applying market-based sourcing for state tax apportionment purposes. Other states, such as Virginia, use cost-of-performance sourcing, which treats services revenue as arising in the state in which costs are incurred to provide the services.

If all states followed the UDITPA formula and defined the three factors in the same manner, the amount of income apportioned across the states in which a firm operated would equal exactly 100 percent. Realistically, state apportionment methods never achieve this mathematical precision. One major reason is that the vast majority of states now use a modified three-factor formula in which sales are double-weighted (the sales factor is counted twice and the factor total is divided by four) or otherwise given greater weight than the payroll and property factors. Over one-half of states either require or permit the use of single-factor apportionment, in which only the sales factor is considered in apportioning income. For example, Missouri permits seven different apportionment methods, including a traditional three-factor formula and a single-factor formula based only on sales.

Another reason state tax results vary is that the definitions of the factors differ from state to state. For instance, the payroll factor under Virginia law includes compensation paid to corporate executive officers, while this compensation is excluded from North Carolina's payroll factor. Similarly, the definition of apportionable income is inconsistent across states. For instance, New Jersey law excludes interest and dividend income from the apportionment base, while New York law includes both as apportionable income. Clearly, states do not conform to a strictly uniform method of apportionment, and the federal courts have not required them to do so.[8] As a result, the division of taxable income among states inevitably results in some overlap or omission.

To demonstrate the mechanics of income apportionment, let's examine the following data for Duo, a corporation conducting business in just two states: North Dakota and Montana.

Apportionment Formulas

Duo's financial records provide the following information (all numbers are in thousands of dollars):

	North Dakota	Montana	Total
Gross receipts from sales	$ 8,200	$ 6,800	$15,000
Payroll expense	1,252	697	1,949
Property costs	18,790	10,004	28,794

Beginning in 2022, Montana uses a three-factor formula that double-weights the sales factor. North Dakota apportions the income of multistate businesses based only on sales. Thus each state's apportionment percentage is computed as follows:

	North Dakota	Montana
Sales factor	54.67% ($8,200 ÷ $15,000)	45.33% ($6,800 ÷ $15,000)
Payroll factor	64.24% ($1,252 ÷ $1,949)	35.76% ($697 ÷ $1,949)
Property factor	65.26% ($18,790 ÷ $28,794)	34.74% ($10,004 ÷ $28,794)

North Dakota $= 54.67\%$

Montana $\dfrac{45.33\% + 45.33\% + 35.76\% + 34.74\%}{4} = 40.29\%$

---

[8] *Moorman Manufacturing Co. v. Bair, Director of Revenue of Iowa,* 437 U.S. 267 (1978).

If Duo's annual income is $40 million, the portion taxable by North Dakota is $21.868 million (54.67 percent × $40 million) and the portion taxable by Montana is $16.116 million (40.29 percent × $40 million). Because of the differences in apportionment between these two states, only 94.96 percent of Duo's income is taxed at the state level. While this result is fortuitous for Duo, apportionment differences can also result in greater than 100 percent taxable across the states in which firms operate.

Tax Planning Implications

Multistate businesses can reduce their overall tax cost to the extent that they can shift income from a high-tax state to a low-tax state. This strategy often involves the manipulation of the state apportionment formulas. Let's refer to our Duo example. Currently, North Dakota's tax rate on corporate income is 2.5 percent, and Montana's tax rate is 6.75 percent. Because of this rate differential, every $100 of income that Duo can shift from Montana's jurisdiction to North Dakota's jurisdiction potentially saves $4.25 of tax.

Manipulating the Property Factor

Duo plans to build a new manufacturing plant at an estimated cost of $25 million. If the plant is built in North Dakota, the corporation's property factors will be revised as follows (all numbers are in thousands of dollars):

	North Dakota	Montana	Total
Property costs	$18,790	$10,004	$28,794
New manufacturing plant	25,000	–0–	25,000
Revised property costs	$43,790	$10,004	$53,794
Revised property factors	81.4%	18.6%	

However, remember that North Dakota uses single-factor sales apportionment! Thus the increase in the North Dakota property factor will have no impact on North Dakota's apportionment percentage. Montana's apportionment percentage will decrease.

North Dakota $= 54.67\%$

Montana $\dfrac{45.33\% + 45.33\% + 35.76\% + 18.6\%}{4} = 36.255\%$

Because Duo's decision to build a new plant in North Dakota decreases Montana's apportionment percentage, the decision shifts income from Montana to North Dakota and saves $108,945 of state tax.

Revised Apportionment

	Original Apportionment	
	North Dakota	Montana
Total taxable income	$40,000,000	$40,000,000
Apportionment percentage	.5467	.4029
State taxable income	$21,868,000	$16,116,000
	.025	.0675
State tax	$ 546,700	$ 1,087,830

(continued)

	Revised Apportionment	
	North Dakota	**Montana**
Total taxable income	$40,000,000	$40,000,000
Apportionment percentage	.5467	.36255
State taxable income	$21,868,000	$14,502,000
	.025	.0675
State tax	$ 546,700	$ 978,885
Total state tax:		
Original apportionment	$ 1,634,530	
Revised apportionment	1,525,585	
Tax savings	$ 108,945	

Of course, the tax savings from the income shift is only one factor in the selection of the optimal site for the plant. Duo should certainly consider how its real and personal property tax costs will be affected by the geographic location of the plant. Nontax factors, such as the local cost of construction and the availability of a skilled workforce, are key elements in the selection process. While Duo may minimize its state income tax cost by locating its new manufacturing facility in North Dakota, this location is not necessarily the best choice for maximizing the value of the facility to the corporation.

TAX CONSEQUENCES OF INTERNATIONAL BUSINESS OPERATIONS

Tax Talk

A recent trend among European Union countries is the enactment of digital services taxes. These taxes, typically on gross income rather than net income, target companies that have no physical presence in a country but earn income from online customers in that country.

In the current business environment, firms operating on a multinational level have become the rule rather than the exception. Globalization creates exciting opportunities for U.S. businesses to expand into the emerging markets of eastern Europe, Africa, Asia, and South America. These opportunities are coupled with formidable obstacles. Firms with international aspirations must cope with differences across currencies, languages, technological sophistication, and cultural and political traditions.

Firms must be aware of the foreign tax implications of international operations. When a U.S. firm plans to expand its activities into another country, it should identify the taxes included in the country's fiscal structure. The firm's liability for these taxes will depend on the nature and extent of its activity within the country and whether such activity triggers the country's taxing jurisdiction. If the foreign country imposes a net income tax, its jurisdiction may depend on whether a tax treaty is in effect between the country and the United States.

Income Tax Treaties

LO 13-4

Explain the significance of a permanent establishment.

An **income tax treaty** is a bilateral agreement between the governments of two countries defining and limiting each country's respective tax jurisdiction. The treaty provisions pertain only to individuals and corporations that are residents of either country and override the countries' general jurisdictional rules.[9] Under a typical treaty, a firm's income is taxable only by the country of residence (the home country) *unless* the firm maintains a **permanent establishment** in the other country (the host country). In this case, income attributable to the permanent establishment can be taxed by the host country. A permanent establishment is a fixed location, such as

[9] The term *resident* includes individuals who are citizens or permanent residents of a country and corporations formed under the laws of the country or a political subdivision thereof.

an office or factory, at which the firm carries on its regular commercial operations.[10] Because of this rule, a U.S. firm conducting business in a treaty country avoids that country's income tax if it does not maintain a fixed place of business in the host country.

Permanent Establishment	Adam, Inc., a U.S. manufacturer, sells its products to many major customers in Italy. The United States and Italy have an income tax treaty under which Italy does not have jurisdiction to tax Adam unless the corporation maintains a permanent establishment within Italy. If Adam maintains a permanent establishment (such as a sales office in Rome), Italy has jurisdiction to tax the portion of Adam's income attributable to such establishment.

Tax Talk
At last count, the United States has entered into or is in the process of negotiating tax treaties with nearly 70 foreign countries.

If a U.S. firm conducts any business in a country that does not have an income tax treaty with the United States, the host country's jurisdiction depends on its unique tax laws. Consequently, the U.S. firm must research these laws to determine the level of activity that triggers jurisdiction. This determination is often subjective and results in considerable uncertainty for the firm. Moreover, the requisite level of business activity in nontreaty countries is often much less than the maintenance of a permanent establishment in the country.

U.S. Jurisdiction to Tax Global Income

The United States has a global tax system under which its citizens, permanent residents, and domestic corporations are taxed on *worldwide* income. In other words, when the United States is the home country, it claims jurisdiction to tax income regardless of where the income is earned. The United States does not surrender this primary jurisdiction when a U.S. firm engages in **outbound transactions** with residents of other nations, even if the income from the transaction is taxed by a foreign government.[11] Thus, a fundamental issue confronting U.S. firms operating abroad is the potential double taxation of their income.

The Tax Cuts and Jobs Act of 2017 made significant changes to the U.S. tax treatment of multinational businesses. Under these provisions, businesses conducted directly by a U.S. taxpayer (citizen, permanent resident, or domestic corporation) are still subject to U.S. tax on global earnings. However, new rules apply after 2017 to foreign operations conducted through foreign subsidiaries and to dividends received by U.S. corporations from foreign-controlled corporations. These new rules are discussed in more detail later in this chapter.

As we learned in Chapter 6, firms can deduct foreign income taxes paid or accrued during the taxable year. However, a deduction is an imperfect remedy for double taxation.

Deduction of Foreign Income Tax	Corporation Q, which pays a 21 percent U.S. income tax, generates $1 million income subject to another nation's 12 percent income tax. Even with a deduction for the foreign income tax (and disregarding state tax), Corporation Q's global tax rate on this foreign income is 30.5 percent:

Foreign tax ($1 million taxable income × 12%)	$120,000
U.S. tax ($880,000 taxable income × 21%)	184,800
Global income tax	$304,800

$$\$304,800 \div \$1 \text{ million before-tax income} = 30.5\%$$

---

[10] U.S. Treasury Department, Model Income Tax Treaty, article 5.

[11] The United States also taxes business income earned in this country by nonresident aliens and foreign corporations. §871(b) and §882. Any discussion of the tax rules applying to these *inbound transactions* is beyond the scope of this text.

The federal government understands that U.S. firms facing this tax burden could be at a competitive disadvantage in the global marketplace. Therefore, the tax law contains the powerful mechanism of a foreign tax credit to alleviate double taxation at the international level.

FOREIGN TAX CREDIT

Tax Talk
In 2013, the U.S. Supreme Court resolved a disagreement between the Third and Fifth Circuit Courts, holding that the UK windfall profits tax is a creditable income tax.

U.S. citizens, residents, and domestic corporations may elect to credit foreign income tax paid or accrued during the year against their U.S. tax.[12] Taxpayers electing the credit are not allowed a deduction for foreign income taxes.[13] The **foreign tax credit** is available only for income taxes; foreign excise, value-added, sales, property, and transfer taxes are not creditable.[14] Let's refer to the example involving Corporation Q to demonstrate the power of the foreign tax credit.

Credit for Foreign Income Tax

If Corporation Q does not deduct its $120,000 foreign tax payment and elects the tax credit, its U.S. tax decreases to $90,000, and its global tax rate decreases to 21 percent.

Precredit U.S. tax ($1 million taxable income × 21%)	$210,000
Foreign tax credit	(120,000)
U.S. tax	$ 90,000
Foreign tax ($1 million taxable income × 12%)	$120,000
U.S. tax	90,000
Global income tax	$210,000

$210,000 ÷ $1 million before-tax income = 21%

Tax Talk
In 2019, U.S. corporations claimed over $73 billion in foreign tax credits.

By permitting Corporation Q to claim the foreign tax credit, the United States relinquished its taxing jurisdiction to the extent that another nation exercised its jurisdiction. In other words, the United States reduced its 21 percent rate by the 12 percent foreign rate so that Corporation Q paid only 9 percent U.S. tax on its foreign income.

Limitation on the Annual Credit

LO 13-5
Compute a foreign tax credit.

The foreign tax credit is subject to a major limitation: The annual credit cannot exceed a specific percentage of the precredit U.S. tax for the year. This percentage is computed by dividing the taxpayer's **foreign source income** by taxable income.[15]

---

[12] §901(a). The election to claim a foreign tax credit is made annually so that taxpayers can choose either the credit or the deduction on a year-to-year basis.

[13] §275(a)(4).

[14] Firms either deduct or capitalize their noncreditable taxes relating to their foreign business activities.

[15] §904(a). The Internal Revenue Code contains elaborate and lengthy rules for distinguishing between foreign source and U.S. source income. See §861 through §865.

Foreign	In 2023, Corporation RH had $800,000 taxable income, $300,000 of which was generated

Foreign Tax Credit Limitation

In 2023, Corporation RH had $800,000 taxable income, $300,000 of which was generated by business activities in Country M. RH paid $123,900 foreign tax (at more than a 40 percent rate) to Country M.[16] Its U.S. income tax is computed as follows:

U.S. source income	$500,000	
Foreign source income	300,000	
Taxable income		$800,000
U.S. tax rate		.21
Precredit U.S. tax		$168,000
Foreign tax credit (limited)		(63,000)
U.S. tax		$105,000

RH's foreign tax credit is *limited* to the precredit U.S. tax of $168,000 multiplied by the ratio of foreign source income to taxable income.

$$\$63,000 = \$168,000 \times \frac{\$300,000 \text{ foreign source income}}{\$800,000 \text{ taxable income}}$$

Even though RH paid $123,900 foreign income tax, only $63,000 is creditable against U.S. tax. Note that the limited credit equals the *entire precredit U.S. tax* on RH's foreign source income ($300,000 × 21 percent = $102,000). Note also that the U.S. tax equals 21 percent of $500,000 U.S. source income. Because of the foreign tax credit, RH pays no U.S. tax on its foreign source income. Because of the limitation on that credit, it pays the full U.S. tax on its *domestic* income.

Excess Credit Carrybacks and Carryforwards

When a firm is subject to the foreign tax credit limitation, the **excess foreign tax credit** (foreign tax paid but not credited) can be carried back 1 year and forward 10 years.[17] The firm can use its excess credits in a carryback or carryforward year, subject to the annual limitation.

Excess Credit Carryback

In the preceding example, RH had a $60,900 excess credit ($123,900 foreign tax paid − $63,000 limited credit) in 2023. Its 2022 U.S. tax return showed the following:

U.S. source income	$350,000	
Foreign source income	250,000	
Taxable income		$600,000
U.S. tax rate		.21
Precredit U.S. tax		$126,000
Foreign tax credit (actual tax paid)		(47,500)
U.S. tax		$ 78,500

(continued)

---

[16] The statement assumes that Country M and the United States use the same definition of taxable income. Actually, the definition of taxable income varies considerably from country to country.

[17] §904(c) as amended by the American Jobs Creation Act of 2004.

The credit limitation did not apply because the $47,500 foreign tax paid was less than the $52,500 limitation.

$$\$52,500 = \$126,000 \times \frac{\$250,000 \text{ foreign source income}}{\$600,000 \text{ taxable income}}$$

Consequently, RH had a $5,000 excess limitation in 2022 ($52,500 limitation − $47,500 credited foreign tax). Because of the excess limitation, RH can carry back $5,000 of its 2023 excess credit and obtain a $5,000 refund of 2022 tax. The remaining $55,900 excess credit is available as a carryforward to 2024.

Cross-Crediting

If a firm's foreign source income is taxed by a foreign jurisdiction at a rate *lower* than the U.S. rate, the firm's global rate on such income is the higher U.S. rate. In such a case, the firm has an excess limitation equal to the U.S. tax paid on its foreign source income. If the foreign source income is taxed by a foreign jurisdiction at a rate *higher* than the U.S. rate, the global rate is the higher foreign rate. In this case, the firm pays no U.S. tax on its foreign source income. It will, however, have an excess foreign tax credit.

If a firm earns income in both low-tax and high-tax foreign jurisdictions, the excess credit from the high-tax income can be used to the extent of the excess limitation from the low-tax income. This **cross-crediting** reduces the firm's global tax rate on its foreign source income. Let's develop a case to illustrate this important result.

Cross-Crediting

CVB, Inc. has the following taxable income:

U.S. source income	$350,000
Foreign source income:	
Country L	100,000
Country H	100,000
Taxable income	$550,000

Country L has a 15 percent income tax, and Country H has a 22 percent income tax. Thus, CVB paid $15,000 income tax to Country L and $22,000 income tax to Country H. Its U.S. tax is $130,000.

Taxable income	$550,000
U.S. tax rate	.21
Precredit U.S. tax	$115,500
Foreign tax credit (actual tax paid)	(37,000)
U.S. tax	$ 78,500

The credit limitation does not apply because the $37,000 foreign tax paid is *less* than the $42,000 limitation.

$$\$42,000 = \$115,500 \times \frac{\$200,000 \text{ foreign source income}}{\$550,000 \text{ taxable income}}$$

In this example, CVB pays only $5,000 U.S. tax on its $200,000 foreign source income:

Foreign source income	$200,000
U.S. tax rate	.21
	$ 42,000
Foreign tax credit	(37,000)
U.S. tax on foreign source income	$ 5,000

Therefore, CVB's global rate on this income is 21 percent, even though the $100,000 earned in Country H was taxed at 22 percent. Because CVB blended low-tax and high-tax income in computing its foreign tax credit limitation, it reduced its U.S. tax bill by every dollar of foreign tax paid for the year.[18]

REDUCED TAX RATE ON FOREIGN-DERIVED INTANGIBLE INCOME

LO 13-6
Describe the tax consequences of export sales, foreign branches, and foreign partnerships.

For tax years beginning after December 31, 2017, the Tax Cuts and Jobs Act provides a reduced rate of taxation on **foreign-derived intangible income (FDII)** earned directly by a U.S. corporation from foreign sales or services. FDII is taxed at an effective tax rate of 13.125 percent, substantially lower than the 21 percent corporate rate applicable after 2017.[19]

Very generally, FDII is income from the sales of goods and services to foreign persons for use outside the United States, to the extent such income exceeds a fixed 10 percent return on depreciable assets. FDII does not include income attributable to operations through a foreign branch office or a controlled foreign corporation. It also excludes sales of property to related parties, unless such property is ultimately sold to an unrelated foreign person.

Tax Savings from Export Sales

Logik Corporation earned $2 million this year from both domestic and international operations and paid no foreign income taxes. If none of this income is considered FDII, Logik owes U.S. income tax of $420,000 ($2 million × 21 percent).

What if $700,000 of Logik's earnings qualify as FDII? Logik's U.S. income tax is reduced to $364,875, computed as follows:

Tax on non-FDII earnings ($1,300,000 × 21%)	$273,000
Tax on FDII ($700,000 × 13.125%)	91,875
Total U.S. income tax due	$364,875

ORGANIZATIONAL FORMS FOR OVERSEAS OPERATIONS

U.S. firms expanding internationally must decide on the form in which to operate their overseas activities. This section of the chapter surveys the basic organizational choices for foreign business ventures.

---

[18] The Tax Cuts and Jobs Act imposes new limitations on cross-crediting of foreign taxes, creating a separate limitation for foreign branch income. Further consideration of these limitations is beyond the scope of this text.

[19] Section 250(a)(1) permits a 37.5 percent deduction against FDII; 21 percent × (1–37.5 percent) yields a 13.125 percent effective rate.

Branch Offices and Foreign Partnerships

U.S. firms wanting to establish a presence in a foreign country can open a branch office. A *branch office* is not a separate legal entity but is merely an extension of the U.S. firm. Any income or loss generated by the foreign branch is commingled with income and losses from the firm's other business activities. If the branch is profitable, its income is subject to U.S. tax. Any foreign tax paid on branch income is included in the computation of the foreign tax credit. The same tax consequences result if a U.S. firm becomes a partner in a foreign partnership. The firm reports its share of the partnership's foreign source income or loss and is entitled to a tax credit for its share of foreign income taxes paid by the partnership.

Foreign Partnership	SC, an Oklahoma corporation engaged in oil and gas drilling, owns a 60 percent interest in a partnership formed under South African law. This year, the foreign partnership generated $3 million income from its drilling activities in Africa and paid $420,000 income tax to various African jurisdictions. SC must include $1.8 million (60 percent × $3 million) foreign source income in its taxable income and may include $252,000 (60 percent × $420,000) of the African taxes paid by the partnership in computing its foreign tax credit.

Domestic Subsidiaries

U.S. corporations often create wholly owned subsidiaries to operate foreign businesses. Because of the parent's limited liability as a shareholder, this strategy confines the risks of the foreign operation to the subsidiary corporation. If the subsidiary is a domestic corporation (one incorporated under U.S. law), the tax consequences are virtually identical to those of a foreign branch. The parent and subsidiary can file a consolidated U.S. tax return so that profits and losses generated by the overseas business are combined with those of the parent and any other domestic subsidiaries.[20] The group can elect a consolidated foreign tax credit for income taxes paid by the subsidiary and any other corporation in the group.

Domestic Subsidiary	SC, the Oklahoma corporation described in the preceding example, owns 100 percent of the outstanding stock of Pacifica, a California corporation. Pacifica conducts oil drilling activities in several countries in Southeast Asia. This year, Pacifica generated $14 million income and paid $3.1 million income tax to its host countries. SC files a consolidated federal tax return that includes Pacifica. Consequently, Pacifica's $14 million foreign source income is included in consolidated taxable income, and the $3.1 million foreign income tax paid by Pacifica is included in the computation of the SC consolidated group's foreign tax credit.

Tax Talk
The IRS has recently increased enforcement of a law that bars companies from avoiding U.S. taxes by moving their headquarters offshore to tax haven countries like Bermuda and the Cayman Islands while maintaining operational control in the United States.

Foreign Subsidiaries

Another alternative is for a U.S. corporation to create a subsidiary under the laws of a foreign jurisdiction. In such a case, the subsidiary is a foreign corporation, although it is completely controlled by a U.S. parent. The foreign jurisdiction is *both* home and host country to the subsidiary even though a U.S. shareholder owns the corporation. Multinational corporations typically have strong political and legal reasons for using foreign subsidiaries, such as the public image of the business in the host country or prohibitions against foreign ownership of real property located in the host country. When a U.S. corporation conducts business through a foreign subsidiary, the subsidiary's activities cannot be combined with those of the parent

[20] See the discussion of consolidated corporate returns in Chapter 11.

because foreign subsidiaries cannot be included in a U.S. consolidated tax return.[21] Thus, income generated by the subsidiary is not included in consolidated taxable income. Losses incurred by the subsidiary are isolated; the parent can't use these losses to shelter its own income from U.S. taxation. Depending on the tax laws of the foreign jurisdiction, the corporation may be allowed to carry the loss back or forward as a net operating loss deduction.

Foreign Subsidiary	SC, our Oklahoma oil and gas corporation, owns 100 percent of the outstanding stock of Latina, a Brazilian corporation. Latina conducts its business activities only in Brazil. This year, Latina generated $9 million income and paid $2.25 million Brazilian income tax. Although SC files a consolidated federal tax return with all its domestic subsidiaries, the return does not include Latina. Because Latina is a foreign corporation operating exclusively in a foreign jurisdiction, it does not pay U.S. income tax.

TAX CONSEQUENCES OF OPERATING ABROAD THROUGH A FOREIGN CORPORATION

Pre-2018 Deferral Regime for Foreign Corporations

LO 13-7
Explain when and how U.S. shareholders are taxed on dividends received from foreign corporations.

Prior to the Tax Cuts and Jobs Act of 2017, foreign source income earned by a foreign corporation was not subject to U.S. tax unless and until the corporation paid a dividend to a U.S. shareholder. Accordingly, U.S. corporations that didn't *repatriate* (bring home) the earnings of their foreign subsidiaries were deferring U.S. tax on such earnings.

When a U.S. corporation receives a dividend from another corporation (the payer), the dividend is included in the recipient's gross income. If the payer is a U.S. corporation, the recipient is allowed a dividends-received deduction. Consequently, little if any of the dividend is included in the recipient's taxable income.[22] If the payer is a foreign corporation, prior to 2018 the recipient was not entitled to a dividends-received deduction.[23] The dividend was included in the recipient's taxable income, and the issue of double taxation again took center stage.

Many countries (including the United States) impose a tax on dividends paid by resident corporations to foreign shareholders. The payer must withhold the tax from the dividend payment and remit it to the government. Consequently, the amount received by the shareholder is net of this **withholding tax.** The withholding tax rates vary across countries and are often specified in a country's income tax treaties. For example, Spain imposes a withholding tax on dividends paid by Spanish corporations to foreign shareholders, and the tax treaty between the United States and Spain specifies that the withholding tax rate is 15 percent. A U.S. corporation that receives a dividend net of a foreign withholding tax is entitled to a foreign tax credit.

Credit for Foreign Withholding Tax	Domino, a U.S. corporation, owns 2 percent of the stock of Carmela, a Spanish corporation. In 2017, Domino received a $265,000 dividend from Carmela net of the 15 percent Spanish withholding tax. Thus, Domino received only $225,250 *cash* ($265,000 dividend − $39,750 withheld foreign tax). The $265,000 dividend is included in Domino's 2017 foreign source taxable income, and the $39,750 withholding tax is a creditable foreign income tax.

[21] §1504(b)(3).

[22] See the discussion of the dividends-received deductions in Chapter 11. Intercompany dividends between members of an affiliated group filing a consolidated return are eliminated from consolidated taxable income. Reg. §1.1502-13(f)(2).

[23] §245 contains several exceptions to this general rule.

Deemed Paid Foreign Tax Credit

Prior to 2018, a U.S. corporation's dividends received from a foreign corporation were included in taxable income and subject to U.S. tax. Regardless of whether the dividends were subject to a foreign withholding tax, they represented after-tax earnings if the foreign corporation had to pay income tax to its home country. If a U.S. corporation owned 10 percent or more of the voting stock of the foreign corporation, it was entitled to a **deemed paid foreign tax credit.**[24] This credit was based on the income tax paid by the foreign corporation and not on any tax paid directly by the U.S. corporation. The best way to explain the computation of the deemed paid foreign tax credit is through an example:

Deemed Paid Credit

YNK, a U.S. corporation, formed FC, Inc. under the laws of Country F. In its first year of operation (prior to 2018), FC generated $100,000 income and paid $25,000 tax to Country F. The foreign subsidiary distributed its $75,000 after-tax income to YNK as a dividend, which was not subject to any withholding tax by Country F. The preliminary step in the computation of YNK's deemed paid credit is to increase (gross up) this dividend by the foreign tax that FC paid. Because FC distributed its entire after-tax income, the $75,000 dividend is grossed up by the entire $25,000 Country F tax. Therefore, YNK reports a $100,000 grossed-up dividend as foreign source income.[25] YNK is now entitled to a credit for the $25,000 foreign tax deemed paid on YNK's behalf by FC. Because of this credit, YNK's U.S. tax on the dividend is only $10,000:

Foreign source income (grossed-up dividend)	$100,000
U.S. tax rate (pre-2018)	.35
Precredit U.S. tax	$ 35,000
Deemed paid foreign tax credit	(25,000)
U.S. tax	$ 10,000

YNK's $25,000 credit is not limited because the 25 percent foreign tax rate is *less* than the U.S. tax rate. Because of the deemed paid credit, the global tax on the $100,000 foreign source income earned by YNK through FC is $35,000: $25,000 foreign tax paid by FC and $10,000 U.S. tax paid by YNK.

Now change the facts by assuming that FC distributed only $10,000 of its $75,000 after-tax income as a dividend. In this case, FC's tax attributable to the dividend is $3,333 [($10,000 ÷ $75,000) × $25,000 Country F tax]. The grossed-up dividend is $13,333, and YNK's U.S. tax on the dividend is $1,333:

Grossed-up dividend	$13,333
U.S. tax rate (pre-2018)	.35
Precredit U.S. tax	$ 4,666
Deemed paid foreign tax credit	(3,333)
U.S. tax	$ 1,333

The global tax on the $13,333 foreign source income earned by YNK through FC is $4,666: $3,333 foreign tax paid by FC and $1,333 U.S. tax paid by YNK.

---

[24] §902(a). This section was repealed by the Tax Cuts and Jobs Act, effective for dividends received after December 31, 2017.

[25] §78.

If the foreign tax rate is less than the U.S. rate, as in the previous example, payment of a dividend by the foreign subsidiary to the U.S. parent resulted in incremental U.S. tax cost. This cost could be avoided by deferring repatriation. If a U.S. parent had no pressing need for cash from its overseas operations, this deferral could go on indefinitely. Such time period variable tax planning created value for firms choosing deferral of repatriation of foreign subsidiary earnings under pre-2018 tax laws.

Post-2017 Participation Exemption for Foreign Corporations

The Tax Cuts and Jobs Act substantially eliminates deferred taxation of foreign income earned by foreign subsidiaries of a U.S. corporation after 2017. Such income is either permanently exempt from tax or taxed when earned.

For distributions received after December 31, 2017, a domestic corporation that owns at least 10 percent voting power of a **specified 10 percent foreign corporation** can take a 100 percent dividends-received deduction (DRD) for the foreign-source portion of dividends received from the foreign corporation.[26] A specified 10 percent foreign corporation is any foreign corporation in which any domestic corporation owns at least 10 percent voting power. In the simplest case, in which the foreign corporation has no U.S. business activity and receives no dividends from U.S. corporations, the foreign-source portion of dividends paid is 100 percent.

In addition to owning at least 10 percent of the voting power of the foreign corporation, a domestic corporation must meet a holding period requirement in order to claim the 100 percent DRD. Specifically, the domestic corporation must own the stock for more than 365 days during the 731-day period beginning 365 days before the date on which the dividend is paid.

Dividends from Foreign Corporations

Vernon, Inc., a Georgia corporation, received dividends from three foreign corporations this year:

Dividend received	
Chaco Corporation	$100,000
Reavie Inc.	250,000
Lyon Corporation	50,000
Total foreign dividend income	$400,000

Vernon owns 5 percent of the stock of Chaco, thus Vernon is not entitled to the 100 percent DRD for this dividend because it does own at least 10 percent of Chaco. Vernon has owned 70 percent of the stock of Reavie for the past 10 years, thus the dividend from Reavie qualifies for the 100 percent DRD. Vernon owns 20 percent of the stock of Lyon, which it purchased six months ago; thus, Vernon cannot claim the 100 percent DRD for the dividend from Lyon because it does not satisfy the holding period requirement.

Vernon may claim a $250,000 DRD for the dividend from Reavie, resulting in $150,000 of net dividend income ($400,000 total foreign dividends − $250,000 DRD) on this year's tax return.

The Tax Cuts and Jobs Act repealed the indirect foreign tax credit permitted when pre-2018 foreign dividends were received by domestic corporations. Thus, any portion of a foreign dividend not qualifying for the 100 percent DRD is fully taxable to the domestic shareholder.

---

[26] §245A.

Transition from Deferral Regime to Participation Exemption

At this point, the astute reader might ask "What about all those foreign earnings deferred prior to 2018? Can they now be repatriated tax free?" Unfortunately, Congress was not that generous in its enactment of the Tax Cuts and Jobs Act. A transition rule provides that the accumulated deferred foreign earnings of a **specified foreign corporation (SFC)** be treated as constructively repatriated in the SFC's last tax year beginning before January 1, 2018.[27] Each **U.S. shareholder** of an SFC includes its pro rata share of the SFC's deferred income as a dividend, referred to in the new law as a **mandatory inclusion** amount. Although this constructive dividend is not eligible for the 100 percent DRD, it is taxed at a reduced rate. A 15.5 percent rate applies to the extent the dividend is attributable to the shareholder's aggregate foreign cash position; otherwise, an 8 percent rate applies.

A specified foreign corporation includes both a specified 10 percent foreign corporation, as previously defined, and a controlled foreign corporation, as defined and discussed further in the next section of this chapter. A U.S. shareholder, for this purpose, includes domestic corporations, partnerships, trusts, estates, and U.S. individuals that own 10 percent or more of the SFC's voting power. The shareholder's aggregate foreign cash position is determined through a complex set of look-through rules that attribute to the shareholder a pro-rata share of the SFC's cash and other liquid assets.

In a valuable relief provision, the new law permits a U.S. shareholder to elect to pay the tax due on its mandatory inclusion over an eight-year period. Specifically, 8 percent of the tax must be paid in each of the first five years, 15 percent in the sixth year, 20 percent in the seventh year, and 25 percent in the eighth year.[28]

Mandatory Inclusion from SFC	RX, Inc., a calendar year domestic corporation, owns 25 percent of the stock of Porto, a calendar year SFC. Prior to 2018, Porto has accumulated deferred foreign earnings of $5.4 million and an aggregate foreign cash position of $830,000. Assume that Porto paid zero foreign tax on these earnings.*

For its tax year ended December 31, 2017, RX is treated as receiving a constructive dividend from Porto of $1,350,000 ($5,400,000 × 25 percent), with $207,500 ($830,000 × 25 percent) of this amount attributable to Porto's foreign cash position. RX's tax liability on this constructive dividend is $123,563, computed as follows:

Tax on portion of distribution deemed from foreign cash position ($207,500 × 15.5 percent rate)	$ 32,163
Tax on remaining distribution [($1,350,000 − $207,500) × 8 percent]	91,400
Total tax due on mandatory inclusion amount	$123,563

* The new law allows a U.S. shareholder to claim a foreign tax credit for a portion of the foreign taxes paid by the SFC associated with the mandatory inclusion amount. Further consideration of this deemed paid credit is beyond the scope of this text.

The installment payment option greatly reduces the current tax cost of the mandatory inclusion. For the previous example, using a 6 percent discount rate, the present value of the required payments is only $95,947.

---

[27] §965(a).
[28] §965(h).

Payment of Tax on Mandatory Inclusion

As shown in the previous example, RX owes $123,563 tax on its mandatory inclusion amount for Porto. This tax will be payable by the initial due date of RX's federal income tax return for each of the following tax years:

2017 tax return ($123,563 × 8 percent)	$ 9,885
2018 tax return ($123,563 × 8 percent)	9,885
2019 tax return ($123,563 × 8 percent)	9,885
2020 tax return ($123,563 × 8 percent)	9,885
2021 tax return ($123,563 × 8 percent)	9,885
2022 tax return ($123,563 × 15 percent)	18,534
2023 tax return ($123,563 × 20 percent)	24,713
2024 tax return ($123,563 × 25 percent)	30,891
Total amount paid	$123,563

Controlled Foreign Corporations

U.S. corporations with foreign subsidiaries in low-tax countries (countries with tax rates less than the U.S. rate) can minimize tax by shifting as much income as possible to those subsidiaries. Before 1962, U.S. corporations routinely created subsidiaries in **tax haven** jurisdictions—countries with minimal or no corporate income tax. In many cases, the tax haven subsidiary existed only on paper, performing no function other than providing tax shelter. Consider the case of a U.S. manufacturer exporting its goods through a French subsidiary for retail sale in the European market. If the U.S. parent sold its goods directly to this marketing subsidiary at an arm's-length price, it would pay U.S. tax on the income from the outbound transaction. Furthermore, the subsidiary would pay French tax on the income from its retail sales of the goods. If, however, the U.S. parent also owned a subsidiary incorporated in the Cayman Islands, a Caribbean nation with no corporate income tax, the parent could sell its goods to this subsidiary for a very low price. The Cayman subsidiary could then sell the goods to the French subsidiary for a very high price. This three-party transaction is diagrammed in Exhibit 13.2.

Even though the U.S. parent sold its goods to the Cayman subsidiary, it shipped the goods directly to the French subsidiary's warehouse outside of Paris. The Cayman subsidiary was

EXHIBIT 13.2
Tax Haven Subsidiary

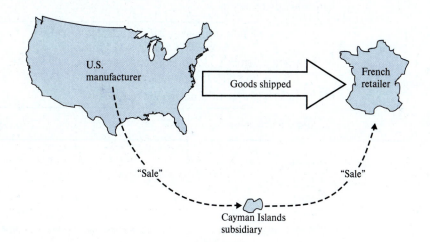

not involved in the actual production or distribution process. Nevertheless, the subsidiary's intermediate legal title to the goods shifted most of the income from the outbound transaction to the Cayman corporation. Until such time as this corporation paid a dividend to its U.S. parent (prior to 2018), no income taxes at all were levied on the income.

LO 13-8
Explain the tax consequences of subpart F income and global intangible low-taxed income earned by a CFC.

This classic tax avoidance scheme is just one example of the creative strategies used by international firms to divert income to tax haven jurisdictions. In 1962, Congress ended the most abusive strategies by enacting a set of "antideferral" rules applying to controlled foreign corporations. A **controlled foreign corporation (CFC)** is a foreign corporation in which U.S. shareholders own more than 50 percent of the voting power or stock value.[29] If a CFC earns certain types of income, the law treats such income as if it were immediately distributed to the CFC's shareholders.[30] Any U.S. shareholder with a 10 percent or more interest must pay tax on its pro rata share of this constructive dividend. These shareholders are entitled to increase the tax basis in their CFC stock by their constructive dividend.[31] If the CFC subsequently makes cash distributions to its shareholders, the distributions are nontaxable to the extent of any prior year constructive dividends and reduce the tax basis in the shareholder's CFC stock.[32]

Subpart F Income

Not all foreign source income earned by a CFC must be constructively repatriated to its U.S. shareholders. Only narrowly defined categories of income (labeled **subpart F income** in the Internal Revenue Code) are treated as constructive dividends. Conceptually, subpart F income is artificial income because it has no commercial or economic connection to the CFC's home country. Subpart F income has many complex components, one of the more important of which is income derived from the sale of goods if (1) the CFC either buys the goods from or sells the goods to a related party and (2) the goods are neither manufactured nor sold for use within the CFC's home country.[33] In our Cayman Islands example, the Cayman CFC is related to both the U.S. manufacturer and the French distributor because all three corporations are members of one controlled group. Moreover, the goods described in the example never touched Cayman soil and have no connection to the country. Quite clearly, the Cayman subsidiary's entire taxable income is subpart F income on which the U.S. parent must pay current tax.

Subpart F Income

Petroni owns 100 percent of the stock of RYM, a CFC operating in Country M. This year, RYM earned $1 million taxable income, $700,000 of which related to RYM's commercial activities within Country M and $300,000 (30 percent) of which was subpart F income. RYM paid $100,000 income tax to Country M and made no cash distributions to Petroni. Nonetheless, Petroni must recognize a constructive dividend equal to RYM's after-tax earnings attributable to its subpart F income.

Petroni's constructive dividend from RYM	
(30% × RYM's $900,000 after-tax earnings)	$270,000
Gross-up for foreign tax paid by RYM	30,000
Petroni's foreign source income from RYM	$300,000
Petroni's deemed paid foreign tax	30,000

Petroni can increase the basis in its RYM stock by the $270,000 constructive dividend.

---

[29] §957(a).

[30] §951(a)(1)(A).

[31] §961.

[32] §959.

[33] Such income constitutes foreign base company sales income per §954(d)(1). Subpart F income is defined in §952 through §954.

Post-2018 Current Year Taxation of Global Intangible Low-Taxed Income

The Tax Cuts and Jobs Act expands the constructive dividend approach of Subpart F to a newly defined type of income earned by a CFC–**global intangible low-taxed income (GILTI).**[34] Conceptually, GILTI is income earned by a CFC, not otherwise subject to U.S. tax, in excess of a fixed 10 percent return on the CFC's tangible business property. Subpart F income is excluded from GILTI, as is any income earned by the CFC associated with U.S. business activities. Tangible business property is measured using adjusted tax basis under the alternative depreciation system discussed in Chapter 7.

Calculating GILTI

FV is a CFC with total foreign earnings of $10 million, of which $3 million is considered sub-part F income. FV owns tangible business property with an adjusted tax basis of $22 million. FV has GILTI of $4.8 million, computed as follows:

Total foreign earnings	$10,000,000
Subpart F income	(3,000,000)
Fixed return on tangible business property	
($22 million × 10 percent)	(2,200,000)
FV's global intangible low-taxed income	$ 4,800,000

Tax Talk

For 2019, IRS data indicates that U.S. shareholders reported more than $495 billion of global intangible low-taxed income.

A U.S. shareholder owning 10 percent or more of a CFC is required to include in income its pro rata share of the CFC's GILTI amount. As with subpart F income, shareholders are permitted to increase the basis of their CFC stock by the constructive dividend. Corporate shareholders are then permitted a deduction equal to 50 percent of GILTI, resulting in an effective tax rate in the United States of 10.5 percent.[35] Corporate shareholders are also entitled to a deemed paid foreign tax credit for any foreign taxes paid by the CFC attributable to the GILTI inclusion. The allowable credit is limited to 80 percent of such deemed paid foreign taxes and cannot be carried back or forward to other tax years if not fully utilized in the year of the GILTI inclusion.

Tax on Subpart F and GILTI Inclusions

Refer to the preceding example involving FV. Suppose that Dykeman, Inc., a U.S. corporation, owns 100 percent of FV's stock. Dykeman's incremental U.S. tax liability as a result of its ownership of FV is $1,134,000, computed as follows:

Subpart F income inclusion	$3,000,000
GILTI inclusion	4,800,000
50 percent GILTI deduction	(2,400,000)
Incremental U.S. taxable income	$5,400,000
U.S. corporate tax rate	.21
Incremental U.S. tax before credits	$1,134,000

(continued)

---

[34] §951A.
[35] §250(a)(1).

In addition, Dykeman is permitted a deemed paid foreign tax credit for FV's foreign taxes paid related to both the subpart F inclusion and the GILTI inclusion. Dykeman will increase the basis in its FV stock by the $7.8 million subpart F and GILTI constructive dividends.

Note that of FV's total earnings of $10 million, $7.8 million is constructively repatriated and taxed in the United States through subpart F and the GILTI provisions. Only $2.2 million avoids current U.S. tax. In the future, if FV makes a cash distribution to Dykeman, up to $2.2 million of such distribution would be considered a dividend eligible for the 100 percent DRD.

Let's briefly summarize the complex web of rules that now apply when a U.S. corporation operates abroad through a CFC. Any income of the CFC considered either subpart F income or GILTI is constructively repatriated and subject to immediate U.S. taxation. Only the 10 percent fixed return on the CFC's tangible business property is excluded from current tax. Subsequent actual distributions to the U.S. corporation are not considered a dividend to the extent made from subpart F income or GILTI. Only distributions of the 10 percent fixed return will be considered dividends, likely qualifying for the 100 percent dividends-received deduction now available for most foreign dividends. Thus, the modified territorial system associated with the 100 percent foreign DRD is, in reality, a very limited exclusion from U.S. tax. Capital-intensive businesses with significant foreign tangible property receive the largest potential exclusion. Service and technology businesses will likely receive very little benefit, with the majority of their income taxable in the United States through subpart F and the GILTI provisions.

Tax on Subpart F and GILTI Inclusions of a Service Business

Refer again to our example involving FV and Dykeman, Inc. Now suppose that FV is a service business whose tangible business property has an adjusted tax basis of only $2 million. In this case, Dykeman's incremental U.S. tax liability as a result of its ownership of FV is $1,344,000, computed as follows:

Subpart F income inclusion	$3,000,000
GILTI inclusion	
($10 million – $3 million – $2 million × 10 percent)	6,800,000
50 percent GILTI deduction	(3,400,000)
Incremental U.S. taxable income	$6,400,000
U.S. corporate tax rate	.21
Incremental U.S. tax before credits	$1,344,000

In addition, Dykeman is permitted a deemed paid foreign tax credit for FV's foreign taxes paid related to both the subpart F inclusion and the GILTI inclusion. Dykeman will increase the basis in its FV stock by the $9.8 million subpart F and GILTI constructive dividends.

Now note that of FV's total earnings of $10 million, $9.8 million is constructively repatriated and taxed in the United States through subpart F and the GILTI provisions. Only $200,000 avoids current U.S. tax.

Limitations on Cross-Border Income Shifting

LO 13-9
Describe limitations on tax benefits from cross-border related party transactions.

While the subpart F and GILTI rules are potent, as we've just determined they do not extend to all types of foreign source income earned by CFCs. Consequently, U.S. parents can still derive some benefit by shifting income to their foreign subsidiaries in low-tax jurisdictions. If a U.S. parent has subsidiaries in high-tax jurisdictions (such as Chad and Brazil), the tax strategy can be reversed. In such cases, the parent wants to use its domestic subsidiaries as tax shelters.

Transfer Pricing

Controlled groups of corporations can shift income among the members through their pricing structure for intercompany transactions. Consider the possibilities for income shifting if a U.S. parent owns an Irish subsidiary that manufactures consumer goods for worldwide export. Although the Irish subsidiary is a CFC, its profit from sales of goods manufactured in Ireland and sold to unrelated purchasers is not subpart F income. As a result, the income is subject only to the much lower Irish corporate tax until the CFC pays dividends to its parent. If the parent (or any domestic subsidiary) sells raw materials to the Irish subsidiary, the lower the price charged for the materials, the greater the income shifted to Ireland. If the U.S. parent provides administrative, marketing, or financial services to the Irish subsidiary, the parent could further inflate the subsidiary's profits (and deflate its own) by charging a nominal fee for the services rendered. Similarly, if the parent owns patents, copyrights, licenses, or other intangible assets that add value to the Irish manufacturing process, it could forgo royalty payments for the subsidiary's use of the intangible.

All of these pricing strategies shift income to the Irish subsidiary. Not surprisingly, the United States and most foreign countries, mindful of the income distortion resulting from artificial **transfer prices,** demand that related entities deal with each other in the same arm's-length manner as they deal with unrelated parties. Under federal tax law, Section 482 gives the IRS the authority to apportion or allocate gross income, deductions, or credits between related parties to correct any perceived distortion resulting from unrealistic transfer prices.[36]

Section 482 Adjustment	BSX, a California corporation, owns a CFC that manufactures and sells goods in the Asian market. The CFC is incorporated in a country with no corporate income tax. Several years ago, BSX sent a team of system engineers to advise the CFC on improving inventory management. BSX did not charge the CFC a fee for this service. In the same year, BSX sold industrial equipment to the CFC for a price of $385,000. During its audit of BSX's tax return, the IRS determined that a reasonable transfer price for the advisory services was $150,000, and a reasonable transfer price for the equipment was $500,000. Consequently, the IRS allocated $265,000 gross income to BSX from its CFC and assessed U.S. tax on this Section 482 adjustment.

Over the past decades, the IRS has not hesitated to use its Section 482 power to ensure that domestic corporations pay U.S. tax on an appropriate amount of their international income. While corporations certainly can challenge the IRS in court, the prevailing judicial attitude is that the IRS's determination of an arm's-length transfer price should be upheld unless the corporation can demonstrate that the determination is "arbitrary, capricious, or unreasonable."[37] Clearly, multinational corporations are in a defensive posture concerning their transfer pricing practices and must be constantly aware of any Section 482 exposure created by their intercompany transactions.

[36] §482 was introduced in Chapter 6.
[37] *Liberty Loan Corp.* v. *U.S.,* 498 F.2d 225 (CA-8, 1974), *cert. denied,* 419 U.S. 1089.

Tax Talk

The Organization for Economic Cooperation and Development (OECD) has spent several years working on a detailed plan to combat what it calls "base erosion and profit sharing" (BEPS). BEPS refers to tax planning strategies that exploit gaps and mismatches in tax rules to artificially shift profits to low- or no-tax locations where there is little or no economic activity. The BEPS action plan, when implemented, attempts to harmonize the enforcement approaches of participating countries, while imposing significant reporting burdens on multinational businesses. Three of the current 15 action areas apply specifically to transfer pricing.

BEAT Minimum Tax

The subjective nature of Section 482 and the transfer pricing rules creates potential for tax planning with related parties transactions. The Tax Cuts and Jobs Act further restricts such planning after 2017 by enacting a **base erosion and anti-abuse tax (BEAT)** aimed at curtailing the U.S. tax benefit of cross-border related party payments made by large multinationals.[38] BEAT targets payments by large U.S. corporations to foreign related parties where a deduction is allowable or in connection with the acquisition of depreciable or amortizable property, excluding payments treated as cost of goods sold. In many cases, such payments are interest costs on related party loans, or royalty payments for the use of intangibles owned by the foreign related party.

BEAT applies only to domestic corporations that (1) are part of a corporate group with at least $500 million average annual domestic gross receipts and (2) have targeted related party payments equaling 3 percent or more of the taxpayer's overall allowable deductions. Thus, smaller corporations and those with few related party payments will not owe this tax.

BEAT is calculated as 10 percent of taxable income computed before base erosion related party payments. BEAT is owed only to the extent the calculated amount exceeds regular tax liability.

BEAT Computation

SMP, Inc. is a domestic corporation with several foreign subsidiaries. This year, SMP has $750 million domestic gross receipts and $500 million of allowable deductions. It made deductible related party payments to its foreign affiliates of $200 million.

SMP is potentially subject to BEAT, because it satisfies the gross receipts test and its deductible-related party payments equal 40 percent of its overall allowable deductions. However, SMP's BEAT liability is zero. SMP's regular tax owed is $52.5 million ($250 million taxable income × 21 percent). Its tentative BEAT amount is $45 million [($250 million taxable income + $200 million cross-border related party payments) × 10 percent]. Because regular tax exceeds tentative BEAT, SMP owes no BEAT.

[38] §59A.

Tax Talk
For 2019, IRS data indicates that U.S. multinationals paid $1.7 billion of BEAT.

Book/Tax Differences Related to Foreign Operations

Under GAAP, financial statements typically include the worldwide operations of a corporate group, including its foreign subsidiaries. However, the U.S. consolidated corporate income tax return will include only U.S. affiliated corporations. To the extent the income of foreign subsidiaries is not currently taxable in the United States, book/tax differences will result. Such differences could be either temporary or permanent, depending on their nature and the tax year to which they relate.

Conclusion

In the preceding chapter, we discussed the tax implications when owners select a particular entity through which to conduct business. In this chapter, we added a new tax planning variable—the jurisdiction in which the entity is taxed. To the extent that owners can manipulate this variable by operating in low-tax jurisdictions, tax costs can be controlled. When a business stretches across jurisdictions, the owners run the risk that double taxation will erode their after-tax profits. If the competing jurisdictions are state governments, income is divided according to each state's apportionment rule. Businesses can often take advantage of anomalies in these rules and differences in state tax rates to reduce their tax burden. If the competing jurisdictions are the United States and a foreign government, the foreign tax credit is an invaluable mechanism for preventing double taxation.

Historically, multinational U.S. corporations could achieve substantial tax savings by incorporating foreign subsidiaries in low-tax jurisdictions. However, changes enacted by the Tax Cuts and Jobs Act have both lowered the U.S corporate tax rate and significantly restricted the opportunities for avoiding U.S. tax on earnings of controlled foreign corporations. Certainly, international tax planning is a complex and challenging specialty that will become more valuable as the global economy continues to develop.

Sources of Book/Tax Differences

Permanent
- Earnings of foreign subsidiaries after 2017, to the extent not subject to subpart F or GILTI provisions

Temporary
- Most unrepatriated earnings of foreign subsidiaries prior to 2018

Key Terms

apportionment *13-5*
base erosion and anti-abuse tax (BEAT) *13-24*
Commerce Clause *13-3*
controlled foreign corporation (CFC) *13-20*
cross-crediting *13-12*
deemed paid foreign tax credit *13-16*
excess foreign tax credit *13-11*
foreign-derived intangible income (FDII) *13-13*

foreign source income *13-10*
foreign tax credit *13-10*
global intangible low-taxed income (GILTI) *13-21*
income tax treaty *13-8*
mandatory inclusion *13-18*
nexus *13-3*
outbound transaction *13-9*
permanent establishment *13-8*

specified foreign corporation (SFC) *13-18*
specified 10 percent foreign corporation *13-17*
subpart F income *13-20*
tax haven *13-19*
transfer price *13-23*
Uniform Division of Income for Tax Purposes Act (UDITPA) *13-5*
U.S. shareholder *13-18*
withholding tax *13-15*

Questions and Problems for Discussion

In the questions, problems, and cases for this chapter, corporations are U.S. corporations unless otherwise stated.

LO 13-1   1. Why does a corporation's state income tax cost depend on its marginal income tax rate for federal purposes?

LO 13-2   2. NY is a New York corporation that manufactures office equipment in a factory located in New York. In which of the following cases does NY have nexus with Pennsylvania?

   a. NY owns two retail outlets for its products in Pennsylvania.

   b. NY owns no tangible property in Pennsylvania. It employs two salespeople who travel throughout Pennsylvania soliciting orders for office equipment from regular customers. NY fills the orders out of its New York factory and ships the equipment to the customers by common carrier.

   c. NY owns no tangible property in Pennsylvania and does not have employees who work in the state. It does have Pennsylvania customers who order equipment directly from the New York factory by telephone or fax.

   d. Refer to the facts in part (*c*). NY employs two technicians who travel throughout Pennsylvania providing repair and maintenance services to NY's customers.

LO 13-2   3. Distinguish between the concepts of physical presence nexus and economic nexus.

LO 13-3   4. Does the federal government require states to use a three-factor formula to apportion the income of an interstate business for state income tax purposes?

LO 13-3   5. Borden, Inc. conducts a business that spans four states. Its total income for the year was $32 million. However, the total of the taxable incomes reported on Borden's four state income tax returns was $34.8 million. Discuss the possible reasons for such a discrepancy.

LO 13-2   6. In what situation would a multistate business deliberately create nexus with a state so that the state has jurisdiction to tax a portion of the business income?

LO 13-4   7. Distinguish between a home country and a host country in the international tax context.

LO 13-4   8. What is the purpose of a bilateral income tax treaty between two countries?

LO 13-4   9. Lefty, Inc. sells its products to customers residing in Country X and Country Y. Both foreign jurisdictions have a 20 percent corporate income tax. This year, Lefty made more than $30 million of sales in both Country X and Country Y. However, it paid income tax only to Country X. What factors could account for this result?

LO 13-6   10. Posse Corporation plans to form a foreign subsidiary through which to conduct a new business in Country J. Posse projects that this business will operate at a loss for several years.

   a. To what extent will the subsidiary's losses generate U.S. tax savings?

   b. To what extent will the subsidiary's losses generate a savings of Country J income tax?

LO 13-7   11. Halifax, Inc. operates its business in Country U through a subsidiary incorporated under Country U law. The subsidiary has never paid a dividend and has accumulated more than $10 million after-tax earnings.

   a. Country U has a 20 percent corporate income tax. Describe the tax consequences to Halifax if it receives a $5 million dividend from the subsidiary in a tax year prior to 2018.

   b. Describe the tax consequence of the subsidiary's pre-2018 unrepatriated earnings as a result of the Tax Cuts and Jobs Act.

LO 13-8   12. Togo, Inc. has a subsidiary incorporated in Country H, which does not have a corporate income tax. Which of the following activities generates subpart F income?

   a. The subsidiary buys woolen clothing products manufactured by a Swedish company and sells the products to unrelated wholesalers in the United States. Togo owns the Swedish company.

   b. The subsidiary buys coffee beans grown on plantations located in Country H and sells the beans to Togo, which makes coffee products.

   c. The subsidiary buys building materials from a Mexican company and sells the materials to construction companies operating in Country H. Togo owns the Mexican company.

LO 13-6, 13-7   13. Column Corporation has a subsidiary operating exclusively in Country A and a subsidiary operating exclusively in Country Z.

   a. Both subsidiaries were incorporated under Delaware law and are therefore U.S. corporations. Can Column use the losses from the Country A subsidiary to reduce the income from the Country Z subsidiary?

   b. Would your answer change if both subsidiaries are foreign corporations?

LO 13-5, 13-6   14. Delta Partnership carries on business in the United States and four other countries. Explain why the ordinary income generated by the foreign business is a separately stated item on Delta's Schedule K, Form 1065.

LO 13-9   15. Kantor, Inc. owns 100 percent of Sub 1 (a CFC in a country with a 50 percent corporate tax) and 90 percent of Sub 2 (a CFC in a country with a 10 percent corporate tax). Kantor sells goods and services to both CFCs. Is the IRS more interested in Kantor's transfer pricing for sales to Sub 1 or sales to Sub 2?

LO 13-5   16. In what situation is the United States a tax haven for an international business operation?

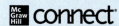 **All applicable Application Problems are available with *Connect*.**

Application Problems

LO 13-1   1. This year, Mesa, Inc.'s before-tax income was $9,877,000. It paid $419,000 income tax to Minnesota and $385,000 income tax to Illinois.

   a. Compute Mesa's federal income tax.

   b. What is Mesa's tax rate on its income?

LO 13-1   2. For the current year, Harbor Corporation earned before-tax income of $776,000. Harbor operates in a single state with a 10 percent state income tax rate.

   a. Compute Harbor's state income tax liability.

   b. Assuming Harbor deducts state income taxes when accrued, compute Harbor's federal taxable income and federal income tax.

   c. Compute the overall income tax rate on Harbor's income.

LO 13-2   3. Bianco, Inc. is headquartered in Pennsylvania. Bianco produces custom stationery for sale to customers in stores located in Pennsylvania and New Jersey. It also sells its products online and ships to customers in other states. Last year, Bianco sold its products to online customers in Maryland, Florida, Iowa, Louisiana, and Georgia. In which of these states does Bianco have nexus for state income tax purposes?

LO 13-3   4. Oldham, Inc. conducts business in State M and State N, which both use the UDITPA three-factor formula to apportion income. State M's corporate tax rate is 4.5 percent, and State N's corporate tax rate is 7 percent. This year, Oldham had the following sales, payroll, and property (in thousands of dollars) in each state:

	State M	State N	Total
Gross receipts from sales	$3,000	$7,500	$10,500
Payroll expense	800	1,200	2,000
Property costs	900	1,000	1,900

If Oldham's before-tax income was $3 million, compute its State M and State N tax.

LO 13-3   5. Refer to the facts in the preceding problem. Compute Oldham's State M and State N tax if State N uses an apportionment formula in which the sales factor is double-weighted.

LO 13-3   6. Refer to the facts in problem 4. Compute the state income tax savings if Oldham could relocate its personnel so that payroll expense in State M increased to $1,900 (thousand) and payroll expense in State N decreased to $100 (thousand).

LO 13-3   7. Cromwell Corporation does business in two states, A and B. State A uses an equal-weighted, three-factor apportionment formula and has a 5 percent state tax rate. State B uses an apportionment formula that double-weights the sales factor and has a 6 percent state tax rate. Cromwell's state-level taxable income, before apportionment, is $2 million. It has identified the following components of its sales, payroll, and property factors:

	State A	State B	Total
Sales	$6,000,000	$4,000,000	$10,000,000
Payroll	2,000,000	1,200,000	3,200,000
Average property	1,000,000	800,000	1,800,000

a. Calculate Cromwell's apportionment factors, income apportioned to each state, and state tax liability.

b. State B is considering changing its apportionment formula to place 100 percent of the weight on the sales factor, ignoring payroll and property for apportionment purposes. Given its current levels of activity, would such a change increase or decrease Cromwell's state income tax burden? Provide calculations to support your conclusion.

LO 13-3   8. Lido, Inc. does business in two states, X and Y. State X uses an equal-weighted, three-factor apportionment formula and has a 4 percent state tax rate. State Y bases its apportionment only on the sales factor and has a 5 percent state tax rate. Lido's state-level taxable income before apportionment is $1,750,000. Based on the following apportionment information, calculate Lido's apportionment factors, income apportioned to each state, and state tax liability.

	State X	State Y	Total
Sales	$4,600,000	$1,300,000	$5,900,000
Payroll	1,200,000	800,000	2,000,000
Average property	2,200,000	700,000	2,900,000

LO 13-1, 13-5 9. Turbo is a U.S. corporation. This year, it earned $5 million before-tax income and paid $175,000 income tax to jurisdictions other than the United States. Compute Turbo's U.S. federal income tax assuming that

    a. The other jurisdictions were Ireland and Germany, and Turbo's foreign tax credit was not limited.

    b. The other jurisdictions were the states of Pennsylvania and New Jersey.

LO 13-1, 13-5 10. Akita is a U.S. corporation. This year, it earned $8 million before-tax income and paid $450,000 income tax to jurisdictions other than the United States. Compute Akita's U.S. income tax assuming that

    a. The other jurisdictions were the states of Montana, Colorado, California, and Arizona.

    b. The other jurisdictions were Italy and Spain, and Akita's foreign tax credit was not limited.

LO 13-5 11. Zenon, Inc. has the following taxable income:

U.S. source income	$1,900,000
Foreign source income	240,000
Taxable income	$2,140,000

    Zenon paid $33,000 foreign income tax. Compute its U.S. income tax, assuming the foreign source income does not qualify as FDII.

LO 13-7 12. Refer to the facts in the preceding problem. How would your answer change if Zenon conducted its foreign operations through a foreign subsidiary that made no shareholder distributions during the current year and had no GILTI or subpart F income?

LO 13-5 13. Basu, Inc. has the following taxable income:

U.S. source income	$18,800,000
Foreign source income	2,690,000
Taxable income	$21,490,000

    Basu paid $1,040,000 foreign income tax. Compute its U.S. income tax, assuming the foreign source income does not qualify as FDII.

LO 13-7 14. Refer to the facts in the preceding problem. Compute U.S. income tax if Basu conducted its foreign operations through a foreign subsidiary that made no shareholder distributions during the current year and had no GILTI or subpart F income.

LO 13-5, 13-6, 13-7 15. Elmo, Inc. is a U.S. corporation with a branch office in foreign Country Z. During the current year, Elmo had $340,000 of U.S. source income and $60,000 of foreign source income from Z, on which Elmo paid $28,000 of Country Z income tax.

    a. Calculate Elmo's U.S. tax liability before foreign tax credit, maximum foreign tax credit allowable, and net U.S. tax liability after foreign tax credit.

    b. If Elmo had paid only $10,000 of Country Z income tax, calculate Elmo's foreign tax credit allowable and net U.S. tax liability after foreign tax credit.

    c. For which fact situation (foreign tax of $28,000 or $10,000) could Elmo have reduced its worldwide tax burden by operating in Country Z using a foreign subsidiary rather than a branch operation? Explain briefly.

LO 13-5 16. Watch Corporation has U.S. source income for the current year of $2 million, foreign source income from Country X of $3 million, and foreign source income from Country

Y of $1 million, for total taxable income of $6 million. Watch paid $900,000 of income tax to Country X and $480,000 of income tax to Country Y. Compute Watch's U.S. income tax, assuming the foreign source income does not qualify as FDII.

LO 13-5 17. Axtell Corporation has the following taxable income:

U.S. source income	$1,620,000
Foreign source income:	
Country A	550,000
Country B	2,000,000
Country C	2,900,000
Taxable income	$7,070,000

Axtell paid $600,000 income tax to Country B and $1.3 million income tax to Country C. Country A does not have a corporate income tax. Compute Axtell's U.S. income tax, assuming the foreign source income does not qualify as FDII.

LO 13-4, 13-5 18. Transcom, an Ohio corporation, earned $700,000 U.S. source income from sales of goods to U.S. customers and $330,000 foreign source income from sales of goods to customers in Canada. Canada's corporate income tax rate is 15 percent, and the United States and Canada have a bilateral tax treaty.

    a. Compute Transcom's U.S. tax if it does not maintain a permanent establishment in Canada. Assume the foreign source income does not qualify as FDII.

    b. Compute Transcom's U.S. tax if it does maintain a permanent establishment in Canada.

LO 13-5, 13-6 19. Aqua, a South Carolina corporation, is a 20 percent partner in a Swiss partnership. This year, Aqua earned $2 million U.S. source income and $190,000 foreign source income. It paid no foreign income tax. The Swiss partnership earned $1.73 million foreign source income and paid $460,000 income tax to Switzerland, France, and Austria. Compute Aqua's U.S. tax, assuming the foreign source income does not qualify as FDII.

LO 13-8 20. The Trio affiliated group consists of Trio, a New Jersey corporation, and its three wholly owned subsidiaries. This year, the four corporations report the following:

	Net Income (Loss)
Trio	$412,000
Subsidiary 1	(180,000)
Subsidiary 2	389,000
Subsidiary 3	600,000

If Trio elects to file a U.S. consolidated return, compute consolidated taxable income assuming that

    a. Subsidiary 1 is a domestic corporation, and Subsidiaries 2 and 3 are foreign corporations.

    b. Subsidiaries 2 and 3 are domestic corporations, and Subsidiary 1 is a foreign corporation.

LO 13-5 21. Comet operates solely within the United States. It owns two subsidiaries conducting business in the United States and several foreign countries. Both subsidiaries are U.S. corporations. This year, the three corporations report the following:

	Foreign Source Income	U.S. Source Income	Foreign Income Tax Paid
Comet	–0–	$600,000	–0–
Sub 1	$3,500,000	150,000	$ 350,000
Sub 2	4,700,000	410,000	1,175,000

    a. If Comet and its two subsidiaries file a consolidated U.S. tax return, compute consolidated income tax.

    b. How would the aggregate tax of the group change if the three corporations file separate U.S. tax returns?

    c. Identify the reason for the difference in the tax liability in parts (*a*) and (*b*).

LO 13-5 22. Velox, Inc. began operations last year. For its first two taxable years, Velox's records show the following:

	Year 1	Year 2
U.S. source income	$300,000	$270,000
Foreign source income	200,000	630,000
Taxable income	$500,000	$900,000
Foreign income tax paid	$ 62,000	$101,000

Compute Velox's U.S. tax for both years, assuming the foreign source income does not qualify as FDII.

LO 13-5 23. Minden Corporation's records show the following results for its first three years of operations:

	Year 1	Year 2	Year 3
U.S. source income	$180,000	$350,000	$ 800,000
Foreign source income	92,000	500,000	680,000
Taxable income	$272,000	$850,000	$1,480,000
Foreign tax paid	$ 17,000	$ 52,000	$ 81,600

In year 4, Minden generated $2 million taxable income ($900,000 of which was foreign source) and paid $370,000 foreign income tax. Assume Minden's foreign source income does not qualify as FDII.

    a. Compute Minden's U.S. tax for years 1, 2, and 3.

    b. Compute Minden's U.S. tax for year 4.

    c. Compute the refund generated by the carryback of the year 4 excess credit.

LO 13-6   24. Cheeta Corporation earned $5 million this year from both domestic and international operations. Assume $2.2 million of this income qualifies as foreign-derived intangible income (FDII). If Cheeta paid no foreign income tax, calculate its U.S. income tax due.

LO 13-6   25. This year, Tuna, Inc., a domestic corporation, earned $3 million from sales of goods to unrelated foreign customers. If Tuna has $12 million of depreciable assets, calculate its foreign-derived intangible income.

LO 13-7   26. Omaha, Inc. owns 100 percent of the stock in Franco, a foreign corporation. All of Franco's income is foreign source, and its foreign income tax rate is 20 percent. During its fiscal year ended June 30, 2017, Franco distributed a $50,000 dividend to Omaha.

   a. Assuming that Omaha had a 35 percent marginal tax rate in 2017, compute its U.S. tax on the dividend.

   b. How would your computation change if Omaha received the dividend from Franco during its fiscal year ended June 30, 2023?

LO 13-7   27. Shao, Inc., a Tennessee corporation, conducts business in South America through two foreign corporations, Shao-Col, Inc. and Shao-Per, Inc. Shao formed Shao-Col six years ago and owns 100 percent of its stock. Shao-Per was formed six months ago and Shao owns 50 percent of its stock. In addition, Shao owns 7 percent of the stock of Albi, Inc., a French corporation. This year, Shao recognized the following dividend distributions from the three foreign corporations:

Shao-Col, Inc.	$249,000
Shao-Per, Inc.	186,000
Albi, Inc.	92,000

   a. Compute Shao's allowable dividends-received deduction with respect to each dividend.

   b. Compute Shao's net dividend income.

LO 13-8   28. Jumper, Inc., which has a 21 percent tax rate, owns 40 percent of the stock of a CFC. At the beginning of 2022, Jumper's basis in its stock was $660,000. The CFC's 2022 income was $1 million, $800,000 of which was subpart F income. The CFC paid no foreign income tax and distributed no dividends.

   a. Compute Jumper's 2022 constructive dividend and related tax cost as a result of its investment in the CFC.

   b. Compute Jumper's basis in its CFC stock at the beginning of 2023.

LO 13-7, 13-8   29. Refer to the facts in the preceding problem. In 2023, the CFC's income was $600,000, none of which was subpart F income or GILTI, and it distributed a $300,000 dividend to its shareholders ($120,000 to Jumper). How much of this actual dividend is taxable to Jumper in 2023? Compute Jumper's basis in its CFC stock at the beginning of 2024.

LO 13-7   30. Yasmin Corporation, a calendar year domestic corporation, owns 100 percent of Luna, Inc., a calendar year controlled foreign corporation. Luna has never paid a dividend and at the end of 2017 has accumulated $18 million undistributed income (none of which is subpart F income). Luna also has $2 million of cash at the end of 2017.

   a. Compute Yasmin's tax due on its mandatory inclusion amount related to ownership of Luna.

   b. Beginning in 2017, determine Yasmin's installment payments of the tax due on its mandatory inclusion amount.

LO 13-7 31. Grandmere, a calendar year domestic corporation, owns 50 percent of Petit, Inc., a calendar year controlled foreign corporation. At the end of 2017, Petit has accumulated $26 million of undistributed income and has $4.2 million of cash.

    a. Compute Grandmere's mandatory inclusion amount related to ownership of Petit.

    b. Compute Grandmere's tax due on its mandatory inclusion amount.

    c. Beginning in 2017, determine Grandmere's installment payments of tax due on its mandatory inclusion amount.

LO 13-8 32. Fairview, Inc. is a CFC with total foreign earnings of $30 million, of which $8 million is considered subpart F income. Fairview owns tangible business property with an adjusted tax basis of $40 million. Collins Corporation, a U.S. corporation, owns 100 percent of the stock of Fairview.

    a. Compute Fairview's global intangible low-taxed income (GILTI).

    b. Compute Collins's incremental U.S. tax liability as a result of its ownership of Fairview.

LO 13-8 33. Leming, Inc. is a CFC with total foreign earnings of $90 million, of which $27 million is considered subpart F income. Leming owns tangible business property with an adjusted tax basis of $70 million. Hare Corporation, a U.S. corporation, owns 30 percent of the stock of Leming.

    a. Compute Leming's global intangible low-taxed income (GILTI).

    b. Compute Hare's pro rata share of Leming's GILTI and subpart F income.

    c. Compute Hare's incremental U.S. tax liability as a result of its ownership of Leming.

LO 13-9 34. Norton, Inc. is a domestic corporation with several foreign subsidiaries. This year, Norton has $940 million domestic gross receipts and $800 million of allowable deductions. It made deductible related party payments to its foreign affiliates of $520 million. Calculate Norton's BEAT liability and total U.S. tax due.

LO 13-9 35. Alamo, a Texas corporation, manufactures plastic components that it sells to Vegas, a Mexican corporation, for assembly into a variety of finished goods. Alamo owns 60 percent of Vegas's stock. Alamo's cost per component is $85, its selling price per component is $100, and it sold 70,000 components to Vegas this year. Alamo's taxable income as reported on its Form 1120 was $900,000, and Vegas's taxable income as reported on its Mexican corporate income tax return was $1.2 million. Compute any increase or decrease in the taxable incomes of both corporations if the IRS determines that an arm's-length transfer price per plastic component is $108.

LO 13-9 36. Cotton Comfort Corporation is a U.S. shirt manufacturer with a foreign subsidiary in Country X. Cloth to make shirts is woven in the United States, at a cost of $14 per shirt, and shipped to Country X where it is cut and sewn at a cost of $15 per shirt. These shirts are sold in Europe for $90 per shirt. The profit on each shirt is $61, a portion of which is U.S. source income and a portion of which is foreign source income, depending on the price at which the cloth is transferred from the United States to Country X.

    a. If the tax rate in Country X is lower than the U.S. tax rate, would Cotton Comfort prefer a high transfer price or a low transfer price? At what transfer price would all of the profit on these shirts be tax in Country X? Explain briefly.

    b. If the tax rate in Country X is higher than the U.S. tax rate, would Cotton Comfort prefer a high transfer price or a low transfer price? At what transfer price would all of the profit on these shirts be tax in the United States? Explain briefly.

LO 13-9   37. Refer to the facts in the preceding problem. Assume that the tax rate in Country X is 15 percent and Cotton Comfort's U.S. marginal tax rate is 21 percent. The corporation and its subsidiary have agreed to a transfer price for the cloth of $30 per shirt.

    a. At this price, how much profit per shirt will be taxed in the United States?

    b. At this price, how much profit per shirt will be taxed in Country X?

    c. If the IRS chooses to challenge Cotton Comfort's transfer price for the cloth, would you expect it to argue for a higher or a lower transfer price? Explain briefly.

Issue Recognition Problems

Identify the tax issue or issues suggested by the following situations and state each issue in the form of a question.

LO 13-1   1. State E wants to encourage the development of a local wine industry. Consequently, it decreased its excise tax rate on retail sales of locally produced wines to 3 percent. The state's excise tax on wines produced out-of-state but sold in-state is 10 percent.

LO 13-1, 13-2   2. ABC operates a meat and poultry business. The corporation distributes its products in six states and pays income tax to each based on the meat and poultry income apportionable to each. Last year, ABC invested in a motion picture. The picture was a commercial success, and ABC received a royalty check for $1,800,000 from the movie's producer.

LO 13-2, 13-3   3. Durbin Corporation is incorporated and has its commercial domicile in State N. This year, Durbin sold its manufactured products to customers in State N (61 percent of sales), State O (28 percent of sales), and State P (11 percent of sales). Durbin has nexus with State N and State O. However, it has no physical presence in State P and therefore is not taxed by that state. Both State N and State O use the three-factor UDITPA formula to apportion income.

LO 13-4   4. The United States has a tax treaty with the United Kingdom that provides certain tax benefits to UK corporations conducting business in the United States. The United States does not have an income tax treaty with Chile. Silas Company, a Chilean firm that exports goods to the United States, decides to operate its export business through a shell corporation formed under UK law.

LO 13-4   5. Benton is a consulting firm with its headquarters in New York City. This year, it entered into a consulting contract with a multinational corporation. Mrs. Kalle, an employee, spent 33 days working at Benton headquarters, 28 days in London, 50 days in Paris, and 14 days in Hong Kong performing the professional services specified in the contract. Benton received a $1 million fee upon completion of Mrs. Kalle's work.

LO 13-5   6. Lim Corporation operates a fleet of oceangoing cargo vessels. During the year, one Lim vessel was docked at its home port in New Orleans for 55 days, was on the high seas for 120 days, and was docked at various foreign ports of call for the remaining 190 days. Lim's net income from operation of this vessel was $620,000.

LO 13-5   7. Funk Corporation conducts business in a foreign jurisdiction that imposes a 1 percent tax on gross receipts from sales within the jurisdiction. This year, Funk paid $750,000 gross receipts tax to the jurisdiction.

LO 13-5   8. Lincoln manufactures paper products in the United States and sells the products internationally. Because most of its foreign sales are in high-tax jurisdictions, Lincoln has excess foreign credits from its paper business. This year, Lincoln earned $8 million interest income on long-term bonds issued by Country NT, which has no income tax.

LO 13-9   9. Hastings Corporation has a foreign subsidiary conducting a manufacturing business in Country Z, which has a 15 percent corporate income tax. The IRS recently challenged the transfer price at which Hastings performs managerial services for the subsidiary and used its Section 482 authority to reallocate $10 million income from the subsidiary to Hastings. The taxing authorities in Country Z maintain the transfer price was perfectly accurate.

LO 13-8, 13-9 10. Williams, Inc. is a U.S. corporation that manufacturers toys in a factory located near Milwaukee, Wisconsin. Williams sells the toys to its foreign subsidiary, which is incorporated in Carnema, a Caribbean country with no corporate income tax. Williams actually ships the toys to a warehouse in Carnema, where the toys are sealed in protective plastic wrappings and labeled. The foreign subsidiary resells the sealed and labeled toys in the European market. This year, the foreign subsidiary's profit from toy sales will exceed $25 million.

LO 13-7 11. For many years, Bertrand, Inc. owned a foreign subsidiary with over $8 million accumulated foreign source income (on which Bertrand has never paid U.S. tax). Immediately prior to December 31, 2017, Bertrand, Inc. sold its investment in the foreign subsidiary to an unrelated U.S. corporation.

Research Problems

LO 13-3 1. Visit the website for Federation of Tax Administrators (**www.taxadmin.org**) under the Taxpayers & Tax Preparers menu, and use the State Tax Agencies link to go to the Illinois Department of Revenue website. Locate a copy of the Corporate Income and Replacement Tax Return (Form IL-1120), scrutinize Step 4, and describe how Illinois's apportionment percentage is computed. Return to the FTA website and link to the New Mexico Department of Revenue website. Locate a copy of the New Mexico Corporation Income and Franchise Tax Return (Form CIT-1), scrutinize Schedule A, and describe how New Mexico's apportionment percentage is computed.

LO 13-5 2. Endless Summer is a Florida corporation that operates a fleet of cruise ships. It offers two categories of cruises. The first category includes round-trip cruises on ships that depart from Miami, visit various Caribbean and South American ports, and then return to Miami at the end of the cruise. The second category includes one-way cruises on ships that depart from Miami and travel to various South American ports. The passengers disembark and are responsible for arranging their return travel from the destination port. The ship then takes on a new group of passengers at the South American port for a one-way journey to Miami. Last year, Endless Summer earned $4,912,000 from its round-trip cruises and $5,018,000 from its one-way cruises. How much of Endless Summer's $9,930,000 total transportation income is U.S. source income, and how much is foreign source income?

LO 13-5 3. In 1995, Jenson Investments, a Delaware corporation with a 35 percent federal tax rate, formed Bestmark, a wholly owned German subsidiary. Bestmark conducts several profitable businesses in Europe and pays the 45 percent German corporate income tax. Bestmark has never paid a dividend to its U.S. parent and has accumulated $8.2 million after-tax earnings. In early 2017, Jenson sold 100 percent of its Bestmark stock to an unrelated purchaser and recognized a $6 million gain. Compute Jenson's U.S. tax on this gain.

LO 13-1 4. Go to the Tax Foundation website (http://taxfoundation.org) and locate the State Business Tax Climate Index for fiscal year 2022. Answer the following questions for your state of residence:

   a. What is the Tax Foundation's overall ranking of your state's business tax climate?

   b. How does your state rank on the components of the tax system? On which component is your state ranked most favorably? Least favorably?

   c. What comments, if any, does the Tax Foundation report provide that are specific to your state?

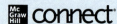 **All applicable Tax Planning Cases are available with *Connect*.**

Tax Planning Cases

LO 13-3

1. Lydell Corporation currently operates in two states, P and Q. State P has a 5 percent tax rate and uses an equally weighted three-factor apportionment formula. State Q has a 9 percent tax rate and uses an apportionment formula that double-weights the sales factor. For the current year, Lydell's state taxable income before apportionment was $1,500,000. Following is information regarding Lydell's current activity within each state:

	State P	State Q	Total
Sales	$3,000,000	$2,000,000	$5,000,000
Payroll	1,000,000	500,000	1,500,000
Average property	1,200,000	800,000	2,000,000

Lydell is considering expanding its operations by constructing a new production facility. The facility would increase Lydell's total property and payroll by $1 million and $400,000, respectively. The company projects that, as a result of the new facility, total sales would increase by $800,000, of which half of these new sales would be to customers in State P and half would be to customers in State Q. Total net income would increase by $300,000. Solely on the basis of state income tax considerations, in which state would you recommend Lydell locate the new facility?

LO 13-5, 13-6

2. Ortega Corporation wants to open a branch operation in eastern Europe and must decide between locating the branch in either Country R or Country S. Labor costs are substantially lower in Country R than in Country S. For this reason, the Country R branch would generate $700,000 annual income, and the Country S branch would generate only $550,000 annual income. However, Country R has a 20 percent corporate income tax, while Country S has a 10 percent corporate income tax. On the basis of these facts, in which country should Ortega locate its eastern European branch?

LO 13-5, 13-6, 13-7

3. Echo, Inc., which has a 21 percent U.S. tax rate, plans to expand its business into Country J. It could open a branch office, or it could create a foreign subsidiary in Country J. The branch office would generate $5,000,000 income in year 0. The foreign subsidiary would incur incremental legal costs and, as a result, would generate only $4,750,000 income in year 0. This income would be taxed at Country J's 15 percent corporate rate. Any repatriation of the subsidiary's earnings would qualify for the 100 percent dividends-received deduction. Assume none of the subsidiary's earnings would be considered GILTI or subpart F income. Should Echo open the branch office or form the subsidiary to maximize year 0 after-tax foreign earnings?

Comprehensive Problems for Part Four

1. Univex is a calendar year, accrual basis retail business. Its financial statements provide the following information for the year:

Revenues from sales of goods	$783,200
Cost of goods sold (FIFO)	(417,500)
Gross profit	$365,700
Interest income from certificates of deposit	1,300
Dividend income from IBM stock	6,720
Gain from sale of IBM stock purchased in 2000	8,615
Bad debt expense	3,900
Administrative salaries and wages	153,400
Business and employment taxes	31,000
Interest expense on debt incurred to buy inventory	5,100
Advertising	7,000
Meals not provided by a restaurant	3,780
Property insurance premiums	4,300
Depreciation	10,800
Repairs and maintenance	18,700
Supplies	4,120
Utilities	21,000
Contributions to charity	5,000

Univex's records reveal the following facts:

- Bad debt expense equals the addition to an allowance for bad debts. Actual write-offs of uncollectible accounts totaled $2,000.
- MACRS depreciation for the year was $21,240.
- Univex made no dispositions of operating assets.
- The owners did not receive compensation or withdraw any funds from Univex.
- Univex is entitled to an $1,800 general business credit.

  a. Assume Univex is a sole proprietorship. Compute net profit on Schedule C, Form 1040, and identify the items from Univex's records that do not appear on Schedule C. Complete Schedule C, Form 1040.

  b. Assume Univex is an LLC. Compute ordinary income on page 1, Form 1065, and complete Schedule K, Form 1065.

  c. Assume Univex is a corporation operating in a state without a corporate income tax. Univex made estimated federal tax payments totaling $23,500. Compute taxable income on page 1, Form 1120, calculate Univex's federal income tax, and complete page 1, Form 1120, and Schedule M-1, page 6, Form 1120.

2. Dollin, Inc. is incorporated under Virginia law and has its corporate headquarters in Richmond. Dollin is a distributor; it purchases tangible goods from manufacturers

and sells the goods to retailers. It has a branch office through which it sells goods in the United Kingdom and owns 100 percent of a French corporation (French Dollin) through which it sells goods in France. Dollin's financial records provide the following information for the year.

Before-tax net income from sales:	
Domestic sales	$ 967,900
UK sales (foreign source income)	415,000
	$1,382,900
Dividend income:	
Brio, Inc.	$ 8,400
French Dollin (foreign source income)	33,800

- Dollin pays state income tax in Virginia, North Carolina, and South Carolina. All three states tax their apportioned share of Dollin's net income from worldwide sales. Because Virginia is Dollin's commercial domicile, it also taxes Dollin's U.S. source (but not foreign source) dividend income net of any federal dividends-received deduction. The states have the following apportionment factors and tax rates:

	Apportionment Factor	Tax Rate
Virginia	43.19%	6.00%
North Carolina	11.02	7.75
South Carolina	39.52	5.00

- Dollin paid $149,200 income tax to the United Kingdom.
- Dollin elects to claim the foreign tax credit rather than to deduct foreign income taxes.

Brio, Inc. is a taxable U.S. corporation. Dollin owns 2.8 percent of Brio's stock.

- Dollin has owned 100 percent of the stock of French Dollin for 10 years. None of French Dollin's earnings are considered GILTI or subpart F income.
- Earnings of the UK branch are not considered FDII.

Solely on the basis of these facts, compute the following:

a. Dollin's state income tax for Virginia, North Carolina, and South Carolina.

b. Dollin's federal income tax. Assume that Dollin paid the state taxes during the year, and no state income tax is allocable to foreign source income.

Part Five

The Individual Taxpayer

Chapter Fourteen

The Individual Tax Formula

Learning Objectives

After studying this chapter, you should be able to:

LO 14-1. Determine an individual's filing status.

LO 14-2. List the four steps for computing individual taxable income.

LO 14-3. Explain the relationship between the standard deduction and itemized deductions.

LO 14-4. Identify the impact of the QBI deduction on taxable income.

LO 14-5. Compute the regular tax on ordinary income.

LO 14-6. Explain why a marriage penalty exists in the federal income tax system.

LO 14-7. Describe four important individual tax credits.

LO 14-8. Compute the individual alternative minimum tax (AMT).

LO 14-9. Describe the individual tax payment and return filing requirements.

Parts Three and Four are concerned with the taxation of business income. In Part Three, we learned how to measure income for federal tax purposes, and we identified the important differences between taxable income and financial statement income determined under generally accepted accounting principles (GAAP). In Part Four, we discovered that the computation of taxable income does not vary significantly across business entities, but the rate at which the income is taxed does depend on the type of entity. Income earned by a sole proprietorship or an S corporation is taxed at the individual rates. Income earned by a regular corporation is taxed at the corporate rates. Income earned by a partnership is allocated to either individual or corporate partners and taxed accordingly.

In Part Four, we observed that a corporation's business income is essentially equivalent to its taxable income. In contrast, an individual's business income is only one component of the total tax base reported on Form 1040 (U.S. Individual Income Tax Return). Unlike corporate taxpayers, people engage in many nonbusiness activities. A person engaged in a nonbusiness activity that results in an economic benefit may have to recognize the value of the benefit as income. If the activity involves an expense or loss, the person may be allowed to deduct it. Therefore, before we can compute individual taxable income and the federal tax on that income, we must turn our attention to the nonbusiness transactions in which people commonly engage.

Part Five of the text is devoted to the individual taxpayer. This chapter lays the groundwork with an overview of the individual tax base and the individual tax computation. This chapter also describes the tax payment and return filing requirements for individuals. Chapter 15 concentrates on the tax implications of compensation arrangements from the perspective of both employer and employee. Chapter 16 turns to the tax consequences of investment activities, and Chapter 17 focuses on personal activities. Throughout Part Five, we will emphasize the planning opportunities and the cash flow consequences for individual taxpayers.

FILING STATUS FOR INDIVIDUALS

Tax Talk
Subsequent to the Supreme Court's decision that the federal Defense of Marriage Act is unconstitutional, the IRS announced that same-sex couples who are legally married in a domestic or foreign jurisdiction will be treated as married for all federal tax purposes.

Every individual who is either a citizen or a permanent resident of the United States is a taxable entity who may be required to file a federal income tax return.[1] One of the first items of information that must be provided on this return is **filing status.** Filing status, which reflects an individual's marital and family situation, affects the computation of taxable income and determines the rates at which income is taxed. A taxpayer's filing status also has implications in determining eligibility for certain tax benefits.

Married Individuals and Surviving Spouses

An individual who is married on the last day of the taxable year can elect to file a **joint return** with their spouse.[2] This filing status is commonly referred to as "married filing jointly" (MFJ). A joint return reflects the combined activities of both spouses for the entire year. A married couple who file a joint return have **joint and several liability** for their tax bill. In other words, each spouse is responsible for paying the entire tax (not just one-half).[3] With respect to a joint return, any reference to the taxpayer is actually a reference to two people.

Married Filing Jointly	Mr. and Mrs. Singh were legally married under Hawaiian law on December 12, 2022. For federal tax purposes, their marital status was determined on December 31. The newlyweds filed a joint return for 2022 that reported their combined incomes for the entire calendar year.

LO 14-1
Determine an individual's filing status.

For the taxable year in which a married person dies, the surviving spouse can file a joint return with the deceased.[4] If the surviving spouse maintains a home for a dependent child, they continue to qualify as a **surviving spouse** for tax purposes for the two taxable years following the year of death.[5] A surviving spouse can use the married filing jointly tax rates for these two years.

---

[1] §7701(b) distinguishes between resident aliens and nonresident aliens. The former are subject to the same tax rules as U.S. citizens. Nonresident aliens are subject to federal income tax only if they earn U.S. source income.

[2] §6013(a).

[3] §6013(d)(3).

[4] §6013(a)(2).

[5] §2(a). A person who remarries within the year of a spouse's death does not qualify as a surviving spouse.

Surviving Spouse	Refer to the facts in the preceding example. Mrs. Singh died on September 14, 2023, and Mr. Singh has not remarried. Mr. Singh filed a 2023 joint return reflecting his deceased spouse's activities from January 1 through September 14 and his activities for the entire year. The couple had two children, ages 6 and 10, who live with their father. Mr. Singh meets the definition of surviving spouse and is entitled to compute 2024 and 2025 income tax using the married filing jointly rates.

As an alternative to joint filing, married individuals can file **separate returns** that reflect each spouse's independent activity and separate taxable income. In a few situations, individuals can derive some negligible tax benefit by filing separately, but most couples who file separate returns do so for nontax reasons.

Married Filing Separately	Mr. and Mrs. Cortez have been legally separated for six years but have not divorced because of their religious faith. They live in different cities and have no joint financial dealings or obligations. Because Mr. and Mrs. Cortez lead independent lives, they choose to file separate tax returns.

Unmarried Individuals

An individual who is unmarried on the last day of the year, who is not a surviving spouse, and who maintains a home that is the principal place of abode for a **dependent** qualifies as **head of household** for filing purposes.[6]

An unmarried individual who is neither a surviving spouse nor a head of household files as an unmarried individual or **single taxpayer.** Note that the tax law does not provide a special filing status for minor or dependent children. Regardless of age, children who earn income in their own name must file as single taxpayers, even if the income is collected and controlled by their parents.[7]

Head of Household	Refer to our example involving Mr. Singh, a surviving spouse with two dependent children living at home. In 2024 and 2025, Mr. Singh will file his tax return as a surviving spouse. In 2026, Mr. Singh's filing status will change to head of household. Mr. Singh will continue to qualify as a head of household until his children no longer qualify as his dependents, no longer live with him, or until he remarries.

Who Qualifies as a Dependent

The classification of an individual as a dependent has important implications in determining filing status. A dependent must be either a **qualifying child** or a **qualifying relative** of the taxpayer. In addition, a dependent cannot file a joint tax return with a spouse and must be a U.S. citizen or a resident of the United States, Mexico, or Canada.

The definition of *qualifying child* is much broader than the term suggests. The definition includes not only the taxpayer's children and their descendants (grandchildren and so on), but also the taxpayer's siblings (including stepsiblings) and their descendants (nieces and nephews and so on). However, for any of these relatives to be a qualifying child, the relative:

[6] §2(b).
[7] §73.

- Must have the same principal place of abode as the taxpayer for more than one-half of the year.
- Must be younger than the taxpayer and less than 19 years old or a student less than 24 years old.
- Must not have provided more than one-half of their own financial support for the year.
- Must not have filed a joint tax return with a spouse unless such return was filed only as a refund claim.

Qualifying Child

Taylor and Robbie White provide a home for their 15-year-old child, Jake, and also for their 17-year-old niece, Kendall, who has lived with the Whites for four years. This year, both Jake and Kendall had summer jobs, but their earnings represented far less than 50 percent of their financial support for the year. Both Jake and Kendall meet the definition of qualifying child and are, thus, considered dependents of the Whites for tax purposes.

Qualifying Married Child

Mr. Wiggen provides a home for his 23-year-old child Richard and Richard's 19-year-old spouse, Colleen. Richard is a full-time student at a local university. Colleen earns minimum wage as a clerk, so Mr. Wiggen provides about 80 percent of the couple's financial support. Richard and Colleen filed a joint income tax return this year only to receive a refund of the $962 tax withheld by Colleen's employer. Although married, Richard meets the definition of a qualifying child and is considered a dependent for tax purposes.

The definition of *qualifying relative* includes specific members of the taxpayer's family or stepfamily (ancestors and descendants, siblings, aunts and uncles, nieces and nephews, and various in-laws) who do not meet the definition of qualifying child. The definition also includes any person who is not related to the taxpayer but has the same principal place of abode and is a member of the taxpayer's household for the year. To qualify, the person must not have gross income in excess of $4,700 (indexed annually for inflation), and must receive more than one-half of their financial support for the year from the taxpayer.

Qualifying Relative

Ms. Vu, a single individual, has provided a home and complete financial support for Rian and Elle Anderson since 2016. Rian and Elle are the children of Ms. Vu's college roommate, who was killed in a plane crash. This year, Rian had a summer job and earned $5,790 gross salary. Elle had no gross income for the year.

Rian and Elle receive more than one-half of their support from Ms. Vu and are members of Ms. Vu's household. Elle has no gross income and meets the definition of a qualifying relative and is considered a dependent of Ms. Vu for tax purposes. At the same time, Rian does not meet the definition of a qualifying relative (and dependent) because Rian's gross income exceeds $4,700.

The classification of an individual as a dependent not only has the potential to affect a taxpayer's filing status, but it may also have implications for other provisions of the tax law, including the availability of certain tax credits.

OVERVIEW OF THE TAXABLE INCOME COMPUTATION

In this section, we will focus on the basic structure of the taxable income computation without devoting much attention to its separate elements. In subsequent chapters, we will examine the more important of these elements in detail. This overview of the taxable income computation offers a practical benefit. It will help you to read and interpret your own federal tax return. It is, after all, a legal document that individuals must sign. By doing so, they are attesting that they have examined the return and that the information on the return is "true, correct, and complete." Therefore, every person, even if using a professional tax return preparer, should understand the flow of information on a Form 1040.

The Four-Step Procedure

LO 14-2
List the four steps for computing individual taxable income.

The computation of taxable income on an individual tax return follows the same four procedural steps that are detailed in this chapter. Form 1040 is the first two pages of the tax return that essentially serve as the summary of an individual's taxable income computation. Beginning in 2018, Form 1040 was shortened and many of the items previously reported directly on Form 1040 are now first reported on separate schedules numbered 1 through 3. These schedules provide additional detail and combine similar items into a single amount to be carried collectively to the tax computation on Form 1040. In addition to these three schedules, various other schedules may be required and attached to the 1040 to provide additional detail or supporting calculations.

Step 1: Calculate Total Income

Tax Talk
In 2019, the IRS introduced the 1040-SR, U.S. Tax Return for Seniors. This form is only available for use by taxpayers who have reached the age of 65 by the last day of the tax year. The intention is to make tax filing simpler for seniors. However, seniors with more complicated tax returns may be required to file the regular 1040.

As the first step in computing taxable income, an individual must report all items of income recognized in the year. Congress has broadly defined gross income to include income realized in any form, whether in money, property, or services, unless excluded by law. Therefore, the list of income items includes salary or wage payments that the individual earned as an employee. It also includes taxable income from the individual's investments, and income from any business in which the individual engaged.

Certain income items such as wages, interest, and dividends are reported directly on Form 1040. Other income items are accumulated on Schedule 1 and then collectively reported as a single line item on Form 1040. For example, if the individual operated a sole proprietorship, the net profit will be reported on Schedule 1. Similarly, if the individual conducted business through a partnership or owned stock in an S corporation, the individual's share of the passthrough entity's income is also reported on Schedule 1. In the end, the sum of all income items on Schedule 1 are combined with those income items directly reported on Form 1040 to arrive at the individual's **total income.**

Mr. and Mrs. Volpe: Step 1

James and Nancy Volpe are a married couple who file a joint income tax return. In 2023, the couple recognized three items of income:

Mr. Volpe's salary from employer	$ 46,600
Interest income on certificates of deposit	1,400
Business income from Mrs. Volpe's sole proprietorship	56,730
Total income	$104,730

(continued)

> Because the 2023 Form 1040 is not available until late in 2023, the 2022 Form 1040 in Exhibit 14.1 is used to reference how the Volpe's 2023 Form 1040 might appear. Mr. Volpe's salary is reported on line 1a and the interest income on line 2b of Form 1040. The net business income is accumulated with other "additional income" items on Schedule 1 (Exhibit 14.2), and the total carried to line 8 of Form 1040 and included in the computation of total income. As previously discussed, Form 1040 serves as a summary of the Volpes' taxable income computation.

Step 2: Calculate Adjusted Gross Income

The second step is the calculation of the individual's adjusted gross income. **Adjusted gross income (AGI)** equals total income less the specific deductions listed on Schedule 1 as "adjustments to income."[8] (See Exhibit 14.2.) One example is the deductible portion of any self-employment tax owed by the individual.[9] We will identify other so-called **above-the-line deductions** throughout the rest of the text. (See Exhibit 17.1 in Chapter 17 for a list of above-the-line deductions.)

While AGI represents an intermediate step in the computation of individual taxable income, it is an important number in its own right. Certain individual deductions and credits are limited by reference to the taxpayer's AGI that is reported on line 11 of Form 1040.

Mr. and Mrs. Volpe: Step 2	Mrs. Volpe's 2023 self-employment tax is $8,016 (line 4, Schedule 2; see Exhibit 14.3), and $4,008 (one-half) of this tax is deductible (line 15, Schedule 1; see Exhibit 14.2) in the computation of AGI. In June, Mr. Volpe cashed in a one-year certificate of deposit after holding it for only 10 months. Because of the early withdrawal, the bank charged a $435 penalty. The Volpes are also allowed to deduct this penalty (line 18, Schedule 1). Both deductions are combined on Schedule 1 (line 26) and then transferred to Form 1040 (lines 10) as an adjustment to AGI. Consequently, line 11, Form 1040 reports that the couple's AGI is $100,287 (see Exhibit 14.1).

[8] §62 provides the list of above-the-line deductions that are subtracted in the AGI calculation.
[9] §164(f).

EXHIBIT 14.1

Source: Internal Revenue Service

Tax Talk

Did you sell sports tickets on Stub Hub? If so, you may have income to report. As part of the American Rescue Plan, Congress changed the tax rules that apply to online market platforms like Stub Hub. The goal is to better track income derived from the online market place. Previously, online companies were only required to report to the IRS income earned by its clients if the seller exceeded 200 transactions and $20,000 in income for that year. The new rules drop the threshold to $600 in income with no minimum number of transactions.

Form 1040 U.S. Individual Income Tax Return 2022 — Department of the Treasury—Internal Revenue Service — OMB No. 1545-0074 — IRS Use Only—Do not write or staple in this space.

Filing Status — Check only one box.
☐ Single ☑ Married filing jointly ☐ Married filing separately (MFS) ☐ Head of household (HOH) ☐ Qualifying surviving spouse (QSS)

If you checked the MFS box, enter the name of your spouse. If you checked the HOH or QSS box, enter the child's name if the qualifying person is a child but not your dependent.

Your first name and middle initial: James L.	Last name: Volpe
Spouse's first name and middle initial: Nancy J.	Last name: Volpe

Your social security number: 4 8 9 4 9 2 4 5 2
Spouse's social security number: 7 2 6 3 3 9 4 5 0

Home address (number and street): 10 St. Martin Circle — Apt. no.
City, town, or post office: Exeter — State: CT — ZIP code: 06429

Presidential Election Campaign — Check here if you, or your spouse if filing jointly, want $3 to go to this fund. ☐ You ☐ Spouse

Digital Assets — At any time during 2022, did you: (a) receive (as a reward, award, or payment for property or services); or (b) sell, exchange, gift, or otherwise dispose of a digital asset (or a financial interest in a digital asset)? ☐ Yes ☑ No

Standard Deduction — Someone can claim: ☐ You as a dependent ☐ Your spouse as a dependent ☐ Spouse itemizes on a separate return or you were a dual-status alien

Age/Blindness — You: ☐ Were born before January 2, 1958 ☐ Are blind — Spouse: ☐ Was born before January 2, 1958 ☐ Is blind

Dependents

(1) First name Last name	(2) Social security number	(3) Relationship to you	(4) Child tax credit	Credit for other dependents
Sara M. Volpe	2 4 9 8 7 1 3 2 2	daughter	☑	☐
Shana E. Volpe	3 1 2 2 2 4 6 7 6	daughter	☑	☐

Income

1a	Total amount from Form(s) W-2, box 1	46,600
1b	Household employee wages not reported on Form(s) W-2	
1c	Tip income not reported on line 1a	
1d	Medicaid waiver payments not reported on Form(s) W-2	
1e	Taxable dependent care benefits from Form 2441, line 26	
1f	Employer-provided adoption benefits from Form 8839, line 29	
1g	Wages from Form 8919, line 6	
1h	Other earned income	
1i	Nontaxable combat pay election	
1z	Add lines 1a through 1h	46,600
2a	Tax-exempt interest	2b Taxable interest: 1,400
3a	Qualified dividends	3b Ordinary dividends
4a	IRA distributions	4b Taxable amount
5a	Pensions and annuities	5b Taxable amount
6a	Social security benefits	6b Taxable amount
7	Capital gain or (loss). Attach Schedule D if required. If not required, check here ☐	
8	Other income from Schedule 1, line 10	56,730
9	Add lines 1z, 2b, 3b, 4b, 5b, 6b, 7, and 8. This is your **total income**	104,730
10	Adjustments to income from Schedule 1, line 26	4,443
11	Subtract line 10 from line 9. This is your **adjusted gross income**	100,287
12	Standard deduction or itemized deductions (from Schedule A)	28,070
13	Qualified business income deduction from Form 8995 or Form 8995-A	10,544
14	Add lines 12 and 13	38,614
15	Subtract line 14 from line 11. If zero or less, enter -0-. This is your **taxable income**	61,673

Standard Deduction for—
• Single or Married filing separately, $12,950
• Married filing jointly or Qualifying surviving spouse, $25,900
• Head of household, $19,400

For Disclosure, Privacy Act, and Paperwork Reduction Act Notice, see separate instructions. Cat. No. 11320B — Form **1040** (2022)

Form 1040 (2022) — Page 2

Tax and Credits

16	Tax (see instructions). Check if any from Form(s): 1 ☐ 8814 2 ☐ 4972 3 ☐	6,961
17	Amount from Schedule 2, line 3	
18	Add lines 16 and 17	6,961
19	Child tax credit or credit for other dependents from Schedule 8812	4,000
20	Amount from Schedule 3, line 8	870
21	Add lines 19 and 20	4,870
22	Subtract line 21 from line 18. If zero or less, enter -0-	2,091
23	Other taxes, including self-employment tax, from Schedule 2, line 21	8,016
24	Add lines 22 and 23. This is your **total tax**	10,107

Payments

25	Federal income tax withheld from:		
25a	Form(s) W-2	3,496	
25b	Form(s) 1099		
25c	Other forms		
25d	Add lines 25a through 25c		3,496
26	2022 estimated tax payments and amount applied from 2021 return		8,000
27	Earned income credit (EIC)		
28	Additional child tax credit from Schedule 8812		
29	American opportunity credit from Form 8863, line 8		
30	Reserved for future use		
31	Amount from Schedule 3, line 15		
32	Add lines 27, 28, 29, and 31. These are your total other payments and refundable credits		
33	Add lines 25d, 26, and 32. These are your **total payments**		11,496

Refund

34	If line 33 is more than line 24, subtract line 24 from line 33. This is the amount you **overpaid**	1,389
35a	Amount of line 34 you want **refunded to you**. If Form 8888 is attached, check here ☐	
b	Routing number — c Type: ☐ Checking ☐ Savings	
d	Account number	
36	Amount of line 34 you want applied to your 2023 estimated tax	1,389

Amount You Owe

37	Subtract line 33 from line 24. This is the **amount you owe**. For details on how to pay, go to www.irs.gov/Payments or see instructions	
38	Estimated tax penalty (see instructions)	

Third Party Designee — Do you want to allow another person to discuss this return with the IRS? See instructions. ☐ Yes. Complete below. ☐ No
Designee's name — Phone no. — Personal identification number (PIN)

Sign Here — Under penalties of perjury, I declare that I have examined this return and accompanying schedules and statements, and to the best of my knowledge and belief, they are true, correct, and complete. Declaration of preparer (other than taxpayer) is based on all information of which preparer has any knowledge.
Your signature — Date — Your occupation — If the IRS sent you an Identity Protection PIN, enter it here
Spouse's signature. If a joint return, both must sign. — Date — Spouse's occupation — If the IRS sent your spouse an Identity Protection PIN, enter it here
Phone no. — Email address

Paid Preparer Use Only
Preparer's name — Preparer's signature — Date — PTIN — Check if: ☐ Self-employed
Firm's name — Phone no.
Firm's address — Firm's EIN

Go to www.irs.gov/Form1040 for instructions and the latest information. — Form **1040** (2022)

EXHIBIT 14.2

Source: Internal Revenue Service

SCHEDULE 1 (Form 1040) Department of the Treasury Internal Revenue Service	**Additional Income and Adjustments to Income** Attach to Form 1040, 1040-SR, or 1040-NR. Go to *www.irs.gov/Form1040* for instructions and the latest information.	OMB No. 1545-0074 **2022** Attachment Sequence No. **01**

Name(s) shown on Form 1040, 1040-SR, or 1040-NR	Your social security number
James L. and Nancy J. Volpe	789 49 2452

Part I Additional Income

1	Taxable refunds, credits, or offsets of state and local income taxes	**1**	
2a	Alimony received	**2a**	
b	Date of original divorce or separation agreement (see instructions): _____		
3	Business income or (loss). Attach Schedule C	**3**	56,730
4	Other gains or (losses). Attach Form 4797	**4**	
5	Rental real estate, royalties, partnerships, S corporations, trusts, etc. Attach Schedule E .	**5**	
6	Farm income or (loss). Attach Schedule F	**6**	
7	Unemployment compensation	**7**	
8	Other income:		
a	Net operating loss	**8a** ( )	
b	Gambling	**8b**	
c	Cancellation of debt	**8c**	
d	Foreign earned income exclusion from Form 2555	**8d** ( )	
e	Income from Form 8853	**8e**	
f	Income from Form 8889	**8f**	
g	Alaska Permanent Fund dividends	**8g**	
h	Jury duty pay	**8h**	
i	Prizes and awards	**8i**	
j	Activity not engaged in for profit income	**8j**	
k	Stock options	**8k**	
l	Income from the rental of personal property if you engaged in the rental for profit but were not in the business of renting such property . . .	**8l**	
m	Olympic and Paralympic medals and USOC prize money (see instructions)	**8m**	
n	Section 951(a) inclusion (see instructions)	**8n**	
o	Section 951A(a) inclusion (see instructions)	**8o**	
p	Section 461(l) excess business loss adjustment	**8p**	
q	Taxable distributions from an ABLE account (see instructions) . . .	**8q**	
r	Scholarship and fellowship grants not reported on Form W-2 . . .	**8r**	
s	Nontaxable amount of Medicaid waiver payments included on Form 1040, line 1a or 1d	**8s** ( )	
t	Pension or annuity from a nonqualifed deferred compensation plan or a nongovernmental section 457 plan	**8t**	
u	Wages earned while incarcerated	**8u**	
z	Other income. List type and amount: _____ _____	**8z**	
9	Total other income. Add lines 8a through 8z	**9**	
10	Combine lines 1 through 7 and 9. Enter here and on Form 1040, 1040-SR, or 1040-NR, line 8	**10**	56,730

For Paperwork Reduction Act Notice, see your tax return instructions.   Cat. No. 71479F   Schedule 1 (Form 1040) 2022

EXHIBIT 14.2
(continued)

Schedule 1 (Form 1040) 2022

Page **2**

Part II Adjustments to Income

11	Educator expenses	**11**	
12	Certain business expenses of reservists, performing artists, and fee-basis government officials. Attach Form 2106	**12**	
13	Health savings account deduction. Attach Form 8889	**13**	
14	Moving expenses for members of the Armed Forces. Attach Form 3903	**14**	
15	Deductible part of self-employment tax. Attach **Schedule SE**	**15**	4,008
16	Self-employed SEP, SIMPLE, and qualified plans	**16**	
17	Self-employed health insurance deduction	**17**	
18	Penalty on early withdrawal of savings	**18**	435
19a	Alimony paid	**19a**	
b	Recipient's SSN		
c	Date of original divorce or separation agreement (see instructions): _____		
20	IRA deduction	**20**	
21	Student loan interest deduction	**21**	
22	Reserved for future use	**22**	
23	Archer MSA deduction	**23**	
24	Other adjustments:		

a	Jury duty pay (see instructions)	**24a**	
b	Deductible expenses related to income reported on line 8l from the rental of personal property engaged in for profit	**24b**	
c	Nontaxable amount of the value of Olympic and Paralympic medals and USOC prize money reported on line 8m	**24c**	
d	Reforestation amortization and expenses	**24d**	
e	Repayment of supplemental unemployment benefits under the Trade Act of 1974	**24e**	
f	Contributions to section 501(c)(18)(D) pension plans	**24f**	
g	Contributions by certain chaplains to section 403(b) plans	**24g**	
h	Attorney fees and court costs for actions involving certain unlawful discrimination claims (see instructions)	**24h**	
i	Attorney fees and court costs you paid in connection with an award from the IRS for information you provided that helped the IRS detect tax law violations	**24i**	
j	Housing deduction from Form 2555	**24j**	
k	Excess deductions of section 67(e) expenses from Schedule K-1 (Form 1041)	**24k**	
z	Other adjustments. List type and amount: _____	**24z**	

25	Total other adjustments. Add lines 24a through 24z	**25**	
26	Add lines 11 through 23 and 25. These are your **adjustments to income**. Enter here and on Form 1040 or 1040-SR, line 10, or Form 1040-NR, line 10a	**26**	4,443

Schedule 1 (Form 1040) 2022

EXHIBIT 14.3

Source: Internal Revenue
Service

SCHEDULE 2			
(Form 1040)			OMB No. 1545-0074

SCHEDULE 2 (Form 1040) Department of the Treasury Internal Revenue Service	**Additional Taxes** Attach to Form 1040, 1040-SR, or 1040-NR. Go to *www.irs.gov/Form1040* for instructions and the latest information.	OMB No. 1545-0074 **2022** Attachment Sequence No. **02**
Name(s) shown on Form 1040, 1040-SR, or 1040-NR James L. and Nancy J. Volpe		Your social security number 789 49 2452

Part I   Tax

1	Alternative minimum tax. Attach Form 6251	**1**	
2	Excess advance premium tax credit repayment. Attach Form 8962	**2**	
3	Add lines 1 and 2. Enter here and on Form 1040, 1040-SR, or 1040-NR, line 17 . .	**3**	

Part II   Other Taxes

4	Self-employment tax. Attach Schedule SE		**4**	8,016
5	Social security and Medicare tax on unreported tip income. Attach Form 4137	**5**		
6	Uncollected social security and Medicare tax on wages. Attach Form 8919	**6**		
7	Total additional social security and Medicare tax. Add lines 5 and 6		**7**	
8	Additional tax on IRAs or other tax-favored accounts. Attach Form 5329 if required. If not required, check here . . . . ☐		**8**	
9	Household employment taxes. Attach Schedule H		**9**	
10	Repayment of first-time homebuyer credit. Attach Form 5405 if required		**10**	
11	Additional Medicare Tax. Attach Form 8959		**11**	
12	Net investment income tax. Attach Form 8960		**12**	
13	Uncollected social security and Medicare or RRTA tax on tips or group-term life insurance from Form W-2, box 12		**13**	
14	Interest on tax due on installment income from the sale of certain residential lots and timeshares		**14**	
15	Interest on the deferred tax on gain from certain installment sales with a sales price over $150,000		**15**	
16	Recapture of low-income housing credit. Attach Form 8611		**16**	

(continued on page 2)

For Paperwork Reduction Act Notice, see your tax return instructions.   Cat. No. 71478U   Schedule 2 (Form 1040) 2022

Step 3: Subtract Standard Deduction or Itemized Deductions

LO 14-3

Explain the relationship between the standard deduction and itemized deductions.

In the third step of the taxable income computation, AGI is reduced by the *greater of* a standard deduction or allowable itemized deductions.

Standard Deduction

The **standard deduction** is a function of filing status. The basic deductions for 2023 are

Married filing jointly and surviving spouses	$27,700
Married filing separately	13,850
Head of household	20,800
Single	13,850

An individual who has reached age 65 by the last day of the year is entitled to an additional deduction. An individual who is legally blind is also entitled to an additional deduction. For 2023, the additional deductions are

Married filing jointly or separately and surviving spouse	$1,500
Head of household or single	1,850

Both the basic and the additional standard deductions are indexed for inflation and may change every year.[10]

---
[10] §63(c) and (f).

Standard Deduction	Thomas and Tyrell O'Neill are legally married and file a joint return. Thomas is 67 years old and legally blind; Tyrell is 66. Their standard deduction for 2023 is $30,100.

Basic standard deduction	$27,700
Additional deductions for Thomas:	
Age 65 or older	1,500
Legally blind	1,500
Additional deduction for Tyrell:	
Age 65 or older	1,500
	$32,200

Limited Standard Deduction for Dependent

In the case of an individual who qualifies as a dependent of another taxpayer (see discussion of dependents on page 14–5), the basic standard deduction on the dependent's own return may be limited. In 2023, the basic standard deduction may not exceed the *greater* of (1) $1,250 or (2) the dependent's earned income (wages, salary, or self-employment income) plus $400. (Both numbers in this limitation are indexed annually for inflation.)

Limited Standard Deduction	Jamar, age 17, and Janelle, age 15, are claimed as dependents on their parents' 2023 tax return. In 2023, Jamar earned $3,940 wages from a summer job, and Janelle earned $586 from babysitting. Jamar and Janelle each own a savings account funded with a small inheritance from their grandmother. The 2023 interest income on each account was $712.
	Jamar's AGI is $4,652 ($3,940 wages + $712 interest income), and Jamar's standard deduction as a single taxpayer ($13,850) is limited to $4,340 ($3,940 earned income + $400). Janelle's AGI is $1,298 ($586 babysitting income + $712 interest income), and Janelle's standard deduction is limited to $1,250.

Itemized Deductions

As a category, **itemized deductions** include any deduction allowed to an individual that cannot be subtracted in the calculation of AGI.[11] Individuals elect to itemize (i.e., subtract itemized deductions from AGI) only if their total deduction amount exceeds the standard deduction for the year. This situation is the exception rather than the rule, with only a minority of taxpayers benefiting by itemizing. Itemized deductions are reported on Schedule A, Form 1040. (See Exhibit 17.1 in Chapter 17 for a list of itemized deductions.)

Itemized deductions create a tax savings only if the individual elects to itemize. In a year in which the individual claims the standard deduction, any itemized deductions yield no tax benefit.

Election to Itemize	Assume that the O'Neills in a previous example accumulated $19,250 of itemized deductions in 2023. Because this total is less than their $32,200 standard deduction ($27,700 + $1,500 + $1,500 + $1,500), they use the standard deduction to compute taxable income, and their itemized deductions yield no tax benefit.
	Now assume that their itemized deductions totaled $36,400. In this case, they would elect to itemize by subtracting this amount from AGI. If their marginal tax rate is 32 percent, their itemized deductions save $11,648 in tax ($36,400 × 32 percent). However, if they had not itemized, their standard deduction would have saved $10,304 ($32,200 × 32 percent). Consequently, the incremental tax savings from the itemized deductions is only $1,344 ($4,200 excess itemized deductions × 32 percent).

---

[11] §63(d).

This example leads to a key observation about individual tax deductions. A deduction listed as an above-the-line deduction *always* reduces taxable income. A deduction that must be itemized may have limited or even no effect on taxable income. Congress decides which deductions are above-the-line and which deductions are itemized. The classification often reflects tax policy concerns and can change from year to year. For example, individuals are allowed to deduct attorney fees and other costs of lawsuits based on unlawful discrimination by the individual's employer. Before the enactment of the American Jobs Creation Act of 2004, this deduction was an itemized deduction. The act reclassified it as an above-the-line deduction was intended to improve the equity of the tax law for individuals involved in such lawsuits.

Bunching Itemized Deductions

People can often maximize the value of their itemized deductions through a tax planning technique called **bunching.** By controlling the timing of their deductible expenses, they can concentrate the deductions into a single year. The objective is to create a critical mass of itemized deductions, the total of which exceeds their standard deduction. The following example illustrates this technique.

Bunching of Itemized Deductions	Rasheed, a single taxpayer with a 24 percent marginal tax rate, routinely incurs $12,200 annual expenses qualifying as itemized deductions. This amount is less than the standard deduction. If Rasheed's pattern of expenses is level from year to year, the standard deductions provide more benefit than itemizing, and no tax benefit is derived from the expenses. In contrast, if Rasheed can shift $4,000 of the expenses from 2023 to 2024, it makes sense to take the standard deduction in 2023 and elect to itemize in 2024.

	Level Pattern of Itemized Deductions	**Bunched Deductions**
2023:		
Itemized deductions	$12,200	$ 8,200
Standard deduction (single)	13,850	13,850
2024:		
Itemized deductions	$12,200	$16,200
Standard deduction (single)	13,850	(13,850)
Itemized deductions in excess of standard deduction		$ 2,350
		.24
Tax savings from bunching		$ 564

How can Rasheed shift deductible expenses from 2023 to 2024? As a cash basis taxpayer, deductions are recognized in the year of payment. By *postponing* payment of an expense from December of 2023 until January of 2024, the deduction is shifted to the next year. At the end of 2024, Rasheed may want to *accelerate* payment of deductible expenses that would normally be paid in 2025, when Rasheed will again take the standard deduction under a cyclical bunching strategy.

Mr. and Mrs. Volpe: Step 3	During 2023, Mr. and Mrs. Volpe incurred the following expenses that qualify as itemized deductions:

Connecticut individual income tax	$5,140
Real estate tax on the Volpes' personal residence	3,920
Home mortgage interest	12,080
Charitable donations	6,930

These deductions are specifically listed and totaled on Schedule A, a supporting statement to their Form 1040, intended to provide additional detail. Because the total itemized deductions of $28,070 exceeded the standard deduction of $27,700, they elect to itemize and this total is carried to their Form 1040, line 12, as a subtraction from AGI (Exhibit 14.1).

Step 4: Subtract the QBI Deduction Amount

LO 14-4
Identify the impact of the QBI deduction on taxable income.

As the fourth and last step in the computation of taxable income, AGI is reduced by the QBI deduction amount. This below-the-line deduction was added under the Tax Cuts and Jobs Act of 2017 with the objective of lowering the effective tax rate on business profits earned by a passthrough entity. In broad terms, the deduction is equal to 20 percent of **qualified business income,** or **QBI.** QBI is calculated as the amount earned by an individual taxpayer through a sole proprietorship, partnership, or S corporation less (1) the deductible portion of self-employment taxes, (2) the self-employed health insurance deduction, and (3) the deduction for contributions to qualified retirement plans.

Various other limitations and exceptions apply in the determination and computation of qualified business income. However, they are beyond the scope of this chapter. Chapter 10 describes the QBI deduction in more detail.

Mr. and Mrs. Volpe: Step 4	Mrs. Volpe has a small flower shop, operated as a sole proprietorship. In 2023, this business generated $56,730 of taxable income, which meets the definition of qualified business income. The Volpes claim a QBI deduction of $10,544 (20 percent of QBI) on line 13 of their Form 1040 (Exhibit 14.1). QBI is $52,722 ($56,730 less the $4,008 deduction for self-employment tax).

The Taxable Income Formula

The four-step procedure for computing individual taxable income can be summarized as follows:[12]

Total income
(Above-the-line deductions)
Adjusted gross income
(Standard or itemized deductions)
(QBI deduction)
Taxable income

While the computation of taxable income may not be completely intuitive, it reflects policy objectives. The AGI reported on Form 1040 is the closest gauge of a taxpayer's

[12] The Consolidated Appropriations Act of 2021 provides a narrowly defined opportunity for individual taxpayers to increase their standard deduction for net disaster losses. Additional details provided in Chapter 17.

disposable income. As such, it serves as the measure used to determine eligibility for a variety of tax benefits. On the other hand, the standard deduction is not based on monetary expenses or economic losses and is unrelated to specific cash flows. The purpose of the standard deduction is to shelter a base amount of disposable income from tax. The QBI deduction is intended to satisfy yet a completely different objective of lowering the effective tax rate on business profits earned by passthrough entities. If a person's AGI is less than the tax-free threshold represented by the combined standard deduction and the QBI deduction, taxable income is zero.

Mr. and Mrs. Volpe: Taxable Income

Using the previous examples (Steps 1 through 4), Mr. and Mrs. Volpe's Form 1040 (Exhibit 14.1) would reflect the following computation of taxable income:

Total income (line 9, 1040)	$104,730
Above-the-line deductions (line 10, 1040)	(4,443)
AGI (line 11, 1040)	$100,287
Itemized deductions (line 12, 1040)	(28,070)
QBI deduction (line 13, 1040)	(10,544)
Taxable income (line 15, 1040)	$ 61,673

COMPUTING INDIVIDUAL TAX

The tax on individual taxable income is computed under the rate schedule determined by the taxpayer's filing status.[13] These rate schedules are adjusted annually for inflation. Below are the 2023 rate schedules.

Individual Tax Rate Schedules

Married Filing Jointly and Surviving Spouse

If taxable income is:	The tax is:
Not over $22,000	10% of taxable income
Over $22,200 but not over $89,450	$2,200 + 12% of excess over $22,000
Over $89,450 but not over $190,750	$10,294 + 22% of excess over $89,450
Over $190,750 but not over $364,200	$32,580 + 24% of excess over $190,750
Over $364,200 but not over $462,500	$74,208 + 32% of excess over $364,200
Over $462,500 but not over $693,750	$105,664 + 35% of excess over $462,500
Over $693,750	$186,601.5 + 37% of excess over $693,750

Married Filing Separately

If taxable income is:	The tax is:
Not over $11,000	10% of taxable income
Over $11,000 but not over $44,725	$1,100 + 12% of excess over $11,000
Over $44,725 but not over $95,375	$5,147 + 22% of excess over $44,725
Over $95,375 but not over $182,100	$16,290 + 24% of excess over $95,375
Over $182,100 but not over $231,250	$37,104 + 32% of excess over $182,100
Over $231,250 but not over $346,875	$52,832 + 35% of excess over $231,250
Over $346,875	$93,300.75 + 37% of excess over $346,875

[13] Form 1040 instructions require individuals with taxable incomes less than $100,000 to use a Tax Table to compute tax. These tables are derived from the rate schedules and eliminate the arithmetic required to use the schedules.

Heads of Household

If taxable income is:	The tax is:
Not over $15,700	10% of taxable income
Over $15,700 but not over $59,850	$1,570 + 12% of excess over $15,700
Over $59,850 but not over $95,350	$6,868 + 22% of excess over $59,850
Over $95,350 but not over $182,100	$14,678 + 24% of excess over $95,350
Over $182,100 but not over $231,250	$35,498 + 32% of excess over $182,100
Over $231,250 but not over $578,100	$51,226 + 35% of excess over $231,250
Over $578,100	$172,623.5 + 37% of excess over $578,100

Single

If taxable income is:	The tax is:
Not over $11,000	10% of taxable income
Over $11,000 but not over $44,725	$1,100 + 12% of excess over $11,000
Over $44,725 but not over $95,375	$5,147 + 22% of excess over $44,725
Over $95,375 but not over $182,100	$16,290 + 24% of excess over $95,375
Over $182,100 but not over $231,250	$37,104 + 32% of excess over $182,100
Over $231,250 but not over $578,125	$52,832+ 35% of excess over $231,250
Over $578,125	$174,238.25 + 37% of excess over $578,125

LO 14-5
Compute the regular tax on ordinary income.

Each tax rate schedule consists of seven income brackets with progressively higher rates. These brackets are listed in the left column. The right column gives the *cumulative* tax on the income in all lower brackets and the marginal rate for the bracket. To compute the tax on a given amount of income, refer to the left column to determine the income bracket and the *excess* taxable income over the bracket floor. Refer to the right column and multiply the *excess* by the marginal rate for the bracket. Add the result to the cumulative tax to equal the total tax on the income.

Tax on Ordinary Income

Mr. and Mrs. Agawa (married filing jointly), Mr. Benevides (head of household), and Ms. Croll (single) each report $203,000 taxable income for 2023. Their tax (rounding up to whole dollars) is computed as follows:

	Mr. and Mrs. Agawa (Married Filing Jointly)	Mr. Benevides (Head of Household)	Ms. Croll (Single)
Taxable income	$203,000	$203,000	$203,000
Bracket floor	(190,750)	(182,100)	(182,100)
Excess over floor	$ 12,250	$ 20,900	$ 20,900
Bracket rate	.24	.32	.32
	$ 2,940	$ 6,688	$ 6,688
Cumulative tax	32,580	35,498	37,104
Tax	$ 35,520	$ 42,186	$ 43,792

Preferential Rates

The tax computation must take into account any preferential rate applying to dividends or capital gains included in taxable income. The complicated preferential rate structure is discussed in detail in Chapter 16. This next example illustrates the basic effect of a preferential rate on the tax computation.

Tax on Ordinary Income and Capital Gain

Assume that Ms. Croll (single) recognized a $25,000 capital gain as part of taxable income. This gain is eligible for a 15 percent preferential tax rate. Consequently, Ms. Croll's 2023 tax is computed as follows:

Taxable income	$203,000
Capital gain	(25,000)
Ordinary income portion of taxable income	$178,000
Bracket floor	(95,375)
Excess over floor	$ 82,625
Bracket rate	.24
	$ 19,830
Cumulative tax	16,290
Tax on ordinary income	$ 36,128
Tax on capital gain ($25,000 × 15%)	3,750
Tax	$ 39,870

The 15 percent capital gains rate reduced Ms. Croll's tax from $43,792 to $39,870 for a $3,922 tax savings.

The Elusive Marginal Tax Rate

The marginal tax rate is the percentage applying to the *next* dollar of taxable income. Obviously, taxpayers must know their marginal rate to compute tax costs and after-tax cash flows from any income-generating transaction. Individuals can determine their apparent marginal rate by comparing their projected taxable income for the year to the applicable rate schedule. For instance, if a single taxpayer estimates 2023 income to be $250,000, referring to the rate schedule suggests a statutory marginal rate of 35 percent. However, this apparent marginal rate is not necessarily the actual marginal rate.

When an individual recognizes an additional dollar of income, AGI generally increases by one dollar. This increase changes the calculation of any deduction or credit limited by reference to AGI. Later in this chapter, we will learn about several important tax credits that are reduced or even eliminated as AGI climbs above a threshold level. In subsequent chapters, we will encounter more of these AGI-sensitive items. If an additional dollar of AGI triggers a decrease in one or more deductions or credits, the tax cost of such dollar is greater than the apparent marginal rate would suggest.

Increased AGI and Marginal Tax Rate

Priya, a single individual with an apparent 35 percent marginal rate, needs to calculate the estimated after-tax cash flow from a transaction expected to generate $10,000 taxable cash flow. The $10,000 increase in AGI will cause a certain itemized deduction to decrease by $700. Consequently, the $10,000 incremental income will result in $10,700 more taxable income and $3,745 more tax ($10,700 × 35 percent). Priya's actual marginal rate on the incremental income will be 37.45 percent, and the estimated after-tax cash flow from the transaction will be $6,255 ($10,000 cash − $3,745 tax cost).

The lesson of this example is that the individual marginal tax rate can be an elusive number. The inverse relationship between AGI and certain deductions and credits can cause a hidden surtax not reflected by the apparent statutory rate. The only sure way to calculate the incremental tax from a proposed transaction is to "run the numbers" by incorporating the tax consequences of the transaction into a complete tax calculation.

Some Perspective on Marginal Rate	Currently, the top statutory rate for the U.S. individual income tax is 37 percent. This rate compares favorably with the national rates in other industrialized countries. For instance, the top rate in Austria is 55 percent and 45 percent in the United Kingdom, Germany, and Australia. From a historical perspective, the 37 percent rate seems like a bargain compared to the top federal rate in 1951 (92 percent), 1964 (77 percent), and even 1981 (50 percent).

Marginal Rate on Child's Unearned Income

Before leaving the topic of marginal tax rate, we introduce the special rule for computing tax on the unearned income of certain children. Recall from earlier in the chapter that the law is quite restrictive with respect to individuals who file a tax return in their own right but who are a dependent of another taxpayer. Such individuals (typically children) are allowed only a limited standard deduction. For any child under the age of 19, the tax law contains an additional restriction.[14] The child's unearned (investment) income in excess of an inflation-adjusted base amount ($2,500 in 2023) is taxed at the parent's marginal tax rate. This particular computation is popularly described as the **kiddie tax.**

Enacted in the 1980s, the intent of the kiddie tax is to limit the ability of wealthy parents to shift income from their high tax bracket to a child's low tax bracket by gifting investment assets to the child. The Tax Cuts and Jobs Act made significant modifications to the computation of the kiddie tax. Arguably, the most significant modification was that, effective in 2018, net unearned income would be taxed at the same rate as estates and trusts rather than the parent's marginal tax rate. The result was a significant increase in tax liability for certain taxpayers. This change was quickly repealed, largely because of the negative tax consequence to certain types of government payments. In December 2019, Congress voted to return to the old kiddie tax rules starting in 2020, also allowing taxpayers to retroactively apply the old rules to tax years 2018 and 2019.

Kiddie Tax	Ben Lee, 17 years old, meets the definition of a dependent for tax purposes. In 2023, Ben reported $500 of income from working at a summer camp and $12,750 interest from a trust fund established by Ben's grandparents. Ben's parents are subject to a 35 percent marginal tax rate. Ben's tax is computed as follows:

Ben's total income	$13,250
Ben's standard deduction	(1,250)
Ben's total taxable income	$12,000
Ben's unearned income	$12,750
Base amount	(2,500)
Taxable income subject to kiddie tax	$10,250
Parents marginal rate	35%
Kiddie tax	$ 3,588
Tax on remaining income — Single rate 10% ($12,000 − $10,250 subject to kiddie tax)	175
Total tax on Ben's Form 1040	$ 3,763

[14] §1(g). The kiddie tax also applies to certain children between the ages of 18 and 24 whose annual earned income doesn't exceed 50 percent of their annual support. It doesn't apply to a child if both parents are deceased at the close of the year or if the child files a joint return with a spouse.

The Marriage Penalty Dilemma

LO 14-6
Explain why a marriage penalty exists in the federal income tax system.

In our example in which a married couple (Mr. and Mrs. Agawa) and a single individual (Ms. Croll) both had $203,000 ordinary taxable income, the couple's tax was $35,520, while the single's tax was $43,792. The rationale for this difference is straightforward: Two people cannot live as well as one on the same income. Mr. and Mrs. Agawa presumably have less financial ability to pay than Ms. Croll and should pay less tax.

Now consider the following situation. Elijah and Destiny are unmarried individuals with identical salaries and no other sources of income. They each report taxable income of $350,000 on their respective returns and are subject to tax of $94,395. Between these two single individuals, their combined tax liability is $188,790. If instead, they were to marry and file a joint return reporting $700,000 of taxable income, their joint tax liability would be $188,914. Comparing this number with the combined tax of $188,790 that they would pay as two single taxpayers, the couple might reasonably assert that they are paying a $124 penalty for being married. Overall, this comparison shows that the federal income tax system is not marriage neutral. However, the majority of taxpayers are not subject to this marriage penalty because, under the current system, the amount of income in all but the 35 percent and 37 percent brackets for married couples is exactly twice the amount of income in the same brackets for single taxpayers. Furthermore, the standard deduction for married couples is exactly twice the standard deduction for single taxpayers. The following example provides the same analysis for lower-income taxpayers and illustrates that the combined tax (each filing as a single individual) is the same as if married filing a joint return.

Why can't Congress design an income tax system that is *completely* marriage neutral? The answer to this tax policy conundrum can be demonstrated by a simple set of facts. Assume that four people—A, B, C, and D—are taxed under a hypothetical system consisting of a 20 percent rate on income up to $30,000 and a 30 percent rate on income in excess of $30,000. The following table presents the relevant information if A, B, C, and D each file their own tax return:

Taxpayer	Taxable Income	Tax
A	$30,000	$ 6,000
B	30,000	6,000
C	10,000	2,000
D	50,000	12,000

Marriage Penalty Relief

In 2023, Kelli earned a $36,000 salary, and Kelli's fiancé, Bob, earned $32,300 in wages. They have no other income. Here is a comparison of their combined tax burden if they marry before the end of the year or if they remain single.

	Married Filing Jointly	Single (Kelli)	Single (Bob)
AGI	$ 68,300	$36,000	$32,300
Standard deduction	(27,700)	(13,850)	(13,850)
Taxable income	$ 40,600	$22,150	$18,450
Tax	$ 4,432	= $ 2,438	+ $ 1,194

The couple's tax if they marry and file a joint return would equal their combined tax if they don't marry and file as single taxpayers. Thus, the income tax is a neutral factor in their wedding plans.

Now assume that A marries B and C marries D. If the system requires the couples to file joint returns, the result is as follows:

Taxpayer	Taxable Income	Tax
AB	$60,000	$15,000
CD	60,000	15,000

As married couples, AB and CD have equal taxable incomes and equal tax. For couple AB, this tax is $3,000 more than their combined tax as single people. Because A and B aggregated their incomes on the joint return, $30,000 of that income was boosted out of the 20 percent bracket into the 30 percent bracket. As a result, the tax increased by $3,000. For couple CD, the tax on their joint return is $1,000 more than their combined single tax. In CD's case, the aggregation of their incomes boosted only $10,000 into the higher tax bracket.

The marriage penalties on AB and CD disappear if each spouse could file as a single taxpayer. Couple AB would file two returns, each reporting $6,000 tax, for a $12,000 combined tax burden. Couple CD would also file two returns, with C's return reporting $2,000 tax, and D's return reporting $12,000 tax. Couple CD's tax burden would be $14,000, *$2,000 more than Couple AB's tax burden.* Couple CD could certainly protest that this result is unfair because it violates the standard of horizontal equity. In our society, married couples are regarded as an economic unit, and their financial ability to pay tax should be a function of their aggregate income. Therefore, couples with the same aggregate income (such as AB and CD) should pay the same tax, regardless of which spouse earned the income. As this set of facts illustrates, a progressive income tax system that allows married couples to file joint returns can be marriage neutral or horizontally equitable—but not both.

INDIVIDUAL TAX CREDITS

Individuals can reduce their tax by tax credits for which they are eligible. A credit reduces the tax liability one dollar for each dollar of credit. Most credits are *nonrefundable,* meaning that the tax credit may only reduce the taxpayers liability to zero and any remaining amount is forfeited. In the case of a *refundable* credit, taxpayers may receive a refund of the credit that exceeds precredit income tax.

People who conduct business as a sole proprietorship or in a passthrough entity are entitled to the general business credit discussed in Chapter 11. People who pay foreign income tax are entitled to the foreign tax credit discussed in Chapter 13. In addition to these credits, individuals may qualify for many other credits, four of which are described in the following paragraphs.

Child Credit

The **child credit** was first created in 1997 to ease the financial burden of families with children. In 2018, the Tax Cuts and Jobs Act made important changes to this provision. Not only was the maximum credit increased to $2,000 per child, the Act also provided that up to $1,400 of the credit may be a refundable credit. In the wake of financial challenges induced by the COVID-19 pandemic, the American Rescue Plan of 2021 further expanded the credit **for one year** by again increasing the size of the available credit, making the credit fully refundable, and providing a mechanism where families could receive government payments toward the credit during the tax year, rather than waiting to claim when filing their taxes.

Because the child credit has broad political appeal, it has repeatedly been a key initiative in legislation targeted at providing financial relief to taxpayers.

The child tax credit expansion under the American Rescue Plan of 2021 was not extended in 2022. Therefore, the child credit reverted back to the structure before changes under the Tax Cuts and Job Act. This means **that eligible taxpayers may claim** a maximum available credit of $2,000 for each dependent child under the age of 17 at the close of the taxable year, and a $500 credit for certain non-child dependents.[15] The credit will phase out for high-income taxpayers. For taxpayers filing a joint return, the total credit is reduced by $50 for every $1,000 increment (or portion thereof) of AGI in excess of $400,000. For single individuals and heads of households, the credit phaseout begins when AGI exceeds $200,000. Up to $1,500 of the credit is fully refundable for certain taxpayers.

Child Credit	Mr. and Mrs. Athanasiou reported $420,890 AGI on their Form 1040. They have three qualifying children, ages 14, 12, and 5, on December 31, and one qualifying non-child dependent age 19. Mr. and Mrs. Athanaiou's child credit is $5,450.

Adjusted gross income	$ 420,890
AGI threshold	(400,000)
Excess AGI	$ 20,890
Excess AGI divided by $1,000 and rounded up to nearest whole number	21
Maximum total credit ($2,000 for three children + $500 for non-child dependent)	$ 6,500
Phaseout ($50 × 21)	(1,050)
Child credit	$ 5,450

Dependent Care Credit

LO 14-7
Describe four important individual tax credits.

Individuals with one or more dependents who are either under age 13 or physically or mentally incapable of caring for themselves may be eligible for a **dependent care credit.**[16] The credit is based on the cost of caring for these dependents. Such costs include compensation paid to caregivers who work in the home (nannies, housekeepers, and babysitters) and fees paid to child care or day care centers. The purpose of the credit is to provide tax relief to people who must incur these costs to be gainfully employed. Consequently, the annual cost on which the credit is based is limited to the taxpayer's earned income for the year. On a joint return, the limit is based on the *lesser* of the two spouse's earned income. The cost is further limited to $3,000 if the taxpayer has only one dependent and $6,000 if the taxpayer has two or more dependents.

The credit equals a percentage of dependent care costs (subject to the limitation described in the preceding paragraph). The percentage is determined by reference to AGI and equals 35 percent reduced by 1 percent for each $2,000 (or fraction thereof) by which AGI exceeds $15,000. The percentage is reduced to a minimum of 20 percent taxpayers with AGI over $43,000 but less than $438,000. Taxpayers with AGI in excess of $438,000 may not claim the credit.

---

[15] §24. The child credit may be refundable for low-income families. Any credit attributable to non-child dependents is nonrefundable.

[16] §21.

Dependent Care Credit	Mr. and Mrs. Axel spent $1,300 this year on child care for their 6-year-old child. Their AGI is $25,400, and their dependent care credit percentage is 29 percent, computed as follows:

AGI	$25,400
AGI floor	(15,000)
Excess AGI	$10,400
Reduction (excess AGI divided by $2,000)	5.2
Maximum credit percentage	35%
Reduction (rounded up to whole point)	(6)
Mr. and Mrs. Axel's percentage	29%

The Axels' dependent care credit is $377 ($1,300 cost × 29%).

Tax Talk

According to former Treasury Secretary Henry Paulson, the earned income credit helps "people who are often on the first step of the economic ladder, gaining the experience and skills to land a better job and earn a higher income in the future."

Source: Henry Paulson

Earned Income Credit

Many individuals pay no federal income tax because of the shelter provided by the standard deduction. However, low-income families are not sheltered from the employee payroll tax, which is levied on the first dollar of wages or salary earned. Congress enacted the **earned income credit** to offset the burden of the payroll tax on low-income workers and to encourage individuals to seek employment rather than to depend on welfare.

The credit is based on a percentage of the individual's earned income.[17] The percentage depends on whether the individual has no children, one child, or more than one child. For 2023, the maximum credit available to a family with one qualifying child is $3,995. If earned income exceeds a dollar threshold, the credit is phased out. For a married couple with one child, the 2023 phaseout threshold is $28,120, and the credit is reduced to zero when earned income reaches $53,120. The earned income credit is a *refundable credit*. Taxpayers may receive a refund of the credit that exceeds precredit income tax.

Refund of Earned Income Credit	Mr. and Mrs. Wong's precredit income tax liability for 2023 was $2,215, and the income tax withheld by Mr. Wong's employer was $2,000. Based on their earned income and the number of their children, the Wongs were entitled to a $3,480 earned income credit. The credit reduced their income tax liability to zero and resulted in a $3,265 refund ($1,265 credit in excess of tax + $2,000 withholding).

The IRS estimates that in 2019 approximately 26.7 million families received about $64.5 billion in earned income tax credit. The average credit was $2,461. As a service, the IRS computes the credit for those taxpayers who request assistance when filing their income tax returns.

Excess Social Security Tax Withholding Credit

The federal employee Social Security tax equals 6.2 percent of an employee's compensation, up to a base amount, or maximum. In 2023, the base amount is $160,200. Employers are required to withhold this tax from their employees' paychecks and remit the withholding to the Treasury. When an employee changes jobs, the new employer must withhold Social Security tax without regard to the amount withheld by any former employer. As a result, the employee may indirectly overpay Social Security tax for the year.

[17] §32.

Excess Social Security Tax Withholding	Jiang worked for FM, Inc. for the first nine months of 2023 and then resigned to take a job with CN Company. Jiang's 2023 salary from FM was $100,000 from which FM withheld $6,200 Social Security tax (6.2% × $100,000). Jiang's 2023 salary from CN was $66,000 from which CN withheld $4,092 Social Security tax (6.2% × $66,000). Consequently, a total of $360 excess Social Security tax was withheld in 2023.

Jiang's Social Security tax withholding:	
FM, Inc.	$ 6,200
CN Company	4,092
	$10,292
Maximum 2022 tax:	
(6.2% × $160,200 annual base)	(9,932)
Excess tax withheld	$ 360

Jiang is allowed to claim this **excess Social Security tax withholding credit** as a *refundable credit* against 2023 income tax.[18] The tax credit has no effect on the two firms that employed Jiang during the year. Neither FM, Inc. nor CN Company is entitled to any refund of the employer Social Security tax on Jiang's compensation.

Mr. and Mrs. Volpe: Credits	Refer to the Volpes' Form 1040 (Exhibit 14.1). The Volpes report $61,673 taxable income on line 15. This translates into $6,961 of federal income tax reported on line 16.

During the year, the Volpes paid $4,350 to an after-school activities program for their two young children. This dependent care cost was less than Mr. Volpe's $46,600 salary (lesser of either spouse's earned income) and less than the $6,000 limit for two dependents. Consequently, the Volpes are entitled to an $870 dependent care credit ($4,350 cost × 20%). This amount is reported on line 2 of Schedule 3 (see Exhibit 14.4) and then carried to Form 1040 (line 20).

The Volpes are also entitled to a $4,000 child tax credit reported on Form 1040 (line 19). The effect of these credits is a reduction of the Volpes' income tax liability to $2,091, reported on line 22 of Form 1040 (Exhibit 14.1).

ALTERNATIVE MINIMUM TAX

Individuals are subject to the **alternative minimum tax (AMT)** system and may owe AMT in addition to their regular income tax.[19] The individual AMT is based on **alternative minimum taxable income (AMTI),** which is computed under the formula introduced in Chapter 11:

Taxable income for regular tax purposes
+ or − AMT adjustments
+ AMT tax preferences
Alternative minimum taxable income

LO 14-8
Compute the individual alternative minimum tax (AMT).

Taxable income for regular tax purposes is the starting point for computing AMTI. AMT adjustments can be positive or negative with the effect of either increasing or decreasing AMTI. For instance, the standard deduction is a positive AMT adjustment that must be added back to taxable income in the AMTI computation. We will identify other individual AMT items in subsequent chapters.

[18] §31. The excess Social Security tax withholding credit is refundable.
[19] §55.

EXHIBIT 14.4

Source: Internal Revenue
Service

SCHEDULE 3 (Form 1040) Department of the Treasury Internal Revenue Service	**Additional Credits and Payments** Attach to Form 1040, 1040-SR, or 1040-NR. Go to *www.irs.gov/Form1040* for instructions and the latest information.	OMB No. 1545-0074 20**22** Attachment Sequence No. **03**
Name(s) shown on Form 1040, 1040-SR, or 1040-NR James L. and Nancy J. Volpe		Your social security number 789 49 2452

Part I   Nonrefundable Credits

1	Foreign tax credit. Attach Form 1116 if required	**1**	
2	Credit for child and dependent care expenses from Form 2441, line 11. Attach Form 2441	**2**	870
3	Education credits from Form 8863, line 19	**3**	
4	Retirement savings contributions credit. Attach Form 8880	**4**	
5	Residential energy credits. Attach Form 5695	**5**	
6	Other nonrefundable credits:		
a	General business credit. Attach Form 3800 . . . . **6a**		
b	Credit for prior year minimum tax. Attach Form 8801 . . . . **6b**		
c	Adoption credit. Attach Form 8839 . . . . **6c**		
d	Credit for the elderly or disabled. Attach Schedule R **6d**		
e	Alternative motor vehicle credit. Attach Form 8910 . . . . . **6e**		
f	Qualified plug-in motor vehicle credit. Attach Form 8936 . . . **6f**		
g	Mortgage interest credit. Attach Form 8396 . . . . **6g**		
h	District of Columbia first-time homebuyer credit. Attach Form 8859 **6h**		
i	Qualified electric vehicle credit. Attach Form 8834 . . . . . **6i**		
j	Alternative fuel vehicle refueling property credit. Attach Form 8911 **6j**		
k	Credit to holders of tax credit bonds. Attach Form 8912 . . . **6k**		
l	Amount on Form 8978, line 14. See instructions **6l**		
z	Other nonrefundable credits. List type and amount: _____ **6z**		
7	Total other nonrefundable credits. Add lines 6a through 6z	**7**	
8	Add lines 1 through 5 and 7. Enter here and on Form 1040, 1040-SR, or 1040-NR, line 20	**8**	870

(continued on page 2)

For Paperwork Reduction Act Notice, see your tax return instructions.	Cat. No. 71480G	Schedule 3 (Form 1040) 2022

Individual AMT is based on AMTI in excess of an exemption amount, which is determined by the individual's filing status. The AMT exemption is phased out for high-income taxpayers. Specifically, the exemption amount is reduced by 25 percent of AMTI in excess of a threshold. The following table presents the 2023 exemption amounts, the AMTI threshold, and the AMTI at which the exemption is reduced to zero (AMTI maximum):

	Exemption	AMTI Threshold	AMTI Maximum
Married filing jointly and surviving spouses	$126,500	$1,156,300	$1,662,300
Married filing separately	63,250	578,150	831,150
Head of household or single	81,300	578,150	903,350

Computing AMT

The individual AMT equals any *excess* of tentative minimum tax over the individual's precredit regular income tax. Tentative minimum tax is based on a rate structure consisting of two brackets:

- 26 percent on the first $220,700 AMTI in excess of the exemption ($110,350 for married filing separately). This 26 percent rate bracket is indexed annually for inflation.
- 28 percent of any additional excess AMTI.

AMT Exemption

Ella Epps, a head of household, has $91,000 AMTI. Because AMTI is below the threshold, Ella's exemption is $81,300.

Farah and Finn Floyd are married and file a joint return. They report $1,850,000 AMTI. Because their AMTI is greater than the AMTI maximum, their exemption is reduced to zero.

Gerhardt and Graham Giles are married and file a joint return. They report $1,296,500 AMTI, which falls in the phaseout range. Consequently, their exemption is $91,450, computed as follows:

AMTI	$1,296,500
AMTI threshold	(1,156,300)
AMTI in excess of threshold	$ 140,200
	.25
Reduction in exemption	$ 35,050
Exemption for married filing jointly	$ 126,500
Reduction in exemption	(35,050)
Exemption for the Giles	$ 91,450

If an individual's taxable income includes dividend income and capital gain taxed at a preferential rate (0, 15, or 20 percent), the same preferential rate applies in computing the tentative minimum tax on the dividend income/capital gain component of AMTI.[20]

Tentative Minimum Tax

Refer to the three taxpayers in the preceding example. Assuming their AMTI doesn't include dividend income or capital gain, their tentative minimum tax is calculated as follows:

	Epps	Floyd	Giles
AMTI	$91,000	$1,850,000	$1,296,500
Exemption	(81,300)	–0–	(91,450)
AMTI in excess of exemption	$ 9,700	$1,850,000	$1,205,050
26% of first $220,700 excess AMTI	$ 2,522	$ 57,382	$ 57,382
28% of additional excess AMTI	–0–	456,204	275,618
Tentative minimum tax	$ 2,522	$ 513,586	$ 330,000

After computing AMTI and tentative minimum tax, individuals compare their tentative minimum tax to their regular income tax to determine if they owe any AMT. If they do, they must pay the AMT *in addition to* their regular tax.

AMT

The three taxpayers in the preceding example must compare their tentative minimum tax with their regular income tax. Here is the comparison:

	Epps	Floyd	Giles
Tentative minimum tax	$ 2,522	$513,586	$330,000
Regular income tax	(14,216)	(525,125)	(302,554)
AMT	–0–	–0–	$ 27,446

While Ella and the Floyds pay only regular income tax, the Giles pay both regular tax *and* AMT, for a total tax bill of $330,000.

---

[20] §55(b)(3).

Individuals who pay AMT may be allowed to carry some portion of the payment forward as a credit against future regular tax.[21] The amount of the minimum tax credit used in any future year generally is limited to the excess of regular tax over tentative minimum tax for that year.

Minimum Tax Credit	Assume that the Giles can carry $5,490 of their current year $27,446 AMT into next year as a minimum tax credit. Next year, their regular tax is $315,718, while their tentative minimum tax is only $313,228. The Giles owe no AMT (because regular tax exceeds tentative minimum tax), and they can use $2,490 of the credit to reduce their *regular tax* to $313,228. The couple has a $3,000 remaining minimum tax credit carryforward ($5,490 − $2,490) into future years.

The original purpose of the AMT was to ensure that a handful of high-income individuals who dramatically reduced their regular tax by overindulging in tax preferences would still pay a fair share of tax. Following its enactment in 1969, the AMT evolved into a broad-based tax. As a result, millions of individuals faced the annual aggravation of computing both their regular tax and their tentative minimum tax to determine if they were liable for any AMT or eligible for any minimum tax credit. The Tax Cuts and Jobs Act significantly increased both the AMT exemption and threshold amounts. As a result, the majority of taxpayers are relieved of the burden of computing this alternate definition of taxable income, and are no longer subject to this additional component of the federal income tax.

PAYMENT AND FILING REQUIREMENTS

LO 14-9

Describe the individual tax payment and return filing requirements.

Tax Talk

The withholding requirement was introduced during WWII. According to the Department of Treasury archive, "This greatly eased the collection of the tax for both the taxpayer and the Bureau of Internal Revenue. However, it also greatly reduced the taxpayer's awareness of the amount of tax being collected . . . which made it easier to raise taxes in the future."

Department of Treasury Archive

Individuals are required to pay their income and self-employment tax to the federal government periodically over the course of the year. The income tax on compensation is paid automatically; employers are required to withhold income tax from each wage or salary payment and remit this withholding to the Treasury on their employees' behalf.[22] The tax on other income items, such as net profit from a sole proprietorship, distributive shares of partnership income, or investment income must be paid in four equal installments.[23] The first three of these **estimated tax payments** are due on April 15, June 15, and September 15 of the current year, while the fourth installment is due on January 15 of the following year.

Individuals who fail to make timely payments of at least 90 percent of their current tax in the form of withholding and quarterly payments may incur an underpayment penalty.[24] Because of the uncertainty inherent in estimating the tax owed for the year in progress, the law provides a **safe-harbor estimate.** Individuals with AGI of $150,000 or less in the preceding year may pay current tax equal to 100 percent of the preceding year's tax.[25] By doing so, they avoid any underpayment penalty, regardless of their actual current tax. The safe-harbor estimate for individuals with AGI *in excess* of $150,000 is 110 percent of the preceding year's tax.[26]

---

[21] See §53 for the complicated calculation of the precise amount of the minimum tax credit.

[22] §3402. The withholding is based on the information concerning marital and family status provided by the employee to the employer on Form W-4. Employees can also specify a dollar amount of income tax to be withheld during the year.

[23] §6654(c).

[24] §6654(a) and (d)(1)(B)(i).

[25] §6654(d)(1)(B)(ii).

[26] §6654(d)(1)(C).

Safe-Harbor Estimate	Mrs. Ruiz, an employee of a small corporation, will have $14,000 of income tax withholding this year. Mr. Ruiz recently started a new business venture and does not know how much income it might generate. The couple knows that their AGI for the preceding year was $92,000, and they paid $25,116 income and self-employment tax. Therefore, they can make a safe-harbor estimate for this year by paying in $25,116. If they make four estimated tax payments of $2,779 each, their total payments plus Mrs. Ruiz's withholding will equal $25,116, and they are immune to penalty regardless of their actual tax for the year.

Form 1040 must be filed by the 15th day of the 4th month following the close of the taxable year; for calendar year taxpayers, this is the familiar April 15 due date.[27] If the tax paid throughout the year (withholding and estimated payments) is *less* than the tax computed on the return, the taxpayer must pay the balance due with the return.[28] If the prepayment is *more* than the tax, the return serves as a claim for refund of the overpayment.

Tax Filing Extension— COVID-19	In response to the COVID-19 emergency declared by former President Trump on March 13, 2020, the 2019 Form 1040 filing deadline for calendar year individual taxpayers was postponed from April 15, 2020, to July 15, 2020. The postponement was automatic and also permitted taxpayers to defer certain payments due on April 15, 2020, to July 15, 2020.

Individuals who are not ready to file a completed return by the due date may request an automatic six-month extension of the filing deadline (October 15 for a calendar year taxpayer).[29] This extension applies only to the return filing requirement; individuals who estimate that they still owe tax should pay the estimated balance due with the extension request to avoid interest and penalties.

Automatic Extension	Mr. Sanchez simply couldn't find the time to complete a 2022 Form 1040 before April 17, 2023. (April 15, 2023 falls on a Saturday so the filing deadline is moved to April 17, 2023.) Mr. Sanchez estimated his 2022 tax liability would be no more than $14,500. Because his 2022 withholding was $13,850, Mr. Sanchez concluded that he owed $650 additional tax. So Mr. Sanchez filed Form 4686 (Application of Time to File U.S. Individual Income Tax Return) on April 12 and attached a check for $650 with the application. Consequently, the filing date for his 2022 Form 1040 was extended until Monday, October 16, 2023. Mr. Sanchez filed his return on July 29. The return showed an actual tax liability of $14,210, so Mr. Sanchez was due a $290 refund ($14,500 tax paid − $14,210 tax owed) from the government.

Let's conclude the discussion of payment and filing requirements by returning one last time to our comprehensive Form 1040 example.

Mr. and Mrs. Volpe: Tax Refund	Refer again to the Volpes' Form 1040 (Exhibit 14.1). Mrs. Volpe's $8,016 self-employment tax is reported on line 4 of Schedule 2 (Exhibit 14.3) and carried to line 23 of Form 1040. The couple's $10,107 total tax ($2,091 of federal income tax and $8,016 self-employment tax) is reported on line 24. During the year, Mr. Volpe's employer withheld $3,496 income tax (line 25a) from Mr. Volpe's salary, and the couple made $8,000 estimated tax payments shown on line 26 of Form 1040. These two payments total $11,496 on line 33, Form 1040. Because the Volpes overpaid their tax by $1,389, the Treasury owes the Volpes a refund (line 34). The Volpes may either request a refund (line 35a) or choose to apply this refund to their estimated tax payments **for the following taxable year** by indicating the refund amount on line 36.

---

[27] §6072(a).

[28] §6151(a).

[29] Reg. §1.6081-4T.

Conclusion

This chapter provides the "big picture" with respect to individual taxpayers. We developed the formula for the computation of taxable income and discussed the significance of AGI in this formula. We learned how to compute the regular tax on individual income, identified the most common individual tax credits, and considered the threat of the alternative minimum tax. This chapter closed with a synopsis of the payment and filing requirements for individual taxpayers.

In the next three chapters, we will explore the incredible variety of transactions that affect the computation of individual taxable income. Our discussions of the tax consequences of many specific transactions will reinforce your understanding of the individual tax formula and will lead to new tax planning ideas. Hopefully, the material in these chapters will also give you a real appreciation of the complexities and nuances that make the study of individual taxation so challenging and yet so fascinating.

Key Terms

above-the-line deduction   *14–8*
adjusted gross income (AGI)   *14–8*
alternative minimum tax (AMT)   *14–24*
alternative minimum taxable income (AMTI)   *14–24*
bunching   *14–14*
child credit   *14–21*
dependent   *14–5*

dependent care credit   *14–22*
earned income credit   *14–23*
estimated tax payments   *14–27*
excess Social Security tax withholding credit   *14–24*
filing status   *14–4*
head of household   *14–5*
itemized deduction   *14–13*
joint and several liability   *14–4*

joint return   *14–4*
kiddie tax   *14–19*
qualified business income (QBI)   *14–15*
qualifying child   *14–5*
qualifying relative   *14–5*
safe-harbor estimate   *14–27*
separate returns   *14–5*
single taxpayer   *14–5*
standard deduction   *14–12*
surviving spouse   *14–4*
total income   *14–7*

Questions and Problems for Discussion

LO 14-2   1. Discuss the extent to which adjusted gross income (AGI) is actually a net income number.

LO 14-2   2. Explain why AGI is considered a better measure of individual disposable income than taxable income.

LO 14-2   3. Why is the formula for computing individual taxable income so much more complicated than the formula for computing corporate taxable income?

LO 14-3   4. Discuss possible tax policy reasons why individuals who are age 65 or older receive an additional standard deduction.

LO 14-3   5. Individuals who are legally blind receive an additional standard deduction, while individuals with other disabilities, such as deafness or paralysis, are not entitled to an additional deduction. Is there a tax policy justification for the different treatment?

LO 14-3   6. Identify the reasons why individual taxpayers benefit more from above-the-line deductions than from itemized deductions.

LO 14-3   7. While checking the computations, Geraldo Gordon realized that a $10,800 expense had been misclassified as a business deduction on Schedule C. The expense should have been an itemized deduction on Schedule A. Geraldo did not correct the error, assuming that the correction would not affect taxable income. Is this assumption correct?

LO 14-3   8. Individuals who plan to bunch itemized deductions into one year can either postpone the payment of expenses from an earlier year or accelerate the payment of expenses from a later year. Which technique is preferable from a cash flow standpoint?

LO 14-3, 14-4   9. Describe the restrictions on tax benefits available to an individual taxpayer who is claimed as a dependent on another taxpayer's Form 1040.

LO 14-3, 14-4, 14-7, 14-8   10. Single individuals Sam and Zelle were married this year and filed their first joint return. To what extent did this change in filing status affect the following?

     a. Sam and Zelle's aggregate standard deduction.

     b. Sam and Zelle's aggregate child credit.

     c. Sam and Zelle's aggregate AMT exemption.

LO 14-3, 14-4, 14-5   11. Explain why an individual's combined standard deduction can be considered a bracket of income taxed at a zero rate.

LO 14-6   12. Under the current rate structure, a high-income single person could pay more tax than a married couple on the same income. What economic circumstances might a single person cite to argue that an unmarried person's ability to pay tax is not necessarily greater than a married couple's ability to pay tax on the same income?

LO 14-7   13. The tax law provides for both refundable and nonrefundable credits. What is the difference between the two types of credit?

LO 14-7   14. Congress enacted the earned income credit to relieve the burden of the payroll tax on low-income workers. Why didn't Congress accomplish this goal by providing a payroll tax exemption for a base amount of annual compensation paid by an employer to an employee?

LO 14-9   15. Mr. Martinez instructed his employer to withhold substantially more federal income tax from his monthly paycheck than was indicated by his marital and family situation. As a result, Mr. Martinez routinely overpays his tax, receives a refund each spring, and invests the refund in a mutual fund. Mr. Martinez views this strategy as an efficient means of enforced savings. Do you agree?

LO 14-9   16. Ms. Jobe has been very ill since the beginning of the year and unable to attend to any financial matters. Ms. Jobe was advised by a CPA to request an automatic extension of time to file a prior year Form 1040. Ms. Jobe wants to avoid paying this tax for as long as possible so likes this idea. Ms. Jobe believes the balance of tax due with the return will be at least $20,000. By requesting the extension, how long can Ms. Jobe delay paying the $20,000 to the Treasury?

Mc Graw Hill **connect**®   **All applicable Application Problems are available with *Connect*.**

Application Problems

For the following problems, assume the taxable year is 2023.

LO 14-1   1. Determine Lilly's 2023 filing status in each of the following independent cases:

     a. Lilly and Paul have been living together since 2021. They were married on December 13, 2023.

     b. Lilly married Paul in 2016. They were divorced on November 8, 2023, and have no dependent children.

     c. Lilly married Paul in 2016. They separated in 2022 and have not lived together since, but they have not divorced.

     d. Lilly divorced Paul in 2022. Lilly's grandparent is considered a dependent and lives with Lilly.

LO 14-1   2. Determine Juan's 2023 filing status in each of the following independent cases:

    a. Juan and his spouse were divorced on November 18. Juan has not remarried and has no dependent children.

    b. Juan and his first spouse were divorced on April 2. Juan remarried on December 15. Juan has no dependent children.

    c. Juan's spouse died on July 23. Juan has not remarried and has no dependent children.

    d. Juan's spouse died on October 1, 2021. Juan has not remarried and maintains a home for one dependent child.

    e. Juan's spouse died on May 30, 2022. Juan has not remarried and has no dependent children.

    f. Juan and his spouse were divorced on May 30, 2020. Juan has not remarried and maintains a home for two dependent children.

LO 14-3   3. The Keppners file a joint income tax return. Compute their standard deduction assuming that

    a. Mr. Keppner is age 68, and Ms. Keppner is age 60.

    b. Mr. Keppner is age 70, and Ms. Keppner is age 68.

    c. Mr. Keppner is age 70, and Ms. Keppner is age 68 and legally blind.

LO 14-3   4. Marnie, a single taxpayer, projects $14,450 of expenses qualifying as itemized deductions in both 2023 and 2024. Assuming that the standard deduction is $13,850 in both years, compute the effect on taxable income for each year if Marnie can shift $2,500 of deductible expenses from 2023 to 2024.

LO 14-1   5. Dana is an unmarried individual. Determine if each of the following unmarried individuals is either a qualifying child or a qualifying relative:

    a. Dee, age 20, is Dana's adoptive child and a student at State University. Dana's home is Dee's permanent residence. Dana provides 80 percent of Dee's financial support. Dee earned $6,650 from a summer internship with a bank.

    b. Lulu is Dana's sibling, 39 years old, and disabled. Lulu lives in a privately operated group home, and Dana provides 100 percent financial support. Lulu has no gross income.

    c. Bryan, age 13, is Dana's child and lives in Dana's home but receives the majority of financial support from Bryan's other parent.

    d. Betsy, age 25, is Dana's niece and lives in Dana's home. Dana provides 60 percent of Betsy's financial support. Betsy is a part-time student and holds a part-time job, earning $10,450 this year.

LO 14-1   6. Mr. and Mrs. Nguyen file a joint income tax return. Determine if each of the following unmarried individuals is either a qualifying child or a qualifying relative:

    a. The Nguyens' child, Jinn, age 20, lives in their home and works full-time as an auto mechanic. Although the Nguyens do not receive rent, Jinn is otherwise self-supporting.

    b. The Nguyens' child, Beth, age 22, is a full-time college student. Beth lives in a dormitory during the school year but lists the Nguyens' home as permanent residence. The Nguyens provide 100 percent of Beth's financial support.

    c. The Nguyens' nephew, Ezra, age 16, has lived in the Nguyens' home since 2016. Ezra is a high school student who earned $6,690 this summer working for a plumber. Ezra is able to save for college because the Nguyens provide 100 percent of Ezra's financial support.

    d. Mr. Nguyen's parent, Minnie, age 64, lives in a retirement community. The Nguyens provide about 65 percent of Minnie's financial support. Minnie earned $5,650 this year as a part-time librarian.

    e. Ms. Nguyen's parent, Bao, age 76, has lived in the Nguyens' home since 2018. The Nguyens provide about 30 percent of Bao's financial support, with the remainder coming from Social Security.

LO 14-1, 14-5

7. Ms. Hill earned a $91,250 salary, and Mr. Gomez earned a $171,000 salary. Neither individual had any other income, and neither can itemize deductions.

    a. Compute Mr. Gomez and Ms. Hill's combined tax if they file as single individuals.

    b. Compute Mr. Gomez and Ms. Hill's tax if they are married and file a joint return.

LO 14-5

8. Mr. Olaf earned an $89,000 salary, and Ms. Olaf earned a $40,330 salary. The couple had no other income and cannot itemize deductions.

    a. Compute their combined tax if they choose to file separate returns.

    b. Compute their tax if they file a joint return.

LO 14-3, 14-4, 14-5

9. Alex and Addison are married and have the following income items:

Alex's salary	$52,500
Addison's Schedule C net profit	41,800
Interest income	1,300

Addison's self-employment tax was $5,906. Addison's Schedule C net business profit is qualified business income (non-service). The couple have $8,070 itemized deductions and no children or other dependents. Compute their income tax on a joint return.

LO 14-3, 14-4, 14-5

10. Mr. and Ms. Sumara have the following income items:

Mr. Sumara's Schedule C net profit	$91,320
Ms. Sumara's Schedule C net loss	(7,480)
Ms. Sumara's taxable pension	32,300
Interest income	21,200

Mr. Sumara's self-employment tax was $12,903. The couple has $29,050 itemized deductions. Mrs. Sumara's Schedule C net business profit is qualified business income (non-service). Compute the couple's income tax on a joint return.

LO 14-3, 14-4, 14-5

11. Terrell, an unmarried individual, has the following income items:

Schedule C net profit	$31,900
Salary	55,120
NOL carryforward deduction	(9,190)
Interest income	725

Terrell's self-employment tax was $4,507. Terrell had $6,270 in itemized deductions and one dependent child (age 9) who lives with Terrell. Terrell's Schedule C net business profit is qualified business income (non-service). Compute Terrell's income tax (before credits).

LO 14-3, 14-4, 14-5   12. Kaori, an unmarried individual with no dependent children, reports the following information:

Wages	$65,000
Schedule C net profit	11,650
Interest from savings account	500
Self-employment tax on Schedule C net profit	1,646

    a. Assume that Kaori's itemized deductions total $9,000 and Schedule C net business profit is qualified business income (non-service). Compute AGI and taxable income.

    b. Assume that Kaori's itemized deductions total $14,000 and Schedule C net business profit is qualified business income (non-service). Compute AGI and taxable income.

LO 14-3, 14-4, 14-5   13. Cole, an unmarried individual with no dependents, has the following income items:

Interest income	$24,200
Schedule C net profit	50,600

Cole has $9,300 itemized deductions and the Schedule C income is qualified business income (non-service). Compute Cole's income tax.

LO 14-3, 14-5   14. Chandler and Cassidy are married and file a joint return. Chandler is age 66, and Cassidy is age 68. They report the following income items:

Dividend eligible for 0% preferential rate	$ 3,400
Capital gain eligible for 0% preferential rate	2,900
Chandler's salary	44,325

Their itemized deductions totaled $6,390, and they have no dependents. Compute their income tax on a joint return.

LO 14-3, 14-5   15. Rashad, an unmarried individual with four dependent children (ages 5 to 15) had the following income items:

Salary	$512,100
Interest income	19,700
Dividend eligible for 20% rate	31,000

Rashad had $34,000 in itemized deductions. Compute Rashad's income tax (before credits).

LO 14-5   16. Lara, a single individual, has $145,000 taxable income. Compute income tax assuming that

    a. Taxable income includes no capital gain.

    b. Taxable income includes $22,000 capital gain eligible for the 15 percent preferential rate.

LO 14-1, 14-5   17. Brandon, an unmarried individual, has $196,400 taxable income. Compute income tax in each of the following cases:

    a. Brandon is a single taxpayer.

    b. Brandon is a head of household.

    c. Brandon is a surviving spouse.

LO 14-5   18. Refer to your computations for Brandon in the previous problem. For each case, identify Brandon's statutory marginal rate and average tax rate.

LO 14-3, 14-5   19. Taylor, a single taxpayer, has $16,700 AGI. Compute taxable income in each of the following cases:

    a. Taylor is 19 years old and a dependent of his parents for tax purposes. AGI consists entirely of interest income.

    b. Taylor is 19 years old and is considered a dependent of his parents for tax purposes. Taylor's AGI consists entirely of wage income.

    c. Taylor is 70 years old and lives with his grown child who provides more than one-half of Taylor's financial support. Taylor's AGI consists entirely of interest income.

LO 14-3   20. Dena Liu is 20 years old and is considered a dependent of Dena's parents for tax purposes. Compute Dena's taxable income in each of the following cases:

    a. Dena's only income item was $2,712 interest earned on a certificate of deposit.

    b. Dena had two income items: $2,712 interest earned on a certificate of deposit and $3,276 wages from a part-time job.

    c. How would your answers change if Dena was not considered a dependent for tax purposes?

LO 14-7   21. The Palios celebrated the birth of their first and only child on November 18. Compute the effect of this event on their tax liability, assuming that

    a. Their AGI was $99,000, and their taxable income before considering the new dependent was $84,200.

    b. Their AGI was $412,000, and their taxable income before considering the new dependent was $345,000.

    c. Their AGI was $830,000, and their taxable income before considering the new dependent was $714,000.

LO 14-6   22. Mr. Ali's salary was $387,000, and Mrs. Ali's salary was $354,000. They had no other income items, no above-the-line or itemized deductions, and no dependents.

    a. Compute their tax on a joint return.

    b. Compute their combined tax if they file separate returns (married filing separately).

    c. Compute their marriage penalty (excess of tax on a joint return over combined tax on two returns filed as single taxpayers).

LO 14-3, 14-5   23. Dakota is an unmarried taxpayer with one dependent child, age 18, living in Dakota's home. Dakota does not itemize deductions and reports AGI of $40,000. The dependent child earned $16,200 from a part-time job and incurred no deductible expenses.

    a. Compute Dakota's income tax (before credits).

    b. Compute the child's income tax.

LO 14-5   24. Callie is the 11-year-old dependent of the Sanders. This year, Callie filed a Form 1040 on which the only item of gross income was $10,557 interest from an investment bond portfolio that Callie inherited from a relative. Assume the Sanders are subject to a 24 percent marginal tax rate. Compute Callie's income tax.

LO 14-5, 14-7   25. Avery, an unmarried taxpayer, had the following income items:

Salary	$38,000
Net income from a rental house	3,200

Avery has a 4-year-old child who attends a child care center. Compute Avery's child tax credit and dependent care credit.

a. Assume Avery paid $1,280 to the child care facility.

b. Assume Avery paid $4,800 to the child care facility.

LO 14-7 26. Jeremiah and Jonnie Chaulk are married and have three dependent children, ages 3, 6, and 9. Compute their child credit if AGI on their joint return is

a. $88,300.

b. $462,700.

c. $200,000, and assume that they also have one non-child dependent who meets the requirements for the child credit.

LO 14-7 27. Vijay and Lina Mehta are married with two dependent children. They paid $7,200 of wages to a nanny to care for their children and $549 employer payroll tax on these wages. The Mehtas file a joint return. In each of the following cases, compute their dependent care credit:

a. The children are ages 10 and 15. Vijay's earned income is $75,000 and Lina has no earned income. Their AGI is $81,300.

b. The children are ages 2 and 6. Vijay's earned income is $45,000 and Lina's earned income is $28,000. Their AGI is $81,300.

c. The children are ages 2 and 6. Vijay's earned income is $245,000 and Lina's earned income is $280,000. Their AGI is $475,000.

LO 14-7 28. Juan Carlos and Roberta Rodriguez have four dependent children, ages 1, 4, 7, and 11. Juan Carlos's salary was $16,200, Roberta's wages totaled $21,400. The couple had no other income or above-the-line deductions this year. The Rodriguezes paid $3,600 for day care and after-school child care.

a. Compute the Rodriguezes child credit.

b. Compute the Rodriguezes dependent care credit.

c. Recompute the Rodriguezes child and dependent care credits if Roberta's salary was $200,000, Juan Carlos's wages totaled $232,000, and the couple earned $5,700 taxable interest income.

LO 14-7 29. On March 31, Milo resigned a position with MT, Inc. and began a new job with PK Company. Milo's salary was $82,600 from MT and $93,000 from PK. Compute Milo's excess Social Security tax withholding credit.

LO 14-3, 14-5, 14-7 30. Ali and Alex Arnaud are married with no dependent children. Ali worked for Smart Tech Corporation January through March and for Computer Associates the remainder of the year. Alex completed a degree in November and immediately began as an associate with Smith and Weber. They report the following information:

Ali's salary from Smart Tech	$32,000
Ali's salary from Computer Associates	142,000
Alex's salary from Smith and Weber	15,550
Interest from savings account	700
Itemized deductions	9,000
Dividends eligible for 15% rate	2,200

a. Compute AGI.

b. Compute taxable income.

c. Compute net tax liability (after credits).

LO 14-7 31. The Kigalis are married and file a joint return. Their AGI (earned income) was $14,610 and federal income tax withholding was $850. They had no itemized deductions and two dependent children, ages 18 and 19. If the Kigalis are entitled to a $4,716 earned income credit, compute their income tax refund.

LO 14-8 32. In each of the following cases, compute AMT (if any). For all cases, assume that taxable income does not include any dividend income or capital gain.

  a. Mr. and Mrs. Baker, married filing jointly, reported taxable income of $200,000 and AMTI before exemption of $203,000.

  b. Mr. Costa, single taxpayer, reported taxable income of $177,300 and AMTI before exemption of $198,000.

  c. Ms. Juma, a single taxpayer, reported taxable income of $650,675 and AMTI before exemption of $795,000.

LO 14-8 33. Jaclyn, who files as a head of household, never paid AMT before 2023. In 2023, Jaclyn's regular tax liability was $102,220, which included $39,900 capital gain taxed at 20 percent, and AMTI in excess of the exemption amount was $422,500. Compute Jaclyn's total income tax for 2023.

LO 14-9 34. In January, Win Lu's employer withheld $25,000 from Win's 2023 salary. Win has also income from several other sources and must make quarterly estimated tax payments. Compute the quarterly payments that result in a 2024 safe-harbor estimate assuming that

  a. Win's 2023 AGI is $176,000 and income tax is $47,200.

  b. Win's 2023 AGI is $139,000 and income tax is $36,800.

LO 14-9 35. Christian and Tyler are married and file a joint return. They report taxable income of $130,000 in 2023. In addition, they report the following:

Excess Social Security withholding credit	$ 2,200
Estimate tax payments	4,000
Withholding	14,200

Compute the amount due or refund claimed when Christian and Tyler file their 2023 federal income tax return.

Issue Recognition Problems

Identify the tax issue or issues suggested by the following situations, and state each issue in the form of a question.

LO 14-1 1. Mr. Leonard died on April 16. Mr. and Mrs. Leonard had been married for 11 years and had always filed a joint return. Mrs. Leonard remarried on December 21.

LO 14-1 2. Thad and Timmie were married in 2001. This year they traveled to Reno, Nevada, immediately after Christmas and obtained a divorce on December 29. They spent two weeks vacationing in California, returned to their home in Texas on January 13, and remarried the next day.

LO 14-4 3. Until March of this year, Pat Chen's invalid parent lived with Pat. Pat also provided 100 percent of the financial support. In March, Pat's parent became eligible for Medicaid and moved into a state-provided room in a nursing home.

LO 14-4 4. Marcus is a 20-year-old college student. This year Marcus lived on campus for nine months and at his parents' home during the summer. Marcus's parents paid for all of his living and educational expenses, with the exception of his tuition which was covered by a $22,000 scholarship.

LO 14-4 5. The Cilettis have an 11-year-old child. The couple is divorced, and Mrs. Ciletti has sole custody of the child. However, Mr. Ciletti pays his former spouse $1,200 child support each month.

LO 14-4 6. Mr. Glenn, age 90, lives in a nursing home. He has no gross income and is financially dependent on his four adult children, each of whom pays 25 percent of the cost of the home.

LO 14-5   7. Raul's AGI includes an $8,700 dividend paid by a German corporation and $11,600 interest paid by a Canadian bank. Raul paid $3,000 foreign income tax this year.

LO 14-7   8. Mr. and Mrs. Wynne have full-time jobs. They employ Mrs. Wynne's 18-year-old sister as an after-school babysitter for their 10-year-old son.

LO 14-7   9. Mr. Severson, a self-employed attorney, has sole custody of his 9-year-old daughter. This year she spent eight weeks during the summer at a recreational camp. The total cost was $3,800.

LO 14-7   10. During the first eight months of the year, Ms. Layne was self-employed and earned $63,200 net income. In September, she accepted a job with MW Company and earned $75,000 salary through the end of the year.

LO 14-9   11. Tatiana and Tony Marceleno own a sole proprietorship that generates approximately $60,000 annual net profit. This business is the couple's only source of income. In April, June, and September, they paid their estimated tax payments. In December, they won $250,000 in a state lottery.

LO 14-9   12. In November, Bao discovered that his combined income tax withholding and estimated tax payments would be less than Bao's prior year tax and, therefore, would not be a safe-harbor estimate. Bao immediately requested that his employer withhold enough tax from his December paycheck to result in a safe-harbor estimate.

Research Problems

LO 14-1   1. Bert Baker and Ernestine Moffet were never formally married but have lived together for the last 14 years. Bert and Ernestine reside in Washington, D.C., a jurisdiction that recognizes common law marriages as valid. Consequently, they filed both a joint district income tax return and a joint federal income tax return for the last eight years. Bert and Ernestine are planning to move their household to Frederick, Maryland, and become permanent residents of that state. Maryland doesn't recognize common law marriages. Will Bert and Ernestine's change in residence allow them to avoid the marriage penalty by filing as single individuals?

LO 14-4   2. Tim is the 5-year-old godchild of the Bryants. Tim's parents died in an accident on December 18 of last year. Tim was seriously injured in the accident and remained hospitalized until August 12 of this year. After being discharged from the hospital, Tim moved into the Bryants' home. The Bryants have provided 100 percent of Tim's financial support since the accident and intend to raise Tim as their own child. For tax purposes, is Tim considered a dependent of the Bryants?

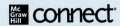 **All applicable Tax Planning Cases are available with *Connect*.**

Tax Planning Cases

LO 14-2, 14-3, 14-4, 14-5, 14-7   1. The Chungs are married with one dependent child. They report the following information for 2023:

Schedule C net profit	$66,650
Interest income from certificate of deposit (CD)	2,100
Self-employment tax on Schedule C net profit	9,418
Dividend eligible for 15% rate	12,000
Lila Chung's salary from Brants Company	75,000
Dependent care credit	500
Itemized deductions	31,000

Compute AGI, taxable income, and total tax liability (including self-employment tax). Assume that Schedule C net profit is qualified business income (non-service income) under Section 199A.

LO 14-3 2. Assume that the tax law allows individuals to claim an itemized deduction for the cost of music lessons for the taxpayer or any member of his family. Instead of this deduction, individuals may claim the first $1,000 of the cost as a nonrefundable tax credit (no carryforward or carryback of any excess credit). In each of the following situations, advise the taxpayer as to whether she should take the deduction or credit. In each situation, the taxpayer is single.

   a. Ms. Margo has $92,000 AGI. Before consideration of the $5,000 cost of music lessons, Ms. Margo has no itemized deductions.

   b. Ms. Nelson has $42,000 AGI. Before consideration of the $5,000 cost of music lessons, Ms. Nelson has $14,000 itemized deductions.

   c. Ms. Omar has $225,000 AGI. Before consideration of the $5,000 cost of music lessons, Ms. Omar has $13,200 itemized deductions.

Chapter Fifteen

Compensation and Retirement Planning

Learning Objectives

After studying this chapter, you should be able to:

LO 15-1. Differentiate between employees and independent contractors.

LO 15-2. Summarize the tax consequences of wage and salary payments to employees and employers.

LO 15-3. Identify the most common nontaxable employee fringe benefits.

LO 15-4. Describe the tax and financial accounting consequences of equity-based compensation.

LO 15-5. Explain the tax advantages of qualified over nonqualified retirement plans.

LO 15-6. Contrast defined-benefit, defined-contribution, and nonqualified deferred compensation plans.

LO 15-7. Describe the tax benefits offered by IRAs and Roth IRAs.

The first item of income listed on page 1, Form 1040, and the most important (if not the only) item of income recognized by millions of individuals is the compensation they earn as employees.[1] Such compensation can consist of an hourly wage, an annual salary, sales commissions, tips, fees, fringe benefits, bonuses, severance pay, or any other economic benefit received for services rendered in the course of employment.[2] In the first part of this chapter, we will concentrate on this broad category of income by describing some popular compensation techniques and analyzing the tax and cash flow implications of each. In the second part of this chapter, we will consider the arrangements through which people convert current compensation into retirement income. Through long-range tax planning, individuals can maximize the cash flow available for consumption and enjoyment during their post-employment years.

---

[1] According to IRS data, wages and salaries constitute about 70 percent of the total income reported by individual taxpayers.

[2] Reg. §1.61-2.

THE COMPENSATION TRANSACTION

Tax Talk
The U.S. Bureau of Labor Statistics reports that in 2021, 55.8 percent of all wage and salary workers were paid at hourly rates. This amounts to 76.1 million workers. Of those paid by the hour, 181,000 earned exactly $7.25 per hour, the federal minimum wage rate at that time.

The payment of compensation is a transaction with tax consequences to two parties: the employer making the payment and the employee receiving the payment. The nature and the amount of the compensation are determined by contractual agreement between these parties. The employer's objective in negotiating the contract is to minimize the after-tax cost of the compensation paid; the employee's objective is to maximize the after-tax value of the compensation received. High-ranking employees can usually negotiate with their employers on a personal basis. Because they are transacting in a private market, employer and employee can work together to achieve their objectives. Specifically, they can compare different compensation arrangements and evaluate the tax consequences to both parties. By doing so, the employer and employee can design a package offering the greatest overall tax savings divided between them on a mutually satisfactory basis.

In contrast, rank-and-file employees typically transact with their employers in an impersonal public market. These employees can only accept or reject the compensation arrangement offered by the employer. In such cases, both employee and employer must pursue their tax planning objectives independently.

CEO Compensation versus Average Wage	The difference in transactional markets may help explain the fact that in 1965, the ratio between CEO compensation and compensation earned by the average employee was about 21 to 1. In 2020, the ratio between compensation of the CEOs of the 350 largest companies and the average employee in their companies was 351 to 1, up from 307 to 1 in 2019. *Source: The Economic Policy Institute*

Competing for Employees	In 2021, Costco raised its minimum wage to $17 per hour. This wage increase raises the stakes for all retailers competing for workers in a tight labor market. *Source: CNN Business (October 27, 2021)*

EMPLOYEE OR INDEPENDENT CONTRACTOR?

LO 15-1
Differentiate between employees and independent contractors.

The employer/employee relationship is characterized by the employer's right to direct and control how, when, and where the employee's duties are performed.[3] The relationship is continual because an **employee** works according to a regular schedule in return for periodic payments from the employer. The relationship is also exclusive because an employee provides services for one employer rather than the general public.

Tax Talk
A record number of senior citizens participate in the U.S. labor force. As of February 2019, more than 20 percent of people over the age of 65 are still working, compared to 10 percent in 1985.

Source: The U.S. Bureau of Labor Statistics.

As an alternative to hiring an employee, a firm can engage an independent contractor to do the job. An **independent contractor** is a self-employed individual who performs services for monetary consideration and who controls the way the services are performed. The independent contractor's clients don't oversee the work in process but can only accept or reject the final product. The relationship between client and independent contractor is impermanent, and the contractor can have any number of clients at the same time.

Tax Consequences of Worker Classification

The distinction between employee and independent contractor is critical for tax purposes. As you learned in Chapter 10, employers must pay federal and state payroll taxes on the

---

[3] Reg. §31.3401(c)-1(b).

compensation paid to their employees. In addition, employers are required to withhold both employee payroll tax and federal, state, and local income tax from their employees' wages and salaries. At the end of the calendar year, employers must issue a Form W-2 (Wage and Tax Statement) to each employee.[4] This form provides detailed information about the various taxes withheld by the employer on the employee's behalf.

Form W-2	Robin Simms is employed by Crockett Products. During 2022, Robin earned a $147,600 salary. Robin's average monthly *net* paycheck was $8,151, which equaled $12,300 monthly *gross* salary less federal income tax, federal Social Security and Medicare tax, and state income tax withheld by Crockett Products. Robin's Form W-2 is shown in Exhibit 15.1.

When clients engage independent contractors, the fees paid aren't subject to FICA payroll taxes, and clients aren't required to withhold income tax. At the end of the year, clients must issue a Form 1099-MISC (Miscellaneous Income) or 1099-NEC (Non-Employee Compensation) to each independent contractor stating the annual compensation paid. The 1099-MISC is used when total annual payments are less than $600. In 2020, the 1099-NEC was reintroduced and is required when total payments exceed $600 for a given year. Independent contractors who are sole proprietors (rather than in partnership with other individuals) report this compensation as business income on Schedule C, Form 1040. Independent contractors pay self-employment tax on the net profit from their business and make quarterly estimated payments of both self-employment and federal income tax.

EXHIBIT 15.1

Source: Department of the Treasury, Internal Revenue Service

Form 1099-MISC	Sam Ling is an independent contractor who performs occasional professional services for Crockett Products. During 2022, Sam earned total fees of $34,700 from Crockett. The Form 1099-NEC on which these fees are reported is shown in Exhibit 15.2.

[4] §6051(a). Employers must issue Form W-2s by January 31. If an employee who terminates employment during the year submits a written request for a Form W-2, the employer must issue the form within 30 days of receipt of the request.

EXHIBIT 15.2

Source: Department of the
Treasury, Internal Revenue
Service

☐ CORRECTED (if checked)

PAYER'S name, street address, city or town, state or province, country, ZIP or foreign postal code, and telephone no.		OMB No. 1545-0116	**Nonemployee Compensation**
Crockett Products PO Box 92252 Wilmington, DE 12899		Form **1099-NEC** (Rev. January 2022) For calendar year 20 **22**	

PAYER'S TIN	RECIPIENT'S TIN	1 Nonemployee compensation	Copy B
87-4009325	165-39-2238	$ 34,700	**For Recipient**

RECIPIENT'S name

Sam Ling
Street address (including apt. no.)

88 Fernglade #316
City or town, state or province, country, and ZIP or foreign postal code

Stafford, DE 12891
Account number (see instructions)

2 Payer made direct sales totaling $5,000 or more of consumer products to recipient for resale ☐

3

4 Federal income tax withheld $

5 State tax withheld $ 6 State/Payer's state no. 7 State income $

This is important tax information and is being furnished to the IRS. If you are required to file a return, a negligence penalty or other sanction may be imposed on you if this income is taxable and the IRS determines that it has not been reported.

Form **1099-NEC** (Rev. 1-2022) (keep for your records) www.irs.gov/Form1099NEC Department of the Treasury - Internal Revenue Service

Worker Classification Controversy

The classification of a worker as either employee or independent contractor depends on the facts and circumstances of each case.[5] The classification is usually straightforward. But occasionally, the nature of the working relationship doesn't clearly indicate whether the worker is an employee or an independent contractor.

The Firm's Viewpoint

When a firm hires a worker whose classification is ambiguous, it has a financial incentive to treat the worker as an independent contractor. By doing so, the firm avoids both the employer payroll tax and the administrative cost of the various withholding requirements. Moreover, it doesn't have to provide independent contractors with the fringe benefits available to its permanent workforce. The payroll cost for an employee includes both base compensation (wage or salary) and any benefits (medical and life insurance, paid vacation, sick leave, retirement pensions, etc.) for which the employee is eligible. If the firm can engage an independent contractor for the same base compensation, it eliminates the incremental cost of the benefits.

The IRS's Viewpoint

In theory, the federal government should be indifferent as to whether workers are employees or independent contractors. The IRS should collect the same employment tax on the worker's compensation, either as payroll tax or self-employment tax. Similarly, the compensation is subject to income tax in either case. Realistically, the IRS has a higher probability of collecting these taxes if the worker is an employee. In this case, the employer is legally responsible for remitting both the employment tax and the income tax on the compensation to the government.

If a firm classifies a worker as an independent contractor, the responsibility for paying tax shifts to the contractor. The IRS has determined that self-employed individuals as a group have a relatively low level of compliance, either because they fail to file a tax return or because they understate their business income. For this reason, the IRS takes an aggressive stance with respect to worker classification. Firms that classify workers as independent

Tax Talk
In 2019, the IRS released the "tax gap" between what taxpayers legally owe and what they actually pay is about $441 billion annually based on 2011, 2012, and 2013 data. A substantial portion is attributable to the misclassification of workers as independent contractors instead of employees. In a speech to the Senate Finance Committee, IRS commissioner Chuck Rettig estimated the gap at approximately $1 trillion.

[5] In Rev. Rul. 87-41, 1987-1 C.B. 296, the IRS lists 20 factors for determining whether an individual is an employee or an independent contractor.

contractors must be aware of the risk that a revenue agent may challenge this classification on audit. If the agent concludes that facts and circumstances tip the scales in favor of employee status, the firm may find itself liable for unpaid taxes, interest, and penalties because it failed to carry out its withholding responsibilities as an employer.

| *Talking the Talk* | Companies that use independent contractors may head off a dispute with the IRS by making sure that all written references to such contractors contain the proper terminology. For example, independent contractors are not "hired" or "fired" or paid "wages" or "salaries." Instead, they are "retained" or "discontinued" and paid "remuneration" or "fees." The company should never refer to itself as the "employer" but as the "principal" or "client." Finally, the department that deals with independent contractors should not be labeled "human resources" but "contractor relations."[6] |

WAGE AND SALARY PAYMENTS

Tax Consequences to Employees

LO 15-2
Summarize the tax consequences of wage and salary payments to employees and employers.

Employees typically are cash basis taxpayers who recognize wages or salary as income in the year in which payment is actually or constructively received. In terms of cash flow, payments are net of employee payroll tax and income tax withheld by the employer. While payroll tax withholding usually equals the individual's payroll tax liability, the income tax withholding is an approximate number. If the annual withholding exceeds the individual's actual income tax, the Treasury owes the individual a refund. Alternatively, withholding may be less than the actual tax, in which case the individual pays the balance due when filing the Form 1040 or extension request.

Tax Consequences to Employers

Tax Talk
In 2020, average U.S. wage earners faced a 28.3 percent total income tax burden (federal, state, and local) on their earnings. This U.S. tax burden has been consistently below the OECD average of 34.6%.

Source: Tax Foundation.

The employer's income tax consequences of wage or salary payments depend on the nature of the employee's services. If the employer is an individual and the services are *not* business related, the payment for such services is a nondeductible personal expense. For instance, people who employ private housekeepers, or gardeners, or nannies for their children can't deduct the compensation paid to these household employees. Of course, the fact that employees are performing domestic services doesn't excuse employers from their payroll tax obligations with respect to the compensation paid.[7]

For sole proprietorships, partnerships, and corporations that hire business employees, the compensation paid is either a deductible expense or a capitalized cost. This distinction depends on the nature of the service and the employer's method of accounting.

---

[6] Daniel P. O'Meara and Jeffrey L. Braff, "A Preventative Approach to Using Independent Contractors," *Journal of Accountancy,* September 1997, p. 43.

[7] In 2021, household employers are not required to pay or withhold payroll tax unless they pay $2,300 or more in wages to an employee during the year. §3121(a)(7)(B) and Subsection (x). Household employers are not required to withhold federal income tax unless the employee requests it and the employer agrees. §3401(a)(3).

Accounting for Compensation Paid	Berring Corporation paid a $165,000 salary to its in-house attorney, an expense that it deducted in the computation of taxable income. It also paid $2,679,000 wages to workers on its production line, a direct labor cost that Berring capitalized to manufactured inventory.

Employers are allowed to deduct compensation expense in the year the compensation is paid, and the employee includes the payment in gross income. Accrual basis employers can deduct accrued compensation expense only if the compensation is paid within two and one-half months after the close of the year.[8]

Reasonable Compensation

The tax law stipulates that only *reasonable* compensation for services rendered is deductible as a business expense. This stipulation is subjective: "Reasonable and true compensation is only such amount as would ordinarily be paid for like services by like enterprises under like circumstances."[9] The IRS generally assumes that compensation resulting from an arm's-length negotiation between employer and employee is reasonable. In other words, the IRS doesn't challenge compensation determined in the competitive marketplace.

The law does limit the compensation *deduction* allowed to publicly held corporations. These corporations can deduct no more than $1 million of the annual compensation paid to their principal executive officer (PEO), their principal financial officer (PFO), and the three other most highly paid officers.[10]

Deduction Limit on Executive Compensation	Shawn Pierce is the PEO of Furst, Inc., a publicly held corporation. According to Shawn's 2023 compensation contract, Shawn will receive a $675,000 base salary and a $600,000 bonus if 2023 gross sales exceed 110 percent of 2022 gross sales. By year-end, 2023 sales were 113 percent of 2022 sales, and Furst paid a bonus to Shawn. Furst, Inc. can deduct only $1 million of Shawn's $1,275,000 2023 compensation.

Closely Held Corporations

The payment of compensation by a closely held corporation to an employee who is also a shareholder may not be an arm's-length transaction. To the extent the employee influences or even controls corporate policy in their capacity as a shareholder, salary negotiations occur in a fictitious market.[11] As a result, the IRS looks closely to determine if the compensation is reasonable. If it concludes that the compensation is unreasonably high, it will reclassify the unreasonable portion as a constructive dividend.[12]

Reasonable compensation is based on the facts and circumstances of each particular employer/employee relationship, and the federal courts have heard thousands of cases in which the IRS and a corporate employer disagreed on this issue. In an often-cited decision, the Second Circuit Court of Appeals described five factors relevant to the reasonableness of employee compensation:

1. The shareholder/employee's role in the corporate business, including the number of hours worked and the duties performed.

[8] See the discussion of compensation accruals in Chapter 6.
[9] Source: Reg. &1.162-7 (b)(3).
[10] §162(m) as amended by the Tax Cuts and Jobs Act.
[11] See the discussion of fictitious markets involving related parties in Chapter 3.
[12] See the discussion of constructive dividends in Chapter 12.

2. External comparisons with other companies: specifically, compensation paid to the employee relative to compensation paid to comparable employees by unrelated employers in a similar business.

3. The financial condition of the corporate employer, including sales, net income, capital value, and general economic fitness.

4. The employee's degree of control over dividend policy in the employee's capacity as shareholder.

5. The internal consistency of the corporation's compensation system throughout the employee ranks.[13]

The appellate court pointed out that no single factor determines the issue and that it must "assess the entire tableau from the perspective of an independent investor—that is, given the dividends and return on equity enjoyed by a disinterested stockholder, would that stockholder approve the compensation paid to the employee?"[14] If unrelated shareholders acting in their economic self-interest would agree to the compensation paid to a shareholder/employee, that compensation should be considered reasonable.

$20 Million Man   John Menard was the CEO and controlling shareholder of Menard, Inc., the third-largest chain of home improvement stores in the country. In 1998, John received total compensation of more than $20 million. After the IRS challenged the reasonableness of this compensation, the corporation took its case to court. The Tax Court concluded that only $7 million was reasonable and that the remainder was a nondeductible dividend. The Tax Court's decision emphasized that Lowe's and Home Depot (Menard, Inc.'s chief competitors) paid their CEOs only $6.1 million and $2.8 million, respectively, in 1998. The Seventh Circuit Court of Appeals reversed the Tax Court's decision, criticizing it as "arbitrary as well as dizzying." The appellate court was impressed by John's "workaholic, micromanaging ways" and the fact that he worked "12 to 16 hours a day, 6 or 7 days a week, taking only 7 days of vacation a year, involving himself in every detail of his firm's operations." Based on this evidence, the court ruled that John was worth every penny of $20 million.[15]

S Corporations

The IRS views the issue of reasonable compensation in an entirely different light when the employment relationship is between an S corporation and its sole shareholder. In this case, the entire corporate income is taxed to the individual who owns the corporation. If the corporation pays the owner a salary as compensation for services rendered as an employee, the corporation's income decreases by the salary deduction, but the owner's income from the business (salary plus corporate income) is unchanged. The only significant tax consequence is the *payroll tax* burden on the salary. Therefore, the owner can minimize this payroll tax cost by having the S corporation pay an unreasonably low (or even no) salary. The IRS may counter this payroll tax avoidance tactic by treating any cash distributed by the S corporation to its shareholder as a constructive salary payment.[16]

[13] *Rapco, Inc.* v. *Commissioner,* 85 F.3d 950 (CA-2, 1996). See also *E.J. Harrison & Sons, Inc.* v. *Commissioner,* 138 Fed. Appx. 994 (CA-9, 2005), and *Aries Communication Inc. & Subs.,* T.C. Memo 2013-97.

[14] *Rapco, Inc.* v. *Commissioner,* 85 F.3d 950 (CA-2, 1996).

[15] *Menard Inc.* v. *Commissioner,* 560 F.3d 620 (CA-7, 2009).

[16] See *David E. Watson, P.C.* v. *United States,* 668 F.3d 1008 (CA-8, 2012), *cert. denied* (U.S., 2012).

Unreasonably Low Compensation	Jaime Perez is the sole shareholder and CEO of PML, Inc., a calendar year S corporation. The IRS recently audited PML's 2020 tax return on which the corporation deducted a $15,000 salary paid to Jaime as CEO. The corporation's taxable income was $741,240, and it distributed $400,000 cash to Jaime as a shareholder. Jaime reported both this salary and 100 percent of PML's taxable income on Form 1040. After comparing Jaime's salary with the salaries paid to CEOs of comparable corporate businesses, the IRS concluded that Jaime's salary should have been $125,000. Consequently, it reclassified $110,000 of Jaime's taxable income from PML as compensation and assessed Social Security and Medicare taxes accordingly.

Family Members as Employees

While the tax law doesn't prohibit closely held businesses from hiring employees who are related to the owners, the compensation paid to these relatives must be reasonable for the services actually performed. Subject to this constraint, business owners can effectively shift income to family members who work in the business.

Family Members as Employees	Lou Young, who owns a sole proprietorship, is in the 35 percent income tax bracket. Lou has two children, ages 14 and 17, who work in Lou's business after school and during the summer. The younger child performs clerical chores and runs errands, while the older child drives a delivery van. Lou pays the children a reasonable wage based on the actual number of hours worked each week. This year, the younger child earned $3,100, the older child earned $14,500, and the family saved $6,095 income tax.

Tax savings of business deduction to Lou ($17,600 wages paid × 35%)		$6,160

Tax consequences to	**Younger Child**	**Older Child**
Wage income	$ 3,100	$14,500
Standard deduction (single)	(3,100)	($13,850)
Taxable income	–0–	$ 650
Tax rate (single)		.10
Tax cost of compensation to children		$ 65

Tax savings to family	
Lou's savings	$ 6,160
Older child's cost	(65)
Net tax savings to family	$ 6,095

The income shift in this example had a second beneficial tax effect. The $17,600 business deduction reduced Lou's net earnings from self-employment and, therefore, her self-employment tax. However, wages paid to an employer's child under age 18 are not subject to FICA or unemployment tax.[17] Consequently, the wage payments to the two children didn't create an additional payroll tax cost for the business.

[17] §3121(b)(3)(A) and §3306(c)(5).

Foreign Earned Income Exclusion

Tax Talk

According to U.S. tax law, Antarctica is not a foreign country because it is not under the sovereignty of any government. Consequently, U.S. citizens working at a scientific station in Antarctica were denied a foreign earned income exclusion for their salaries.

Before leaving the topic of wages and salaries, we should consider the special case of individuals who are U.S. citizens but who reside and work on an extended basis in another country. These individuals, referred to as **expatriates,** may face a higher cost of living because of their overseas assignment or may incur additional costs such as foreign income taxes. Because of these financial concerns, U.S. firms with international operations may have difficulty staffing their foreign offices. To help U.S. firms compete in the labor market and to encourage them to employ U.S. citizens to work abroad, the tax law allows expatriates to exclude foreign wages or salary from taxable income. This **foreign earned income exclusion** for 2023 is $120,000.[18] Expatriates may not claim a foreign tax credit for any foreign income tax paid on the excluded income.[19]

Foreign Earned Income Exclusion

PBG operates a branch office in Portugal, which is managed by Malik Harris. Although a U.S. citizen, Malik has been a resident of Lisbon since 2009. In 2023, Malik earned $146,800 salary from PBG and paid $13,280 Portuguese income tax. In preparing Form 1040, Malik may exclude $120,000 of foreign-earned income from taxable income. Consequently, only $26,800 of salary is subject to U.S. tax. Malik may also claim a foreign tax credit based on the Portuguese income tax paid on the *taxable* portion of the salary.

EMPLOYEE FRINGE BENEFITS

Tax Talk

Certain employers have allowed employees to give up their accumulated vacation, sick leave, or personal leave days in exchange for the employer's cash payments to charities providing relief to hurricane victims. The IRS announced that such cash payments are not an indirect taxable benefit to the employees, and the employers can deduct the payments as a business expense.

As a general rule, individuals are taxed on any economic benefit received as compensation for services rendered to their employers, even if the benefit doesn't result in any direct cash flow.[20] However, the tax law allows employees to exclude the value of certain statutorily defined **fringe benefits** from income. These fringe benefits not only escape the income tax but also are exempt from payroll tax. Firms that provide fringe benefits account for the cost of the benefits in the same manner as the base compensation paid. If the salary or wage paid to an employee is currently deductible, the cost of the employee's fringe benefits is also deductible.[21] This section of this chapter describes several important nontaxable fringe benefits and discusses how employers and employees include these benefits in their compensation arrangements to mutual advantage.

LO 15-3
Identify the most common nontaxable employee fringe benefits.

Employer-Provided Benefits

Health and Accident Insurance

Employees can exclude the value of health and accident insurance coverage provided by their employers.[22] Hence, premiums that employers pay directly to insurance carriers on behalf of their employees aren't taxable to the employees. Similarly, if an employer has a self-insured medical reimbursement plan, participating employees don't recognize the imputed value of their coverage under the plan as income. This fringe benefit has tremendous significance to the U.S. workforce. Millions of employees rely on their employers for insurance protection. A worker's decision to accept or reject a job offer may depend on whether

---

[18] §911(a) and (b). The exclusion is adjusted annually for inflation.

[19] §911(d)(6).

[20] Reg. §1.61-21(a)(1).

[21] Reg. §1.263A-1(e)(3)(ii)(D).

[22] §106. This exclusion extends to the value of employer-provided, long-term-care insurance.

the prospective employer provides a comprehensive health and accident insurance plan. The tax law encourages employers to do so by making this form of compensation nontaxable. Such preferential treatment is costly; the Treasury loses over $220 billion of annual income tax revenue because of the exclusion for employer-provided medical insurance, making it the largest item in the government's tax expenditures budget.

Group Term Life Insurance

Employees can exclude the value of term life insurance coverage provided under a group policy carried by their employers, but only to the extent the coverage doesn't exceed $50,000. If the coverage exceeds $50,000, the employee is taxed on the cost of the excess. This cost is determined by reference to a uniform premium table provided by the Treasury rather than by reference to the actual insurance premiums paid by the employer.[23]

Group Term Life Insurance	Mr. Kung, a 46-year-old employee of ABC Corporation, has $200,000 life insurance coverage under ABC's group term plan. According to the Treasury's table, the cost of $1,000 of life insurance to a 46-year-old person is 15 cents a month. The annual cost of Mr. Kung's $150,000 excess coverage is $270 (150 × $.15 × 12 months). This amount is a taxable fringe benefit to Mr. Kung, and ABC must report $270 as part of Mr. Kung's compensation on his Form W-2.

Dependent Care Assistance Programs

Employees can exclude amounts paid or incurred by their employers for dependent care assistance.[24] Thus, employers may provide onsite day care for their employees' children (or other dependents) as a nontaxable fringe benefit. Alternatively, employers may contract with a third party to provide dependent care or may reimburse employees directly for their dependent care expenses. The annual exclusion is limited to $5,000 ($2,500 in the case of a separate return filed by a married individual). If the value of employer-provided dependent care exceeds $5,000, the employee must recognize the excess as taxable income.

Other Nontaxable Fringe Benefits

Most firms provide their employees with a variety of fringe benefits. The benefits that a particular firm offers depend on the nature of its business and the composition of its workforce. The list of possible benefits includes employee use of company cars, employer-provided cell phones, on-premise dining facilities, parking and public transportation, professional dues and subscriptions, and company-sponsored picnics and holiday parties. Each item on this list (as well as many other employee perks) can qualify as a nontaxable fringe benefit, but only if the item meets the detailed, and sometimes strict, requirements specified in the Internal Revenue Code and Treasury regulations.[25]

Reimbursed Employee Business Expenses

It is not unusual for individuals to incur out-of-pocket expenses relating to their employment. Common examples are union dues, subscriptions to professional or trade journals, uniforms, continuing education courses that maintain or improve job skills, and transportation and travel costs incurred while conducting business for an employer. Employers routinely reimburse employees for substantiated employment-related expenses,

[23] Reg. §1.79-3. The employer's actual cost of group term life insurance is a §162 expense. Reg. §1.162-10 and Rev. Rul. 69-478, 1969-2 C.B. 29.

[24] §129.

[25] See §132 and accompanying regulations.

thereby assuming the economic burden of the expense. In such cases, the employee simply excludes the cash reimbursement from gross income, and the expense/reimbursement transaction is a wash without any effect on the employee's taxable income.[26]

The tax consequence of *unreimbursed* employment-related expenses is much less benign. Congress has expressed its belief that individuals should not be allowed to deduct such expenses. If the expenses are truly necessary to the successful performance of an employee's duties, the employer should be willing to provide reimbursement. Consequently, unreimbursed employment-related expenses are nondeductible by the employee.

Reimbursed Employee Expenses	Anaru, who is employed by an advertising firm, spent $1,500 to attend a seminar on computer graphics. Anaru's employer agreed to provide reimbursement for this employment-related expense and direct deposited $1,500 to Anaru's bank account in the same way the company direct deposits employee paychecks. Anaru excludes the reimbursement from gross income. If instead Anaru's employer refused to provide reimbursement, the $1,500 is a nondeductible expense of Anaru's.

Prior to enactment of the Tax Cuts and Jobs Act, individuals were allowed an above-the-line deduction for employment-related moving expenses. If an employer reimbursed an employee for moving expenses eligible for deduction, the reimbursement was excluded from the employee's gross income as a nontaxable fringe benefit. Beginning in 2018, employment-related moving expenses are not deductible, and any reimbursement by the employer is included in the employee's gross income.[27]

Reimbursed Moving Expenses	BV Corporation transferred an employee from its San Diego office to its San Antonio office. The employee paid $5,800 to a moving company to transport household goods from California to Texas, and $2,400 in airfare to relocate the employee's family. BV Corporation reimbursed the employee $8,200 for moving expenses, a payment that the employee must include in gross income.

Fringe Benefits and Self-Employed Individuals

The tax-exempt status of many employee fringe benefits doesn't extend to benefits that self-employed individuals provide for themselves. As a result, self-employed individuals must spend after-tax dollars to pay for certain commodities that employees can obtain with before-tax dollars (as nontaxable compensation). For example, if a self-employed person pays $750 to purchase a $50,000 life insurance policy to protect their family, the payment is a nondeductible personal expense. The same disadvantage applies to individual partners and shareholders in S corporations. If a partnership has a group term life insurance plan covering both employees and partners, the cost of a partner's insurance is a guaranteed payment that the partner must recognize as taxable income.[28] If an S corporation has a group term life insurance plan, the cost of a shareholder/employee's insurance is similarly taxable compensation instead of a nontaxable fringe benefit.[29]

---

[26] Reg. §1.162-2(c)(4).

[27] §217(k) and §132(g)(2). Disallowance of the deduction and exclusion doesn't apply to members of the Armed Forces on active duty who move pursuant to a military order and incident to a permanent change of station.

[28] Rev. Rul. 91-26, 1991-1 C.B. 184.

[29] §1372 prevents any shareholder who owns more than 2 percent of an S corporation's stock from excluding employee fringe benefits from taxable income.

Although, self-employed individuals, partners, and S corporation shareholders do receive special consideration with respect to medical and accident insurance for themselves and their families. These taxpayers are allowed an above-the-line deduction for the cost of this insurance.[30]

Deduction of Health Insurance Costs	Vernon LLC has 38 employees and five individual members who work for the LLC. The LLC provides a group medical insurance plan that covers both employees and members. The cost of the insurance is a nontaxable fringe benefit to Vernon's employees and taxable compensation to the members. This year, George, an LLC member, recognizes the $2,650 cost of medical insurance as an income item. However, George is allowed an above-the-line deduction of the same amount, so the net effect of this fringe benefit on her AGI is zero.

Compensation Planning with Fringe Benefits

Fringe benefits are an extremely popular form of compensation. One reason is that the employer's cost of providing the benefit is usually less than the benefit's value to the employee. This differential is attributable to the employer's economy of scale: The cost per person of providing a commodity such as health insurance or child care to a large group is less than the cost of the commodity to one individual.

Cost versus Value of Fringe Benefit	Contex Corporation, which has 1,200 employees, maintains a group medical plan with a commercial insurance company. Jian participates in this plan, and the annual cost of coverage is $2,400. If Jian were not a participant, comparable private insurance would cost $3,600. Contex operates an on-premise day care facility in which employees can enroll their preschool children at no charge. Contex's annual operating cost is $1,750 per child. Jian's child attends this facility. If the facility were not available, Jian would pay $2,100 per year for private day care. The aggregate value of these two fringe benefits to Jian is $5,700. Contex's cost to provide the benefits is only $4,150.

Cafeteria Plans

Because employees have varying financial needs and consumption preferences, each one places a different value on any noncash benefit offered by their employer.

Valuing Fringe Benefits	In the preceding example, Jian placed a $2,100 value on the child care provided by Contex and was willing to pay $2,100 for this commodity. Blair, another corporate employee, has no children. Therefore, Blair places a zero value on employer-provided child care and would prefer a different fringe benefit or even additional salary from Contex rather than a worthless fringe benefit.

Employers can maximize the aggregate value of their fringe-benefit programs to their employees through a **cafeteria plan.** Under a cafeteria plan, each employee may select noncash benefits from a menu of benefit choices. In lieu of noncash benefits, employees may simply select additional taxable salary.[31] By participating in a cafeteria plan, employees can combine both nontaxable and taxable benefits to result in the greatest after-tax compensation based on their individual needs and preferences.

[30] §162(l).
[31] Cafeteria plans are described in §125.

Negotiating with Nontaxable Fringe Benefits

Employers are aware that employees may enjoy substantial tax savings because of nontaxable fringe benefits. By substituting nontaxable benefits for taxable compensation, employers can capture some portion of these savings for themselves and reduce the after-tax cost of the compensation. The examples that follow demonstrate this important point.

Salary Payment

Leyton Corporation is negotiating a one-year employment contract with Ms. King, who begins the negotiation by requesting a $200,000 salary. Leyton's tax rate is 21 percent, and Ms. King's marginal tax rate is 35 percent. The after-tax cost of this salary to Leyton and the after-tax value of this salary to Ms. King are computed as follows:

	Leyton	Ms. King
Salary payment	$(200,000)	$200,000
Employer/employee payroll tax (2023)	(12,833)	(12,833)
Income tax savings (cost):		
Salary deduction × 21%	42,000	
Payroll tax deduction × 21%	2,695	
Salary income × 35%		(70,000)
After-tax (cost) value	$(168,138)	$117,117

Now assume that Leyton makes a counteroffer to Ms. King. Leyton will pay a $185,000 salary and provide complete medical and dental insurance coverage for Ms. King and a membership in its on-premises health spa. Assume that the value of these nontaxable fringe benefits to Ms. King is $12,000, but their incremental cost to Leyton is only $9,000.[32]

Reduced Salary plus Fringe Benefits

The after-tax cost of the compensation package (salary plus fringe benefits) to Leyton and the after-tax value of this package to Ms. King are computed as follows:

	Leyton	Ms. King
Salary payment	$(185,000)	$185,000
Fringe-benefit (cost) value	(9,000)	12,000
Employer/employee payroll tax (2023)	(12,616)	(12,616)
Income tax savings (cost):		
Salary deduction × 21%	38,850	
Fringe-benefit deduction × 21%	1,890	
Payroll tax deduction × 21%	2,649	
Salary income × 35%		(64,750)
After-tax (cost) value	$(163,227)	$119,634

The substitution of nontaxable fringe benefits for salary *decreased* Leyton's after-tax cost by $4,911 and *increased* Ms. King's after-tax compensation by $2,517. Thus, both parties to this negotiation benefited from the nontaxable fringe benefits.

---

[32] The value of an on-premises athletic facility can qualify as a nontaxable fringe benefit. §132(j)(4).

EQUITY-BASED COMPENSATION

LO 15-4
Describe the tax and
financial accounting
consequences of equity-
based compensation.

Corporate employers often include some form of equity in the compensation package offered to key employees. Such equity-based compensation can consist of shares of corporate stock or options to purchase such stock. The recipient employees who become stockholders have a financial interest in the corporation's long-term success and a powerful incentive to contribute to that success. From the employer's perspective, the payment of equity-based compensation requires no cash outlay and, in the case of stock options, may result in an infusion of capital.

Restricted Stock

Tax Talk

Early in 2018, Apple, Inc. pledged to grant a $2,500 restricted stock award to all eligible part-time and full-time employees, described by CEO Tim Cook as "the heart and soul of Apple."

Corporations that transfer their own stock as compensation typically place restrictions on the recipient employee's rights of ownership. The employee may be prohibited from selling or disposing of the stock for a specified time period. Or the employee may be required to return (forfeit) the stock back to the corporation if the employee terminates employment within a specified time period. In theory, the use of compensatory **restricted stock** provides assurance to the corporation of the employee's continued commitment to their job.

An employee who receives stock as compensation for services must include the fair market value of the stock in gross income at the time the employee's rights to the stock are transferable or such rights are not subject to a substantial risk of forfeiture, whichever occurs earlier.[33] The employee's tax basis in the stock equals the amount of income recognized.[34]

Receipt of Restricted Stock

Drew is an employee of Kylo Industries, a publicly held corporation. As part of the 2017 compensation package, the company issued Drew 4,000 shares of Kylo common stock. On the June 30 issuance date, the stock's fair market value was $29,000. According to the terms of the compensation contract, Drew's rights in the stock weren't transferable until July 1, 2023. If employment was terminated before this date, Drew would forfeit the stock back to Kylo. Because the rights in the stock were nontransferable and subject to a substantial risk of forfeiture, Drew did not include the $29,000 value of the stock in 2017 gross income.

On July 1, 2023, Drew's rights in the 4,000 shares of Kylo stock became fully vested (such rights became transferable and were no longer subject to forfeiture). The fair market value of the stock on this date was $45,500, which Drew included in 2023 gross income and took as the tax basis in the stock. Note that Drew recognized $45,500 of *noncash* compensation subject to both income tax and employee payroll tax.[35] Drew generated the cash to pay this tax bill by selling some shares for fair market value. Because the selling price equaled the tax basis in the shares, the sale did not result in any additional 2023 income.

Tax Talk

In 2020, Eric Wu, CEO of Opendoor Technologies, earned over $388.7 million compensation, which included only $189,600 in salary and the remainder in stock awards.

Source: Bloomberg

Because of the restrictions on Drew's ownership of the 4,000 shares, recognition of income could be deferred from 2017 until 2023. However, the *amount* of income Drew recognized in 2023 was significantly more than the 2017 value of the stock. In retrospect, Drew might have reduced the tax cost (in present value terms) by foregoing the deferral and recognizing $29,000 of income in 2017. The tax law does give recipients of restricted stock this very

[33] §83(a). Restricted stock units (RSUs) are a popular variation of restricted stock. RSUs give the recipient employee the right to receive stock at a future date after the employee has worked for a specified period of time or satisfied other performance obligations. RSUs are deferred compensation; employees recognize income in the future year in which they actually receive unrestricted stock in an amount equal to the FMV of the stock at that time.

[34] Reg. §1.61-2(d).

[35] §3121(a).

choice. By filing a written election with the IRS, an employee can choose to include the value of restricted stock in gross income on the date the stock is received, even though the stock is nontransferable or subject to risk of forfeiture.[36] This election must be filed not later than 30 days after the receipt, a point in time when the employee doesn't know what the stock will be worth in the future. There is a second risky aspect of this election. If the employee subsequently has to forfeit the stock, no deduction is allowed because of the forfeiture.

Election to Accelerate Income Recognition	Refer to the preceding example in which Drew received 4,000 shares of restricted Kylo stock on June 30, 2017. Now assume that Drew filed an election by July 30 to include the $29,000 value of the stock in 2017 gross income. Assume also that when the stock became fully vested on July 1, 2023, its fair market value was only $32,500. The vesting has no tax consequences to Drew. However, the tax benefit of recognizing only $29,000 instead of $32,500 of income may be less than the tax cost of accelerating the recognition of that income (and tax cost) by six years.
	The worst-case scenario is that Drew elected to recognize $29,000 of income in 2017, and then, due to unforeseen circumstances, terminated employment with Kylo Industries before July 1, 2023. In such case, the 4,000 shares of stock would be forfeited back to Kylo. Even though income was recognized when the restricted stock was received, Drew would not be allowed an offsetting deduction upon its forfeiture.

Stock Options

Corporate employers often include stock options as a major component of the compensation package offered to key employees. A **stock option** is the right to purchase the corporation's stock for a stated price (the strike price) for a given period of time. From the employee's perspective, stock options are an opportunity to acquire equity at a bargain price.

To analyze the tax consequences of compensatory stock options, consider the case of BRT and its employee, Liam Bell. In year 1, BRT grants Liam had an option to buy 2,000 shares of BRT stock for a strike price of $30 per share at any time during the next eight years. On the date of grant, BRT stock is selling for $28 per share. Because the strike price exceeds the market price, the option has no readily ascertainable value, and Liam doesn't recognize income on receipt of the option.[37] The risk that Liam assumes in accepting the option is that the market price will not climb above $30 per share over the term of the option. In this case, the option is worthless, and Liam will simply let it lapse.

Liam's expectation is that the market price of BRT stock will increase over the option period. Suppose that by year 8, the stock is selling at $75 per share. Liam exercises the option by paying $60,000 cash to BRT for 2,000 shares with a market value of $150,000. Liam must recognize the $90,000 **bargain element** (excess of market value over cost) as ordinary income in year 8. These results are shown in Exhibit 15.3 in which the vertical axis is BRT stock price and the horizontal axis is the eight-year option period.

The shaded area in Exhibit 15.3 represents the value of Liam's option, which increased over time as the BRT stock price climbed from $28 to $75. Liam defers income recognition until realization of this value by converting the option to actual shares of stock. Liam's tax basis in the 2,000 shares is $150,000: $60,000 out-of-pocket cost plus $90,000 income recognized on the exercise of the option.

Note that in year 8, Liam has *negative* cash flow; Liam must pay $60,000 for the stock plus both income and payroll tax on $90,000 compensation. Liam can generate cash by

---

[36] §83(b).

[37] Reg. §1.83-7.

EXHIBIT 15.3
Tax Consequences of Ms. Bell's Stock Option

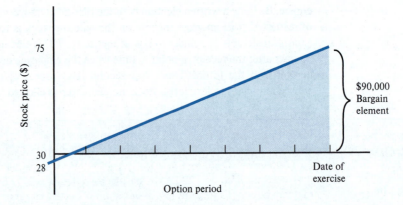

selling some shares of BRT.[38] This sale won't trigger additional income unless the selling price exceeds Liam's $75 basis per share. On the other hand, BRT received $60,000 cash as paid-in capital when Liam exercised the stock option.

Consequences to Corporate Employer

Corporations that use restricted stock or stock options to compensate an employee can take a business deduction equal to the amount of gross income recognized by the employee.[39] This deduction is allowed for the corporate taxable year in which the employee's taxable year of recognition ends.

Corporate Deduction: Restricted Stock	On September 30, 2019, Bantam, Inc. issued 20,000 shares of restricted stock to its PFO, Jose Martinez. On October 1, 2023, the restrictions lapsed, and Jose included the $70,000 fair market value of the shares in gross income reported on Jose's 2023 calendar year Form 1040. Because Bantam also uses a calendar year for tax purposes, it reported a $70,000 compensation deduction on its 2023 Form 1120.

Corporate Deduction: Stock Options	In 2017, Yadon, Inc. granted an option to purchase 10,000 shares of common stock to its vice president, Sophie Laub. Sophie exercised the option in 2023 and included the $63,000 bargain element in gross income reported on Sophie's 2023 calendar year Form 1040. Because Yadon uses a fiscal year ending May 30, it reported a $63,000 compensation deduction on its Form 1120 for the taxable year ending May 30, 2024, the year *within which* Sophie's taxable year ended.

Book/Tax Differences

The treatment of equity-based compensation for financial statement purposes can be radically different from the treatment for tax purposes.[40] In the case of restricted stock, the value of the stock determined on the date of transfer to the employee becomes the corporation's compensation cost. This cost is amortized as an expense over the time period during which the restrictions are in force (the vesting or service period). In contrast, the amount and timing of the corporation's tax deduction is based on the amount of gross income recognized by

[38] If an employee acquires stock in a *closely held* corporation by exercising an option, the employee might be prohibited from selling shares to generate cash. In the case of such nontransferable stock, the employee can elect to defer income recognition for up to five years from the date of exercise. §83(i) as amended by the Tax Cuts and Jobs Act.

[39] §83(h) and Reg. §1.83-6. If compensation to the employee is a capital cost (e.g., an inventory cost under UNICAP) rather than a period expense, capitalization occurs according to the same timing rule.

[40] ASC Topic 718, *Compensation-Stock Compensation,* provides the financial accounting rules with respect to restricted stock and stock options.

the employee and the taxable year in which recognition occurs. This difference in accounting treatment results in temporary differences between book income and taxable income.

| *Book/Tax Difference: Restricted Stock* | On December 31, 2020, Parma Corporation issued 8,000 shares of restricted stock to a key employee. If the employee terminates employment before January 1, 2023, the shares must be forfeited back to Parma. On the date of issuance, the fair market value of the shares was $50,000. For book purposes, Parma amortized this compensation cost over the two-year vesting period ($25,000 expense on its 2021 and 2022 income statements).

The employee deferred income recognition until the restrictions on the stock lapsed on January 1, 2023. The fair market value of the 8,000 shares on that date was $59,400, which the employee included in 2023 gross income. Consequently, Parma reported a $59,400 compensation deduction on its 2023 Form 1120. The difference in accounting treatment caused a temporary excess of taxable over book income in 2021 and 2022, which reversed as an excess of book income over taxable income in 2023. |
|---|---|

For financial statement purposes, corporations must record the estimated value of stock options as compensation expense in the year of grant. For tax purposes, the corporation is not allowed a compensation deduction until the year of exercise. This difference in accounting treatment causes a temporary excess of taxable income over book income in the year of grant that reverses in the year of exercise.

Book/Tax Difference from Stock Options	Four years ago, Perino, Inc. granted stock options to 16 key employees and expensed the $2.84 million total estimated value of the options on its income statement. This nondeductible expense resulted in a temporary excess of taxable over book income. In the current year, one of Perino's employees exercised an option and included the $103,100 bargain element (excess of market value over option price) in gross income. Perino's $103,100 current year deduction of the bargain element is a partial reversal of the original temporary difference.

Incentive Stock Options

The tax law creates a special type of employee stock option called an **incentive stock option (ISO).** The qualification requirements for ISOs are narrow and complex, but the preferential treatment of ISOs as compared to nonqualifying options is straightforward.[41] When an employee exercises an ISO, they do not recognize the bargain element as taxable income.[42] The tax basis in the purchased shares is the employee's out-of-pocket cost, and the employee recognizes no income with respect to these shares unless and until the employee disposes of them in a taxable transaction. Furthermore, any gain recognized on disposition is capital gain.

Refer back to the facts concerning Liam's option to purchase 2,000 shares of BRT common stock and assume that the option qualified as an ISO. In year 8, Liam does not recognize any income with the purchase of 2,000 shares worth $150,000 for only $60,000. Suppose that Liam holds these shares until year 15, and then sells for $225,000. Liam's capital gain on sale is $165,000 ($225,000 amount realized − $60,000 basis), $90,000 of which represents the untaxed bargain element on exercise of the option.

| *ISO versus Nonqualified Option: Ms. Bell's Perspective* | The following table contrasts Liam's income tax cost from this sequence of transactions to the tax cost if the stock option had not qualified as an ISO. The table assumes a 37 percent rate on ordinary income and a 20 percent rate on capital gain.

(continued) |
|---|---|

[41] Incentive stock options are defined in §422(b).
[42] §421(a).

	ISO	Nonqualified Option
Year 8 (exercise of option):		
Ordinary income recognized	–0–	$ 90,000
Tax cost at 37%	**–0–**	**33,300**
Basis in 2,000 shares	$ 60,000	$ 150,000
Year 15 (sale of stock):		
Selling price	$225,000	$ 225,000
Basis	(60,000)	(150,000)
Capital gain recognized	$165,000	$ 75,000
Tax cost at 20%	**$ 33,000**	**$ 15,000**

This table shows the dual advantage of ISOs compared to nonqualified stock options: the extension of the *tax-deferral* period until the year of sale and the *conversion* of the option's bargain element from ordinary income to capital gain. However, individuals who are planning to exercise ISOs must be cautious. The untaxed bargain element is an alternative minimum tax (AMT) adjustment added to taxable income in the computation of alternative minimum taxable income (AMTI).[43] Accordingly, individuals may want to avoid exercising ISOs in a year in which they have any exposure to the AMT.

AMT on ISO

Maya Craig, a single taxpayer, plans to exercise an ISO in 2023. The bargain element (excess of market value over cost) would be $380,000. Maya estimates that the taxable income on Form 1040 will be $760,000, and AMTI (without the bargain element) will be $785,000. Consequently, regular income tax would be $241,532, tentative minimum tax would be only $204,100, and Maya would owe no AMT. If Maya exercises the ISO, the bargain element would not increase taxable income. However, it would be a tax preference item that would increase AMTI to $1,165,000. Tentative AMT would increase to $321,786 and Maya would owe $80,254 AMT ($321,786 – $241,532 regular income tax).

A negative feature of ISOs is that employers never receive a tax deduction for the option's bargain element. Consequently, they derive no tax benefit when an employee exercises an ISO. The book/tax difference that originates in the year of grant of an ISO doesn't reverse in the year of exercise and results in a permanent excess of taxable income over book income.

ISO versus Nonqualified Option: BRT's Perspective

Refer to the example concerning Liam's exercise of his BRT stock option. The following table compares BRT's cash flow consequences of compensating Liam with an ISO rather than with a nonqualified stock option.

	ISO	Nonqualified Option
Year 8 (Liam's exercise of option):		
BRT's paid-in capital from issuance of shares	$60,000	$60,000
Deduction for bargain element	–0–	$90,000
BRT's tax rate		.21
Tax savings from deduction	–0–	18,900
BRT's net cash flow in year 8	$60,000	$78,900

Liam's sale of BRT stock in year 15 has no effect on BRT.

[43] §56(b)(3).

RETIREMENT PLANNING

At some point in their lives, most people confront the need to plan for retirement. Given the life expectancy for the average American, individuals who want to retire by age 65 know that they might live 20 to 30 years after leaving the workforce. They also know that they should take action now to maintain their standard of living during this post-employment period. Specifically, they must invest some portion of their current income in financial assets that will provide future income. In this section of this chapter, we will learn how the tax laws encourage people to save for retirement. By taking advantage of tax-favored retirement plans, individuals can maximize the future value of their investments and enhance their prospects for long-term security.[44]

Retirement Planning Is Top Priority	On the basis of a survey of employee benefit specialists, retirement planning has replaced health care as the top priority for today's labor force. The tidal wave of baby boomers approaching retirement age is recognizing the need to evaluate the adequacy of retirement savings. Many firms have initiated investment education programs to help their employees assess their investment options and develop strategies to increase their retirement income. Better still, the value of these retirement planning services is a nontaxable fringe benefit to the employees.[45]

LO 15-5
Explain the tax advantages of qualified over nonqualified retirement plans.

Tax Advantages of Qualified Retirement Plans

The tax law confers a generous set of advantages on an array of retirement savings plans, described generically as **qualified retirement plans.** While the statutory requirements and the financial and legal structures of the plans vary considerably, they all offer two basic benefits to the individuals who participate.[46]

- Dollars of earned income contributed to the plan (or contributed by an employer on an employee's behalf) are not taxed currently.
- The plan itself is tax-exempt, so the earnings generated by the contributed dollars are not taxed currently.

The effect of these two benefits on the rate at which the contributed dollars grow over time is tremendous. The next example highlights this effect.

Qualified Retirement Plan Contributions	Mr. Quincy and Mrs. Russ, who are both in the 35 percent marginal tax bracket, have decided to contribute $20,000 annual before-tax earned income to a retirement fund. Both funds earn an annual 5 percent rate of return and involve the same financial risk. The only difference is that Mr. Quincy's fund is a qualified retirement plan, while Mrs. Russ's fund is not. The following table shows the calculation of the balances in the two funds after 25 years:
	(continued)

---

[44] While many people anticipate that they will receive Social Security benefits during their retirement years, they can't undertake any type of individualized tax planning to increase these benefits. The tax consequences of Social Security are covered in Chapter 17 as part of the discussion of government transfer payments.

[45] Qualified retirement planning services are a nontaxable fringe benefit per §132(a)(7).

[46] The tax law provides another inducement for individuals to save for retirement: a nonrefundable tax credit for low-income taxpayers. This "saver's credit" equals a percentage of the taxpayer's *elective* contributions to a qualified retirement plan [including a Section 401(k) plan or an IRA]. The maximum annual contribution eligible for the credit is $2,000, and the maximum credit percentage is 50 percent. §25B.

	Mr. Quincy	Mrs. Russ
Before-tax annual contribution	$ 20,000	$ 20,000
Income tax cost	–0–	(7,000)
After-tax annual contribution	$ 20,000	$ 13,000
Before-tax rate of return on contributions	.05	.05
After-tax rate of return on contributions	.05	.0325
Fund balance after 25 years	$1,002,269	$505,759

The balance in Mr. Quincy's fund does not represent the disposable wealth available on retirement. The law allows Mr. Quincy to *defer* the tax on retirement savings—but not to escape taxation entirely. When Mr. Quincy withdraws money from the fund, the withdrawals are taxable.[47] In contrast, Mrs. Russ's fund balance consists of after-tax dollars that may be withdrawn without further tax cost. The next example provides a final comparison of the two funds.

Qualified Retirement Plan Withdrawals

At the end of 25 years, both Mr. Quincy and Mrs. Russ withdraw the balance from their retirement fund. Assume that Mr. Quincy pays 35 percent tax on the entire withdrawal.

	Mr. Quincy	Mrs. Russ
Fund balance after 25 years	$1,002,269	$505,759
Income tax cost of withdrawal	(350,794)	–0–
After-tax disposable wealth	$ 651,475	$505,759

This comparison of after-tax wealth is testimony to the power of tax deferral. Moreover, Mr. Quincy can prolong the deferral by liquidating his retirement fund gradually over a number of years rather than in a single lump sum. Depending on the type of plan, Mr. Quincy may have the option of receiving the fund balance in the form of an annuity, a series of fixed payments over a specific period of time. In such a case, Mr. Quincy will pay tax on the retirement dollars received each year.

The tax law limits the duration of the deferral that people can achieve by investing in qualified retirement plans. Plan participants generally must begin receiving distributions from their plans no later than April 1 of the year following the year in which they reach the age of 72. The entire interest in the plan must be distributed over a period of years based on the participant's life expectancy and the life expectancy of the designated beneficiary of the plan.[48] Treasury regulations provide life expectancy tables for computing a participant's annual **minimum distribution** from a plan.

Tax Talk
In response to the COVID-19 pandemic, the CARES Act waived the 2020 required minimum distribution from IRAs and retirement plans for all taxpayers regardless of whether the taxpayer was affected by the pandemic.

Minimum Distribution

Ms. Ramone participated in a qualified retirement plan for 28 years before retiring eight years ago at age 63. Mr. Ramone is the beneficiary who would receive Ms. Ramone's interest in the plan if Ms. Ramone dies. Because the Ramones have sufficient annual income, they haven't withdrawn any funds from the qualified plan. However, Ms. Ramone reached age 72 in 2023 and must receive a minimum distribution by April 1 of 2024. According to Treasury regulations and the Ramones' ages, their distribution period is 27.4 years, and their minimum distribution must be 3.64 percent of the plan balance at the beginning of the taxable year. For example, if the plan balance at the beginning of a year is $319,200, the Ramones must withdraw $11,651 ($319,200 × .0365) and include this distribution in taxable income.

---

[47] §402(a) provides that distributions from qualified retirement plans are taxable to the recipient under §72.

[48] §401(a)(9). In the case of employer-sponsored retirement plans, employees who continue to work after age 72 may postpone receiving distributions until they retire.

Premature Withdrawals

When Congress decided to allow individuals to defer income tax through participation in qualified plans, the intent was that participants use the plans to save for retirement. To discourage people from withdrawing funds before retirement, the Internal Revenue Code imposes a 10 percent penalty on any **premature withdrawal** from a qualified plan.[49]

Generally, a withdrawal is premature unless the participant has reached the age of 59½ by the date of withdrawal. This rule is subject to a number of important exceptions. For instance, the penalty is waived if the owner is totally or permanently disabled; if the owner has reached age 55 and has terminated employment with the plan sponsor; or if the withdrawal is made by the owner's estate or beneficiary after the owner's death.

Premature Withdrawal	Jung Soo, age 51, withdrew $16,000 cash from a qualified retirement plan to fund an investment in a start-up company. Jung must include the $16,000 distribution in gross income and also pay a $1,600 premature withdrawal penalty. Now change the facts by assuming that Jung is age 63. In this case, Jung must still include the $16,000 in gross income, but the 10 percent penalty is avoided because Jung has reached the age of 59½.

A Question of Age	Wilfred Omoloh was born in Kenya but became a naturalized U.S. citizen in 1997. In 2010, Mr. Omoloh withdrew $35,000 from his IRA but failed to report it as income on his tax return. The IRS discovered the omission and assessed both income tax and the 10 percent penalty on the withdrawal. Mr. Omoloh conceded that the withdrawal was taxable, but argued in the Tax Court that he was 60 years old on the date of withdrawal and owed no penalty. As proof, he presented a recently issued Kenyan birth certificate showing that he was born in 1950. However, Mr. Omoloh's Texas driver's license, his certificate of naturalization, and his academic transcript from the University of Georgia showed that he was born in 1952. After weighing the evidence, the Tax Court was not persuaded that Mr. Omoloh was 60 years old at the date of withdrawal and upheld the 10 percent penalty.[50]

The 10 percent penalty applies only to the portion of a withdrawal included in the participant's income. Individuals who withdraw funds from a qualified plan can avoid both the income tax and any premature withdrawal penalty by rolling over the funds to *another* qualified plan (including an IRA) within 60 days of the withdrawal.

Rollover of Plan Withdrawal	Harrison, age 48, participated for 14 years in an employer-sponsored qualified retirement plan through Acton, Inc. and generated a $35,000 balance. This year, Harrison resigned from Acton to accept a new job with Zuma, Inc. Because of the termination of employment, Harrison received a cash distribution from the Acton plan equal to the $35,000 balance. Harrison spent $12,000 of these funds to buy a new car and made a **rollover contribution** of the $23,000 remainder to Zuma's qualified retirement plan. Consequently, Harrison recognized only $12,000 of the distribution as taxable income. Applying Harrison's 24 percent marginal rate, the total tax cost of the withdrawal was $4,080:

Income tax ($12,000 × 24%)	$2,880
Premature withdrawal penalty ($12,000 × 10%)	1,200
Total tax cost	$4,080

[49] §72(t).

[50] *Omoloh*, T.C. Summary Opinion 2017-64.

TYPES OF QUALIFIED PLANS

LO 15-6
Contrast defined-benefit, defined-contribution, and nonqualified deferred compensation plans.

Qualified retirement plans fall into three categories:

1. Plans that employers provide for their employees.
2. Plans available to self-employed individuals (Keogh, SEP, or Simple IRA).
3. Individual retirement accounts (IRAs) available to any person who recognizes compensation or earned income.

This section of this chapter describes the plans included in each category. As you will observe, qualified plans come in a variety of shapes and sizes. But regardless of the differences in structure or operation, qualified retirement plans share a common characteristic: They all are vehicles for tax-favored savings.

Employer-Provided Plans

One of the more common fringe benefits offered to employees is participation in one or more retirement plans sponsored and maintained by their employer. For an **employer-provided plan** to be qualified for federal tax purposes, it must satisfy a formidable list of statutory requirements.[51] These requirements reflect two underlying policy objectives. The first objective is that *employer-provided plans should carry minimum risk for participating employees.* To meet this objective, the law requires that

- Qualified plans must be written permanent arrangements and must be administered in trust form so that the plan assets are invested by an independent trustee for the exclusive benefit of the employees and their families.
- Qualified plans must be funded; annual contributions made to a plan by an employer on behalf of the employees must consist of cash or other valuable property.
- Employees must have a nonforfeitable (vested) right to 100 percent of their retirement benefits under a qualified plan after no more than six years (defined-contribution plan) or seven years (defined-benefit plan) of service with the employer.

The second objective is that *employer-provided plans should offer benefits in an equitable manner to all participating employees.* Accordingly, plans may not discriminate in favor of officers, owner-employees, or highly compensated employees.[52] In other words, rank-and-file employees must be entitled to participate in qualified retirement plans on essentially the same basis as the chief executive officer.

Defined-Benefit Plans

Employer-provided plans may take the form of a pension plan under which participating employees are promised a targeted or defined benefit when they retire. Firms make annual contributions to their pension plans based on the actuarially determined cost of funding the future retirement benefits to which the current workforce is entitled.[53] These contributions are deductible payroll expenses, even though the employees don't recognize the

Tax Talk

In response to the COVID-19 pandemic, the CARES Act allowed for increased access to retirement savings without the normal penalties. Qualified individuals could take a distribution of up to $100,000 from an eligible retirement plan between January 1 and December 30, 2020. This coronavirus-related distribution was not subject to the 10 percent additional tax that generally applies to distributions taken before age 59½. The taxpayer could then choose to repay the distribution within three years to avoid the tax consequences of the distribution. Alternatively, the taxpayer could choose not to repay the retirement account and include the withdrawal in income in equal installments over a three-year period.

Tax Talk

According to the Federal Reserve data, the retirement landscape in the U.S. continues to shift with defined contribution plans becoming the predominant form of plan. Defined contribution plans account for about 55 percent of retirement savings among nonretirees, while defined benefits plans represent less than half that amount at 22 percent.

---

[51] §401 through §415.

[52] §401(a)(17) provides that an employer-provided plan is not qualified unless the annual compensation of each employee taken into account for determining benefits under the plan is limited to an inflation-adjusted amount. In 2020, the annual limitation is $285,000. See also §404(l).

[53] In 1974, Congress created the Pension Benefit Guaranty Corporation (PBGC) to insure defined benefit plans and to guarantee that participating employees receive their promised pension, even if the plan is underfunded or is terminated by the employer. Qualified plans must pay annual premiums to the PBGC for such insurance.

contributions as income.[54] For tax purposes, firms must comply with a minimum funding standard for their qualified pension plans.[55] Because of this standard, a firm may be required to make contributions to the retirement trust in years in which it operates at a loss or experiences cash flow difficulties. For this reason, employers should regard employee pension plans as long-term financial obligations.

Funding a Defined-Benefit Plan	BN, Inc. provides a qualified defined-benefit plan for its employees. This year, an independent actuary determined that BN must contribute $4.28 million to the retirement trust to fund the future pension benefits to which its workforce is entitled. The contribution doesn't represent taxable compensation to the employees participating in the plan. However, BN can deduct the $4.28 million contribution on its Form 1120.

The annual pension that employers can provide through a qualified **defined-benefit plan** is limited to the *lesser* of 100 percent of the retiree's average compensation for their three highest compensation years or an annual base amount.[56] In 2023, the base amount is $265,000. Firms wanting to provide more generous pensions must do so through nonqualified retirement plans. The tax consequences of nonqualified plans are discussed later in this section.

Contribution Limit on Defined-Benefit Plan	Damien, a corporate officer of BN, Inc., currently earns a $252,000 salary and anticipates a salary increase every year until retirement. Damien participates in BN's qualified pension plan. Damien's average compensation for the three highest compensation years is projected to be at least $300,000. Therefore, BN's 2023 plan contribution on Damien's behalf is limited to the amount necessary to fund an annual pension benefit of $265,000.

Defined-Contribution Plans

Employer-provided plans may be structured as **defined-contribution plans** under which the retirement trust maintains a separate account for each participating employee. Each year, the employer contributes a specified amount to each account. The yearly contribution for each employee is limited to the *lesser* of 100 percent of annual compensation or an annual base amount.[57] In 2023, this base amount is $66,000. Employers may deduct their yearly contributions even though these contributions aren't taxable to the employees.

Contribution Limit on Defined-Contribution Plan	Leyla, a midlevel manager with JH Corporation, earned $266,750 salary in 2023 and participates in JH's qualified defined-contribution plan. JH's contribution to Leyla's plan account is limited to $66,000.

Profit-sharing plans under which firms contribute a percentage of current earnings to a retirement trust are a common type of defined-contribution plan. A firm has no obligation to contribute to the trust in a year in which it operates at a loss. As a result, profit-sharing plans are favored by new companies with volatile earnings and uncertain cash flows.

---

[54] Employer contributions to qualified plans are not subject to FICA payroll tax. §3121(a)(5).

[55] §412 contains the minimum funding standards that employers must satisfy every year for qualified defined-benefit plans.

[56] §415(b).

[57] §415(c).

From the employees' perspective, these plans require them to share the risk associated with their employer's business because the retirement savings available to each employee depend on the long-term success of that business.

Profit-Sharing Plan	Solange, Inc. has a profit-sharing plan under which it contributes 1.5 percent of annual book income to a qualified retirement plan. The annual contribution is allocated among participating employees in proportion to the base compensation of each employee. In 2022, Solange's book income was $81.3 million, and its profit-sharing contribution was $1.22 million. The contribution was allocated among 93 employees participating in the retirement plan. In 2023, Solange reported a $9.7 million loss on its financial statements and made no contribution to its qualified retirement plan.

Employee stock ownership plans (ESOPs) are a second type of defined-contribution plan that gives corporate employees a vested interest in their employer's long-term financial success. Employer contributions to ESOPs are invested primarily in the employer's own common stock.[58] Consequently, employees who participate in ESOPs become shareholders, and the value of their retirement benefits depends on the market value of their employer's stock. When participants retire, they receive distributions of the stock held in their ESOP accounts. Such distributions represent taxable income only to the extent of the ESOP's aggregate basis in the stock. Any excess of the stock's market value over basis is excluded from the recipient's income.[59]

Participation in an ESOP	Taylor was employed by BD, Inc. for 29 years. During this time, BD made annual contributions to an ESOP on Taylor's behalf. Taylor retired this year and received a lump-sum distribution of the balance in this retirement account: 14,987 shares of BD common stock. The ESOP's aggregate basis in the shares was $79,250, and the market value of the shares at date of distribution was $299,600. Taylor recognized $79,250 ordinary income because of the distribution and took a $79,250 basis in his BD shares. Taylor will not recognize the $220,350 unrealized appreciation in the shares until the shares are sold.

Tax Talk *More than 62 million Americans, about a third of the U.S. adult population, participate in their company's Section 401(k) plan.*	**Section 401(k) plans,** also described as *salary reduction plans* or *cash-or-deferred arrangements,* have become the most popular qualified plan. Under these plans, each participating employee defines their contribution by electing to divert some amount of current salary or wage to the employee's retirement account. The compensation diverted to the account is tax-deferred to the employee even though it is deductible by the employer.[60] In 2023, the maximum compensation that employees can contribute to a Section 401(k) plan is $22,500.[61] This amount is increased by $7,500 for taxpayers over age 50. Employers often agree to make additional contributions or even match their employees' elective contributions to Section 401(k) plans.

Section 401(k) Plan Contribution	Terrell, age 49 and a financial analyst with PW, Inc., earned a $92,000 salary in 2023. Terrell elected to contribute the $22,500 maximum to PW's Section 401(k) plan. Consequently, only $69,500 of Terrell's salary was taxable. PW's policy is to match each employee's elective contribution up to 5 percent of the employee's salary. So PW contributed $4,600 (5 percent of $92,000) to Terrell's retirement account, increasing the total tax-deferred contribution to $27,100.

---

[58] §409.

[59] §402(e)(4)(B).

[60] This compensation is subject to payroll tax in the year of contribution. §3121(v)(1)(A).

[61] §402(g)(1)(B).

Changing Times for Qualified Plans

Tax Talk

Many states, such as Kentucky, that face huge shortfalls in their employee pension funds are switching from traditional pension plans to Section 401(k)-type plans. Unlike private companies, most states are legally barred from changing their retirement plans without the consent of their current employees.

Three decades ago, 40 percent of the U.S. private sector workforce participated in traditional employer-sponsored pension plans. Today, that percentage is only 12 percent. Over the same 30-year period, the percentage of the workforce participating in defined-contribution plans increased from 17 percent to 47 percent.[62] Clearly, the financial tide is turning in favor of profit-sharing and Section 401(k) plans. One reason is that employers are increasingly leery of the long-term financial commitment represented by a pension plan, particularly in light of the increased longevity of retired employees.

A second reason is that participants in traditional pension plans receive the maximum retirement benefit only after working for the company for a long period of time—perhaps 20 or 30 years. A participant who leaves the company before qualifying for a full pension may be entitled to a relatively insignificant cash settlement. In contrast, participants in defined-contribution plans quickly earn a vested right to the entire value of their plan account. Today's workforce is characterized by its mobility. Unlike their grandparents, young employees do not expect to work for the same company for their entire careers. Instead, they expect to move from employer to employer and prefer the portable retirement savings offered by defined-contribution plans.

Nonqualified Deferred Compensation Plans

Qualified retirement plans offer a win–win outcome. Employers can deduct contributions made to the plans on their employees' behalf, while employees defer income recognition until they receive distributions from the plans at retirement. But as we learned in our discussion of pension plans, profit-sharing plans, and Section 401(k) plans, the dollar amount of compensation that employers can offer on a tax-deferred basis is limited. Moreover, because of the nondiscrimination requirements, employers can't be overly selective as to the employees who may participate in a qualified retirement plan. Finally, most employers need professional help to cope with the morass of federal rules and regulations governing qualified plans. Hence, these plans can be expensive to maintain, even for the smallest employer.

These negative aspects of qualified plans have prompted many employers to establish nonqualified retirement plans. Employers use these plans to offer unlimited **deferred compensation** to key employees, such as highly paid corporate executives, without extending the benefits of the plan to other employees. In their simplest form, deferred compensation plans are nothing more than contractual arrangements under which an employer agrees to pay some portion of the employee's compensation at a specific future date. The arrangement is unfunded: The employer accrues its liability for the deferred compensation but doesn't set aside any cash or property to secure the liability.

Employees who agree to this arrangement don't recognize their deferred compensation as income because they aren't in actual or constructive receipt of any payment.[63] These employees will recognize income in the future year in which their employer makes good on its obligation to pay the deferred compensation. On the employer's side of the arrangement, the accrued liability for deferred compensation is a current expense for financial statement purposes. However, employers aren't allowed to deduct deferred compensation until the year of payment when the employee includes the compensation in income.[64]

[62] U.S. Bureau of Labor Statistics, National Compensation Survey, March 2019.

[63] Rev. Rul. 60-31, 1960-1 C.B. 174. See also §409A.

[64] §404(a)(5). Deferred compensation plans typically require the employer to accrue interest on its liability to the employee. Employers may not deduct this interest until the year it is actually paid to the employee. *Albertson's Inc.* v. *Commissioner*, 42 F.3d 537 (CA-9, 1994), *cert. denied,* 516 U.S. 807 (1995).

Deferred Compensation	Hannan Ahmad, age 49 and NY's chief financial officer, received a $300,000 salary in 2023. At its December meeting, NY's board of directors awarded Hannan a $150,000 bonus to be paid in three annual installments, beginning at age 60 upon retirement. NY did not set aside any cash or property to fund the deferred compensation but accrued a $150,000 liability on its balance sheet. Hannan did not recognize the deferred compensation as 2023 income, nor did NY deduct the deferred compensation expense on its 2023 Form 1120. Hannan will recognize income and NY will claim a deduction over the three years during which the deferred compensation is actually paid.

Employees who consider saving for retirement through a deferred compensation plan must weigh the tax advantages against the financial risk inherent in the plan. In the case of an unfunded plan, the employee is an unsecured creditor of the employer with respect to the deferred compensation. If the employer is financially secure, the employee's retirement is equally secure. But if the employer's business should fail and the employer defaults on its liabilities, the employee may discover that their right to deferred compensation has little or no value as a source of retirement income.

Plans for Self-Employed Individuals

Individuals who earn self-employment income can make annual contributions to a retirement plan. These plans were originally referred to as a **Keogh plan** (named after the Congressional representative who sponsored the legislation that created this qualified plan).[65] The law no longer distinguishes between corporate or other plan sponsors, therefore the term Keogh is used less often. However, small business owners and the self-employed continue to have a variety of choices for retirement savings depending on their savings goals and the number of employees in the business. As an example, a self-employed, small-business owner with no or few employees may choose a **SEP** plan because of the ease in administration—low fees, limited paperwork, but potentially high contribution limits. On the other hand, an employer of a midsize business (typically fewer than 100 employees), may elect to offer a **Simple IRA,** a small-company version of the 401(k).

For the sole proprietor or partner, contributions to these plans are deductible as an above-the-line deduction in the computation of AGI. Thus, individuals pay no income tax on the business earnings invested in these retirement plans.[66] Because these plans are qualified retirement plans, the earnings generated by the financial assets held in the plan are tax-exempt. Accordingly, self-employed individuals can take advantage of self-employed retirement plans to accumulate tax-deferred savings in the same way that employees take advantage of their employer-provided plans.

Like employer-provided plans, these qualified plans must be administered by an independent trustee. Commercial banks, credit unions, brokerage firms, and other financial institutions typically serve as trustees for the plans they maintain and manage for their individual clients. These plans also have contribution limits. For example, tax deductible contributions to SEPs are limited to the *lesser* of 20 percent of self-employment income or an inflation-adjusted base amount ($66,000 in 2023) each year.[67] For purposes of computing this limitation, self-employment income is reduced by the deduction for one-half of the individual's self-employment tax. For the sole proprietor or partner, contributions to

---

[65] §401(c) and §404(a)(8).

[66] They do, however, pay self-employment tax on this income. *Gale* v. *United States,* 768 F. Supp. 1305 (ND Ill, 1991).

[67] IRS Publication 560, *Retirement Plans for Small Business* pp. 23–24.

these plans are deductible as an above-the-line deduction in the computation of AGI. Thus, individuals pay no income tax on the business earnings invested in these retirement plans.[68]

SEP Plan Contribution	Lin Levine's sole proprietorship generated $63,000 net profit in 2023. Lin paid self-employment tax of $4,451 and deducted this amount in the computation of AGI. The self-employment income is computed as follows:

Net profit from sole proprietorship	$63,000
SE tax deduction	(4,451)
Self-employment income	$58,549

Lin's 2023 contribution to a SEP is limited to the lesser of 20 percent of self-employment income or $66,000. Therefore, the maximum deductible contribution to the plan is $11,710 (20 percent of $58,549).

There is a downside to plans for self-employed individuals who hire employees to work in their business: In general, the plan must provide retirement benefits to such employees on a nondiscriminatory basis. In other words, the owner cannot use the plan to defer tax on their earnings unless the plan allows the employees to do the same with respect to their compensation. The owner's tax savings from these plans can be eroded by the incremental cost of including employees in the plan.

INDIVIDUAL RETIREMENT ACCOUNTS

LO 15-7
Describe the tax benefits offered by IRAs and Roth IRAs.

Every person who earns employee compensation or self-employment income can save for retirement through a tax-favored individual retirement account (IRA). People establish IRAs with commercial banks or other financial institutions that serve as trustee of the account. IRAs are tax-exempt so that the earnings on the account grow at a before-tax rate of return. When an owner withdraws funds from the account, the tax consequences depend on whether the account is a **traditional IRA** or a **Roth IRA.** In very general terms, withdrawals from traditional IRAs are taxable as ordinary income, so the earnings on the account are *tax-deferred*. Withdrawals from Roth IRAs are nontaxable, so the earnings on the account are *tax-exempt*. The differences between traditional and Roth IRAs are described in detail in this section.

Limits on IRA Contributions

In 2023, individuals can contribute up to $6,500 to their IRAs, and those who have reached age 50 by the end of the year can contribute an additional $1,000 *catch-up* contribution. The annual contribution amount can't exceed 100 percent of the individual's compensation/self-employment income.[69] For married couples filing jointly, this limit is based on their combined compensation/self-employment income.[70]

Tax Talk
A 2022 Congressional Research Service Report (8/10/222) indicates that in 2019 about 25% of all households owned either a traditional or Roth IRA. The rate of ownership varies by income level: Approximately 50% of all households with income exceeding $125,000 report owning an IRA compared with just 6.7% of households with income less than $30,000.

[68] Self-employed individuals can maintain Section 401(k) plans. By making elective contributions to these "solo" or "mini" 401(k) plans in addition to deductible contributions to their Keogh plans, self-employed individuals can defer tax on the maximum annual amount of their self-employment income. See Reg. §1.401(k)-1(a)(6)(i).

[69] §408(a)(1), 408A(c)(2), and §219(b). Contribution amounts are adjusted annually for inflation.

[70] §219(c). Married individuals filing separate returns are subject to special restrictions regarding IRA contributions. However, such individuals who live apart at all times during a taxable year are considered single taxpayers for IRA purposes. §219(g)(4).

IRA Contributions

Shannon Swazey (age 19 and single) earned $3,725 self-employment income. Shannon's maximum IRA contribution is $3,725.

Lynn Kwan (age 25 and single) earned $22,050 in wages. Lynn's maximum IRA contribution is $6,500.

Laurant and Chris are married. Laurant (age 36) earned a $47,200 salary, and Chris (age 37) earned $4,180 from a part-time job. Because Laurant and Chris file a joint return and their combined compensation exceeds $13,000, they each can contribute the $6,500 maximum to their IRAs.

Ali (age 64) earned $41,950 self-employment income. Ali's maximum IRA contribution is $7,500 ($6,500 + $1,000 catch-up contribution).

Individuals can contribute the maximum to their traditional IRAs regardless of their income level. However, the maximum annual contribution to a Roth IRA may be limited based on the contributor's AGI. If AGI exceeds a phaseout threshold, the maximum contribution is reduced by a phaseout percentage. This percentage equals the excess AGI divided by a phaseout range. The 2023 phaseout threshold is $218,000 for married individuals filing jointly and $138,000 for unmarried individuals. The phaseout range is $10,000 for married individuals filing jointly and $15,000 for unmarried individuals.[71]

Limited Roth IRA Contribution

Tom Tran (age 40 and single) wants to contribute to a Roth IRA. Because Tom's AGI is $144,670, this contribution is limited to $3,607.

AGI	$144,670
Phaseout threshold (unmarried)	(138,000)
Excess AGI	$ 6,670

$6,670 ÷ $15,000 = .445 phaseout percentage

Maximum contribution	$6,500
	.445
Contribution phaseout	$2,893
Limited contribution ($6,500 − $2,893)	$3,607

In addition to a $3,607 contribution to a Roth IRA, Tom can make a $2,893 contribution to a traditional IRA. Thus, total IRA contributions for the year equal the $6,500 maximum.

Deduction of IRA Contributions

Traditional IRAs

Deductibility of contributions to traditional IRAs is governed by a complex web of rules. Such contributions can be fully deductible, partially deductible, or nondeductible; any allowable IRA deduction is above-the-line in the computation of AGI. Note that any deductible portion of a contribution consists of before-tax dollars, while any nondeductible portion consists of after-tax dollars. Deductibility depends on two factors: the contributor's status as an *active participant* in any other qualified retirement plan, and the contributor's AGI.[72]

---

[71] §408A(c)(3). Phaseout thresholds are adjusted annually for inflation.

[72] §219(g).

For individuals *who actively participate* in an employer-sponsored defined benefit, defined contribution, or self-employed plan, the rules for deducting a contribution to a traditional IRA can be summarized as follows:

- If AGI is below a phaseout threshold, contributions are fully deductible. The 2023 phaseout threshold is $116,000 for married individuals filing jointly and $73,000 for unmarried individuals.[73]

- If AGI exceeds the phaseout threshold, the maximum deduction dollar amount ($6,500 + $1,000 catch-up contribution in 2023) is reduced by a percentage equal to the excess AGI divided by a phaseout range. The phaseout range is $20,000 for married individuals filing jointly and $10,000 for unmarried individuals.

- The maximum deduction dollar amount is reduced to zero for married individuals filing jointly with AGI in excess of $136,000 and unmarried individuals with AGI in excess of $83,000.

Deduction Phaseout for Active Participant

Rian and Tessa Howard each made the $6,500 maximum contribution to their traditional IRAs. Both spouses are active participants in their respective employer's profit-sharing plan. Before any deduction for their IRA contributions, the AGI on their joint return is $125,700. Because their excess AGI falls in the phaseout range, their IRA contributions are partially deductible.

AGI before IRA deduction	$125,700
Phaseout threshold (MFJ)	(116,000)
Excess AGI	$ 9,700

$9,700 ÷ $20,000 = .485 phaseout percentage

Maximum deduction	$6,500
	.485
Deduction phaseout	$3,153

Consequently, the maximum deductible contribution for Rian and Tessa is only $3,347 each ($6,500 – $3,153 phaseout), and their AGI is $119,006. The IRA deduction is reported on Form 1040, Schedule 1, line 20.

AGI before IRA deduction	$125,700
IRA deduction ($3,347 × 2)	(6,694)
AGI	$119,006

How would Rian and Tessa's IRA deduction change if they each contributed only $2,500 (instead of the $6,500 maximum) to their IRA? In that case, each contribution is less than the $3,347 maximum deduction, so their entire contributions are deductible. In this case, their AGI is $120,700.

AGI before IRA deduction	$125,700
IRA deduction ($2,500 × 2)	(5,000)
AGI	$120,700

For individuals *who do not actively participate* in any other qualified retirement plan, the general rule is that IRA contributions are fully deductible, regardless of the contributor's AGI.

[73] Phaseout thresholds are adjusted annually for inflation.

Deduction for Nonparticipant	Ari Radick, age 48 and single, made a $6,500 contribution to a traditional IRA. Ari is not an active participant in any other qualified retirement plan. Ari's AGI before any IRA deduction is $364,600. Because this IRA contribution is fully deductible, Ari's AGI is $358,100 ($364,600 – $6,500).

The general rule is subject to a major exception for a nonparticipant who files a joint return *with a spouse* who is an active participant in a qualified retirement plan. In this case, the nonparticipant's maximum deduction dollar amount is reduced by a percentage equal to the couple's AGI in excess of a phaseout threshold ($218,000 in 2023) divided by $10,000. Thus, the maximum deduction is reduced to zero when AGI exceeds $228,000.[74]

Deduction for Nonparticipant Spouse	Mr. and Ms. Dowd (both age 60) each made the $7,500 maximum contribution ($6,500 + $1,000 catch-up contribution) to their traditional IRAs. Mr. Dowd is an active participant in a SEP, but Ms. Dowd is not an active participant in any other qualified plan. The couple files a joint return.
	• Assume the Dowds' AGI before any IRA deduction is $83,800. This AGI is below the $116,000 phaseout threshold (MFJ) for active participants, so Mr. Dowd's contribution is fully deductible. The AGI is also below the $218,000 phaseout threshold for a nonparticipant spouse, so Ms. Dowd's contribution is fully deductible. The Dowds' AGI is $68,800 ($83,800 – $15,000 IRA deduction).
	• Now assume the Dowds' AGI before any IRA deduction is $173,700. This AGI is above the AGI phaseout range (MFJ) for active participants, so Mr. Dowd's contribution is nondeductible. However, the AGI is below the $216,000 phaseout threshold for a nonparticipant spouse, so Ms. Dowd's contribution is fully deductible. The Dowds' AGI is $166,200 ($173,700 – $7,500 IRA deduction).
	• Now assume the Dowds' AGI before any IRA deduction is $229,600. This AGI is above the AGI phaseout range (MFJ) for active participants, so Mr. Dowd's contribution is nondeductible. The AGI is also above the AGI phaseout range for a nonparticipant spouse, so Ms. Dowd's contribution is nondeductible. The Dowds' AGI is $229,600.

Roth IRAs

Contributions to Roth IRAs are subject to one simple rule: Such contributions aren't deductible and therefore consist only of after-tax dollars.[75]

Nondeductible Roth IRA Contribution	Lou and Lana Bartlett each made a $2,000 contribution to their Roth IRAs. Regardless of their AGI and whether either spouse actively participates in another qualified retirement plan, their $4,000 contribution is nondeductible on their joint return.

Withdrawals from IRAs

Traditional IRAs

Owners of traditional IRAs must begin withdrawing funds no later than April 1 of the year following the year in which they reach age 72. Annual withdrawals are subject to the minimum distribution requirement.[76] Any portion of the withdrawal attributable to the owner's nondeductible contributions is a nontaxable return of investment. The remainder of the withdrawal

---

[74] §219(g)(7).

[75] §408A(c)(1).

[76] §408(a)(6).

(the portion attributable to deductible contributions and accumulated earnings) is ordinary income. The nontaxable portion of an annual withdrawal is based on the ratio of the owner's unrecovered investment at the beginning of the year to the current year value of the IRA. The current year value is defined as the year-end IRA balance *plus* current year withdrawals.[77]

Traditional IRA Withdrawals	Helmie owns a traditional IRA. Helmie made $44,000 of contributions to this IRA, $19,000 of which were nondeductible. In 2022, Helmie retired at age 63 and made a $15,000 withdrawal from this IRA. The account balance at year-end was $73,220. In 2023, Helmie withdrew $17,500 from the IRA. The account balance at year-end was $60,200. (Note that the IRA continued to earn tax-exempt income during both years.) The yearly withdrawals that Helmie must recognize as ordinary income are computed as follows:

		2022		**2023**
Year-end balance in IRA		$73,220		$60,200
Plus withdrawals during the year		15,000		17,500
Current year value of IRA		$88,220		$77,700
Nondeductible contributions	$19,000		$19,000	
Prior year recoveries	(–0–)		(3,231)	
Unrecovered investment	$19,000		$15,769	
Ratio of unrecovered investment to current year value	.2154		.2029	
Withdrawal during the year		$15,000		$17,500
		.2154		.2029
Nontaxable recovery of investment		$ 3,231		$ 3,551
Ordinary income (withdrawal − nontaxable recovery)		$11,769		$13,949

As Helmie continues to withdraw funds from the IRA, a portion of each withdrawal will be treated as a nontaxable return of investment. By the time Helmie completely liquidates the account, all of the $19,000 in nondeductible contributions will be recouped on a tax-free basis.

Owners who make withdrawals from their IRAs before reaching age 59½ must pay the 10 percent penalty described earlier in the chapter. However, this penalty is waived in a number of situations. For instance, an individual can withdraw funds from an IRA to pay higher education expenses (tuition, fees, books, supplies, and equipment). An individual who qualifies as a first-time homebuyer can withdraw up to $10,000 to finance the purchase of a home. While some or all of the withdrawal must be included in the owner's taxable income, the taxable portion escapes the premature withdrawal penalty.[78]

Roth IRAs

Owners of Roth IRAs are not subject to the minimum distribution requirement. Consequently, they don't have to begin withdrawing funds at age 72 and can allow the account to grow at a tax-free rate until death.[79] When the owner makes a *qualified* withdrawal from a Roth IRA, the entire withdrawal is tax-exempt. Thus, the owner is never taxed on the portion of the withdrawal attributable to accumulated earnings in the account. A withdrawal is qualified only if it occurs after the owner reaches age 59½ *and* after the five-year period beginning with the first year in which the owner contributed to the account.[80]

---

[77] §408(d)(2).

[78] §72(t)(2)(E) and (F).

[79] §408A(c)(5).

[80] §408A(d)(1) and (2). First-time homebuyers can make a qualified withdrawal of $10,000 to finance the purchase of a home.

Roth IRA Withdrawals	This year, Alex withdrew $14,000 from a Roth IRA to pay for a family vacation. Alex made the first contribution to this account in 2001. If Alex is older than 59½, the withdrawal is qualified, and the entire $14,000 is tax-exempt. If Alex is younger than age 59½, the withdrawal is not qualified. As a result, Alex must include the taxable portion (attributable to accumulated earnings) in gross income and pay the 10 percent premature withdrawal penalty on the inclusion.

Rollovers to IRAs

Individuals who receive distributions from qualified retirement plans can avoid income recognition by rolling the distribution over into a traditional IRA.[81] Individuals wanting to take advantage of this tax-planning opportunity have only 60 days from the date of receipt to contribute the distributed funds to an IRA. Individuals who fail to meet this 60-day requirement must include the distribution in income. The 60-day requirement doesn't apply to rollovers in which the retirement plan makes the distribution *directly* to the IRA (trustee-to-trustee transfer).[82] The use of so-called **rollover IRAs** to prolong tax deferral has been a standard planning technique for decades.

Rollover IRA	Victor Vega, age 49, participated in his corporate employer's Section 401(k) plan for 23 years. This year, Victor quit his corporate job to go into business for himself. Victor instructed his former employer to transfer the $148,800 balance in his Section 401(k) account to a new rollover IRA that he opened with a local bank. Victor does not include any amount of this direct rollover in gross income.

Individuals can convert a traditional IRA to a Roth IRA or roll over distributions from qualified retirement plans into a Roth IRA, *regardless of the income level of the taxpayer.* Consequently, Roth IRAs are available to millions of individuals who are precluded from contributing directly to a Roth IRA because their AGI is too high.[83]

Individuals who move funds from a traditional IRA or an employer-sponsored plan into a Roth IRA are converting a *tax-deferred* investment to a *tax-exempt* investment. Consequently, they must treat this conversion as a taxable event by including the taxable portion of the rollover amount in gross income.[84]

Conversion of Traditional IRA to Roth IRA	Erin, age 68, owns a traditional IRA and has made only nondeductible contributions to this account. The current balance in the IRA is $78,000, composed of Erin's $67,000 contributions and $11,000 accumulated earnings. Consequently, if Erin withdrew the current balance in a lump-sum, the entire $67,000 investment could be recovered tax-free and Erin would pay tax only on the $11,000 earnings. Erin has other sources of retirement income and would like to indefinitely avoid mandatory distributions from this IRA. However, if Erin converts the IRA into a Roth IRA, $11,000 must be included in current year gross income and the taxes on that income must be paid.

[81] §402(c)(1).
[82] §402(c)(3) and (e)(6).
[83] §408A(c)(6) and (e)(1).
[84] §408A(d)(3)(A). The amount included in gross income is not subject to any premature withdrawal penalty.

Rollover of Plan Distribution to Roth IRA	Ms. Lenz, age 69, plans to retire this year and will be entitled to a $175,000 distribution from an employer-sponsored, qualified profit-sharing plan. Because Ms. Lenz was not subject to tax on the employer's annual contributions to the plan, and the accumulated earnings in the plan were tax-exempt, Ms. Lenz has no unrecovered investment in the plan, and the entire distribution would be included in gross income. Ms. Lenz can continue the deferral of tax on the $175,000 by rolling the distribution over into a traditional IRA. However, this conversion will trigger required minimum distributions when Ms. Lenz reaches age 72. If the distribution is rolled into a Roth IRA, the entire $175,000 must be included in current year gross income and taxes paid accordingly.

As these examples demonstrate, individuals who move retirement funds into a Roth IRA incur an upfront, and perhaps exorbitant, tax cost. In return, the future earnings on the account are tax-exempt, and the owner is not required to begin liquidating the account at age 72. Whether a transfer of funds to a Roth IRA is advantageous depends on the individual's unique tax circumstances. Individuals who are considering such a transfer should seek the advice of a tax professional to make a well-informed investment decision.

Conclusion

In this chapter, we've explored the tax consequences of compensation arrangements between employer and employee. These arrangements can consist of a mix of cash payments and noncash fringe benefits, many of which are excluded from the recipient's income. Corporate employers frequently include equity-based compensation in the packages offered to key employees. By understanding both the economic implications and the tax consequences of the various forms of compensation, employers and employees can negotiate to improve their respective after-tax positions.

No area of the tax law offers a better opportunity for effective long-term planning than qualified retirement plans. The tax deferral available through these plans is one of the surest routes toward wealth maximization. Young adults who are just beginning their careers should take immediate advantage of any qualified retirement plans sponsored by their employers. Entrepreneurs who own their own businesses should consider their options for investing through qualified retirement plans. And every working person, regardless of age, who can afford to save even a few dollars each year toward retirement should open an IRA.

Sources of Book/Tax Differences

Permanent
- Incentive stock options
- Nondeductible compensation

Temporary
- Restricted stock
- Nonqualified stock options
- Nonqualified deferred compensation

Key Terms

bargain element *15-15*
cafeteria plan *15-12*
deferred compensation *15-25*
defined-benefit plan *15-23*
defined-contribution plan *15-23*
employee *15-2*
employee stock ownership plan (ESOP) *15-24*
employer-provided plan *15-22*

expatriate *15-9*
foreign earned income exclusion *15-9*
fringe benefits *15-9*
incentive stock option (ISO) *15-17*
independent contractor *15-2*
Keogh plan *15-26*
minimum distribution *15-20*
premature withdrawal *15-21*
profit-sharing plans *15-23*

qualified retirement plans *15-19*
restricted stock *15-14*
rollover contribution *15-21*
rollover IRA *15-32*
Roth IRA *15-27*
Section 401(k) plan *15-24*
SEP *15-26*
Simple IRA *15-26*
stock option *15-15*
traditional IRA *15-27*

Questions and Problems for Discussion

LO 15-1 1. Discuss how the presence of a strong labor union may change the nature of the market in which rank-and-file employees negotiate with their employer.

LO 15-1 2. Discuss the difference in the relationship between an employer and an employee and a client and an independent contractor.

LO 15-1 3. Mr. Updike accepted an engagement to perform consulting services for MK Company. The engagement will last at least 18 months. Identify any reasons Mr. Updike might prefer to be classified as an MK employee rather than as an independent contractor.

LO 15-1 4. Discuss the practical reasons why the tax law authorizes the IRS to collect unwithheld employee payroll tax from the employer rather than the employees who were liable for the tax.

LO 15-2 5. A reasonable compensation problem for the sole shareholder of a C corporation is quite different from the reasonable compensation problem for the sole shareholder of an S corporation. What is the difference?

LO 15-3 6. Bobbie owns 10 percent of the stock of ABC, Inc. and is the corporation's director of marketing. ABC has a medical insurance plan for its employees. This year, it paid $1,400 in premiums to the insurance carrier for Bobbie's coverage. Contrast the treatment of this payment to Bobbie if ABC is a C corporation or an S corporation.

LO 15-2, 15-7 7. This year, publicly held Corporation DF paid its PFO a $1.4 million salary, only $1 million of which was deductible. It also accrued a $200,000 liability for deferred compensation payable in the year 2025 (when the PFO must retire). To what extent does either transaction result in a difference between DF's book income and taxable income? Is the difference permanent or temporary?

LO 15-3 8. Zane Zelig was recently promoted to an executive position. The corporation now requires Zane to frequently entertain clients, likely resulting in at least $1,000 of out-of-pocket business entertainment expenses each month. The corporation will either provide reimbursement for these expenses or provide a salary bonus at year-end that indirectly covers these annual expenses. Which option should Zane choose and why?

LO 15-4 9. Employees who are compensated with restricted stock or stock options face financial risks not associated with cash compensation. Describe and compare the financial risks of these two types of equity-based compensation.

LO 15-4 10. Six years ago, Corporation AT granted a stock option to an employee to purchase 1,000 shares of AT stock for $15 per share. At date of grant, AT stock was selling for $14.10 per share. Over the last six years, the market price has steadily declined to $11.80 per share. What are the tax consequences to the employee when the option lapses?

LO 15-4 11. Two years ago, Corporation WZ granted a stock option to an employee to purchase 2,500 shares of WZ stock for $30 per share. Since the date of grant, the market price of the stock has risen steadily and reached $31 just days ago. However, the option period is 10 years. Should the employee exercise the option immediately to minimize the income that must be recognized or wait for eight more years before exercising the option?

LO 15-6 12. Describe the differences between a defined-benefit plan and a defined-contribution plan.

LO 15-6 13. How does the fact that employees have a vested right to their benefits reduce the risk of participating in an employer-sponsored qualified retirement plan?

LO 15-6 14. How does the fact that an employer-sponsored qualified retirement plan is administered by an independent trustee reduce the employees' risk of participating in the plan?

 **All applicable Application Problems are available with *Connect*.**

Application Problems

For the following problems, assume the taxable year is 2023.

LO 15-1   1. Greg Company agreed to pay Blayne $45,000 compensation for services performed for the company.

    a. Compare the income tax consequences to Greg and Blayne if Blayne is an employee or an independent contractor.

    b. Compare the payroll tax consequences to Greg and Blayne if Blayne is an employee or an independent contractor.

    c. Compare the income tax *payment* requirements to Blayne if Blayne is an employee or an independent contractor.

LO 15-1   2. Trent, Inc. needs an additional worker on a multiyear project. It could hire an employee for a $65,000 annual salary. Alternatively, it could engage an independent contractor for a $72,000 annual fee. If Trent's income tax rate is 21 percent, which option minimizes the after-tax cost of obtaining the worker?

LO 15-2   3. Marlo, a publicly held corporation with a 21 percent tax rate, has agreed to pay an annual salary of $1.3 million to its employee, Lindsey. In each of the following cases, compute Marlo's after-tax cost of the salary. In making your calculation, ignore the employer payroll tax.

    a. Lindsey is Marlo's principal executive officer (PEO).

    b. Lindsey is Marlo's director of marketing and the sixth most highly compensated employee in the company.

LO 15-2   4. Thomas and Christian Brock own a bakery. Their marginal tax rate on the bakery's income is 32 percent. The Brocks' 18-year-old child, Megan, works part-time in the bakery. This year, Megan's only income was $15,284 of wages earned at the bakery.

    a. Compute Megan's income tax this year.

    b. Compute the Brock family's income tax savings from Megan's employment.

LO 15-2   5. Mr. and Ms. Soon are the sole shareholders of SW, Inc. For the last three years, SW has employed their child as a sales representative, paying a $30,000 annual salary. During a recent IRS audit, the revenue agent discovered that the child has never made a sale and spends the majority of time playing saxophone in a jazz band. Determine the potential effect of this discovery on SW's taxable income and on the Soons' taxable income under the following assumptions:

    a. SW, Inc. is an S corporation.

    b. SW, Inc. is a C corporation.

LO 15-2   6. Kim Jung is a U.S. citizen working for Byte Corporation. For the last six years, Kim has been stationed in the company's Tokyo office.

    a. Compute AGI if Kim's only income for the year is $65,000 in wages.

    b. Compute AGI if Kim's only income for the year is $169,000 in wages.

    c. Under Japanese law, Kim is a permanent resident and must pay Japanese income tax on the salary earned in Tokyo. Assuming that the Japanese individual tax rates exceed the U.S. rates, will Kim owe U.S. tax on any portion of the salary?

LO 15-3   7. Dominique, age 57, participates in an employer-sponsored group term life insurance plan. According to Treasury tables, the cost of $1,000 of life insurance for a 57-year-old person is 43 cents per month. Determine the taxable income that Dominique must recognize assuming that

    a. The plan provides $40,000 coverage.

    b. The plan provides $275,000 coverage.

LO 15-3   8. Fran Eller's corporate employer has a cafeteria plan under which its employees can receive a $3,000 year-end holiday bonus or enroll in a qualified medical reimbursement plan that pays up to $3,000 of annual medical bills. Fran is in a 24 percent tax bracket and averages $2,300 in medical bills each year.

    a. Should Fran choose the cash bonus or the nontaxable fringe benefit? (Ignore any payroll tax implications.)

    b. Does your answer change if Fran is in the 12 percent tax bracket?

LO 15-3   9. Aleena and Ike are employed by HD, Inc., which provides its employees with free parking. If the parking was not available, Aleena would pay $35 a month to a city garage. Ike uses public transportation to commute. HD offers a complete family medical plan to its employees in which both Aleena and Ike participate. Aleena's family consists of five people, while Ike is single. Consequently, Aleena's annual cost of comparable medical insurance would be $9,000, and Ike's cost would be just $4,100.

    a. Aleena has a 24 percent marginal tax rate. How much additional salary must Aleena earn to individually purchase and cover the cost of parking and medical insurance?

    b. Ike has a 37 percent marginal tax rate. How much additional salary must Ike earn to individually purchase and cover the cost of parking and medical insurance?

LO 15-3   10. Peet Company provides free on-site day care for employees with preschool children. Determine the pretax value of the care for each of the following employees:

    a. Ms. Udolf has a 32 percent marginal tax rate and pays $10,675 annually for day care for three children.

    b. Mr. Zuo has a 12 percent marginal tax rate and pays $3,300 annually for day care for one child.

LO 15-4   11. This year, Faro, Inc., a calendar year taxpayer, issued 500 shares of its publicly traded stock as a bonus to its employee, Darius. On the date of issuance, the stock's fair market value was $16,750. What are the tax consequences to Darius and Faro if

    a. Ownership of the stock was fully vested on the date of issuance (the stock was transferable and not subject to risk of forfeiture).

    b. The terms of the bonus require that Darius must hold the stock five years from the date of issuance. If employment is terminated before that date, the stock must be forfeited back to Faro. Darius made no election with respect to the restricted stock.

LO 15-4   12. On September 30, 2018, Stalling, Inc. issued 2,000 shares of its publicly traded stock as compensation to its employee, Harry. On the date of issuance, the stock's fair market value was $40,000. Under the terms of his 2018 compensation contract, Harry could not dispose of the stock before October 1, 2023, and if employment with Stalling was terminated before that date, the stock is returned to the corporation. On October 1, 2023, Harry, who still worked for Stalling, sold all 2,000 shares for $57,500.

    a. Assume that Harry made no election with respect to the restricted stock in 2018. How much compensation income does Harry recognize in 2023 because the restrictions lapsed? How much gain or loss is recognized on sale of the stock?

    b. Assume that Harry filed a timely election in 2018 to accelerate income recognition with respect to the 2,000 shares of restricted stock. How much compensation income does Harry recognize in 2023 because the restrictions lapsed? How much gain or loss is recognized on sale of the stock?

LO 15-4 13. Refer to the facts in the preceding problem. Stalling, Inc. uses a fiscal year ending August 31 for tax purposes. Determine the amount of Stalling's deduction and the taxable year in which Stalling is allowed the deduction with respect to the 2,000 shares issued to Harry under the assumptions in parts (*a*) and (*b*).

LO 15-4 14. This year, Gogo, Inc. granted a nonqualified stock option to Mwana to buy 10,000 shares of Gogo stock for $8 per share for five years. At date of grant, Gogo stock was selling on a regional securities market for $7.87 per share. Gogo recorded $26,700 compensation expense for the estimated value of the option.

    a. How much income must Mwana recognize this year?

    b. Can Gogo deduct the $26,700 expense on this year's tax return?

    c. Assuming a 21 percent tax rate, compute Gogo's deferred tax asset or deferred tax liability (identify which) resulting from the $26,700 compensation expense.

LO 15-4 15. Refer to the facts in the preceding problem. Five years after the option grant, Mwana exercised the option when Gogo stock was selling for $10.31 per share.

    a. How much income must Mwana recognize in the year of exercise?

    b. What is Gogo's tax deduction in the year of exercise?

    c. What is the effect of the exercise on Gogo's book income and deferred taxes?

LO 15-4 16. In 2018, BT granted a nonqualified stock option to Pieter to buy 500 shares of BT stock at $20 per share for five years. At date of grant, BT stock was trading on Nasdaq for $18.62 per share. In 2023, Pieter exercised the option when BT's stock was trading at $31.40 per share.

    a. How much income did Pieter recognize in 2018 and 2023 because of the stock option?

    b. Compute Pieter's basis in the 500 shares.

    c. What are the tax consequences of the stock option to BT in 2018 and 2023?

LO 15-4 17. In 2014, BB granted an incentive stock option (ISO) to Raul to buy 8,000 shares of BB stock at $7 per share for 10 years. At date of grant, BB stock was trading on the AMEX for $6.23 per share. In 2023, Raul exercised the option when BB's stock was trading at $22.81 per share.

    a. How much income did Raul recognize in 2014 and 2023 because of the ISO?

    b. Compute Raul's basis in the 8,000 shares.

    c. What are the tax consequences of the stock option to BB in 2014 and 2023?

LO 15-4 18. Two years ago, Ms. Erb was granted an employee stock option from Sunny, Inc. At date of grant, the stock was selling at $14 per share, and the strike price was $18 per share. This year, Ms. Erb sold the option to an unrelated party for $26,000. How much gain does Ms. Erb recognize on this transaction?

LO 15-4 19. In 2016 (year 0), Jessee exercised a stock option by paying $100 per share for 225 shares of ABC stock. The market price at date of exercise was $312 per share. In 2023, Jessee sold the 225 shares for $480 per share. Assuming that Jessee is in the 35 percent tax bracket, has a 15 percent capital gains rate, and uses a 6 percent discount rate, compute the 2016 NPV of the cash flows from the exercise and sale if

    a. The stock option was nonqualified.

    b. The stock option was an ISO.

LO 15-4 20. Mr. Toomey (a 45-year-old single taxpayer) exercised an ISO to purchase $380,000 of company stock for only $113,000. Mr. Toomey does not itemize deductions and has no income other than $158,500 salary. Compute Mr. Toomey's income tax including any AMT.

LO 15-5 21. Kirsten withdrew $30,000 from a retirement account and used the money to furnish a new home. Kirsten's marginal tax rate is 24 percent. Compute the tax cost of the withdrawal in each of the following cases:

    a. Kirsten is 56 years old, and withdrew the money from a personal savings account.

    b. Kirsten is 56 years old, and withdrew the money from an employer-sponsored qualified plan upon retirement from the company. Kirsten made no after-tax contributions to this plan.

    c. Kirsten is 56 years old, and withdrew the money from an employer-sponsored qualified plan. Kirsten intends to work for the employer for at least 10 more years. Kirsten made no after-tax contributions to this plan.

    d. Kirsten is 61 years old and withdrew the money from an employer-sponsored qualified plan. Kirsten intends to work for the employer for at least four more years. Kirsten made no after-tax contributions to this plan.

LO 15-6 22. Evan participates in his corporate employer's qualified defined benefits plan and will be entitled to receive an annual pension upon retirement in five years. What is the maximum contribution that the employer can make to the plan on Evan's behalf assuming that

    a. Evan's average compensation for the three highest compensation years is $145,000?

    b. Evan's average compensation for the three highest compensation years is $375,000?

LO 15-6 23. Ms. Garza participates in an employer's qualified profit-sharing plan. What is the maximum contribution that the employer can make to Ms. Garza's retirement account, assuming that

    a. annual compensation was $38,200?

    b. annual compensation was $180,000?

LO 15-6 24. Ramesh participates in an employer's Section 401(k) plan, which obligates the employer to contribute 25 cents for every dollar that an employee elects to contribute to the plan. This year, Ramesh elects to contribute the maximum allowable to this plan and has salary of $110,000.

    a. How much of Ramesh's salary is taxable this year?

    b. Compute the total contribution to Ramesh's plan.

    c. Compute the employer's deduction for compensation paid to Ramesh.

LO 15-6 25. Gilly is the PFO of Petro, Inc. This year, Gilly's compensation package was $625,000, which included $500,000 salary and an accrued, unfunded liability to pay the $125,000 balance upon retirement at age 60.

    a. How much compensation income does Gilly recognize this year?

    b. What is Petro's book expense for Gilly's current compensation?

    c. What is Petro's tax deduction for Gilly's current compensation?

    d. Assuming a 21 percent tax rate, compute Petro's deferred tax asset or deferred tax liability (identify which) resulting from the compensation expense.

LO 15-6 26. Refer to the facts in the preceding problem. Petro, Inc. pays $125,000 deferred compensation to Gilly in 2028, the year of retirement.

    a. How much compensation income does Gilly recognize in 2028?

    b. What is Petro's 2028 tax deduction for the payment to Mr. Gilly?

    c. What is the effect of the payment on Petro's 2028 book income and deferred taxes?

LO 15-6 27. This year, Brianna, who is head of Lyton Industries' accounting and tax department, received a compensation package of $360,000. The package consisted of $300,000 current salary and $60,000 deferred compensation. Lyton will pay the deferred compensation in three annual $20,000 installments beginning with the year in which Brianna retires. Lyton accrued a $60,000 unfunded liability for the deferred compensation on its current year financial statements.

    a. How much compensation income does Brianna recognize this year?

    b. What is Lyton Industries' book expense for Brianna's current compensation?

    c. What is Lyton Industries' tax deduction for Brianna's current compensation?

    d. Assuming a 21 percent tax rate, compute Lyton Industries' deferred tax asset or deferred tax liability (identify which) resulting from the compensation expense.

LO 15-6 28. Refer to the facts in the preceding problem. Assume Brianna retires in 2026 and receives the first $20,000 payment from Lyton Industries.

    a. How much compensation income does Brianna recognize in 2026?

    b. What is Lyton Industries' 2026 tax deduction for the payment to Brianna?

    c. What is the effect of the payment on Lyton Industries' 2026 book income and deferred tax asset or liability?

LO 15-6 29. MN's compensation package for its PEO consisted of a $600,000 salary plus $200,000 unfunded deferred compensation. The PEO will receive the $200,000 upon retirement in 2027. The PEO is also a participant in MN's qualified pension plan. MN contributed $21,000 to fund a $90,000 annual pension that the PEO will begin to receive in 2029.

    a. Compute MN's current year financial statement expense for the PEO's compensation.

    b. Compute MN's current year tax deduction for the PEO's compensation.

    c. Compute the PEO's taxable compensation income.

    d. How much taxable income will the PEO recognize in 2029?

LO 15-6, 15-7 30. Elton Weiss and Reyna Herrera-Weiss are married and report the following income items:

Elton's salary	$254,000
Reyna's Schedule C net profit	50,000

The income tax deduction for Reyna's SE tax was $3,532. Elton contributed the maximum to a Section 401(k) plan, and Reyna contributed the maximum to a SEP plan. Both spouses contributed $2,750 to their IRAs. Compute their AGI.

LO 15-7 31. What is the maximum IRA contribution that Josh can make under each of the following assumptions?

    a. Josh is age 20 and single. Josh's only income item is $13,200 interest from a trust fund.

    b. Josh is age 40 and single. Josh's only income item is a $31,900 share of ordinary income from a partnership.

    c. Josh is age 60 and single. Josh's only income item is $24,200 wages.

    d. Josh is age 46 and files a joint return with a spouse. Josh's sole proprietorship generates a $7,720 loss, and the spouse's salary is $43,000.

LO 15-7 32. Chandra is age 48 and single. What is the maximum contribution that Chandra can make to a Roth IRA if

    a. AGI consists of a $99,400 salary?

    b. AGI consists of a $99,400 salary plus $44,000 interest and dividends from a trust fund?

    c. AGI consists of a $145,000 salary plus a $19,250 share of ordinary income from a partnership?

LO 15-7 33. Ms. Ray is age 46 and single. This year, Ms. Ray's retirement savings included a $2,895 employer contribution to a qualified profit-sharing plan account, and a contribution by Ms. Ray to a traditional IRA. Ms. Ray contributed the maximum allowed. Compute Ms. Ray's IRA deduction if current year income includes

   a. 50,000 salary.

   b. $81,250 salary.

   c. $81,250 salary and $7,970 dividend income.

LO 15-7 34. Micah and Lin Davos file a joint tax return. Each spouse contributed the maximum $6,500 to a traditional IRA. In each of the following cases, compute the deduction for these contributions. The AGI in each case is *before* any deduction.

   a. Neither spouse is an active participant in a qualified retirement plan, and their AGI is $138,400.

   b. Micah is an active participant, but Lin is not. Their AGI is $148,400.

   c. Both spouses are active participants, and their AGI is $89,200.

   d. Micah is self-employed and does not have a SEP plan. Lin is an active participant. Their AGI is $124,400.

LO 15-7 35. Mr. and Ms. Marlo, ages 39 and 35, file a joint tax return. Each spouse contributed only $2,000 to a traditional IRA. In each of the following cases, compute the deduction for these contributions. The AGI in each case is *before* any deduction.

   a. Mr. Marlo is an active participant in an employer's qualified profit-sharing plan. Ms. Marlo is self-employed and does not have a SEP plan. Their AGI is $128,000.

   b. Both spouses are active participants in their employer's qualified pension plan. Their AGI is $73,000.

   c. Both spouses are active participants in their employer's qualified Section 401(k) plan. Their AGI is $218,500.

   d. Neither spouse is an active participant in their employer's qualified ESOP. Their AGI is $469,000.

LO 15-7 36. Mr. Gilbert is self-employed and makes annual contributions to a SEP plan. Ms. Gilbert's employer doesn't offer any type of qualified retirement plan. Each spouse contributes the maximum $6,500 to a traditional IRA. In each of the following cases, compute the AGI on their joint return:

   a. AGI before an IRA deduction is $144,500.

   b. AGI before an IRA deduction is $224,100.

LO 15-7 37. Ms. Shin retired in 2022 at age 63 and made the first withdrawal of $20,000 from a traditional IRA. At year-end, the IRA balance was $89,200. In 2023, Ms. Shin withdrew $22,000 from the IRA. At year-end, the account balance was $71,100. Determine how much of each annual withdrawal was taxable assuming that

   a. Contributions to the IRA were fully deductible.

   b. Ms. Shin made $26,500 nondeductible contributions to the IRA.

   c. Ms. Shin made $37,950 nondeductible contributions to the IRA.

LO 15-7 38. Eloise retired in 2022 at age 69 and made a first withdrawal of $35,000 from a traditional IRA. At year-end, the IRA balance was $441,000. In 2023, Eloise withdrew $60,000 from the IRA. At year-end, the account balance was $407,000. Determine how much of each annual withdrawal was taxable assuming that

   a. Eloise made $320,000 nondeductible contributions to the IRA.

   b. Eloise's contributions to the IRA were fully deductible.

LO 15-7   39. Kwan Fu withdrew the entire $8,000 balance from a Roth IRA this year. The total contributions to the account were $6,070, and Kwan has a 12 percent marginal tax rate. Determine the tax cost of the withdrawal if

    a. Kwan is age 63 and opened the Roth IRA three years ago.

    b. Kwan is age 63 and opened the Roth IRA seven years ago.

    c. Kwan is age 48 and opened the Roth IRA seven years ago.

LO 15-7   40. Levi Lohan, age 64, plans to retire this December. Levi intends to withdraw funds from an IRA to finance the purchase of a condominium and is projecting a balance of $86,500 in the account at retirement. Assuming a 24 percent marginal tax rate, compute the after-tax cash from the IRA liquidation assuming that

    a. The IRA is a Roth IRA and was opened in 2003.

    b. The IRA is a traditional IRA and all contributions were deductible.

    c. The IRA is a traditional IRA in which $20,400 were deductible and $32,600 were nondeductible contributions.

LO 15-7   41. Shelby owns a tax-deferred retirement account with a $200,000 current balance. Shelby intends to roll over this balance into a new Roth IRA before the end of the year. Assuming a 35 percent marginal tax rate, compute both the tax cost of converting the existing retirement account to a Roth IRA and also the after-tax amount of the rollover if

    a. The existing account is a Section 401(k) plan funded by Shelby's elective contributions and employer's matching contributions.

    b. The existing account is a traditional IRA and Shelby made $38,400 of nondeductible contributions.

Issue Recognition Problems

Identify the tax issue or issues suggested by the following situations, and state each issue in the form of a question.

LO 15-2   1. Trung and Thomas founded TV Corporation six years ago and have devoted every waking hour to the corporate business. During the first four years, neither shareholder received a salary. During the last two years, each shareholder received a $400,000 salary, which is about 180 percent of the average salary paid by comparable corporations to their unrelated officers.

LO 15-3   2. Lizzy Bourne, an executive with GG, Inc., flies more than 150,000 business miles each year and accumulates considerable frequent-flier points from the airlines. GG allows its employees to use their frequent-flier points for personal travel. In March, Lizzy used 300,000 points to obtain two first-class, round-trip tickets to Paris for a family vacation. The value of the tickets was $12,000.

LO 15-3   3. Randall is a professor at a private university. The university waives the tuition for a faculty member's child who meets the entrance requirements. Randall's two children are enrolled in degree programs at the university. If not for the waiver, Randall would pay $16,000 annual tuition for each child.

LO 15-3   4. Devonte has the full-time use of an automobile owned and maintained by his employer. This year, Devonte drove this company car 48,000 miles on business and 22,000 for personal reasons. Devonte is not required to report this information to his employer.

LO 15-3   5. Lex is employed at VD's corporate headquarters and often works late hours. The headquarters building is located in a high-crime urban area. As a result, corporate policy is that any employee leaving the premises after 7:00 P.M. must take a cab home rather than walk or use the subway. VD pays the cab fare. However, it doesn't pay employee commuting expenses under any other circumstances. This year, VD spent $1,080 on cab fare for Lex.

LO 15-3, 15-4   6. Mr. Granger, an employee of a closely held corporation, was awarded a year-end bonus of 50 shares of stock worth $200 per share. Mr. Granger's ownership of the stock was nontransferable and restricted. If Mr. Granger resigned from the job within four years of the date of issuance, the stock would be forfeited back to the corporation. Mr. Granger died in a traffic accident two years after receiving the restricted stock. Under the terms of Mr. Granger's will, the ownership interest in the stock passes to Mr. Granger's spouse.

LO 15-4   7. GHK recently granted a stock option to an employee to purchase 20,000 shares of stock for $11 per share. On the date of grant, GHK stock was selling for $12 on the NYSE.

LO 15-4   8. Six years ago, Deepti paid $20 per share for 1,000 shares of stock in her company. This stock is now worth $58 per share. Deepti wants to exercise a stock option to buy 1,000 more shares at a strike price of $29 per share. Deepti does not have $29,000 cash readily available. Therefore, Deepti has requested that the corporation allow her to exchange 500 of the original shares (valued at $29,000) for the 1,000 new shares.

LO 15-2   9. Mr. and Ms. Schill are CPAs. Mr. Schill is an employee of a national accounting firm, while Ms. Schill operates her own professional practice. Each year, the couple pays approximately $1,300 to subscribe to professional publications and research services that they both read and use in their work.

LO 15-3   10. Jordan recently moved from Boston to Pittsburgh to take a job with OP, Inc. As part of the relocation, Jordan sold a home in Boston, and OP paid the $14,500 realtor's commission on the sale.

LO 15-6   11. This year, TT Corporation agreed to defer $100,000 compensation owed to Ms. Blass, the director of research. TT funded its obligation by transferring $100,000 cash to a trust administered by a local bank. TT cannot reclaim these funds. However, the trust fund is subject to the claims of TT's general creditors. Ms. Blass has no right to the funds unless she works for TT until age 59, the mandatory retirement age.

LO 15-6   12. Corporation J sponsors a qualified profit-sharing plan for its employees that Paul has participated in for more than 12 years. This year, Paul abruptly resigned from Corporation J and left town without leaving a forwarding address. The corporation has tried to locate Paul to send a Form W-2 and a final paycheck. So far, these efforts have been unsuccessful.

LO 15-6   13. Watts McNeil, age 50, is a self-employed writer who published 11 novels in the past 20 years. Each year, Watts makes the maximum contribution to a SEP plan. This year, Watts borrowed $200,000 from the plan to finance the construction of a new home. Under the borrowing agreement, the market rate of interest is assessed and Watts must repay the debt in five years.

LO 15-6   14. Mr. and Mrs. Vishnu are the sole shareholders of VC Enterprises. They are also employed by VC and participate in its qualified pension plan. VC is experiencing cash flow difficulties. To ease the strain, Mr. and Mrs. Vishnu voluntarily forfeited their vested benefits under the plan and instructed the plan administrator to transfer the $219,000 value of such benefits back to VC.

LO 15-7   15. Reynaldo, age 53, owns a traditional IRA with a $215,000 current balance. Reynaldo is recently divorced and transferred this IRA to the ex-spouse as part of the property settlement.

Research Problems

LO 15-2   1. Curtis Bedford, age 73, is a professor of English at a private university. Curtis holds a tenured position, which represents a lifetime employment contract. The university has offered Curtis a $75,000 lump-sum payment as an early retirement package. If accepted, Curtis must give up any legal claim against the university for age discrimination and must forfeit all privileges as a faculty member. If Curtis accepts the university's offer, will the $75,000 payment represent compensation that is subject to employer and employee payroll (Social Security and Medicare) tax?

LO 15-3   2. Cameron Kline was recently elected mayor of a large midwestern city that furnishes its mayor with an official residence for occupancy during the term of office. The residence (house and gardens) is owned and maintained by the city, and the mayor does not pay rent. To facilitate the social and ceremonial obligations of the office, Cameron is required to live in the residence. Many of these obligations occur in the evenings and on weekends. The fair rental value of the mayoral residence is $60,000 annually. Must Cameron recognize the value of the employer-provided housing as taxable compensation?

LO 15-7   3. Helene Toolson, age 67, is an avid collector of historical documents and signatures. Helene's collection is worth more than $300,000 and, by any measure, is an excellent investment. Helene also owns an IRA with First State Bank. Recently learning that a letter written by Thomas Jefferson was available for purchase out of a private collection, Helene met with a bank vice president to discuss having the IRA acquire the letter. The vice president determined that state banking laws would not prohibit such an acquisition by an IRA. The asking price of the letter is $32,500. Would the purchase of the letter by Helene's IRA have any adverse tax consequence to Helene?

LO 15-7   4. Early this year, Scott Lowe, age 54, became dissatisfied with the service he was receiving from the broker who managed his traditional IRA. Scott requested a distribution of the $48,200 balance in the account and received a check for this amount from the broker on May 23. Scott planned to roll over the distribution into a new IRA with a different broker. Before he could do so, he received news that his son-in-law had died in a hunting accident. Scott immediately traveled to his daughter's home to console her and his grandchildren. During this period of trauma and confusion, Scott wrote a check for $48,200 to his new broker but failed to instruct the broker to put the money into an IRA. Instead, the broker invested it in a taxable money market account. Scott and his broker did not discover the mistake until late December. Must Scott include the $48,200 withdrawal in his gross income and pay a $4,820 premature withdrawal penalty?

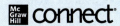 All applicable Tax Planning Cases are available with *Connect*.

Tax Planning Cases

LO 15-6, 15-7   1. This year, Jordan accepted a job with BL, Inc. Jordan intends to work for only eight years and then start a business. Jordan has two options for accumulating the money needed to start this business:

- *Option 1:* Jordan is eligible to participate in BL's Section 401(k) plan and can afford to save $5,000 of salary each year by diverting it to this plan. The plan earns 5 percent a year. Consequently, the plan balance in eight years will be $47,746 ($5,000 for eight years compounded at 5 percent).

- *Option 2:* Jordan can take the entire salary in cash, pay income tax, and save $3,600 ($5,000 less $1,400 tax) in an investment fund that earns 5 percent a year. Because the annual earnings are taxable, the savings in the fund will grow at only 3.6 percent a year. Consequently, the fund balance in eight years will be $32,702 ($3,600 for eight years compounded at 3.6 percent).

Assuming a constant 28 percent combined federal and state tax rate, which option results in the greatest after-tax cash for Jordan to begin this business?

LO 15-6, 15-7

2. Layne is entitled to a $5,200 bonus this year (year 0). Layne's employer provides two options. Layne can either receive a $5,200 bonus in cash or $4,500 deferred compensation. Under the deferral option, the employer will accrue 6 percent annual interest on the deferred compensation. Consequently, the employer will pay $8,059 ($4,500 plus compounded interest) to Layne upon retirement in year 10. Which option has the greater NPV under each of the following assumptions? In making your calculations, use a 5 percent discount rate.

    a. Assume a current 32 percent marginal tax rate and a 12 percent marginal tax rate at retirement.

    b. Assume a 32 percent marginal tax rate both currently and upon retirement.

LO 15-6, 15-7

3. Priya, age 51, plans to save $5,000 this year toward retirement. Priya is considering three different investments. First, a nondeductible contribution to a traditional IRA earning 5 percent a year. Second, the purchase of a certificate of deposit paying 5 percent annual interest. Third, the purchase of corporate stock paying a 5 percent annual dividend. In each case, Priya will reinvest after-tax earnings. (Each investment will grow at an after-tax rate of return.) Priya anticipates liquidating the investment after 15 years and using the after-tax cash to make a down payment on a condominium.

    Determine which investment has the greatest after-tax *future* value. To compute the future value of a sum invested in year 0, use the discount factors in Appendix A. Simply multiply the sum by (1 ÷ discount factor). For example, the future value of $100 invested at 9 percent after five years is $154 [$100 × 1.538 (1 ÷ .650 discount factor)]. In making your computations, assume that over the 15-year investment period, Priya's combined federal and state tax rate is 20 percent on ordinary income and 10 percent on dividends.

LO 15-7

4. Mr. and Mrs. Boltono, ages 64 and 65, are both retired and live on Social Security plus the interest and dividends from several investments. Their taxable income averages $35,000 a year. Mrs. Boltono owns a traditional IRA that she funded entirely with deductible contributions. The couple plans to withdraw $75,000 from the IRA to make some much-needed improvements to their home. How should they time the withdrawal (or series of withdrawals) to maximize the cash available from the IRA?

Chapter **Sixteen**

Investment and Personal Financial Planning

Learning Objectives

After studying this chapter, you should be able to:

LO 16-1. Determine the tax treatment of dividend and interest income.

LO 16-2. Explain how life insurance policies and annuity contracts defer income recognition.

LO 16-3. Compute gain or loss recognized on security transactions.

LO 16-4. Summarize the tax consequences of net capital gain and net capital loss.

LO 16-5. Describe the preferential tax treatment of investments in small corporate businesses.

LO 16-6. Determine the deduction for investment interest expense.

LO 16-7. Summarize the tax consequences of investments in real property.

LO 16-8. Apply the passive activity loss limitation.

LO 16-9. Compute the Medicare contribution tax on unearned income.

LO 16-10. Explain the transfer tax and income tax consequences of inter vivos and testamentary transfers.

This chapter focuses on the tax consequences of investment activities involving the acquisition, holding, and disposition of income-producing property. Individuals engage in investment activities, expecting them to be profitable. In financial terms, they expect the investment to yield a positive return on capital. This return can take the form of current income and cash flow generated by the property or appreciation in the property's value. This chapter explores the tax consequences of both types of returns. Of course, not every investment is profitable, and this chapter also deals with the tax consequences of investment losses.

Many individuals who accumulate significant wealth through their business and investment activities want their children and grandchildren to benefit from their good fortune.

These individuals must develop personal financial planning strategies to achieve this goal in the most cost-effective manner. In the final section of this chapter, we will discover that federal transfer taxes can impede this planning process. However, we will also consider some techniques by which people can minimize these taxes and maximize the wealth available to their younger-generation family members.

BUSINESS VERSUS INVESTMENT ACTIVITIES

The tax consequences of investment activities are very different from the tax consequences of business activities. Individuals engage in the two types of activities for the same purpose: to make a profit. The distinction between business and investment activities lies in the extent of the individual's personal involvement in the activity. An individual engaging in a business activity commits time and talent to the activity on a regular basis, and the business profit is partially attributable to this personal involvement.[1] In contrast, an individual engaging in an investment activity takes a passive role as the owner of income-producing property. The profit from the activity is primarily attributable to the invested capital rather than to the owner's personal involvement. For tax purposes, this distinction holds true even when individuals devote substantial time to managing income-producing property. "A taxpayer who merely manages his investments seeking long-term gain is not carrying on a trade or business. This is so irrespective of the extent or continuity of the transactions or the work required in managing the portfolio."[2]

INVESTMENTS IN FINANCIAL ASSETS

Financial assets are legal claims on the production assets owned by a business entity or other organization. Financial assets include equity interests such as common and preferred corporate stock and creditor interests such as savings accounts, certificates of deposit, notes, bonds, and other debt instruments. These types of financial assets are commonly referred to as **securities.** Financial assets are intangible property rights. They have no intrinsic value; their worth depends on the underlying value of the production assets subject to their claim. Financial assets may be publicly traded on an established market or may be privately placed.

LO 16-1
Determine the tax treatment of dividend and interest income.

Individuals who invest in financial assets can own the assets directly or indirectly through a mutual fund. A **mutual fund** is a diversified portfolio of securities owned and managed by a *regulated investment company (RIC)*. RICs sell shares in their funds to the public—specifically to purchasers wanting to diversify their financial holdings and take advantage of the professional expertise of the fund managers. A mutual fund portfolio can consist of equity stocks, debt instruments, or a combination of both, depending on the investment objectives of the particular fund. Currently, more than 100 million people, about 45 percent of the households in America, hold over $20 trillion of financial assets in mutual funds, making them the most popular investment vehicle on the market.

Dividend and Interest Income

Individuals who invest in securities receive a return on their investment in the form of dividends (paid on equity interests) or interest (paid on creditor interests). As cash basis taxpayers, individuals recognize dividend or interest income in the year in which they actually or

---

[1] In capital-intensive businesses, profit is attributable to the business assets as well as to the personal involvement of the owners.

[2] *Moller* v. *United States,* 721 F.2d 810, 814 (CA FC,1983).

constructively receive payment. Investors in stocks and mutual funds often have a dividend reinvestment option under which their dividends are used to purchase additional shares for their account. Even though shareholders who elect this option receive no cash payments, they are in constructive receipt of the dividends reinvested on their behalf.

Dividends and interest are characterized as ordinary income, and interest income is taxed at the regular individual rates. However, qualified dividend income earned by noncorporate (individual) taxpayers is subject to the same preferential rate structure that applies to long-term capital gains. **Qualified dividend income** is broadly defined as dividends from taxable domestic corporations and qualified foreign corporations. The preferential tax rates are 0, 15, and 20 percent.[3] Computation of the tax is explained in the section Preferential Rates on Long-Term Capital Gains. In addition to the income tax, dividends and interest also may be subject to the Medicare contribution tax discussed later in this chapter.

Preferential Rates on Qualified Dividends	Mr. Hassan's $29,500 taxable income includes $179 interest income and $245 qualified dividend income. The interest income is subject to Mr. Hassan's regular tax rate of 12 percent. However, his dividend income is taxed at the 0 percent preferential rate. Ms. Diaz's $640,000 taxable income includes $13,800 interest income and $22,000 qualified dividend income. The interest income is subject to Ms. Diaz's regular tax rate of 37 percent. However, her dividend income is taxed at the 20 percent preferential rate.

Organizations that pay dividends or interest issue annual Forms 1099-DIV (Dividends and Distributions) and Forms 1099-INT (Interest Income) to inform investors of their total payments for the year. The IRS receives copies of these forms and cross-checks to make sure that the payment reported on each form matches the income reported on the investor's Form 1040. Investors must pay careful attention to the detailed information on their Form 1099s to determine the correct tax treatment of their payments. For example, corporations occasionally make distributions to their shareholders that are tax-free returns of capital rather than taxable dividends. These distributions, which are identified on Form 1099, are not included in the recipient's gross income but instead reduce the recipient's tax basis in the corporate stock.

Corporate Distributions	Rocko, Inc., a New York corporation, distributed $935,700 cash to its shareholders this year. Rocko's tax department determined that only $894,100 (95.55 percent) of the distribution was a dividend paid from corporate earnings. The $41,600 remainder was a return of corporate capital. Mr. Jude Isley received a $44,800 cash distribution from Rocko. According to his Form 1099, only $42,806 (95.55 percent) of his distribution was qualified dividend income, and the $1,994 remainder was a nontaxable reduction in the basis of Mr. Isley's Rocko stock.

Distributions from mutual funds are typically labeled as dividends but actually represent a payout of the various types of income generated by the fund's investment portfolio. Consequently, a mutual fund dividend could include qualified dividend income generated by the fund's investment in equities, interest income generated by the fund's investment in debt instruments, and a **capital gain distribution** of the net long-term capital gain recognized by the fund on sales of securities. Form 1099s issued by mutual funds must report any qualified dividend or capital gain distributions for the year so that individual investors can benefit from the preferential rates on these types of income.

[3] §1(h)(3)(B) and (h)(11).

| Mutual Fund Dividend | Stargaze Mutual Fund manages a diversified portfolio consisting of 60 percent stock in taxable domestic corporations, 35 percent corporate bonds, and 5 percent cash. This year, Stargaze's portfolio earned $8 million of qualified dividends, $3.6 million of interest, and $1.9 million net long-term capital gain on security sales. Stargaze distributed a $13.5 million dividend to its investors that consisted of an $8 million qualified dividend distribution, a $3.6 million ordinary dividend, and a $1.9 million capital gain distribution.

Ms. Cindy Jung received a $9,930 distribution from Stargaze. According to her Form 1099, $5,884 was a qualified dividend distribution, $2,648 was an ordinary dividend, and $1,398 was a capital gain distribution. |

Individuals report interest and dividend income on Schedule B of their Form 1040. Here is a comprehensive example showing how these types of income flow through this schedule.

| Mr. and Mrs. David: Schedule B | Ronald and Janet David, who file a joint return, have a savings account with Midwest Credit Union. They own a $75,000 certificate of deposit with Second Union Bank and a $100,000 bond issued by Tryton, Inc. This year, they earned $161 interest on the savings account, $4,712 interest on the CD, and $6,200 interest on the bond. Shortly after year-end, they received a Form 1099-INT from each payer on which their annual interest income was reported. They entered this information on Part I of their Schedule B (shown as Exhibit 16.1). Their $11,073 total interest (line 4) was carried as an income item to Form 1040, line 2b.

At the beginning of the year, Mr. and Mrs. David owned 5,122 shares of Prime Growth mutual fund. They elected to reinvest their annual dividends in additional Prime Growth shares. Consequently, they received no cash from the mutual fund during the year. Mr. and Mrs. David received a Form 1099-DIV from Prime Growth containing the following information. |

Ordinary dividend	$ 2,316
Qualified dividend distribution	4,775
Capital gain distribution	5,383
Gross distribution	$12,474
Shares owned on January 1	5,122
Additional shares purchased for investor's account (198 shares at $63 per share = $12,474)	198
Shares owned on December 31	5,320

Mr. and Mrs. David also own 16,780 shares of Mortimer Industries common stock. At the beginning of the year, their cost basis in these shares was $59,000. During the year, they received cash distributions totaling $19,000 from Mortimer. Their Form 1099-DIV contained the following information.

Qualified dividend income	$17,980
Nontaxable distribution	1,020
Gross distribution	$19,000

Mr. and Mrs. David entered their ordinary and qualified dividends from Prime Growth and Mortimer on Part II, Schedule B. The capital gain distribution of the Prime Growth fund ($5,383) was reported on Schedule D for inclusion with their other capital gains and losses. The nontaxable distribution reduced the tax basis in the Mortimer stock to $57,980. Their $25,071 total ordinary dividend (line 6) was carried as an income item to Form 1040, line 3b, and their total qualified dividend income ($22,755) was entered on line 3a.

EXHIBIT 16.1

Department of the Treasury, Internal Revenue Service

SCHEDULE B
(Form 1040)

Department of the Treasury
Internal Revenue Service

Interest and Ordinary Dividends

Go to *www.irs.gov/ScheduleB* for instructions and the latest information.
Attach to Form 1040 or 1040-SR.

OMB No. 1545-0074

2022

Attachment
Sequence No. **08**

Name(s) shown on return
Ronald and Janet David

Your social security number
498-31-1240

Part I

Interest

(See instructions and the Instructions for Form 1040, line 2b.)

Note: If you received a Form 1099-INT, Form 1099-OID, or substitute statement from a brokerage firm, list the firm's name as the payer and enter the total interest shown on that form.

		Amount
1	List name of payer. If any interest is from a seller-financed mortgage and the buyer used the property as a personal residence, see the instructions and list this interest first. Also, show that buyer's social security number and address:	
	Savings account - Midwest Credit Union	161
	Certificate of deposit - Second Union Bank	4,712
	6.2% Tryton Inc. corporate bond	6,200

2	Add the amounts on line 1	**2**	11,073
3	Excludable interest on series EE and I U.S. savings bonds issued after 1989. Attach Form 8815	**3**	
4	Subtract line 3 from line 2. Enter the result here and on Form 1040 or 1040-SR, line 2b	**4**	11,073

Note: If line 4 is over $1,500, you must complete Part III.

Part II

Ordinary Dividends

(See instructions and the Instructions for Form 1040, line 3b.)

Note: If you received a Form 1099-DIV or substitute statement from a brokerage firm, list the firm's name as the payer and enter the ordinary dividends shown on that form.

		Amount
5	List name of payer:	
	Prime Growth mutual fund - ordinary dividend	2,316
	Prime Growth mutual fund - qualified dividend distribution	4,775
	Mortimer Industries - qualified dividend	17,980

6	Add the amounts on line 5. Enter the total here and on Form 1040 or 1040-SR, line 3b	**6**	25,071

Note: If line 6 is over $1,500, you must complete Part III.

Part III

Foreign Accounts and Trusts

Caution: If required, failure to file FinCEN Form 114 may result in substantial penalties. Additionally, you may be required to file Form 8938, Statement of Specified Foreign Financial Assets. See instructions.

You must complete this part if you **(a)** had over $1,500 of taxable interest or ordinary dividends; **(b)** had a foreign account; or **(c)** received a distribution from, or were a grantor of, or a transferor to, a foreign trust.

		Yes	No
7a	At any time during 2022, did you have a financial interest in or signature authority over a financial account (such as a bank account, securities account, or brokerage account) located in a foreign country? See instructions		✓
	If "Yes," are you required to file FinCEN Form 114, Report of Foreign Bank and Financial Accounts (FBAR), to report that financial interest or signature authority? See FinCEN Form 114 and its instructions for filing requirements and exceptions to those requirements		
b	If you are required to file FinCEN Form 114, list the name(s) of the foreign country(-ies) where the financial account(s) are located:		
8	During 2022, did you receive a distribution from, or were you the grantor of, or transferor to, a foreign trust? If "Yes," you may have to file Form 3520. See instructions		✓

For Paperwork Reduction Act Notice, see your tax return instructions.   Cat. No. 17146N   Schedule B (Form 1040) 2022

Tax-Exempt Interest

The public security markets offer thousands of financial assets that individuals can select to meet their particular investment needs. In making their selection, investors should consider their overall tax situation, as well as any preferential tax characteristics of the assets under consideration. One such characteristic is the tax-exempt status of interest on certain debt instruments.

State and Local Bonds

For federal tax purposes, interest income earned on investments in debt instruments issued by state and local governments, including the District of Columbia, is excluded from income.[4] The interest rate on these tax-exempt bonds is typically lower than the rate on taxable bonds with a comparable degree of risk; investors who purchase tax-exempt bonds pay an implicit tax equal to this rate differential.[5] Moreover, state and local bond interest may be taxed by the state or locality in which the investor resides. Finally, the interest on tax-exempt **private activity bonds** issued by any state or local government after August 7, 1986, is a preference item for alternative minimum tax purposes.[6] Because of these variables, even individuals in high marginal tax brackets can't assume that they will benefit by buying tax-exempt bonds until they evaluate the investment on an after-tax basis.

U.S. Debt Obligations

The U.S. government issues a variety of debt instruments for investors. Treasury bills are issued on a discount basis and are payable at a fixed maturity date not exceeding 1 year from date of issue. Treasury notes have maturity periods ranging from 1 to 10 years, while Treasury bonds have maturity periods from 10 to 30 years. Both are issued at face value and bear a fixed rate of interest, payable at six-month intervals. **Treasury inflation-protected securities (TIPS)** are long-term debt instruments that pay a fixed rate of interest on a principal amount adjusted semiannually for inflation or deflation based on the Consumer Price Index. **Series EE savings bonds** are long-term debt instruments issued at a discount.

The interest on all these debt instruments is subject to federal income tax. However, the interest is exempt from income tax levied by any state or local government. Because state and local tax rates are generally much lower than federal rates, exemption from such taxes may result in only a modest benefit. Nonetheless, investors should be aware of this preferential state tax characteristic of U.S. debt obligations.

Tax-Exempt Interest	Ms. Staton is a Connecticut resident. Her investment portfolio includes City of Chicago municipal bonds and U.S. Treasury bonds. This year, she earned $9,100 interest on the municipal bonds and $17,900 interest on the Treasury bonds. The municipal bond interest is exempt from federal income tax but subject to a 6 percent Connecticut income tax. So Ms. Staton's after-tax income from the municipal bonds is $8,554 ($9,100 − $546 state tax). The Treasury bond interest is subject to a 32 percent federal income tax but is exempt from Connecticut income tax. So Ms. Staton's after-tax income from the Treasury bonds is $12,172 ($17,900 − $5,728 federal tax).

Deferred Interest Income

The tax law offers investors a few narrow opportunities to defer the recognition of interest income. For instance, cash basis taxpayers who purchase short-term debt obligations at a discount don't recognize income until the obligation matures.[7]

---

[4] §103. This exclusion extends to any portion of a mutual fund dividend attributable to the fund's investment in tax-exempt bonds.

[5] See the discussion of implicit tax in Chapter 4.

[6] §57(a)(5). The proceeds from private activity bonds are used for nongovernmental purposes, such as industrial development.

[7] See §454 and §1271(a)(3) and (4). Short-term debt obligations have fixed maturity periods of one year or less.

Interest Deferral	In July 2022, Mrs. Webb bought a $50,000 U.S. Treasury bill for $48,900; the bill matured 26 weeks after date of issue. She reported no 2022 income from this investment, even though most of the interest on the bill accrued in 2022. When Mrs. Webb redeemed the bill in January 2023 for $50,000, she recognized the entire $1,100 interest income.

Individuals can achieve the same type of deferral if they purchase Series EE savings bonds. Even though these discount bonds have long-term maturity periods, individuals postpone recognition of any interest income until they cash in the bonds. In the unusual case in which an investor prefers to take the discount into annual income on an accrual basis, he may elect to do so by reporting the accrued interest on Schedule B.

Market Discount

Cash basis investors who purchase bonds *in a market transaction* at a price lower than the bond's stated redemption value at maturity aren't required to accrue the **market discount** as interest income over the life of the bond.[8] Instead, they recognize the discount as interest in the future year in which they sell the bond or the bond is redeemed.[9]

Deferral of Market Discount	Mr. Barry bought a publicly traded corporate bond through his broker for $21,300. Although the bond is redeemable at maturity for $25,000, it traded at a discounted price because the stated interest rate (3.5 percent) was below the market rate (4.4 percent). Mr. Barry will include the 3.5 percent interest payments in his annual income but will not include any portion of the market discount. If he holds the bond until maturity, Mr. Barry will recognize the entire $3,700 excess of the $25,000 redemption proceeds over his $21,300 cost basis as ordinary income in the year of redemption.

Original Issue Discount

Investors who purchase *newly issued* corporate debt instruments at a discount can't defer recognition of the interest income represented by the original issue discount. **Original issue discount (OID)** equals the excess of the bond's stated redemption value at maturity (face value) over the issue price. Even cash basis investors must recognize accrued income by amortizing this discount over the life of the bond.[10]

Amortization of OID	Jacks, Inc. made a new public offering of 15-year bonds with a stated interest rate of only 1.5 percent of face value. Mr. Barry, our investor in the previous example, bought $50,000 of these bonds for their discounted issue price of $27,000. Mr. Barry's return on his investment consists of the $750 yearly interest payments *plus* the $23,000 difference between his cost and the cash he will collect when the bonds mature. Every year, Jacks sends Mr. Barry the following: • Form 1099-INT reporting the $750 interest payment. • Form 1099-OID reporting the amortized discount he must recognize as additional interest income.[11] <div align="right">*(continued)*</div>

[8] Investors may elect to accrue interest income under §1278(b).

[9] §1276(a)(1). This rule extends to any market discount on state and local bonds. While the periodic interest payments on these bonds are tax-exempt, the accrued discount is fully taxable as ordinary income.

[10] §1272(a). This income recognition rule doesn't apply to tax-exempt state and local obligations.

[11] The annual OID income on debt instruments issued after July 1, 1992, is based on the instrument's constant yield to maturity. §1272(a)(3). This calculation results in increasing annual OID income over the life of the instrument. Corporations may take an annual interest deduction for amortized OID. §163(e)(1).

> Over the 15-year term of the bonds, Mr. Barry will recognize $23,000 OID income with no corresponding cash flow. However, he will not recognize additional income when he redeems the bonds at maturity for $50,000.

Inflation-Adjusted Debt Instruments

Investors who purchase inflation-adjusted debt instruments (such as TIPS issued by the U.S. government) receive interest payments computed at a fixed rate on an inflation-adjusted principal amount. Investors must include both the interest received and any annual increase in the principal in current income. The tax treatment of the inflation adjustment is similar to the treatment of OID because the adjustment creates taxable income without corresponding cash flow.[12] In other words, recognition of interest income is accelerated rather than deferred.

Inflation Adjustment	At the beginning of 2022, Mrs. Salina invested $200,000 in TIPS paying 4 percent yearly interest. On the first semiannual interest payment date, the inflation adjustment to principal was 1 percent. Consequently, Mrs. Salina received $4,040 interest ($202,000 adjusted principal × .04 × one-half year). On the second interest payment date, the cumulative inflation adjustment to principal was 2.5 percent, and Mrs. Salina received $4,100 interest ($205,000 adjusted principal × .04 × one-half year). Mrs. Salina's 2022 taxable income from the TIPS totals $13,140 ($8,140 interest payments + $5,000 annual increase in principal).

Assume that Mrs. Salina holds the TIPS until maturity and receives $233,400 redemption proceeds equal to the inflation-adjusted value of her original $200,000 investment.[13] Because she has recognized the cumulative $33,400 adjustment as interest income over the life of the TIPS, she won't recognize additional income upon redemption. |

Life Insurance Policies and Annuity Contracts

Life Insurance Policies

LO 16-2
Explain how life insurance policies and annuity contracts defer income recognition.

Tax Talk
According to Forbes magazine, life insurance should play an important role in any financial plan. After all, "you can't invest your way out of an untimely death."

A life insurance policy is a legal contract between a purchaser (the owner) and a commercial insurance company. The owner pays a premium or series of premiums for the company's commitment to pay a specific sum of money (death benefit) on the death of the person whose life is insured. The owner has the right to name the beneficiary (the person or organization that will receive the death benefit). An individual purchases insurance on his or her own life primarily to provide financial protection for dependent family members. However, many life insurance contracts offer both protection against premature death and an investment element. The investment element is called the **cash surrender value,** which increases every year that the policy remains in effect. The owner does not recognize this annual increase in value, called the **inside buildup,** as taxable income. If the owner eventually decides that his family no longer needs insurance protection, he may liquidate the policy for its cash surrender value. In this case, the owner recognizes the *excess* cash surrender value over his investment in the policy (total premiums paid) as ordinary income.[14]

---

[12] Reg. §1.1275-7.

[13] TIPS provide a *minimum guarantee* feature to protect investors against deflation of the value of their investment: When TIPS mature, investors receive the *greater* of the original principal amount or the inflation-adjusted amount at maturity.

[14] §72(e)(2).

Liquidation of Life Insurance Policy	Twenty years ago, Mr. Wilde purchased an insurance policy on his own life. The policy provided a $350,000 death benefit payable to Mr. Wilde's wife and children. To date, Mr. Wilde has paid $38,000 of premiums. Because his wife predeceased him and his children are financially independent, Mr. Wilde liquidated the policy for its $42,800 cash surrender value. The insurance company sent Mr. Wilde a Form 1099-R reporting $4,800 ordinary income ($42,800 − $38,000 aggregate premiums).[15]

The deferral of tax on the inside buildup certainly makes life insurance contracts a tax-preferred investment. The tax consequences are even more favorable if the policy is held until it matures on the death of the insured. In this case, the beneficiary excludes the death benefit from gross income, and the accumulated return on the owner's investment in the life insurance contract escapes tax entirely.[16]

Life Insurance Proceeds	Twenty years ago, Mrs. Muzo purchased an insurance policy on her own life. The policy provided a $350,000 death benefit payable to Mrs. Muzo's children. Mrs. Muzo paid $38,000 of premiums, and the policy's cash surrender value was $42,800. Mrs. Muzo died on May 4 with the policy still in effect. On September 3, her children received $350,000 from the insurance company and excluded the entire payment from their gross income.

This highly advantageous tax treatment also applies to **accelerated death benefits:** payments made under the contract to insured individuals who are terminally or chronically ill.[17] Such individuals may be forced to draw against or even liquidate their life insurance policies to pay medical expenses resulting from an extended illness. The tax law alleviates this financial hardship by classifying these premature payments as nontaxable death benefits.

Annuity Contracts

Individuals purchase annuity contracts from commercial insurance companies to provide themselves with a fixed stream of income for a future period of time. The owner pays a premium or series of premiums that the insurance company invests on the owner's behalf. The owner is not taxed on the yearly inside buildup in the value of her investment. Instead, tax is deferred until the owner begins receiving periodic payments under the contract. The portion of each annuity payment representing a distribution of accumulated earnings is taxed as ordinary income, while the portion representing a return of the owner's investment is nontaxable.

Annuity Payments	Mrs. Water purchased an annuity for a $75,000 single premium when she was 51 years old. This year, Mrs. Water reached age 65 and began receiving annuity payments. Under the terms of her contract, she will receive $1,100 per month for the rest of her life. The portion of each payment representing a return of her investment is based on the ratio of that investment to the expected return under the contract.[18] On the basis of life expectancy *(continued)*

[15] Form 1099-R reports distributions from insurance contracts, annuities, and pension, profit sharing, IRAs, and other retirement plans.

[16] §101.

[17] §101(g). Accelerated death benefits include the proceeds of the sale or assignment of a contract to a *viatical settlement provider,* which is a company licensed to engage in the business of purchasing life insurance contracts from individuals who are terminally or chronically ill.

[18] §72(b)(1).

tables provided in Treasury regulations, Mrs. Water can expect to receive 240 payments ($264,000). Consequently, her exclusion ratio is 28.41 percent:

$$\frac{\$75,000 \text{ investment (single premium)}}{\$264,000 \text{ expected return}} = .2841$$

Mrs. Water received eight monthly payments totaling $8,800 this year, and her nontaxable return of investment is $2,500:

Total annuity payments received	$8,800
Exclusion ratio	.2841
	$2,500

Mrs. Water must recognize the remaining $6,300 of the total payments as ordinary income.

Each year, Mrs. Water will apply the exclusion ratio to determine the nontaxable portion of her total payments until she recovers her entire $75,000 investment. Any additional payments will be fully taxable.[19] If Mrs. Water dies before recovering her investment, the uncovered portion is allowed as an itemized deduction on her final Form 1040.[20]

Death of Annuitant	Assume that Mrs. Water in the previous example collected 203 annuity payments totaling $223,300 before her death. Consequently, she recovered $63,440 of her $75,000 investment ($223,300 × .2841 exclusion ratio) in the annuity contract. Mrs. Water's executor can report her $11,560 unrecovered investment as an itemized deduction on her final Form 1040.

Nontax Considerations

People buy life insurance policies to protect against dying too soon and annuity contracts to protect against living too long. In addition to their protection element, both assets offer a tax-deferred financial return. However, life insurance policies and annuity contracts may have lower before-tax rates of return and higher transaction costs than investment opportunities that are not tax favored. For instance, life insurance policies have the highest commission charges of any financial product—typically more than 50 percent of the first-year premium paid by the investor. Annuity contracts routinely charge an annual fee and impose early surrender charges on individuals who liquidate their investment in the contract before the annuity starting date. These nontax costs can outweigh the benefit of tax deferral, particularly for individuals in the lower tax brackets or who aren't prepared to commit to these investments for the long haul.

GAINS AND LOSSES FROM SECURITY TRANSACTIONS

Tax Talk

A recent proposal from Senate Finance Committee chairman Ron Wyden, labeled the "Billionaires Income Tax," would require extremely high net worth individuals to mark-to-market the value of their tradeable investment assets annually, recognizing taxable gain or loss.

A key principle of federal tax law is that *unrealized* gains and losses are not taxed. Increases or decreases in the value of property over time are not recognized until an external transaction triggers gain or loss realization. Accordingly, individuals who invest in financial assets defer paying tax on any appreciation in value until they dispose of the assets in a taxable transaction. In this section of the chapter, we will examine the tax rules that apply to dispositions of securities. By paying attention to these rules, individuals can control their tax costs and enhance the after-tax return on such investments.

[19] §72(b)(2).

[20] §72(b)(3).

Computing Gains and Losses

LO 16-3
Compute gain or loss recognized on security transactions.

Realized gain from the sale of securities equals the excess of the amount realized over the seller's basis in the securities. Realized loss equals the excess of basis over the amount realized. Amount realized is the sum of any money plus the fair market value (FMV) of any property received by the seller. If the investor incurred any selling expenses, such as brokerage fees and commissions, these expenses reduce the amount realized on sale. A seller's basis in a security depends on the transaction in which the security was acquired. Securities acquired by purchase have a cost basis including both the price of the securities plus any front-end fees or load charges. Investors who sell securities purchased through a broker receive a Form 1099-B (Proceeds from Broker and Barter Exchange Transactions) reporting the amount realized on sale and other relevant information about the transaction.

Tracking Security Basis

Tax Talk

Investors who bought $5,000 worth of Amazon stock when the company went public in 1997 made a spectacular investment. Today, that stock is worth over $6 million.

Individuals should keep careful record of the initial cost of the securities in their investment portfolios and the effect of any subsequent transactions on such basis. For instance, if an investor elects to reinvest dividends in additional shares of stock or a mutual fund, the dividend becomes the cost basis in the new shares. If an investor receives a nontaxable distribution with respect to shares of stock, the basis in the shares must be reduced by this return of capital. Investors who own debt instruments with original issue discount should increase their basis in the securities by the OID income accrued each year. Investors who own inflation-adjusted debt instruments should increase their basis by the annual increase in the principal. Failure to keep track of these common basis adjustments results in overstatement or understatement of gain or loss realized on the eventual disposition of the securities.

Basis Adjustments for Reinvested Dividends

Nine years ago, Ms. Farley paid $25,000 for 3,400 shares of Fastrack mutual fund. She elected to reinvest her dividends in additional shares. As of June 4, Ms. Farley had recognized $19,100 dividend income (without corresponding cash flow) and acquired 2,816 additional shares. On June 4, she sold all 6,216 shares for $58,000. Her realized gain is computed as follows:

Amount realized on sale		$58,000
Adjusted basis:		
Cost of 3,400 shares	$25,000	
Cost of 2,816 shares (reinvested dividends)	19,100	
		(44,100)
Gain realized on sale		$13,900

Identifying Basis on Sale

When an investor sells a specific security with an identifiable basis, gain or loss is determined with reference to such basis. However, investment portfolios often contain identical securities acquired at different times and for different prices. If the investor sells some of the securities but can't identify which specific ones were sold, the basis is determined by a first-in, first-out (FIFO) method.[21] In other words, the investor is presumed to have sold the securities with the earliest acquisition date.

[21] Reg. §1.1012-1(c).

Individuals who sell mutual fund shares or shares of stock acquired after 2010 pursuant to a dividend reinvestment plan may also use an average cost basis method for calculating gain or loss.[22] Under the simplest version of this method, the basis of each share equals the aggregate cost of all shares divided by the total number of shares. Mutual funds typically provide average cost basis information on their year-end statements as a service to their investors.

Average Basis Method

At the beginning of the year, Mr. Yao owned 1,000 shares of TNT Mutual Fund with a $52,000 aggregate basis. Every month, he invested $1,000 in the fund. Because of fluctuations in the market price of TNT shares, he acquired a different number of shares with a different cost basis each month. By September, Mr. Yao owned 1,155 shares with a $60,000 aggregate basis. On September 9, he sold 300 shares for $56 per share ($16,800 total price). He can determine his basis in the 300 shares as follows:

$60,000 aggregate basis ÷ 1,155 shares = $51.948 basis per share
300 shares sold × $51.948 basis per share = $15,584

Consequently, Mr. Yao's gain on sale is $1,216 ($16,800 amount realized − $15,584 basis), and his aggregate basis in his 855 remaining shares is $44,416 ($60,000 − $15,584).

Worthless Securities and Nonbusiness Bad Debts

Securities are capital assets in the hands of individual investors. Therefore, gains and losses realized on security sales are capital gains and losses subject to the special tax rules presented in the next section of the chapter. According to the statutory definition, capital gains and losses result from the sale or exchange of capital assets.[23] The Internal Revenue Code provides that two other events result in capital loss.

The first event occurs when an investor determines that a security has become worthless during the year. This event is treated as a deemed sale of the security on the last day of the year for an amount realized of zero.[24] In other words, the investor recognizes his unrecovered basis in the worthless security as a capital loss.

Worthless Security

Eight years ago, Mrs. Lax paid $77,500 for 3,900 shares of PPK common stock. This year, PPK declared bankruptcy and informed its shareholders that their stock had no value. Mrs. Lax can recognize a $77,500 capital loss on the December 31 deemed sale of her worthless PPK stock.

The second event occurs when an individual who loaned money to another party determines that the debt is uncollectible. In such a case, the individual recognizes the unpaid balance of the **nonbusiness bad debt** as a short-term capital loss.[25]

Nonbusiness Bad Debt

Six years ago, Mr. Jared loaned $25,000 to PT Partnership in exchange for PT's interest-bearing note. PT has repaid $9,000 of the debt. However, PT recently announced that it is hopelessly insolvent and can't pay any of its creditors. Mr. Jared can recognize his $16,000 nonbusiness bad debt as a capital loss.

---

[22] Reg. §1.1012-1(e).
[23] §1222.
[24] §165(g).
[25] §166(d). If an individual lends money or extends credit *as part of his business,* any resulting bad debt is a deductible business expense.

Nontaxable Exchanges of Securities

As a general rule, the exchange of one security for another security is a taxable event. For instance, if an investor exchanges stock in Corporation A for a long-term bond issued by Corporation Z, the investor recognizes the difference between his amount realized (FMV of the bond) and the basis of the stock as capital gain or loss. The tax law does contain several nontaxable exchange provisions applying to security transactions. No gain or loss is recognized on the exchange of one class of common stock for a different class of common stock *in the same corporation.* Similarly, preferred stock can be exchanged for preferred stock *in the same corporation* at no current tax cost.[26] If an investor exchanges stock or securities in one corporation for stock or securities in a different corporation, no gain or loss is recognized only if the exchange is pursuant to a **reorganization** involving the two corporations.[27] In each of these nontaxable exchanges, the investor's basis in the newly acquired security equals the basis of the security surrendered. Because of this substituted basis rule, gain or loss realized on the exchange is merely deferred, not eliminated.[28]

Exchange of Securities	The shareholders of LG, Inc. voted to merge their corporation into SM, Inc. under Missouri law. Pursuant to the merger, Ms. Gwin exchanged her 813 shares of LG stock for 12,300 shares of SM stock. Her realized gain on the exchange is computed as follows:

Amount realized (FMV of SM stock received)	$945,200
Basis in LG stock surrendered	(550,300)
Gain realized on exchange	$394,900

If the merger of LG and SM qualifies as a reorganization for federal tax purposes, Ms. Gwin doesn't recognize any of her realized gain. In this case, the basis in her 12,300 shares of SM stock is $550,300 (basis of LG stock surrendered in the nontaxable exchange). If the merger doesn't qualify as a reorganization, Ms. Gwin must recognize a $394,900 taxable gain on the exchange. In this case, the basis in her 12,300 shares of SM stock is their $945,200 cost (FMV of LG stock surrendered).

TAX CONSEQUENCES OF CAPITAL GAINS AND LOSSES

LO 16-4
Summarize the tax consequences of net capital gain and net capital loss.

Individuals who recognize both capital gains and losses during the year can deduct the losses to the extent of the gains. In other words, individuals can combine their capital gains and losses to result in either a net gain or a net loss. A net gain is included in adjusted gross income and may be taxed at a preferential rate. A net loss results in a limited deduction in the AGI computation. Before focusing on these outcomes, we must examine the rules governing the netting of capital gains and losses.

Netting Capital Gains and Losses

Individuals report the sale or other disposition of a capital asset on Form 8949. Each sale or disposition is classified on Form 8949 as either short-term (Part I) or long-term (Part II).[29]

---

[26] §1036.

[27] Reorganizations are a set of precisely defined transactions in which one corporation acquires another, one corporation divides into two corporations, or one corporation changes its capital structure. Reorganizations are defined in §368.

[28] See the discussion of generic nontaxable exchanges in Chapter 9.

[29] See §1222.

- **Short-term capital gains or losses** result from the sale or exchange of capital assets owned for one year or less. The capital loss from a nonbusiness bad debt is classified as a short-term loss, regardless of the time period of the debt.

- **Long-term capital gains or losses** result from the sale or exchange of capital assets owned for more than one year. There is a narrow subcategory of long-term gains and losses, described as **28 percent rate gains or losses,** that includes recognized gains and losses from the sale or exchange of **collectibles** (tangible assets such as works of art, antiques, gems, stamps, and coins) and the taxable gain recognized on the sale of qualified small business stock (defined later in the chapter).[30]

The aggregate information from Form 8949 for both short-term and long-term transactions is carried to Schedule D, Form 1040. This information is used to compute *net* short-term and *net* long-term capital gain or loss for the year.

Mr. and Mrs. Dixon: Schedule D	In 2022, Mark and Sue Dixon made the following four sales of marketable securities:				
		Date Acquired	**Sales Price**	**Tax Basis**	**Gain or Loss**
	11,812 shares of Oslo Mutual Fund	04/15/22	$28,400	$22,750	$ 5,650
	Zephyr corporate bonds	06/22/22	8,340	10,000	(1,660)
	2,065 shares of BLP preferred stock	09/12/05	59,000	67,900	(8,900)
	335 shares of Elsco common	07/18/02	71,000	44,200	26,800

Shortly after year-end, the Dixons received a Form 1099-B from their broker reporting the relevant information for the four sales and a Form 1099-DIV from Oslo Mutual Fund reporting that the fund had made a $7,800 capital gain distribution to the Dixons in 2022.

The Dixons reported the details of each sale on Form 8949 and then entered the aggregate short-term and long-term information on their Schedule D. They also reported their $7,800 capital gain distribution on line 13 of Schedule D. Page 1 of the Dixons' Schedule D is shown in Exhibit 16.2.

The short-term and long-term outcomes reported on Part I, line 7, and Part II, line 15, of Schedule D are combined, and the resulting net capital gain or loss is reported on line 16, Part III, Schedule D (not shown). If the result is a net gain, such gain is carried to Form 1040, line 7, for inclusion in taxable income. The Dixons' Schedule D reports a $3,990 net short-term capital gain and a $25,700 net long-term gain, which combine to a $29,690 net capital gain includable in their taxable income.

The following examples illustrate two other combinations of short-term and long-term outcomes resulting in a taxable capital gain.

Taxable Short-Term Capital Gain	Mr. Boyle's Schedule D reflects a $12,200 net short-term gain and a $4,700 net long-term loss. Because the loss can be deducted (netted) against the gain, he has a $7,500 short-term capital gain included in taxable income.

[30] §1(h)(5) and (7). When an individual sells or exchanges a collectible held for personal use (rather than as an investment), a realized gain is recognized (taxable) but a realized loss is not recognized (nondeductible). For further discussion, see Chapter 17.

EXHIBIT 16.2

Department of the Treasury, Internal Revenue Service

SCHEDULE D **(Form 1040)** Department of the Treasury Internal Revenue Service	**Capital Gains and Losses** Attach to Form 1040, 1040-SR, or 1040-NR. Go to *www.irs.gov/ScheduleD* for instructions and the latest information. Use Form 8949 to list your transactions for lines 1b, 2, 3, 8b, 9, and 10.	OMB No. 1545-0074 **2022** Attachment Sequence No. **12**

Name(s) shown on return — **Mark and Sue Dixon**   Your social security number

Did you dispose of any investment(s) in a qualified opportunity fund during the tax year? ☐ Yes ☑ No
If "Yes," attach Form 8949 and see its instructions for additional requirements for reporting your gain or loss.

Part I Short-Term Capital Gains and Losses—Generally Assets Held One Year or Less (see instructions)

See instructions for how to figure the amounts to enter on the lines below. This form may be easier to complete if you round off cents to whole dollars.	(d) Proceeds (sales price)	(e) Cost (or other basis)	(g) Adjustments to gain or loss from Form(s) 8949, Part I, line 2, column (g)	(h) Gain or (loss) Subtract column (e) from column (d) and combine the result with column (g)
1a Totals for all short-term transactions reported on Form 1099-B for which basis was reported to the IRS and for which you have no adjustments (see instructions). However, if you choose to report all these transactions on Form 8949, leave this line blank and go to line 1b .	36,740	32,750		3,990
1b Totals for all transactions reported on Form(s) 8949 with **Box A** checked				
2 Totals for all transactions reported on Form(s) 8949 with **Box B** checked				
3 Totals for all transactions reported on Form(s) 8949 with **Box C** checked				

4 Short-term gain from Form 6252 and short-term gain or (loss) from Forms 4684, 6781, and 8824 . .	**4**	
5 Net short-term gain or (loss) from partnerships, S corporations, estates, and trusts from Schedule(s) K-1	**5**	
6 Short-term capital loss carryover. Enter the amount, if any, from line 8 of your **Capital Loss Carryover Worksheet** in the instructions	**6** ( )	
7 **Net short-term capital gain or (loss).** Combine lines 1a through 6 in column (h). If you have any long-term capital gains or losses, go to Part II below. Otherwise, go to Part III on the back	**7**	3,990

Part II Long-Term Capital Gains and Losses—Generally Assets Held More Than One Year (see instructions)

See instructions for how to figure the amounts to enter on the lines below. This form may be easier to complete if you round off cents to whole dollars.	(d) Proceeds (sales price)	(e) Cost (or other basis)	(g) Adjustments to gain or loss from Form(s) 8949, Part II, line 2, column (g)	(h) Gain or (loss) Subtract column (e) from column (d) and combine the result with column (g)
8a Totals for all long-term transactions reported on Form 1099-B for which basis was reported to the IRS and for which you have no adjustments (see instructions). However, if you choose to report all these transactions on Form 8949, leave this line blank and go to line 8b .	130,000	112,100		17,900
8b Totals for all transactions reported on Form(s) 8949 with **Box D** checked				
9 Totals for all transactions reported on Form(s) 8949 with **Box E** checked				
10 Totals for all transactions reported on Form(s) 8949 with **Box F** checked.				

11 Gain from Form 4797, Part I; long-term gain from Forms 2439 and 6252; and long-term gain or (loss) from Forms 4684, 6781, and 8824	**11**	
12 Net long-term gain or (loss) from partnerships, S corporations, estates, and trusts from Schedule(s) K-1	**12**	
13 Capital gain distributions. See the instructions	**13**	7,800
14 Long-term capital loss carryover. Enter the amount, if any, from line 13 of your **Capital Loss Carryover Worksheet** in the instructions	**14** ( )	
15 **Net long-term capital gain or (loss).** Combine lines 8a through 14 in column (h). Then, go to Part III on the back	**15**	25,700

For Paperwork Reduction Act Notice, see your tax return instructions. Cat. No. 11338H Schedule D (Form 1040) 2022

Taxable Long-Term Capital Gain

Ms. Coller's Schedule D reflects an $8,500 net short-term loss and a $20,000 net long-term gain. Because the loss can be deducted (netted) against the gain, she has an $11,500 long-term capital gain included in taxable income.[31]

[31] If a net long-term capital gain includes any 28 percent rate gain, a short-term capital loss reduces the 28 percent rate gain before other long-term gain. §1(h)(4)(B)(ii).

Preferential Rates on Long-Term Capital Gains

If individual taxable income includes capital gain, such gain is taxed under a complicated rate structure[32]:

- Short-term capital gain is taxed at the regular rates applying to ordinary income.
- Long-term capital gain categorized as 28 percent rate gain is taxed at a *maximum* rate of 28 percent. Thus, this rate is beneficial only if the regular rate that would apply to such gain exceeds 28 percent.
- Other long-term gain plus the taxpayer's qualified dividend income (the total labeled **adjusted net capital gain**) is taxed at preferential rates of 0, 15, or 20 percent.

Adjusted Net Capital Gain	This year, Marjory Dunlop recognized $2,400 short-term capital gain and $13,870 long-term capital gain from sales of mutual fund shares. She also earned $3,200 qualified dividend income from her mutual fund investments. Her adjusted net capital gain eligible for the preferential tax rates is $17,070 (long-term capital gain plus qualified dividend income).

Conceptually, the zero percent preferential rate applies to adjusted net capital gain to the extent such gain doesn't result in taxable income in excess of the **maximum zero rate amount.** In 2023, this amount is $89,250 for married filing jointly, $59,750 for heads of household, and $44,625 for married filing separately and single taxpayers.

Zero Preferential Rate	Gina Guiterrez, a single taxpayer, has $29,000 taxable income that includes an $890 adjusted net capital gain. Because her taxable income is less than $44,625, Gina's preferential rate on the $890 capital gain is 0 percent. Gina's 2023 marginal tax rate on her $28,110 ordinary income is 12 percent.

The 15 percent preferential rate applies to adjusted net capital gain resulting in taxable income in excess of the maximum zero rate amount but not exceeding the **maximum 15 percent rate amount.** In 2023, the maximum 15 percent rate amount is $553,850 for married filing jointly ($276,900 for married filing separately), $523,050 for heads of household, and $492,300 for single taxpayers.[33]

15 Percent Preferential Rate	Ben Lopez, a single taxpayer, has $184,000 taxable income that includes a $10,000 adjusted net capital gain. Because his taxable income exceeds $44,625 but is less than $492,300, Ben's preferential rate on the $10,000 gain is 15 percent, and the tax on the gain is $1,500. Ben's 2023 marginal tax rate on his $174,000 ordinary income is 24 percent.

The 20 percent preferential rate applies to adjusted net capital gain resulting in taxable income in excess of the maximum 15 percent rate amount.

---

[32] §1(h) and (j)(5) modifications for taxable years 2018–2025. The conceptual discussion of the preferential capital gains rates and the examples do not address the computational complexity in situations in which taxable income without adjusted net capital gain is *less* than the maximum zero or 15 percent rate amount, but taxable income with the adjusted net capital gain is *more* than the maximum 0 or 15 percent rate amount.

[33] The maximum 0 and 15 percent rate amounts are indexed annually for inflation.

20 Percent Preferential Rate	Sloan Digby, a single taxpayer, has $703,000 taxable income that includes a $50,000 adjusted net capital gain. Because her taxable income exceeds $492,300, Sloan's preferential rate on the $50,000 gain is 20 percent, and the tax on the gain is $10,000. Sloan's 2023 marginal tax rate on her $653,000 ordinary income is 37 percent.

As the previous three examples illustrate, the preferential rate on an individual's adjusted net capital gain is lower than his or her marginal rate on ordinary income at any income level. However, in addition to the capital gains tax, both short-term and long-term gains may be subject to the Medicare contribution tax, discussed later in this chapter.

Unrecaptured Section 1250 Gain

Real property used in a business (including rental real estate) and held for more than one year is a Section 1231 asset rather than a capital asset. When an individual sells or exchanges business or rental realty, recognized gain is subject to the Section 1250 partial depreciation recapture rule discussed in Chapter 8. Any additional gain (subject to the Section 1231 netting process) is treated as long-term capital gain. Such long-term gain is taxed according to the following rules:

- Any unrecaptured Section 1250 gain is taxed at a *maximum* rate of 25 percent. Thus, this rate is beneficial only if the regular rate that would apply to such gain exceeds 25 percent. **Unrecaptured Section 1250 gain** is defined as Section 1231 gain that would be recaptured as ordinary income under a full depreciation recapture rule.[34]

- Any remaining gain is included in adjusted net capital gain and taxed at 0, 15, or 20 percent.

Unrecaptured Section 1250 Gain	Mr. Lilley sold two tracts of real estate, Property A and Property B, both of which he held for more than one year. He didn't sell any other capital or Section 1231 asset, and his marginal tax rate on ordinary income is 37 percent.

	Property A		Property B	
Sales price		$800,000		$475,000
Original cost	$ 950,000		$ 440,000	
Depreciation (straight-line)	(190,000)		(32,000)	
Adjusted basis		(760,000)		(408,000)
Section 1231 gain recognized		$ 40,000		$ 67,000

Because Mr. Lilley used the straight-line method to compute depreciation, the Section 1250 partial recapture rule is inapplicable, and the gain recognized on both sales is Section 1231 gain. However, the $40,000 gain recognized on the sale of Property A is less than the accumulated depreciation. Consequently, the entire gain is classified as unrecaptured Section 1250 gain. The $67,000 gain recognized on the sale of Property B includes only $32,000 unrecaptured 1250 gain (equal to accumulated depreciation). Thus, Mr. Lilley's real estate sales resulted in $72,000 unrecaptured Section 1250 gain (taxed at 25 percent) and $35,000 adjusted net capital gain (taxed at 20 percent).[35]

[34] §1(h)(6).

[35] Net short-term capital loss or net 28 percent rate loss is netted against unrecaptured Section 1250 gain before other long-term gain. §1(h)(6)(A).

Even simple examples of the various preferential capital gains rates reflect the complexity of this tax rate structure. Individuals who must use the capital gains rates to compute their tax can follow the procedure contained in Part III of Schedule D. Use of this procedure is illustrated in the Comprehensive Schedule D Problem included as in Appendix 16–A to this chapter.

Policy Reasons for a Preferential Rate

Capital gains have been taxed at lower rates than ordinary income since 1922. The greatest spread was in the 1950s when the highest marginal rate on ordinary income hovered at 90 percent, and the rate on capital gains was 25 percent. What is the theory justifying a preferential tax rate on capital gains? This tax policy question is relevant in assessing the vertical equity of the income tax system because capital gains are recognized most frequently by high-income individuals who engage in significant investment activities.

Supporters of the preferential rate observe that individuals don't pay tax on capital gain each year as the gain accrues but only in the year in which the gain is realized. This bunching effect could cause the gain to be taxed at a higher rate than if it were taxed in annual increments. Critics of the preferential rate respond that the bunching problem is mitigated by the deferral of tax on the capital gain until the year of realization.

A second argument is that the preferential rate on long-term gains counteracts the effect of inflation. An investor's tax basis in capital assets isn't adjusted for changes in the purchasing power of the dollar. If an investor holds an asset for a long time, the dollars realized on sale may exceed the historical basis of the asset, but some or even all the realized gain may be inflationary rather than real. The counterargument is that a preferential rate on all long-term gains, regardless of the duration of the investor's holding period, is a crude solution to this problem. Congress periodically considers indexing the tax basis of assets to reflect changes in the value of the dollar but has backed away from this solution because of the complexity it would add to the tax law.

Many economists contend that the preferential rate on capital gains encourages the mobility of capital. Without a tax break on realized gains, individuals owning appreciated assets might be reluctant to liquidate or convert such assets because of the tax cost. This locking-in effect distorts financial decision making and hinders the efficiency of the stock and bond markets. A variation on this argument is that the preferential rate reduces the risk of financial investments and thereby increases the supply of venture capital to the economy. A counterargument is that the preferential rate lures wealthy individuals to invest in convoluted tax shelters designed for one purpose: to convert ordinary income into capital gain. As a result, venture capital is diverted from productive investments that could actually bolster the economy.

Capital Loss Limitation

Recall from our earlier discussion that an individual's net short-term capital gain or loss is combined with net long-term capital gain or loss to result in a final net capital gain or loss for the year. If the final result is a net gain, some or all of the gain may be taxed at a preferential rate. But what if the final result reported on line 16, Part III, Schedule D is a net loss? In this case, only $3,000 of the net capital loss can be carried to line 7, Form 1040, to reduce taxable income.[36] The nondeductible portion of the loss is carried forward indefinitely to be combined with the individual's future capital gains and losses. Carryforwards retain their character as short-term or long-term loss.[37]

---

[36] §1211(b).

[37] §1212(b). If the net capital loss consists of both short-term and long-term loss, the $3,000 deduction is attributed to the short-term loss first.

Net Capital Loss	Ms. Nash sold four blocks of securities this year with the following results:

Short-term capital loss	$ (4,000)
Short-term capital gain	6,100
Long-term capital loss	(11,500)
Long-term capital gain	1,250

She has a $2,100 net short-term gain and a $10,250 net long-term loss that combine to an $8,150 long-term loss. She can deduct $3,000 of this loss in the computation of AGI; the $5,150 nondeductible portion becomes a long-term capital loss carryforward.

The netting of capital gains and losses on Schedule D reflects the basic rule that capital losses are deductible to the extent of capital gains. Thus, the tax savings from a capital loss depend on the amount of capital gain recognized during the year.

Tax Savings from Capital Losses	Refer to the facts in the preceding example. Ms. Nash's capital losses sheltered $6,100 short-term capital gain, $1,250 long-term capital gain, and $3,000 ordinary income from tax. If Ms. Nash's marginal tax rate on ordinary income is 37 percent and her preferential tax rate on adjusted net capital gain is 20 percent, the losses saved $3,617 tax:

Tax savings on:	
Short-term gain ($6,100 × 37%)	$2,257
Long-term gain ($1,250 × 20%)	250
Ordinary income ($3,000 × 37%)	1,110
	$3,617

Ms. Nash's $5,150 capital loss carryforward will save tax in future years to the extent she can deduct it against capital gains or ordinary income.

Capital Loss Carryforward	In the following year, Ms. Nash has only one capital transaction that generates an $1,800 short-term capital gain. Consequently, she has an $1,800 net short-term gain and a $5,150 net long-term loss (her carryforward) that net to a $3,350 long-term loss. She can deduct $3,000 of this loss in computing AGI and carry the $350 nondeductible portion forward to the next year.

Tax Talk
Investors who strategically buy and sell stocks at the end of their taxable year contribute to a flurry of December trading activity in the stock market called the Santa Claus rally.

In present value terms, the tax savings from a capital loss diminish with each year that the investor must wait to deduct it. The obvious tax planning strategy is for the investor to generate capital gains to absorb the loss as soon as possible. Of course, even without capital gains, individuals can deduct their capital losses at the rate of $3,000 per year. But for investors who suffer large losses, the value of this stream of annual deductions may be negligible.

INVESTMENTS IN SMALL CORPORATE BUSINESSES

LO 16-5
Describe the preferential tax treatment of investments in small corporate businesses.

Investments in small corporate businesses that are struggling to grow are riskier than investments in well-established corporations with proven track records. To encourage individuals to accept this higher level of risk, the tax law contains two preferential provisions for investments in small corporate businesses.

Qualified Small Business Stock

Individuals who realize capital gain on the sale or exchange of **qualified small business stock** held for more than *five years* may exclude 50 percent of such gain from gross income.[38] The remaining capital gain is classified as 28 percent rate gain. The stock must have been issued after August 10, 1993, and issued directly to the individual in exchange for money, property, or services rendered to the issuing corporation. In other words, individuals can't purchase qualified small business stock from other shareholders.

Congress has attempted to stimulate investment in the small business sector of the economy by increasing the 50 percent exclusion rate. The rate jumps to 75 percent for qualified stock acquired after February 17, 2009, and before September 28, 2010, and to 100 percent for qualified stock acquired after September 27, 2010. Individuals must still hold the stock for more than five years to take advantage of the exclusion.[39]

Gain on Qualified Small Business Stock

QB, Inc. is a qualified small business corporation. In November 2002, Mrs. Horne contributed $200,000 to QB, Inc. in exchange for 1,000 shares of stock. This year, she sold these QB shares for $560,000, realizing a $360,000 long-term capital gain. Mrs. Horne may exclude $180,000 of this gain from gross income. The $180,000 gain included in income is a 28 percent rate gain.

On November 18, 2015, Mrs. Horne contributed $500,000 to QB, Inc. in exchange for 2,500 shares of stock. If Mrs. Horne sells this stock after November 18, 2020, she may exclude 100 percent of her gain from gross income.

A qualified small business is a regular corporation with no more than $50 million of gross assets immediately after the qualified stock was issued. The corporation must conduct an active trade or business other than a financial, leasing, real estate, farming, mining, hospitality, or professional service business.[40]

Section 1244 Stock

Individuals who realize a loss on the disposition of **Section 1244 stock** may deduct a limited portion as ordinary, rather than capital, loss. Married couples filing jointly are limited to an annual $100,000 ordinary deduction, while unmarried individuals or married individuals filing separate returns are limited to an annual $50,000 ordinary deduction. Any loss in excess of these limits retains its character as capital loss.[41]

[38] §1202. For any tax year, the gain eligible for this exclusion is limited to the *greater* of (1) 10 times the aggregate basis in the stock disposed of during the year or (2) $10 million reduced by eligible gain recognized in prior taxable years.

[39] According to §57(a)(7), 7 percent of the gain excluded from gross income under §1202 is an AMT preference that must be added to taxable income to compute the individual's AMTI. However, §1202(a)(4)(C) provides that no amount of a 100 percent excluded gain is an AMT preference item.

[40] A pending tax proposal in Congress would potentially eliminate the availability of the 75% and 100% exclusion for taxpayers with AGI exceeding $400,000 of a qualified small business.

[41] §1244(a) and (b).

Loss on Section 1244 Stock	Six years ago, Mr. and Mrs. Phipp contributed $200,000 to NW, Inc. in exchange for 1,000 shares of stock, which qualified as Section 1244 stock. This year, they sold all 1,000 shares for $30,000. This was their only asset sale. Their salary, interest, and dividend income totaled $319,000, and the AGI on their joint return is $216,000:

Salary, interest, dividends	$ 319,000
Maximum Section 1244 loss	(100,000)
Capital loss deduction	(3,000)
AGI	$ 216,000

Mr. and Mrs. Phipp can carry their $67,000 nondeductible long-term capital loss ($170,000 recognized loss − $100,000 Section 1244 loss − $3,000 deductible capital loss) forward to next year.

As a general rule, the first $1 million of stock issued by a corporation that derives more than 50 percent of its annual gross receipts from the conduct of an active business qualifies as Section 1244 stock.[42] This special character applies only to stock issued directly by the corporation to an individual investor in exchange for money or property. Stock issued for services rendered to the issuing corporation does not qualify as Section 1244 stock. The Section 1244 label has no downside. If the fledgling corporate venture is a success and the investor eventually sells the stock at a gain, that gain is characterized as capital gain. On the other hand, if the investor sells the stock at a loss or if the stock becomes worthless, a significant portion (if not all) of the loss yields an immediate benefit as an above-the-line deduction.

INVESTMENT EXPENSES

LO 16-6
Determine the deduction for investment interest expense.

Individuals may incur a variety of expenses relating to the acquisition and management of their investment property. Such expenses include the cost of subscriptions to investment publications and newsletters, investment management fees, and the rental of a safety deposit box to hold securities or investment-related documents. Although these expenses are incurred pursuant to an income-producing activity, they are not deductible. The major exception to this rule is **investment interest expense.**

Investment Interest Expense

Individuals are allowed to deduct interest paid on debt incurred to purchase investment property. However, the deduction is subject to limitations. If an individual borrows money and uses the funds to purchase tax-exempt state and local bonds, the interest on the debt is nondeductible.[43] The logic of this rule is apparent: Congress doesn't want the tax law to subsidize the purchase of investments generating nontaxable income. If an individual incurs debt to purchase other investment property, the interest on the debt is an itemized deduction but only to the extent of the debtor's net investment income from any source.[44] The nondeductible portion of the interest expense is carried forward to future taxable years.

[42] §1244(c).
[43] §265.
[44] §163(d).

Investment Interest Expense	Mr. Guss borrowed $80,000 at 4.5 percent and invested the loan proceeds in a mutual fund that paid a $5,000 ordinary dividend. He paid $3,600 of investment interest expense for the year. Because his net investment income exceeded $3,600, the entire interest payment is an itemized deduction. Now assume that Mr. Guss used the loan proceeds to purchase common stock in a corporation that didn't pay a dividend. His only investment income was $750 interest earned on a savings account. In this case, he can deduct only $750 investment interest expense. The $2,850 nondeductible expense carries forward to next year, when Mr. Guss can deduct it subject to the net investment income limitation.

Net Investment Income

Net investment income is generated by property held for investment purposes and includes interest, dividends, annuity payments, and net gain on the sale of investment assets. However, if an individual recognizes income that is taxed at a preferential rate (qualified dividend income and long-term capital gain), the tax law offers an interesting choice. The individual may elect to treat such income (or any portion thereof) as investment income, thereby securing a deduction for investment interest. But by making this election, the individual forfeits any preferential tax rate on the income.[45] This election prevents investors from enjoying a double benefit. Their dividends and long-term capital gains can increase the investment interest expense deduction or be taxed at a preferential rate, but not both.

Election to Treat Capital Gain as Investment Income	Ms. Small paid $5,000 investment interest this year. She didn't earn any interest, dividends, or other investment income. She did, however, recognize a $6,000 long-term capital gain from the sale of investment assets. Ms. Small can elect to treat $5,000 of this gain as investment income to deduct her investment interest expense. If she makes the election, only $1,000 of the $6,000 long-term capital gain included in taxable income is eligible for the 0, 15, or 20 percent preferential rate.

INVESTMENTS IN REAL PROPERTY

LO 16-7
Summarize the tax consequences of investments in real property.

As an alternative to financial assets, individuals may put their money into real estate. In this section of this chapter, we examine the tax consequences of investing in real property.

Undeveloped Land

Individuals who invest in undeveloped land expect a return in the form of appreciation in value because land typically doesn't generate significant revenue or cash flow.[46] However, owners may incur out-of-pocket expenses with respect to their land. Real property taxes can be a considerable annual expense; these tax payments are itemized deductions.[47] If the owner financed the purchase of the land through a mortgage, the interest payments are investment interest, deductible to the extent of the owner's net investment income. Instead

---

[45] §1(h)(2).

[46] Owners might receive revenues from grazing, hunting, mineral, or crop leases.

[47] §164(a)(1).

of treating property taxes and interest as current expenses, the owner may make an annual election to capitalize these carrying charges to the basis of the land.[48] Another important consideration is that undeveloped land may be a very illiquid asset. All in all, land may be a poor investment choice for individuals who want ready access to cash.

Capitalized Interest and Tax	Ms. Jamison recently purchased a 15-acre tract of undeveloped land as a long-term investment. She financed the purchase through a mortgage. This year, she paid $1,780 interest on the mortgage and $492 local property tax on the land. Ms. Jamison took the standard deduction on her income tax return and, therefore, derived no tax benefit from itemized deductions, including her mortgage interest and property tax. So she elected to capitalize the interest and tax, thereby increasing her basis in the land by $2,272. In any future year in which she itemizes deductions, Ms. Jamison can deduct the mortgage interest and property tax paid during such year instead of making the annual election.

The tax advantage of holding investment land is that appreciation in value is not recognized as income until the owner disposes of the land in a taxable transaction.[49] Moreover, any gain recognized on the sale of land held for at least a year qualifies for a preferential tax rate.

This conclusion, of course, presumes that the land was a capital asset in the owner's hands. Individuals who make periodic sales of land run the risk that the IRS may treat this activity as a business and the land as an inventory asset held primarily for sale to customers. In such cases, the gains recognized on the sale are ordinary income rather than capital gain.

The question of whether an individual who sells land is engaging in an investment or a business is subjective; the answer depends on the facts and circumstances of each case. When called on to decide the issue, the federal courts consider the number, frequency, and regularity of the sales and the extent to which the individual actively solicited buyers, either through advertising or a real estate agent. In cases in which the individual added substantial improvements to the land, such as roads and drainage ditches, or subdivided a single tract of land into smaller parcels, the courts have generally agreed with the IRS that the individual engaged in a business.[50]

Rental Real Estate

Developed real estate consists of land with some type of building or structure permanently attached. Individuals who own developed real estate receive rents paid by tenants or lessees who occupy the property. In many respects, a rental real estate activity is treated as a business for tax purposes. The owner recognizes the rents as ordinary income and deducts operating and maintenance expenses.[51] These items are reported on Part I, Schedule E, Form 1040. Consequently, only net profit from the rental activity is included in the owner's AGI. Rental real estate is a Section 1231 asset, and the building component is depreciable property with either a 27.5-year or a 39-year MACRS recovery period. Therefore, the owner can recover his investment in the building through annual depreciation deductions.

---

[48] §266.

[49] Individuals frequently enter into like-kind exchanges of investment real property. See the discussion of these nontaxable exchanges in Chapter 9.

[50] See, for example, *Phelan,* T.C. Memo 2004-206, and *Rice,* T.C. Memo 2009-142.

[51] Reg. §1.212-1.

Mr. and Mrs. David: Schedule E	Ronald and Janet David own residential real estate that they have leased to the same tenant since 2014. This year, their revenue and expenses were as follows:

Rents received ($2,250 per month)	$27,000
Monthly yard maintenance	1,480
Property and liability insurance	2,880
Interest on mortgage	1,720
Repairs and painting	4,140
Local property tax	2,075
Monthly utilities	2,900
Legal fee for consultation on zoning restriction	675

MACRS depreciation for the year was $6,400. This information is summarized on their Schedule E, shown in Exhibit 16.3. Their $4,730 net income (line 26) was carried as an income item to Form 1040, Schedule 1, line 5.

While rental real estate activities have many business characteristics, they actually fall into the special class of *passive activities.*[52] This classification doesn't affect the regular tax consequences of profitable rental activities. However, rental income may be subject to the Medicare contribution tax. For rental real estate activities *operating at a loss,* the passive activity classification has major income tax consequences.

INVESTMENTS IN PASSIVE ACTIVITIES

LO 16-8
Apply the passive activity loss limitation.

Individuals can own equity interests in business entities without rendering personal services to the business. Many partners and shareholders have no involvement in the business conducted by their partnership or S corporation. Nevertheless, these owners are allocated a share of business income. Even the owner of a sole proprietorship might choose to leave the business operation entirely in the hands of employees. But regardless of such a lack of participation, net profits belong to the proprietor. In these situations, the income to which the partner, shareholder, or sole proprietor is entitled is primarily a return on invested capital. Although such income retains its ordinary business character when reported on the owner's individual tax return, it is economically equivalent to investment income.

If an individual owns an interest in a business but doesn't materially participate in that business, the interest is a **passive activity** for federal tax purposes. **Material participation** means that the individual is involved in day-to-day operations on a regular, continual, and substantial basis.[53]

Passive Activity	JKL Partnership consists of three equal individual partners. Mr. Jett and Ms. Kyle are general partners who work full-time in JKL's business, while Mr. Lamb is a limited partner who has no personal involvement at all. For the two general partners, their interest in JKL is clearly a business activity. Because Mr. Lamb doesn't materially participate in the business, his interest in JKL is a passive activity.[54]

---

[52] §469(c)(2).

[53] §469(c)(1). Reg. §1.469-5T provides several objective tests for determining material participation.

[54] The statute creates a presumption that a *limited* partnership interest is a passive activity. §469(h)(2).

EXHIBIT 16.3

Department of the Treasury, Internal Revenue Service

SCHEDULE E (Form 1040)	Supplemental Income and Loss	OMB No. 1545-0074
Department of the Treasury Internal Revenue Service	(From rental real estate, royalties, partnerships, S corporations, estates, trusts, REMICs, etc.) Attach to Form 1040, 1040-SR, 1040-NR, or 1041. Go to *www.irs.gov/ScheduleE* for instructions and the latest information.	2022 Attachment Sequence No. **13**

Name(s) shown on return: **Ronald and Janet David**   Your social security number: **498-31-1240**

Part I   Income or Loss From Rental Real Estate and Royalties

Note: If you are in the business of renting personal property, use **Schedule C**. See instructions. If you are an individual, report farm rental income or loss from **Form 4835** on page 2, line 40.

A Did you make any payments in 2022 that would require you to file Form(s) 1099? See instructions . . . . . ☐ Yes ☑ No
B If "Yes," did you or will you file required Form(s) 1099? . . . . ☐ Yes ☐ No

1a Physical address of each property (street, city, state, ZIP code)

A **1412 West Reeder Avenue, Omaha, NE 51102**
B
C

1b Type of Property (from list below)	2 For each rental real estate property listed above, report the number of fair rental and personal use days. Check the QJV box only if you meet the requirements to file as a qualified joint venture. See instructions.		Fair Rental Days	Personal Use Days	QJV
A 1		A	365	0	☐
B		B			☐
C		C			☐

Type of Property:
1 Single Family Residence   3 Vacation/Short-Term Rental   5 Land   7 Self-Rental
2 Multi-Family Residence   4 Commercial   6 Royalties   8 Other (describe) _____

Income:			A	B	C
3	Rents received	3	27,000		
4	Royalties received	4			
Expenses:					
5	Advertising	5			
6	Auto and travel (see instructions)	6			
7	Cleaning and maintenance	7	1,480		
8	Commissions	8			
9	Insurance	9	2,880		
10	Legal and other professional fees	10	675		
11	Management fees	11			
12	Mortgage interest paid to banks, etc. (see instructions)	12	1,720		
13	Other interest	13			
14	Repairs	14	4,140		
15	Supplies	15			
16	Taxes	16	2,075		
17	Utilities	17	2,900		
18	Depreciation expense or depletion	18	6,400		
19	Other (list) _____	19			
20	Total expenses. Add lines 5 through 19	20	22,270		
21	Subtract line 20 from line 3 (rents) and/or 4 (royalties). If result is a (loss), see instructions to find out if you must file **Form 6198**	21	4,730		
22	Deductible rental real estate loss after limitation, if any, on **Form 8582** (see instructions)	22	(	)( )( )

23a	Total of all amounts reported on line 3 for all rental properties	23a	27,000
b	Total of all amounts reported on line 4 for all royalty properties	23b	
c	Total of all amounts reported on line 12 for all properties	23c	1,720
d	Total of all amounts reported on line 18 for all properties	23d	6,400
e	Total of all amounts reported on line 20 for all properties	23e	22,270
24	**Income.** Add positive amounts shown on line 21. **Do not** include any losses	24	4,730
25	**Losses.** Add royalty losses from line 21 and rental real estate losses from line 22. Enter total losses here	25	( )
26	**Total rental real estate and royalty income or (loss).** Combine lines 24 and 25. Enter the result here. If Parts II, III, IV, and line 40 on page 2 do not apply to you, also enter this amount on Schedule 1 (Form 1040), line 5. Otherwise, include this amount in the total on line 41 on page 2	26	4,730

For Paperwork Reduction Act Notice, see the separate instructions.   Cat. No. 11344L   Schedule E (Form 1040) 2022

The classification of an interest as a passive activity doesn't affect the regular tax consequences of a profitable business interest. Assume that JKL Partnership generated $129,000 business income. Each of the three partners received a Schedule K-1 reporting a $43,000 share of this income. All three included this share as ordinary income on their Form 1040 and paid tax accordingly. The fact that Mr. Lamb's share was passive activity income had no effect on the computation of his regular tax on the income. However, his passive activity income may be subject to the Medicare contribution tax discussed later in this chapter.

Passive Activity Loss Limitation

The classification of business interest as a passive activity has profound tax consequences if the business *operates at a loss*. Specifically, the owner of the passive activity can deduct the loss only to the extent of income generated by other passive activities.[55] Any disallowed loss is carried forward as a suspended passive activity loss. Suspended losses are deductible in any future year to the extent of the owner's passive activity income in that year.[56]

Passive Activity Loss Limitation	Refer to the facts in the preceding example and assume that JKL Partnership generated a $90,000 operating loss. Each partner received a Schedule K-1 reporting a $30,000 share. Mr. Jett and Ms. Kyle, the general partners who work in the business, can deduct their loss in the computation of AGI.[57] Mr. Lamb, the limited partner, is subject to the passive activity loss limitation. If his JKL interest is his only passive activity, he can't deduct any of his $30,000 loss. If he owns another passive activity that generated income, he can deduct the loss to the extent of such income. Any disallowed loss is carried forward as a suspended passive activity loss. Mr. Lamb can deduct the suspended loss in a future year to the extent he recognizes income from either JKL Partnership or any other passive activity.

Rental Activities

The definition of passive activity includes any **rental activity** in which revenues are principally derived from the lease of tangible property for an extended period of time.[58] Activities in which revenues are principally derived from the provision of customer services are not rental activities. For instance, the operation of a hotel is a business rather than a rental activity. Similarly, businesses providing short-term use of property such as automobiles, carpet-cleaning equipment, or Halloween costumes are not rental activities. If an individual owns a rental activity, that activity is passive, *regardless of the extent of the owner's participation in the activity.*

As mentioned earlier in this chapter, rental real estate activities are passive activities.[59] Accordingly, individuals who invest in rental real estate can deduct losses only to the extent of their passive activity income. However, the law provides an important exception under which individuals can deduct up to $25,000 annual loss from rental real estate without regard to the passive activity loss limitation.[60] To qualify for the full $25,000 exception, the individual's AGI (before consideration of any rental loss) must not exceed $100,000. If AGI exceeds this threshold, the $25,000 exception is reduced by 50 percent of the excess. Thus, the exception shrinks to zero for taxpayers with AGI greater than $150,000.

---

[55] §469(a)(1) and (d)(1).

[56] §469(b).

[57] This statement presumes that the partners have sufficient basis in their partnership interests to absorb their loss. See Chapter 10.

[58] Reg. §1.469-1T(e)(3).

[59] Real estate professionals who devote more than one-half of their work effort each year and at least 750 hours annually to a real property business are engaged in an active business rather than a passive rental activity. A real property business includes the development, redevelopment, construction, reconstruction, acquisition, conversion, rental, operation, management, leasing, or brokering of real property. §469(c)(7).

[60] §469(i). The individual must own at least a 10 percent interest in the real estate and must be significantly involved in its management.

Rental Real Estate Exception

Mr. and Mrs. Ennis own and manage three duplexes that they rent to college students. They don't own other passive activities. The duplexes generated a $31,000 loss this year. Before deduction of this loss, the couple's AGI was $95,000. Because of the rental real estate exception, they can deduct $25,000 of the rental loss to reduce AGI to $70,000. The $6,000 excess loss is a nondeductible passive activity loss that carries forward to next year.

If Mr. and Mrs. Ennis's AGI before deduction of their rental loss was $141,000, their exception is reduced to $4,500.

AGI before loss	$141,000
AGI threshold	(100,000)
Excess AGI	$ 41,000
	.50
Reduction in $25,000 exception	$ 20,500

Consequently, they can deduct $4,500 of their rental loss to reduce AGI to $136,500. The $26,500 excess loss is a nondeductible passive activity loss that carries forward to next year.

Dispositions of Passive Activities

The passive activity loss limitation is not a *permanent* loss disallowance rule. When an investor disposes of her entire interest in a passive activity in a taxable transaction (generally a sale or exchange), any suspended losses with respect to the interest are fully deductible in the year of disposition. As a result, the investor finally reaps a tax benefit from every dollar of loss disallowed in an earlier year. Of course, in present value terms, the tax savings from the deferred deduction are less than the savings from a deduction in such earlier year.

Deduction of Suspended PAL

Mr. Zhou invested in a limited partnership that generated a substantial business loss in 2016 (year 0). Mr. Zhou couldn't deduct his $48,300 share of this loss because the loss was passive and he had no passive activity income. Nor did he have passive activity income in 2017 through 2022. Mr. Zhou sold his partnership interest in 2023. Because of this disposition, he was allowed to deduct his $48,300 suspended loss in 2023.

If Mr. Zhou had a 39.6 percent marginal tax rate in 2016 and a 37 percent marginal tax rate in 2023 and uses a 5 percent discount rate to compute NPV, deferral of the tax savings from the deduction cost him $6,421 in present value terms:

Tax savings from 2016 deduction	
$48,300 × 39.6%	$19,127
PV of tax savings from 2023 deduction	
$48,300 × 37% × .711 discount factor	(12,706)
Cost of deferral of tax savings	$ 6,421

Planning with Passive Activity Losses

Suppose that Mrs. Queen, a practicing attorney, paid $50,000 to buy stock in an S corporation operating a chain of Mexican restaurants. Because she doesn't materially participate in the S corporation's business, Mrs. Queen's interest is a passive activity. On her first Schedule K-1, she is allocated a $9,000 ordinary business loss, which reduces the basis in her stock to $41,000.[61] She owns no other passive activities and therefore recognized no passive

[61] §1367(a)(2)(B).

activity income this year. Consequently, she can't deduct her $9,000 loss in computing AGI. Stated another way, Mrs. Queen's passive activity loss doesn't shelter the income generated by her legal practice (or any other income) from tax.

Sale of the Passive Activity

What are Mrs. Queen's options with respect to her $9,000 suspended loss? Given that the restaurant business apparently is losing money, her best option may be to sell the stock as quickly as possible! Suppose that early in the next year Mrs. Queen finds a buyer who offers $30,000 for her shares. If she sells, she will recognize an $11,000 capital loss *and* can deduct her $9,000 suspended passive activity loss as an ordinary business loss.[62] The total of the two losses ($11,000 capital loss + $9,000 ordinary loss) corresponds to her $20,000 economic loss on this unfortunate investment. The only effect of the passive activity loss limitation was to defer the deduction of the ordinary loss (and the tax benefit therefrom) for one year.

Purchase of a PIG

If Mrs. Queen believes that the restaurant business is a solid long-term investment, her second option is to find a source of passive activity income. Perhaps the restaurant will become profitable so that Mrs. Queen eventually can deduct her suspended loss against her share of the S corporation's future taxable income. If this possibility is too uncertain, she could invest in a moneymaking passive activity (dubbed a **passive income generator [PIG]** by the financial press). For instance, if she buys an interest in a profitable commercial office building, she can deduct her suspended loss from the S corporation to the extent of her rental income from the PIG.

UNEARNED INCOME MEDICARE CONTRIBUTION TAX

LO 16-9
Compute the Medicare contribution tax on unearned income.

High-income taxpayers with significant investment income may pay the **unearned income Medicare contribution tax,** the revenues from which are earmarked for the Medicare trust fund. This tax complements the Medicare taxes imposed on the earned income of employees and self-employed individuals.

The Medicare contribution tax equals 3.8 percent of the *lesser* of an individual's net investment income or the excess of AGI over a threshold amount.[63] The threshold amount is $250,000 for married individuals filing jointly ($125,000 for married filing separately) and $200,000 for unmarried individuals.

Medicare Tax on Unearned Income

This year, Mr. and Mrs. Yuan's net investment income totals $43,000. If the AGI on their joint return is $269,400, their unearned income Medicare contribution tax is $737 (3.8 percent of $19,400 excess AGI). If their AGI is $309,200, their Medicare contribution tax is $1,634 (3.8 percent of $43,000 net investment income).

For purposes of the Medicare contribution tax, investment income includes taxable interest, dividends, annuities, royalties, and rents. It also includes net income from a passive activity (a business in which the individual taxpayer doesn't materially participate) and net

---

[62] This calculation of loss is based on Mrs. Queen's basis in the stock on January 1 without adjustment for any pro rata share of the corporation's income or loss for the year of sale.

[63] §1411. For purposes of this computation, AGI is increased by any §911 foreign earned income exclusion.

taxable gain from the disposition of nonbusiness property. Net investment income is the excess of investment income over any deductions properly allocated to such income.

Net Investment Income	Ms. Dahl's taxable income includes $12,700 interest and dividends from her portfolio of marketable securities and a $29,000 share of net business income from a partnership. Ms. Dahl is a limited partner who doesn't materially participate in the partnership business. Her taxable income also includes an $11,000 net capital gain from the sale of securities. She had no deductions properly allocable to these three income items. Ms. Dahl's net investment income for purposes of the Medicare contribution tax is $52,700.

WEALTH TRANSFER PLANNING

LO 16-10
Explain the transfer tax and income tax consequences of inter vivos and testamentary transfers.

Individuals who engage in successful business and investment activities inevitably accumulate wealth in the process. At some point in their lives, these individuals begin to think about transferring wealth to other parties—usually to their children and grandchildren. The decision to part with property can be intensely personal; the property owner may be more concerned with private family matters than with the financial implications of the decision. However, once the decision is made, most people are eager to adopt financial strategies to maximize the wealth available to younger-generation family members. As we will learn in this final section of this chapter, the federal transfer taxes are a primary consideration in the development of such strategies.

The Transfer Tax System

The federal transfer tax system has three components: the gift tax, the estate tax, and the generation-skipping transfer tax (which we don't discuss in this text). Congress enacted the original estate tax in 1916 as a way to redistribute a portion of the private fortunes amassed by society's richest families to the public domain. Historically, only a small percentage of the U.S. population has ever paid a federal transfer tax. Nonetheless, these taxes have always been a political flash point.

In 2001, Congress took the bold step of prospectively repealing the estate tax effective on January 1, 2010. This repeal actually went into effect, but in December 2010, Congress did an about-face by reinstating the estate tax retroactive to the beginning of the year. In 2017, the House of Representatives's version of the Tax Cuts and Jobs Act again repealed the estate tax effective on January 1, 2025. However, the Senate didn't agree to the repeal, and the final version of the act maintained the estate tax, but with a greatly reduced scope.

The Gift Tax

The gift tax is levied on the transfer of property by an individual during life **(inter vivos transfer)** for which the transferor doesn't receive adequate consideration in money or money's worth. The amount of the gift equals the property's fair market value.[64] The tax is paid by the **donor** making the gift. Donors are usually motivated by generosity or affection toward the **donee** receiving the gift. In other words, a gift incurs in a personal rather than a business context. Certain transfers are not treated as taxable gifts. Transfers of property to a spouse or to a qualified charity or political organization aren't taxable.[65] Similarly, tuition payments to

---

[64] §2501 and §2512.
[65] §2501(a)(4), §2522, and §2523.

an educational organization or payments of medical expenses on behalf of another person aren't taxable.[66]

Nontaxable Transfers	Maria Vargas recently transferred her equity interest in a real estate partnership to her husband Luis. She made a $100,000 donation to her church's building fund and a $50,000 donation to the American Cancer Society. Maria made a $4,500 tuition payment to the University of Oklahoma on behalf of her nephew Robert, and she paid $7,100 of medical expenses incurred by her sister Beth. None of these transfers are subject to federal gift tax.

Gift Tax Computation

Every donor can give a *de minimis* amount to a donee that is excluded from the donor's taxable gifts for the year. In 2023, this **annual gift tax exclusion** is $17,000 per donee.[67] The exclusion removes most routine birthday, graduation, wedding, and holiday presents from the gift tax base. Married couples can elect to treat a gift made by either spouse as a gift made equally by both spouses.[68] By making this gift-splitting election, the couple doubles the exclusion for the gift. The first rule of transfer tax planning is that individuals should take full advantage of the annual gift tax exclusion.

Annual Exclusion	Mr. and Mrs. Archer have two adult sons, who are both married, and six unmarried grandchildren. In 2023, Mr. Archer gave $34,000 cash to each of the 10 donees (two sons, two daughters-in-law, and six grandchildren). Mr. and Mrs. Archer elected to split the gifts so that each could claim a $17,000 annual exclusion. As a result, none of the gifts were taxable, and the Archers transferred $340,000 at no tax cost. The couple plans to make this systematic nontaxable transfer of wealth to younger-generation family members every year.

If the value of a gift to a donee exceeds the donor's annual exclusion, the donor has made a taxable gift. The donor must report the gift on Form 709, United States Gift Tax Return, which must be filed with the IRS by April 15 following the calendar year in which the gift was made.[69] However, a donor doesn't owe tax until the cumulative amount of taxable gifts made during the donor's lifetime exceeds a **lifetime transfer tax exclusion**.[70] The $10 million statutory exclusion amount is indexed annually for inflation. In 2023, the lifetime exclusion is $12,920,000. The tax on the amount of gifts in excess of the lifetime exclusion is computed at a flat 40 percent rate.

Lifetime Exclusion and Tax Computation	Tina Wood made her first taxable gift and filed her first Form 709 in 2007. The amount of this gift in excess of the annual exclusion was $850,000. Because this amount was less than Tina's lifetime exclusion, she owed no gift tax in 2007.
	Tina made a second taxable gift and filed her second Form 709 in 2015. The amount of this gift in excess of the annual exclusion was $3 million. Because the $3.85 million cumulative amount of the 2007 and 2015 gifts was less than Tina's lifetime exclusion, Tina owed no gift tax in 2015.

[66] §2503(e).
[67] §2503(b). The annual exclusion is indexed for inflation.
[68] §2513.
[69] §6075(b)(1).
[70] §2505(a)(1). The lifetime transfer tax exclusion is accomplished by a credit offsetting the transfer tax on the exclusion amount.

Tina made a third taxable gift and filed her third Form 709 in 2023. The amount of the gift in excess of the annual exclusion was $10 million. Because the $13.85 million cumulative value of the 2007, 2015, and 2023 gifts exceeded the $12.92 million lifetime exclusion, Tina owes $372,000 gift tax ($930,000 excess × 40%), which she must pay by April 15, 2024, filing date of the return.

Income Tax Consequences of Gifts

When a donee receives a gift from a donor, the gift is excluded from the donee's gross income.[71] If the gift includes any noncash property, the donor's adjusted basis in the property carries over to become the donee's basis.[72] Similarly, the donor's holding period for the property is included in the donee's holding period.[73] Because of the carryover basis rule, unrealized appreciation in the value of the property is shifted from donor to donee.

Carryover Basis and Holding Period

Six years ago, Mr. Solano paid $25,000 to purchase stock in SBB Corporation. This year, he gave the SBB stock to his 26-year-old daughter Eva. The fair market value of the stock at date of gift was $53,000. Mr. Solano paid no gift tax on this transfer. Eva held the stock for seven months before selling it for $57,000 cash. Eva's carryover basis in the SBB stock was $25,000, and her holding period was six years and seven months. Consequently, she recognized a $32,000 long-term capital gain on the sale.

A gift of income-producing property (such as marketable securities) shifts the future income from the property (interest, dividends, capital gain) from the donor to the donee. If the donee's marginal tax rate is lower than the donor's, the income shift should result in a tax savings.

Income Shift

Before selling the SBB stock, Eva Solano received $1,100 of qualified dividends. Eva's preferential rate on the dividend income and capital gain was zero. If her father had received the dividends and recognized the capital gain, he would have paid tax at a 23.8 percent rate (20 percent preferential income tax rate + 3.8 percent Medicare contribution tax rate). Consequently, the income shift saved $7,878 tax for the Solano family ($33,100 dividends and capital gain × 23.8%).

The tax savings from transfers of income-producing property to minor children is severely limited by the kiddie tax rules described in Chapter 14. Recall that the income tax on investment income of children under the age of 19 is computed by reference to the marginal tax rates that would apply if that income were included on their parents' tax return.

Kiddie Tax

Refer to the facts in the previous two examples. Now assume that Eva Solano is only age 13. In this case, Eva's tax on her dividend income and capital gain is computed at 20 percent (Mr. Solano's preferential income tax rate). Note the kiddie tax rules *don't* apply for purposes of the Medicare contribution tax.

[71] §102.

[72] §1015 governs the tax basis of gifted property. If the donor pays gift tax, the carryover basis is increased by the tax attributable to the appreciation in the gifted property. If the FMV of gifted property is less than the donor's basis, the donee's basis is limited to FMV, and the donor's unrealized loss in the property disappears. As a result, donors avoid giving away loss property.

[73] §1223(2).

While the kiddie tax certainly reduces the potential tax savings from an income shift to children, families can avoid it by transferring assets that yield deferred rather than current income. For instance, children can be given stock in a growth corporation that doesn't pay regular dividends. Similarly, children can be given Series EE savings bonds that won't generate interest income until the year of redemption.

The Estate Tax

Wealthy individuals who choose not to give away property during life are postponing the inevitable. No one can avoid the final transfer of property that must occur at death. It is this **testamentary transfer** that may be subject to the federal estate tax.

The federal estate tax is levied on the fair market value of a deceased individual's taxable estate.[74] The **taxable estate** includes the decedent's **probate estate,** which consists of the assets bequeathed to individuals or organizations named in the decedent's will. The taxable estate also includes property not included in the probate estate but which transfers by reason of the decedent's death. For example, a decedent may have owned an insurance policy on his own life that pays a death benefit to the beneficiary named in the policy. Similarly, a decedent may have owned an interest in a retirement plan that distributes the plan balance to the beneficiary named in the plan. Both the insurance death benefit and the retirement plan distribution are included in the decedent's taxable estate.[75]

The taxable estate is reduced by the decedent's debts, funeral expenses, and any administrative costs of settling the estate.[76] It is also reduced by testamentary transfers to religious, charitable, educational, government, or other nonprofit organizations.[77] Consequently, a decedent could leave her or his entire fortune to charity and avoid the estate tax altogether. Finally, the taxable estate is reduced by any transfer to a surviving spouse.[78] Because of this **unlimited marital deduction,** the estate tax on the wealth accumulated by a married couple can be deferred until the death of the second spouse.

Taxable Estate

Mr. Webb died on May 3 and was survived by his wife Imelda and two children from a previous marriage. At date of death, Mr. Webb owned property with a $7.27 million fair market value and had $938,100 of debts. Funeral expenses and legal fees incurred by his estate totaled $94,300. In his will, Mr. Webb left his art collection worth $1.825 million to the Metropolitan Museum and financial assets and real estate worth $3 million to Imelda. His remaining property transferred in equal shares to his children. Mr. Webb's taxable estate is $1,412,600:

FMV of property transferred at death	$7,270,000
Decedent's debts	(938,100)
Funeral and administrative costs	(94,300)
Net estate	$6,237,600
Charitable bequest	(1,825,000)
Marital deduction	(3,000,000)
Taxable estate	$1,412,600

[74] §2001(a) and §2031(a).

[75] §2039 and §2042.

[76] §2053.

[77] §2055.

[78] §2056. Because of the repeal of the federal Defense of Marriage Act, transfers to a same-sex surviving spouse are eligible for the unlimited marital deduction.

Estate Tax Computation

Any amount of a decedent's taxable estate in excess of the decedent's lifetime transfer tax exclusion ($12.92 million in 2023) is taxed at a flat 40 percent rate. The transfer tax exclusion available at death is reduced by any amount of lifetime transfer tax exclusion used by the decedent during life for gift tax purposes.[79]

| Estate Tax Computation | In 2009, 2014, and 2018, Helen Nash made substantial taxable gifts to her children and grandchildren. She used $2.9 million of her lifetime transfer tax exclusion to reduce the amount on which gift tax was owed to zero. Helen died in 2023, leaving a taxable estate of $13.923 million. The estate tax was computed as follows: |

Taxable estate	$13,923,000
Transfer tax exclusion ($12,920,000 − $2,900,000)	(10,020,000)
Excess taxable estate	$ 3,903,000
Tax rate	.40
Estate tax	$ 1,561,200

Tax Talk

After the 2017 enactment of the Tax Cuts and Jobs Act, fewer than one out of every 1,000 estates will owe federal estate tax.

Note that every individual, irrespective of marital status, is allowed a lifetime transfer tax exclusion to reduce the amount of transfers subject to the gift and estate taxes. When a married individual dies, any unused amount of the decedent's lifetime exclusion becomes available for use by the surviving spouse. Because of this portability of the exclusion between spouses, a married couple obtains the benefit of two lifetime transfer tax exclusions regardless of the order of their deaths or the amount of wealth transferred by each.[80]

| Portability of Exclusion between Spouses | Ben and Edna Piper, who were married for 22 years, made no taxable gifts during their lifetimes. Ben died on November 9, 2010. His net estate was $7.2 million, half of which he left to Edna and half of which he left to his son from a previous marriage. In 2010, the lifetime transfer tax exclusion was $5 million. Ben's estate used $3.6 million of his exclusion to reduce Ben's excess taxable estate to zero. As a result, his estate owed no estate tax: |

Net estate	$7,200,000
Marital deduction for transfer to Edna	(3,600,000)
Taxable estate	$3,600,000
Transfer tax exclusion	(3,600,000)
Excess taxable estate	–0–

Ben's unused $1.4 million exclusion became available to his surviving spouse Edna.

Edna Piper died on May 14, 2023. She left her $18.9 million net estate to various nieces and nephews. Edna's transfer tax exclusion totaled $14.32 million ($12.92 million + $1.4 million portable exclusion from Ben), and her estate tax was computed as follows:

Taxable estate	$ 18,900,000
Transfer tax exclusion	(14,320,000)
Excess taxable estate	4,580,000
Tax rate	.40
Estate tax	$ 1,832,000

---

[79] §2001(b) and §2010.

[80] §2010(c)(2)(B) and (c)(4).

The executor of a decedent's estate must file Form 706, United States Estate Tax Return, and pay any estate tax due within nine months of the date of death. However, the law provides a number of generous extensions of both the filing and the payment deadlines.[81]

Income Tax Consequences of Inherited Property

When a beneficiary inherits property from a decedent, the inheritance is excluded from the beneficiary's gross income. If the inheritance includes any noncash property, the beneficiary's basis equals the property's fair market value at date of death.[82] Because of this step-up (or step-down) basis rule, any unrealized appreciation (or depreciation) in the property simply vanishes and is never recognized for income tax purposes.

Stepped-Up Basis	Nancy Carter inherited undeveloped land from her deceased father. The father's basis in the land was $400,000, but its fair market value at the date of his death was $5.25 million. Nancy's basis in the land became $5.25 million. Two years after her father's death, Nancy sold the land for $5.6 million and recognized a $350,000 long-term capital gain.

Conclusion

Millions of individuals work conscientiously to provide financial comfort for their families. They pay close attention to the income tax consequences of their business and investment decisions and implement strategies to minimize income tax cost. Unfortunately, many of these same individuals give little thought to long-range transfer tax planning. They have no idea of the size of the tax bill that would be triggered by their death. Such shortsightedness can have disastrous financial consequences, particularly in cases of unexpected and untimely death.[83] The moral of this story should be clear: People with wealth should consult a tax professional to determine their exposure to the federal transfer tax. In virtually every case, the application of fundamental planning principles can reduce that exposure and guarantee a brighter financial future.

[81] §6075(a) and §6151(a). See §6161(a)(2) and §6166.

[82] §1014.

[83] A case in point: When Joe Robbie (former owner of the Miami Dolphins) died, his estate was hit with a $47 million tax bill. The estate had insufficient liquid assets, and the family was forced to sell both the football team and the Dolphins' stadium to raise cash to pay the tax.

Key Terms

accelerated death benefits *16-9*
adjusted net capital gain *16-16*
annual gift tax exclusion *16-30*
capital gain distribution *16-3*
cash surrender value *16-8*
collectibles *16-14*
donee *16-29*
donor *16-29*
inside buildup *16-8*
inter vivos transfer *16-29*

investment interest expense *16-21*
lifetime transfer tax exclusion *16-30*
long-term capital gain or loss *16-14*
market discount *16-7*
material participation *16-24*
maximum 15 percent rate amount *16-16*
maximum zero rate amount *16-16*
mutual fund *16-2*

net investment income *16-22*
nonbusiness bad debt *16-12*
original issue discount (OID) *16-7*
passive activity *16-24*
passive income generator (PIG) *16-28*
private activity bonds *16-6*
probate estate *16-32*
qualified dividend income *16-3*

Questions and Problems for Discussion

LO 16-1 1. Contrast the income tax consequences of the yields on the following investments:
   a. U.S. Treasury bonds.
   b. Bonds issued by the State of Illinois.
   c. Bonds issued by a publicly held corporation at their face value.
   d. Bonds issued by a publicly held corporation at a discounted value.
   e. Preferred stock issued by a publicly held corporation.
   f. Shares issued by a mutual fund.

LO 16-2 2. Term life insurance has no investment element and no cash surrender value. As a result, a term policy represents pure insurance protection. What are the tax consequences when the owner lets a term policy lapse by discontinuing premium payments?

LO 16-2 3. Mrs. Buckley, age 74, has $100,000 in a certificate of deposit paying 1.5 percent annual interest. In addition to this interest income, she receives Social Security and a modest pension from her former employer. Her marginal tax rate is 10 percent. Mrs. Buckley lives independently, but she anticipates that in several years she will need to liquidate the certificate of deposit to buy into an assisted-living retirement home. She recently read a magazine article on the benefits of tax-deferred annuities and wonders if she should transfer her $100,000 savings into an annuity. Discuss whether this tax planning strategy is advisable for Mrs. Buckley.

LO 16-3 4. Ms. Quint sadly concluded that a $7,500 debt owed to her by Mr. and Mrs. Lammas is uncollectible. Compare the tax consequences to Ms. Quint if the debt arose because she extended credit to Mr. and Mrs. Lammas in a business transaction or if the debt arose because she loaned them money for personal reasons.

LO 16-8 5. What is the logic for the presumption that a limited interest in a business partnership is a passive activity?

LO 16-8 6. Mrs. King is a shareholder in TK, an S corporation. What fact would be the strongest indicator that she materially participates in TK's business?

LO 16-8 7. Discuss the potential effect of the passive activity loss limitation on the market value of *profitable* rental real estate activities.

LO 16-4, 16-6, 16-8 8. Identify the structural similarity between the capital loss limitation, the investment interest expense limitation, and the passive activity loss limitation.

LO 16-10 9. Mr. and Mrs. Rath each own 30 percent of the voting common stock of FB, Inc. Four unrelated investors each own 10 percent. Based on a recent appraisal, FB's net worth is $80 million. Discuss the *valuation* issue suggested if
   a. Mr. and Mrs. Rath give their combined 60 percent stock interest to their son.
   b. An unrelated investor gives her 10 percent stock interest to her son.

LO 16-10   10. Discuss the tax policy rationale behind the unlimited federal estate tax deduction for testamentary transfers to religious, charitable, educational, government, or other non-profit organizations.

LO 16-10   11. Mr. and Mrs. Greer earn a combined annual salary of $150,000. What *two* basic economic choices do they have with respect to this income (i.e., what can they do with their money)? Now assume that Mr. and Mrs. Greer own property worth $2 million. What *three* basic economic choices do they have with respect to this wealth?

McGraw Hill connect   **All applicable Application Problems are available with *Connect*.**

Application Problems

For the following problems, assume the taxable year is 2023.

LO 16-1   1. Ms. Shaver, a single taxpayer, has $213,000 taxable income, which includes a $19,580 qualified dividend from Benbow, Inc. Compute her income tax on this dividend assuming that
   a. On the basis of Ms. Shaver's instruction, Benbow made a $19,580 direct deposit into her bank account.
   b. On the basis of Ms. Shaver's instruction, Benbow reinvested the dividend in additional Benbow shares.

LO 16-1, 16-9   2. Mr. and Mrs. Lay's taxable income is $779,000, which includes a $22,030 dividend on their investment in Rexford Mutual Fund. Mr. and Mrs. Lay's marginal rate on ordinary income is 37 percent, and their entire Rexford dividend is subject to the Medicare contribution tax. Compute the Lays' total tax on this dividend if their Form 1099 from Rexford reported that
   a. The entire $22,030 was an ordinary dividend.
   b. $17,540 was an ordinary dividend and $4,490 was a capital gain distribution.
   c. $6,920 was an ordinary dividend, $10,620 was a qualified dividend distribution, and $4,490 was a capital gain distribution.

LO 16-1, 16-9   3. Dianne Stacy, a single taxpayer, has $372,000 taxable income, which includes an $88,400 dividend from Tobler Mutual Fund. Ms. Stacy's marginal tax rate on ordinary income is 35 percent, and her entire Tobler dividend is subject to the Medicare contribution tax. Compute Ms. Stacy's total tax on this income if her Form 1099 from Tobler reported that
   a. The entire dividend was a qualified dividend distribution.
   b. $61,000 was an ordinary dividend and $27,400 was a qualified dividend distribution.
   c. $45,500 was a qualified dividend distribution and $42,900 was a capital gain distribution.

LO 16-1   4. At the beginning of the year, Mr. Olsen paid $15 per share for 620 shares of Carmel common stock. He received cash distributions totaling $840. His Form 1099 reported that $700 was a qualified dividend and $140 was a nontaxable distribution. Compute his basis in his 620 shares at year-end.

LO 16-1   5. Mrs. Nunn, who has a 24 percent marginal tax rate on ordinary income, earned $2,690 interest on a debt instrument this year. Compute her *federal* income tax on this interest assuming that the debt instrument was
   a. An unsecured note from her son, who borrowed money from his mother to finance the construction of his home.
   b. A certificate of deposit from a federal bank.

    c. A 30-year General Electric corporate bond.

    d. A U.S. Treasury note.

    e. A City of Memphis municipal bond.

LO 16-1   6. Refer to the preceding problem and assume that Mrs. Nunn lives in New Jersey, which taxes the interest on bonds issued by state and local jurisdictions outside New Jersey. If Mrs. Nunn's state income tax rate is 7 percent, compute her *New Jersey* tax on the $2,690 interest assuming that the debt instrument was

    a. A 30-year General Electric corporate bond.

    b. A U.S. Treasury note.

    c. A City of Memphis municipal bond.

LO 16-1   7. Mrs. Yue, a resident of Virginia, paid $50,000 for a bond issued by Pennsylvania that paid $3,400 interest this year. Her marginal state income tax rate is 6 percent. Under Virginia law, interest on debt obligations issued by another state is taxable. Mrs. Yue can deduct her state income tax on her Form 1040, and her marginal federal income tax rate is 24 percent. Compute her after-tax rate of return on the bond.

LO 16-1, 16-9   8. Ms. Pay, who has a 40.8 percent marginal tax rate on interest income (37 percent income tax + 3.8 percent Medicare contribution tax), owns HHL corporate bonds in her investment portfolio. She earned $74,800 interest this year on her HHL bonds. Compute her after-tax cash flow assuming that

    a. She received two semiannual cash payments of $37,400 each.

    b. She instructed HHL to reinvest her interest payments in additional bonds.

    c. The entire $74,800 represented amortization of OID.

LO 16-1   9. Mr. Jolly received the $100,000 face amount on the redemption of a matured corporate bond. How much interest income does he recognize on redemption if

    a. He purchased the publicly traded bond through his broker for $93,100?

    b. He purchased the bond from the corporate issuer at its $72,900 original discount price?

LO 16-1   10. In 2021, Mrs. Ulm paid $80,000 for a corporate bond with a $100,000 stated redemption value. Based on the bond's yield to maturity, amortization of the $20,000 discount was $1,512 in 2021, $1,480 in 2022, and $295 in 2023. Mrs. Ulm sold the bond for $84,180 in March 2023. What are her tax consequences in each year assuming that

    a. She bought the newly issued bond from the corporation?

    b. She bought the bond in the public market through her broker?

LO 16-1   11. On February 13, Mr. Dega invested $75,000 in TIPS paying 3.5 percent yearly interest. During the year, Mr. Dega received two cash interest payments totaling $2,742. On December 31, the adjusted principal amount of the TIPS was $76,038.

    a. How much interest income from the TIPS does Mr. Dega recognize this year?

    b. What is Mr. Dega's tax basis in his TIPS investment at the beginning of next year?

LO 16-2   12. Sixteen years ago, Ms. Cole purchased a $500,000 insurance policy on her own life and named her son as sole beneficiary. She has paid $31,280 total premiums to keep this policy in force.

    a. This year, she liquidates the policy for its $38,500 cash surrender value. Does she recognize income on the liquidation?

    b. Now assume that Ms. Cole is terminally ill. The insurance policy provides that a person with a life expectancy of less than one year can liquidate the policy and receive 80 percent of the death benefit. She does so and receives a $400,000 accelerated death benefit. Does she recognize income on the liquidation?

LO 16-2   13. Ira Munro owns a life insurance policy that will pay $750,000 to his granddaughter, Ginnie, upon Ira's death. To date, Ira has paid $69,200 total premiums on the policy, which has a current cash surrender value of $82,500.

  a. Assume that Ira dies and Ginnie receives a $750,000 payment from the insurance company. How much of the payment does Ginnie include in her gross income?

  b. Assume that Ira liquidates the policy for its cash surrender value and receives an $82,500 payment from the insurance company. How much of the payment does Ira include in his gross income?

LO 16-2   14. Fifteen years ago, Mr. Fairhold paid $50,000 for a single-premium annuity contract. This year, he began receiving a $1,300 monthly payment that will continue for his life. On the basis of his age, he can expect to receive $312,000. How much of each monthly payment is taxable income to Mr. Fairhold?

LO 16-2   15. Refer to the facts in the preceding problem. Assume that on January 1, 2028, Mr. Fairhold's unrecovered investment in the annuity is $1,875.

  a. How much of his total 2028 annuity payments ($15,600) are taxable?

  b. Assume that he dies in February after receiving only one $1,300 payment. What are the tax consequences on his final Form 1040?

LO 16-3   16. In 2021, Mr. Dale paid $47,600 for 3,400 shares of GKL Mutual Fund and elected to reinvest his year-end dividends in additional shares. In 2021 and 2022, he received Form 1099s reporting the following:

	Dividends Reinvested	Shares Purchased	Price per Share	Total Shares Owned
2021	$4,920	312	$15.769	3,712
2022	5,873	340	17.274	4,052

  a. If Mr. Dale sells his 4,052 shares for $18 per share, compute his recognized gain.

  b. If he sells only 800 shares for $18 per share and uses the FIFO method to determine basis, compute his recognized gain.

  c. If he sells only 800 shares for $18 per share and uses the average basis method, compute his recognized gain.

LO 16-3   17. Ten years ago, Mr. Pott paid $8 per share for 1,800 shares of Drago stock. Mr. Pott learned that Drago is in bankruptcy and can pay only 30 percent of its debt. What are the tax consequences to Mr. Pott of Drago's bankruptcy?

LO 16-3   18. Three years ago, Mrs. Gattis loaned $10,000 to Mr. Wren in return for his interest-bearing note. She made the loan to enable him to begin his own business. This year, Mr. Wren informed Mrs. Gattis that his business had failed and he was unable to repay the debt. Mrs. Gattis decided not to take legal action to enforce the debt. What are her tax consequences of this bad debt?

LO 16-3   19. CVF Company owned 2,000 shares of Jarvis nonvoting common stock with a $225,000 basis. In each of the following cases, determine CVF's recognized gain or loss on the disposition of this stock:

  a. CVF exchanged it for 1,300 shares of Jarvis voting common stock worth $387,000.

  b. CVF exchanged it for U.S. long-term bonds worth $317,500.

  c. CVF exchanged it for 900 shares of Newton common stock worth $280,000. This exchange was not pursuant to a corporate reorganization involving Jarvis and Newton.

  d. CVF exchanged it for 900 shares of Newton common stock worth $280,000. This exchange was pursuant to a corporate reorganization involving Jarvis and Newton.

LO 16-3 20. Refer to the preceding problem. For each case, determine CVF's tax basis in the security received in the exchange.

LO 16-4 21. Mrs. Beard recognized a $12,290 capital loss on the sale of corporate stock this year. How much loss can she deduct in each of the following cases?

    a. She had no other capital transactions this year.

    b. She recognized a $3,780 capital gain on the sale of an antique rug and had no other capital transaction this year.

    c. She recognized a $15,610 capital gain on the sale of investment land and had no other capital transaction this year.

LO 16-4 22. Mr. Alm earned a $61,850 salary and recognized a $5,600 capital loss on the sale of corporate stock this year. Compute Mr. Alm's AGI and any capital loss carryforward into future years in each of the following cases:

    a. Mr. Alm had no other capital transactions this year.

    b. Mr. Alm recognized a $12,250 capital gain on the sale of mutual fund shares.

    c. Mr. Alm received an $8,000 capital gain distribution from a mutual fund and had a $3,900 capital loss carryforward from a previous year.

LO 16-4 23. This year, Linda Moore earned a $112,000 salary and $2,200 interest income from a jumbo certificate of deposit. She recognized a $15,300 capital loss on the sale of undeveloped land. Compute Linda's AGI and any capital loss carryforward into future years in each of the following cases:

    a. She also recognized a $10,500 capital gain from the sale of corporate stock.

    b. She also received a $16,000 capital gain distribution from a mutual fund.

    c. She had no other capital transactions this year but has a $17,000 capital loss carryforward from a previous year.

LO 16-4 24. Mr. and Mrs. Revel had $206,200 AGI before considering capital gains and losses. For each of the following cases, compute their AGI:

    a. On May 8, they recognized an $8,900 short-term capital gain. On June 25, they recognized a $15,000 long-term capital loss.

    b. On February 11, they recognized a $2,100 long-term capital gain. On November 3, they recognized a $1,720 long-term capital loss.

    c. On April 2, they recognized a $5,000 long-term capital loss. On September 30, they recognized a $4,800 short-term capital loss.

    d. On January 12, they recognized a $5,600 short-term capital loss. On July 5, they recognized a $1,500 long-term capital gain.

LO 16-4 25. Refer to the preceding problem. Determine which of the four cases results in a capital loss carryforward for Mr. and Mrs. Revel. What is the amount and character of each carryforward?

LO 16-4, 16-9 26. Mr. Fox, a single taxpayer, recognized a $64,000 long-term capital gain, a $14,300 short-term capital gain, and a $12,900 long-term capital loss. Compute Mr. Fox's income tax and Medicare contribution tax if his taxable income *before* consideration of his capital transactions is $501,000.

LO 16-4 27. Mrs. Cox, a head of household, earned a $313,000 salary and recognized a $29,300 net long-term capital gain this year. Compute the income tax on the gain if

    a. None of the gain is collectibles gain or unrecaptured Section 1250 gain.

    b. $10,000 is collectibles gain.

    c. $15,500 is unrecaptured Section 1250 gain.

    d. $1,700 is collectibles gain and $22,000 is unrecaptured Section 1250 gain.

LO 16-4, 16-9   28. Mr. and Mrs. Scoler sold commercial real estate for $685,000. Their adjusted basis at date of sale was $544,700 ($596,600 cost − $51,900 straight-line accumulated depreciation). Compute the Scolers' income tax and Medicare contribution tax on their recognized gain assuming that this sale was their only property disposition this year and their marginal tax rate on ordinary income is 37 percent.

LO 16-4, 16-9   29. Mr. Scott, a head of household, sold rental real estate that had a $186,200 adjusted basis ($200,000 cost − $13,800 straight-line accumulated depreciation). The sales price was $210,000. This was his only property disposition for the year. Compute Mr. Scott's income tax on his recognized gain assuming that

   a. His marginal tax rate on ordinary income is 10 percent.

   b. His marginal tax rate on ordinary income is 37 percent.

LO 16-4   30. Mr. Dunn, who has a 32 percent marginal rate on ordinary income and a 15 percent marginal rate on adjusted net capital gain, recognized a $15,000 capital loss in 2023. Compute the tax savings from this loss assuming that

   a. He also recognized an $18,000 short-term capital gain.

   b. He also recognized an $18,000 long-term capital gain.

   c. He also recognized an $18,000 28 percent rate gain.

   d. He recognized no capital gain in 2023 and doesn't expect to recognize capital gain in 2024 through 2027. Mr. Dunn uses a 5 percent discount rate to compute NPV.

LO 16-5, 16-9   31. In 2000, Ms. Ennis, a head of household, contributed $50,000 in exchange for 500 shares of Seta stock. Seta is a qualified small business. This year, Ms. Ennis sold all 500 shares for $117,400. Her only other investment income was an $8,600 long-term capital gain from the sale of land. Her taxable income *before* consideration of her two capital transactions is $590,000.

   a. Compute Ms. Ennis's income tax and Medicare contribution tax for the year.

   b. How would the computation change if Ms. Ennis acquired the Seta stock in 2011 instead of 2000?

   c. How would the computation change if Ms. Ennis acquired the Seta stock in 2020 instead of 2000?

LO 16-5   32. In 2005, Mr. Earl, a single taxpayer, contributed $45,000 in exchange for 500 shares of DB stock. In 2008, he paid $40,000 to another shareholder to purchase 1,000 more DB shares. All DB's stock qualified as Section 1244 stock when it was issued. This year, Mr. Earl sold all 1,500 DB shares for $16 per share. His only income item was his $80,000 salary.

   a. Compute Mr. Earl's AGI.

   b. How would AGI change if he recognized a $20,000 capital gain on the sale of other securities?

LO 16-6   33. Ms. Reid borrowed $50,000 from a broker to purchase Lero, Inc. common stock. This year, she paid $3,900 interest on the debt. Compute her itemized deduction for this interest in each of the following cases:

   a. The Lero stock paid a $1,100 dividend this year, and Ms. Reid had no other investment income.

   b. Ms. Reid's only investment income was $690 interest on a certificate of deposit.

   c. Ms. Reid's only investment income was a $4,900 ordinary dividend from her investment in Koal Mutual Fund.

LO 16-6   34. Mr. and Mrs. Poe earned $135,900 compensation income and $963 interest this year and recognized a $600 short-term capital gain and a $7,200 long-term capital gain on the sale of securities. They incurred $4,400 investment interest expense and $28,500 other itemized deductions.

a. Compute the Poes' income tax on a joint return if they don't elect to treat long-term capital gain as investment income.

b. Compute the Poes' income tax if they elect to treat enough long-term capital gain as investment income to allow them to deduct their investment interest.

LO 16-8   35. Mr. and Mrs. Morris own a grocery store as a sole proprietorship. Their net profit and other relevant items for the year are as follows:

Grocery store net profit	$44,000
Deduction for SE tax	(3,109)
Dividends and interest income	1,080
Loss from a rental house	(6,470)
Loss from a limited partnership interest	(3,400)

Compute Mr. and Mrs. Morris's AGI.

LO 16-8   36. Mr. Kelly owns stock in VP and in BL, both of which are S corporations. This year, he had the following income and loss items:

Salary	$ 62,300
Business income from VP	19,000
Business loss from BL	(25,000)

Compute Mr. Kelly's AGI under each of the following assumptions:

a. He materially participates in VP's business but not in BL's business.

b. He materially participates in BL's business but not in VP's business.

c. He materially participates in both corporate businesses.

d. He does not materially participate in either corporate business.

LO 16-8   37. Ms. Turney owns a one-half interest in an apartment complex, which is her only passive activity. The complex operated at a $53,000 loss this year. In addition to her share of this loss, Ms. Turney had the following income items:

Salary	$59,000
Interest and dividends	4,400

a. Compute her AGI.

b. How would AGI change if her salary was $113,400 rather than $59,000?

c. How would AGI change if her salary was $168,250 rather than $59,000?

LO 16-8   38. Ms. Adams owns an interest in ABCD Partnership, which is a passive activity. At the beginning of the year, she projects that her share of ABCD's business loss will be $16,000 and that she will have the following additional items:

Net profit from her consulting business	$75,000
Deduction for SE tax	(5,299)
Interest and dividends	1,500

Ms. Adams plans to buy a rental house that should generate $9,500 income this year. Compute her AGI and the tax cost of her projected rent income.

LO 16-8 39. Mr. Garza earned an $85,000 salary and recognized a $12,000 loss on a security sale and a $14,000 gain on the sale of a limited partnership interest. His share of the partnership's business income through date of sale was $2,100. (Both the gain and the business income are passive activity income.) Mr. Garza was allocated a $13,900 passive activity loss from an S corporation. Compute his AGI.

LO 16-9 40. Boyd Salzer, an unmarried individual, has $212,950 AGI consisting of the following items:

Salary	$188,000
Interest income	2,900
Dividend income	8,300
Rental income from real property	13,750

     a. Compute Mr. Salzer's Medicare contribution tax.

     b. How would the computation change if Boyd Salzer files a joint income tax return with his wife, Harriet?

LO 16-9 41. Mr. Erwin's marginal tax rate on ordinary income is 37 percent. His $958,000 AGI included a $24,900 net long-term capital gain and $37,600 business income from a passive activity.

     a. Compute Mr. Erwin's income tax on the $62,500 investment income from these two sources.

     b. Compute Mr. Erwin's Medicare contribution tax if the $62,500 is his net investment income for the year. What is Mr. Erwin's marginal tax rate on long-term capital gain and on passive activity income?

LO 16-10 42. Mr. Zeplin wants to make a cash gift to each of his 5 children, to each of their 5 spouses, and to each of his 13 grandchildren. How much total wealth can he transfer to his descendants without making a taxable gift if

     a. He is an unmarried individual?

     b. He is married to Mrs. Zeplin?

LO 16-10 43. Mr. Ito, an unmarried individual, made a gift of real estate to his son. Compute the amount subject to federal gift tax in each of the following situations:

     a. The FMV of the real estate was $4.75 million, and the transfer was Mr. Ito's first taxable gift.

     b. The FMV of the real estate was $15 million, and the transfer was Mr. Ito's first taxable gift.

     c. The FMV of the real estate was $15 million. Two years ago, Mr. Ito made his first taxable gift: marketable securities with a $3 million FMV in excess of the annual exclusion.

LO 16-10 44. Mr. Jackson died on June 19 when the total FMV of his property was $24 million and his debts totaled $2.789 million. His executor paid $23,000 funeral expenses and $172,000 accounting and legal fees to settle the estate. Mr. Jackson bequeathed $500,000 to the First Lutheran Church of Milwaukee and $1 million to Western Wisconsin College. He bequeathed his art collection (FMV $6.4 million) to his wife and the residual of his estate to his three children.

     a. Compute Mr. Jackson's taxable estate.

     b. Compute the estate tax payable by Mr. Jackson's executor if Mr. Jackson made no taxable gifts during his lifetime.

    c. Compute the estate tax payable by Mr. Jackson's executor if Mr. Jackson made a substantial taxable gift in 2011 and used $5 million of his lifetime transfer tax exclusion to reduce the amount on which gift tax was owed to zero.

LO 16-10   45. Mrs. Turner died this year at age 83. On the date of death, the FMV of Mrs. Turner's property was $46.3 million, and she owed $2.491 million to various creditors. The executor of her estate paid $17,800 funeral expenses and $294,200 legal and accounting fees to settle the estate. Mrs. Turner bequeathed $1 million to the local SPCA and $2.5 million to the March of Dimes (both of which are qualified charities for federal tax purposes). She bequeathed $25 million to her surviving husband, Jeffrey, and the residual of her estate to her brother, Marcus.

    a. Compute Mrs. Turner's taxable estate.

    b. Compute the estate tax payable by Mrs. Turner's executor if Mrs. Turner made $4.8 million taxable gifts during her lifetime but paid no gift tax because of her lifetime transfer tax exclusion.

    c. Assume the facts in part (*b*). Compute the estate tax payable by Mrs. Turner's executor assuming that Jeffrey predeceased his wife and had an unused $1.91 million lifetime transfer tax exclusion. In this case, Marcus inherited the residual of Mrs. Turner's estate net of charitable bequests.

LO 16-10   46. Mrs. Wolter, an unmarried individual, owns investment land with a $138,000 basis, a nine-year holding period, and a $200,000 FMV. Compute the after-tax (income tax and Medicare contribution tax) sale proceeds in each of the following cases:

    a. She sells the land herself. Her taxable income *before* considering the gain on sale is $310,000.

    b. She gives a 25 percent interest in the land to each of her four single adult grandchildren (without incurring a gift tax) who immediately sell it. Each grandchild's taxable income *before* considering the gain on sale is $8,000.

    c. She dies while still owning the land. Her single daughter inherits the land and immediately sells it. The daughter's taxable income before considering the gain on sale is $79,000.

Issue Recognition Problems

Identify the tax issue or issues suggested by the following situations and state each issue in the form of a question.

LO 16-1   1. Mr. Clem invests in Series EE savings bonds. He projects that his sole proprietorship will generate a sizable loss, and he wants to accelerate income from other sources to offset it. He could elect to recognize $28,000 accrued interest on the savings bonds he now owns. However, he doesn't want to recognize current income on the bonds he will purchase in future years.

LO 16-1   2. At the beginning of the year, Ms. Alston owned 2,900 shares of SBS stock with a basis of $32 per share. SBS paid a 50 percent stock dividend, and Ms. Alston received 1,450 additional SBS shares. Before this dividend, the market price per share was $90. After the dividend, the price fell to $65.

LO 16-1   3. In 2003, Mr. Lloyd paid $18,000 for a newly issued BN bond with a $30,000 stated redemption value. He has recognized $6,000 of the original issue discount (OID) as ordinary interest income. This year, BN went bankrupt and informed Mr. Lloyd that his bond was worthless.

LO 16-1   4. Mr. and Mrs. Gamble paid $53,000 for a corporate bond with a $50,000 stated redemption value. They paid the $3,000 premium because the bond's annual interest rate is higher than the market interest rate.

LO 16-3   5. Three years ago, Mrs. Best purchased 1,000 shares of NN stock from an unrelated party for $12 per share. After her purchase, the value of the shares steadily declined. Two weeks ago, an unrelated party offered to buy the shares for 30 cents per share. Mrs. Best declined the offer and immediately mailed her shares to NN's secretary-treasurer with a note declaring her intention to abandon them.

LO 16-3   6. Two years ago, Ms. Eager loaned $3,500 to her 20-year-old daughter, who used the loan proceeds to buy a used car. This year, the daughter informed her mother that she could not repay the debt.

LO 16-8   7. Mr. Morales was a 25 percent partner in MNOP Partnership, which operated a gift and souvenir shop. He materially participated in the partnership business. Several years ago, Mr. Morales loaned $10,000 to MNOP in return for a written interest-bearing note. Unfortunately, MNOP went bankrupt before the loan was repaid.

LO 16-4, 16-8   8. This year, Ms. Tan had a $29,000 capital loss carryforward and an $8,200 suspended passive activity loss carryforward. She died on September 12 and didn't recognize any capital gain or passive activity income during the year.

LO 16-8   9. Ms. Nassam has $60,000 suspended passive activity losses from her interest in the EZ Limited Partnership. In December, she sold this interest to N, Inc., a regular corporation in which she is the sole shareholder.

LO 16-8   10. Mr. Pugh has a $7,900 adjusted basis in his limited interest in PKO Partnership. He also has $22,000 suspended passive activity losses from PKO. Mr. Pugh recently sent a letter to PKO's corporate general partner formally abandoning his equity in the partnership.

LO 16-10   11. Mr. Oakem, a 66-year-old divorced individual, has two children with his former wife. He recently married a 45-year-old woman with no property of her own. Therefore, Mr. Oakem plans to change his will to provide that when he dies, his fortune will be placed in a trust. His new wife will receive the income for as long as she lives, but she has no direct ownership in the trust property. When she dies, Mr. Oakem's two children will inherit everything.

LO 16-10   12. Mr. Durst died on March 8. His taxable estate includes a traditional IRA with a $140,000 balance. Mr. Durst's contributions to this IRA were fully deductible. His son is the beneficiary of the IRA.

LO 16-10   13. Mrs. Allen died on June 1. She and her surviving husband were co-owners of real property with a $200,000 adjusted basis and a $1.6 million FMV. Mr. Allen inherited his wife's half of the property.

Research Problems

LO 16-4   1. Mrs. Evelyn Baker sued her stockbroker for mismanagement of her account. The broker ultimately settled the case by paying her $250,000. The payment represented the loss in value of Mrs. Baker's stock portfolio attributable to the mismanagement. Because the payment was made with respect to capital assets, Mrs. Baker could report the payment as a $250,000 capital gain (rather than ordinary income) on her Form 1040. Her legal fees for the lawsuit totaled $70,000. Can Mrs. Baker treat the fees as a capital loss by simply offsetting them against the settlement and thereby include only $180,000 net capital gain in her AGI?

LO 16-5   2. Todd Zimler, who files a joint income tax return with his wife, Stella, owns 85 percent of the outstanding stock of Zimler Manufacturing. In January of last year, Todd transferred a tract of investment land to the corporation in exchange for 600 shares of nonvoting preferred stock, which qualified as Section 1244 stock. At date of transfer, Todd's basis in the land was $185,000, and the land's FMV was $60,000. The exchange of land for stock was nontaxable under Section 351. Consequently, Todd recognized no loss and took a $185,000 substituted basis in the 100 shares of stock. In May of this year, Todd sold the 100 shares to an unrelated investor for $62,000. What is the character of Todd's $123,000 recognized loss?

LO 16-8   3. Rachel Sanchez is a limited partner in HN Partnership, which operates a souvenir shop, and a member in Jams-n-Jellies LLC, which makes specialty food items and sells them at retail. Rachel has no involvement in the partnership business, but she handles all the advertising for the LLC. The LLC compensates her at the rate of $45 per hour, and she billed the LLC for 592 hours of work this year. Rachel's only other income-generating activity is her part-time employment as a librarian.

Rachel's Schedule K-1 from HN Partnership reported that her share of ordinary business loss was $3,810. Her Schedule K-1 from Jams-n-Jellies LLC reported that her share of ordinary business income was $15,082. How much of her share of the partnership loss can Rachel deduct on her current year Form 1040?

McGraw Hill **connect**   **All applicable Tax Planning Cases are available with *Connect*.**

Tax Planning Cases

LO 16-2   1. Ms. Echols is the owner and beneficiary of a $150,000 insurance policy on her mother's life. Ms. Echols has paid $46,000 premiums, and the policy is fully paid up (no more premiums are due). She needs money and is considering cashing in the policy for its $95,000 cash surrender value. Alternatively, she can borrow $70,000 against the policy from the insurance company. She will pay 5 percent annual interest (a nondeductible personal expense) and repay the loan from the death benefit. Ms. Echols's mother is in poor health and should live no more than 10 years. Ms. Echols's marginal tax rate on ordinary income is 24 percent. Assuming a 6 percent discount rate, should she cash in the policy or borrow against it?

LO 16-3, 16-4, 16-5   2. Ms. Kaspari, who has a 24 percent marginal rate on ordinary income and a 15 percent marginal rate on adjusted net capital gain, acquired the following blocks of stock in KDS, a closely held corporation:

July 12, 2006	1,400 shares at $41 per share
December 3, 2010	800 shares at $46 per share
September 30, 2019	2,000 shares at $49 per share*
May 2, 2023	750 shares at $53 per share

*Qualified small business stock.

In November 2023, Ms. Kaspari agreed to sell 1,000 KDS shares to Mr. Nolan for $60 per share. Which shares should she sell to maximize her after-tax cash from the sale?

LO 16-5   3. As of November 30, Ms. Brett had $12,000 capital losses and no capital gains. She owns 4,900 shares of GG stock with a $15 basis and a $45 FMV per share. Ms. Brett plans to hold her stock for three more years before selling it and using the proceeds to buy a home. However, she could easily sell 400 shares to trigger a $12,000 capital gain and then immediately repurchase them. If Ms. Brett's marginal tax rate on ordinary income is 37 percent, she is subject to the Medicare contribution tax, and she uses a 4 percent discount rate to compute NPV, should she implement this year-end tax planning strategy?

LO 16-7
4. Mr. and Mrs. Prinze are evaluating an investment in undeveloped land. The year 0 cost is $100,000, and they can borrow $60,000 of the purchase price at 8 percent. They will pay interest only in years 1 through 5. The annual property tax on the land will be $1,200 in years 1 through 5. Mr. and Mrs. Prinze project that they can sell the land in year 5 for $160,000 and repay the $60,000 loan from the sales proceeds. They have a 37 percent marginal tax rate on ordinary income, are subject to the Medicare contribution tax, and use a 4 percent discount rate to compute NPV. Determine the NPV of this investment under the following assumptions:

   a. The Prinzes have enough net investment income and other itemized deductions so that the $6,000 annual carrying charge (interest plus property tax) is fully deductible in years 1 through 5.

   b. Because the Prinzes don't itemize deductions, they elect to capitalize the annual carrying charge to the basis of the land.

LO 16-8
5. Ms. Barstow purchased a limited interest in Quinnel Partnership in 2023. Her share of the partnership's 2023 business loss was $5,000. Unfortunately, Ms. Barstow couldn't deduct this loss because she had no passive activity income, so she is carrying it forward into 2024. Quinnel Partnership projects that it will operate at breakeven (no income or loss) for several years. However, Ms. Barstow believes that her partnership interest is a solid long-term investment, and she has no plans to sell it.

   On January 1, 2024, Ms. Barstow must decide between two new investments that are comparable in terms of risk and liquidity. She could invest $100,000 in TNB Limited Partnership, and her share of the partnership's 2024 business income would be $8,000. Alternatively, she could invest $100,000 in a high-yield bond fund that promises a 10 percent return. (Ms. Barstow would receive $10,000 interest income in 2024.) Which investment would result in a better after-tax return for 2024, assuming that

   a. Ms. Barstow has a 24 percent marginal tax rate on ordinary income and is not subject to the Medicare contribution tax?

   b. Ms. Barstow has a 37 percent marginal tax rate on ordinary income and is subject to the Medicare contribution tax on either the $8,000 partnership income or the $10,000 interest income?

Appendix **16–A**

Comprehensive Schedule D Problem

According to the year-end statement provided by their stockbroker, Martin and Deanna Lowell made the following security sales in 2022:

	Date Acquired	Date Sold	Sales Price	Tax Basis
45 shares Pluto mutual fund	08/03/22	12/30/22	$13,500	$13,100
2,040 shares GG stock	05/14/16	10/06/22	42,400	37,500
13,199 shares MN stock	02/11/05	09/12/22	17,050	21,200
1,782 shares ZT stock	01/08/02	12/29/22	36,900	4,400

- Mrs. Lowell is a limited partner in Cohen LP. Her Schedule K-1 reported a $7,610 share of long-term capital gain.
- The Lowells received a Form 1099 from Pluto mutual fund reporting a $700 long-term capital gain distribution.
- In 2019, Mrs. Lowell loaned $7,500 to her cousin, Cynthia Graetz, who needed the money for a new business venture. Cynthia recently declared personal bankruptcy, and Mrs. Lowell decided not to pursue collection of the $7,500 debt in court.
- The Lowells have a $630 short-term capital loss carryforward and a $2,900 long-term capital loss carryforward.
- The Lowells' taxable income (Form 1040, line 15) is $495,332, which includes $26,200 qualified dividend income (line 3(a)).

The given information and the calculation of Mr. and Mrs. Lowell's regular tax are shown on the following Form 8949, Schedule D, and Qualified Dividends and Capital Gain Tax Worksheet. (For simplicity of presentation, the required multiple Forms 8949 are condensed into one form.)

Form **8949**	Sales and Other Dispositions of Capital Assets	OMB No. 1545-0074
Department of the Treasury Internal Revenue Service	Go to *www.irs.gov/Form8949* for instructions and the latest information. File with your Schedule D to list your transactions for lines 1b, 2, 3, 8b, 9, and 10 of Schedule D.	**2022** Attachment Sequence No. **12A**

Name(s) shown on return	Social security number or taxpayer identification number
Martin and Deanna Lowell	598-65-5150

Before you check Box A, B, or C below, see whether you received any Form(s) 1099-B or substitute statement(s) from your broker. A substitute statement will have the same information as Form 1099-B. Either will show whether your basis (usually your cost) was reported to the IRS by your broker and may even tell you which box to check.

Part I **Short-Term.** Transactions involving capital assets you held 1 year or less are generally short-term (see instructions). For long-term transactions, see page 2.

Note: You may aggregate all short-term transactions reported on Form(s) 1099-B showing basis was reported to the IRS and for which no adjustments or codes are required. Enter the totals directly on Schedule D, line 1a; you aren't required to report these transactions on Form 8949 (see instructions).

You **must** check Box A, B, **or** C below. **Check only one box.** If more than one box applies for your short-term transactions, complete a separate Form 8949, page 1, for each applicable box. If you have more short-term transactions than will fit on this page for one or more of the boxes, complete as many forms with the same box checked as you need.

☐ **(A)** Short-term transactions reported on Form(s) 1099-B showing basis was reported to the IRS (see **Note** above)
☐ **(B)** Short-term transactions reported on Form(s) 1099-B showing basis **wasn't** reported to the IRS
☐ **(C)** Short-term transactions not reported to you on Form 1099-B

1

(a) Description of property (Example: 100 sh. XYZ Co.)	(b) Date acquired (Mo., day, yr.)	(c) Date sold or disposed of (Mo., day, yr.)	(d) Proceeds (sales price) (see instructions)	(e) Cost or other basis See the **Note** below and see *Column (e)* in the separate instructions.	Adjustment, if any, to gain or loss If you enter an amount in column (g), enter a code in column (f). **See the separate instructions.**		(h) Gain or (loss) Subtract column (e) from column (d) and combine the result with column (g).
					(f) Code(s) from instructions	(g) Amount of adjustment	
45 sh. Pluto mutual fund (Box A)	08/03/2022	12/30/2022	13,500	13,100			400
Nonbusiness bad debt (Box C) (see attached explanation)			0	7,500			(7,500)
2 Totals. Add the amounts in columns (d), (e), (g), and (h) (subtract negative amounts). Enter each total here and include on your Schedule D, **line 1b** (if Box A above is checked), **line 2** (if Box B above is checked), or **line 3** (if Box C above is checked) . .			13,500	20,600			(7,100)

Note: If you checked Box A above but the basis reported to the IRS was incorrect, enter in column (e) the basis as reported to the IRS, and enter an adjustment in column (g) to correct the basis. See *Column (g)* in the separate instructions for how to figure the amount of the adjustment.

For Paperwork Reduction Act Notice, see your tax return instructions.   Cat. No. 37768Z   Form **8949** (2022)

Source: Internal Revenue Service

Name(s) shown on return. Name and SSN or taxpayer identification no. not required if shown on other side	Social security number or taxpayer identification number

Before you check Box D, E, or F below, see whether you received any Form(s) 1099-B or substitute statement(s) from your broker. A substitute statement will have the same information as Form 1099-B. Either will show whether your basis (usually your cost) was reported to the IRS by your broker and may even tell you which box to check.

Part II   **Long-Term.** Transactions involving capital assets you held more than 1 year are generally long-term (see instructions). For short-term transactions, see page 1.

> **Note:** You may aggregate all long-term transactions reported on Form(s) 1099-B showing basis was reported to the IRS and for which no adjustments or codes are required. Enter the totals directly on Schedule D, line 8a; you aren't required to report these transactions on Form 8949 (see instructions).

You *must* **check Box D, E,** *or* **F below. Check only one box.** If more than one box applies for your long-term transactions, complete a separate Form 8949, page 2, for each applicable box. If you have more long-term transactions than will fit on this page for one or more of the boxes, complete as many forms with the same box checked as you need.

- ☑ **(D)** Long-term transactions reported on Form(s) 1099-B showing basis was reported to the IRS (see **Note** above)
- ☐ **(E)** Long-term transactions reported on Form(s) 1099-B showing basis **wasn't** reported to the IRS
- ☐ **(F)** Long-term transactions not reported to you on Form 1099-B

1 (a) Description of property (Example: 100 sh. XYZ Co.)	(b) Date acquired (Mo., day, yr.)	(c) Date sold or disposed of (Mo., day, yr.)	(d) Proceeds (sales price) (see instructions)	(e) Cost or other basis See the **Note** below and see *Column (e)* in the separate instructions.	(f) Code(s) from instructions	(g) Amount of adjustment	(h) Gain or (loss) Subtract column (e) from column (d) and combine the result with column (g).
2,040 sh. GG stock	05/14/2016	10/06/2022	42,400	37,500			4,900
13,199 sh. MN stock	02/11/2005	09/12/2022	17,050	21,200			(4,150)
1,782 sh. ZT stock	01/08/2002	12/29/2022	36,900	4,400			32,500
2 Totals. Add the amounts in columns (d), (e), (g), and (h) (subtract negative amounts). Enter each total here and include on your Schedule D, **line 8b** (if **Box D** above is checked), **line 9** (if **Box E** above is checked), or **line 10** (if **Box F** above is checked) . .			96,350	63,100			33,250

Note: If you checked Box D above but the basis reported to the IRS was incorrect, enter in column (e) the basis as reported to the IRS, and enter an adjustment in column (g) to correct the basis. See *Column (g)* in the separate instructions for how to figure the amount of the adjustment.

Form **8949** (2022)

SCHEDULE D
(Form 1040)

Department of the Treasury
Internal Revenue Service

Capital Gains and Losses

Attach to Form 1040, 1040-SR, or 1040-NR.
Go to *www.irs.gov/ScheduleD* for instructions and the latest information.
Use Form 8949 to list your transactions for lines 1b, 2, 3, 8b, 9, and 10.

OMB No. 1545-0074

2022

Attachment
Sequence No. **12**

Name(s) shown on return
Martin and Deanna Lowell

Your social security number
598-65-5150

Did you dispose of any investment(s) in a qualified opportunity fund during the tax year? ☐ Yes ☐ No
If "Yes," attach Form 8949 and see its instructions for additional requirements for reporting your gain or loss.

Part I **Short-Term Capital Gains and Losses—Generally Assets Held One Year or Less** (see instructions)

See instructions for how to figure the amounts to enter on the lines below. This form may be easier to complete if you round off cents to whole dollars.	(d) Proceeds (sales price)	(e) Cost (or other basis)	(g) Adjustments to gain or loss from Form(s) 8949, Part I, line 2, column (g)	(h) Gain or (loss) Subtract column (e) from column (d) and combine the result with column (g)
1a Totals for all short-term transactions reported on Form 1099-B for which basis was reported to the IRS and for which you have no adjustments (see instructions). However, if you choose to report all these transactions on Form 8949, leave this line blank and go to line 1b .				
1b Totals for all transactions reported on Form(s) 8949 with **Box A** checked	13,500	13,100		400
2 Totals for all transactions reported on Form(s) 8949 with **Box B** checked				
3 Totals for all transactions reported on Form(s) 8949 with **Box C** checked	0	7,500		(7,500)

4 Short-term gain from Form 6252 and short-term gain or (loss) from Forms 4684, 6781, and 8824 . .	**4**	
5 Net short-term gain or (loss) from partnerships, S corporations, estates, and trusts from Schedule(s) K-1	**5**	
6 Short-term capital loss carryover. Enter the amount, if any, from line 8 of your **Capital Loss Carryover Worksheet** in the instructions	**6** (	630)
7 **Net short-term capital gain or (loss).** Combine lines 1a through 6 in column (h). If you have any long-term capital gains or losses, go to Part II below. Otherwise, go to Part III on the back	**7**	(7,730)

Part II **Long-Term Capital Gains and Losses—Generally Assets Held More Than One Year** (see instructions)

See instructions for how to figure the amounts to enter on the lines below. This form may be easier to complete if you round off cents to whole dollars.	(d) Proceeds (sales price)	(e) Cost (or other basis)	(g) Adjustments to gain or loss from Form(s) 8949, Part II, line 2, column (g)	(h) Gain or (loss) Subtract column (e) from column (d) and combine the result with column (g)
8a Totals for all long-term transactions reported on Form 1099-B for which basis was reported to the IRS and for which you have no adjustments (see instructions). However, if you choose to report all these transactions on Form 8949, leave this line blank and go to line 8b .				
8b Totals for all transactions reported on Form(s) 8949 with **Box D** checked	96,350	63,100		33,250
9 Totals for all transactions reported on Form(s) 8949 with **Box E** checked				
10 Totals for all transactions reported on Form(s) 8949 with **Box F** checked.				

11 Gain from Form 4797, Part I; long-term gain from Forms 2439 and 6252; and long-term gain or (loss) from Forms 4684, 6781, and 8824	**11**	
12 Net long-term gain or (loss) from partnerships, S corporations, estates, and trusts from Schedule(s) K-1	**12**	7,610
13 Capital gain distributions. See the instructions	**13**	700
14 Long-term capital loss carryover. Enter the amount, if any, from line 13 of your **Capital Loss Carryover Worksheet** in the instructions	**14** (	2,900)
15 **Net long-term capital gain or (loss).** Combine lines 8a through 14 in column (h). Then, go to Part III on the back	**15**	38,660

For Paperwork Reduction Act Notice, see your tax return instructions.   Cat. No. 11338H   Schedule D (Form 1040) 2022

Schedule D (Form 1040) 2022

Page **2**

Part III	**Summary**

16 Combine lines 7 and 15 and enter the result **16**   30,930

- If line 16 is a **gain**, enter the amount from line 16 on Form 1040, 1040-SR, or 1040-NR, line 7. Then, go to line 17 below.
- If line 16 is a **loss**, skip lines 17 through 20 below. Then, go to line 21. Also be sure to complete line 22.
- If line 16 is **zero**, skip lines 17 through 21 below and enter -0- on Form 1040, 1040-SR, or 1040-NR, line 7. Then, go to line 22.

17 Are lines 15 and 16 **both** gains?
☑ **Yes.** Go to line 18.
☐ **No.** Skip lines 18 through 21, and go to line 22.

18 If you are required to complete the **28% Rate Gain Worksheet** (see instructions), enter the amount, if any, from line 7 of that worksheet **18**

19 If you are required to complete the **Unrecaptured Section 1250 Gain Worksheet** (see instructions), enter the amount, if any, from line 18 of that worksheet **19**

20 Are lines 18 and 19 both zero or blank and you are not filing Form 4952?
☐ **Yes.** Complete the **Qualified Dividends and Capital Gain Tax Worksheet** in the instructions for Form 1040, line 16. **Don't** complete lines 21 and 22 below.

☐ **No.** Complete the **Schedule D Tax Worksheet** in the instructions. **Don't** complete lines 21 and 22 below.

21 If line 16 is a loss, enter here and on Form 1040, 1040-SR, or 1040-NR, line 7, the **smaller** of:

- The loss on line 16; or
- ($3,000), or if married filing separately, ($1,500) } . . . .   **21** (   )

Note: When figuring which amount is smaller, treat both amounts as positive numbers.

22 Do you have qualified dividends on Form 1040, 1040-SR, or 1040-NR, line 3a?

☐ **Yes.** Complete the **Qualified Dividends and Capital Gain Tax Worksheet** in the instructions for Form 1040, line 16.

☐ **No.** Complete the rest of Form 1040, 1040-SR, or 1040-NR.

Schedule D (Form 1040) 2022

2022 Qualified Dividends and Capital Gain Tax Worksheet – Line 16

1. Enter the amount from Form 1040, line 15............................ 1. <u>495,332</u>
2. Enter the amount from Form 1040, line 3a....... 2. <u>26,200</u>
3. Are you filing Schedule D?
    Yes. Enter the smaller of line 15 or 16 of
        Schedule D. If either line 15 or 16 is
        Blank or a loss, enter -0-
    No. Enter the amount from Form 1040, ... 3. <u>30,930</u>
        Line 7.
4. Add lines 2 and 3 .... 4. <u>57,130</u>
5. Subtract line 4 from line 1 .... 5. <u>438,202</u>
6. Enter:
    $41,675 if single or married filing separately,
    $83,350 if married filing jointly or qualifying widow(er),
    $55,800 if head of household ....6. <u>83,350</u>
7. Enter the smaller of line 1 or line 6 ....7. <u>83,350</u>
8. Enter the smaller of line 5 or line 7 ....8. <u>83,350</u>
9. Subtract line 8 from line 7. This amount is taxed at 0% ....9. <u>0</u>
10. Enter the smaller of line 1 or line 4 .... 10. <u>57,130</u>
11. Enter the amount from line 9 .... 11. <u>0</u>
12. Subtract line 11 from line 10 .... 12. <u>57,130</u>
13. Enter:
    $459,750 if single,
    $258,600 if married filing separately,
    $517,200 if married filing jointly or qualifying widow(er),
    $488,500 if head of household .... 13. <u>517,200</u>
14. Enter the smaller of line 1 or line 13 .... 14. <u>495,332</u>
15. Add lines 5 and 9 .... 15. <u>438,202</u>
16. Subtract line 15 from line 14. If zero or less, enter -0- .... 16. <u>57,130</u>
17. Enter the smaller of line 12 or line 16 .... 17. <u>57,130</u>
18. Multiply line 17 by 15% (0.15) .... 18. <u>8,570</u>
19. Add lines 9 and 17 .... 19. <u>57,130</u>
20. Subtract line 19 from line 10 .... 20. <u>0</u>
21. Multiply line 20 by 20% (0.20) ....21. <u>0</u>
22. Figure the tax on the amount on line 5. If the amount on line 1 is
    less than $100,000, use the Tax Table to figure the tax. If the
    amount on line 1 is $100,000 or more, use the Tax Computation
    Worksheet.. 22. <u>100,877</u>
23. Add lines 18, 21, and 22 .... 23. <u>109,447</u>
24. Figure the tax on the amount on line 1. If the amount on line 1 is
    less than $100,000, use the Tax Table to figure the tax. If the
    amount on line 1 is $100,000 or more, use the Tax Computation
    Worksheet.. 24. <u>120,872</u>
25. **Tax on all income**. Enter the smaller of line 23 or 24
    Also include this amount on Form 1040, line 16.................................. 25. <u>109,447</u>

Chapter Seventeen

Tax Consequences of Personal Activities

Learning Objectives

After studying this chapter, you should be able to:

LO 17-1. Determine the extent to which prizes, awards, gifts, and inheritances are included in the recipient's gross income.

LO 17-2. Summarize the tax consequences of legal settlements and government transfer payments.

LO 17-3. Compute the tax on gain from the sale of personal assets.

LO 17-4. Identify personal expenses that result in tax deductions or credits.

LO 17-5. Determine the deductibility of personal losses.

LO 17-6. Describe the tax benefits resulting from homeownership.

To this point, Part Five has focused on the tax consequences of profit-motivated activities. We learned how to compute taxable income from business, employment, and investment activities and discovered effective techniques for reducing the tax on such income. This chapter introduces a new topic: the tax consequences of activities in which people engage for personal reasons. The first section of this chapter discusses the taxation of economic benefits that aren't derived from business, employment, or investment activities. The second section of this chapter concentrates on the tax rules for personal expenses or losses and identifies the limited circumstances under which they result in a tax savings. The third section explains the significant tax advantages of homeownership.

GROSS INCOME FROM WHATEVER SOURCE DERIVED

Section 61 of the Internal Revenue Code states that gross income means all income from whatever source derived. This statement creates a presumption that any receipt of an economic benefit that increases an individual's net worth is subject to income tax. The context in which the receipt occurred or the source of the receipt is irrelevant.[1] The tax law does make exceptions to this inclusive rule, and we will identify a number of them in this chapter. Nevertheless, an individual who receives an economic benefit should assume that the benefit is included in gross income, even if it was derived from a purely personal or private activity.

Property Tax Abatements for Senior Volunteers	More than 50 Massachusetts cities have adopted a state-sponsored program under which senior citizens who perform voluntary civic services receive local property tax abatements of up to $1,500. The IRS ruled that the amount of the abatements is gross income to the senior citizens for federal tax purposes because no exception to the general rule of inclusion applies to this particular economic benefit.[2]

Restitution for Shooting Victims	The surviving victims and the families of slain victims of the 2007 Virginia Tech shootings are eligible to receive restitution payments from the Hokie Spirit Memorial Fund. Congress passed special legislation to provide that such payments are excluded from the recipient's gross income for federal tax purposes.[3]

Prizes, Awards, Gifts, and Inheritances

LO 17-1
Determine the extent to which prizes, awards, gifts, and inheritances are included in the recipient's gross income.

People who receive prizes or awards must include the value of the prize or award in gross income.[4] This general rule applies to awards based on professional achievement or merit, such as the Nobel and Pulitzer Prizes. It also applies to academic and athletic awards. However, students who are degree candidates at educational institutions may exclude scholarship or fellowship awards but only to the extent the award pays for tuition, fees, books, supplies, and equipment.[5]

Going for the Gold, Silver, or Bronze	On October 7, 2016, President Obama signed into law an exclusion from gross income for the value of medals or prize money awarded to athletes by the U.S. Olympic Committee on account of competition in the Olympic or Paralympic Games. The exclusion doesn't apply if the athlete's AGI exceeds $1 million.[6]

Scholarships	Mary Dillon received a four-year scholarship from the University of Kansas that pays her $12,250 annual tuition (including all fees and books) plus her $10,300 annual room and board. She also received a $2,000 alumni association scholarship that she used to buy her college wardrobe. Mary can exclude the tuition scholarship but must include the $12,300 other scholarship awards in gross income.

[1] This presumption applies to receipts derived from unlawful activities such as embezzlement or extortion. Consequently, even illegal income is subject to income tax. *James* v. *United States,* 366 U.S. 213 (1961).

[2] Chief Counsel Advice Memorandum 200227003 (July 5, 2002).

[3] 2007 Virginia Tech Victims Act §1.

[4] §74(a). The law provides a narrow exception for certain employee achievement awards to the extent the award consists of tangible property worth no more than $1,600. This is called *the gold watch exception.*

[5] §117.

[6] §74(d).

The general rule of taxability also applies to receipts attributable entirely to good luck, such as lottery jackpots, raffle or door prizes, and gambling winnings. The prize or award need not consist of cash; the game show contestant who wins a trip to Paris must include the value of the trip in gross income.[7]

Oprah's Giveaway	During one of her last daytime television shows, Oprah Winfrey gave every member in the audience a gift bag, which included an iPad, a $1,000 Nordstrom gift certificate, a diamond encrusted wristwatch, and a Volkswagen Beetle. Because the recipients had to include the value of this bag of swag in gross income, Oprah also paid each recipient's estimated tax cost to the IRS.

Finally, the general rule applies to rewards that people receive for performing a special or noteworthy service.

Reward for Whistle-blowing	Albert Campbell acted as a whistle-blower by suing his former employer, Lockheed Martin, for contract fraud committed against the United States. Lockheed Martin settled the case by paying $37.9 million to the federal government and $8.75 million to Albert in his role as whistle-blower. Albert failed to report this payment on his tax return and argued that the payment was simply his share of a nontaxable recovery of federal funds. The courts concluded that the payment was a reward for meritorious service that was clearly includable in Albert's gross income.[8]

The major exception to the rule that personal receipts are taxable applies to gifts and inheritances.[9] Individuals who receive gifts of cash or property from a donor or who inherit cash or property from a decedent don't report the receipt as income on Form 1040. Similarly, life insurance proceeds are nontaxable. The beneficiary of a life insurance policy doesn't include the death benefit in gross income.[10]

Personal Receipts	This year, Ms. Hardy received the following items:	
	Birthday gift of cash from her dad	$ 1,500
	Set of dishes won at a church raffle (retail value)	600
	Pearl ring inherited from her grandmother (appraised FMV)	2,600
	Insurance proceeds from a policy on her grandmother's life	50,000
	The only item that she must report on her Form 1040 is the $600 raffle prize.	

| *Gift or Compensation Income?* | Reverend Lloyd Goodwin received an annual salary plus the use of a parsonage from the church at which he served as pastor. The church held three "special occasion" Sundays each year when the congregation was invited to make anonymous cash contributions to their pastor and his family. For the three tax years in question, the contributions totaled $42,250, and Reverend Goodwin didn't report them on his tax return. The IRS concluded that the contributions represented employment compensation and should be included in gross income. Members of the congregation who testified on behalf of Reverend Goodwin described the contributions as gifts made out of "love, respect, and admiration" for him.

(continued) |
|---|---|

[7] *Reginald Turner*, T.C. Memo 1954-38.

[8] *Campbell* v. *Commissioner*, 658 F.3d 1255 (CA-11, 2011).

[9] §102.

[10] §101(a).

The court, however, concluded that the contributions were regular payments made by persons to whom Reverend Goodwin provided professional services and, therefore, were taxable compensation rather than nontaxable gifts.[11]

LO 17-2
Summarize the tax consequences of legal settlements and government transfer payments.

Legal Settlements

Individuals may receive economic benefits under legal agreements or settlements. For instance, a person who suffered an injury or detriment because of the fault of another party may be awarded damages by a court of law. The general rule is that legal damages are gross income unless they represent compensation for physical injury or illness.[12]

Legal Damages

Mr. Kaleb was a candidate for public office when he was accused of being a racist and neo-Nazi in an editorial published in a local newspaper. Mr. Kaleb successfully sued the paper for libel and defamation of character and was awarded $1 million in compensatory damages in a jury trial. Mr. Kaleb must include the $1 million in gross income.

Compensation for Physical Injury

Mrs. Spears was walking along a city sidewalk when she was struck by falling debris from a construction project. She sued the construction company for negligence and was awarded a $300,000 settlement: $100,000 for her physical injuries plus $200,000 punitive damages (damages intended to punish a defendant for extreme misconduct). Mrs. Spears may exclude $100,000 of this settlement from gross income but must report and pay tax on the $200,000 punitive damages.[13]

Tax Talk
Nichelle Perez argued that the $20,000 she received for donating her eggs to an infertile couple was excludable from income as damages for her physical pain from the medical procedure. The Tax Court concluded that her pain was "a by-product of performing a service contract," and the payment was taxable compensation.

Divorce

The divorce of a married couple is a personal event that may have profound economic consequences. The divorce decree, which specifies the rights and obligations of the divorcing parties, may require one party to transfer ownership of valuable property to the other. For *income tax* purposes, this transfer is treated as a gift, regardless of any affection or animosity underlying the transfer.[14] As a result, the transferor recognizes no gain or loss on the disposition of the property. The transferee recognizes no gross income on receipt of the property and takes a carryover tax basis from the transferor.

The divorce decree may require one party to pay alimony to the other. Alimony consists of a series of payments by which a person discharges a legal obligation to support an ex-spouse. Under pre–Tax Cuts and Jobs Act law, the recipient must include the alimony in gross income, while the payer is allowed to deduct it above-the-line in computing adjusted gross income (AGI).[15] The new law upended this long-standing treatment of alimony payments. For divorce decrees executed after December 31, 2018, the recipient excludes alimony payments from gross income, while the payer is not allowed to deduct the payments.

---

[11] *Goodwin* v. *United States,* 67 F.3d 149 (CA-8, 1995). For a similar case, see *White,* T.C. Memo 2016-167.

[12] §104(a)(2).

[13] Mrs. Spears's legal fees paid in connection with the lawsuit are nondeductible.

[14] §1041. The transfer is not subject to gift tax.

[15] Legal fees paid in connection with a divorce are nondeductible.

If the divorcing couple has dependent children, the parent who surrenders custody may be required to pay child support to the custodial parent. Child support payments are not gross income to the recipient and are nondeductible by the payer. Child support raises the question of which parent can claim the child tax credit for a dependent child. Regardless of the support involved, the custodial parent is entitled to the credit *unless* they sign a written declaration releasing the credit to the noncustodial parent.[16]

| *Payments Pursuant to a Divorce* | Mr. and Mrs. Watson are divorced. Under the terms of the divorce decree, Mr. Watson transferred $600,000 worth of marketable securities to Mrs. Watson as a property settlement. His basis in the securities was $319,000. He is also required to pay $1,500 a month to his ex-wife: $900 alimony and $600 child support for their 5-year-old daughter, who lives with Mrs. Watson.

   Mr. Watson didn't recognize gain on disposition of the appreciated securities, and Mrs. Watson didn't recognize gross income on their receipt. She has a $319,000 basis in the securities. If the divorce decree was executed on or before December 31, 2018, Mrs. Watson includes the $900 monthly alimony payment in her gross income for the current and subsequent years, and Mr. Watson is allowed a corresponding deduction. If the decree was executed after December 31, 2018, the annual alimony payments are not taxable to Mrs. Watson and not deductible by Mr. Watson. Regardless of the tax treatment of the alimony payments, the child support payments are not taxable to Mrs. Watson and not deductible by Mr. Watson. As the custodial parent, Mrs. Watson is entitled to the child tax credit for the daughter on her Form 1040 unless she releases the credit to Mr. Watson. |

Government Transfer Payments

Tax Talk
To provide relief to suffering businesses during the coronavirus pandemic, certain government loans that are forgiven under the Paycheck Protection Program are not considered gross income.

People who receive need-based payments from a local, state, or federal government agency may exclude the payments from gross income.[17] Consequently, benefits provided through public assistance programs such as school lunches, food stamps, and welfare are nontaxable. In contrast, people who are entitled to receive government transfer payments irrespective of any demonstrated economic need must include the payments in gross income. For instance, unemployed workers must pay federal income tax on unemployment compensation received from their state government.[18]

| *Government Transfer Payments* | For the first six months of the year, Mr. Gilly worked as the custodian of an elementary school. When the school was permanently closed, Mr. Gilly lost his job and applied for unemployment benefits from the state of Wisconsin. He received $8,240 unemployment compensation this year. He also applied for help from the federal food assistance program. Based on financial need, Mr. Gilly was eligible to receive $2,050 worth of food stamps. Mr. Gilly must report his $8,240 unemployment compensation on his Form 1040 but may exclude the value of the food stamps from gross income. |

Social Security

Individuals who paid employee payroll tax or self-employment tax during their working lives are entitled to receive Social Security and Medicare benefits when they retire. The Social Security system is often described as a safety net that protects the elderly from poverty by providing a guaranteed, if minimal, income during their waning years. Unfortunately, many

[16] §152(e) and §24(c)(1).
[17] See Rev. Rul. 71-425, 1971-2 C.B. 76.
[18] §85.

senior citizens depend on this minimal income to survive. According to Social Security Administration data, half of Americans age 65 and older receive at least 50 percent of their income from Social Security, and nearly 25 percent depend almost entirely on Social Security.

One Leg of the Stool	The Social Security Administration's website cautions that Social Security was never intended to be the sole source of income in retirement and that "a comfortable and stable retirement is based on a three-legged stool of Social Security, private pensions, and savings and investment." Source: Social Security Administration

Tax Talk
Based on a recent survey conducted by Northwestern Mutual, 24 percent of respondents believe that "it is not at all likely" that Social Security will be available when they retire. According to the most recent trustee report, the Social Security trust fund will be unable to pay full benefits by 2037.

The question of whether Social Security benefits should be taxable is controversial. One political camp argues that these benefits should be taxed because they are not based on financial need. The opposing camp argues that Social Security benefits should be immune to the income tax. After all, aren't retirees entitled to their benefits because they paid non-deductible employee payroll tax or self-employment tax during their working years? The federal government's complicated approach to taxing Social Security benefits reflects a cautious compromise between these polar positions. In very general terms

- Married couples with less than $32,000 and single individuals with less than $25,000 of modified AGI don't pay tax on their benefits.
- Married couples with modified AGI between $32,000 and $44,000 and single individuals with modified AGI between $25,000 and $34,000 pay tax on 50 percent of their benefits.
- Married couples with more than $44,000 and single individuals with more than $34,000 of modified AGI pay tax on 85 percent of their benefits.[19]

According to the Congressional Research Service, about 50 percent of Social Security recipients do pay some income tax on their benefits. The complete details of the computation of taxable benefits are incorporated into a Social Security Worksheet included as Appendix 17–A to this chapter.

Social Security	Mr. and Mrs. Dean received $22,800 of Social Security this year. Their only other source of income was Mr. Dean's $18,000 annual pension from his former employer. Because their modified AGI is so low, none of the Deans' Social Security benefit is included in gross income. Mr. and Mrs. Lutz also received $22,800 of Social Security this year. Mr. and Mrs. Lutz earned $79,600 of interest and dividends from their investment portfolio. Because their modified AGI is so high, $19,380 ($22,800 × 85%) of their Social Security benefit is included in gross income.

The Silver Tsunami	Kathleen Casey-Kirschling, born at one second after midnight on January 1, 1946, became the first baby boomer to receive a Social Security check. Kathleen is part of the earliest wave of America's "silver tsunami." Over the next two decades, nearly 80 million boomers will become eligible for Social Security, at the rate of more than 10,000 per day.

LO 17-3
Compute the tax on gain from the sale of personal assets.

Gains on Sales of Personal Assets

Individuals who realize gain on the sale of an asset generally must include the gain in gross income, even if the asset was not held for business or investment purposes. The character of

[19] §86. For purposes of this summary, modified AGI includes one-half of any Social Security benefits received and any tax-exempt interest earned during the year.

gain recognized on the sale of a personal asset depends on whether the asset was a capital or a noncapital asset in the hands of the seller. Most personal assets meet the definition of capital asset so that gain recognized on sale is characterized as capital gain. Recall from Chapter 16 that capital gains are taxed at preferential rates. Specifically, long-term capital gain from the sale of collectibles (works of art, antiques, gems, postage stamps, rare coins, and similar tangible personal property) is taxed at a maximum rate of 28 percent, while long-term capital gain from the sale of other personal assets is taxed at 0, 15, or 20 percent.

Gain on Sale of Collectibles	During the last 15 years, Boyd Lovett purchased more than 700 bottles of French wine, which he stored in his personal wine cellar. This year, Boyd moved to a small apartment and sold his entire wine collection to a local restaurant for $112,500. Boyd's cost basis in the collection was $73,600. Therefore, he recognized a $38,900 long-term capital gain. Because Boyd's marginal rate on ordinary income was 32 percent, this collectibles gain was taxed at the 28 percent preferential rate, resulting in $10,892 federal income tax ($38,900 × 28%).

A narrow exception to the rule that personal assets are capital assets applies to certain **creative assets:** copyrights; literary or artistic compositions; letters or memoranda; or similar assets. A creative asset is not a capital asset in the hands of the person who created it. In the case of a letter, memorandum, or similar property, the asset is not a capital asset in the hands of the person for whom it was written. Finally, a creative asset is not a capital asset in the hands of a donee who received it as a gift from either the creator or (in the case of letters and memoranda) the person for whom it was written.[20]

A Letter from Michael Jackson	In 1981, Darla Roth wrote a fan letter to Michael Jackson and received a handwritten letter from Michael in return. Darla kept Michael's letter until 2003 when she gave it to her daughter, Kathy. This year, Kathy sold the letter on eBay to a collector in Oregon for $55,000. Although the letter is a personal asset, it wasn't a capital asset to Michael Jackson (its creator), Darla (the person for whom it was written), or Kathy (Darla's donee). Consequently, Kathy's $55,000 gain recognized on sale of the letter is ordinary income. If the collector in Oregon holds the letter as a personal asset, it is a capital asset to the collector.

Most personal assets fall into the category of *consumer durables*—tangible assets that people buy for their private use and enjoyment. Individuals can't recover the cost of these assets through depreciation. Thus, the initial cost basis of consumer durables is not adjusted downward, even though the market value of such goods invariably decreases over time. For this reason, people who sell consumer durables usually realize a loss on the transaction. As we will discuss later in this chapter, these personal losses are nondeductible.

Garage Sale	Emma Pena decided to clean out her basement and attic by selling an accumulation of clothing, books, toys, exercise equipment, and other used household items at a multifamily garage sale. Emma was delighted to clear $1,175 from the sale of these personal assets, even though this amount was substantially less than her original cost. Emma's realized loss on the sale (whatever the amount) is nondeductible.

[20] §1221(a)(3). Individuals who create a musical composition or who receive a musical composition as a gift from the creator can elect to treat the composition as a capital asset. §1221(b)(3).

PERSONAL EXPENSES

LO 17-4
Identify personal expenses that result in tax deductions or credits.

The Internal Revenue Code states that no deduction is allowed for personal, living, or family expenses.[21] Accordingly, the everyday costs of managing a household, raising a family, pursuing social or civic interests, and enjoying leisure time don't result in any tax benefit. Even expenses with a tangential connection to a business or employment activity, such as the cost of a professional wardrobe, the daily commute to work, or routine noonday lunches, are inherently personal in nature and thus nondeductible.

Business or Personal Expenses?

Jeffrey Stone operated an appliance repair business out of a shop located about eight miles from his home. On the Schedule C on which he computed business income, he reported several thousand dollars of miscellaneous expenses. The IRS discovered that the miscellaneous expenses included payments for his children's birthday parties; Christmas presents to his nephews; trips to visit Mrs. Stone's parents; family trips to baseball tournaments; a fishing license; subscriptions to *People, Ladies' Home Journal,* and *Family Circle* magazines; and veterinary bills for the family dog and cat. The judge who tried Mr. Stone's case agreed with the IRS that his miscellaneous expenses were clearly nondeductible. "In differentiating between personal and business expenses, there may be some 'grey' areas, but the expenditures here do not fall within those areas, at least not without a Herculean effort of delusion."[22]

The tax law relaxes the no-deduction rule for three major categories of personal expenses: medical expenses; local, state, and foreign tax payments; and charitable contributions. Individuals who incur such expenses may be allowed an itemized deduction on Schedule A. (See Exhibit 17.1 for a quick reference as to whether an individual deduction is allowed above-the-line or only as an itemized deduction.)

Medical Expenses

Individuals may claim an itemized deduction for the unreimbursed cost of medical care for themselves and their family.[23] Medical care includes payments to healthcare practitioners (doctors, dentists, chiropractors, etc.) and treatment facilities (outpatient clinics, hospitals, and long-term-care facilities), certain travel expenses related to medical treatment, the cost of medical aids (eyeglasses, hearing aids, crutches, wheelchairs, etc.), and prescription drugs. Premiums paid to purchase health, accident, and long-term-care insurance also qualify as medical care expenses.[24]

Medical Travel Expense

Donny Lang, the 12-year-old son of Ben and Mary Pat Lang, lost a leg in a boating accident last year. This year, the family made 12 one-day visits to a regional rehabilitation center where Donny received physical therapy to improve the use of his artificial limb. The total driving distance for each round trip was 160 miles. On each visit, the family ate lunch in the rehab center cafeteria. Their total cost of the meals was $408. The cost of Donny's prosthesis and the cost of his physical therapy qualify as medical expenses. The family's travel expenses also qualify. The Langs used the IRS-provided standard mileage rate to compute their $422 transportation expense. Their total medical travel expense was $830 ($422 transportation expense + $408 meals).

---

[21] §262(a).

[22] Kendall L. Houghton and Jeffrey A. Friedman, "Lost in (Cyber) Space?" *State Tax Notes,* September 15, 1997, pp. 173–25.

[23] §213. IRS Publication 502 *Medical and Dental Expenses* includes a detailed list of expenses that qualify for the deduction.

[24] Medical insurance reimbursements are excluded from gross income under §105(b).

EXHIBIT 17.1
Classification of Individual Deductions

Above-the-Line Deductions on Form 1040, Schedule 1, Part II

- One-half self-employment tax [Chapters 10 and 14]
- Penalty on early withdrawal of savings [Chapter 15]
- Self-employed health insurance premiums [Chapter 15]
- Contribution to self-employed qualified retirement plan [Chapter 15]
- Contribution to IRA [Chapter 15]
- Net capital loss ($3,000 maximum) [Chapter 16]
- Alimony paid under pre-2019 divorce decree [Chapter 17]
- Interest on student (qualified education) loans [Chapter 17]

Itemized Deductions on Form 1040, Schedule A

- Real estate tax on investment land [Chapter 16]
- Investment interest expense [Chapter 16]
- Medical expenses [Chapter 17]
- State and local income *or* sales tax [Chapter 17]
- Personal property tax [Chapter 17]
- Foreign income tax [Chapter 17]
- Real estate tax on personal residences [Chapter 17]
- Charitable contributions [Chapter 17]
- Casualty loss from federally declared disasters [Chapter 17]
- Gambling losses and expenses [Chapter 17]
- Home mortgage interest expense [Chapter 17]

Long-Term-Care Expense

For the last five years, Ruth Meyer, age 86, lived in her daughter Becky Gleason's home. Ruth has no financial resources other than Social Security, and Becky claims her as a dependent for federal tax purposes. Ruth suffers from Alzheimer's disease, and from January through May of this year, Becky paid a licensed healthcare practitioner $2,900 per month to tend to Ruth while Becky was at work. By June, Becky could no longer meet her mother's medical needs at home and moved her into the memory care unit of a nursing home. Becky pays $6,100 a month to the home, which covers the cost of meals and lodging, personal care services, medical treatment, and supervision to protect Ruth from threats to her health and safety. Both the cost of the in-home nursing care and the cost of the nursing home qualify as medical expenses.

Tax Talk
The Tax Court ruled that a taxpayer's gender identity disorder (GID) qualified as a disease, and the cost of her sex realignment surgery was a deductible medical expense.

Medical care doesn't include the cost of cosmetic surgery unless the surgery is necessary to correct a congenital deformity or damage from a traumatic injury or disfiguring disease. Thus, the costs of procedures intended solely to improve or enhance physical appearance (face lifts, tummy tucks, body piercings, tattoos) are not deductible.

The medical care deduction is limited to the excess of total *unreimbursed* expenses over 7.5 percent of AGI.

Limited Medical Care Deduction

Mr. and Mrs. Chester incurred $5,150 of medical expenses (including insurance premiums) during the year. They received a payment of $1,800 from their insurance company in partial reimbursement of these expenses. If their AGI is $30,000, they are allowed a $1,100 itemized deduction.

(continued)

Medical expenses	$5,150
Insurance reimbursement	(1,800)
Unreimbursed expenses	$3,350
AGI threshold ($30,000 AGI × 7.5%)	(2,250)
Medical care deduction	$1,100

If the Chesters' AGI exceeds $44,667, the 7.5 percent threshold exceeds unreimbursed expenses, and the Chesters have no medical care deduction this year.

As this example demonstrates, the AGI limitation restricts the number of taxpayers who actually receive a tax benefit from their medical expenses. Only those unfortunate families that bear unusually high healthcare costs receive any tax relief from this particular itemized deduction.

Local, State, and Foreign Tax Payments

Tax Talk

Recent tax proposals have considered increasing the deduction limit for state and local taxes to $80,000. Critics argue that this would provide a disproportionate benefit to wealthier taxpayers and those living in high-tax states.

Individuals may deduct state and local real or personal property taxes paid on nonbusiness (personal or investment) assets such as their home, family automobile, or land held for investment.[25] They may elect to deduct *either* state and local income taxes *or* state and local sales taxes (but not both).[26] The election to deduct sales taxes is particularly beneficial to residents of the seven states that have a sales tax but no individual income tax (Alaska, Florida, Nevada, South Dakota, Texas, Washington, and Wyoming). Individuals who pay income tax to a foreign jurisdiction may either deduct such tax or (as generally is the case) claim a foreign tax credit.

Beginning in 2018, the aggregate itemized deduction for state and local property taxes, state and local income or sales taxes, and foreign income taxes is limited to $10,000 annually ($5,000 for married filing separately).[27] This itemized deduction (whether limited or not) is disallowed for purposes of the individual AMT.[28]

Several common taxes that individuals pay are not deductible for federal income tax purposes. Gift and estate taxes, employee payroll taxes, and employment taxes paid for household employees are all nondeductible personal expenses.[29] Of course, the federal income tax itself is a nondeductible expense.

Limited Deduction for Taxes

This year, Ruthie Green paid $2,013 local property tax, $15,119 Ohio income tax, $2,899 federal gift tax, and $1,240 employer payroll tax on the wages paid to her housekeeper. She also paid $118 Canadian income tax on dividends received from a Canadian corporation.

Ruthie's itemized deduction for the $17,132 aggregate amount of her local property tax and state income tax is limited to $10,000. However, this deduction is disallowed in the computation of Ruthie's alternative minimum taxable income (AMTI). Ruthie took a foreign tax credit for the Canadian income tax. The federal gift tax and employer payroll tax are nondeductible.

[25] §164(a). §164(b)(6)(A) provides that nonbusiness foreign real property taxes are not deductible.

[26] §164(b)(5). The IRS provides tables that individuals can use to estimate their general sales tax for the year based on AGI.

[27] §164(b)(6).

[28] §56(b)(1)(A)(ii).

[29] §275.

State or Local Income Tax Refunds

Individuals who overpay their state or local income tax in one year will receive a refund of the overpayment in the following year. If the individual deducted the state or local income tax in the year of payment, the tax payment reduced the individual's federal income tax for that year. Consequently, under the tax benefit rule, the individual must include the tax refund in gross income. If the individual didn't deduct the tax payment, the refund is excluded from gross income.[30]

State Tax Refund	This year, Mr. and Mrs. Bartino received a $1,418 refund of New York state income tax and a Form 1099-G (Certain Government Payments) documenting the refund. Last year, the Bartinos deducted the entire amount of state income tax paid on their Schedule A. As a result, they must report the state income tax refund as gross income on their Form 1040. If the Bartinos had taken the standard deduction last year, they would have received no federal tax benefit from their state income tax payment, and the refund would have been nontaxable.

Charitable Contributions

Tax Talk
Apple's charitable giving program matches every hour an employee volunteers or dollars they donate with a monetary donation to the same organization. Since the program's inception, Apple employees have raised almost $600 million in total donations for more than 34,000 organizations.

People who contribute money or property to nonprofit organizations that have been granted tax-exempt status by the IRS can claim the contribution as an itemized deduction.[31] The policy rationale is that this deduction encourages private citizens to support worthy causes that benefit society as a whole. By allowing the charitable contribution deduction, the federal government indirectly subsidizes thousands of social, civic, cultural, religious, scientific, environmental, and educational institutions. This subsidy represents a tax expenditure of about $50 billion annually. Individuals who want to ensure that their contribution to a particular organization is deductible can use the IRS's online search tool *Exempt Organizations Select Check* to determine if that organization has tax-exempt status.

There are broad (and extremely complicated) limits on the charitable contribution deduction. For example, the annual deduction for cash contributions to public charities can't exceed 60 percent of AGI (50 percent for tax years before 2018). Any contribution in excess of such limit is carried forward as an itemized deduction for five years. However, the CARES Act of 2020 and Consolidated Appropriations Act of 2021 temporarily removed the AGI limitation for cash contributions to qualified charities for tax years 2020 and 2021.

Charitable Contribution Limitation	In 1996, Hillary Rodham Clinton earned $742,000 royalties from her book *It Takes a Village,* kept $152,000 to pay state and federal tax on the income, and donated the $590,000 remainder to charity. However, because the Clintons' AGI on their joint return was $1,065,101, their charitable contribution deduction was limited to $532,551.

Tax Talk
An investment banker with a passion for designer dresses and shoes claimed a $48,954 deduction for the value of used clothing donated to charity. A highly skeptical Tax Court reduced the deduction to $8,949.

When an individual contributes property to charity, the amount of the deduction depends on the character of the property.[32] If the property is a long-term capital asset to the contributor, the deduction generally equals FMV. As a result, individuals who own highly appreciated capital assets enjoy a significant tax benefit if they give the assets to charity.

[30] The tax benefit of the deduction for state and local taxes is reduced if the taxpayer is in an AMT situation. Individuals can use the State and Local Income Tax Refund Worksheet in the Instructions for Form 1040 to compute the tax benefit attributable to a state tax refund.

[31] §170. Contributions of $250 or more to a single charity must be substantiated by a written acknowledgment from the charity. §170(f)(8).

[32] Reg. §1.170A-1(c)(1) and §170(e)(1).

Contribution	Mr. Nelke, who is in the 37 percent marginal tax bracket, owns an oil painting that he bought
of Appreciated	15 years ago for $50,000. The painting's value was recently appraised at $400,000. If
Capital Asset	Mr. Nelke gives this painting to the Metropolitan Museum of Art, his itemized deduction is
	$400,000, and his tax savings are $148,000 (37 percent of $400,000). Most of the savings
	is attributable to the $350,000 appreciation in the painting's FMV, an unrealized gain on
	which Mr. Nelke never paid income tax.

If an individual contributes property that is not a capital asset to charity, the deduction is limited to the *lesser* of FMV or the contributor's basis in the property. In this case, the contributor doesn't enjoy a deduction for any unrealized appreciation in the property.

Contribution of	Ms. Holk owns and operates a pet store. She contributed 5,000 bags of cat and dog food
Noncapital Asset	from her inventory to the local Society for Prevention of Cruelty to Animals. Her cost basis in
	the pet food was $6,300, and its FMV (retail) was $9,500. Ms. Holk's itemized deduction for
	this contribution is limited to $6,300.

Tax Subsidies for Education

The costs incurred by individuals for their own education and the education of their children are nondeductible personal expenses. However, Congress subsidizes the cost of education through a profusion of tax incentives available to low-income and middle-income families. Here is a bullet-point summary of the major education incentives. Students who want more details should refer to IRS Publication 970, *Tax Benefits for Education.*

- Individuals can exclude the interest earned on the redemption of qualified Series EE savings bonds (**education savings bonds**) to the extent of tuition and fees paid to a postsecondary educational institution. This exclusion is phased out for high-income taxpayers.[33]

- Individuals can report interest paid on **qualified education loans** as an above-the-line deduction.[34] A loan is qualified if the proceeds were used to pay for the cost of postsecondary education, such as college tuition, room, and board. This deduction is limited to $2,500 and is phased out for high-income taxpayers.

- Individuals can claim an **American Opportunity Credit** based on the cost of tuition, fees, and course materials paid during the first four years of postsecondary education.[35] The maximum annual credit is $2,500 per eligible student. Alternatively, individuals may claim a **Lifetime Learning Credit** based on 20 percent of their qualified tuition expenses. The maximum annual credit is $2,000. Both credits are phased out for high-income taxpayers.

- Individuals can contribute a maximum of $2,000 every year to a tax-exempt **Coverdell education savings account** established for a beneficiary (typically a child or grandchild) under the age of 18. Withdrawals from the account are nontaxable to the extent of the beneficiary's elementary, secondary, and higher education expenses. The contribution is phased out for high-income taxpayers.[36]

---

[33] §135.

[34] §221 and §62(a)(17).

[35] §25A.

[36] §530.

- Individuals can contribute to tax-exempt **qualified tuition programs** (also referred to as 529 plans) sponsored by states or by private colleges and universities. Distributions from qualified tuition programs are nontaxable to the extent used to pay qualified education expenses.[37]

PERSONAL LOSSES

Losses on Sales of Personal Assets

LO 17-5
Determine the deductibility of personal losses.

In earlier chapters of this text, we learned that individuals can deduct losses realized on the disposition of business or investment assets. While the capital loss and passive activity loss limitations may defer recognition of such losses to future years, sooner or later the losses reduce AGI and result in a tax savings. If an individual realizes a loss on the disposition of a personal asset, such loss is nondeductible.[38] In many instances, this rule has little economic significance. Suppose a person pays $1,500 for a new refrigerator, uses it for eight years, and then sells it to a college student for $200. The $1,300 realized loss ($200 amount realized less $1,500 cost basis) is nondeductible, and the sale of the personal asset is a nonevent for tax purposes.

Nondeductible Personal Loss

Mr. Rooker purchased a membership in a private country club for $20,000. Over the past 13 years, he was assessed $7,000 for the cost of capital improvements to the club's swimming pool, tennis courts, and golf course. This year, he sold his membership to an unrelated party for $15,000. The IRS acknowledged that the club membership was a capital asset and that Mr. Rooker realized a $12,000 loss on the sale ($15,000 amount realized − $27,000 original cost plus assessments). However, the IRS ruled that the loss was nondeductible because he held the membership primarily for personal use rather than for investment purposes.[39]

A loss realized on the sale of a personal residence can result in severe economic distress. For many people, their residence is their most valuable asset, and they consider it as a long-term investment. Even so, owner-occupied housing is a personal rather than an investment asset for tax purposes, and a loss on sale is nondeductible.

Loss on Sale of Personal Residence

Mr. and Mrs. Zuma purchased their family home in Colorado Springs for $278,000 in 2005. This year, the Zumas had to relocate to Minnesota. Because of the depressed housing market in their locality, they sold their home for only $250,000. Their $28,000 loss realized on the sale is a nondeductible personal loss.

Casualty Losses

Individuals are allowed an itemized deduction for property losses attributable to a federally declared disaster.[40] A **federally declared disaster** is a destructive event such as a hurricane or wildfire that is determined by the U.S. president to warrant federal assistance by agencies such as the Federal Emergency Management Agency (FEMA). For tax purposes, the amount of casualty loss equals the *lesser* of the tax basis in the property or the decrease in value from the casualty. The cost of repairs to the property is acceptable as evidence of the decrease in value if the taxpayer shows that the repairs are necessary to restore the property to its condition immediately before the casualty.[41]

[37] §529.

[38] Rev. Rul. 54-268, 1954-2 C.B. 88, and *Arlen L. Rower,* T.C. Memo 1998-117.

[39] This example is based on IRS Letter Ruling 8205045.

[40] §165(h)(5)(A) as amended by the Tax Cuts and Jobs Act.

[41] Reg. §1.165-7(a) and (b).

A casualty loss is reduced by any insurance proceeds received by the taxpayer so that only the *unreimbursed* loss is deductible.[42] Furthermore, the loss from each casualty is reduced by a $100 floor. Finally, only the aggregate loss for the year in excess of 10 percent of AGI is deductible.[43]

Casualty Loss Deduction	

Mr. and Mrs. Duke reside in a coastal community hit by a hurricane that the president designated as a federally declared disaster. The Dukes' sailboat, which they purchased 12 years ago for $86,000, was completely destroyed. The fair market value of the boat prior to its destruction was $100,000, and the Dukes received a $70,000 reimbursement from their insurance company.

For tax purposes, the Dukes' casualty loss attributable to the hurricane is $86,000 (*lesser* of $86,000 tax basis or $100,000 decrease in value). If this loss is the Dukes' only casualty loss for the year and their AGI is $118,400, their casualty loss deduction is limited to $4,060:

Casualty loss	$ 86,000
Insurance proceeds	(70,000)
Unreimbursed loss	$ 16,000
$100 floor per casualty	(100)
	$ 15,900
10% AGI threshold	(11,840)
Casualty loss deduction	$ 4,060

Hobby and Gambling Losses

Activities in which people engage primarily for personal enjoyment may generate gross income. Consider the case of Dr. Cox, a practicing dentist, who breeds toy poodles as his hobby. Not only does he exhibit his own animals in local and regional dog shows, but he also sells puppies and shows poodles owned by other people. This year, Dr. Cox earned $6,100 from his canine-related activities. His annual expenses, such as dog food, veterinary fees, and travel to shows, totaled $10,400. What are the tax rules concerning his $4,300 **hobby loss?** Because of the inclusive rule for gross income recognition, he must report his $6,100 revenue as "other income" on page 1, Form 1040. However, his $10,400 expenses are nondeductible personal expenses.[44]

To say the least, this is a disappointing result for Dr. Cox. His hobby expenses exceeded his revenues by $4,300, but his taxable income from the hobby equaled his $6,100 gross income. The tax consequences would be much more favorable if Dr. Cox could treat his dog-breeding activity as a business. In such a case, he would account for revenues and expenses on Schedule C and could deduct his $4,300 net loss in the computation of AGI. To do so, he must demonstrate that he breeds poodles with the "actual and honest objective" of making a profit rather than for recreation.[45] To this end, he should operate in a businesslike manner by maintaining a separate bank account and proper accounting records. He should actively seek out customers by advertising in the appropriate trade journals and should charge the market rate for his products and services.

Tax Talk
Bruce Phillips, a U.S. postal employee, deducted a $28,243 loss from his "business" of bowling. Not only did Mr. Phillips fail to win any prize money during the year, he failed to enter a single bowling tournament. Based on all the facts, the Tax Court concluded Mr. Phillips incurred a $28,243 nondeductible hobby loss.

[42] If the insurance proceeds exceed the basis of the property, the owner may defer recognition of such gain by replacing the property. See the discussion of involuntary conversions in Chapter 9.

[43] §165(h)(1) and (2).

[44] Prior to enactment of the Tax Cuts and Jobs Act, §183(b) allowed a deduction for hobby expenses to the extent of hobby revenues. This deduction was a miscellaneous itemized deduction, all of which were repealed for tax years ending after December 31, 2017.

[45] *Ronnen*, 90 T.C. 74, 91 (1988). For recent cases, see *Susan Crile*, T.C. Memo 2014-202, *Terry G. Akey*, T.C. Memo 2014-211, and *Finis R. Welch*, T.C. Memo 2017-229.

Of course, the best way for Dr. Cox to demonstrate a profit motive is to actually make a profit. The tax law establishes a *presumption* that any activity generating net income (gross income over deductible expenses) in three out of the five consecutive years ending with the year of the questionable loss is a business.[46] In such a case, the IRS must prove that the activity is a hobby, and it rarely tries to do so.

Presumption of a Business	Mrs. Saltzman, a practicing corporate attorney, spends a significant amount of time running a travel consulting activity out of her home. In 2023, her consulting fees totaled $18,700, while her expenses, such as promotional materials, professional seminars, and subscriptions to industry publications, totaled $21,750. She reported the results of this activity as a business on Schedule C and deducted her $3,050 net loss in the computation of her 2023 AGI. Although she incurred a loss in 2023, her consulting activity generated a profit in 2020, 2021, and 2022. As a result, the legal presumption is that her travel consulting activity is a business and not a hobby.

For tax purposes, gambling activities are treated more favorably than other hobbies. Individuals must report their winnings as gross income but may deduct their losses and any gambling-related expenses to the extent of such winnings.[47]

Gambling Losses	Mrs. Toomey, a full-time school teacher, loves playing the dollar slot machines in Atlantic City. She keeps a diary in which she records the date, the casino, and her winnings or losses for that day. This year, Mrs. Toomey won a $15,000 jackpot. Because the payout exceeded $1,200, the casino was required to issue a Form W-2G (Certain Gambling Winnings) to Mrs. Toomey and provide a copy to the IRS.[48] According to her diary, Mrs. Toomey won $18,917 (including the $15,000 jackpot) and lost $5,368 during the year. She reported the $18,917 winnings as "other income" on page 1, Form 1040, and the $5,368 loss as an itemized deduction on Schedule A.
	Now assume that Mrs. Toomey didn't win the jackpot. According to her diary, Mrs. Toomey won only $3,917 and lost $5,368 during the year. She must report her $3,917 winnings as other income and can report only $3,917 of her losses as an itemized deduction on Schedule A. In other words, her $1,451 *net* gambling loss is nondeductible.

TAX CONSEQUENCES OF HOMEOWNERSHIP

LO 17-6
Describe the tax benefits resulting from homeownership.

Even though an owner-occupied residence is a personal asset, the Internal Revenue Code contains several preferential rules that can make such a residence a fine investment. In fact, one of the greatest economic advantages of homeownership is that the tax law treats owner-occupied real property as a nonproductive personal asset. Consider the relative economic situations of Mrs. Hicks and Ms. Gray. Neither individual owns her own home, and each pays $24,000 a year to rent a dwelling. These rent payments are nondeductible personal expenses. This year, each woman inherits $400,000. Mrs. Hicks uses the money to buy a home, while Ms. Gray invests her money in a financial asset yielding 6 percent a year. What are the cash flow implications of their respective purchases?

[46] §183(d).
[47] §165(d).
[48] Reg. §1.6041-10.

*Comparative
Cash Flows*

Mrs. Hicks now lives in her own home and no longer pays rent. Consequently, her annual after-tax cash outflow is zero. Ms. Gray continues to pay rent but also receives $24,000 income on her investment. If Mrs. Gray is in a 32 percent marginal tax bracket, her after-tax cash outflow is $7,680, the tax on her investment income:

	Mrs. Hicks	**Ms. Gray**
Cash outflow before purchase:		
Rent expense	$ (24,000)	$ (24,000)
Cash outflow after purchase:		
Rent expense	–0–	(24,000)
Taxable income from investment	–0–	24,000
Tax cost of income	–0–	(7,680)
	–0–	$ (7,680)

How can the purchase of a personal asset have a better financial result than the purchase of income-producing investment property? Observe that Mrs. Hicks's personal residence provides a $24,000 annual benefit—the rent she avoids paying. Economists refer to this benefit as the **imputed income from owner-occupied housing.** The federal tax system has never required homeowners to include such imputed income in their tax base. This preferential treatment creates an economic incentive for people to purchase a home. In our example, both Mrs. Hicks and Ms. Gray invested $400,000 in assets yielding a 6 percent before-tax return. Because Mrs. Hicks's return consists of nontaxable imputed income, her after-tax return is also 6 percent, making her purchase of a personal residence the superior investment.

Home Mortgage Interest Deduction

Individuals who incur debt to finance a personal expenditure can't deduct the interest paid on the debt.[49] The major exception to this rule applies to **qualified residence interest,** which individuals may claim as an itemized deduction.[50] This popular home mortgage interest deduction represents a tax expenditure of over $25 billion annually. People living in areas where housing prices are high tend to have bigger mortgages and pay more mortgage interest than people living in areas where housing prices are low. It follows that the states benefiting most from the home mortgage interest deduction are Maryland (Washington, D.C., suburbs) and California, while the states that benefit the least are South Dakota and West Virginia.

Subsequent to enactment of the Tax Cuts and Jobs Act, qualified residence interest includes only interest paid on **acquisition debt.** Acquisition debt is incurred to acquire, construct, or substantially improve a personal residence and must be secured by the residence. For debt incurred after December 15, 2017, the amount treated as acquisition debt is limited to $750,000 ($375,000 for married filing separately). For debt incurred on or before this date, the limit is $1 million ($500,000 for married filing separately).

*Qualified
Residence
Interest*

In 2012, Mr. and Mrs. Early financed the construction of their home through a mortgage secured by the residence. In 2023, the average balance on this mortgage was $890,000, and the Earlys paid $44,500 interest. The mortgage qualifies as acquisition debt incurred before December 15, 2017. Because this debt is less than $1 million, the entire $44,500 is deductible qualified residence interest.

[49] §163(h)(1).
[50] §163(h)(3).

On April 19, 2023, Mr. and Mrs. Clark financed the purchase of their home through a mortgage secured by the residence. In 2023, the average balance on this mortgage was $890,000, and the Clarks paid $33,600 interest. Only $750,000 of the mortgage qualifies as acquisition debt. Consequently, only $28,315 of the interest is deductible qualified residence interest.[51]

$$\frac{\$750,000 \text{ acquisition debt}}{\$890,000 \text{ total debt}} \times \$33,600 \text{ total interest} = \$28,315$$

If a taxpayer has pre–December 15, 2017, acquisition debt and incurs additional debt after this date, the $750,000 limit on acquisition debt must be reduced (but not below zero) by the amount of the pre–December 15, 2017, acquisition debt.

Reduced Limit on Acquisition Debt

In 2004, Mr. Mill, a single taxpayer, financed the purchase of his home through a mortgage secured by the residence. In 2023, the average balance on this mortgage was $420,000, and Mr. Mill paid $19,600 interest. The mortgage qualifies as acquisition debt incurred before December 15, 2017. Because this debt is less than $1 million, the entire $19,600 is deductible qualified residence interest.

Early in 2023, Mr. Mill took out a second mortgage secured by his residence and used the funds to add a second story and a garage to the residence. The average balance of this second mortgage was $500,000, and Mr. Mill paid $16,400 interest. The $750,000 limit with respect to the second mortgage is reduced by $420,000 to $330,000. Consequently, only $10,824 of the interest on the second mortgage is deductible qualified residence interest:

$$\frac{\$330,000 \text{ acquisition debt}}{\$500,000 \text{ total debt}} \times \$16,400 \text{ total interest} = \$10,824$$

Individuals may take into account the interest paid with respect to their **principal residence** *and* one other personal residence (second home) in computing their deduction for qualified residence interest.[52] A residence can be a house, condominium, mobile home, boat, or house trailer that contains sleeping space and toilet and cooking facilities.[53]

Principal Residence and Second Home

In 2015, Kevin and Kendra Holt purchased a home in Baton Rouge, Louisiana, where they live with their son, Bart, during the school year. The Holts financed the purchase of this home with a $465,000 mortgage secured by the home. In 2016, the Holts purchased a two-bedroom houseboat moored on Lake Pontchartrain. The Holts assumed a $175,000 mortgage secured by the houseboat when they bought the boat from a friend. The Holt family spends most weekends, holidays, and the entire summer on their boat. Both mortgages qualify as acquisition debt. Because the Holts' $640,000 total acquisition debt is less than $1 million, the interest they pay on both mortgages is deductible as qualified residence interest.

Vacation Home Rental

Many people (like the Holts in the preceding example) own more than one personal residence. In addition to their principal residence, they may own a second or **vacation home** for occasional use. Owners of vacation homes often rent the property to other individuals for some limited period of time. In such cases, they can deduct the expenses of maintaining

[51] IRS Publication 936 *Home Mortgage Interest Deduction* explains the computation of average mortgage balance and provides a worksheet to calculate deductible home mortgage interest.
[52] §163(h)(4).
[53] Reg. §1.163-10T(p)(3)(ii).

the home (utilities, homeowners insurance, repairs, etc.) allocable to the rental period on Schedule E.[54] They are also allowed a depreciation deduction based on the number of days of rental usage. The aggregate of these deductions is limited to the gross rents less any home mortgage interest or property taxes allocable to the rental period.[55]

| *Vacation Home Rental* | Ms. DeSilva owns a vacation home on Cape Cod. She and her family use the home on weekends and during June and July. During August and September, she rents the home to tourists. This year, this rental activity resulted in the following: |

Rent revenue	$6,400
Home mortgage interest and real property tax for August and September	3,505
Maintenance expenses for August and September	3,760
MACRS depreciation for August and September	1,200

Ms. DeSilva reports this rental activity on Schedule E as follows:

Gross rents	$ 6,400
Interest and property tax deduction	(3,505)
	$ 2,895
Deductible maintenance expenses	(2,895)
MACRS depreciation deduction	–0–
Net rental income	–0–

Ms. DeSilva can carry the $865 disallowed maintenance expenses and the $1,200 disallowed depreciation forward and include them in future calculations of her Schedule E deductions.[56] While such deductions may decrease or even eliminate the rental revenue included in Ms. DeSilva's AGI, they can never generate a *net* rental loss. Note that Ms. Silva can deduct both the home mortgage interest and property tax allocable to the other 10 months of the year, but only as itemized deductions.

Exclusion of Gain on Sale of Principal Residence

Individuals who realize gain on the sale (or exchange) of a home can exclude the gain from gross income if the home was owned and used as the principal residence for periods aggregating at least two years during the five-year period ending on the date of sale.[57] The exclusion applies to only one sale every two years. The exclusion is limited to $250,000 for each sale. The maximum exclusion is doubled (to $500,000) for a married couple filing jointly if *either* spouse meets the two-out-of-five-year ownership requirement and *both* spouses meet the two-out-of-five-year use requirement for the residence.

| *Maximum Exclusion* | Mr. and Mrs. Sutton, who file a joint tax return, purchased a principal residence as co-tenants in 2006 and have lived there ever since. On October 6, 2022, they realized a $618,000 gain on sale of the residence. Because they met the ownership/use requirement and didn't sell another principal residence within the two-year period prior to the sale, they excluded $500,000 of the gain from their 2022 gross income. The $118,000 recognized gain was long-term capital gain taxed at 15 percent. |

---

[54] §280A(e)(1). If an owner rents a personal residence for less than 15 days during a year, the revenue is nontaxable and the related expenses are nondeductible. §280A(g).

[55] §280A(c)(5).

[56] §280A(c)(5) flush language.

[57] §121.

A person who realizes a gain on sale of a principal residence but fails to meet the ownership/use requirement or violates the two-year/one-sale rule may be eligible for a reduced exclusion. If the person sold the residence because of a change in place of employment, for health reasons, or because of unforeseen circumstances, the allowable exclusion equals the maximum exclusion multiplied by a reduction ratio. The numerator of the ratio equals the *shorter* of (1) the aggregate time period of ownership/use of the residence or (2) the time period between the earlier sale of a residence for which gain was excluded and the current sale. The denominator of the ratio is two years.

Reduced Exclusion

Refer to the facts in the preceding example. Mr. and Mrs. Sutton purchased and moved into a new principal residence on December 13, 2022. In June 2023, Mr. Sutton suffered a major heart attack. To accommodate his physical condition, the couple sold their new residence on August 10, 2023, and moved into an assisted-living apartment. The gain realized on this sale was $15,200. Mr. and Mrs. Sutton owned *and* occupied their new residence for only 240 days and sold it just 308 days after the sale of their former residence. Consequently, they fail the ownership/use requirement *and* violate the two-year/one-sale rule. However, because they sold the new residence for health reasons, they are eligible for a reduced exclusion of $164,384:

$$\$500,000 \times \frac{240 \text{ days of ownership/use}}{730 \text{ days (two years)}} = \$164,384$$

Consequently, they may exclude the entire $15,200 gain on the second sale from their 2023 gross income.

Unforeseen Circumstances

Eleven months ago, Ralph Small, a single father of two children, purchased a condominium as his family's principal residence. Last week, Ralph became engaged to Gloria Kyle, a single mother of four children. Ralph plans to sell his condominium and purchase a much larger home with enough bedrooms to accommodate the blended family. According to the IRS, Ralph's sale of his condominium before meeting the two-year use/ownership requirement is justified by the "unforeseen circumstance" of his remarriage. Consequently, Ralph is entitled to a reduced exclusion of gain recognized on the condominium sale.[58]

Conclusion

When people engage in personal transactions with no connection to any business, employment, or investment activity, they should be mindful of possible tax consequences. Of course, most personal transactions are nonevents for tax purposes. But, occasionally, a personal transaction will have significant tax consequences. If any transaction results in an economic benefit, the individual must consider the prospect that such benefit is taxable. He or she should also determine if the transaction can be structured so that part or all of the benefit escapes taxation. If a transaction involves an expense or loss, the individual might be allowed to deduct some or even the entire expense or loss. Through an awareness of this possibility, the individual can plan to maximize the deduction and minimize their tax bill.

[58] IRS Letter Ruling 200725018 (June 22, 2007).

Key Terms

acquisition debt *17-16*

American Opportunity Credit *17-12*

Coverdell education savings account *17-12*

creative assets *17-7*

education savings bonds *17-12*

federally declared disaster *17-13*

hobby loss *17-14*

imputed income from owner-occupied housing *17-16*

Lifetime Learning Credit *17-12*

principal residence *17-17*

qualified education loan *17-12*

qualified residence interest *17-16*

qualified tuition program *17-13*

vacation home *17-17*

Questions and Problems for Discussion

LO 17-1, 17-4 1. Contrast the general rule concerning the recognition of gross income from personal activities with the general rule concerning the deductibility of personal expenses and losses.

LO 17-1 2. Discuss the tax policy reasons why gifts and inheritances aren't included in gross income.

LO 17-2 3. In what way does the tax law give preferential treatment to the divorced spouse with custody of the children?

LO 17-2 4. Why are welfare payments from a state social services agency nontaxable to the recipient while state unemployment benefits are taxable?

LO 17-2 5. A basic principle of federal tax law is that a return of investment is nontaxable. Discuss the application of this principle to Social Security payments.

LO 17-3 6. People frequently sell used appliances, old furniture and clothing, books, toys, and other personal goods through an online service such as Craigslist or eBay. Should these people recognize the cash proceeds from such sales as gross income?

LO 17-4 7. If an individual purchases property insurance on business equipment, the premiums are deductible, but if that same individual purchases property insurance on his home, the premiums are nondeductible. Can you explain this inconsistent tax treatment?

LO 17-4 8. Assume that Congress amended the tax law to limit the itemized deduction for cash contributions to charity to 5 percent (rather than 60 percent) of AGI. Discuss the incidence of the tax increase represented by this expansion of the tax base.

LO 17-4 9. Last year, both the Burton family and the Awad family incurred $8,000 unreimbursed medical expenses. Mr. and Mrs. Burton deducted $6,000 of their expenses, but Mr. and Mrs. Awad were unable to deduct any of their expenses. How do you explain this apparently inequitable result?

LO 17-4 10. Wealthy individuals can reduce their taxable estate by donating property to charity either during life or at death. Discuss the reasons why an inter vivos charitable donation is the preferable option for tax planning purposes.

LO 17-5 11. Mrs. Leland's profession is dentistry, but she has quite a reputation as a master gardener. Last year, she won $990 in prize money from entering her roses in competitions and earned $800 in lecture fees from garden clubs. Should Mrs. Leland pay self-employment tax on her prize money and fees?

LO 17-5, 17-6 12. Discuss the similarities and differences in the structure of the gambling loss rule and the vacation home rule.

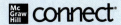 **All applicable Application Problems are available with *Connect*.**

Application Problems

For the following problems, assume the taxable year is 2023.

LO 17-1, 17-2

1. Marcy Tucker received the following items this year. Determine to what extent each item is included in her AGI.
   a. A $25,000 cash gift from her parents.
   b. A $500 cash award from the local Chamber of Commerce for her winning entry in a contest to name a new public park.
   c. $8,000 alimony from her former husband, which he paid under the terms of their 2011 divorce decree.
   d. $100,000 cash inheritance from her grandfather.

LO 17-1

2. Ms. Queen, age 21, is a full-time college student with an athletic scholarship that provides the following annual benefits:

Tuition payment	$12,800
Fees and books	3,500
Room and board	10,000

Ms. Queen works in the athletic department as a trainer for a $4,200 salary. She also receives a $6,000 annual allowance from her grandmother. Compute Ms. Queen's AGI.

LO 17-1

3. Buddy Bushey is a student at a local community college. This year, he received a $20,000 living allowance from his parents and an $11,500 academic scholarship from a civic club. This scholarship paid $8,200 for Buddy's tuition, $1,300 for his textbooks, and $2,000 for his commuting expenses. Buddy also won $5,000 playing the Texas state lottery. Compute Buddy's AGI.

LO 17-2

4. Four years ago, Lyle Mercer was injured in a railroad accident and sued the railroad for damages. The jury required the railroad to pay $600,000 compensation for his physical injuries, $150,000 for lost wages during his long recuperation, and $1,000,000 punitive damages. How much of the $1,750,000 settlement is included in Lyle's gross income?

LO 17-2

5. Ann Moore receives a $1,000 monthly payment from her former husband Bill. How much of the $12,000 annual receipt is included in Ann's AGI under each of the following assumptions?
   a. The monthly payment is alimony that Bill is required to pay under the Moores' 2017 divorce decree.
   b. The monthly payment consists of $600 alimony and $400 child support that Bill is required to pay under the Moores' 2017 divorce decree.
   c. The monthly payment is a gift from Bill, who is not legally obligated to pay anything to Ann under their divorce decree.
   d. How would your answers to parts (*a*), (*b*), and (*c*) change if the Moores' divorce decree was executed in March 2020?

LO 17-2

6. Will and Sandra Emmet were divorced this year. As part of the property settlement, Sandra transferred marketable securities to Will. Her basis in the securities was $89,800, and their FMV was $168,000. Four months after the divorce, Will sold the securities for $175,250.

       a. How much income does Will recognize on receipt of the securities from Sandra?

       b. How much gain does Will recognize on the sale of the securities?

       c. Does Sandra recognize any gain on the transfer of the securities to Will?

LO 17-1, 17-2   7. Mr. Lynch had the following items of financial support this year:

Unemployment compensation	$9,279
State welfare payments	4,060
Food stamps	1,948
Proceeds from a life insurance policy on his deceased wife	50,000

Compute Mr. Lynch's AGI.

LO 17-2   8. Mr. and Mrs. Nester had the following items of financial support this year:

Social Security benefits	$26,890
Dividends and interest	78,600
Pension from Mr. Nester's former employer	28,200
Pension from Mrs. Nester's former employer	34,700

Both pensions were paid by a qualified defined-benefit plan. Compute Mr. and Mrs. Nester's AGI.

LO 17-2   9. Mrs. Small, a widow, had the following items of financial support this year:

Social Security benefits	$13,670
Pension from her former employer	10,800
Cash gifts from her grandchildren	12,000

Mrs. Small's pension was paid by a qualified defined-benefit plan. Compute Mrs. Small's AGI.

LO 17-3, 17-5   10. Milt Payner purchased an automobile several years ago for $40,000 and has held it as a personal asset ever since. This year he sold the automobile. Compute Milt's recognized gain or loss on the sale if

       a. Milt's amount realized on sale was $28,300.

       b. Milt's amount realized on sale was $55,000. The automobile was a classic Thunderbird and was purchased by a vintage car collector in Boston.

LO 17-3, 17-5   11. Conrad Smith, a business executive, is an avid collector of vintage comic books. In February, he sold a 1938 Superman comic for $3,700 that he had purchased six years ago for $625. In December, Conrad sold a 1950 Donald Duck comic for $575 that he had purchased two years ago for $900. What is the effect of these two sales on Conrad's AGI?

LO 17-4   12. Ms. Lincoln paid $14,340 of medical expenses this year that were not reimbursed by her insurance provider. Compute the after-tax cost of these expenses assuming that

       a. Ms. Lincoln doesn't itemize deductions on her Form 1040.

       b. Ms. Lincoln itemizes deductions, her AGI is $64,400, and her marginal tax rate is 22 percent.

       c. Ms. Lincoln itemizes deductions, her AGI is $209,200, and her marginal tax rate is 32 percent.

LO 17-4   13. Mr. and Mrs. Compton paid $9,280 of medical expenses that were not reimbursed by their private insurance provider. Compute the after-tax cost of these expenses assuming that

 a. The Comptons itemize deductions on their joint tax return, their AGI is $97,000, and their marginal tax rate is 22 percent.

 b. The Comptons itemize deductions on their joint tax return, their AGI is $424,000, and their marginal tax rate is 32 percent.

 c. The Comptons take the standard deduction on their joint tax return, their AGI is $39,000, and their marginal tax rate is 12 percent.

LO 17-4   14. Mr. and Mrs. Moss have major medical and dental insurance provided by Mrs. Moss's employer. This year, they incurred the following *unreimbursed* expenses:

Routine office visits to doctors and dentists	$940
Emergency room visits	415
Disposable contact lenses for Mr. M	360
Prescription drugs	500

Compute their itemized deduction for medical expenses if AGI is

 a. $16,000.

 b. $50,000.

LO 17-4   15. Mr. Curtis paid the following taxes:

Federal income tax	$50,789
Federal gift tax	285
Federal employer payroll tax for housekeeper	920
Indiana income tax	5,710
Indiana sales tax on consumer goods and services	2,040
Local property tax on:	
Principal residence	2,800
Vacation home	1,800
Two automobiles	900

To what extent (if any) can Mr. Curtis deduct each of these payments?

LO 17-4   16. Mrs. Stuart paid the following taxes:

Local property tax on:	
20 acres of land held for investment	$ 1,500
Condominium used as principal residence	2,825
Sailboat used as vacation residence	1,975
Florida sales tax on consumer goods	3,400
Federal employee payroll tax on salary	15,200
Federal income tax	30,800

To what extent (if any) can Mrs. Stuart deduct each of these payments?

LO 17-4   17. Perry Bell paid $6,438 of state and local property and income tax this year. Compute the after-tax cost of these payments assuming

 a. Perry doesn't itemize deductions on his Form 1040.

 b. Perry itemizes deductions, has a 24 percent marginal tax rate on regular taxable income, and didn't pay AMT.

 c. Perry itemizes deductions, has a 32 percent marginal tax rate on regular taxable income, and paid $2,875 AMT.

LO 17-3   18. Mary Vale contributed a bronze statuette to a local museum. Mary received the statuette as a gift from her grandmother 35 years ago, and her tax basis was only $200. However, the statue's appraised fair market value at date of contribution was $8,500. Compute Mary's tax savings from the contribution assuming

    a. Mary doesn't itemize deductions on her Form 1040.

    b. Mary itemizes deductions and has a 24 percent marginal tax rate.

    c. Mary itemizes deductions and has a 37 percent marginal tax rate.

LO 17-4   19. Diane Bauman, a professional artist with AGI in excess of $75,000, made the following donations. Determine to what extent each donation is deductible on her Schedule A.

    a. $2,000 cash to the First Methodist Church of Chicago.

    b. $50 cash to a homeless person.

    c. One of Diane's own oil paintings to the local chapter of Meals on Wheels, a tax-exempt charity. The charity sold the painting for $3,900 at a silent auction.

    d. $10,000 cash to the Democratic political party.

    e. Used household furniture to the Salvation Army. Diane's original cost was $6,800, and the furniture was reasonably worth $1,200.

LO 17-4   20. Ms. Prince wants to create a scholarship in honor of her parents at the law school from which she received her degree. She could endow the scholarship with $500,000 cash or with $500,000 worth of marketable securities with a cost basis of $318,000. If her AGI is $3.8 million, compare the after-tax cost of the two endowment options.

LO 17-4, 17-5   21. Mr. and Mrs. Remy have the following *allowable* itemized deductions this year:

Medical expenses	$2,310
State and local taxes	4,019
Casualty loss	8,000
Charitable contributions	2,500

    Determine the effect on the amount of each deduction if the Remys engage in a transaction generating $20,000 additional AGI on this year's Form 1040.

LO 17-4, 17-6   22. Mr. Tolen made the following interest payments. Determine the extent to which he can deduct each payment on his Form 1040.

    a. $4,600 on credit card debt.

    b. $14,100 on a $210,000 mortgage secured by his vacation home in Key West. Mr. Tolen incurred the mortgage to purchase this second home.

    c. $1,300 on a $22,000 unsecured loan from a credit union. Mr. Tolen used the loan proceeds to add a boat dock to his Key West home.

    d. $3,700 on a $100,000 unsecured loan from his mother-in-law. Mr. Tolen used the loan proceeds as working capital for his business as an independent insurance agent.

    e. $2,400 on a $50,000 loan from a bank. Mr. Tolen used the loan proceeds to purchase an interest in Farlee Limited Partnership, which is his only investment asset. This year, Mr. Tolen was allocated a $790 ordinary loss from the partnership.

    f. $800 in a $35,000 loan from a car dealership that financed the purchase of Mr. Tolen's new family automobile.

LO 17-4, 17-6   23. Mrs. Carr made the following interest payments. Determine the extent to which she can deduct each payment on her Form 1040.

    a. $21,000 on a $280,000 mortgage incurred to construct (and secured by) her personal residence.

b. $3,000 on a $34,000 second mortgage secured by her personal residence. Mrs. Carr used the proceeds to pay off her credit card debt.

c. $2,290 on credit card debt.

d. $15,000 on a $200,000 bank loan incurred to purchase inventory for her sole proprietorship.

e. $1,610 on a bank loan incurred to purchase a car for her son.

f. $1,750 on a bank loan incurred to purchase mutual fund shares that generated $1,900 dividend income this year.

LO 17-5 24. Mr. and Mrs. Marcum live in Southern California in an area devastated by wildfires that the president designated a federally declared disaster. Because of fire damage, the Marcums had to replace the roof of their home at a cost of $55,000. Their homeowners insurance reimbursed them for only $32,500 of the cost. The Marcums' $22,500 unreimbursed loss was their only casualty loss this year. Compute their deductible casualty loss if their AGI is

a. $163,000.

b. $380,000.

LO 17-5 25. Refer to the preceding problem. How would your answers change if the fire that damaged the Marcums' roof was attributable to faulty electrical wiring in their attic?

LO 17-5 26. Mr. Monk is a self-employed computer consultant who earns more than $100,000 each year. He also is an enthusiastic artist. This year, he spent $4,900 on oil paints, canvasses, supplies, and lessons at a local studio. Mr. Monk made several trips to the National Gallery in Washington, D.C., to attend lectures on painting technique. His total travel costs were $3,350. Compute the effect of Mr. Monk's painting revenue and expenses on his AGI under each of the following assumptions:

a. Mr. Monk earned $13,290 from sales of his paintings. This was the sixth consecutive year that the painting activity generated a profit.

b. Mr. Monk earned $2,000 from sales of his paintings. The painting activity has never generated a profit.

c. Mr. Monk earned $2,000 from sales of his paintings. The painting activity also generated a net loss four years ago but was profitable in each of the past three years.

LO 17-5 27. Sandy Assam enjoys betting on horse and dog races. This year, she won $4,308 and lost $6,735 on her gambling activities. If Sandy's marginal tax rate is 24 percent, compute the after-tax cost of her gambling assuming that

a. She does itemize deductions.

b. She doesn't itemize deductions.

LO 17-6 28. Mr. and Mrs. Udall live in a home that Mrs. Udall inherited from her parents. This year, the Udalls took out a first mortgage secured by the home. Determine their itemized deduction for interest paid on the mortgage in each of the following cases:

a. The interest payment was $2,775, the average balance of the mortgage was $60,000, and the Udalls used the borrowed funds to pay for their daughter's wedding and honeymoon.

b. The interest payment was $10,506, the average balance of the mortgage was $162,000, and the Udalls used the borrowed funds to add a new screened porch to their home.

LO 17-6   29. Mr. and Mrs. Kim, married filing jointly, own a principal residence and a vacation home. Each residence is subject to a mortgage that qualifies as acquisition debt, and both mortgages were incurred before December 15, 2017. This year, the mortgage holders provided the following information:

	Mortgage Interest Paid	Average Balance of Mortgage
Principal residence	$38,000	$941,800
Vacation home	22,100	340,000

Compute Mr. and Mrs. Kim's qualified residence interest.

LO 17-6   30. Ms. Imo, who is single, purchased her first home in 1991 for $85,000 and sold it in May 2000 for $178,500. She purchased her second home in July 2000 for $385,000 and sold it this year for $700,000.

a. Compute Ms. Imo's taxable gain on the 2000 sale and on this year's sale.

b. Compute the income tax and Medicare contribution tax on her gain this year if her preferential rate on long-term capital gain is 20 percent.

LO 17-4, 17-6   31. Mr. and Mrs. Kilo, married filing jointly, purchased their first home in 2003 for $240,000. They sold this home in 2007 for $210,000. They purchased their second home in 2008 for $435,000 and sold it this year for $1,150,000.

a. Did the Kilos recognize a deductible loss on the 2007 sale of their first home?

b. Compute the income tax and Medicare contribution tax on the Kilos' gain on the sale of their home this year if their preferential rate on long-term capital gain is 20 percent.

LO 17-6   32. On January 12, 2021, Mr. and Mrs. Nixon moved out of their old residence (where they had lived for 22 years) and into a new residence purchased nine days earlier on January 3. They finally sold their old residence on June 7, 2021, for a $278,000 realized gain.

a. How much gain did they recognize on the sale of their old residence?

b. On February 26, 2023, Mr. and Mrs. Nixon sold their new residence for a $48,000 realized gain and moved into a nearby house because it had a swimming pool. How much gain would they recognize?

c. How much gain would they recognize if they sold the new residence because Mrs. Nixon accepted a job in a different state and the family had to relocate?

LO 17-6   33. Mrs. Gomez, a widow, paid $148,000 for her home 20 years ago. She recently sold this home and moved in with her son on a permanent basis. Compute Mrs. Gomez's recognized gain or loss on the sale assuming that her amount realized was

a. $140,000.

b. $262,500.

c. $467,000.

Issue Recognition Problems

Identify the tax issue or issues suggested by the following situations and state each issue in the form of a question.

LO 17-1   1. A local radio station offers a $5,000 reward for information leading to the arrest of vandals and other petty criminals. Mr. Jenks received the reward for identifying three people who spray-painted graffiti on a public building.

LO 17-1   2. Mr. Saul, a real estate broker, just negotiated the sale of a home for a wealthy client. Two days after the sale closed, he received a beautiful leather briefcase from the client with a card reading: "In grateful appreciation of your efforts over the past year."

LO 17-1   3. Mr. Tinsler was a contestant on a game show and won a vacuum cleaner with a retail price of $365. Three months later, he sold the unused appliance in a garage sale for $275.

LO 17-1   4. Ms. Lewis, a bartender and aspiring actress, won a statewide beauty pageant and was awarded a $15,000 cash scholarship to further her education and career goals. She used the money to pay for private acting lessons.

LO 17-1   5. On a recent scuba dive, Mr. Underhill located a shipwreck and recovered a Spanish sword inlaid with precious stones. The sword's appraised value is $11,500. Mr. Underhill mounted the sword over his fireplace.

LO 17-2   6. The pilots of Skyway Airlines have been on strike for four months. Ms. Biggs received a $2,700 benefit from her union, the Airline Pilots Association International. The union funded the benefits for Skyway pilots through a solicitation from union members flying for other airlines.

LO 17-2   7. Mrs. Overton, age 60, won an age discrimination suit against her former employer. The court awarded her $100,000 in damages for mental anguish and $200,000 for the violation of her civil rights.

LO 17-4   8. Mrs. Newton, who is a self-employed author, paid $3,200 for a new computer system. She uses the system to write her books, and her two children use it for their schoolwork and video games.

LO 17-4   9. Mr. Tahoma, who is a member of the Navajo tribe of Native Americans, developed severe arthritis this year. He paid $1,100 to a tribal medicine man who performed a series of traditional Navajo healing ceremonies called "sings."

LO 17-4   10. Mr. Sheraton suffers from severe arthritis. His physician advised him to swim for at least one hour every day in a heated pool. Because such a facility is not conveniently located in his area, he paid $25,000 to build a heated lap pool in his backyard.

LO 17-4   11. Mr. Ruskin, a CPA who charges $150 per hour for his professional services, keeps the financial records for a local charity. Although he spends at least 10 hours each month at this task, he doesn't charge the charity a fee for his services.

LO 17-4   12. Mr. and Mrs. Fitch bought $500 worth of Girl Scout cookies from their godchild. Because they don't eat sweets, they gave away every box to various friends and family members.

LO 17-5, 17-6   13. Mr. Dix borrowed $600,000 to purchase 162 acres of undeveloped land and secured the debt with the land. He converted a three-room log cabin on the land to his principal residence. This year, he paid $39,910 interest on the mortgage.

LO 17-6   14. For the past 10 years, Mr. Bianco lived on his sailboat for five months of the year and spent the other seven months living in his daughter's home. This year, he realized a $35,200 gain on sale of the boat and moved into his own apartment.

LO 17-6   15. Ms. Seagram paid $155,000 for a house that she occupied as her principal residence until February 1, when she moved out and converted the house to rental property. The appraised FMV of the house was $140,000. She leased the house to tenants who purchased it on November 18. Her realized loss on the sale was $24,700, computed as follows:

Amount realized		$125,000
Original cost basis	$155,000	
MACRS depreciation during rental period	(5,300)	
Adjusted basis		(149,700)
		$ (24,700)

LO 17-6   16. Mr. and Mrs. Ayala purchased their home one year ago. This year, a local government attempted to seize the home because the former residents had failed to pay their property taxes for 12 years. Mr. and Mrs. Ayala paid $1,700 to an attorney who resolved the dispute in their favor.

Research Problems

LO 17-1   1. Eighteen months ago, Barry Shelton won a $2 million Maryland state lottery jackpot and chose to receive it as $120,000 annual annuity for the rest of his life. This year his brothers persuaded him to sell the annuity to a financial institution for $1.79 million and invest the sales proceeds in a new family business. How much gain did Barry recognize on sale of his annuity, and is it ordinary income or long-term capital gain?

LO 17-4   2. Mr. Clark Besson is undergoing extensive chemotherapy treatment for cancer. His oncologist recommended that he ingest marijuana to relieve the painful side effects. However, possession or use of marijuana is illegal in Mr. Besson's state of residence. Therefore, he makes a weekly trip to a neighboring state in which the medically prescribed use of marijuana is legal. Since beginning his treatment, he has spent $2,730 to buy marijuana. Is this a deductible medical expense?

LO 17-4   3. Mr. and Mrs. Lukert own a sole proprietorship and have no other source of income. This year, they paid $11,674 Massachusetts income tax, all of which is attributable to their business profit. Can they deduct their state income tax as a business expense on Schedule C, or must they report it as an itemized deduction on Schedule A?

LO 17-6   4. Betsy and Larry Lorch own and reside in an apartment in midtown Manhattan. They left the city to avoid the uproar surrounding New Year's Eve and spent a long holiday with Larry's parents in upstate New York. They sublet their apartment to a German couple who wanted to join the throng in Times Square. They paid the Lorches $500 per night ($11,000 total) to stay in the apartment from December 21 through January 11. What are the tax consequences of this rental arrangement?

LO 17-6   5. Howard Wilson, a single individual, sold his principal residence in Cleveland eight months ago and excluded his entire $148,000 gain on the sale from gross income. He purchased and moved into a new home in a suburb of Chicago. Shortly thereafter, Howard's 20-year-old son moved in with him. The son was on probation from a prison sentence for drug dealing and assault with a deadly weapon. Howard's neighbors learned about the son's criminal record and have organized protests against the son's presence in the community. Howard has received several verbal and written threats, and his house has been spray-painted with graffiti. The atmosphere has become so hostile that Howard has decided to sell his new home and relocate in a different city. Will he be eligible to exclude any of his gain on this second sale?

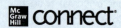 **All applicable Tax Planning Cases are available with *Connect*.**

Tax Planning Cases

LO 17-2   1. Ms. French is a successful attorney in the 37 percent marginal tax bracket. During the past several years, she provided legal services to her great-uncle, who is 78 years old and in failing health. Although the uncle offered to pay for her work, she refused any compensation, requesting instead that her uncle remember her appropriately in his will. The uncle recently added a codicil providing for a $250,000 cash bequest to Ms. French. The remainder of his estate will pass to his two children and seven grandchildren.

        a. What tax planning objective may Ms. French have accomplished through her request of her uncle?

        b. Can you identify both the opportunity cost and the risk inherent in her plan?

LO 17-4

2. Mr. and Mrs. Isaacs, ages 68 and 66, always claim the standard deduction on their joint return. They own a local restaurant, the Shoreline Grill, as a sole proprietorship. They are both graduates of State University and make regular donations to their alma mater. Their method for doing so is a bit unusual. At the beginning of each State University home football game, the public address system informs the crowd that the Shoreline Grill will contribute $50 to the athletic scholarship fund for every first down the home team makes. As a result of this commitment, Mr. and Mrs. Isaacs contributed $6,950 to State University this year. What tax planning objective may they have accomplished by structuring their donation in this manner?

LO 17-6

3. Mr. Massey, who is in the 32 percent marginal tax bracket and itemizes deductions, recently inherited $30,000. He is considering three alternative uses for this windfall:

- He could buy shares in a mutual bond fund paying 6 percent interest a year.
- He could pay off a $30,000 personal debt to a local bank on which he pays $2,350 interest each year.
- He could pay off $30,000 of the mortgage incurred to buy his home. This principal repayment would decrease his annual home mortgage interest expense by $2,900.

Compute the annual increase in Mr. Massey's after-tax cash flow for each of these three alternatives. Which alternative would you recommend and why?

Comprehensive Problems for Part Five

1. Blake and Valerie Meyer (both age 30) are married with one dependent child (age 5). On the basis of the following information, compute the Meyers' 2023 federal income tax (including any AMT) on their joint return.

- Blake's gross salary from his corporate employer was $70,000, and his Section 401(k) contribution was $6,300.
- Valerie's salary from GuiTech, an S corporation, was $29,400.
- Valerie owns 16 percent of GuiTech's outstanding stock. Her pro rata share of GuiTech's ordinary business income was $13,790, her pro rata share of GuiTech's net loss from rental real estate was $8,100, and she received a $7,000 cash distribution from GuiTech. The ordinary income from GuiTech is qualified business income.
- Blake received a $15,000 cash gift from his grandmother.
- Valerie won $6,400 in the Maryland state lottery.
- The Meyers received a distribution from their investment in Pawnee Mutual Fund that consisted of a $712 qualifying dividend and a $3,020 long-term capital gain.
- Blake paid $12,000 alimony to a former spouse under a divorce agreement executed in 2011.
- The Meyers paid $17,200 home mortgage interest on acquisition debt and $2,780 property tax on their personal residence.
- The Meyers paid $7,000 state income tax and $4,200 state and local sales tax.
- Valerie contributed $1,945 to the First Baptist Church.

2. Mrs. Cora Yank (age 42) is divorced and has full custody of her 10-year-old son, William. From the following information, compute Mrs. Yank's 2023 federal income

tax (including any AMT) and the amount due with her Form 1040 *or* the refund she should receive.

- Mrs. Yank works as a medical technician in a Chicago hospital. Her salary was $38,400, from which her employer withheld $1,045 federal income tax and $2,938 employee FICA tax.

- Several years ago, Mrs. Yank was seriously injured in a traffic accident caused by another driver's negligence. This year, she received a $25,000 settlement from the driver's insurance company: $20,000 as compensation for her physical injuries and $5,000 for lost wages during her convalescent period. Because she was unable to work for the first seven weeks of the year, she collected $1,400 unemployment compensation from the state of Illinois.

- Mrs. Yank earned $629 interest on a savings account. She contributed $800 to a traditional IRA. She is not an active participant in any other qualified retirement plan.

- Mrs. Yank paid $10,800 rent on the apartment in which she and William live. She received $1,600 alimony and $2,350 child support from her former husband under a divorce agreement executed in 2015.

- Mrs. Yank is covered under her employer's medical reimbursement plan. However, this year's medical bills exceeded her reimbursement limit by $1,630.

- Mrs. Yank paid $1,062 income tax to Illinois.

- Mrs. Yank spent $470 on hospital shoes and uniforms. Her employer didn't reimburse her for this expense.

- Mrs. Yank paid $1,300 for after-school child care for William.

3. Tom and Allie Benson (ages 53 and 46) are residents of Fort Worth, Texas, and file a joint federal income tax return. They provide the entire support for their two children, ages 19 and 17. On the basis of the following information, compute Mr. and Mrs. Benson's 2023 federal income tax (including any AMT), self-employment tax, and Medicare contribution tax, and the amount due with their Form 1040 *or* the refund they should receive.

- Mr. Benson is an attorney who practices in partnership with 18 other attorneys. His ordinary income was $268,300, and his net earnings from self-employment were $247,775 (92.35 percent of $268,300). The ordinary income from the partnership is qualified business income for purposes of the QBI deduction.

- The Bensons made estimated tax payments totaling $45,000 to the IRS and a $30,000 contribution to the qualified Keogh plan maintained by the partnership.

- The Bensons earned $10,365 interest income and $28,060 qualified dividend income from their investment portfolio. They also received a $4,218 long-term capital gain distribution from a mutual fund. They have a $9,723 long-term capital loss carryforward from last year.

- The Bensons received a Schedule K-1 from an S corporation in which they own 6 percent of the stock. Their share of the corporation's business loss was $4,930. The S corporation operates a mink farm in Maine.

- Mrs. Benson received a $50,000 cash inheritance from her great-aunt.

- The Bensons moved from San Antonio to Fort Worth in April so that Mr. Benson could manage the Fort Worth office. The cost of moving their household goods was $11,260. The law firm reimbursed Mr. Benson for $10,000 of this expense.

- The Bensons paid $33,890 interest on a $573,000 first mortgage and $6,120 interest on a $90,000 second mortgage on their personal residence. They incurred the first mortgage to buy the home and the second mortgage to buy new furniture.
- The Bensons paid $12,400 real property tax on their home and $2,920 for home-owners insurance.
- Mrs. Benson underwent extensive dental work that cost $28,900, only $15,000 of which was reimbursed under the Bensons' health insurance plan. They had no other unreimbursed medical expenses.
- The Bensons made $21,980 cash donations to various qualified charities.
- The Bensons paid $7,911 state and local sales tax. (Texas has no individual income tax.)
- The Bensons paid $3,350 to the CPA who prepared their Form 1040.

Appendix 17–A

Social Security Worksheet (Adapted from IRS Publication 915)

1. Social Security benefits received	_____	1. Social Security benefits received	14,400
2. One-half of line 1	_____	2. One-half of line 1	7,200
3. Adjusted gross income (AGI) (without Social Security benefits)	_____	3. Adjusted gross income (AGI) (without Social Security benefits)	43,000
4. Tax-exempt interest income	_____	4. Tax-exempt interest income	600
5. Add lines 2, 3, and 4	_____	5. Add lines 2, 3, and 4	50,800
6. Enter:	_____	6. Enter:	32,000
$32,000 (married filing jointly)		$32,000 (married filing jointly)	
$25,000 (single or head of household)		$25,000 (single or head of household)	
-0- (married filing separately)*		-0- (married filing separately)*	
7. Subtract line 6 from line 5	_____	7. Subtract line 6 from line 5	18,800

If line 7 is zero or less, the Social Security benefits are nontaxable. / **If line 7 is zero or less, the Social Security benefits are nontaxable.**

8. Enter:	_____	8. Enter:	12,000
$12,000 (married filing jointly)		$12,000 (married filing jointly)	
$9,000 (single or head of household)		$9,000 (single or head of household)	
-0- (married filing separately)		-0- (married filing separately)	
9. Subtract line 8 from line 7. If zero or less, enter zero	_____	9. Subtract line 8 from line 7. If zero or less, enter zero	6,800
10. Enter the lesser of line 7 or line 8	_____	10. Enter the lesser of line 7 or line 8	12,000
11. Enter one-half of line 10	_____	11. Enter one-half of line 10	6,000
12. Enter the lesser of line 2 or line 11	_____	12. Enter the lesser of line 2 or line 11	6,000
13. Multiply line 9 by 85 percent	_____	13. Multiply line 9 by 85 percent	5,780
14. Add line 12 and line 13	_____	14. Add line 12 and line 13	11,780
15. Multiply line 1 by 85 percent	_____	15. Multiply line 1 by 85 percent	12,240
16. Enter the lesser of line 14 or line 15	_____	16. Enter the lesser of line 14 or line 15	11,780

Line 16 is the taxable portion of the Social Security benefits. / **Line 16 is the taxable portion of the Social Security benefits.**

*Married individuals filing separate returns who live apart at all times during the year are considered single for purposes of this computation.

Example	Mr. and Mrs. PB received $14,400 Social Security benefits this year. The AGI on their joint return before considering these benefits was $43,000, and they received $600 tax-exempt interest. The taxable portion of their Social Security benefits is $11,780.

The Tax Compliance Process

Chapter Eighteen

The Tax Compliance Process

Learning Objectives

After studying this chapter, you should be able to:

LO 18-1. Determine the filing date and extended filing date for income tax returns.

LO 18-2. Compute a late-filing and late-payment penalty.

LO 18-3. Describe the statute of limitations for a tax return.

LO 18-4. Identify the three types of IRS audits.

LO 18-5. Summarize the noncompliance penalties that can be imposed on taxpayers and tax return preparers.

LO 18-6. Identify the three judicial levels in the tax litigation process.

LO 18-7. Discuss the various IRS collection procedures.

LO 18-8. Explain the purpose of the innocent spouse rule.

The federal income, payroll, self-employment, and transfer taxes are all self-assessed taxes. Each person who is required to pay or collect any of these taxes must compute the amount of tax due, file the proper return, and maintain adequate records supporting the calculations presented on the return.[1] As a practical matter, the tax laws are sufficiently complex that the majority of taxpayers engage a tax practitioner to assist in the preparation of their returns. Nevertheless, even taxpayers who rely entirely on professional help are responsible for complying with the law and must bear the consequences of failure to comply.

This final chapter is an overview of the federal tax compliance system. The procedural rules for payment of tax and filing of income tax returns and the IRS's audit process are explained. Your rights as a taxpayer in dealing with the IRS, as well as the penalties the IRS may impose, are described. This chapter ends with a discussion of the judicial process by which both individuals and corporations may challenge the outcome of an IRS audit in federal court.

[1] §6001 and §6011.

FILING AND PAYMENT REQUIREMENTS

LO 18-1
Determine the filing date and extended filing date for income tax returns.

Tax Talk
Due to the COVID pandemic, the IRS issued relief to the filing and payment deadlines by granting an automatic extension to July 15, 2020, for any income tax return or any payment of income tax, self-employment tax, or estimated tax due on April 15, 2020. This blanket exception to the filing and payment deadlines was limited to forms and payments specified under Notice 2020-18, IRB 2020-15, March 23, 2020.

Most individuals report income on the basis of a calendar year and are required to file their Form 1040 for the current year by April 15 of the following year. The few individuals who have adopted a fiscal year must file their returns by the 15th day of the fourth month following the close of the year. Similarly, the Form 1120 deadline for corporations reporting income on a calendar year-basis is the 15th day of the fourth month following the close of the year.[2] However, corporations with a fiscal year ending June 30, as well as Partnerships (Form 1065) and S-Corporation (1120-S), must file their returns by the 15th day of the *third* month (September 15) following the close of the year.[3] If the 15th day of the relevant month is a Saturday, Sunday, or legal holiday, the filing date is moved to the next succeeding day that is not a weekend or a holiday.[4] For example, the filing date for calendar year 2017 income tax returns was Tuesday, April 17, 2018, because Monday was Emancipation Day, a legal holiday in the District of Columbia.

As we discussed in earlier chapters, individuals and corporations must pay their income tax periodically over the course of the year, either in the form of withholding (individuals) or quarterly estimated tax payments. Taxpayers who fail to pay their total tax liability during the year must pay the balance due by the filing date of the return for the year.[5]

Both individual and corporate taxpayers may apply for a six-month extension of time to file their income tax return by submitting an application for extension with the IRS by the due date of the return.[6] The extensions are automatic; taxpayers do not have to explain to the IRS why they need additional time to file. An automatic extension of time for filing a return doesn't extend the time for payment of any tax due. Consequently, taxpayers are required to pay any estimated balance of tax due by the *unextended* filing date of the return.

Application for Extension	On April 8, 2023, Laurie Crawford submitted an application to extend the 2022 Form 1040 filing date from April 15 to October 15, 2023. Laurie's estimated 2022 tax liability was $62,100. Withholding for 2022 totaled $57,000. Consequently, Laurie paid the $5,100 estimated balance of tax due with the extension application.

Interest Payments

Taxpayers who pay any amount of income tax after the required payment date are charged interest by the federal government. The interest is based on the number of days from the required payment date to the actual payment date.[7] The annual interest rate, referred to as the *underpayment rate,* equals the federal short-term rate plus three percentage points. Interest is compounded daily, and the federal rate is adjusted quarterly.[8]

---

[2] §6072(a). Partnerships and S corporations must file their returns by the 15th day of the fourth month following the close of the year. §6072(b).

[3] Reg. §1.6072-2T(a)(2).

[4] §7503.

[5] §6151(a).

[6] §6081. Corporations with a taxable year ending December 31 (calendar year) are allowed only a five-month automatic filing extension; corporations with a fiscal year ending June 30 are allowed a seven-month automatic filing extension.

[7] §6601(a).

[8] §6621(a)(2) and §6622. The underpayment rate for corporate underpayments exceeding $100,000 equals the federal short-term rate plus five percentage points. §6621(c).

Interest Charge	On March 29, 2023, Maria Benavides applied for an automatic six-month extension of time to file a 2022 Form 1040. Maria's 2022 withholding totaled $23,750. Although, Maria's estimated 2022 tax liability was only $23,000. Consequently, Maria did not pay additional tax with the extension application. Maria filed a completed Form 1040 on June 18, 2023. The correct tax liability reported on the return was $24,400, so Maria paid the $650 balance of tax due with the return. Because Maria failed to pay the total 2022 tax by April 15, 2023, the IRS will send a bill for interest on the $650 late payment. The interest period runs from April 16 through June 18. If the federal short-term rate during this period was 1 percent, the IRS will compute the interest charge at a 4 percent annual rate compounded daily.

Millions of taxpayers overpay their annual income tax in the form of excess withholding or estimated tax payments. These taxpayers report the overpayment on their tax returns and request a refund from the government. The IRS is not required to pay interest on any income tax overpayment refunded within 45 days after the filing date of the return.[9] As a result, the millions of taxpayers who receive their refunds within this grace period do not earn interest. In the rare case when the IRS fails to mail a refund check on a timely basis, the government must pay interest to the taxpayer.

The annual overpayment rate for individuals equals the federal short-term rate plus 3 percent, which is the same as the underpayment rate. The overpayment rate for corporations depends on the size of the overpayment. If the corporate overpayment is $10,000 or less, the interest rate equals the short-term rate plus 2 percent. If the overpayment exceeds $10,000, the interest rate equals the short-term rate plus only one-half percent.[10]

Interest on Refunds	Refer to the previous example in which Maria Benavides filed a 2022 Form 1040 on June 18, 2023. Now assume that Maria's correct tax liability reported on the return was only $21,000. Consequently, Maria overpaid 2022 tax by $2,750 ($23,750 withholding − $21,000 tax liability). If the IRS refunds this overpayment within 45 days after June 18, 2023, Maria will not receive interest from the government. However, if the refund is unusually delayed, Maria will receive the refund plus interest.

Late-Filing and Late-Payment Penalty

LO 18-2
Compute a late-filing and late-payment penalty.

A taxpayer who fails to file an income tax return by the required due date and cannot provide a good excuse for such failure must pay a **late-filing and late-payment penalty.**[11] This penalty equals 5 percent of the balance of tax due with the return for each month (or portion thereof) that the return is delinquent.

Late-Filing and Late-Payment Penalty	Mr. Toomey failed to request an extension of time to file a 2022 return and delayed filing until July 29, 2022. The return reported a $45,890 tax liability and $42,000 tax withheld by Mr. Toomey's employer. Mr. Toomey enclosed a check for the $3,890 balance due with the late return. Because the balance due was not paid by April 15, 2023, the IRS charged interest on $3,890 from April 16 through July 29. Because the return was delinquent, the IRS also assessed a $778 late-filing and late-payment penalty ($3,890 × 5% for three full months and a portion of a fourth month). The IRS may waive this penalty (but not the interest) if Mr. Toomey can show reasonable cause for filing late.

[9] §6611(e)(1). The filing date is the later of the statutory filing date or the date the return is actually filed.
[10] §6611(a) and §6621(a)(1).
[11] §6651. For 2021, the *minimum* penalty for failure to file an income tax return within 60 days of the filing date is the *lesser* of $435 or 100 percent of the balance of tax due with the return.

The 5 percent penalty runs for only five months (until the penalty equals 25 percent of the balance due). After five months, the penalty rate drops to one-half percent of the balance due. This reduced penalty can run for an additional 45 months.

Reduced Penalty	Ms. Rojas filed an unextended 2022 Form 1040 on November 22, 2023, and had no reasonable cause for the delinquency. The return showed a $9,094 balance of tax due, which Ms. Rojas paid with the return. The IRS charged Ms. Rojas interest on $9,094 from April 16 through November 22 and assessed a $2,410 late-filing and late-payment penalty:

Penalty for April 16–September 15	
$9,094 × 5% for five months	$2,274
Penalty for September 16–November 22	
$9,094 × .5% for three months	136
Total penalty	$2,410

Reasonable Cause for a Delinquent Return?	David McMahan, an investment broker, engaged James Russell, a tax attorney, to file his individual income tax return. Mr. Russell told his client that he would file the necessary paperwork to extend the filing date of the return. Months later, Mr. McMahan discovered that his attorney had neglected to file the extension request. The IRS assessed a $141,028 late-filing and late-payment penalty, which he contested in court. Mr. McMahan argued that his reliance on a tax professional to file an extension request was reasonable cause for the delinquent return. The court was not persuaded by his argument, observing that a "taxpayer has an affirmative nondelegable duty to ensure that the appropriate forms—whether a tax return or an extension request—are actually filed by the statutory deadline." Consequently, Mr. McMahan was liable for the penalty.[12]

One feature of the late-filing penalty deserves emphasis. The penalty is based on the balance of tax due with a delinquent return. If a taxpayer overpays tax, the return will show a refund due instead of a balance due. In this case, the government cannot assess a penalty if such return is filed after the due date. Of course, for as long as the return is delinquent, the government is enjoying an interest-free loan from the taxpayer that it doesn't repay until the taxpayer finally decides to file.[13]

Poor Money Management	Donna Tao finally filed a 2021 Form 1040 on May 9, 2023. The return showed that Donna's employer withheld $1,640 income tax. However, Donna's 2021 tax liability was only $930. Within 45 days after filing this return, Donna received a $710 refund of 2021 income tax. Even though the return was delinquent, Donna was not charged a late-filing penalty. Despite the belated refund, Donna did not receive any interest from the government.

Return Processing

Each year more than 260 million tax returns are filed with the IRS by individuals, corporations, partnerships, and fiduciaries. These returns pour into the five IRS service centers

---

[12] *McMahan* v. *Commissioner*, 114 F.3d 366 (CA-2, 1997).

[13] Generally, a taxpayer must file a return claiming an income tax refund within two years from the date the tax was paid. Withheld tax and estimated tax payments are deemed paid on the unextended required filing date for the return. After the two-year filing period, the taxpayer is no longer entitled to any refund. §6511(a) and §6513(b).

Tax Talk

Computer matching of Form W-2s and 1099s results in a 99 percent compliance rate for taxpayers who must report the income documented on these information returns.

located throughout the country. The service centers are information-processing facilities where each return is checked for mathematical accuracy and logged into the IRS's computer system. This system cross-checks each return against information returns filed with respect to the taxpayer, such as Form W-2s filed by employers; Form 1099s filed by payers of interest, dividend, rents, or other types of income; and Schedule K-1s filed by partnerships and S corporations. If a return reflects a math error or a discrepancy with an information return, the service center mails a letter to the taxpayer explaining the problem and calculating the additional tax or refund. The service centers are responsible for collecting tax payments and authorizing tax refunds for the U.S. Treasury.

Statute of Limitations

LO 18-3
Describe the statute of limitations for a tax return.

Many taxpayers place unjustified significance on the fact that the government received their tax payment or issued a tax refund. While these events prove that their tax return was processed, they don't mean that the IRS has accepted the accuracy of the return. A **statute of limitations** gives the IRS three years from the later of the statutory filing date (April 15 for calendar year individuals) or the date on which the return was actually filed to examine that return for mistakes and to assess additional tax.[14]

Three-Year Statute of Limitations	Mr. and Mrs. Epps filed their 2022 Form 1040 on March 5, 2023. The IRS has until April 15, 2026, to audit this return and assess any additional tax. Mr. Procter requested an extension of time to file a 2022 return and actually filed the return on August 2, 2023. In his case, the IRS has until August 2, 2026, to audit the return and assess additional tax.

If a taxpayer files a return and omits an amount of gross income exceeding 25 percent of the gross income reported on the return, the normal three-year statute of limitations is extended to six years.

Extended Statute of Limitations	Ms. Yang, a self-employed consultant, failed to include a $13,200 business receipt in the income reported on a 2022 return filed on February 8, 2023. The gross income on the return was $52,000, and the omitted income was more than 25 percent of this income: $13,200 > $13,000 ($52,000 gross income × 25%) Consequently, Ms. Yang's return remains open until April 15, 2029.

If the IRS determines that a return is fraudulent (a concept discussed later in this chapter), the return remains open (subject to audit) indefinitely.

No Statute of Limitations	Dr. Kohan practiced as a dentist in New York. Mr. Kohan failed to report over $760,000 of payments received from patients on the appropriate 2009 and 2010 income tax returns. The IRS audited these returns and did not assess tax deficiencies until 2018. Dr. Kohan argued that the assessments of additional tax for 2009 and 2010 were barred by the three-year statute of limitations. The Tax Court concluded that the assessments were not time-barred because Dr. Kohan's underpayments of tax were due to fraud.[15]

---

[14] §6501.
[15] *Kohan,* T.C. Memo 2019-85.

Because of the possibility of audit, taxpayers should keep all supporting paperwork such as receipts and proof of payment for at least three years after the return is filed. Records substantiating the tax basis of property, any legal documents containing tax information (closing statement on a property sale, divorce decree, etc.), and a copy of the return should be retained permanently.

THE AUDIT PROCESS

LO 18-4
Identify the three types of IRS audits.

The IRS selects corporate tax returns for audit primarily on the basis of the size of the business, measured in terms of taxable income and net worth as reported on Form 1120. Individual returns are usually selected by a highly classified computer program that analyzes the contents of each return and assigns a **discriminate inventory function (DIF) score.** This score theoretically measures the return's potential for generating additional tax revenue on audit. The higher the score, the greater the likelihood that the return contains an error causing an understatement of tax. Obviously, returns with the highest DIF scores are chosen for examination. Although the details of the DIF selection process are a closely guarded secret, tax practitioners assume that highly speculative investment activities, unusually large itemized deductions, and deductions that are prone to manipulation or abuse (travel and entertainment expenses, nonbusiness bad debts, losses generated by a secondary business, etc.) inflate DIF scores. Similarly, high-income returns are much more likely to be selected for audit than returns reflecting modest incomes.

Audit Coverage

According to the 2021 IRS Data Book, the IRS examined just under 158 million individual income tax returns filed for 2019, an average audit coverage rate of 0.2 percent. The rate was highest for returns reporting income in excess of $10,000,000 at 2.0 percent as compared to a rate of 0.1 percent for taxpayers reporting income between $75,000 and $500,000.

In her 2018 statement to Congress, the National Taxpayer Advocate Nina Olsen identified IRS funding as a challenge facing the IRS. Since fiscal year 2010, the agency's budget has been reduced by 20 percent, and its workforce has declined by about the same percentage. According to the statement: "These reductions have led to significant cuts in taxpayer service levels and have prevented the IRS from deploying new technology that would improve the taxpayer experience."[16]

Tax Talk
The IRS uses social media tools and platforms to share the latest information on tax changes, initiatives, products, and services. A list of these social media resources, which includes Facebook, YouTube, and Twitter, is available on IRS.gov.

Types of Audits

Routine audits are conducted by personnel working out of the IRS area offices located throughout the United States. The simplest audit, called a **correspondence examination,** may be handled entirely by telephone or through the mail. More complex audits take place at the IRS office (an **office examination** conducted by a tax auditor) or at the taxpayer's place of business (a **field examination** conducted by a revenue agent). Office audits focus on a few questionable items on a return. Field audits are broader in scope and may involve a complete analysis of the taxpayer's books and records for the year or years under investigation.

If the IRS requests a personal interview with a taxpayer or if the taxpayer requests an interview during an audit, the IRS must schedule the interview at a reasonable time and a convenient location. Individuals who must deal with the IRS can represent themselves or authorize an attorney, certified public accountant, or enrolled agent to represent them.

[16] Joe Davidson, "IRS Chief Says Trump's Budget Would Sharply Cut Taxpayer Service," *The Washington Post,* 2018.

While attorneys and CPAs are licensed to practice by state boards or agencies, **enrolled agents** receive certification to practice before the IRS by passing an exam on tax law written and administered by the IRS itself.

Assessments of Deficiencies and Interest

Individuals who are notified that they are being audited may panic unnecessarily. Any person who made a good-faith effort to comply with the laws in preparing the return and has maintained adequate records has nothing to fear. In a best-case scenario, the audit will be concluded with no change in tax, or even with a refund (plus interest) due to the taxpayer. Of course, the return was selected for audit because of its high probability of error. Consequently, the probable outcome is that the IRS will discover that the return contains a mistake that resulted in an understatement of tax. In this case, the taxpayer is assessed a **deficiency** (the additional tax owed) and is billed for interest based on the number of days between the time the return was filed and the date the deficiency is paid.

Corporations may deduct the interest paid on federal income tax deficiencies as a business expense. However, Treasury regulations state that interest paid by an individual on a federal income tax deficiency is nondeductible personal interest "regardless of the source of the income generating the tax liability."[17]

Interest Paid on Tax Deficiency	Lin Doh owns a sole proprietorship that makes custom-designed patio furniture. This year, Lin received a deficiency notice from the IRS. The notice indicated Lin owed $42,760 additional income tax for 2021 in addition to $6,157 interest. The entire deficiency resulted from an understatement of net profit on Lin's Schedule C. The $6,157 interest payment is a nondeductible personal expense.

Your Rights as a Taxpayer

Tax Talk
In 2021, the IRS provided taxpayer information in response to more than 2 billion visits to its website and assisted 88 million taxpayers through its toll-free telephone helpline or at walk-in sites. In 2021, taxpayers made more than 632 million inquiries to the recently established "Where's My Refund?" portal at IRS.gov.

In 1989, Congress enacted the first **Taxpayer Bill of Rights,** which requires the IRS to deal with every citizen and resident in a fair, professional, prompt, and courteous manner and to provide the technical assistance needed by taxpayers to comply with the law. To assist taxpayers, the IRS publishes more than 100 free information booklets and maintains a website (IRS.gov) that provides guidance for people who need help with the tax return filing and payment process.

In 1998, Congress created the office of National Taxpayer Advocate, the purpose of which is to assist taxpayers in resolving problems and to help taxpayers who suffer hardship because of IRS actions. The National Taxpayer Advocate heads a team of local Taxpayer Advocates who operate independently of the IRS's audit, assessment, and collection functions.[18]

In 2014, the IRS adopted an expanded Taxpayer Bill of Rights, which is now featured on page 1 of Publication 1 *Your Rights as a Taxpayer.* The following are the 10 provisions included in the Taxpayer Bill of Rights:

1. The right to be informed.
2. The right to quality service.
3. The right to pay no more than the correct amount of tax.
4. The right to challenge the IRS's position and be heard.

---

[17] Reg. §1.163-9T(b)(2)(i)(A).

[18] For more information, see IRS Publication 1546, *Taxpayer Advocate Service: We Are Here to Help You.*

5. The right to appeal an IRS decision in an independent forum.
6. The right to finality.
7. The right to privacy.
8. The right to confidentiality.
9. The right to retain representation.
10. The right to a fair and just tax system.

According to the IRS Commissioner, these 10 provisions embody "core concepts about which taxpayers should be aware. Respecting taxpayer rights continues to be a top priority for IRS employees, and the new Taxpayer Bill of Rights summarizes these important protections in a clearer, more understandable format than ever before."[19]

IRS Mission Statement	As part of its ongoing public relations effort, the IRS adopted the following mission statement: "Provide America's taxpayers top-quality service by helping them understand and meet their tax responsibilities and enforce the law with integrity and fairness to all."[20]

Noncompliance Penalties

LO 18-5
Summarize the noncompliance penalties that can be imposed on taxpayers and tax return preparers.

As stated in the beginning of this chapter, individuals are legally responsible for computing and paying their income tax, and most people make a good-faith effort to do so. In a 2020 IRS survey, individuals were asked this question: "How much, if any, do you think is an acceptable amount to cheat on your income taxes?" An impressive 88 percent responded that it is not at all acceptable to cheat, while only 7 percent responded that cheating "a little here and there" or "as much as possible" is acceptable. Ninety-three percent of respondents said that it is a civic duty to report and pay taxes honestly. These survey results suggest that the overwhelming majority of American taxpayers play by the rules and expect everyone else to do the same.[21]

Tax Talk
As a federal judge observed, "Like moths to a flame, some people find themselves irresistibly drawn to the tax protester movement's illusory claim that there is no legal requirement to pay federal income tax. And, like moths, these people sometimes get burned."

Source: Internal Revenue Service.

Those individuals who don't play by the rules may face a variety of monetary penalties. The IRS can assess these penalties, singly or in combination, on any taxpayer who doesn't make a good-faith effort to comply with the tax law. In this section, we will examine several of the more common penalties.

Frivolous Tax Returns

The occasional tax protester defies the federal self-assessment system by filing a blatantly incorrect or incomplete return on the basis of a legal argument with absolutely no merit. The IRS can retaliate by imposing a $5,000 penalty for the filing of a frivolous tax return.[22] The IRS is required to publish a list of legal arguments that it considers frivolous. The current list includes 46 such arguments, including: The federal income tax is unconstitutional because the Sixteenth Amendment to the Constitution was not properly ratified; payment of the individual income tax is purely voluntary; and wages, tips, and other compensation received for personal services are not taxable income.[23] In an introduction to this list, the IRS Commissioner cautioned people

---

[19] IRS Adopts "Taxpayer Bill of Rights"; 10 Provisions to Be Highlighted on IRS.gov, Publication 1, John A. Koskinen, Commissioner, Washington, D.C.: U.S. Internal Revenue Service.

[20] Internal Revenue Service.

[21] 2021 IRS Data Book, Comprehensive Taxpayer Attitude Survey.

[22] §6702.

[23] Notice 2010-33, 2010-17 I.R.B. 609.

that "they are ultimately responsible for what is on their tax return even if some unscrupulous preparers have steered them in the wrong direction. The truth about these frivolous arguments is simple: They don't work."[24]

Frivolous Argument	Norbert Yolandu filed a 2008 Form 1040 on which he entered zeros on every line. Across page 1 of the return, Norbert wrote: "I refuse to pay income tax because of my religious and moral conviction that the war in Iraq is a sin against mankind." He went on to explain that his refusal to pay tax was based on the First Amendment to the United States Constitution that protects his freedom of religion. This legal argument was rejected by the Supreme Court more than 35 years ago, and the IRS has listed it as a frivolous argument.[25] Consequently, the IRS imposed a $5,000 penalty on Mr. Yolandu.

Accuracy-Related Penalty

If the IRS determines that a taxpayer underpaid the amount of tax required on a return, the IRS can impose an **accuracy-related penalty** equal to 20 percent of any portion of the underpayment attributable to any one of eight reasons. The two most common reasons are negligence and any substantial understatement of income tax.[26]

Negligence includes any failure on the part of the taxpayer to make a reasonable attempt to comply with the tax laws or exercise ordinary care in the preparation of a tax return. Negligence is strongly indicated when a taxpayer doesn't try to ascertain the correctness of a deduction, credit, or exclusion that would seem to a prudent person to be "too good to be true."[27]

Negligence	The IRS agent who audited Ms. Purl's Form 1040 discovered three errors that collectively resulted in a $45,000 understatement of tax. The agent believed that two of the errors reflected a sincere misunderstanding of the law but that the third error was caused by Ms. Purl's disregard of a clear instruction on the return. The portion of the understatement caused by the third error was $13,000. The agent could impose a $2,600 negligence penalty (20 percent of $13,000). Ms. Purl must pay this penalty *in addition to* the $45,000 deficiency and the interest thereon.

An understatement of income tax equals the excess of the correct amount of tax for the year over the amount of tax reported on the return. For individuals, an understatement is substantial if it exceeds the *greater* of 10 percent of the correct tax, or $5,000.[28] Note that the test for a **substantial understatement of income tax** is mechanical because it is not based on the taxpayer's actions or intent.[29]

A taxpayer who is facing an accuracy-related penalty may avoid the penalty by convincing the IRS that there was a reasonable cause for, and the taxpayer acted in good faith with

[24] Internal Revenue Service.

[25] *United States* v. *Lee,* 455 U.S. 252 (1982).

[26] §6662(a) and (b).

[27] Reg. §1.6662-3(b)(1).

[28] §6662(d)(1). For corporations, an underpayment is substantial if it exceeds the *lesser* of 10 percent of the correct tax (or if greater, $10,000) or $10 million.

[29] Per §6662(d)(2)(B), an understatement of tax is reduced by any portion attributable to the tax treatment of any item on the return for which there is substantial statutory, administrative, or judicial authority. An understatement of tax is also reduced by any portion attributable to an item the tax treatment of which is reasonable and adequately disclosed in the return.

Substantial Understatement	Mr. and Mrs. Sisco filed a Form 1040 that failed to include interest income that was reported by the payer to the IRS on a Form 1099 INT. As a result of the omission, the Siscos owed an additional $8,740 of income tax in addition to the $54,200 tax reported on their Form 1040. Thus, their correct tax liability for the year was $62,940 and their understatement was $8,740. This understatement is substantial because it exceeds the greater of $6,294 (10 percent of $62,940) or $5,000. The Siscos' accuracy-related penalty is $1,748 (20 percent of $8,740), which they must pay in addition to the $8,740 deficiency and the interest thereon.
	Now assume that the income tax reported on the Siscos' Form 1040 was $104,700 instead of only $54,200. In this case, their correct tax liability for the year was $113,440 ($104,700 + $8,740). Their $8,740 understatement is not substantial because it does not exceed the greater of $11,344 (10 percent of $113,440), or $5,000.

respect to, the underpayment.[30] The determination of whether a taxpayer acted with reasonable cause and in good faith is made on a case-by-case basis, taking into account all pertinent facts and circumstances. Pertinent facts include the taxpayer's genuine effort to compute the correct tax liability and the taxpayer's experience, knowledge, and education.[31]

An Unlikely Story	Benjamin Smith was a teacher for the New York State Board of Education and a licensed attorney. On his 1992 and 1993 tax returns, he reported $8 gross receipts and deducted $57,938 business expenses in connection with his law practice. When the IRS requested written substantiation of these expenses, Mr. Smith explained that he kept his business records and receipts in a U-Haul trailer. Unfortunately, the trailer had unhitched from his car and had overturned, destroying all its contents. After he failed to provide evidence of this accident, the IRS disallowed his business deductions and slapped him with a negligence penalty. The Tax Court observed that: "Petitioner is an attorney. He claims he had been in private practice for several years. Although petitioner contends that he lacks any proficiency with regard to the tax matters, we believe that as a member of the legal profession, he should have recognized the importance of substantiating his expenses. Petitioner was given ample time and opportunity to procure and reconstruct the necessary records. Petitioner chose not to do so." The Tax Court agreed with the IRS that Mr. Smith acted in bad faith in filing his tax returns and was guilty of negligence.[32]

When the IRS imposes an accuracy-related penalty and the taxpayer challenges the penalty in court, the IRS has the *burden of production* in the litigation. In other words, the IRS must present a *preponderance of evidence* before the court will sustain the penalty.[33]

Civil Fraud

The harshest administrative penalty that the IRS may impose is the **civil fraud** penalty, which equals 75 percent of the portion of a tax underpayment attributable to fraud.[34] Fraud can be defined as the intent to cheat the government by deliberately understating tax. Fraud is characterized by the systematic omission of substantial amounts of income from the tax return or by the deduction of nonexistent expenses or losses. Revenue agents often assess a

Tax Talk
In 2020, the IRS assessed $31.4 billion in civil penalties. Approximately $14.1 billion was assessed on individual and estate and trust income tax returns.

[30] §6664(c).
[31] Reg. §1.6664-4(b).
[32] *Benjamin H. Smith,* T.C. Memo 1998-33.
[33] §7491(c).
[34] §6663.

fraud penalty when they discover that a taxpayer keeps two sets of financial records: one for tax purposes and one reflecting the taxpayer's true income. The fact that a taxpayer altered or destroyed business records and documents, concealed assets, or can't account for large cash receipts or deposits is a strong indication of fraud.

Civil Fraud	The IRS agent who audited Mr. Lowe's Form 1040 discovered large monthly cash deposits made to a bank account under a fictitious name. Mr. Lowe told the agent the cash deposits were gifts received from a friend. When asked to reveal the friend's identity, Mr. Lowe became verbally abusive and refused to answer. After further investigation, the agent discovered that the cash represented $62,000 unreported income from Mr. Lowe's lawn service business and estimated $23,220 of federal tax owed on this income. Because the agent concluded that Mr. Lowe intended to cheat the government by failing to report the income, the IRS assessed a $17,415 fraud penalty (75 percent of $23,220).

Because of the severity of the penalty, the burden of proof in establishing fraud falls on the IRS.[35] To sustain a fraud penalty, the IRS must have more than just a preponderance of evidence; it must show by *clear and convincing evidence* that the fraud occurred.[36]

A Clear Case of Fraud	Mr. Luan Nguyen was the sole shareholder of Hi-Q Personnel, Inc., an employment agency that provided skilled and nonskilled temporary workers to more than 250 clients. Mr. Nguyen offered company employees the choice of being paid by check or in cash. The corporation treated those workers paid by check as employees and paid federal employment tax on their wages. The corporation ignored those workers paid in cash. During the years in question, Hi-Q paid $14,845,019 cash wages on which it failed to pay employment tax. When the IRS imposed the civil fraud penalty, Mr. Nguyen argued that it was necessary to pay these workers in cash to be competitive in the temporary labor market and that this practice was simply honoring workers' wishes to maximize their earnings. The Tax Court was unmoved by this argument, concluding that Hi-Q needed to supplement the workers' earnings "either at its own expense or at the expense of the U.S. Treasury." By choosing the latter course, the corporation and its owner committed tax fraud.[37]

False in One Thing, False in All	Margaret Knowles was a psychiatrist who graduated from Johns Hopkins Medical School. The IRS audited her income tax returns for 2011 and 2012 and concluded that Margaret claimed false deductions (among other transgressions) and filed as a single taxpayer, even though she was married during these two years. The IRS imposed the civil fraud penalty, which Margaret contested in the Tax Court. In support of her assertion that she was single, Margaret provided a copy of a decree of divorce from her husband issued by a state court. However, the state court had no record of the alleged divorce, and the Tax Court determined that the decree was a fabrication. As a result, the court applied the maxim "False in one thing, false in all," stated that "If she was not truthful about her filing status, it leads us to conclude that she was not truthful about the various deductions she claimed," and upheld the fraud penalty.[38]

[35] §7454(a).

[36] *Richard McGirl*, T.C. Memo 1996-313, *aff'd per curiam*, 131 F.3d 143 (CA-8, 1997).

[37] *HI-Q Personnel, Inc.*, 132 T.C. 279 (2009).

[38] *Knowles*, T.C. Memo 2017-152.

Criminal Fraud

If a revenue agent uncovers a particularly egregious incident of fraud, the IRS may turn the matter over to its Criminal Investigation office. Criminal Investigation will assign a **special agent** to determine if the government has enough evidence to indict the taxpayer for **criminal fraud,** also known as tax evasion. **Tax evasion** is a felony offense, punishable by severe monetary fines (up to $100,000 in the case of an individual and $500,000 in the case of a corporation) and by imprisonment in a federal penitentiary.[39] A person must be convicted of tax evasion in a court of law, and the prosecution must establish guilt *beyond a reasonable doubt.*[40] If Criminal Investigation decides that the case against the taxpayer doesn't meet this strict evidential standard and is too weak to prosecute, the IRS may have to settle for the civil fraud penalty.

Celebrity Tax Fraud	The federal government prosecuted actor Wesley Snipes for multiple charges of federal tax evasion, including willful failure to file income tax returns and falsely claiming a $12 million tax refund. The jury acquitted Mr. Snipes of the felony charges but found him guilty of three misdemeanors for which the court sentenced the actor to the maximum three years in prison. After serving his time in a minimum security federal prison in Pennsylvania, Mr. Snipes was released from prison on April 2, 2013.

Tax Return Preparer Penalties

Tax Talk

Any tax return preparer who expects to file 11 or more returns during a year is required to file the returns electronically. E-filed returns can include electronic taxpayer signatures, so that the e-filing process can be completely digital and paperless.

Circular 230 contains the rules and regulations governing practice before the Internal Revenue Service. This publication includes both rules and duties related to practice as well as disciplinary actions and sanctions for violating these rules. The Internal Revenue Code further imposes penalties on tax return preparers who fail to comply with certain statutory rules of professional conduct.[41]

The term **tax return preparer** refers to any person who prepares returns (or who employs other people to prepare returns) for compensation, regardless of whether such a person is a licensed attorney, certified public accountant, or enrolled agent. Legal precedence and other authoritative legal positions have established that the common law duty of tax preparer is to perform the task they were engaged to do, in a timely manner and with the skill and care that can be expected of a prudent tax preparer under the same circumstances.

Preparers are required to

- Sign (as Paid Preparer) the tax returns prepared for their clients.
- Include their identifying number on such returns.
- Furnish clients with copies of their completed returns.
- Retain copies of all returns or a list of the names and identifying numbers of all clients.

In addition, preparers are prohibited from endorsing or negotiating tax refund checks. Violation of any of these procedural rules without reasonable cause results in a monetary penalty. For instance, a preparer who fails to sign a tax return may be assessed $50 for each failure. The maximum penalty with respect to returns filed during any calendar year is limited to $25,000.

Tax return preparers must make every effort to prepare accurate returns that report their clients' correct tax. If a preparer takes an unreasonable legal position in preparing a return and that position results in an understatement of the client's tax liability, the IRS

---

[39] §7201.

[40] *Bonansinga,* T.C. Memo 1987-586.

[41] §6694 through §6696. The American Bar Association and the American Institute of Certified Public Accountants also have standards of professional conduct for their members in tax practice.

Tax Talk

IRC Sec. 7525 provides a limited privilege for communications between a tax preparer and the client, similar to the privilege recognized between an attorney and a taxpayer-client. For the privilege to apply, the communication must be for the purpose of securing tax advice and must have occurred with an expectation of confidentiality, among other things. The privilege does not generally extend to criminal matters or to communications regarding tax shelters.

may impose a penalty on the preparer. The penalty for an unreasonable position equals the *greater* of $1,000, or 50 percent of the preparer's compensation with respect to the return. A preparer can avoid the penalty by demonstrating that there was a reasonable cause for the understatement and that the preparer was acting in good faith.

If the IRS determines that a tax return preparer willfully understated a client's tax liability or intentionally disregarded the tax law in preparing a return, it can impose a penalty for willful and reckless conduct. This more serious penalty equals the *greater* of $5,000 or 75 percent of the compensation for the return.

Clearly, the return preparer penalties are intended to discourage tax return preparers from taking overly aggressive positions on behalf of their clients. Even though the monetary penalties are modest, they can result in adverse publicity that could damage the preparer's professional reputation.

In addition to statutory requirements, the Statement on Standards for Tax Services (SSTS) No. 1, Tax Return Positions (AICPA, Professional Standards); and Interpretation 1-1, Reporting and Disclosure Standards (AICPA, Professional Standards) are enforceable ethical standards that all CPAs must adhere to. The Standards and Interpretation of the AICPA prescribe professional standards on tax reporting when recommending tax positions or preparing or signing returns. Interpretation 1-1 is particularly helpful in providing guidance on whether a tax position meets reporting standards and disclosure requirements for common tax issues.

Preparer Penalty

Lionel Mackey is a self-employed enrolled agent who prepared Mr. and Mrs. Boyen's Form 1040. The fee for the preparation was $6,300. The IRS agent who audited the Boyens' return disallowed a $75,000 itemized deduction, which increased the Boyens' tax liability by $14,475. The agent concluded that Mr. Mackey had no reasonable basis for claiming the deduction and was not acting in good faith by doing so. Consequently, the agent imposed a $3,150 preparer penalty (greater of $1,000, or 50 percent of $6,300) on Mr. Mackey. If the agent had concluded that Mr. Mackey's conduct was willful and reckless, the preparer penalty would increase to $5,000 (greater of $5,000, or 75 percent of $6,300).

CONTESTING THE RESULT OF AN AUDIT

Tax Talk

The IRS Appeals Office receives about 100,000 cases annually and brings about 80 percent of the cases to a successful resolution.

Taxpayers who disagree with all of or any part of the outcome of an audit (including penalties) may appeal the disputed issue to the Appeals Office of the IRS. An appeal leads to an administrative conference between the taxpayer (or more typically, the taxpayer's representative) and a specially trained IRS appeals officer. The purpose of the conference is to resolve the controversy in a fair and impartial manner. Appeal officers have broad latitude in settling disputes and may negotiate a compromise between the contestants on questionable issues. IRS Publication 5, *Your Appeal Rights and How to Prepare a Protest If You Don't Agree,* and IRS Publication 556, *Examination of Returns, Appeal Rights, and Claims for Refund,* explain a taxpayer's appeal rights and the appeal procedure in detail.

Litigation
Trial Court

LO 18-6
Identify the three judicial levels in the tax litigation process.

When a taxpayer and the government fail to resolve their differences in an administrative conference, the taxpayer can take the case to federal court for judicial review. In federal tax matters, one of three trial courts has original jurisdiction. A taxpayer may refuse to pay the deficiency determined by the IRS and file a petition with the **U.S. Tax Court** to hear the case.

Alternatively, the taxpayer may pay the deficiency and then immediately sue the government for a refund in either the local **U.S. District Court** or the **U.S. Court of Federal Claims** located in Washington, D.C. The tax litigation process is illustrated in Exhibit 18.1.

The selection of the appropriate judicial forum is an important matter of strategy for the taxpayer's legal counsel. Each of the courts is different in operation, and one may be more advantageous than the others depending on the nature of the controversy. The Tax Court adjudicates only federal income, gift, and estate tax issues and is comprised of judges who are acknowledged experts in the tax law. By contrast, judges in the district courts and Court of Federal Claims preside over cases involving many legal issues and typically have no special expertise in the tax area.

Taxpayers who want a jury trial must take their case to district court. In both the Tax Court and Court of Federal Claims, a single judge or a panel of judges tries the case and renders a verdict. If the controversy is one of fact rather than the technical application of the law, the taxpayer's attorney may recommend that the matter be put to a jury in the hope that the jury panel (who, after all, are taxpayers themselves) may be sympathetic. Of course, the viability of this strategy depends on the particular issue at hand. For instance, if the parent of a chronically ill child is arguing that the cost of a nontraditional treatment should qualify as a deductible medical expense, a jury trial seems a wise choice. However, if a taxpayer is trying to prove that a $750,000 annual salary from the taxpayer's closely held corporation is reasonable compensation, they may be better off pleading the case before a Tax Court judge.

EXHIBIT 18.1
The Tax Litigation Process

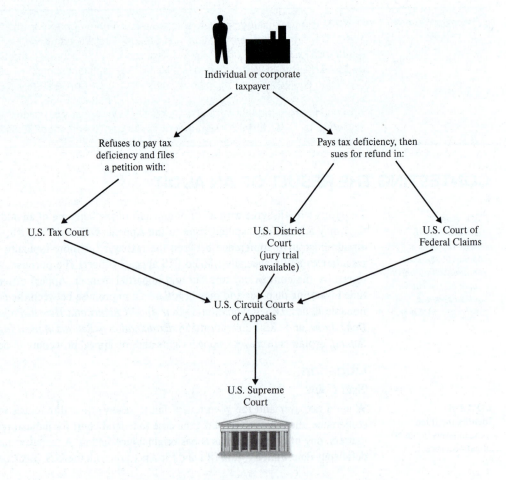

Appellate and Supreme Court

The losing party at the trial court level (taxpayer or government) may appeal the verdict to one of 13 **U.S. Circuit Courts of Appeals.** The geographic location of the trial court determines which appellate court has jurisdiction. These courts generally don't review findings of fact by a lower court, but they will consider if the lower court properly applied the relevant law to the facts. After the appellate court has either affirmed or reversed the trial court's decision, the losing party may appeal the case to the **U.S. Supreme Court.** This Court may agree to hear the case (grant *certiorari*) or refuse to hear it (deny *certiorari*). When the Supreme Court denies *certiorari,* the decision of the appellate court is final. During an average term, the Supreme Court hears no more than a dozen federal tax cases, which are selected either because the Court believes that the case involves a significant principle of law or because two or more appellate courts have rendered conflicting opinions on the proper resolution of a tax issue.

A Case History: *Lori Williams* v. *United States*

To summarize our discussion of the tax litigation process, consider the sequence of events in which Ms. Lori Williams took her case to the Supreme Court.

Facts of the Case

During Lori Williams's marriage to Jerrold Rabin, Rabin failed to pay $41,000 of federal employment tax related to his business. The government assessed a deficiency for the unpaid tax against Mr. Rabin and placed a lien on all his property, including the personal residence jointly owned with his wife. However, just one month before the lien was recorded, Mr. Rabin transferred his interest in the residence to Lori Williams as part of a divorce settlement. Nine months later, she contracted to sell the residence. Although Ms. Williams was not personally liable for her former husband's $41,000 tax deficiency, she paid it under protest. Her payment was the only way to remove the government's lien on the residence so that she could convey clear title to the purchasers.

Trial Court Decision

After paying her former husband's tax bill, Ms. Williams filed a claim for refund, arguing that the government had "erroneously or illegally assessed or collected" the tax. The IRS refused to even consider her claim, responding that Ms. Williams could not seek a refund of tax assessed against another person, even though she paid the tax. Ms. Williams then brought suit against the United States for her refund in district court.[42] The district court accepted the government's argument and held that Ms. Williams lacked standing to seek a refund. In making its decision, the district court relied on precedent established in decisions by the Fifth and Seventh Circuit Courts of Appeals.[43]

Lori Williams's Appeal

Lori Williams appealed the trial court's verdict to the Ninth Circuit Court of Appeals. This court analyzed a very similar case decided in the taxpayer's favor by the Fourth Circuit Court.[44] The Ninth Circuit Court was persuaded by the Fourth Circuit Court's reasoning and decided that Lori Williams had the right to seek a refund, thereby reversing the district court's verdict.[45]

---

[42] *Lori Rabin Williams* v. *United States,* Civil No. 91–5286 WMB (DC CA, September 2, 1992).

[43] *Snodgrass* v. *United States,* 834 F.2d 537 (CA-5, 1987) and *Busse* v. *United States,* 542 F.2d 421 (CA-7, 1976).

[44] *Martin* v. *United States,* 895 F.2d 992 (CA-4, 1990).

[45] *Williams* v. *United States,* 24 F.3d 1143 (CA-9, 1994).

The Government's Appeal

Now it was the government's turn to appeal the case to the Supreme Court, which granted *certiorari* to resolve the conflict among the appellate courts. In a decision in which six justices concurred and three justices dissented, the Court affirmed the Ninth Circuit Court's decision by holding that any person who pays a tax has the right to seek a refund of such tax.[46] Justice Ruth Bader Ginsburg, writing for the majority, concluded that federal statute does not expressly restrict refund claims to those persons against which the tax was assessed. Ms. Williams had no realistic alternative to paying the tax assessed against her former husband if she ever wanted to sell the residence. Congress didn't intend to leave people in Ms. Williams's predicament without legal remedy, and equity demands that the IRS consider her claim.

Making the Legal System More Taxpayer Friendly

While every taxpayer who disagrees with the IRS has the right to a day in court, many people are reluctant to bear the emotional and financial cost of litigation. To make the legal system more accessible to the average person, Congress established a **Small Tax Case Division** of the Tax Court.[47] A taxpayer who is disputing a deficiency of $50,000 or less may request an informal hearing presided over by an officer of the court. The filing fee for such hearing is only $60, and the taxpayer may plead their case without an attorney. After the presiding officer has heard the taxpayer's side of the story and rendered judgment, the matter is settled—neither taxpayer nor government may appeal the case to any other court.

Taxpayers who win their tax case may be entitled to recover litigation expenses from the government.[48] Such expenses include court costs, attorney fees, fees paid to expert witnesses, and payments for technical studies, analyses, tests, and reports necessary for the preparation of the taxpayer's case. Taxpayers are reimbursed for these expenses unless the IRS can convince the court that its position in the case was substantially justified. If the IRS failed to follow any of its own published rules, regulations, and procedures during the taxpayer's audit, the legal presumption is that the IRS's position was unjustified. Another factor that the courts consider is whether the IRS pursued the litigation to harass or embarrass the taxpayer or for political reasons.

Recovery of Litigation Expenses	St. David's Health Care System is a nonprofit corporation that provides medical services to the public. The IRS challenged St. David's charitable purpose and attempted to revoke its tax-exempt status, and the corporation fought the revocation in court. The Texas district court sided with the corporation by concluding that "there is absolutely no issue as to whether St. David's has a charitable purpose, and any argument to the contrary appears at least mildly disingenuous."[49] The court then ordered the federal government to pay the corporation's $950,000 of litigation expenses because the IRS's position in the case was not substantially justified.

The existence of the Small Tax Case Division and the right of taxpayers to recover litigation costs reflect congressional sympathy for individuals who sincerely believe that they are right and the IRS is wrong. On the other hand, Congress has little tolerance for people who waste federal time and money by initiating foolish lawsuits against the IRS. The Internal Revenue Code authorizes the Tax Court to impose a monetary penalty up to $25,000 on a taxpayer who takes a frivolous or groundless position before the court or institutes a case primarily for delay.[50]

[46] *United States* v. *Williams*, 514 U.S. 527 (1995).
[47] §7463.
[48] §7430. Taxpayers may also be entitled to recover reasonable administrative costs incurred when dealing with the IRS.
[49] *St. David's Health Care System Inc.* v. *United States*, 90 AFTR 2d 2002–6878 (DC TX, 2002).
[50] §6673.

A Frivolous Lawsuit	During 2011, Bruno Bruhwiler worked as a self-employed film compositor in Hollywood. The IRS discovered that Bruno failed to file a tax return for that year, and, in fact, had not filed a return for any year during the last decade. Based on an examination of Form 1099s issued by his clients, the IRS concluded that Bruno owed $2,834 of 2011 income and self-employment tax. In response, Bruno petitioned the Tax Court to hear his case. In his petition, Bruno advanced 27 reasons why he owed no tax, including the assertions that he "is not a U.S. citizen but in fact is a California National" and that the Internal Revenue Code "is not law." At the beginning of his trial, the Tax Court warned Bruno that he could be penalized for making frivolous arguments. When he persisted, the court lost patience, declared that Bruno had "deluged this Court with gibberish," and imposed a $3,500 penalty for wasting the court's time.[51]

Warning from the Tax Court	In 2012, Paul Staples earned $18,954 nonemployee compensation, which the payer reported to him on Form 1099-MISC. Mr. Staples failed to file a 2012 income tax return and contested the IRS's notice of deficiency for that year. In front of the Tax Court, he argued that as an independent contractor, he was not required to pay tax because "Congress has not enacted a law making it mandatory for him as a U.S. citizen to either file a tax return or pay Federal income tax." Not only did the court uphold the deficiency but also imposed a $1,000 penalty. The court warned Mr. Staples that if he did not abandon his "misguided and rejected positions," it may impose a heavier penalty in the future. "If the penalty does not dissuade him, imposing the penalty on him for his hardheaded persistence in making frivolous arguments may serve as a warning to other taxpayers."[52]

IRS Collection Procedures

LO 18-7
Discuss the various IRS collection procedures.

Taxpayers who have exhausted every avenue of appeal must finally pay their tax deficiency (including interest and penalties) to the government. The IRS is authorized to collect the deficiency by whatever means necessary, including seizing the taxpayer's assets and selling them at auction, levying bank accounts, and garnishing the taxpayer's salary or wage.[53] A taxpayer who lacks the current resources to pay a tax bill may request an **installment agreement** that provides for monthly payments over a reasonable period of time. The IRS must approve an installment agreement for an *individual* if the income tax owed is not more than $10,000, the agreement requires full payment within three years, and the IRS determines that the individual is financially unable to make immediate payment.[54] If a taxpayer's financial condition is so bad that it is unlikely that a tax bill will ever be paid in full, the IRS may accept the taxpayer's **offer in compromise** to settle the bill for a lesser amount.[55] The government's goal in accepting the settlement is to collect the most feasible amount at the earliest possible time and at the least cost to the government.

A question sometimes arises as to which person is legally responsible for the payment of a federal tax deficiency. If the taxpayer is a corporation, the deficiency must be satisfied with corporate assets; shareholders are not liable for their corporation's unpaid taxes. A major exception to this limited shareholder liability arises when the corporation no longer exists. In this case, the shareholders have **transferee liability** for the corporation's unsatisfied debts, including federal taxes, to the extent of the value of any assets received on liquidation of the corporation.[56]

Tax Talk
In 2021, taxpayers proposed 49,285 offers in compromise to settle their tax liabilities for less than the full amount owed. The IRS accepted 15,154 of these offers, amounting to just over $200 million.

[51] *Bruno Bruhwiler,* T.C. Memo 2016-18.

[52] *Staples,* T.C. Memo 2019-75.

[53] See *United States* v. *Davis,* 815 F.3d 253 (CA-6, 2016).

[54] §6159(c).

[55] §7122.

[56] §6901. See *Kardash,* T.C. Memo 2015-51.

Transferee Liability	Ms. Morgan owned 30 percent of the stock of KLM, Inc., which was dissolved under state law in 2020. Ms. Morgan received a $55,000 cash distribution from KLM in complete liquidation of her equity interest. The IRS audited KLM's tax returns for 2018, 2019, and 2020, and determined that the corporation underpaid its income tax by $114,800. The IRS can assess $55,000 of this deficiency against Ms. Morgan.

The Innocent Spouse Rule

LO 18-8
Explain the purpose of the innocent spouse rule.

When individuals sign their Form 1040s, they become liable for any tax deficiency with respect to that return. In the case of a joint return, both husband and wife must sign, thereby becoming jointly and severally liable.[57] As a result, the IRS may assess either person for the entire deficiency determined on subsequent audit of the return. Occasionally, this rule can work a real hardship on a person who is liable for unpaid taxes on a joint return that they signed without any knowledge of the information on the return. Such a person may be relieved of liability under the **innocent spouse rule**.[58] Such relief is dependent on three conditions:

1. The deficiency must be attributable to erroneous items (such as omitted income or bogus deductions) of the person's spouse.
2. The person must establish that in signing the return they did not know, and had no reason to know, that the return understated the correct tax.
3. Taking into account all the facts and circumstances, it is inequitable to hold the person liable for the deficiency.

Tax Talk
Aggressive phone calls by criminals impersonating IRS agents have become a major threat to taxpayers. The callers typically demand immediate payment for bogus tax bills. The IRS commissioner advises, "Don't be fooled by callers pretending to be from the IRS. We continue to say that if you are surprised to be hearing from us, then you are not hearing from us."

Source: Internal Revenue Service

One factor that the courts weigh very heavily in analyzing the third condition is whether the person significantly benefited, directly or indirectly, from any income omitted from the return. If a court concludes that a significant benefit existed, innocent spouse relief is denied, even if the person was ignorant of the omission. Normal spousal support is not considered a significant benefit, but an unusually lavish or extravagant lifestyle may indicate that both spouses enjoyed the omitted income. Another factor that the courts consider is whether the person seeking relief has been deserted by or is divorced from their spouse.

Innocent Spouse Relief	Kathleen and Joe Alioto were married for 20 years before his death at age 82. Kathleen, who was 30 years younger than her husband, was Joe's second wife. Joe was an antitrust attorney who served for eight years as mayor of San Francisco. During their marriage, Mrs. Alioto "attended to" Mayor Alioto, kept their home, and raised their two children. Mayor Alioto did not want his wife to work outside the home, and he never discussed finances or business matters with her. Mrs. Alioto reasonably believed that her husband was a successful lawyer with substantial earning capacity, a man of wealth, and a "man who was on top of everything and who was in control." After Mayor Alioto's death in 1998, Mrs. Alioto was stunned to learn that his creditors had filed claims in excess of $74 million against his estate. The IRS's claim for unpaid federal tax totaled $4,239,834. Mrs. Alioto struggled for eight years to settle her husband's debts while working to support her family before she petitioned the Tax Court for relief from the $1,998,551 balance of unpaid federal tax. At the date of trial, Mrs. Alioto was 64 years old and had $7,000 in a savings account, $99,000 deposited in retirement plans, and did not own a car. The Tax Court concluded that further payment of the unpaid tax would represent a substantial hardship for Mrs. Alioto and that she was entitled to relief as an innocent spouse.[59]

[57] §6013(d)(3).
[58] §6015.
[59] *Kathleen S. Alioto*, T.C. Memo 2008-185.

Conclusion

This chapter has provided a brief summary of the tax compliance process. After reading this chapter, you should have a much better sense of the rights and responsibilities of corporate and individual taxpayers. You should be aware that noncompliance with the tax laws can result in monetary penalties and, in extreme cases, criminal prosecution. Finally, you should understand the roles played by the IRS and the federal courts in administering our nation's tax laws. The information contained in this chapter, which culminates our study of the federal tax system, should serve you in good stead in your role as a taxpaying citizen or resident of the United States.

Key Terms

accuracy-related penalty *18-11*
civil fraud *18-12*
correspondence examination *18-8*
criminal fraud *18-14*
deficiency *18-9*
discriminate inventory function (DIF) score *18-8*
enrolled agent *18-9*
field examination *18-8*
innocent spouse rule *18-20*

installment agreement *18-19*
late-filing and late-payment penalty *18-5*
negligence *18-11*
offer in compromise *18-19*
office examination *18-8*
Small Tax Case Division *18-18*
special agent *18-14*
statute of limitations *18-7*
substantial understatement of income tax *18-11*

tax evasion *18-14*
tax return preparer *18-14*
Taxpayer Bill of Rights *18-9*
transferee liability *18-19*
U.S. Circuit Courts of Appeals *18-17*
U.S. Court of Federal Claims *18-16*
U.S. District Court *18-16*
U.S. Supreme Court *18-17*
U.S. Tax Court *18-15*

Questions and Problems for Discussion

LO 18-1

1. During an IRS audit, Ms. Heller provided the revenue agent with a meticulous set of records substantiating every number on the return. The agent actually complimented Ms. Heller on the quality of the records. Nevertheless, Ms. Heller did make an error that resulted in an underpayment of taxes. The formal notification from the IRS indicated an additional tax due of $4,350. Ms. Heller was dismayed that the IRS also billed for $920 interest on the deficiency, given the good-faith effort to comply with the tax law. Can you explain to Ms. Heller?

LO 18-3

2. During a field examination of GNT's income tax returns for 2019 and 2020, the revenue agent discovered that the treasurer had systematically omitted substantial income items and inflated deductions to minimize the corporation's tax. The agent suspects that the treasurer adopted this deliberate course of action as early as 2012. Can the IRS initiate an audit of GNT's tax returns all the way back to 2012? Explain briefly.

LO 18-3

3. Discuss the policy reasons for a statute of limitations for tax returns.

LO 18-4

4. Historically, about 1 percent of Form 1040s are audited. Why does a Form 1040 reflecting $31,000 AGI and a standard deduction have much *less* than a 1 percent chance, while a Form 1040 reflecting $912,800 AGI and $214,790 itemized deductions has a much *greater* than 1 percent chance of audit?

LO 18-4

5. Which has the greater chance of audit: a Form 1040 with $200,000 AGI, all of which is salary income, or a Form 1040 with $200,000 AGI, all of which is net profit from a sole proprietorship?

LO 18-4 6. Vitronix Corporation's net worth exceeds $160 million, its stock is publicly traded, and a national CPA firm audits its financial statements. Wilson Corporation's net worth also exceeds $160 million. However, it is closely held by members of the Wilson family. Discuss the reasons that the IRS might choose to audit Wilson Corporation rather than Vitronix Corporation.

LO 18-4 7. Both NK and CS are closely held corporations. NK's tax returns for the last five years reflect average taxable income of $90 million. CS's tax returns for the same period reflect average taxable income of $90,000. Discuss the reasons that the IRS might choose to audit NK rather than CS.

LO 18-5 8. Mrs. Merrick received a letter from the IRS asking for written substantiation of a $1,500 charitable contribution deduction. Discuss the probable tax consequences to Mrs. Merrick if

   a. Mrs. Merrick sends the IRS copies of the canceled check for $1,500 made out to the charitable organization and the thank-you letter in which the organization acknowledged the contribution.

   b. Mrs. Merrick cannot provide substantiation and, therefore, ignores the IRS request.

LO 18-5 9. Is it easier for the IRS to determine that an individual omitted an income item from a return or overstated deductions?

LO 18-5 10. Discuss the burden of proof as it relates to the penalties for

   a. Negligence.

   b. Civil fraud.

   c. Criminal fraud.

LO 18-5 11. Mr. Daly, a commercial artist, engaged Mr. Ramirez, a local attorney, to prepare an income tax return. Mr. Daly provided the attorney with a check register, deposit slips, receipts, and pertinent financial documents and read through the completed return before signing it. This year, the return was selected for audit. The IRS agent discovered that Mr. Ramirez incorrectly deducted certain of Mr. Daly's personal living expenses. Consequently, Mr. Daly's tax was understated by $8,900. The agent decided that the deduction was based on an unreasonable legal position.

   a. Is Mr. Daly liable for payment of the $8,900 tax deficiency plus interest?

   b. Could the IRS impose a negligence penalty on Mr. Daly?

   c. Could Mr. Ramirez be penalized because of the error made in preparing Mr. Daly's income tax return?

   d. Would your answer to the preceding questions change if Mr. Ramirez were Mr. Daly's brother-in-law, who prepared the return as a favor rather than for compensation?

LO 18-5 12. Mr. Nugent is an enrolled agent in tax practice. Last year, the IRS imposed a $1,000 preparer penalty on Mr. Nugent. In response, Mr. Nugent engaged an attorney to contest the penalty. Mr. Nugent's legal fee was $7,900. Was it rational to spend so much money to avoid the penalty?

LO 18-6 13. Mrs. Emmet has decided to contest a $28,650 tax deficiency, and understands that litigation can be initiated in district court or the Tax Court. Identify reasons why Mrs. Emmet might prefer one trial court over the other.

LO 18-8 14. Mr. and Mrs. Braun divorced this year. Several years ago, the couple filed a joint tax return reporting $24,000 AGI. During that year, Mr. Braun was extremely ill and was hospitalized for four months. Mrs. Braun, desperate for funds to pay medical bills, took a night job as a bartender and earned approximately $7,000 in tips. These tips were not reported on the return. Mr. Braun had no idea his wife had gone to such lengths to meet their financial obligations. After auditing this return, the IRS notified Mr. Braun of $1,100 deficiency plus interest because of the unreported tip income. Can Mr. Braun avoid liability as an innocent spouse? Explain your conclusion.

All applicable Application Problems are available with *Connect*.

Application Problems

LO 18-1   1. Percy Wilson is a calendar year taxpayer. What is the unextended filing date of Percy Wilson's 2023 federal income tax return if

     a. Percy Wilson, Inc. is a corporation?

     b. Mr. Percy Wilson is an individual?

LO 18-1   2. Mr. and Mrs. Kim Soo use a fiscal year ending July 31 as the taxable year for filing their joint Form 1040.

     a. What is the last date on which the Soos can apply for an automatic extension of time to file their return for fiscal year ending July 31, 2023?

     b. Assuming that the Soos make a timely application, what is the extended filing date for the return?

LO 18-1   3. Zucker, Inc. uses a fiscal year as the taxable year for filing its Form 1120.

     a. If Zucker's fiscal year ends on March 31, what is the filing date and the extended filing date for Zucker's Form 1120 for the fiscal year ending March 31, 2023?

     b. If Zucker's fiscal year ends on June 30, what is the filing date and the extended filing date for Zucker's Form 1120 for the fiscal year ending June 30, 2023?

LO 18-1   4. Collin Products received notice of a $21,000 income tax deficiency plus $4,300 interest. The deficiency related to an incorrect method of accounting for business inventory. Compute the after-tax cost of the $4,300 interest payment assuming that

     a. Collin Products is a corporate taxpayer with a 21 percent marginal tax rate.

     b. Collin Products is a sole proprietorship owned by Leslie Collin. Leslie's marginal tax rate is 37 percent.

LO 18-2   5. Mr. and Mrs. Gomez failed to apply for an extension of time to file their 2022 Form 1040 and didn't mail the return to the IRS until May 29, 2023. Assuming the Gomez's had no excuse for filing a delinquent return, compute their late-filing and late-payment penalty if

     a. The return showed a $19,758 balance of tax due.

     b. The return showed a $7,098 refund due.

LO 18-2   6. Mr. and Mrs. Wickham did not apply for an extension of time to file their 2022 Form 1040. Because they were vacationing outside the United States, they neglected to file their Form 1040 until July 14, 2023. Compute the Wickhams' late-filing and late-payment penalty if

     a. Their Form 1040 showed a $1,160 refund due.

     b. Their Form 1040 showed a $7,300 balance of tax due.

LO 18-2   7. Keyshawn Brown prepared and signed last year's tax return on April 3 but forgot to mail the return until the morning of April 20. Keyshawn enclosed a check for the $3,612 balance of tax due with the return. Compute the late-filing and late-payment penalty.

LO 18-2   8. Ms. Schmidt didn't request an extension of time to file a 2022 income tax return and didn't mail the completed return to the IRS until August 8, 2023. Ms. Schmidt enclosed a check for $2,380, the correct balance of tax due with the return.

  a. Assuming that Ms. Schmidt can't show reasonable cause for filing a delinquent return, compute the late-filing and late-payment penalty.

  b. How would your answer change if the return was not mailed until November 21?

LO 18-2 9. Mr. Abdul filed a delinquent tax return on July 27. The return reflected $3,700 total tax, $4,000 withholding, and a $300 refund due. Compute the late-filing penalty.

LO 18-3 10. LZ Corporation uses a fiscal year ending September 30. The controller filed LZ's Form 1120 for the year ending September 30, 2023, on October 23, 2023.

  a. What is the last day on which the IRS may assess additional tax for this fiscal year?

  b. How would your answer change if LZ's return was timely filed on its extended due date of July 15, 2024?

LO 18-3 11. Mrs. Fugate failed to include $28,000 lottery winnings on a 2022 Form 1040. The only gross income reported was $78,000 salary. Mrs. Fugate filed the return on January 19, 2023.

  a. What is the last date on which the IRS can assess additional tax for 2022?

  b. Would your answer change if Mrs. Fugate also reported $37,500 dividend income on the 2022 Form 1040?

LO 18-3 12. Egolf Corporation failed to include $300,000 of taxable interest income on its 2022 calendar year Form 1120. The gross income reported on the return was $4.7 million, and the return was filed on February 20, 2023.

  a. What is the last day on which the IRS may assess additional tax for Egolf's 2022 taxable year?

  b. How would your answer change if Egolf's gross income reported on the 2022 return was only $1 million?

LO 18-5 13. A revenue agent determined that Ms. Osaka underpaid income tax by $48,100 and concluded that $9,200 was caused by inadequate record keeping while the remainder was caused by an understandable misapplication of a complex rule of law. Compute the negligence penalty that the revenue agent can impose on Ms. Osaka.

LO 18-5 14. Mr. Stanhope has an MBA degree from Stanford University and has successfully operated a business for 18 years. The revenue agent who audited Mr. Stanhope's Form 1040 discovered a glaring error resulting in a $16,200 underpayment of tax. When questioned by the revenue agent about the error, Mr. Stanhope just shrugged and offered no logical explanation.

  a. If the error resulted from Mr. Stanhope's blatant disregard of a tax rule, compute the penalty for negligence.

  b. Should the fact of Mr. Stanhope's education and business experience influence the agent's decision to impose the penalty?

LO 18-5 15. The revenue agent who audited Ms. Hsui's Form 1040 discovered a $15,250 deduction that wasn't allowed by the tax law. The improper deduction reduced Ms. Hsui's tax by $5,033. The total tax deficiency for the year under audit was $6,490.

  a. Compute the maximum penalty if the agent concludes that the improper deduction was due to Ms. Hsui's negligence in preparing the tax return.

  b. Compute the maximum penalty if the agent concludes that the improper deduction represented Ms. Hsui's deliberate attempt to cheat the government by underpaying tax.

LO 18-5 16. Upon audit of Ms. Evelyn Carlyle's Form 1040, the revenue agent determined a $17,000 understatement of the tax liability. Compute Ms. Carlyle's penalty for substantial understatement if the correct tax liability was

  a. $218,500.

  b. $142,900.

LO 18-5 17. Upon audit of Mr. Tom Staton's Form 1040, the revenue agent identified a $4,300 understatement of the tax liability. Compute Mr. Staton's penalty for substantial understatement if the correct tax liability for was

    a. $40,800.

    b. $69,700.

LO 18-5 18. The revenue agent who audited Mr. and Mrs. Hamad's Form 1040 concluded that the couple failed to report $16,900 of taxable income for the year. As a result, the IRS assessed a $4,225 deficiency of the tax on the omitted income. Compute the penalty that the IRS can impose if the revenue agent concludes that

    a. The Hamads made an honest mistake in omitting the income from their return.

    b. The Hamads failed to make a reasonable attempt to determine the correct tax treatment of the omitted income.

    c. The Hamads deliberately omitted the income in an attempt to cheat the government out of $4,225 tax.

LO 18-5 19. During the audit of Mr. and Mrs. Jessel's 2020 and 2021 tax returns, the revenue agent learned that they kept two sets of books for their sole proprietorship. A comparison of the two revealed that Mr. and Mrs. Jessel earned more than $80,000 unreported income. The tax deficiency on the unreported income was $32,000.

    a. Compute the civil fraud penalty the IRS may impose.

    b. Describe the procedural steps the IRS must take to charge the couple with criminal fraud.

    c. Why might the IRS decide to impose a civil fraud penalty on Mr. and Mrs. Jessel but not charge them with criminal fraud?

LO 18-1, 18-5 20. Mr. and Mrs. Lear filed their 2021 Form 1040 on April 1, 2022. In November 2023, they received a notice of deficiency in which the IRS assessed $19,044 of additional 2021 income tax. Compute the total amount that the Lears owe the federal government assuming

    a. The annual interest rate (underpayment rate) throughout the 18-month period between the required filing date and the payment date was 3 percent. Ignore the effect of interest compounding.

    b. The revenue agent who audited the return imposed an accuracy-related penalty on the entire deficiency.

    c. The revenue agent who audited the return imposed a civil fraud penalty on the entire deficiency.

LO 18-1, 18-5 21. Mr. Leon filed a 2021 Form 1040 on March 29, 2022. In 2024, the IRS issued a notice of deficiency to Mr. Leon, in which it assessed $7,700 of additional 2021 income tax. Compute the total amount that Mr. Leon owes to the federal government assuming

    a. The annual interest rate (underpayment rate) throughout the 24-month period between the required filing date and the payment date was 4 percent. Ignore the effect of interest compounding.

    b. The IRS imposed an accuracy-related penalty on the entire deficiency.

    c. The IRS imposed a civil fraud penalty on the entire deficiency.

LO 18-5 22. Ms. Perez is a professional tax return preparer. Three years ago, Ms. Perez prepared Form 1120 for Denver, Inc. The tax preparation fee was $14,850. Upon audit of the return, the IRS disallowed a $112,000 deduction, which increased the corporation's tax liability by $39,200. Compute Ms. Perez's preparer penalty if the IRS concludes that

    a. Ms. Perez had no reasonable legal basis for claiming the deduction and was not acting in good faith by doing so.

>   *b.* Ms. Perez intentionally disregarded the tax law by claiming the deduction in a willful attempt to understate Denver's tax.
>
>   *c.* How would your answers to parts (*a*) and (*b*) change if Ms. Perez's preparation fee was only $3,500?

LO 18-6 23. The IRS assessed a $32,800 income tax deficiency plus $4,015 interest against Mr. and Mrs. Reczyk because of an alleged understatement of investment income. They refused to pay and took their case to the U.S. Tax Court. The Reczyks incurred $7,829 attorney fees and other costs of the litigation. Determine their after-tax cost assuming that

    a. The Reczyks won their case, and the IRS failed to demonstrate that its position was substantially justified.

    b. The Reczyks won their case, but the IRS convinced the court that its position was substantially justified.

    c. The Reczyks lost their case.

LO 18-7 24. Two years ago, Lodi, Inc.'s shareholders voted to dissolve the corporation. Pursuant to the dissolution, Lodi sold all its assets, paid off its outstanding debts, and distributed $789,000 remaining cash to its shareholders in complete liquidation of their equity. This year, the IRS determined that Lodi underpaid its corporate income tax for its last three years. The tax deficiency totaled $1.4 million.

    a. To what extent can the IRS collect the deficiency from the former Lodi shareholders?

    b. MN Partnership was a 5 percent shareholder that received a $39,450 liquidating distribution from Lodi. How much tax can the IRS collect from MN partnership?

Issue Recognition Problems

Identify the tax issue or issues suggested by the following situations, and state each issue in the form of a question.

LO 18-1 1. On April 3, Mr. and Mrs. Rath traveled to Japan. They made the trip because their son, who lives in Tokyo, was injured in an accident and needed their care. After nursing their son back to health, they returned home on June 11. On June 17, Mrs. Rath mailed their delinquent Form 1040 and paid the $18,262 balance of tax due with the return.

LO 18-1 2. On July 2, Mrs. Nandu received a notice assessing a $10,861 tax deficiency. Mrs. Nandu did not pay this tax bill within 10 days as required by the notice, and instead waited until September 29 to mail a check for $10,861 to the IRS.

LO 18-1 3. On April 13, Mr. Price applied for an automatic extension of time to file a Form 1040. At this time, Mr. Price estimated that the balance of tax due was $3,800, which was paid with the extension request. The return was filed on June 20 and reflected an actual tax liability of $6,900. Therefore, Mr. Price paid an additional $3,100 when the return was filed.

LO 18-1 4. Nunoz, Inc., a calendar year taxpayer, incurred a net operating loss in 2022 that it carried back as a deduction against 2020 income. Nunoz's treasurer filed a claim for a $712,600 refund of 2020 tax and expects to receive a check from the government any day now.

LO 18-3 5. Mr. Tillotson has not paid income tax or filed a tax return for the last eight years. Mr. Tillotson believes that the IRS can no longer assess back taxes for the first five of those years.

LO 18-3 6. KP, a calendar year corporation, filed its 2019 return on May 1, 2020. On February 19, 2023, it filed an amended 2019 return reflecting $2.61 million *less* taxable income than the original return and requesting a $913,000 tax refund.

LO 18-4   7. Mr. Barlow, a self-employed consultant, charged a client a $15,000 fee plus $3,900 reimbursable business expenses. The client paid the $18,900 bill and sent a Form 1099 reporting $18,900 income. Mr. Barlow's Schedule C reports $15,000 income from the client. Mr. Barlow did not report the $3,900 reimbursement or deduct the expenses.

LO 18-4   8. Mrs. Luce died on February 12, and left her entire estate (including a portfolio of marketable securities) to her son. After the end of the year, the son received a Form 1099s showing Mrs. Luce's name and Social Security number. This 1099s reported $29,788 dividend income that the son simply reported on his Form 1040.

LO 18-7   9. Mr. Martinez died, leaving all assets and property to an only grandchild. After the estate was settled, the grandchild received the inheritance worth $942,000. Nine months later, the IRS audited Mr. Martinez's final Form 1040 and discovered underreported income taxes of $18,450.

Research Problems

LO 18-4   1. Using an electronic tax library that contains IRS publications, determine the purpose of Publication 334, Publication 504, and Publication 907.

LO 18-4   2. Locate information on the procedure by which an individual taxpayer can request a photocopy of a prior year federal income tax return. What is the number of the form to request a photocopy? Does the IRS charge a fee for this service?

LO 18-5   3. Using an electronic tax library, locate a recent judicial decision involving taxpayer negligence and a different decision involving taxpayer fraud. Describe the actions of the taxpayers that resulted in these penalties.

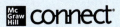 **All applicable Tax Planning Cases are available with *Connect*.**

Tax Planning Cases

LO 18-4   1. Mr. Rouse's tax situation for the year is very complicated, including several multimillion-dollar investment transactions involving unresolved tax issues. Mr. Rouse's accountants have been instructed to take the most aggressive position possible with respect to these transactions. Mr. Rouse also wants to take a business travel deduction for a trip that included Mr. Rouse's family. The deduction would be $7,293. Can you suggest any strategic reason to forgo the business travel deduction?

LO 18-6   2. The IRS recently assessed a $290,800 income tax deficiency on CMP Corporation. The deficiency is attributable to a complicated accounting issue involving CMP's investment in a controlled foreign corporation. CMP plans to contest the deficiency in court. CMP is located in the Third Circuit. Neither the local district court, the Tax Court, nor the Third Circuit Court of Appeals has considered the accounting issue. The Court of Federal Claims and the Eighth Circuit Court of Appeals have decided the issue in favor of the government. However, the Ninth and Tenth Circuit Courts of Appeals have decided the identical issue in favor of the taxpayer. Discuss CMP's litigation strategy in selecting a trial court.

Appendixes

Appendix A

Present Value of $1

Periods	3%	4%	5%	6%	7%	8%	9%
1	.971	.962	.952	.943	.935	.926	.917
2	.943	.925	.907	.890	.873	.857	.842
3	.915	.889	.864	.840	.816	.794	.772
4	.888	.855	.823	.792	.763	.735	.708
5	.863	.822	.784	.747	.713	.681	.650
6	.837	.790	.746	.705	.666	.630	.596
7	.813	.760	.711	.665	.623	.583	.547
8	.789	.731	.677	.627	.582	.540	.502
9	.766	.703	.645	.592	.544	.500	.460
10	.744	.676	.614	.558	.508	.463	.422
11	.722	.650	.585	.527	.475	.429	.388
12	.701	.625	.557	.497	.444	.397	.356
13	.681	.601	.530	.469	.415	.368	.326
14	.661	.577	.505	.442	.388	.340	.299
15	.642	.555	.481	.417	.362	.315	.275
16	.623	.534	.458	.394	.339	.292	.252
17	.605	.513	.436	.371	.317	.270	.231
18	.587	.494	.416	.350	.296	.250	.212
19	.570	.475	.396	.331	.277	.232	.194
20	.554	.456	.377	.312	.258	.215	.178

Periods	10%	11%	12%	13%	14%	15%	20%
1	.909	.901	.893	.885	.877	.870	.833
2	.826	.812	.797	.783	.769	.756	.694
3	.751	.731	.712	.693	.675	.658	.579
4	.683	.659	.636	.613	.592	.572	.482
5	.621	.593	.567	.543	.519	.497	.402
6	.564	.535	.507	.480	.456	.432	.335
7	.513	.482	.452	.425	.400	.376	.279
8	.467	.434	.404	.376	.351	.327	.233
9	.424	.391	.361	.333	.308	.284	.194
10	.386	.352	.322	.295	.270	.247	.162
11	.350	.317	.287	.261	.237	.215	.135
12	.319	.286	.257	.231	.208	.187	.112
13	.290	.258	.229	.204	.182	.163	.093
14	.263	.232	.205	.181	.160	.141	.078
15	.239	.209	.183	.160	.140	.123	.065
16	.218	.188	.163	.141	.123	.107	.054
17	.198	.170	.146	.125	.108	.093	.045
18	.180	.153	.130	.111	.095	.081	.038
19	.164	.138	.116	.098	.083	.070	.031
20	.149	.124	.104	.087	.073	.061	.026

Appendix B

Present Value of Annuity of $1

Periods	3%	4%	5%	6%	7%	8%	9%
1	.971	.962	.952	.943	.935	.926	.917
2	1.913	1.886	1.859	1.833	1.808	1.783	1.759
3	2.829	2.775	2.723	2.673	2.624	2.577	2.531
4	3.717	3.630	3.546	3.465	3.387	3.312	3.240
5	4.580	4.452	4.329	4.212	4.100	3.993	3.890
6	5.417	5.242	5.076	4.917	4.767	4.623	4.486
7	6.230	6.002	5.786	5.582	5.389	5.206	5.033
8	7.020	6.733	6.463	6.210	5.971	5.747	5.535
9	7.786	7.435	7.108	6.802	6.515	6.247	5.995
10	8.530	8.111	7.722	7.360	7.024	6.710	6.418
11	9.253	8.760	8.306	7.887	7.499	7.139	6.805
12	9.954	9.385	8.863	8.384	7.943	7.536	7.161
13	10.635	9.986	9.394	8.853	8.358	7.904	7.487
14	11.296	10.563	9.899	9.295	8.745	8.244	7.786
15	11.938	11.118	10.380	9.712	9.108	8.559	8.061
16	12.561	11.652	10.838	10.106	9.447	8.851	8.313
17	13.166	12.166	11.274	10.477	9.763	9.122	8.544
18	13.754	12.659	11.690	10.828	10.059	9.372	8.756
19	14.324	13.134	12.085	11.158	10.336	9.604	8.950
20	14.877	13.590	12.462	11.470	10.594	9.818	9.129

Periods	10%	11%	12%	13%	14%	15%	20%
1	.909	.901	.893	.885	.877	.870	.833
2	1.736	1.713	1.690	1.668	1.647	1.626	1.528
3	2.487	2.444	2.402	2.361	2.322	2.283	2.106
4	3.170	3.102	3.037	2.974	2.914	2.855	2.589
5	3.791	3.696	3.605	3.517	3.433	3.352	2.991
6	4.355	4.231	4.111	3.998	3.889	3.784	3.326
7	4.868	4.712	4.564	4.423	4.288	4.160	3.605
8	5.335	5.146	4.968	4.799	4.639	4.487	3.837
9	5.759	5.537	5.328	5.132	4.946	4.772	4.031
10	6.145	5.889	5.650	5.426	5.216	5.019	4.192
11	6.495	6.207	5.938	5.687	5.453	5.234	4.327
12	6.814	6.492	6.194	5.918	5.660	5.421	4.439
13	7.103	6.750	6.424	6.122	5.842	5.583	4.533
14	7.367	6.982	6.628	6.302	6.002	5.724	4.611
15	7.606	7.191	6.811	6.462	6.142	5.847	4.675
16	7.824	7.379	6.974	6.604	6.265	5.954	4.730
17	8.022	7.549	7.120	6.729	6.373	6.047	4.775
18	8.201	7.702	7.250	6.840	6.467	6.128	4.812
19	8.365	7.839	7.366	6.938	6.550	6.198	4.843
20	8.514	7.963	7.469	7.025	6.623	6.259	4.870

2023 Income Tax Rates

INDIVIDUAL TAX RATES

Married Filing Jointly and Surviving Spouse

If taxable income is	The tax is
Not over $22,000	10% of taxable income
Over $22,000 but not over $89,450	$2,200.00 + 12% of excess over $22,000
Over $89,450 but not over $190,750	$10,294.00 + 22% of excess over $89,450
Over $190,750 but not over $364,200	$32,580.00 + 24% of excess over $190,750
Over $364,200 but not over $462,500	$74,208.00 + 32% of excess over $364,200
Over $462,500 but not over $693,750	$105,664.00 + 35% of excess over $462,500
Over $693,750	$186,601.50 + 37% of excess over $693,750

Married Filing Separately

If taxable income is	The tax is
Not over $11,000	10% of taxable income
Over $11,000 but not over $44,725	$1,100.00 + 12% of excess over $11,000
Over $44,725 but not over $95,375	$5,147.00 + 22% of excess over $44,725
Over $95,375 but not over $182,100	$16,290.00 + 24% of excess over $95,375
Over $182,100 but not over $231,250	$37,104.00 + 32% of excess over $182,100
Over $231,250 but not over $346,875	$52,832.00 + 35% of excess over $231,250
Over $346,875	$93,300.75+ 37% of excess over $346,875

Head of Household

If taxable income is	The tax is
Not over $15,700	10% of taxable income
Over $15,700 but not over $59,850	$1,570.00 + 12% of excess over $15,700
Over $59,850 but not over $95,350	$6,868.00 + 22% of excess over $59,850
Over $95,350 but not over $182,100	$14,678.00 + 24% of excess over $95,350
Over $182,100 but not over $231,250	$35,498.00 + 32% of excess over $182,100
Over $231,250 but not over $578,100	$51,226.00 + 35% of excess over $ 231,250
Over $578,100	$172,623.50 + 37% of excess over $578,100

Single

If taxable income is	The tax is
Not over $11,000	10% of taxable income
Over $11,000 but not over $44,725	$1,100.00 + 12% of excess over $11,000
Over $44,725 but not over $95,375	$5,147.00 + 22% of excess over $44,725
Over $95,375 but not over $182,100	$16,290.00 + 24% of excess over $95,375
Over $182,100 but not over $231,250	$37,104.00 + 32% of excess over $182,100
Over $231,250 but not over $578,125	$52,832.00 + 35% of excess over $231,250
Over $578,125	$174,238.25 + 37% of excess over $578,125

ESTATE AND TRUST TAX RATES

If taxable income is	The tax is
Not over $2,900	10% of taxable income
Over $2,900 but not over $10,550	$290.00 + 24% of excess over $2,900
Over $10,550 but not over $14,450	$2,126.00 + 35% of excess over $10,550
Over $14,450	$3,491.00 + 37% of excess over $14,450

Visit *Principles of Taxation for Business and Investment Planning* in *Connect.*

Glossary

20 percent recapture   Twenty percent of the excess of Section 1245 recapture over Section 1250 recapture for buildings owned by corporations.

28 percent rate gain or loss   Long-term capital gain or loss from the sale or exchange of collectibles or qualified small business stock.

abandonment loss   The unrecovered basis in an abandoned asset. Abandonment losses with respect to business assets are ordinary deductions.

abatement   A property tax exemption granted by a government for a limited period of time.

ability to pay   Economic resources under a person's control from which he or she can pay tax.

above-the-line deduction   An allowable deduction for an individual taxpayer that can be subtracted from total income to compute AGI.

accelerated death benefits   Payments made under a life insurance contract to insured individuals who are terminally or chronically ill.

accrual method of accounting   An overall method of accounting under which revenues are realized in the year the earnings process is complete and expenses are matched against revenues in the year the liability for the expense is incurred.

accumulated earnings tax   A penalty tax levied on corporations accumulating income beyond the reasonable needs of the business to avoid paying dividends to their shareholders. The tax is levied in addition to the regular income tax.

accuracy-related penalty   Noncompliance penalty equal to 20 percent of an underpayment of tax attributable to any one of eight reasons, including negligence or a substantial understatement of income tax.

acquisition debt   Debt incurred to acquire, construct, or substantially improve a personal residence. The debt must be secured by the residence.

activity-based tax   A tax imposed on the results of an ongoing activity in which persons or organizations engage.

ad valorem tax   A tax based on the value of property.

adjusted basis   The initial tax basis of an asset reduced by cost recovery deductions allowable with respect to the basis.

adjusted gross income (AGI)   Total income less adjustments as computed on page 1, Form 1040. AGI is an intermediate step in the calculation of individual taxable income.

adjusted net capital gain   Net long-term capital gain (reduced by any 28 percent rate gain or any unrecaptured Section 1250 gain) plus qualified dividend income.

affiliated corporation   For purposes of the tax rules governing worthless securities, any 80 percent or more controlled domestic subsidiary that has always derived more than 90 percent of annual gross receipts from the conduct of an active business.

affiliated group   A parent corporation and its 80 percent or more controlled subsidiaries.

all-events test   The test for determining if an accrued expense is deductible. The test is satisfied if the liability on which the accrued expense is based is fixed, the amount of the liability is determinable with reasonable accuracy, and economic performance with respect to the liability has occurred.

allowance method   The GAAP method for computing bad debt expense. The expense is based on the estimated losses from current year receivables.

alternative minimum tax (AMT)   A second federal tax system parallel to the regular tax system. Congress enacted the AMT to ensure that every individual pays at least a minimal tax every year.

American Opportunity Credit   An individual tax credit based on the cost of tuition, fees, and course materials paid during the first four years of postsecondary education.

amortization   The ratable deduction of the capitalized cost of an intangible asset over its determinable life.

amount realized   The sum of any money plus the fair market value of any property received by a seller on the sale or exchange of property.

annual gift tax exclusion   The annual amount that a donor can give to each donee that is excluded from taxable gifts.

annuity   A cash flow consisting of a constant dollar amount for a specific number of time periods.

apportionment   A method of dividing a firm's taxable income among the various states with jurisdiction to tax the firm's business activities.

arm's-length transaction   A transaction occurring between unrelated parties who are dealing in their own self-interest.

assignment of income doctrine   Income must be taxed to the entity that renders the service or owns the capital with respect to which the income is paid.

average rate   The tax rate determined by dividing the total tax liability by the total tax base.

bargain element   The excess of fair market value over cost of stock acquired on exercise of a stock option.

base erosion and anti-abuse tax (BEAT)   A minimum tax on cross-border related party payments made by large multinationals.

bonus depreciation   Accelerated deduction in the year placed in service of 50 percent or 100 percent of the cost of qualified tangible personal property.

boot   Cash or other nonqualifying property included as part of a nontaxable exchange.

bracket   The portion of a tax base subject to a given percentage rate in a graduated rate structure.

bunching   A tax planning technique to concentrate itemized deductions into one year so that the total exceeds the standard deduction for the year.

business interest limitation   Business interest in excess of 30 percent of adjusted taxable income is not currently deductible.

business purpose doctrine   A transaction should not be effective for tax purposes unless it is intended to achieve a genuine and independent business purpose other than tax avoidance.

buy-sell agreement   A binding agreement that restricts the conditions and terms under which shareholders may dispose of corporate stock.

cafeteria plan   A compensation plan under which employees may choose among two or more benefits, including both cash and noncash items.

calendar year   The 12-month period from January 1 through December 31.

capital asset   Any asset that does not fall into one of eight statutory categories of noncapital assets. Most business assets (accounts receivable, supplies, inventories, tangible personalty, realty, and purchased intangibles) are noncapital assets.

capital gain distribution   A distribution of long-term capital gain recognized by a mutual fund to investors in the fund.

capital gain   Gain realized on the sale or exchange of a capital asset and that may be eligible for a preferential tax rate.

capital gain or loss   Gain or loss realized on the sale or exchange of a capital asset. Capital gain may be eligible for a preferential tax rate.

capitalization   An accounting requirement that an expenditure be charged to a balance sheet account rather than against the firm's current income.

carryover basis   The basis of transferred property in the hands of the recipient equal to the basis of the property in the hands of the transferor.

cash method of accounting   An overall method of accounting under which revenue is accounted for when payment is received and expenses are accounted for when payment is made.

cash surrender value   The amount paid to the owner of a life insurance policy on the liquidation of the policy.

centralized management   A legal characteristic of the corporate form of business: Corporations are managed by a board of directors appointed by and acting on behalf of the shareholders.

child credit   A credit based on both the number of dependent children under the age of 17, as well as other nonchild dependents of the taxpayer.

Citator   A resource used to determine the status of tax judicial decisions, revenue rulings, and revenue procedures.

civil fraud   The intention to cheat the government by deliberately understating tax liability.

closely held corporation   Corporation privately owned by a relatively small number of shareholders.

collectibles   Tangible capital assets such as works of art, antiques, gems, stamps, and coins.

Commerce Clause   Article 1 of the U.S. Constitution that grants the federal government the power to regulate interstate commerce.

Conference Committee   A committee composed of House and Senate members formed for the purpose of reconciling differences in the House and Senate versions of new tax legislation.

consolidated tax return   A single Form 1120 reporting the combined results of the operations of an affiliated group of corporations.

constructive dividend   A distribution by a corporation to a shareholder that the corporation classifies as salary, interest, rent, or some other type of payment but that the IRS classifies as a dividend.

constructive receipt   The point at which a taxpayer has unrestricted access to and control of income, even if the income item is not in the taxpayer's actual possession.

controlled foreign corporation (CFC)   A foreign corporation in which U.S. shareholders own more than 50 percent of the voting power or stock value.

convenience   The second standard for a good tax. A tax should be convenient for the government to administer and for people to pay.

correspondence examination   The simplest type of audit that can be handled entirely by telephone or through the mail.

cost basis   The purchase price of an asset, including any sales tax paid by the purchaser and any incidental costs related to getting the asset in place and into production.

cost depletion   The method for recovering the capitalized cost of an exhaustible natural resource. Cost depletion equals unrecovered basis in the resource (mine or well) multiplied by the ratio of units of production sold during the year to the estimated total units of production at the beginning of the year.

cost of goods sold   The capitalized cost of inventory sold during the taxable year and subtracted from gross receipts in the computation of gross income.

Coverdell education savings account   An investment account through which individuals can save for education expenses on a tax-exempt basis.

creative assets   Copyrights; literary, musical, or artistic compositions; letters or memoranda; or similar assets.

criminal fraud   A felony offense involving the willful attempt to evade or defeat any federal tax.

cross-crediting   Crediting the excess foreign tax paid in high-tax jurisdictions against the excess limitation attributable to income earned in low-tax jurisdictions.

Cumulative Bulletin (C.B.)   Semiannual compilation of weekly Internal Revenue Bulletins.

declining marginal utility of income   The theory that the financial importance associated with each dollar of income diminishes as the total income increases.

deduction   An offset or subtraction in the calculation of taxable income.

deemed paid foreign tax credit   A credit available to U.S. corporations that receive dividends from a foreign subsidiary. The credit is based on foreign income tax paid by the subsidiary.

deferred compensation   A nonqualified plan under which an employer promises to pay a portion of an employee's current compensation in a future year.

deferred tax asset   The excess of tax payable over tax expense per books resulting from a temporary difference between book income and taxable income.

deferred tax liability   The excess of tax expense per books over tax payable resulting from a temporary difference between book income and taxable income.

deficiency   An underpayment of tax determined on audit and assessed by the IRS.

defined-benefit plan   A qualified plan under which participants are promised a targeted benefit, usually in the form of a pension, when they retire.

defined-contribution plan   A qualified plan under which an annual contribution is made to each participant's retirement account.

dependent   A member of a taxpayer's family or household who receives more than half of their financial support from the taxpayer.

dependent care credit   A credit based on the taxpayer's cost of caring for dependents either under age 13 or physically or mentally incapable of caring for themselves.

depreciation   The systematic deduction of the capitalized cost of tangible property over a specific period of time.

depreciation recapture   Recapture computed with reference to depreciation or amortization deductions claimed with respect to property surrendered in a sale or exchange.

direct write-off method   The method for determining a bad debt deduction required by the tax law. Only receivables that are written off as uncollectible during the year are deductible.

discount rate   The rate of interest used to calculate the present value of future cash flows.

discriminate inventory function (DIF) score   A numeric score assigned to individual tax returns that measures the return's potential for generating additional tax on audit.

distributive share   A partner's share of any item of income, gain, deduction, loss, or credit recognized by the partnership. Distributive shares are usually expressed as a percentage and specified in the partnership agreement.

dividends-received deduction   A corporate deduction equal to a percentage of dividend income received from other taxable domestic corporations and certain foreign corporations.

donee   An individual or organization that receives a gift.

donor   An individual who makes a gift.

dynamic forecast   A projection of revenue gain or loss resulting from a tax rate change that assumes that the change will affect the tax base.

earmarked tax   A tax that generates revenues for a designated project or program rather than for the government's general fund.

earned income credit   A refundable income tax credit that offsets the impact of the payroll tax on low-income workers.

economic performance   The third requirement of the all-events test.

economic substance doctrine   A transaction that doesn't change the taxpayer's economic situation except by the tax savings from the transaction should be disregarded for tax purposes.

education savings bonds   Qualified Series EE savings bonds that can be redeemed tax-free to pay for certain education expenses.

efficiency   The third standard for a good tax. Classical economic theory holds that an efficient tax is neutral and has no effect on economic behavior. In contrast, Keynesian theory holds that an efficient tax is a fiscal policy tool by which the government can affect economic behavior.

employee   An individual who performs services for compensation and who works under the direction and control of an employer.

employee payroll tax   The FICA tax (Social Security and Medicare tax) levied on employees who receive compensation during the year.

employee stock ownership plan (ESOP)   A qualified defined contribution plan in which contributions are invested primarily in the corporate employer's common stock.

employer identification number   A number assigned to an employer by the IRS to identify the employer for employment tax purposes.

employer payroll tax   The FICA tax (Social Security and Medicare tax) levied on employers that pay compensation during the year.

employer-provided plan   A retirement plan sponsored and maintained by an employer for the benefit of the employees.

employment tax   A tax based on wages, salaries, and self-employment income. Federal employment taxes are earmarked to fund Social Security and Medicare.

enrolled agent   A tax practitioner certified by the IRS to represent clients in IRS proceedings.

estimated tax payments   Quarterly installment payments of estimated current year tax liability required of both corporate and individual taxpayers.

event- or transaction-based tax   A tax imposed on the occurrence of a certain event or transaction.

excess business loss limitation   Limit on the deductibility of excess business losses of noncorporate taxpayers.

excess foreign tax credit   Foreign tax paid or accrued during the year but not credited against U.S. tax because of the foreign tax credit limitation.

excess Social Security tax withholding credit   An overpayment of employee Social Security tax allowed as a credit against income tax.

excise tax   A tax levied on the retail sale of specific goods or services. An excise tax may be in addition to or instead of a general sales tax.

expansion costs   Costs of enlarging the scope of operations of an existing business.

expatriate   An individual who is a U.S. citizen and resides and works for an extended period in a foreign country.

explicit tax   An actual tax liability paid directly to the taxing jurisdiction.

federally declared disaster   A destructive event such as a hurricane or wildfire that is determined by the U.S. president to warrant federal assistance by agencies such as the Federal Emergency Management Agency (FEMA). For tax purposes, the amount of casualty loss equals the lesser of the tax basis in the property or the decrease in value from the casualty. The cost of repairs to the property is acceptable as evidence of the decrease in value if the taxpayer shows that the repairs are necessary to restore the property to its condition immediately before the casualty.

field examination   An audit conducted by a revenue agent at the taxpayer's place of business.

FIFO (first-in, first-out)   The inventory costing convention under which the first goods manufactured or purchased are assumed to be the first goods sold.

filing status   A classification for individual taxpayers reflecting marital and family situation and determining the rate schedule for the computation of tax liability.

fiscal year   Any 12-month period ending on the last day of any month except December.

flat rate   A single percentage that applies to the entire tax base.

foreign earned income exclusion   An annual amount of foreign source earned income on which expatriates are not required to pay federal income tax.

foreign source income   Taxable income attributable to a U.S. firm's business activities carried on in a foreign jurisdiction.

foreign tax credit   A credit against U.S. tax based on foreign income tax paid or accrued during the year.

foreign-derived intangible income (FDII)   Export income of a U.S. corporation from foreign sales and services that qualifies for a reduced effective tax rate of 13.125 percent.

free transferability   A legal characteristic of the corporate form of business: Shareholders can buy and sell corporate stock with maximum convenience and minimal transaction cost.

fringe benefits   Any economic benefit subject to valuation received by an employee as additional compensation.

general business credit   The aggregate of numerous different tax credits available to business enterprises.

general partnership   A partnership in which all the partners have unlimited personal liability for the debts incurred by the partnership.

generally accepted accounting principles (GAAP)   The set of accounting rules developed by the Financial Accounting Standards Board (FASB) and adhered to by the public accounting profession.

global intangible low-taxed income (GILTI)   Foreign earnings of a CFC (excluding subpart F income) in excess of 10 percent of the adjusted tax basis of the CFC's tangible business property.

going-concern value   Value attributable to the synergism of business assets working in coordination.

goodwill   Value created by the expectancy that customers will continue to patronize a business.

graduated rates   Multiple percentages that apply to specified brackets of the tax base.

gross income   Realized increases in wealth from whatever source derived. In the business context, gross profit from sales of goods, performance of services, and investments of capital.

gross profit percentage   The ratio of gain realized to total contract price in an installment sale.

guaranteed payment   A distribution from a partnership to a partner to compensate the partner for ongoing services performed for the partnership.

half-year convention   Property placed in service on any day of the taxable year is treated as placed in service halfway through the year for MACRS purposes.

head of household   Filing status for an unmarried individual who maintains a home for a child or dependent family member.

hobby loss   Excess of expenses over revenue from a personal activity not engaged in for profit.

horizontal equity   One aspect of the fourth standard of a good tax: A tax is fair if persons with the same ability to pay (as measured by the tax base) owe the same tax.

House Ways and Means Committee   The committee of the U.S. House of Representatives responsible for originating and drafting tax legislation.

hybrid method of accounting   An overall method of accounting that combines the accrual method for purchases and sales of inventory and the cash method for all other transactions.

implicit tax   The reduction in before-tax rate of return that investors are willing to accept because of the tax-favored characteristics of an investment.

imputed income from owner-occupied housing   The nontaxable economic benefit (fair rental value) derived by the owner of a home.

incentive stock option (ISO)   A qualified stock option for federal tax purposes. Individuals do not recognize the bargain element as income on the exercise of an ISO.

incidence   The ultimate economic burden represented by a tax.

income effect   A behavioral response to an income tax rate increase. Taxpayers engage in more income-producing activities to maintain their level of disposable income.

income tax   A tax imposed on the periodic increases in wealth resulting from a person's economic activities.

income tax treaty   A bilateral agreement between the governments of two countries defining and limiting each country's respective tax jurisdiction.

independent contractor   A self-employed individual who performs services for compensation and who retains control over the manner in which the services are performed.

innocent spouse rule   The rule of law under which a person who filed a joint return with a spouse is not held liable for any deficiency of tax with respect to the return.

inside buildup   Annual increase in value of a life insurance or annuity contract.

installment agreement   An agreement with the IRS under which a taxpayer can make monthly payments to settle a tax deficiency over a reasonable period of time.

installment sale method   A method of accounting for gains realized on the sale of property when some part of the amount realized consists of the buyer's note. Under the installment sale method, gain recognition is linked to the seller's receipt of cash over the life of the note.

intangible drilling and development costs (IDCs)   Expenses such as wages, fuel, repairs to drilling equipment, hauling, and supplies associated with locating and preparing oil and gas wells for production. IDCs are deductible for federal tax purposes.

inter vivos transfer   A transfer of property occurring during the life of the property owner.

Internal Revenue Bulletin (I.R.B.)   The IRS's weekly publication containing revenue rulings and revenue procedures.

Internal Revenue Code of 1986   The compilation of statutory tax laws written and enacted by the Congress of the United States.

Internal Revenue Service (IRS)   The subdivision of the U.S. Treasury Department responsible for the enforcement of the federal tax laws and the collection of federal taxes.

investment interest expense   Interest paid by an individual on debt incurred to purchase or carry investment property.

involuntary conversion   The receipt of insurance or condemnation proceeds with respect to property destroyed by theft or casualty or taken by eminent domain.

itemized deduction   An allowable deduction for an individual taxpayer that cannot be subtracted in the calculation of AGI.

joint and several liability   Each spouse on a joint tax return is individually liable for the entire tax for the year.

joint return   A return filed by husband and wife reflecting their combined activities for the year.

jurisdiction   The right of a government to levy tax on a specific person or organization.

Keogh plan   A qualified retirement plan for self-employed individuals.

key-person life insurance policies   Insurance purchased by a firm on the life of a high-level employee. The firm is the beneficiary of the policy.

kiddie tax   The tax on a child's unearned income based on the tax rate applicable to estates and trusts.

late-filing and late-payment penalty   The penalty imposed on taxpayers who fail to file their returns and pay the balance of tax due on a timely basis.

leasehold costs   Up-front costs incurred to acquire a lease on tangible business property.

leasehold improvements   Physical improvements made by a lessee to leased real property.

leverage   The use of borrowed funds to create a tax basis.

Lifetime Learning Credit   An individual tax credit based on 20 percent of the cost of tuition, fees, and course materials.

lifetime transfer tax exclusion   The cumulative amount of transfers that an individual can make during life or at death without incurring federal transfer tax.

LIFO (last-in, first-out)   The inventory costing convention under which the last goods manufactured or purchased are assumed to be the first goods sold.

like-kind property   Qualifying business or investment property that can be exchanged on a nontaxable basis.

limited liability   A legal characteristic of the corporate form of business: Corporate shareholders are not personally liable for the unpaid debts of the corporation.

limited liability company (LLC)   A form of unincorporated business organization in which the members have limited liability for business debt. LLCs are generally treated as partnerships for federal tax purposes.

limited liability partnership (LLP)   A partnership in which the general partners are not personally liable for malpractice-related claims arising from the professional misconduct of another general partner.

limited partnership   A partnership in which one or more partners are liable for partnership debt only to the extent of their capital contributions to the partnership. Limited partnerships must have at least one general partner.

long-term capital gain or loss   Gain or loss resulting from the sale or exchange of a capital asset owned for more than one year.

mandatory inclusion   A U.S. shareholder's share of a specified foreign corporation's deferred foreign earnings subject to mandatory repatriation following the Tax Cuts and Jobs Act.

marginal rate   The tax rate that applies to the next dollar of taxable income.

market   A forum for commercial interaction between two or more parties for the purpose of exchanging goods or services.

market discount   The excess of a bond's stated redemption value over the price paid for the bond in a market transaction.

material participation   An owner's regular, continual, and substantial involvement in the day-to-day operation of an active business.

maximum 15 percent rate amount   The maximum amount of adjusted net capital gain (in excess of any zero rate amount) subject to the 15 percent preferential rate.

maximum zero rate amount   The maximum amount of adjusted net capital gain taxed at the zero percent preferential rate.

method of accounting   A consistent system for determining the point in time at which items of income and deduction are recognized for tax purposes.

midmonth convention   Property placed in service on any day of a month is treated as placed in service at the midpoint of the month for MACRS purposes.

midquarter convention   Property placed in service on any day of a quarter is treated as placed in service at the midpoint of the quarter for MACRS purposes.

minimum distribution   The annual withdrawal an individual must make from a qualified retirement plan beginning no later than April 1 of the year following the year in which he/she reaches age 70½.

minimum tax credit   AMT liability carried forward indefinitely as a credit against future regular tax liability.

Modified Accelerated Cost Recovery System (MACRS)   The statutory and regulatory rules governing the computation of depreciation for tax purposes.

mutual fund   A diversified portfolio of securities owned and managed by a regulated investment company.

negative externality   An undesirable by-product of the free enterprise system.

negligence   Failure to make a prudent attempt to comply with the tax law or the intentional disregard of tax rules and regulations.

net capital loss   The excess of current year capital losses over capital gains.

net cash flow   The difference between cash received and cash disbursed.

net investment income   Income from investment assets reduced by expenses directly related to the production of investment income.

net operating loss (NOL)   An excess of allowable deductions over gross income.

net present value (NPV)   The sum of the present values of all cash inflows and outflows relating to a transaction.

nexus   The degree of contact between a business and a state necessary to establish the state's jurisdiction to tax the business.

NOL carryforward   A net operating loss allowed as a deduction in the years following the year of loss. The amount deductible in any carryforward year is limited to 80 percent of taxable income.

nonbusiness bad debt   An uncollectible debt held by an individual creditor that is unrelated to the individual's business.

nonprofit corporation   A corporation formed for philanthropic purposes and, as a result, exempt from the federal income tax.

nonrecaptured Section 1231 loss   A net Section 1231 loss recognized in any of the five preceding taxable years that has not caused recharacterization of Section 1231 gain as ordinary income.

nonrecourse debt   A debt secured by specific collateral for which the debtor is not personally liable.

nontaxable exchange   A transaction resulting in realized gain or loss that is not recognized (in whole or part) in the current year.

offer in compromise   A negotiated settlement with the IRS in which the taxpayer pays less than the entire deficiency.

office examination   An audit conducted by a tax auditor at an IRS district office.

ordinary gain or loss   Any realized gain or loss that is not a capital gain or loss.

ordinary income   Any income that is not capital gain. Ordinary income is taxed at the regular individual or corporate tax rates.

organizational costs   Expenditures incurred in connection with the formation of a partnership or corporate entity.

original issue discount (OID)   The excess of a bond's stated redemption value over the issue price.

outbound transaction   A transaction by which a U.S. firm engages in business in a foreign jurisdiction.

partnership   An unincorporated association of two or more persons to conduct business as co-owners.

passenger automobiles   Four-wheeled vehicles manufactured primarily for use on public roads with an unloaded gross vehicle weight of 6,000 pounds or less.

passive activity   An individual's interest in (1) an active business in which the individual does not materially participate or (2) a rental activity.

passive income generator (PIG)   An interest in a profitable passive activity.

passthrough entity   A business entity that is not a taxable entity. The income, gains, deductions, and losses recognized by a passthrough entity are reported by the entity's owners and taxed only once at the owner level.

payment liabilities   Accrued liabilities for which economic performance does not occur until payment is made.

percentage depletion   An annual deduction based on the gross income generated by a depletable property multiplied by a statutory depletion rate.

permanent difference   A difference between financial statement income and taxable income that does not reverse over time.

permanent establishment   A fixed location at which a firm carries on its regular commercial activities. For income tax treaty purposes, a country has no jurisdiction to tax a foreign business entity unless the entity maintains a permanent establishment in the country.

personal holding company   A corporation owned by a small number of individuals that receives taxable income consisting primarily of nonbusiness income such as dividends, interest, rents, and royalties.

personal holding company tax   A penalty tax levied on personal holding companies in addition to the regular corporate income tax.

personal service corporation   Closely held corporation owned by individuals who perform services in the fields of health, law, engineering, architecture, accounting, actuarial science, performing arts, or consulting for the corporation's clientele. Personal service corporations are subject to a flat 35 percent tax rate.

personalty   Any asset that is not realty.

premature withdrawal   A withdrawal from a qualified retirement plan made before the individual reaches age 59½.

prepaid income   Payment for goods and services made in advance of the provision of the goods or performance of the services.

primary authorities   Statutory, administrative, and judicial authorities.

principal residence   The home in which an individual resides for most of the year and considers his permanent address.

private activity bonds   Tax-exempt bonds issued by state or local governments for nongovernmental purposes such as industrial development.

private letter ruling (PLR)   The IRS's written response to a taxpayer's inquiry as to how the tax law applies to a proposed transaction.

private market   A market in which the parties deal directly with each other and can customize the terms of their agreement to meet their respective objectives.

pro rata share   A shareholder's share of any item of income, gain, deduction, loss, or credit recognized by an S corporation. Pro rata shares are based on the number of shares of outstanding stock owned by the shareholders.

probate estate   Property owned by a decedent and disposed of according to the terms of a valid will or state intestacy laws.

profit-sharing plan   A defined-contribution plan under which an employer regularly contributes a percentage of current earnings to the employee's retirement accounts.

progressive rate structure   A graduated rate structure with rates that increase as the base increases.

property similar or related in service or use   Qualifying replacement property in a nontaxable involuntary conversion.

proportionate rate structure   A rate structure with a single, or flat, rate.

public market   A market in which the parties deal indirectly through an intermediary such as a broker or a financial institution.

publicly held corporation   Corporation with outstanding stock traded on an established securities market.

QBI deduction   A deduction permitted to noncorporate taxpayers, generally equaling 20 percent of qualified business income. Wage and taxable income limitations may apply to reduce the allowable deduction.

qualified business income (QBI)   Active trade or business income from nonservice businesses eligible for the Section 199A deduction.

qualified dividend income   Dividends received from taxable domestic corporations and certain qualified foreign corporations eligible for a preferential individual tax rate.

qualified education loan   Any debt incurred to pay higher education expenses.

qualified improvement property   Certain nonstructural improvement to the interior of nonresidential real property, qualifying for a 15-year recovery life and the Section 179 election.

qualified residence interest   Interest paid on acquisition debt or home equity debt allowed as an itemized deduction.

qualified retirement plans   Retirement plans that meet certain statutory requirements and that allow participants to save for retirement on a tax-deferred basis.

qualified small business stock   Stock in a corporate business that meets certain statutory requirements. Individuals who recognize gain on the sale of qualified small business stock may be eligible to exclude 50, 75, or 100 percent of the gain from income.

qualified tuition expenses   Tuition and fees paid for postsecondary education.

qualified tuition program   A savings program sponsored by a state or private educational institution in which individuals can invest to pay future college expenses.

qualifying child   A child (or specified family member) who has the same principal residence as the taxpayer, who does not provide more than one-half of their own financial support, and who is younger than 19 years old or a student younger than 24 years old.

qualifying property   The specific property eligible for a particular nontaxable exchange.

qualifying relative   A specified family member or member of the taxpayer's household who receives more than one-half of their financial support from the taxpayer and whose annual gross income is less than an amount prescribed by Congress (indexed annually for inflation).

real property tax   A tax levied on the ownership of realty and based on the property's assessed market value.

realization   Income is taken into account when the earnings process with respect to the income is complete and an event or transaction occurs that provides an objective measurement of the income.

realized gain or loss   The positive or negative difference between the amount realized on the disposition of property and the adjusted basis of the property.

realty   Land and whatever is erected or growing on the land or permanently affixed to it.

recapture   Recharacterization of Section 1231 or capital gain as ordinary income.

recognition   Inclusion of an item of income or deduction in the computation of taxable income.

recognized gain or loss   Realized gain or loss taken into account for tax purposes in the current year.

recourse debt   A debt for which the debtor is personally liable.

recovery period   The number of years prescribed by statute over which the basis of tangible business property is depreciated under MACRS.

recurring item exception   An exception to the economic performance requirement under which a liability is considered incurred in a taxable year in which it meets the first two requirements of the all-events test and economic performance occurs within 8½ months after year-end.

regressive rate structure   A graduated rate structure with rates that decrease as the base increases.

rehabilitation credit   A business credit equal to a percentage of the cost of rehabilitating certified historic structures.

related party transaction   A transaction between parties who share a common economic interest or objective and who may not be dealing at arm's length.

rental activity   An activity where payments are principally for the use of tangible property for an extended period of time. Rental activities are passive activities.

reorganization   A statutorily defined transaction in which one corporation acquires another, one corporation divides into two corporations, or a corporation changes its capital structure.

research and experimental expenditures   A preferential deduction for costs of basic research designed to encourage businesses to conduct such research.

revenue   Total tax collected by the government and available for public use.

restricted stock   Corporate stock transferred as compensation to an employee that is either nontransferable or subject to a substantial risk of forfeiture.

revenue procedure   An IRS pronouncement advising taxpayers how to comply with IRS procedural or administrative matters.

revenue ruling   An IRS pronouncement explaining how the IRS applies the tax law to a particular set of facts.

rollover contribution   A distribution from one qualified plan contributed to another qualified plan within 60 days.

rollover IRA   An IRA created to receive a distribution from another qualified retirement plan.

Roth IRA   An investment account through which individuals with compensation or earned income can save for retirement on a tax-exempt basis.

safe-harbor estimate   Estimated current year tax payments based on the preceding year's tax liability that protect the taxpayer from the underpayment penalty.

sales tax   A general tax levied on the retail sale of goods and services.

Sample Key Term   This is sample key term definition.

secondary authorities   Textbooks, treatises, professional journals, and commercial tax services.

Section 1231 asset   Real or depreciable property used in a trade or business (including rental real estate) and intangible business assets subject to amortization held by the owner for more than one year.

Section 1244 stock   The first $1 million of stock issued by a corporation for cash or property. Some portion of the loss on the disposition of Section 1244 stock is ordinary to individual investors.

Section 1245 recapture   Full recapture of depreciation or amortization allowed for tangible personalty or purchased intangibles.

Section 1250 recapture   Recapture of excess accelerated depreciation over straight-line depreciation allowed for buildings placed in service before 1987.

Section 179 election   The election under which firms can expense a limited dollar amount of the cost of tangible personalty placed in service during the taxable year.

Section 401(k) plan   A defined-contribution plan under which employees elect to contribute a portion of current year compensation to an employer-provided retirement plan.

section   Numerically labeled subdivision of the Internal Revenue Code. Each section contains an operational, definitional, or procedural rule relating to one of the federal taxes.

securities   Financial instruments including equity interests in business organizations and creditor interests such as savings accounts, notes, and bonds.

self-employment (SE) tax   Employment tax levied on an individual's net earnings from self-employment.

seller-financed sale   A sale transaction in which the seller accepts the purchaser's debt obligation as part of the sale price.

Senate Finance Committee   The committee of the U.S. Senate responsible for drafting tax legislation.

SEP   A SEP is a retirement plan that allows an employer (sole proprietor, partnership, or corporation) to administer and contribute to a qualified plan for themself or their employees.

separate return   A return filed by a married individual reflecting his or her independent activity and tax liability for the year. The tax liability is based on the married filing separately rate schedule.

separately stated item   An item of income, gain, deduction, or loss recognized by a passthrough entity that retains its character as it flows through to the owners. Separately stated items are not included in the computation of the entity's ordinary business income or loss.

Series EE savings bonds   Long-term debt instruments issued by the U.S. government at a discount.

short-period return   A tax return for a taxable year consisting of less than 12 months.

short-term capital gain or loss   Gain or loss resulting from the sale or exchange of a capital asset owned for one year or less.

Simple IRA   A Simple IRA is a retirement plan established by a small business owner (typically less than 100 employees) on behalf of the businesses owner or employees.

single taxpayer   An unmarried individual who is neither a surviving spouse nor a head of household.

Small Tax Case Division   A division of the U.S. Tax Court that holds informal hearings of disputes involving tax deficiencies of $50,000 or less.

sole proprietorship   An unincorporated business owned by one individual.

special agent   A revenue agent who handles criminal fraud investigations.

specific identification method   An accounting method under which cost of goods sold includes the actual cost of specific items of inventory sold during the year.

specified 10 percent foreign corporation   A foreign corportion in which any domestic corporation owns at least 10 percent.

specified foreign corporation (SFC)   A foreign corporation whose previously deferred earnings are subject to mandatory repatriation to U.S. shareholders during the last tax year beginning before January 1, 2018.

standard deduction   A deduction from AGI based on filing status. The standard deduction amounts are indexed annually for inflation.

start-up expenditures   Up-front costs of investigating the creation or purchase of a business and the routine expenses incurred during the preoperating phase of a business.

static forecast   A projection of revenue gain or loss resulting from a tax rate change that assumes that the change will have no effect on the tax base.

statute of limitations   The statutory limit on the time period after a tax return is filed during which the IRS can audit the return and assess additional tax.

step transaction doctrine   The IRS can collapse a series of intermediate transactions into a single transaction to determine the tax consequences of the arrangement in its entirety.

stock option   The right to purchase corporate stock for a stated price (the strike price) for a given period of time.

subchapter S corporation   A corporation with a subchapter S election in effect. The corporation is a passthrough entity for federal tax purposes and does not pay federal income tax.

subpart F income   A category of foreign source income earned by a CFC constructively distributed to U.S. shareholders in the year earned. Conceptually, subpart F income is artificial income in that it has no commercial or economic connection to the country in which the CFC is incorporated.

substance over form doctrine   The IRS can look through the legal formalities to determine the economic substance (if any) of a transaction and to base the tax consequences on the substance instead of the form.

substantial understatement of income tax   An understatement of individual income tax exceeding the greater of 10 percent of the tax required to be reported on the return, or $5,000.

substituted basis   The basis of qualifying property received in a nontaxable exchange determined by reference to the basis of the property surrendered in the exchange.

substitution effect   A behavioral response to an income tax rate increase. Taxpayers engage in fewer income-producing activities and more non–income-producing activities.

sufficiency   The first standard for a good tax. A tax should generate enough revenue to pay for the public goods and services provided by the government levying the tax.

supply-side economic theory   A decrease in the highest income tax rates should stimulate economic growth and ultimately result in an increase in government revenues.

surviving spouse   Filing status that permits a widow or widower to use the married filing jointly rate schedule for two taxable years following the death of a spouse.

tax   A payment to support the cost of government. A tax is nonpenal but compulsory and is not directly related to any specific benefit provided by the government.

tax assessor   An elected or appointed government official responsible for deriving the value of realty located within a taxing jurisdiction.

tax avoidance   The implementation of legal strategies for reducing taxes.

tax base   An item, occurrence, transaction, or activity with respect to which a tax is levied. Tax bases are usually expressed in monetary terms.

tax basis   A taxpayer's investment in any asset or property right and the measure of unrecovered dollars represented by the asset.

tax benefit rule   The recovery of an amount deducted in an earlier year must be included in gross income in the year of recovery.

tax cost   An increase in tax liability for any period resulting from a transaction.

tax credit   A direct reduction in tax liability.

tax evasion   The willful and deliberate attempt to defraud the government by understating a tax liability through illegal means; also see *criminal fraud.*

Tax Expenditures Budget   Part of the federal budget that quantifies the annual revenue loss attributable to each major tax preference.

tax haven   A foreign jurisdiction with minimal or no income tax.

tax law   The body of legal authority consisting of statutory laws, administrative pronouncements, and judicial decisions.

tax planning   The structuring of transactions to reduce tax costs or increase tax savings to maximize net present value.

tax policy   A government's attitude, objectives, and actions with respect to its tax system.

tax preferences   In the general context, provisions included in the federal tax law as incentives to encourage certain behaviors or as subsidies for certain activities; in AMT context, specific items added to regular taxable income in the computation of AMTI.

tax return preparer   Any person who prepares returns (or who employs other people to prepare returns) for compensation, regardless of whether such person is a licensed attorney, certified public accountant, or enrolled agent.

tax savings   A decrease in tax liability for any period resulting from a transaction.

taxable estate   The aggregate fair market value of property owned by a decedent or transferred because of the decedent's death reduced by allowable deductions.

taxable income   Gross income minus allowable deductions for the taxable year.

taxpayer   Any person or organization required by law to pay tax to a governmental authority.

Taxpayer Bill of Rights   Part of the federal law requiring the IRS to deal with every citizen and resident in a fair, professional, prompt, and courteous manner.

technical advice memorandum (TAM)   The IRS position on a disputed item on a tax return.

temporary difference   A difference between financial statement income and taxable income that reverses over time.

testamentary transfer   A transfer of property occurring on the death of the property owner.

thin capitalization   A corporate capital structure with a high ratio of debt to equity.

time value of money   A dollar available today is worth more than a dollar available tomorrow because the current dollar can be invested to start earning interest immediately.

total income   The sum of the income items recognized by an individual during the year and listed on page 1, Form 1040.

traditional IRA   An investment account through which individuals with compensation or earned income can save for retirement on a tax-deferred basis.

transfer price   In the international area, the price at which goods or services are exchanged between controlled corporations operating in different taxing jurisdictions.

transfer tax   A tax levied on the transfer of wealth by gift or at death and based on the market value of the transferred assets.

transferee liability   Liability of a recipient of property (transferee) for the unpaid tax of the transferor of the property.

Treasury inflation-protected securities (TIPS)   Long-term U.S. debt instruments with a fixed interest rate on an inflation-adjusted principal amount.

Treasury regulation   The official interpretation of a statutory tax rule written and published by the U.S. Treasury.

U.S. Circuit Courts of Appeals   Thirteen federal courts that hear appeals of trial court decisions.

U.S. Court of Federal Claims   A federal trial court located in Washington, D.C., in which taxpayers can sue the government for a refund of tax.

U.S. District Courts   Federal trial courts in which taxpayers can sue the government for a refund of tax.

U.S. shareholder   Domestic corporations, partnerships, trusts, estates, and U.S. individuals that own 10 percent or more of a specified foreign corporation's voting power.

U.S. Supreme Court   The highest federal court. The Supreme Court hears appeals of circuit court decisions.

U.S. Tax Court   A federal court that tries only federal income, gift, and estate tax cases.

underpayment penalty   The penalty imposed by the Internal Revenue Code on both individuals and corporations that fail to make required estimated payments of current tax on a timely basis.

unearned income Medicare contribution tax   A 3.8 percent tax on an individual taxpayer's net investment income, the revenues from which are earmarked for the Medicare trust funds.

unemployment tax   A tax levied by both the federal and the state governments on compensation paid by employers to their employees. Unemployment taxes are earmarked to fund the national unemployment insurance program.

uniform capitalization (UNICAP) rules   The set of tax rules governing the type of current expenditures that must be capitalized to inventory.

Uniform Division of Income for Tax Purposes Act (UDITPA)   A model act describing a recommended method for apportioning a firm's taxable income among multiple state jurisdictions.

unlimited life   A legal characteristic of the corporate form of business: A corporation's legal existence is not affected by changes in the identity of its shareholders.

unlimited marital deduction   A deduction in the computation of a decedent's taxable estate equal to the value of property transferred to the decedent's surviving spouse.

unrecaptured Section 1250 gain   Section 1231 gain on the sale of business realty that would be recaptured as ordinary income under the full recapture rule.

use tax   A tax levied on the ownership, possession, or consumption of goods if the owner did not pay the jurisdiction's sales tax when the goods were purchased.

vacation home   A personal residence other than the owner's principal residence.

value-added tax (VAT)   A tax levied on firms engaged in any phase of the production or manufacture of goods and based on the incremental value added by the firm to the goods.

vertical equity   One aspect of the fourth standard of a good tax: A tax is fair if persons with a greater ability to pay (as measured by the tax base) owe more tax than persons with a lesser ability to pay.

wash sale   A sale of marketable securities if the seller reacquires substantially the same securities within 30 days after (or 30 days before) the sale.

withholding tax   A tax on dividends paid to foreign shareholders that is withheld by the corporation paying the dividend.

Index

Page numbers followed by n refer to notes.

State Business Climate Index
    (Tax Foundation), 13-7
State jurisdiction, constitutional
    restrictions, 13-3–13-5
State registration, 1-8
State taxes. *See also* Local taxes
    corporate income taxes, 1-10–1-11
    deduction of, 17-10–17-11
    excise tax, 1-10
    governments, 1-9
    personal income taxes, 1-10
    pervasive nature of, 1-9–1-11
    refunds, 17-11
    retail sales tax, 1-9
    sales tax, 1-9
    use tax, 1-9
Static forecast, 2-4
Statute of limitations, 18-7–18-8
    for the IRS, 18-7–18-8
Statutory authority, as tax law source,
    1-17
Statutory restrictions, 12-5–12-7
St. David's Health Care System, 18-18
*St. David's Health Care System Inc. v.
    United States* (2002), 18-18n49
Stepped-up basis, 16-34
Step transaction doctrine, 4-17
Stewart, Potter, 1-7
Stock. *See also* Equity-based
    compensation corporate
    exchange of property for, 9-12
    qualified small business stock, 16-20
    in S corporations, 10-32
    Section 1244, 16-20–16-21
Stock options, 15-15–15-16
Stone, Jeffrey, 17-8
Straight-line depreciation, 8-19
Subchapter K corporations, 12-9
Subchapter S corporations, 10-28, 12-9
    adjusting the basis of S corporation
        stock, 10-34–10-36
    eligible corporations, 10-31–10-32
    Faux Antiques-S corporation, 10-28
    passthrough entity, 10-28
    tax consequences to shareholders,
        10-32–10-34
Subchapter S election, 10-31
Subpart F income, 13-20
Subsidiaries
    corporations as, 11-3
    domestic, 13-14
    foreign, 13-14–13-15
    tax, for education, 17-12–17-13
    tax havens and, 13-19

Subsidies
    deductions of capital expenditures as,
        7-5–7-6
    for education, 17-12–17-13
    government, to Boeing, 1-8
Substance over form doctrine, 4-16
Substantial understatement of income
    tax, 18-11, 18-12
Substituted basis rule, for generic
    nontaxable exchanges, 9-3–9-4
Substitution effect, of tax rate increase,
    2-5–2-6
SueLee Company, 6-19
Sufficiency, as revenue raiser, 2-2–2-7
Sufficiency, good tax
    behavioral responses, rate changes,
        2-5–2-7
    debt financing, 2-2
    insufficient tax system, 2-2
    legalized gambling, 2-2
    national debt, 2-3
    public goods and services, 2-2
    static versus dynamic forecasting, 2-4
    tax revenues, 2-3
Sugary soft drinks, excise taxes
    on, 1-10
Supplies, disposition of, 8-14–8-15
Supply-side economic theory, 2-6–2-7
Surcharge taxes, 13-3
Surviving spouse, joint tax returns and,
    14-4–14-5, 14-16
Susan Crile (2014), 17-14n45
Swazey, Shannon, 15-28
Swig Investment Co. v. United States
    (1996), 7-3n11

T

Talmadge Partnership, 9-8
TAM. *See* Technical advice
    memorandum (TAM)
Tangible business assets
    bonus depreciation, 7-21–7-22
    depreciation, definition, 7-11
    generally accepted accounting
        principles (GAAP), 7-11
    purchase versus leasing decision,
        7-22–7-23
    Section 179 expensing election,
        7-19–7-20
Tangible property, 1-8, 1-8n5
Tao, Donna, 18-6
Taxable estate, 16-32–16-34

Taxable exchange of property for stock,
    9-12
Taxable income. *See also* Business
    operations, taxable income from
    definition of, 6-4
    federal definition of, 1-10
    limitation, 7-20
Taxable income, business operations,
    6-4
    calendar year, 6-5
    cost recovery deductions, 6-5
    discharge of debt income, 6-4
    fiscal year, 6-5, 6-6
    gross income, 6-4
    Internal Revenue Code, 6-3
    methods of accounting. *See* Methods
        of accounting
    net operating loss (NOL)
        accounting for, 6-27
        average tax rate, 6-25
        carryforward, 6-25
        deduction, 6-26–6-27
        excess business loss limitation,
            6-27–6-28
        excess deductions problem,
            6-24–6-25
    net present value (NPV), 6-3
    short-period return, 6-6
    taxable year, 6-5–6-6
    Treasury regulations, 6-3
Taxable income computation. *See*
    Individual tax formula
Taxable income formula, 14-15–14-16
Taxable income limitation, 7-20
Taxable long-term capital gain, 16-15
Taxable personalty, 1-8
Taxable year, 6-5–6-6
Tax advantages, retirement planning,
    15-19–15-20
Tax adviser, 5-1
Tax assessor, 1-7
Taxation of capital gains, 8-12
Tax audit, 1-10
Tax avoidance, 3-18n11, 4-2
Tax base
    changes in, 1-14–1-15
    definition of, 1-5
    expanding, 2-3
    rate and revenue relationship to,
        1-5–1-6
    rate change effect on, 2-4
Tax basis, 1-5, 7-6
    adjusted basis, 7-6
    after-tax cost, 7-7

additional costs versus, 4-14
from capital losses, 16-19
from export sales, 13-13
Tax shelters, 12-14–12-15, 13-19, 13-22, 16-18
Tax shields, 3-8n3
Tax subsidies
for education, 17-12–17-13
government, to Boeing, 1-8
Tax systems, 2-1, 2-9
base changes
legalized gambling, 1-14
nontax revenue, 1-14
revenue-generating power, 1-14
sales tax expansion, 1-15
and data analytics, 1-16
insufficient, 2-2
Keynesian schema, 2-9
and political process, 1-15–1-16
Technical advice memorandum (TAM), 5-5
Temporary differences, 6-16–6-18
Temporary differences in taxable and book income
accrued expenses, 6-19–6-21
bad debts, 6-23–6-24
compensation accruals, 6-21–6-22
overview of, 6-16
prepaid income, 6-18–6-19
related party accruals, 6-22–6-23
reversal of, 6-17
Tentative minimum tax, 14-25
Terms & Connectors method, in keyword searches, 5-9–5-10
Terrorist attacks on United States, 2-7
Testamentary transfer, 16-32
Texas margin tax (TMT), 13-3
TG Corporation, 8-3
Theft and casualty losses, 8-25, 17-13–17-14
Thin capitalization, 12-13–12-14
Thomson Reuters, 5-8, 5-10–5-11
Thor Power Tool Co. v. Comm. (1979), 6-15n35
Three-party exchanges, 9-7–9-8
Time period variable, in income tax planning, 4-6–4-9
Time value of money, 3-4
TIPS (Treasure inflation-protected securities), 16-6, 16-8, 16-8n13
TMT (Texas margin tax), 13-3
TNT Mutual Fund, 16-12
Todd, Ghani, 10-34
Topically arranged tax services, 5-8

Total income, 14-7–14-8
Total Tax Index (KPMG), 2-11
Trade Facilitation and Trade Enforcement Act of 2015, 13-5
Trademarks, 6-4
Trade secret misappropriation, 8-9
Traditional IRA, 15-27–15-30. *See also* Individual retirement accounts (IRAs)
Transactional markets, 3-14–3-18, 15-2
arm's-length presumption, 3-16–3-17
private market transactions
compensation package, 3-15, 3-16
health insurance factor, 3-15
legal and financial characteristics, 3-14
tax cost to government, 3-16
tax planning, 3-14–3-16
public market transactions, 3-17
related party transactions, 3-17–3-18
Transaction-based taxes, 1-6
Transaction costs
business decision-making process, 3-3
net present value (NPV), 3-4–3-7
partnerships, S corporations, and, 12-7
tax reduction, 3-13–3-18
Transaction costs, taxes as, 3-3–3-26
cash flows and
marginal tax rate significance, 3-8–3-9
net present value (NPV) and, 3-9–3-11
tax costs, 3-8
tax savings, 3-8
uncertainty of tax consequences and, 3-11–3-13
different tax treatments across transactions, 3-10
net present value (NPV) in decision making, 3-4–3-7
structuring, to reduce taxes, 3-13–3-18
Transaction- or activity-based taxes, 1-6
Transactions. *See also* Business transactions
private market transactions
compensation package, 3-15, 3-16
health insurance factor, 3-15
legal and financial characteristics, 3-14
tax cost to government, 3-16
tax planning, 3-14–3-16
public market transactions, 3-17
related party transactions, 3-17–3-18

revenue-generating transactions, 3-4
Transferee liability, 18-19
Transfer payments, 17-5–17-6
Transfer prices, 13-23
Transfer pricing, Section 482 and, 13-23–13-24
Transfer tax system, 1-12, 16-29
Transportation Act of 2015, 11-15
Tran, Tom, 15-28
Treasury inflation-protected securities (TIPS), 16-6, 16-8
Treasury regulations, 1-17, 5-5, 5-7, 6-3, 10-17
TresChic Company, 7-25
Trial court, 18-15–18-16
Trump administration, 2-7
Trump, Donald J., 1-11, 2-10, 8-4
Tunley, Inc., 8-15
Turner, Reginald, 17-3n7
TUV, Inc., 6-25, 6-26
"12-month rule," 6-12
28 percent rate gains or losses, 16-14
20 percent preferential rate, 16-16, 16-17
20 percent recapture rule, 8-19–8-20
Twitter, 18-8
2023 income tax rates, A-4–A-5
2023 phaseout threshold, 15-28–15-30

U

Uncertainty, of tax consequences, 3-11–3-13
Underpayment penalty, 11-15
Underpayment rate, 18-4
Undeveloped land, investment in, 16-22–16-23
Unearned income medicare contribution tax, 16-28–16-29
Unearned income, of children, 14-19
Unemployment taxes, 1-12, 10-11–10-12
Unforeseen circumstances, 17-19
Uniform capitalization (UNICAP) rules, 7-10, 10-13n17
Uniform Division of Income for Tax Purposes Act (UDITPA), 13-5
United States Gift Tax Return (Form 709), 16-30
United States Tax Reporter, 5-8
United States v. Bisceglia (1975), 1-7n3
United States v. Davis (2016), 18-19n53
United States v. General Dynamics Corp. (1987), 6-20n43
United States v. Lee (1982), 18-11n25